# CHILD MALTREATMENT

## A COMPREHENSIVE PHOTOGRAPHIC REFERENCE IDENTIFYING POTENTIAL CHILD ABUSE

THIRD EDITION

**G.W. Medical Publishing, Inc.**
St. Louis

*To the staff at the Center for Children's Support at the*
*University of Medicine and Dentistry of New Jersey, School of Osteopathic Medicine*
*under the leadership of Martin A. Finkel, DO, FACOP (Medical Director) and*
*Esther Deblinger, PhD (Clinical Director), who continue to develop and*
*study best practices that serve the interests of children, families, and professionals at large.*
*— APG*

*To Ray Helfer, David Chadwick, Robert Reece,*
*Jay Whitworth, and the other pioneers of child abuse advocacy*
*for deeply caring about children in a world that sometimes does not care as well as it should.*
*— RA*

# CHILD MALTREATMENT

## A COMPREHENSIVE PHOTOGRAPHIC REFERENCE IDENTIFYING POTENTIAL CHILD ABUSE

THIRD EDITION

**Randell Alexander, MD, PhD, FAAP**
Professor of Pediatrics, and Chief
Division of Child Protection and Forensic Pediatrics
Department of Pediatrics
University of Florida
Jacksonville, Florida
Professor of Pediatrics
Morehouse School of Medicine
Atlanta, Georgia

**Angelo P. Giardino, MD, PhD, FAAP**
Associate Chair – Pediatrics
Associate Physician-in-Chief/Vice President, Clinical Affairs
St. Christopher's Hospital for Children
Professor in Pediatrics
Drexel University College of Medicine
Adjunct Professor of Pediatric Nursing
LaSalle University School of Nursing
Philadelphia, Pennsylvania

**G.W. Medical Publishing, Inc.**
St. Louis

Publishers: Glenn E. Whaley and Marianne V. Whaley

Design Director: Glenn E. Whaley

Managing Editors: Megan E. Ferrell
Karen C. Maurer

Associate Editors: Jonathan M. Taylor
Christine Bauer

Book Design/Page Layout: G.W. Graphics
Charles J. Seibel, III
Sudon Choe

Print/Production Coordinator: Charles J. Seibel, III

Cover Design: G.W. Graphics

Color Prepress Specialist: G.W. Graphics
Richard C. Stockard

Copy Editor: Jonathan M. Taylor

Developmental Editor: Elaine Steinborn
Jeanne Allison

Indexer: Nelle Garrecht

Proofreader: Michael S. McConnell



Printed in Canada.

Publisher:
**G.W. Medical Publishing, Inc.**
**77 Westport Plaza, Suite 366, St. Louis, Missouri, 63146-3124 U.S.A.**
**Phone: (314) 542-4213 Fax: (314) 542-4239 Toll Free: 1-800-600-0330**
**http://www.gwmedical.com**

Library of Congress Cataloging-in-Publication Data

Child maltreatment : a comprehensive photographic reference identifying potential child abuse /
[edited by] Randell Alexander and Angelo P. Giardino . -- 3rd ed.
p. ; cm.
Includes bibliographical references and index.
ISBN 1-878060-56-2 (hardcover : alk. paper)
1. Child abuse -- Atlases. 2. Battered child syndrome -- Atlases.
[DNLM: 1. Child Abuse -- Atlases. 2. Child Abuse -- Case Reports. ] I. Alexander, Randell, 1950- II. Giardino, Angelo P.,
RJ375C488 2005
618.92 ' 858223 -- dc22

2005003367

# Contributors

**Sandra P. Alexander, MEd**
Prevention Consultant
Atlanta, Georgia

**Kathleen M. Benasutti, MCAT, ATR-BC, LPC**
Registered and Board Certified Art Therapist
Trauma Consultant
Treatment Research Institute at the University of Pennsylvania
Philadelphia, Pennsylvania

**Thomas L. Bennett, MD**
Forensic Medicine and Pathology
Associate Montana State Medical Examiner
Billings, Montana

**Joseph S. Bova Conti, BA**
Detective Sergeant
Maryland Heights Police Department
Maryland Heights, Missouri
Crimes Against Children Specialist
Certified Juvenile Specialist – State of Missouri
Member MPJOA, MJJA, SLCJJA
Lecturer, Author, Consultant

**Paul T. Clements, PhD, APRN, BC, DF-IAFN**
Assistant Professor
College of Nursing
University of New Mexico
Albuquerque, New Mexico
Distinguished Fellow
International Association of Forensic Nurses

**Donna L. Evans, MD, FAAP**
Assistant Professor of Pediatrics
Backus Children's Hospital
Savannah, Georgia

**Eric N. Faerber, MD**
Chief, Section of Neuroradiology
Director, Department of Radiology
St. Christopher's Hospital for Children
Philadelphia, Pennsylvania
Professor of Radiologic Sciences
Drexel University College of Medicine
Philadelphia, Pennsylvania

**Brian J. Forbes, MD, PhD**
Assistant Professor of Ophthalmology
The Childrens' Hospital of Philadelphia
University of Pennsylvania School of Medicine
Philadelphia, Pennsylvania

**Lori D. Frasier, MD, FAAP**
Associate Professor of Pediatrics
University of Utah School of Medicine
Medical Director, Medical Assessment Team
Center for Safe and Healthy Families
Primary Children's Medical Center
Salt Lake City, Utah

**Edward Goldson, MD, FAAP**
Professor
Department of Pediatrics
University of Colorado Health Sciences Center
Developmental and Behavioral Pediatrics
The Children's Hospital
Denver, Colorado

**Michael Graham, MD**
Professor of Pathology
St. Louis University School of Medicine
Chief Medical Examiner
St. Louis, Missouri

**Sam P. Gulino, MD**
Associate Medical Examiner
Hillsborough County Medical Examiner Department
Tampa, Florida
Assistant Professor of Pathology and Laboratory Medicine
University of South Florida School of Medicine

**Gloria C. Henry**
Bereavement Specialist
Philadelphia, Pennsylvania

**Charles F. Johnson, MD, FAAP**
Professor of Pediatrics
Ohio State University College of Medicine and Public Health
Staff Physician Child and Family Advocacy Program
Children's Hospital
Columbus, Ohio

**John P. Kenney, DDS, MS, D-ABFO, FACD, FAAPD, FAAFS**
Associate Professor of Clinical Surgery
Northwestern University Medical School
Deputy Coroner/Director Identification Services
DuPage County, Illinois Coroner's Office
Wheaton, Illinois

**Swati Mody, MD, MBBS**
Staff Radiologist
Department of Pediatric Imaging
Children's Hospital of Michigan
Assistant Professor of Radiology
Wayne State University School of Medicine
Detroit, Michigan

**Lynn Douglas Mouden, DDS, MPH**
Director
Office of Oral Health
Arkansas Department of Health
Professor
University of Arkansas Medical Sciences (UAMS) College of Public Health
Department of Maternal and Child Health
Associate Professor
University of Tennessee College of Dentistry
Department of Pediatrics and Community Oral Health
Adjunct Clinical Assistant Professor
UAMS College of Medicine
Department of Pediatrics
Associate Professor
UAMS College of Health Related Professions
School of Hygiene

**Lawrence R. Ricci, MD**
Director
The Spurwink Child Abuse Program
Portland, Maine

**Andrew Sirotnak, MD, FAAP**
Associate Professor of Pediatrics
University of Colorado School of Medicine
Director
Kempe Child Protection Team
The Children's Hospital & Kempe Children's Center
Denver, Colorado

**Craig Smith**
C.B. Smith Training & Consulting Ltd.
Nanaimo, British Columbia
Canada

**Wilbur L. Smith, MD**
Children's Hospital of Michigan
Detroit Receiving Hospital
Professor and Chairman
Department of Radiology
Wayne State University
Detroit, Michigan

**J. M. Whitworth, MD, FAAP**
Professor
Division of Child Protection and Forensic Pediatrics
Department of Pediatrics
University of Florida
Jacksonville, Florida

**Matt Young, MD, MPH, FAAP**
Director of Pediatrics
Assistant Medical Director
Director of Outpatient Burn Services
Director of Hyperbaric Medicine
Grossman Burn Center
Sherman Oaks Hospital
Sherman Oaks, California

**Supplemental Photo Contributions**

**John R. Brewer, MD**
**Joan M. Boyer**
**Jon C. Boyer**
**Phillip M. Burch, MD**
**Mary E. S. Case, MD**
**Oscar A. Cruz, MD**
**Timothy J. Fete, MD**
**Jane B. Geiler**
**Det Gary W. Guinn**
**Sgt Milton Jones, Ret**
**Vicki McNeese, MS**
**Missouri Police Juvenile Officer's Association**
**James A. Monteleone, MD**
**Christian E. Paletta, MD**
**Colette M. Rickert, LPCC, ATR-BC**
**Anthony J. Scalzo, MD**
**Elaine C. Siegfried, MD**
**George F. Steinhardt, MD**
**Det Gary L. Thompson**

# FOREWORD

Child maltreatment is a universal problem. Throughout the world there are parents, neighbors, friends, relatives, school or church workers, and others who fail to value children. Cases of maltreatment involve all socioeconomic classes; no one is exempt.

With a scope this all-encompassing, how does one intervene effectively? These children and their families are best served when there is a collective effort by all who are called upon to respond to cases of child maltreatment. Those involved need to understand their respective roles and work together constructively. This means mutual respect and knowledge of how all parts of the system intertwine to provide the best protection for the child and family.

The knowledge base in child maltreatment is expanding each day. Whereas in the 1970s there was a paucity of literature devoted to this field, last year there were hundreds of peer-reviewed journal articles written to inform professionals of new findings. These include articles about abuse or neglect as well as conditions that can be mistaken for maltreatment, issues arising in the context of child maltreatment cases, the economic consequences of adverse childhood experiences, the long-term psychological and medical consequences of maltreatment, and the legal aspects of this epidemic. The need for reliable information has never been greater.

In this 2-volume set, child maltreatment is thoroughly described. Information necessary to understand the medical aspects of child maltreatment and the specific role of each team member is presented clearly. Included are chapters specific to healthcare providers, law enforcement personnel, child protection workers, attorneys, and others. The text attempts to reflect the most current and comprehensive knowledge base in each area.

The third edition of *Child Maltreatment: A Clinical Guide and Reference* and *A Comprehensive Photographic Reference Identifying Potential Child Abuse* represents the collaboration of many dedicated professionals. Their overarching purposes are to educate every professional involved with children about the problem of maltreatment, to elucidate the approaches that have been successful, and to provide the best outcome possible for the involved children and their families. The practical applications presented are designed to provide all that is necessary to manage complex issues surrounding child maltreatment.

**Robert M. Reece, MD**
Clinical Professor of Pediatrics
Tufts University School of Medicine
Visiting Professor of Pediatrics
Dartmouth Medical School
Editor, *The Quarterly Update*
Norwich, Vermont

# Foreword

Recognition of child maltreatment is essential to safeguard the well-being of children. In 1961 Henry Kempe first brought this problem to world attention, yet it still remains largely unaccepted as an epidemic. The recognition of certain findings that lead to the identification of child maltreatment is vital in its detection, treatment, and prosecution.

The Convention on the Rights of the Child guarantees children the right to a name, family, state, education, and safety, among others. However, parts of the world remain where children are not granted these basic rights. In many contexts, children are no more than commercial commodities, under the control of the adults around them. As such, they can be bought and sold and may be subjected to cruelties to enhance their commercial value, such as having their limbs cut off or their eyes blinded so they are more appealing as beggars. Harsh treatments of children may include inadequate food or shelter and punishments that threaten their life, physical integrity, or psychological well-being. Child trafficking for the purpose of enforced labor, soldiering, or prostitution is widely practiced. It affects not only nations with limited resources, but also those whose resources are almost limitless, since globalization facilitates children being traded on the world market. The facts and signs of maltreatment are plain to see in these cases, yet what is lacking is the will to name the problem and act against it. Cultural practices, lack of awareness, and systems that are geared solely to the economic gain of a few perpetuate the problem. Challenging these practices is a daunting undertaking that requires considerable resources, political will, and systemic change.

In countries where child maltreatment is manifestly illegal and where sanctions exist against the abuser, the challenge of recognition is one of detection and identification. Instances of maltreatment can be hidden, or caregivers may claim that injuries are caused by accidental events or organic illnesses. The veracity of children who disclose abuse and the expertise of professionals who testify to the features of maltreatment may be called into question. The lack of rigorous experimental studies may be cited as evidence of the unreliability of child witnesses or the ingenuousness of forensic professionals. When lies, misunderstandings, or lack of sufficient knowledge or evidence prevent a clear distinction between abuse and a more benign explanation, it is the task of the responsible professional to make this distinction clear. However, when signs of maltreatment exist or they indicate that maltreatment is at least a strong possibility, professionals must make that case and advocate for measures to ensure the child's safety. To increase the likelihood of reaching accurate conclusions, the professional must have a clear understanding of the harm attributable to maltreatment, of the mechanisms that cause injury, and of the signs that identify the lesions they produce.

Reference to this atlas will contribute to the accurate identification of abuse and, in so doing, will contribute to the wider recognition of maltreatment as a violation of children's rights, safety, and well-being. One of the benefits of globalization is that this knowledge and attitude may be disseminated so that the world can become a safer place for children everywhere.

**Marcellina Mian, MDCM, FRCPC, FAAP**
Pediatrician, Suspected Child Abuse and Neglect (SCAN) Program
Director, Undergraduate Medical Education
Hospital for Sick Children
Professor, Faculty of Medicine
University of Toronto
Toronto, Canada

# Preface

Child maltreatment evokes visual images, real or imagined, in the minds of professionals and the public. Some of these images are easily anticipated: the child with bruises, radiographs of broken bones, pictures of damaged hymens, and even the autopsy findings of the deceased child. Often they are horrific even though most child maltreatment cases are not the worst extremes. But many images are less obvious: the equipment used in child maltreatment cases, drawings by abused children, the many faces of neglect, or child maltreatment prevention images. Several of the photographic chapters in this book are relatively unique to child maltreatment texts. The goal of this photographic atlas is to give life to the content and process of child maltreatment in an attempt to expand upon the traditional ways in which child maltreatment is portrayed.

One of the advantages of visual media is that they add exactness to some situations that cannot otherwise be easily described. Seeing a photograph of an abused child informs the viewer of more than notations on a line drawing of a figure. Too often, professionals attempt to communicate by words alone, believing that they are communicating the same point, but ultimately fail to completely grasp what the other is saying. This "parallel play" can have important consequences for abused children and those at risk. One example that may be familiar to many professionals is the shaking seen with shaken baby syndrome. Many in the public, and many beginning professionals, believe they know what the shaking looks like. This is belied by some of their questions ("Couldn't it be accidental?" "Could it happen by jogging with a child in a backpack?") that show that they are thinking of "jiggle baby syndrome" instead. This belief can persist for years as the professional imagines what experts are saying. Seeing an actual doll demonstration or computer animation depicting the extreme violence that actually occurs is much better for these professionals and perhaps the public. When juries see this, they know exactly what the expert is referring to and can make their own decisions without being ignorant of what is being proposed.

Different modes of visualization can inform us in ways we are just beginning to explore. One visual aspect that should emerge more strongly in the future is the videotaping of a child who has been maltreated. While pictures of a child who is dirty, disheveled, and listless are very informative, it is even more revealing to watch a videotape of a child who is apathetic, has a sad affect, or may have various developmental delays. Still photographs of hymens have increased in quality both with an increase in photographic equipment detail and with greater experience of examiners, yet a static photograph of a genital exam evokes the question of whether a "finding" or "lack of finding" is an artifact of that instance in time. Even more importantly for the beginner, it can be hard to judge foreground and background—the problem most of us have when looking at aerial reconnaissance photographs. Put into motion, the examination looks like what we see with the real child. A product of the greater depth perception seen with motion parallax, visual perception is enhanced by retinal and visual cortex motion "detectors." Another visual modality that will become increasingly informative will be the results of "nanny cams"—the home videotapes that are beginning to capture physical abuses committed by a person when it is thought no one is looking. In a future edition, we hope to begin to incorporate some of these video possibilities into the library of what is known.

It is our hope that this atlas will be seen as providing an overview of the possibilities within the world of child maltreatment today. Read straight through, or used as a reference, the information contained within should help broaden horizons and help professionals in the field more clearly understand the many aspects of child maltreatment.

**Randell Alexander, MD, PhD, FAAP**
Atlanta, Georgia

**Angelo P. Giardino, MD, PhD, FAAP**
Philadelphia, Pennslyvania

# Reviews of the Third Edition

*Whether in an intensive care unit caring for a child abuse victim, providing training, or testifying as an expert witness, there is one resource that I know I can cite as a reliable reference, and that is* Child Maltreatment. *This is the most outstanding text of its kind, and provides a complete review with relevant references on all aspects of the medical diagnosis and treatment of child abuse and neglect. I recommend* Child Maltreatment *to all members of an investigative multidisciplinary team and consider it a mandatory resource in any medical, social science, or criminal justice library.*

Sharon Cooper, MD, FAAP
Adjunct Associate Professor of Pediatrics
University of North Carolina School of Medicine
Chapel Hill, North Carolina
Clinical Assistant Professor of Pediatrics
Uniformed Services University of Health Sciences
Bethesda, Maryland
Chief, Developmental Pediatric Service
Womack Army Medical Center
Fort Bragg, North Carolina

*This publication presents a comprehensive look at the issues involved in cases of child maltreatment, emphasizing the contemporary importance of this subject together with reviewing the multidisciplinary techniques for forensically detecting as well as addressing the needs of victims of such maltreatment. The text provides professionals in the fields of law, social science and the healthcare industry with invaluable source materials when confronted with suspected child maltreatment.*

Faye Battiste-Otto, RN, SANE
President, American Forensic Nurses
Palm Springs, California

*Angelo Giardino and his interdisciplinary team of colleagues have continued to improve on an already exceptional collection of essays focused on the nature, extent and seriousness of child maltreatment in the United States and other economically advanced countries. In addition to providing the reader with a deep understanding of the complex forces that contribute to child maltreatment, the volume's chapters offer clinicians and policy makers alike state-of-the-art guidance in preventing and caring for children who become victims of abuse and neglect. Dr. Giardino and his colleagues are to be congratulated for their pioneering contributions in helping to halt the current epidemic of child maltreatment cases.*

Richard J. Estes, DSW, ACSW
Professor
Chair, Concentration in Social and Economic Development
Director, International Programs
University of Pennsylvania School of Social Work
Philadelphia, Pennsylvania

*This edition of* Child Maltreatment *builds on the terrific start provided by James Monteleone with an expansion that is up-to-date, complete, and provides the best available information from an extraordinary group of contributors. It is a "must," not only for specialists in the field of child abuse and neglect, but for all health professionals who provide care to children.*

Richard Krugman, MD
Dean of Medicine
University of Colorado School of Medicine
Denver, Colorado

*This 3rd edition of* Child Maltreatment *includes the very latest in research and clinical issues related to the injury and exploitation of children. The editors have gathered the best and the brightest authors in the field to write the chapters and the volumes contain essential knowledge for students and clinicians. It is designed to be a reference and resource for all agencies that assist and manage child maltreatment issues.*

Ann Wolbert Burgess, RN, DNSc, CS
Boston College Connell School of Nursing

*The third edition of this vital reference designed for child maltreatment professionals contains new, cutting-edge, and evidence-based information. Comprised of 2 volumes with a total of 62 chapters,* Child Maltreatment: A Clinical Guide and Reference *and* A Comprehensive Photographic Reference Identifying Potential Child Abuse *covers virtually every aspect of child physical, sexual, and psychological abuse, child neglect, and service delivery systems that either encounter or address child maltreatment. This reference work should be in the library of every professional concerned with the problem of child maltreatment.*

Kathleen Coulborn Faller, PhD, ACSW
Professor, School of Social Work
Director, Family Assessment Clinic
University of Michigan
Ann Arbor, Michigan

**G.W. Medical Publishing, Inc.**
St. Louis

## Our Mission

To become the world leader in publishing and information services on child abuse, maltreatment and diseases, and domestic violence. We seek to heighten awareness of these issues and provide relevant information to professionals and consumers.

*A portion of our profits is contributed to nonprofit organizations dedicated to the prevention of child abuse and the care of victims of abuse and other children and family charities.*

# Contents in Brief

# Contents in Detail

# CHILD MALTREATMENT

## A COMPREHENSIVE PHOTOGRAPHIC REFERENCE IDENTIFYING POTENTIAL CHILD ABUSE

THIRD EDITION

**G.W. Medical Publishing, Inc.**
St. Louis

Chapter 1

# Bruises and Other Skin Injuries

Charles Felzen Johnson, MD

## Manifestations of Physical Maltreatment on the Skin: Impacts and Other Contacts

Parents' or caretakers' reactions to unwanted behaviors from a child may be manifested by an unplanned and immediate physical or verbal attack on the child. If the attack does not result in any persistent tissue injuries, such as a bruise, there will be no record of the injury. Consequently, the injury may be considered insignificant or not serious enough to constitute a report of suspected abuse. For example, a slap to the face should be considered inappropriate because of the vulnerability of the delicate structures of the face and the impact's potential to harm the brain. Erythema from a slap to the face will fade in minutes to hours depending on the force used.

The objects used in a physical attack generally are readily available. The hand requires no preparation for an attack on a child. It can be used in an open manner as a slap or in a fist as a punch. The hand can grab, pinch, and twist the skin. Nails can gouge and scratch. Common objects around the house varying in size and shape can be wielded by hand. Depending on where and how they impact the skin, the marks they leave may be in silhouette or outline form. For example, a flat object impacting the buttocks, lower back, or chest will leave varying marks on each surface, such as a round mark on the buttocks, a row of round marks on the lower back from the spinous processes that are under the skin of the back, or a series of lines mirroring the underlying ribs.

Other parts of the body may be used to injure a child. Mouths may be used to bite or suck on a child's skin. Occasionally, a knee may kick or strike a child or arms may be used to crush a child against a caretaker's chest. Impacts to areas of the body where bones are not immediately under the skin, such as the abdomen, may not show topical marks. Parents may apply folk remedies to the skin that result in tissue injury. Physicians who care for children must be familiar with the marks left by various objects that indicate abuse and those skin conditions that may mimic intentional injury.

# Bruises

### Case Study 1-1

This boy of 2 years and 7 months was removed from his home because of neglect. The mother is HIV positive. The caseworker saw bruises on the child's face and referred him for evaluation. During the examination the child had a grand mal seizure.

***Figures 1-1-a** and **b**. 2 cm oval brown bruises on both sides of the face, lacerations on both ear lobes, and red abrasions are seen on the lower lip and under the left chin.*

***Figure 1-1-c**. The pattern of the bruises is best seen by applying circles over the bruises in a computer graphics program. The pattern is compatible with blunt impact from fingertips. The other injuries are indicated with applied arrows.*

***Figure 1-1-d.** Further examination revealed bruises on the hips, penis, and scrotum. It may be difficult to determine if bruises to the genitalia result from a physical or sexual assault. The marks on the penis and scrotum are likely to be from pinching. The cause of the hip bruises is unknown. Bruises from impacts are more likely to manifest on the hips because they, like the shins, brow, chin, and forehead, are areas where the skin is close to underlying bone.*

***Figure 1-1-e**. The examination for findings of physical abuse should include thorough examination of the genitalia and anus. In this child, new fissures surround the anus. The perianal area is erythematous. A red and blue bruise is seen on the right buttock. This boy has been anally penetrated.*

Review of the chart revealed a seizure disorder on medication. Blood studies were ordered to determine if the child was being given prescribed medication. A failure to give prescribed medication should be reported as medical neglect. A head CT scan was normal. Bruises on different surfaces cannot be compared with each other for dating. The brown bruises on the cheeks may have been older than the red purple bruises seen on other body parts. It is possible that the injuries to the cheeks and hips occurred in the process of attempted rectal penetration. The fingertip marks on the face are likely to have been caused as a way to hold the child still. They are not slap marks. (See **Figure 1-17** for an example of slap marks.) To determine if the marks on the scrotum and penis were from sexual abuse, one would need to know the intent of the perpetrator. Suspect physical abuse and sexual abuse were reported. The child was too young to interview. There were no other children in the home.

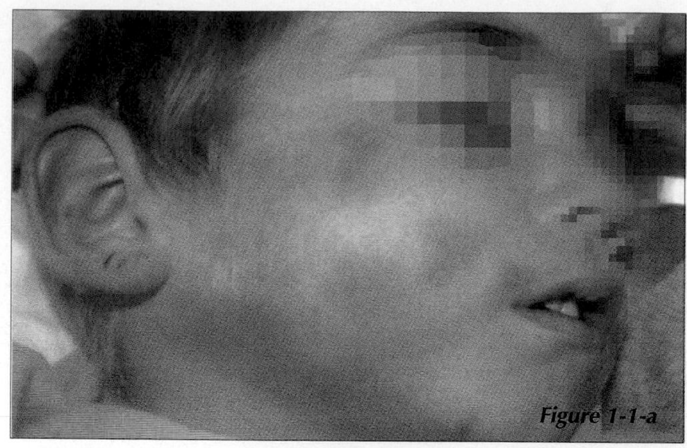

Figure 1-1-a

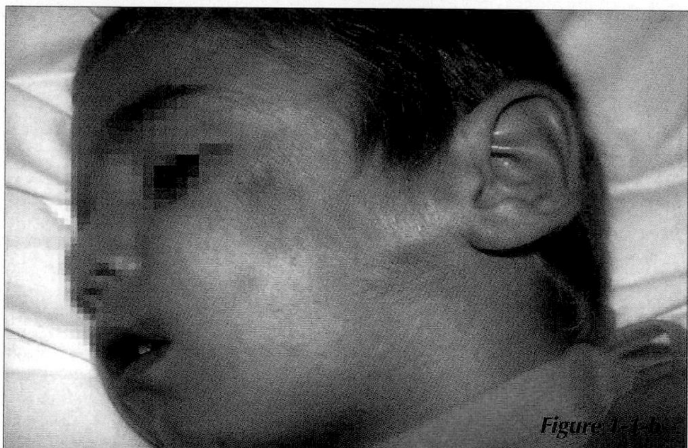

Figure 1-1-b

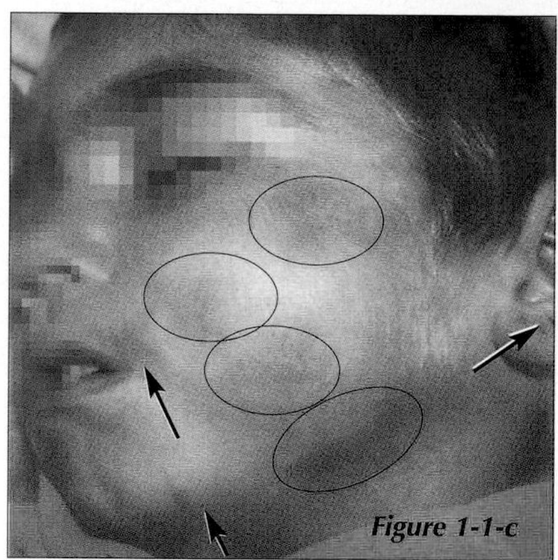

Figure 1-1-c

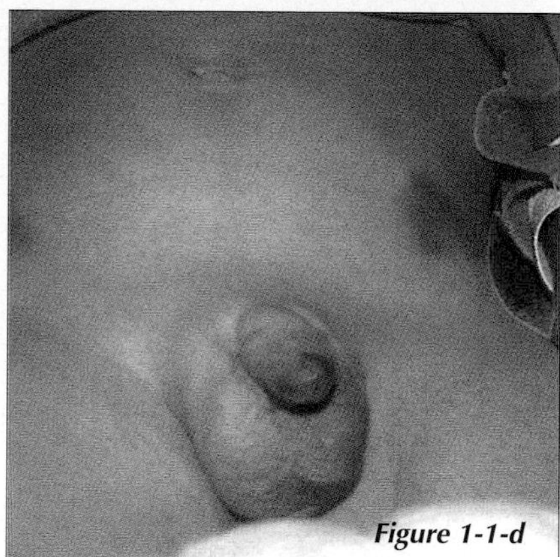

Figure 1-1-d

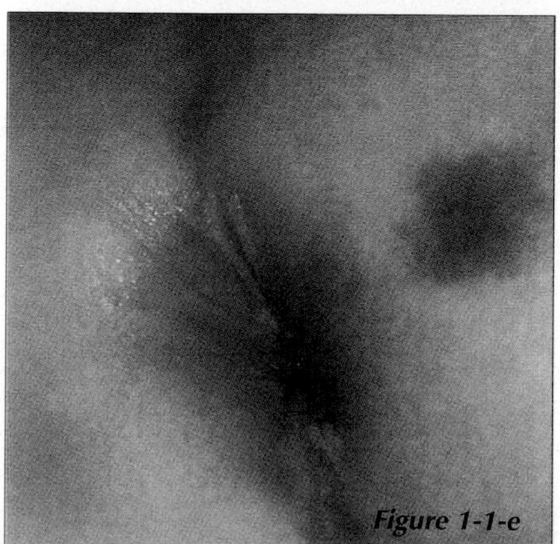

Figure 1-1-e

# Bruises

**Case Study 1-2**

While the mother of a this 2-year-old boy was at work, the father was the caretaker. The mother returned from work to find bruises on the child's buttocks. The father said that the bruises were caused by placing the child on a potty-chair with force. He also claimed that he had thrown the child onto a couch in play. A photograph was made of the toilet but the covering of the couch was not documented.

***Figure 1-2-a.*** *Petechiae on the right side of the face, behind the right ear, and on the left side of the back. A subconjunctival hemorrhage is seen in the right eye.*

***Figure 1-2-b.*** *The petechiae are mapped on an anatomical form to determine if there is a pattern.*

A suspect physical abuse report was filed, and law enforcement personnel made a home visit.

Anal penetration could not be ruled out. Although there was no evidence of penetration of the anus with an object larger than the anal orifice, as there were no fissures, enlargement of the anus or erythema, the anus can be penetrated by a small object, which leaves no physical evidence. The impact mark was not toward the anal opening, as one might expect with attempted penetration with a larger object. The lone, linear mark lateral to the anus was not the shape or size of a pinch. It was not curved in the shape of the potty bowl. The pattern of the petechial areas was not similar to those seen in a Valsalva maneuver or from choking or vomiting. Because more than one body surface was involved, it was possible that multiple impacts from the resilient surface of a couch caused the petechiae. The intent of the father was not material. His acts resulted in trauma to the child. It was appropriate to report suspect physical abuse.

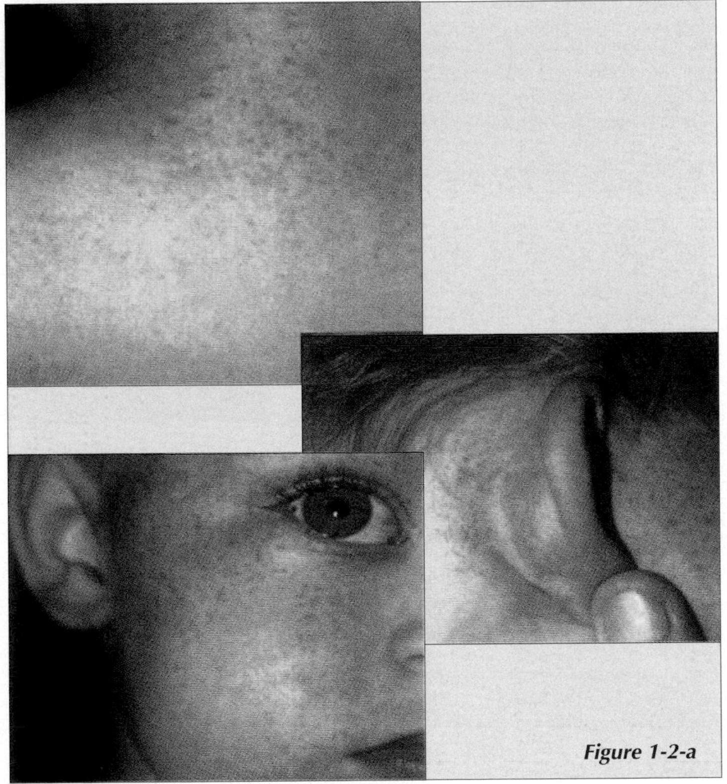

**Figure 1-2-a**

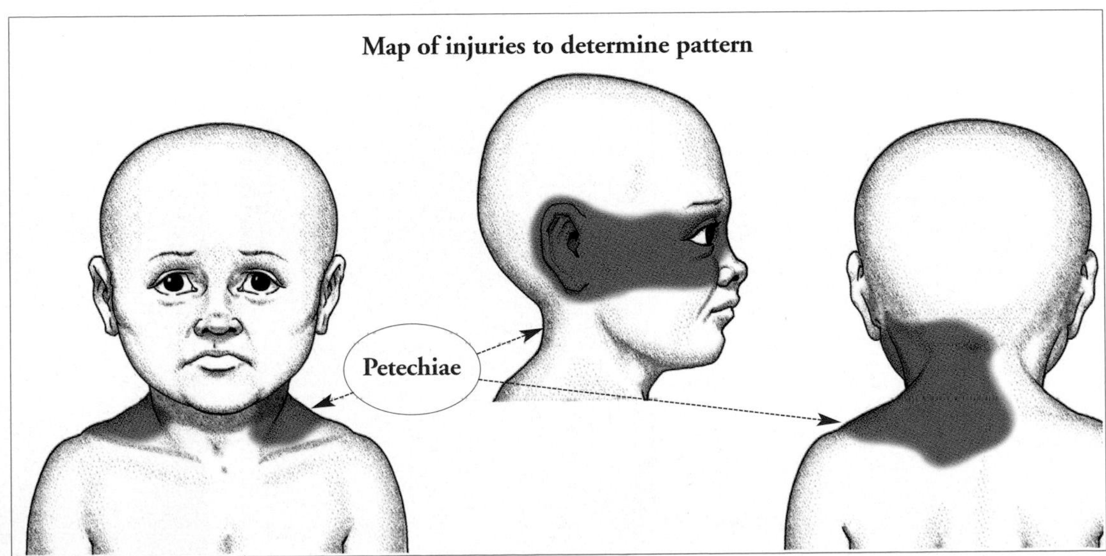

# Bruises

### Case Study 1-3

The caretaker claimed that this child fell to a carpeted floor. The absence of any midline impact mark indicated that this history was not accurate. The injuries were reported as suspect physical abuse. The presence of multiple colors in a bruise is not unusual after the first few days of an injury. The uncertainty of the timing of color change and the persistence of the red, blue, and purple colors throughout the history of a bruise makes dating bruises problematic.

***Figure 1-3.*** *Brown, blue, green, and purple discoloration below each eye of this child.*

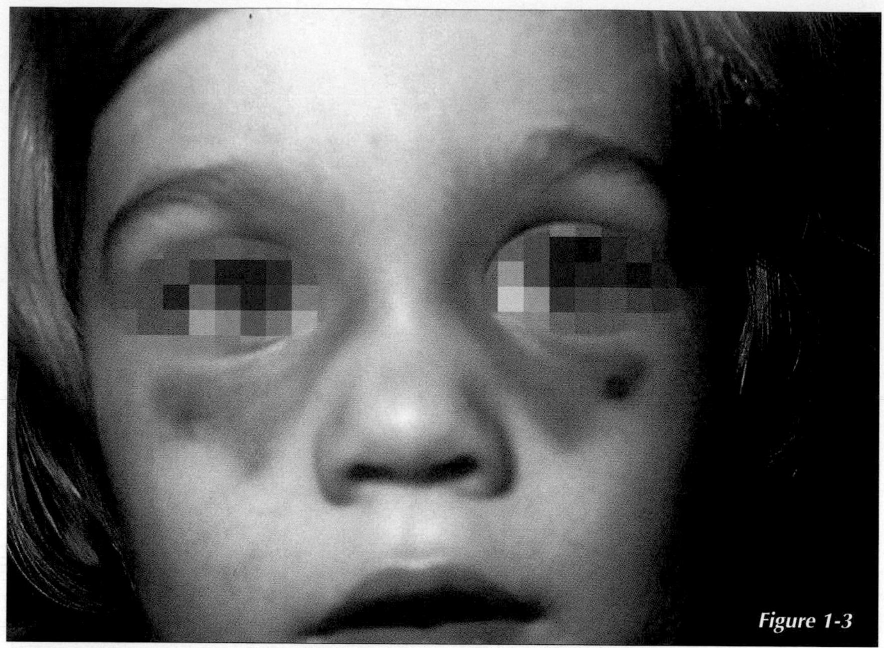

Figure 1-3

### Case Study 1-4

The following 3 cases exhibit bruising in usual and unusual locations. It is important to note the location and nature of bruising in order to correctly identify the source. Such information can verify or contradict a caregiver's history of the injury.

***Figure 1-4-a.*** *This 3-year-old child's mother reported that he must have bruised his arm while playing. An oval bruise is seen on the right lower arm where the ulna lies close to the skin surface. The bruise shape resembles the oval mark from a fingertip. No other finger-shaped marks are seen on the arm, as one would expect if the child were grabbed. Therefore, the mark is consistent with the history. It is possible to interview a verbal 3-year-old. The child gave no history of intentional trauma.*

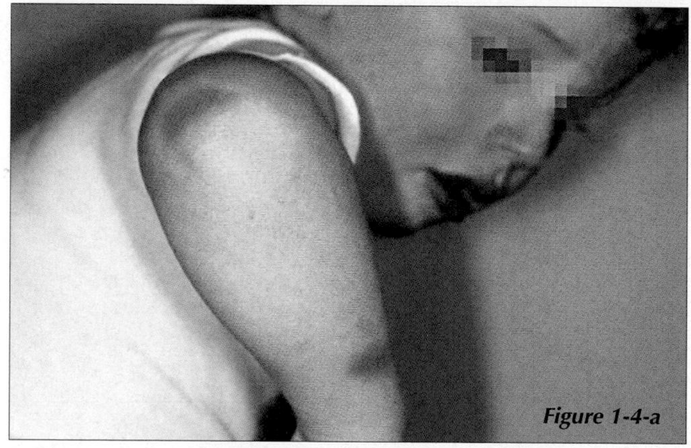

Figure 1-4-a

***Figure 1-4-b.*** *Bruises on the shins and right lateral knee. These are common places for impact injuries from normal play.*

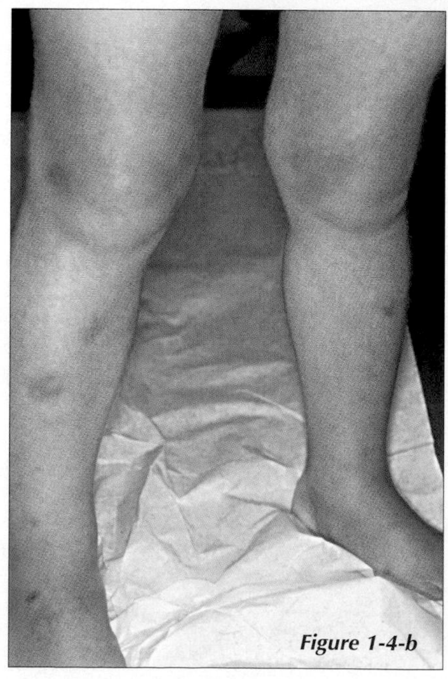

Figure 1-4-b

***Figure 1-4-c.*** *Circular bruise on the buttocks and a bruise on the left of the popliteal fossa of this child with hemophilia. Children with hemophilia can have bleeding into joints and into the skin from minor trauma. Their behavior may cause stress for caretakers who are admonished against striking them. The mark on the buttocks is round and the central area is clear. Buttocks are relatively protected from accidental injury. This child with hemophilia was struck with a saucepan. Children with chronic illness may stress their parents, causing them to react by physically abusing the child.*

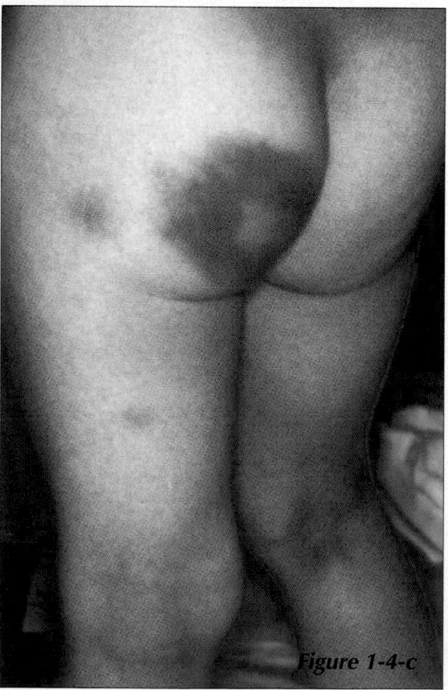

Figure 1-4-c

# Bruises

**Case Study 1-5**

This 5-year-old boy was seen in the ER. He was unconscious after what was explained as a body slam by a male caretaker who claimed he was wrestling with the boy. There were numerous marks on the skin and new subdural blood.

***Figure 1-5-a.*** *The marks on the shoulders seen in this image, shown with the boy on his back and the arm pulled across the chest, are caused by extended fingers grasping rather than striking the shoulder.*

***Figure 1-5-b.*** *The adult hands placed over the injury marks illustrate grasping of the shoulder. If the shoulder were struck, it is likely that the marks would be in an outline instead of the silhouette that is seen.*

***Figure 1-5-c.*** *Impact trauma to the helix of the right ear and pitting edema of the scalp. The tissue over both orbits is bruised (black eyes).*

Multiple impacts to several body surfaces were suffered. The boy did not survive the assault.

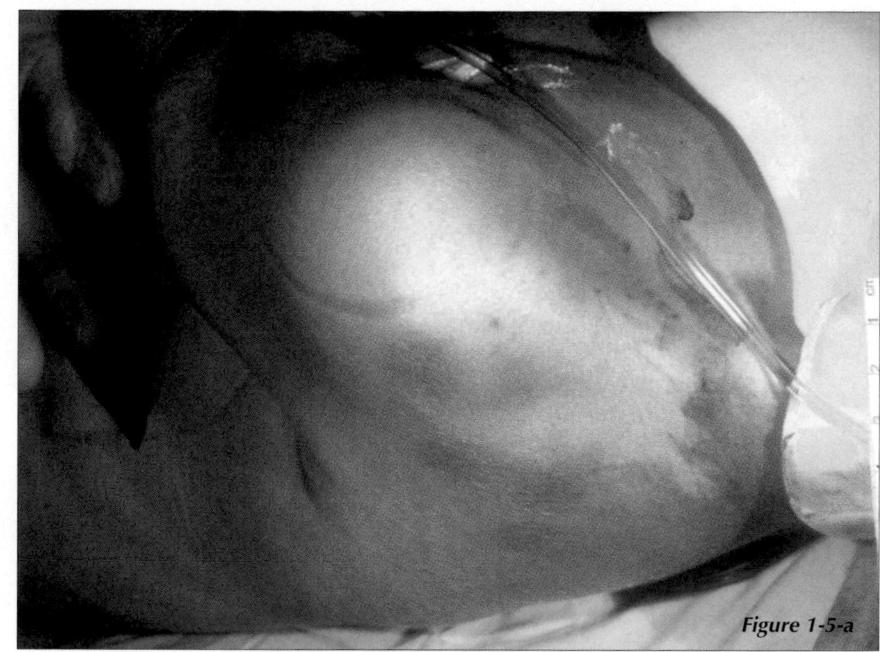

**Figure 1-5-a**

**Figure 1-5-b**

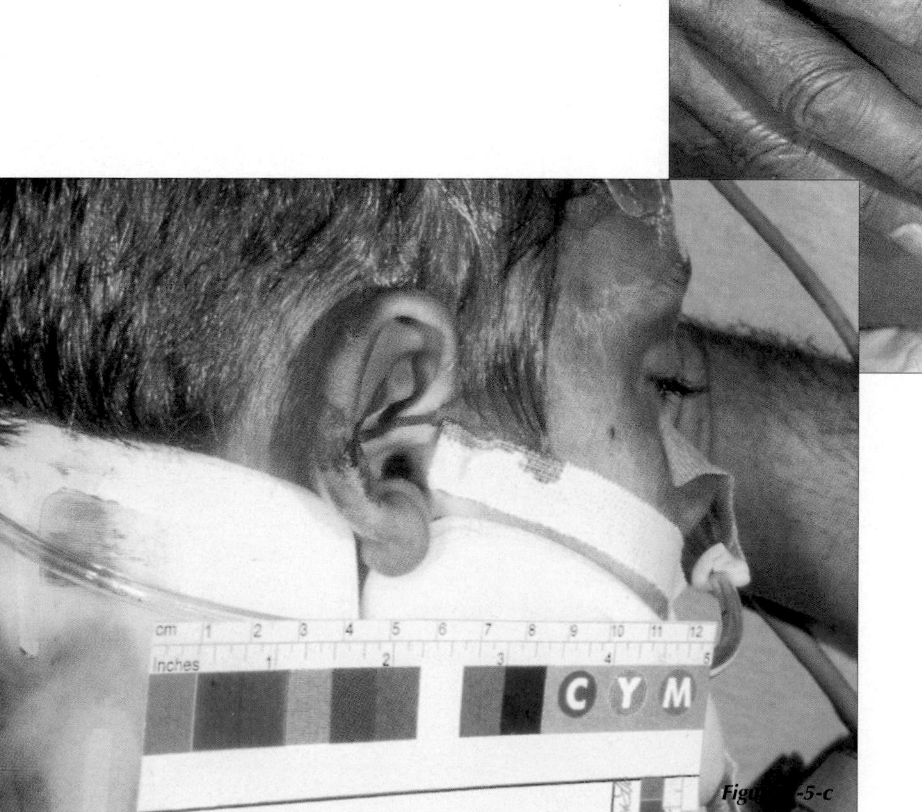


**Figure 1-5-c**

# Bruises

### Case Study 1-6

The mother brought this 7-year-old child to the ER. She gave a history of domestic violence by her husband who "tended to lose control when he was drunk." The child indicated that the father had hit her on the face and slammed her to the floor.

***Figure 1-6.*** *In addition to the marks and sutured laceration of the cheek that are seen here, the child has bruises to the shoulder, back, and left arm.*

When asked why this happened she stated that the father had attempted to insert his finger into her genitalia. When she resisted, he hit her. The genital examination was normal.

It is important that the history in suspect physical abuse includes questions about alcoholism and other substance abuse, domestic violence, mental illness, animal abuse, and sexual abuse, because all of these issues may be related.

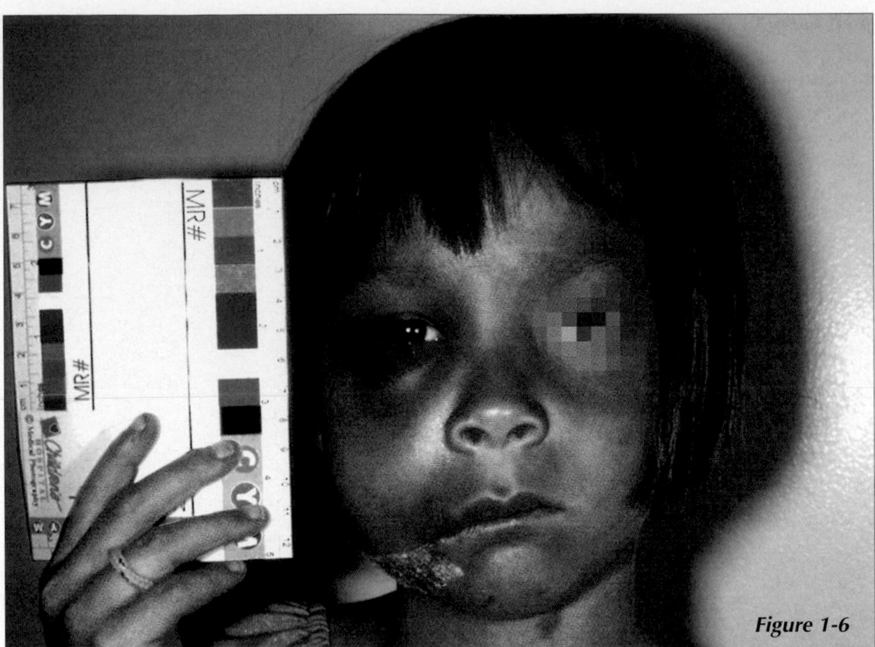


**Figure 1-6**

### Case Study 1-7

This infant was comatose and on life support as a result of injury to her brain. The caretakers indicated that the child fell down the stairs. The severity of the head injury was not in keeping with the history.

***Figure 1-7.*** *Bruise to the chin of this infant. Other bruises are scattered on the skin of the trunk, back, and abdomen.*

It is unusual for children to bruise the underside of their chins in a fall. Generally the forward edge of the chin will sustain injury when it strikes a firm surface. A laceration may result from the impact. If a stair edge struck the undersurface of the chin, this injury could occur.

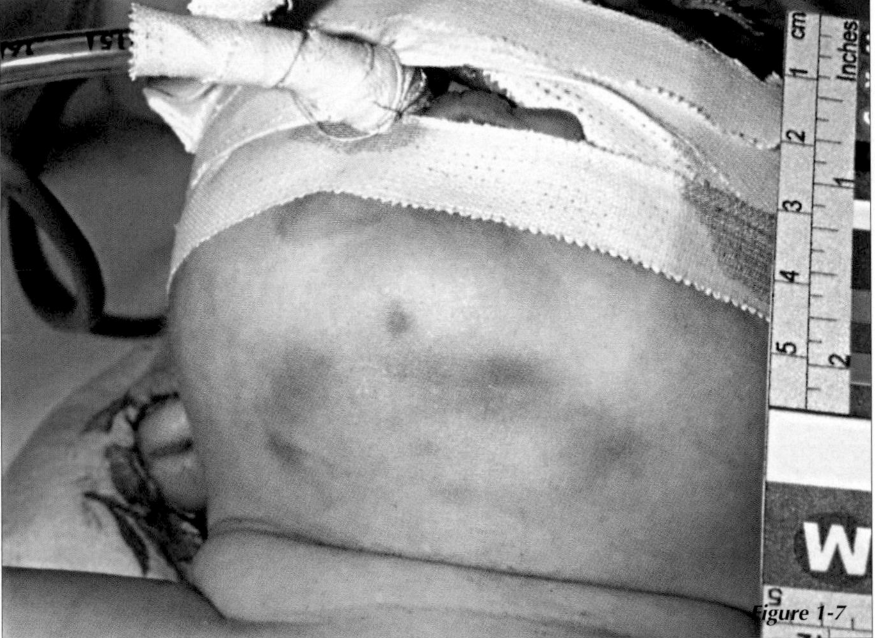


**Figure 1-7**

# Bruises

**Case Study 1-8**

Older children may escape injury from caretakers by running away. Their larger size may dissipate the force of blows. They may be able to protect delicate parts of the body, such as the face, with their arms. This adolescent was beaten by the fist and kicked with the shoes of his father.

***Figure 1-8-a.*** *Facial injuries to this child.*

***Figure 1-8-b.*** *Bruises to the back, which are unusual from falls but may occur as a result of impact from sports activities. A series of 3 marks also appearing on the back may have been effected by the underlying ribs. The linear marks could be from the edge of the shoe.*

**Case Study 1-9**

This 2-year-old girl was examined with bilateral black eyes. The history given by the caregiver was that she walked into a door. Her nose was not broken. Impact to the nose or central forehead may cause bilateral black eyes.

***Figure 1-9.*** *Bilateral black eyes, which can be seen in basal skull fractures.*

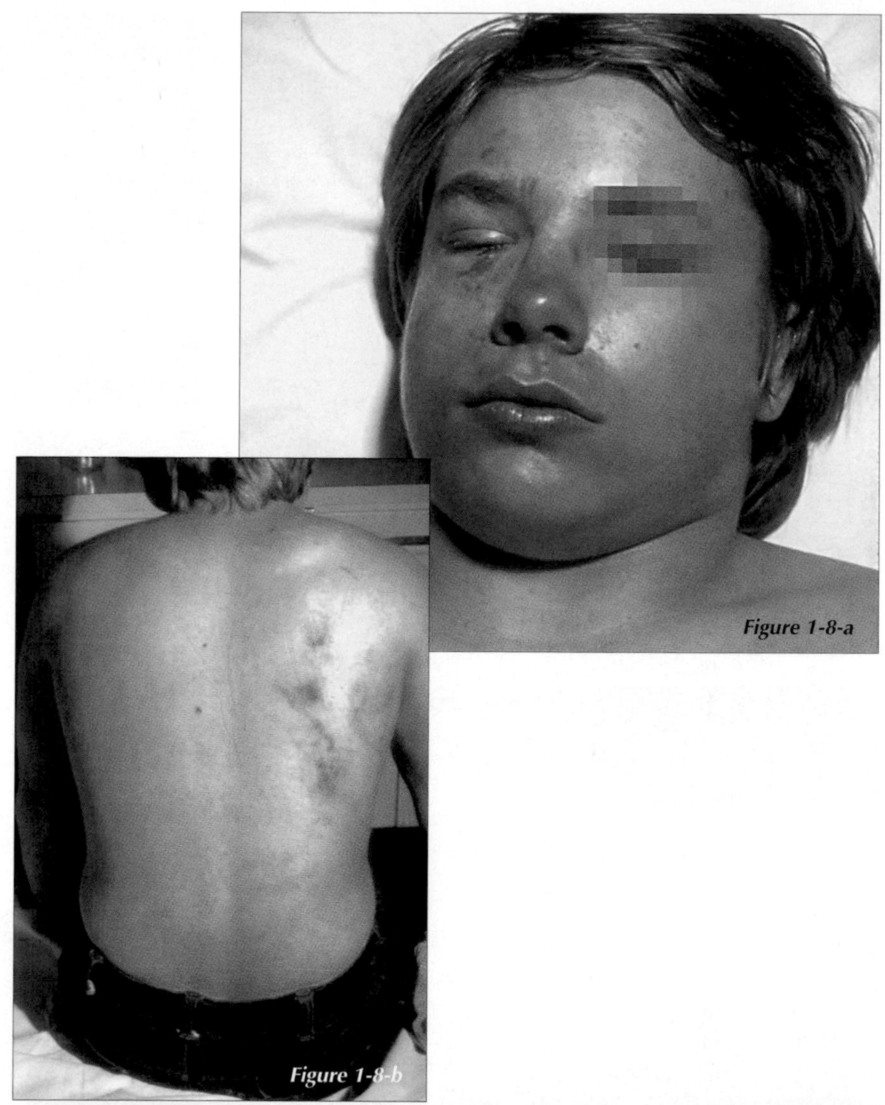

Figure 1-8-a

Figure 1-8-b

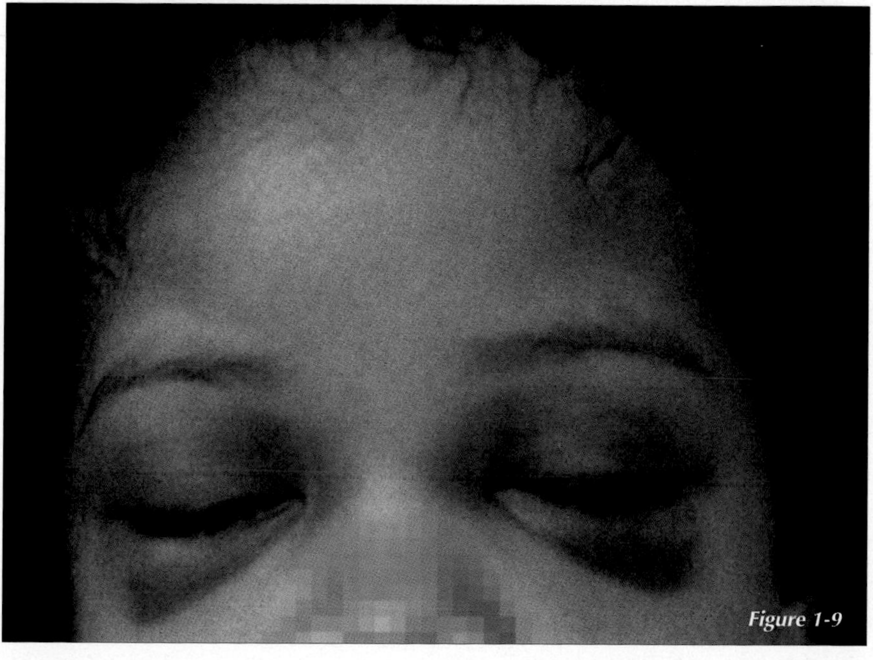

Figure 1-9

# Bruises

**Case Study 1-10**

This 4-year-old girl was brought to the ER by her father and his girlfriend, who said she was found unconscious after falling down the stairs. She had a subdural hematoma from blunt trauma to the head, retinal hemorrhages, a plenic hematoma, a liver laceration, and a contusion of the duodenum. She was also anemic.

***Figure 1-10-a.*** *The child is severely malnourished with patchy and thin hair. When the caretakers were asked how the child had lost so much hair, they said that she had a metabolic disease.*

***Figures 1-10-b, c, d,*** *and* ***e.*** *Numerous bruises, which are not fresh, on multiple surface areas.*

The girl died shortly after admission. The girlfriend was convicted of homicide. Death rarely, if ever, results from a fall down stairs.

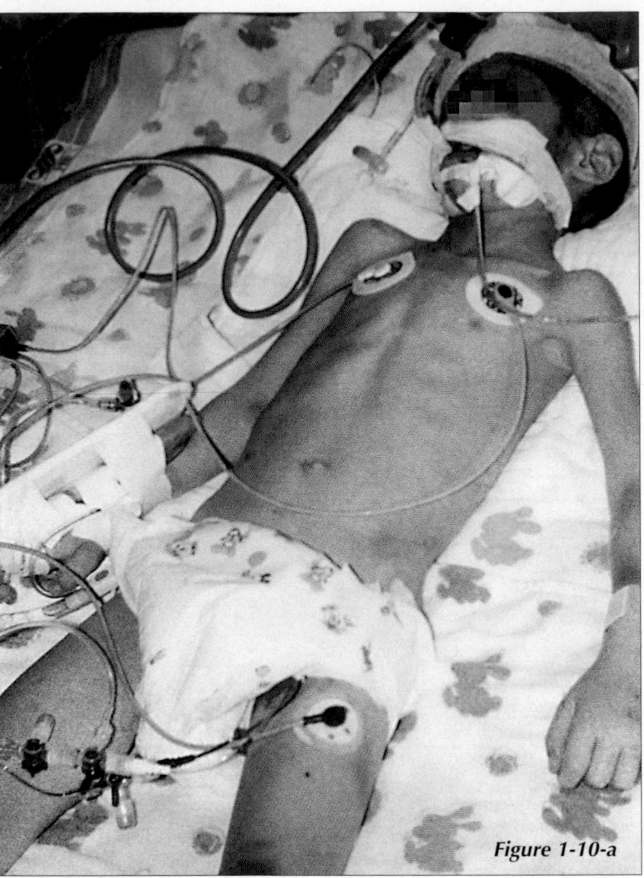

**Figure 1-10-a**

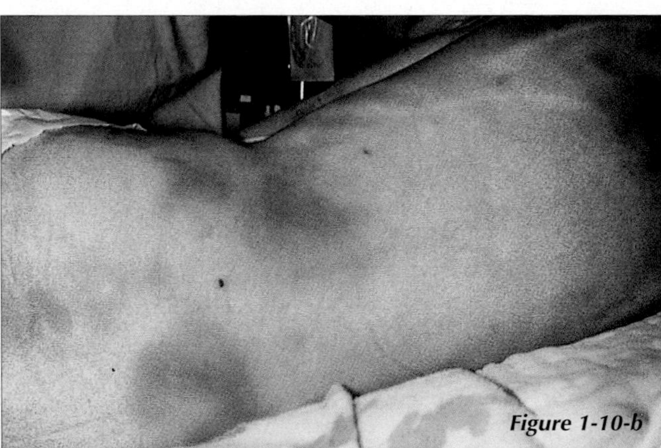

**Figure 1-10-b**

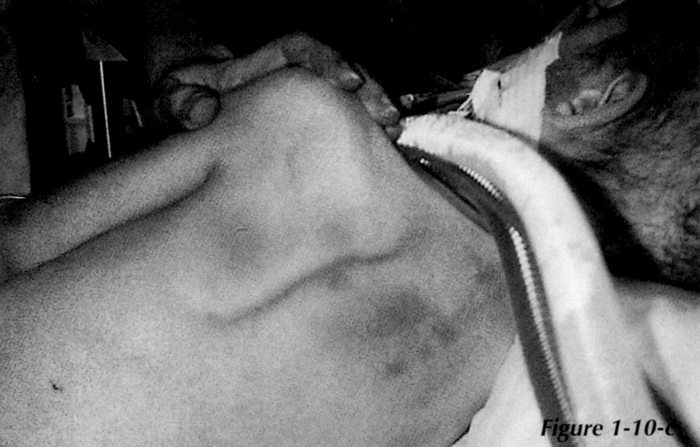

**Figure 1-10-c**

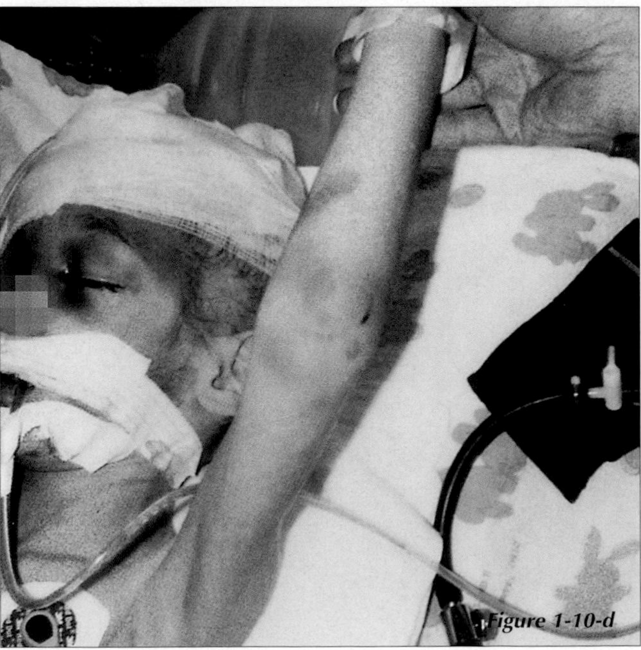

**Figure 1-10-d**

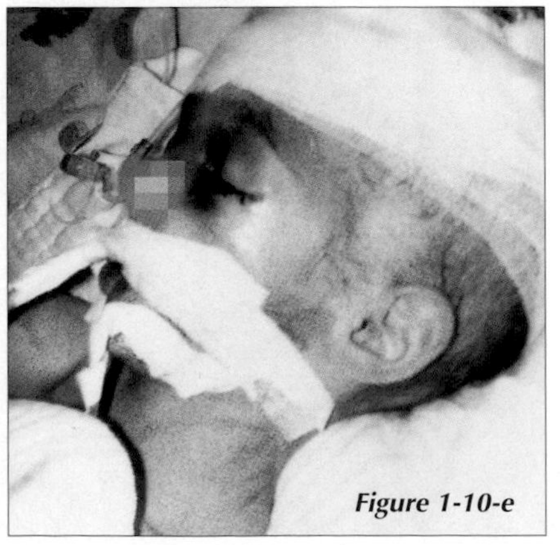

**Figure 1-10-e**

# Bruises

### Case Study 1-11

This 2-year-old boy was examined for facial bruising. When confronted, the child's father admitted to losing patience with the child and beating him. Blows to the abdomen can rupture internal organs. Abdominal trauma is the second most common manifestation of child maltreatment. Blows to the abdomen that cause internal organ damage may not result in bruising.

***Figure 1-11-a.*** *Facial bruising.*

***Figure 1-11-b.*** *A large ecchymotic area on the abdomen.*

***Figure 1-11-c.*** *An avulsed tooth.*

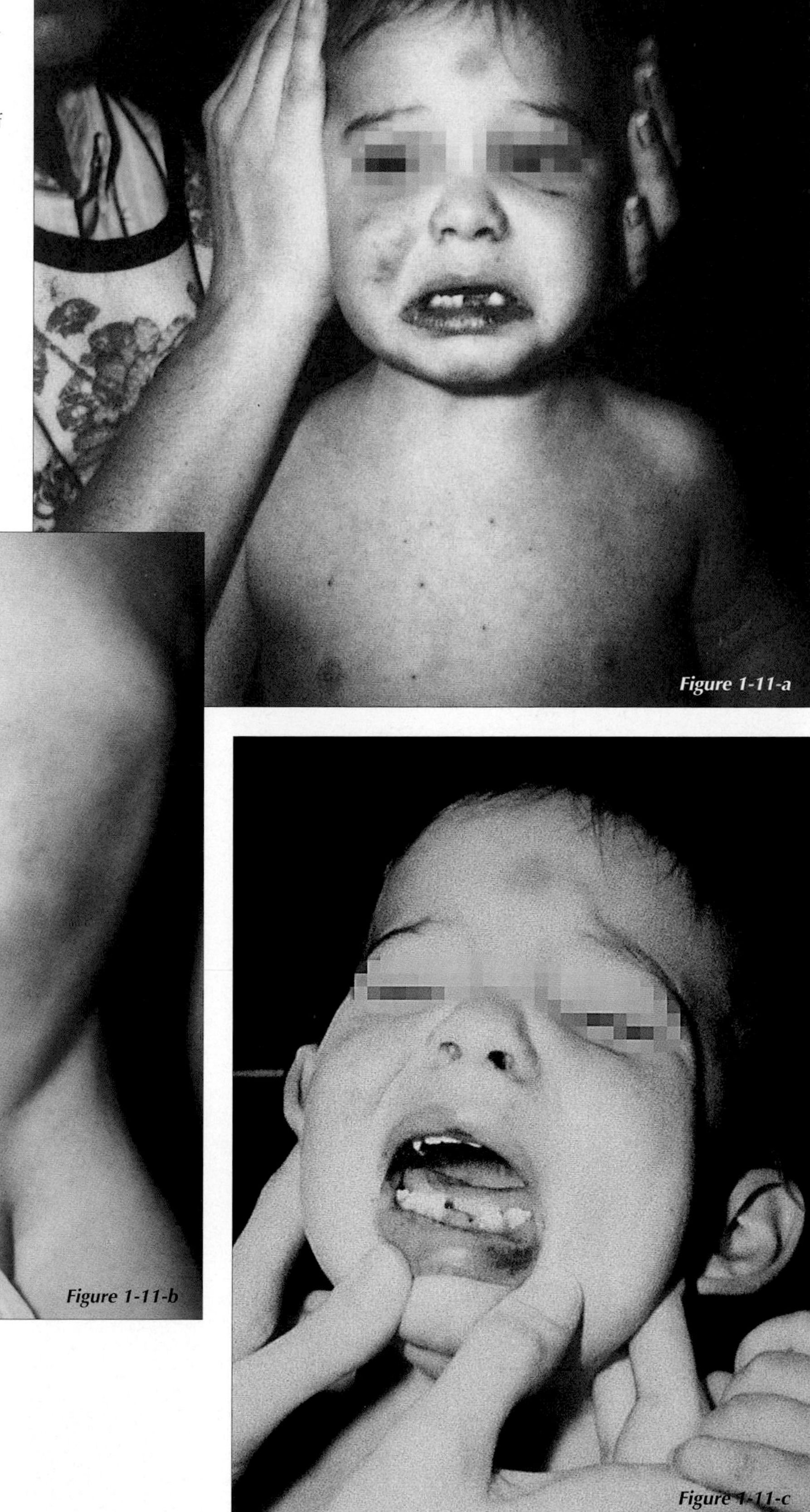

Figure 1-11-a

Figure 1-11-b

Figure 1-11-c

# Bruises

**Case Study 1-12**

This 3-year-old boy was examined with multiple bruises. The history initially given by the caregiver was that the bruises were sustained in a fall.

***Figure 1-12-a.*** *Injuries involving the lateral face.*

***Figures 1-12-b, c,*** *and* ***d.*** *Injuries seen on the genital area, which is relatively protected from accidental impact injury. Injuries to this area of the body may be due to physical or sexual abuse.*

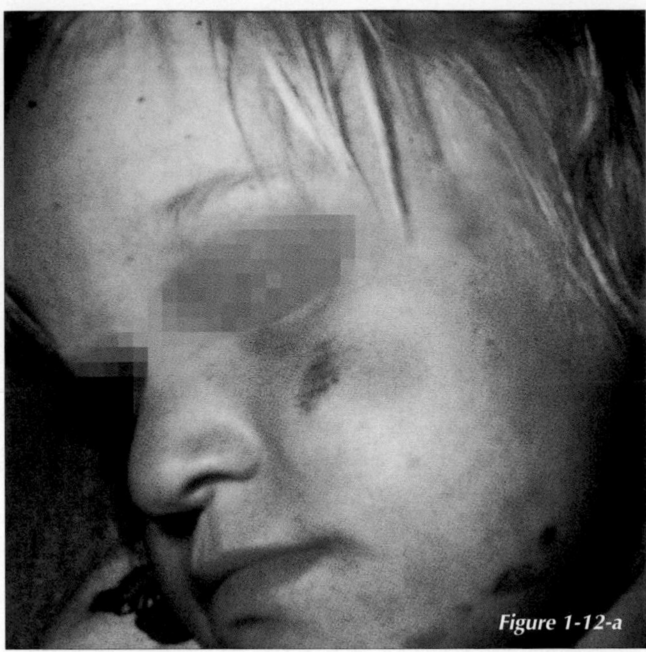

Figure 1-12-a

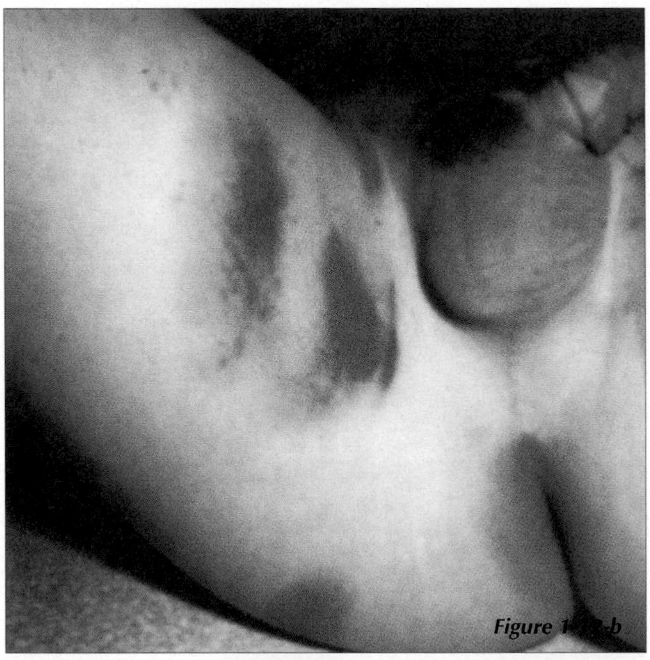

Figure 1-12-b

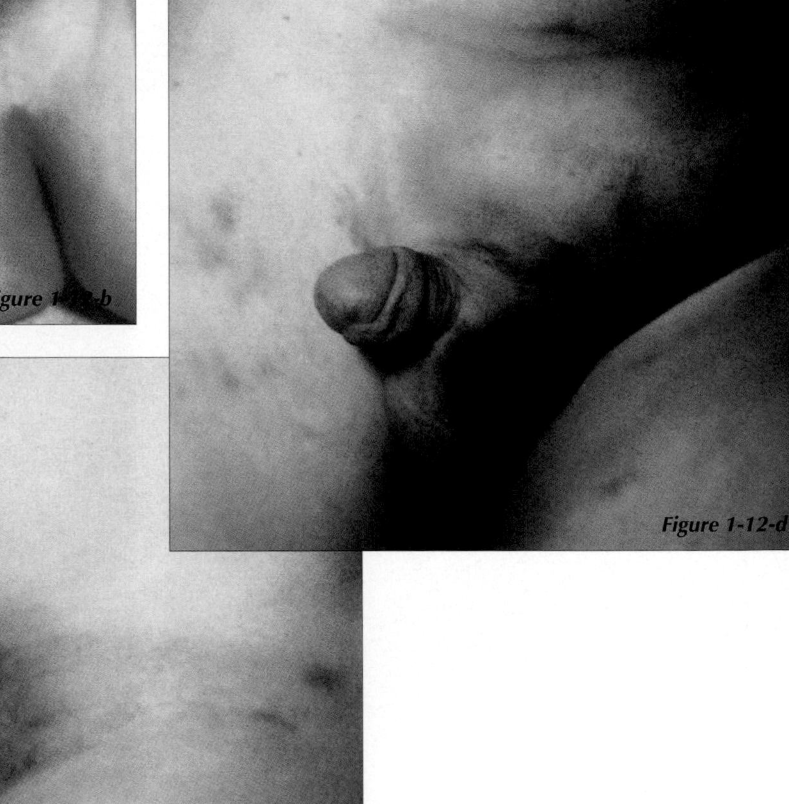

Figure 1-12-d

Figure 1-12-c

# Bruises

**Case Study 1-13**

This 9-year-old had multiple bruises in various stages of healing. She had also been sexually abused.

***Figures 1-13-a, b, c,*** *and* ***d.*** *Bruises on multiple surfaces of the skin of a 9-year-old girl.*

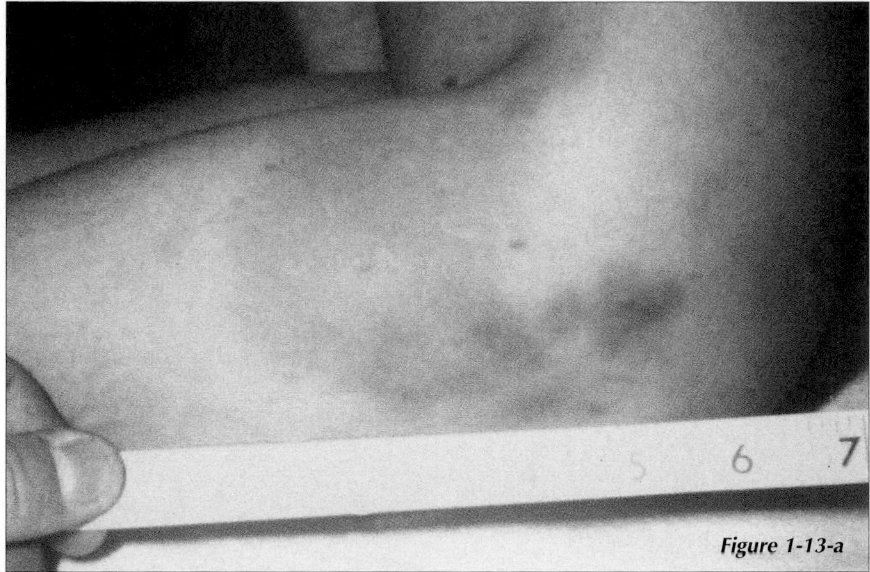

**Figure 1-13-a**

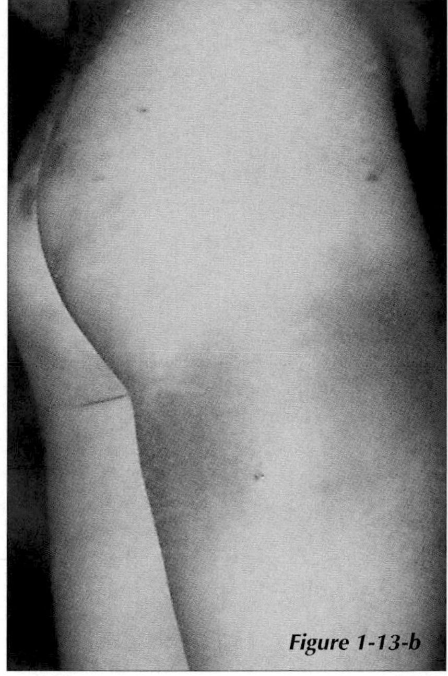

**Figure 1-13-b**

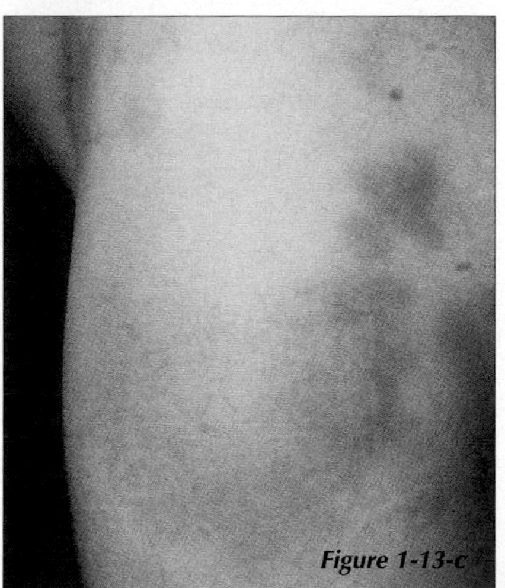

**Figure 1-13-c**

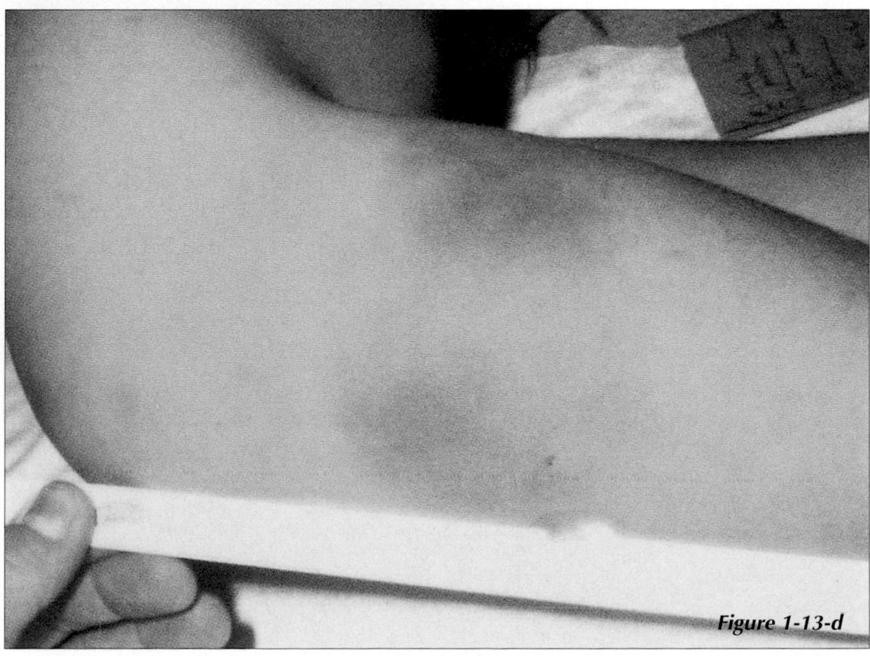

**Figure 1-13-d**

# Bruises

**Case Study 1-14**

This 4-month-old girl was seen by social services and found to have linear bruising on her neck. The mother's boyfriend admitted to picking her up by the back of her shirt and suspending her in the air until she stopped crying. (Photographs courtesy of Officer S. Krakowiecki and Investigator S. Blair.)

***Figure 1-14-a.*** *Anterior line of bruising on the neck of this infant.*

***Figure 1-14-b.*** *With a sweep upward, the bruising ends at the posterior base of the ear.*

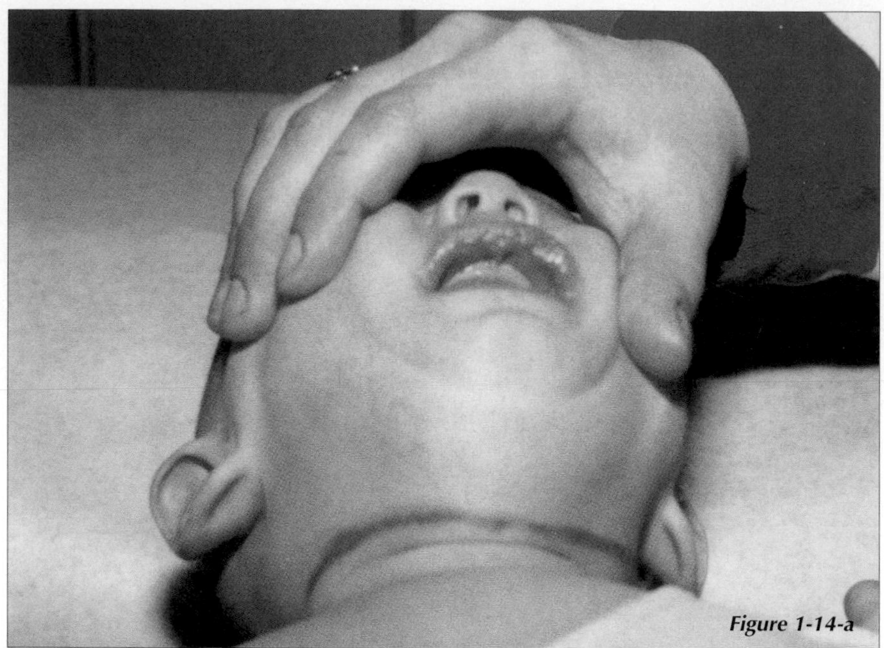

Figure 1-14-a

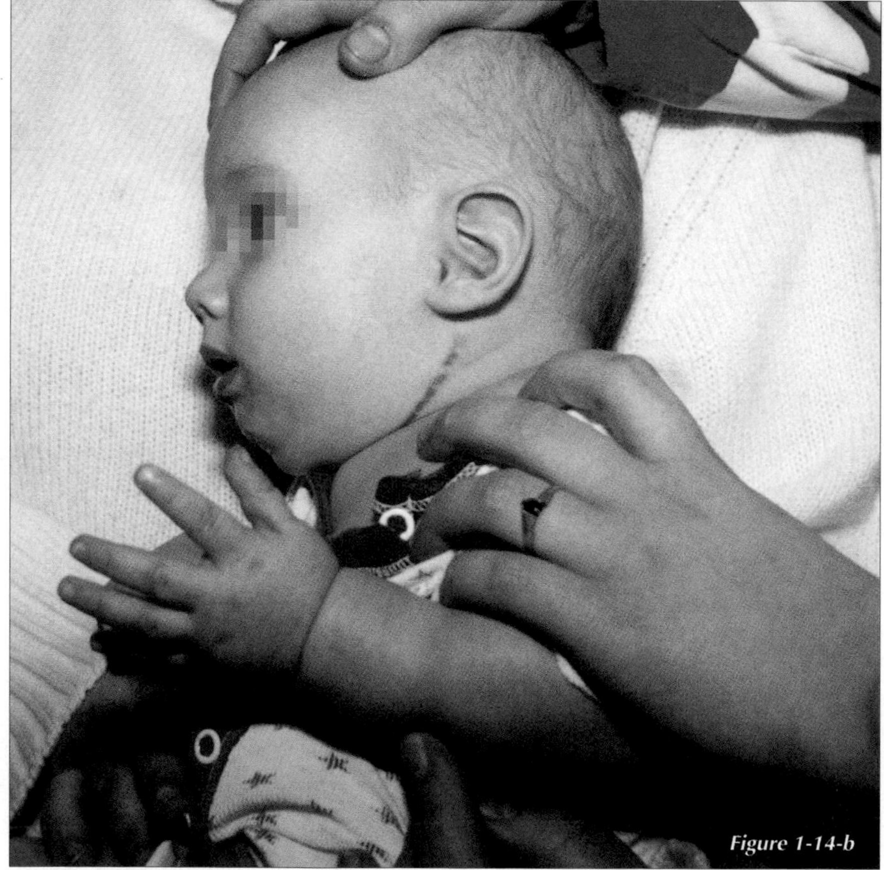

Figure 1-14-b

# Bruises

### Case Study 1-15

This 10-month-old boy was taken to the ER by his parents because he was irritable. They noted bruising of his abdomen and chest and abrasions to the side of his face. He had been left in the care of an adolescent male. The injuries to his face were done by a pick comb. Liver enzyme levels were elevated as a result of blunt trauma to the abdomen. MRI of the evaluation was needed to clarify the cause of the elevated liver enzymes. Liver lacerations may result from blows to the abdomen.

***Figure 1-15-a.*** *Bruising of the abdomen and chest.*

***Figure 1-15-b.*** *Abrasions to the side of the boy's face.*

***Figure 1-15-c.*** *Pick comb causing injuries to this boy's face.*

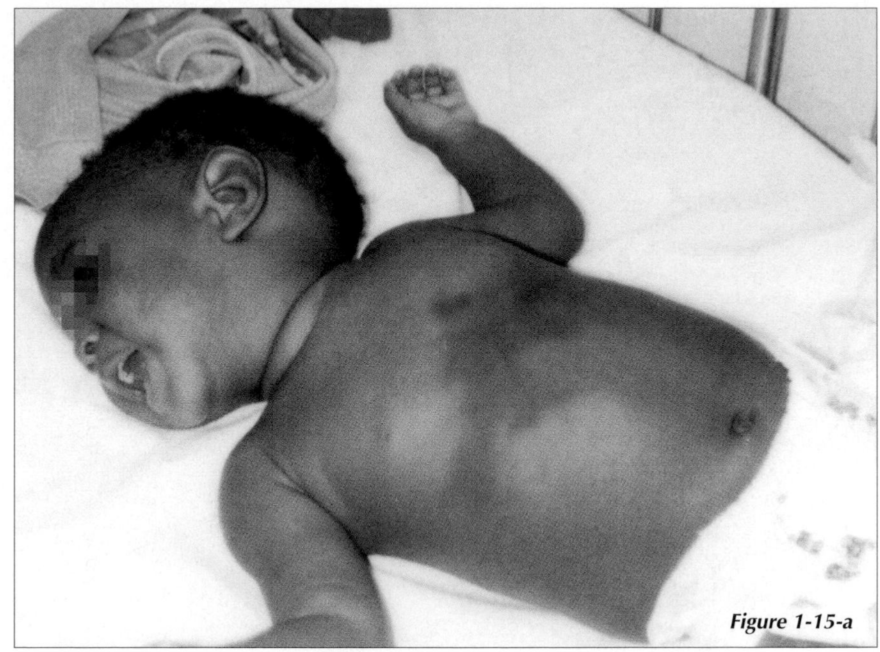

**Figure 1-15-a**

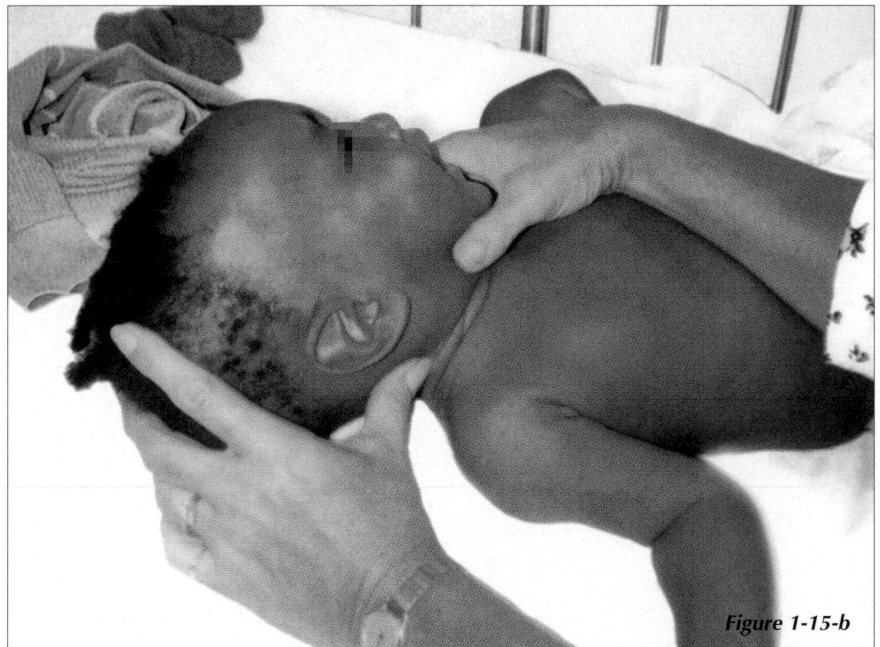

**Figure 1-15-b**

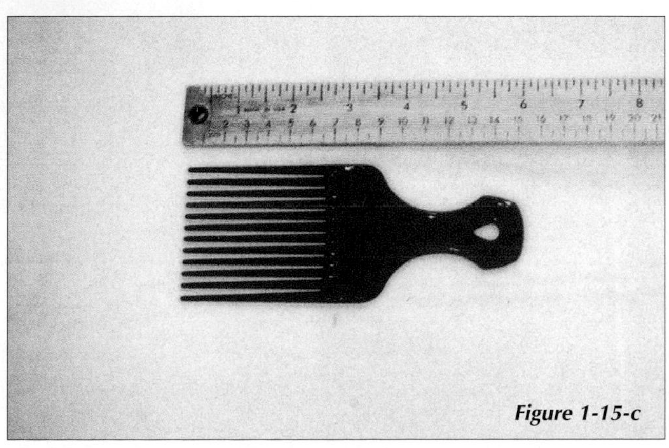

**Figure 1-15-c**

# Patterned Injuries

**Case Study 1-16**

This child had a series of marks on the buttocks. These were seen after a return from a visit with the child's mother. There were no other children in the home. The buttocks are relatively protected from injury, especially in children who are wearing diapers. It is unusual for a child to fall on the buttocks with sufficient force to cause a bruise unless the force of the fall is concentrated on a small area by an object on which the child lands. The object can be a hand, a hand-wielded object, or, more rarely, an object on which the child lands.

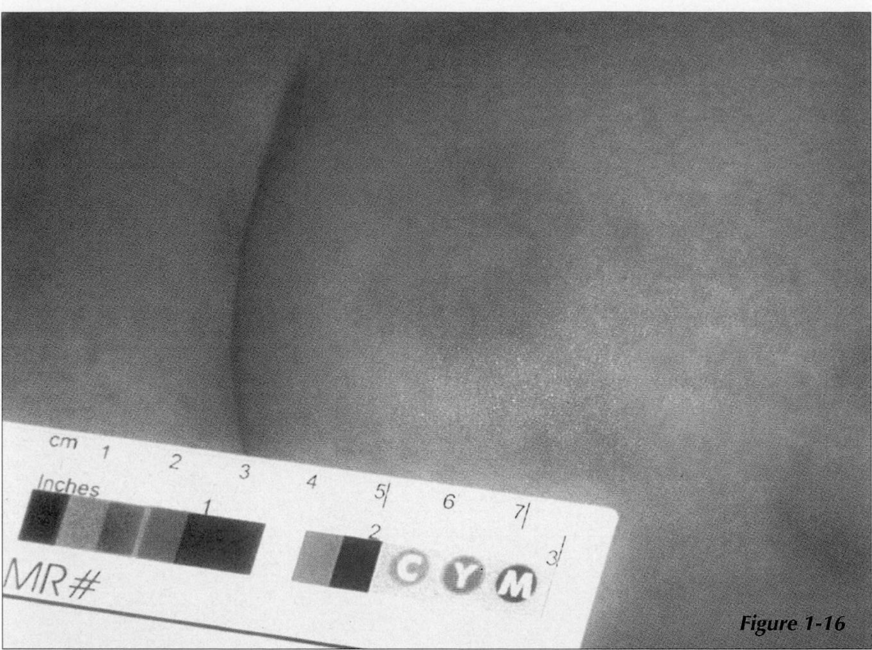


Figure 1-16

***Figure 1-16.*** *Typical C-shaped bruises composed of a series of smaller bruises made by teeth. The challenge is not so much in determining that the marks are from a bite, but rather in determining who made the mark.*

**Case Study 1-17**

This 6-month-old child's mother claimed that he had fallen against the leg of a swing. The marks were not in keeping with that history unless the swing had many closely spaced legs. At 6 months of age it is unlikely that he was pulling himself up to a standing position from which he could fall. Marks on the face other than those on the brow and chin from falling forward and impacting a hard object should raise suspicion of intentional trauma.

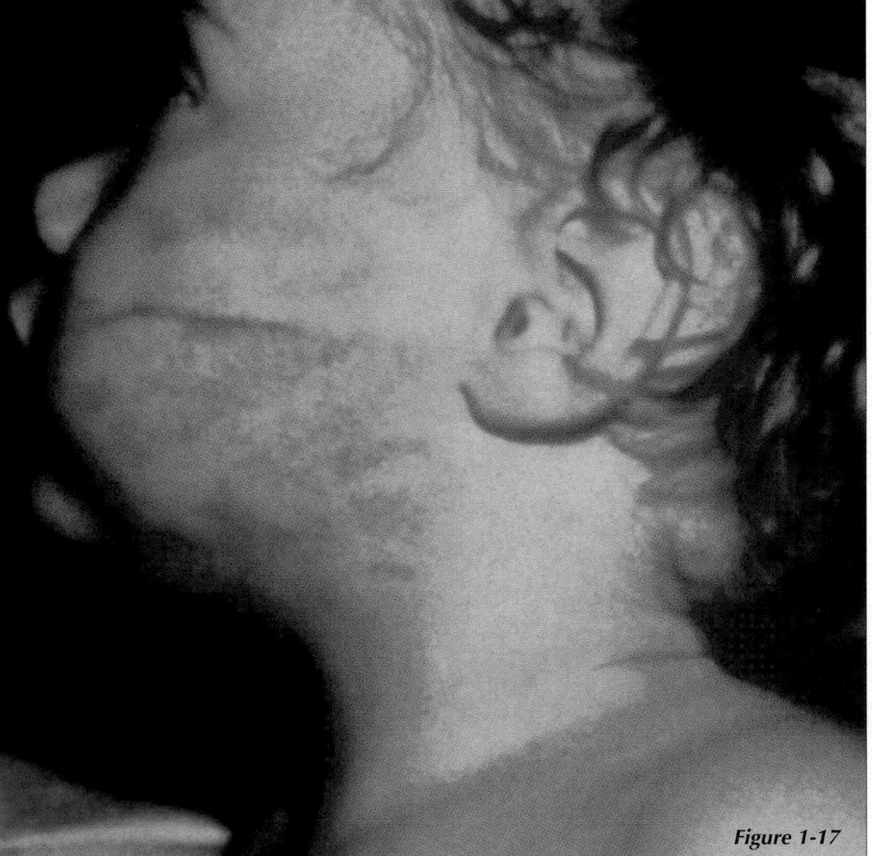

Figure 1-17

***Figure 1-17.*** *Blood coming from the left ear canal from an eardrum ruptured by impact. The markings on this child's face are typical of slap marks and medically diagnostic for child abuse. The direction of the parallel marks from the fingers indicates that the child has been struck at least 3 times.*

# Patterned Injuries

**Case Study 1-18**

This 7-year-old mentally impaired boy was brought to the ER following a bout of unconsciousness. According to his caretaker he had fallen against a wooden stair edge and became unresponsive. When EMS arrived the child was breathing and responsive. He could not be interviewed because of his developmental problems.

***Figure 1-18-a.*** *A linear mark around the anterior and lateral sides of the neck.*

***Figure 1-18-b.*** *Mark on the child's neck can be seen from the right side.*

***Figure 1-18-c.*** *A polystyrene model of a head from a wig supplier. The neck of the model has been pressed against the stair edge. The dent is colored with a marker to reveal an oval shape. The linear red mark on the model is copied from photographs of the child.*

It would be unusual for accidental impact with an object to injure 3 body surfaces. In addition, the mark did not look like what would be expected from an impact with a stair edge. Unless there was interference with respiration, the child should not have lost consciousness from impact.

It was concluded that the child was garroted with a rope because of the abrasions that surrounded the linear marks. A variety of body parts including legs, wrists, and the penis can be tied with objects. This banding may be accidental or intentional. The legs and arms may be bound during a beating or sexual abuse (**Figures 1-25-a** and **b**). The inability of the boy to communicate made it more difficult to determine if the history of the injury was in keeping with the marks seen. The ability of the older child to talk about the cause of an injury is countered by the ability to invent a history. This possibility is more likely if the child is old enough to realize the consequences that may arise from an untruth.

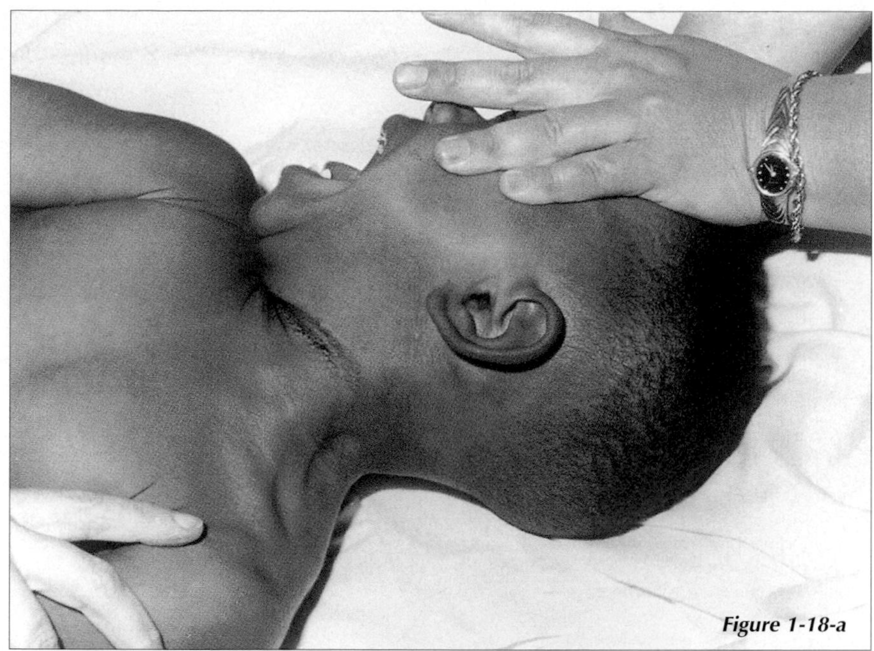

*Figure 1-18-a*

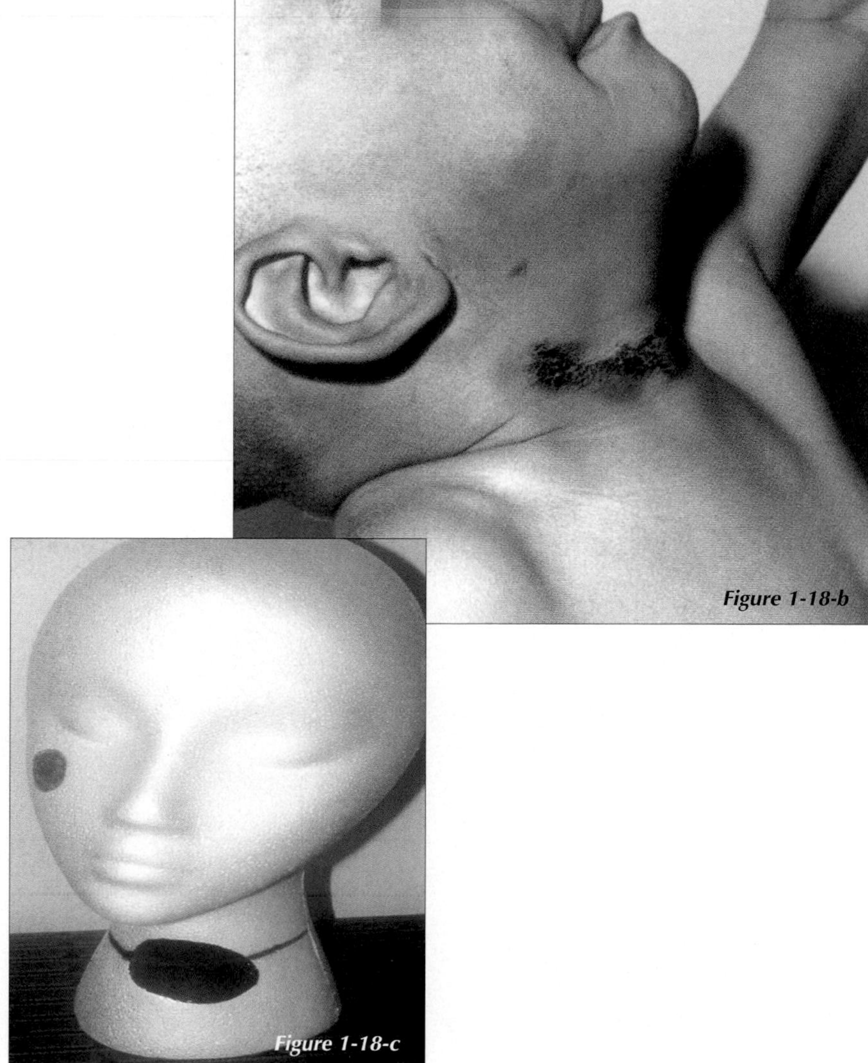

*Figure 1-18-b*

*Figure 1-18-c*

# Patterned Injuries

**Case Study 1-19**

This 7-year-old boy's teacher noted a parallel red mark on the boy's right hand and reported him to the school nurse. The boy said that he was hit by his father with a belt.

***Figure 1-19.*** *Three other marks on his left thigh found by the school nurse. The marks are in keeping with the history.*

A mark on the left thigh was found to be a continuation of the thigh mark when the leg was flexed. This indicated that he was in a crouched position while being beaten.

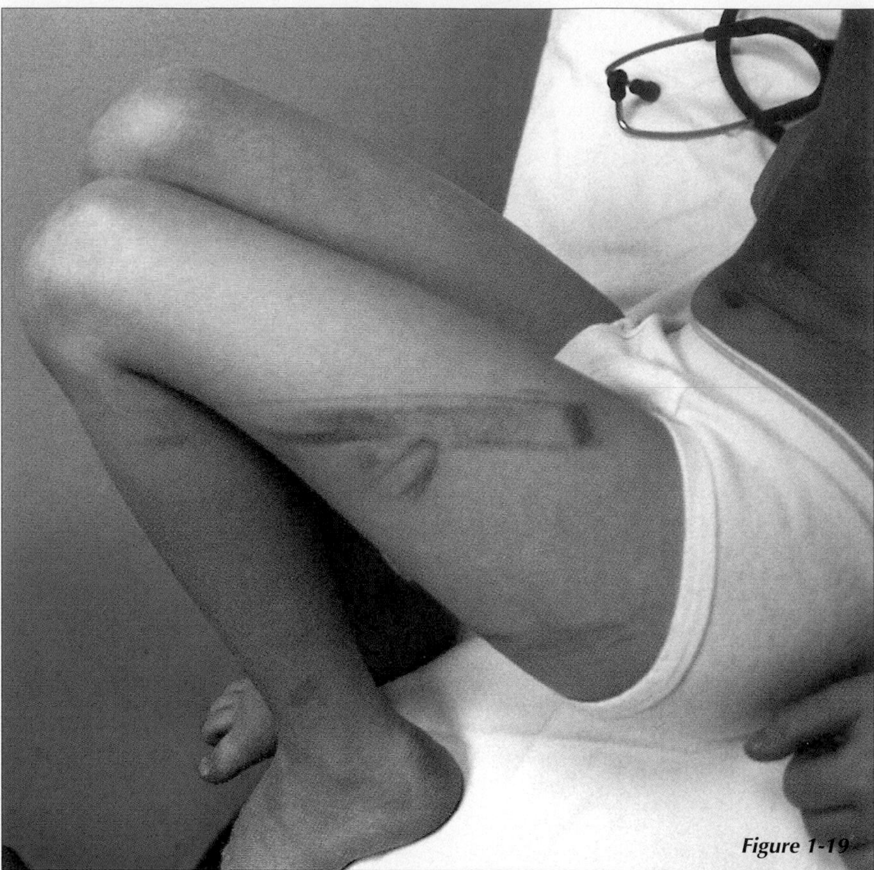

Figure 1-19

**Case Study 1-20**

This moderately emotionally disturbed and cognitively impaired young adult was examined for patterned injuries to his chest. A photo of the man's chest was taken, processed by a digital copier, and sent to a child abuse program for consultation. Although deaf, the man was verbal and able to write with limited proficiency. Law enforcement personnel interviewed him and he said that he was hit with a belt and kicked by a staff member at his sheltered workshop. There were no witnesses to speak on his behalf, and a search of the premises failed to find a weapon with the pattern of the marks. Staff members denied injuring the man. His credibility was challenged because of his cognitive disability. He had no previous history of self-injurious behavior.

***Figure 1-20.*** *The marks are compatible with those that would result from the impact of a hard, geometrically shaped object. There are 5 separate impact marks, which appear to be triangular in shape. It is possible that the overlapping marks to the left of the nipple came from different directions.*

It is interesting that the object used to injure the patient was not found. It is unlikely that this adult was sophisticated enough to injure himself and consequently create a story blaming others. It is not unusual for agencies to consult child abuse experts about unusual marks in adults who are cognitively disabled. These individuals are at increased risk for being abused.

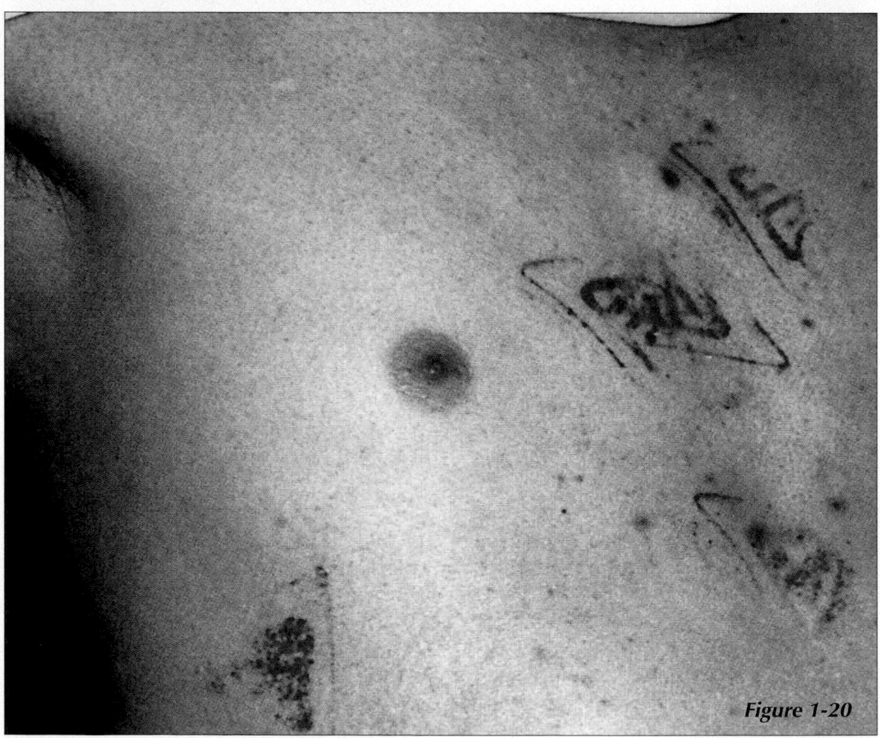

Figure 1-20

## PATTERNED INJURIES

**Case Study 1-21**

This 5-year-old boy was examined with approximately 50 marks scattered on most parts of the body except for the back and face. He told a caseworker that the marks resulted from being pinched by a caretaker. The caretaker stated that the marks were self-induced. The child was not seen, but instead, 20 photographs were reviewed.

***Figure 1-21-a.*** *Purple-brown irregular shaped bruises on the arms, 2 linear red marks on the chest, and a red mark on the chin. Two of the marks on the left arm have the linear appearance of pinch marks.*

***Figure 1-21-b.*** *Bruises are also seen on the thighs. Marks on the lateral left thigh and inner right thigh have an excoriated mark in their centers.*

***Figure 1-21-c.*** *The marks on the posterior rear left thigh are thickened or lichenified. Marks are not seen on the back.*

The marks varied in shape from round and oval to irregular. They were not geometric in shape and the child could reach all of the marks. The cause of the marks was unclear. It is possible that there were marks from eczema on the thighs, pinch marks on the arms, and marks from a blunt object such as finger tips on the lateral upper left thigh. The child's statements had to be relied upon to protect the child. Observation in a controlled environment and a dermatology consultation would clarify the cause. The astute observer will note that the child has abnormalities of the external ears. He has hearing problems, mild developmental delay, and speech problems. A review of the photographs is not as satisfactory as an examination of the child.

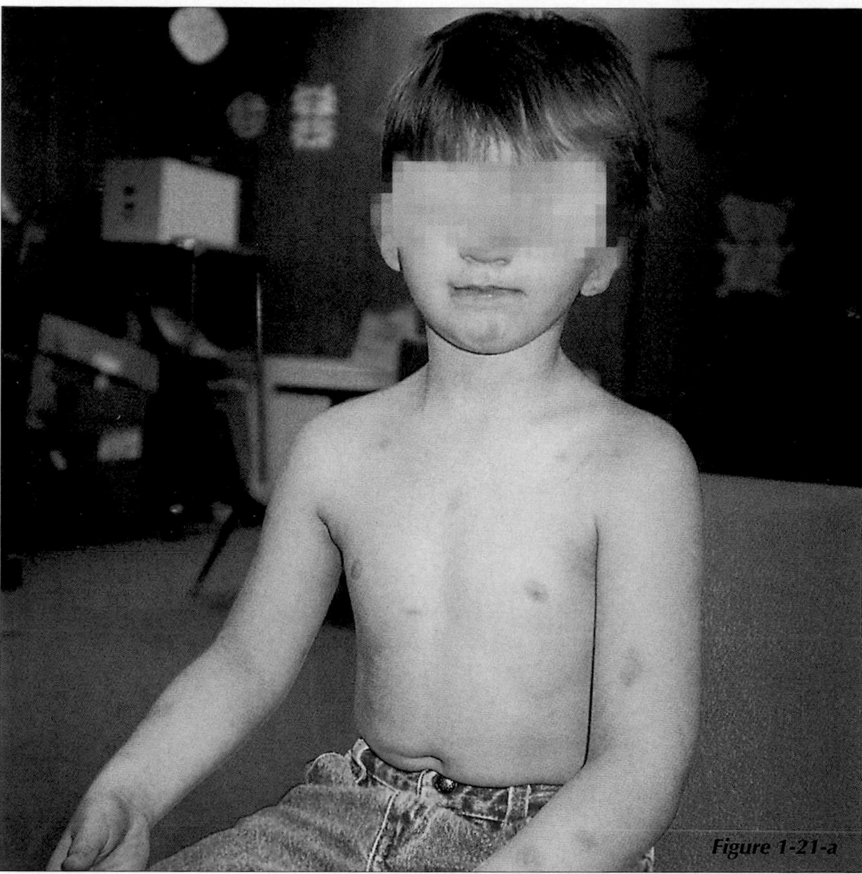
Figure 1-21-a

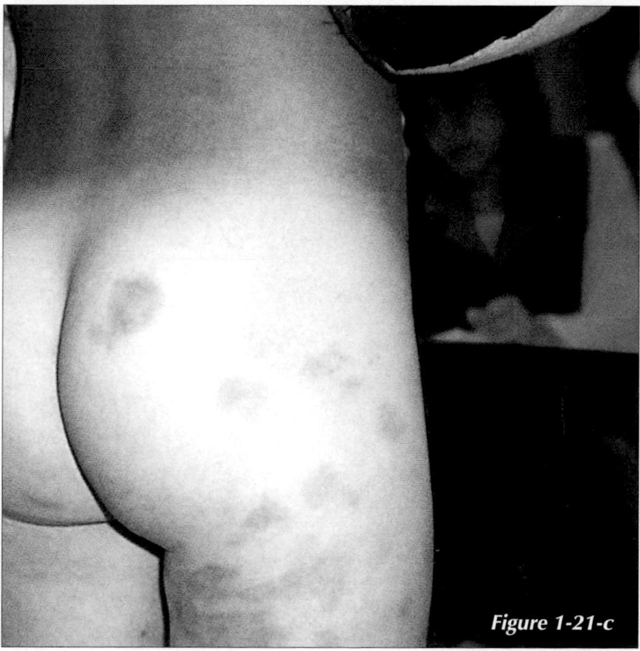
Figure 1-21-c

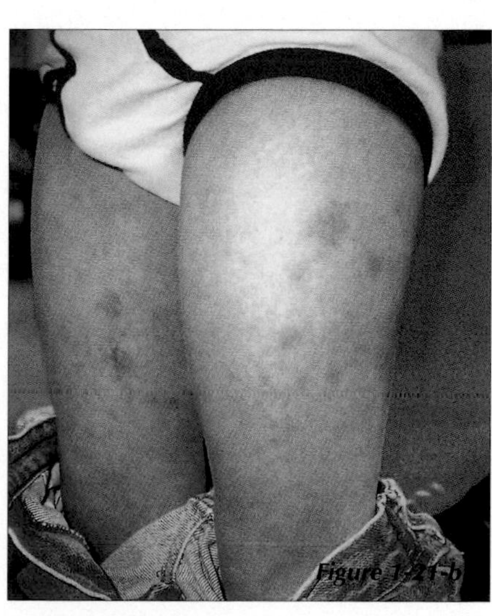
Figure 1-21-b

## Patterned Injuries

**Case Study 1-22**

This child's teacher noted that he had a loop mark on his left hand. He also had difficulty sitting.

***Figure 1-22-a.*** *Loop mark found on the child's hand.*

***Figure 1-22-b.*** *Linear and looped marks and lacerations on the child's arms, back, buttocks, and thighs found when the child was examined without his clothes. The skin was denuded from his left buttock and thigh and had the appearance of second- or third-degree burns.*

The boy was placed on antibiotics for what was perceived to be an infection complicating the skin lacerations resulting from a beating with a looped cord. The denuded areas of his skin required grafting. At first he was unable to be interviewed because he was obtunded by pain relief medication. Later he stated that he had been beaten with a cord. The parents treated the burn with peroxide as they delayed seeking medical attention for several weeks. This may have accounted for the fact that cultures came back without pathogen growth. This was not reported as child abuse; it was reported as torture. This term has legal significance relative to charges that can be filed and the consequences of a conviction. This child will have significant scarring of his skin and psyche from the beating.

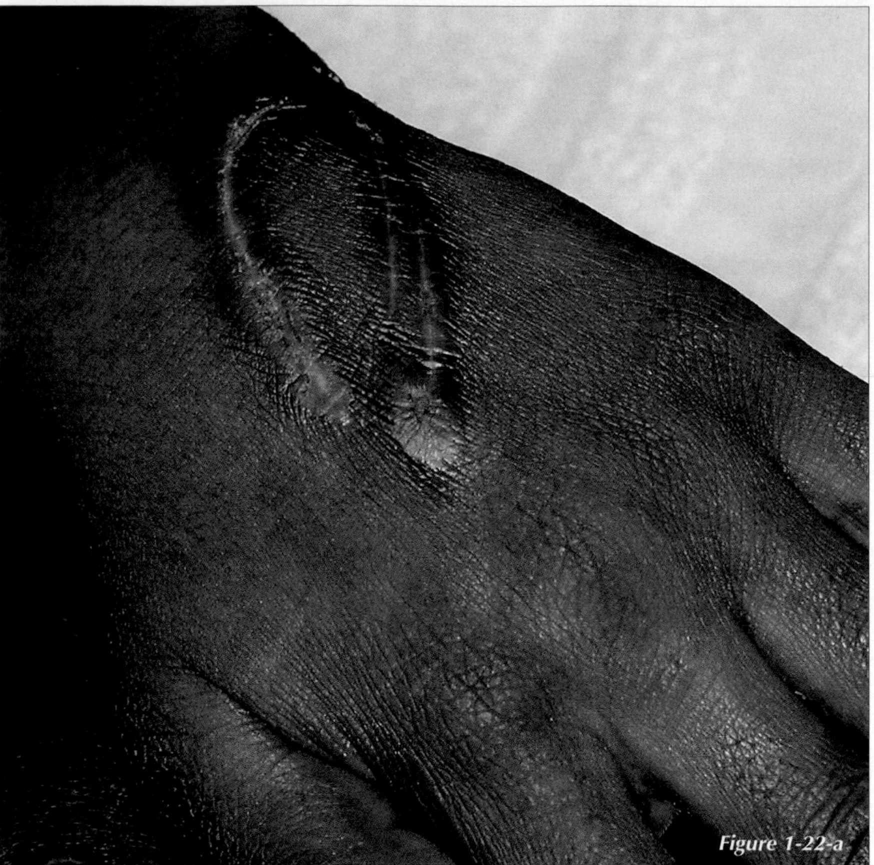

Figure 1-22-a

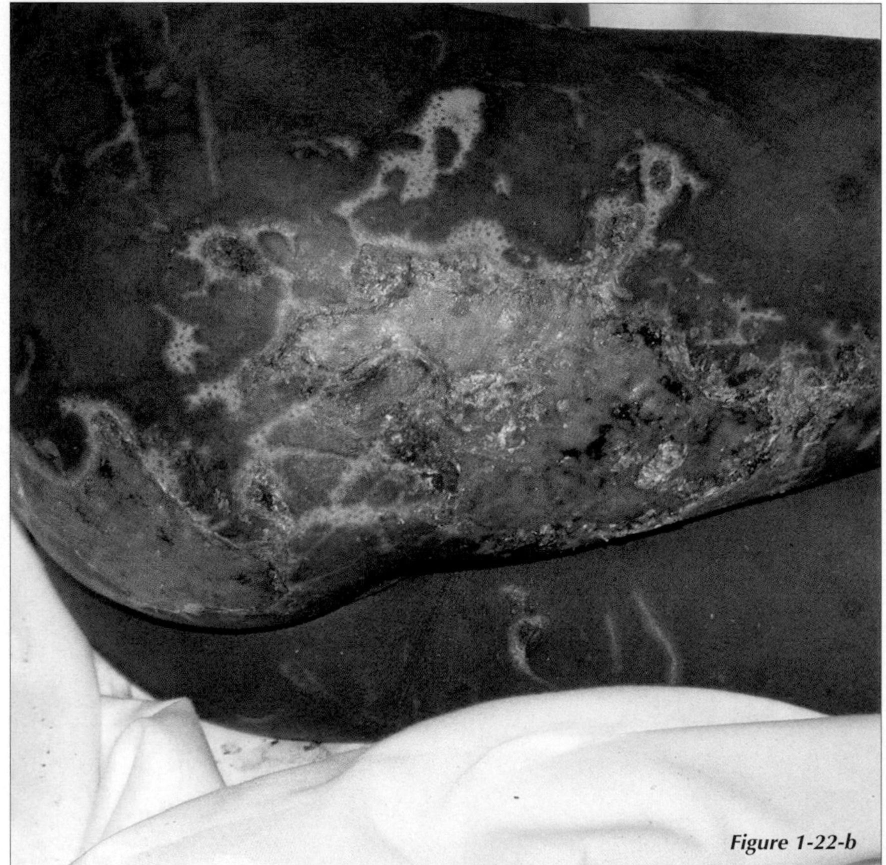

Figure 1-22-b

# Patterned Injuries

**Case Study 1-23**

Not all adolescents are able to escape physical abuse. This teenage girl was struck on several different occasions with a looped cord.

While a paddle or belt may leave linear marks if only the edge of the object strikes the child, it is possible that the child's movements to escape resulted in marks in different directions. Caretakers may state that the marks were caused by a fall from a bicycle or playground equipment.

***Figure 1-23-a.*** *Linear marks in many directions on the back of this girl.*

***Figure 1-23-b.*** *There is an eschar from a loop impact on the right cheek. Although the cord narrowly missed her eye, there is a laceration of the lower lid.*

**Case Study 1-24**

It is unusual for curved marks to appear on children's skin as the result of falling onto an object, unless the object is curved. The shape of the mark should match the shape of the object.

***Figure 1-24-a.*** *A narrow, 2–3 mm wide curved eschar on the left shoulder of a child who was struck with a belt. The belt curved about the shoulder.*

***Figure 1-24-b.*** *A J-shaped mark on this child's cheek. This was caused by the edges of one side of the end of a belt.*

***Figure 1-24-c.*** *A narrow C-shaped eschar caused by the end of the belt lacerating the skin.*

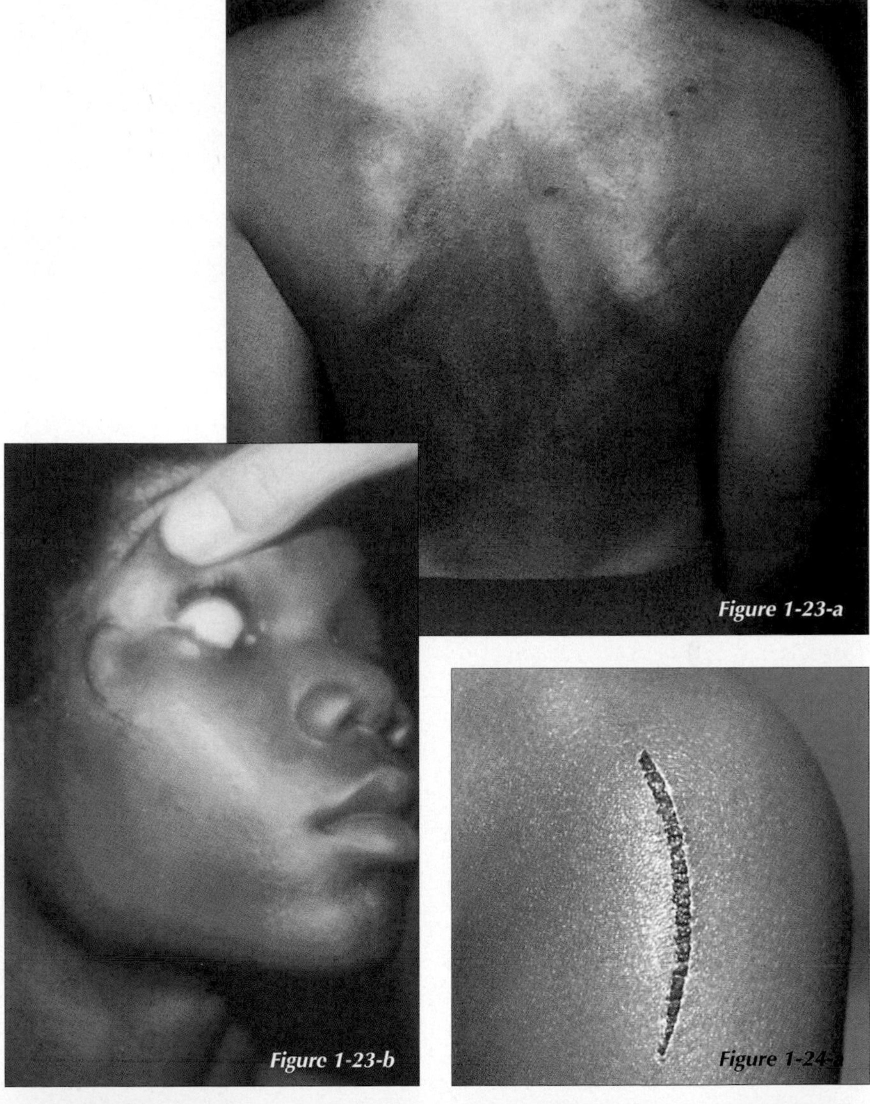

Figure 1-23-a

Figure 1-23-b

Figure 1-24-a

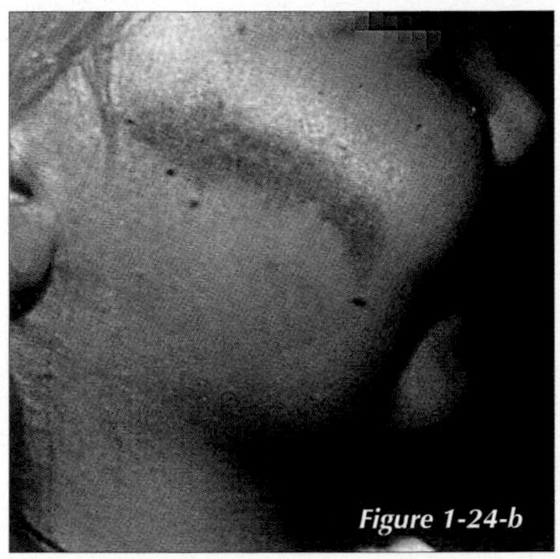

Figure 1-24-b

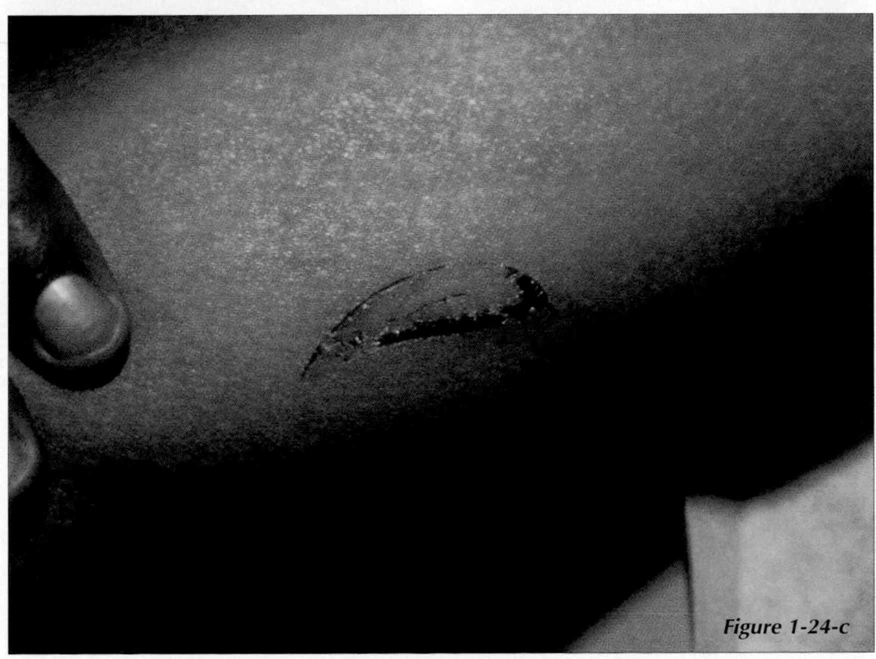

Figure 1-24-c

# Patterned Injuries

**Case Study 1-25**

Intentional injuries are most likely to be caused by the hand or by common objects wielded by hand. Banding is an unusual form of intentional injury and must be distinguished from accidental banding or banding that has taken place in utero. Toes may become wrapped in loose threads from socks or booties. It is important to examine the object that binds an appendage in determining whether or not the case is suspicious for abuse.

***Figure 1-25-a.*** *The object binding the base of the middle 3 toes of this 14-week-old infant was found to be the mother's hair. This raises suspicions of intentional injury.*

***Figure 1-25-b.*** *The wrists and ankles of this 13-year-old girl were bound while she was beaten. The narrow mark that encircles the wrist is denuded. Larger ropes may cause a "braided" band.*

***Figure 1-25-c.*** *The marks on the arms of this 5-month-old child were determined to have been caused by an allergic reaction to the rubber of the bands in the sleeves of her clothing.*

***Figure 1-25-d.*** *This child was referred for evaluation of a band encircling the ankle and a bruise, which is seen immediately distal to the band. The elastic in the child's sock had caused the band and the bruise was a mongolian spot.*

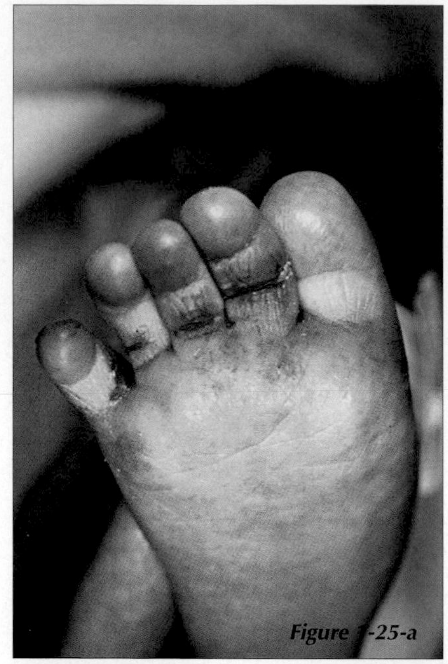

***Figure 1-25-a***

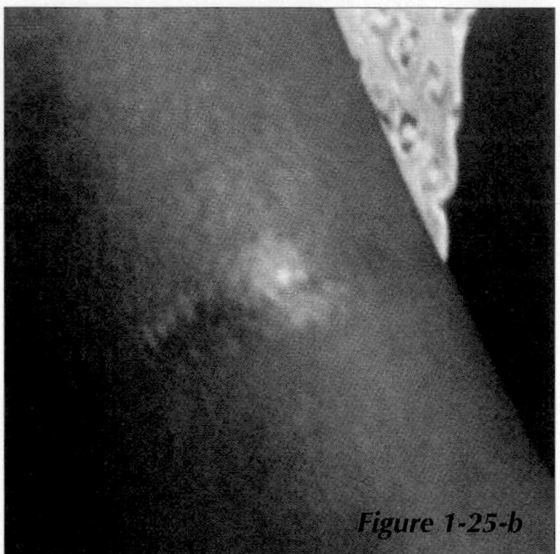

***Figure 1-25-b***

***Figure 1-25-c***

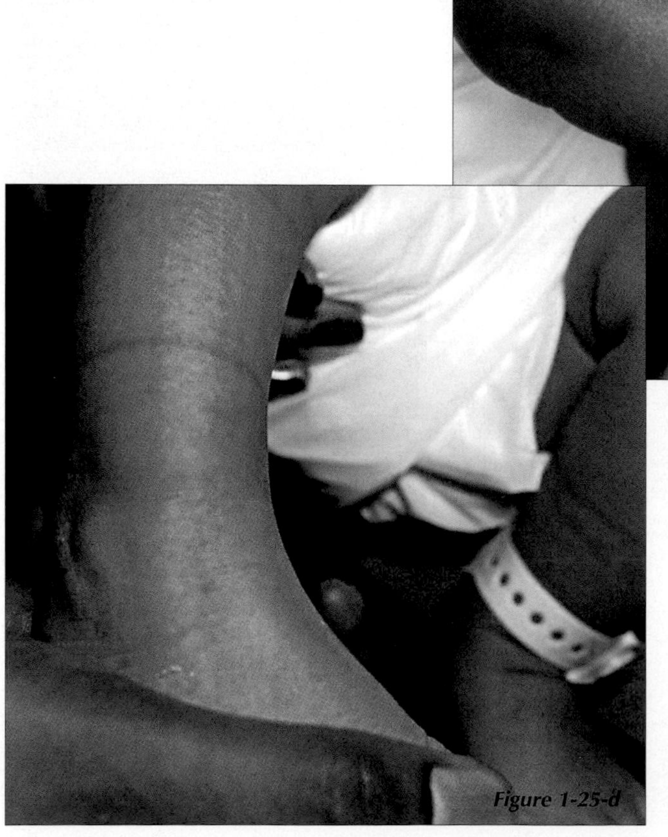

***Figure 1-25-d***

## Patterned Injuries

### Case Study 1-26

The arms may be struck intentionally with a variety of objects. In the process of beating a child, the object may wrap around the child being struck from behind and injure anterior surfaces. A child's arms may be held while a beating or shaking takes place. Although investigation of the geometric mark left on the skin by the object often leads to discovery of the causative object, it cannot determine if the child hit the object or the object hit the child. The location of the mark and the object causing the mark should be considered in raising suspicion of intentional injury.

This child experienced traumas to the right arm. Stating that the child has been burned or has experienced an impact should be avoided before carefully describing the injury. In this case, the pattern of injury identifies the causative object.

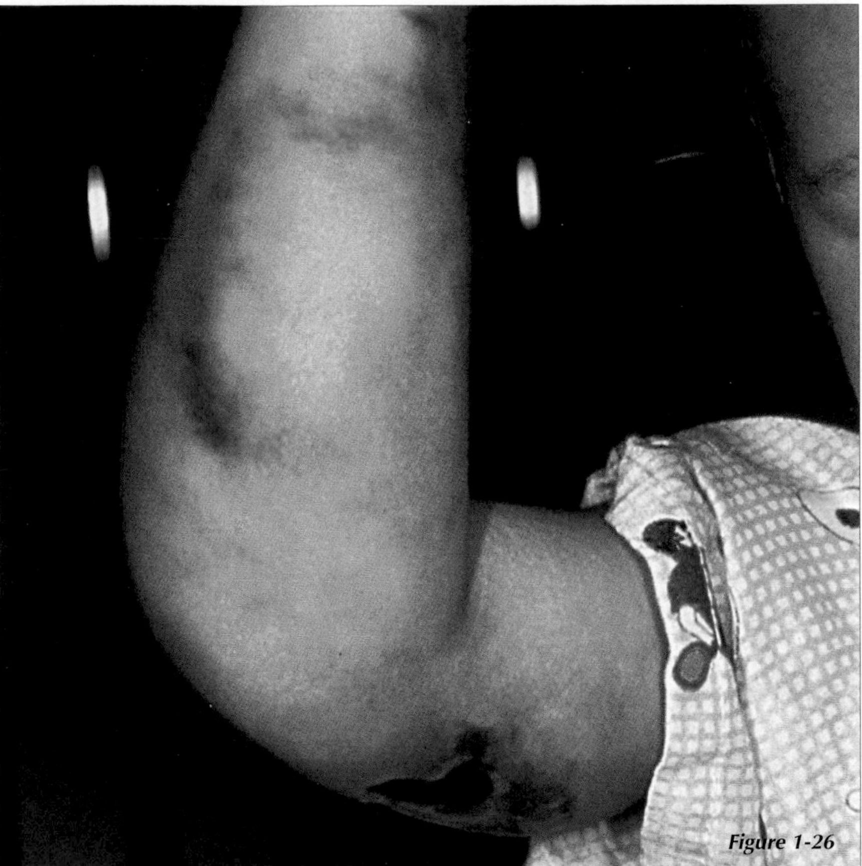

Figure 1-26

***Figure 1-26.*** *There is a backward C-shaped ring of erythema on the swollen forearm. There is an area of black eschar under the arm.*

The child had not been burned or experienced impact. The arm was caught in the wringer of an old washing machine. The wringers crushed the forearm and then eroded the tissue under the arm. It would be unusual for this to be an intentional injury; rather, it was mostly likely the result of safety neglect.

### Case Study 1-27

Children may suffer a variety of intentional traumas to the skin. The instruments used to injure the skin may vary with accessibility and culture. In Germany a wooden spoon is a common tool of intentional injury. In Israel children may be pinched. The head is a common target for parental anger and frustration and the child's hair may become a target as well.

Child hair loss may result from children pulling out their own hair, as in trichotillomania, or rubbing it out as may be seen in the case of neglected children. The practice of placing children on their back as a sleeping position to prevent SIDS also may result in thinning of hair over the occiput.

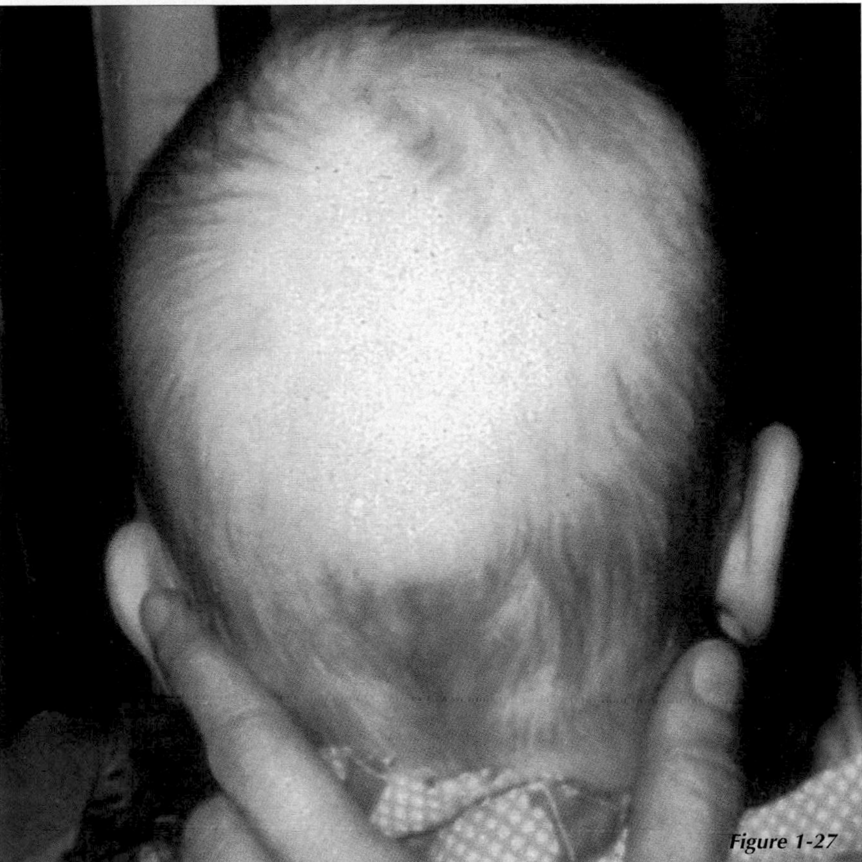

Figure 1-27

***Figure 1-27.*** *The caretaker in this case admitted to pulling the child's hair.*

# Patterned Injuries

**Case Study 1-28**

The skin has a limited number of responses to trauma. Erythema may result from impact, infection, or contact with a caustic or hot object.

This child, according to the siblings, was held by the father on a metal heating vent in the floor to teach the child that the vent was hot. Multiple directions of the marks suggest 3 different contacts with the hot grid.

***Figure 1-28.*** *A series of linear marks on the back and side of this infant that are similar to those that could result from being struck with a straight cord or thin stick (cane). The geometric pattern of the marks suggests contact with a hot linear object.*

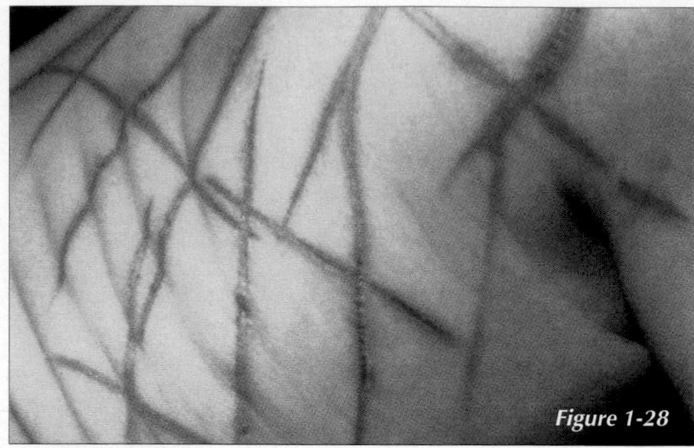

Figure 1-28

**Case Study 1-29**

This child was examined with a 1-cm linear scar on the forearm. The caretaker claimed that the child did this to himself.

***Figure 1-29.*** *Note that the child's fingernails are bitten or trimmed short. The mark is longer than would be expected from the size of the child's nails. Marks from nails may have a very slight curve and are easier to recognize when they are in a series.*

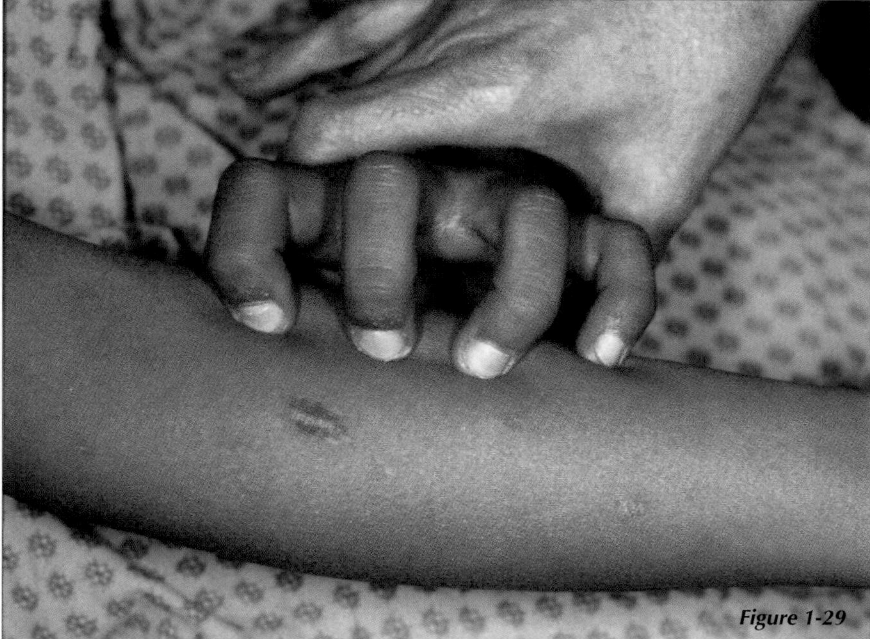

Figure 1-29

**Case Study 1-30**

This 3-year-old boy was seen in the ER. According to the father the child fell from a high chair and became unconscious. Suspicion about the credibility of the father's history should have been raised due to by the typical consequences of a fall from a high chair fall. Unconsciousness after such a fall would be unusual.

***Figure 1-30.*** *Injuries on 2 body surfaces; erythema to the helix of the left ear, a laceration to the left side of the nose, and a mark on the mid neck. Careful inspection of the child reveals patches of red dots in front of the left ear and on the left cheek. Red "dots" may be petechiae; however, these dots are in a geometric pattern.*

It was suspected that the child was struck with a hairbrush or similar object that would leave the 1-mm dots in a geometric array. The mark on the ear came from impact with an object that did not leave a pattern. The left ear could have been "boxed" with an open hand. The eardrum should have been examined to determine if the blow had injured it. Inspection of the home revealed a pair of slippers belonging to the father that had a matching pattern on the soles.

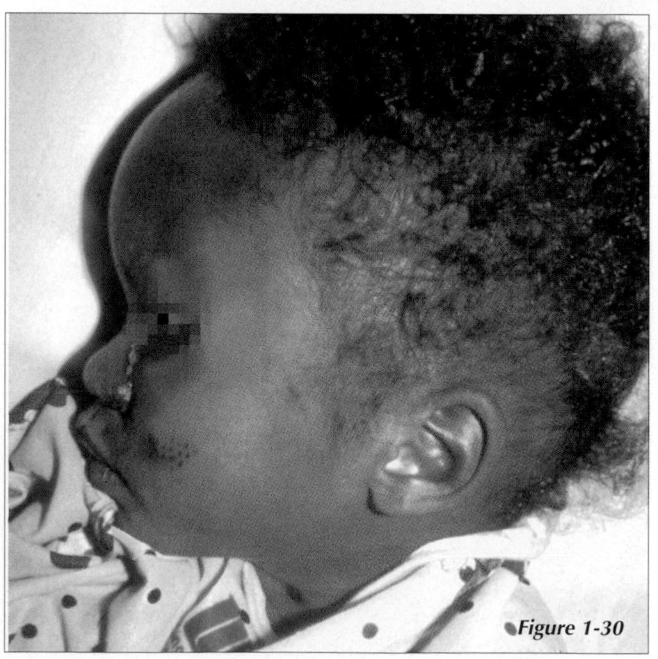

Figure 1-30

## Patterned Injuries

**Case study 1-31**

In an examination for the Department of Family Services, this 4-month-old child was noted to have multiple pinch marks on his back and arms. Pinch marks may look like butterfly-shaped bruises. In some countries pinching is a common form of "discipline."

***Figures 1-31-a** and **b**. These pinch marks consist of 2 centrally placed, narrow, vertical reddish clusters of petechiae surrounded by contusion.*

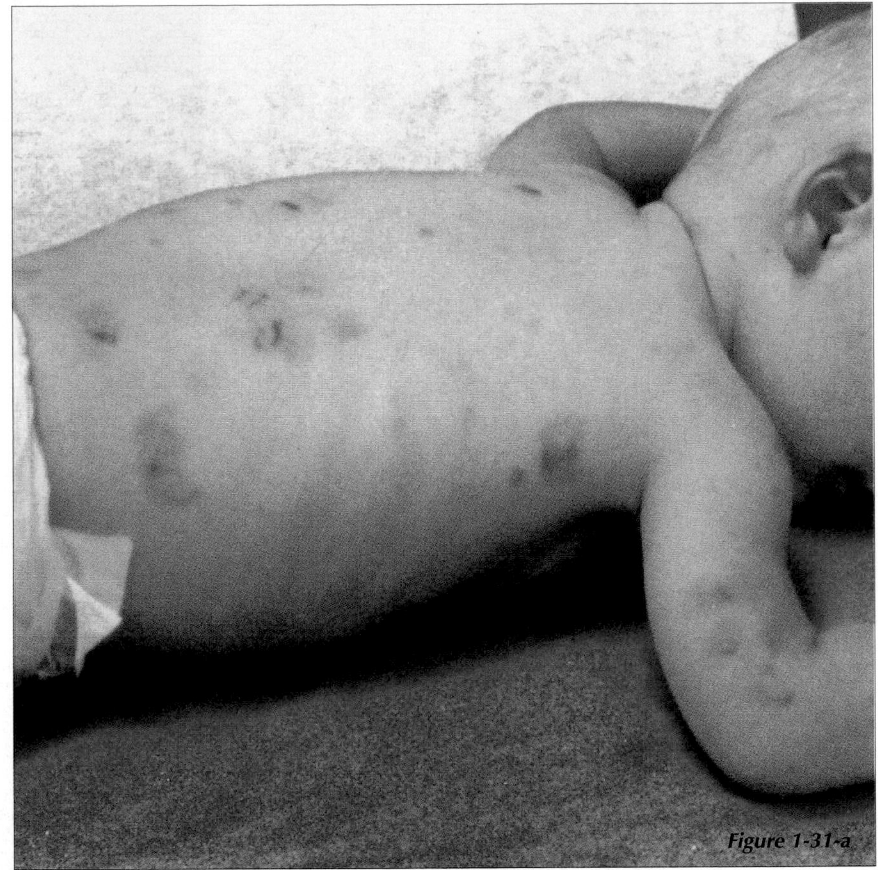

*Figure 1-31-a*

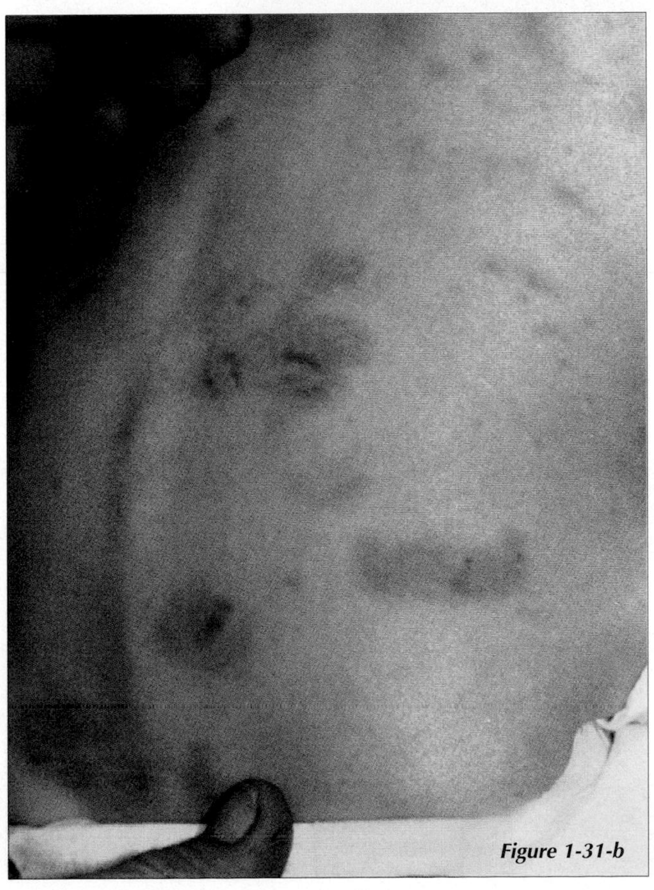

*Figure 1-31-b*

# Patterned Injuries

**Case Study 1-32**

This 26-month-old girl was reported by her mother to have died suddenly. At autopsy the child weighed 19 pounds, which is well below the 5th percentile for her age, and had multiple contusions about her face, neck, scalp, extremities, abdomen, back, and buttocks.

***Figure 1-32-a.*** *Multiple bruises to the face.*

***Figure 1-32-b.*** *A large healing laceration of the frenulum (arrow) above the tooth line.*

***Figure 1-32-c.*** *A fresh loop mark on the inner thigh from a belt.*

***Figure 1-32-d.*** *The belt used in abuse correlates to the loop marks on the child's legs.*

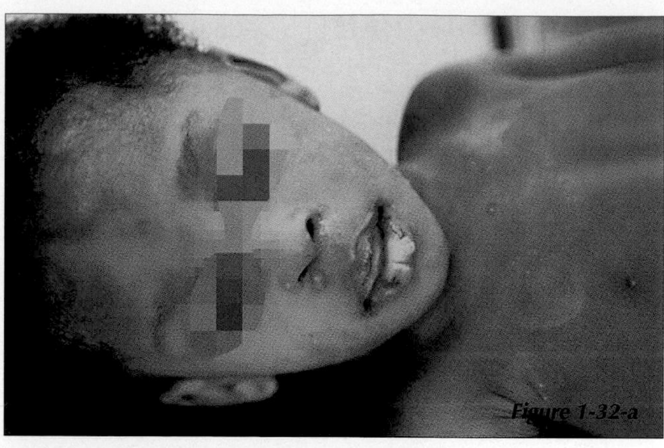

Figure 1-32-a

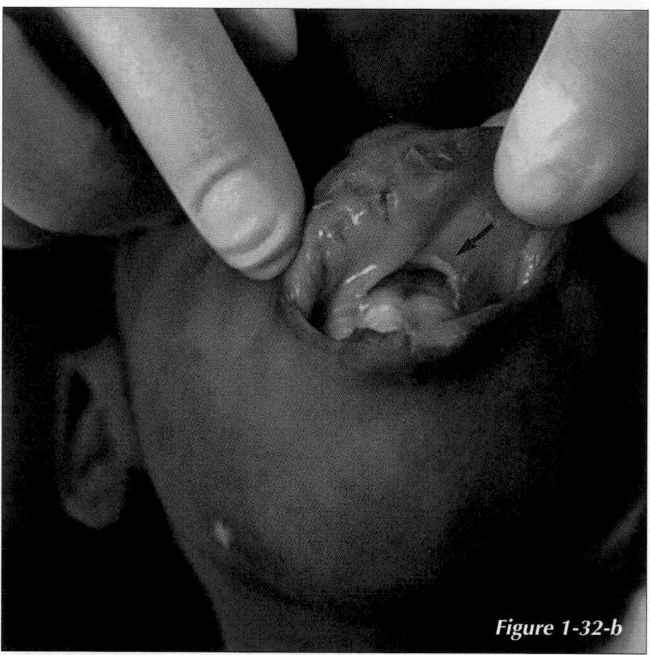

Figure 1-32-b

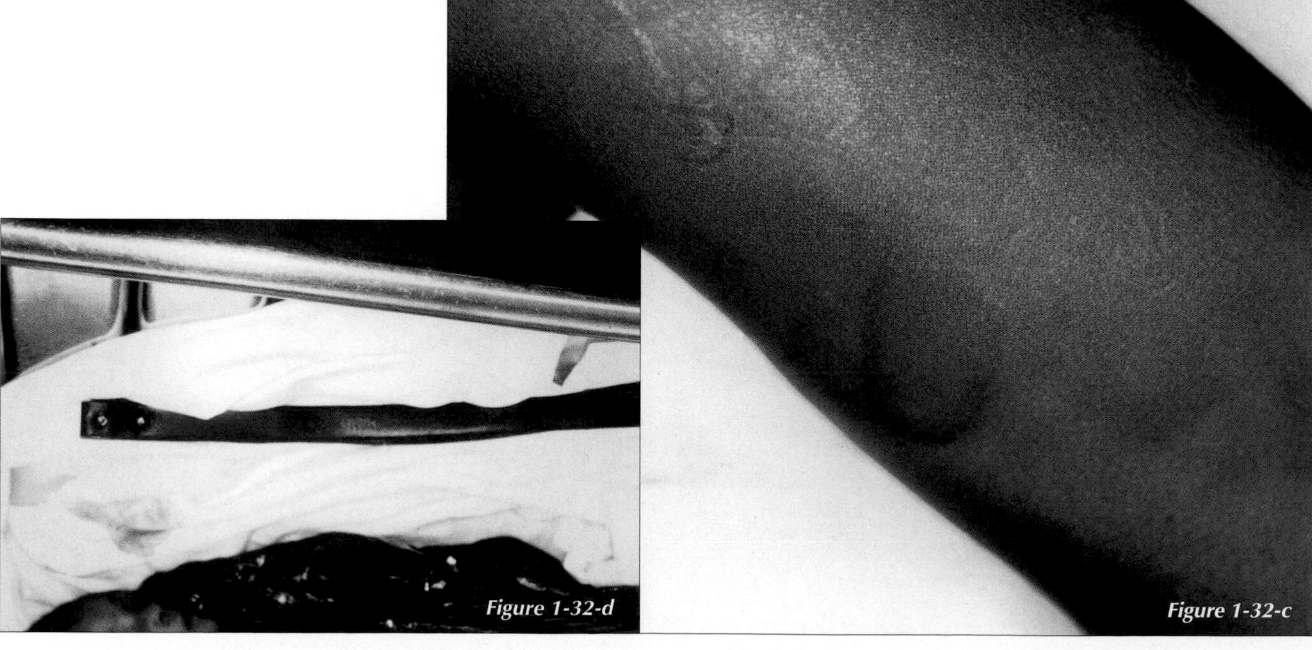

Figure 1-32-d

Figure 1-32-c

# Patterned Injuries

**Case Study 1-32** *(continued)*

***Figures 1-32-e** and **f.** Old scars related to belt marks indicate previous incidences of abuse with the belt.*

***Figure 1-32-g.** Incisions of the lower extremities show contusions of soft tissues.*

The cause of death was blunt soft tissue trauma.

Figure 1-32-e

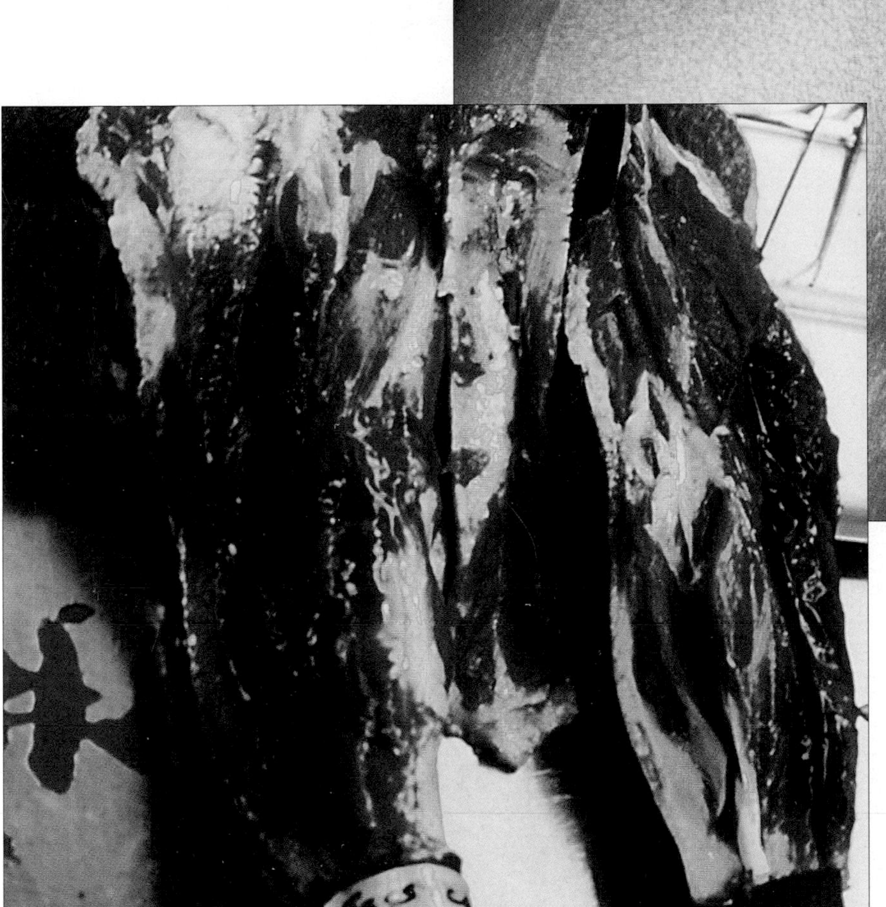

Figure 1-32-g

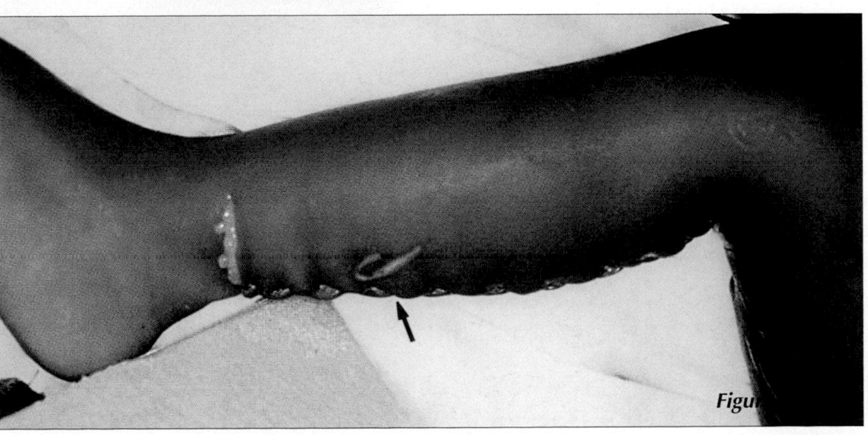

Figu

## Patterned Injuries

**Case Study 1-33**

This 5-year-old girl was beaten by her father with a variety of instruments, including a cord, a belt, a paddle, a fan belt, and tree branches. The child was dead on arrival at the hospital.

***Figure 1-33-a.*** *Instruments used to beat the girl.*

***Figures 1-33-b, c, d,*** *and* ***e.*** *Injuries include multiple abrasions and contusions of head, face, neck, chest, and abdomen. Patterned injuries of loops from belt marks and notches from the fan belt are recognizable.*

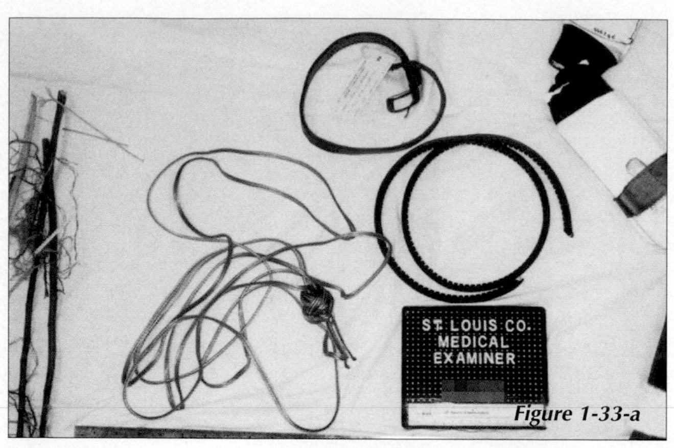


***Figure 1-33-a***

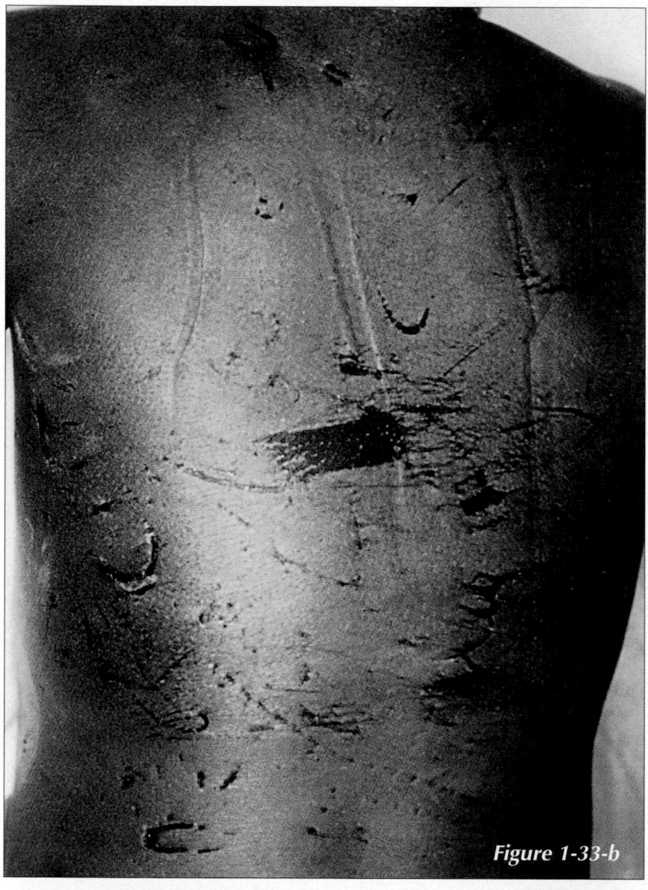

***Figure 1-33-b***

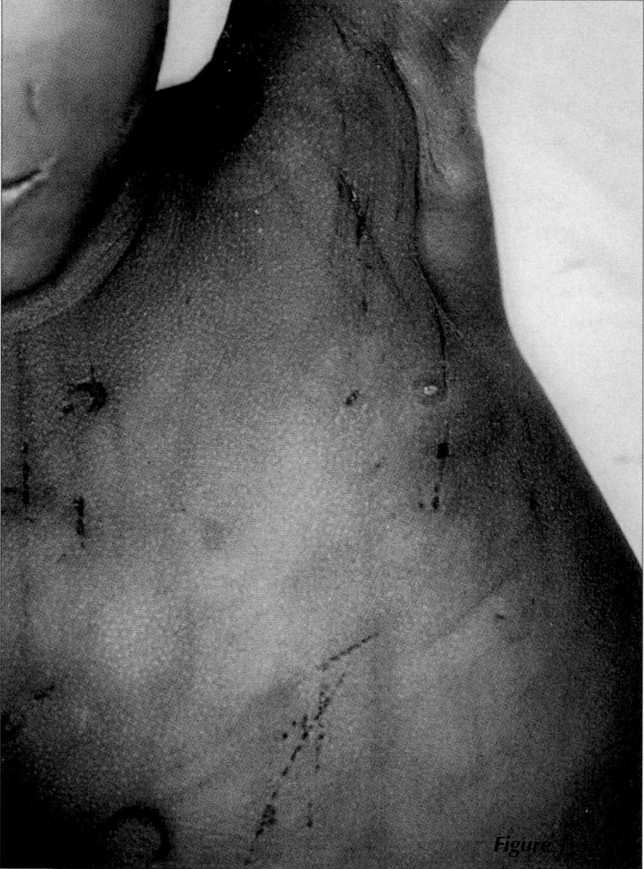

***Figure***

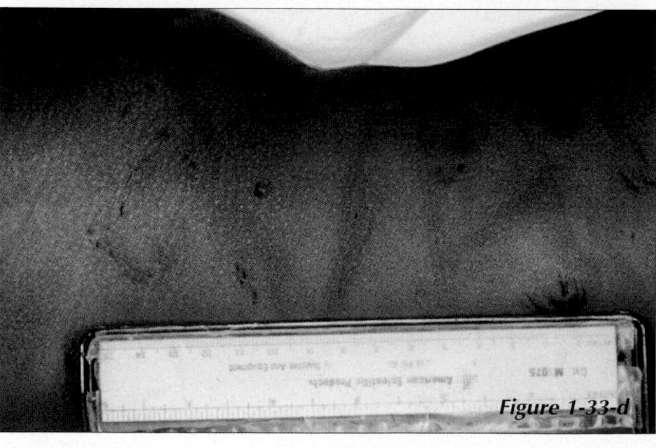

***Figure 1-33-d***

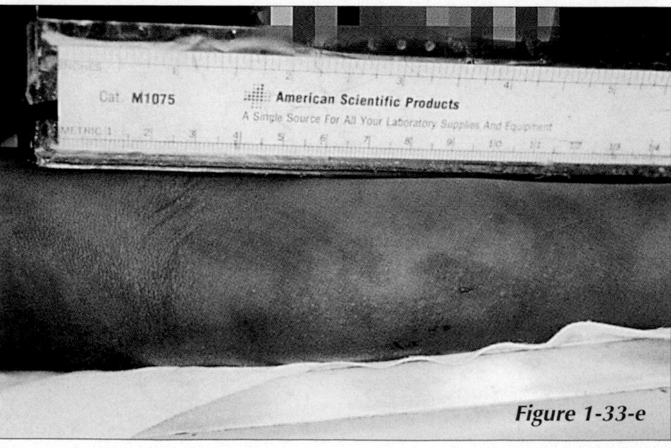


***Figure 1-33-e***

## Patterned Injuries

**Case Study 1-33** *(continued)*

***Figures 1-33-f*** *and* ***g.*** *Multiple abrasions and contusions of back and extremities.*

***Figures 1-33-h*** *and* ***i.*** *Blunt soft tissue trauma.*

The cause of death was determined to be blunt soft tissue trauma.

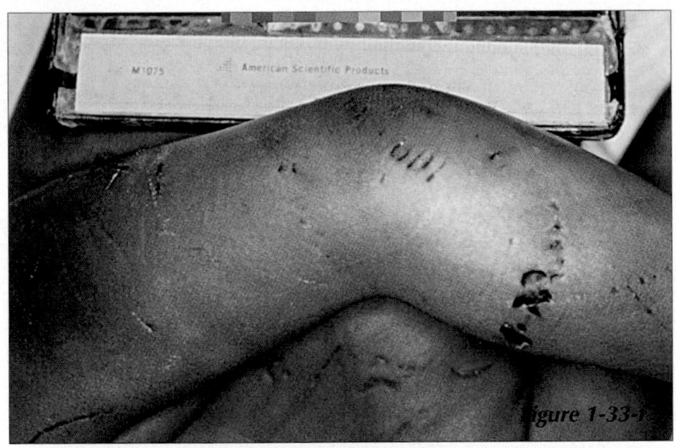


Figure 1-33-f

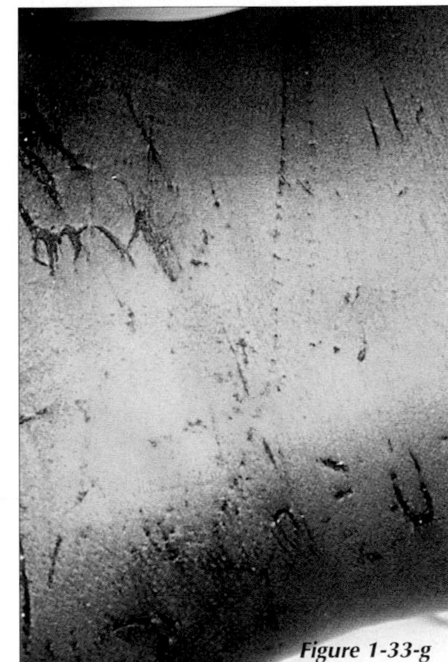

Figure 1-33-g

Figure 1-33-h

Figure 1-33-i

# Patterned Injuries

**Case Study 1-34**

This 2-year-old girl and her mother were visiting from another city and staying with friends. The child was sleeping on a couch in the living room and was found dead in the morning. The cause of death was determined to be traumatic asphyxia. All children should have an autopsy and their cause of death reviewed by a death review team when they die. In SIDS, a site investigation is also mandatory.

***Figure 1-34-a.*** *Petechial hemorrhages can be seen over the eyelids and beneath the eyes.*

***Figure 1-34-b.*** *Petechial hemorrhages on the palpebral conjunctivae.*

***Figure 1-34-c.*** *Petechial hemorrhages on the gingival of the upper gum.*

***Figure 1-34-d.*** *Petechial hemorrhages along the left side of the neck.*

A male member of the host family eventually admitted to lying down on top of the child to keep her from crying, and he said that after about 15 minutes the child appeared to be sleeping.

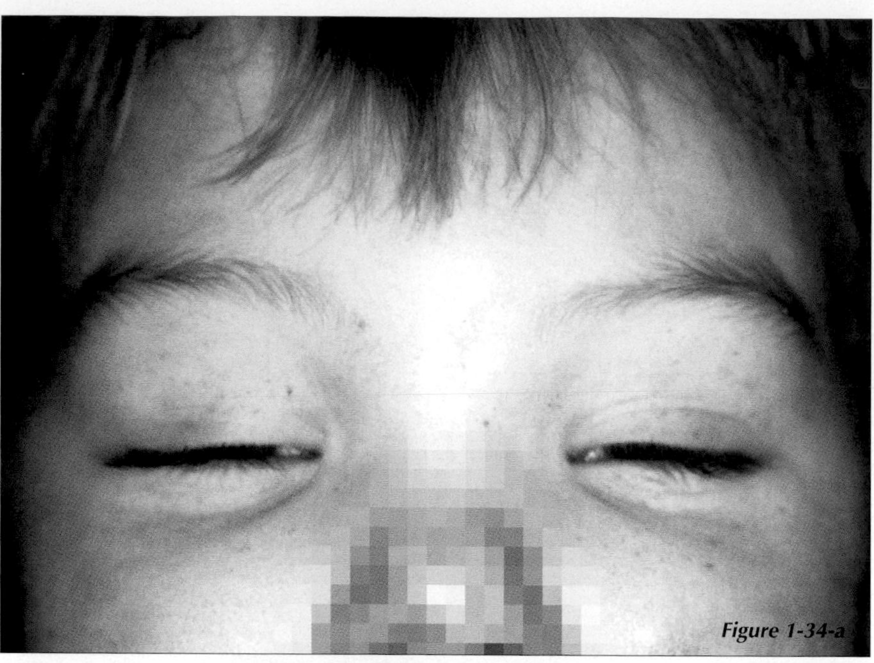

Figure 1-34-a

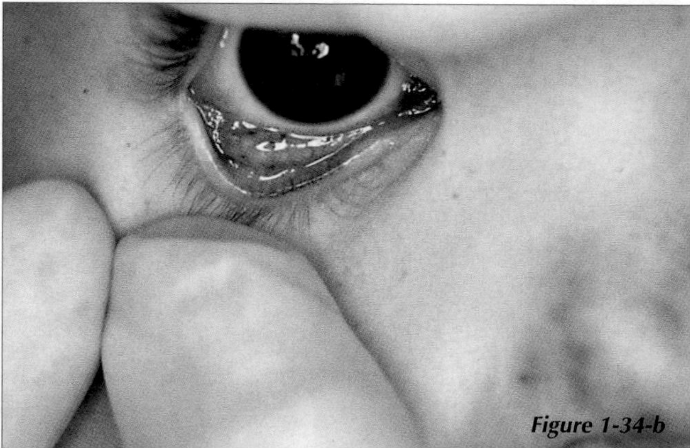

Figure 1-34-b

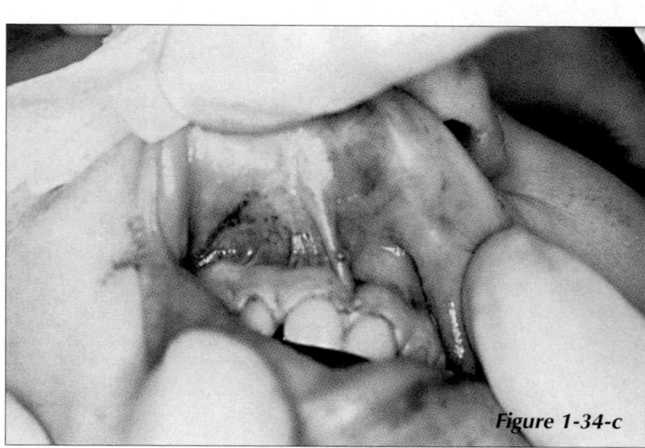

Figure 1-34-c

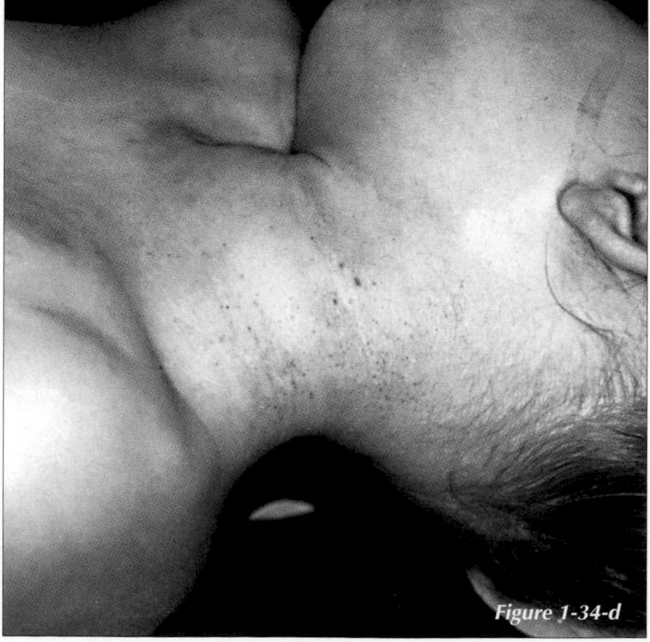

Figure 1-34-d

## Patterned Injuries

**Case Study 1-35**

This 13-month-old boy was seen with bruises to his face and buttocks. The injuries were found during a routine examination. The linear appearance of the petechiae on the left side of the face suggested impact with a hand.

***Figure 1-35-a.*** *Bruises to the face.*

***Figure 1-35-b.*** *Bruises to the buttocks.*

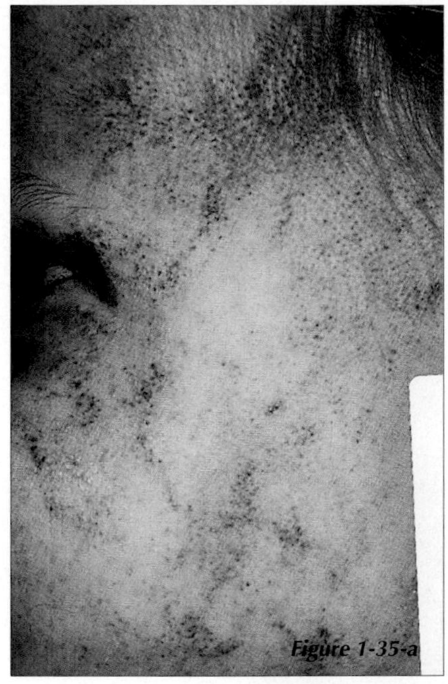

Figure 1-35-a

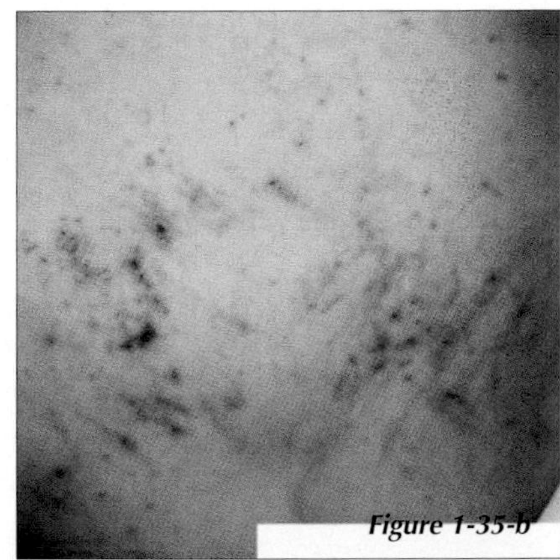

Figure 1-35-b

**Case Study 1-36**

This 3-year-old girl was seen in the ER for an upper respiratory infection. The child was found to have numerous old loop and linear marks, some leaving scars, on both the back and the front of her body. She was also developmentally delayed and deaf. Disabled children are more at risk for abuse and neglect. This beating may be classified as torture—a term recognized in the courts with more serious consequences to the perpetrator.

***Figure 1-36-a.*** *Old loop and linear marks on the back of the girl's body.*

***Figure 1-36-b.*** *Old loop and linear marks on the front of her body.*

Note that the lashings came from many directions perhaps as a consequence of the child trying to escape. Keloid formation is a possible physical consequence. Emotional consequences are more likely and this child will need psychiatric services.

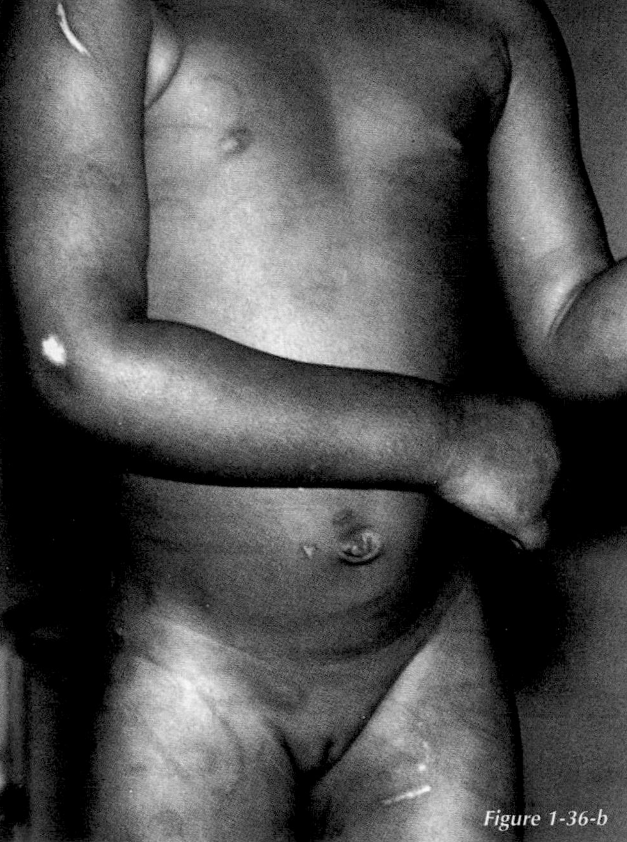

Figure 1-36-b

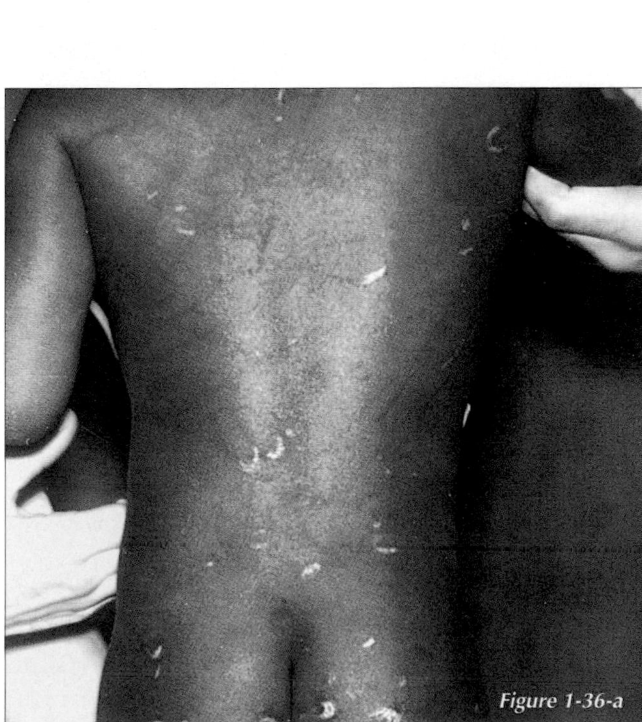

Figure 1-36-a

# Patterned Injuries

**Case Study 1-37**

This 6-year-old boy was examined for evidence of a recent beating by a belt and a fist. There was no evidence of old lesions. Belt marks are linear marks and may appear as outlines or silhouettes of the belt, depending on the surface of the belt that hits the skin. Fist marks are generally a series of teardrop marks in an arc. The thickness of overlying tissue and proximity to bone influences the shape of the bruise.

***Figure 1-37-a.*** *The boy's back.*

***Figure 1-37-b.*** *The boy's right side.*

***Figure 1-37-c.*** *The left upper leg and hip of the boy.*

Figure 1-37-a

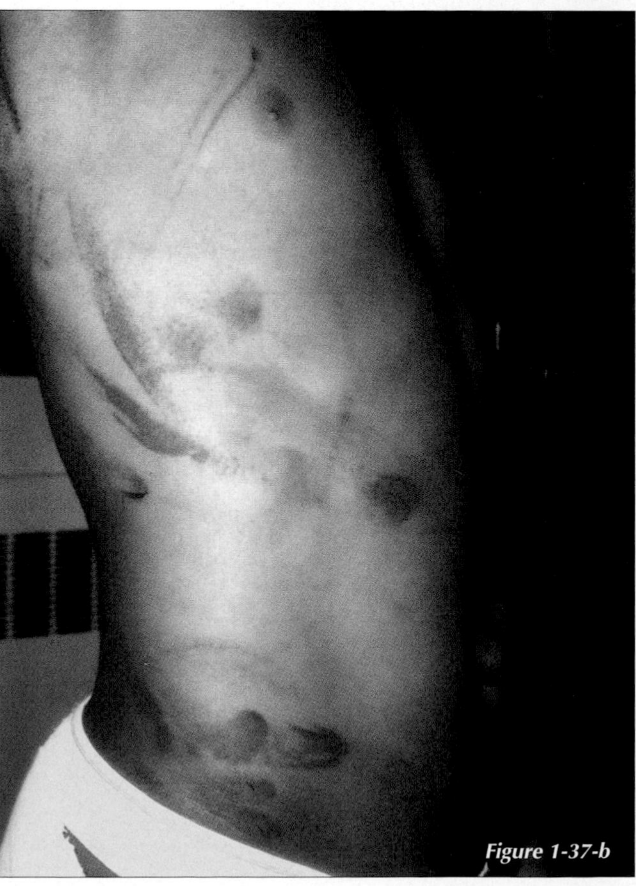

Figure 1-37-b

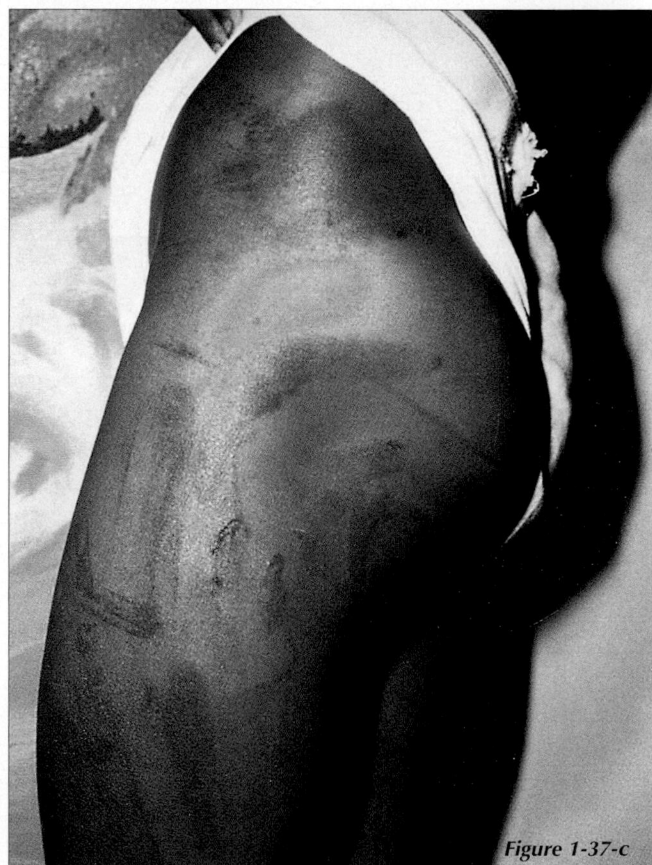

Figure 1-37-c

# Patterned Injuries

**Case Study 1-38**

This 2-year-old boy was taken to the ER because of a swollen prepuce, or foreskin. The mother reported that she did not know how he had suffered the injury. The child was found to have several other lesions, including a loop mark on his right thigh, linear marks on his left thigh and lower abdomen, and a small rounded, healed burn scar on his left shoulder that resembled a cigarette burn. The prepuce lesions were suspected to be due to pinching or clamping as punishment for the child soiling himself. The loop mark on his thigh was exemplary of the type of mark that results from a looped phone cord or extension cord. Swelling of the prepuce can result from manipulation and poor hygiene. Forced retraction of the foreskin may result in erythema.

***Figure 1-38-a.*** *Swollen prepuce.*

***Figure 1-38-b.*** *Loop mark on the child's right thigh.*

***Figure 1-38-c.*** *Linear marks on his lower abdomen.*

***Figure 1-38-d.*** *Linear marks also appear on his left thigh.*

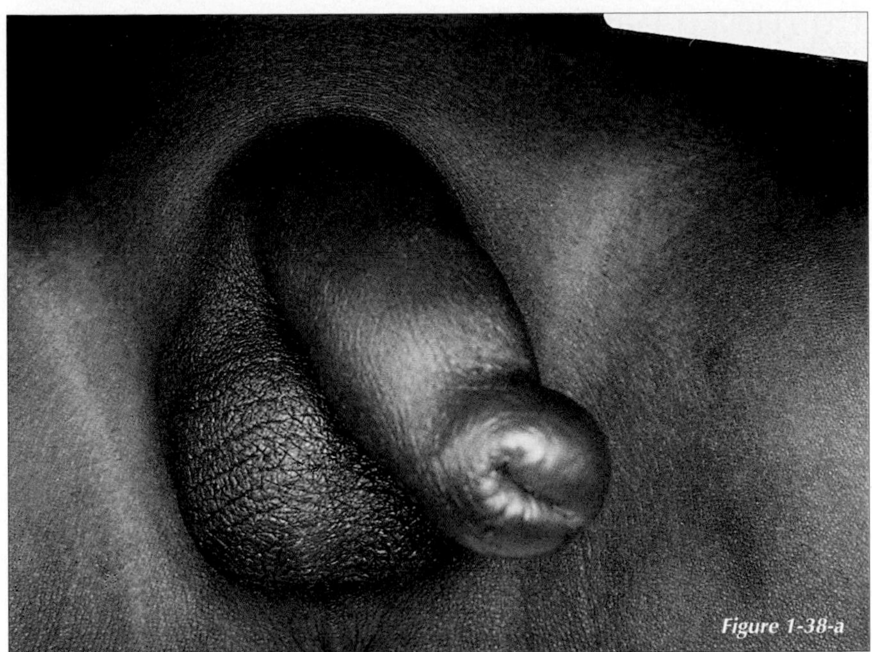

*Figure 1-38-a*

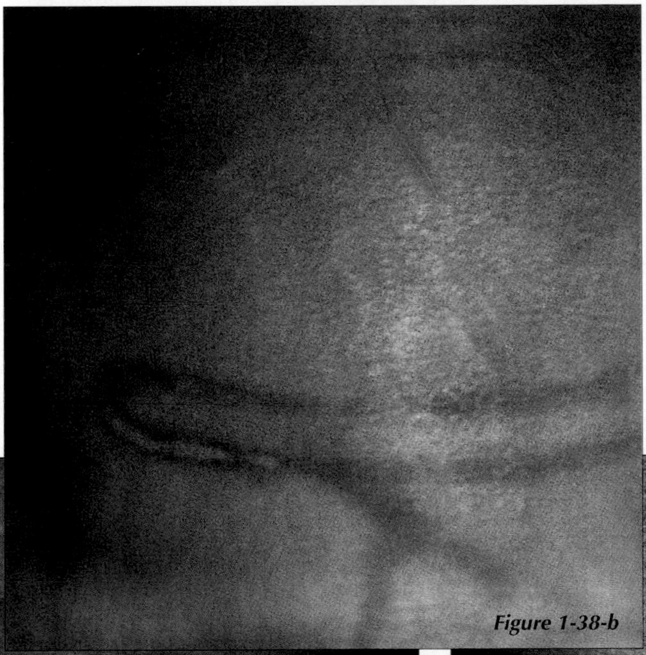

*Figure 1-38-b*

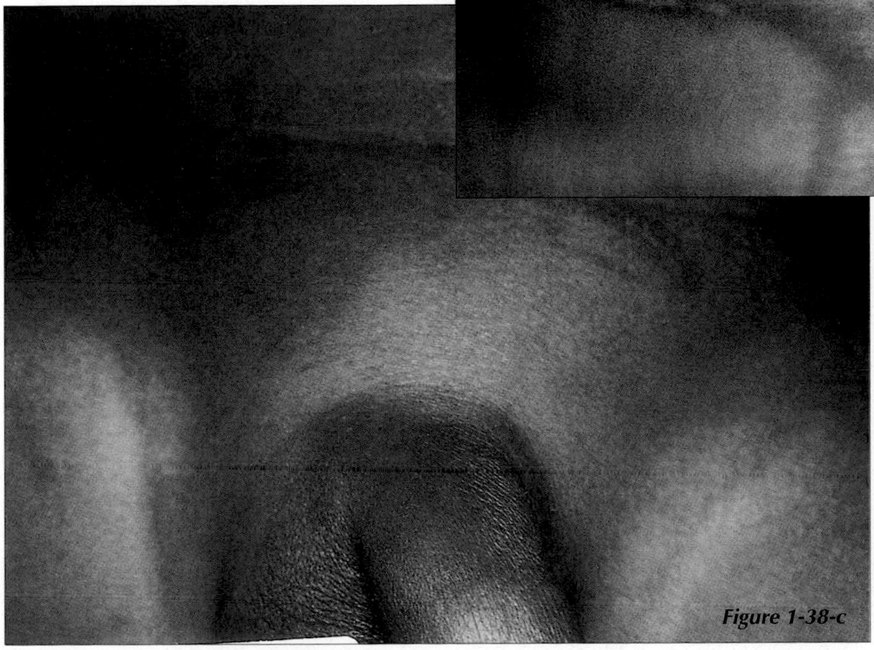

*Figure 1-38-c*

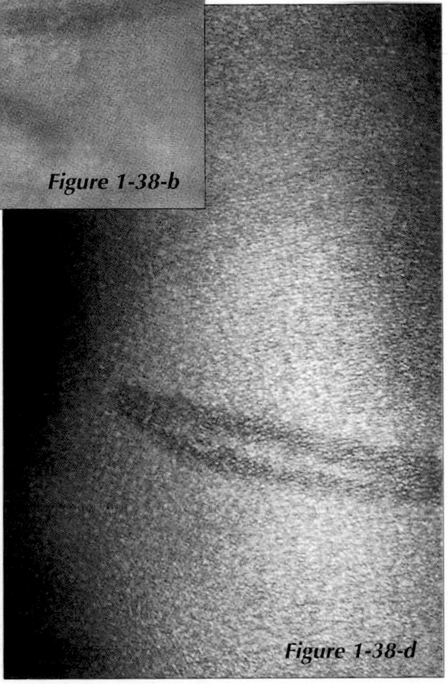

*Figure 1-38-d*

# Patterned Injuries

**Case Study 1-39**

This 11-month-old child was taken to the ER by his mother. She had been at work when the babysitter dropped him off saying that he had just fallen out of his crib and injured his right eye. The child's 6-year-old sibling corroborated that the child had fallen out of his crib.

***Figure 1-39-a.*** *Ecchymotic area involving the right upper lid and temporal area. The left eye shows no injury.*

***Figure 1-39-b.*** *An injury to the left side of the head with an abrasion.*

***Figure 1-39-c.*** *A band of punctate, petechial-looking lesions across the side of the left leg.*

***Figure 1-39-d.*** *A bite mark behind the left leg.*

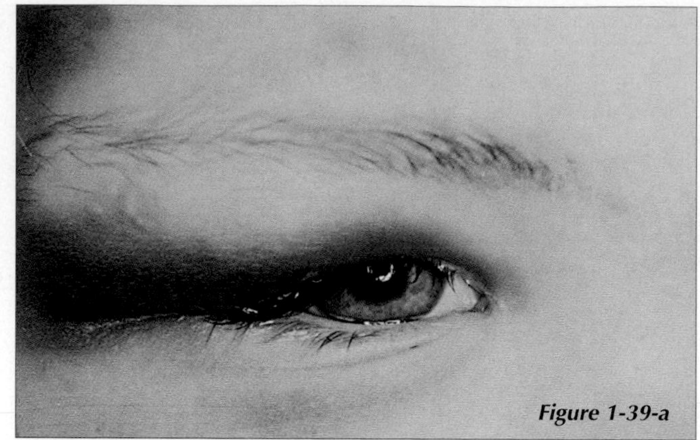

**Figure 1-39-a**

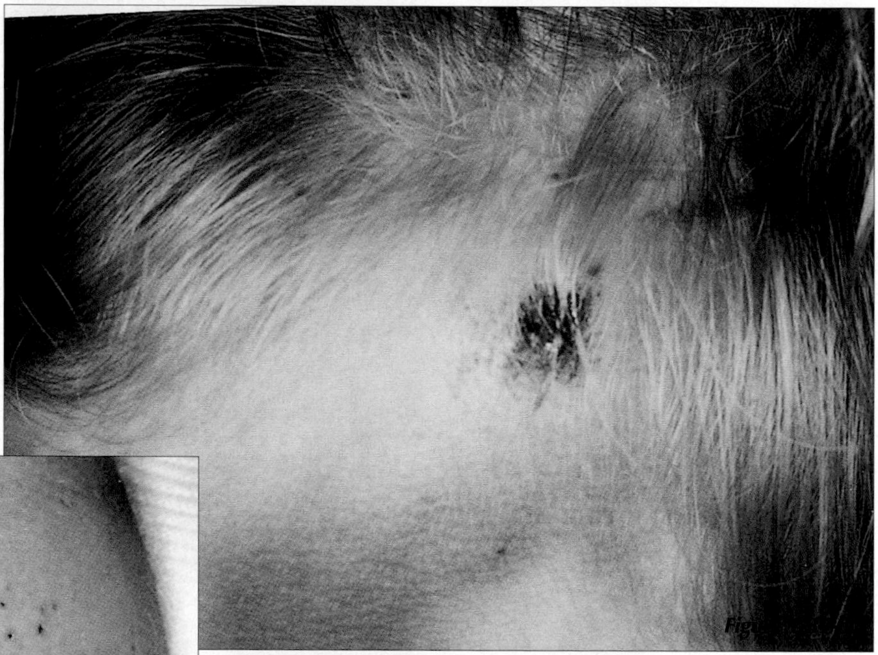

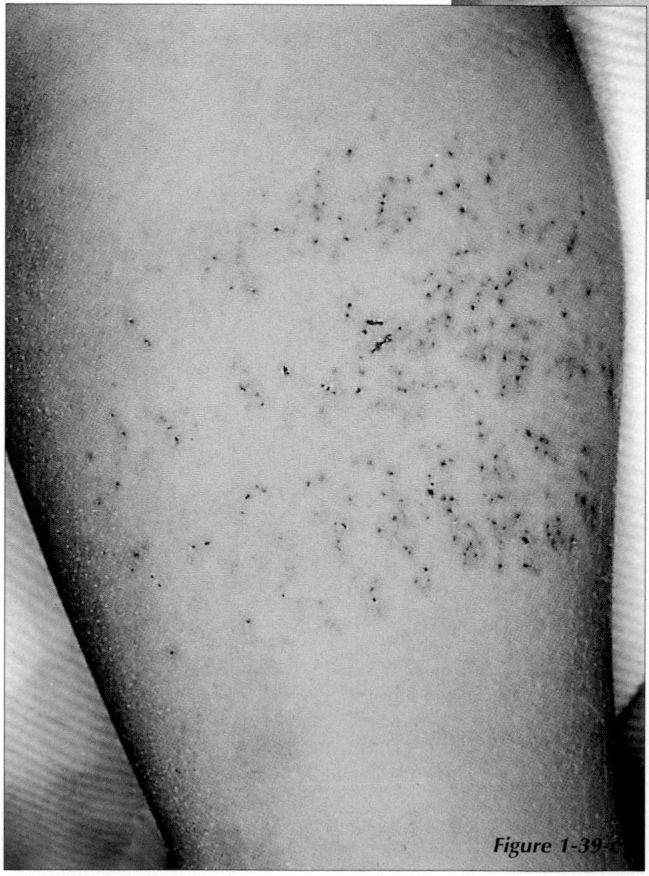

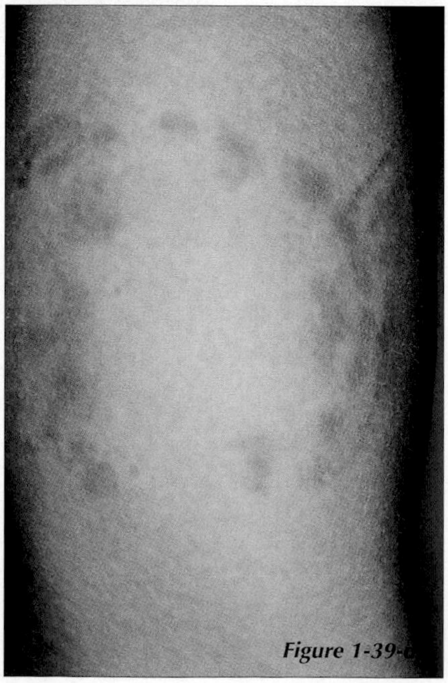

## Patterned Injuries

**Case Study 1-39** *(continued)*

***Figure 1-39-e.*** *Ecchymotic area behind the right ear with punctate ecchymotic lesions.*

***Figure 1-39-f.*** *Rudimentary bite marks to the buttocks.*

***Figure 1-39-g.*** *Pinch lesion to the glans penis.*

***Figure 1-39-h.*** *A band of bruising across the back of the right forearm.*

The child was admitted to the hospital and reported to the Division of Family Services as a case of suspected child abuse.

***Figures 1-39-i** and **j.** The following morning the child shows changes with marked bilateral periorbital edema and ecchymosis and now had bruising to the left check.*

There can be a delay in the development of ecchymotic changes and blood can follow fascial planes and surface in distal areas. The blood accumulation in the left eye originated from the injury of the left side of the head. The child did not have a bleeding disorder and bleeding and clotting studies were normal.

The Division of Family Services investigated the case. The sibling revealed that he had lied and the child did not fall out of his crib, but rather was beaten with a paddle by the babysitter. It is important to interview all children and adults who may have witnessed the trauma. Injuries to more than one body surface are unusual in falls. Forensic investigations, with measurement photographs and molds, if practical, can help identify the perpetrator of bite marks. It is important to keep in mind that children do bite each other—especially in unsupervised situations.

Medical evaluation of any child with injuries should include workup for bleeding disorders, a skeletal survey—which is repeated in 10 days, and a CT or MRI scan of the structures' underlying impact marks in the head, chest, or abdomen.

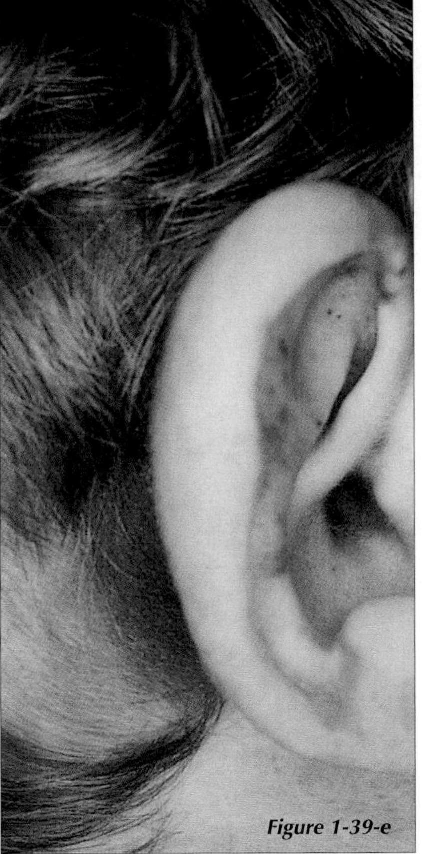

**Figure 1-39-e**

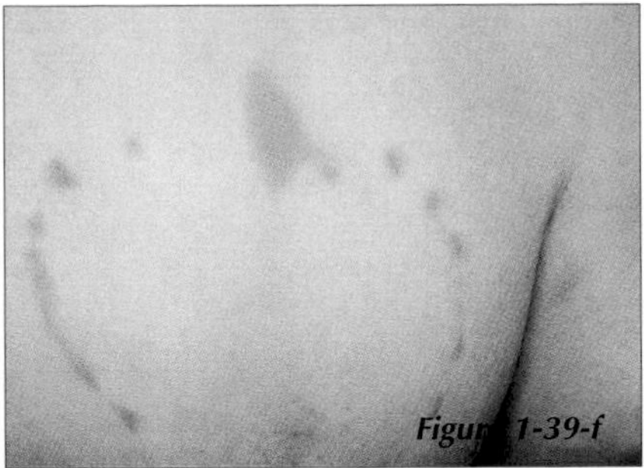

**Figure 1-39-f**

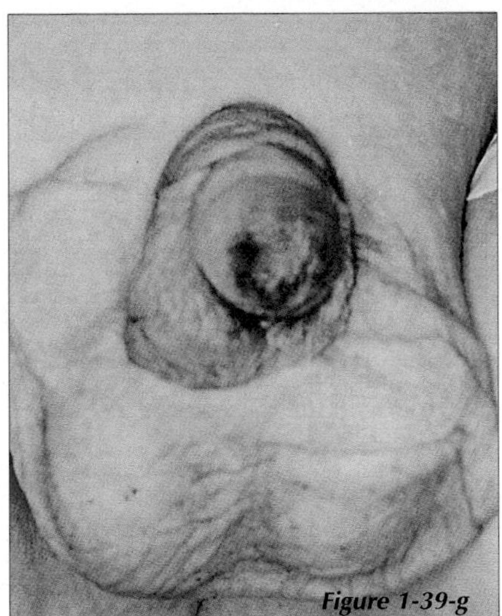

**Figure 1-39-g**

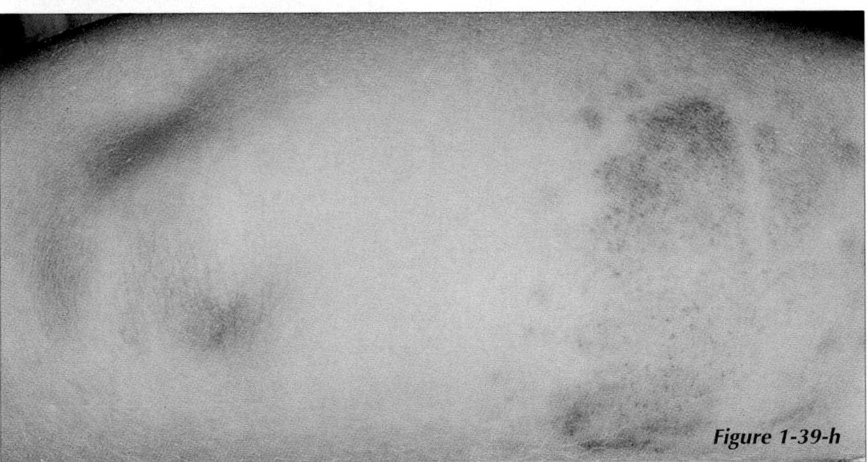

**Figure 1-39-h**

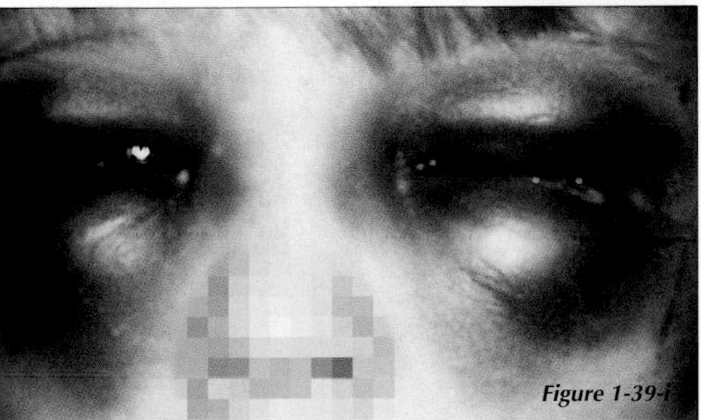

**Figure 1-39-i**

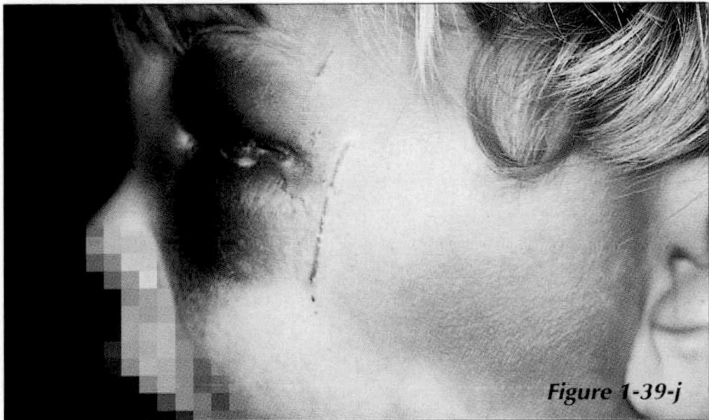

**Figure 1-39-j**

# PATTERNED INJURIES

**Case Study 1-40**

This 4-year-old boy was seen in the ER with a history provided by the caregiver of having fallen down the stairs. He had bruising on multiple surface areas of his body in various stages of healing. He also had an ecchymotic area on the right cheek and a five-pointed abrasion that was repeated lateral to the right eye and on the chin. These were believed to be left by a ring. He had perioral ecchymosis with older lip injuries and conjunctival hemorrhages in the right eye. Other findings included scrotal ecchymosis and an ecchymotic area on the upper right thigh, scalp injury, and injuries to his arms and legs. The child had a past history of spiral fracture of the humerus, lead toxicity, and hearing deficiency. He was developmentally delayed and considered to have a behavior problem. Children with developmental and behavioral disorders are more at risk for abuse and neglect. Stair injuries are rarely, if ever, fatal. If the stairs are padded, injury may be limited to abrasions and bruises. The stair edge imparts a series of linear impacts on the body. The final landing or surface will likely be the cause of injury. Cement is unyielding and more likely to cause a fracture. Fractures of distal extremities are more likely in falls down stairs.

An internal eye examination by an ophthalmologist is mandatory in any injury to the eye or head. A retininoscope photo will provide a wide field of examination and a permanent record of the findings.

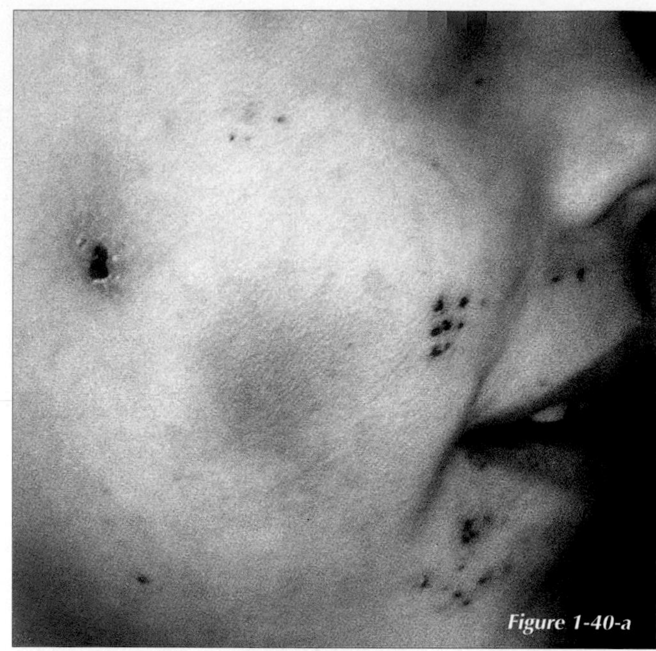

Figure 1-40-a

*Figure 1-40-a.* Five-pointed abrasion and ecchymotic area on the right cheek.

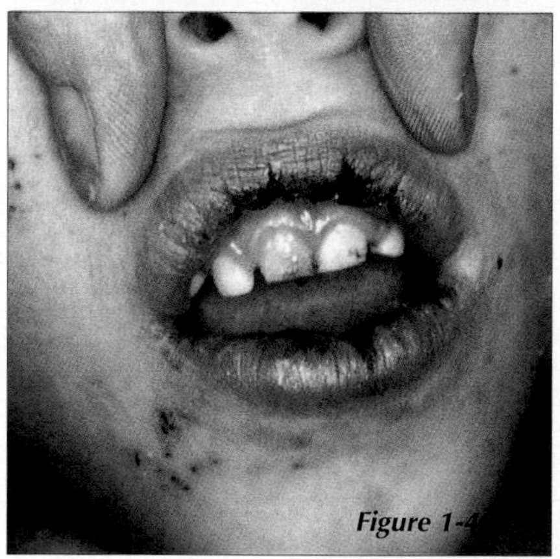

Figure 1-4

*Figure 1-40-b.* The five-pointed abrasion is repeated on the chin.

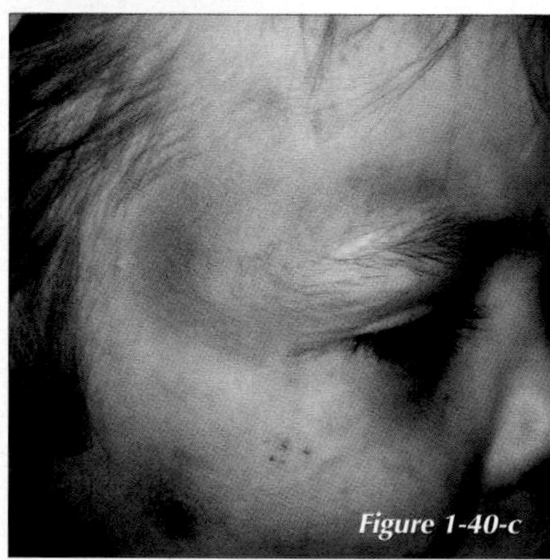

Figure 1-40-c

*Figure 1-40-c.* Another five-pointed abrasion near the right eye.

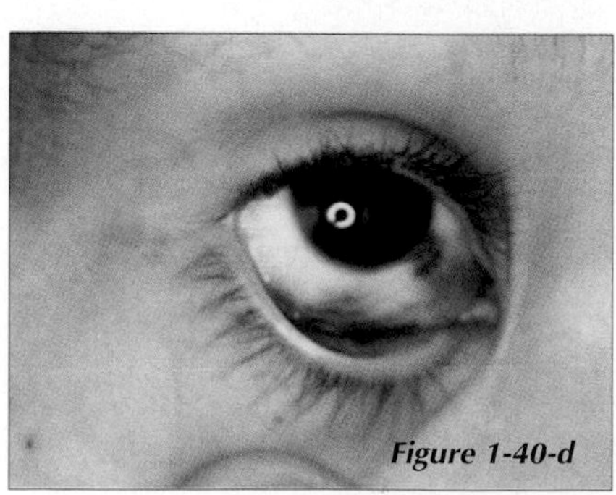

Figure 1-40-d

*Figure 1-40-d.* Conjunctival hemorrhages in the right eye.

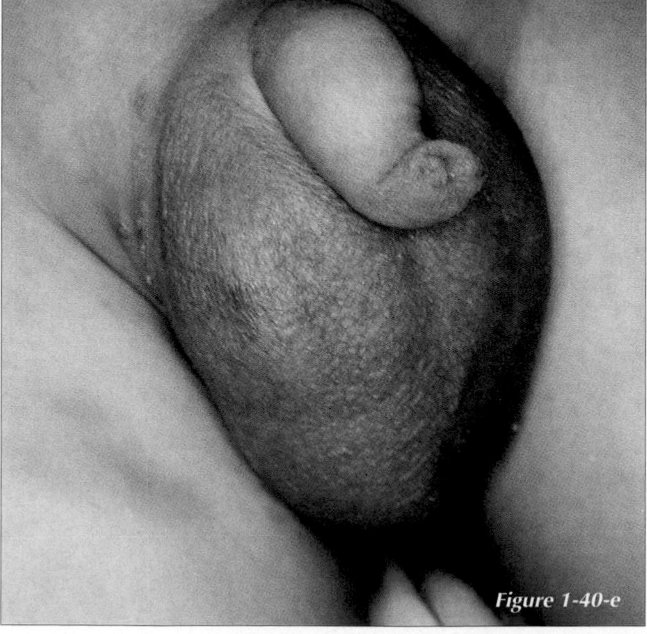

Figure 1-40-e

*Figure 1-40-e.* Other findings include scrotal ecchymosis and an ecchymotic area on the upper right thigh.

# Patterned Injuries

**Case Study 1-41**

This 12-year-old girl was examined for multiple loop and linear marks.

***Figure 1-41.*** *Fresh loop and linear marks on this 12-year-old girl.*

**Case Study 1-42**

This 15-year-old boy was seen for an eye injury caused by a beating with a stick. Impact may be directed to a less vulnerable part of the body, eg, children may be injured on the face or hands as they dodge and try to protect themselves. The use of an instrument on any part of the body, as well as impacts to the face and head, should be reported as abuse. This also includes slap marks.

***Figure 1-42.*** *The imprint of the instrument is central, with ecchymosis extending beyond the area of impact.*

**Case Study 1-43**

This 8-year-old boy was seen with dog bites. When questioning the appearance of a bite, consultation with a veterinarian may be useful because they are experts in bites from various types of animals. Safety neglect should be considered in all animal bites.

***Figure 1-43.*** *Prominent canine teeth marks as seen on the leg of this boy.*

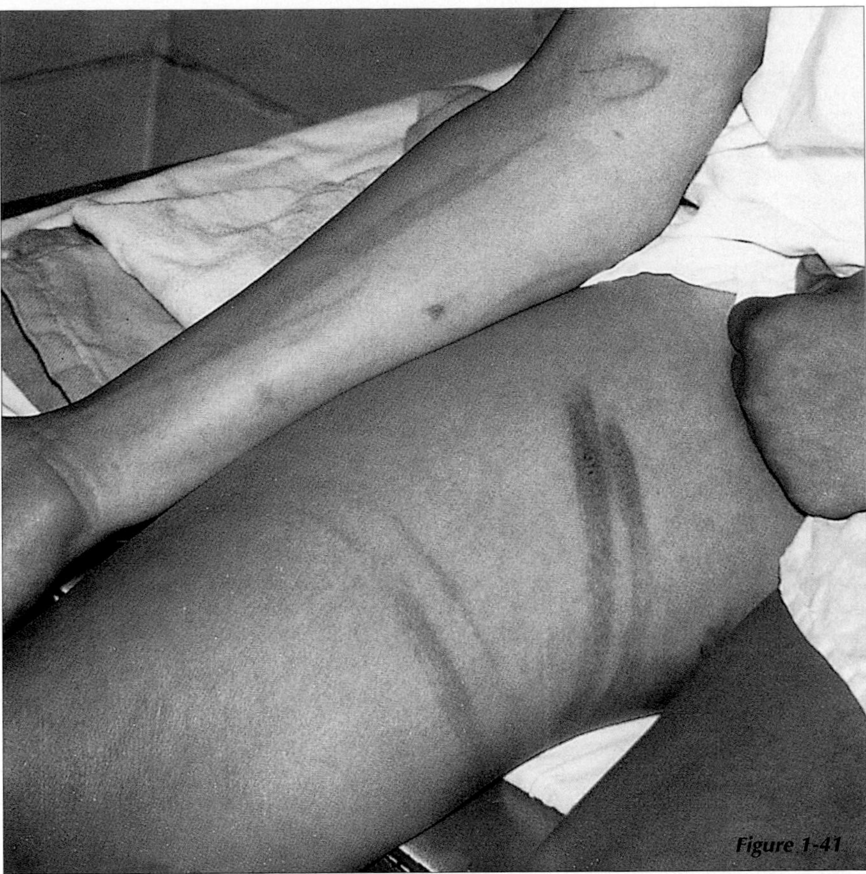


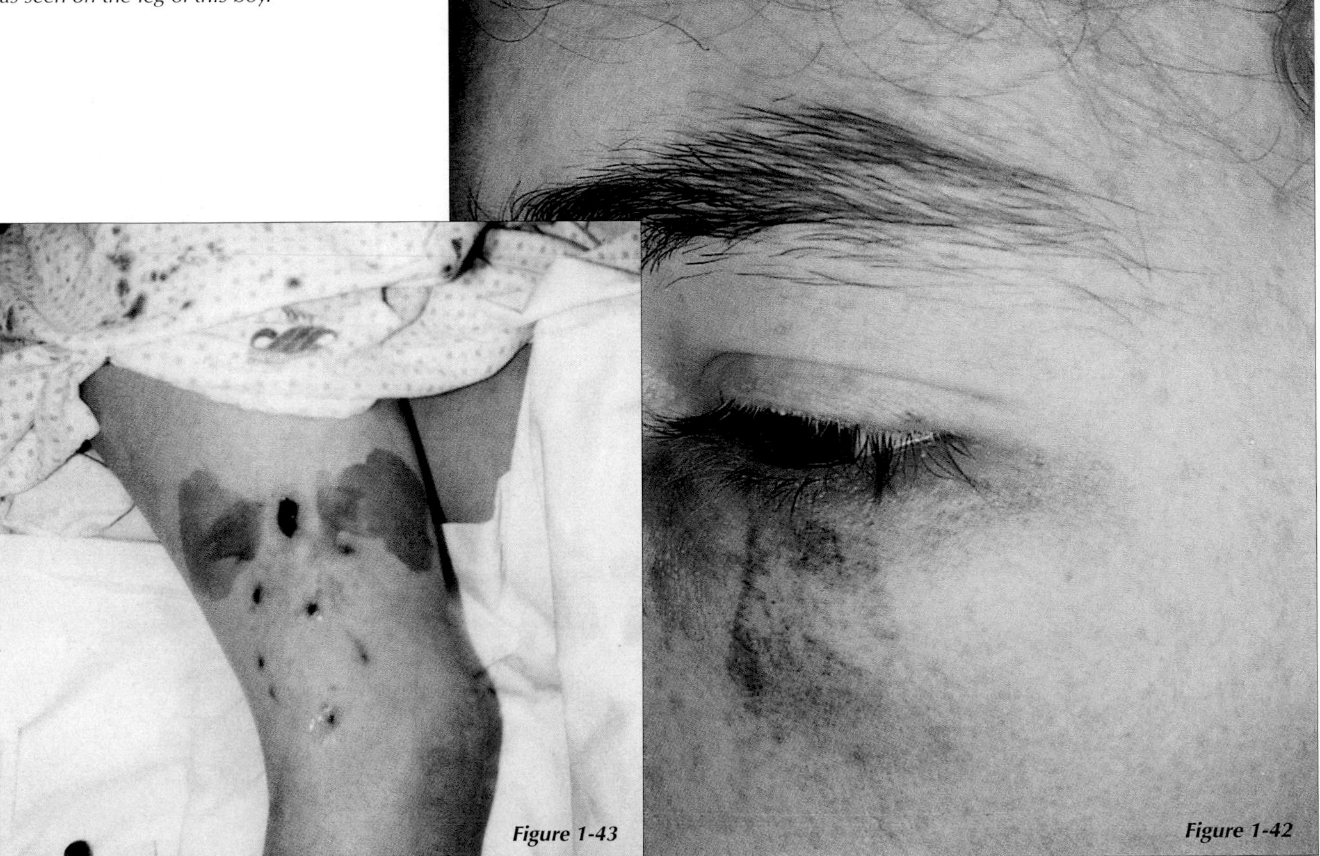

# Patterned Injuries

**Case Study 1-44**

This exhibit was used in a criminal trial to demonstrate a human bite on the back of a 9-month-old boy. A forensic dentist was able to match the bite injury with the bite of the mother's boyfriend.

***Figure 1-44.*** *Marking injuries with a ball-point pen will highlight them for photography. All photographs in suspected child abuse must include the child's identification, a color chart, and a measuring device.*

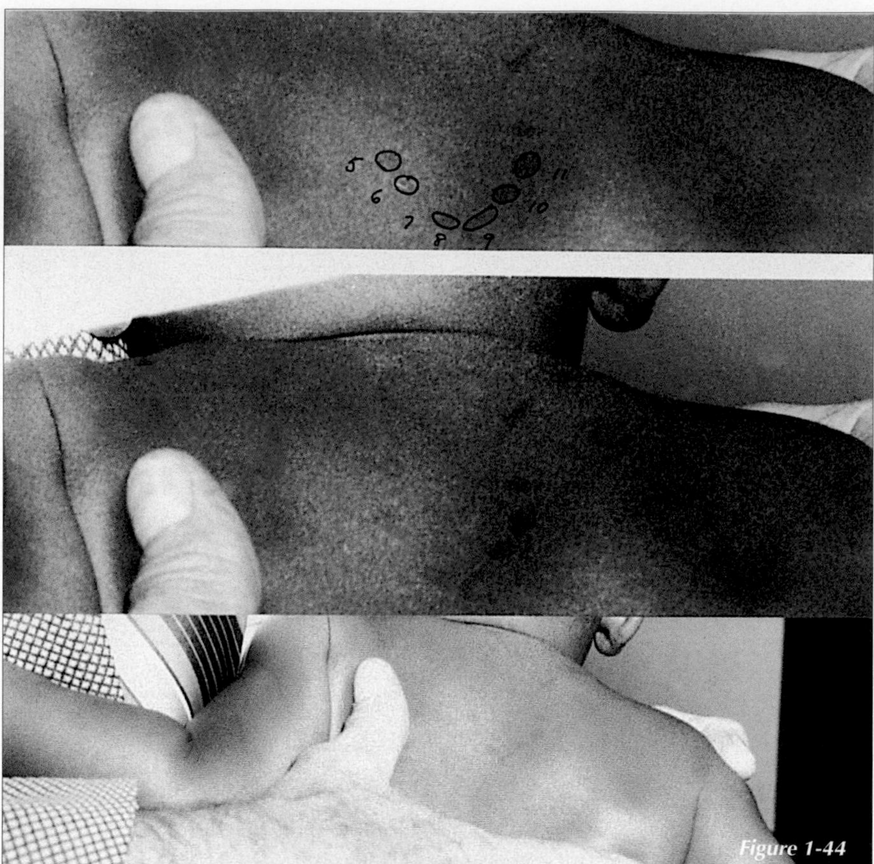


Figure 1-44

**Case Study 1-45**

This 4-year-old boy was left in the care of his 16-year-old cousin while his father went to the store. When the father returned, the boy complained of anal pain. The father noted blood in the child's underwear and took him to the hospital. The boy was found to have a severe laceration of the anus extending into the rectum. He also had anal laxity and dilation. He initially said that he did not know how it happened but later described anal intercourse by the cousin. The cousin stated that the boy had fallen on an exercise bike. Anal and vaginal/hymen tears from straddle injuries rarely occur. Underwear generally protects these anatomic areas. The object the cousin claimed penetrated the boy should have been investigated for the boy's blood to confirm the cousin's history.

***Figures 1-45-a*** *and* ***b.*** *Severe laceration of the anus extending into the rectum.*

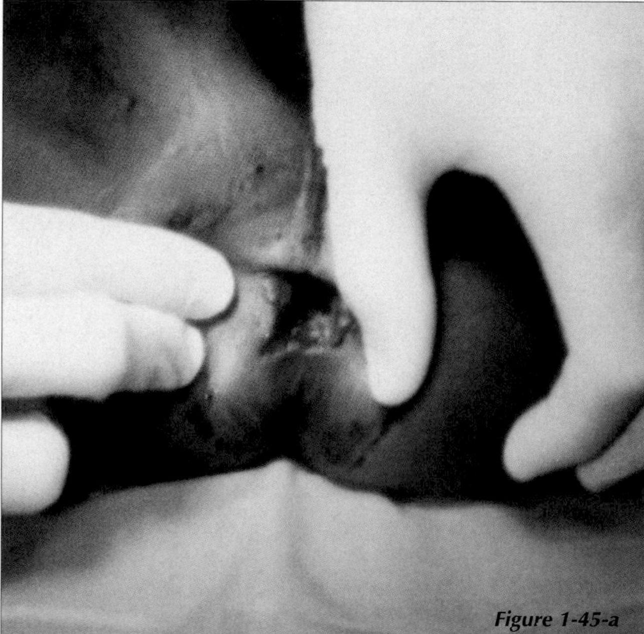

Figure 1-45-a

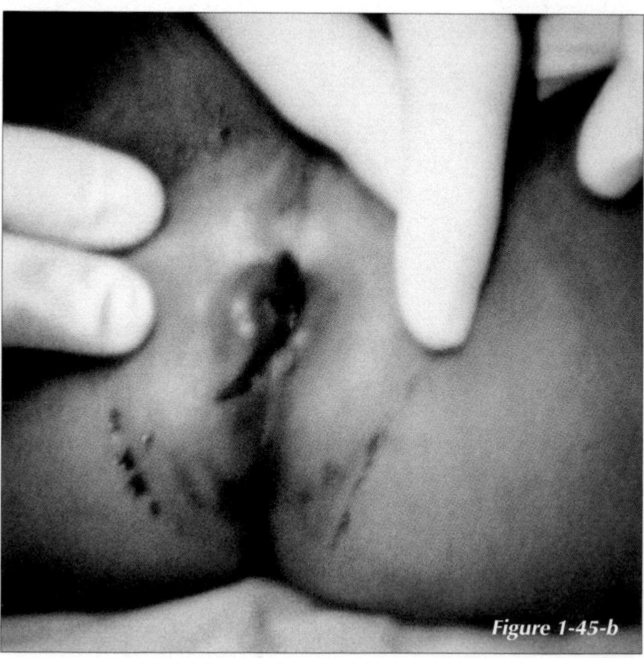

Figure 1-45-b

## Patterned Injuries

**Case Study 1-46**

This 4-year-old boy was examined for scarred marks.

***Figure 1-46.*** *Scarred linear and loop marks as seen on the outside of the upper right leg.*

## Target Organs

**Case Study 1-47**

The hand is a frequent target organ in intentional injury. The activities of hands get children into trouble, and those hands are readily accessible for intentional impact and burning. Marks to the hands may bring an abused child to the attention of others because clothing does not cover them.

***Figure 1-47-a.*** *A mother brought her newborn baby to the ER, claiming that she had just delivered the baby. The infant had erythema of both palms and what appeared to be black dirt on the hands and other body parts. After careful questioning, the mother admitted to delivering the baby in a ravine and throwing it onto the ground afterwards. This action could explain the impact bruises on the hands. The mother apparently had a change of heart over time and brought the baby to the ER without bathing the infant.*

***Figure 1-47-b.*** *This child was seen with unusual marks on the hands. The coloration was dark red, with a pattern that does not suggest immersion, contact burn, or impact. Areas of the skin are friable and bleed with minimal contact. A dermatology consultation was sought, and a diagnosis of reticuloendotheliosis was made.*

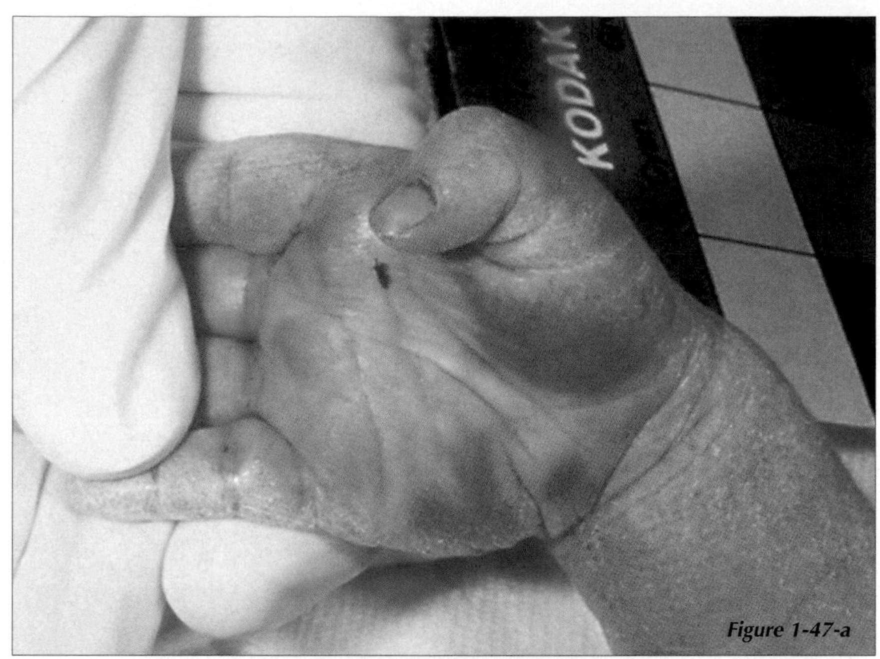

**Figure 1-47-a**

**Figure 1-47-b**

**Figure 1-46**

# Target Organs

**Case Study 1-48**

Some areas of the body, including the genitalia, neck, axillae, and popliteal fossae, are relatively protected from injury in falls. Children generally lead with the anterior surface of the body when they run and fall. Consequently, they generally only land on one body surface when they strike an object. Marks on the buttocks—a relatively protected area of the body—should raise concern about intentional injury. The buttocks are common targets for intentional injury because they are considered safe targets by those who accept intentional injury as corporal punishment.

***Figure 1-48-a.*** *The mother of this 20-month-old child stated that the gray-blue marks on the buttocks were present at birth. These were mongolian spots, which may appear at birth on any body part in dark-skinned individuals.*

***Figure 1-48-b.*** *The marks on this child are darker and are the more typical slate blue of Mongolian spots. If there is any question that the mark on the skin is a birthmark, time provides the diagnosis. Bruises can be expected to resolve within 21 days, but birthmarks persist. Marks from objects will depend on the shape and consistency of the object and the anatomy of the underlying surface.*

***Figure 1-48-c.*** *This child was struck with a looped cord. The marks on the buttocks are scars from impact with a paddle. Dark-skinned children may have scars with increased or decreased pigmentation, and impact to the buttocks can result in more severe injuries.*

***Figure 1-48-d.*** *This child developed necrosis as the result of impacts from a belt. A significant amount of blood can accumulate in tissues of the buttocks or thighs as the result of impact and may be seen on CT scan or at autopsy. As a result, there may be evidence of anemia and rhabdomyolysis may occur from muscle trauma, with an adverse effect on renal function. In the case of necrosis, Creatine phosphokinase (CPK) would be elevated and a urine dipstick would be positive for blood. Myoglobinuria is confirmed by a specific urine test.*

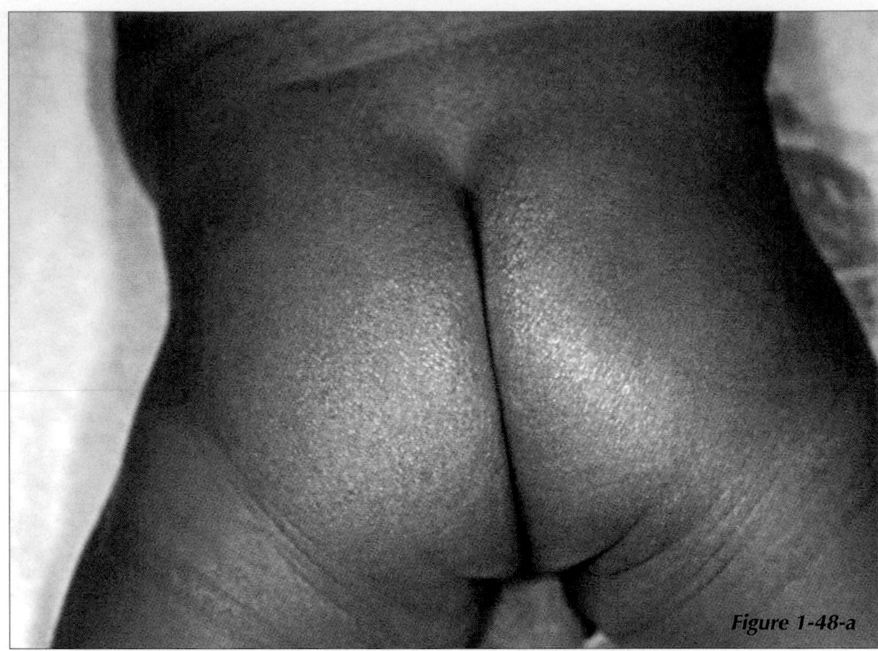

Figure 1-48-a

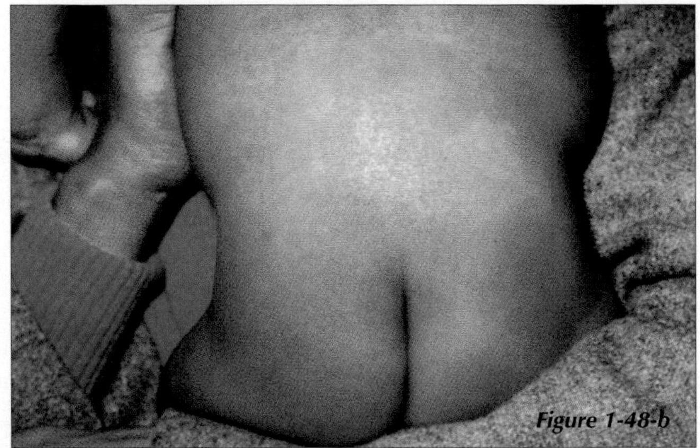

Figure 1-48-b

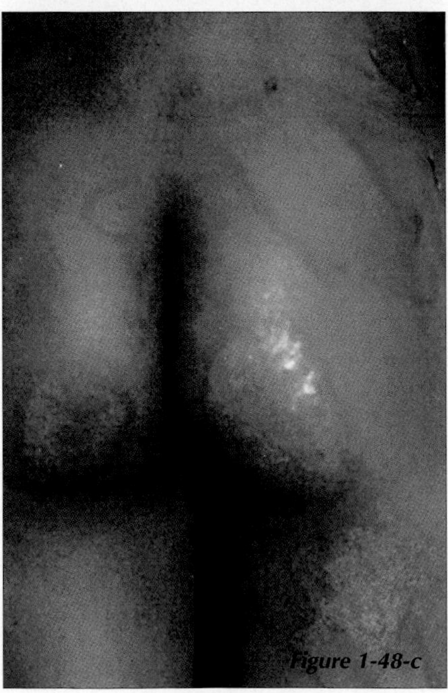

Figure 1-48-c

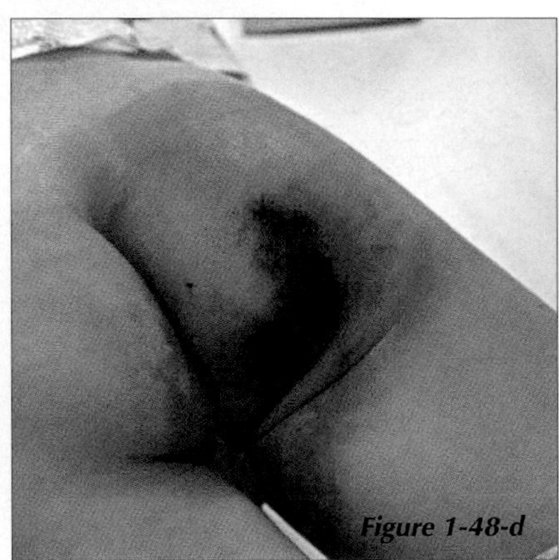

Figure 1-48-d

# Target Organs

**Case Study 1-49**

It is unusual for children to fall on their ears. Injured ears are more likely boxed or hit with an object.

***Figure 1-49-a.*** *The ear of this child was twisted. Unless the child's long hair was lifted and the back of the ear examined, this injury would have been missed.*

***Figure 1-49-b.*** *The bruise seen on the back of this child's ear and over the mastoid process is not considered to be from a direct blow. It is considered to be Battle's sign, or a manifestation of a basal skull fracture from disruption of the posterior auricular artery. However, it is possible that the blow that resulted in the basal skull fracture was directed to the ear.*

**Case Study 1-50**

Noises from a child that disturb a parent are more likely to come from the mouth. Crying, refusing to take food from a spoon or nipple, or swearing may result in a blow to the mouth or forced feeding. As with other impacts, it may be impossible to determine if the mouth hit the object in a fall or if a hand or wielded object hit the mouth. If children are communicating, they should be separated from parents to obtain a history. The object responsible for the impact can be forensically examined for traces of the child's blood.

***Figure 1-50.*** *The impact to this child's mouth was so severe it resulted in a laceration of the lip that required suturing.*

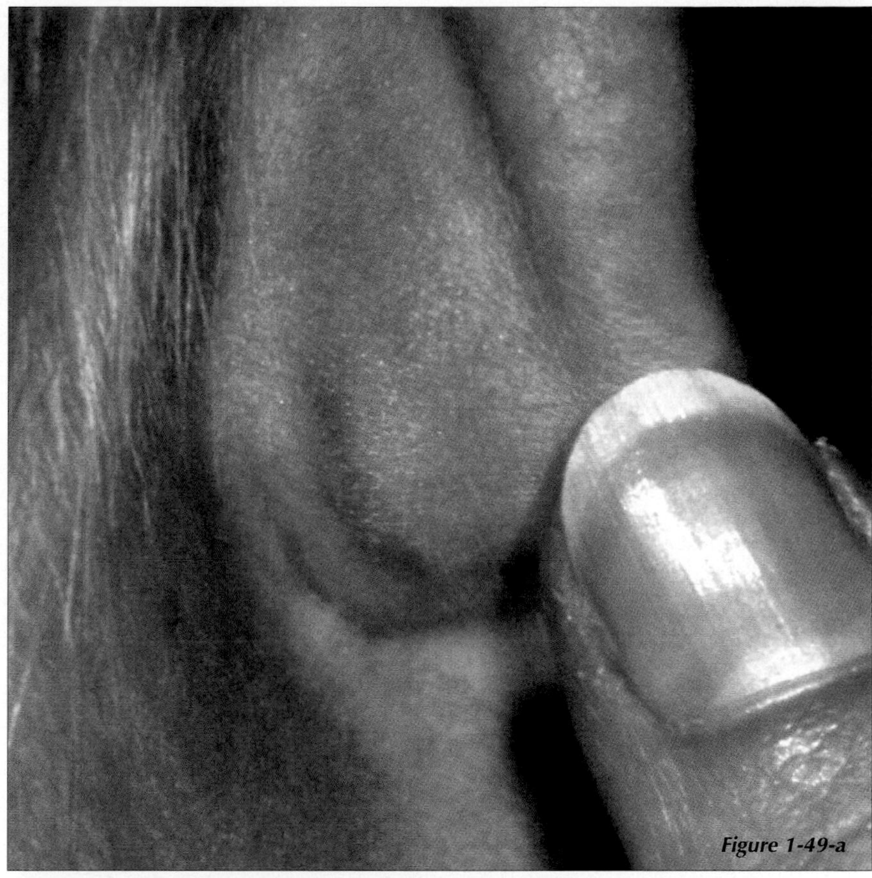

**Figure 1-49-a**

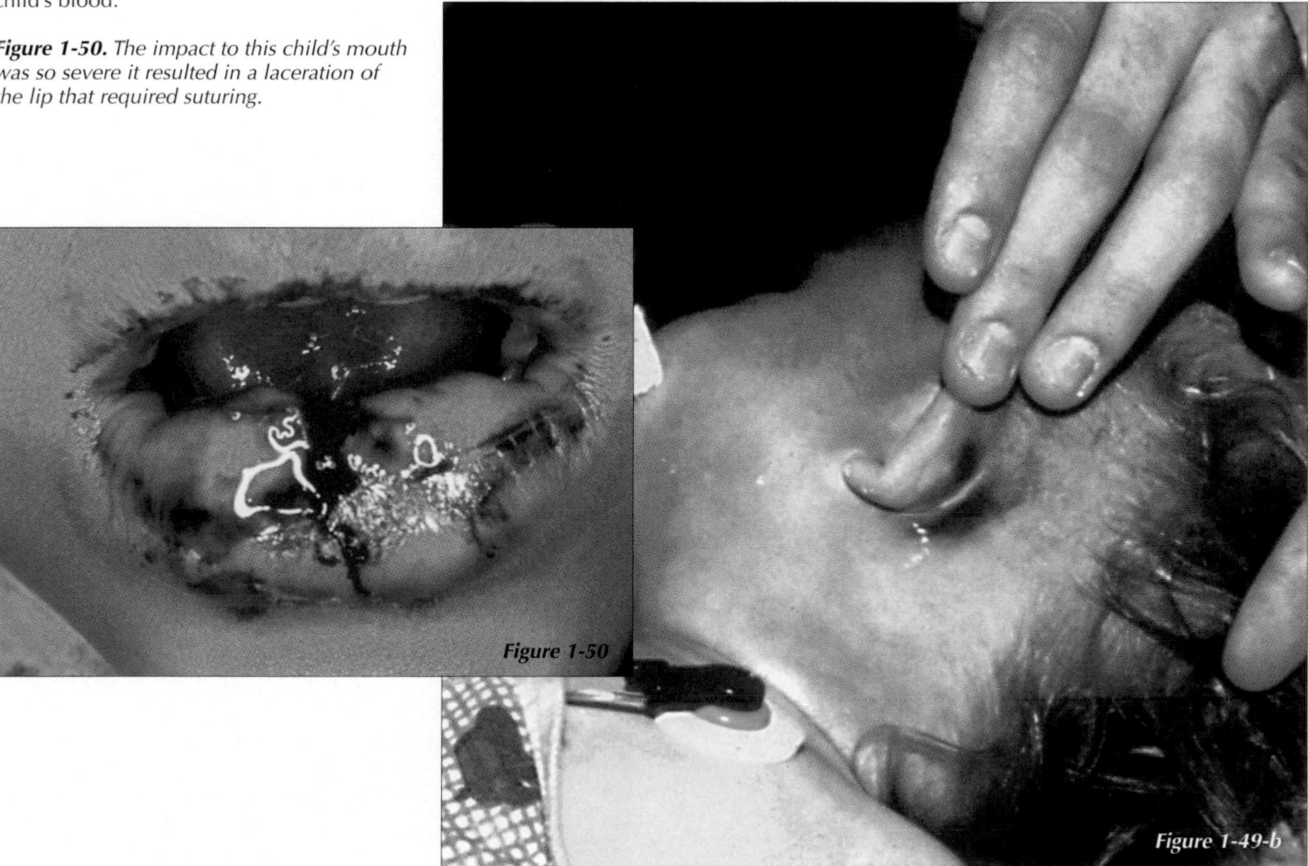

**Figure 1-50**

**Figure 1-49-b**

# Target Organs

**Case Study 1-51**

This 2-year-old child had a fatal head injury and evidence of previous traumatic chipping of the anterior enamel of the upper central incisor that is thought to have resulted from abuse.

***Figure 1-51.*** *Injury to teeth, lips, and gums may result from intentional or non-intentional impact trauma.*

**Case Study 1-52**

This 12-year-old boy was taken to the ER by the police after a domestic argument. The child's father had disciplined the boy, injuring his lower lip and ear.

***Figure 1-52-a.*** *A tooth has lacerated the lower lip. A similar injury could take place from an accidental impact.*

***Figure 1-52-b.*** *The child's ear is injured as well.*

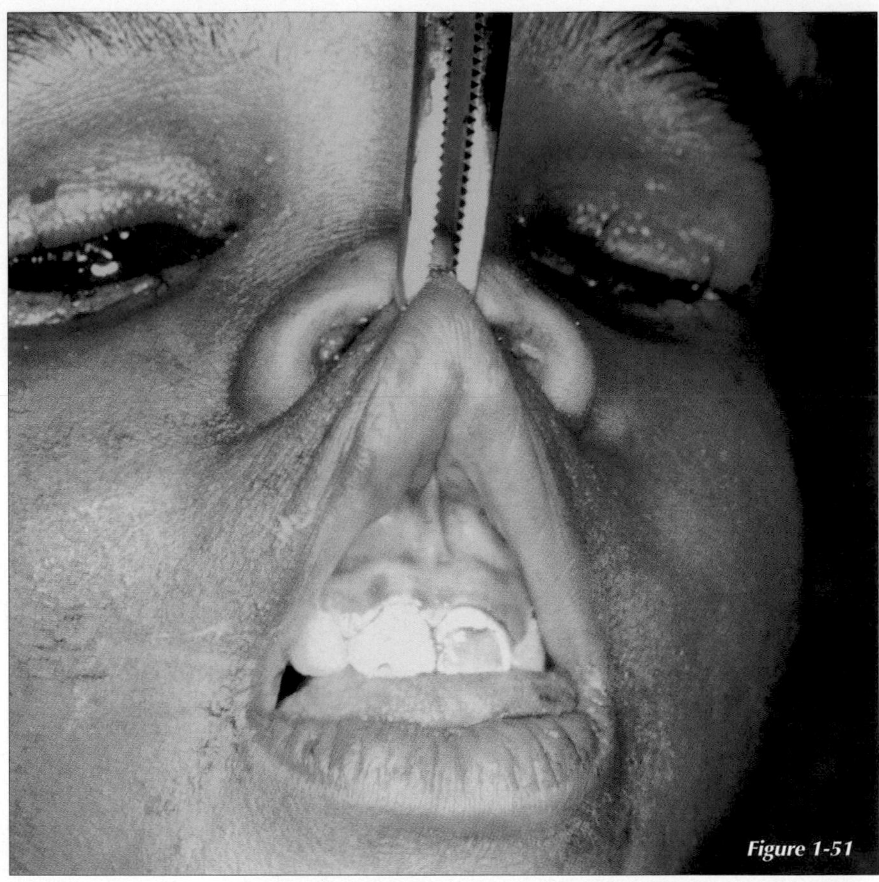

Figure 1-51

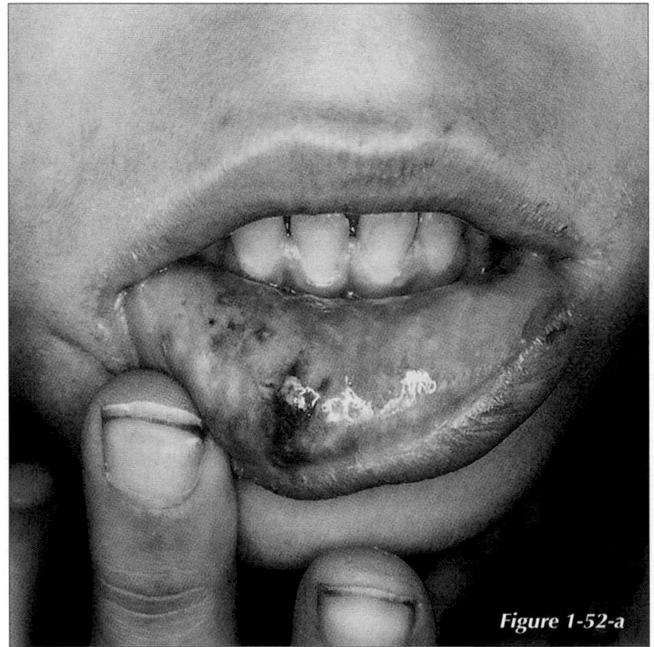

Figure 1-52-a

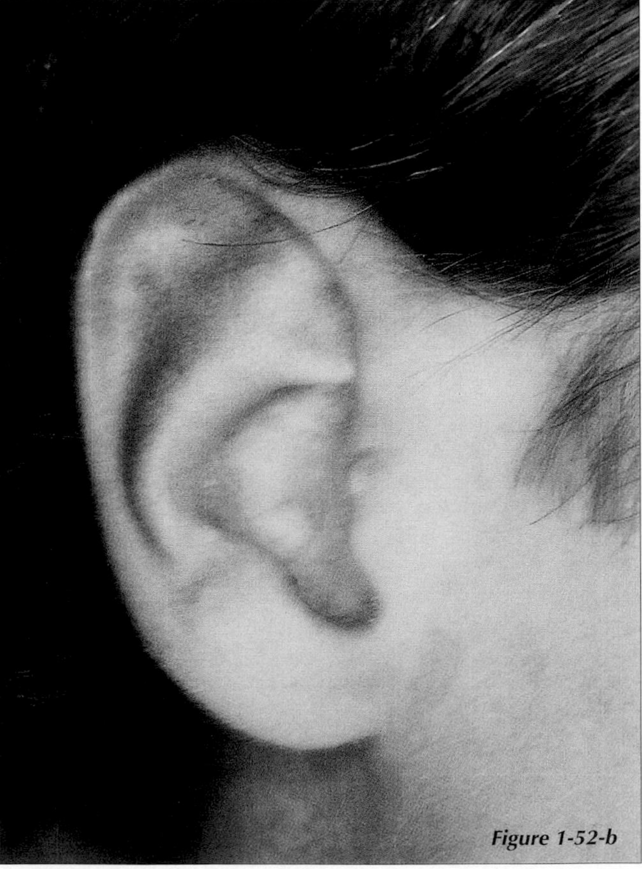

Figure 1-52-b

# Target Organs

**Case Study 1-53**

This 8-month-old boy was examined for multiple coalesced, short, linear lesions principally on the dorsum of both hands. The caregiver said that he saw a rat coming out of the child's room and thought that was probably how the injuries occurred. When the caregiver's history was challenged by saying that the injuries did not appear to be rat bites, the caregiver said that they had a puppy in the house that the child liked to play with, and the injuries were most likely caused by the puppy scratching the child. Healthcare workers believed that the injuries were secondary to disciplining the child with a hairbrush or similar instrument. Injuries resulting from a bite would appear distinct and punctate.

Though the marks were limited to the hands, a detailed examination of all body surfaces and orifices was needed, including a skeletal survey with follow-up in 7-10 days. Any symptoms of concern should have resulted in a CT or MRI scan of the head.

***Figures 1-53-a, b, c,** and **d.** Multiple coalesced, short, linear lesions on the dorsum of both hands.*

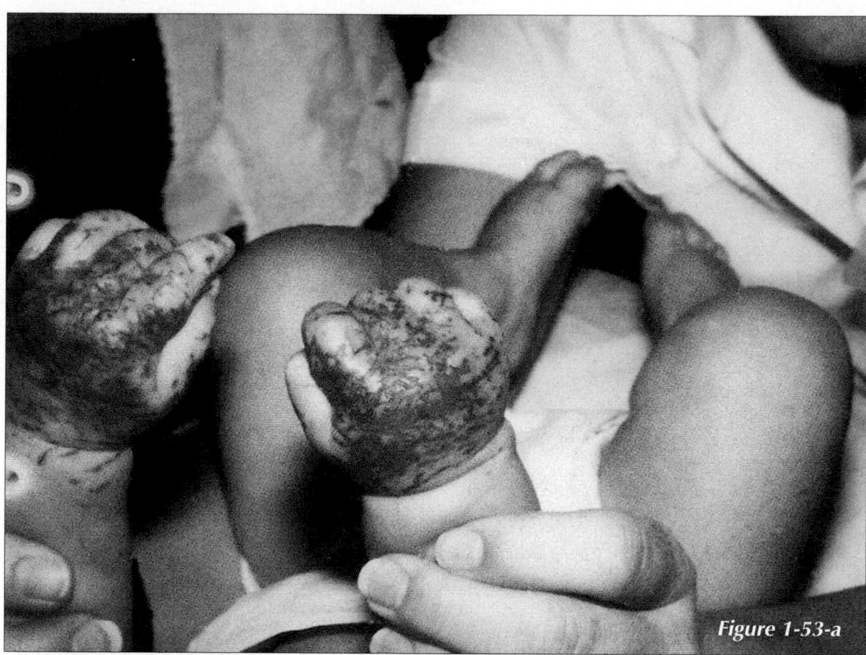

Figure 1-53-a

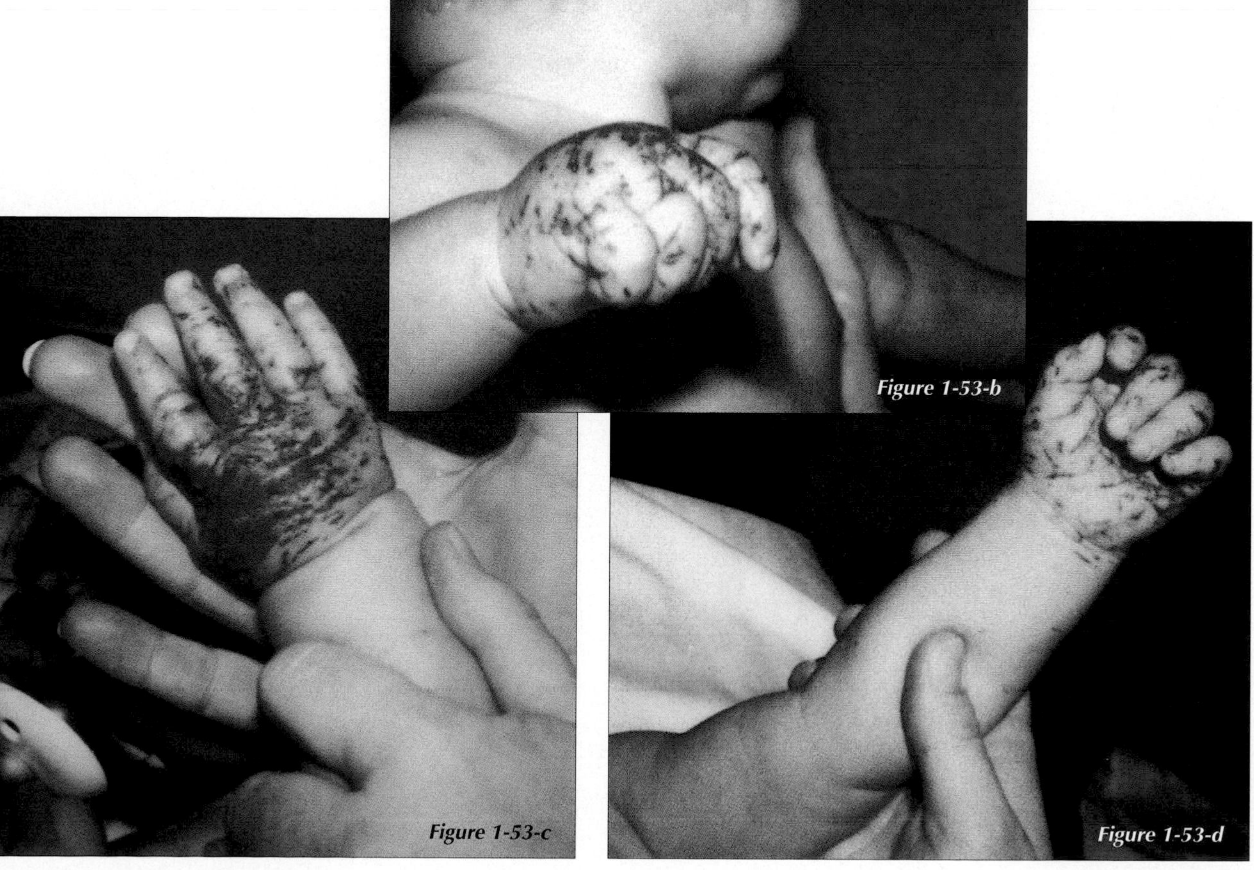

Figure 1-53-b

Figure 1-53-c

Figure 1-53-d

# Target Organs

**Case Study 1-54**

This 15-year-old girl was seen oral and eye injuries resulting from being beaten by her father. The oral injuries were not noticeable when her mouth was closed. All verbal children appearing with an injury should be separated from their caretakers and interviewed when possible to obtain their history of the injury. Children may fear giving an account of an intentional injury unless they can be convinced that they will be protected. As a routine, children and caretakers should be interviewed about domestic violence and animal abuse as these 3 forms of violence are related to each other.

***Figure 1-54-a.*** *Eye injuries.*

***Figures 1-54-b*** *and* ***c.*** *Oral injuries.*

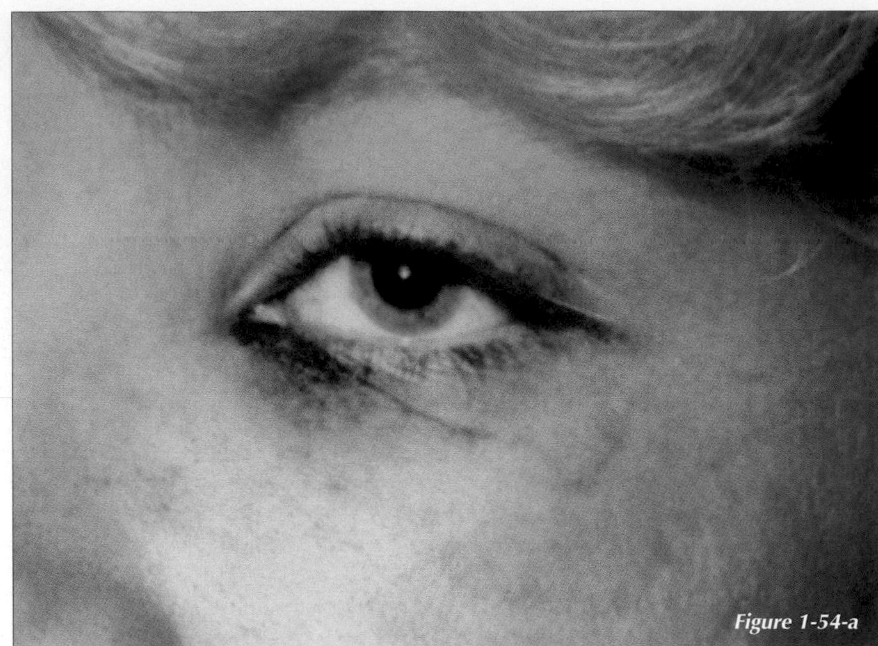

*Figure 1-54-a*

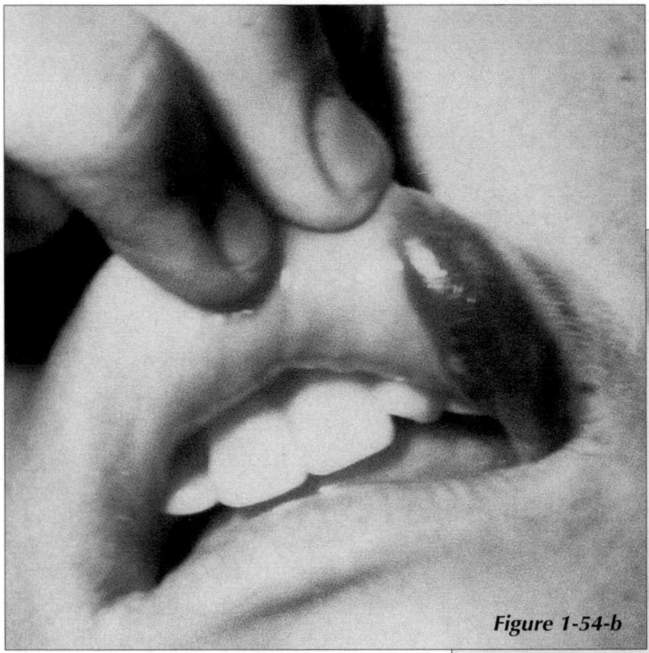

*Figure 1-54-b*

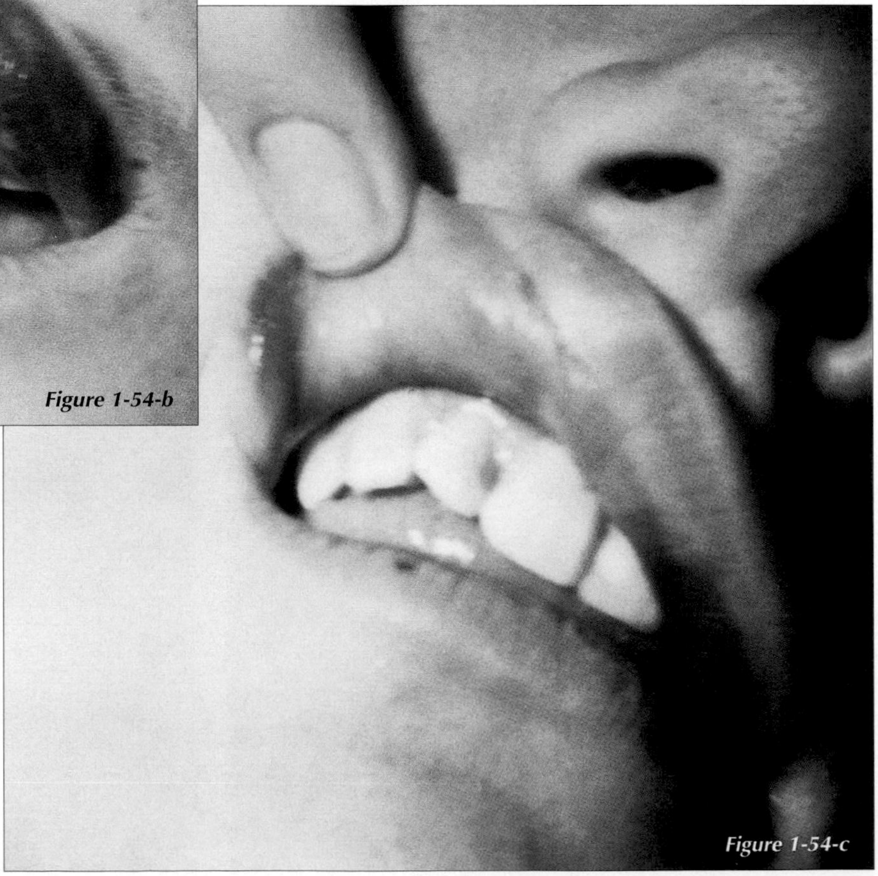

*Figure 1-54-c*

# Target Organs

**Case Study 1-55**

This 23-month-old boy was seen with multiple injuries as a result of a beating.

***Figures 1-55-a** and **b.** Loop marks appear on the child's face.*

***Figure 1-55-c.** An eye injury can also be seen on the boy.*

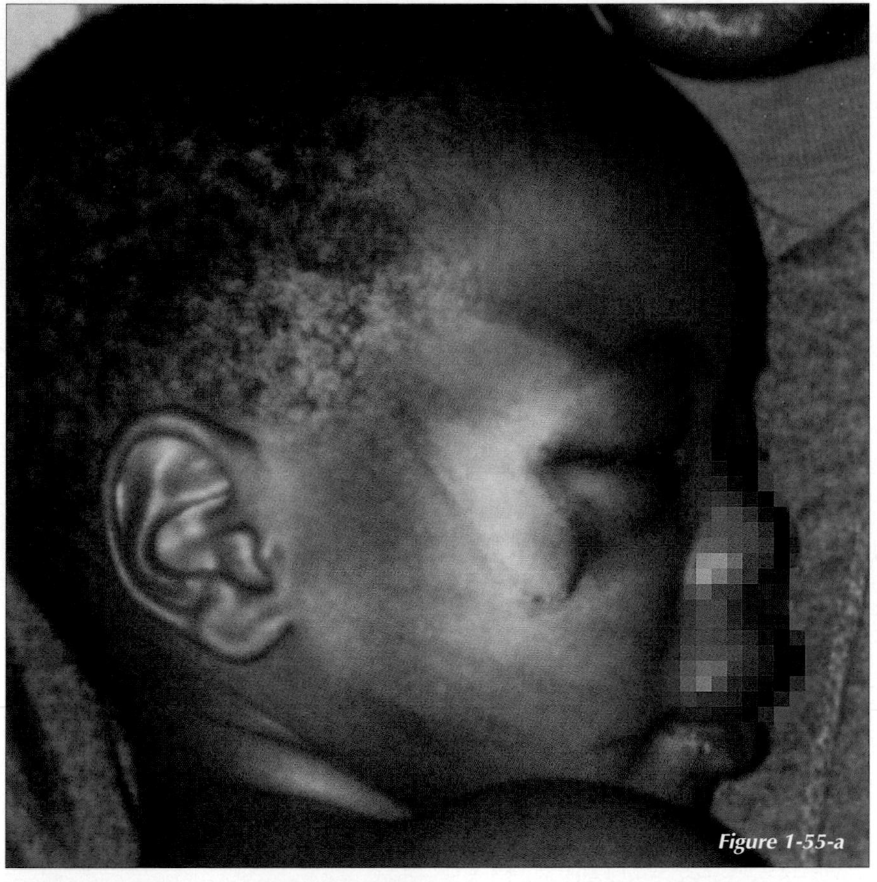

Figure 1-55-a

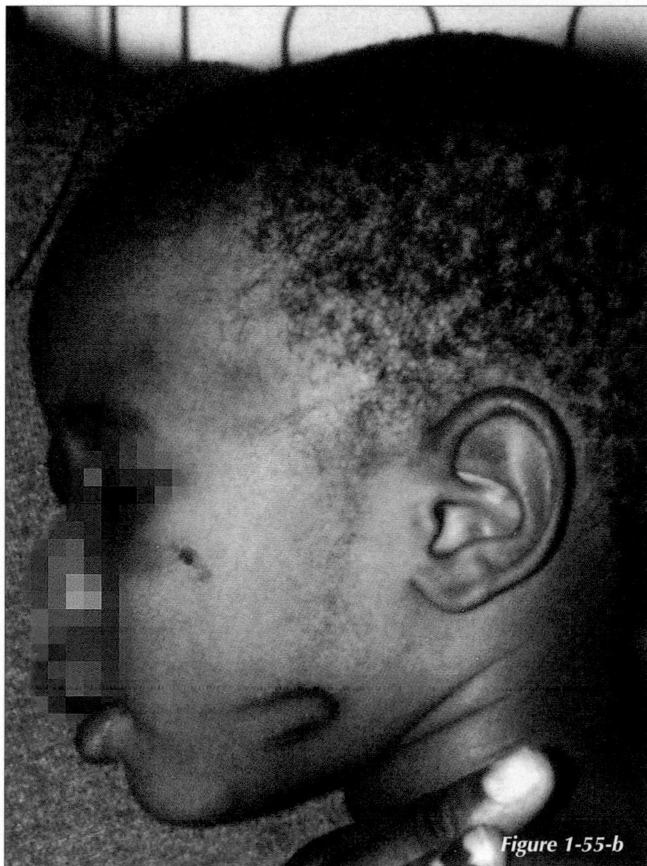

Figure 1-55-b

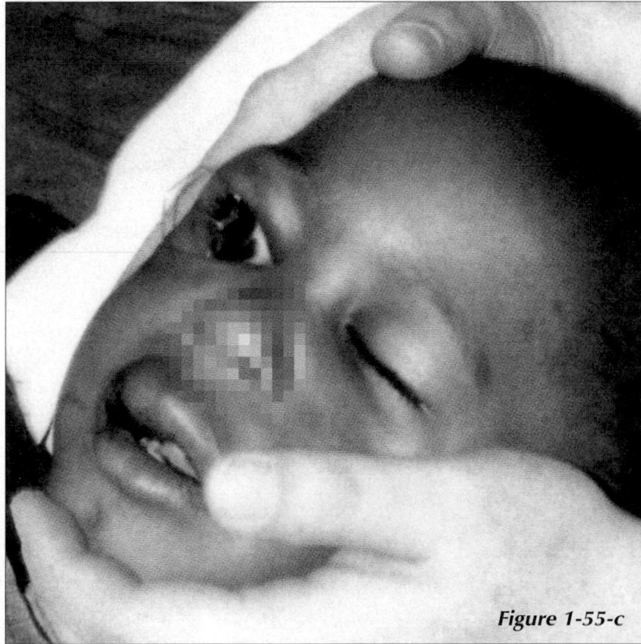

Figure 1-55-c

# TARGET ORGANS

**Case Study 1-56**

This 3-year-old boy was first seen in a small community hospital ER with the history that he had a fever and had been vomiting for 2 days. Before coming to the hospital he had suffered a convulsion. The child had a large hematoma of the left ear that the caregiver claimed occurred because he had been jumping on the bed and struck his ear against the bedpost. He had bruises on his chin and leg and a torn frenulum. He had a skull fracture with a subdural hematoma, a lacerated liver and pancreas, a fractured humerus, and large patches of his hair had been pulled out. In addition, he showed evidence of nutritional neglect.

The mother had 3 children: the patient, a 4-year-old brother, and a 9-year-old sister. They had been living and traveling across the country with a man and his 3-year-old son. The older sister related how the man had killed the younger brother and buried him somewhere in Oregon. Although the man severely abused the patient, his brother, and his sister, the man's own child had not been physically abused.

After several days in the hospital the patient was recovering. All children in the care of a suspect perpetrators of child maltreatment should receive a detailed physical examination. Additionally, children less than 2 years of age should have a skeletal survey, to be repeated in 7-10 days.

***Figures 1-56-a** and **b.** Bruises on this boy's chin and a torn frenulum.*

***Figure 1-56-c.** Bruising on this boy's legs.*

***Figures 1-56-d** and **e.** Note the lid lag and flat affect as well as the wasted extremities.*

***Figure 1-56-f.** Recent injury to ear caused by a blow to the side of the face. When an ear injury heals without medical intervention it leaves a distortion of the cartilage often called cauliflower ear.*

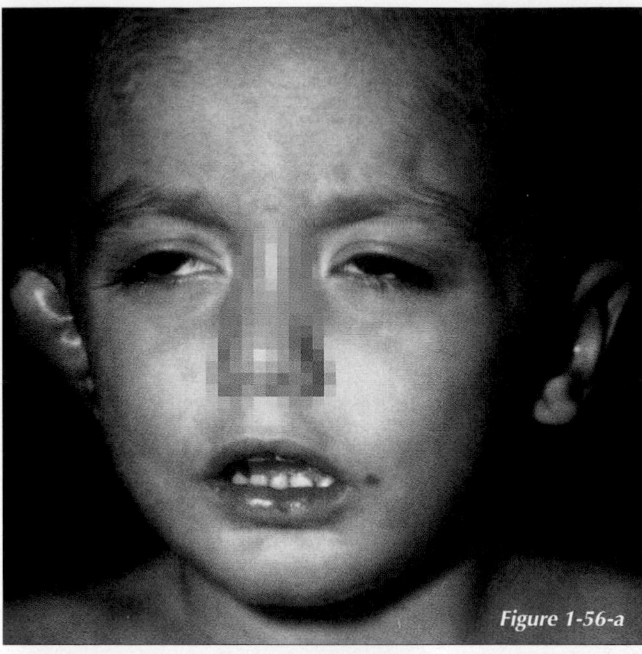

Figure 1-56-a

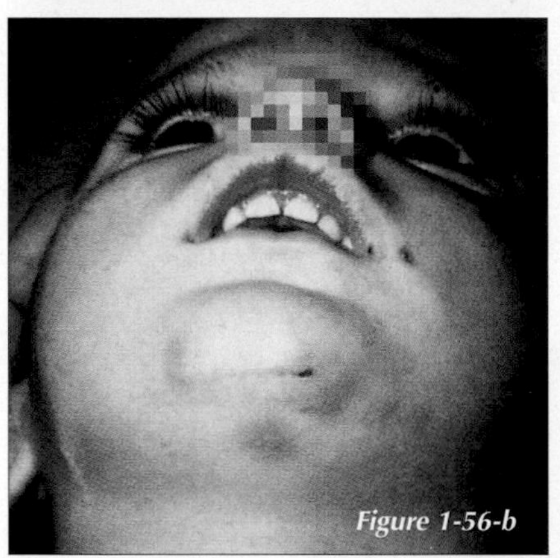

Figure 1-56-b

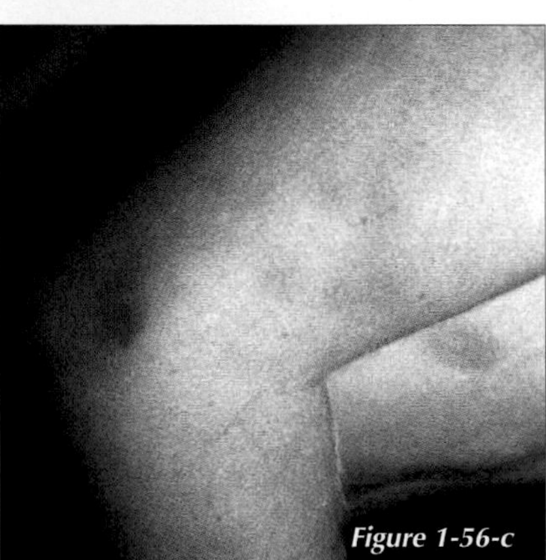

Figure 1-56-c

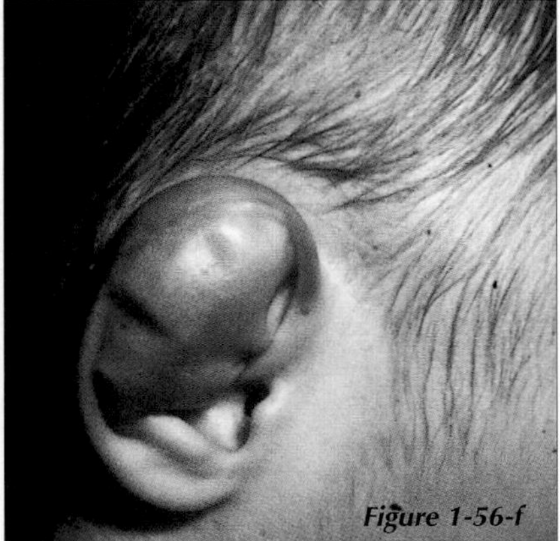

Figure 1-56-f

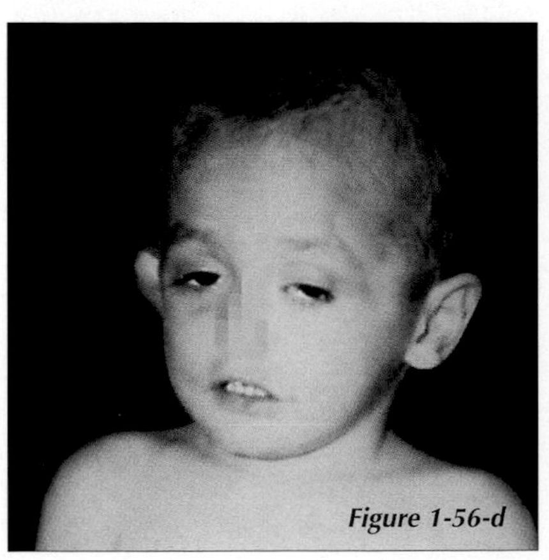

Figure 1-56-d

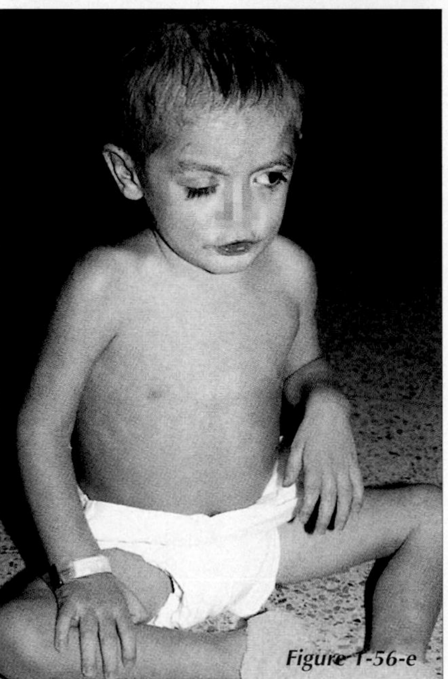

Figure 1-56-e

# Target Organs

**Case Study 1-57**

This 3-year-old boy was examined for a closed head injury caused by abuse. He previously had suffered a hematoma of the right ear that had gone untreated and left a residual deformation of the cartilage that could be seen when compared with his normal left ear. This deformity can be congenital.

***Figure 1-57-a***. *Cauliflower ear.*

***Figure 1-57-b.*** *Normal left ear.*

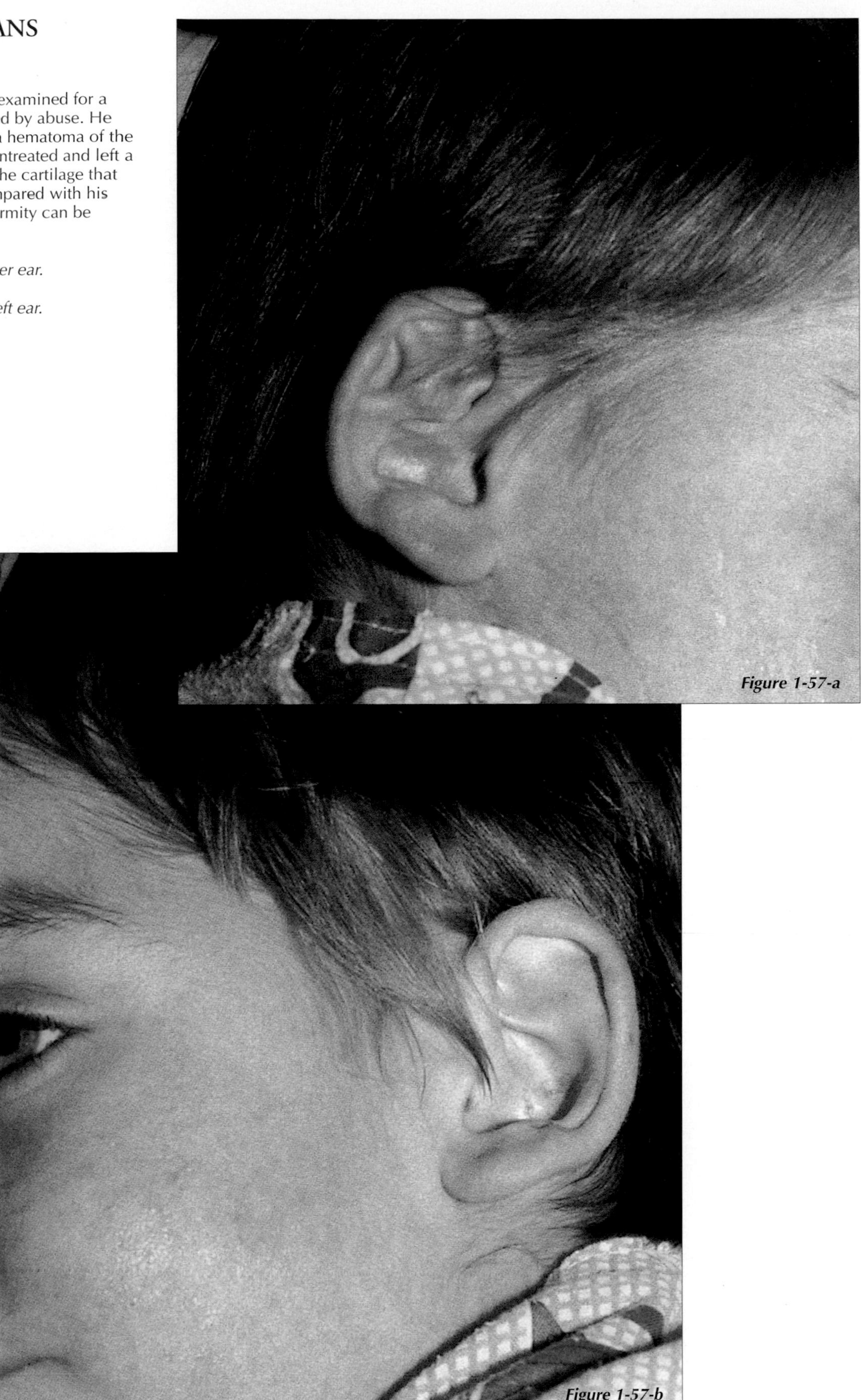

**Figure 1-57-a**

**Figure 1-57-b**

# Target Organs

**Case Study 1-58**

This 6-year-old boy came to the ER with a history that he had accidentally injured his eye. An alert resident noted fresh loop marks and the child stated that his eye was struck while he was being whipped. He had a corneal abrasion.

***Figure 1-58-a.*** *Corneal abrasion to the eye.*

***Figure 1-58-b.*** *Fresh loop marks on the boy's hip and abdomen.*

**Case Study 1-59**

This 3-year-old boy presented with dried blood in his external ear canal.

***Figure 1-59.*** *The boy's ruptured eardrum due to a slap to the side of the head.*

**Case Study 1-60**

This child was examined for bruising of the buttocks. Diapers protect the buttocks of pre–toilet-trained children. Impact must be hard enough to carry the blow through the diaper to the underlying skin, unless the child is struck while the diapers are off.

***Figure 1-60.*** *Bruising of the buttocks. The lesion in the upper right area of the buttocks is a nevus and not related to the abuse.*

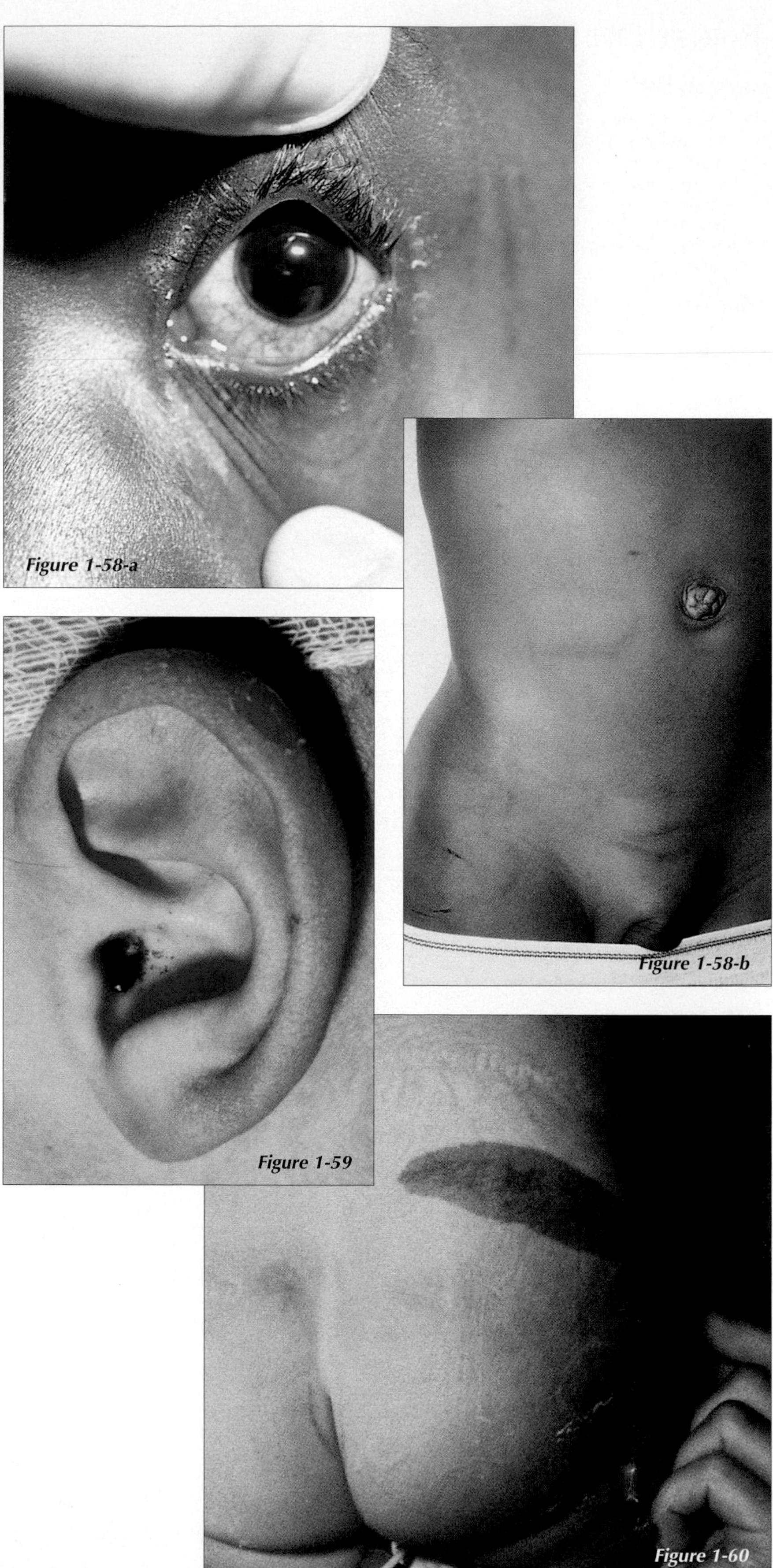
Figure 1-58-a
Figure 1-58-b
Figure 1-59
Figure 1-60

# Multiple Injuries

### Case Study 1-61

This 2-year-old boy's parents gave the history that they noted blood coming out of his ear after he had fallen out of his high chair. Abuse was suspected and reported. The child had a perforated right eardrum and circumferential markings to his arm where he was restrained. Other old and fresh bruises were noted on his forehead. The marks on the arm suggested that a cord was used for restraining the child. Marks from fingers are generally parallel. It is unusual to impact 2 body surfaces in a fall, eg, the left eye and right ear.

***Figure 1-61-a.*** *Bruising to the right cheek and blood in the right ear.*

***Figure 1-61-b.*** *Bruising was also found on the left eye.*

***Figure 1-61-c.*** *Circumferential markings on his arm, suggesting a cord used as a means of restraint.*

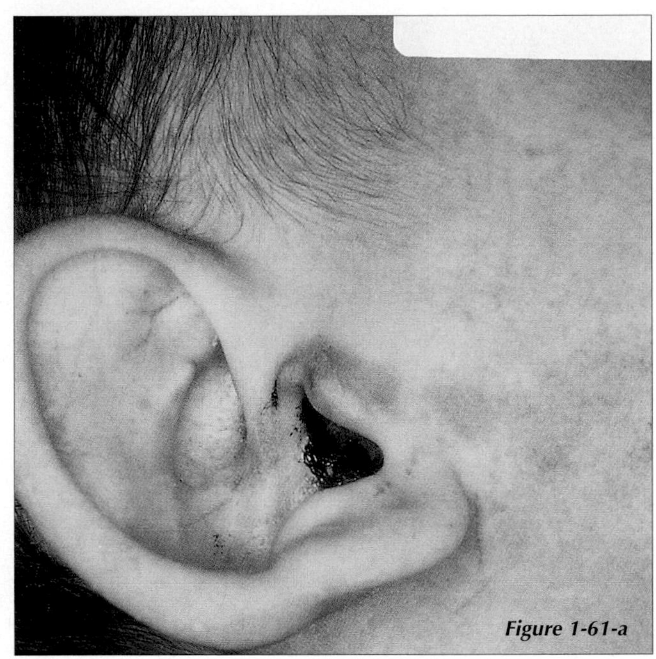

**Figure 1-61-a**

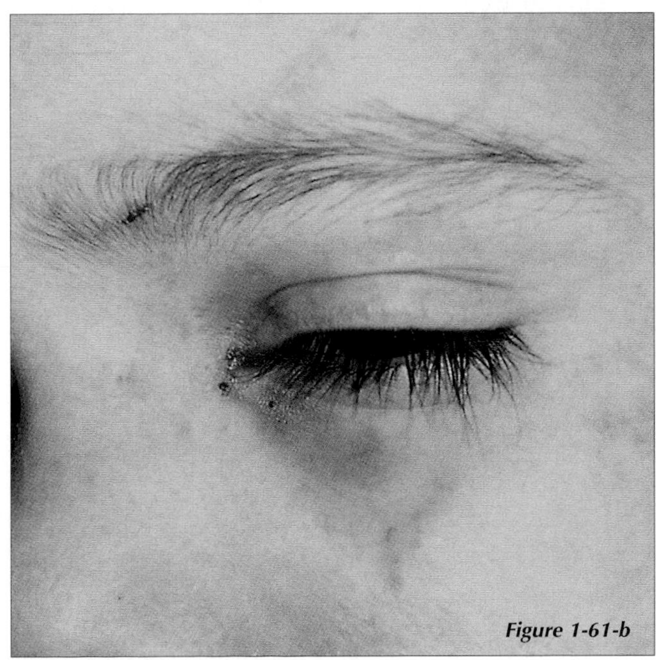

**Figure 1-61-b**

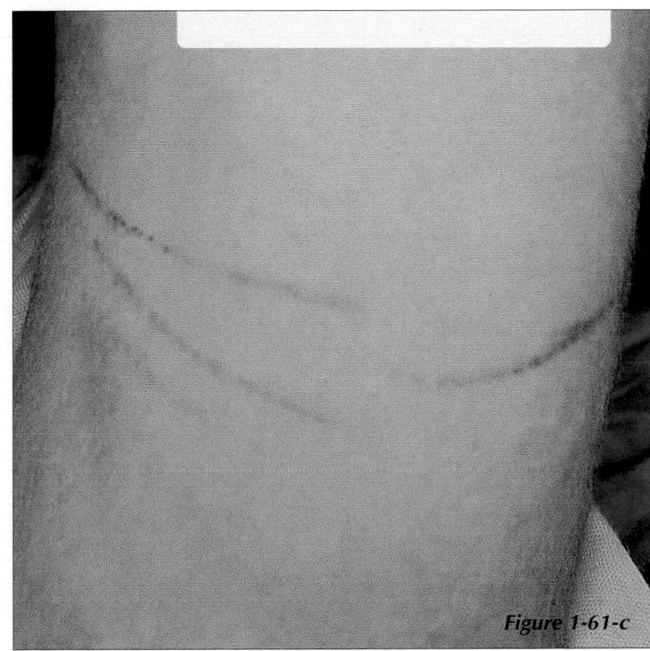

**Figure 1-61-c**

# Multiple Injuries

**Case Study 1-62**

This 24-month-old girl was brought to the ER by the police. Her mother had left her in the care of a 4-year-old sibling while she ran to answer a phone call next door. This was a form of abandonment and reportable as such. The 4-year-old ran after the mother, leaving the child unattended. According to the history given by the mother, the 2-year-old child tried to follow them. A neighbor found the child naked in the middle of the yard, sitting in a dog run. The dog was a puppy. The neighbor said that the dog was to the side, away from the child, at the time. The mother stated that the child's injuries were inflicted by the dog. None of the injuries were bites, and none resembled dog scratches. The cause of the injuries was not determined. The caregiver was reported for abuse. The history given by the mother did not match the nature or extent of the injuries.

***Figure 1-62-a.*** *Lateral facial bruising and ecchymoses.*

***Figure 1-62-b.*** *The ecchymotic areas of the back were parallel to one another.*

***Figure 1-62-c.*** *The abrasions on the back and chest were all singular and linear.*

***Figures 1-62-d*** *and* ***e.*** *More wounds appearing on the 2-year-old child.*

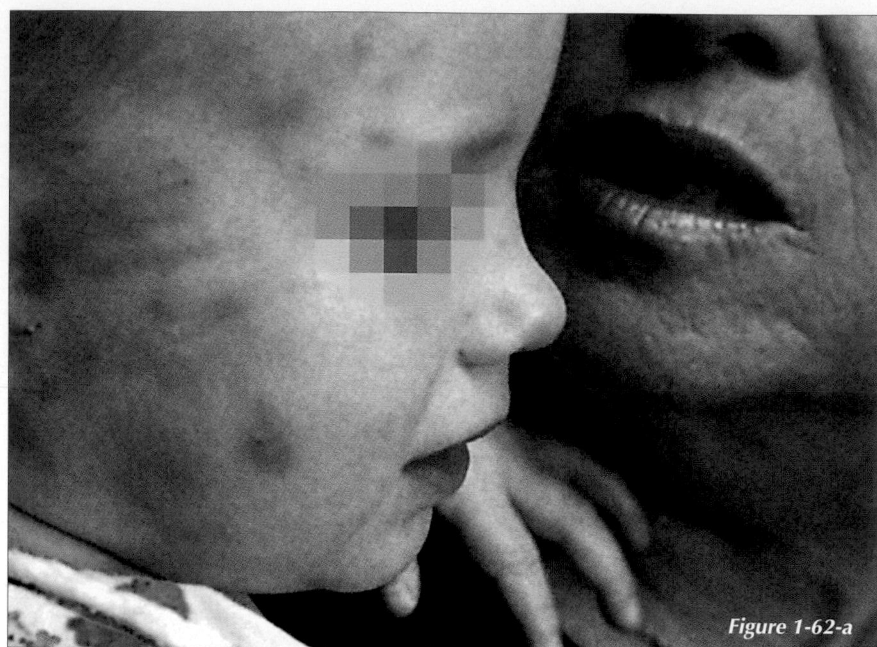
Figure 1-62-a

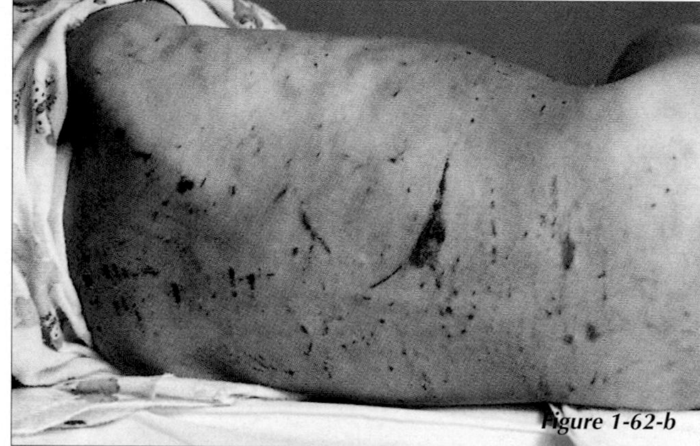
Figure 1-62-b

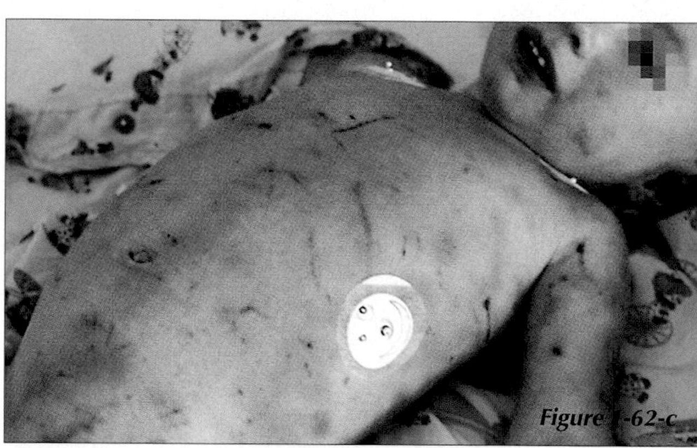
Figure 1-62-c

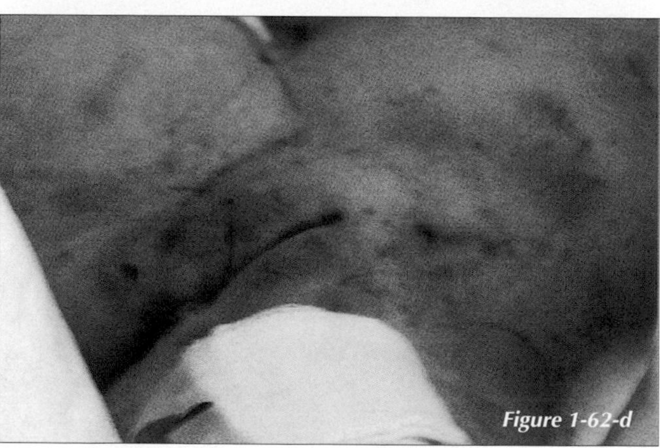
Figure 1-62-d

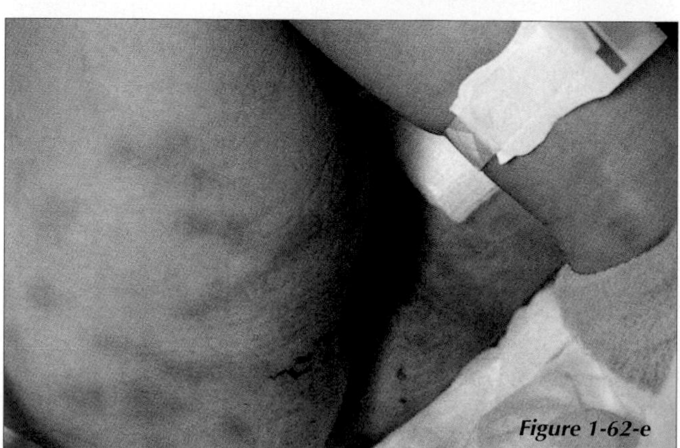
Figure 1-62-e

# Multiple Injuries

**Case Study 1-62** *(continued)*

***Figure 1-62-f.*** *This 3-year-old child is shown for comparison, illustrating a child who was bitten numerous times by a dog on a chain. None of the injuries appear to be made by the chain.*

***Figure 1-62-g.*** *The 24-month-old child also has an anal tear and several puncture wounds of the perianal area. Rectal fissures may result from a large, hard stool exiting the anus, or from an object larger than the anal opening entering the anus.*

***Figure 1-62-h.*** *Vaginal examination show an imperforate hymen (under low power).*

***Figure 1-62-i.*** *The anal fissures appear to be fresher than the other wounds, which are in the process of healing.*

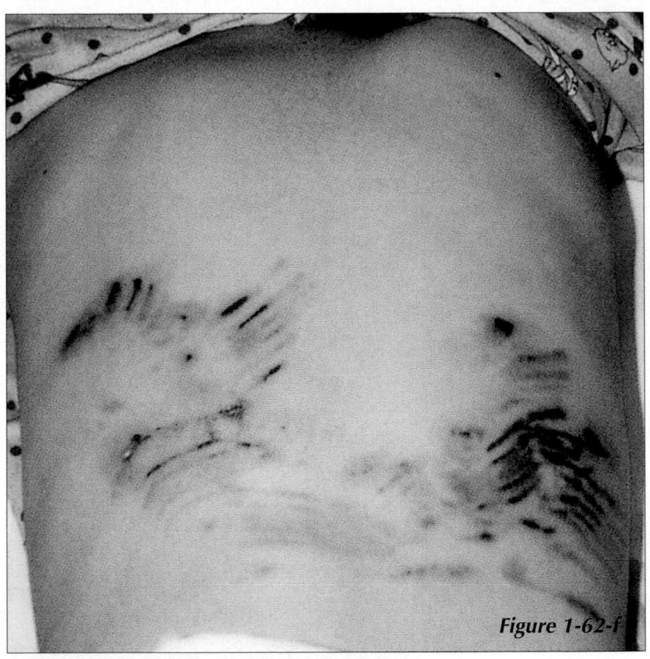

Figure 1-62-f

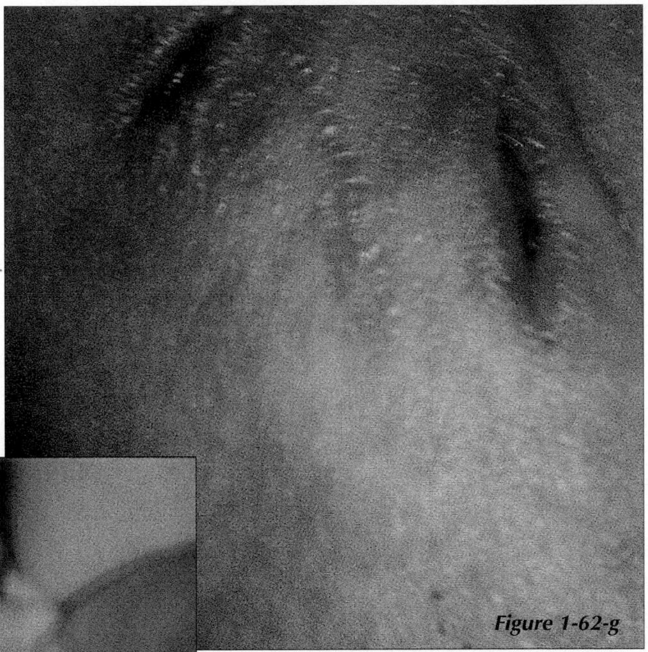

Figure 1-62-g

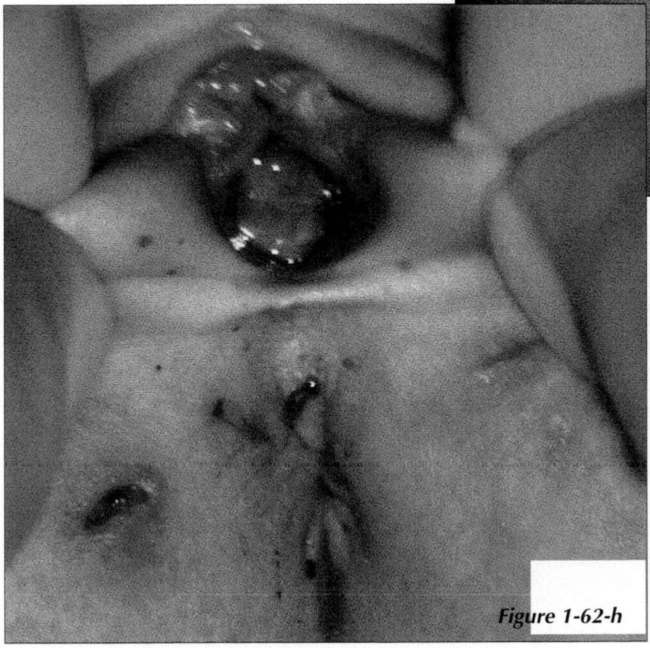

Figure 1-62-h

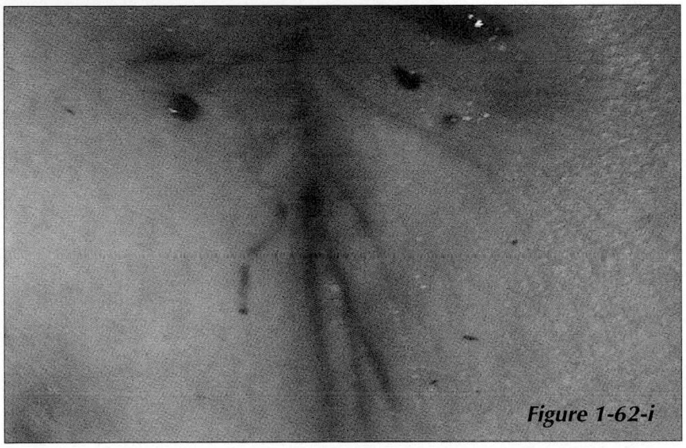

Figure 1-62-i

## Multiple Injuries

**Case Study 1-63**

This 5-month-old infant was seen in acute care for a fever. She was found to have several small ecchymotic areas on the chest and one on the hip, as well as a torn frenulum. A torn frenulum can be the result of forced bottle-feeding or laceration from an adult fingernail. A 5 month old is not able to ambulate and falls to the face would not be expected to cause lacerations of the tongue frenulum.

***Figure 1-63-a.*** *Ecchymotic areas on the chest.*

***Figure 1-63-b.*** *Torn frenulum.*

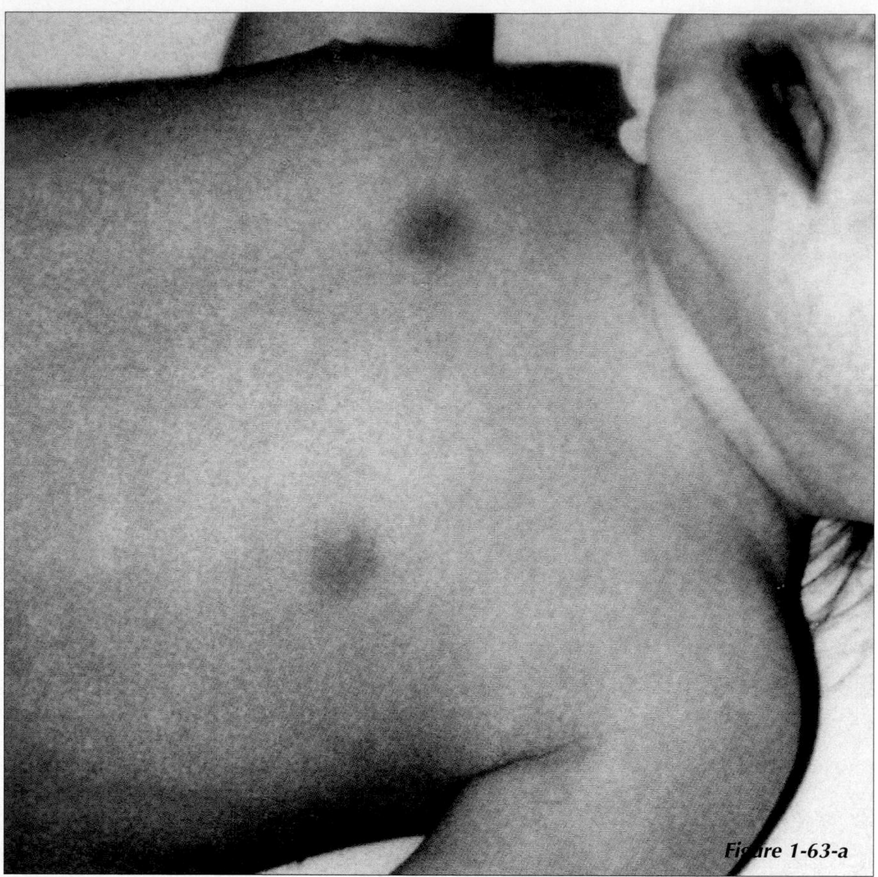

**Figure 1-63-a**

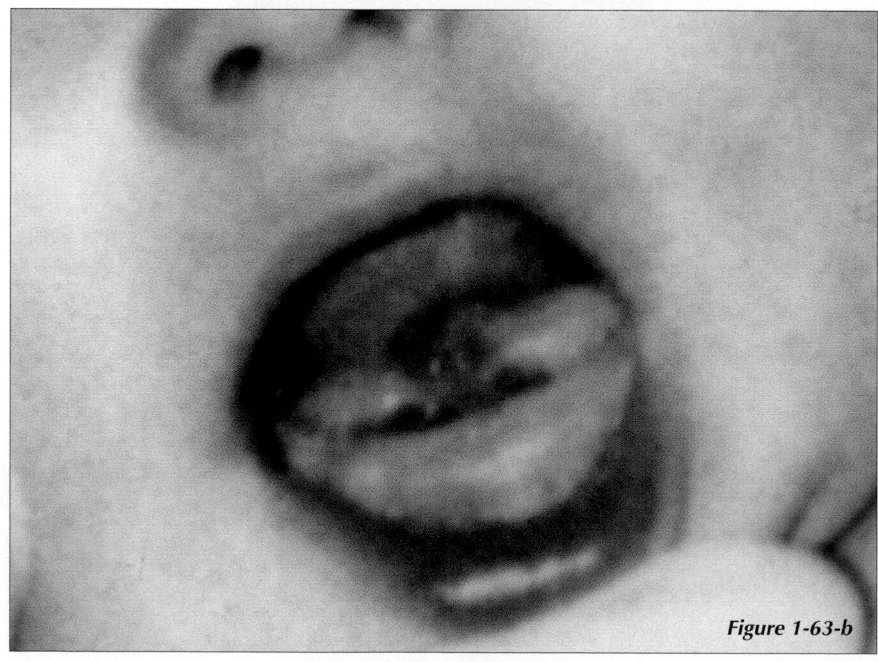

**Figure 1-63-b**

# Multiple Injuries

**Case Study 1-64**

This 2-year-old boy was taken to the ER by his mother and her boyfriend. The mother said that the child had been vomiting for the past day, was unable to hold any food or liquids down, and had a fever. The child had multiple bruises in various stages of healing and on multiple surface areas, including the genitalia. When asked why the child had so many bruises, the mother said that he had been injured by their dog. The child had a laceration of the pancreas and a post-traumatic pancreatic pseudocyst, which required surgery. The child was well below the third percentile in height and weight. He was in the care of his mother's boyfriend while the mother worked. It is important to note that although he had a severe intra-abdominal injury, there was no evidence of injury to the external abdominal wall. Persistent vomiting in a child with other signs of maltreatment requires surgical consultation and an MRI examination of the abdominal anatomy and laboratory investigation for signs of organ damage. The most common cause of oval marks in a series is from fingertips. Overlying the photo with a transparent outline of the hand belonging to the adult in question may clarify this suspicion.

***Figure 1-64-a.*** *Bruises in various stages of healing on the neck and shoulder.*

***Figure 1-64-b.*** *Bruises on the boy's leg.*

***Figure 1-64-c.*** *Bruises on the boy's buttocks.*

***Figure 1-64-d.*** *Brusies on the boy's toe.*

***Figure 1-64-e.*** *Bruises on the genitalia.*

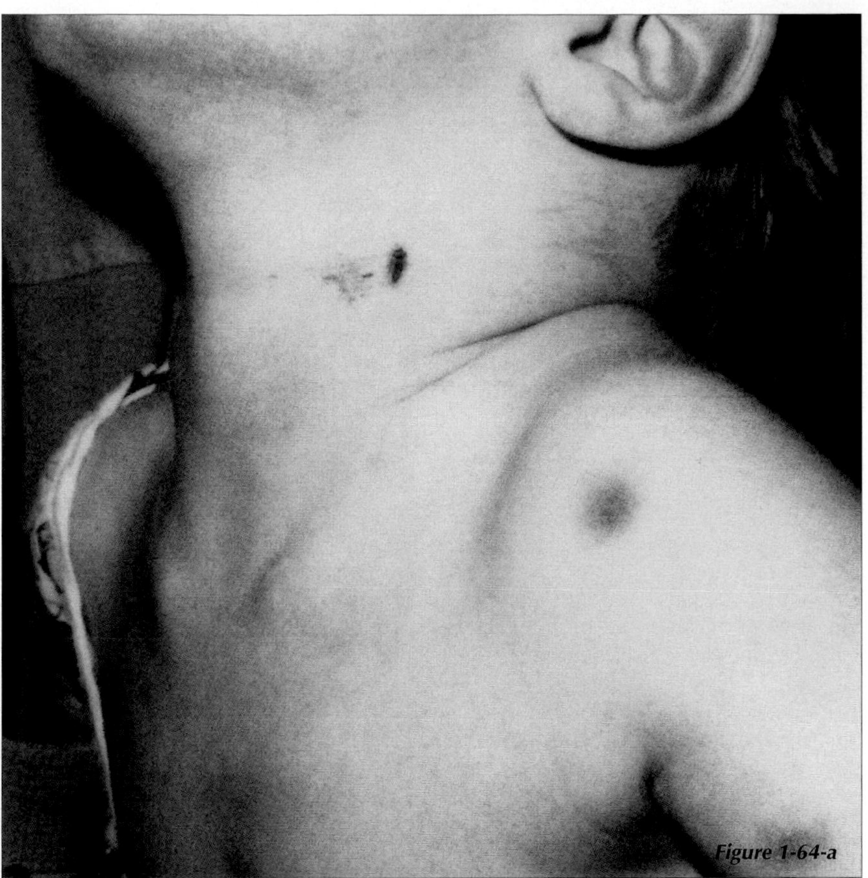
Figure 1-64-a

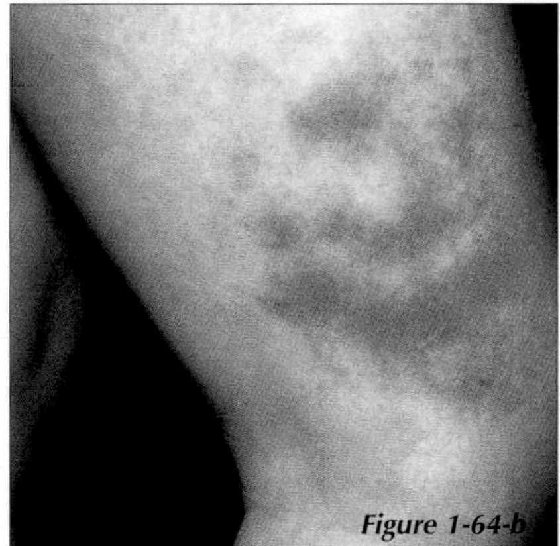
Figure 1-64-b

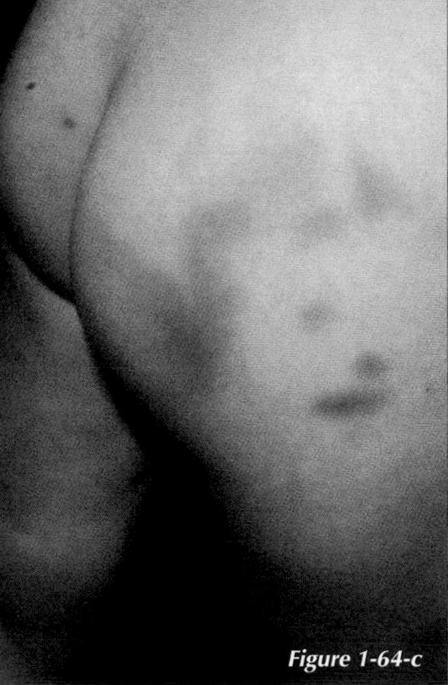
Figure 1-64-c

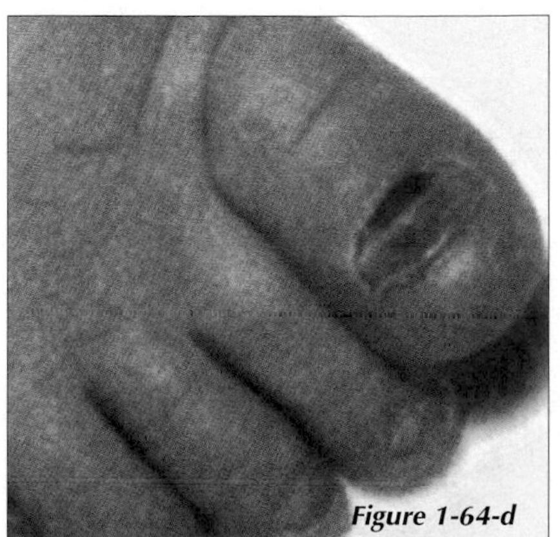
Figure 1-64-d

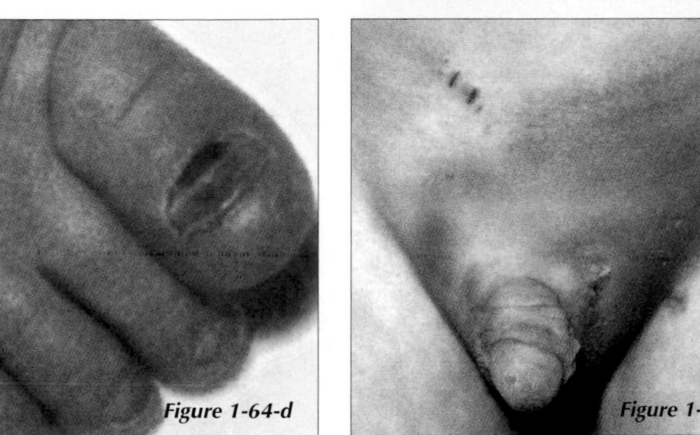
Figure 1-64-e

## Multiple Injuries

**Case Study 1-65**

The history given by the caregivers of this 3-year-old girl was that she fell down the stairs. She had fresh bruises that were all the same age on every body surface, in addition to a closed head injury with a cerebral hemorrhage and blunt trauma to the abdomen. The 18-year-old mother was living with a 21-year-old man. When the history given was challenged, the mother admitted that she and her boyfriend "got stoned" and beat the child. Six weeks before this admission the child was seen in another hospital with similar but less serious injuries. The child was sent home with the understanding that the boyfriend would no longer have access to her daughter. However, the family was not monitored closely enough and the boyfriend returned. The child was sent to a rehabilitative hospital in a chronic vegetative state. The failure to adequately protect this child was an institutional one, or a form of institutional safety neglect requiring review and policy revision.

***Figures 1-65-a, b,*** *and* ***c.*** *Multiple bruises appearing on this 3-year-old girl with a closed head injury with a cerebral hemorrhage and trauma to the abdomen.*

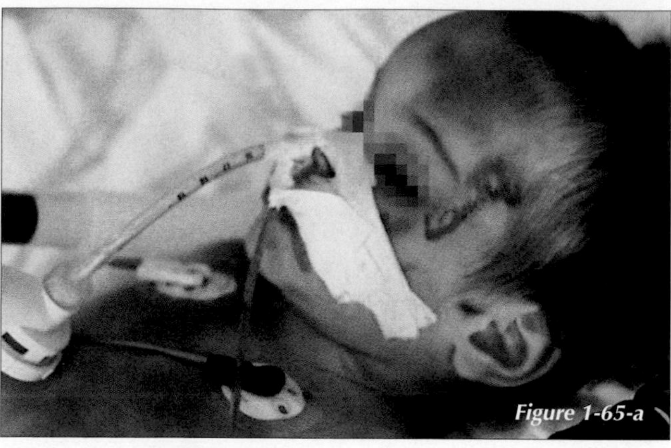

**Figure 1-65-a**

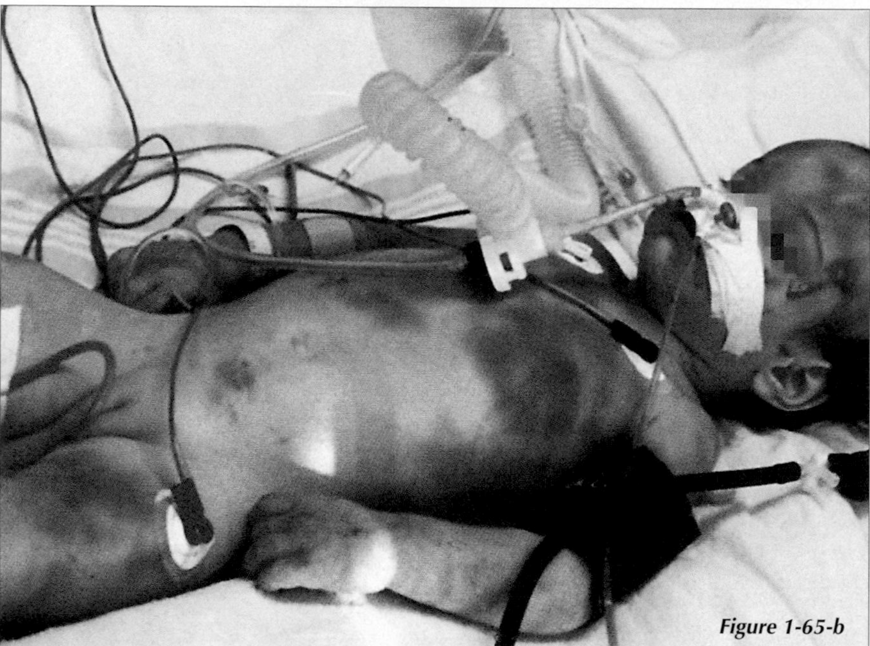

**Figure 1-65-b**

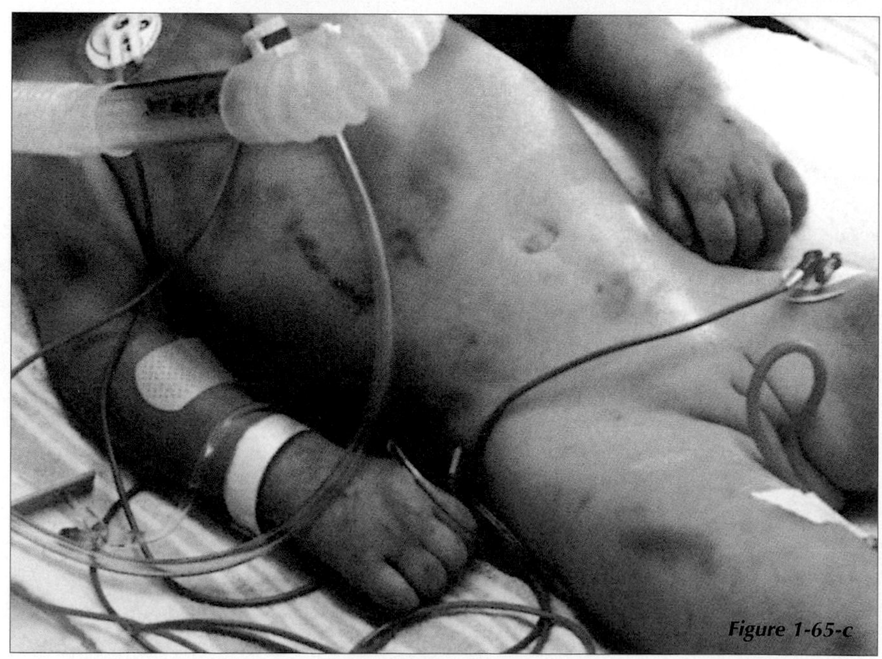

**Figure 1-65-c**

## Multiple Injuries

**Case Study 1-66**

This 11-week-old boy was left in the care of his teenage father who said he found the child unresponsive. He called the mother to come home. They took the child to the hospital where he survived 2 days, although he was brain dead.

***Figures 1-66-a*** *and* ***b.*** *Contusion of the penis determined at autopsy.*

***Figure 1-66-c.*** *A large contusion of the frontoparietal scalp is seen as subgaleal hemorrhage. Marks that result from impact to the skull which are not apparent on physical examination may be seen at autopsy when the scalp is retracted.*

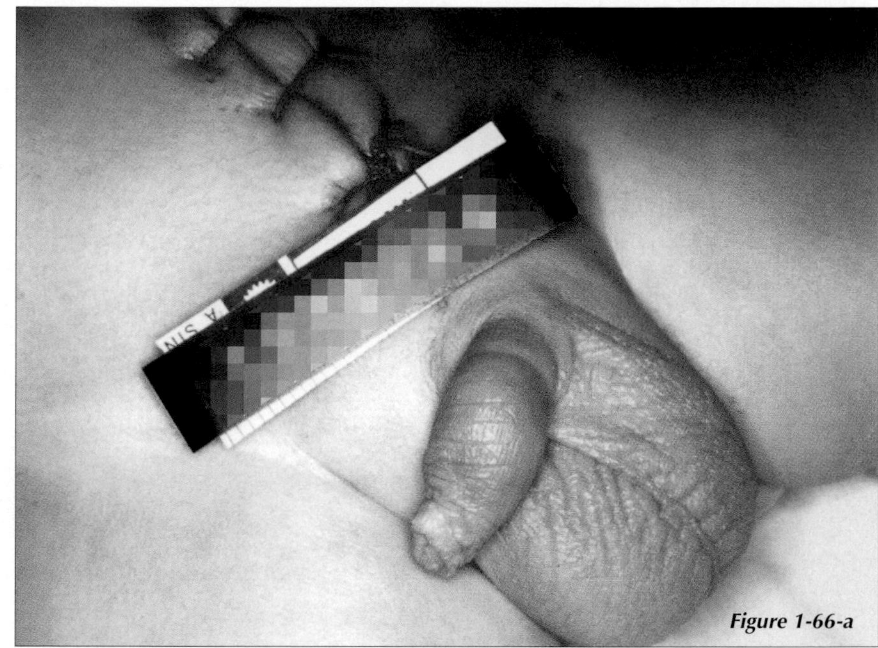

**Figure 1-66-a**

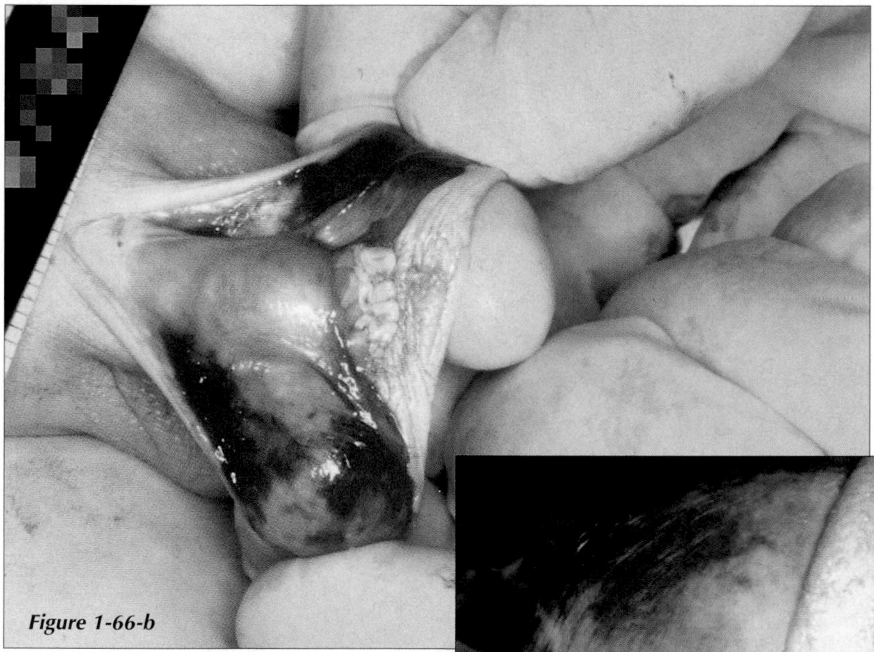

**Figure 1-66-b**

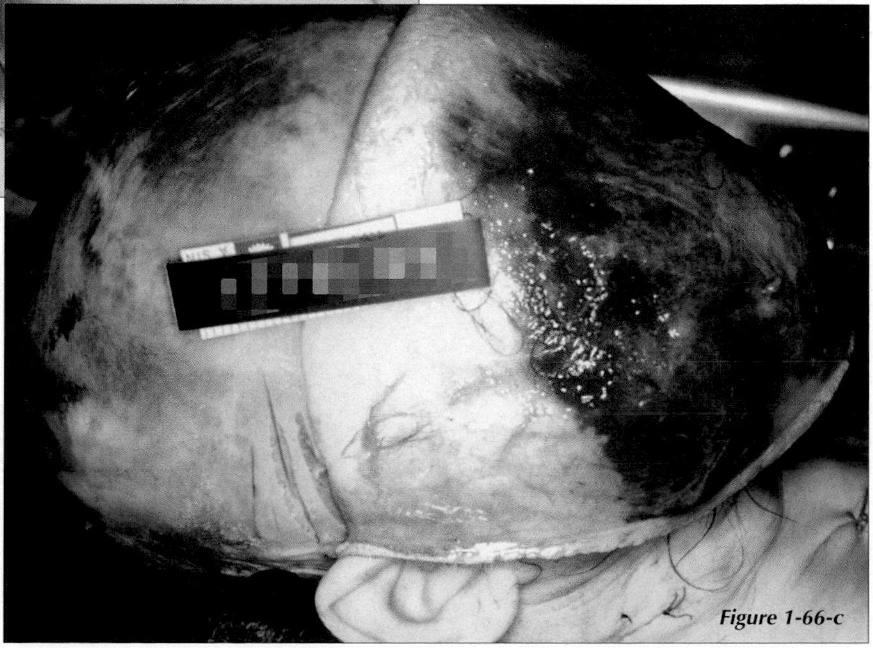

**Figure 1-66-c**

# Multiple Injuries

**Case Study 1-66** *(continued)*

***Figure 1-66-d.*** *Small amounts of subdural hemorrhage over the cerebral convexities*

***Figure 1-66-e.*** *Healing fractures of left ribs 3, 4, 5, and 6 posteriorly (arrows)*

***Figure 1-66-f.*** *Three of the excised ribs show early callus formation.*

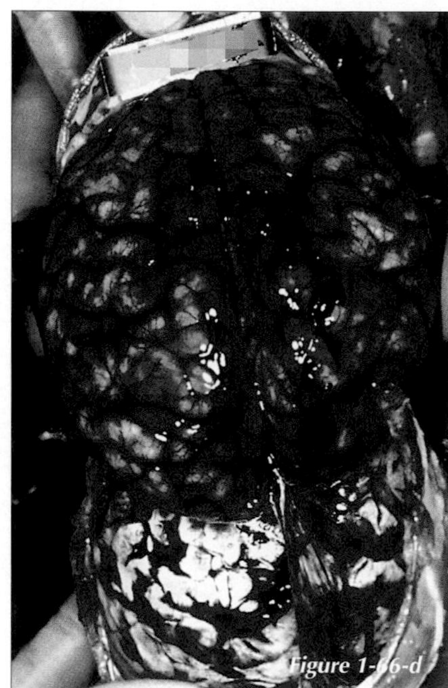

Figure 1-66-d

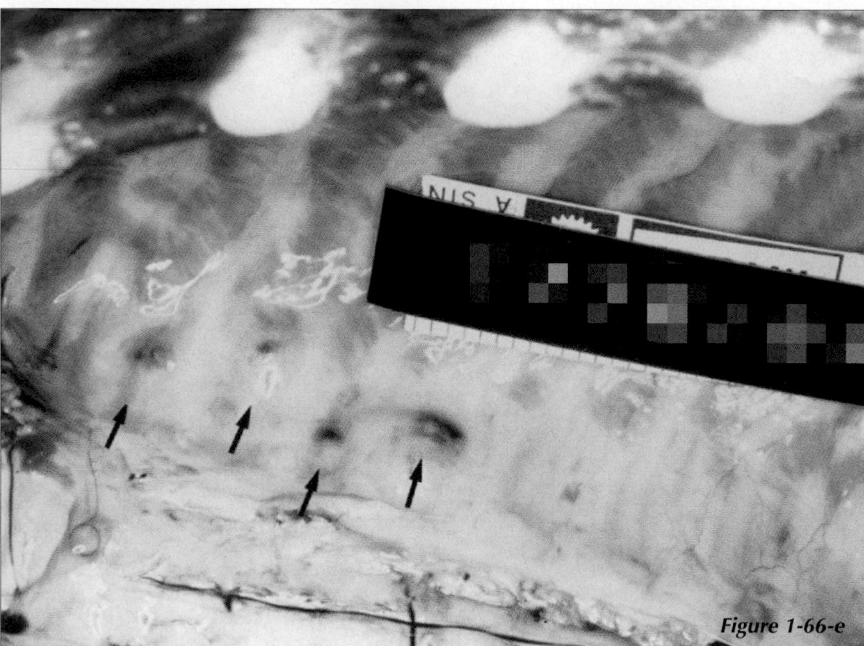

Figure 1-66-e

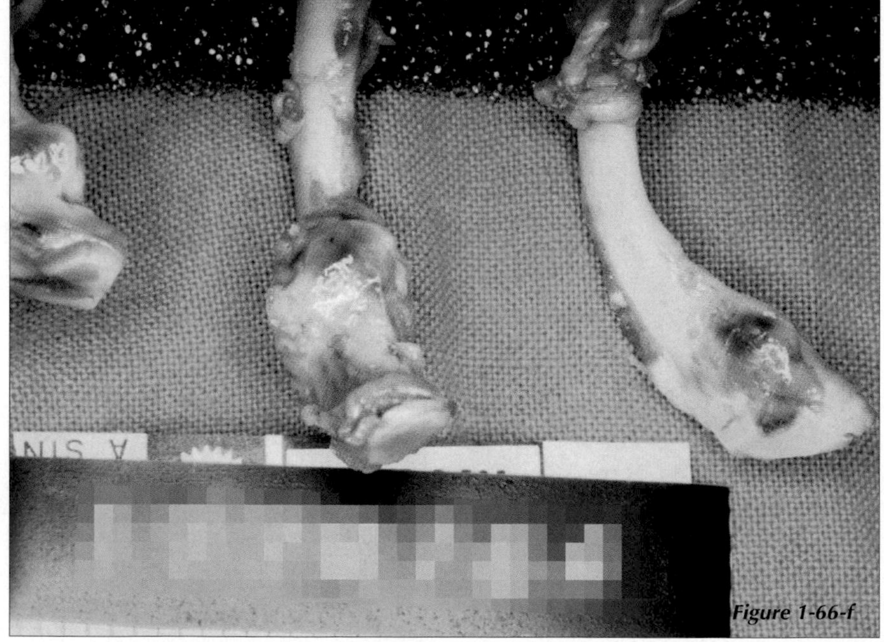

Figure 1-66-f

## Strangulation

**Case Study 1-67**

This 12-year-old was seen as a result of an attempted strangualtion. Children may attempt self-strangulation with a cord looped around their neck and tied to another object such as a doorknob. This has been reported in conjunction with masturbation.

***Figure 1-67-a.*** *A lateral view of attempted strangulation is seen. Note the small petechial hemorrhages above the injury. The single linear mark suggests that a cord was used in strangulation. Finger outlines are seen in attempted strangulation with hands.*

***Figure 1-67-b.*** *Frontal view of attempted strangulation.*

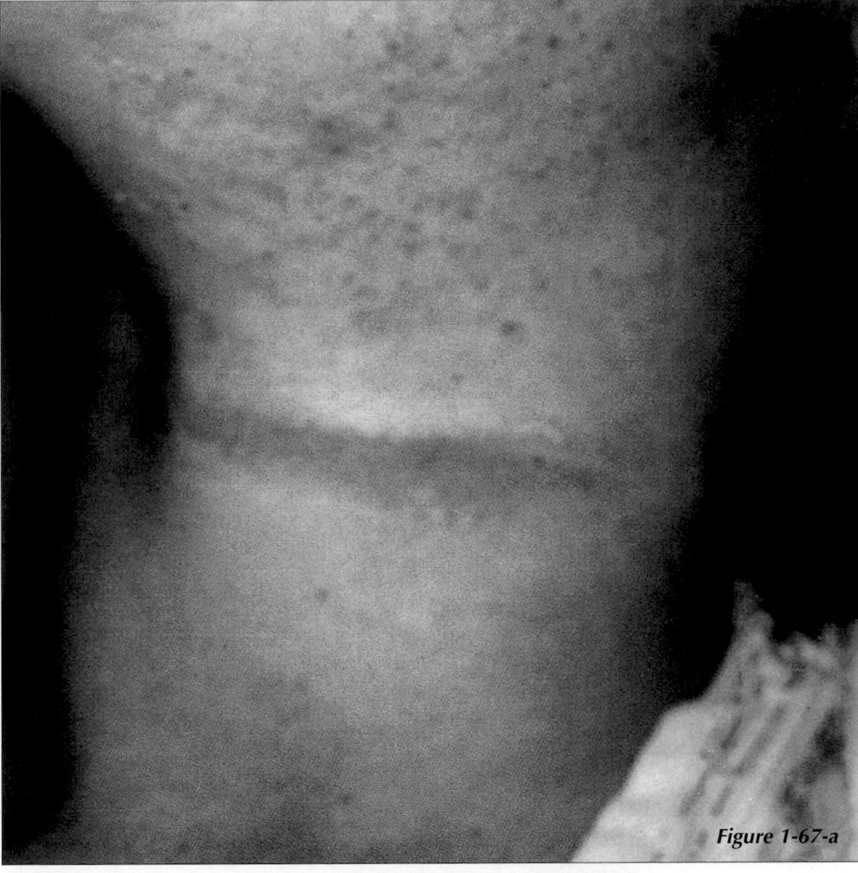

**Figure 1-67-a**

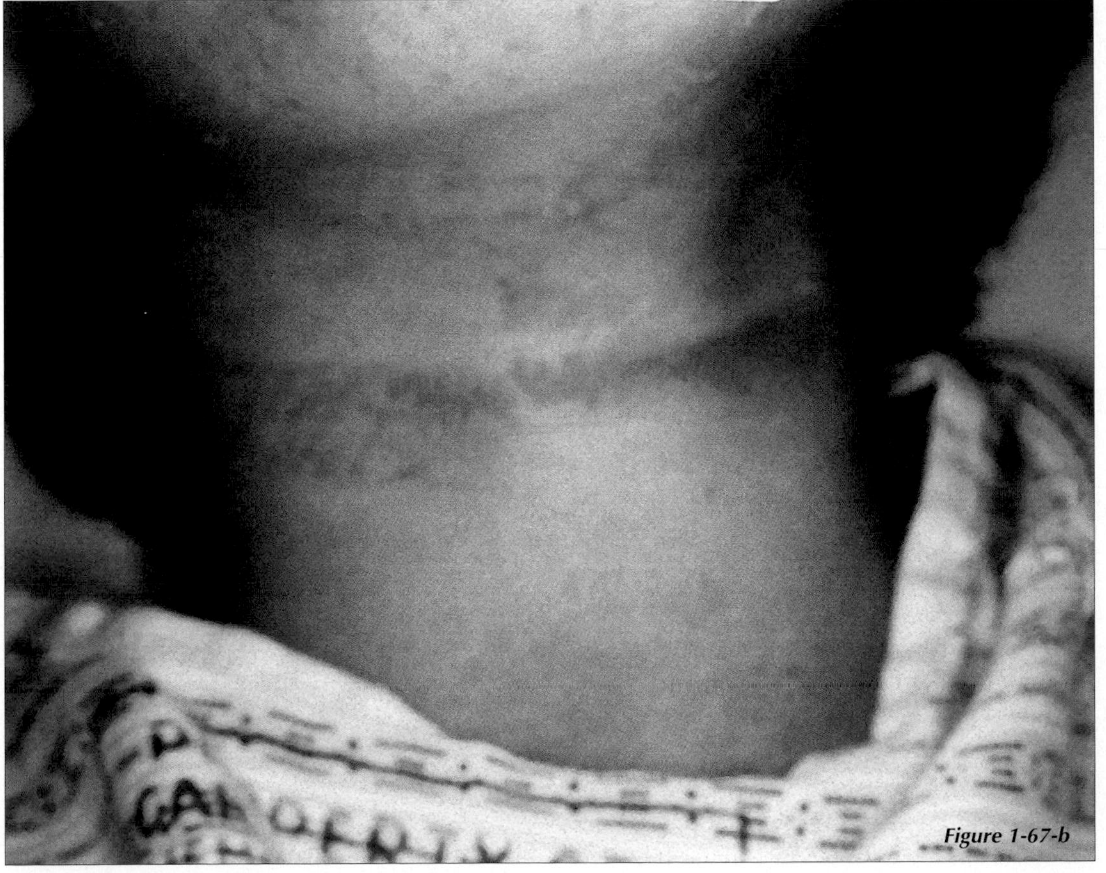

**Figure 1-67-b**

# STRANGULATION

**Case Study 1-68**

This 4-year-old boy was seen in the ER following a near strangulation. He and his family were waiting in line at a restaurant and the boy was playing with a restraining rope when he was pushed into the rope by a sibling. He did not lose consiousness and the event was witnessed by others. In intentional strangulation, the person generally loses consciousness and suffers facial petechiae. Witnessed accidental injuries, such as this one, help document their cause and consequence. The mark was linear and not keeping with the parallel marks expected from strangulation with hands. Elastic bands (***Figures 1-17 a*** and ***b***) cause similar marks.

***Figures 1-68-a, b,*** *and* ***c.*** *Marks on the boy's neck indicating that the rope encircled his neck and burned him, but did not occlude the airway or blood supply.*

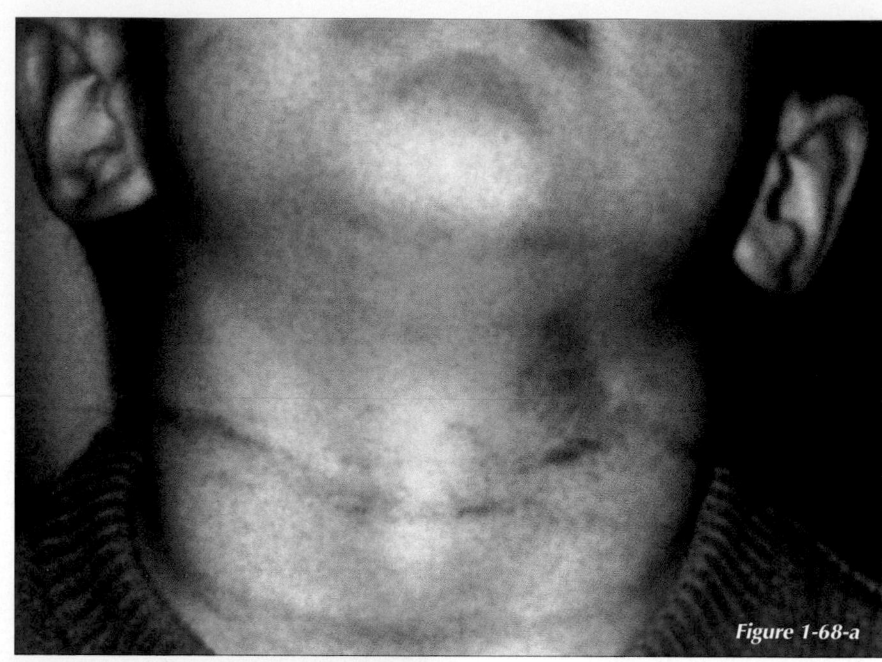

Figure 1-68-a

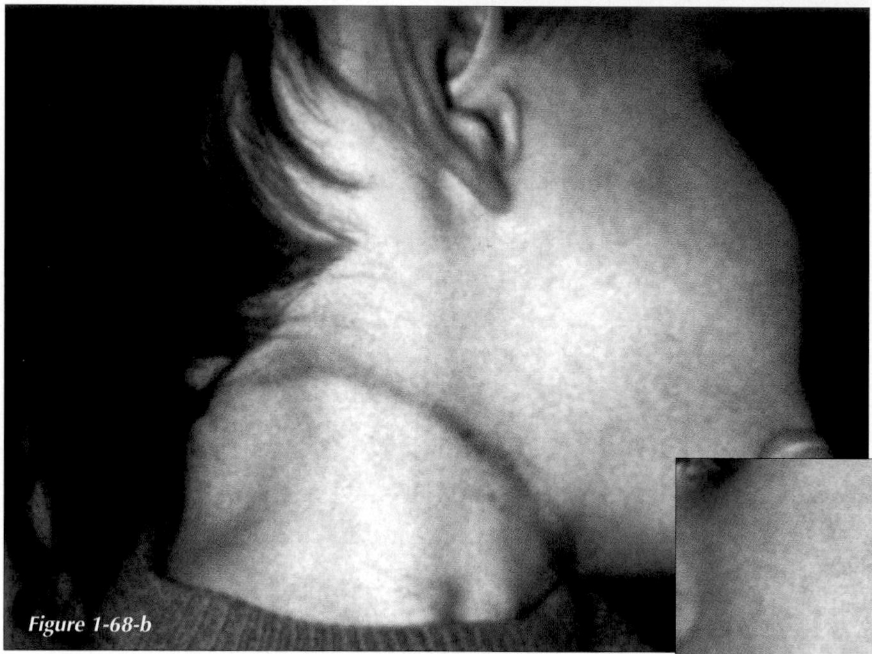

Figure 1-68-b

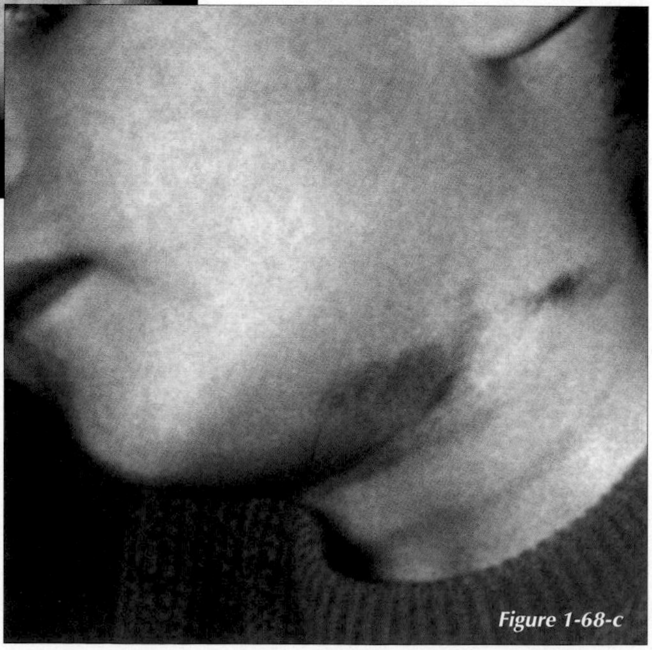

Figure 1-68-c

# Folk Medicine Practices

**Case Study 1-69**

This 14-month-old Southeast Asian boy was seen in the ER because he was having difficulty breathing. The mother said that the bruising to the back was due to her treating him for his illness with a Chinese rub, a form of folk medicine referred to as cao gio. In this folk medicine practice, a coin is rubbed against the skin in a linear pattern following the posterior ribs. Hot oil may be used as lubricant. However, this was not what is typically seen with this practice. These families should be referred for counseling about the need to keep physicians' recommendations for treatment. Failure to follow medical recommendations with or without resorting to folk medicine practice should result in a report of medical neglect.

***Figures 1-69-a** and **b.** The bruising follows a bony pattern, lying over the ribs, sternum, and spine.*

***Figure 1-69-c.** There is a hint of a pattern indicative of malpractice of cao gio on the child's back.*

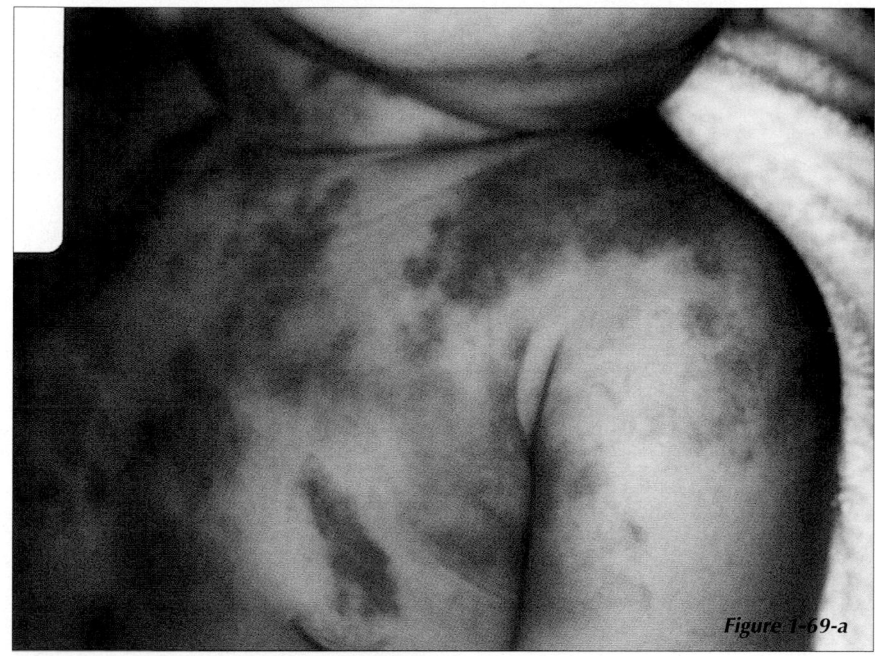

*Figure 1-69-a*

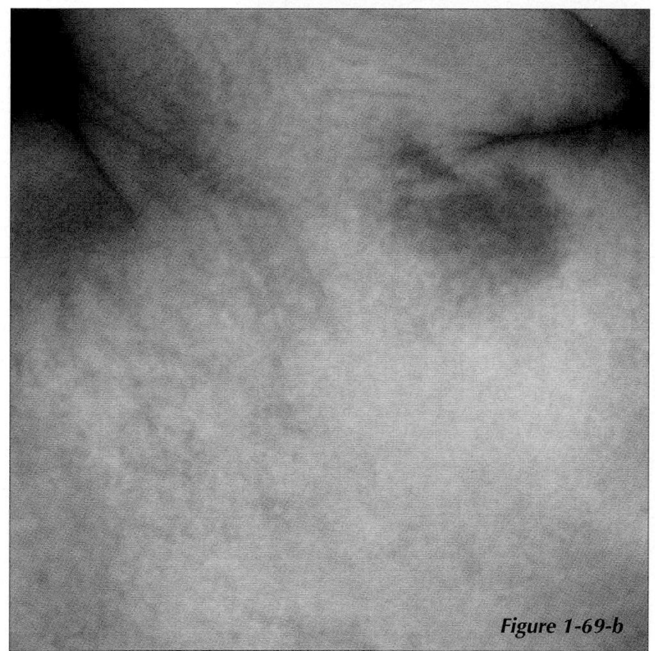

*Figure 1-69-b*

*Figure 1-69-c*

# Folk Medicine Practices

**Case Study 1-70**

According to practitioners of cao gio, the folk treatment should not result in burns or abrasions. If a burn, bruise, or abrasion does take place, this should be reported as suspect abuse. The parents will need counseling about treatment that is acceptable in their community.

***Figure 1-70-a.*** *The marks on the back of this Vietnamese child are symmetrical, brownish red, and follow the directions of the ribs. The marks are too wide to have resulted from impacts to the ribs.*

Cupping, another folk medicine practice, may leave suction or burn marks. The marks from cupping are perfectly round and result from heating a cup or glass and applying it to the skin. A relative vacuum is created as the heated air cools. This vacuum "sucks" the skin surface in a manner similar to a hickey or sucker bite (**Figure 1-2**).

***Figure 1-70-b.*** *This teenager was undergoing cupping when the alcohol that was used to flame the cups splashed on her skin and ignited. The cupping caused the perfect circles on her back. An overheated object may burn the skin as the air inside cools. As a result there may be a burn in a distinct circle and erythema or ecchymosis from the suction created by the cooling air. The parents of this teenager filed assault charges against the cupping practitioner.*

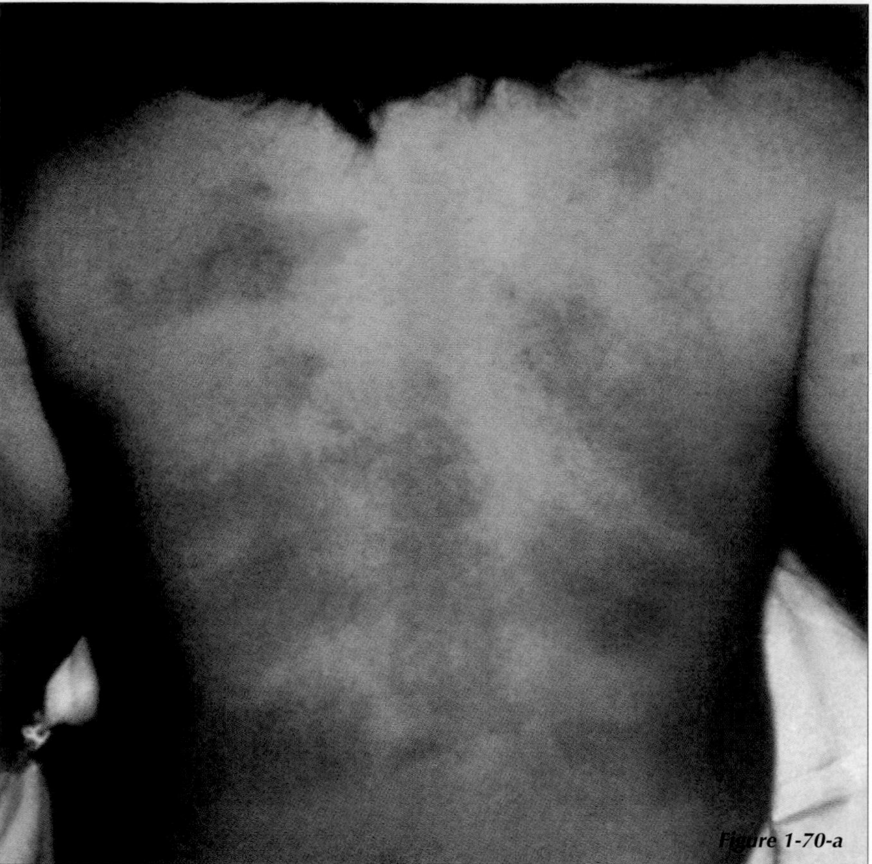

**Figure 1-70-a**

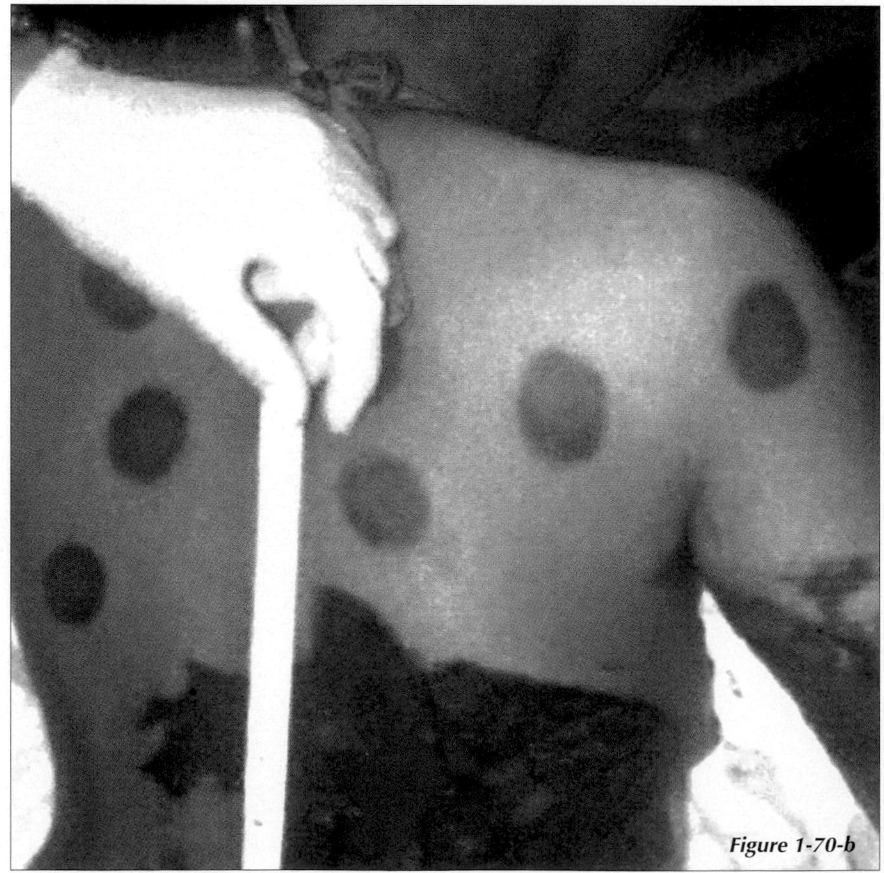

**Figure 1-70-b**

# Mimics of Abuse

**Case Study 1-71**

This 11-month-old biracial boy was reported to a child abuse hotline by a new daycare employee for bruising on his buttocks. The child was healthy and happy and the mother said that the discoloration was present from birth. The staff determined that the discoloration was a Mongolian spot, which is a slate blue birthmark and may appear on any body surface in dark-skinned children. Review of medical records may not reveal a description of birthmarks from the delivery, but a bruise can be expected to resolve in 21 days.

***Figure 1-71*** *The Mongolian spot appears on the buttocks of this boy.*

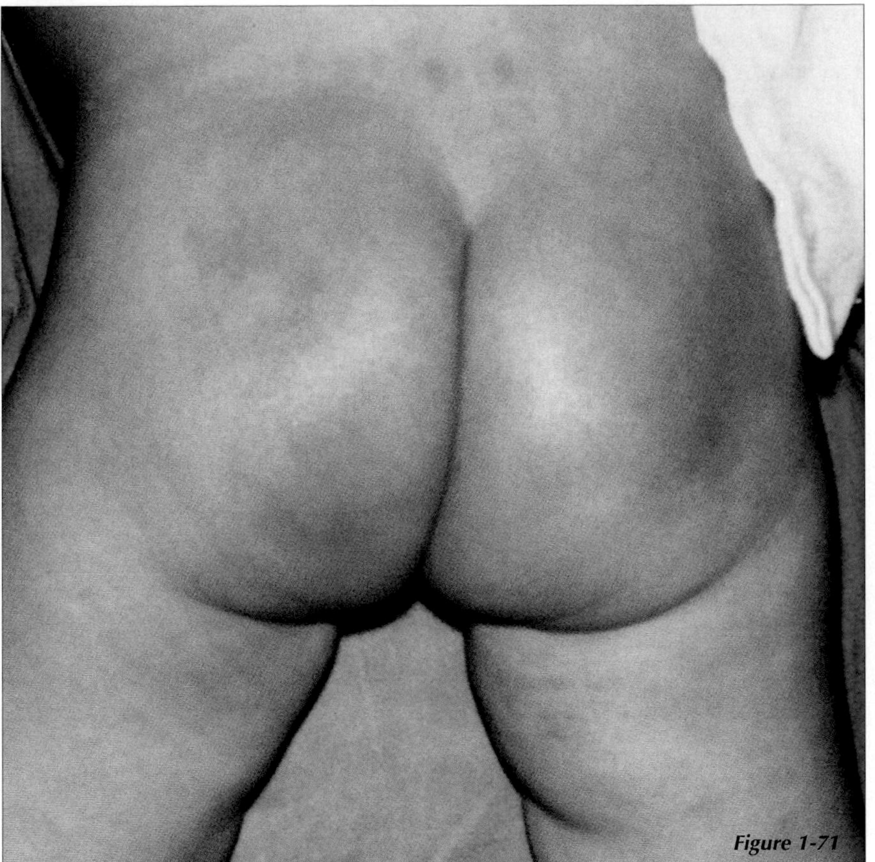

Figure 1-71

**Case Study 1-72**

The parents of this 2-year-old child claimed that the child fell onto a vinyl-covered wooden floor. One would not expect a fall from standing onto a vinyl-covered floor to cause such extensive bruising.

***Figure 1-72.*** *Extensive bruise involving the left periorbital area and left cheek and a subconjunctival hemorrhage of the left eye.*

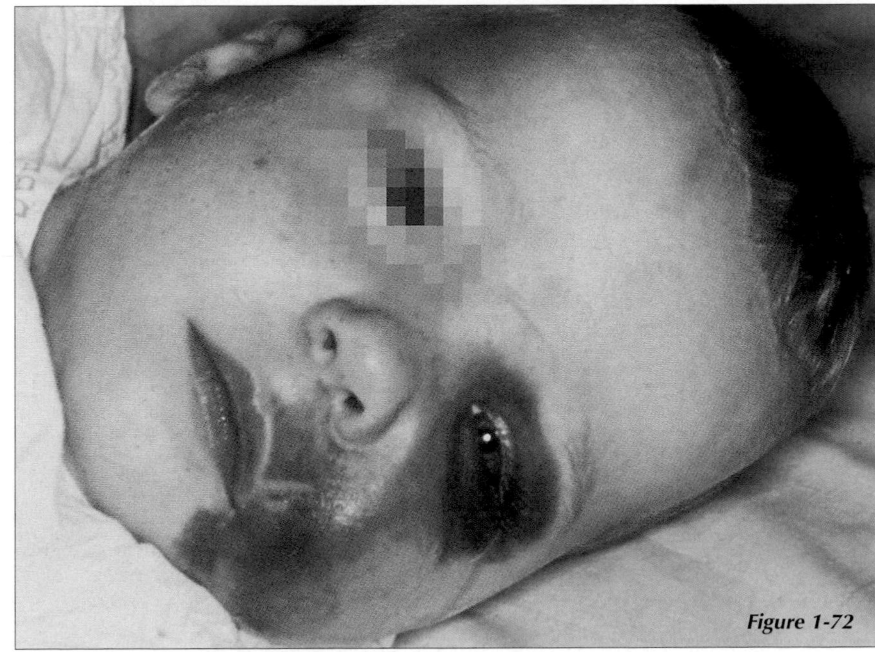

Figure 1-72

In the process of examining this child for suspect abuse, the hematological studies indicated leukemia. It is imperative to always do a bleeding examination for any child with bruises. The caretaker's claim that the child bruises resulted from a fall may be true. If examination is delayed, it may be claimed that the bruises were due to a viral disease with temporarily decreased platelets or another cause of clotting delay.

## Mimics of Abuse

**Case Study 1-73**

This 1-week-old infant was delivered at home. At the first examination a slightly red-purple midline swelling was seen. The mother claimed that the swelling was present at birth and had been enlarging. It is important for physicians and midwives who deliver babies to carefully document all birthmarks and other skin findings.

***Figure 1-73.*** *The mass has a wormlike consistency compatible with a capillary hemangioma.*

**Case Study 1-74**

This 7-month-old boy was taken to the ER by his babysitter. He had an upper respiratory infection and the sitter was concerned that the child had been abused because of the linear bruises on his legs. A child abuse hotline was called to report suspected abuse, but it was determined that the injuries were caused by tight elastic in his socks.

***Figure 1-74-a*** *and* ***b.*** *Linear bruises on the legs was caused by tight elastic.*

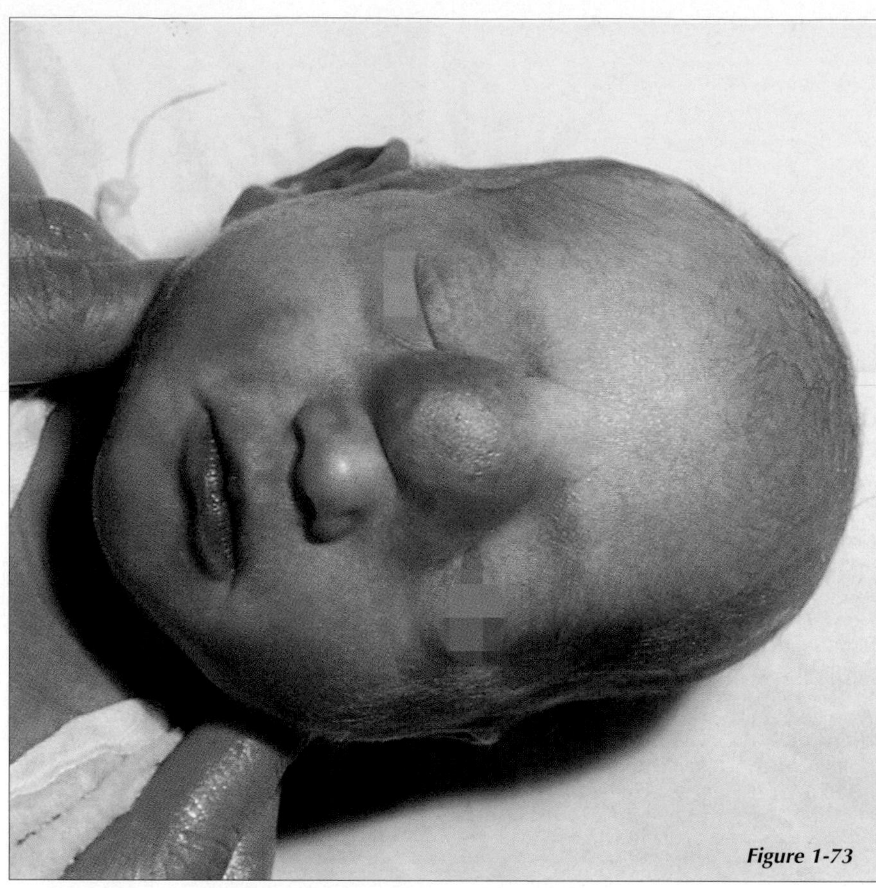

Figure 1-73

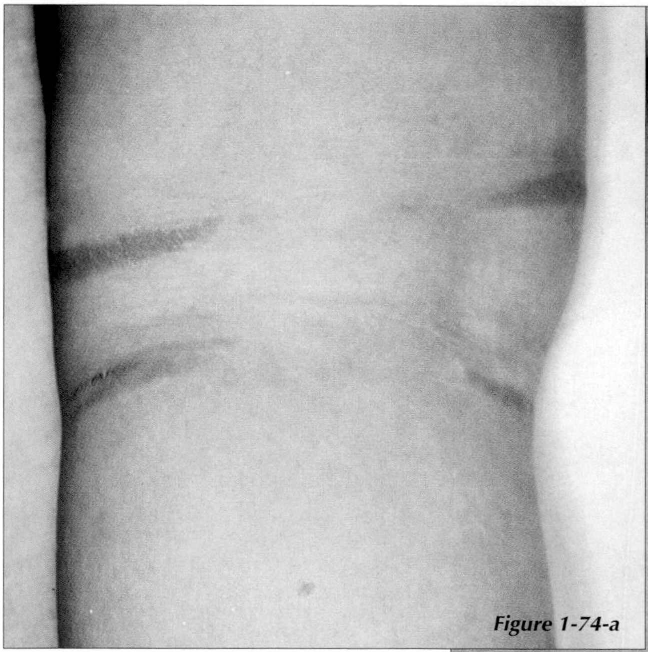

Figure 1-74-a

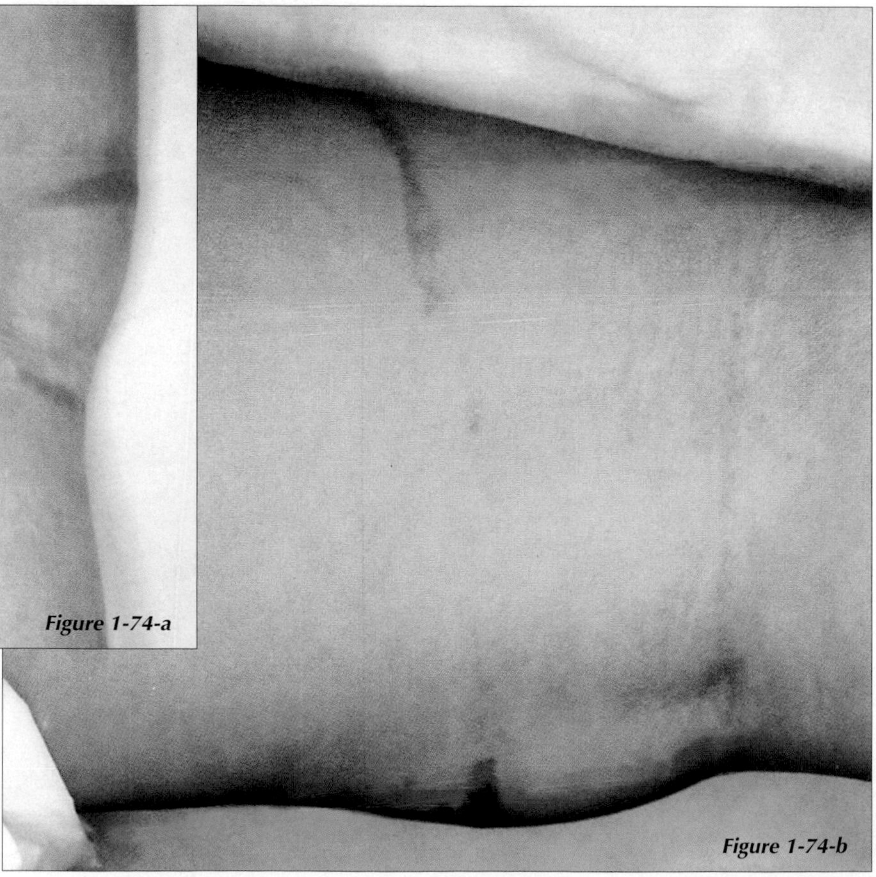

Figure 1-74-b

# Mimics of Abuse

**Case Study 1-75**

This 4-year-old girl was taken to the ER with swelling and ecchymosis of both hands. Within hours a more familiar pattern of trauma appeared on her buttocks and legs, indicating early Henoch-Schonlein purpura. A variety of skin conditions may mimic intentional injury. Patterned lesions on protected parts of the body are most likely due to abuse. All abuse evaluations should include a bleeding workup. A dermatology consultation may be advised in unusual skin conditions. Nature rarely causes geometrical marks.

***Figure 1-75-a.*** *Swelling and ecchymosis of both hands. Note the beginning of lesions on her lower legs.*

***Figure 1-75-b.*** *Buttocks and legs demonstrating a more typical pattern of skin trauma indicative of early Henoch-Schonlein purpura.*

***Figure 1-75-c.*** *Circumferential lesions of the lower extremities caused by pressure from the elastic of her socks.*

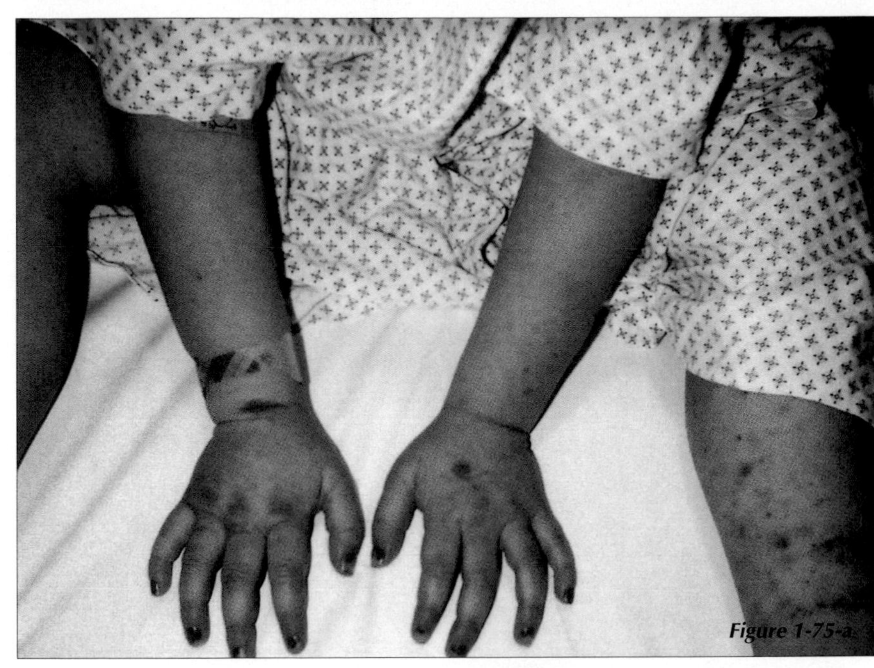

Figure 1-75-a

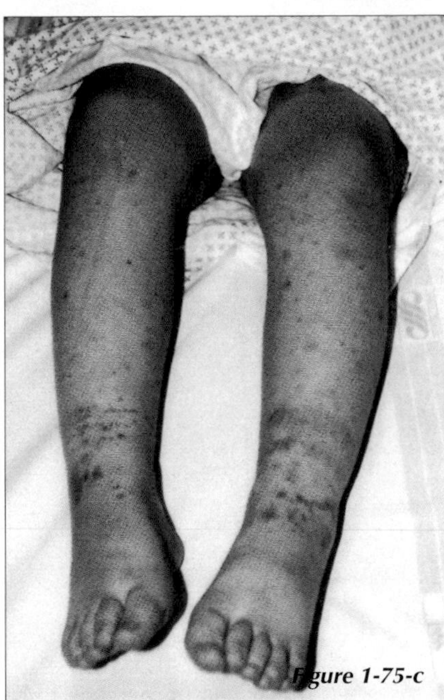

Figure 1-75-c

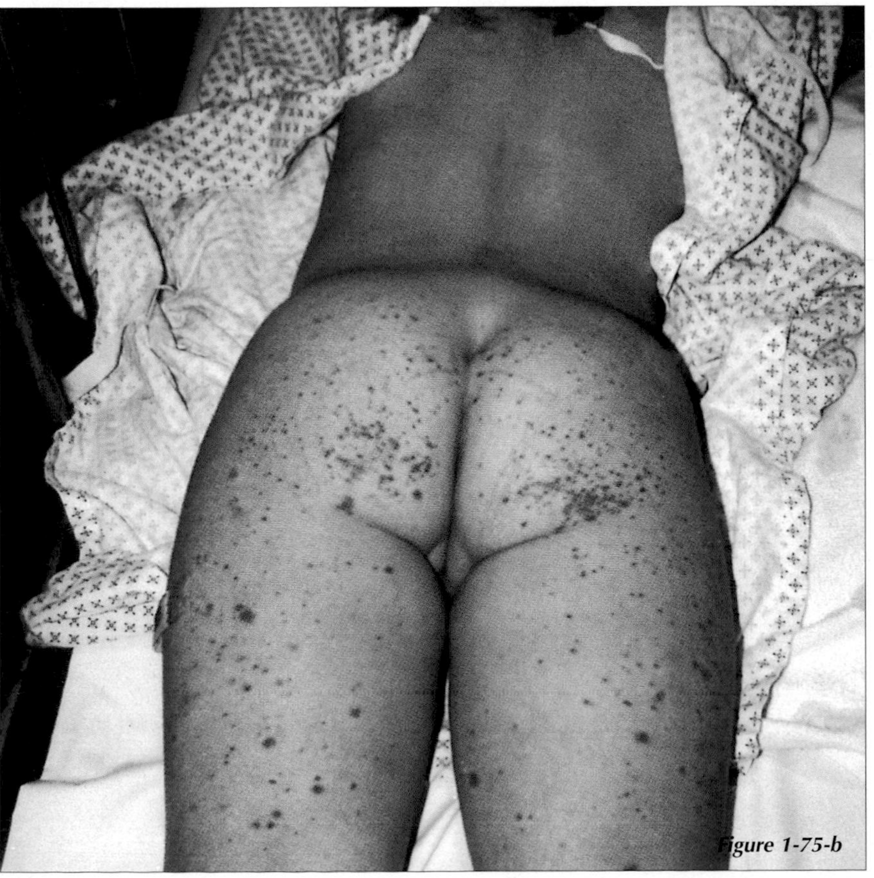

Figure 1-75-b

## Mimics of Abuse

**Case Study 1-76**

These 2 children had Ehlers-Danlos syndrome, which has been mistaken for abuse. Children suffering from this syndrome bruise easily and scar extensively. *(Photographs courtesy of Dorothy K. Grange, MD.)*

***Figures 1-76-a, b, c,*** *and* ***d.*** *Skin on those suffering from Ehlers-Danlos syndrome is fragile, thin, and resembles cigarette paper in consistency.*

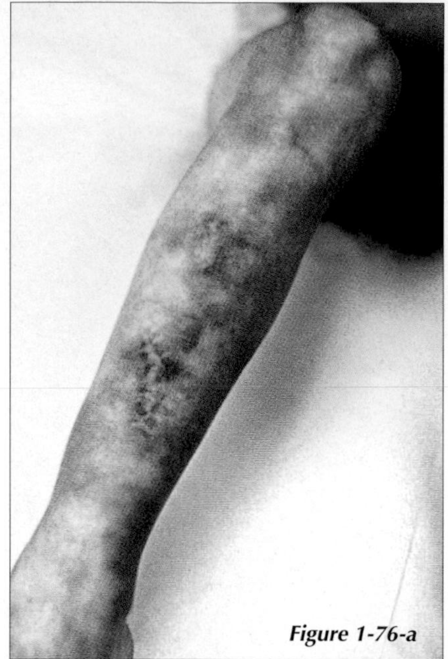

**Figure 1-76-a**

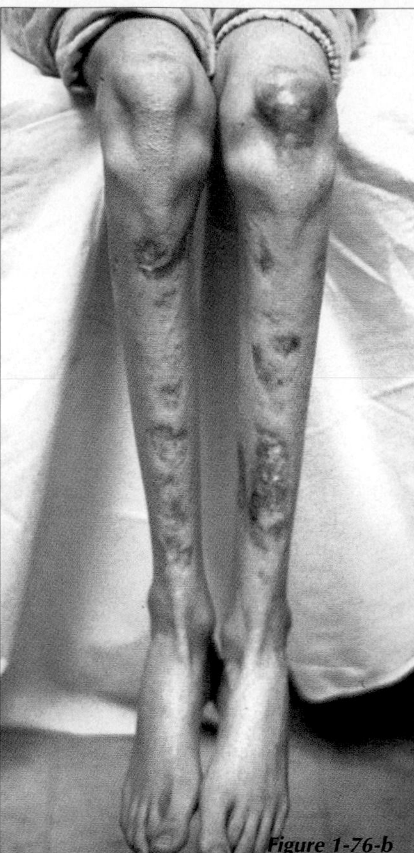

**Figure 1-76-b**

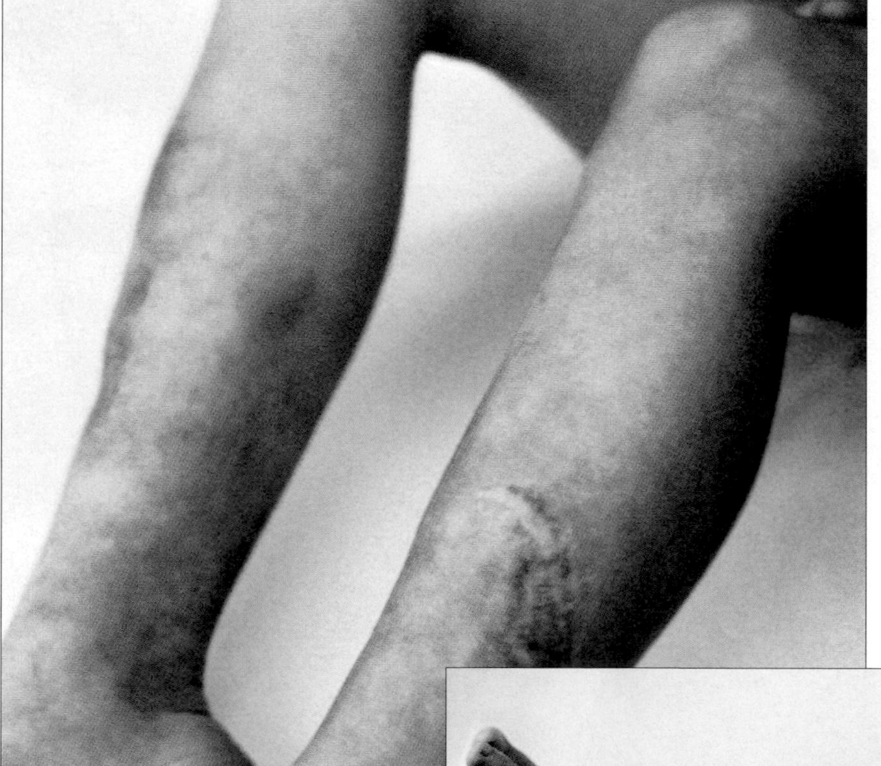

**Figure 1-76-c**

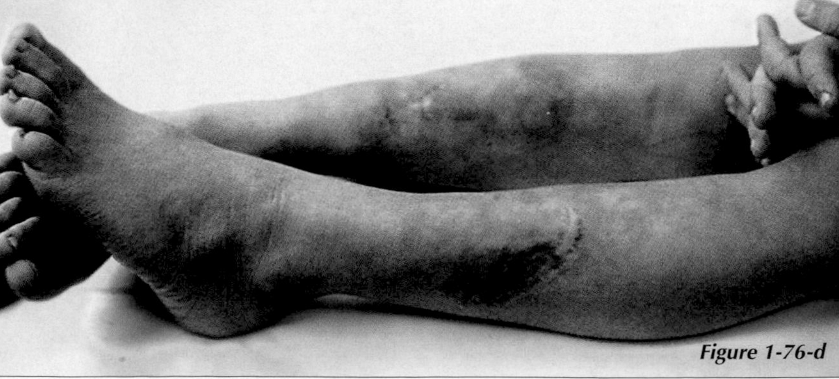

**Figure 1-76-d**

## Mimics of Abuse

**Case Study 1-77**

House staff believed this injury of the upper and lower lip to be abuse; however, further investigation revealed it to be a self-induced suck mark. Older children may tattoo themselves with objects including colored markers.

***Figure 1-77.*** *Suck blisters on the fingers and lips also may be seen in newborns.*

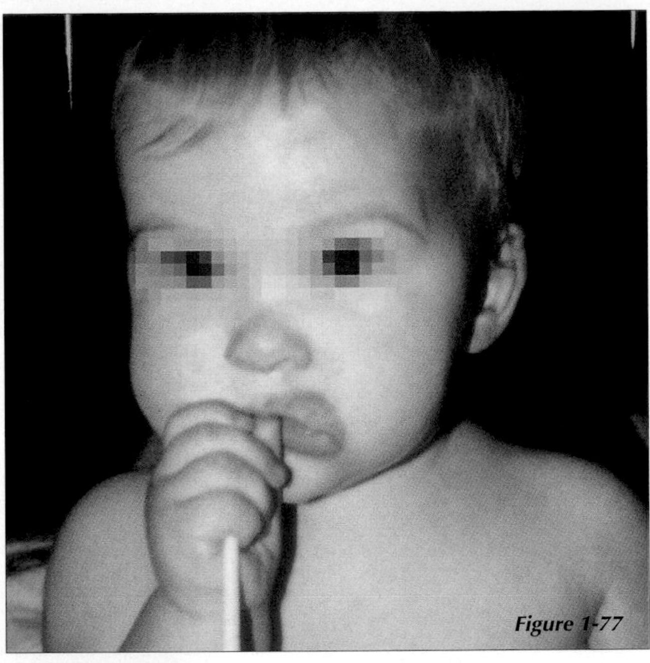

## Accidental Injuries

**Case Study 1-78**

The caretaker of this child gave the history that the child fell onto a bicycle from a porch. The 2-year-old child was too young to interview, and there were no witnesses. It is not possible to determine if the impact resulted from a wielded object impacting the child or from the child impacting an object; however, midline blows to the nose or forehead can result in bilateral black eyes. If there was any doubt about the credibility of the history, the site should have been investigated to confirm that there was a porch and a bicycle as stated.

***Figure 1-78-a.*** *Dark blue discoloration around the nasal side and below both eyes. There is a swelling with blue discoloration above the bregma. Symmetric injuries should raise suspicion of intentional injury.*

Table edges typically are designed at approximately the level of the brow of a 2-year-old child. The proximity of the narrow-edged orbit to the surface of the skin increases the possibility that impacts to that area will result in bruises or lacerations. The area of the force of an impact can be narrowed by the shape of the object or underlying bone. The parent of this child gave the history that the child ran into the edge of a table. This injury is compatible with the history.

***Figure 1-78-b.*** *Laceration to the brow that required suturing.*

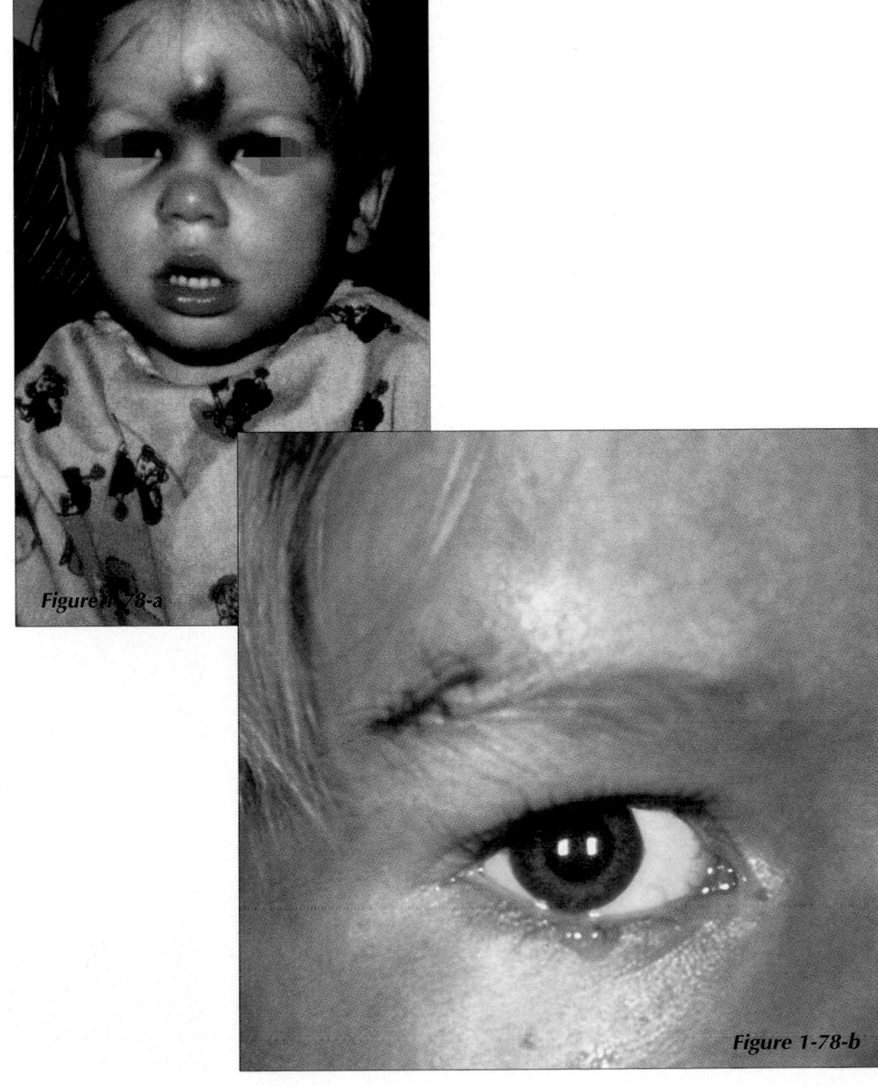

# Accidental Injuries

**Case Study 1-79**

The history given by the caregiver of this 22-month-old boy was that he fell from a second-story window, landing in a wheelbarrow before striking the ground. There were no witnesses and all but one of the injuries were fresh. There was a large ecchymosis of the forehead, a swollen upper lip, and multiple abrasions of the neck, right shoulder and arm, left chin, and left thorax. An abrasion that appeared older on the right elbow had been covered with a bandage. After their investigation, the police determined that the cause of the injury was consistent with the explanation and was accidental, due to a lack of supervision. A site investigation is mandatory in any reported accident to clarify the credibility of the history and do a safety check of the home. Accidental risk factors and abuse risk factors overlap. Injuries to relatively protected parts of the body—such as the neck, popliteal fossae, axilla and genitalia are rare and merit suspicion for intentional trauma and detailed questioning and investigation.

***Figure 1-79-a.*** *Ecchymosis of the forehead.*

***Figure 1-79-b.*** *The boy's right shoulder and arm at examination.*

***Figure 1-79-c.*** *Abrasions to the neck.*

***Figure 1-79-d.*** *The left chin of the boy.*

***Figure 1-79-e.*** *The left thorax.*

***Figure 1-79-f.*** *Old abrasion on the right elbow.*

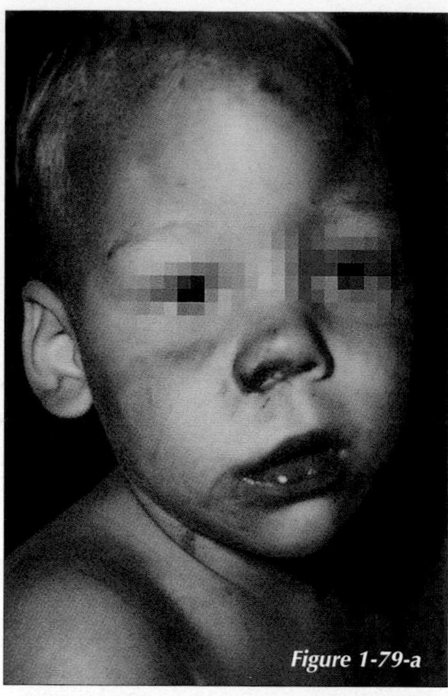
Figure 1-79-a

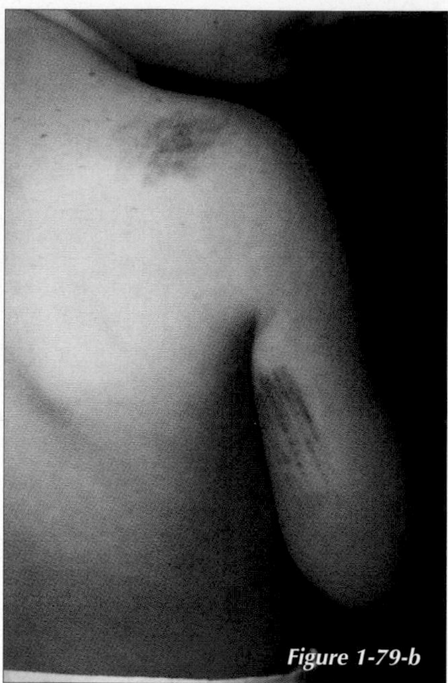
Figure 1-79-b

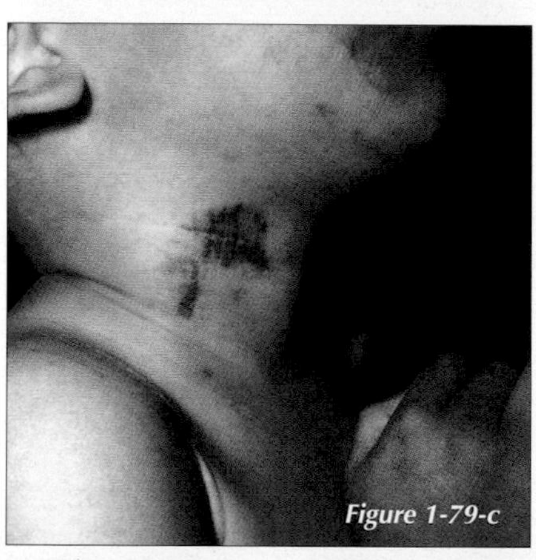
Figure 1-79-c

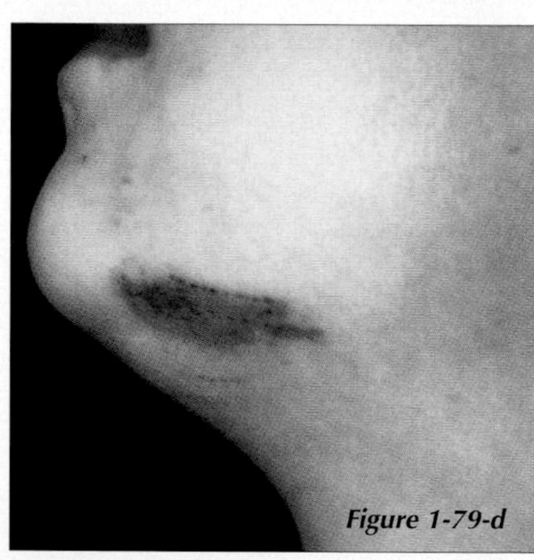
Figure 1-79-d

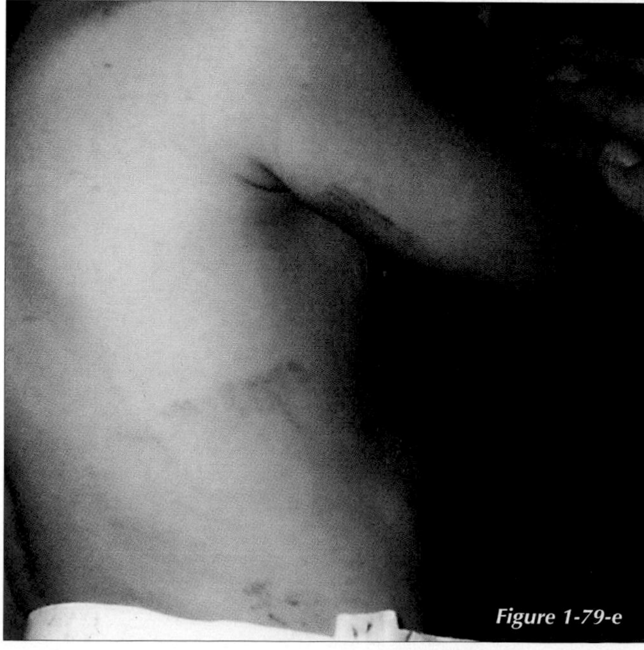
Figure 1-79-e

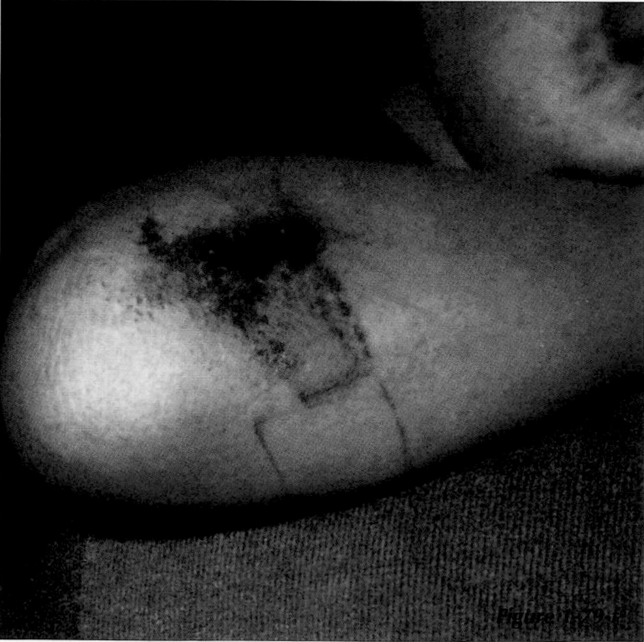
Figure 1-79-f

# Accidental Injuries

**Case Study 1-80**

This 25-month-old boy was in the care of his mother's boyfriend while his mother was asleep. The history given was that the child had climbed up the back of a rocking chair that was propped against the wall. When told to get down, he quickly stepped down and the rocker lunged forward, throwing him over the arm of the rocker. He straddled the arm momentarily as he fell and struck his forehead on the floor. The glans and shaft of the penis were injured. The scrotum was ecchymotic, but not swollen. The blood accumulation in the scrotum was most likely drainage from the penile injury because it followed the fascial planes and settled in a more dependent area. After an investigation of the scene by a state child protection worker, the injury was determined to be consistent with an accidental straddle injury.

***Figures 1-80-a** and **b.** Blood accumulation in the scrotum following fascial planes.*

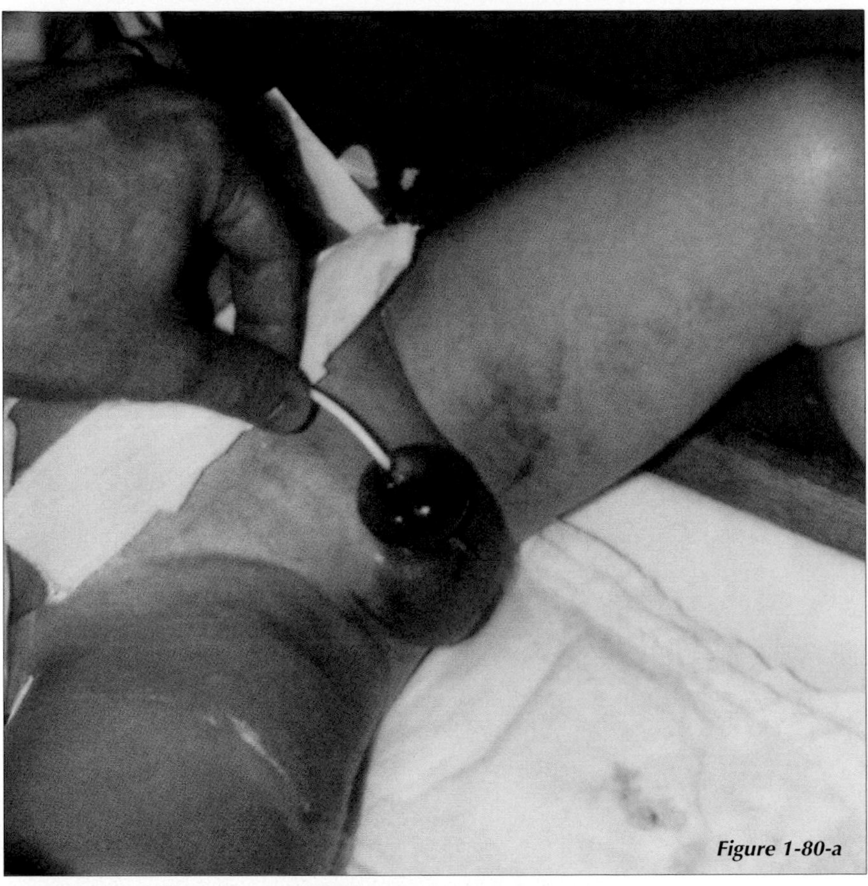

**Figure 1-80-a**

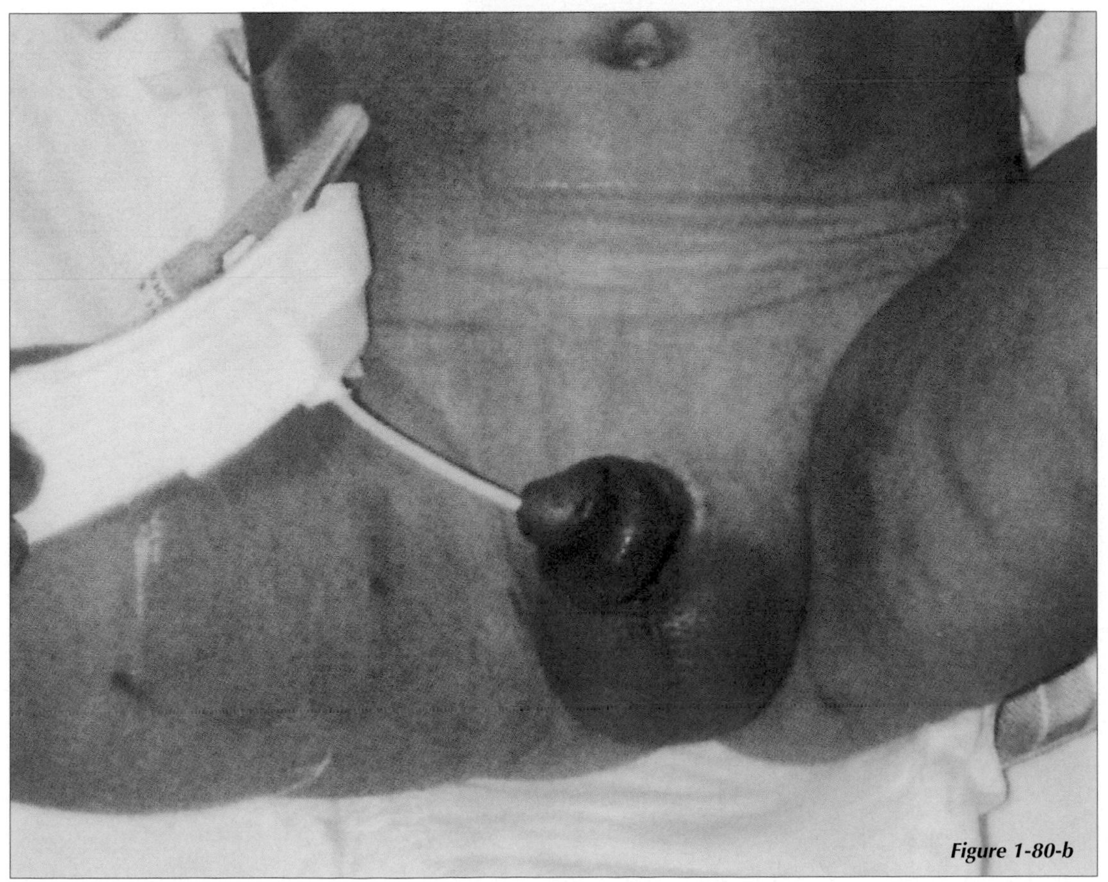

**Figure 1-80-b**

Chapter 2

# BURNS PART 1

Matt Young, MD

Children who are burned abusively are marked or branded with the outward manifestation of parental violence, emotional imbalance, impulsivity, educational and cultural deprivation, and poverty. Intentionally burning a child is controlled and premeditated. Abusive burns cause both physical and emotional trauma at the time of the incident, and often produce long-term physical and psychological scarring.

Abusers who burn typically are educationally deprived, abuse women (if male), and may be isolated, suspicious, rigid, dependent, or immature. They often display more concern for themselves than the child, frequently show little remorse, and are evasive and contradictory. They generally do not volunteer information, seldom visit the child in the hospital, and rarely ask questions about the child's condition. By contrast, parents whose child is accidentally burned usually blame themselves for a lack of supervision and may display a profound sense of guilt.

The 6 categories of burn injuries are: flame, scald, contact, electrical, chemical, and radiation (eg, sunburn from ultraviolet radiation). Abusive burns generally cluster in the scald and contact categories, although there are reports of other types of burns. Children's skin is much thinner than adult skin, so serious burning occurs more rapidly and at lower temperatures. Electrical burns can be deceptive since trauma may not always be outwardly apparent. Electricity follows the path of least resistance, and skin is a natural resistor to electrical flow. Nerves, muscles, and blood vessels, however, are good conductors and more susceptible to electrical trauma. Electrical flash burns are caused when the current is shorted, producing a very brief, high-intensity fireball that causes thermal injury. Flash burns char the superficial layers of skin, but usually do not cause destruction of deep tissues.

Medical treatment of the injury must be the first priority with burn patients. Once these needs are met, efforts can be directed toward obtaining an accurate history from witnesses and family members. Investigators must carefully outline the time, nature, extent, and location where the burn occurred. It also vital that medical personnel note the exact shape, depth, and margins of all wounds, including all body parts involved. Immediate attention to these details can prove to be invaluable when drawing a later distinction between an abusive and accidental injury.

Children need to feel like they are in a safe environment and they are not going to be hurt again. It is best to begin by asking them general questions, such as: How did you get hurt? Specific questions should be asked only after they have had the opportunity to tell their story. Another important question to ask is: Is there anything that you are not supposed to tell me?

Another important factor to consider in the examination of a child is the length of time it takes for a second- or third-degree burn to occur relative to the temperature of a given liquid (**Figure 2-1**). Consideration of time and surface temperature in determining the causation of burns can indicate whether or not the burns are abusive

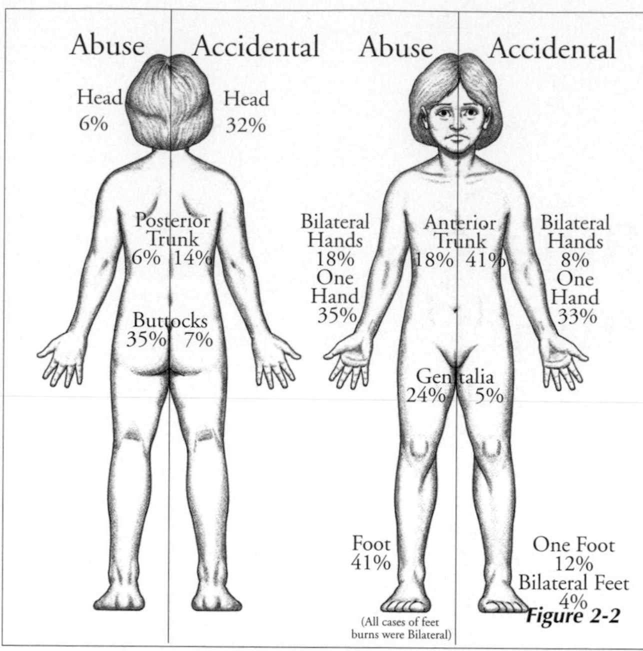


*Figure 2-1. Length of time required for second- and third-degree burns to occur when exposed to liquids of varying temperatures, reinforcing the relative importance of time and surface temperature in the causation of cutaneous burns.*

*Figure 2-2. Diagram of anterior and posterior body surfaces with the results of the Grossman Burn Center Study that was presented at the American Burn Association Annual Meeting in 1999. It represents the frequency of involvement of different body parts with a comparison between accidental and abusive burns.*

or accidental. The location of the burn on the surface of the child's body is also key information when determining if injuries are the result of abuse (**Figure 2-2**). It is significant to note that the head and thoracoabdominal region are more likely to be involved in accidental burns, whereas the buttocks, genitalia, bilateral hand, and bilateral feet burns are much more likely to be related to abuse.

Accidental scald burns of the trunk usually involve the anterior surface of the body. In most cases, hot liquid is spilled onto children when they pull a tablecloth edge, causing a hot liquid to spill over and burn them from the table. Gravity causes a linear burn pattern and clothing affects the burn pattern and severity as it insulates the skin. Hot liquid may pool in the diaper area resulting in an unusual burn pattern.

In a physical exam, the most common indicators of abuse are burns to the genitalia and buttocks, mirror image burns of the extremities, in addition to bruises, welts, or fractures. The most important determination to make in distinguishing between accidental and inflicted burns is whether the pattern of the burn is consistent with the history given by caregivers. When a child presents with a burn and one or more of the following factors are found, the evaluator should consider abuse:

1. Multiple hematomas or scars in various stages of healing
2. Concurrent injuries or evidence of neglect such as malnutrition and failure to thrive (Especially suspicious are bone injuries such as old rib fractures and distal tibial, metaphyseal, or spiral fractures.)
3. History of multiple prior hospitalizations for "accidental" traumas
4. An inexplicable delay between time of injury and first attempt to obtain medical attention (In some cases, if the parent has medical training, such as an RN or MD, the delay may be because the parents initially tried to care for the burn on their own.)
5. Burns appearing older than the alleged day of the accident, similarly indicating ambivalence about seeking care due to the possible risk of exposure of the abuse
6. An account of the incident not consistent with the age or ability of the child

7. Allegations by the responsible adults that there were no witnesses to the incident and the child was merely discovered to be burned, in the hope of discouraging further inquiry
8. History of relatives other than the parents bringing the injured child to the hospital, or a nonrelated adult bringing the child (excepting a proper explanation, such as a babysitter caring for a child while the parents are out of town)
9. Burns attributed to the action of a sibling or other child (Although this is often an explanation from parents or other caregivers for abusive burns, it should also be noted that siblings can be abusive.)
10. An injured child who is excessively withdrawn, submissive, overly polite, or does not cry during painful procedures
11. Scalds of the hands or feet, often symmetrical, that appear to be full thickness in depth, suggesting that the extremities were forcibly immersed and held in hot liquid
12. Isolated burns of the buttocks or perineum and genitalia, or the characteristic "doughnut"-shaped burn of the buttocks, which can hardly ever be produced accidentally by children
13. Conflicting stories offered by the responsible adults as to the cause of the burn that changed when the adults were questioned

The burns presented in this chapter illustrate patterns found in abusive as well as accidental burns. The inability to match the caregivers' description to the patterns observed usually reveals the abusive nature of intentional burns when they have occurred. The young ages of the victims are typical of the findings with abusive burns.

# Immersion Burns

## Stocking-Glove Pattern

### Case Study 2-3

This 11-month-old male presented with bilateral submersion burns of the hands, typically a clear indicator of abuse. The initial history given by the mother was that the child had been burned when he spilled hot coffee on himself. The injury was not consistent with a spill and indicated a submersion burn. The burns were a result of the child's hands being immersed in a pot of scalding water.

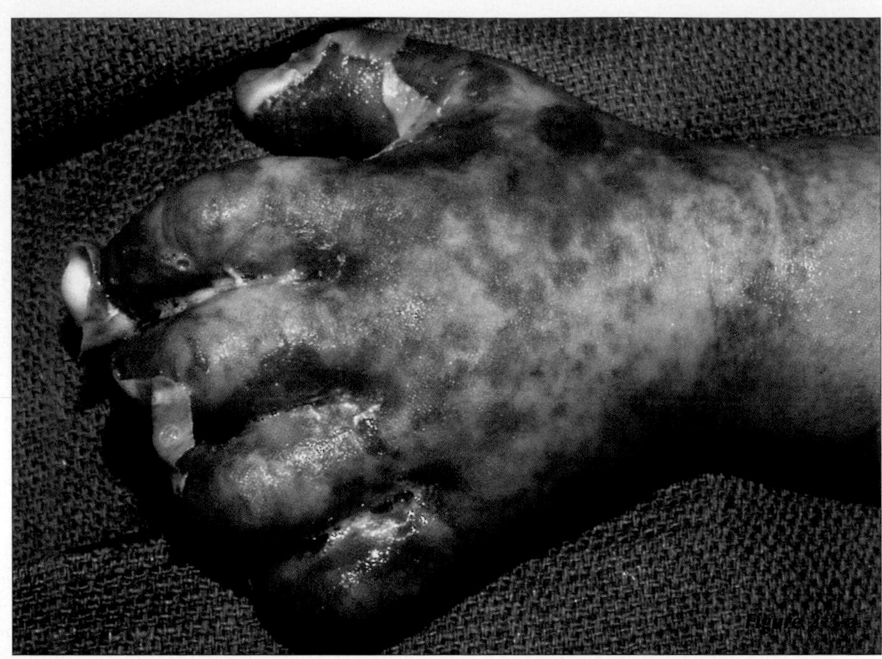

***Figure 2-3-a.*** *Note the distinct line of demarcation between the burned and unburned areas.*

***Figure 2-3-b.*** *Note that all digits of both hands are burned.*

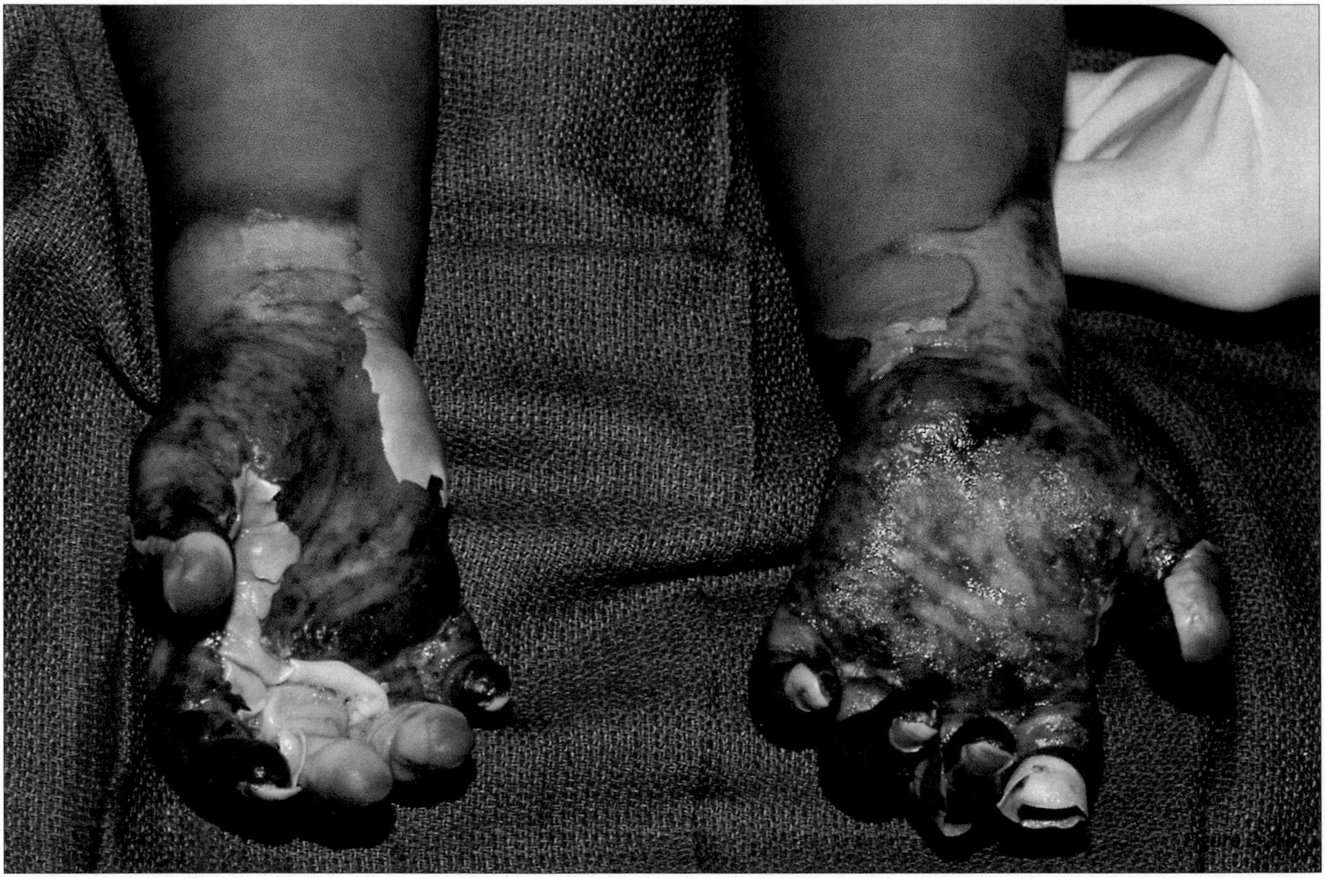

# Immersion Burns

## Stocking-Glove Pattern

### Case Study 2-4

This 20-month-old girl was in the care of her mother's boyfriend. He stated that she was sitting in about 4 inches of bathwater when he left the room momentarily and the girl accidentally turned on the hot water. When he heard her cry, he returned and pulled her out of the water. His story was inconsistent with the injuries, which were clearly caused by submersion. The abusive nature of the injuries was evidenced by the stocking-glove pattern and the spared portion of skin in the popliteal area of the left leg, which was protected by either the girl flexing her leg or the boyfriend's hand as he dipped her into the water.

***Figures 2-4-a, b,*** *and* ***c.*** *Stocking-glove pattern burns on both legs of the infant.*

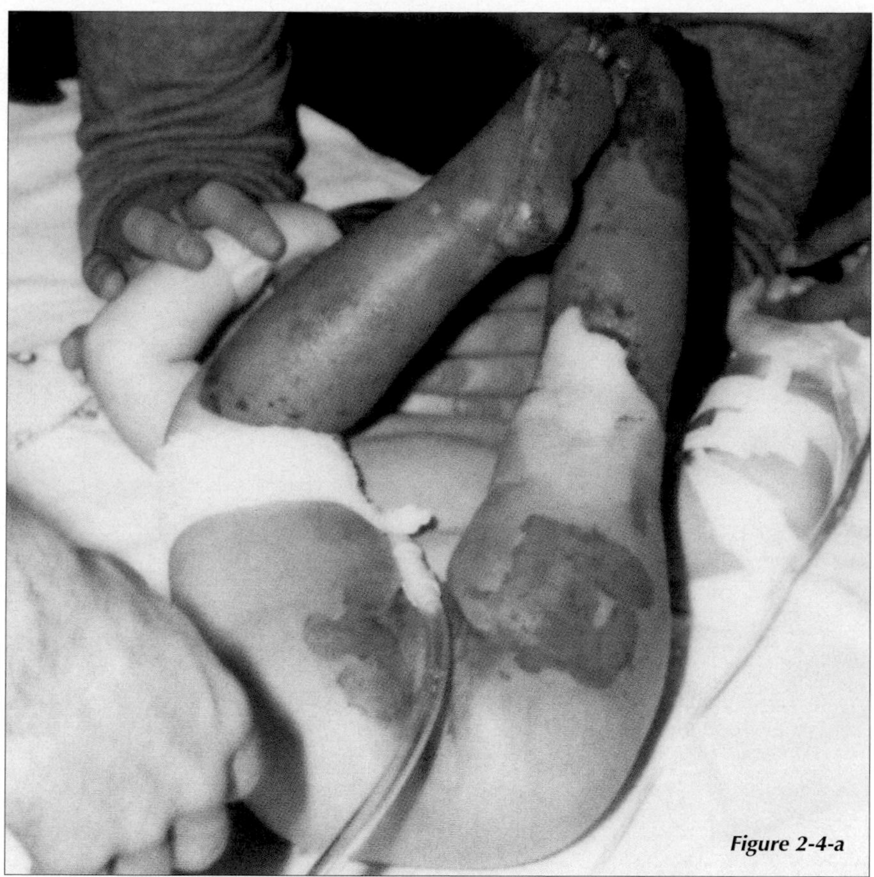

**Figure 2-4-a**

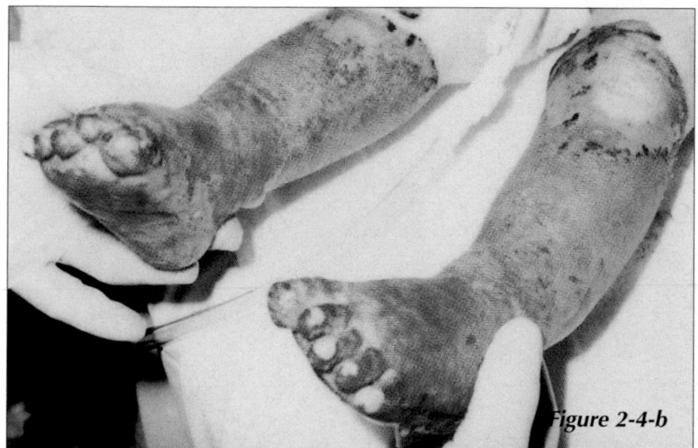

**Figure 2-4-b**

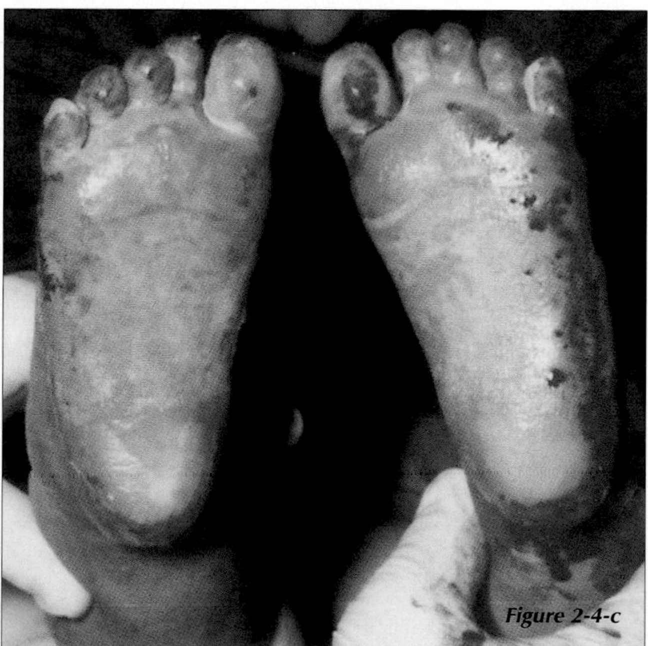

**Figure 2-4-c**

# Immersion Burns

## Stocking-Glove Pattern

### Case Study 2-5

The caregivers of this 18-month-old boy stated that his burns were self-inflicted by accidentally turning on the hot water in the bathroom sink. The bilateral stocking-glove pattern, however, was indicative of immersion burns. The caregivers later admitted to intentionally immersing the boy's hands in hot water as punishment.

***Figure 2-5-a.*** *Bilateral stocking-glove pattern burns on the boy's hands and forearms.*

***Figures 2-5-b*** *and* ***c.*** *The palms of each of the boy's hands are severely burned.*

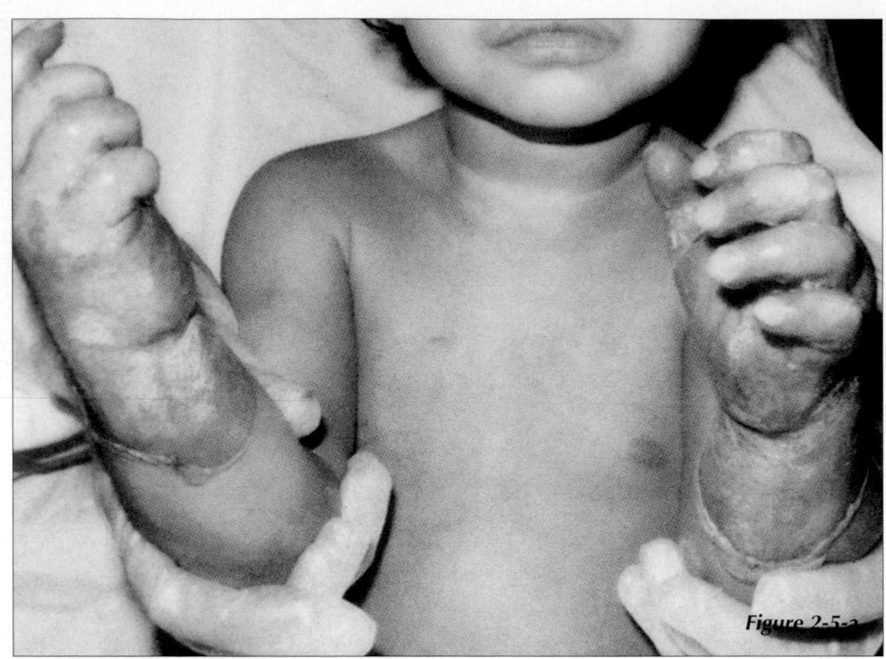

Figure 2-5-a

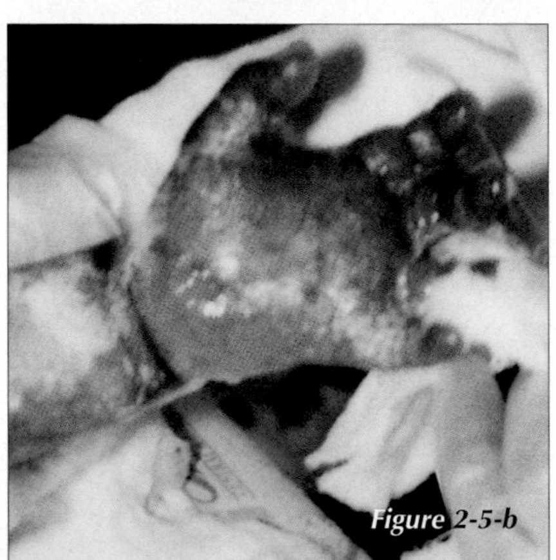

Figure 2-5-b

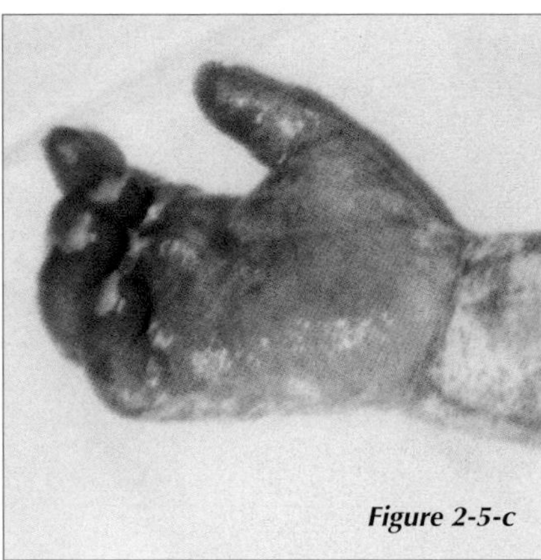

Figure 2-5-c

### Case Study 2-6

This 20-month-old boy was examined with a healed immersion burn. The caregiver stated that it was caused by splashing hot water; however, the stocking-glove pattern was indicative of an immersion burn.

***Figure 2-6.*** *Stocking-glove pattern burn 3 weeks after the injury took place. The skin has been grafted and is healing.*

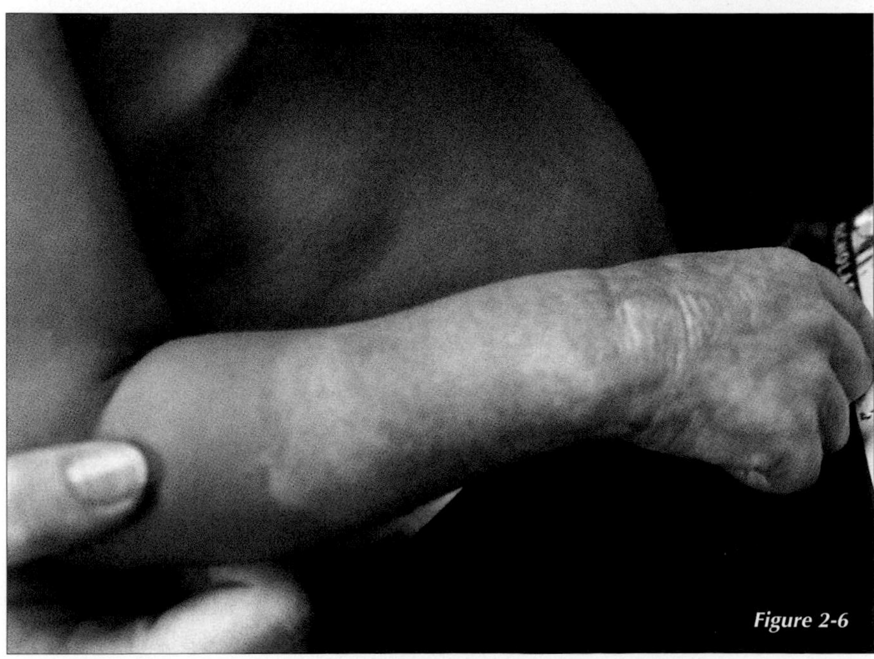

Figure 2-6

# Immersion Burns

## Multiple Injuries

### Case Study 2-7

This 6-year-old girl was held in a bathtub of scalding water by her mother's boyfriend while the mother was away from home. The history given by the mother's boyfriend was that the child had slipped on some soap in the bathtub. The child initially corroborated the history in the presence of the mother and her boyfriend until she was separated from them for an interview. When asked: "When you were in the bathtub, did it hurt?" the child replied, "Yes." When asked: "Did you cry?" she replied, "No." When asked why not, she said: "Because I had tape on my mouth." The child proceeded to state that the boyfriend used electrical tape to cover her mouth and bind her wrists and ankles prior to being submerged in the scalding water.

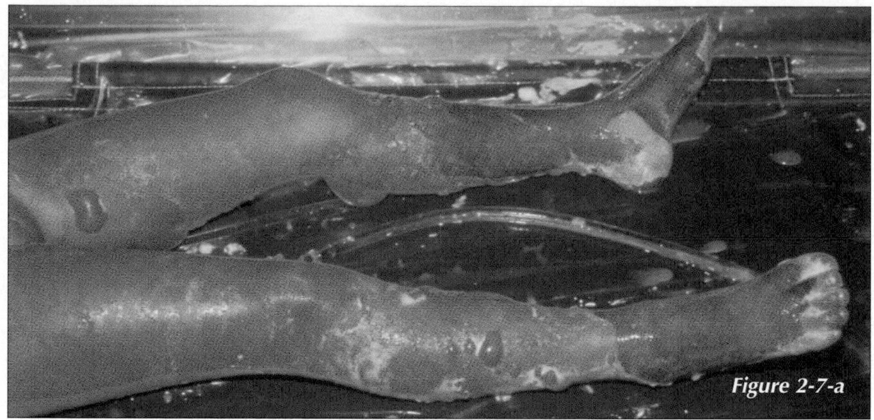

Figure 2-7-a

***Figure 2-7-a.*** *The child's legs at the time of admission, less than 8 hours after the incident, show blistering and redness. The full severity of the scald burn may not show itself until 24 to 48 hours after the event.*

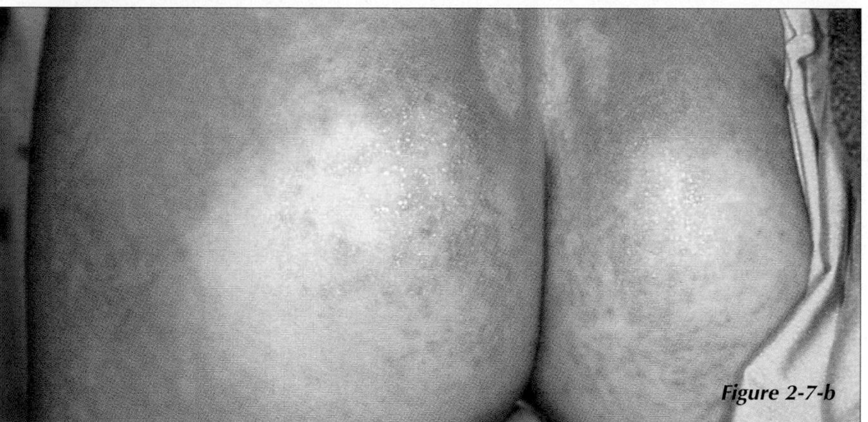

Figure 2-7-b

***Figure 2-7-b.*** *Note the initial appearance of the "doughnut"-shaped pattern, the circular areas of unburned skin on the child's buttocks. This is the result of the buttocks being held forcibly against the cooler surface of the bottom of the bathtub. This "doughnut" pattern is an important indicator of abuse; however, it may not be present in all abusive burn injuries. A child can be held in scalding water without being forced to the bottom of the tub, which would produce burns to the entire buttocks.*

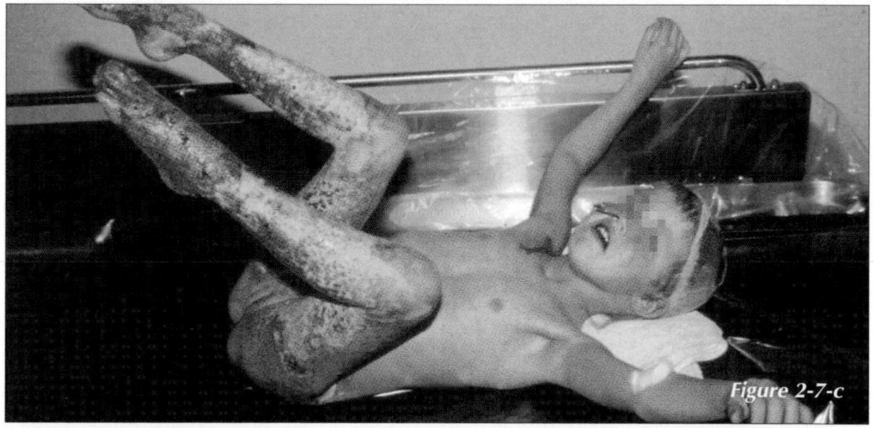

Figure 2-7-c

***Figure 2-7-c.*** *After 24 hours, the burns show evidence of much more necrotic skin, represented by the white areas.*

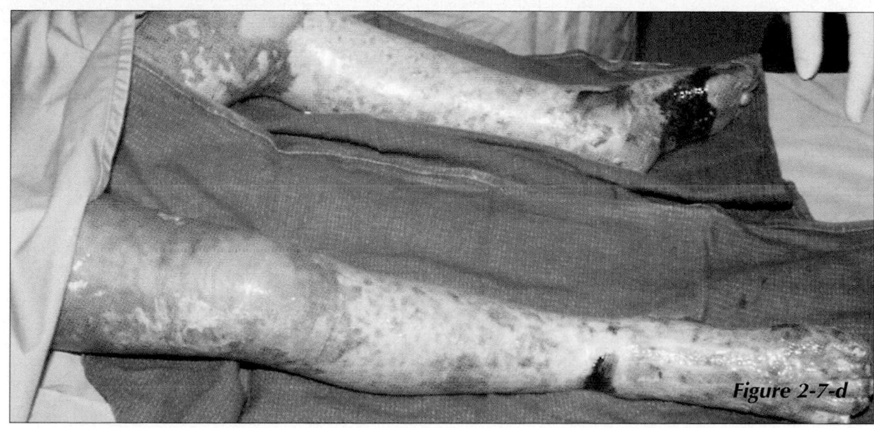

Figure 2-7-d

***Figure 2-7-d.*** *The burns at 48 hours become better demarcated. Note the area of the left ankle that is not burned; this supports the child's statement that her ankles were covered with electrical tape.*

The boyfriend was later convicted and sentenced to a life term.

# Immersion Burns

## Multiple Injuries

### Case Study 2-8

This 6-year-old girl was abused by a daycare worker as punishment for soiling herself. The daycare worker slapped her across the face, whipped her with an electrical cord, and then immersed her in scalding water from the waist down.

***Figure 2-8-a.*** *Pattern bruises on the girl's back caused by being whipped with an electrical cord.*

***Figure 2-8-b.*** *Pattern bruises on the girl's right cheek caused by an open-handed slap.*

***Figure 2-8-c.*** *Note the distinct line of demarcation between the burned and unburned skin.*

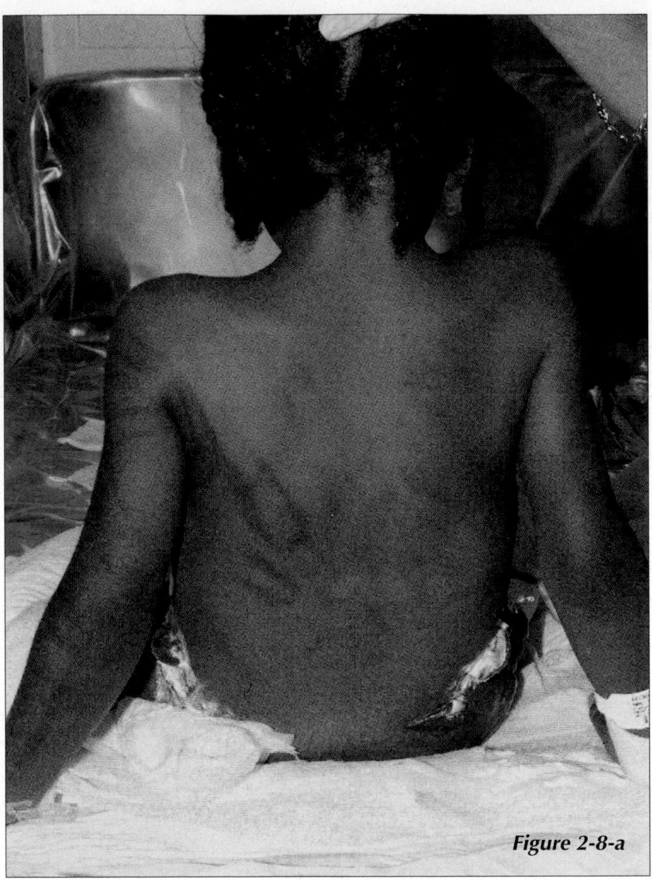

**Figure 2-8-a**

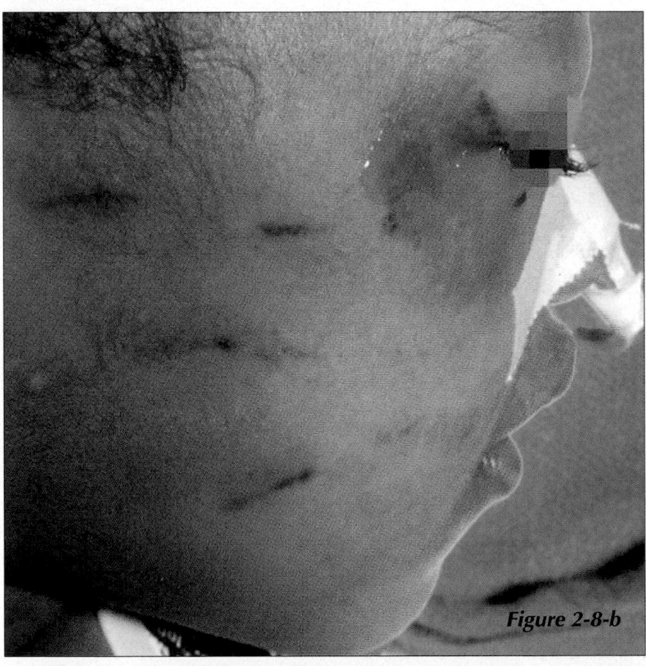

**Figure 2-8-b**

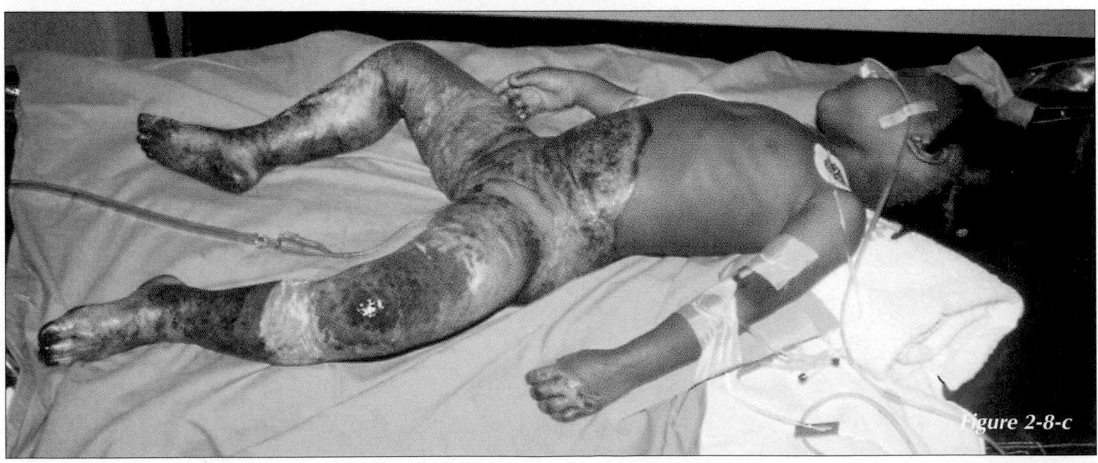

**Figure 2-8-c**

# Immersion Burns

## Multiple Injuries

**Case Study 2-8** *(continued)*

***Figures 2-8-d*** *and* ***e.*** *The child's extremities were flexed during submersion; therefore, there is an absence of injury in the flexion creases of her groin. This is also true of the popliteal areas.*

***Figure 2-8-f.*** *Note the circumferential nature of the immersion burns.*

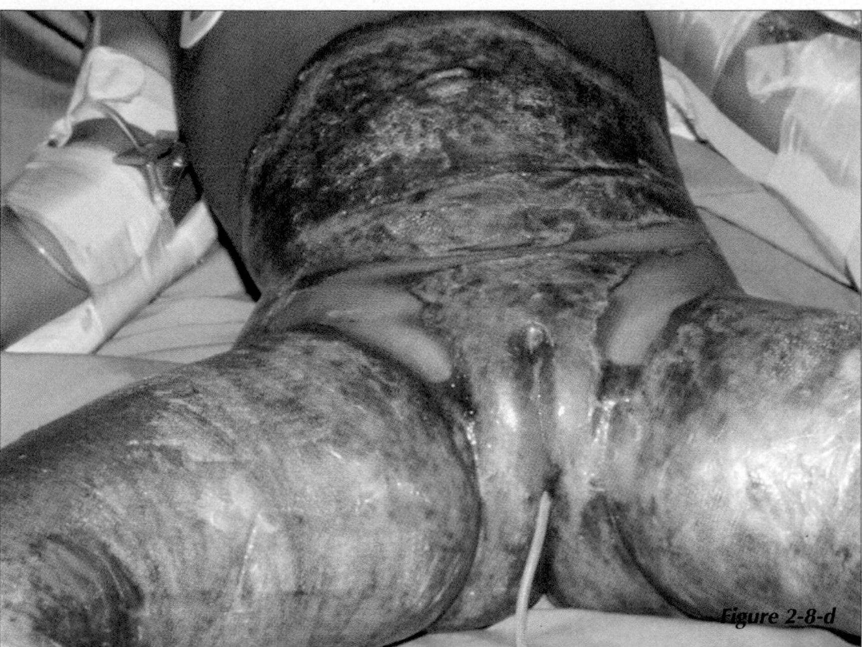

**Figure 2-8-d**

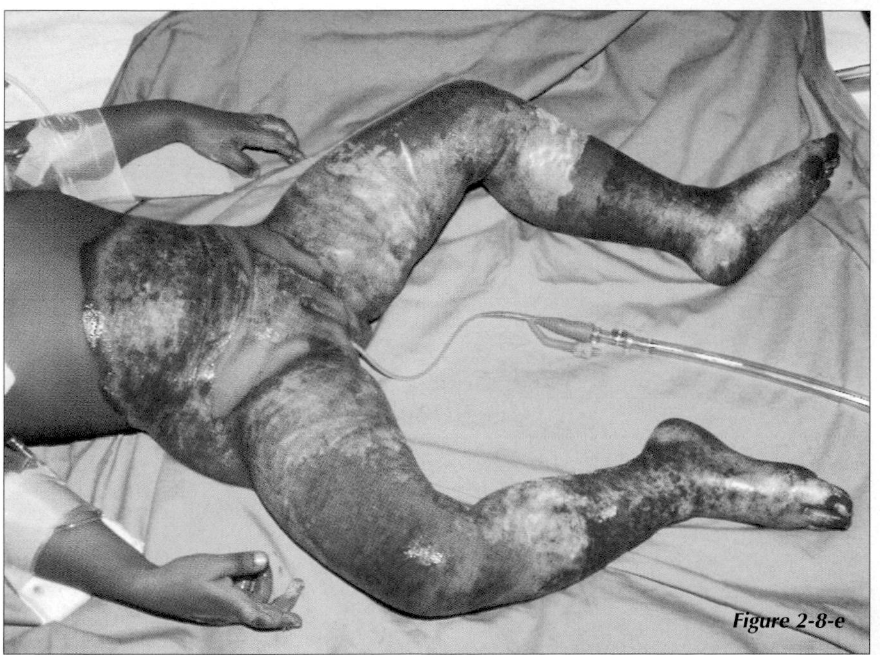

**Figure 2-8-e**

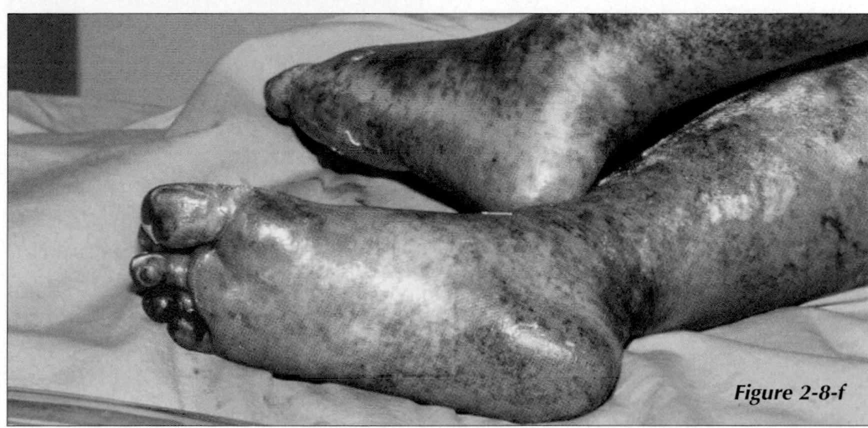

**Figure 2-8-f**

# Immersion Burns

## Multiple Injuries

### Case Study 2-9

This 18-month-old boy was examined with contact burns to the chin caused by a cigarette lighter. Additionally, he had immersion burns to his lower trunk and bilateral lower extremities. His mother held him in a bathtub of scalding water.

***Figure 2-9-a.*** *Contact burn to the chin.*

***Figure 2-9-b.*** *The distribution of the burn can be used to approximate the position in which the child was held in the water. The sharp line of demarcation is evidence that the child's knees were above the water level.*

***Figure 2-9-c.*** *The "doughnut"-shaped pattern on the right buttock is consistent with the lack of burns to the knees. The right buttock would be deeper in the water and against the cooler surface of the tub, whereas the left buttock would have been in the water and received burns to the entire surface. The distinct line of demarcation on the back trunk indicates the water level in the tub.*

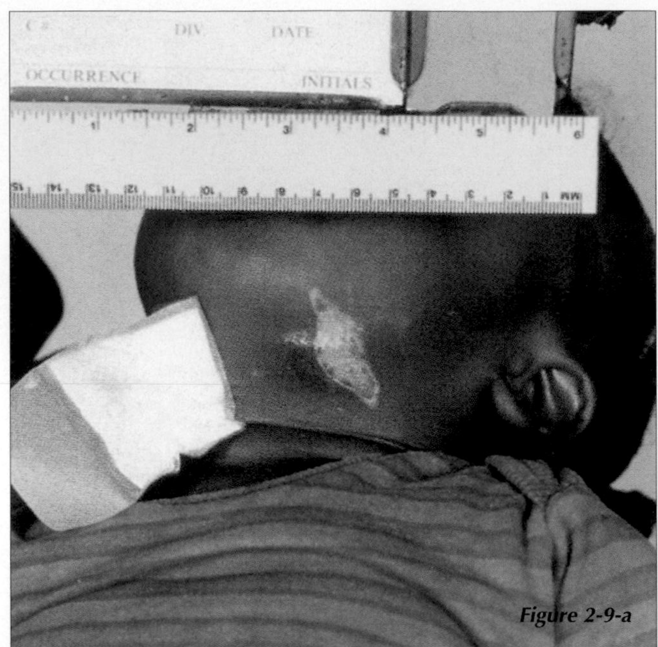


**Figure 2-9-a**

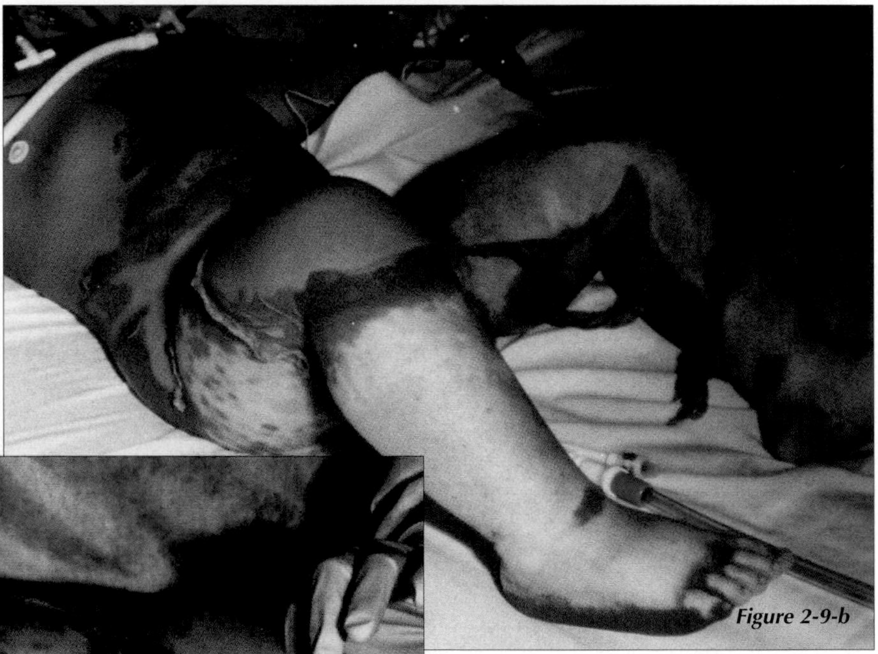

**Figure 2-9-b**

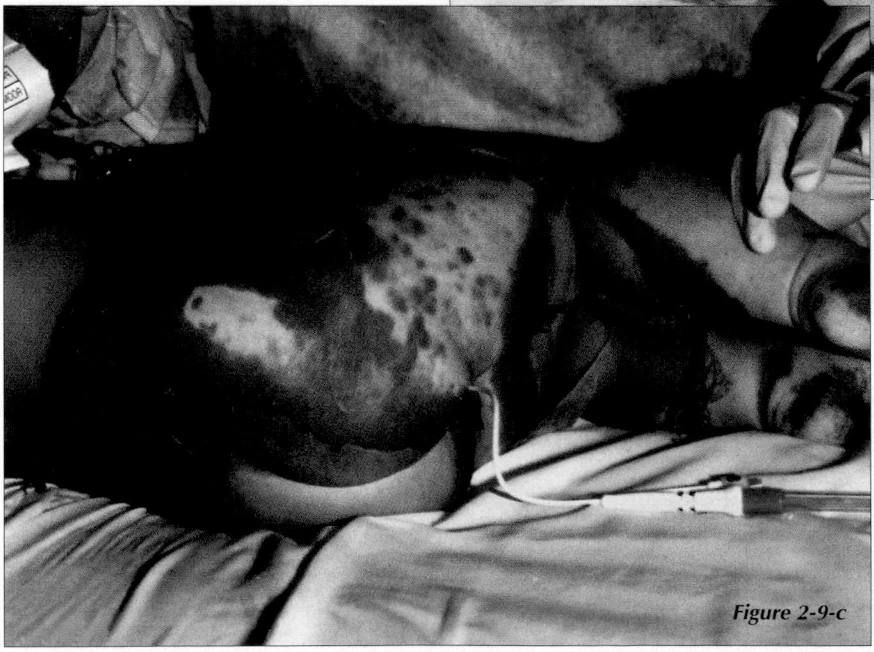

**Figure 2-9-c**

# Immersion Burns

## Multiple Injuries

### Case Study 2-10

This 9-year-old boy was held in scalding water by his mother. His initial description of the incident indicated that he fell into the bathtub. After he learned of his mother's incarceration, he felt safer with the healthcare providers and told the truth. He described being held in the water "until his skin was floating off in the water." He also described his exact position in the bathtub as leaning more to the right side. The child's mother was tried for abuse and torture. She was released with time served.

***Figures 2-10-a** and **b.** The child's description of his position in the bathtub is consistent with his injuries. There are greater burns on his right thigh than on the anterior surface of his left thigh. There are also unburned areas in the popliteal and inguinal flexion creases.*

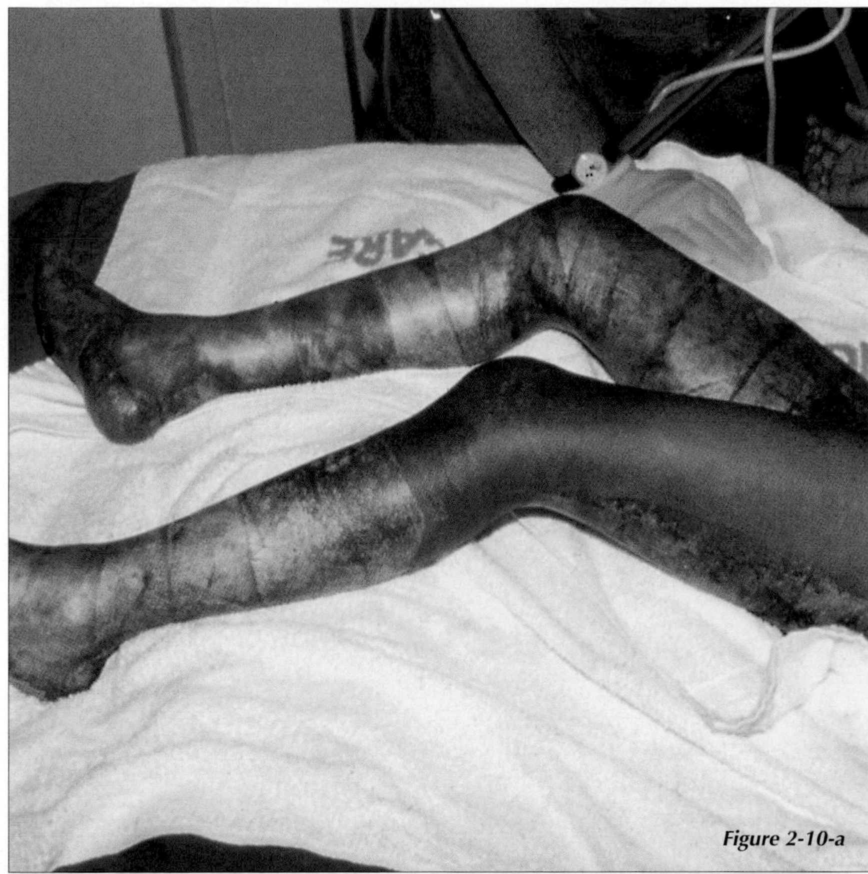

**Figure 2-10-a**

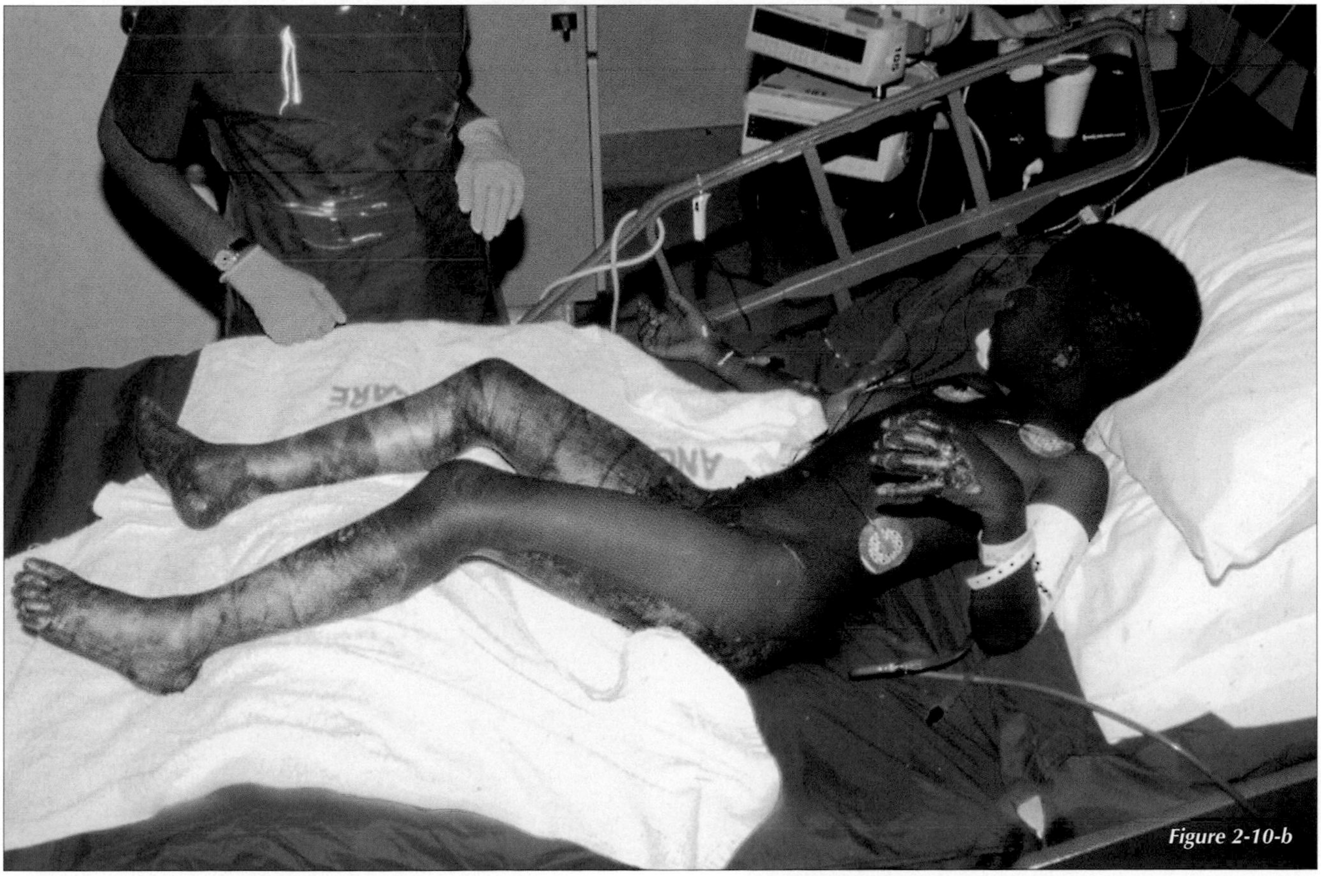

**Figure 2-10-b**

# Immersion Burns

## Multiple Injuries

### Case Study 2-11

This 33-month-old girl was taken to the ER by her parents. They said that they noted the burns to the child's back after returning from a trip. The child was in the backseat of the car. They said that she was restless but did not give any other reason to suspect that she was injured and they initially had no idea how the injury had occurred.

***Figure 2-11-a.*** *Second-degree burns of the back to the gluteal crease on her left side, including the left buttock.*

***Figures 2-11-b** and **c.** The burns extend laterally on the torso to the midchest on her right side and higher on her left side.*

***Figure 2-11-d.*** *Her right arm has a small area of burn medially and at the elbow.*

After examination the parents suggested that it might have been sunburn or that it was caused by the sun heating the back of the car seat. She was also reported to have been wearing a bathing suit. The burns involved multiple surface areas and the patterns were not consistent with sunburn, since there were no clothing lines. For these injuries to be considered contact burns the host surface would have had to have been contoured. They were determined to be immersion burns caused by a hot liquid, and subsequently reported as abuse. The child was placed in foster care for 6 months, and then returned to her parents. She was returned with another similar burn 1 month later. Again, the parents denied abuse and had no idea how she was burned.

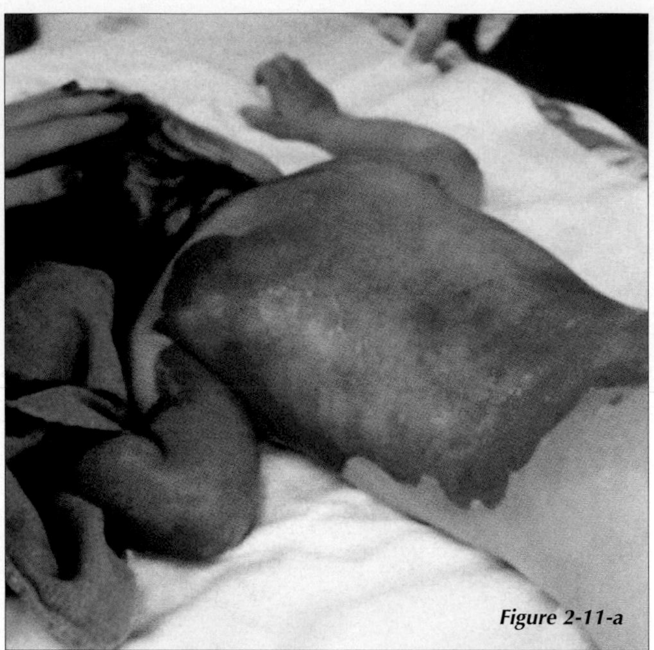

**Figure 2-11-a**

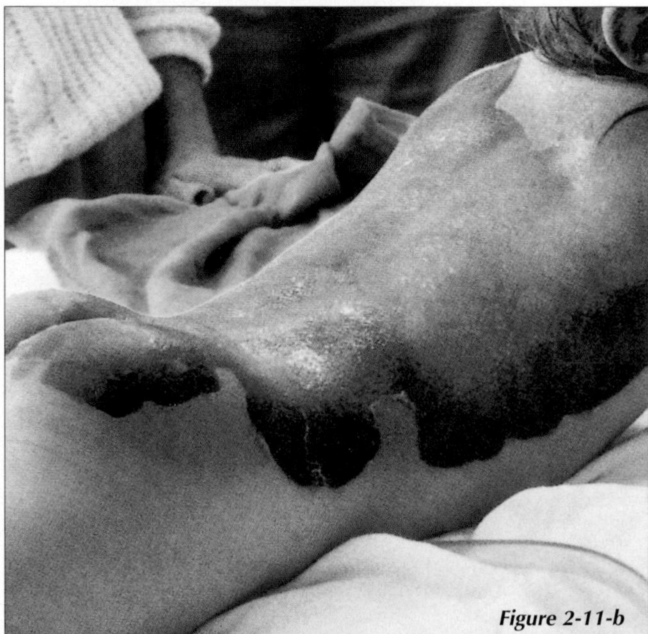

**Figure 2-11-b**

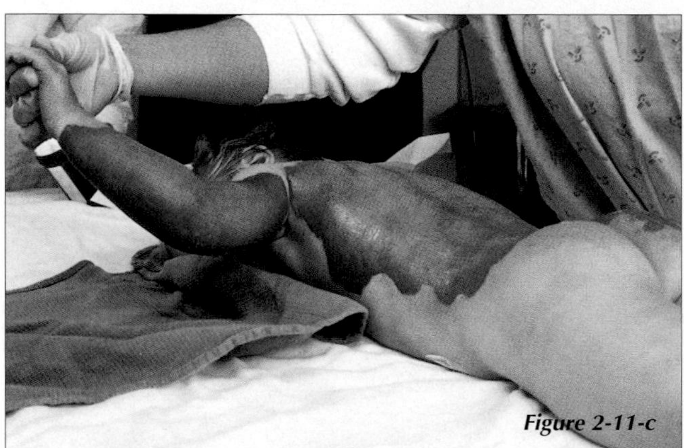

**Figure 2-11-c**

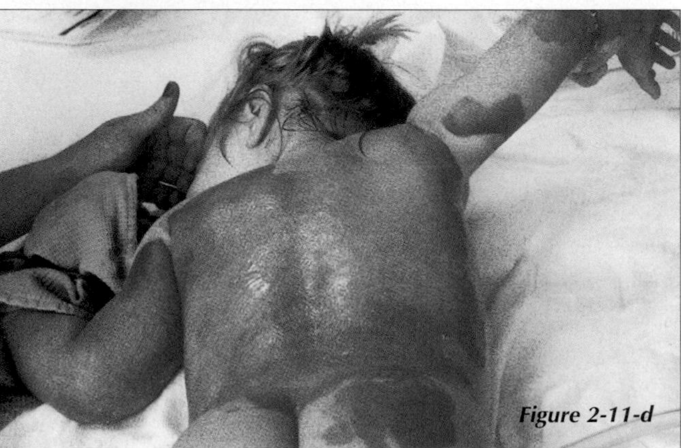

**Figure 2-11-d**

# Immersion Burns

## Multiple Injuries

### Case Study 2-12

This 18-month-old girl was examined for second- and third-degree burns on both legs. She was noted to be malnourished and required nutritional support before skin grafting could be done. Investigation by social services determined that the burns were most likely accidental.

***Figures 2-12-a** and **b.** Sustained second- and third-degree burns of both legs from hot water immersion.*

She was readmitted 6 months later with a large third-degree burn on her back. Her mother and stepfather stated that she was asleep in the back seat of their car when battery acid spilled onto her back. According to their account of the burn, she did not awaken when she was burned. They noted the burn after they arrived home and were getting her ready for bed. After a thorough investigation, it was determined that her stepfather inflicted the burns. She was then placed in foster care and has subsequently been adopted.

***Figure 2-12-c.** Third-degree burn to this child's back that occurred 6 months after the initial burns on her legs were treated.*

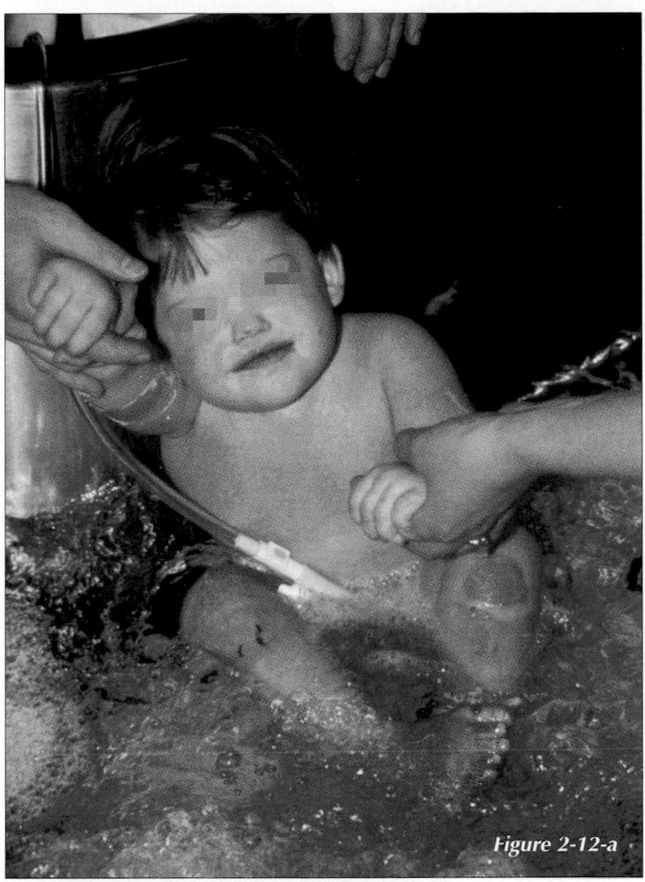

**Figure 2-12-a**

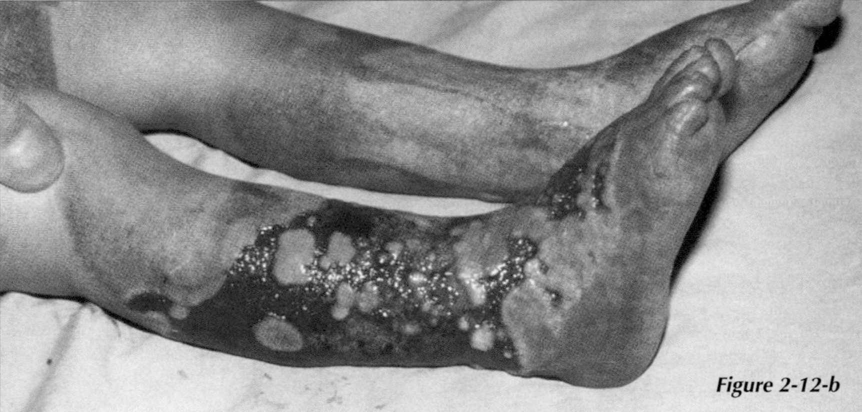

**Figure 2-12-b**

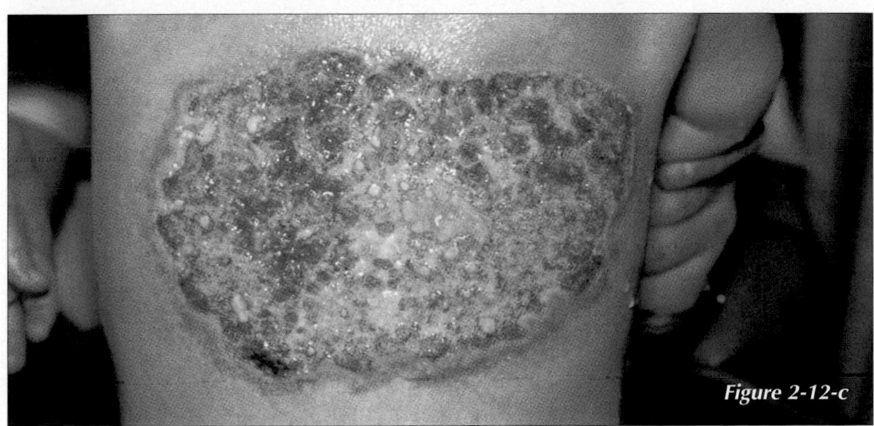

**Figure 2-12-c**

# Immersion Burns

## Multiple Injuries

### Case Study 2-13

This 18-month-old boy had second- and third-degree immersion burns to both lower extremities. He was originally admitted to another hospital and was transferred with the diagnosis of "scalded skin syndrome" believed to be secondary to an infectious process.

***Figures 2-13-a** and **b.** This burn, which shows a combination of thermal and chemical burn characteristics, appears more like an intentional immersion burn.*

Body radiographs revealed a healing tibial plateau fracture. Because of progressive swelling, a compartment syndrome developed in the affected leg and required a fasciotomy. It was later determined that this child was one of several being cared for by a particular caregiver. He had soiled his diaper, and she had run out of clean diapers. She then dipped him in a mixture of hot water, ammonia, and disinfecting cleaning detergent to both cleanse and punish him for soiling his diapers.

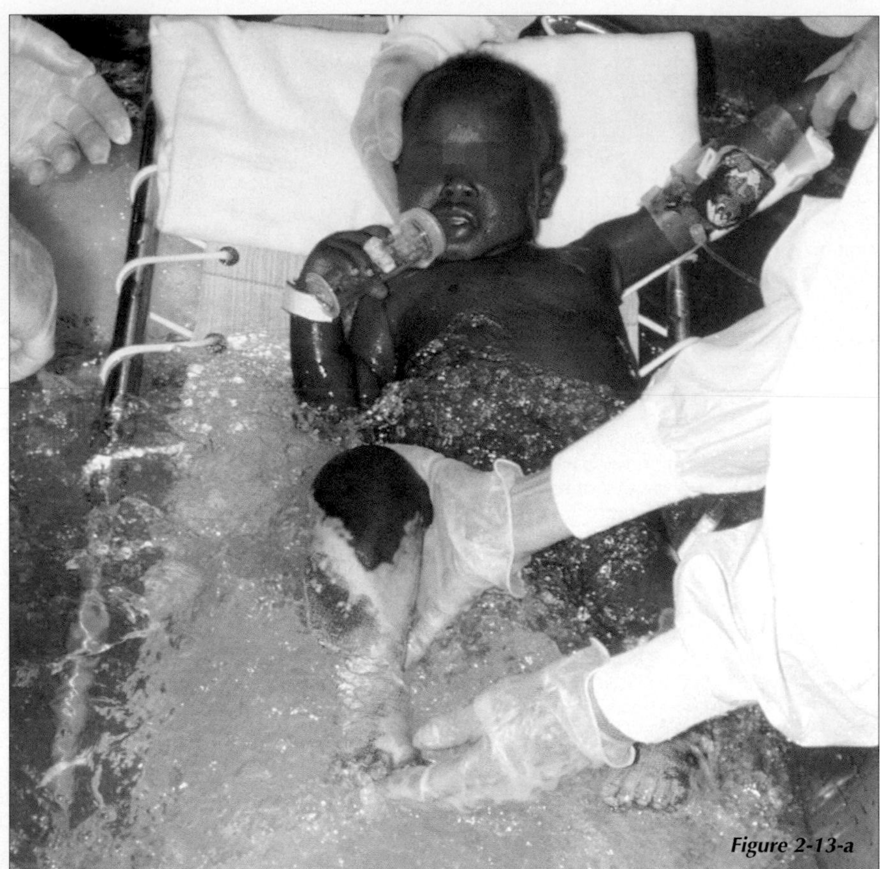

Figure 2-13-a

Figure 2-13-b

# Immersion Burns

## Multiple Injuries

### Case Study 2-14

This child was first seen when he was 26 months old. The history given at the time was that while in the care of a 14-year-old babysitter he burned his right hand on a space heater. It was determined to be an accidental injury. He reappeared in the ER 4 months later and the mother reported that she had given him a bath the evening before. She did not see the burns until the following day when she noticed that the skin on his buttocks was coming off. The burning was determined to be a form of punishment.

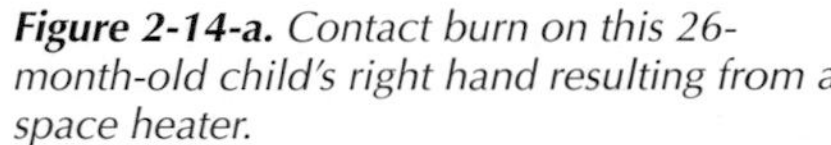

***Figure 2-14-a.*** *Contact burn on this 26-month-old child's right hand resulting from a space heater.*

***Figures 2-14-b, c,*** *and* ***d.*** *This child has a large ecchymotic area on the lower back and a smaller one on the left thigh. These are confluent linear marks.*

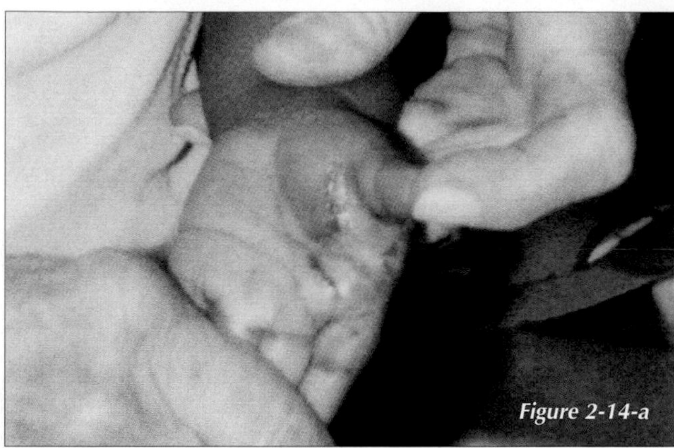

Figure 2-14-a

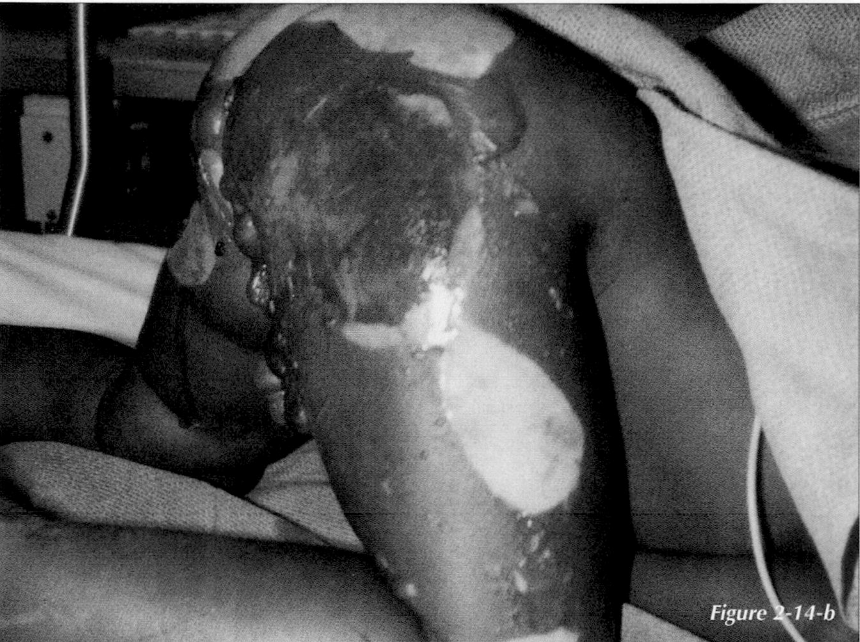

Figure 2-14-b

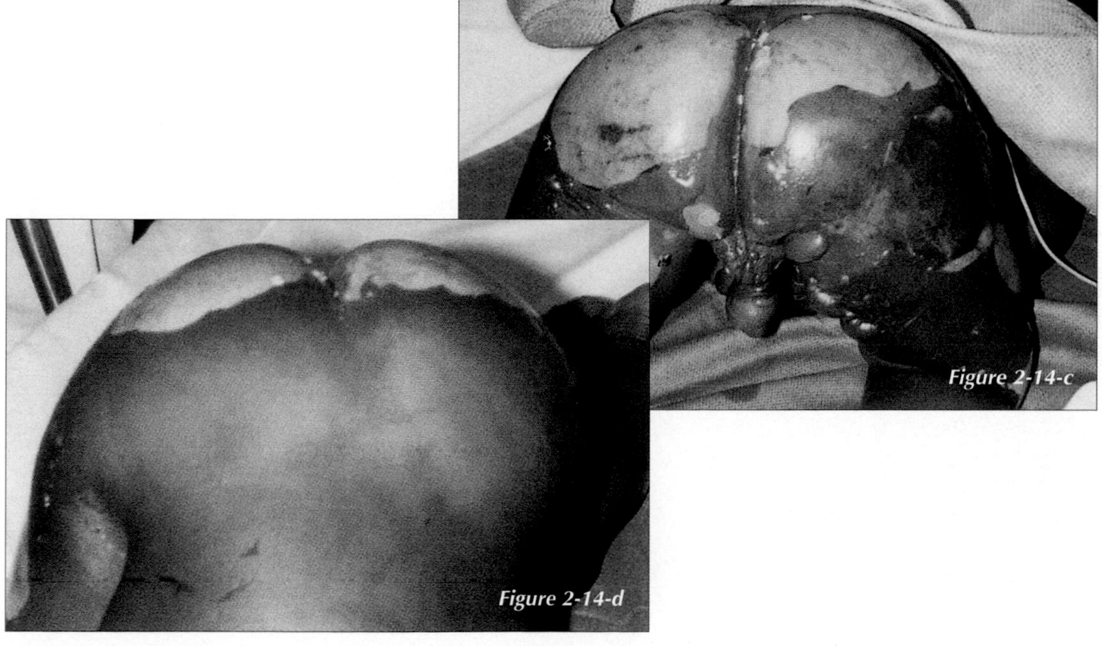

Figure 2-14-c

Figure 2-14-d

# Immersion Burns

## Multiple Injuries

### Case Study 2-15

This 3-year-old girl was taken to the ER for second- and third-degree burns of the hands. The original history given was that she accidentally stuck her hands under running hot water. The child later stated that "mommy was mad at me and put my hands in the water."

***Figures 2-15-a** and **b**. Compare these injuries with typical immersion injuries. There is no stocking-glove sign. The palms are relatively spared.*

In addition to the child's history, a measurement of the water temperature by the investigator confirmed that the water temperature was not hot enough to give an instant burn.

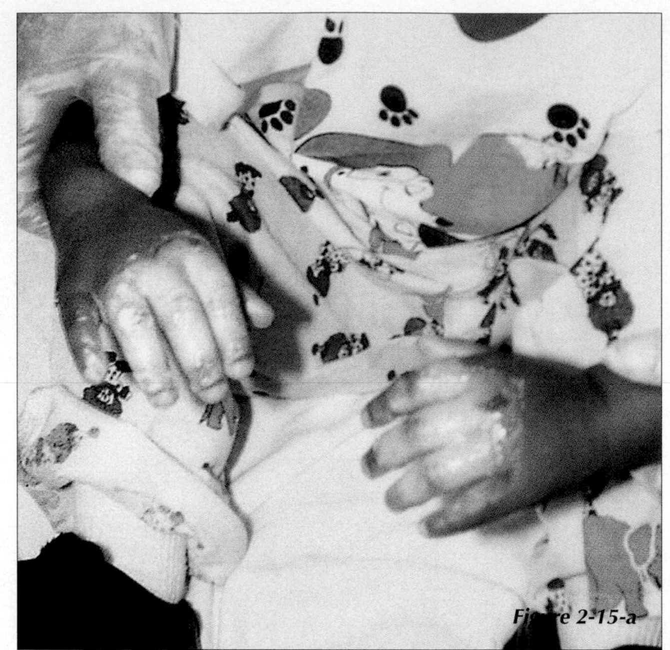

Figure 2-15-a

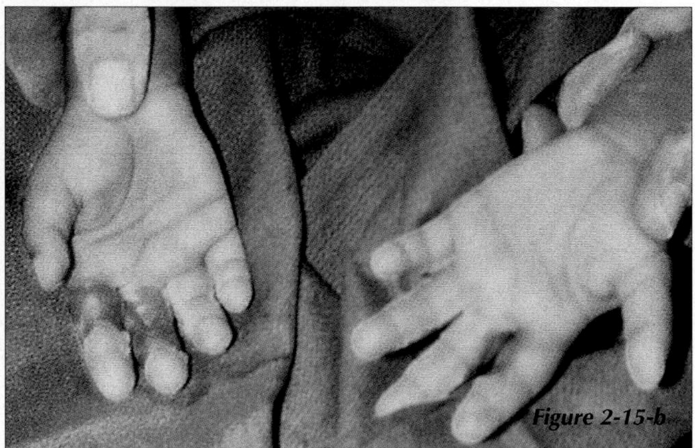

Figure 2-15-b

## Scald Burns

**Case Study 2-16**

This 2-year-old girl died from abdominal trauma. While babysitting, the mother's boyfriend repeatedly kicked the child's abdomen, rupturing her spleen. He also poured hot butter onto her body. The boyfriend was charged with murder. The burns were significant for the prosecution, leading to a charge of torture in addition to the murder charge. Torture is a special circumstance in the state of California that may lead to the death sentence.

***Figure 2-16-a.*** *Burns on the child's face from the hot butter.*

***Figure 2-16-b.*** *Burns on the anterior and posterior of the torso.*

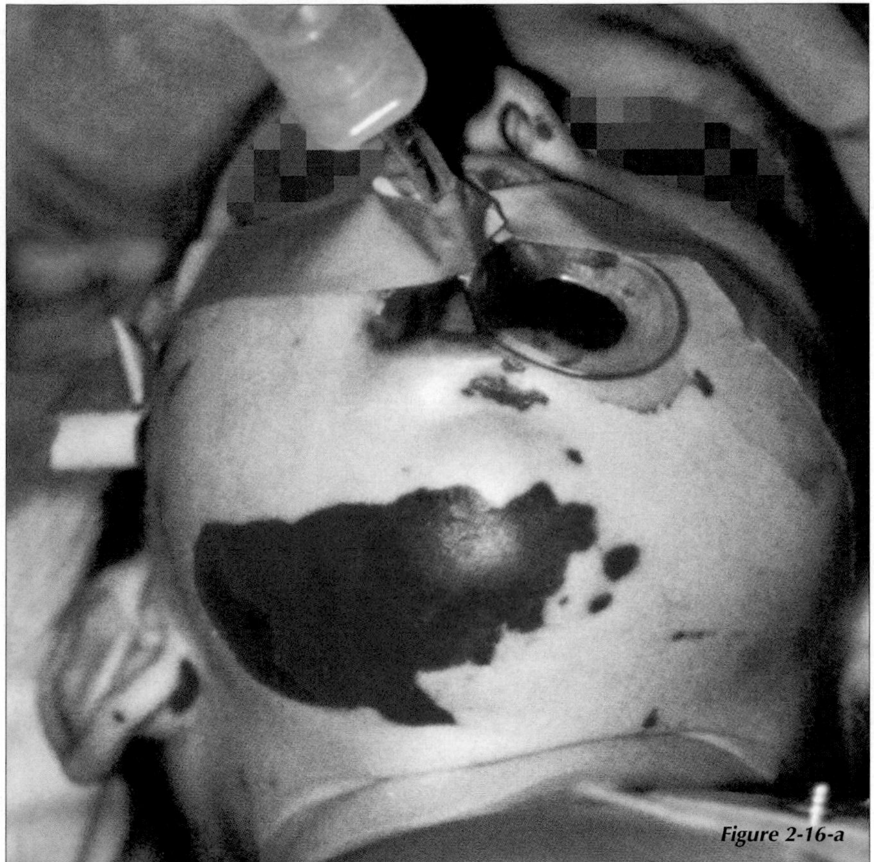

Figure 2-16-a

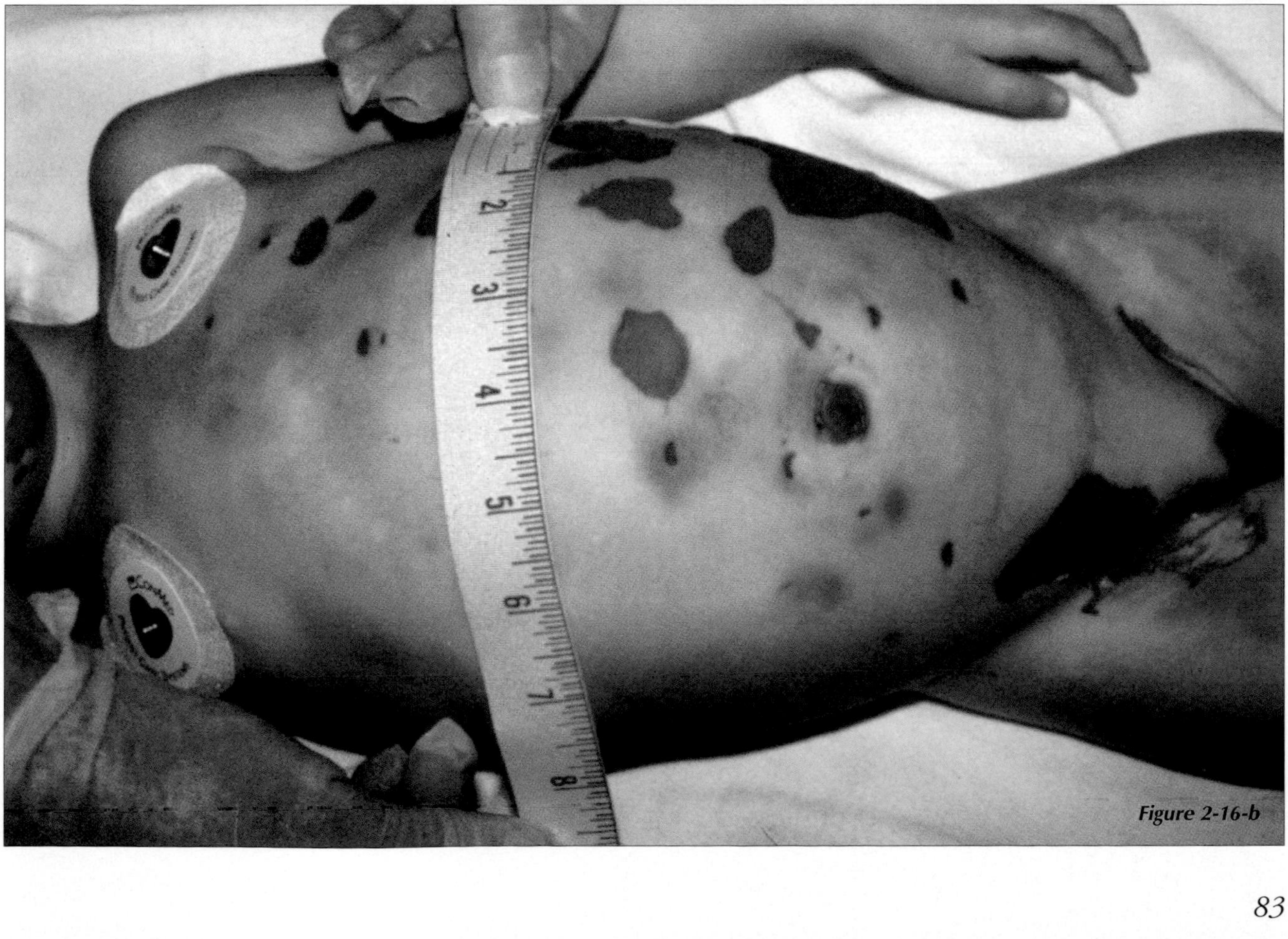

Figure 2-16-b

## Scald Burns

**Case Study 2-17**

This 30-month-old boy was examined for multiple scald burns. The boy's mother said that she had left him in the care of relatives with whom she shared a house. When she returned home they told her the boy had been burned, although no one claimed to have witnessed the incident. They claimed that they found the child crying outside the bathroom and assumed that he had burned himself. The house was overcrowded and the children living there were poorly supervised. The child was unable to speak and could not relate what had happened to him. The injuries were considered to be a result of abuse.

***Figure 2-17-a.*** *Scald burns to the face of the boy.*

***Figure 2-17-b.*** *Scald burns to the buttocks.*

***Figure 2-17-c.*** *Scald burns appearing on the boy's left shoulder.*

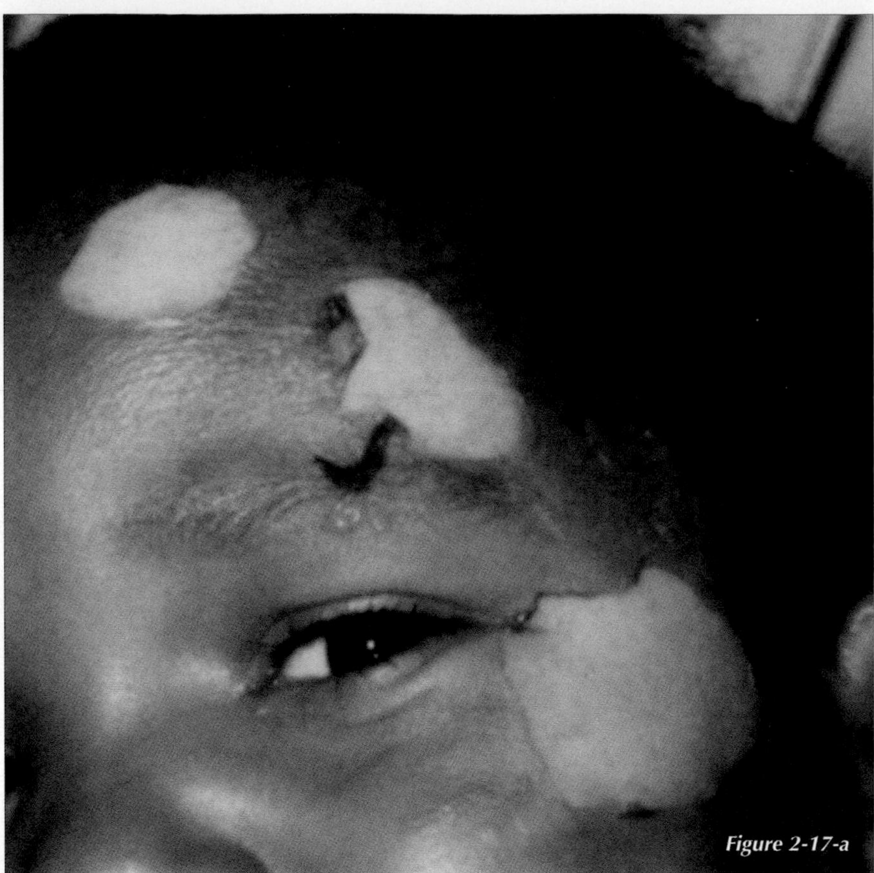

Figure 2-17-a

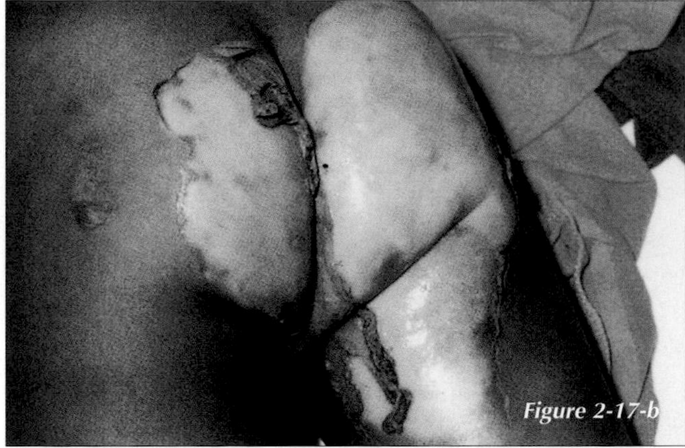

Figure 2-17-b

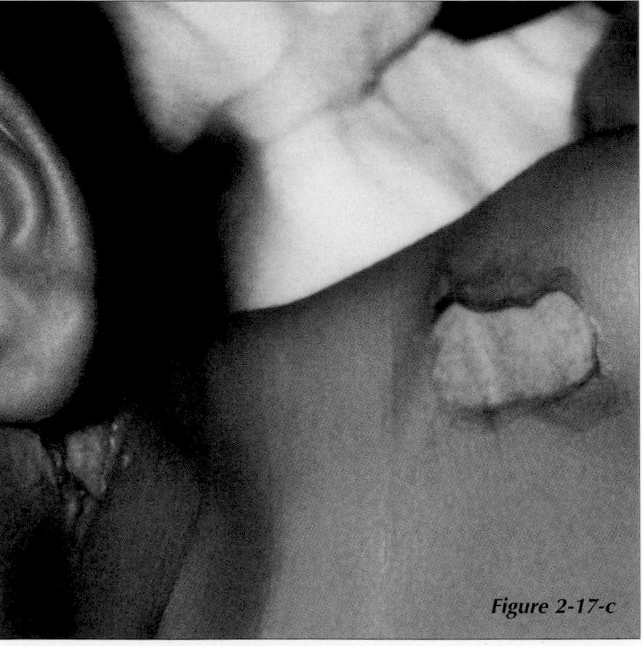

Figure 2-17-c

# SCALD BURNS

**Case Study 2-17** *(continued)*

***Figures 2-17-d*** *and* ***e.*** *Additional burns behind each ear.*

***Figure 2-17-f.*** *The child's feet with embedded dirt and feces.*

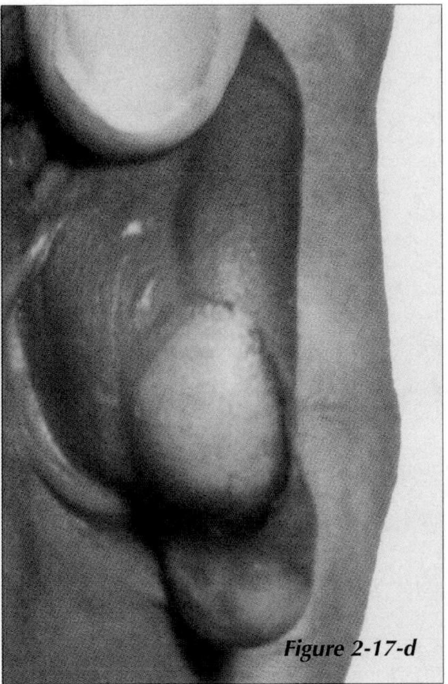

Figure 2-17-d

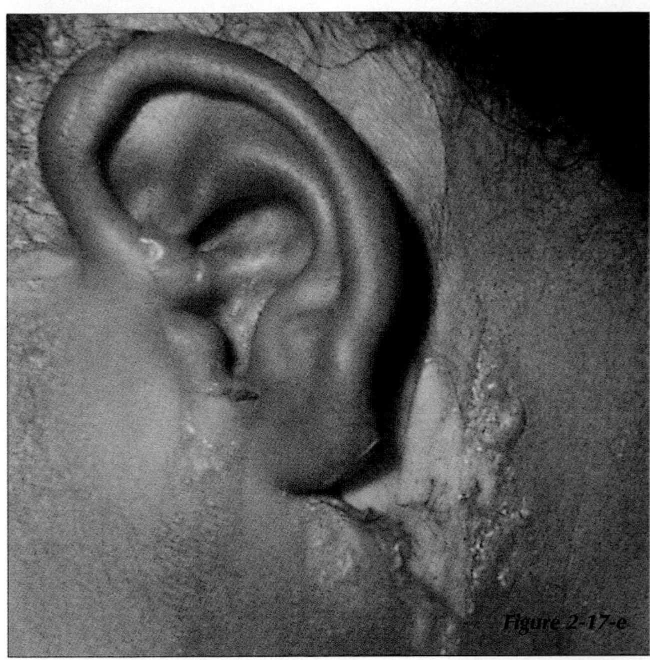

Figure 2-17-e

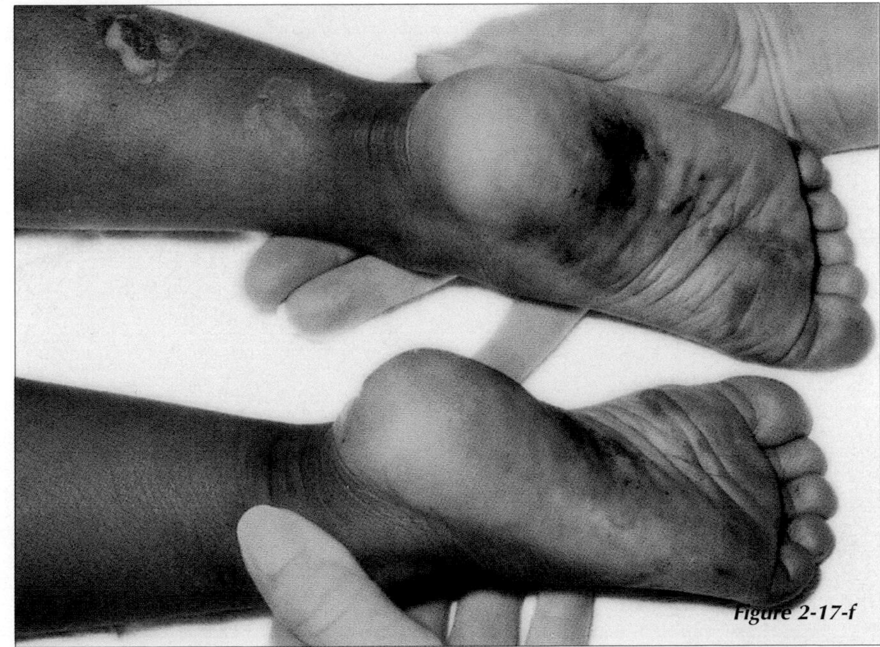

Figure 2-17-f

# Scald Burns

**Case Study 2-18**

This 15-month-old girl was in the care of a babysitter, who said she spilled hot grease and the "hot grease got under her Pampers." The injuries were not consistent with the history. There was no diaper line burn, which would be expected if grease fell cleanly into the diaper area without first touching the abdomen. A diaper would have limited the flow of liquid. Additionally, there was no grease-soaked diaper.

***Figures 2-18-a** and **b**. Second-degree burns to the diaper area.*

***Figure 2-18-c.** A circular burn to her right arm.*

This was determined to be a scald burn from hot water.

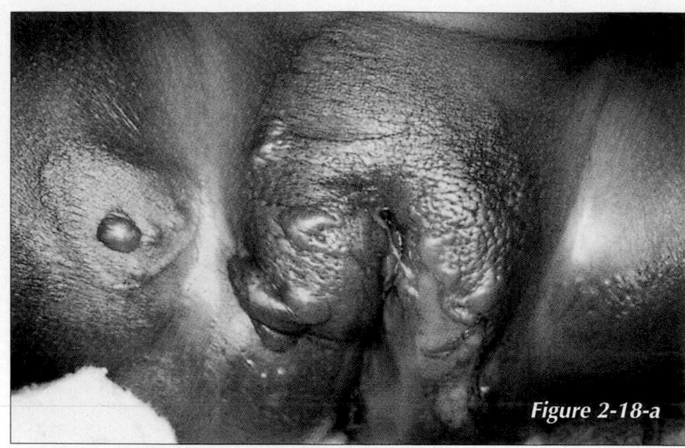

Figure 2-18-a

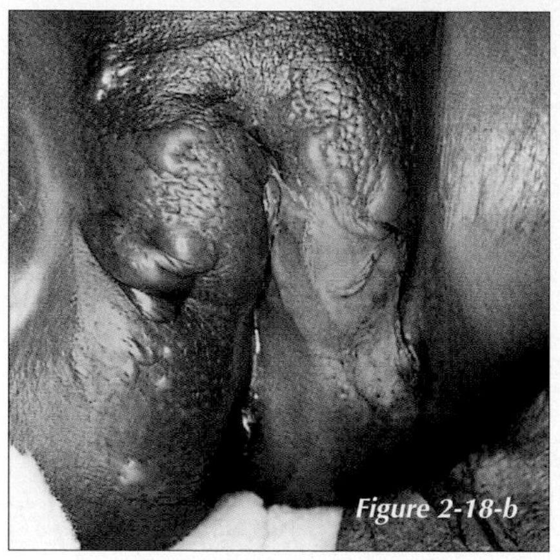

Figure 2-18-b

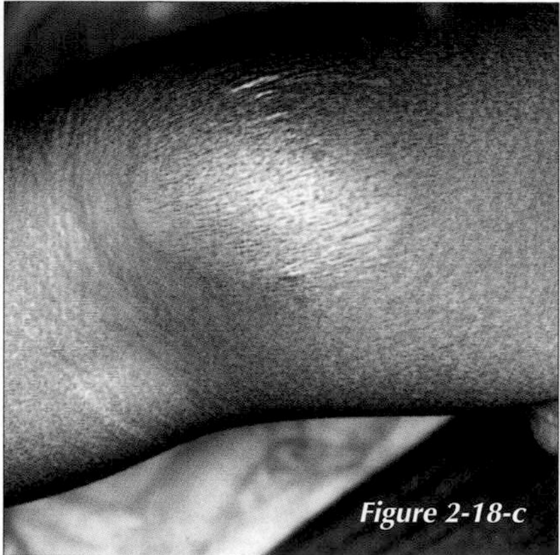

Figure 2-18-c

**Case Study 2-19**

This 18-month-old girl was examined in the ER with a history that she had pulled hot liquid off a table onto her face.

***Figure 2-19.** Second-degree burns of the girl's face with a burn over the bridge of the nose, above her lip, and the sides of her mouth. Note that the chin is not burned.*

Further examination revealed that she had burns on the inside of her lips and on her tongue. It was determined that she was forced to drink hot liquid. She was also found to have a healing fracture of the left radius and ulna.

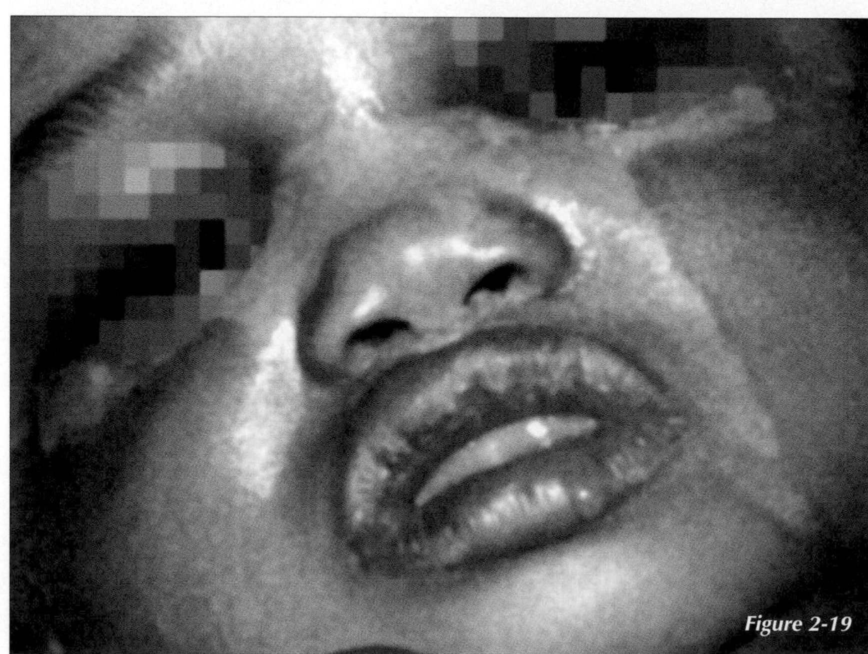

Figure 2-19

# Scald Burns

**Case Study 2-20**

This 17-month-old girl was seen in the ER with swollen feet. She had mild first-degree burns to her feet. The child was in the care of her mother's boyfriend, who said that she received the mild burn when he "gave her a bath after she soiled herself."

***Figure 2-20-a.*** *An ecchymotic area behind the girl's ear.*

***Figure 2-20-b.*** *A deep healing injury on the right foot.*

The case was reported to the hotline as suspected abuse.

**Case Study 2-21**

This 8-month-old was dipped in scalding water.

***Figure 2-21.*** *Scald burns to this child.*

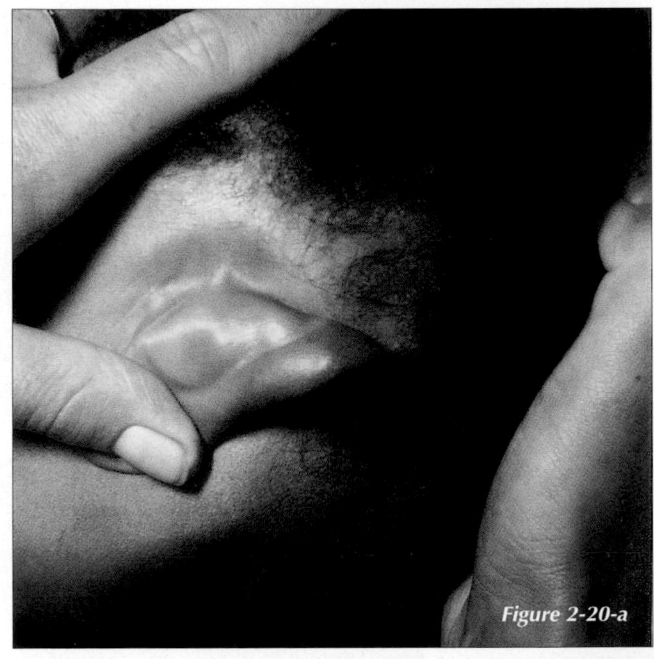

Figure 2-20-a

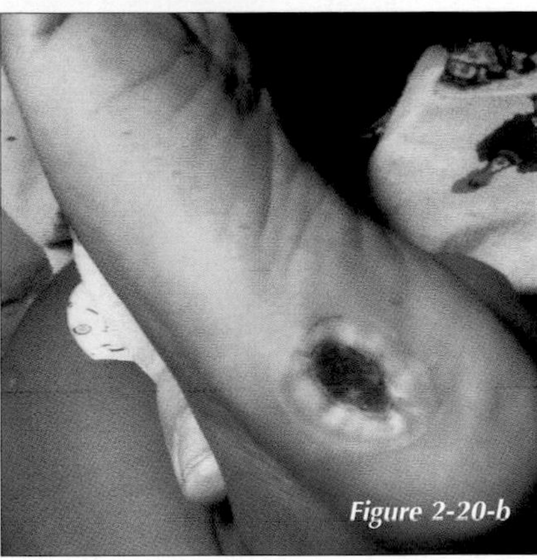

Figure 2-20-b

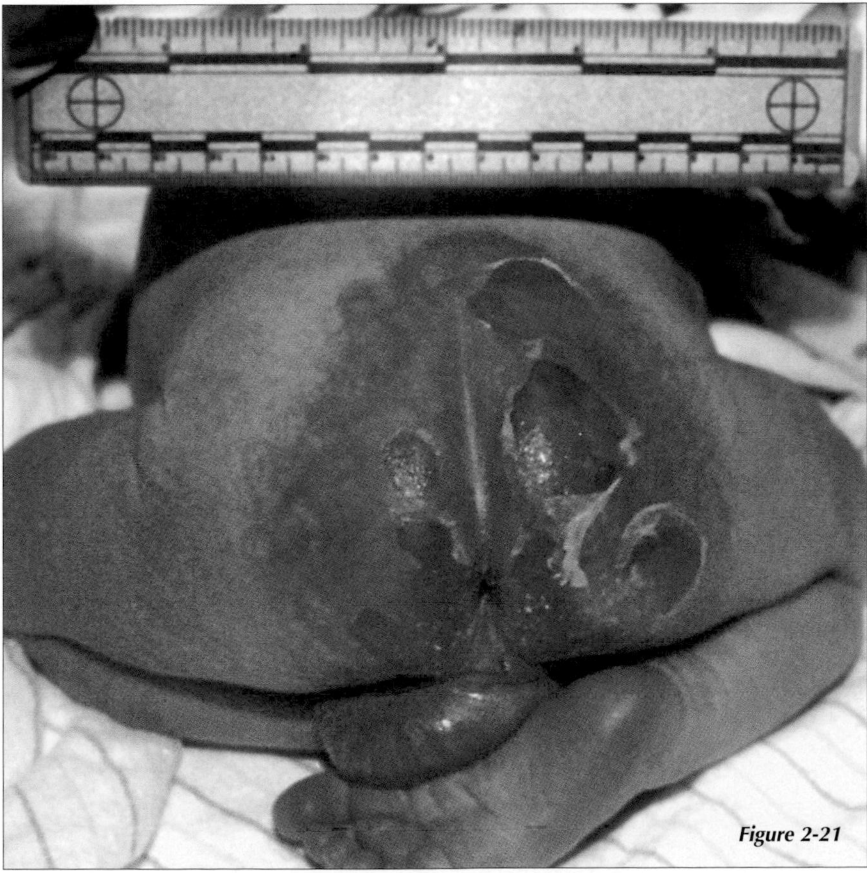

Figure 2-21

# Scald Burns

**Case Study 2-22**

This child was examined in the ER for burns to her left foot, which had been immersed in scalding water.

***Figure 2-22-a.*** *Scald burns to the foot of this child.*

***Figure 2-22-b.*** *Multiple abrasions and scratches from a sharp object to the sole of her foot.*

**Case Study 2-23**

This child's hands were burned by holding them under hot running water.

***Figures 2-23-a*** *and* ***b.*** *Bilateral hand burns resulting from intentional scalding. Note that the severity of the burning is concentrated at the center of the back of the hands, where the running water would have impacted the hands first, and reduces in severity radiating outwardly toward the fingertips, which are spared.*

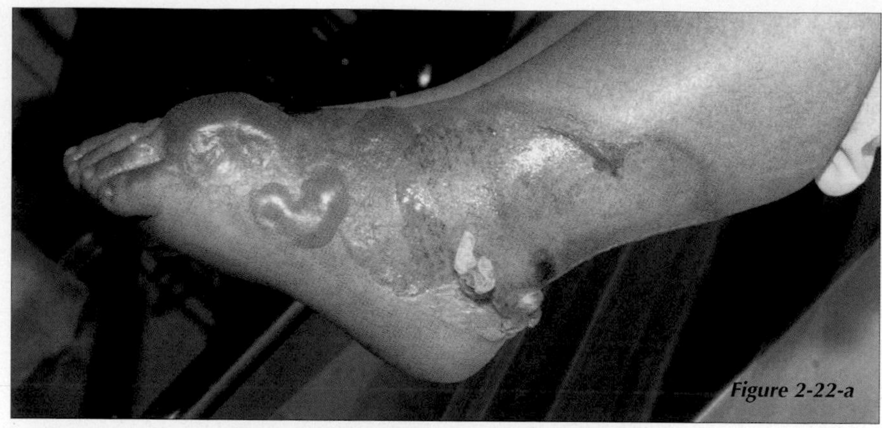

Figure 2-22-a

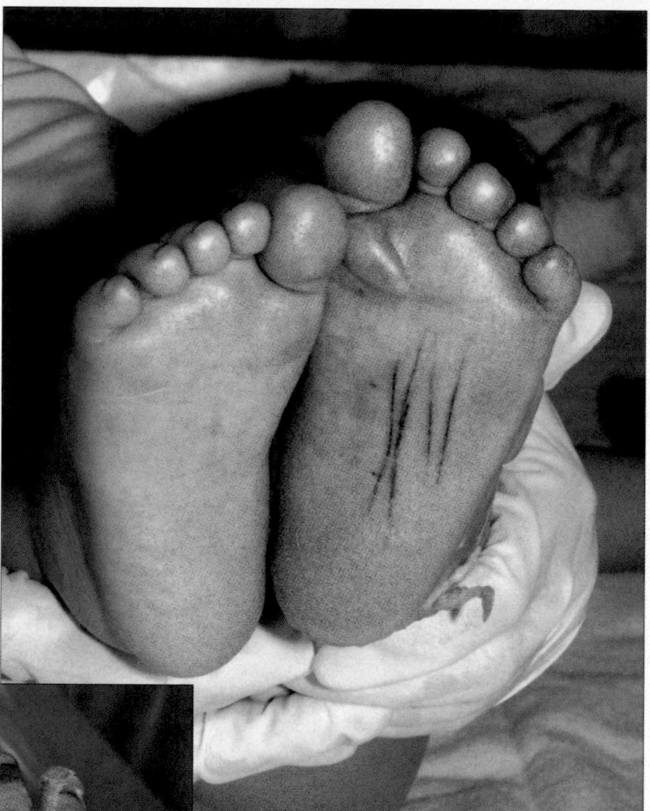

Figure 2-22-b

Figure 2-23-a

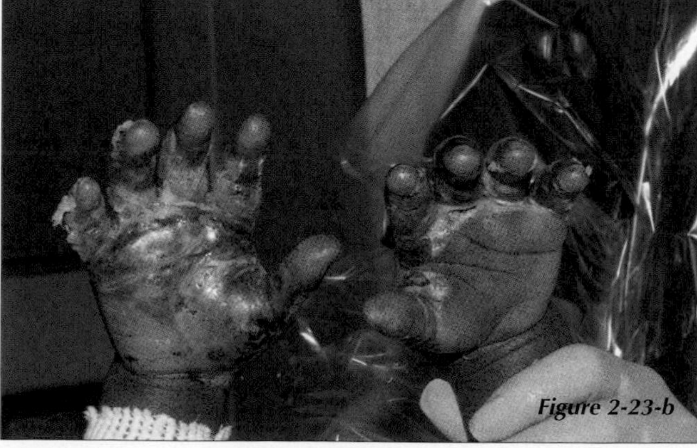

Figure 2-23-b

## Scald Burns

**Case Study 2-24**

This 9-month-old infant was dipped in scalding bath water.

***Figure 2-24.*** *Scald burns from abusive immersion in hot bath water.*

**Case Study 2-25**

This 1-year-old child presented with a scald burn to the thigh and abdomen.

***Figure 2-25.*** *Spared skin in the inguinal area indicates flexion of the hip when the burn occurred.*

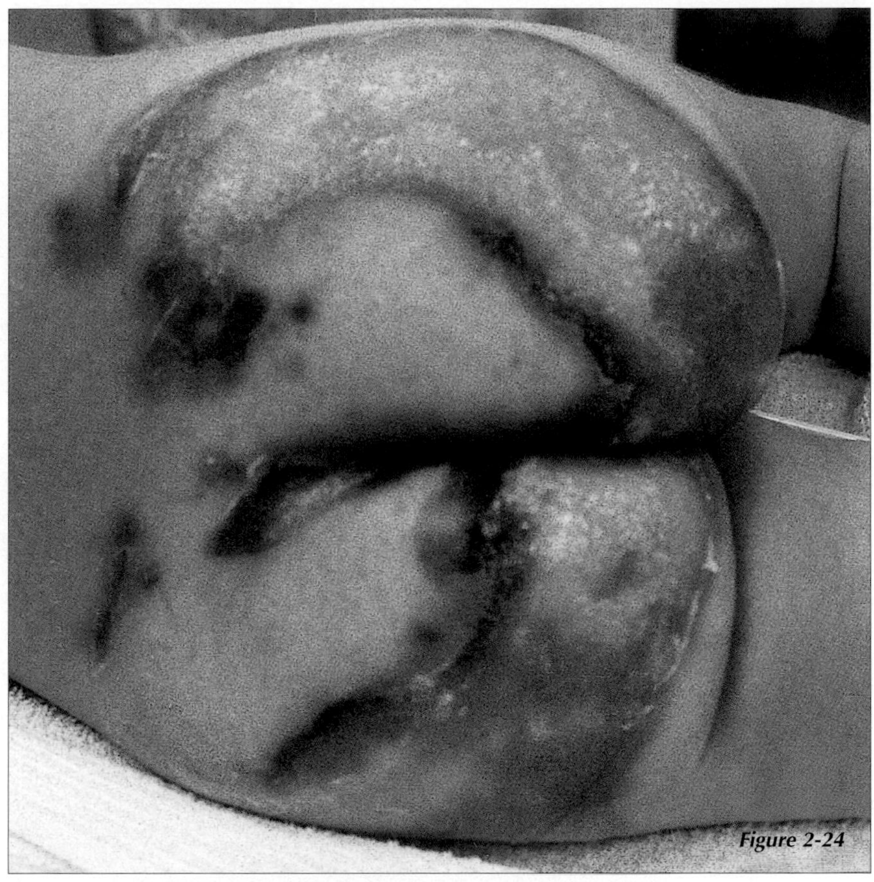

Figure 2-24

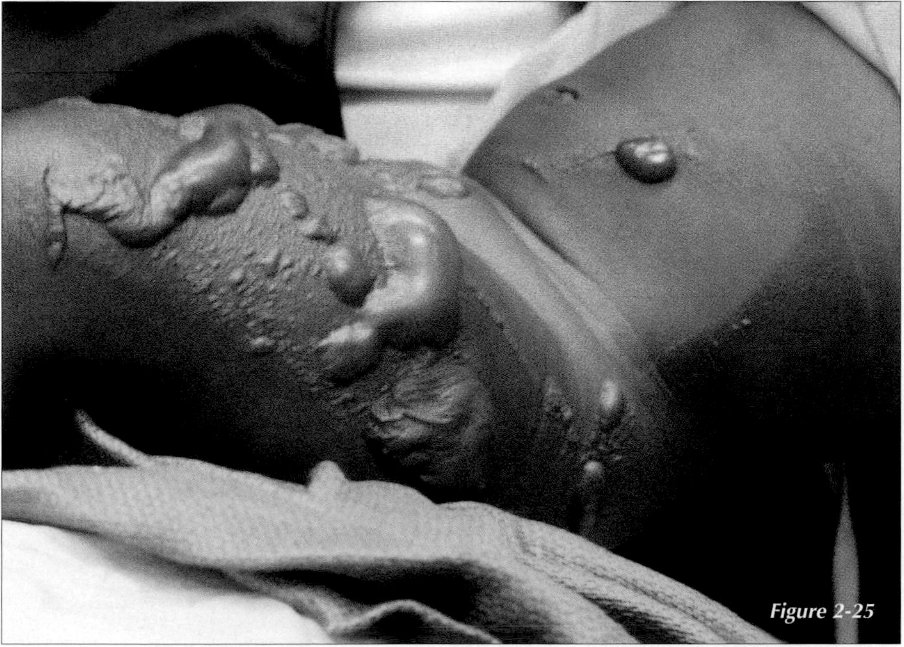

Figure 2-25

# Contact Burns

## Hot Iron / Steam Iron

**Case Study 2-26**

This 2-year-old child was burned on the hand by a hot iron. Other indicators of physical abuse were also present.

***Figure 2-26-a.*** *Abusive burn from a hot iron to the palmar surface of the hand and digits with visible evidence of the steam holes of the iron.*

***Figure 2-26-b.*** *Photograph of iron that corresponds to the pattern of injury.*

***Figure 2-26-c.*** *Multiple bruises to the back and buttocks.*

***Figure 2-26-d.*** *Multiple bruises to the buttocks.*

***Figure 2-26-e.*** *Laceration of the lip from trauma to the mouth.*

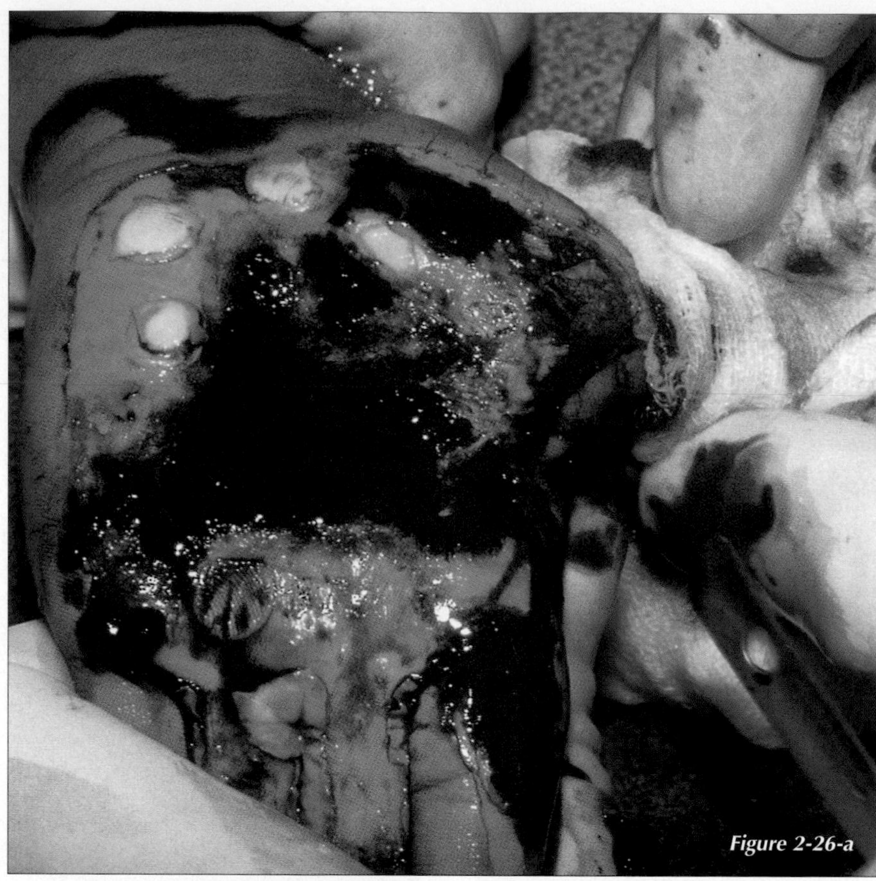

Figure 2-26-a

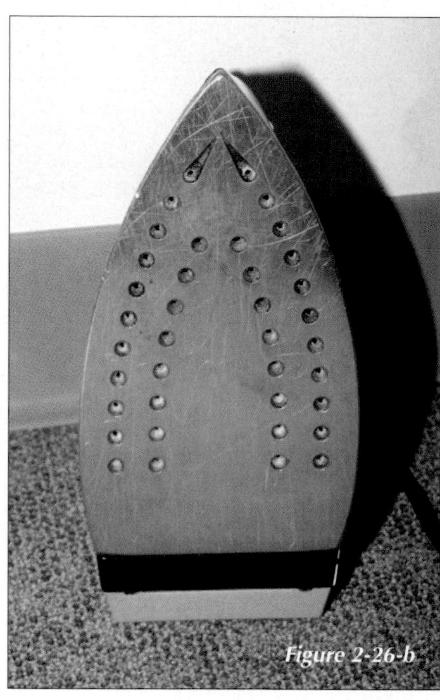

Figure 2-26-b

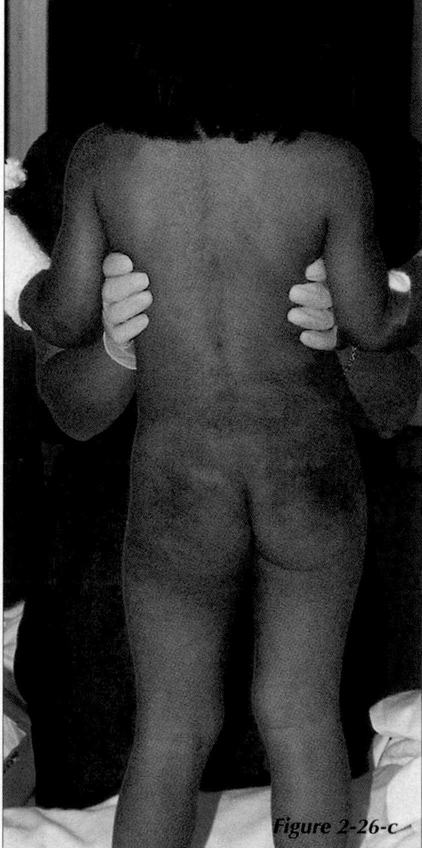

Figure 2-26-c

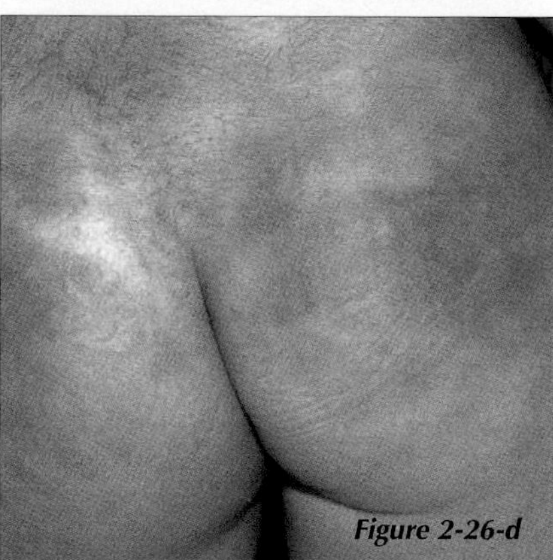

Figure 2-26-d

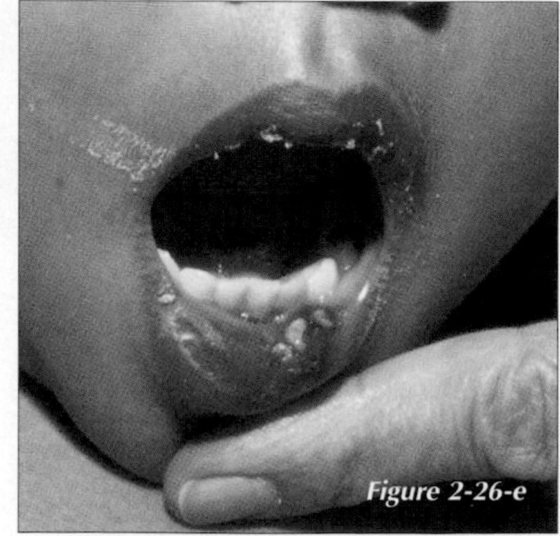

Figure 2-26-e

# Contact Burns

## Hot Iron / Steam Iron

### Case Study 2-27

This 3-year-old boy was examined for second- and third-degree burns made with a hot iron, inflicted as a form of discipline.

***Figure 2-27.*** *Second- and third-degree burns on the dorsum of the left wrist.*

### Case Study 2-28

This 6-year-old boy was burned with a steam iron as a form of discipline.

***Figure 2-28.*** *Note the clarity of the pattern burn resembling the steam jet holes from the iron.*

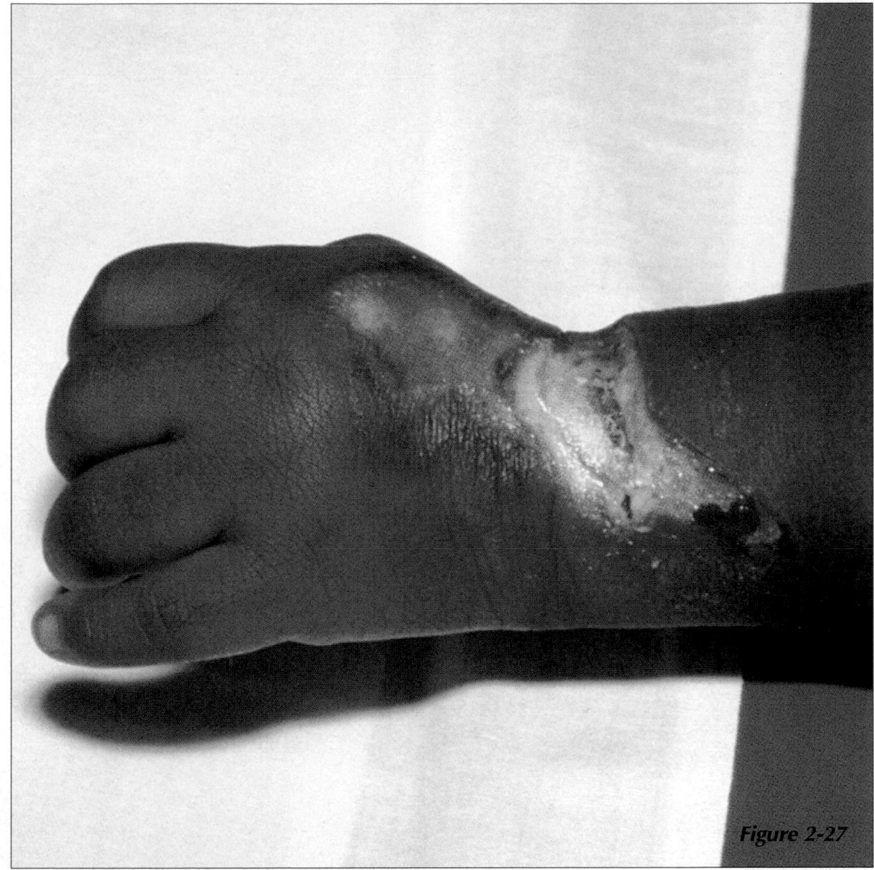

*Figure 2-27*

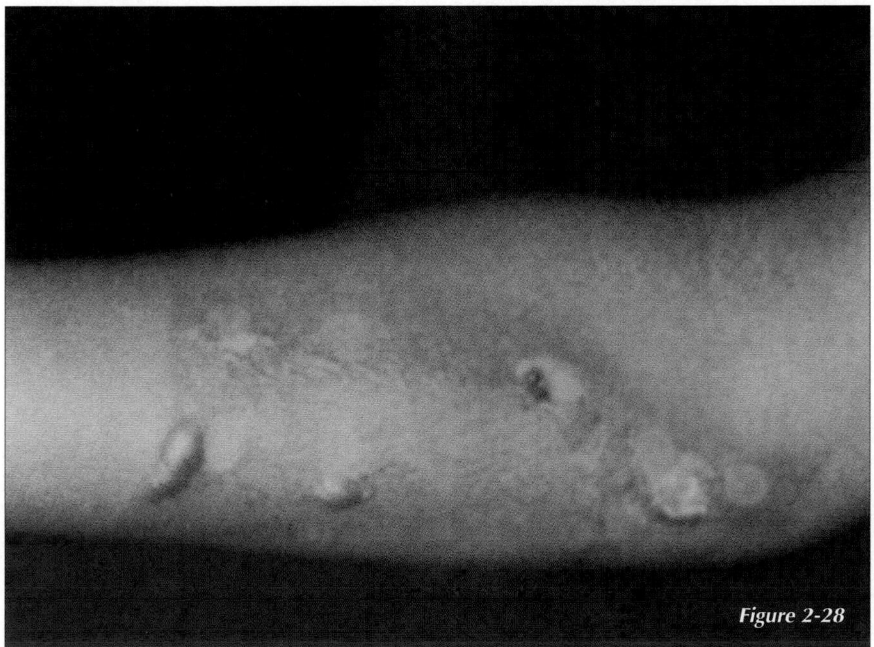

*Figure 2-28*

# Contact Burns

## Curling Iron

### Case Study 2-29

This 9-year-old boy was examined for multiple burns. Upon admission, the patient stated that his mother burned him with a curling iron.

***Figures 2-29-a** and **b**. Contact burns from the curling iron to the torso, legs, and buttocks.*

***Figure 2-29-c.** Contact burns to the abdomen, genitalia, and thigh.*

***Figure 2-29-d.** The logo from the curling iron can be seen branded on the skin of the lower abdomen.*

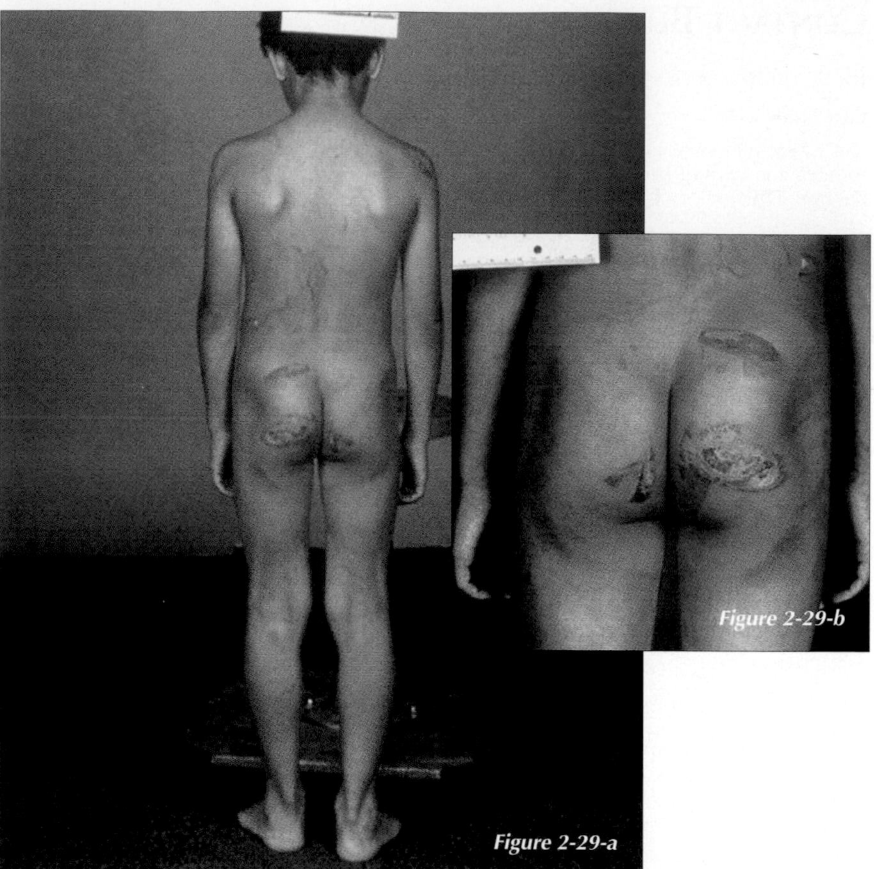

Figure 2-29-a

Figure 2-29-b

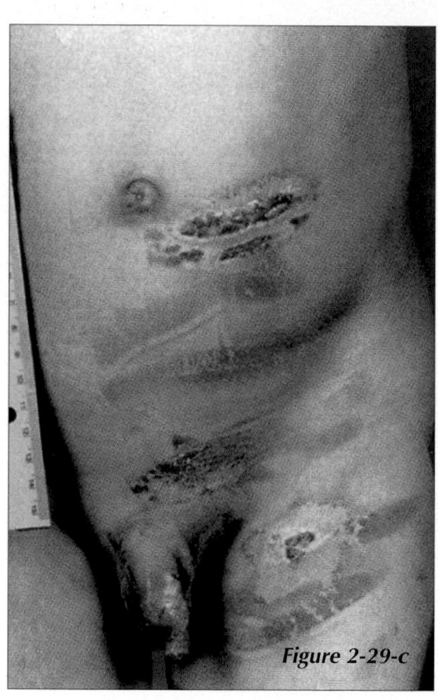

Figure 2-29-c

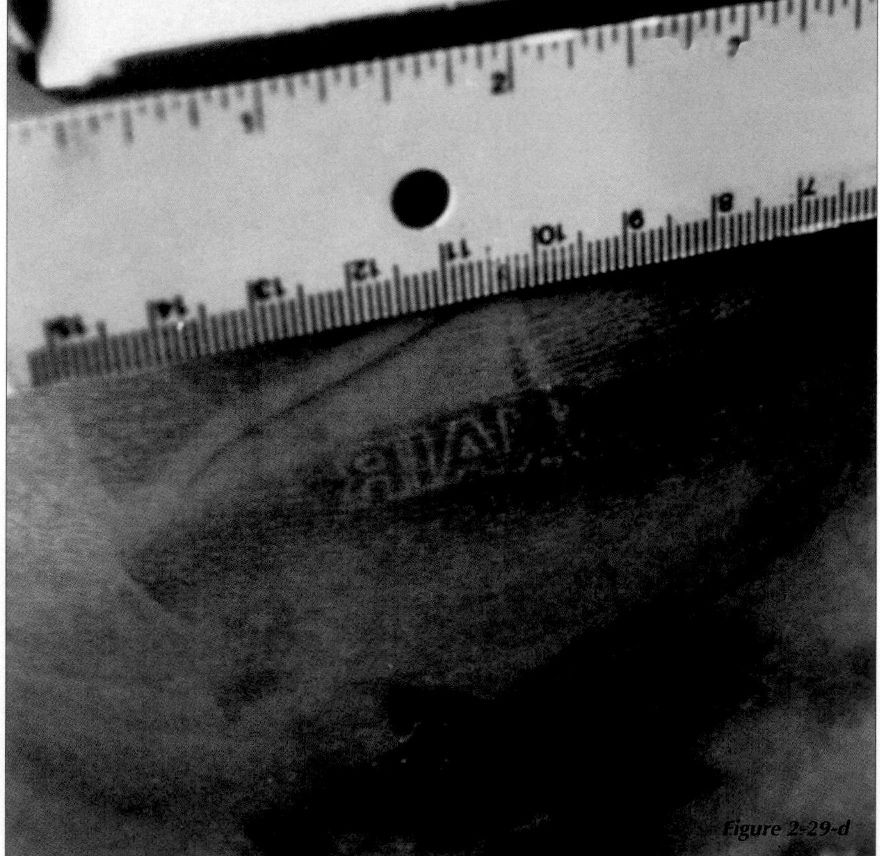

Figure 2-29-d

# Contact Burns

## Curling Iron

### Case Study 2-30

This 13-month-old boy was taken to the ER by his mother, who stated that he had been in the care of a 16-year-old cousin while she went to the grocery store. When she returned, the cousin told her that the boy had been burned by a curling iron, although the cousin did not witness the incident. The curling iron had been left on the kitchen table, and the cousin heard the boy crying from another room. Upon entering the kitchen, the cousin found the boy and assumed that he had taken the curling iron off the table and had accidentally burned himself in the process.

The child had been seen in the ER just a week earlier with a curling iron burn of his left forearm. The incident was reported as suspicious of abuse.

***Figures 2-30-a** and **b.** This child has second-degree burns of the left lateral chest . As can be seen, when the arm is flexed, the two areas are contiguous.*

***Figure 2-30-c.** Curling iron burn to the left forearm as seen upon examination the previous week.*

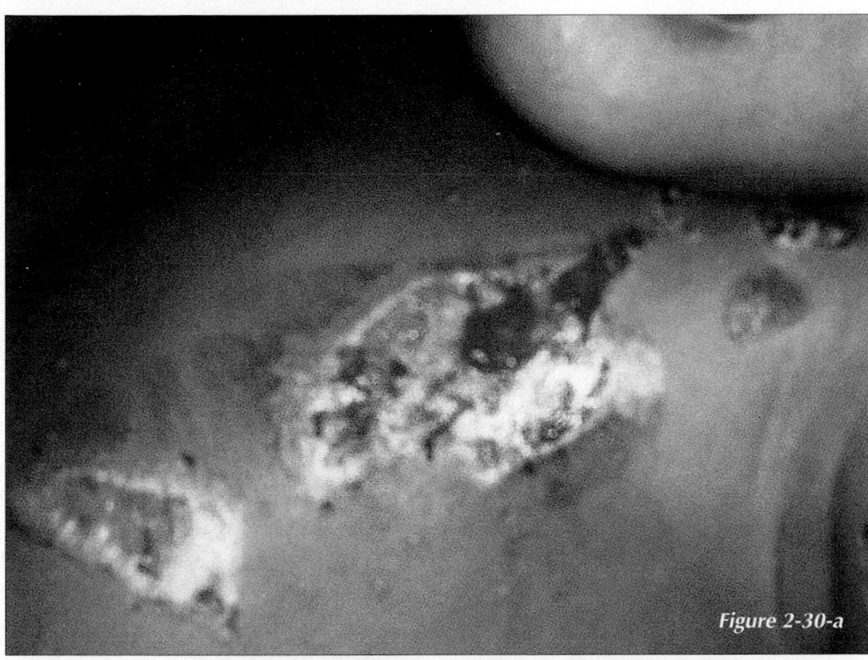

Figure 2-30-a

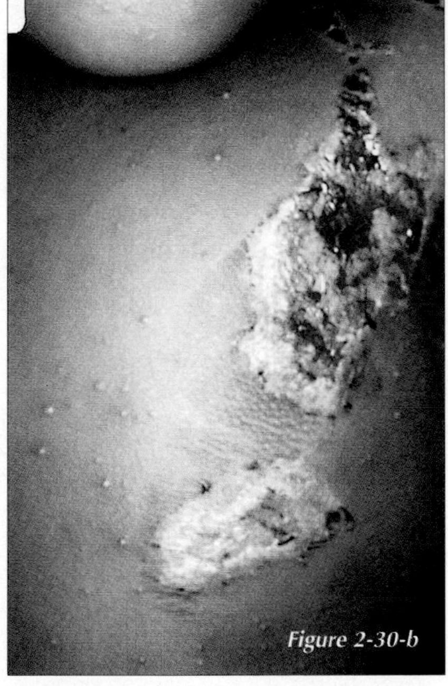

Figure 2-30-b

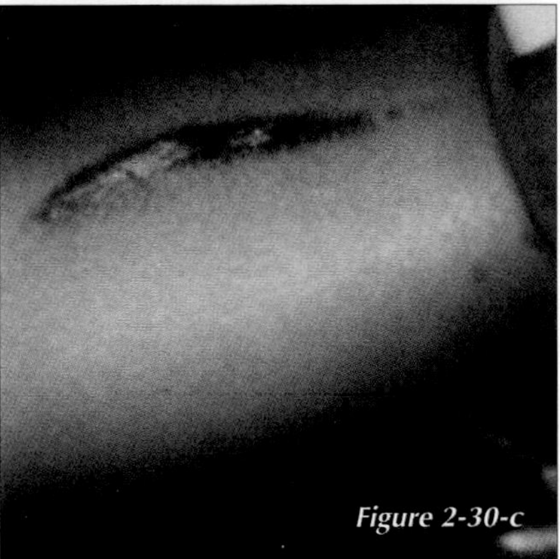

Figure 2-30-c

# Contact Burns

## Curling Iron

### Case Study 2-31

This 2-year-old girl was seen in the ER for respiratory distress. While there, the staff noticed multiple burns in various stages of healing that were said to be accidental burns from a curling iron. The child had a past history of premature birth and a long stay in the intensive care nursery. At 1 year of age she was admitted for a drug ingestion. This injury was reported as abuse.

***Figure 2-31-a.*** *Two burns to the right shoulder.*

***Figure 2-31-b.*** *One healed burn to the right forearm.*

***Figure 2-31-c.*** *A more recent burn to the left lower leg can be seen.*

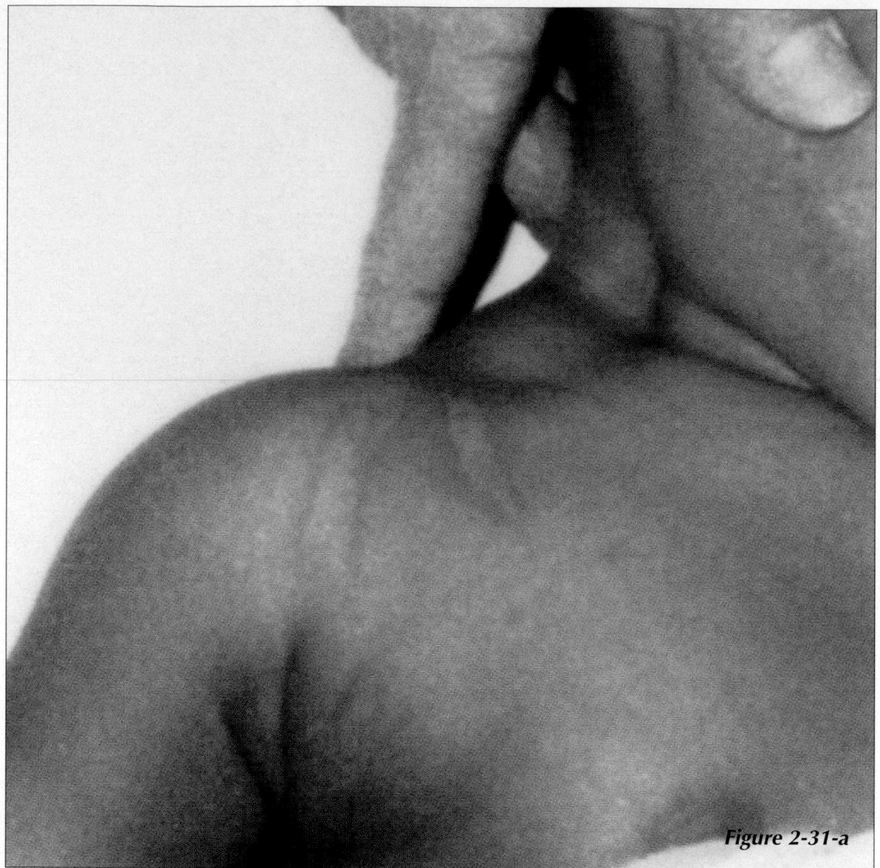
Figure 2-31-a

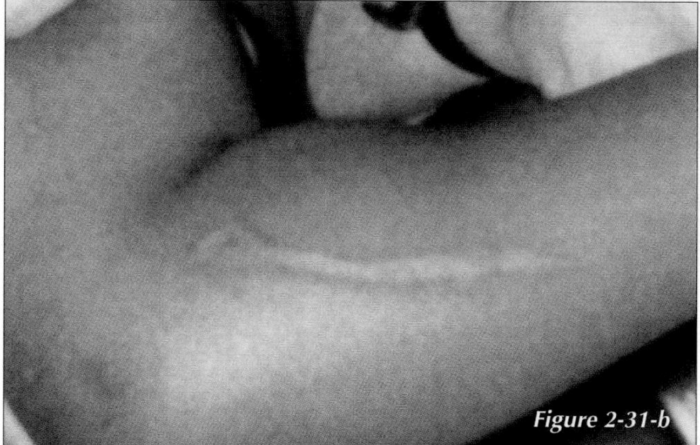
Figure 2-31-b

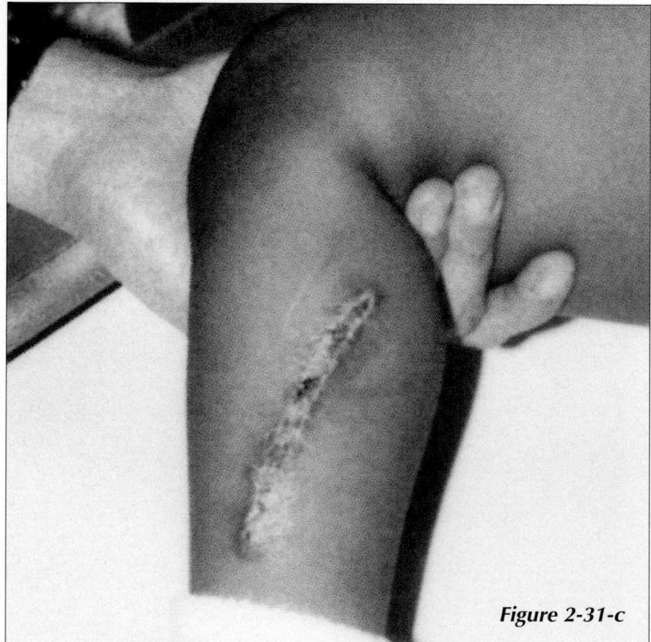
Figure 2-31-c

# Contact Burns

## Curling Iron

### Case Study 2-32

This 6-year-old boy was brought to medical attention by his stepmother with multiple curling iron burns in various stages of healing. At the age of 2 he had been abused by his biological mother, who burned his buttocks and injured his penis.

***Figures 2-32-a, b,** and **c.** Intentional curling iron burns inflicted by the boy's stepmother.*

***Figure 2-32-d.** Note the shape of the burn to the neck. This wound is the most recent, with the configuration being caused by the child flexing his neck on the iron.*

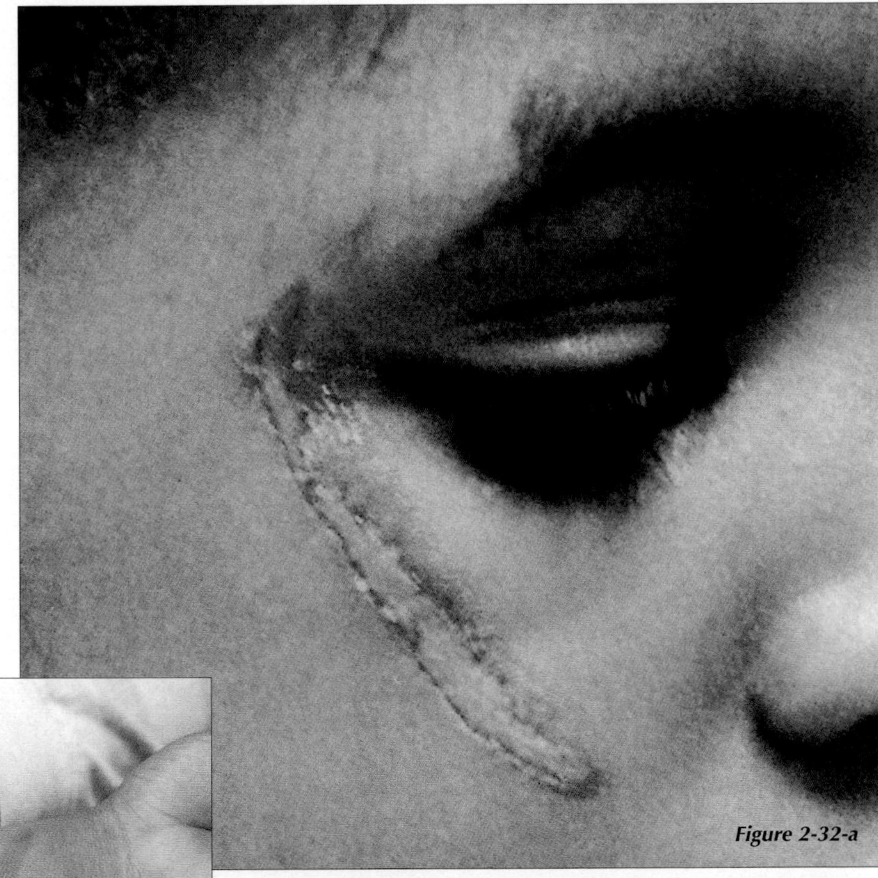

**Figure 2-32-a**

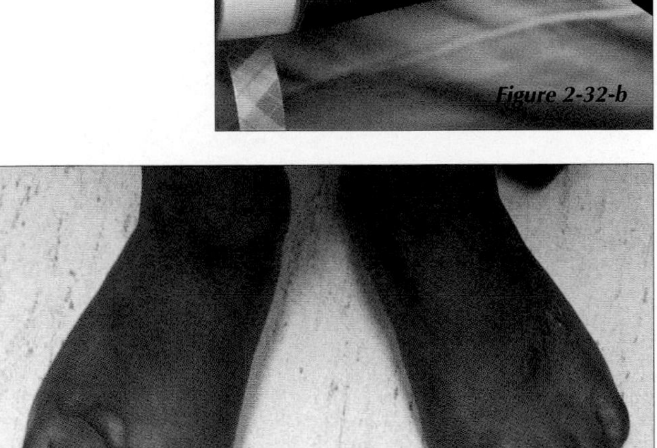

**Figure 2-32-b**

**Figure 2-32-c**

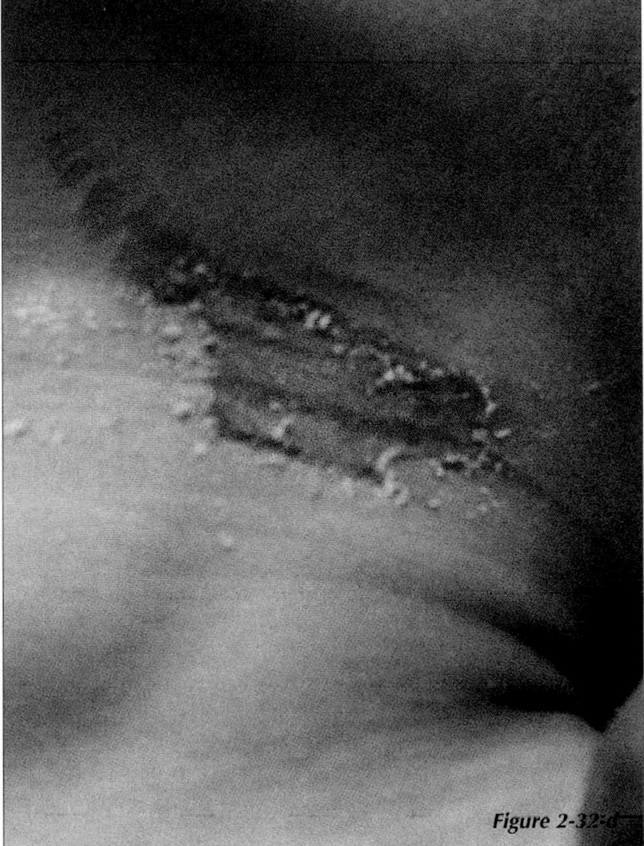

**Figure 2-32-d**

# Contact Burns

## Curling Iron

### Case Study 2-33

This boy was brought in by his mother for burns she noticed on his genitalia after a visit with her estranged husband. The mother could not explain the burns. Although all of the injuries were of the same age, the ER staff thought that each injury represented a separate incident. The instrument was believed to be a curling iron, and the injuries were determined to be the result of discipline for soiling. The father denied injuring the child and the mother had been recently released from a psychiatric hospital.

***Figures 2-33-a, b, c,*** *and* ***d.*** *The injuries to the scrotum and glans penis.*

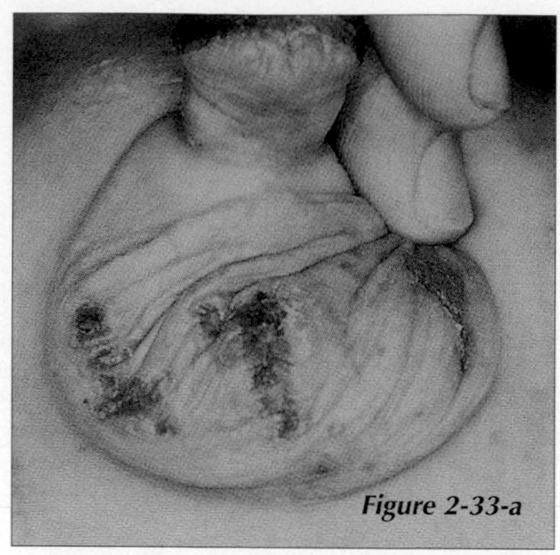

Figure 2-33-a

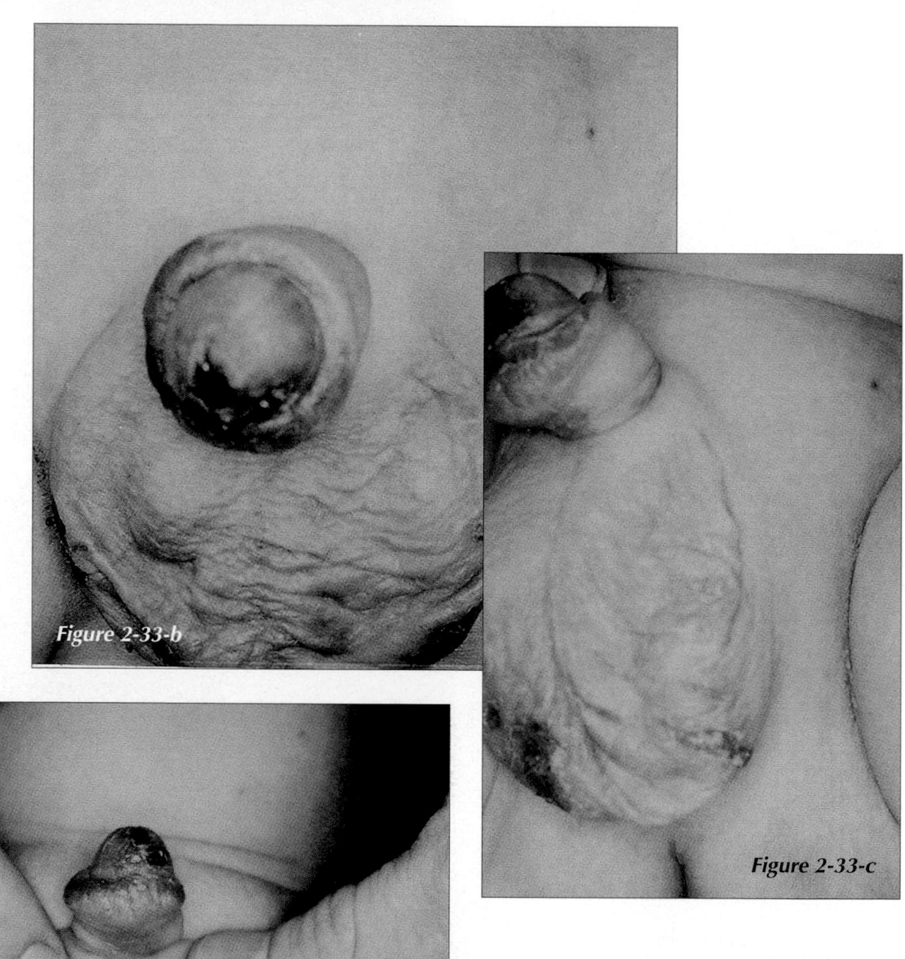

Figure 2-33-b

Figure 2-33-c

Figure 2-33-d

# Contact Burns

## Curling Iron

**Case Study 2-34**

This 28-month-boy was examined for a severe burn to his buttocks. The caretaker stated that he had sat on a hot curling iron. The burn was suspected to be abusive as it was located on the non–weight-bearing portion of the buttocks.

***Figures 2-34-a*** *and* ***b.*** *The burn is above the weight-bearing area of the buttocks, and is therefore suspicious of abuse.*

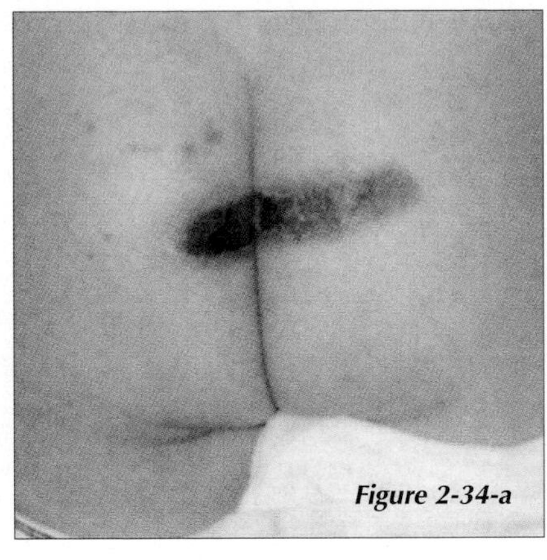

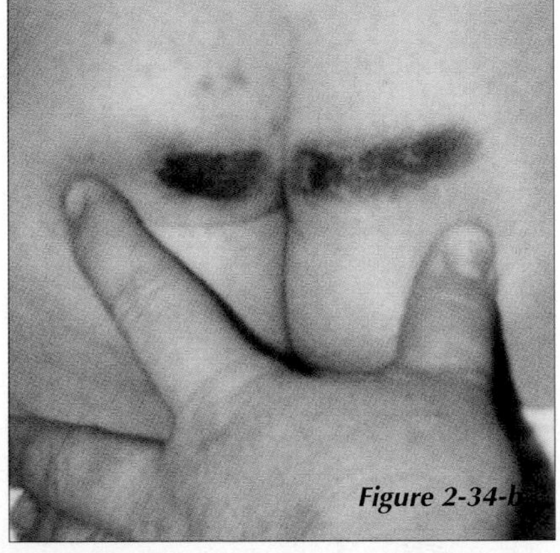

## Cigarettes

**Case Study 2-35**

This 18-month-old child was seen with a cigarette burn to the back. The parents reported that the child walked into a relative who was holding a cigarette. Cigarette burns are always suspicious of abuse, especially when there are multiple burns.

***Figure 2-35.*** *Cigarette burn to child's back.*

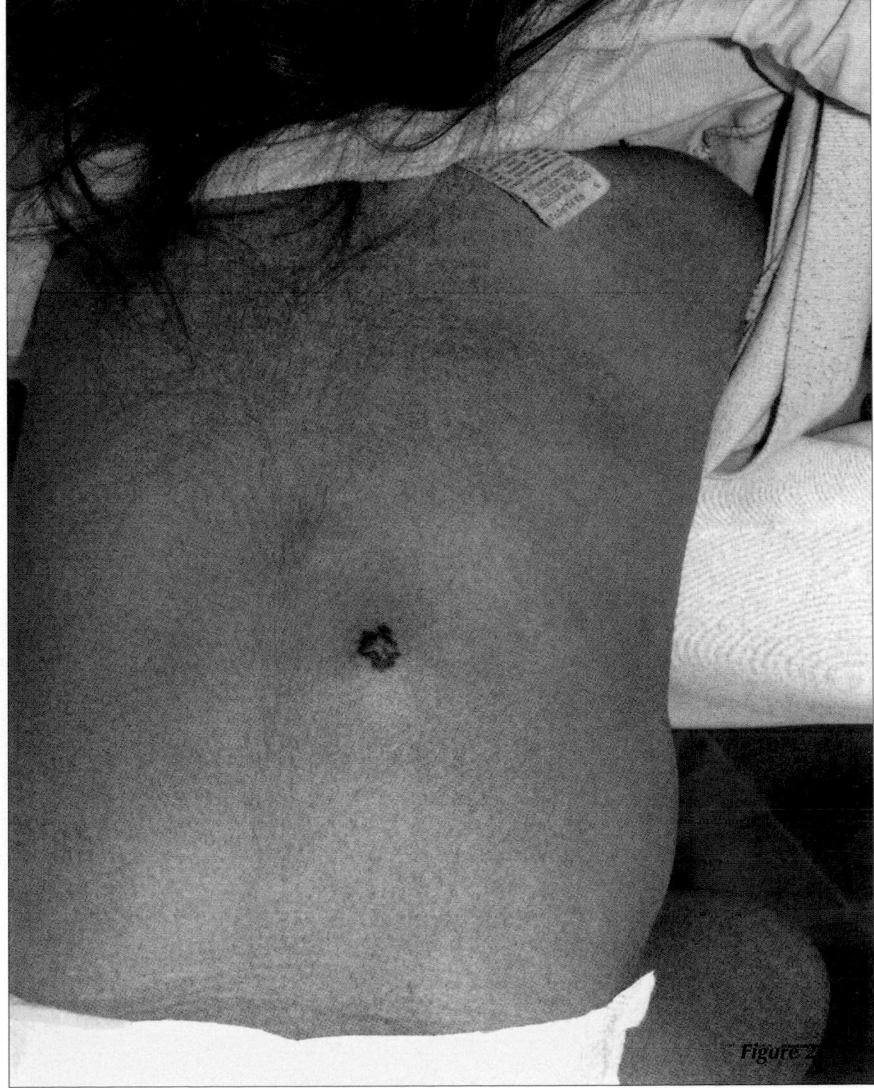

# Contact Burns

## Cigarettes

### Case Study 2-36

This 18-month-old child was examined with a cigarette burn to the wrist. Note the circular pattern of the burn injury. Cigarette burns are sometimes mistaken for impetigo, or vice versa.

***Figures 2-36-a** and **b**. Cigarette burn to a child's wrist.*

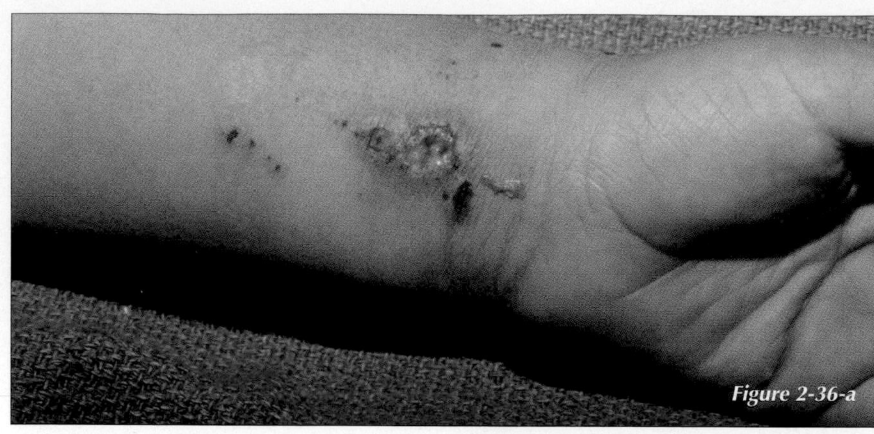

Figure 2-36-a

Figure 2-36-b

### Case Study 2-37

This 9-month-old girl was examined with circular healing burns of different ages. No history was given to explain the injuries. The caregivers stated that they might have been caused by popping grease or a cigarette ash. The poor history, the age of the wounds, and the patient's age made this case suspicious of abuse.

***Figure 2-37**. Circular healing burn to the back of the right upper arm.*

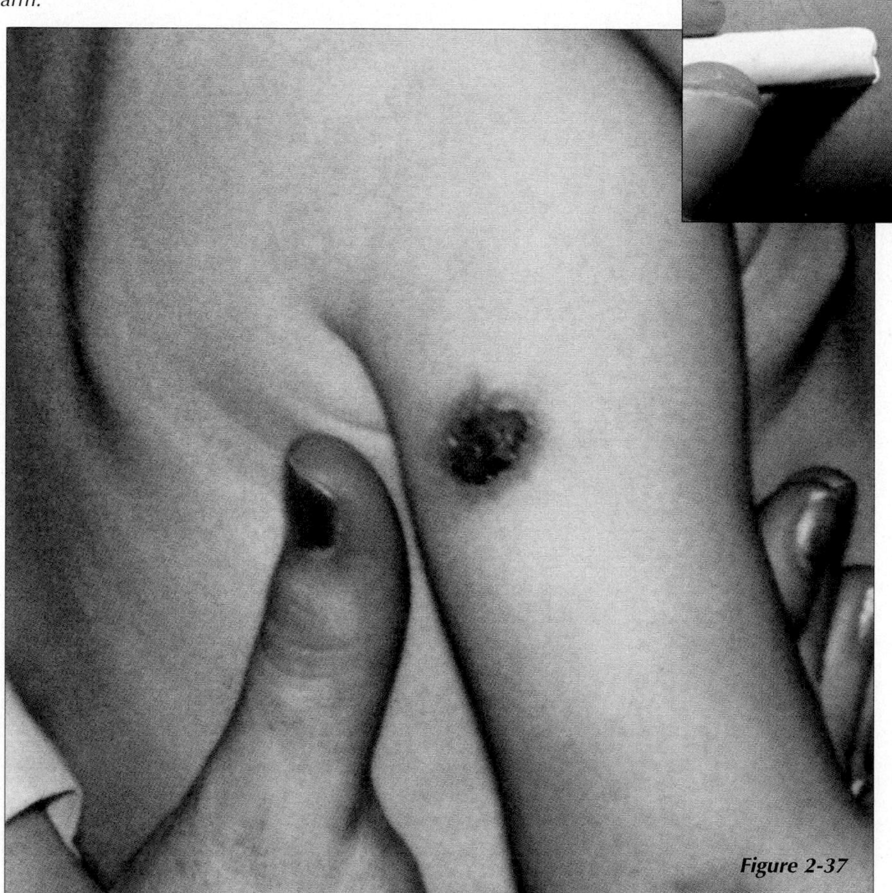

Figure 2-37

# Contact Burns

## Cigarettes

**Case Study 2-38**

This 4-year-old girl was examined with a self-reported history that her stepmother disciplined her with a lit cigarette.

***Figure 2-38-a.*** *A fresh cigarette burn is under the bandage on this girl's right buttock.*

***Figures 2-38-b, c, d,*** *and* ***e.*** *Multiple scarred cigarette burns on this 4-year-old girl.*

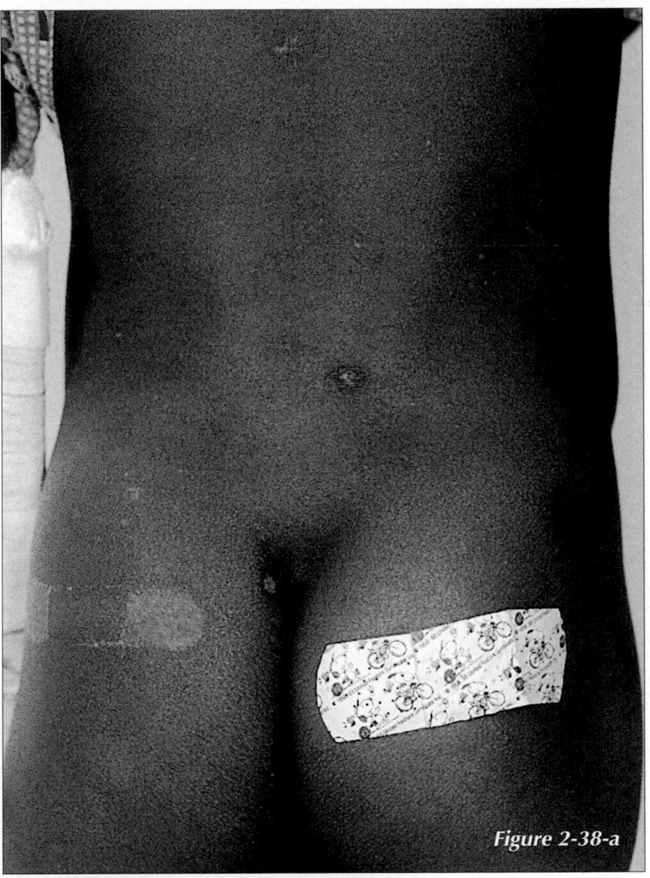

Figure 2-38-a

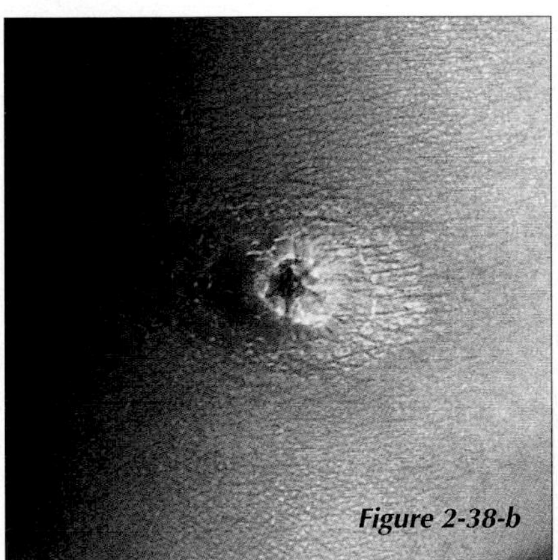

Figure 2-38-b

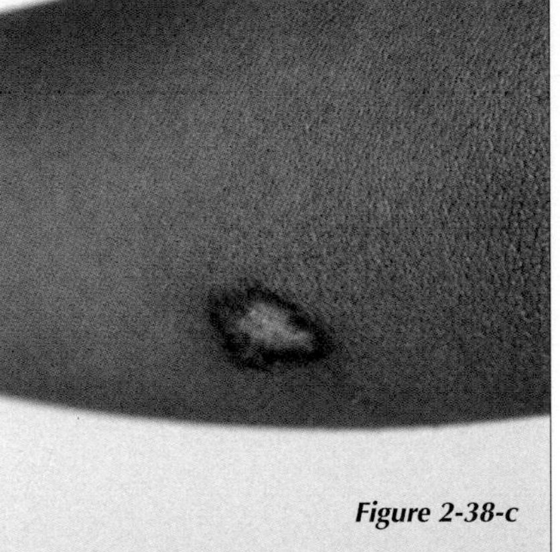

Figure 2-38-c

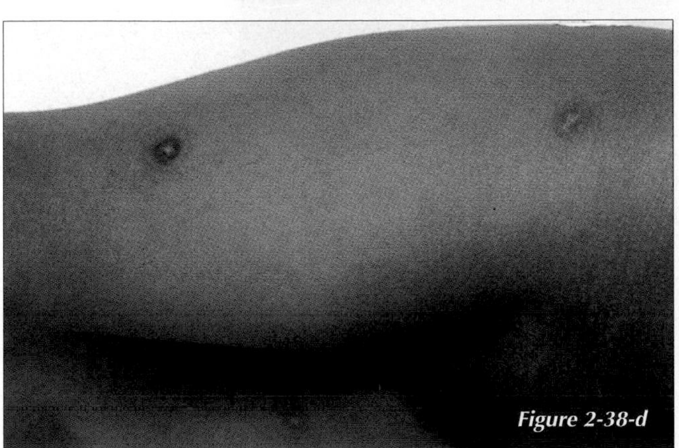

Figure 2-38-d

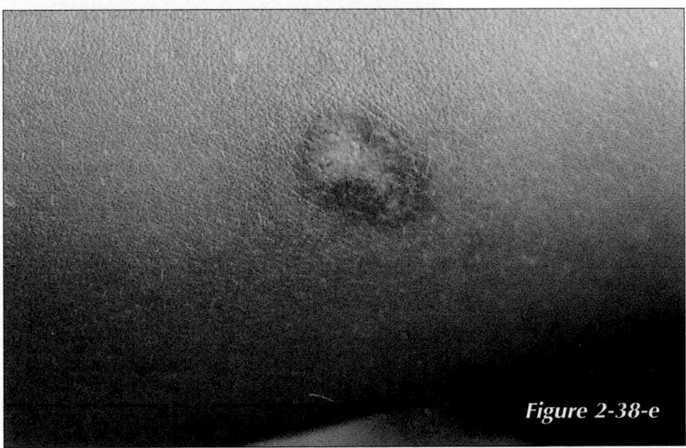

Figure 2-38-e

# Contact Burns

## Cigarettes

### Case Study 2-39

This 2-year-old child was seen with cigarette burns to multiple locations. Multiple cigarette burns in various stages of healing are suspicious of abuse.

**Figure 2-39-a.** *Recent burn.*

**Figure 2-39-b.** *Healing burn.*

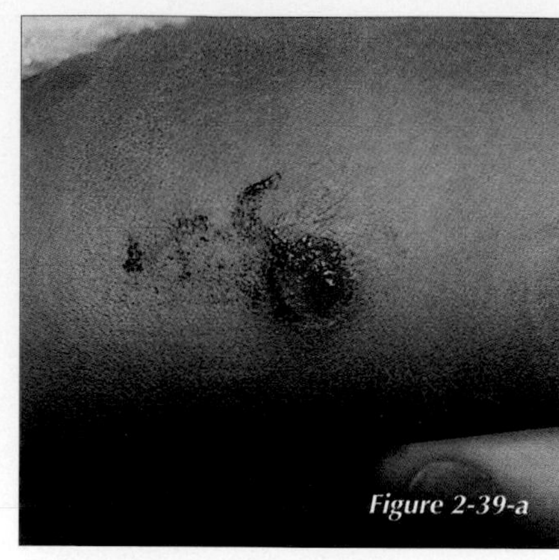

Figure 2-39-a

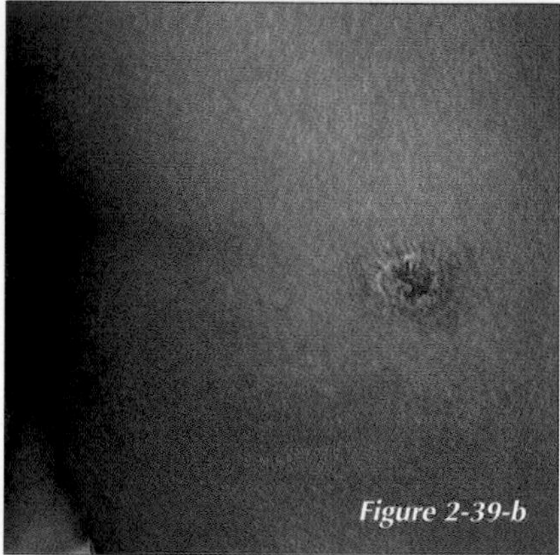

Figure 2-39-b

### Case Study 2-40

This 18-month-old boy was examined for several characteristic burn lesions on his face, abdomen, and thighs. It was determined that the mother's boyfriend would discipline the boy for crying by touching him with the hot metallic top of a cigarette lighter.

**Figure 2-40.** *The pattern burn appearing on the face of this boy, indicating contact with a cigarette lighter.*

Figure 2-40

# Contact Burns

## Fireworks

### Case Study 2-41

This boy was brought to the ER for severe burns to the upper thigh and genital area. He was carrying firecrackers in his pocket and the fuses ignited when they came into contact with sparks from other fireworks, causing the firecrackers to explode in his pocket. While evidence of neglect, this incident was determined to be accidental.

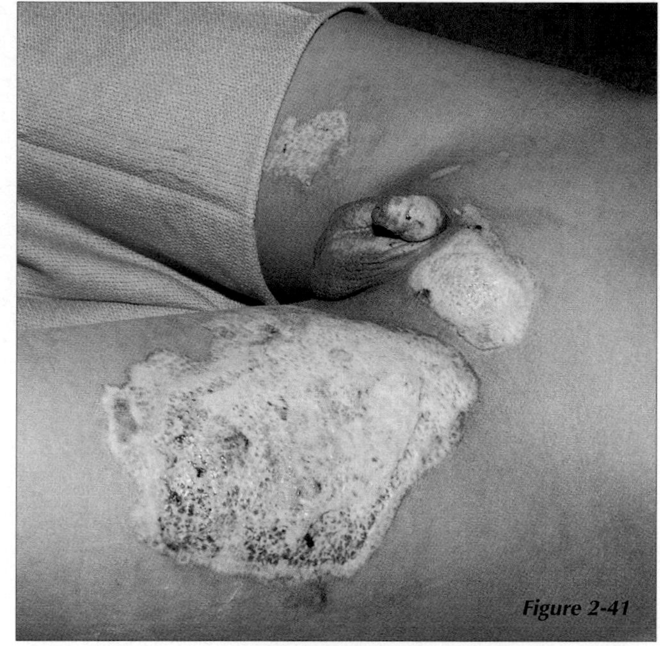

***Figure 2-41.*** *Burn to the thigh from fireworks.*

Figure 2-41

### Case Study 2-42

This infant presented with fireworks burns. According to the caregiver's history, the child had been crawling in a backyard where fireworks were being thrown, when a bottle rocket exploded under her chin, hitting her in the face.

***Figure 2-42.*** *Fireworks burn.*

Figure 2-42

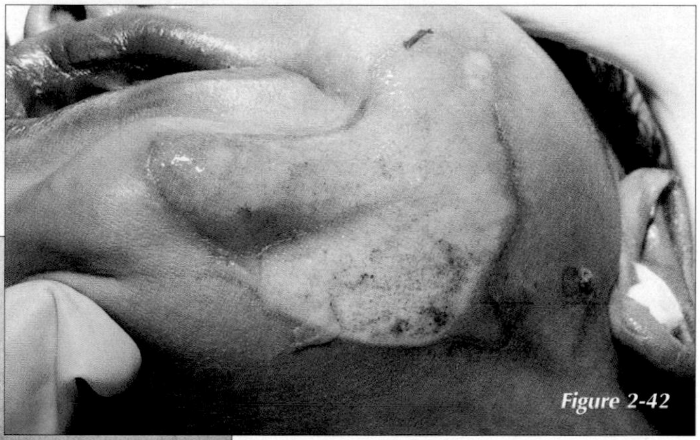

### Case Study 2-43

The caregivers of this 4-year-old boy reported that he was accidentally burned when he ran into someone who was running with a sparkler, which hit him in the eye.

***Figure 2-43.*** *Periorbital burns.*

Figure 2-43

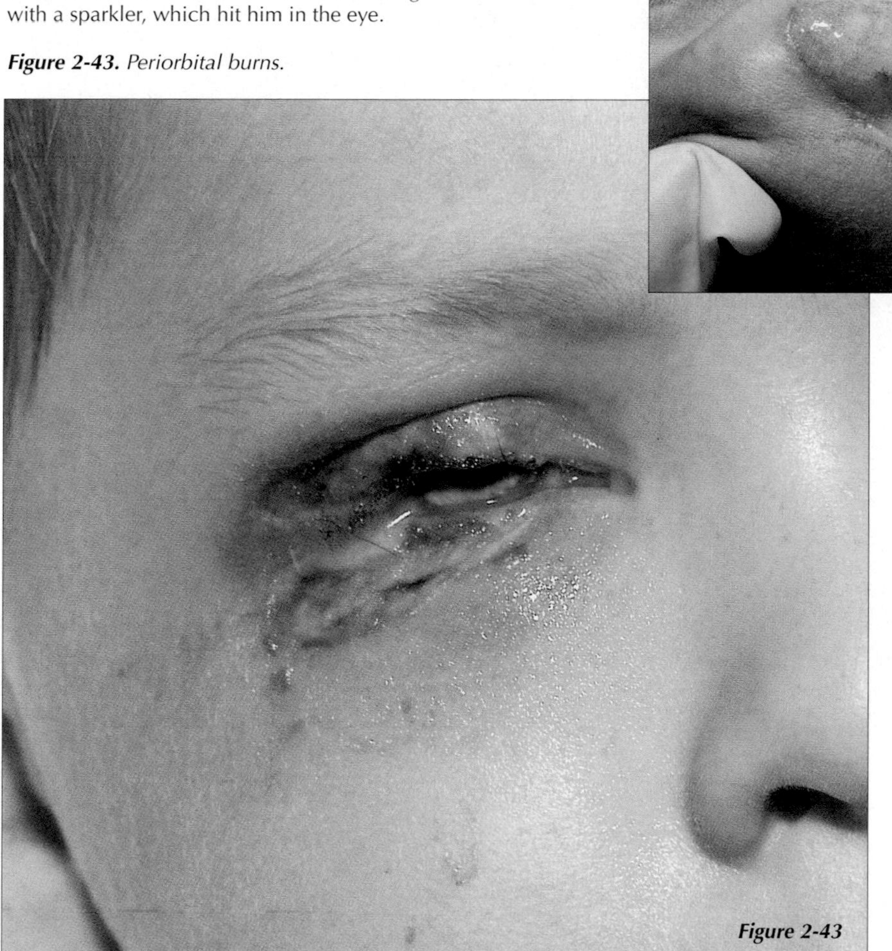

# Contact Burns

## Space Heater/Radiator

### Case Study 2-44

This 4-year-old boy was taken to the ER by his parents for a burn to the dorsum of his right foot. The burn was said to be accidental. The parents gave the history that the child had accidentally placed his foot on the top of a space heater. Abuse was suspected because the injury appeared older than the parents had indicated, it was in an unusual location, and the child had healed loop marks on his back and a well-healed burn scar to his chest.

***Figure 2-44-a.*** *Burn to the dorsum of right foot.*

***Figure 2-44-b.*** *Healed loop marks on the back.*

***Figure 2-44-c.*** *Well-healed burn scar on the chest.*

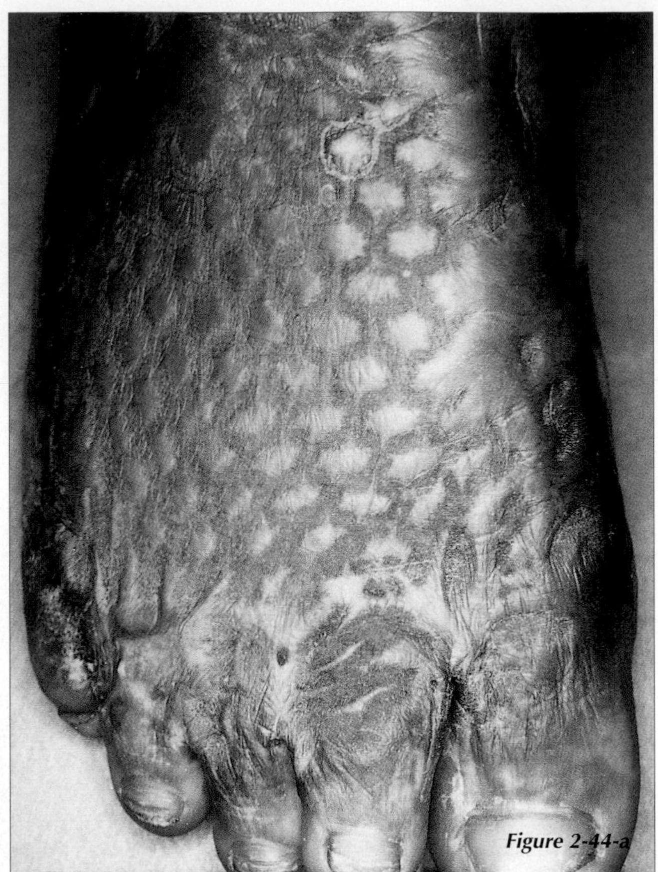
Figure 2-44-a

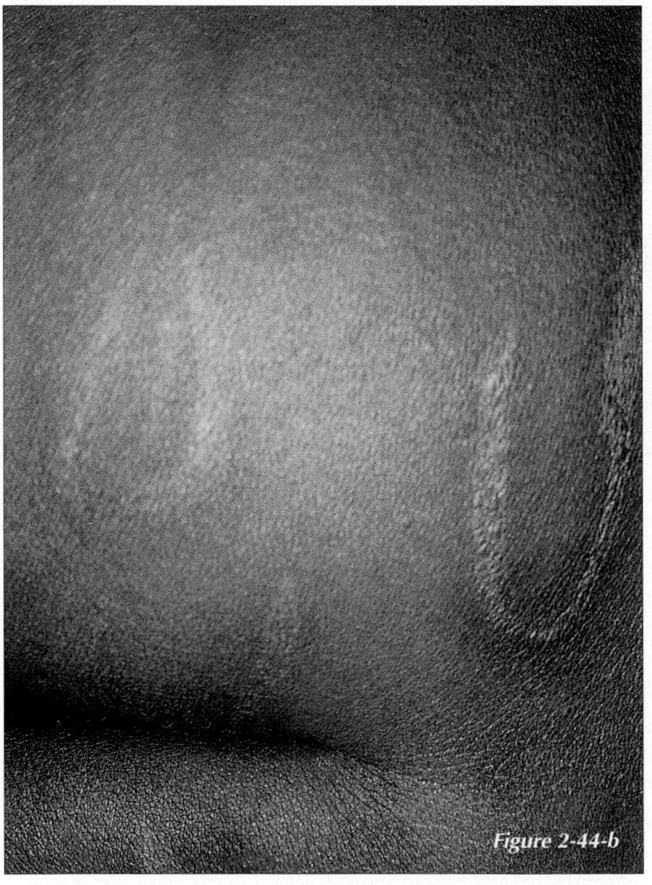
Figure 2-44-b

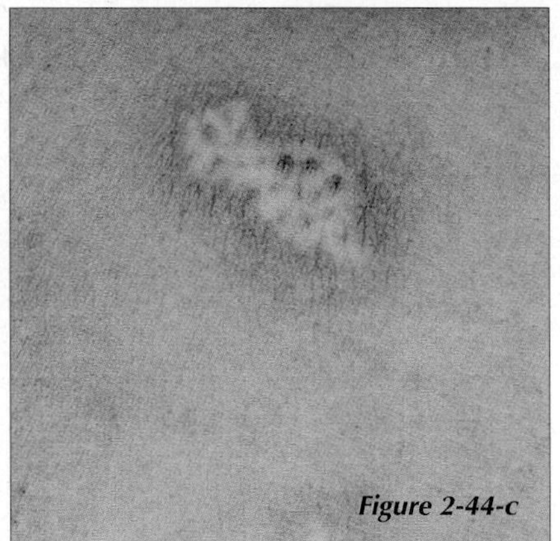
Figure 2-44-c

# Contact Burns

## Space Heater/Radiator

### Case Study 2-45

This 3-year-old boy's caregivers brought him to the ER with the history that he was pushed by his older sibling against the radiator in the bathroom. Three things suggested abuse: there was a delay in seeking help; the injury involved 3 surface areas, including both the buttocks and the back of the hand; and the injury was blamed on a sibling. Although abuse by siblings is common, the constellation of injuries and history provided sufficient cause for suspicion of abuse.

***Figure 2-45-a.*** *Burns to the back of this 3-year-old boy.*

***Figure 2-45-b.*** *Additional burns to the buttocks.*

***Figure 2-45-c.*** *Additional burns to the right hand and left thigh.*

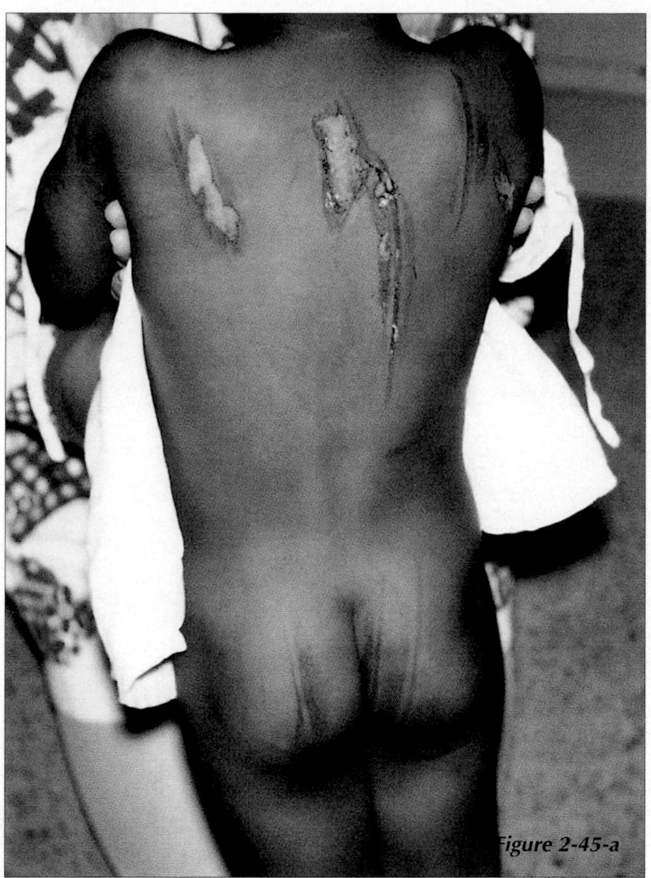

Figure 2-45-a

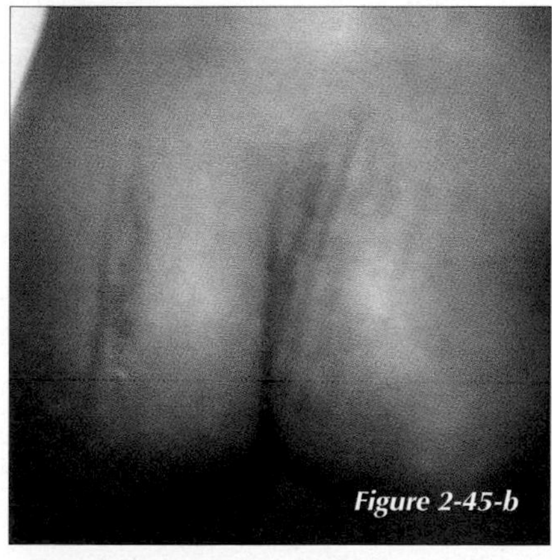

Figure 2-45-b

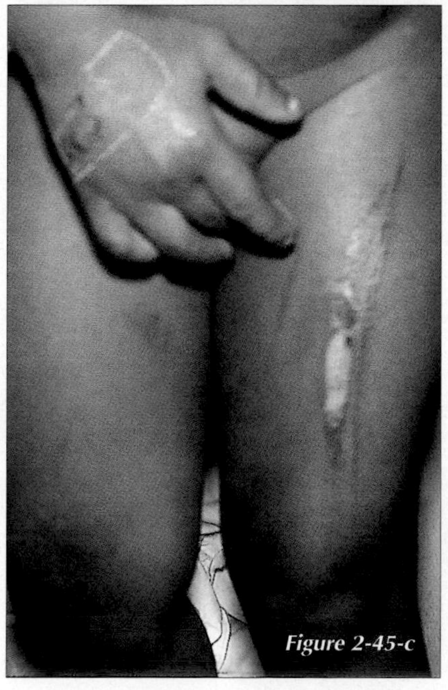

Figure 2-45-c

# Contact Burns

## Space Heater/Radiator

### Case Study 2-46

This 15-month-old girl was examined with the history that she was burned after climbing onto a space heater and sitting on it. The child had no other injuries, and the history was deemed to be suspicious since climbing onto the space heater would have caused additional injuries to her hands and legs. This incident was later determined to be a case of abuse.

***Figure 2-46-a.*** *The burn is not on the weight-bearing portion of the buttocks.*

***Figure 2-46-b.*** *The pattern of the burn is the same as the top of the heater and could only have been made by contact with the top of the heater.*

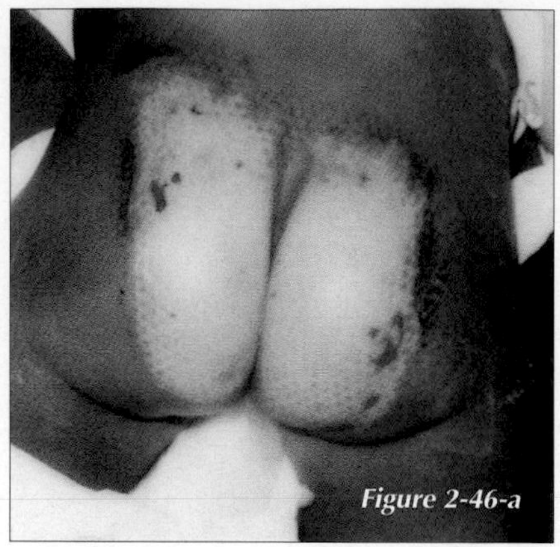

Figure 2-46-a

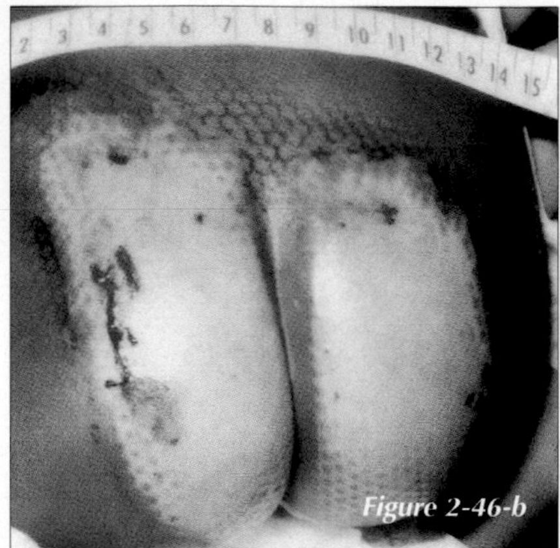


Figure 2-46-b

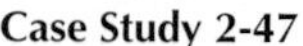

### Case Study 2-47

This 4-year-old child was seen with the history of backing into a space heater, causing a pattern burn to the buttocks.

***Figure 2-47.*** *Pattern burn to buttocks.*

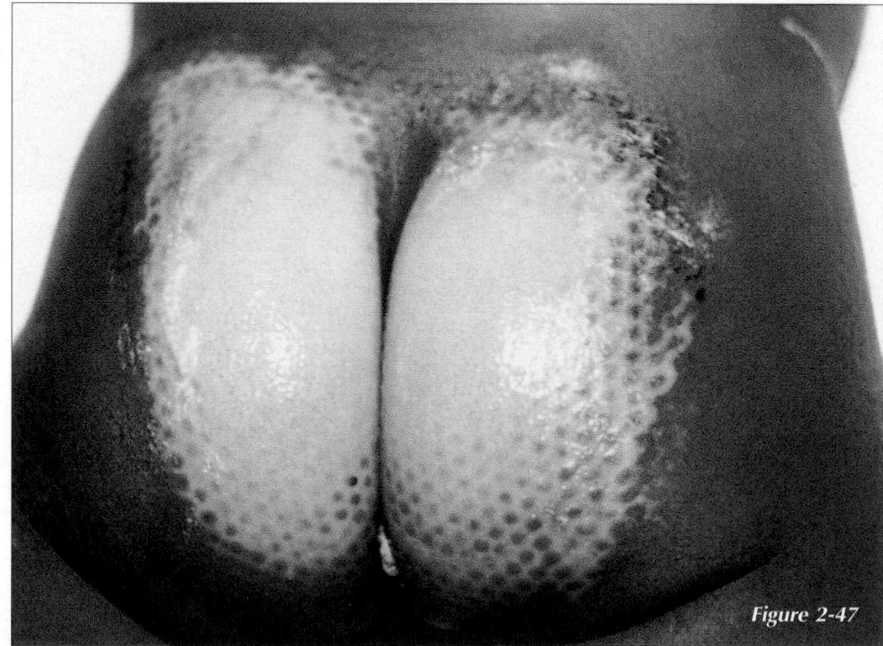

Figure 2-47

## Report from a Third Party

### Case Study 2-48

This 19-month-old boy was taken to the hospital by his grandmother. She noticed the contact burn to his back that was healed over. The child was in the care of his father, who was an alcoholic and had given no explanation for the burn. The burn was reported as a reason to suspect child abuse since there was no explanation for its cause, a third party sought medical attention, and the injury was old.

***Figures 2-48-a*** *and* ***b.*** *Healed contact burn on the back of this 19-month-old boy.*

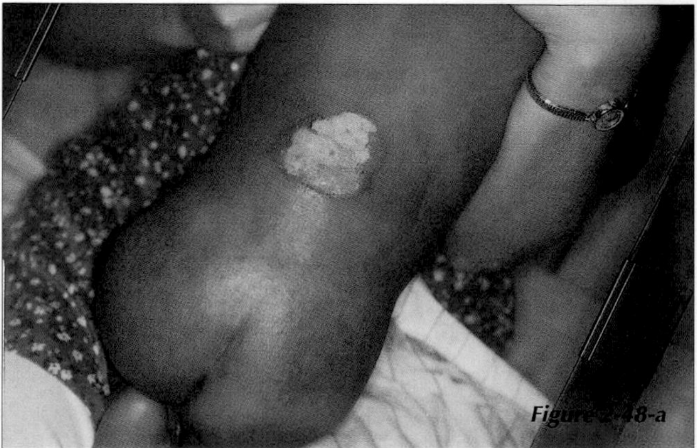

Figure 2-48-a

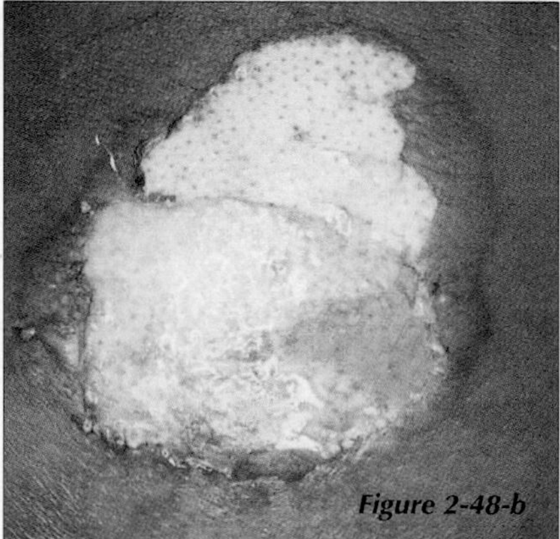

Figure 2-48-b

# Contact Burns

## On-site Investigation of Multiple Burn Surfaces

### Case Study 2-49

This 23-month-old boy was examined 2½ weeks after his injury occurred. According to the initial history, he was riding a tricycle that got caught between a wall and a space heater. The veracity of this story was doubtful due to the location and severity of the burns. After measuring the temperature at the bottom of the heating unit, corresponding to the alleged position of the boy, it was determined that it would have taken 20 minutes of exposure to sustain burns of this magnitude. The burn was suspected to have been caused by direct contact with a source of extreme heat. Further investigation of the home raised suspicions that the stovetop was the source of the burn to his buttocks, since the right side oven door would have been at the proper height to cause the burns to the boy's calves if he were seated on the stove.

***Figure 2-49-a.*** *Bilateral buttocks and posterior calf burns.*

***Figure 2-49-b.*** *The boy's tricycle.*

***Figure 2-49-c.*** *One of the burners on the stove.*

***Figure 2-49-d.*** *The stove shown with a partially open right side oven door.*

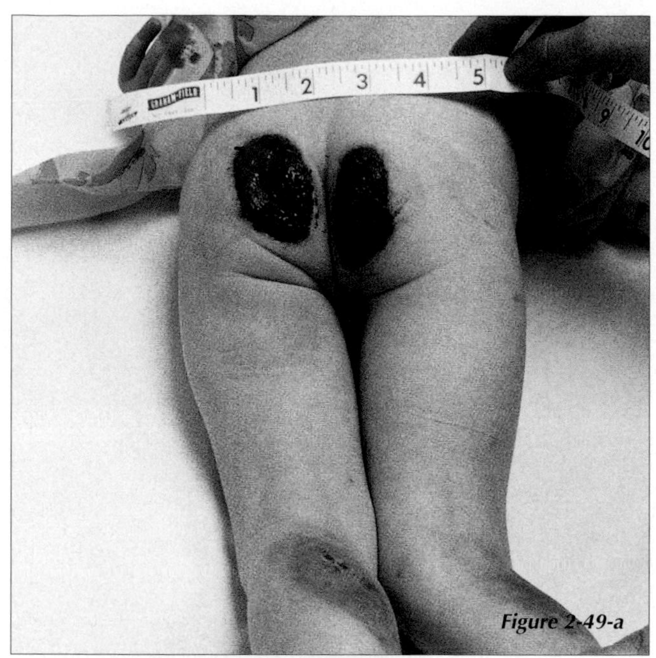
Figure 2-49-a

Figure 2-49-b

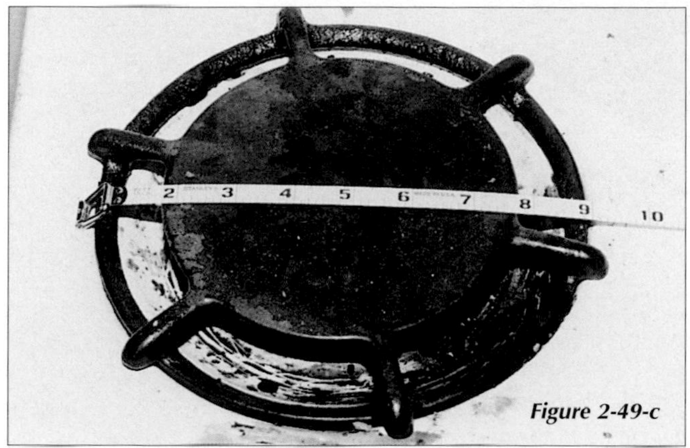
Figure 2-49-c

Figure 2-49-d

# Contact Burns

## Wringer Washer

### Case Study 2-50

This 9-year-old boy was taken to the ER with a second- and third-degree burn to the upper anterior arm and chest. The boy initially stated that it was the result of having put his finger into an electrical socket. This was challenged because the injury was obviously not an electrical burn and there was no evidence of an exit burn or an injury of the finger. Because of the inconsistencies, the incident was reported to state protective services. He finally stated that he had received the burn after he caught his arm in a wringer washer. The apparatus had sprung; the lower roller, which was active, continued to turn and he was unable to free his arm. When asked why he had lied initially, he said that if his grandmother had found out that he was playing with the machine, he would have been in trouble. A torn shirt was recovered to substantiate the history and the case was determined to be accidental.

***Figures 2-50-a.*** *Second- and third-degree burns of the upper anterior arm and chest.*

***Figures 2-50-b.*** *The washing machine that caused the injuries.*

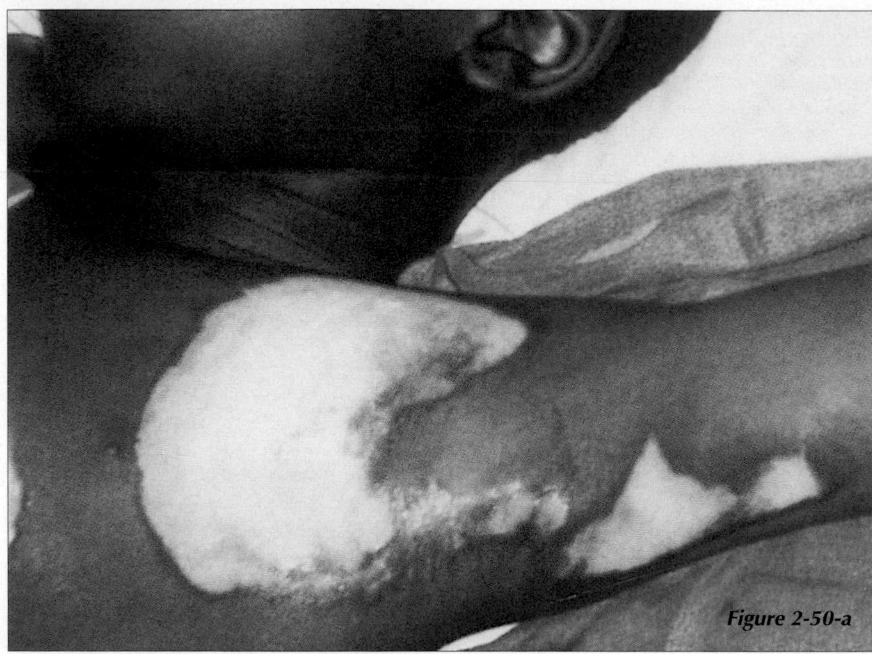

**Figure 2-50-a**

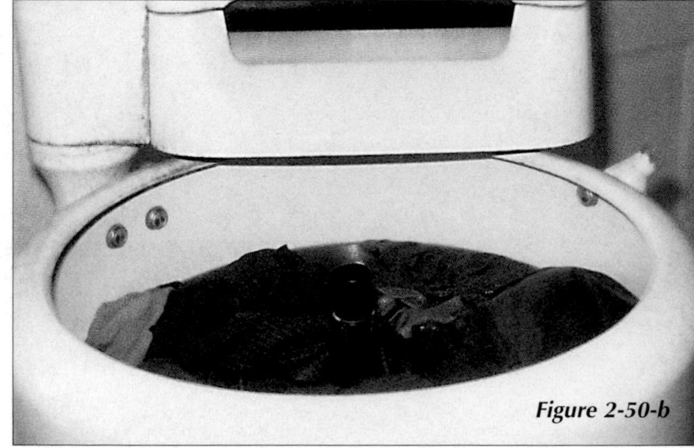

**Figure 2-50-b**

# Contact Burns

## Multiple Burns

### Case Study 2-51

This 1-year-old boy was examined for numerous contact burns on the chest, back, shoulder, and thigh. The mother and her boyfriend both stated that they found the child touching himself with a hot fork. This story was doubtful since the location and direction of some of the burns precluded self-infliction. Additionally, the quantity of burns would have required constant reheating of the fork. The mother's boyfriend was eventually convicted of inflicting these injuries.

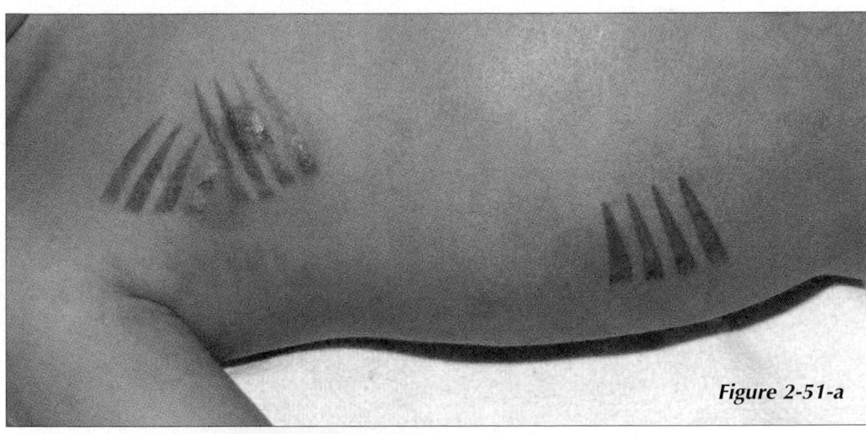

Figure 2-51-a

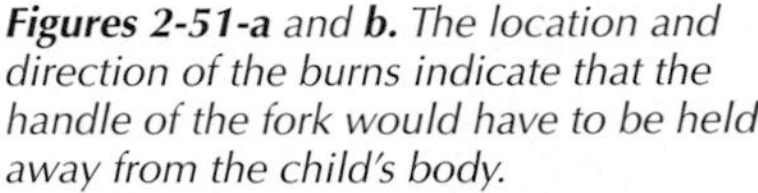

***Figures 2-51-a** and **b.** The location and direction of the burns indicate that the handle of the fork would have to be held away from the child's body.*

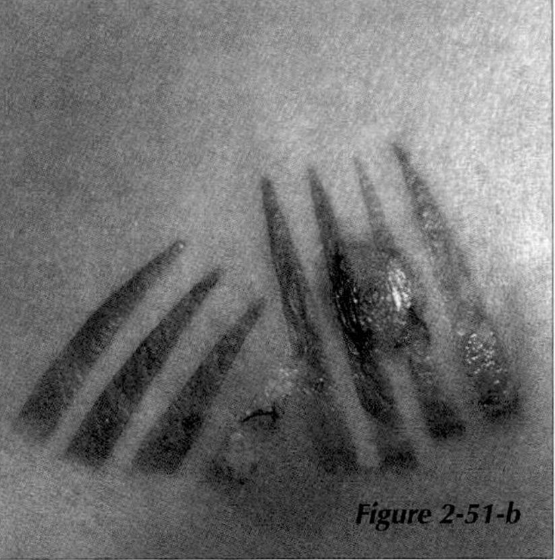

Figure 2-51-b

***Figures 2-51-c** and **d.** Additional burns to the boy's back and upper thighs.*

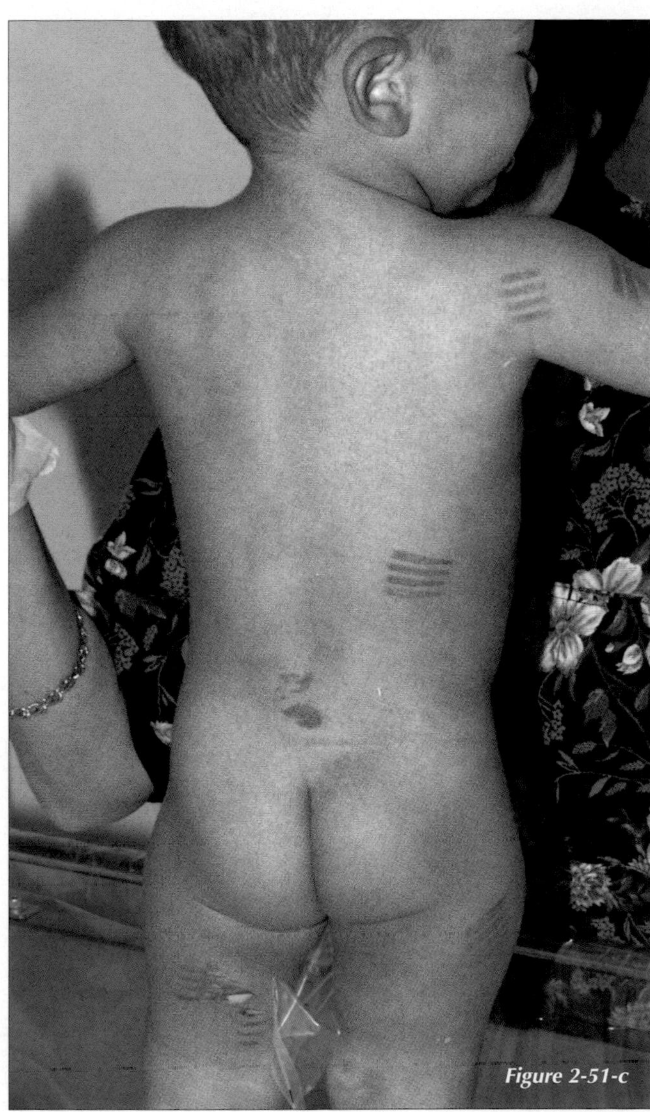

Figure 2-51-c

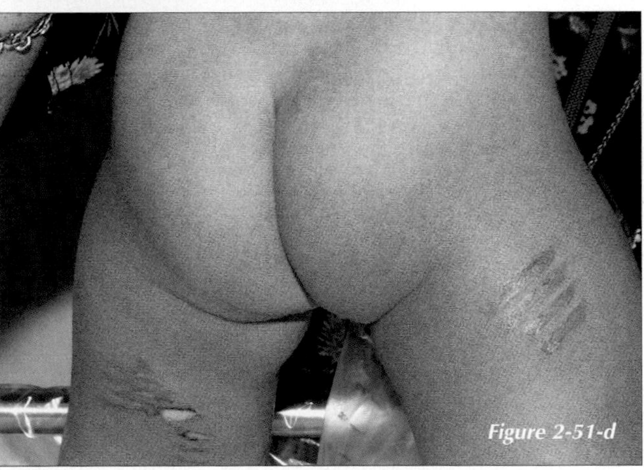

Figure 2-51-d

# Contact Burns

## Multiple Injuries

### Case Study 2-52

This 3½-year-old boy was examined for multiple burns and choke marks. His mother was a former mental hospital patient who had been noncompliant with her antipsychotic medication regimen for several years. She had 2 other children who had been removed permanently a year earlier because of abuse. Although this child was several years old, the mother had successfully concealed him from state protective services. He had not received any immunizations. (Photograph courtesy of James J. Williams, MD)

***Figure 2-52-a.*** *Contact burns to the child's face.*

***Figure 2-52-b.*** *Partially healed burns on the buttocks.*

***Figure 2-52-c.*** *Contact burns to the right shoulder.*

***Figure 2-52-d.*** *Partially healed cigarette burns.*

***Figure 2-52-e.*** *Recent cigarette burns to the scalp.*

***Figure 2-52-f.*** *Evidence of choking on the boy's neck.*

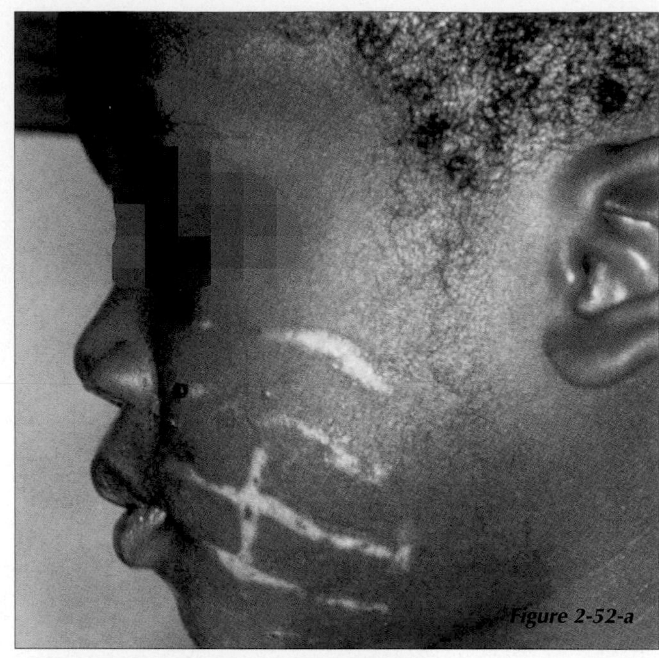

Figure 2-52-a

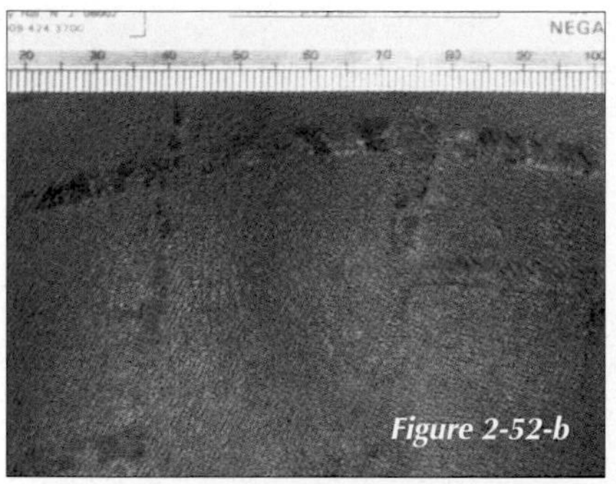


Figure 2-52-b

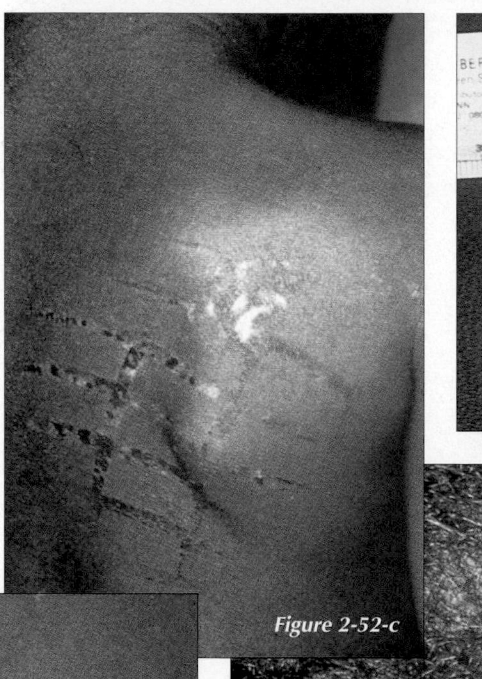

Figure 2-52-c

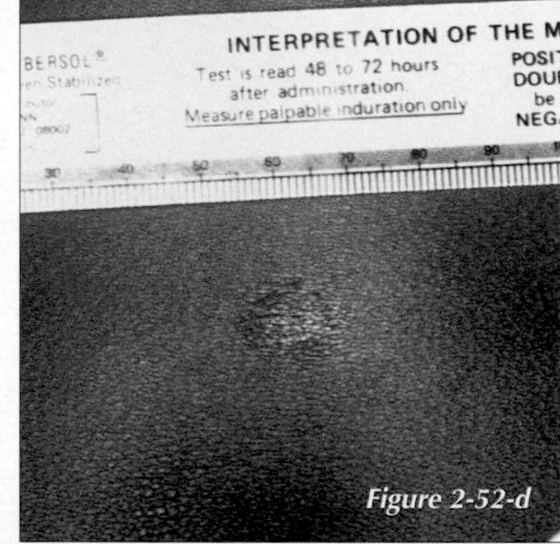


Figure 2-52-d

Figure 2-52-e

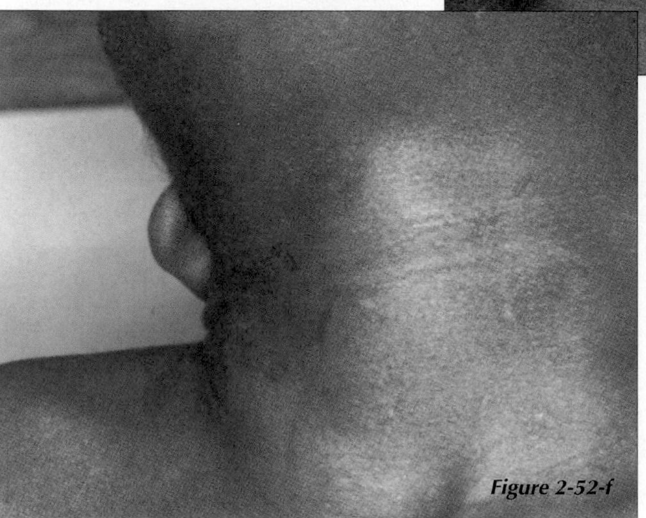

Figure 2-52-f

# Contact Burns

## Multiple Injuries

### Case Study 2-53

This 2½-year-old girl was taken to the ER by her foster mother, who was concerned because the girl was returned with injuries after every visitation with her biological mother. On this particular visit, the child had multiple pattern burns, which the biological mother said were caused by a blow dryer. The biological mother said that the child was clumsy and that she caused the burns by moving too much.

***Figures 2-53-a, b,*** *and* ***c.*** *Multiple pattern burns appearing on the girl's face, chest, and arms.*

***Figure 2-53-d.*** *An additional conjunctival injury.*

***Figure 2-53-e.*** *Bruising to the girl's upper back.*

***Figure 2-53-f.*** *A healed circular burn to the buttocks that was revealed during the examination.*

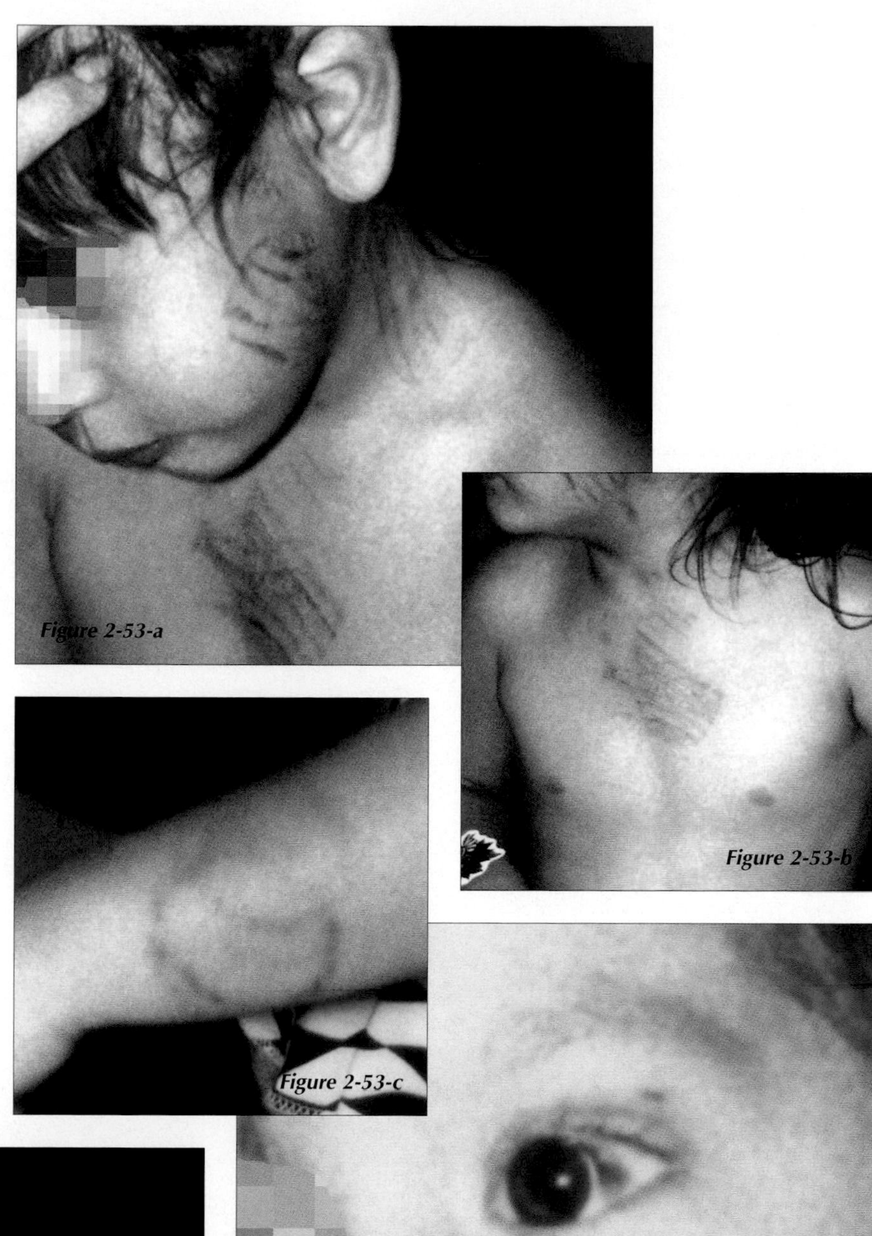

Figure 2-53-a

Figure 2-53-b

Figure 2-53-c

Figure 2-53-d

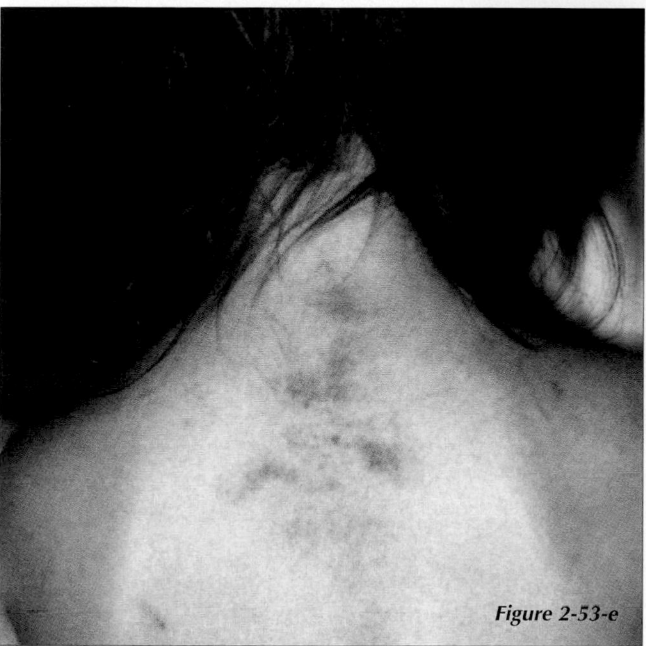

Figure 2-53-e

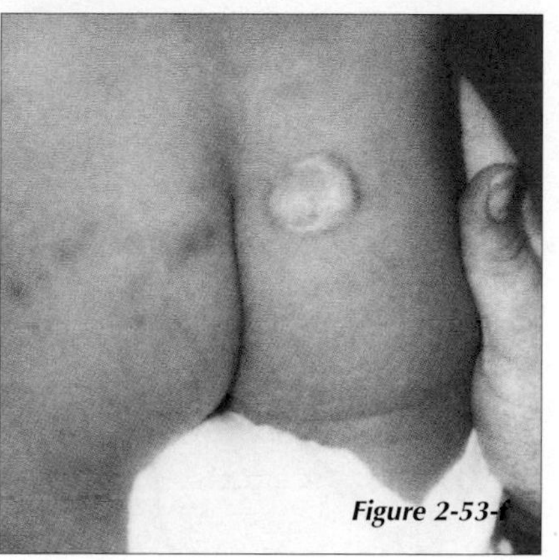

Figure 2-53-f

# CONTACT BURNS

## MULTIPLE INJURIES

### Case Study 2-54

This 2-year-old boy had first-, second-, and third-degree burns of the anterior abdominal wall skin. The cause of the burns was never determined. Skin grafting was required for the central portion of the burned area.

***Figure 2-54.*** *First-, second-, and third-degree burns of the anterior abdominal wall skin.*

The child was lost to follow-up after discharge. It was later learned that the child died at the age of 3 of "natural causes." A funeral director informed police about many bruises on the child's body. A more thorough autopsy revealed a total of 88 blunt wounds and a bite mark, all of which had been inflicted within 36 hours before the child's death. The direct cause of death was found to be peritonitis from a ruptured small intestine. The child's stepfather was later convicted of murder.

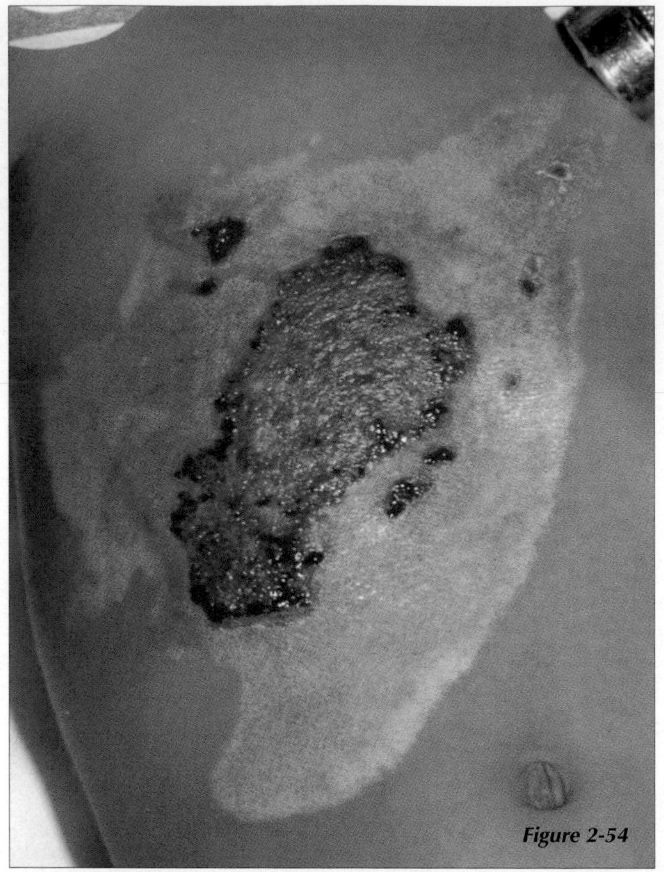

Figure 2-54

### Case Study 2-55

This 22-month-old boy was brought in for convulsions by paramedics. He was found to be hypoglycemic and had an elevated ethanol level. The mother stated that her boyfriend had given the boy alcohol. Additionally, burns were found during the examination. The mother "did not know" how the child had been burned.

***Figures 2-55-a*** *and* ***b.*** *A flow burn to the back of this boy's right hand.*

***Figure 2-55-c.*** *Contact burn to the left forearm.*

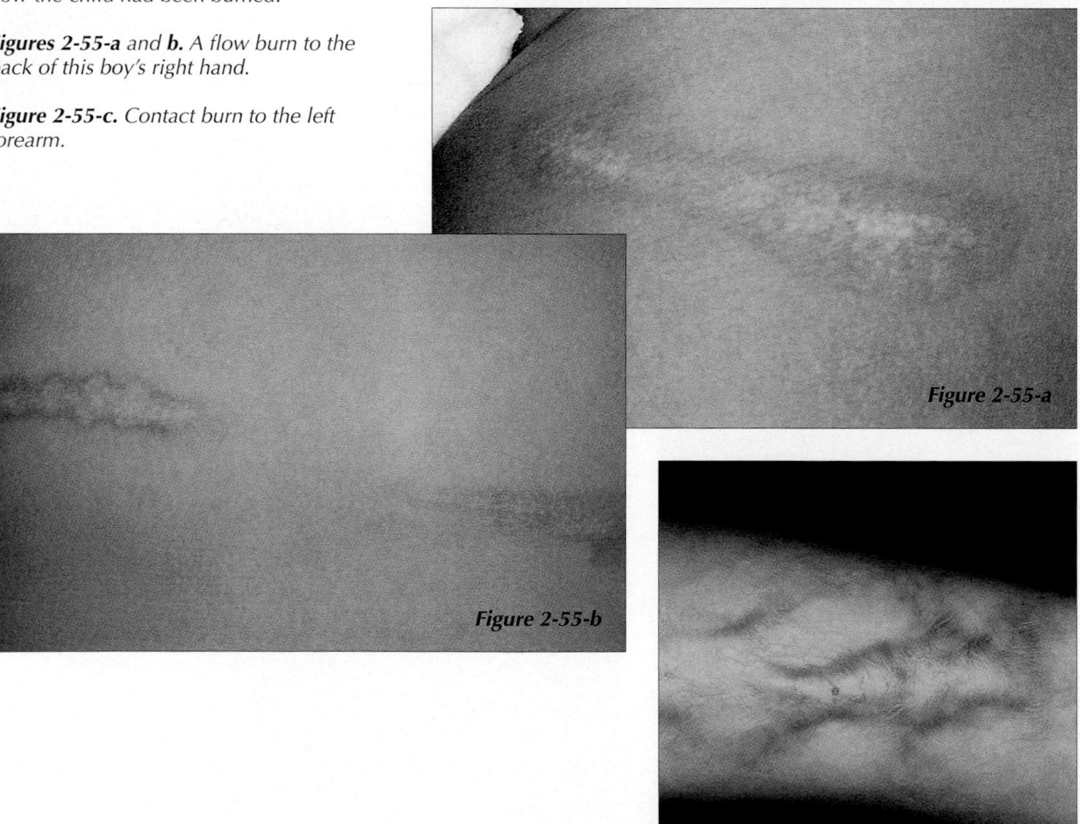

Figure 2-55-a

Figure 2-55-b

Figure 2-55-c

# Contact Burns

## Branding

**Case Study 2-56**

This 6-month-old boy was branded by his mother's boyfriend with a square-shaped object, which was not found. (Photograph courtesy of James J. Williams, MD)

***Figures 2-56-a, b,*** *and* ***c.*** *The object seems to have been carefully applied on the left shoulder with minimal overlapping to form a larger burn pattern.*

## Healed Burns

**Case Study 2-57**

This child presented with healed submersion burn injuries to the bilateral buttocks.

***Figure 2-57.*** *Healed abusive burn to the buttocks.*

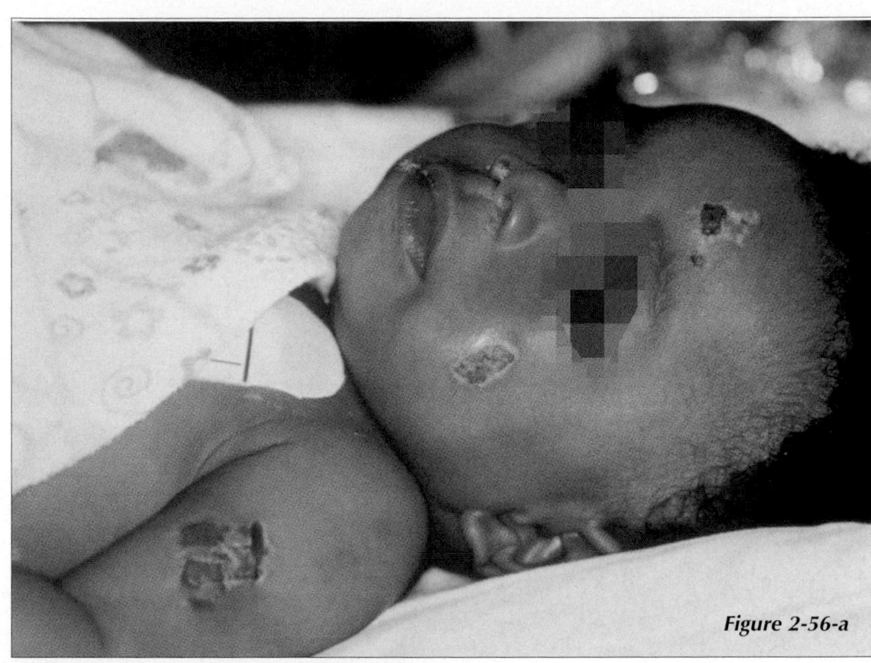

**Figure 2-56-a**

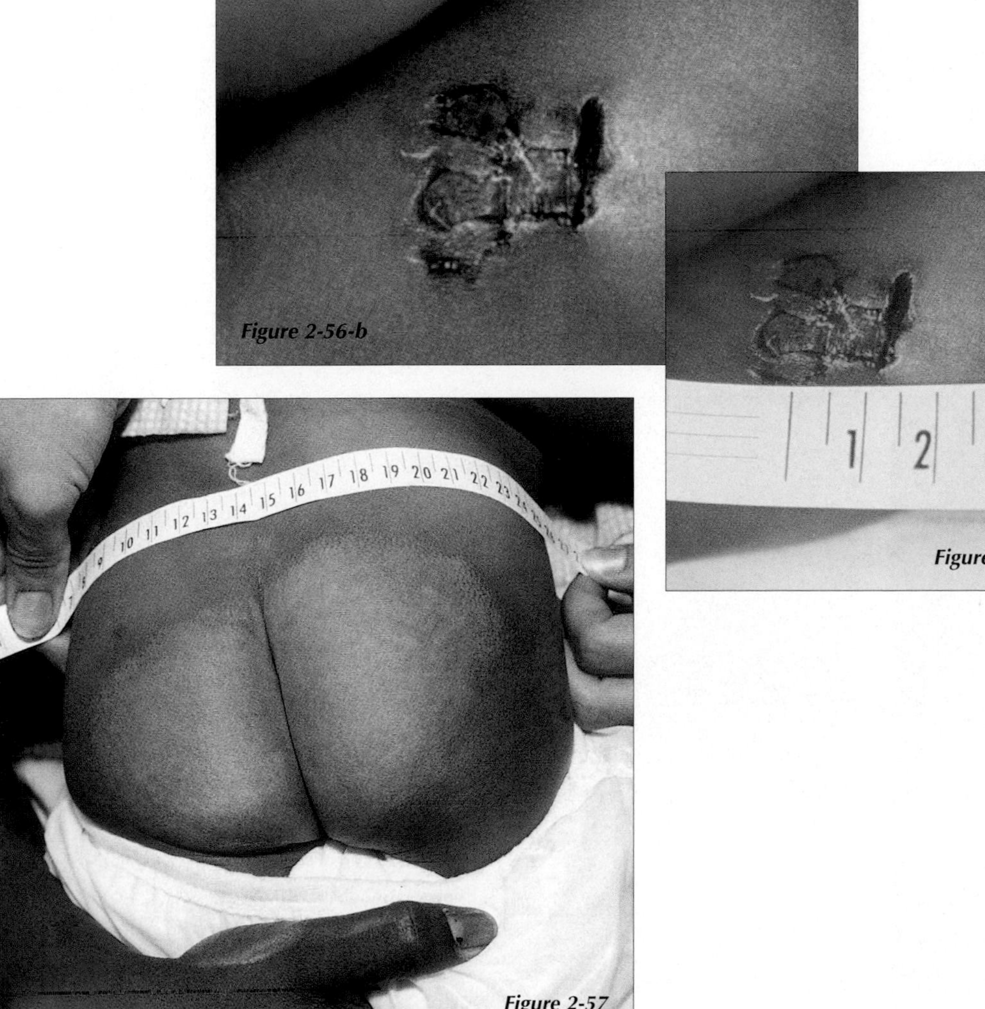


**Figure 2-56-b**

**Figure 2-56-c**

**Figure 2-57**

## FLAME BURNS

**Case Study 2-58**

This 10-year-old boy was brought to the ER with a burn to his thigh. The burn was caused by an ignited lighter, which set his clothes aflame. While they may involve neglect, flame burns are rarely a direct result of physical abuse.

***Figure 2-58.*** *A third-degree burn to the boy's right posterior thigh.*

**Case Study 2-59**

This child was examined for multiple abusive burns. The child's father had held the hand over an open flame on the stove.

***Figure 2-59.*** *Abusive flame burns to the palm and digits.*

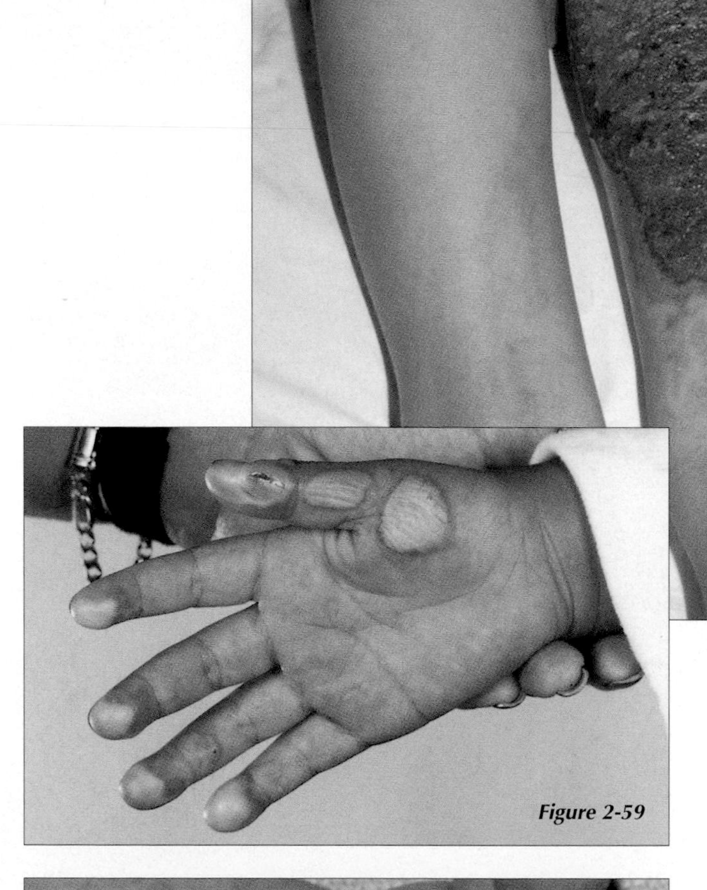

Figure 2-58

Figure 2-59

## CHEMICAL BURNS

**Case Study 2-60**

This child presented with liquid acid burns. Although the type of acid is unknown, they illustrate a typical splash pattern.

***Figure 2-60.*** *Note the splash pattern of this liquid acid burn.*

**Case Study 2-61**

This child was presented with a chemical burn.

***Figure 2-61.*** *Burn from chemical fertilizer.*

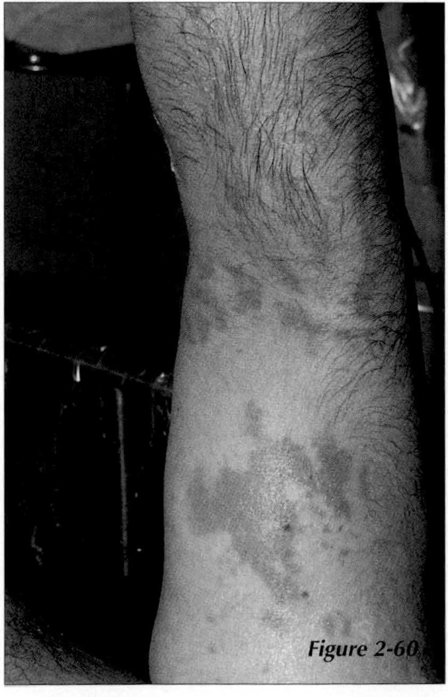

Figure 2-60

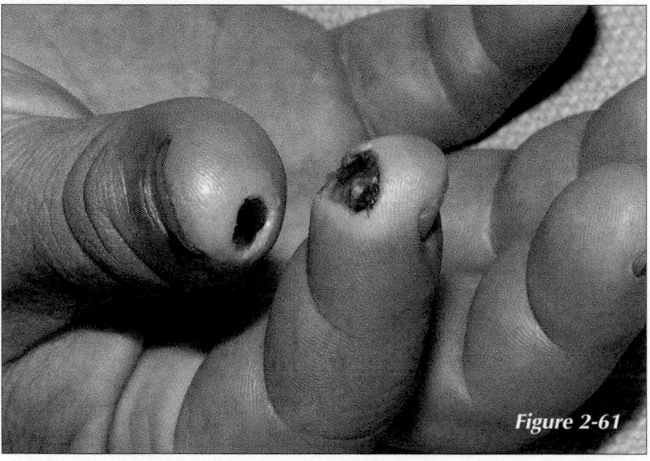

Figure 2-61

## Electrical Burns

**Case Study 2-62**

This young child stepped on exposed electrical wiring. In the United States, household current is alternating and especially dangerous if the path of the current through the body crosses the heart. Burns can vary in severity from mild to those that burn through skin, connective tissues, muscle, and bone. External appearance is not always a clear indication of the extent of the underlying burn.

***Figure 2-62.*** *Burns caused by contact with an electrical current.*

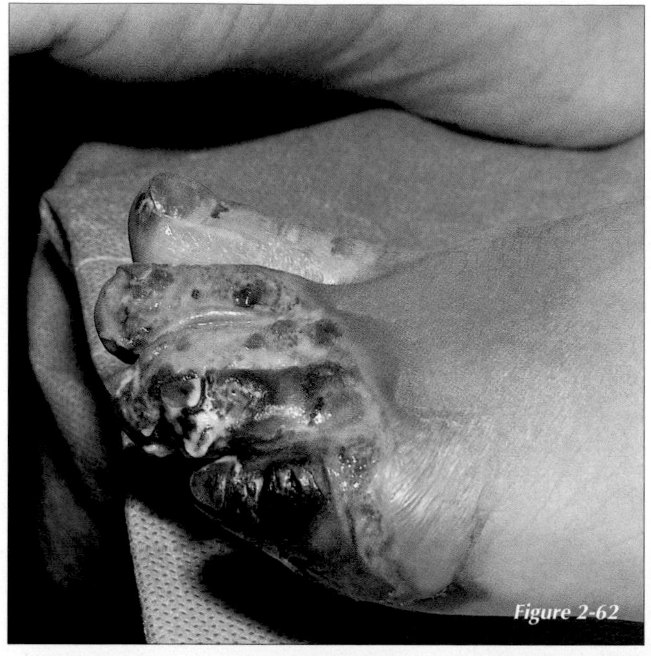

Figure 2-62

**Case Study 2-63**

This child suffered from an electrical flash burn, which frequently occurs when children grab exposed wiring. This action may be at the child's initiative, depending on the age and developmental capabilities of the child. However, neglect should be a consideration, depending on the case history.

***Figures 2-63-a** and **b.** Electrical flash burn.*

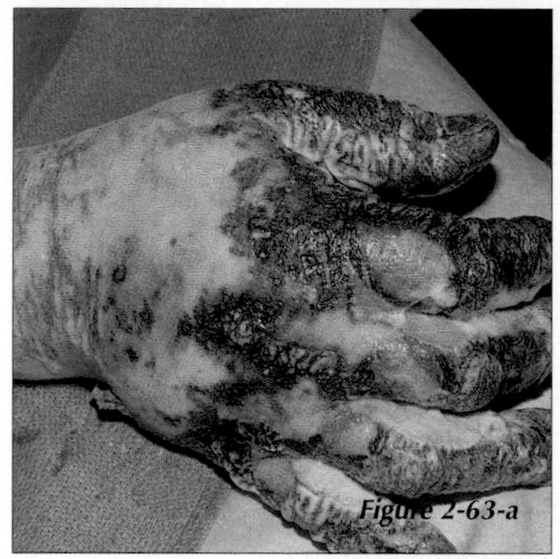

Figure 2-63-a

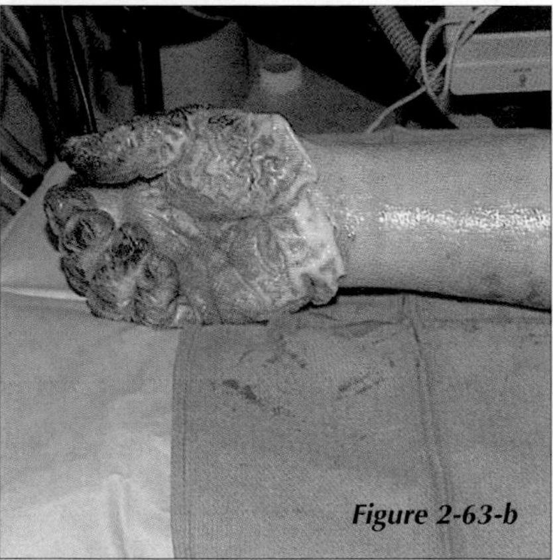

Figure 2-63-b

## Frostbite

**Case Study 2-64**

This child sustained frostbite as a consequence of inadequate clothing. As often with cases of this nature, the appearance of frostbite evolved over time to more fully reveal the extent of the injuries. Severe cases of frostbite are treated in burn units as frostbites are a type of burn. Long-term consequences may include nerve damage and sometimes devitalized tissue leading to amputation.

***Figure 2-64-a.*** *The initial appearance of frostbite in this child.*

***Figure 2-64-b.*** *The appearance 10 days after the initial injury.*

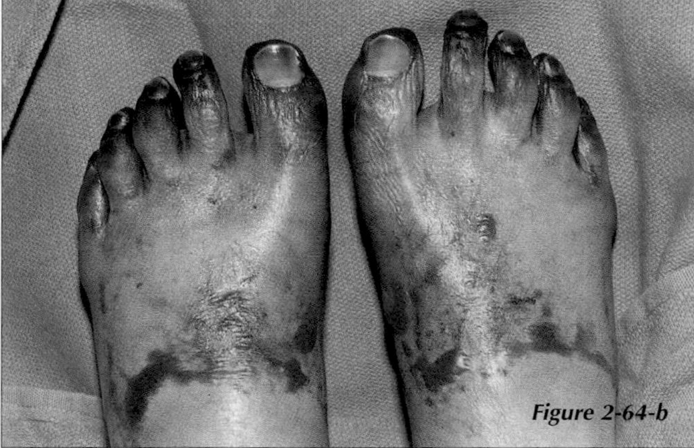

Figure 2-64-b

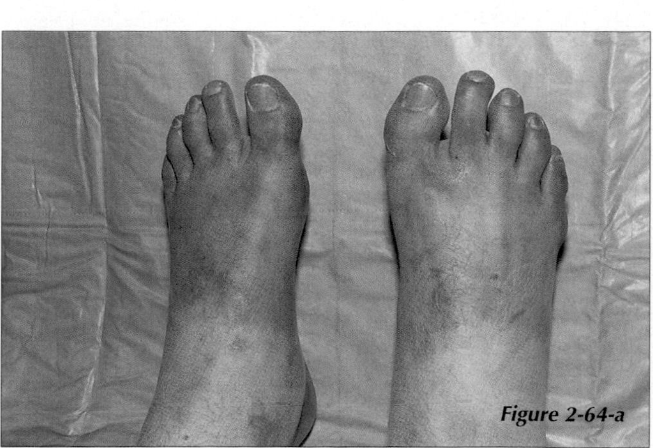

Figure 2-64-a

# Mimics

## Senna

### Case Study 2-65

This boy presented with severe diaper rash and the appearance of a serious burn injury. The father had given him senna-containing laxatives the previous day. The appearance of the injury was limited to the diaper area and was caused by prolonged contact of the senna content in the boy's waste with the skin underneath the diaper.

***Figures 2-65-a, b,*** *and* ***c.*** *The appearance of a burn that is limited to the diaper area and actually caused by a reaction to a laxative.*

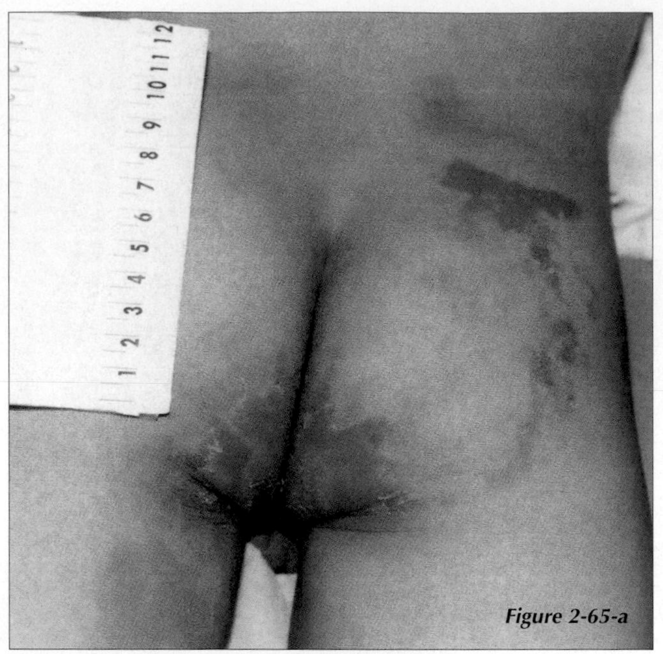


**Figure 2-65-a**

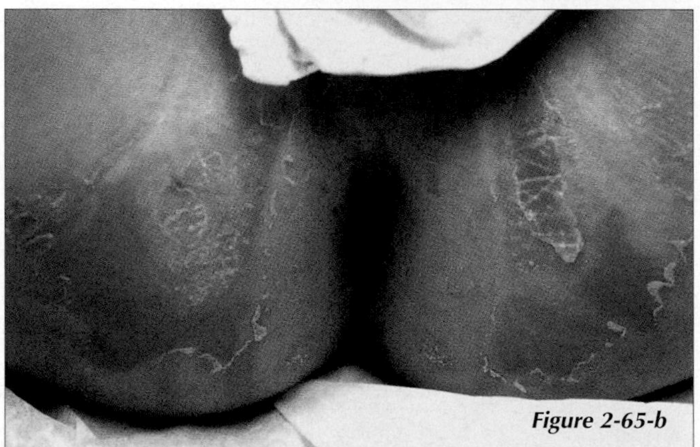

**Figure 2-65-b**

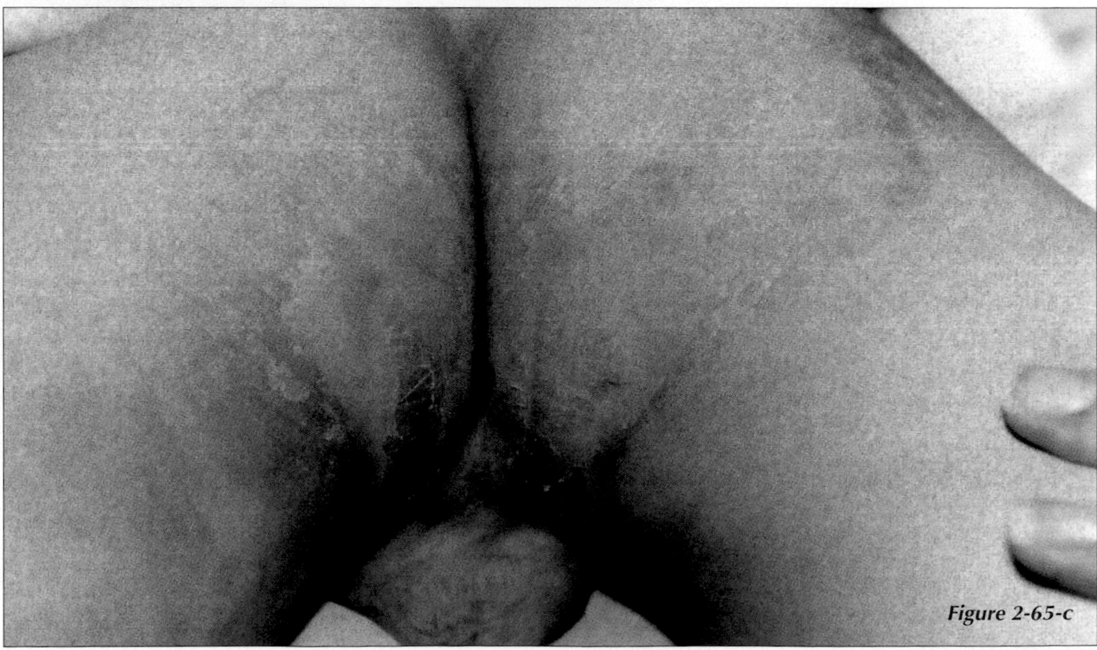

**Figure 2-65-c**

# Accidental Burns

## Contact Burns

### Case Study 2-66

This 11-month-old girl was taken to the ER with a second-degree burn of the left palm and a linear burn at the base of the fingers. She had no other injuries and the burn was fresh. The child supposedly sustained the injury when she grasped a hot curling iron sitting on the table, which was consistent with the injury. There were no indicators suggesting abuse, so the injury was determined to be accidental.

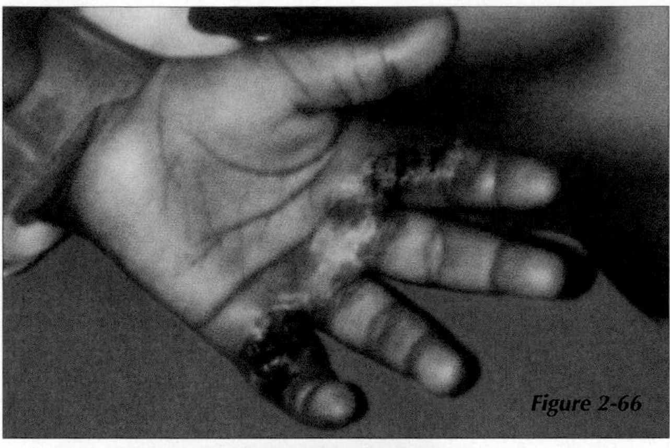

Figure 2-66

***Figure 2-66.*** *Second-degree burn of the left palm and a linear burn at the base of the fingers.*

### Case Study 2-67

This 16-month-old boy was burned by a curling iron sitting on a counter. He grabbed it with his hand, and then released it, striking his upper left arm as it fell. The hand injury and the glancing burn injury to his arm were consistent with the history. The child had a previous admission to the hospital for an ingestion of disinfectant cleaning solution.

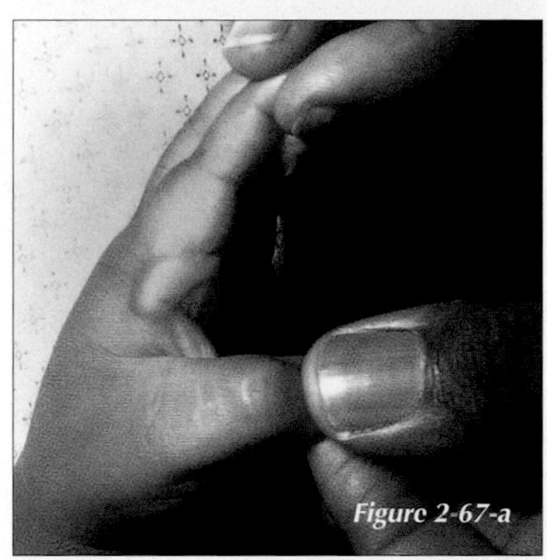

Figure 2-67-a

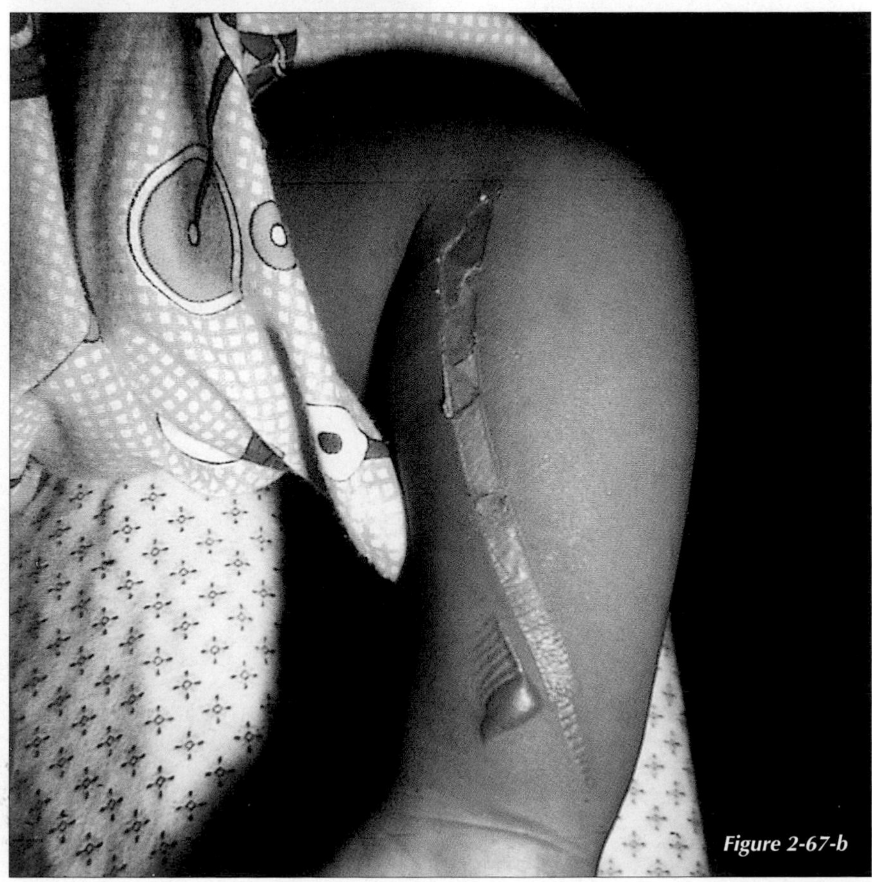

Figure 2-67-b

***Figures 2-67-a** and **b.*** *Note the hand injury and the glancing burn injury to this boy's arm. The injuries are consistent with an accidental burn with a curling iron.*

# Accidental Burns

## Contact Burns

### Case Study 2-68

This 10-month-old boy was in the care of his mother's paramour. The caregiver said that the child accidentally sat on a furnace grid. The grid pattern was present. The case was reported to state child protective services because of a delay in seeking medical assistance. Due to the age of the child and the location of the injury, it was determined to be an accidental burn.

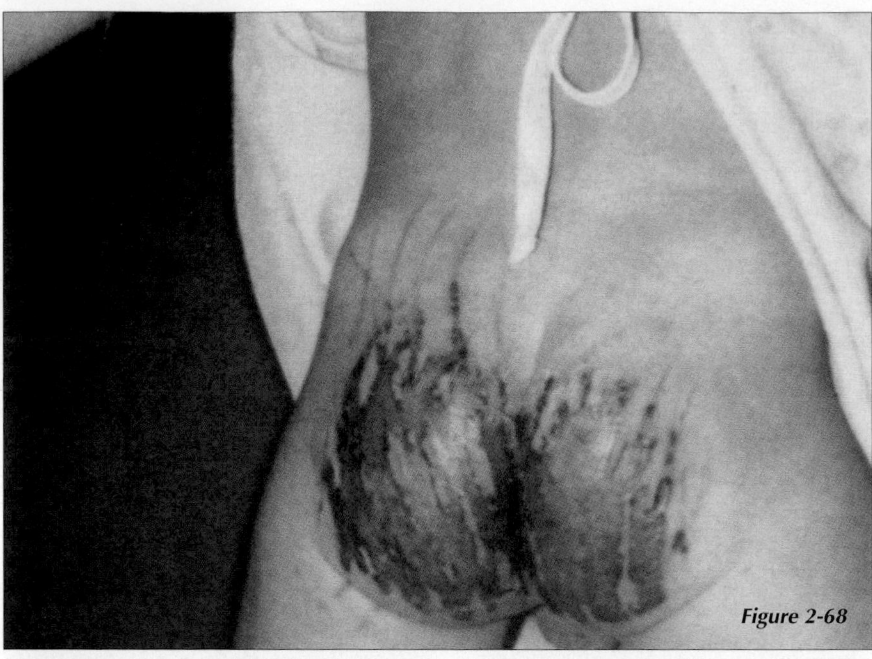

***Figure 2-68.*** *Pattern burn caused by a furnace grid.*

### Case Study 2-69

This 3-month-old girl was examined for a burn to her right forearm. The caregiver stated that she had touched a space heater. The pattern of the burn matched the grids of a space heater. The child was healthy, and there were no other injuries. The case was reported to child protection personnel so that they could inspect the home and make sure that there were no safety hazards.

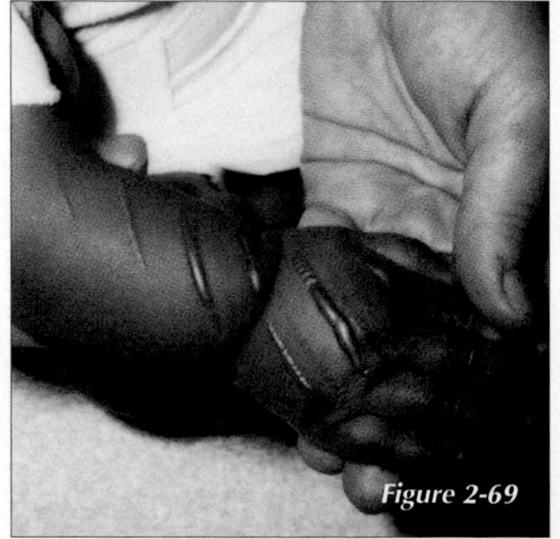

***Figure 2-69.*** *Pattern burn to the dorsum of the right hand and lower arm.*

## Multiple Injuries

### Case Study 2-70

This 5-year-old boy was admitted to the ER with pattern burns and loop marks on his back. The boy eventually revealed that he fell onto a space heater while his mother was chasing him around the house to whip him with an extension cord.

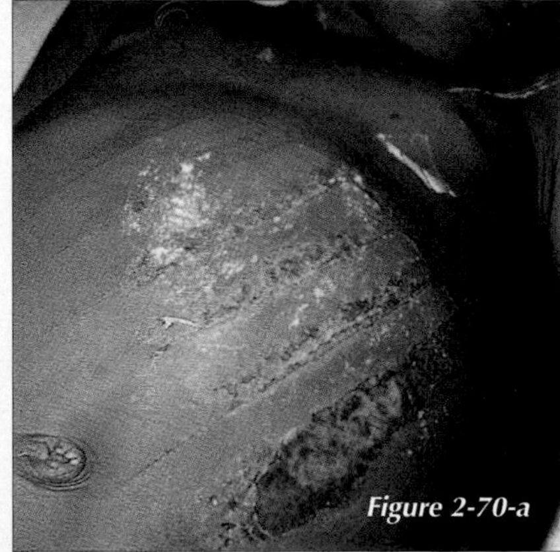

***Figure 2-70-a.*** *Pattern burns from accidental contact with a space heater.*

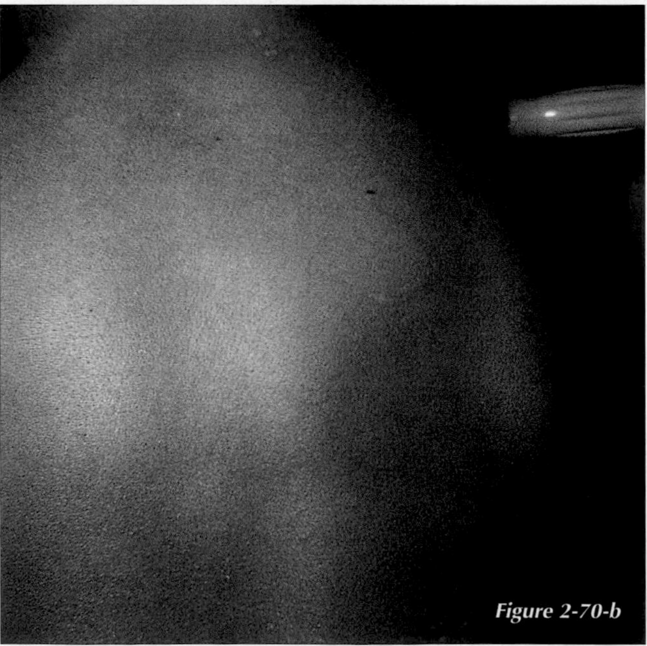

***Figure 2-70-b.*** *Loop marks to the right upper back, indicating contact with an extension cord.*

# Accidental Burns

## Spills

### Case Study 2-71

This 5-year-old boy was brought to the ER with severe scald burns and trauma to his forehead. He explained that he ran into his mother while she was carrying a pot of hot water. It was a suspicious burn because three surface areas were involved, but the boy was steadfast in his insistence that it was accidental. It was postulated that the child struck the pot of hot water with his forehead,causing the water to splash down the front to his flexed leg. The remainder of the liquid spilled down his left neck and back area.

***Figure 2-71-a.*** *Left forehead area that has been struck by a pot of hot water. The scalp is spared of any burns.*

***Figure 2-71-b.*** *The burns on the boy's back, with an arrow sign.*

***Figure 2-71-c.*** *The burn to left thigh, minus an arrow sign.*

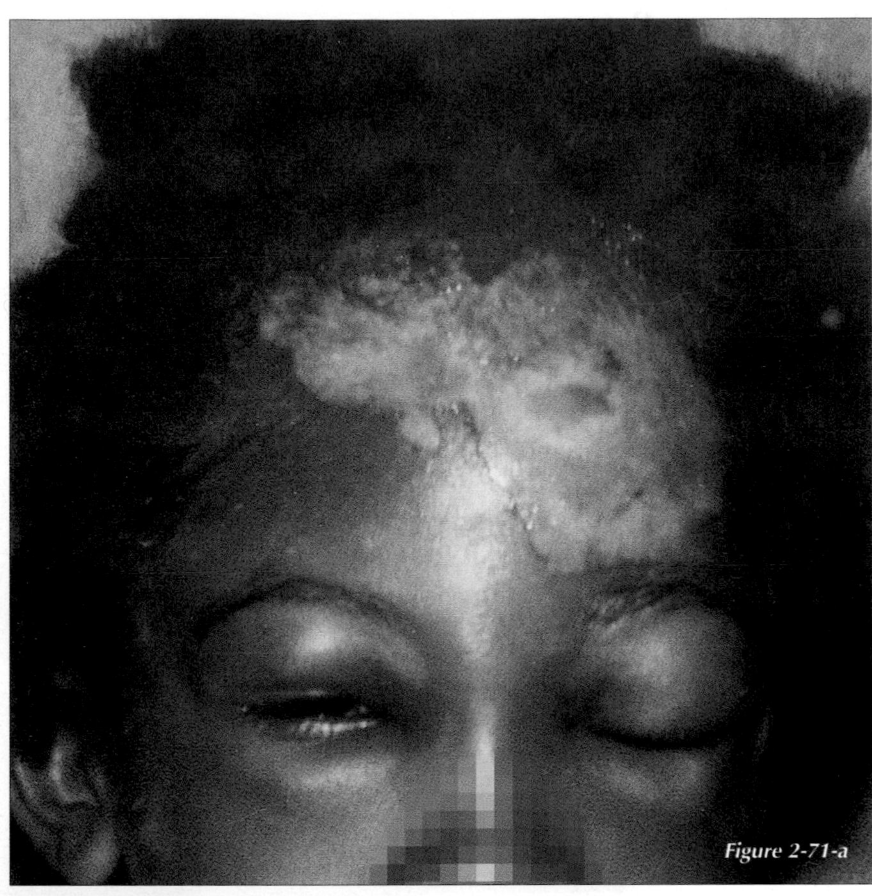

Figure 2-71-a

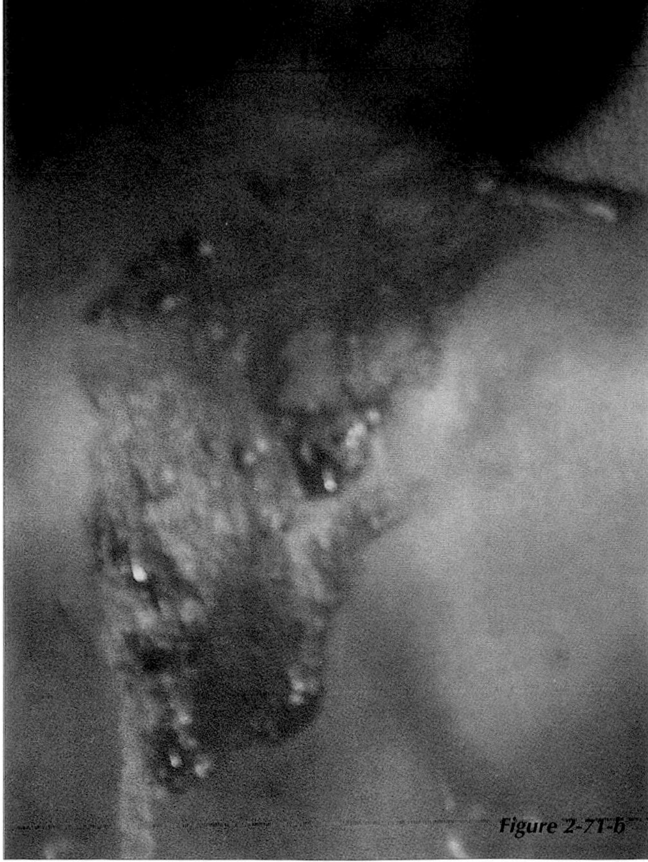

Figure 2-71-b

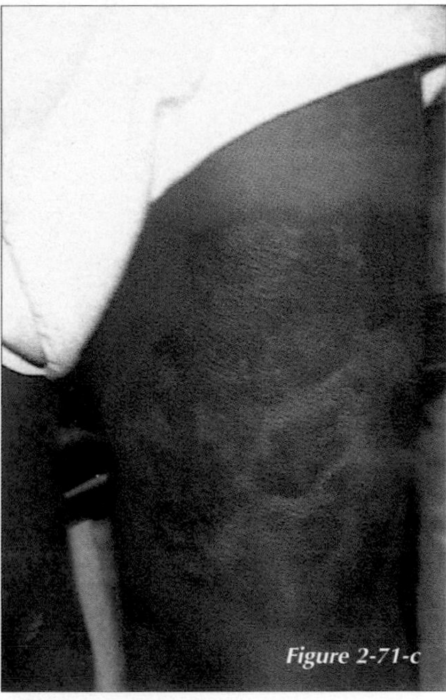

Figure 2-71-c

# IMMERSION BURNS

## EXTENSIVE BATHTUB BURNS

### Case Study 2-77

This 15-month-old boy was brought to the ER for burns that reportedly occurred in a bathtub. The mother stated that she put him into the tub for a bath and left him for just a couple of seconds. She said that the infant turned on the hot water and burned himself. Extensive partial thickness burns resulted.

***Figure 2-77-a.*** *Burns to the right foot and lower leg.*

***Figure 2-77-b.*** *Partial thickness burns to the perineum, buttocks, and scrotum, which are very painful.*

***Figure 2-77-c.*** *The position of this child is similar to the position when burned, but he would have been sitting more upright. The foot is forward into the deeper water with the knee only slightly bent.*

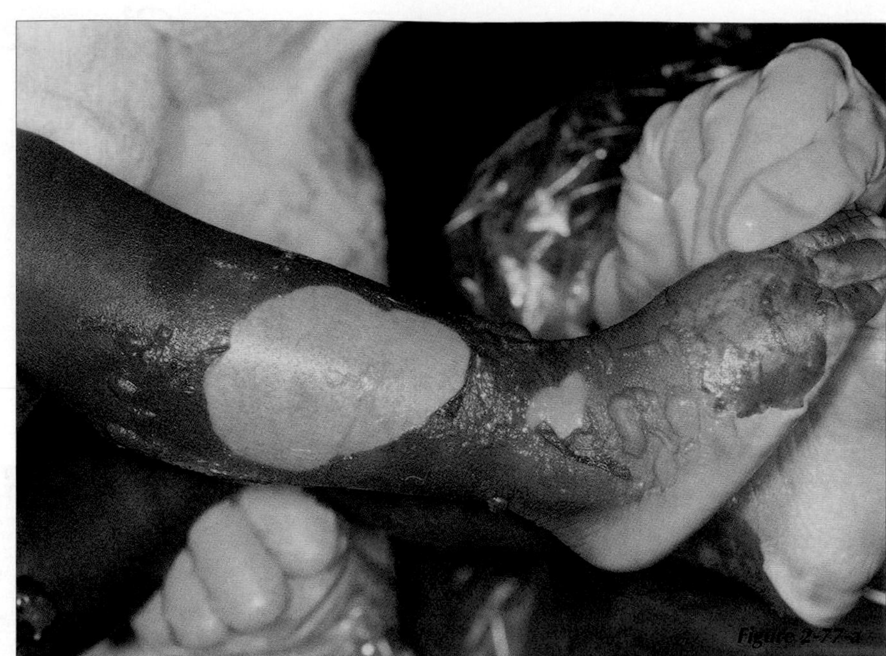

Figure 2-77-a

Figure 2-77-b

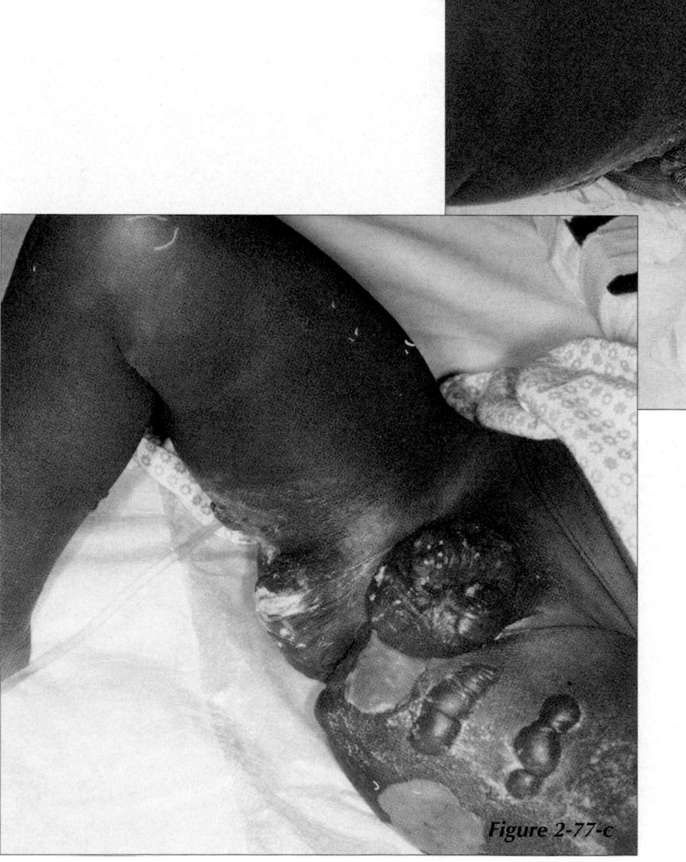

Figure 2-77-c

# Immersion Burns

## Extensive Bathtub Burns

**Case Study 2-77** *(continued)*

***Figure 2-77-d.*** *Pattern reveals that the right foot was in the water more than the left.*

***Figure 2-77-e.*** *The heel of the left foot is burned, but the dorsum spared, indicating the left foot was held up—perhaps as the child was being placed into the hot water.*

***Figure 2-77-f.*** *The thicker skin of the soles is relatively spared. Burns on the right leg indicate it was only slightly bent.*

If there was no water in the bathtub initially, it would have taken a long time to get water to the depth indicated by the burns. If the water had already been in the tub, the mother would be neglectful for leaving the child alone. However, incoming hot water would take a long time to heat the existing water to a temperature that could cause such burns, and the screams of the child would have alerted the mother. Also, it is doubtful that this child would have stayed relatively still in this position, and movement away from the painful stimulus would have prevented these burns. Thus, these burns represent immersion into very hot water that would already have been in the bathtub to this depth. It was determined that this was a case of physical abuse and not neglect—the mother's history was false.

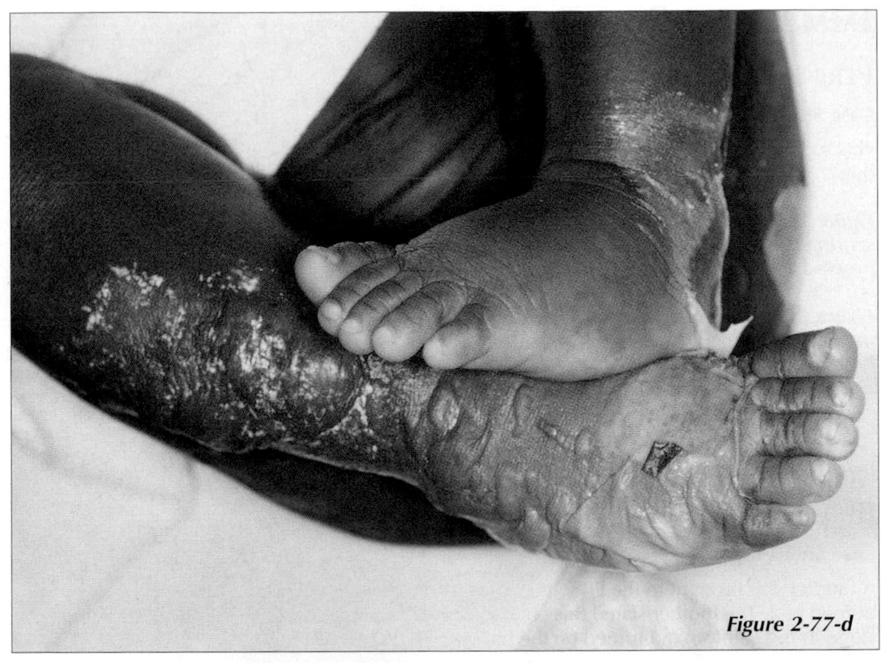

**Figure 2-77-d**

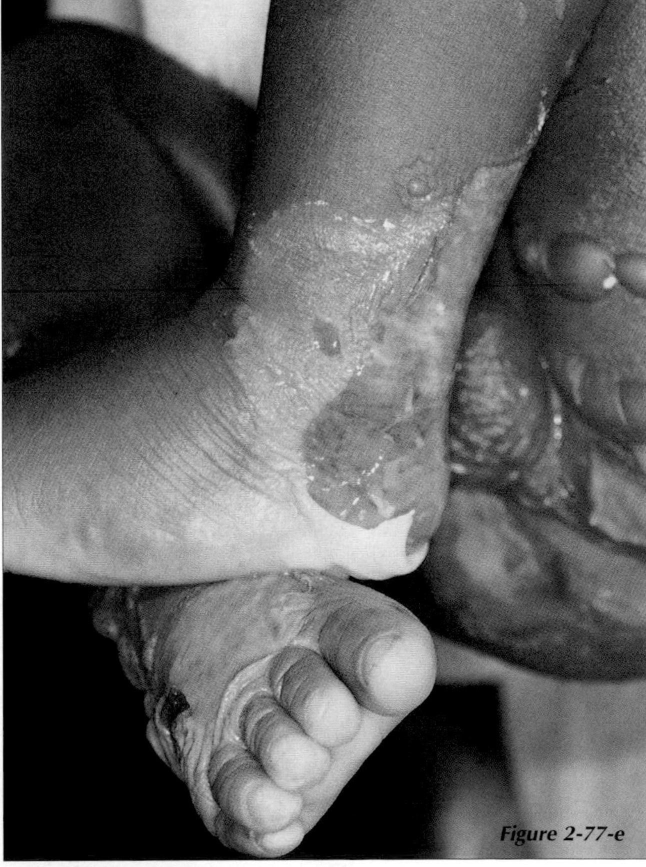

**Figure 2-77-e**

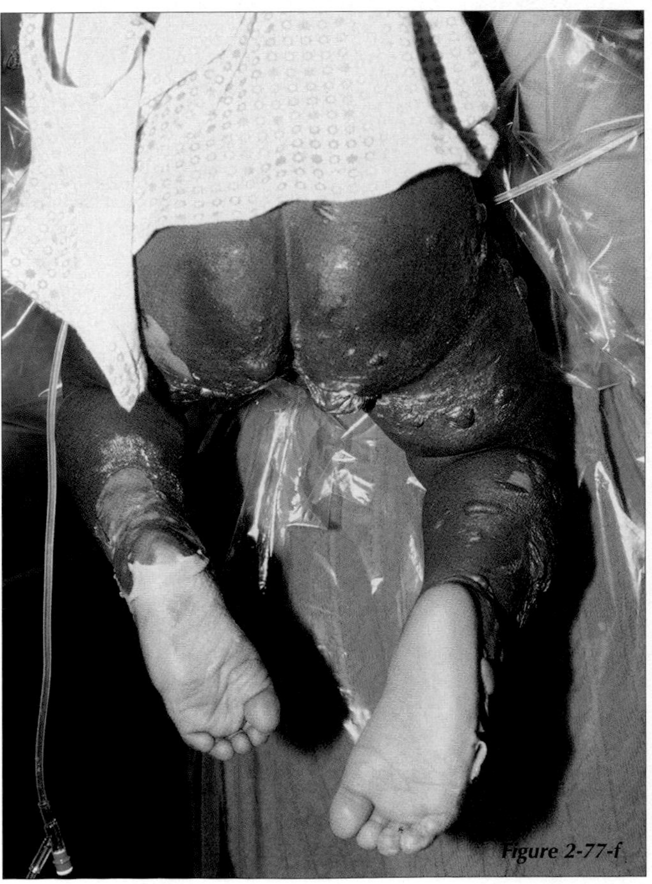

**Figure 2-77-f**

# Immersion Burns

## Scarring

### Case Study 2-84

This 4-year-old boy was being cared for by the mother's paramour. Neighbors called the police when a disturbance was heard. The paramour said that this child got into a tub of very hot water by himself. Reportedly, there was skin in the bathtub when the water was let out. This child suffered burns over 85% of his body. A burn of this magnitude requires prolonged medical and physical therapy and produces considerable long-term pain. In addition, the risk of death as a result of infection is substantial, so meticulous care in a burn unit is required. Photographs were obtained from this child's follow-up examination several months after the incident.

**Figures 2-84-a.** *Scarring over the chest, upper left abdomen, and left arm.*

**Figure 2-84-b.** *Immersion burn to the left foot. Amputation was not necessary.*

**Figure 2-84-c.** *Immersion-burn scarring of both feet. Note the water line on both feet.*

**Figure 2-84-d.** *Considerable scarring of the right hand.*

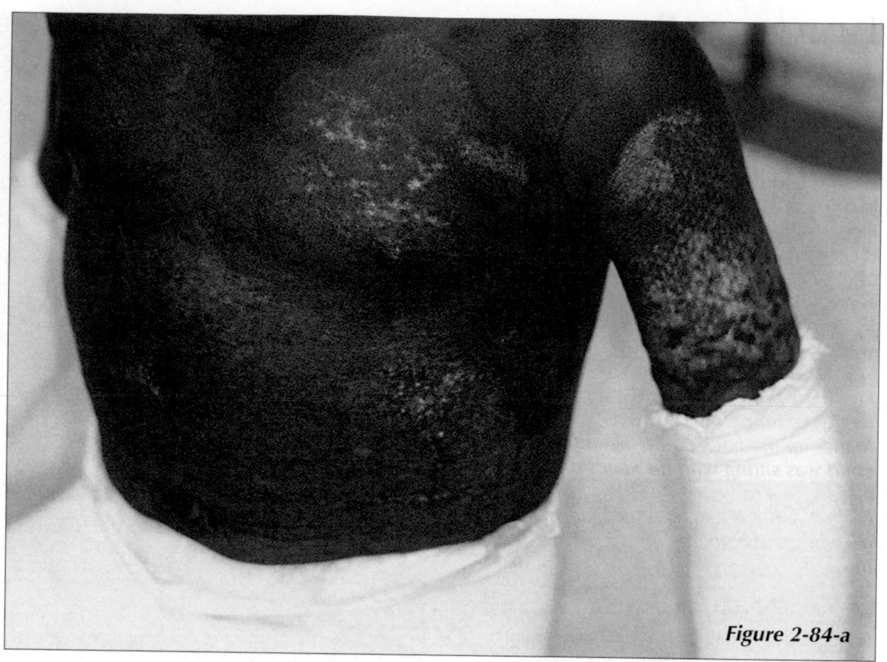

**Figure 2-84-a**

**Figure 2-84-b**

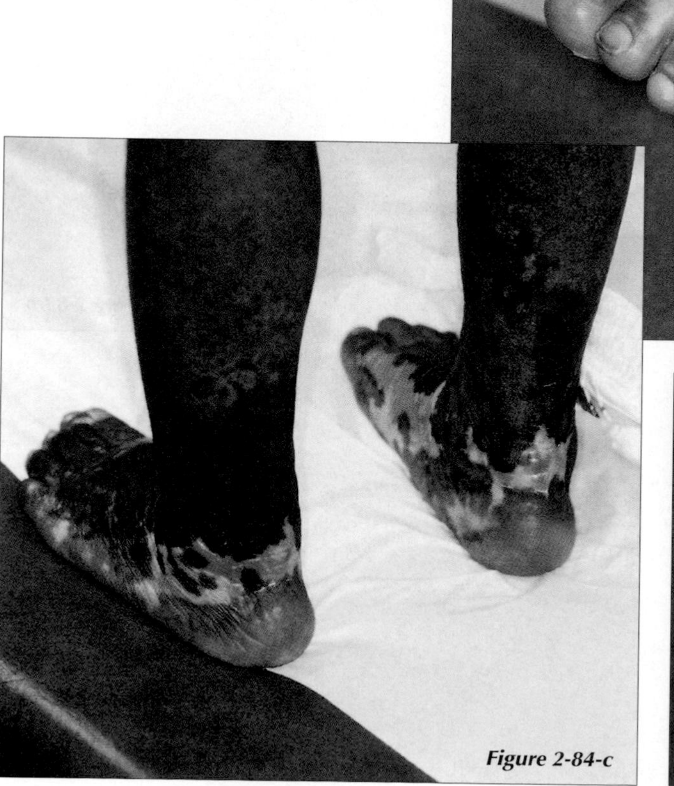

**Figure 2-84-c**

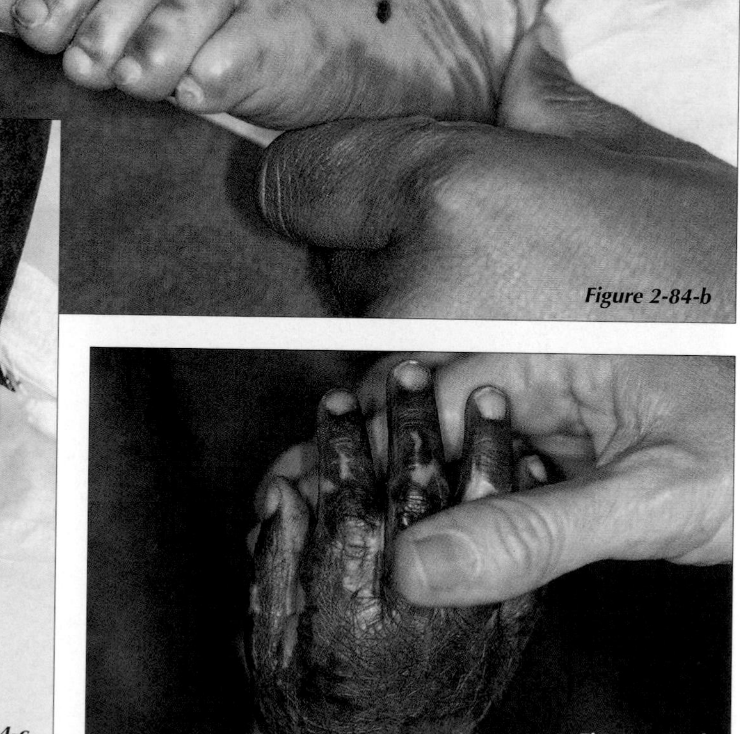

**Figure 2-84-d**

# Immersion Burns

## Scarring

**Case Study 2-84** *(continued)*

***Figure 2-84-e.*** *Scarring along the dorsum of the left arm.*

***Figure 2-84-f.*** *Scarring along the inner surface of the left arm, indicating that the entire left arm was immersed.*

***Figure 2-84-g.*** *Scarring of the back.*

The immersion burns to the feet and left arm and the accompanying burns elsewhere do not correspond to a history of the child voluntarily getting into a bathtub or falling in.

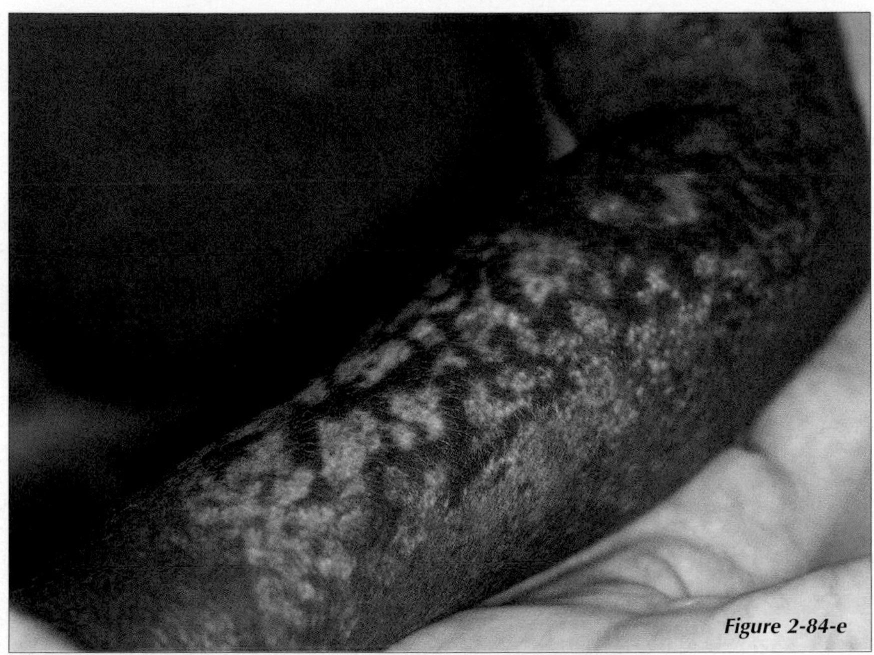

**Figure 2-84-e**

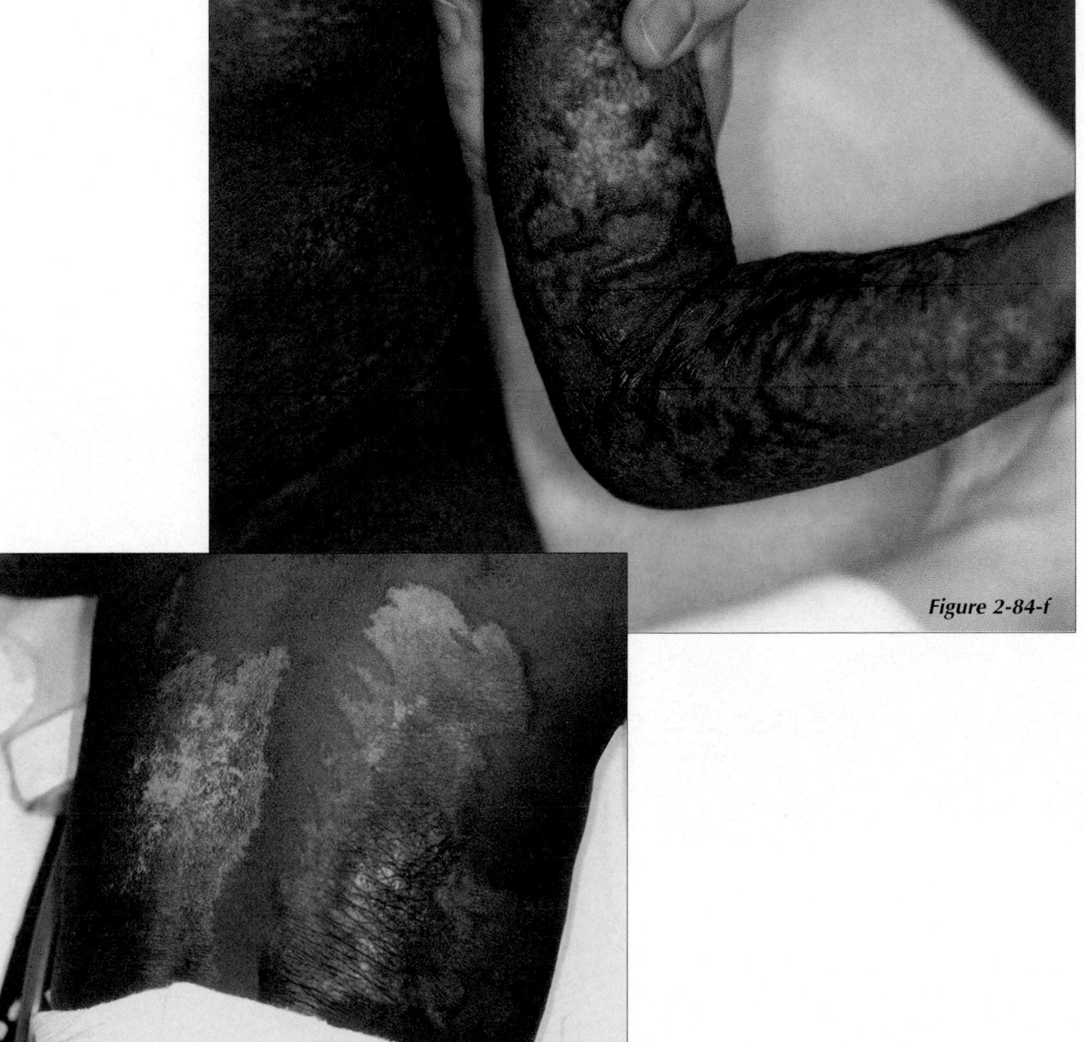

**Figure 2-84-f**

**Figure 2-84-g**

# Immersion Burns

## Water Burn Reported as Chemical Burn

### Case Study 2-85

This 15-month-old with sickle-cell disease had been placed in foster care. The child protective services worker attempted to make a home visit, but the foster mother would not let the worker into the house. The worker later returned with the police. The foster mother said the child was accidentally bathed in bleach and that she was treating the burns at home and did not think it was necessary to seek medical care.

***Figure 2-85-a.*** *The left foot shows granulation. Inevitably such an injury is complicated by some degree of infection and is therefore treated with antibiotics. Note the immersion line above the ankle.*

***Figure 2-85-b.*** *Back of the left leg shows sparing of the back of the knee, which usually results when the knee is flexed and the opposing skin surfaces seal out the water, or because the water is not high enough to reach this area.*

***Figure 2-85-c.*** *The back of the right lower leg shows an immersion line. There is some sparing of tissue along the thicker sole and lateral aspect of the foot.*

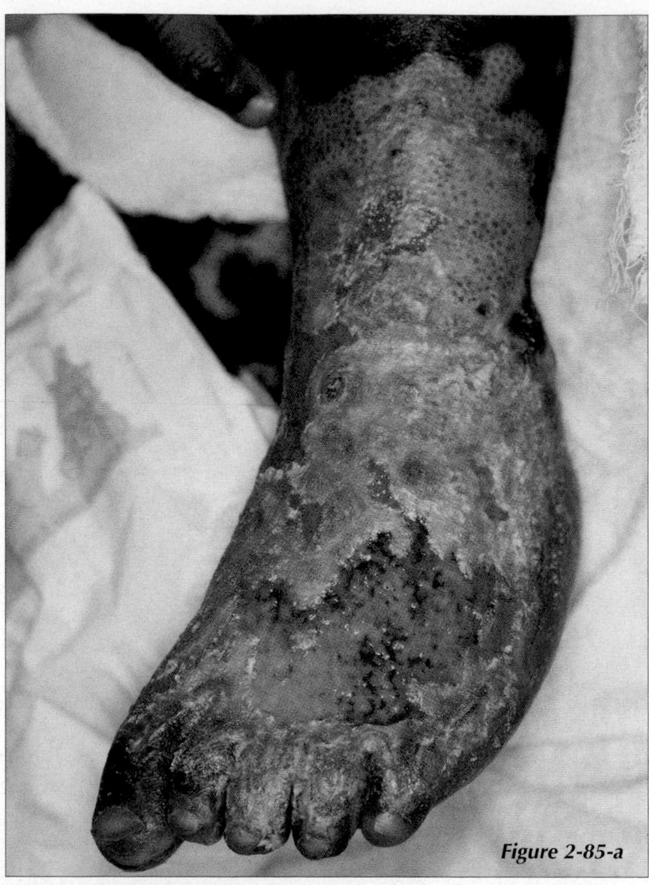

Figure 2-85-a

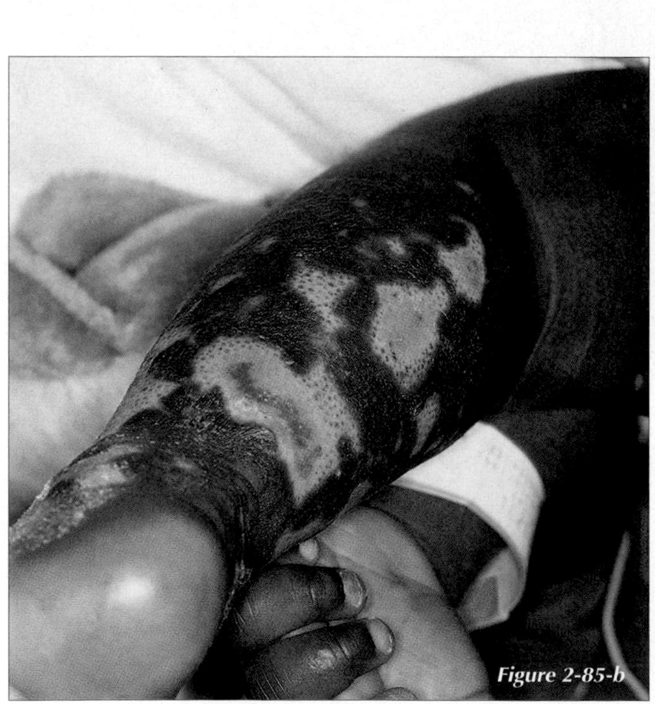

Figure 2-85-b

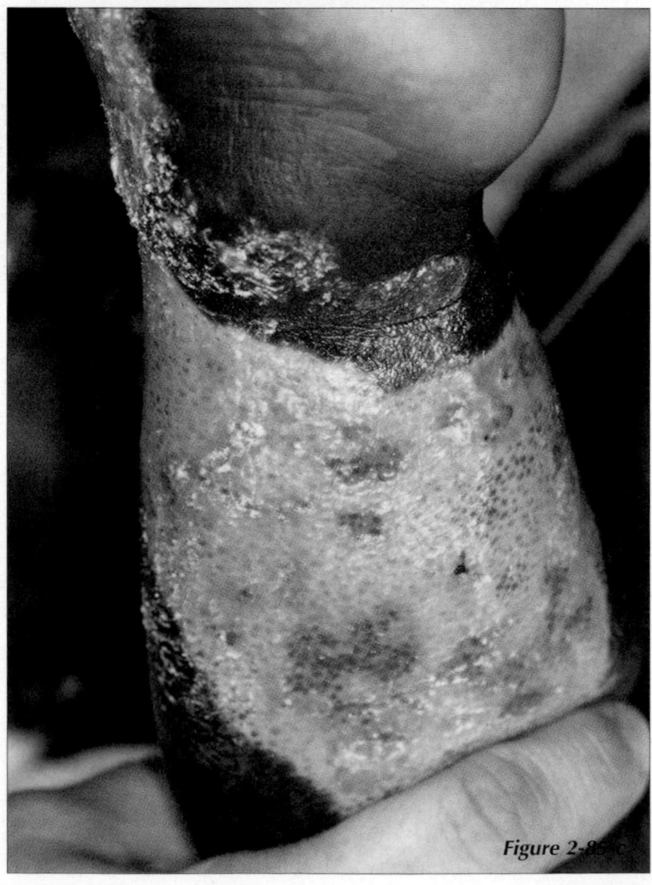

Figure 2-85-c

# Immersion Burns

## Water Burn Reported as Chemical Burn

**Case Study 2-85** *(continued)*

***Figure 2-85-d.*** *View of the right leg reveals the foot was in front of the knee so that a diagonal water line is on the lower leg. Burns to the upper foot heal with scar tissue that is less flexible than skin, requiring physical therapy to keep the foot flexible for dorsiflexion and to avoid dragging of the toes in a dysfunctional gait.*

***Figure 2-85-e.*** *Partial thickness burns are found on the posterior left thigh and the back of the left calf.*

***Figure 2-85-f.*** *The perineum is burned, but the scrotum spared. Pattern reveals the water line is lower at this end than the feet, so this chlld must have been sitting with his feet toward the drain.*

The child protection team felt that this child had been scalded or immersed. The burns were estimated to be more than 7 to 10 days old because of the epithelial budding. Both physical abuse and medical neglect were found.

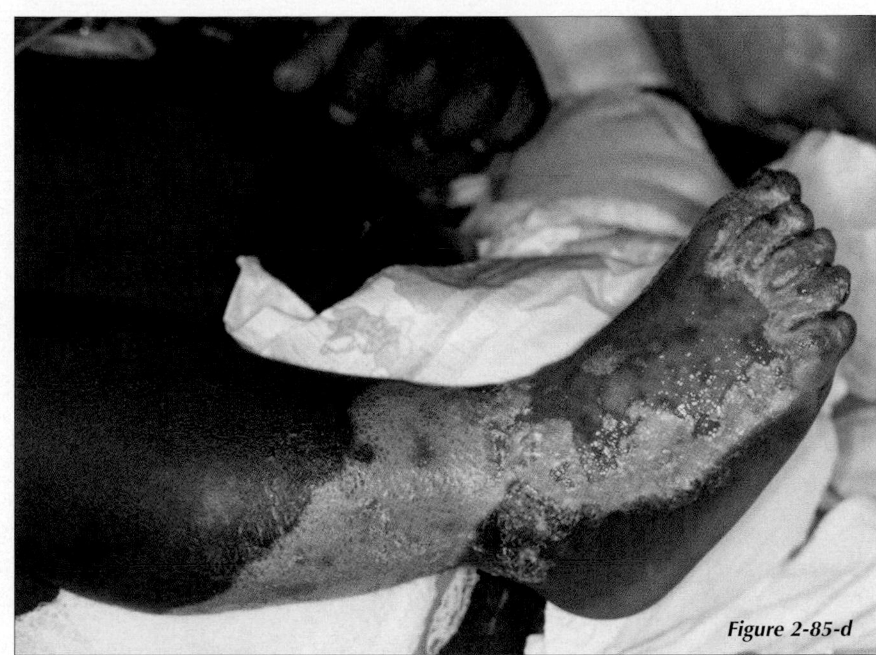

**Figure 2-85-d**

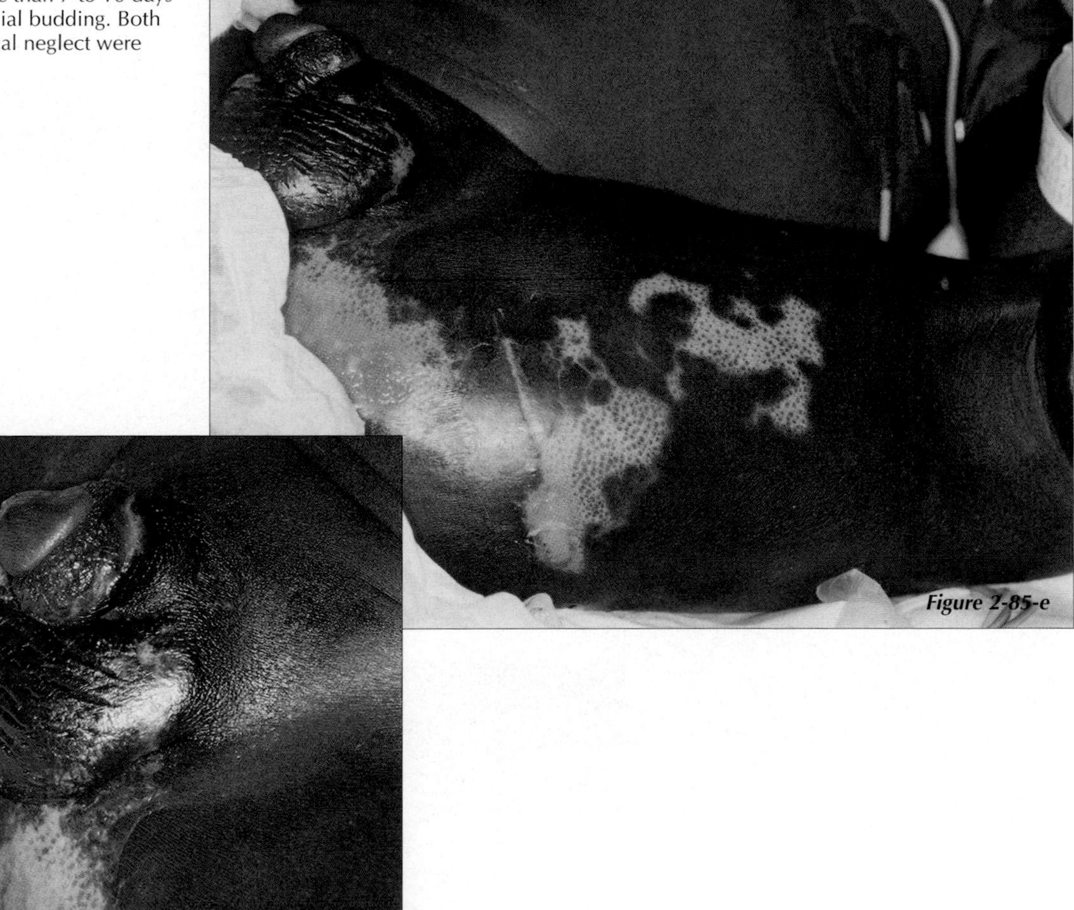

**Figure 2-85-e**

**Figure 2-85-f**

# Scalding

## Pattern with Scalding

**Case Study 2-86**

This infant was being cared for by an older sibling who was cooking. The infant was sitting in his high chair. The history was that hot water was poured on the infant when the pot was taken off the stove.

***Figure 2-86.*** *The burns are consistent with scalding from water coming from above.*

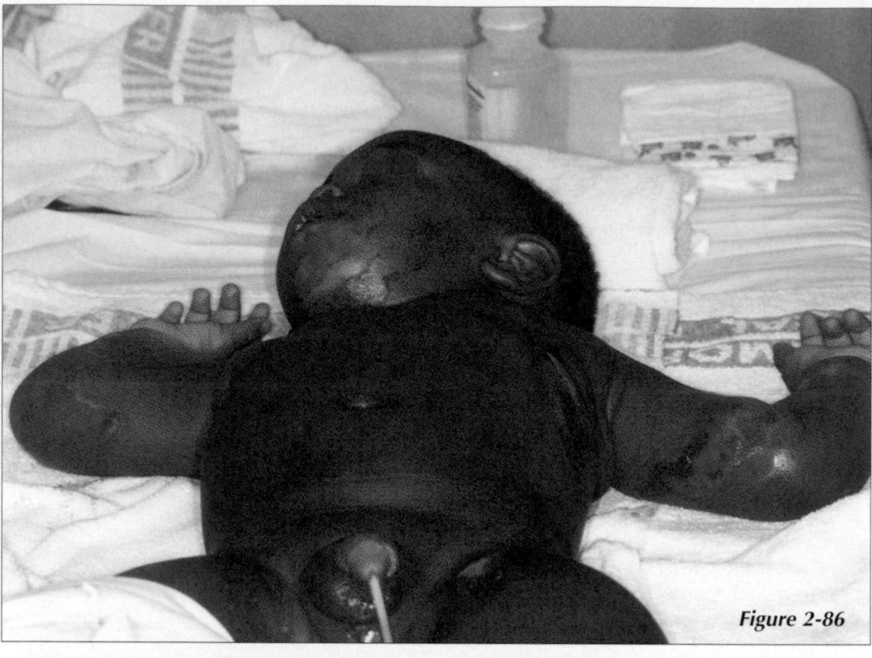

Figure 2-86

**Case Study 2-87**

This infant was sitting in a high chair and scalded by hot water poured on her.

***Figure 2-87-a.*** *Burns to the right ear, cheek, and chest. Note that flexion led to sparing of the neck.*

***Figure 2-87-b.*** *Pattern of burns along the right side indicating flow of water toward the chin and downward on the chest.*

***Figure 2-87-c.*** *Sparing of skin in the armpit.*

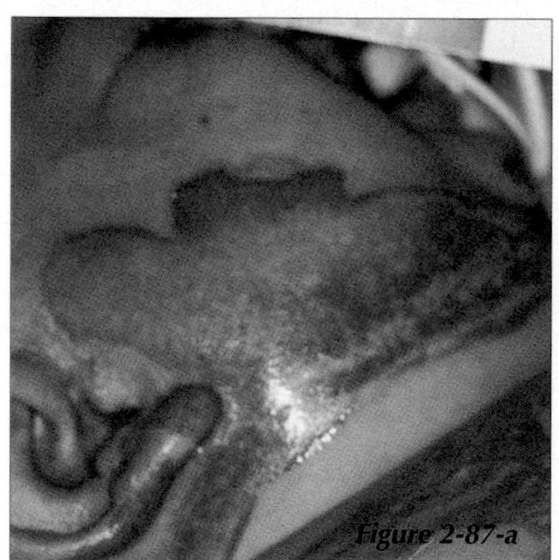

Figure 2-87-a

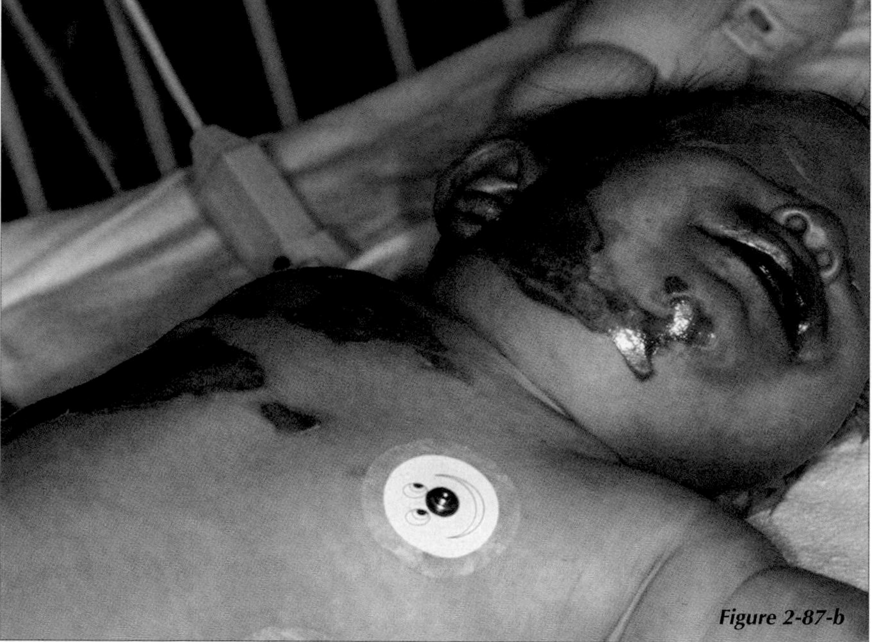

Figure 2-87-b

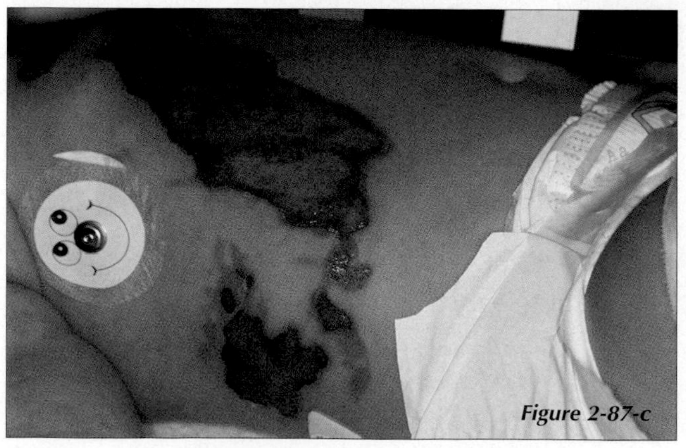

Figure 2-87-c

# Scalding

## Pattern with Scalding

**Case Study 2-86** *(continued)*

***Figure 2-87-d.*** *Pattern indicating flow of water on the shoulder and down the upper back.*

***Figure 2-87-e.*** *Pattern indicating the water also flowed onto the right arm and down the side.*

Burn patterns of inflicted injuries can be similar to patterns seen on children who pull hot water upon themselves. The history offered for the burn, careful inspection of the burn pattern, and the developmental capabilities of the individual child are needed to distinguish between abuse and an accident.

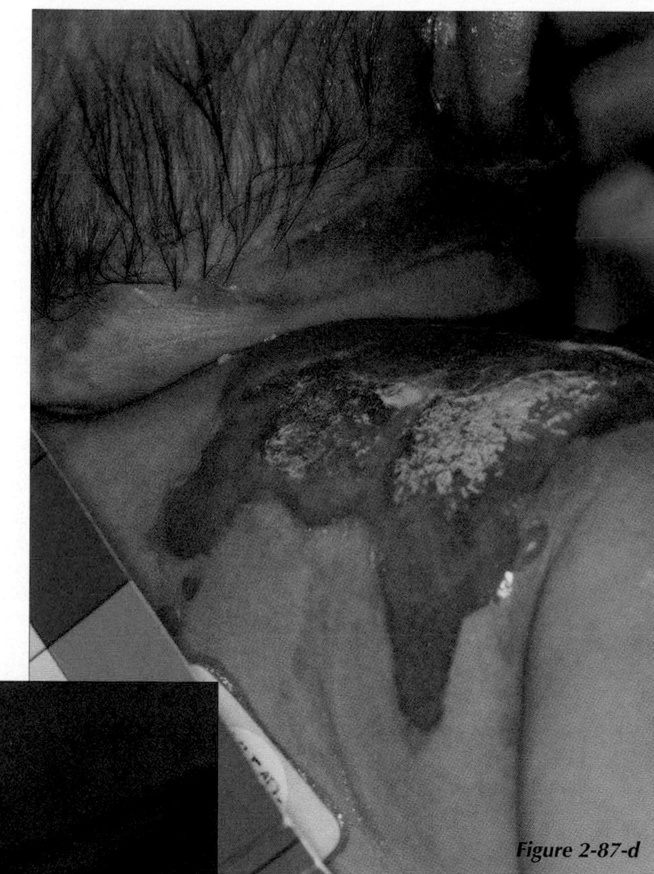

Figure 2-87-d

Figure 2-87-e

# Miscellaneous Burn Cases

## Multiple Burns

**Case Study 2-88**

This 18-month-old boy was brought for care with a history of being burned by hot water from a pot. The toddler was in the care of the mother's paramour who stated that he tripped while holding the pot of hot water and it fell onto this child.

***Figure 2-88-a.*** *Superficial and partial thickness burns are seen in a pattern of water coming from above this child.*

***Figure 2-88-b.*** *Extensive burns on the right back.*

***Figure 2-88-c.*** *Cigarette burn on the right hand.*

***Figure 2-88-d.*** *Extensive anterior burns.*

The case was determined to be one of physical abuse with multiple injuries.

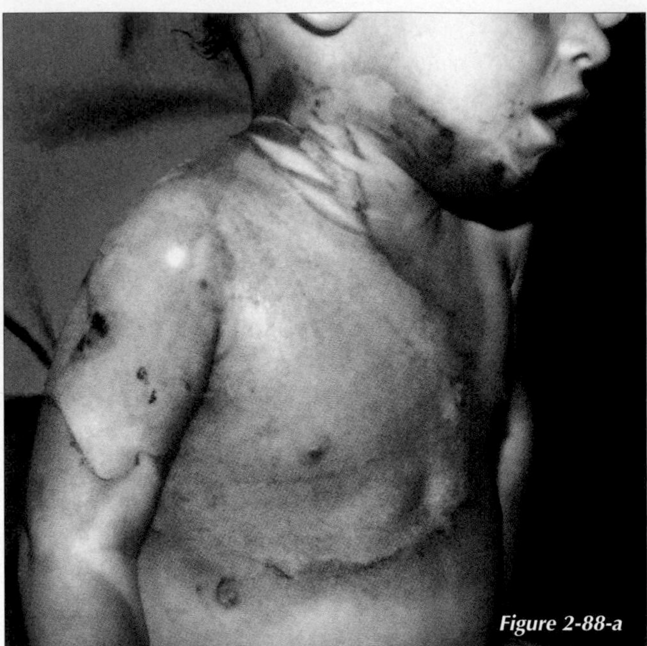

***Figure 2-88-a***

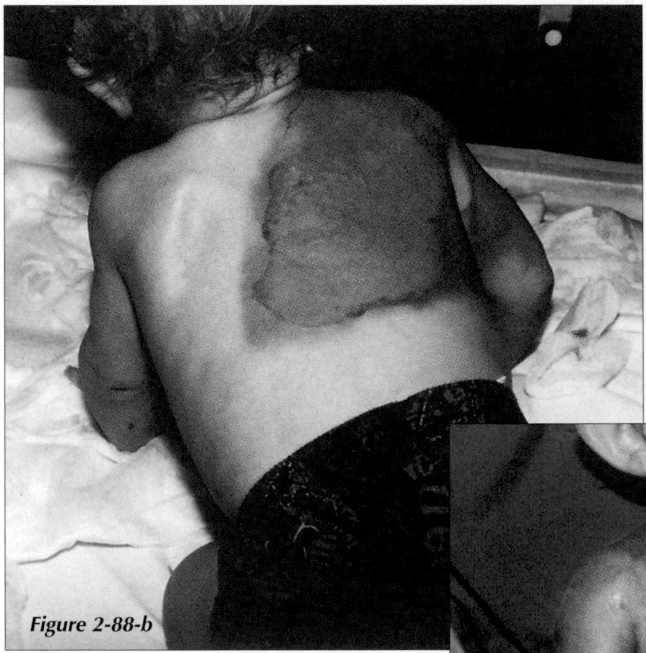

***Figure 2-88-b***

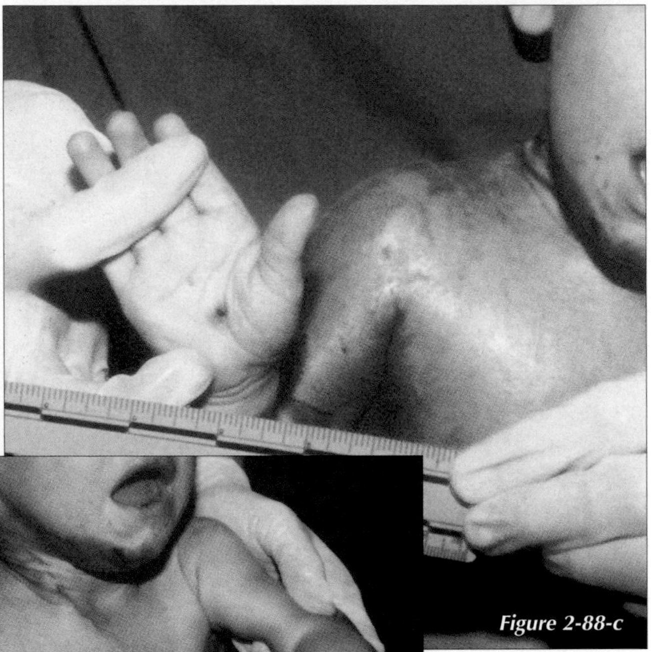

***Figure 2-88-c***

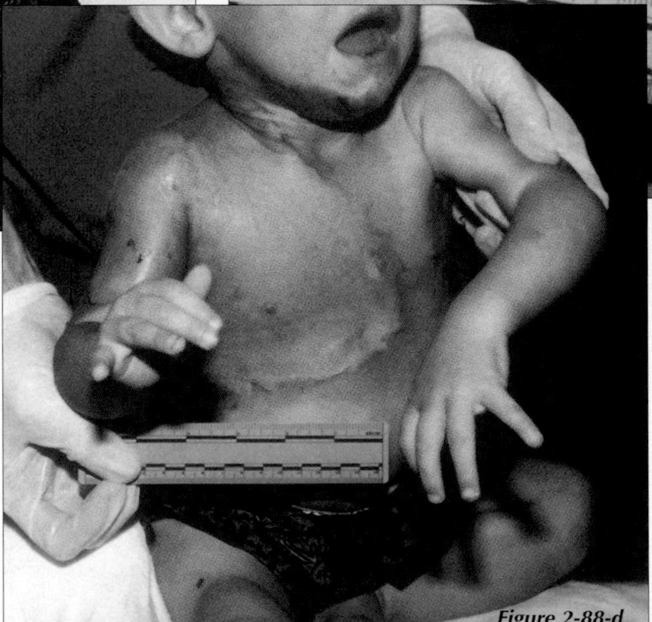

***Figure 2-88-d***

# Miscellaneous Burn Cases

## Burns to Brand a Child

**Case Study 2-89**

This 8-month-old boy was brought to the ER in full cardiorespiratory arrest. He had multiple injuries and died from head trauma. Distinctive burns were noted on his right cheek. (Photograph courtesy of Dr. Tom McKee.)

***Figure 2-89.*** *Burns caused by a cigarette lighter used to "brand" this child. The pattern is indicative of a disposable lighter.*

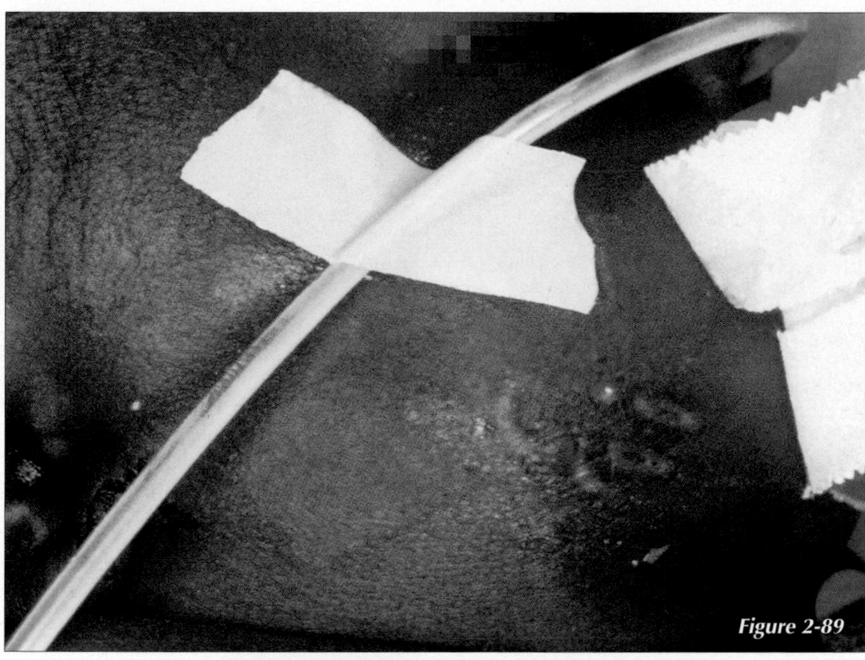

Figure 2-89

## Contact With Hot Stove

**Case Study 2-90**

This 18-month-old boy was left home alone. The history given by caregivers was that he crawled on top of the stove and turned it on.

***Figure 2-90-a.*** *Burn marks on the leg and thigh show a clear pattern of the metal rings of a burner. The burn would have occurred quickly.*

***Figure 2-90-b.*** *Burns seen from another angle. Note that the knee would have been bent.*

***Figure 2-90-c.*** *Partial thickness burns on the bottom of the foot.*

Examination is important to determine if the injuries are consistent with the history or whether they were inflicted by another person.

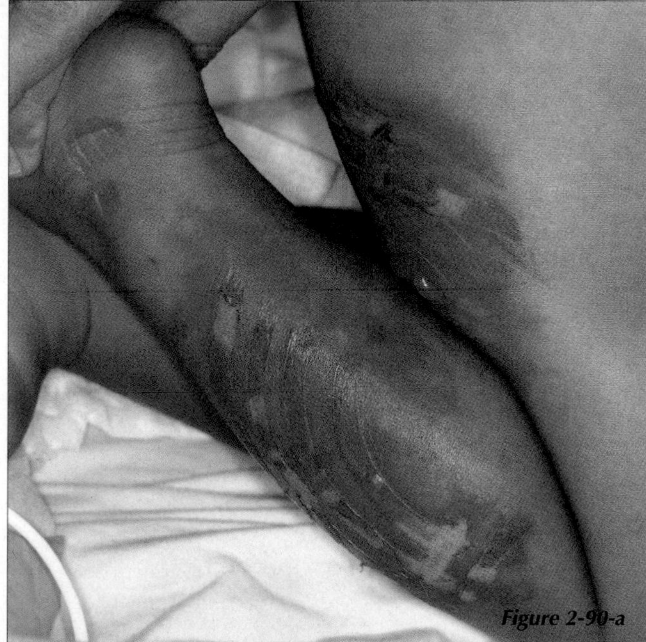

Figure 2-90-a

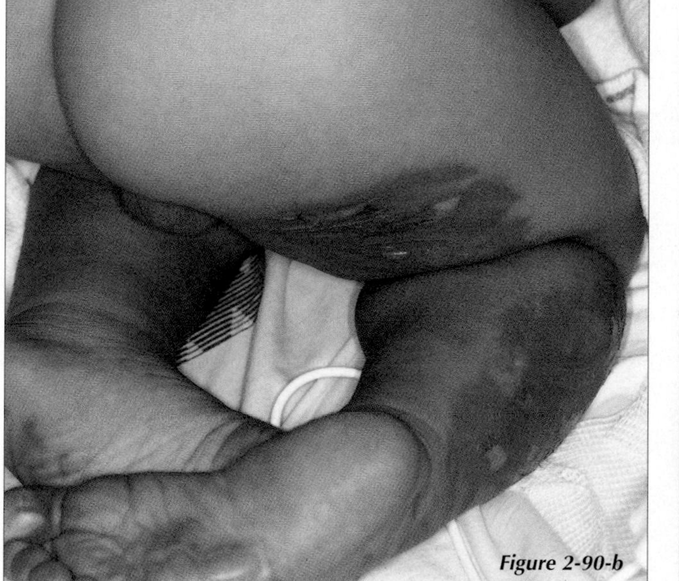

Figure 2-90-b

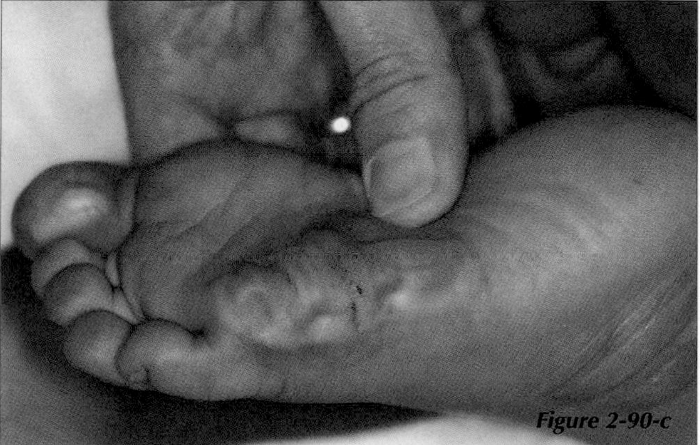

Figure 2-90-c

# Miscellaneous Burn Cases

## Curling Iron Burn

**Case Study 2-91**

This young girl came to the outpatient clinic of a hospital for a health check. Upon examination she was found to have a burn. The history was that she sat on a curling iron.

***Figure 2-91.*** *A healing curling iron burn.*

Such a burn would have been very painful and should have received medical treatment, so neglect was involved. Whether the burn was deliberately inflicted or was as reported requires further investigation, but the curling iron was the undisputed cause of this pattern of injury.

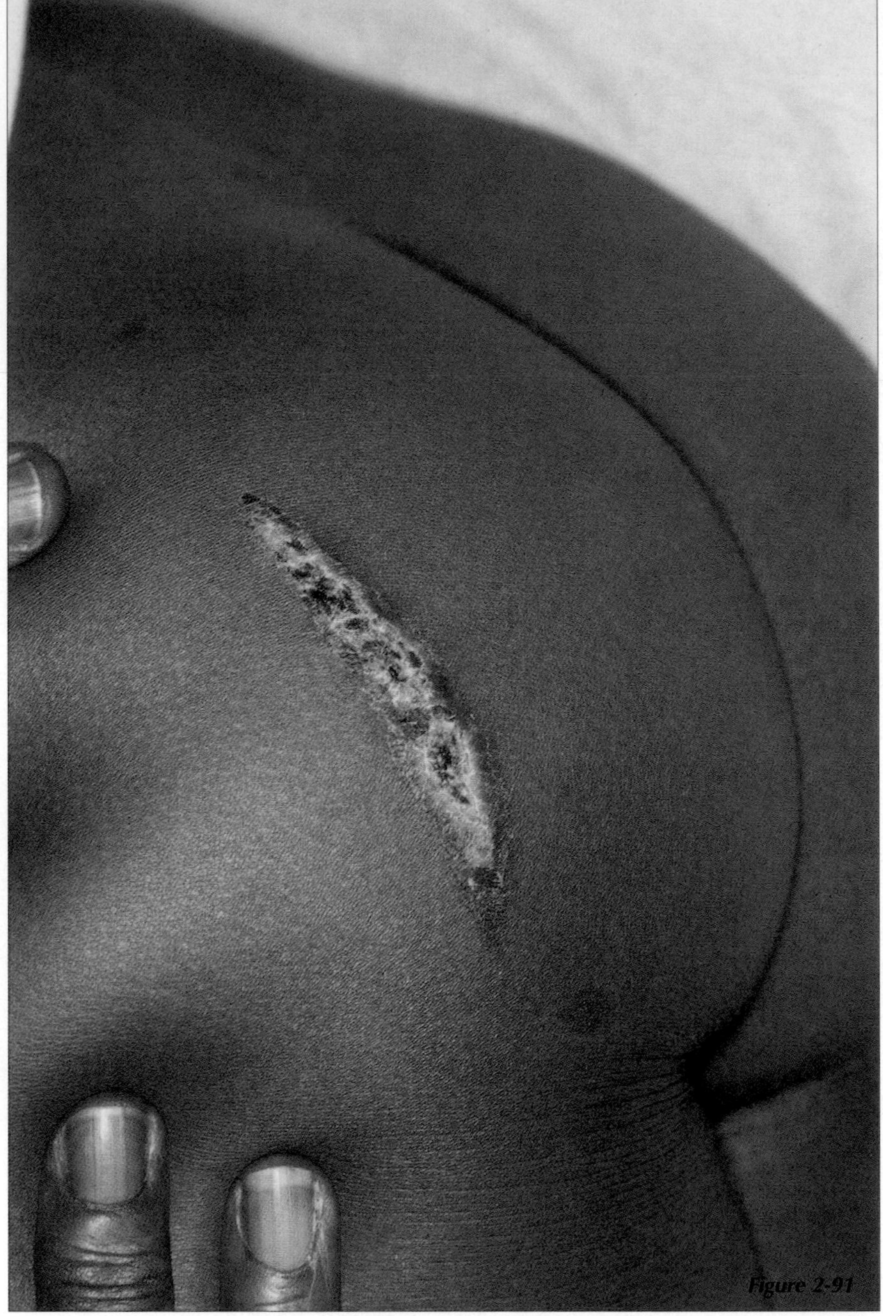

*Figure 2-91*

Chapter 3

# HEAD INJURIES

Sam Gulino, MD
Wilbur Smith, MD
Swati Shah-Mody, MD

Abusive head injury has several synonyms, including shaken baby syndrome, shake impact syndrome, and non-accidental brain trauma. Regardless of the label, abusive head injury frequently results in serious and permanent brain damage. The forces to which the infant's brains are subjected are severe. The prevalence of abusive head injury is highest in children younger than two years of age, probably because the size of an older infant makes it difficult to create the extreme forces necessary to inflict such severe injury to the brain and its coverings.

When evaluating abusive head injury, it is best to consider each injury individually since it involves the internal layers of tissue as well as those surrounding the brain. While this is a logical approach to describing the injuries, it is important to recognize that multiple anatomical areas of injury are the rule, not the exception.

External to the brain, the scalp is often the site of a subgaleal hemorrhage after impact. Hemorrhage into the scalp creates the proverbial "egg" on the scalp. The subgaleal space is a large potential space; therefore, the blood often flows into a dependent region. This explains why the palpable or visible bump is not always in the region of the trauma. Unless the child has a bleeding disorder or some other abnormality, the presence of a subgaleal hematoma always suggests that there was an impact injury. There is another, less common variant of scalp injury: the cephalhematoma, which is a hemorrhage in the subperiosteal space, external to the bone but localized anatomically to the bone since it is confined by the periosteial layer of each bone of the skull. Cephalhematomas are rarely seen in child abuse and always remain local to the area of hemorrhage or impact.

The skull serves to protect the brain and is often fractured if the injury involves impact. Skull fractures typically associated with abusive head injury are similar to those due to high velocity impact. These fractures are long (longer than 5 cm), stellate (many limbs from one point of impact) or diastatic (the edges of the fracture are widely spread). It is possible to have skull fracture from a short fall. In rare cases, some overlap of features between high impact and short fall injuries may occur; however, the presence of long, stellate, or diastatic fractures should lead to enhanced suspicion if they are ascribed to a short fall.

The epidural hematoma is an unusual injury in child abuse. This type of hematoma occurs because of bleeding, usually arterial, into the epidural space between the inner table of the skull and the dura mater. This lesion is classically associated with a lucid interval and skull fracture. The theory of the lucid interval is that the initial impact causes the fracture and concussion, rendering the victim unconscious. The subsequent bleeding from ruptured branches of the middle meningeal artery then causes a hematoma, which subsequently causes further deterioration of mental status after the patient stabilizes from the concussion.

The subdural hematoma (SDH) is a hallmark of abusive head inury and is the most frequently diagnosed intracranial injury in child abuse. Bleeding in the subdural space occurs because of a rupture of the bridging veins that drain blood from the surface of the brain to the dural venous sinuses. The principal route of drainage of surface veins is to the sagittal sinus. As a result, subdural hematomas due to child abuse most often occur over the convexities of the parietal, frontal, and occipital lobes. Frequently, subdural hematomas can be identified as new or old depending upon the characteristics of the blood degradation products on a computed tomographic (CT) scan or magnetic resonance imaging (MRI) scan. The relative insensitivity of CT scans for definition of anatomical spaces has led to some confusion in older literature, particularly regarding benign subdural hygromas, most of which are merely enlarged or prominent subarachnoid spaces, and are of no significance.

Bleeding into the subarachnoid space occurs when the vessels are ruptured between the arachnoid membrane and the pia mater. The subarachnoid space readily communicates with the cerebrospinal fluid (CSF) cisterns and the spinal subarachnoid space. Blood obtained on spinal taps in abused children can be used to indicate subarachnoid hemorrhages (SAH). Subarachnoid hemorrhages can be identified on imaging by bleeding into the cerebrospinal fluid cisterns or by a serpiginous, gyriform pattern of hemorrhage. Subarachnoid blood also accumulates along the cerebral tentorium or within the thecal sack over the spine. Subarachnoid hemorrhages are very important clinically because there is almost universal agreement among experts that they have distinct symptoms. Adults with subarachnoid hemorrhages—the most common victims of ruptures of an intracranial aneurysm—describe a typical "thunderclap" headache as the worst of their lives. In infants, the symptoms are manifest as extreme irritability, discomfort, and pain. An infant with a subarachnoid hemorrhage is highly unlikely to act normally.

Parenchymal injuries to the brain include both bland and hemorrhagic contusions. There is a tendency for the brain to suffer contre coup injuries, an injury opposite the side of impact. The contre coup injury is usually larger than the direct impact injury. The other characteristic hemorrhagic injury to the brain is the ***diffuse axonal injury*** (DAI), an injury to the axons of the neurons that has a high prevalence at areas of differing physical density in the brain such as the watershed areas along the cortex or the deep gray and pericollosal white matter areas. Parenchymal injuries of the brain tend to be rapidly symptomatic.

The final serious injury of the brain ascribable to child abuse is hypoxic ischemic injury. This injury occurs due to a complex interaction of events that leads to either a lack of perfusion of brain tissue or a lack of sufficient oxygenation of the blood perfusing the brain tissue. As the brain tissue begins to die, a complex event called a neuronal cascade begins, further increasing intracranial pressure and compromising both blood flow and oxygen delivery. The visible result is cerebral edema, which, in its extreme, results in a pattern of injury known as the "bad black brain." In this imaging picture the structures of the brain are obscured and the ventricles are often compressed due to the increased intracranial pressure. This results in an extremely poor prognosis.

# Head Trauma

**Case Study 3-1**

This 5-month-old girl was beaten to death with a broom by her father in a domestic argument with her mother. These photographs were taken at autopsy.

***Figures 3-1-a, b, c,*** *and* ***d.*** *Bruises are seen on the face. Pattern injuries, especially on the right eye, are indicative of a broom. Frequently, subgaleal hemorrhage (blood beneath the scalp) is seen with external injuries such as these. If the subgaleal bleeding is extensive enough, it may be seen on CT scans or at autopsy upon reflecting the scalp backwards.*

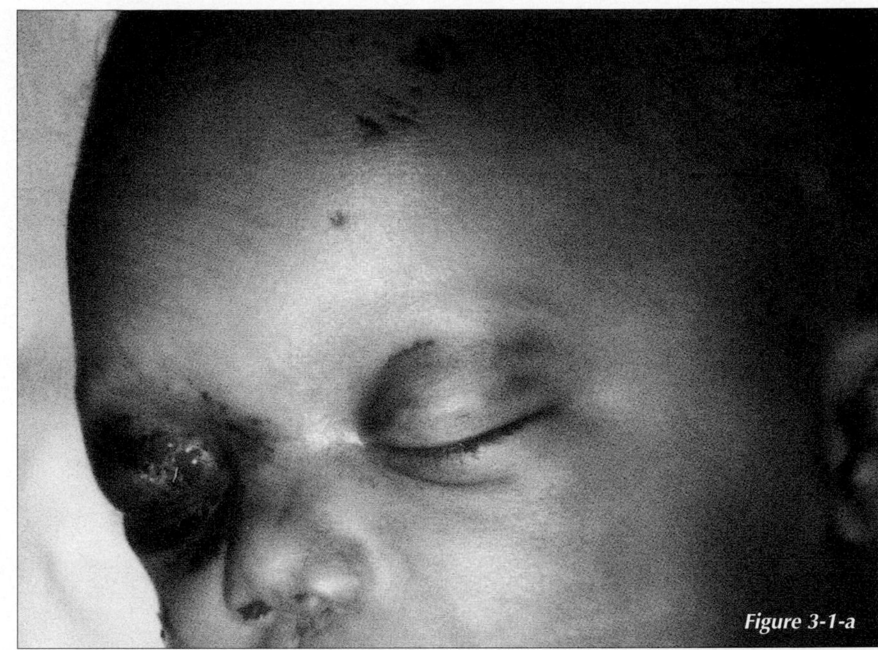

***Figure 3-1-a***

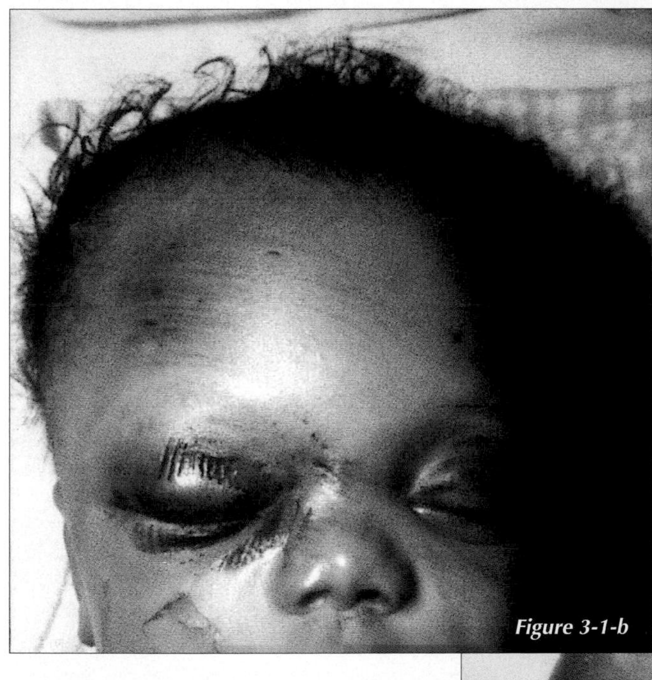

***Figure 3-1-b***

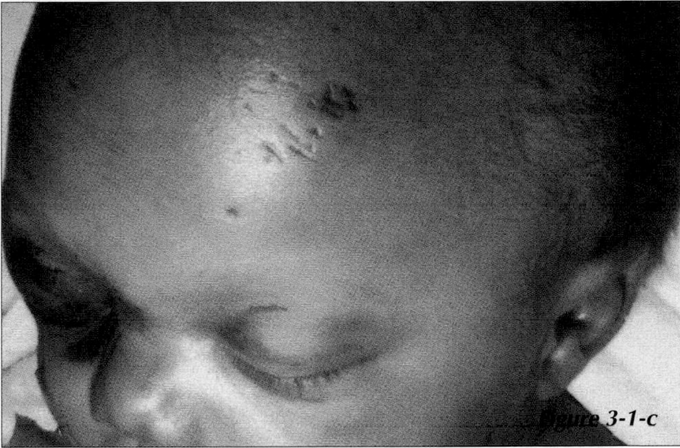

***Figure 3-1-c***

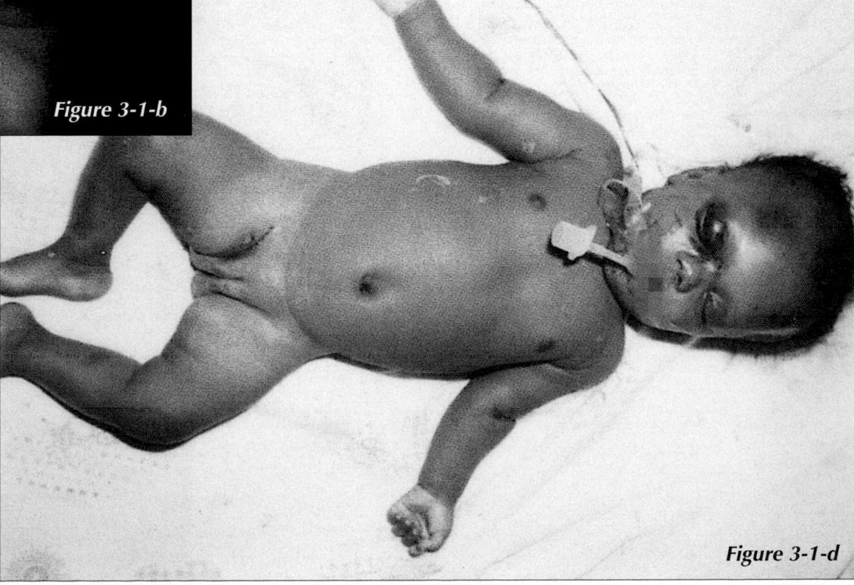

***Figure 3-1-d***

# Head Trauma

**Case Study 3-1** *(continued)*

***Figures 3-1-e, f,*** *and* ***g.*** *Radiographs showing multiple skull fractures. Such fractures would not be the result of a single blow (eg, being "caught in the crossfire" of an argument between two adults), but are the result of a repeated blows to the child's head indicative of a specific beating.*

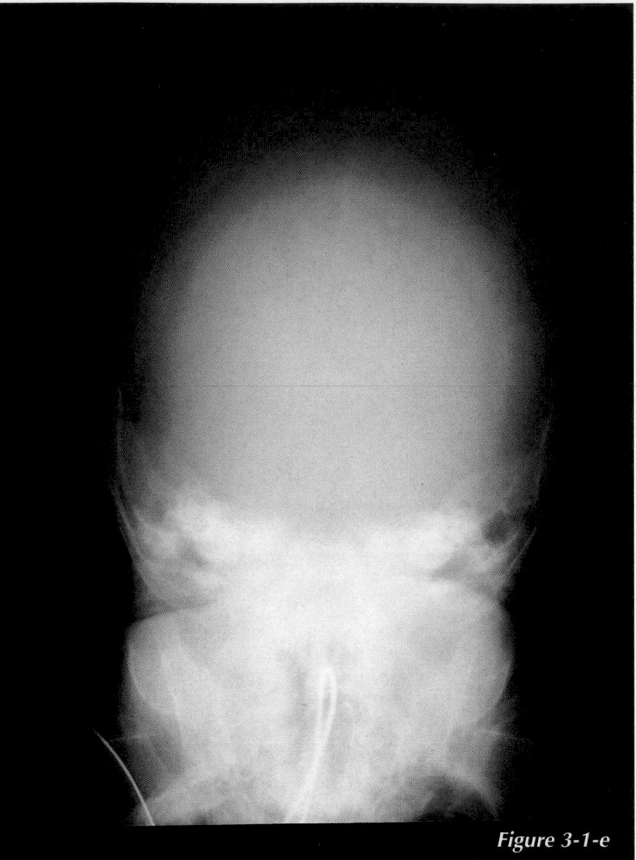

Figure 3-1-e

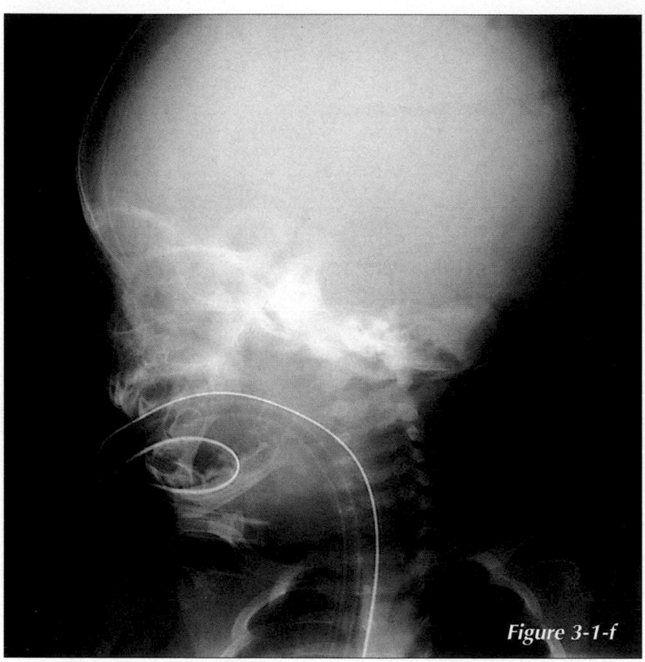

Figure 3-1-f

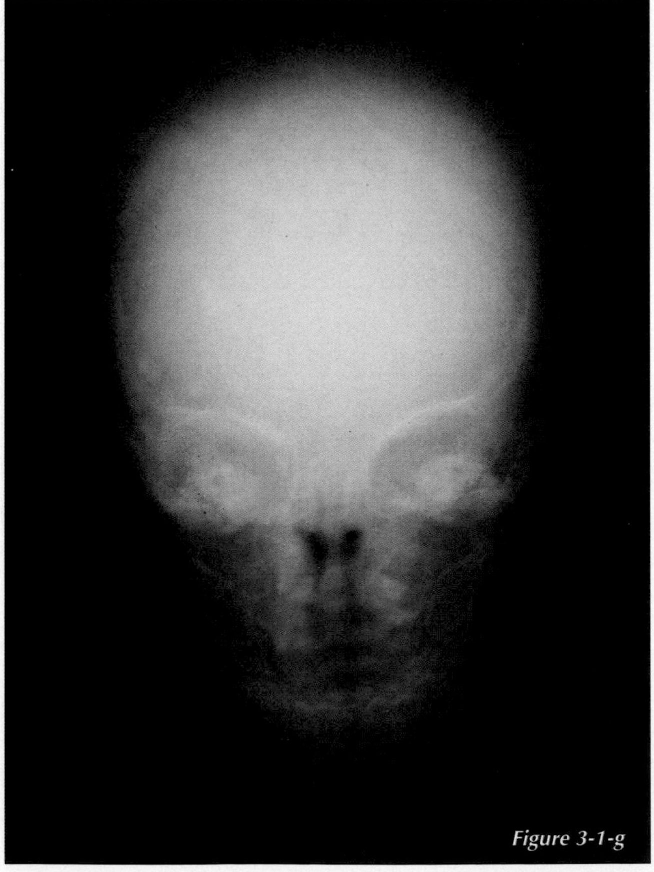

Figure 3-1-g

# Head Trauma

**Case Study 3-2**

This 5-month-old boy was being watched by a caregiver in the living room at night. He was discovered in the early morning to be not breathing. He was pronounced dead shortly after arrival to the ER. Bilateral retinal hemorrhages were noted, as well as multiple bruises around the body and mouth for which no history was provided. The child died relatively suddenly before extensive cerebral edema could develop, due to either the injuries inducing cessation of breathing or additional suffocation.

***Figure 3-2-a.*** *Multiple bruises are evident around the body, especially around the mouth. They are most likely caused by some type of forceful suffocation with a firm surface, such as a hand.*

***Figure 3-2-b.*** *A torn frenulum labii superioris. This is the result of impact, force feeding of food, or shearing secondary to a suffocation attempt.*

***Figure 3-2-c.*** *A right subdural hemorrhage adherent to the skull. The brain is swollen bilaterally, but not to the extent often seen. Note that the gyri are not as flattened as would be expected.*

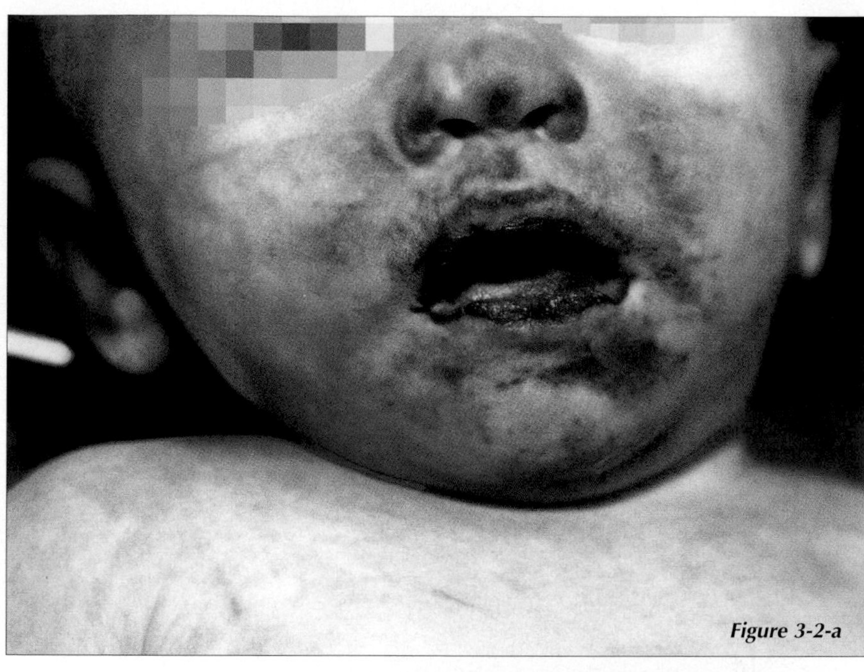

**Figure 3-2-a**

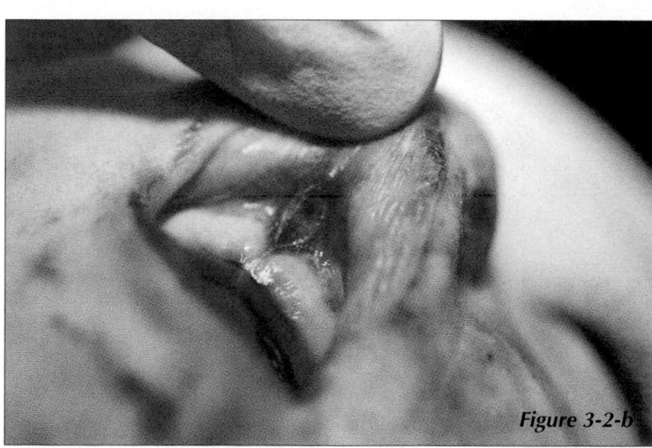

**Figure 3-2-b**

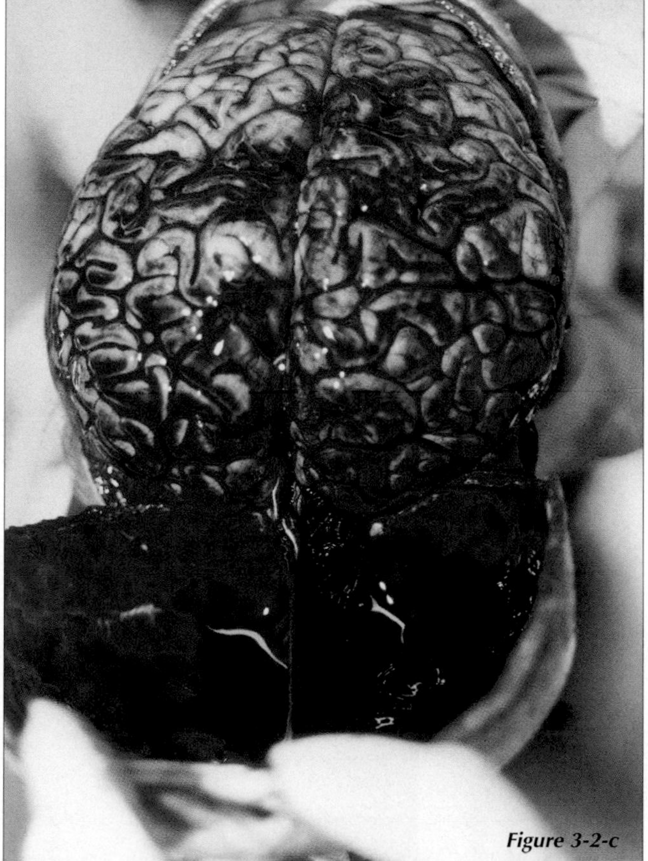

**Figure 3-2-c**

# Head Trauma

### Case Study 3-3

This 7-month-old boy was admitted to the hospital with the history that he fell off a mattress eight inches to the floor, had seizures, and became unresponsive. A thin layer of subdural hemorrhage over both cerebral convexities and small retinal hemorrhages were found.

***Figure 3-3-a.*** *There is substantial bruising to the right forehead.*

***Figure 3-3-b.*** *There is a contusion of the inner lower lip that is the result of impact, force feeding of food, or injury secondary to an attempt at suffocation.*

***Figure 3-3-c.*** *Right frontal subgaleal hemorrhage found during autopsy. This corresponds to the area of bruising noted on the forehead. However, it is possible to have either external bruising or subgaleal hemorrhage without the other being present.*

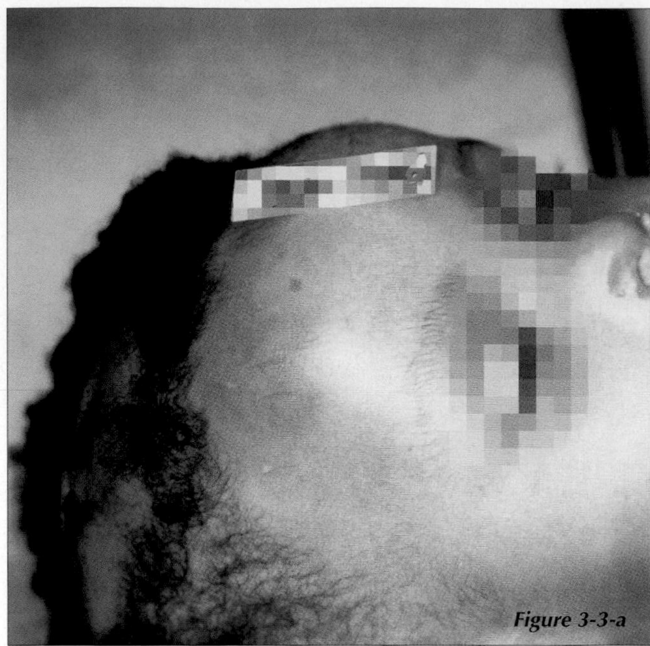

Figure 3-3-a

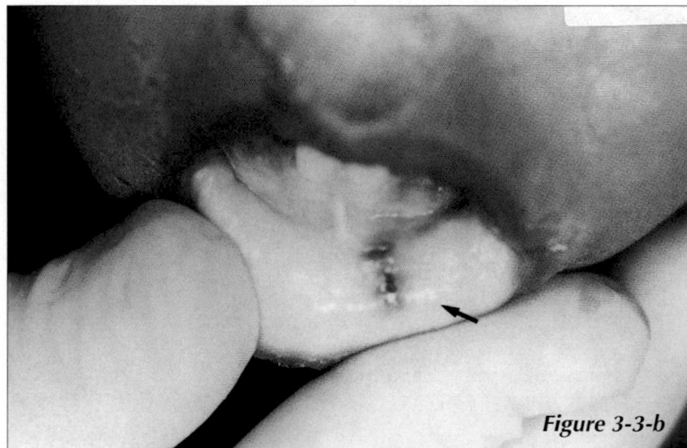

Figure 3-3-b

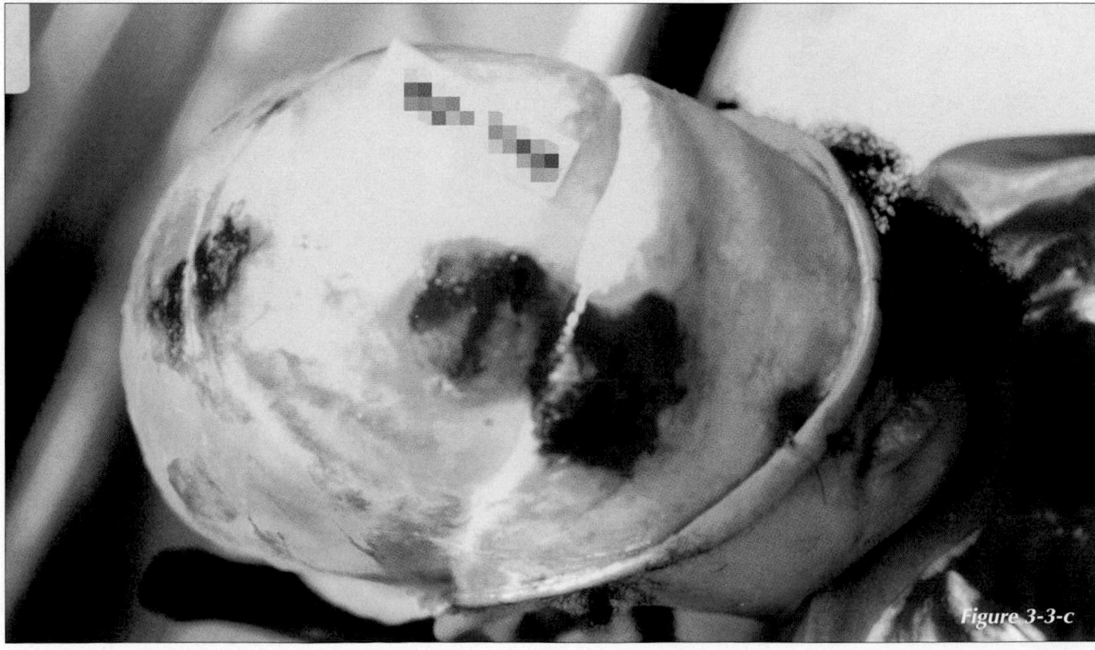

Figure 3-3-c

# Head Trauma

**Case Study 3-4**

A marked hemorrhage was found in the optic nerve of this child, who was the victim of abusive head trauma. Optic nerve sheath hemorrhages are often found at autopsies of children who are victims of shaken baby syndrome, although this finding is not specific to shaken baby syndrome.

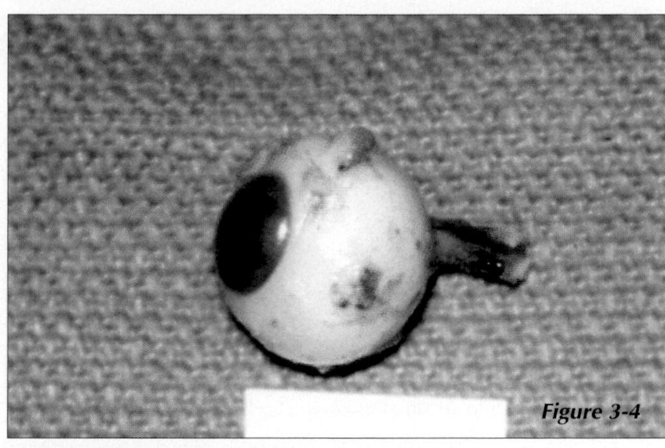

***Figure 3-4.*** *External aspect of the eye with marked hemorrhage in the optic nerve sheath.*

**Case Study 3-5**

This child was dying of abusive head trauma injuries, including numerous and scattered retinal hemorrhages.

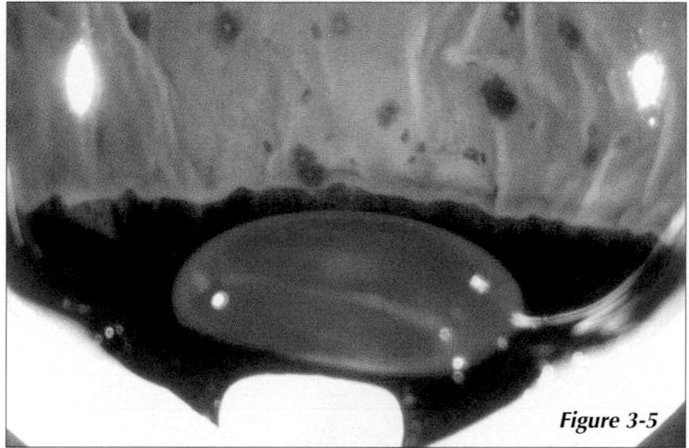

***Figure 3-5.*** *Close-up photograph of the sectioned eye, showing small retinal hemorrhages extending almost to the* **ora serrata** *(junction of the retina extending forward to behind the iris). Retinal hemorrhages that extend to the ora serrata are almost never seen in any condition except shaken baby syndrome. The yellow lens and clear* **vitreous** *(fluid in the center of the eye) are also seen.*

**Case Study 3-6**

This infant suffered an abusive head injury that led to his death.

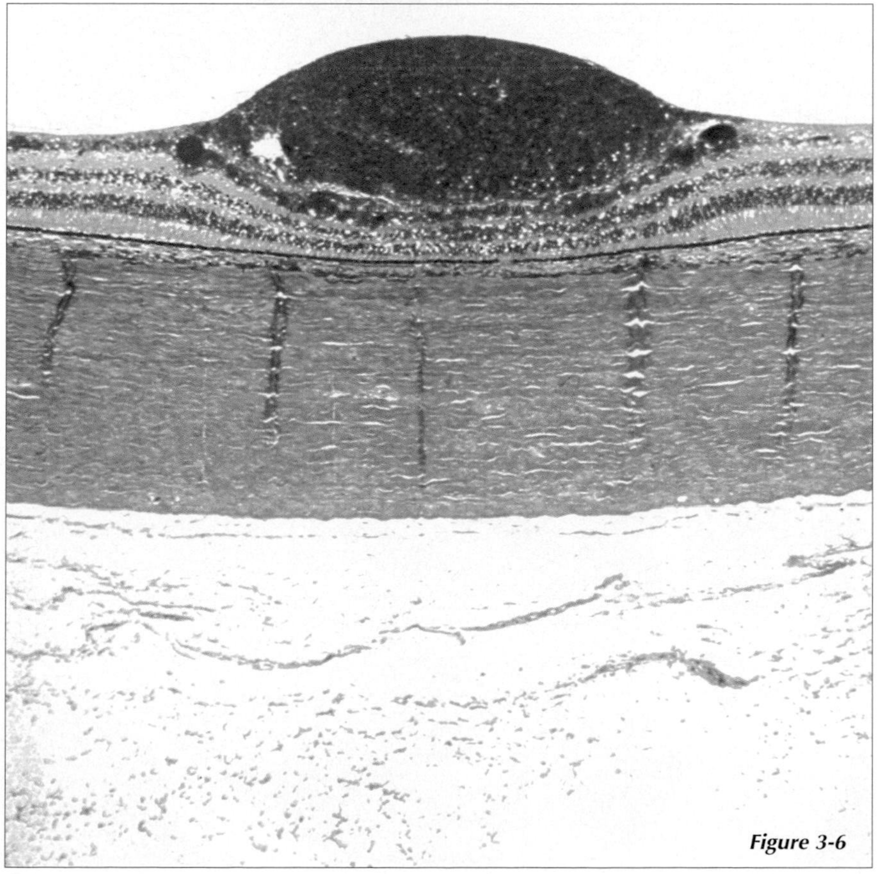

***Figure 3-6.*** *Photomicrograph of a portion of the eye showing a small retinal schisis cavity filled with blood. Note the multiple layers of the retina compressed by this hemorrhage.*

# HEAD TRAUMA

**Case Study 3-7**

This 5-month-old had a history of increasing head circumference and developmental delay. Such findings warrant imaging of the head to determine whether some intracranial explanation exists. Subdural hematomas of multiple ages were subsequently documented.

***Figure 3-7-a** and **b.** CT scans showing large bilateral chronic subdural hematomas with a hyperdense acute component on the patient's left side (appearing on the right side of **Figure 3-7-a** midway along the brain surface).*

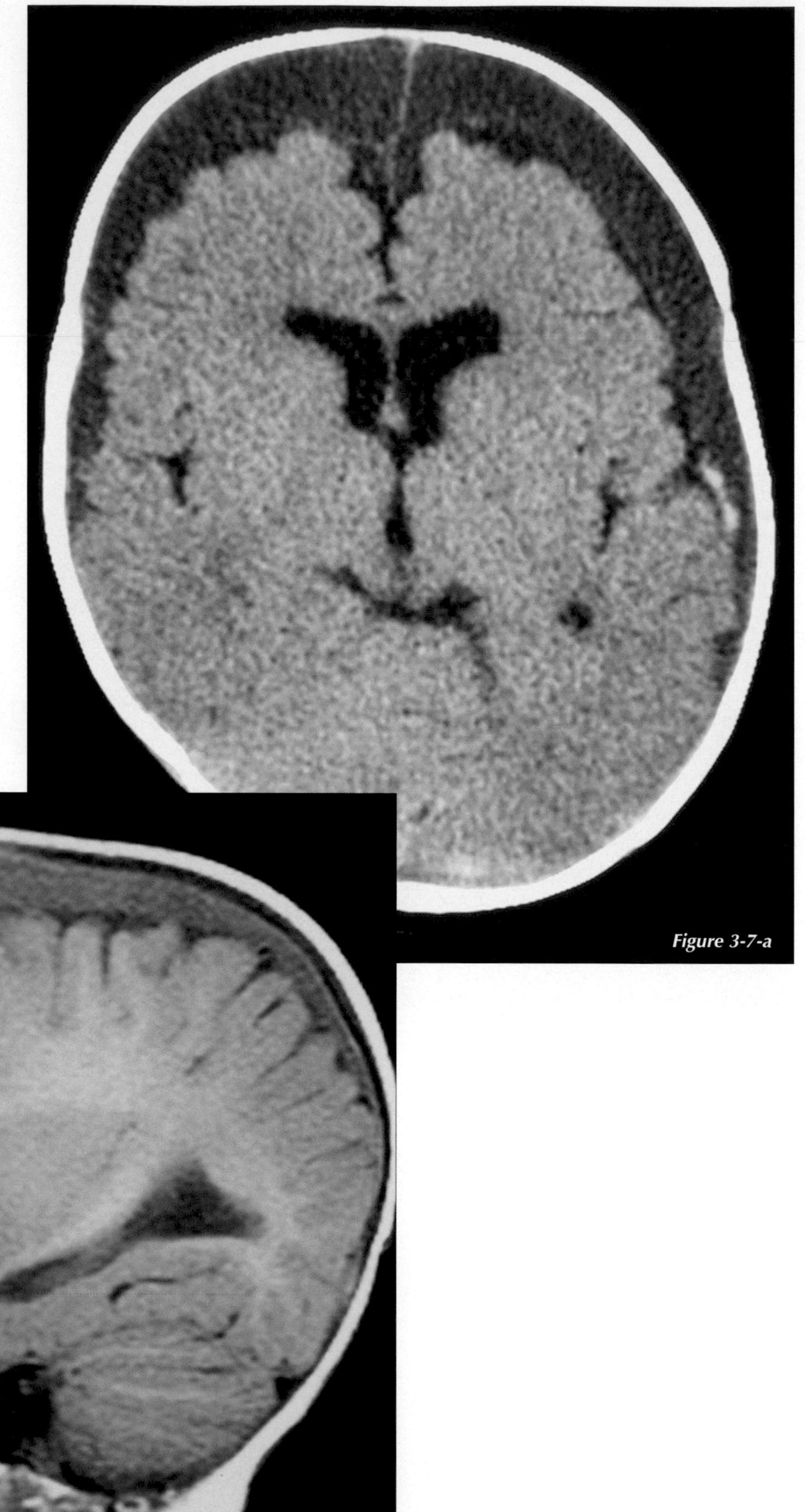

***Figure 3-7-a***

***Figure 3-7-b***

# Head Trauma

**Case Study 3-7** *(continued)*

***Figure 3-7-c.*** *MRI scan with sagittal T1- and axial T2-weighted images confirm these findings.*

***Figure 3-7-d.*** *Gradient echo images best demonstrate different ages of hemorrhage with a dark acute component and hemosiderin staining of the dura mater.*

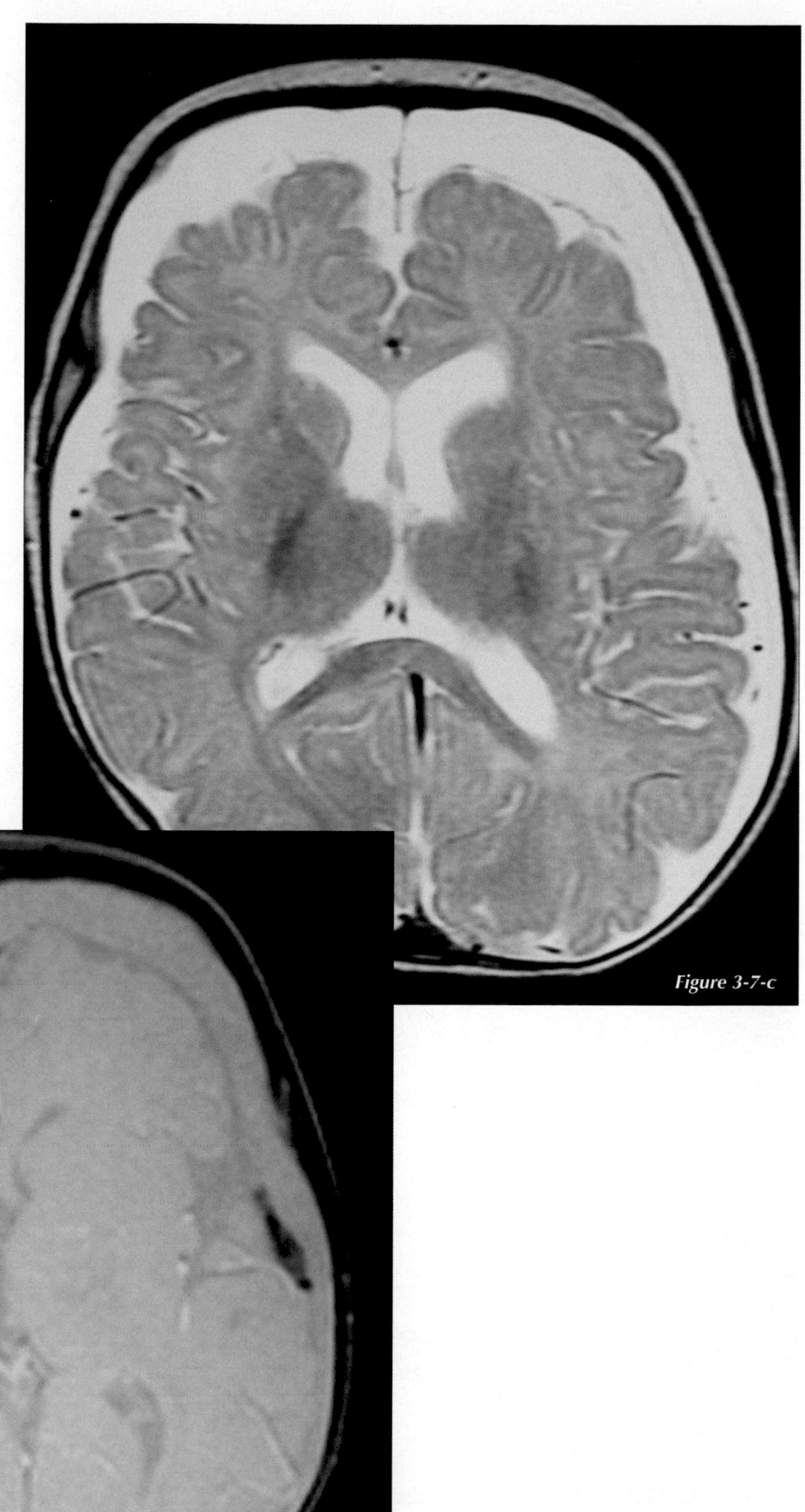

Figure 3-7-c

Figure 3-7-d

# Head Trauma

**Case Study 3-8**

This 16-month-old girl was admitted to the hospital with a closed head injury. Her mother eventually admitted that her boyfriend beat the child and threw her against the metal headboard of a bed. The boyfriend's actions are physical abuse and the mother's failure to initially inform the physicians of the correct history is neglect.

***Figure 3-8-a.*** *There is a large contusion of the right forehead that is consistent with an impact injury.*

***Figure 3-8-b*** *and* ***c.*** *Multiple areas of bruising are seen beneath the scalp when it is pulled back from the skull at autopsy. This subgaleal bleeding does not always correspond with an external bruise.*

***Figure 3-8-d.*** *Thin layers of subdural blood are seen over both cerebral convexities. The external bruising, subgaleal bleeding, and subdural bleeding are not the cause of death. However, they indicate the considerable forces used that were transmitted to the brain, resulting in fatal brain injury.*

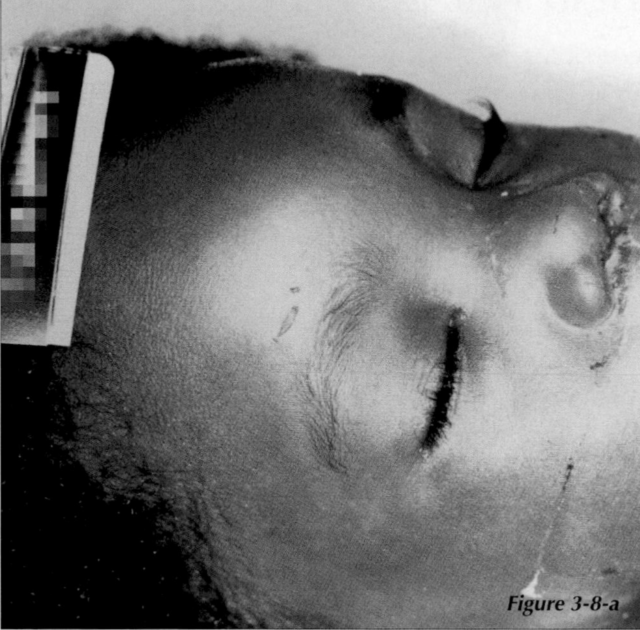

Figure 3-8-a

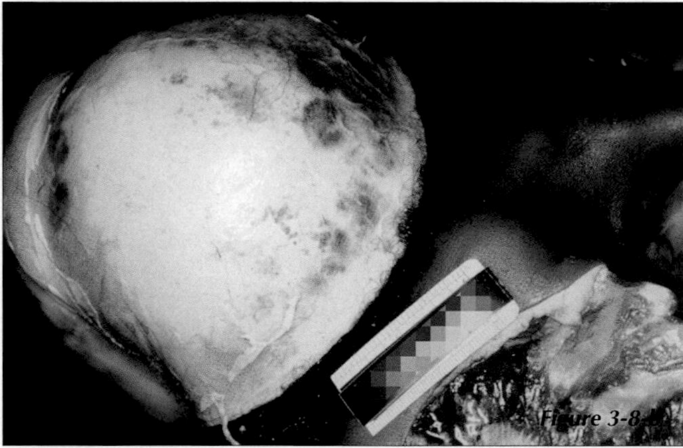

Figure 3-8-b

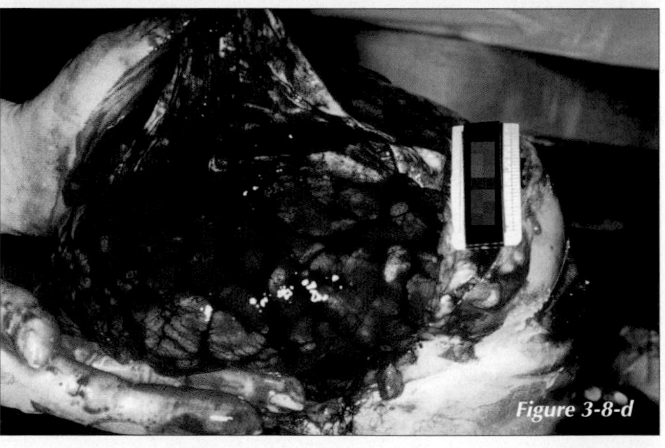

Figure 3-8-d

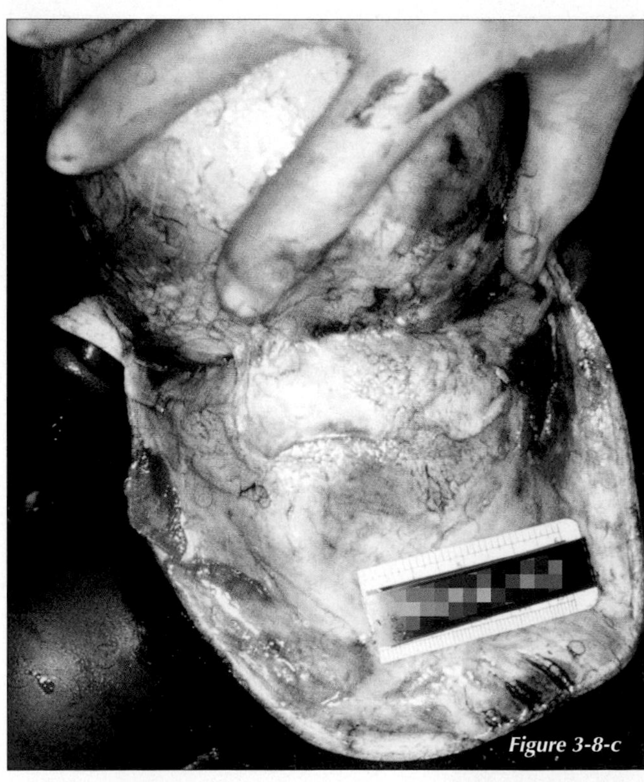

Figure 3-8-c

# Head Trauma

**Case Study 3-9**

This 23-month-old boy was left with the mother's boyfriend who said the child "disappeared." The child was found in a plastic bag on the roof of the apartment building the next day, frozen due to subzero weather. Such "disposal" of children to the elements is more common with infants; older children are more able to move or cry out effectively and be found if they are still alive.

***Figure 3-9-a.*** *The child as found in a black plastic trash bag.*

***Figure 3-9-b.*** *Large subgaleal hemorrhages beneath the scalp indicate multiple blows to the head.*

***Figure 3-9-c.*** *Small amounts of subdural hemorrhage over both cerebral convexities, indicating that the child was alive for a short period of time after the head injuries were sustained, allowing this much bleeding and brain injury to occur. Whether the child died of brain injuries alone or subsequent cold exposure requires further autopsy investigation.*

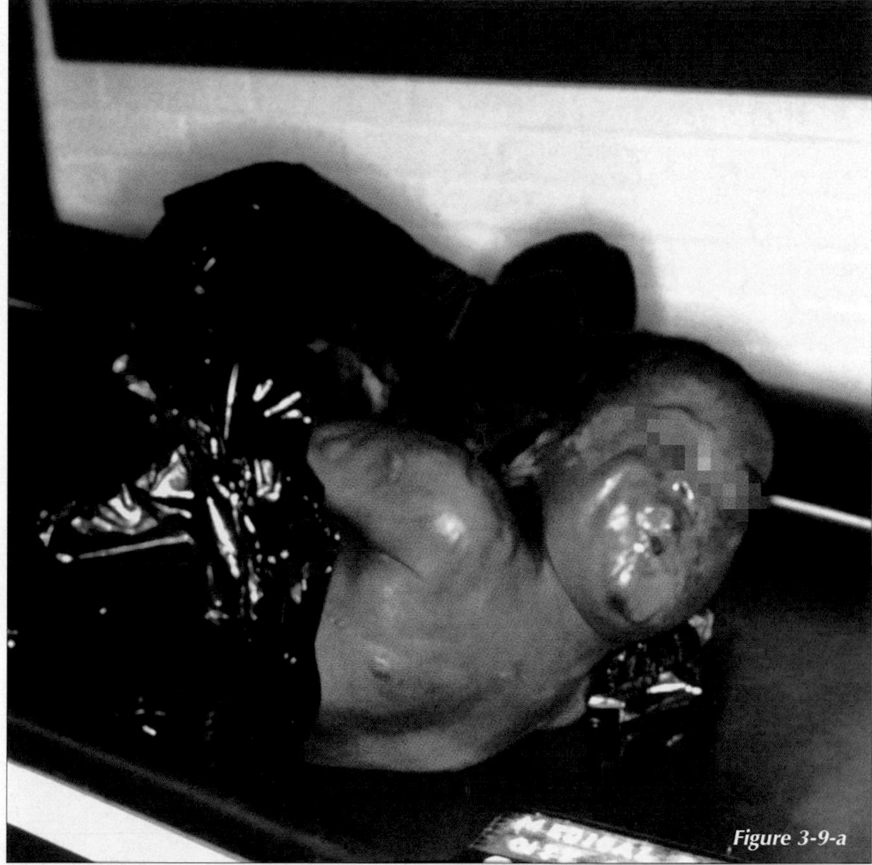
Figure 3-9-a

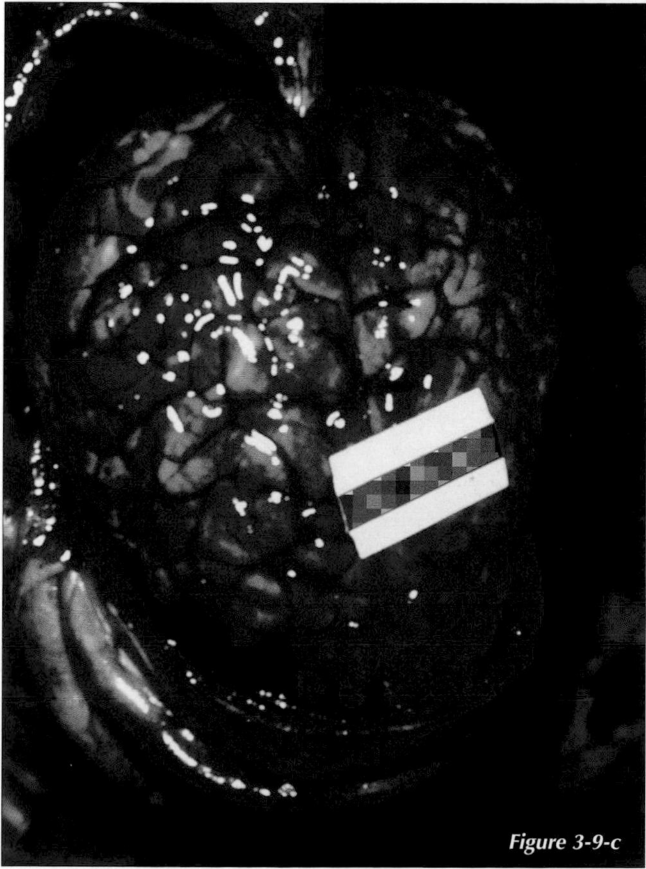
Figure 3-9-c

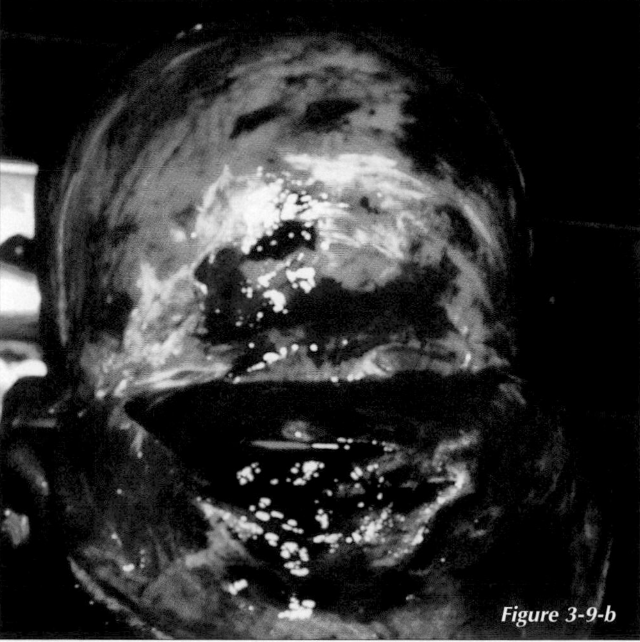
Figure 3-9-b

# Head Trauma

**Case Study 3-10**

This 3-month-old child was severely shaken. The presence of the subgaleal hematoma indicated that this instance of abusive head injury was likely caused by a combination of shaking and impact.

***Figure 3-10.*** *This CT scan shows a right-sided subgaleal hematoma with multiple associated subdural hematomas and brain injury.*

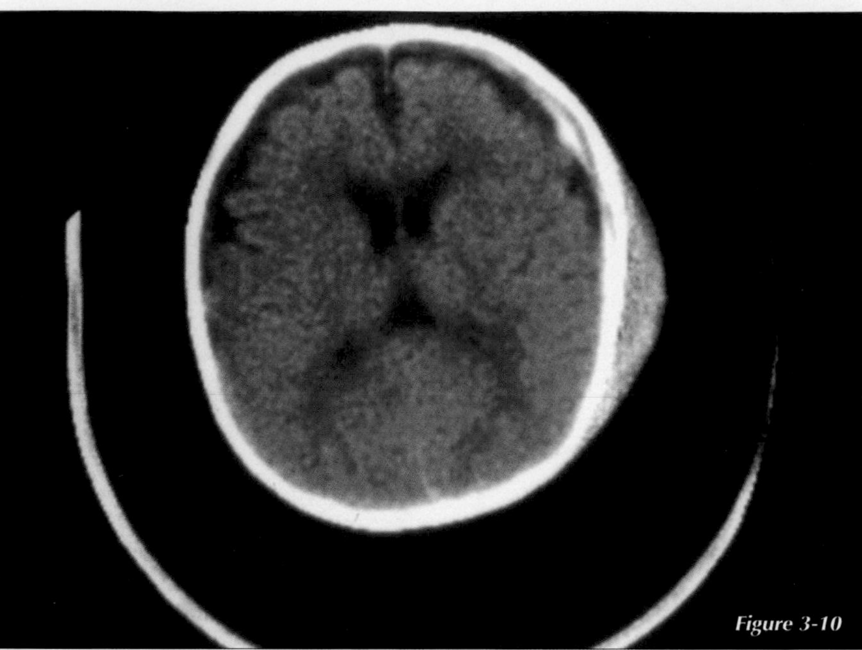

Figure 3-10

**Case Study 3-11**

This young infant showed a large bump on the head and was found to have a cephalhematoma, with bleeding beneath the periosteum external to the occipital bone. A large soft-tissue bump superior to the right parietal bone that stayed in the same location further documented cephalhematoma.

***Figure 3-11.*** *A skull radiograph in this child showing the large soft-tissue bump (hazy area above the skull) located superior to the right parietal bone. Notice that the sutures are also widely separated, indicating increased intracranial pressure secondary to the impact trauma.*

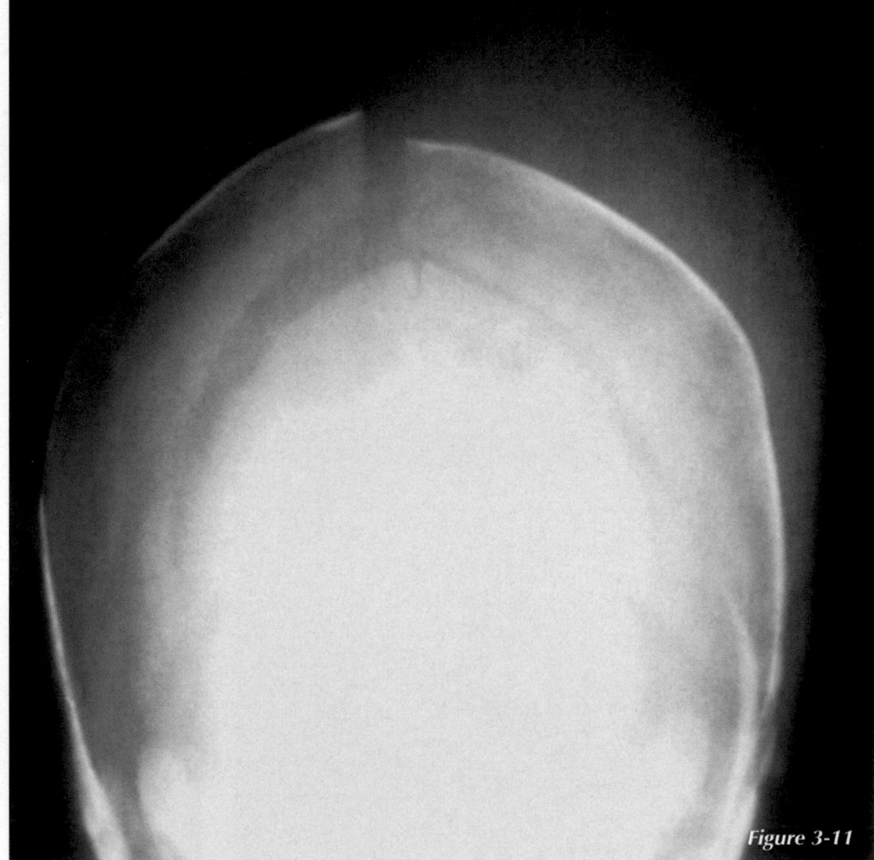

Figure 3-11

# Head Trauma

**Case Study 3-12**

This 4-month-old infant was the victim of abusive head trauma. An impact was seen on the left side of the infant's head toward the back and CT imaging was obtained.

***Figure 3-12.*** *There is a hyperdense (acute) hemorrhagic contusion in the left occipital lobe and a fracture of the overlying left occipital bone with a subgaleal hematoma.*

**Case Study 3-13**

This patient was the victim of a severe head injury that occurred when the child's head was slammed repeatedly against a doorframe.

***Figure 3-13.*** *A large fluid collection beneath the right side of the scalp in the subgaleal space is seen (left side of the image). In addition, there is a fracture of the skull, subdural blood, and brain injury. Subgaleal hematomas occur predominantly due to impact traumas.*

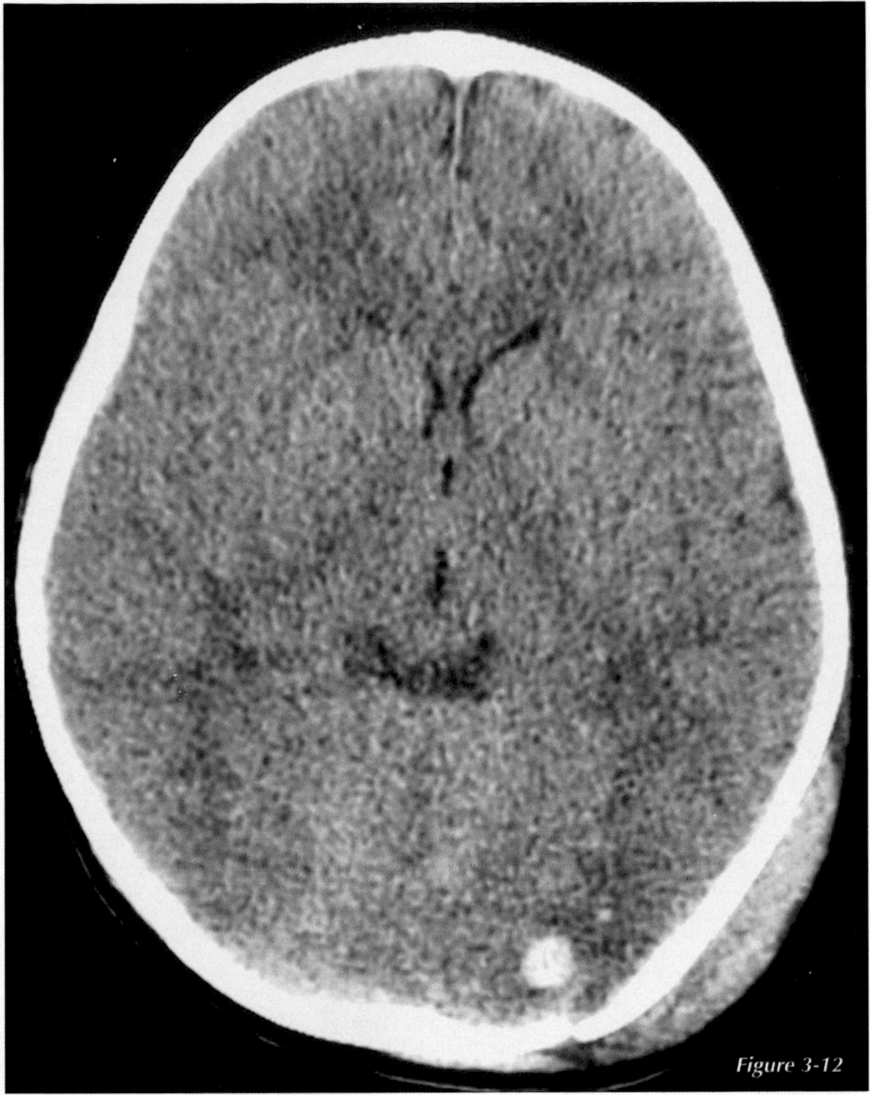

Figure 3-12

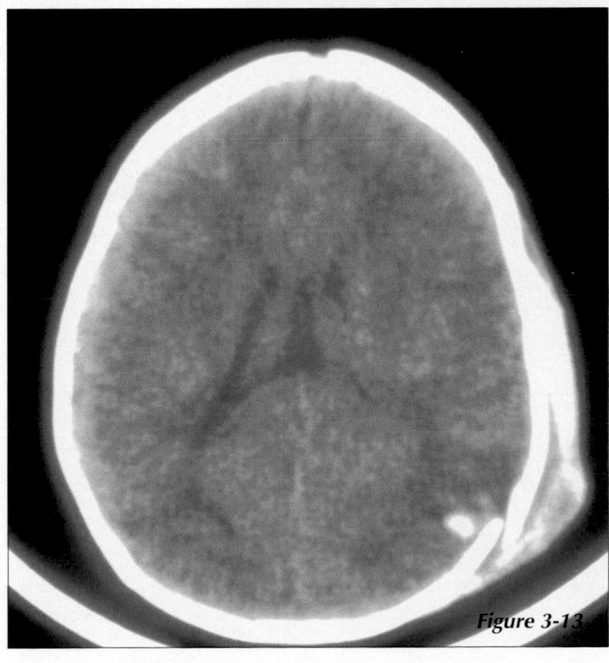

Figure 3-13

# Head Trauma

### Case Study 3-14

This 3-year-old girl reportedly fell from a bathroom counter six days before she was found cold and unconscious at home. Although she had initially vomited and had a fever for several days, she had seemed fine for three days. She was dead on arrival at the ER. It was stated later that she fell in the bathtub just before she died.

At autopsy, multiple scalp contusions were seen. There was a subdural hemorrhage, especially on the left side of the brain, as well as diffuse cerebral edema, bilateral retinal hemorrhages, optic nerve sheath hemorrhages, and a basilar skull fracture.

***Figure 3-14-a.*** *Multiple scalp contusions are evident. Not all of the scalp contusions are evident by external inspection since some are visible only on the undersurface of the scalp.*

***Figure 3-14-b.*** *Brain swelling is noted with smoothing of the gyri on both sides. The child's left side is even more swollen than the right.*

***Figure 3-14-c.*** *The inner portion of the skull shows adherent subdural hemorrhage on the left side of the brain (black-looking blood).*

**Figure 3-14-a**

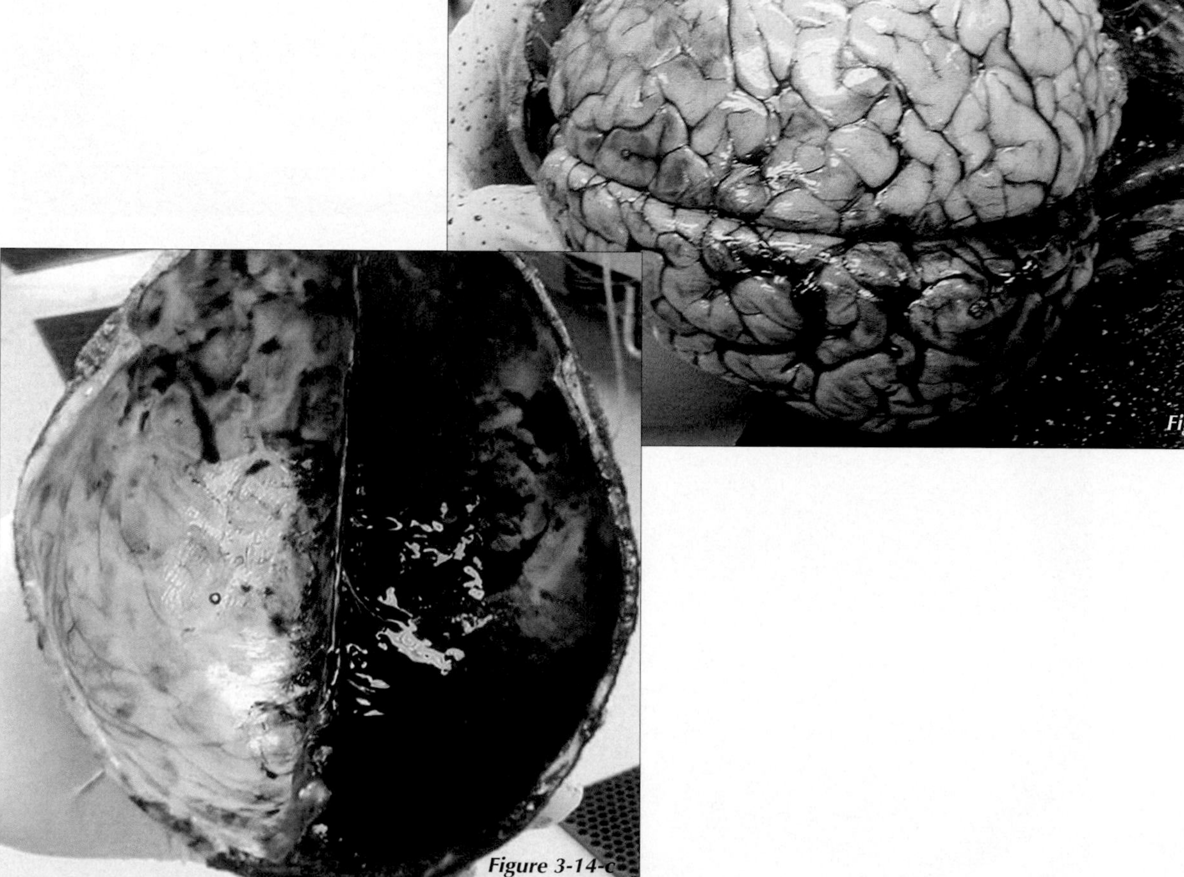

**Figure 3-14-b**

**Figure 3-14-c**

# Head Trauma

**Case Study 3-15**

This 6-month-old child with a lump on his head and flattening of the left occipital bone was left lying on his back after being knocked unconscious during an episode of abuse.

***Figure 3-15.*** *The child has an occult skull fracture and a subgaleal hematoma on the left side of the head. The brain appears relatively normal with no midline shift. The subgaleal hematoma is predominantly located posteriorly because the child was left on his back.*

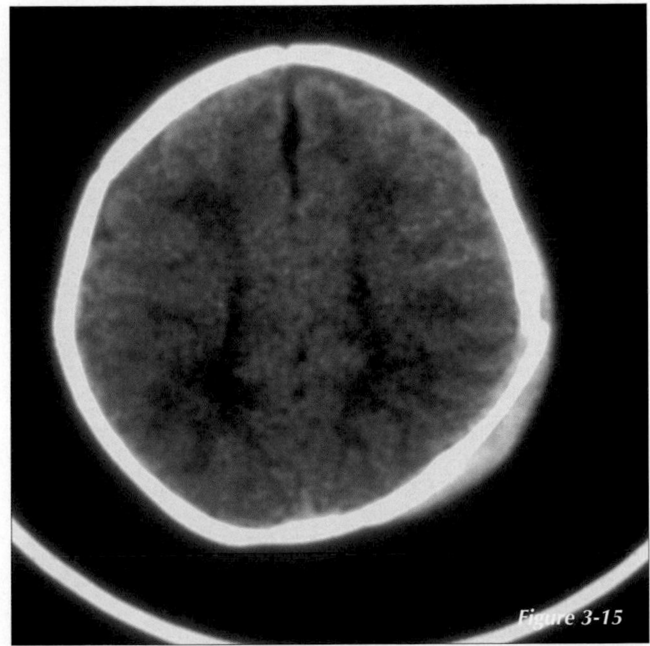

Figure 3-15

**Case 3-16**

This 6-month-old boy was found dead in a crib at the babysitter's home with no history of trauma. Mandatory autopsy laws help to distinguish between sudden infant death syndrome (SIDS) and instances of abuse where the child is alleged to have died in his sleep.

***Figures 3-16-a*** *and* ***b.*** *There is a 5-cm contusion on the right occipital scalp.*

Figure 3-16-a

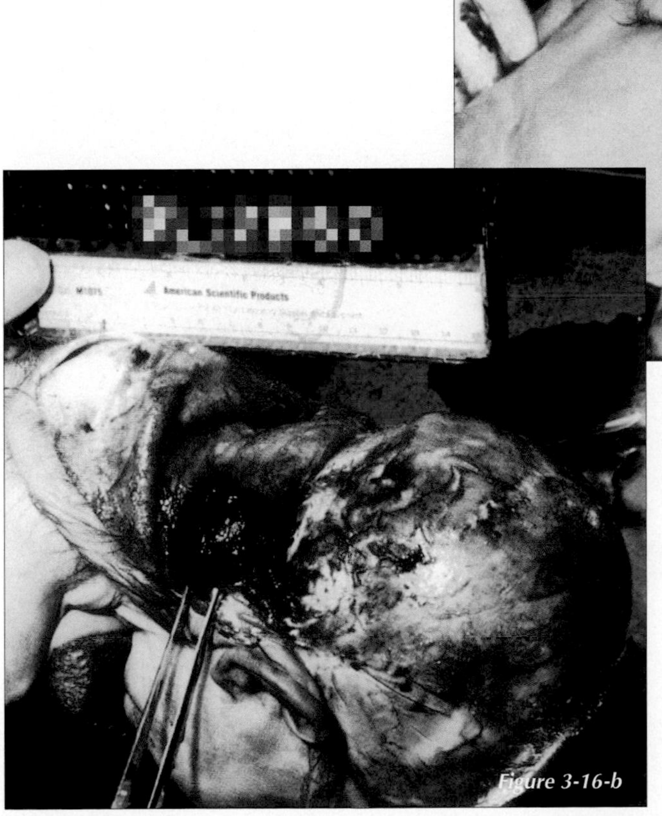


Figure 3-16-b

# Head Trauma

**Case 3-16** *(continued)*

***Figures 3-16-c*** *and* ***d.*** *Autopsy further revealed a linear fracture of the adjacent right posterior fossa and an epidural hemorrhage of 6 to 8 ml in the right posterior.*

***Figure 3-16-e.*** *There is a marked flattening of the adjacent right occipital pole indicating extensive increased intracranial pressure on this side.*

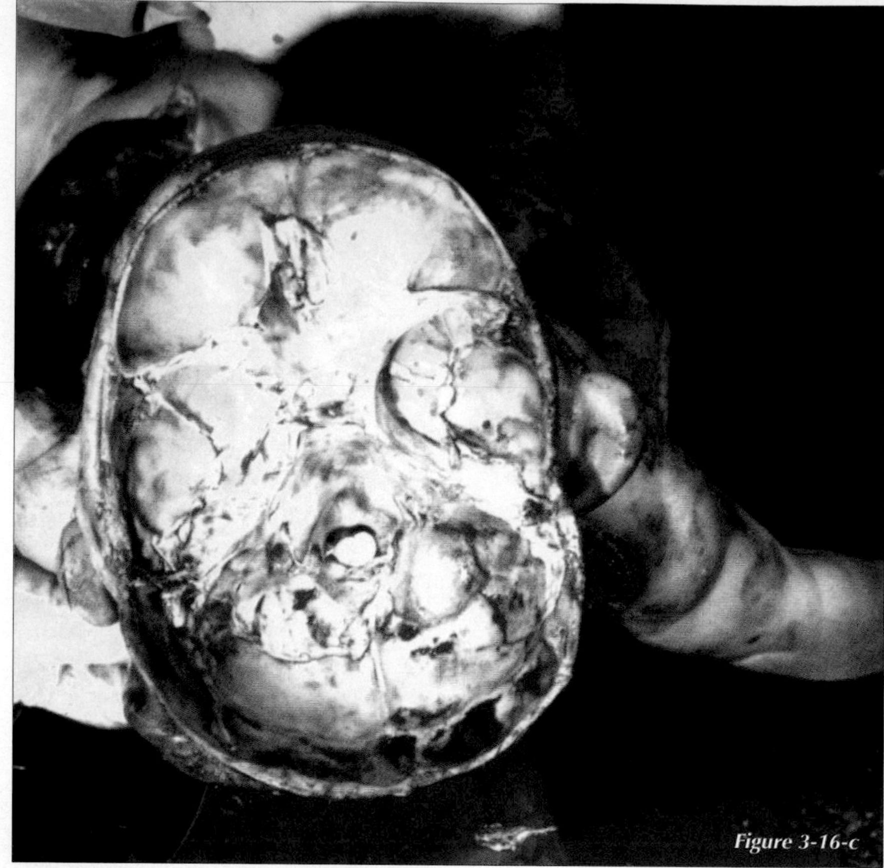

Figure 3-16-c

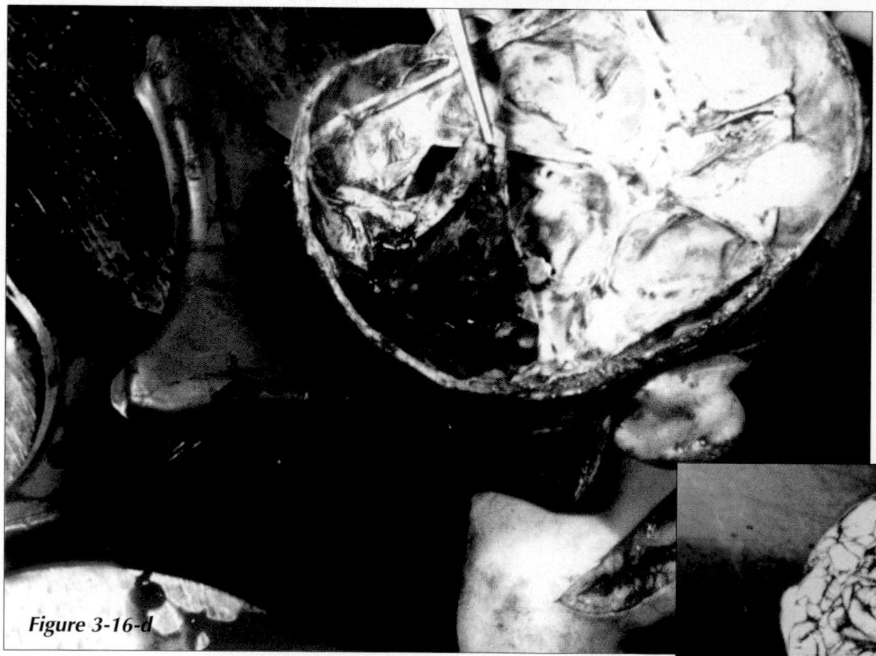

Figure 3-16-d

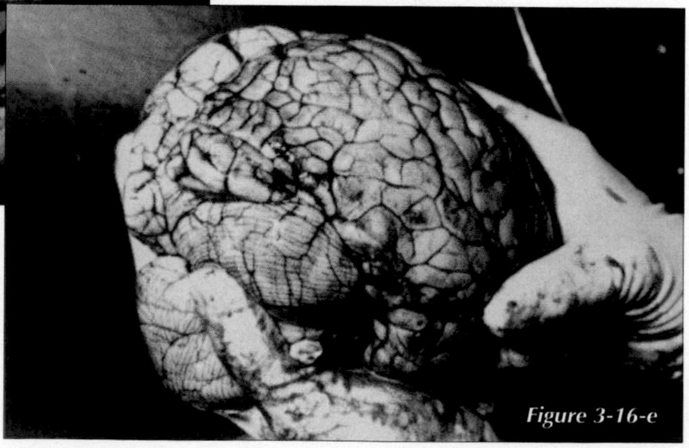

Figure 3-16-e

# Head Trauma

**Case Study 3-17**

This infant suffered a head injury after being involved in an automobile accident.

***Figures 3-17-a*** *and* ***b.*** *The infant has a diastatic fracture of the right parietal bone. Note that the fracture margins are widely separated, indicating a high-velocity impact injury or a severe force applied to the skull. Accidental (short fall) injuries are usually linear, short in length, and pencil-line thin. Short falls to flat surfaces should not be fatal.*

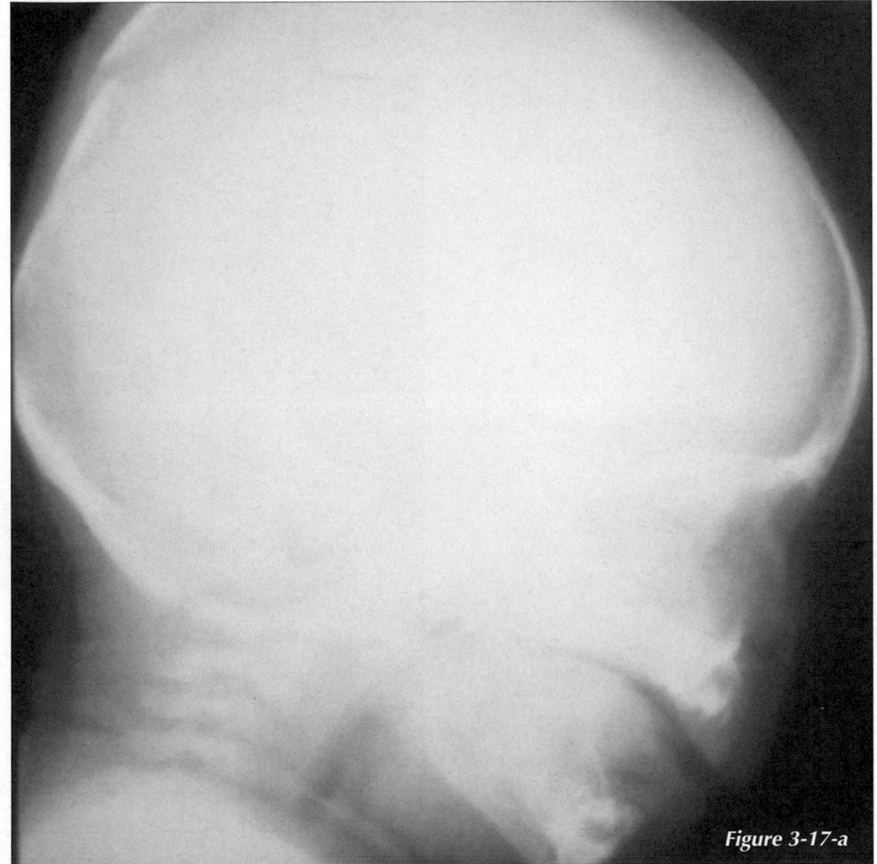

Figure 3-17-a

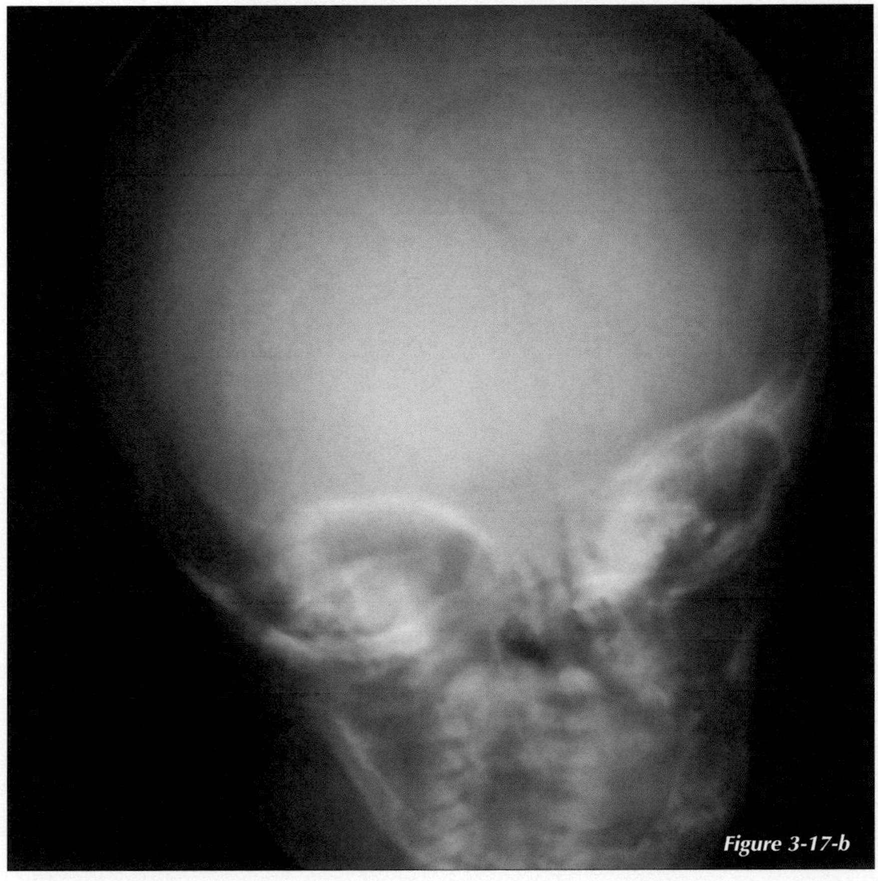

Figure 3-17-b

# Head Trauma

**Case Study 3-18**

This child was found to have multiple skull fractures.

***Figures 3-18-a** and **b.** One of the skull fractures has an associated subgaleal hemorrhage above the fracture.*

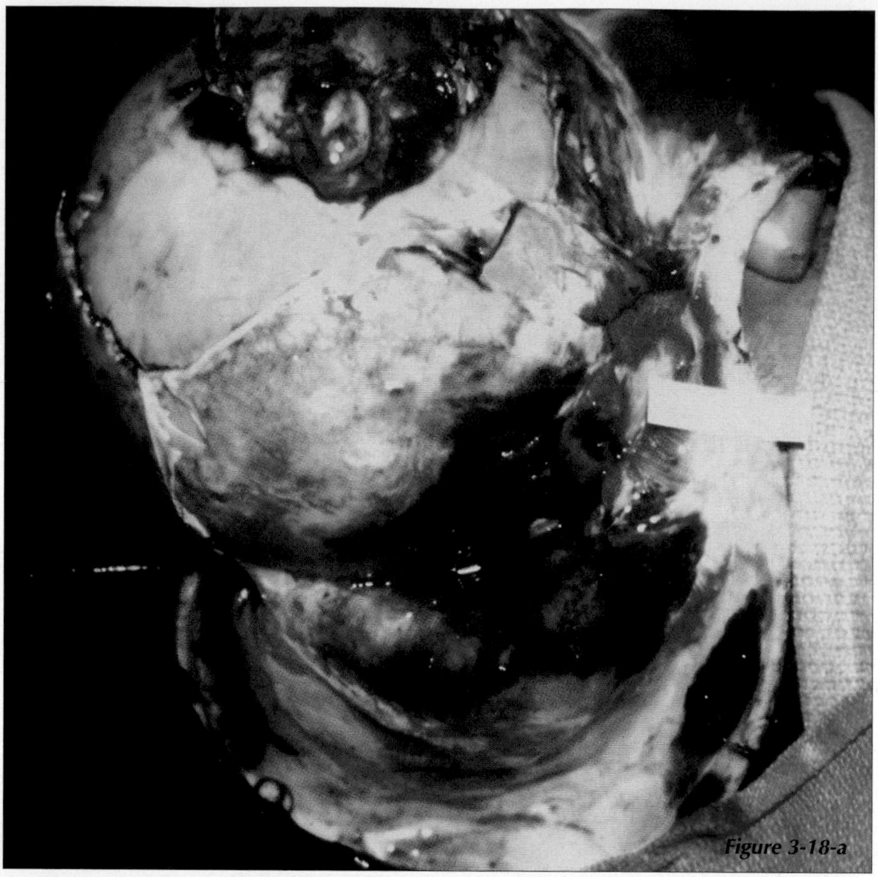

Figure 3-18-a

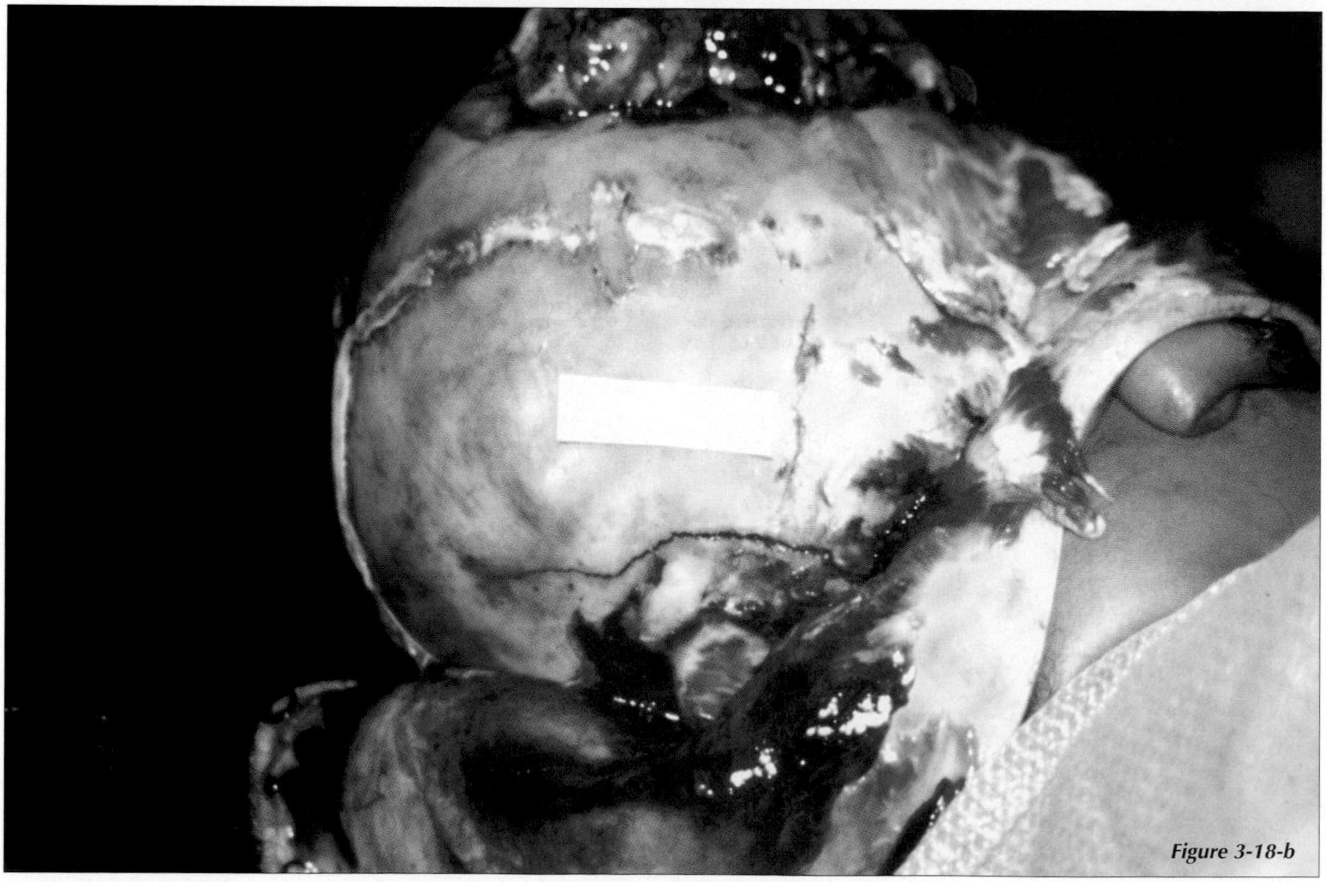

Figure 3-18-b

# Head Trauma

**Case Study 3-18** *(continued)*

***Figures 3-18-c, d,*** *and* **e.** *Another skull fracture with an associated subgaleal hemorrhage and a thin underlying epidural hemorrhage.*

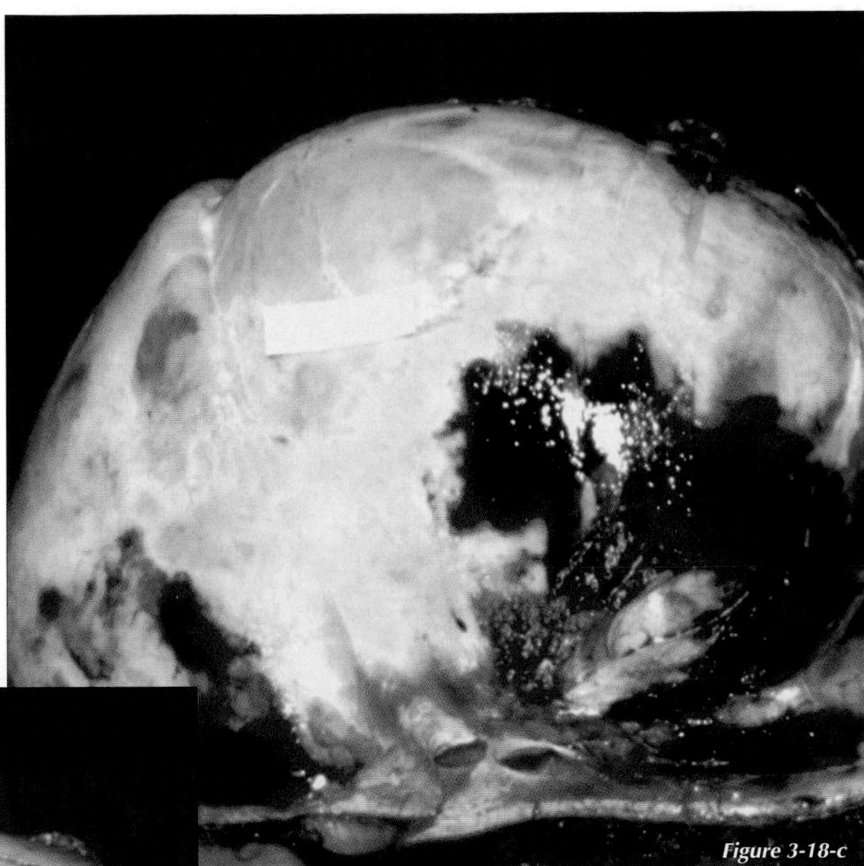

Figure 3-18-c

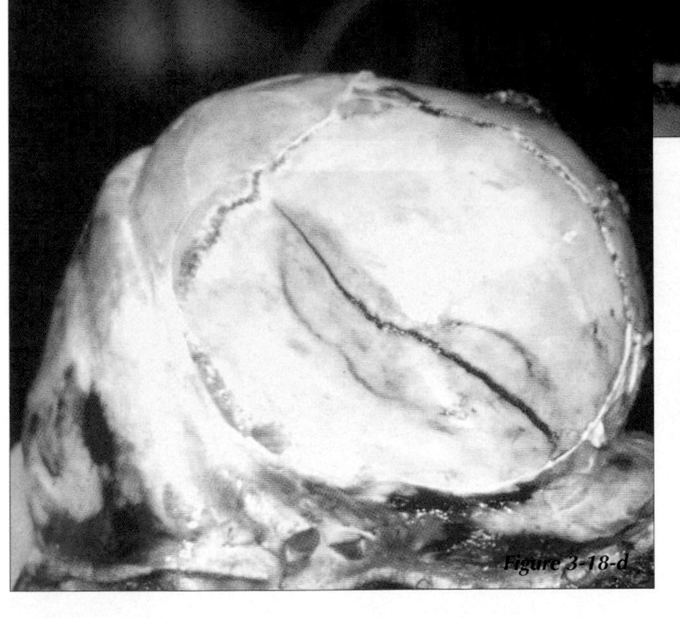

Figure 3-18-d

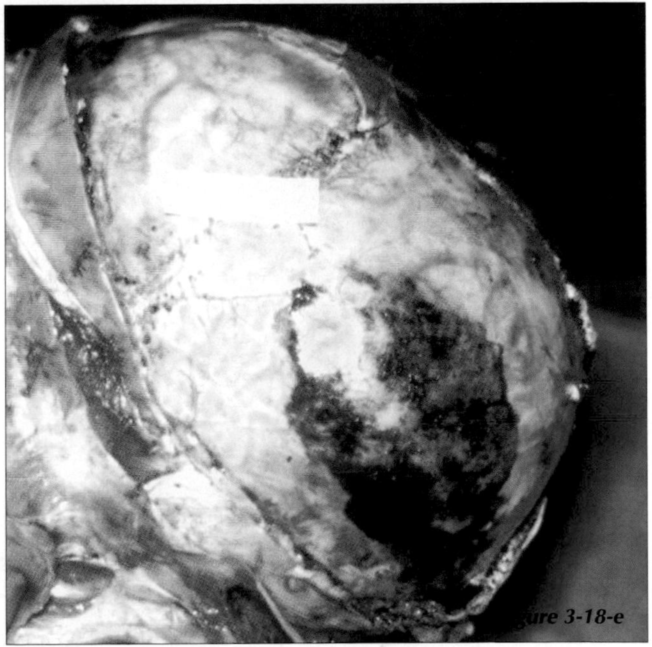

Figure 3-18-e

# Head Trauma

**Case Study 3-23**

Subdural hematomas are seen in many cases of abusive head injury. Infants, who are unable to place themselves in situations where major impact injury can occur, are more likely to be victims of shaken baby syndrome because of their smaller size.

***Figure 3-23.*** *Typically thin, non–space-occupying subdural hematomas in a vicim of abusive head injury.*

**Case 3-24**

This hematoma of small volume completely resorbed rather than becoming a chronic subdural fluid collection.

***Figure 3-24.*** *Yellow-brown discoloration of the inner aspect of the dura mater, indicating a previously resorped subdural hematoma. Resorption is typical of most subdural hematomas.*

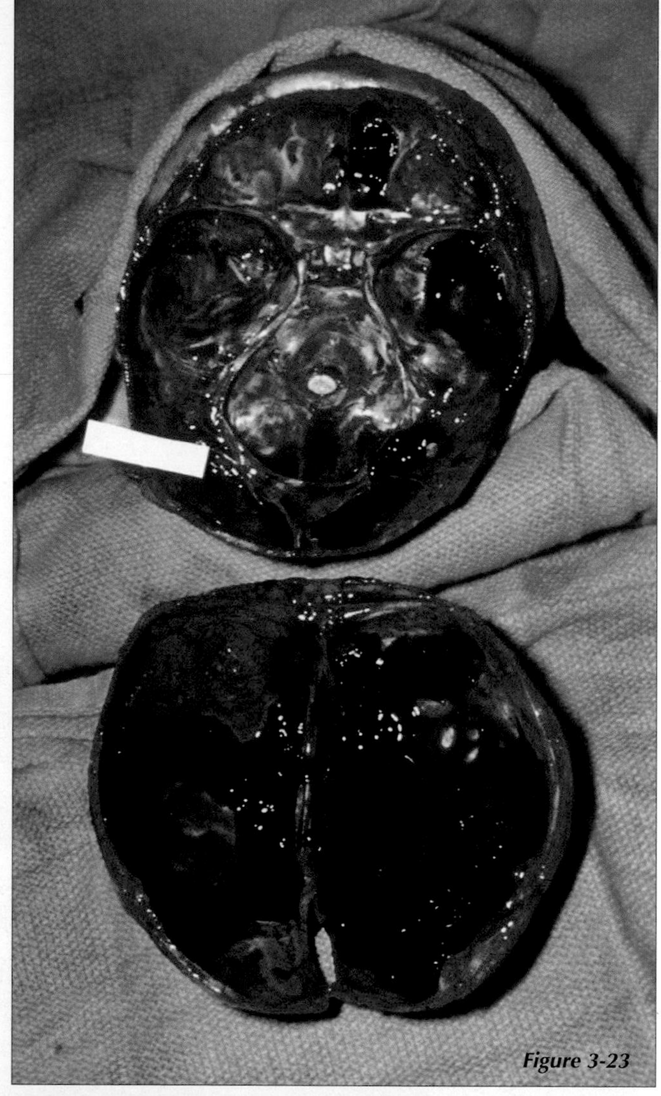

*Figure 3-23*

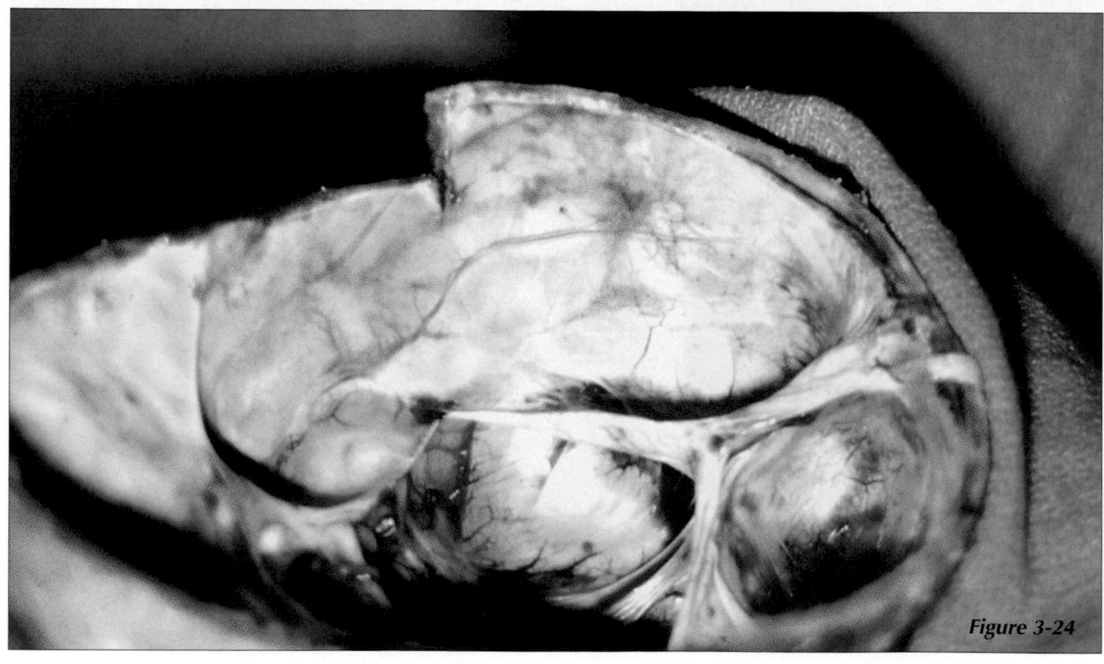

*Figure 3-24*

# Head Trauma

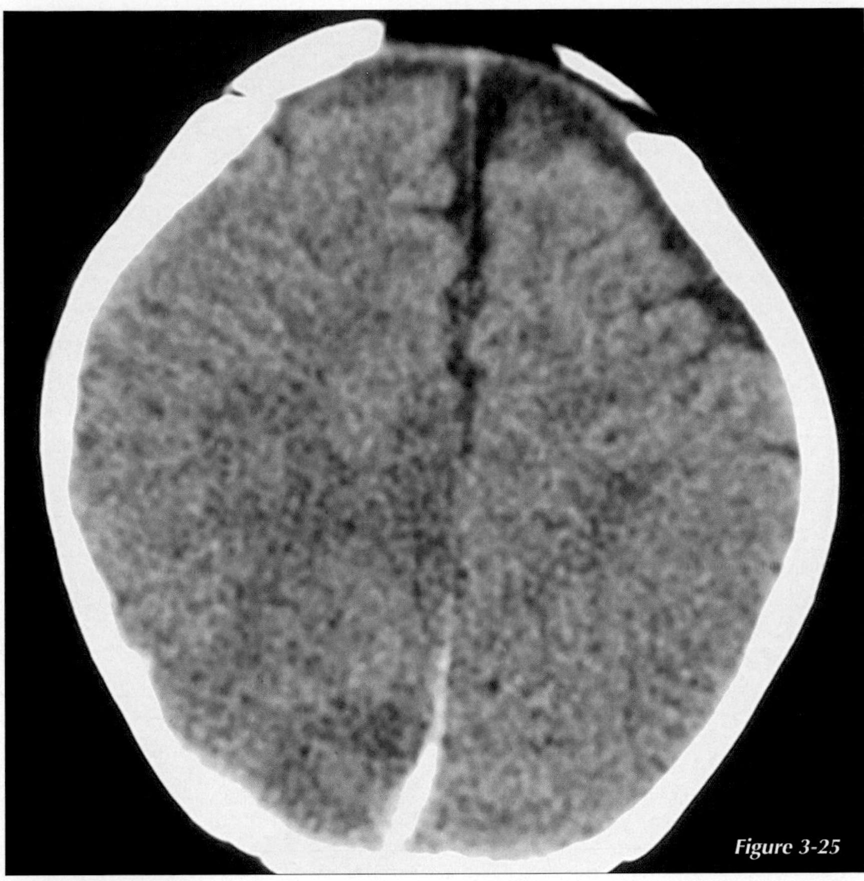
Figure 3-25

### Case Study 3-25

This 4-month-old male had an unsubstantiated history of being dropped by an older sibling. While older siblings may sometimes be old enough and strong enough to carry and drop their siblings, such falls are short and should not cause substantial injury. Siblings are often blamed in cases of abusive head trauma committed by adults.

***Figure 3-25.*** *An acute interhemispheric subdural hematoma in addition to a subtle low-attenuation nonhemorrhagic contusion in the right posterior parietal lobe.*

### Case Study 3-26

This 4-month-old child was brought to the hospital with lethargy and a history of possible sepsis. Since there was a suspicion of trauma, an MRI scan was subsequently performed.

***Figures 3-26-a** and **b.** CT scans showing an asymmetrical subdural fluid collection located in the right high parietal region with density slightly hyperdense to cerebrospinal fluid.*

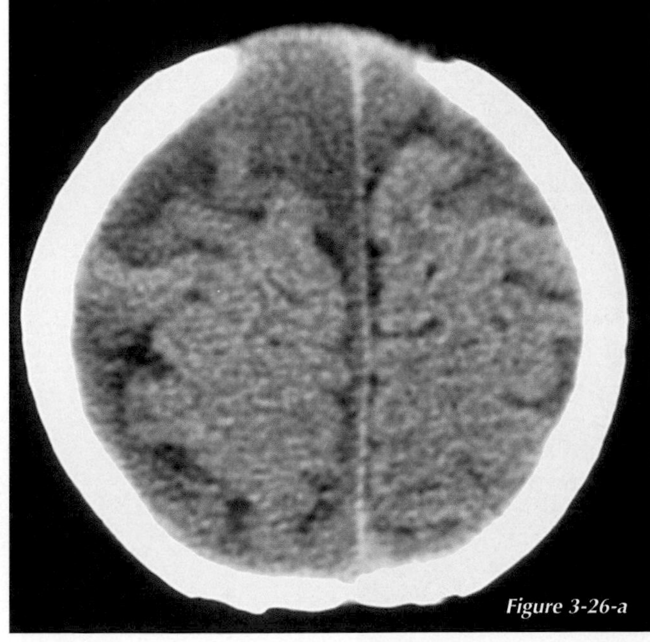
Figure 3-26-a

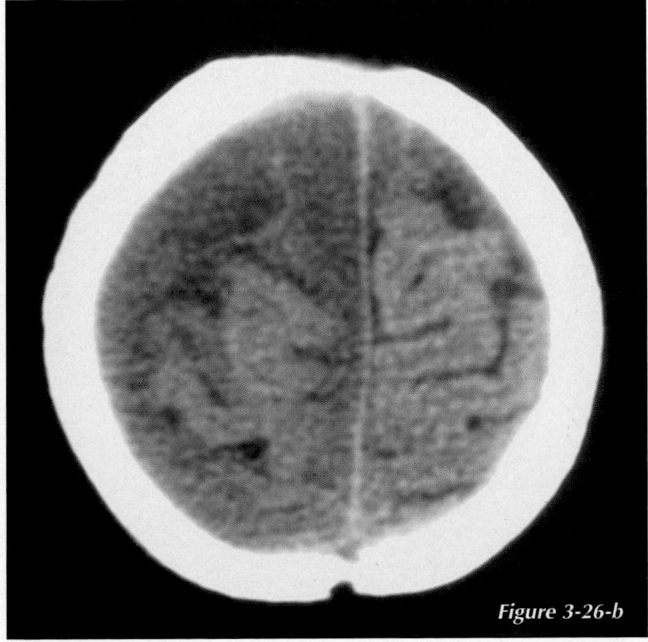
Figure 3-26-b

# Head Trauma

**Case Study 3-26** *(continued)*

***Figure 3-26-c.*** *Sagittal T1-weighted image clearly demonstrating a hyperintense subdural hematoma.*

***Figure 3-26-d.*** *T2-weighted image in coronal plane. The asymmetrical fluid collection has septation, a common finding in older subdural hematomas.*

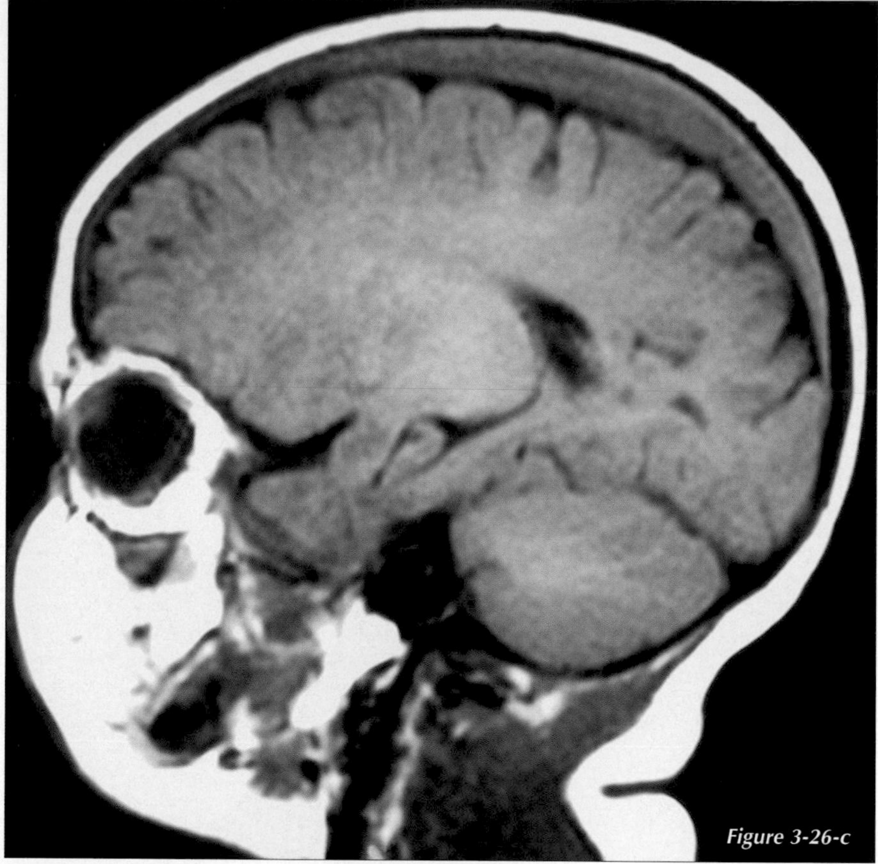

*Figure 3-26-c*

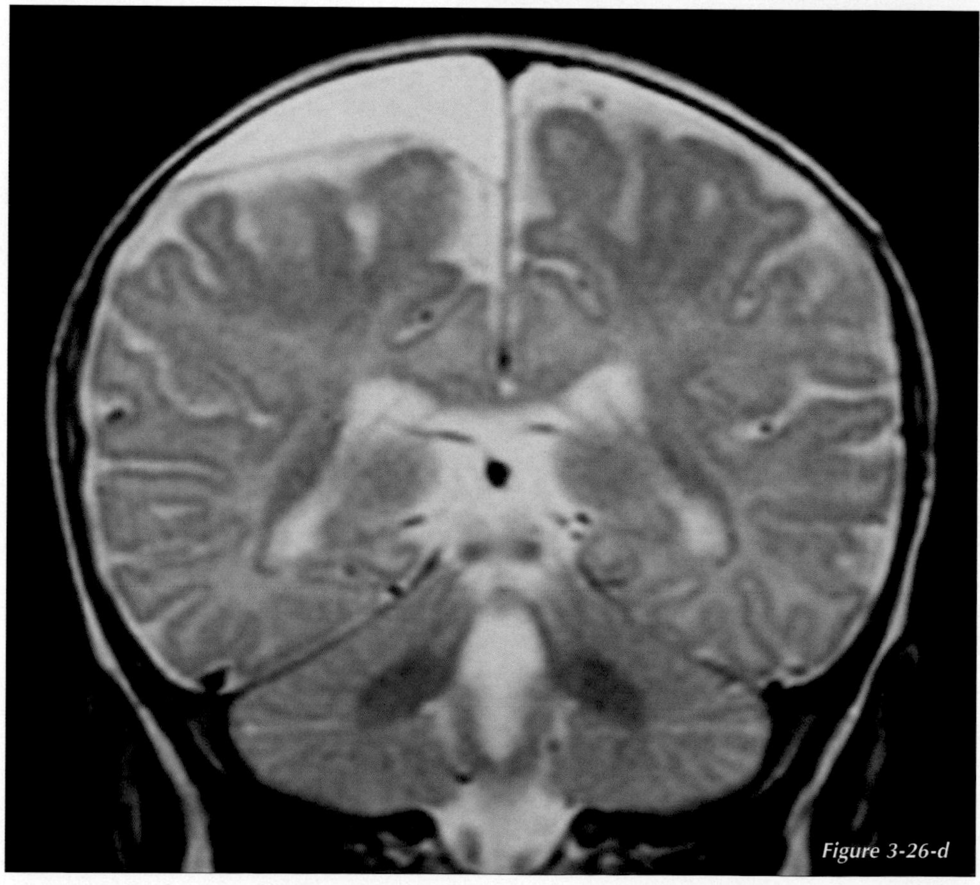

*Figure 3-26-d*

# Head Trauma

**Case Study 3-27**

This 3-month-old infant with an unexplained altered mental state and bulging fontanelle had subdural hematomas of multiple ages.

***Figure 3-27-a.*** *A CT scan demonstrating bilateral subdural hematomas of different ages. The acute component of the hemorrhage is hyperdense (white), and the subacute chronic component is more isodense to cerebrospinal fluid.*

***Figure 3-27-b.*** *On a T1-weighted axial MRI scan, the subacute subdural hematomas are hyperintense to cerebrospinal fluid with layering of fluid owing to blood component separation.*

***Figure 3-27-c.*** *On a T2-weighted scan, the subdural hematomas are hyperintense.*

***Figure 3-27-d.*** *A gradient echo image best demonstrates the hemorrhage as hemoglobin by-products with an acute dark component and hemosiderin staining of the dura mater.*

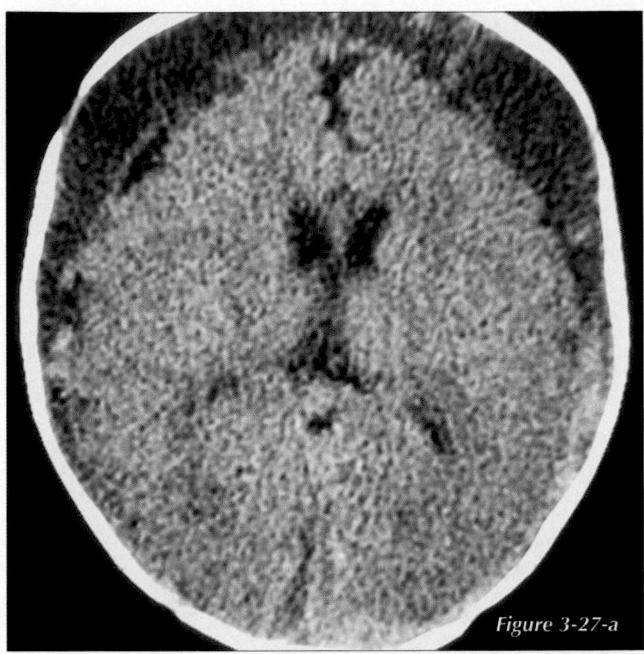
Figure 3-27-a

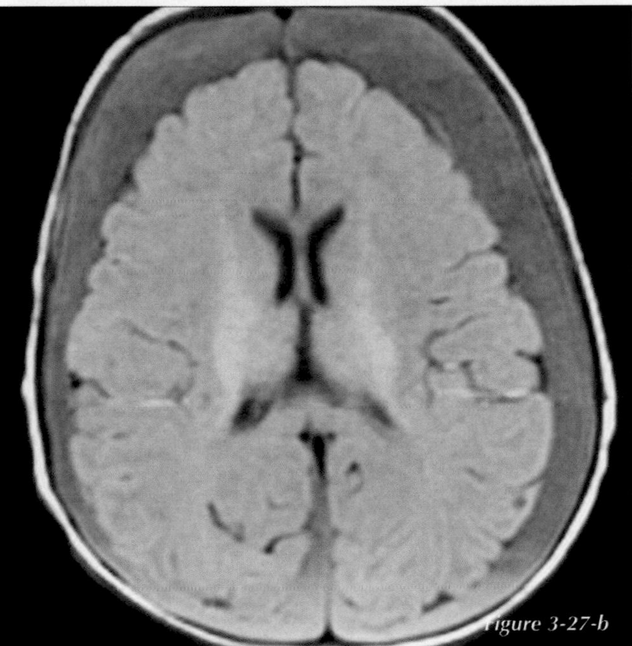
Figure 3-27-b

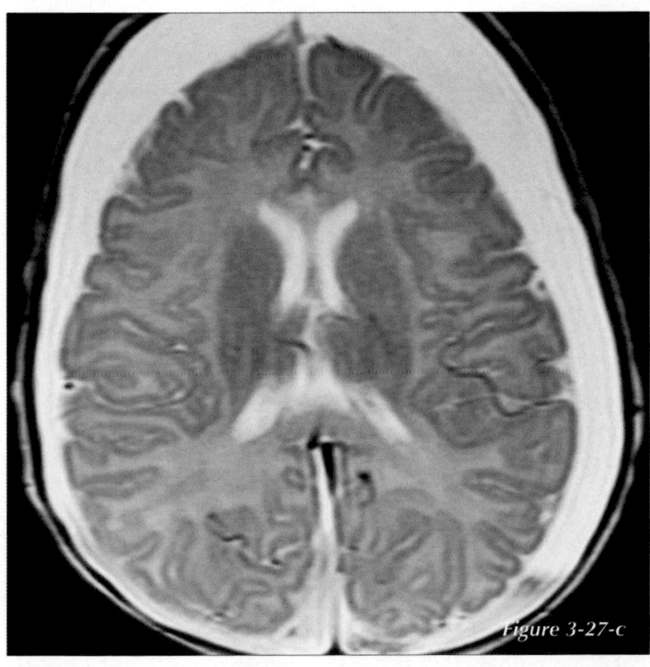
Figure 3-27-c

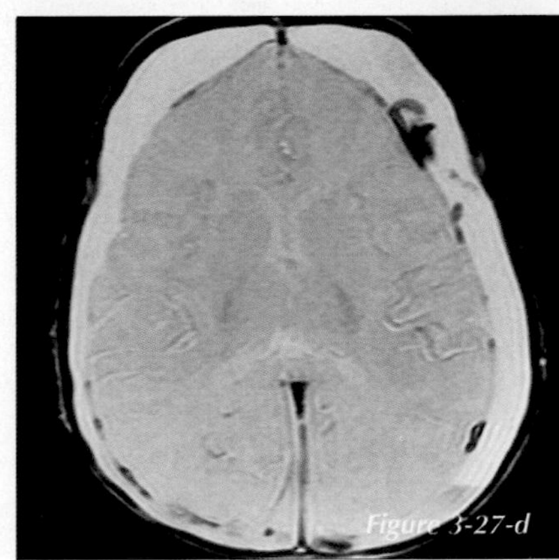
Figure 3-27-d

# Head Trauma

**Case Study 3-28**

This 2-month-old showed blood collections typical for a subarachnoid hemorrhage.

***Figure 3-28.*** *A CT scan showing an acute (white) subarachnoid hemorrhage with indistinct margins in the left sylvian fissure, the interhemispheric fissure, and extended to outline the cortical sulci. These follow the confines of the subarachnoid spaces and are typical for subarachnoid hemorrhages. Also note the large subgaleal hematoma in the left parietal region beneath the scalp.*

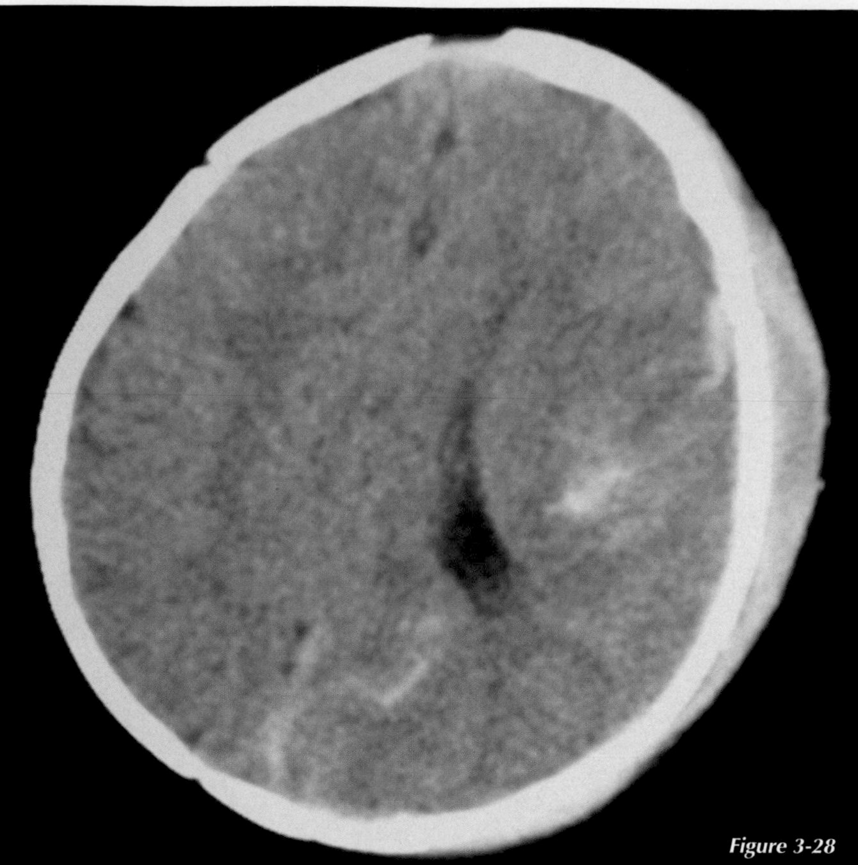

*Figure 3-28*

**Case Study 3-29**

This 11-month-old male had a history of an alleged fall from a car seat.

***Figure 3-29.*** *A CT scan illustrating a large hyperdense acute epidural hematoma in the right parietal region with convex margins. There is effacement of adjacent sulci and the right lateral ventricle with shift of the midline structures. There is a parietal bone fracture on the bone window setting. Epidural hemorrhages are often the result of accidents, but can occur with an abusive impact as well.*

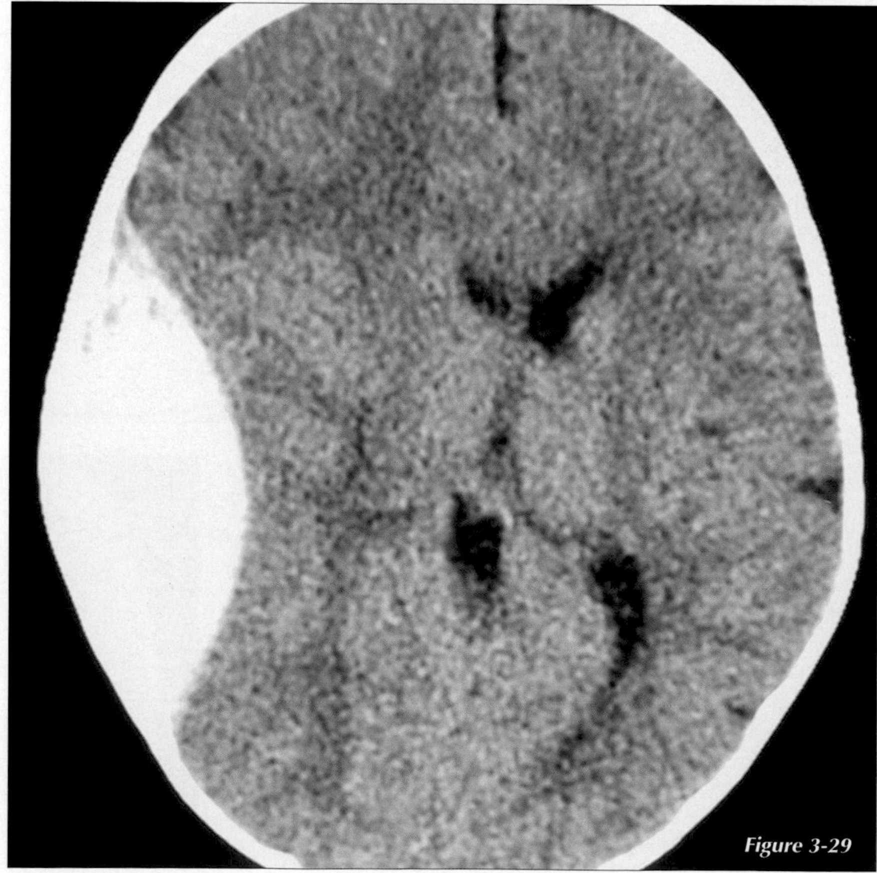

*Figure 3-29*

# Head Trauma

**Case Study 3-30**

This child had patchy subarachnoid hemorrhages in the parasagittal regions, which are typically associated with subdural hematomas.

***Figure 3-30.*** *Patchy subarachnoid hemorrhage in the parasagittal regions of the brain.*

**Case Study 3-31**

This nearly 2-year-old girl was in good health until early evening when her father left the home. His girlfriend reported that she was in the bathroom with the child when she left to attend to another child. She heard a thump and returned to find the child lying on the floor and unresponsive.

***Figure 3-31-a.*** *Note the bilaterally swollen brain and the bilateral subdural hemorrhages adherent to the skull (black-looking areas).*

***Figure 3-31-b.*** *This view of the base of the skull shows a fracture along the right occipital bone extending to the posterior lip of the foramen magnum.*

***Figure 3-31-c.*** *The right eye has optic nerve sheath hemorrhaging. Retinal hemorrhages are present but cannot be seen well in this photograph.*

***Figure 3-31-d.*** *The left eye has several retinal hemorrhages, as well as an optic nerve sheath hemorrhage. The ophthalmologist often has a clear view of the retinal hemorrhages within the eye, but only the pathologist is able to see if optic nerve sheath hemorrhages are present behind the eyeball.*

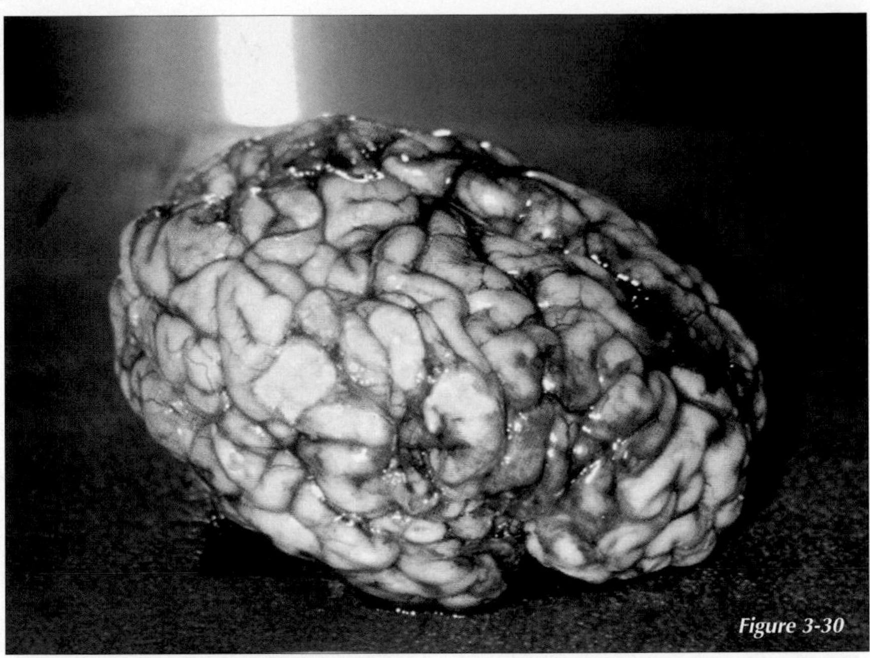

Figure 3-30

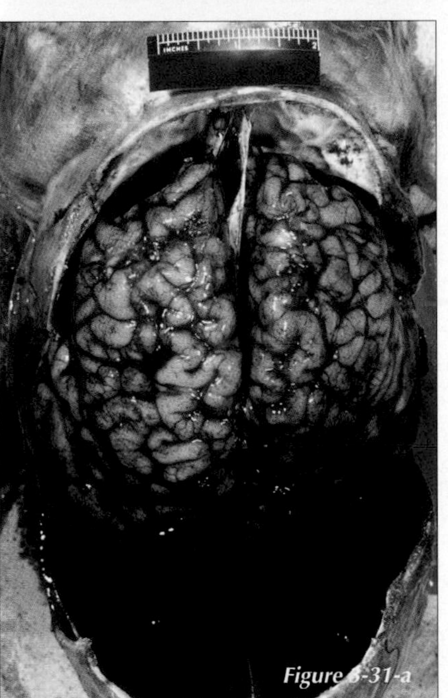


Figure 3-31-a

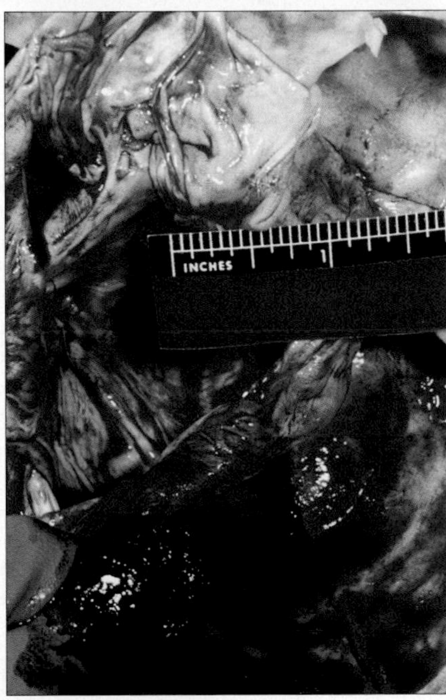


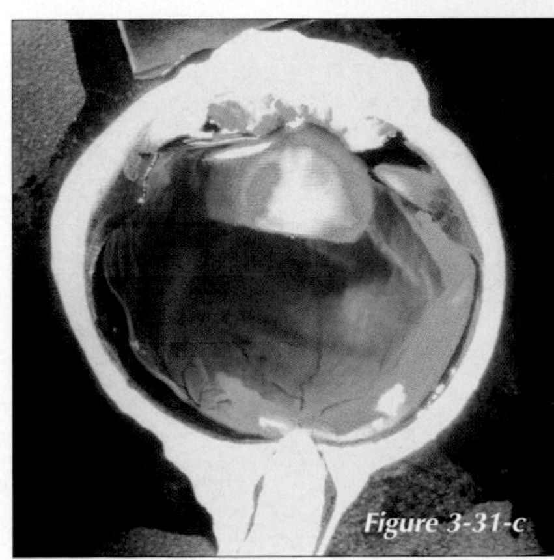

Figure 3-31-c

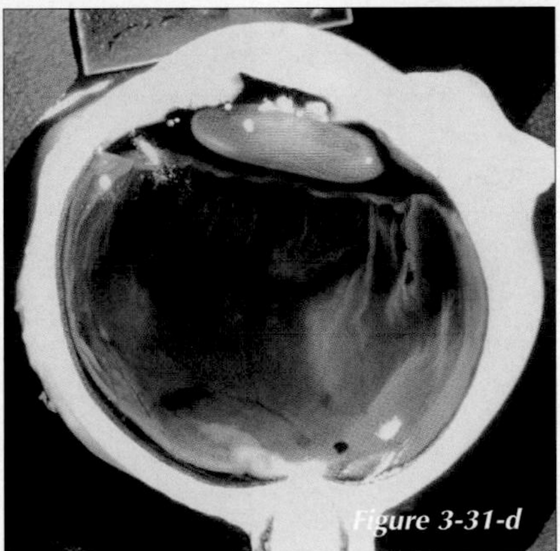

Figure 3-31-d

# HEAD TRAUMA

**Case Study 3-32**

The mother of this 3-year-old said the child was found dead in his bed.

***Figure 3-32-a.*** *There is a hemorrhage in the right temporalis muscle (arrow A) and a linear fracture of the right parietal calvaria (arrow B).*

***Figures 3-32-b*** and ***c.*** *There is 80 ml of epidural blood lying over the right cerebral lateral convexity.*

***Figures 3-32-d*** and ***e.*** *There is a fracture contusion of the right temporal gyri and marked concave compression of the right cerebral hemisphere.*

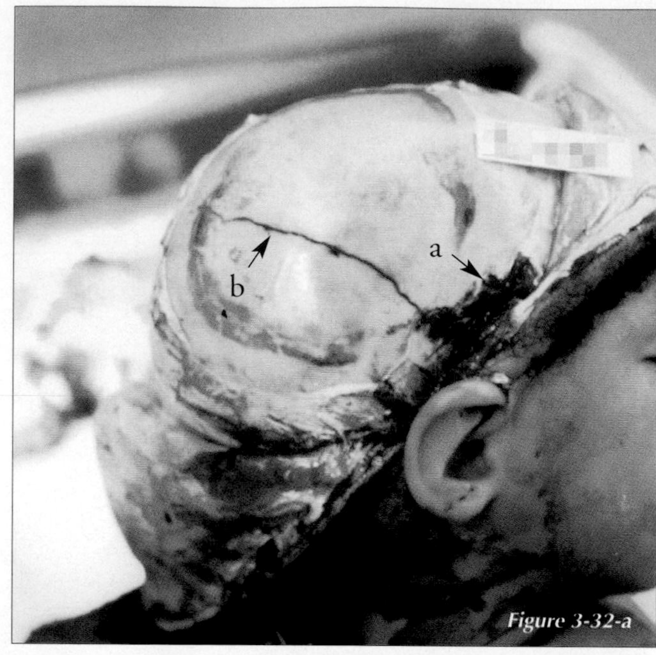

Figure 3-32-a

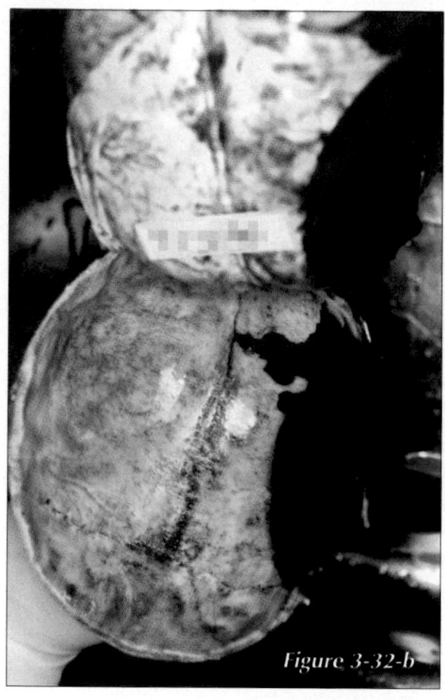
Figure 3-32-b

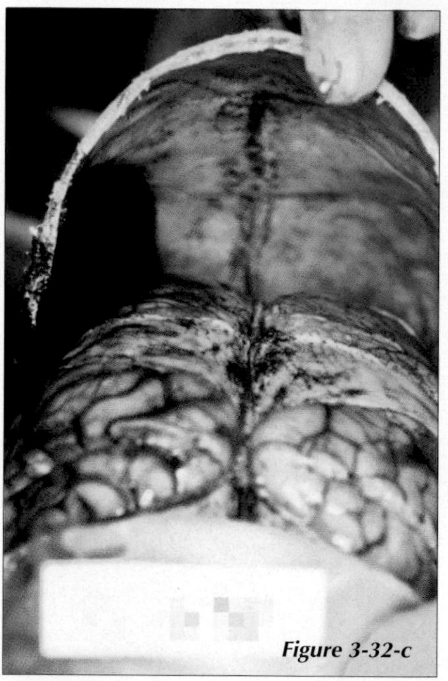
Figure 3-32-c

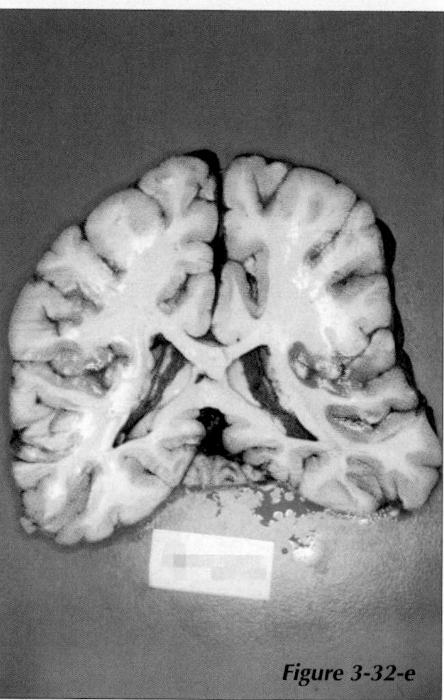
Figure 3-32-e

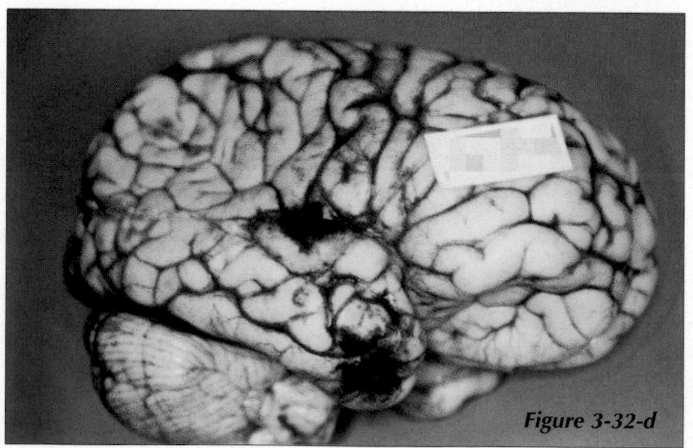
Figure 3-32-d

# Head Trauma

**Case Study 3-33**

This 4-month-old boy was admitted to the hospital obtunded and posturing after the babysitter reported that she found him breathing abnormally. Additionally, he would not open his eyes. The CT scan revealed moderate bilateral subdural hemorrhages and small subarachnoid bleeding. There were also massive retinal and subretinal hemorrhages bilaterally with a small amount of vitreous blood.

***Figure 3-33.*** *The brain is swollen bilaterally with subarachnoid and subdural hemorrhaging.*

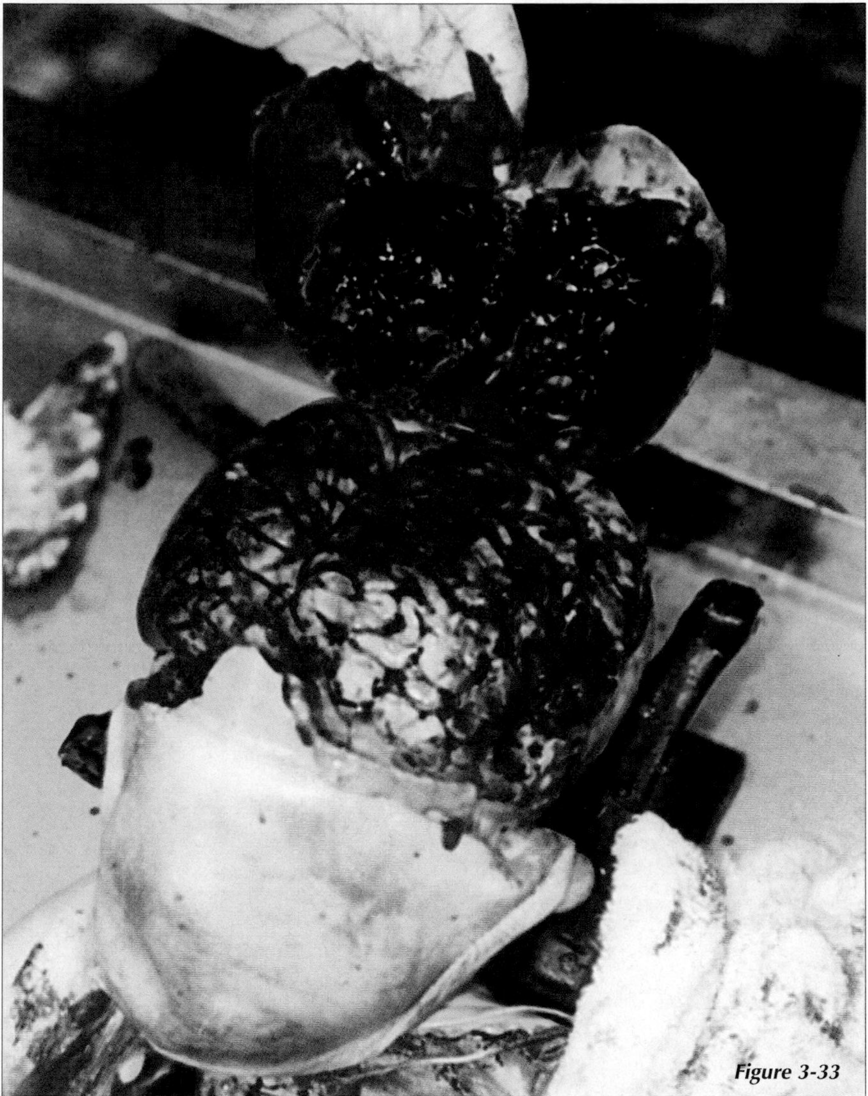

**Figure 3-33**

# Head Trauma

**Case Study 3-34**

This 6-month-old had a profound hypoxic/ischemic injury. Such injuries can occur from any type of asphyxia or interference with blood flow to the brain.

***Figure 3-34-a.*** *CT scan showing a low-attenuation signal bilaterally in the caudate head and basal ganglia.*

***Figure 3-34-b.*** *T2-weighted MRI scan showing a hyperintense signal in the basal ganglia and thalami. Diffuse hyperintensity is also seen throughout the cerebral cortex.*

***Figure 3-34-c.*** *Linear hyperintensities in the parietal occipital cortex on a T1-weighted CT image that are suggestive of cortical laminar necrosis.*

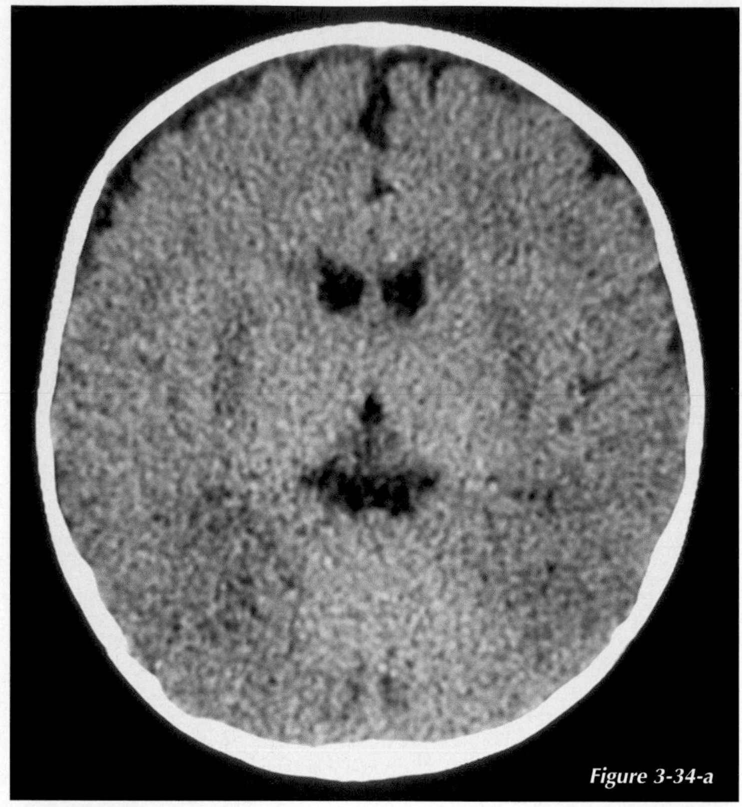

Figure 3-34-a

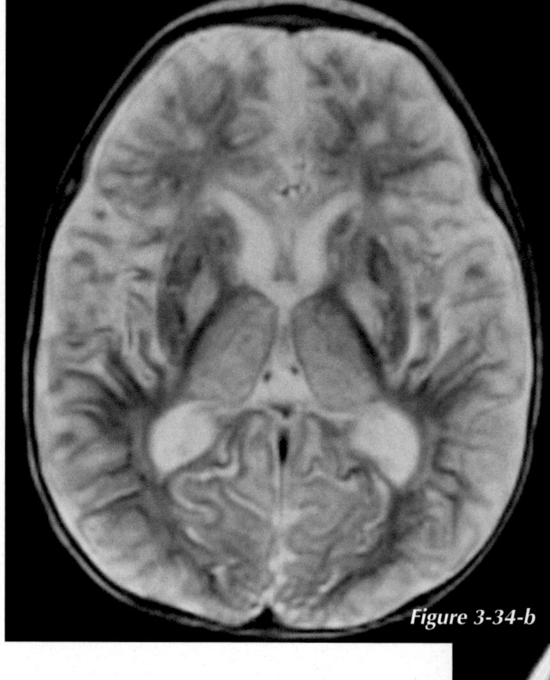

Figure 3-34-b

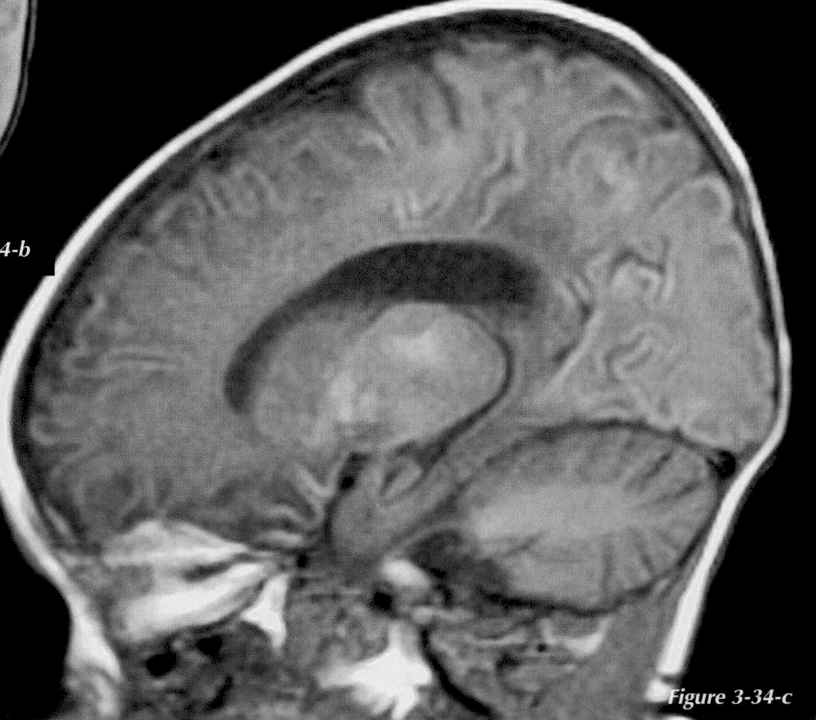

Figure 3-34-c

# HEAD TRAUMA

**Case Study 3-35**

This 6-month-old male child had extensive brain injuries.

***Figure 3-35-a.*** *CT scan showing acute hyperdense interhemispheric subdural hematoma. There is diffuse edema of the left cerebral hemisphere with loss of gray/white matter differential and a midline shift.*

***Figures 3-35-b*** *and* ***c.*** *In the sagittal T1-weighted MRI image, the interhemispheric hematoma appears hyperdense. In the T2-weighted image, there is diffuse hyper-intensity of the cortex with edema and effacement of the cisterns. There is also uncal herniation and mass effect on the midbrain.*

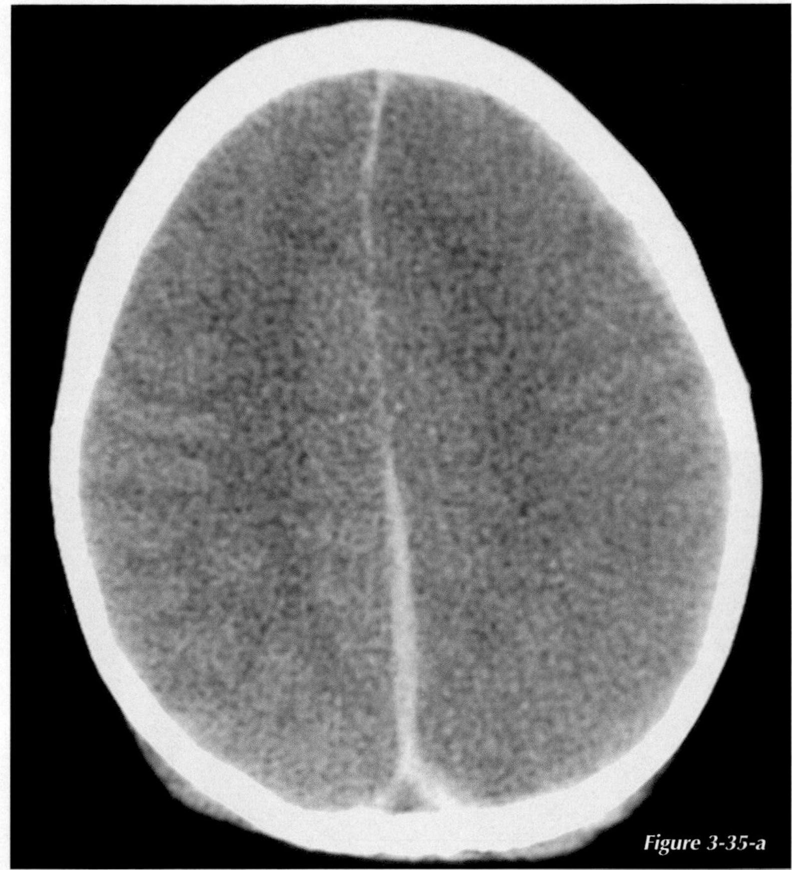

Figure 3-35-a

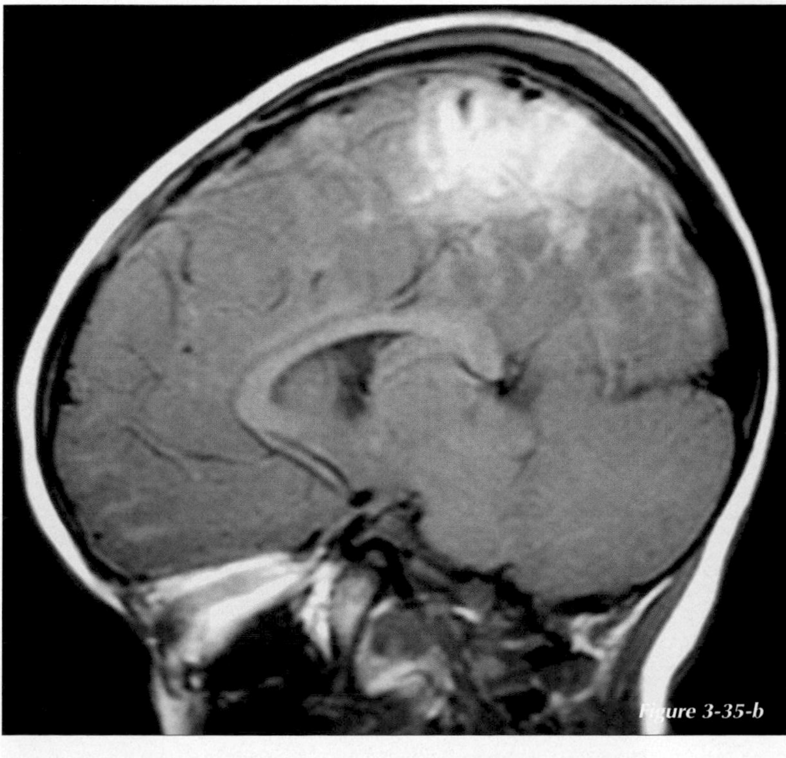

Figure 3-35-b

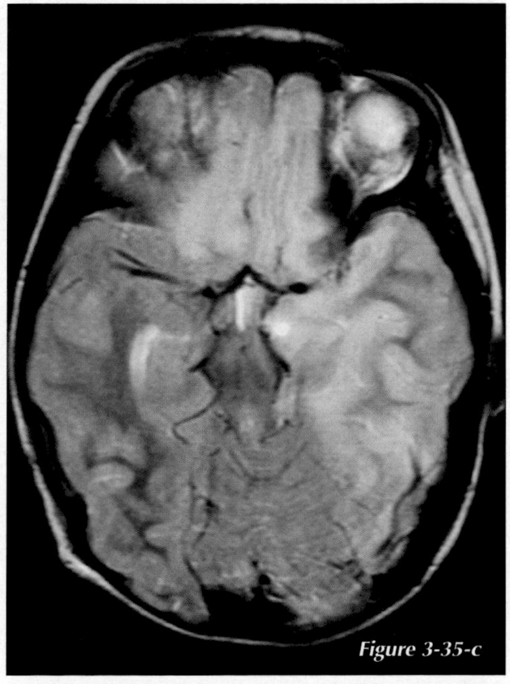

Figure 3-35-c

# Head Trauma

**Case Study 3-36**

This 14-month-old experienced decreased sensorium with the diagnosis of possible sepsis. As the patient deteriorated, both CT and MRI scans were performed.

***Figures 3-36-a** and **b**. There is diffuse brain tissue volume loss on the CT scan with prominence of the sulci and extra-axial fluid spaces.*

***Figure 3-36-c.** MRI scan showing a hyper-intense signal in the caudate head and basal ganglia suggestive of profound hypoxic injury.*

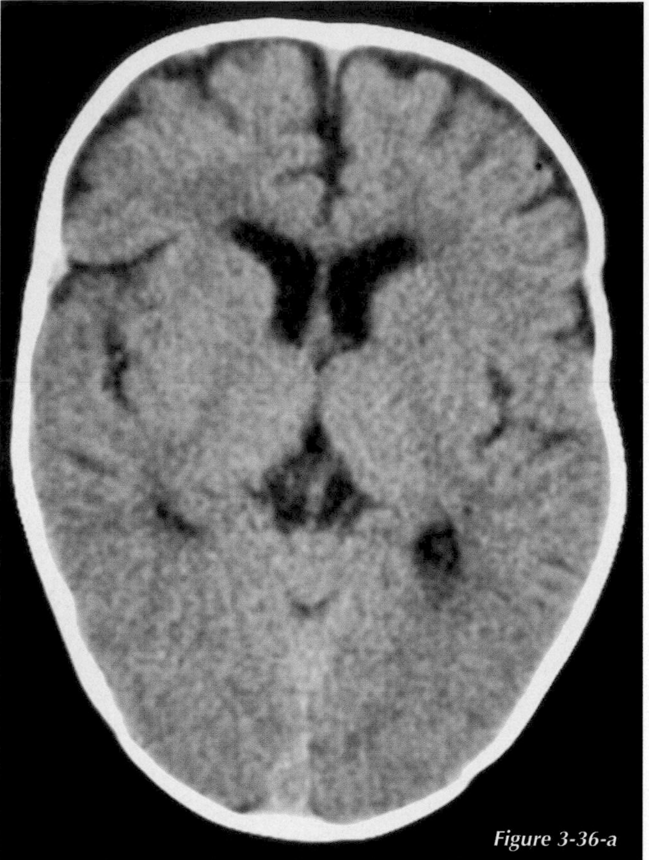

Figure 3-36-a

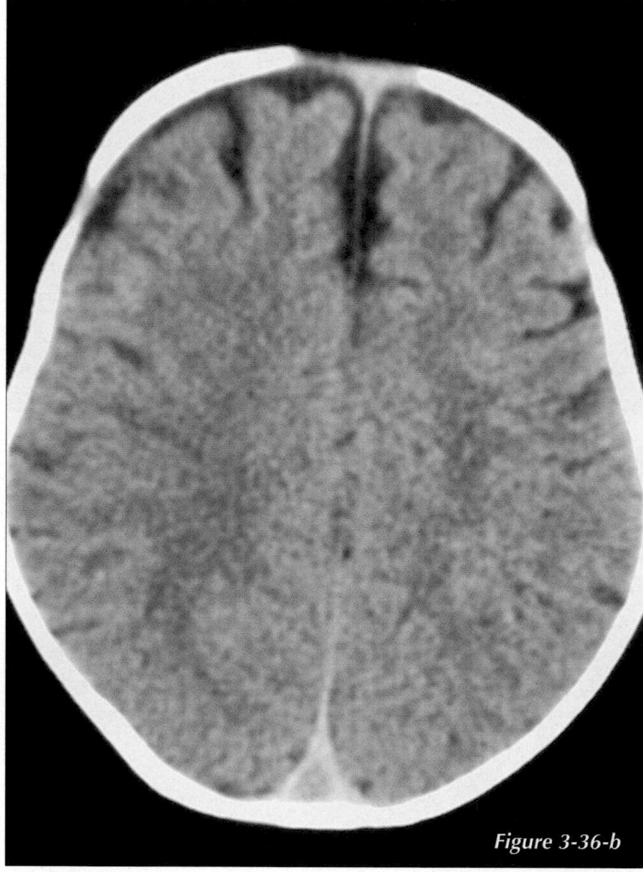

Figure 3-36-b

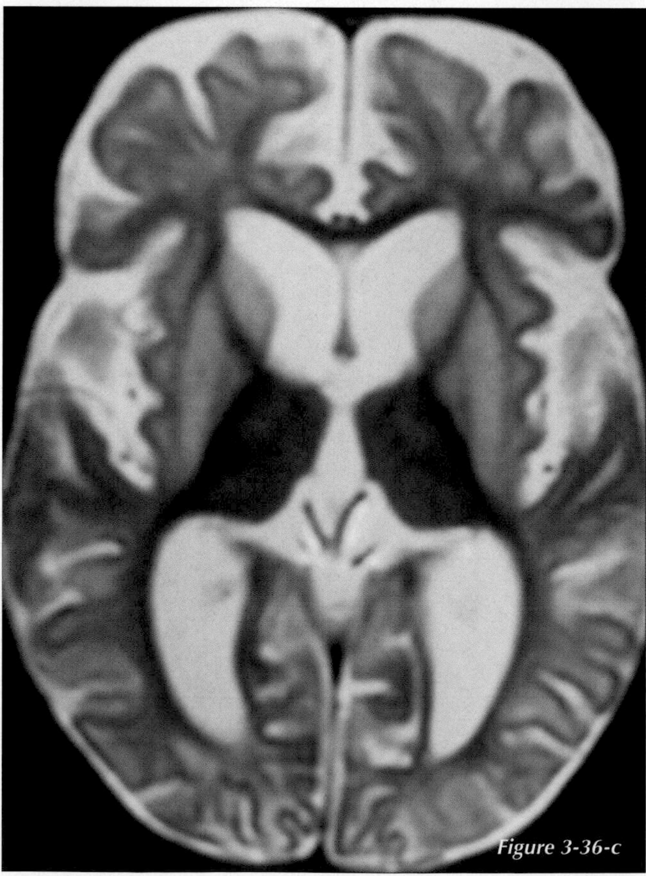

Figure 3-36-c

# HEAD TRAUMA

**Case Study 3-37**

This severely shaken 6-month-old baby was examined with symptoms of profound brain injury. Imaging revealed radiological evidence of DAI.

***Figure 3-37-a.*** *CT scan showing hyperdense foci in the frontal white matter.*

***Figure 3-37-b.*** *Sagittal T1-weighted MRI scan with a focus of acute hemorrhage in the splenium of the corpus callosum.*

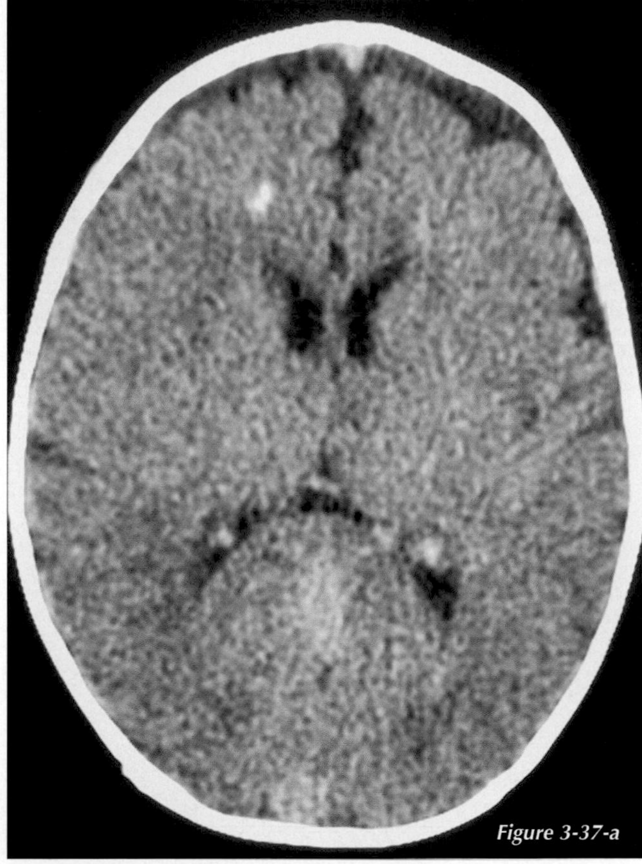

Figure 3-37-a

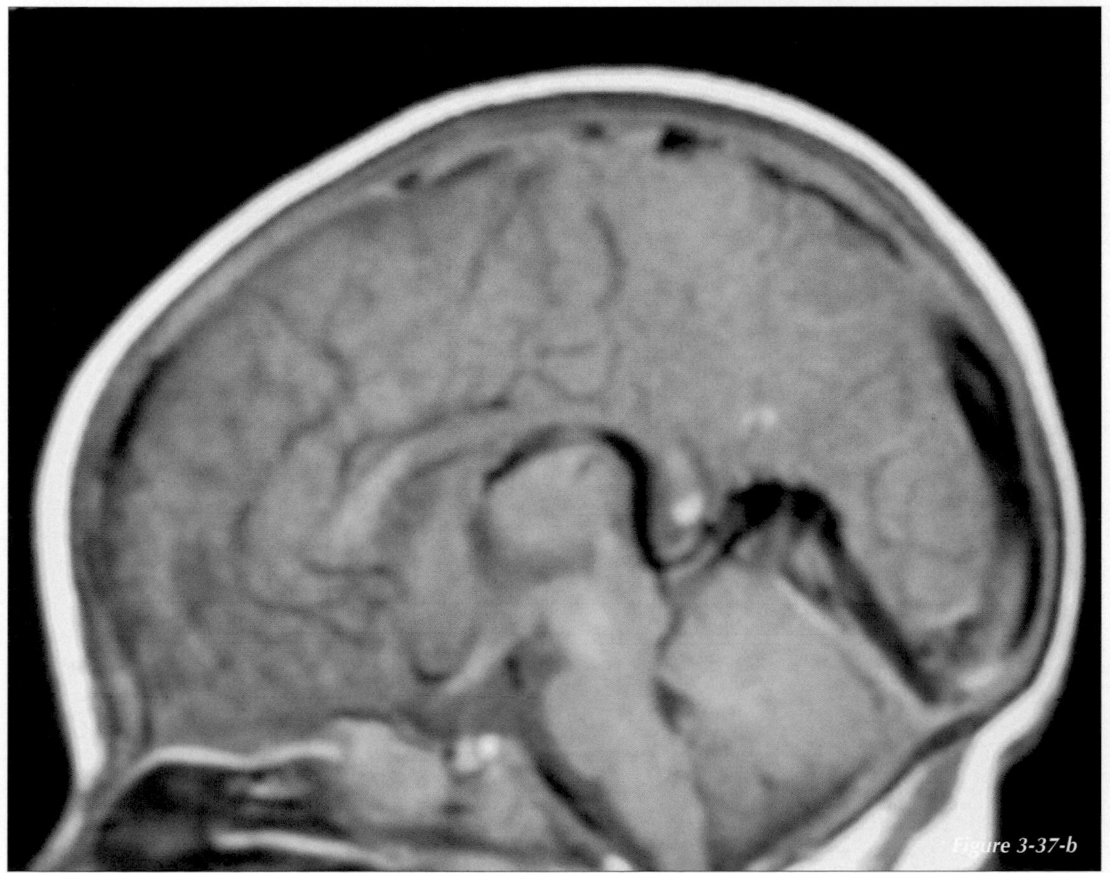

Figure 3-37-b

# Head Trauma

**Case Study 3-38**

This 2-week-old infant had a severely abusive injury that occurred when the baby was slammed against a bed frame.

***Figure 3-38-a.*** *An MRI scan with T1-weighted image in the axial plane showing a hypodense laceration to the left parietal lobe.*

***Figure 3-38-b.*** *A coronal T2-weighted image in which the laceration appears hyperdense and extends through the parietal cortex to the ventricle. There is a parietal bone fracture adjacent to the area of injury and cerebral parenchyma herniated through the fracture defect.*

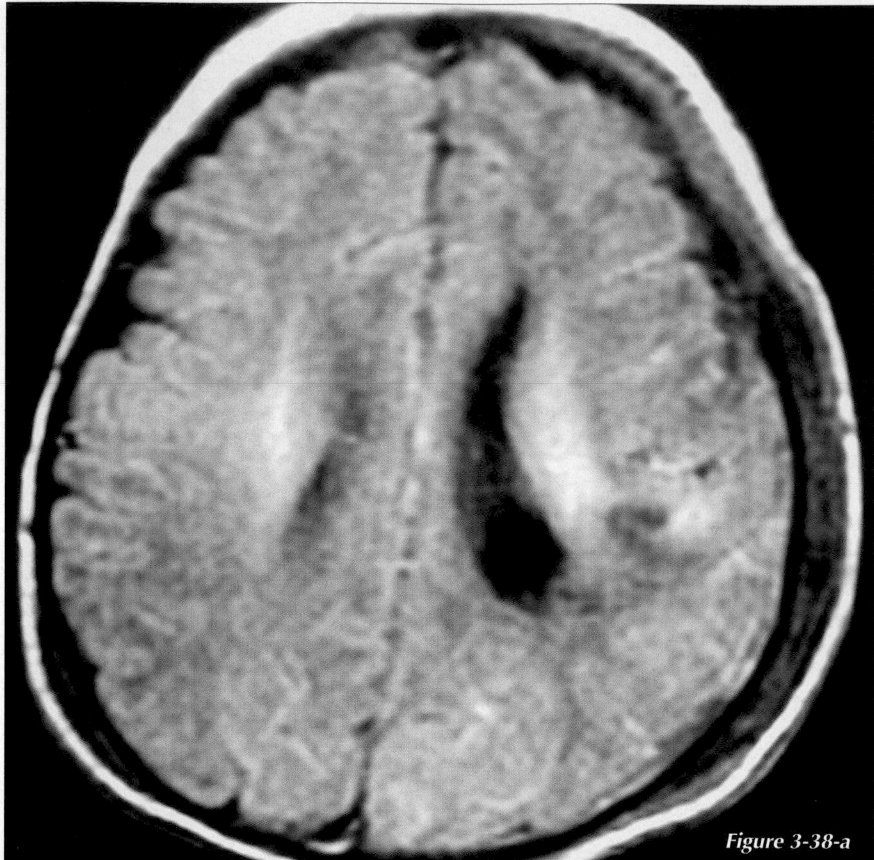

Figure 3-38-a

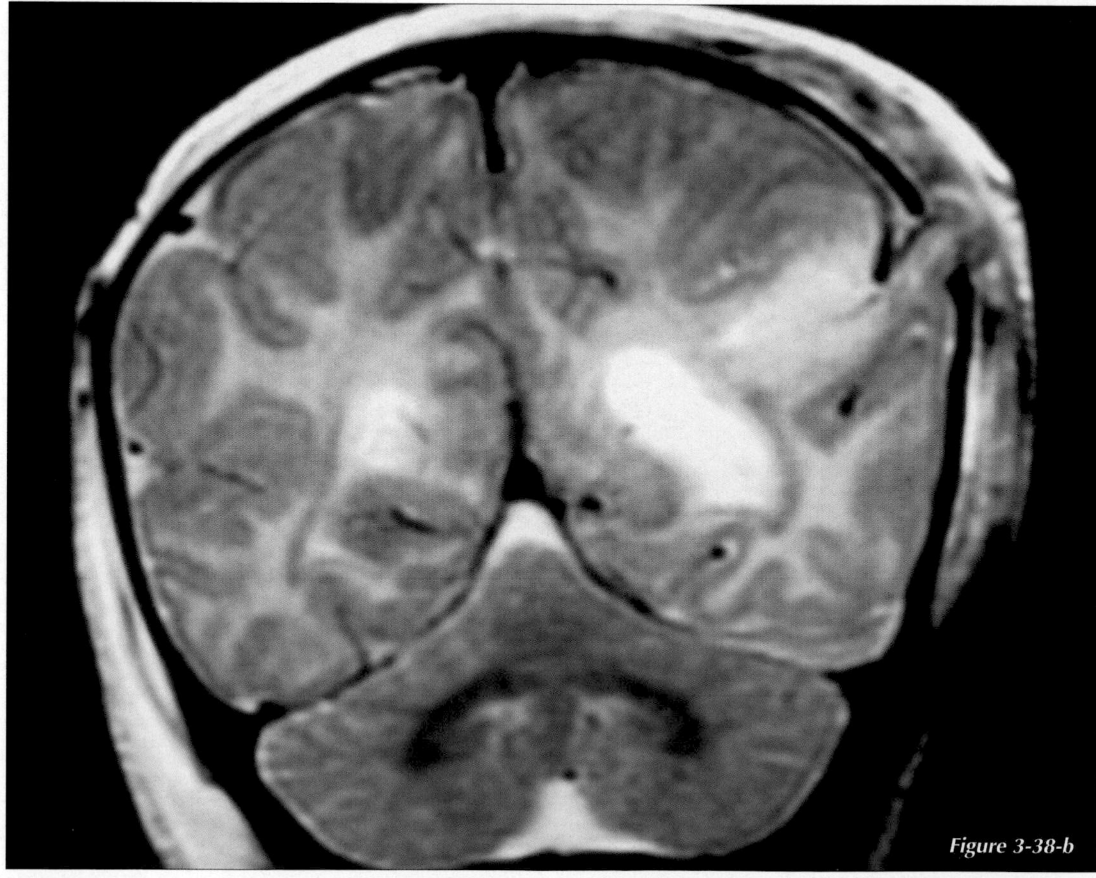

Figure 3-38-b

# Head Trauma

**Case Study 3-39**

This 20-week-old child suffered from diffuse cerebral edema.

***Figure 3-39-a.*** *A CT scan with an indistinct gray/white interface (when compared with more normal right cerebral hemisphere), which evidences the diffuse cerebral edema of the left cerebral hemisphere. There is effacement of the left lateral ventricle, a shift of the midline structures, and a subdural hemorrhage.*

***Figure 3-39-b.*** *No intracranial perfusion is seen on the radioisotope cerebral blood flow study, meaning that the brain is not receiving any blood flow.*

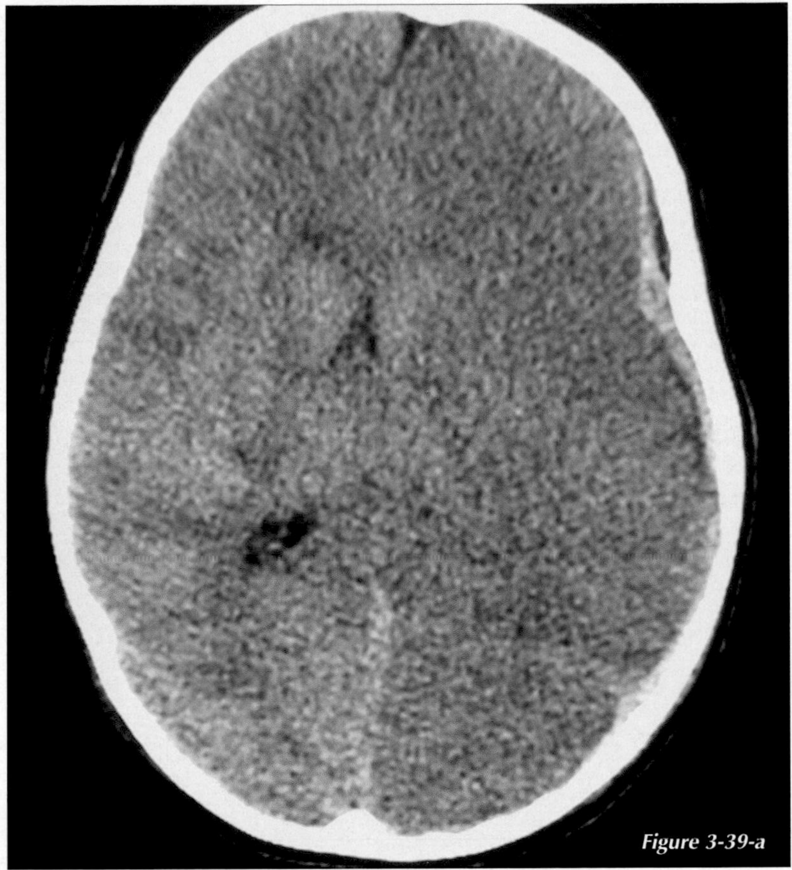

Figure 3-39-a

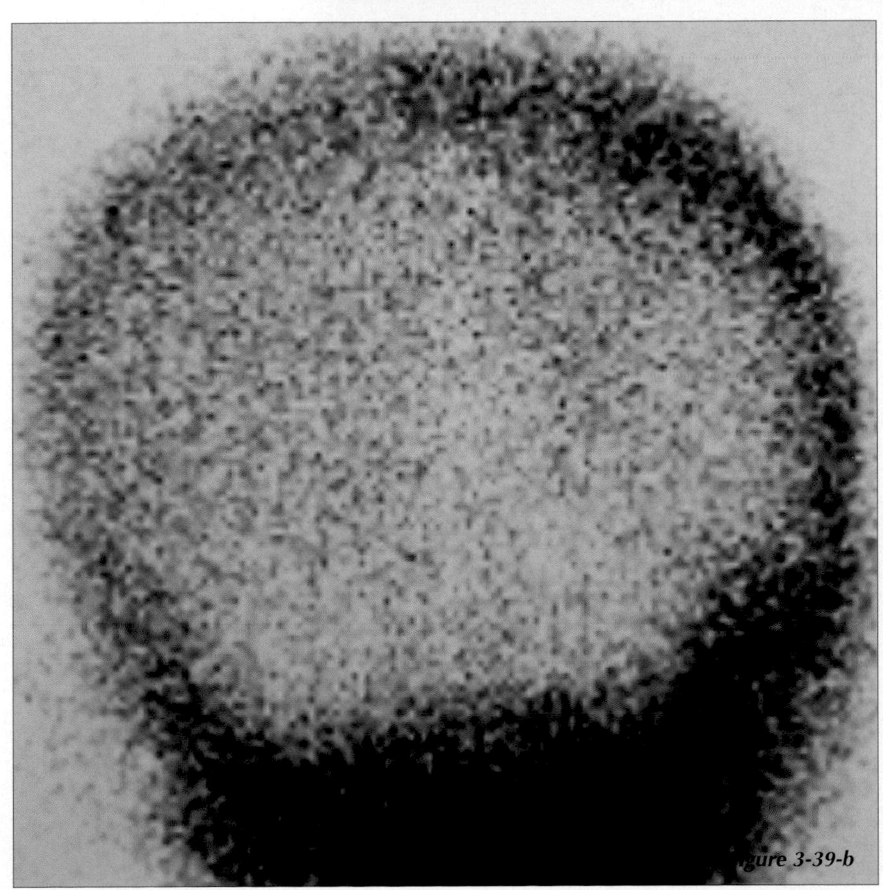

Figure 3-39-b

# Head Trauma

**Case Study 3-40**

This 3-month-old infant was found to have a large knot on the head located over the left parietal bone.

***Figure 3-40-a.*** *A posterior and anterior straight view of the skull showing a lump over the parietal bone on the left.*

***Figure 3-40-b.*** *A close up view illustrating that the lump is calcified and that there is some flattening of the parietal bone. This is a birth injury, a calcified cephalhematoma, and is not related to child abuse. Cephalhematomas begin to calcify approximately 2 weeks after an injury is suffered.*

**Case Study 3-41**

Once thought to be diagnostic of hyperextension injuries of the head, epidural hemorrhages around the cervical spinal cord are now widely regarded as an artifact in most cases.

***Figure 3-41.*** *Epidural hemorrhage overlying the cervical spinal cord.*

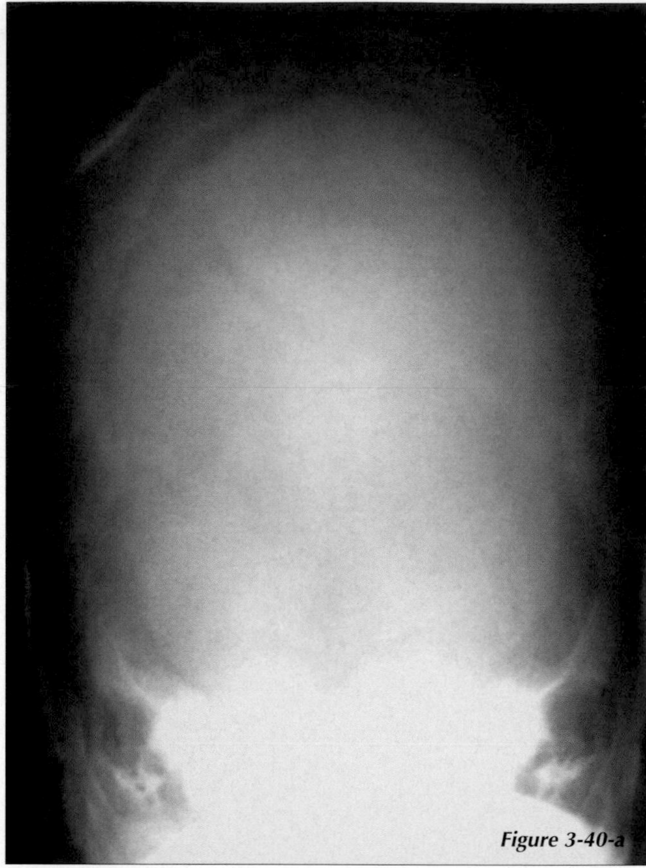

Figure 3-40-a

Figure 3-40-b

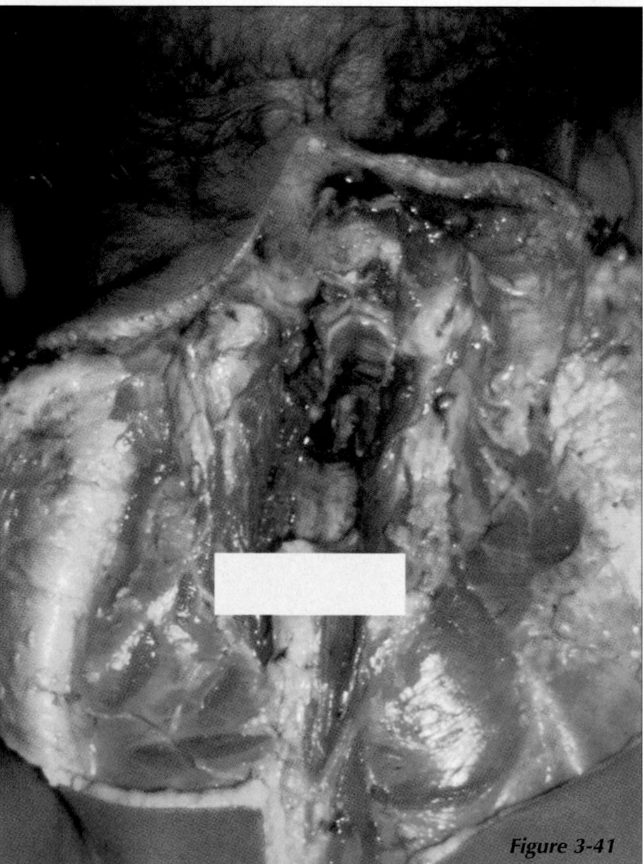

Figure 3-41

Chapter 4

# Thoracoabdominal Trauma

Randell Alexander, MD, PhD
Eric Faerber, MD

Thoracoabdominal trauma is not as common as skin injuries or head injuries. Yet the mortality rate for abusive abdominal trauma exceeds head trauma. Although brain injury has immediate symptoms (eg, neurons directly disrupted and failing to respond normally), abdominal injuries in particular are significant when they cause excessive bleeding or lead to infection; these processes occur over time. In addition, bruising of the abdomen is often absent even with major organ damage. Therefore, the diagnosis of thoracoabdominal trauma is often delayed until major complications result.

Thoracic injuries can consist of organ and other structural damage, including damage to the lungs, heart, thymus, mediastinum, and vascular and lymphatic systems. Injuries can also occur on the skin and other bones in the thoracic region, including the ribs. Ribs are difficult to break in infants as they are more cartilaginous and tend to bend rather than break. Most often rib fractures occur in the context of the grabbing and shaking seen with shaken baby syndrome.

In some cases, perpetrators have admitted to extreme squeezing of the chest only, but deny shaking. In these cases, negative results of head CT, MRI, and ophthalmological examinations have reinforced the presumed isolated mechanism of squeezing without shaking. Abdominal injuries can occur to solid organs (eg, liver, pancreas, kidneys), hollow organs (eg, intestines, bladder), and other structures (eg, mesentery).

Abdominal and thoracic injuries are not suspected often enough because a physical examination is not revealing for these injuries. Once suspected, imaging techniques are very helpful in delineating injuries. To overcome the difficulty in detection, trauma protocols should be adopted that routinely include abdominal and thoracic evaluations in physically abused children. Although this would result in many negative evaluations, the consequences of missing a life-threatening abdominal injury are profound.

# Chest Injuries

## Ribs

### Case Study 4-4

This 4-month-old boy died with an acute contusion of the scalp, acute bilateral subdural hemorrhages, chronic bilateral subdural hemorrhages probably 1 to 2 months old, 3 rib fractures, extensive bilateral retinal hemorrhages, and acute and chronic bilateral optic nerve sheath hemorrhages. The child's scrotum was also swollen, for which the father blamed himself; he stated that the night before calling emergency medical services (EMS) he fell while holding the boy and accidentally grabbed the boy's scrotum when they hit the floor. The father also stated that the boy had fallen from a sofa 2 months prior to his death. The injuries were ultimately determined to be the result of shaken baby syndrome (SBS) and other physical abuse. The father was convicted of homicide.

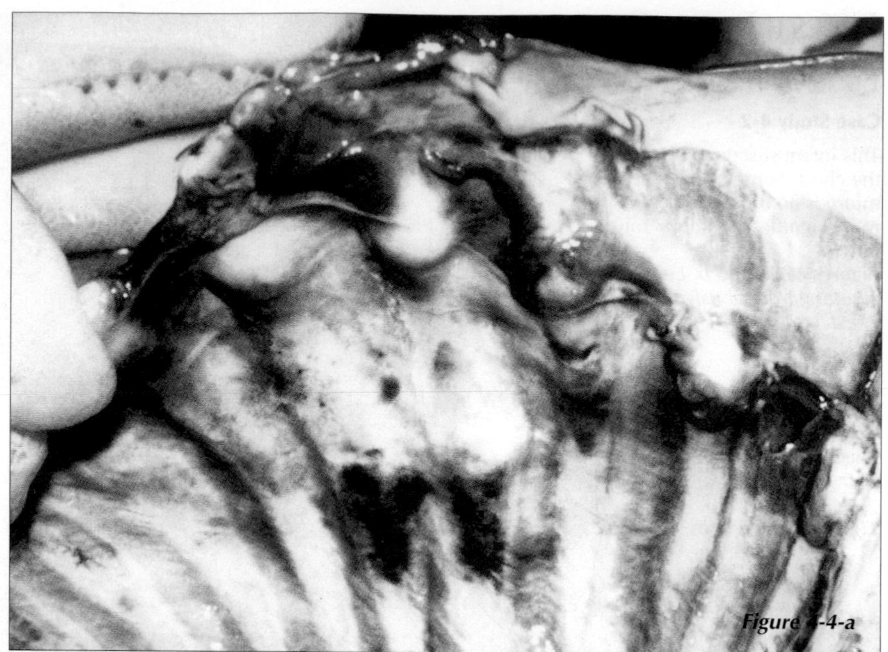

**Figure 4-4-a.** *Two rib fractures with callus formations. To inflict such injuries in infants requires intense force attributable to squeezing during violent shaking.*

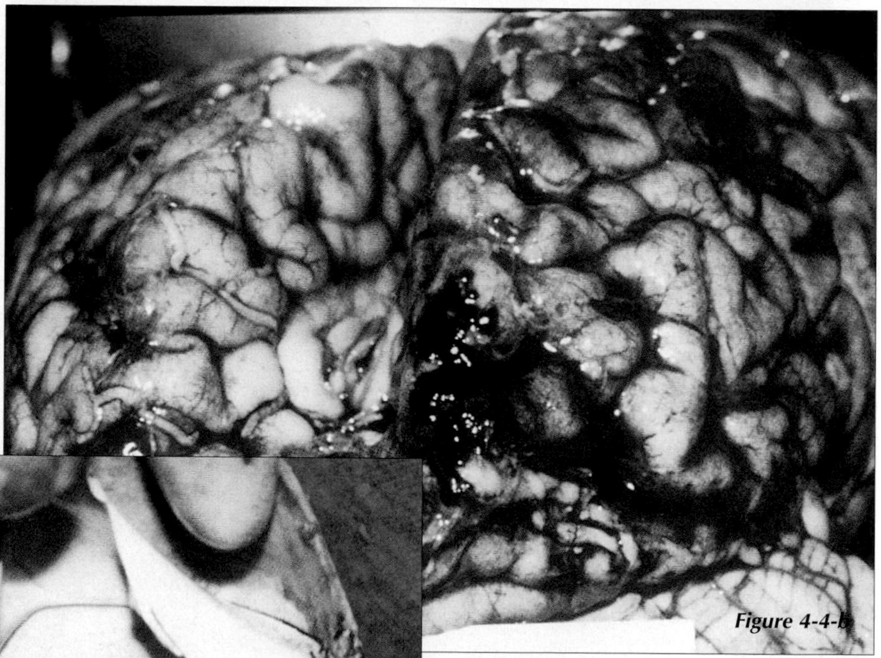

**Figure 4-4-b.** *The brain is grossly swollen bilaterally, especially in the right hemisphere. The dark areas represent some subarachnoid blood.*

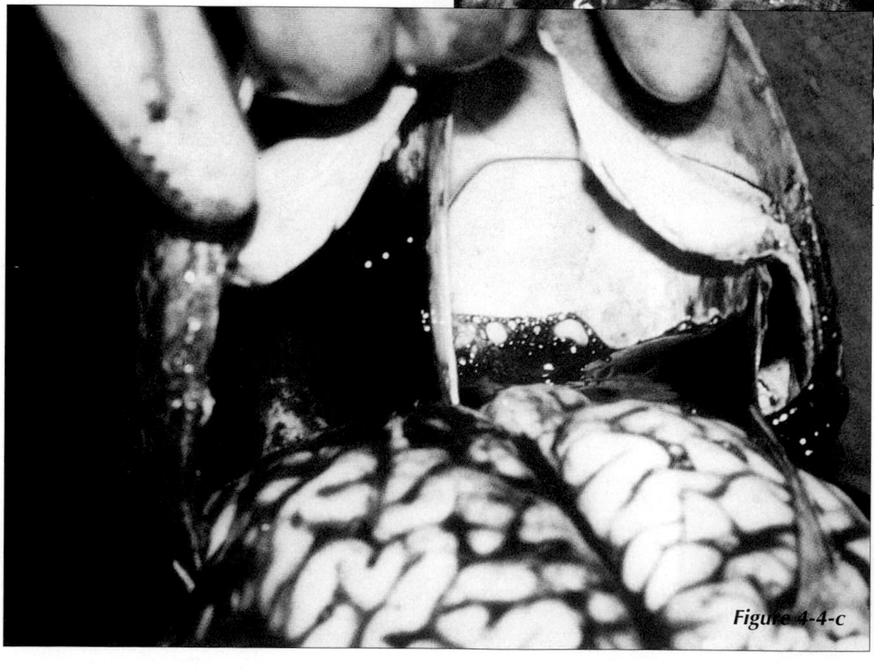

**Figure 4-4-c.** *Black-looking subdural blood is adherent to the skull as it is pulled back. Note the evidence of brain swelling, which is the ultimate cause of death in this case.*

Figure 4-4-a

Figure 4-4-b

Figure 4-4-c

# Chest Injuries

## Contusions

### Case Study 4-5

This 20-month-old girl was reportedly found unconscious in her bedroom. A family member performed CPR prior to bringing her to the ER where she was pronounced dead. The autopsy revealed 2 skull fractures, contusions to the scalp, acute subdural and subarachnoid hemorrhages, diffuse cerebral edema, contusions to the back and chest, a posterior esophageal hemorrhage, and two mesenteric contusions. The cause of death was blunt force trauma to the head.

***Figure 4-5-a.*** *Two areas of mesenteric contusions. These injuries are not the result of inappropriate CPR since they are significantly posterior in the abdomen. One or more blows to the abdomen would account for both injuries.*

***Figure 4-5-b.*** *Multiple contusions to the chest area. They are not the result of CPR, but most likely represent multiple blows to this area.*

***Figure 4-5-c.*** *The dark area is a large acute subgaleal contusion.*

***Figure 4-5-d.*** *The brain is markedly swollen on both sides. Subarachnoid blood is present, and subdural blood is bilaterally adherent to the inside of the skull.*

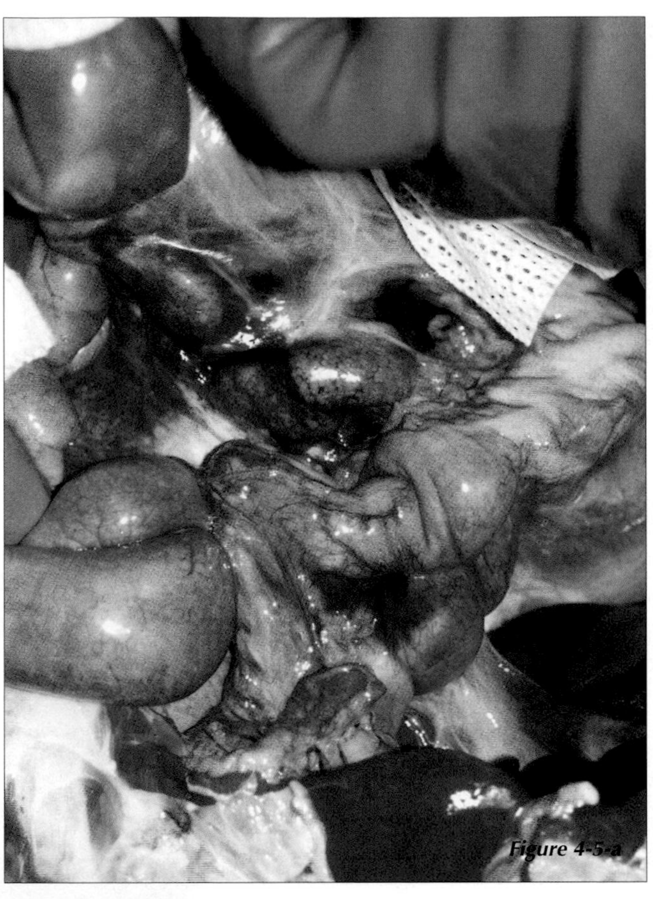

Figure 4-5-a

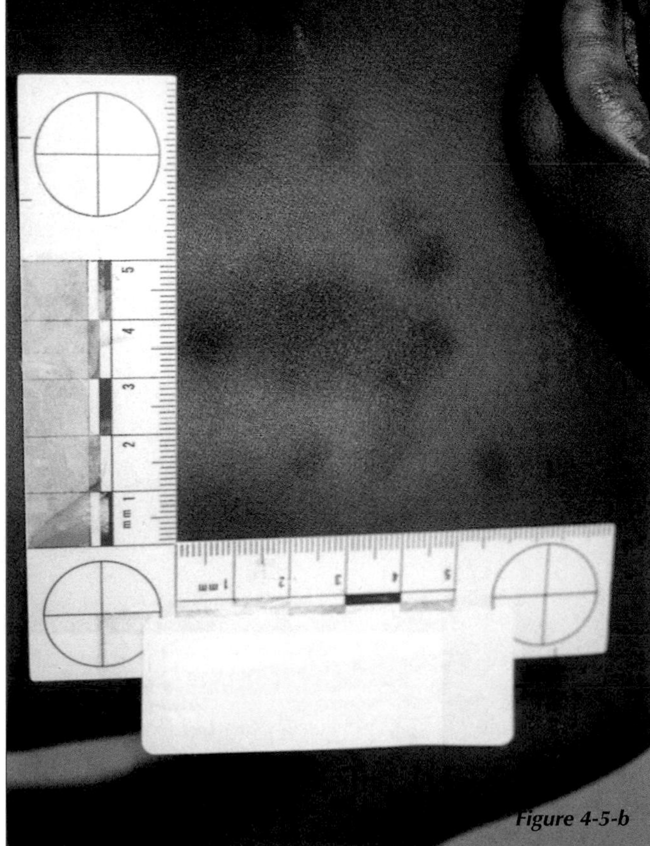


Figure 4-5-b

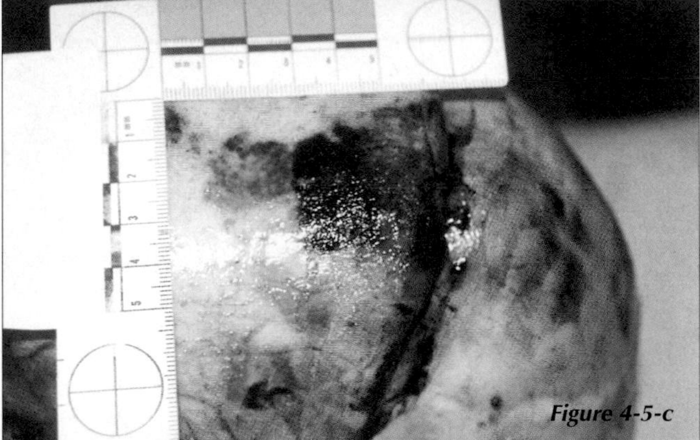


Figure 4-5-c

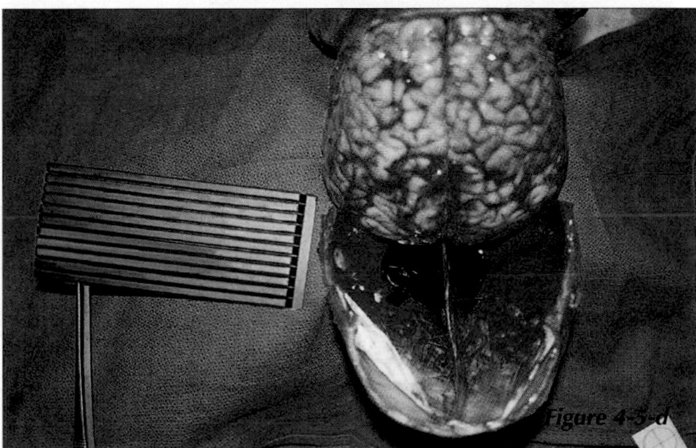

Figure 4-5-d

# Abdominal Injuries

## Multiple Injuries With Insufficient History

**Case Study 4-11** *(continued)*

***Figure 4-11-d.*** *Upon closer inspection with the pleura stripped away, the acute fracture is more visible.*

***Figure 4-11-e.*** *Multiple liver lacerations are present. A piece of the liver has been torn away by multiple impacts.*

***Figure 4-11-f.*** *Hemorrhages are evident in both kidneys. Inflicting these injuries requires considerable anterior or posterior force.*

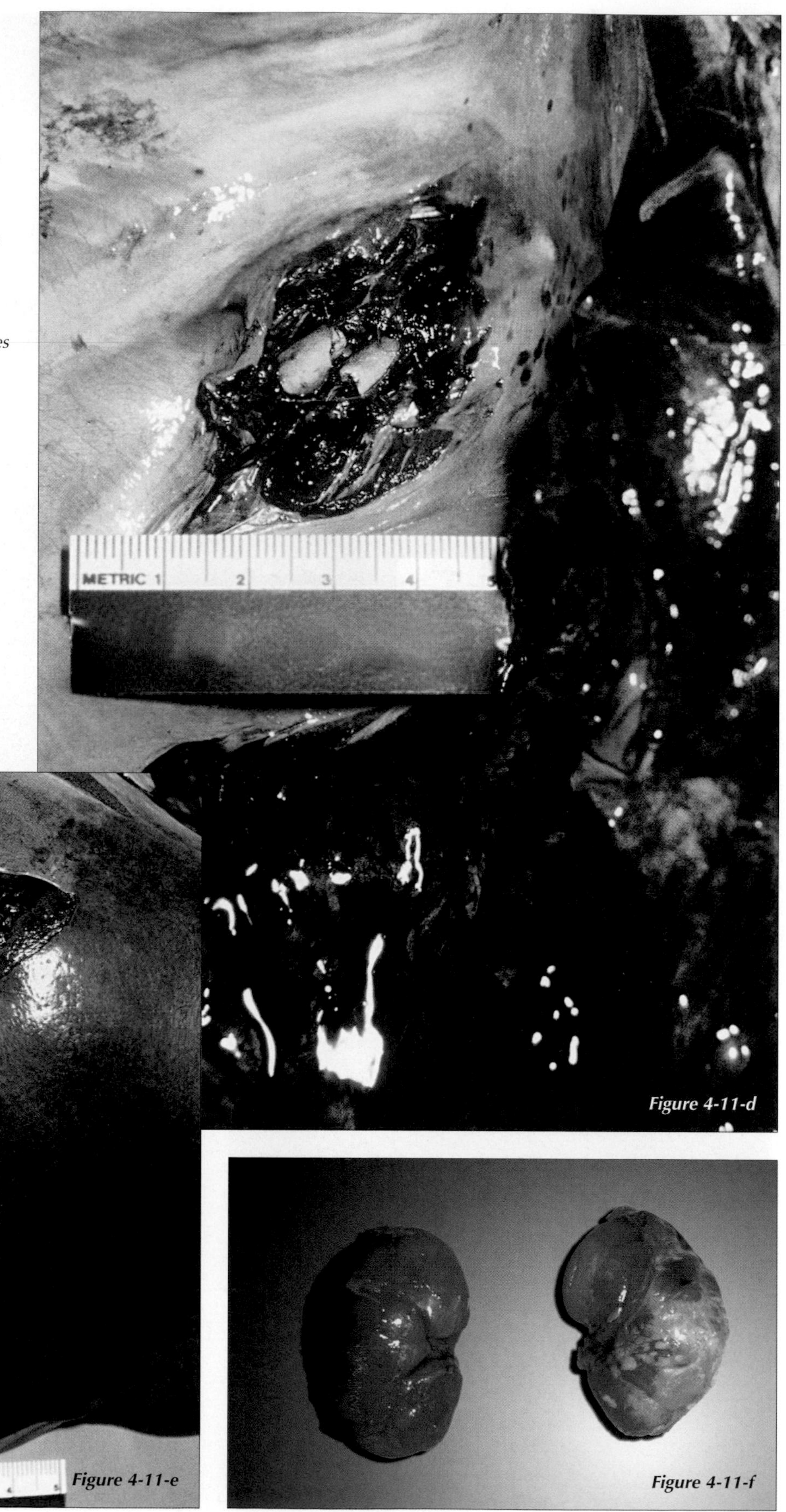


**Figure 4-11-d**

**Figure 4-11-e**

**Figure 4-11-f**

# Imaging

## Computed Tomography (CT) Scans

### Liver Laceration

**Case Study 4-12**

This 2-week-old boy sustained trauma to multiple areas. Such injuries require significant time to inflict.

***Figure 4-12-a.*** *Frontal radiograph of the chest postextubation demonstrates bilateral rib fractures and hemothoraces.*

***Figure 4-12-b.*** *Contrast-enhanced axial CT scan of the abdomen demonstrates a contusion to the liver.*

***Figure 4-12-c.*** *Non-contrast axial head CT scan demonstrates a right frontal subdural hematoma.*

***Figure 4-12-d.*** *Non-contrast axial head CT scans obtained 9 years later demonstrate cerebral atrophy and bilateral areas of encephalomalacia.*

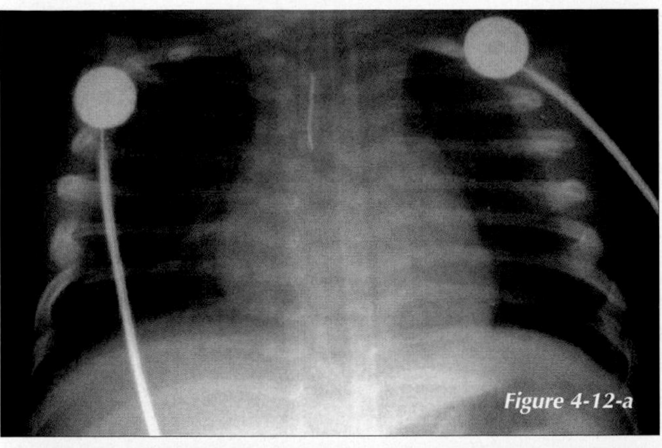

Figure 4-12-a

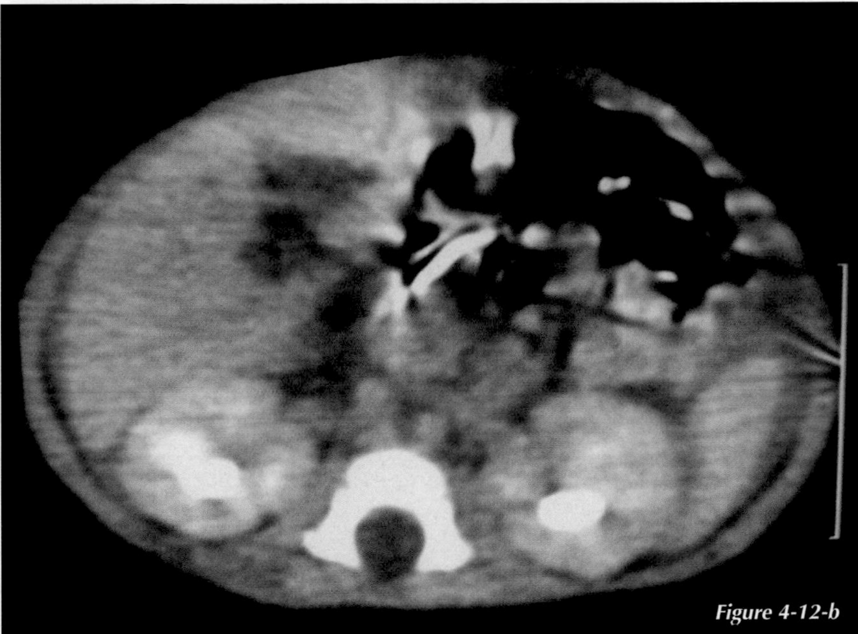

Figure 4-12-b

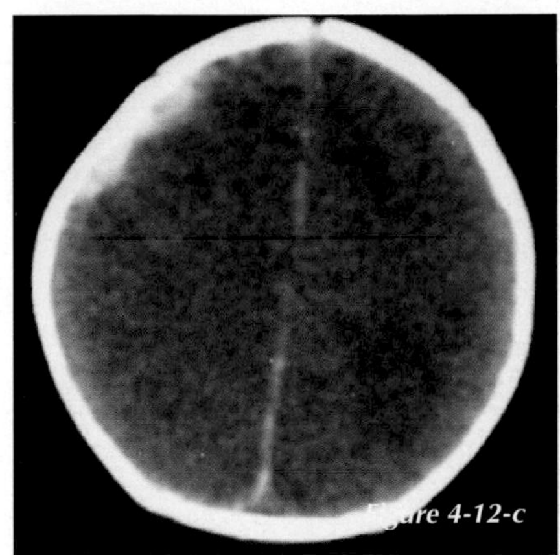

Figure 4-12-c

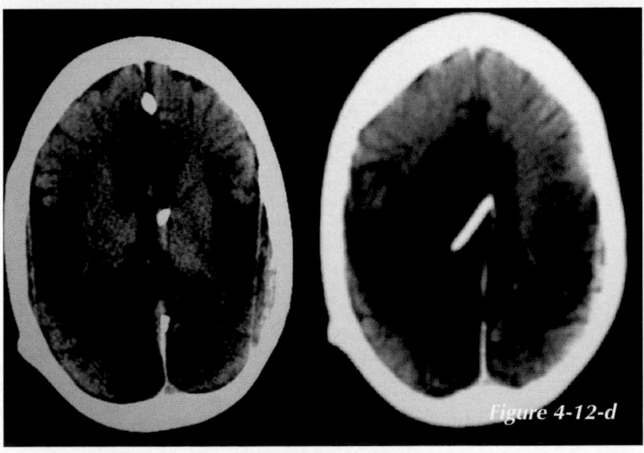

Figure 4-12-d

# Imaging

## Computed Tomography (CT) Scans

### Abdominal Trauma

**Case Study 4-13**

This 3-year-old girl was punched and kicked in the abdomen by her father. She was brought to the ER with increasing abdominal girth and vomiting. Her father was sought by the police immediately after the incident. One week later he was still eluding the police.

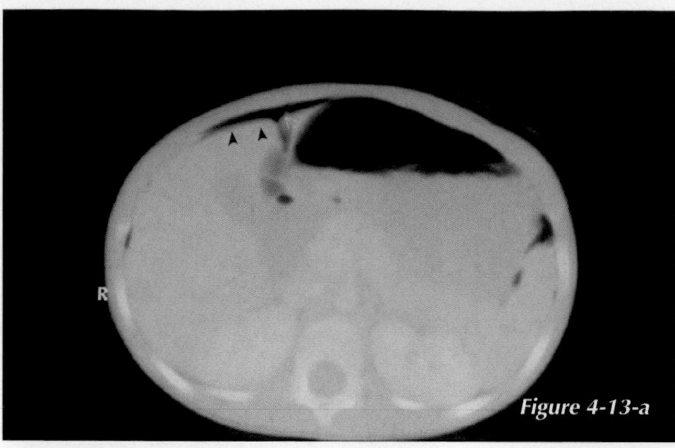

***Figure 4-13-a.*** *Non-contrast axial CT scan of the abdomen demonstrates a pneumoperitoneum.*

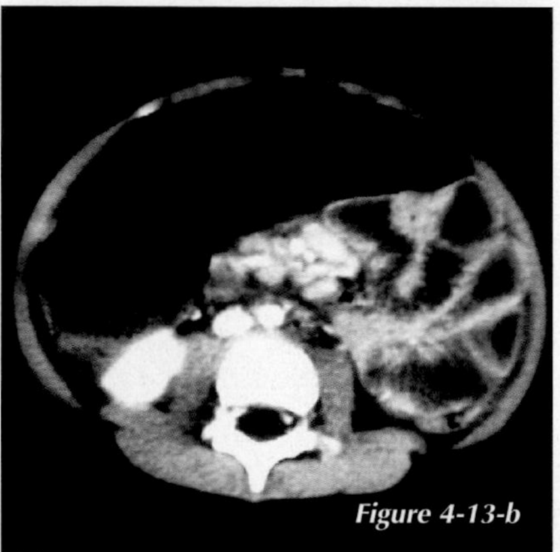

***Figure 4-13-b.*** *Contrast-enhanced axial CT scan of the abdomen demonstrates dilated bowel loops with enhancement of the bowel wall consistent with loss of peristalsis secondary to traumatic intestinal injury.*

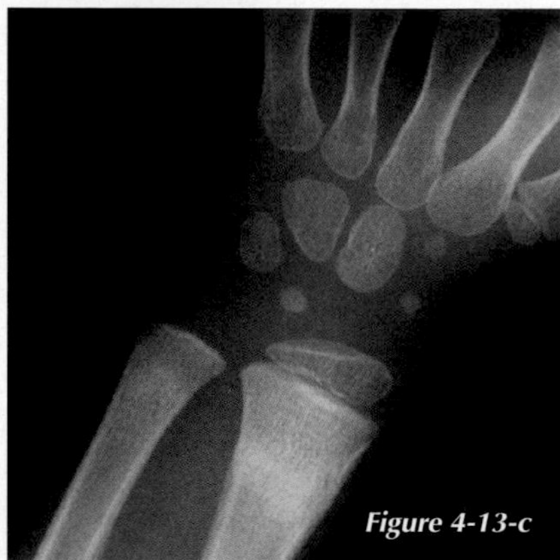

***Figure 4-13-c.*** *Frontal radiograph of the wrist demonstrates healing fractures of the distal radius and ulna.*

### Pancreatic Pseudocyst

**Case Study 4-14**

This 3-year-old boy sustained abdominal trauma from abuse.

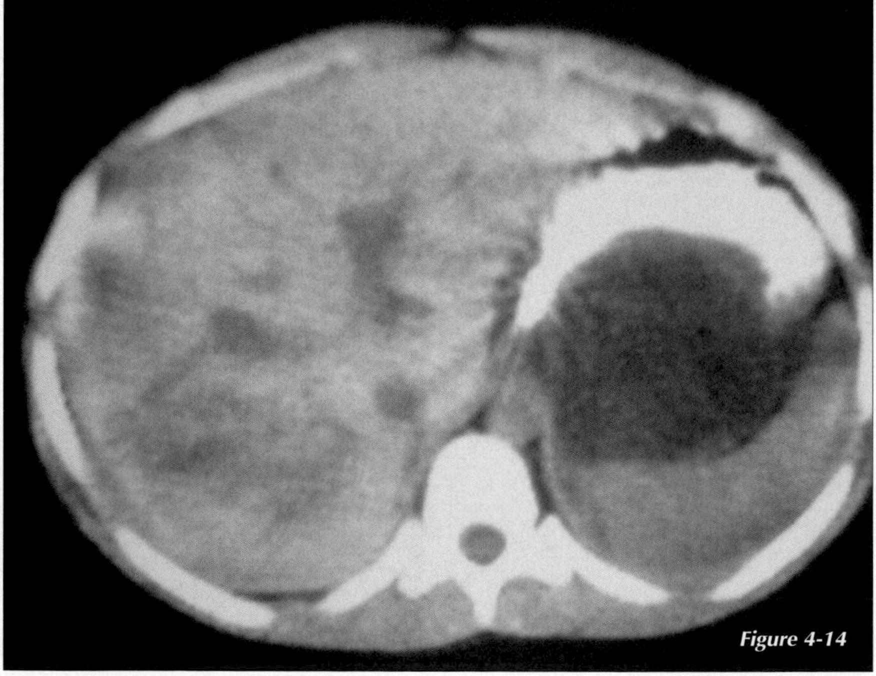

***Figure 4-14.*** *Non-contrast axial CT scan of the abdomen demonstrates a large low-density mass representing a pancreatic pseudocyst.*

# Imaging

## Upper Gastrointestinal (GI) Studies

### Duodenal Hematoma

**Case Study 4-15**

This 4-year-old girl sustained severe abdominal trauma.

***Figure 4-15-a.*** *Upper GI study demonstrates obstruction in the third portion of the duodenum. The duodenum is dilated.*

***Figure 4-15-b.*** *Upper GI study demonstrates the dilated duodenum with "picket fence" appearance of the third portion of the duodenum consistent with hematoma.*

***Figure 4-15-c.*** *Contrast-enhanced axial CT scan demonstrates duodenal hematoma.*

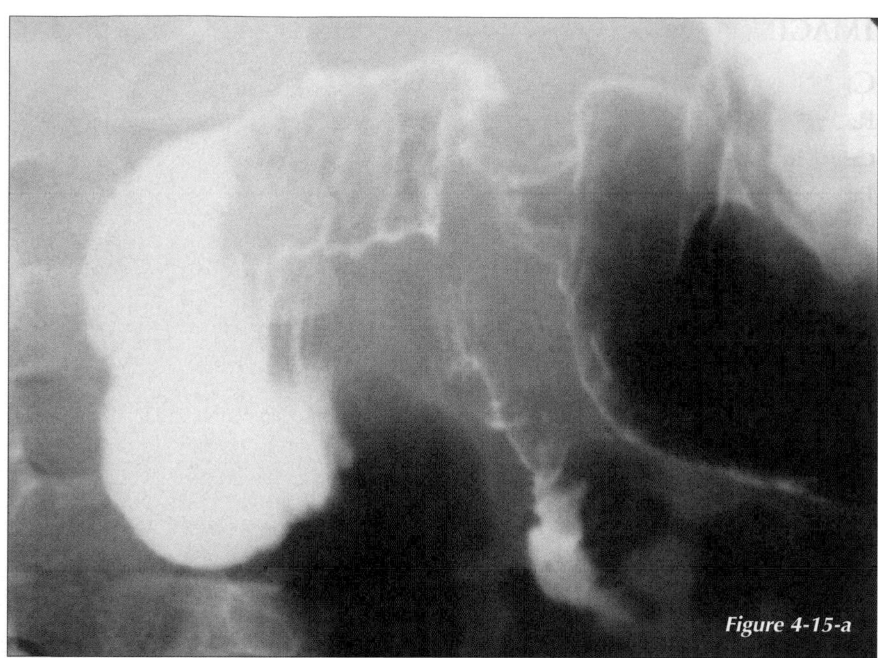

Figure 4-15-a

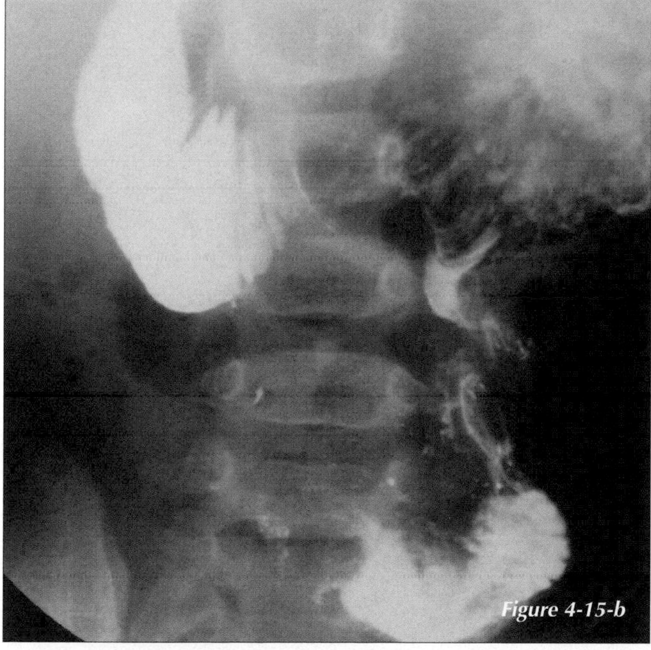

Figure 4-15-b

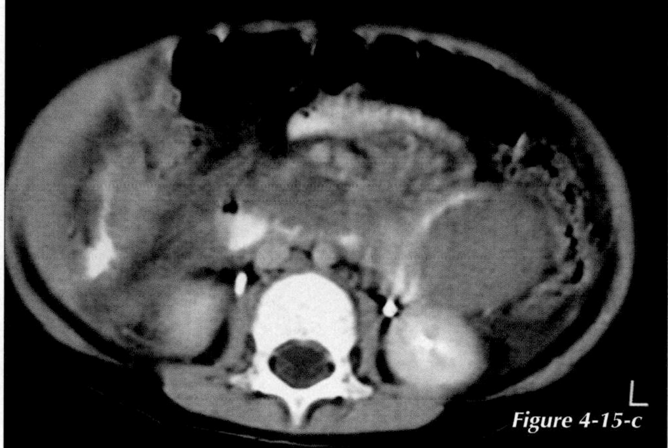


Figure 4-15-c

## Brusies

**Case Study 5-9**

This child suffered a blow to the face.

***Figure 5-9.*** *Bruised upper lip from blow to the face.*

**Case Study 5-10**

This child was examined after being struck with a baby bottle by a sibling. A credible witness was present to verify the story. (Photograph courtesy of Children's Memorial Hospital, Chicago)

***Figure 5-10.*** *Child struck in the face with a baby bottle.*

## Pattern Injuries

**Case Study 5-11**

This child was a victim of child abuse homicide due to multiple trauma cased by the mother's boyfriend. (Photograph courtesy of Cook County Medical Examiner's Office, Chicago.)

***Figure 5-11.*** *Patterned bruise to the cheek, most likely caused by human teeth.*

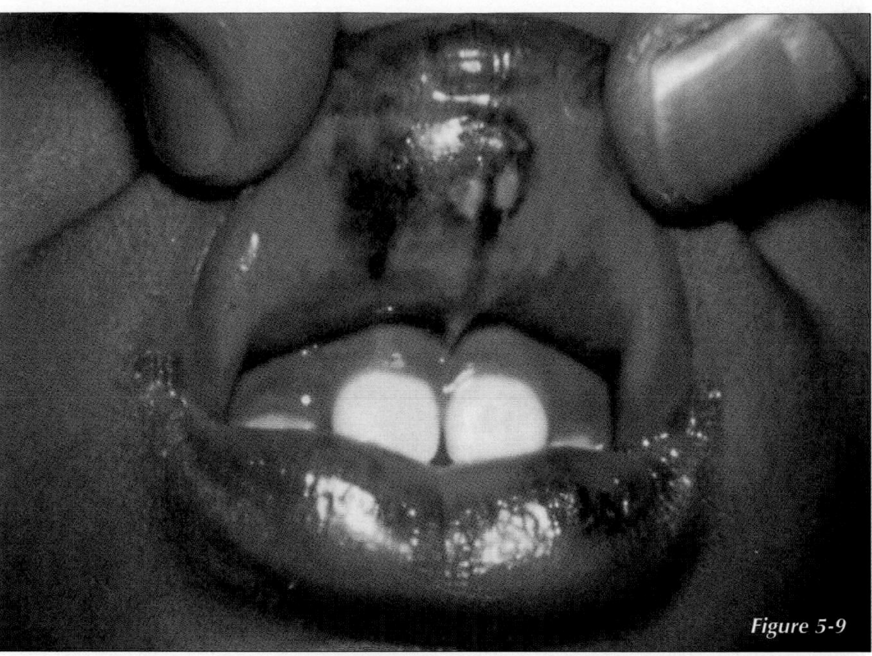

Figure 5-9

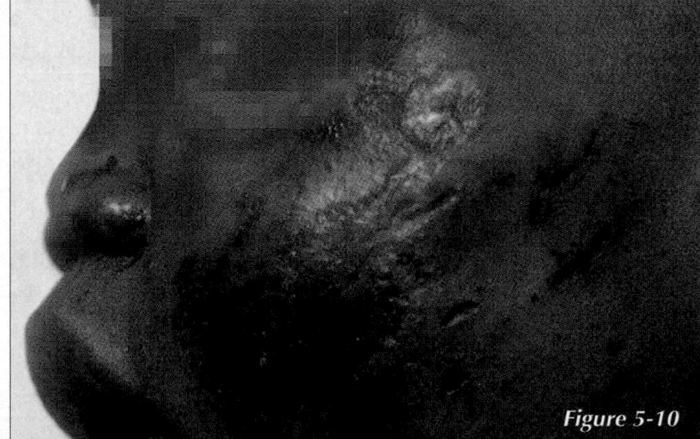

Figure 5-10

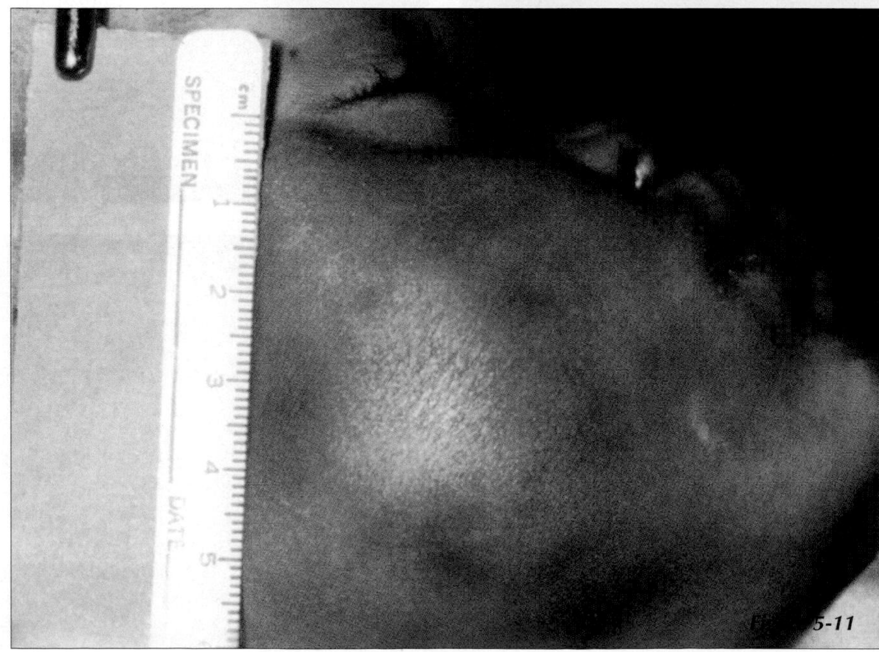

# Pattern Injuries

**Case Study 5-12**

This child was admitted to the Pediatric Intensive Care Unit for trauma resulting from a severe beating by an adult. The child ultimately fell into a coma and died from the multiple injuries. (Photograph courtesy of Children's Memorial Hospital, Chicago.)

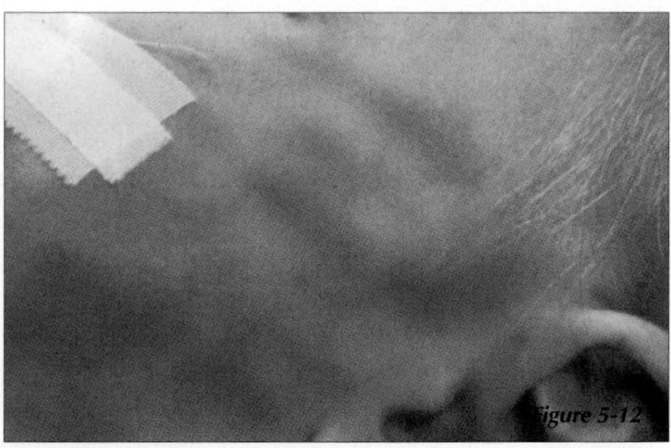


***Figure 5-12.*** *Marks from a belt buckle used to strike this child's face.*

# Bite Marks

## Animal Bite Marks

**Case Study 5-13**

This 5-month-old girl died from multiple animal bites covering her entire body. The family owned two dogs, a Miniature Doberman Pinscher puppy and an adult Rottweiler. According to the parents, the Rottweiler was locked outside on the back porch, and the Miniature Pinscher was inside the apartment where the girl was attacked while sleeping in her baby carrier. The parents, who were alleged to be impaired and claimed to be asleep during the entire incident, said that only the Miniature Pinscher had been inside the apartment and was responsible for the fatal attack. Prior to calling the police and paramedics, the parents washed the girl and dressed her in a clean dress. The baby carrier was devoid of blood when police arrived. Both dogs were euthanized by Animal Control, and the heads were brought to the medical examiner's office in order to examine and compare the dentition of both dogs with the bite marks. Analysis of the dentition determined that both dogs had participated in the attack, with the Rottweiler causing the most severe and fatal injuries. The Miniature Pinscher's permanent teeth were just erupting into the oral cavity, and some primary teeth were loose, so it was not surprising that the bites from the smaller dog were fairly superficial. The Rottweiler had also been abused, evident by the cigarette burns on the dog's muzzle and head. They were somewhat healed when the incident occurred. The parents were charged with neglect.

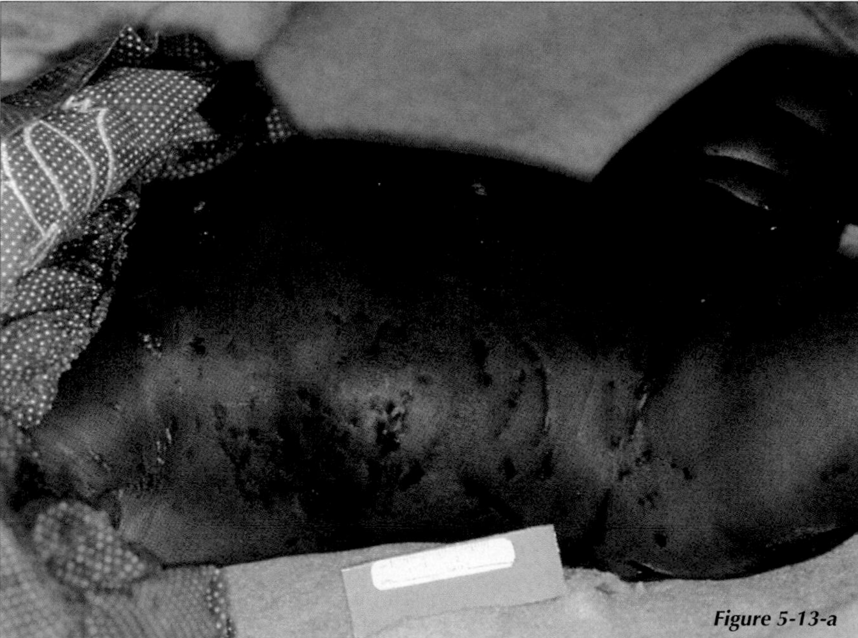


***Figure 5-13-a.*** *Dog bites appearing over the entire body of this child.*

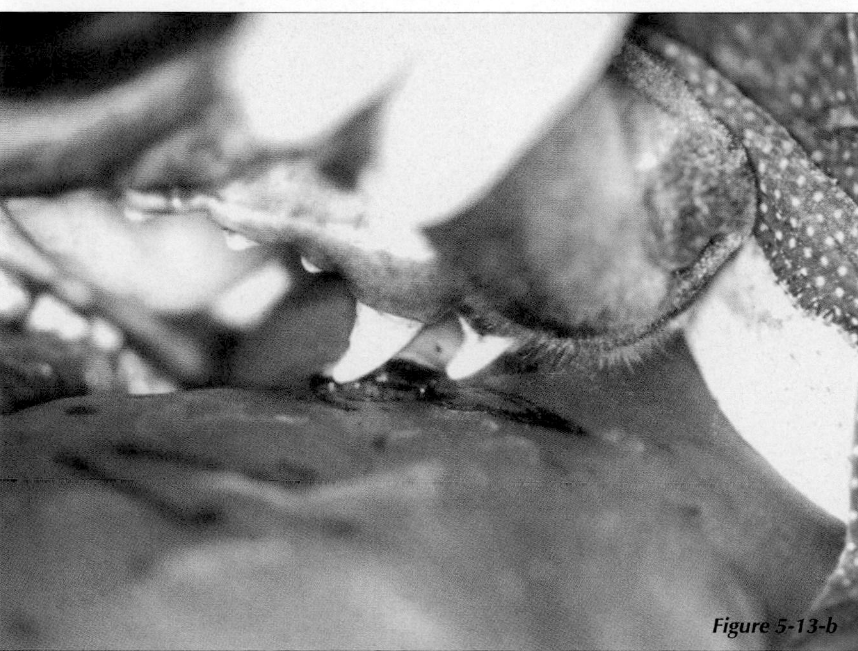


***Figure 5-13-b.*** *Analysis of the dog's dentition and the bite marks.*

# Bite Marks

## Animal Bite Marks

**Case Study 5-14**

This infant died from multiple animal bites. He was left unattended with the family's golden retriever when the dog attacked the infant. The dog inflicted a bite across the boy's upper back in addition to fracturing the boy's skull by biting it.

***Figure 5-14**. Dog bite to the back of the boy, noting the evidence of six incisors and the outside-in pattern of the cuspids.*

## Human Bite Marks

**Case Study 5-15**

This child was bitten by an adult. The father was ultimately implicated by comparing his dentition with the bruised bite marks. (Photograph courtesy of Cook County Medical Examiner's Office, Chicago.)

***Figure 5-15.** Bite mark.*

**Case Study 5-16**

This child was seen at the hospital emergency department with the physician's notation of a "patterned injury of unknown origin" that was not investigated further.

***Figure 5-16.** Bite mark.*

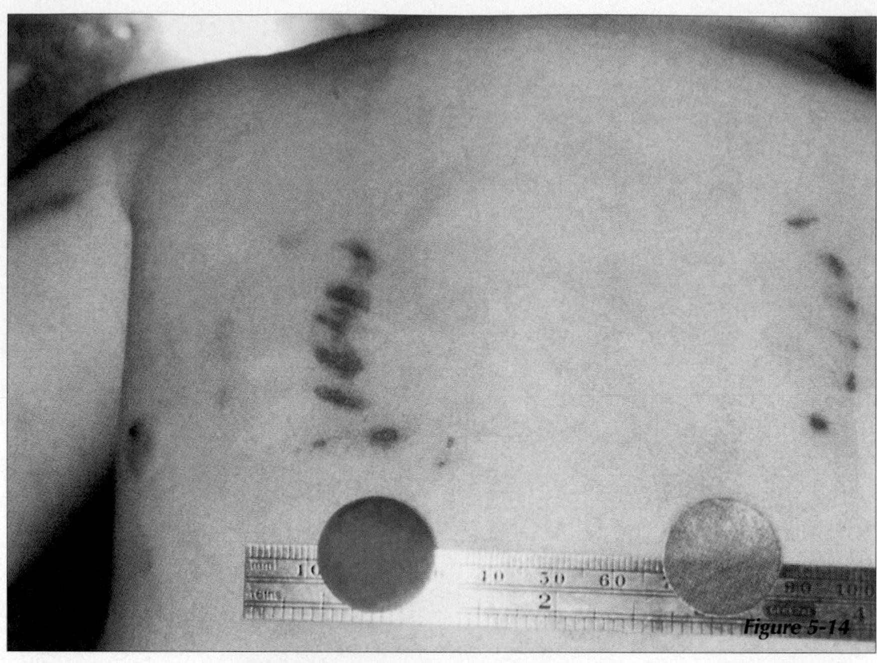

Figure 5-14

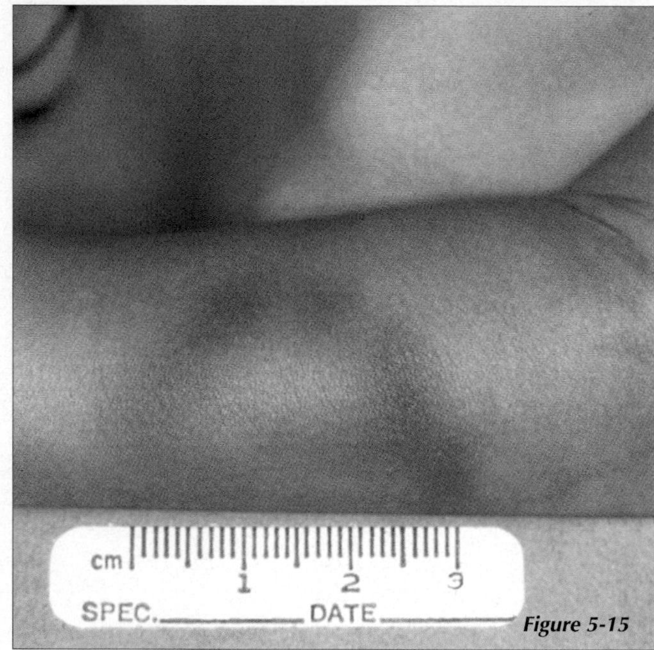


Figure 5-15

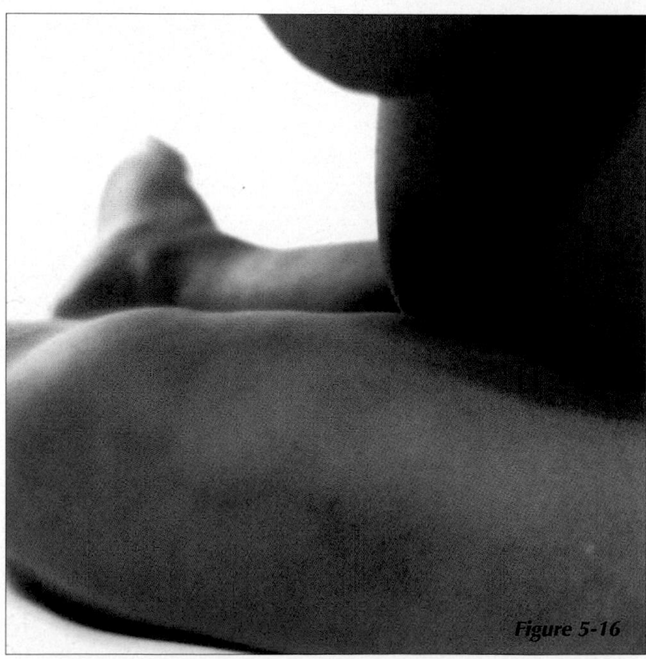

Figure 5-16

# Bite Marks

## Human Bite Marks

**Case Study 5-17**

This child died as a result of severe abuse that included multiple bites by an adult. (Photographs courtesy of Cook County Medical Examiner's Office, Chicago.)

***Figures 5-17-a** and **b.** Multiple bite marks on the arm.*

**Case Study 5-18**

This child was brought to the ER with multiple bite marks on the body. There were opposing bite marks on the top and sole of the foot, most likely caused by the foot being placed in the perpetrator's mouth and being bitten. (Photograph courtesy of Cook County Medical Examiner's Office, Chicago.)

***Figure 5-18.** Bite mark to the top of this child's foot.*

**Case Study 5-19**

This child was examined with a bite mark of unknown origin. (Photgraph courtesy of Children's Memorial Hospital, Chicago.)

***Figure 5-19.** Bite mark to the right calf. Note the absence of a scale or other means to measure the injury for comparison.*

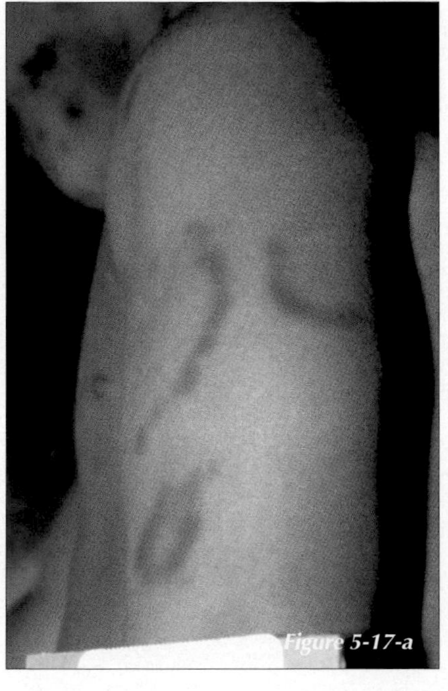

Figure 5-17-a

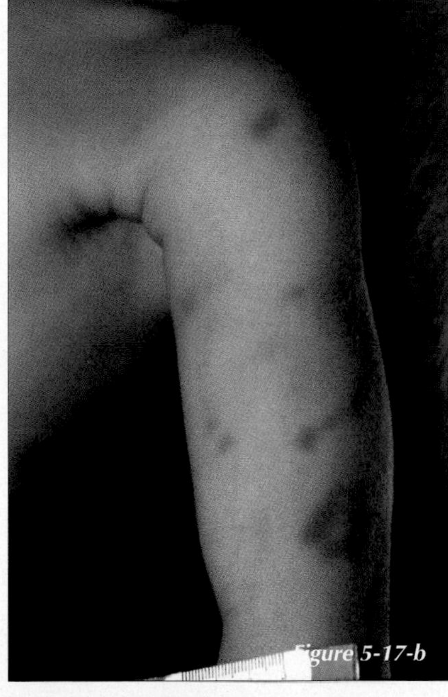

Figure 5-17-b

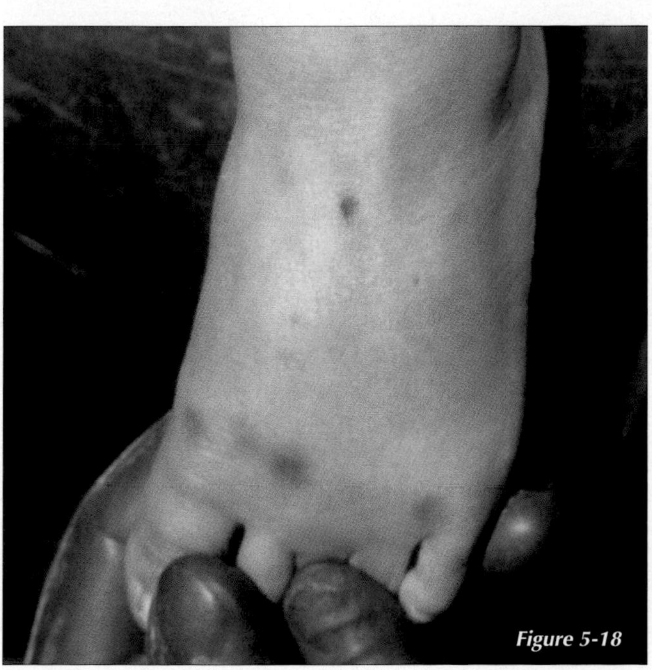

Figure 5-18

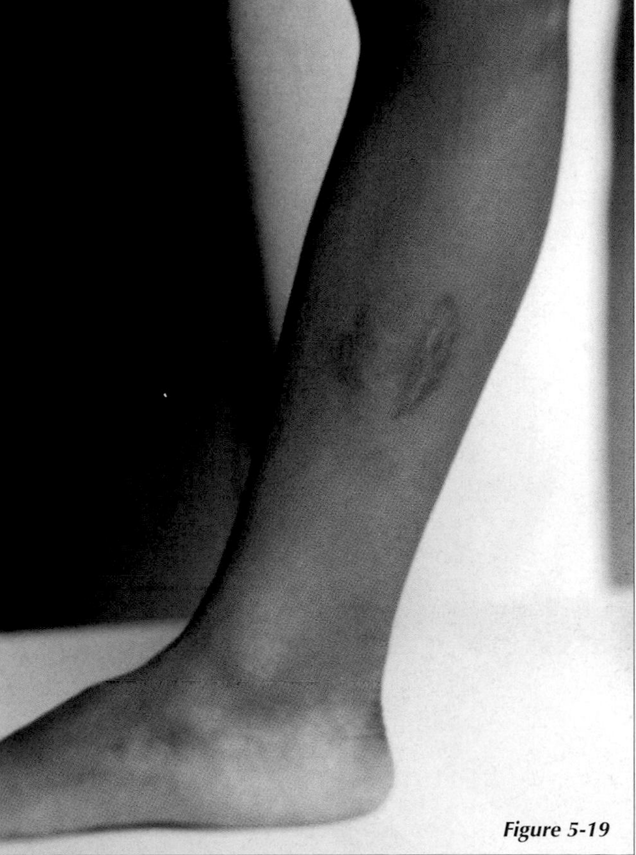

Figure 5-19

# Bite Marks

## Human Bite Marks

**Case Study 5-20**

This child was brought to the pediatric dental clinic approximately 10 days after the injury was inflicted. Due to the scabbing, all that could be determined was that the injury was adult in origin. No further action was taken.

***Figure 5-20.*** *A scabbed-over bite mark approximately 1 week old.*

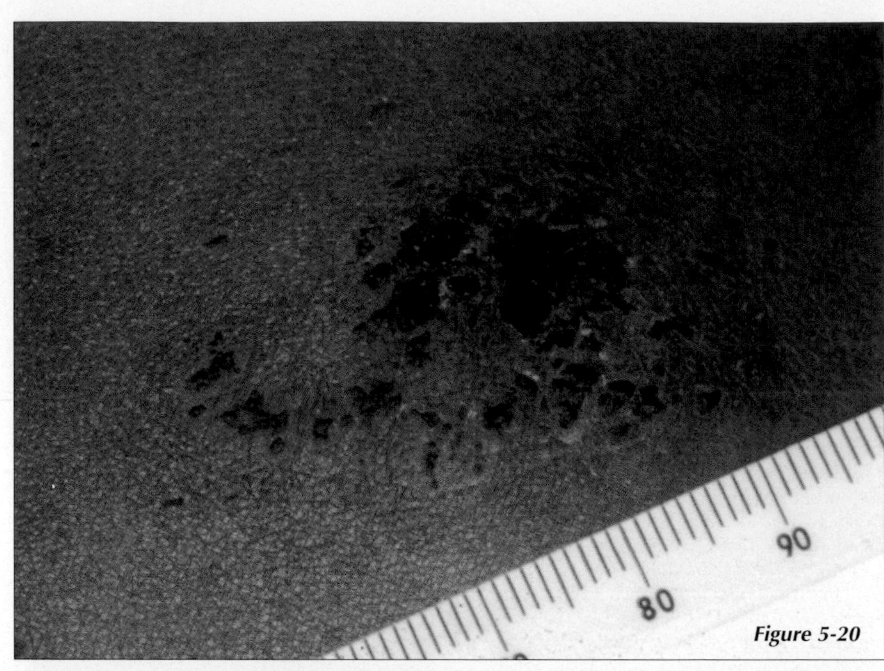

**Case Study 5-21**

This child was examined for multiple abusive injuries, including human bite marks.

***Figure 5-21.*** *Photo of bite mark taken with a 35-mm camera with an architectural grid in the focusing screen and an ABFO No. 2 scale in the frame of the photo. This is an ideal photo document of a bite mark.*

**Case Study 5-22**

This 17-month-old boy was examined for a human bite mark on his right arm.

***Figure 5-22.*** *Human bite mark on the arm.*

**Figure 5-20**

**Figure 5-21**

**Figure 5-22**

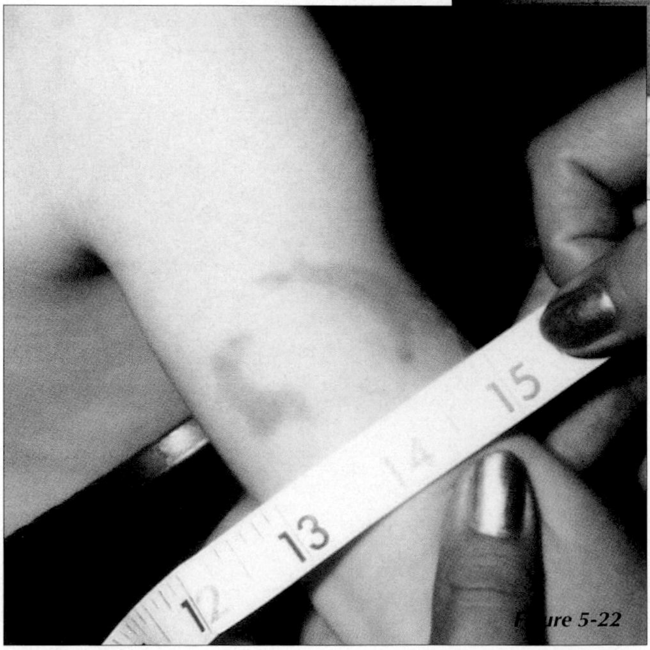

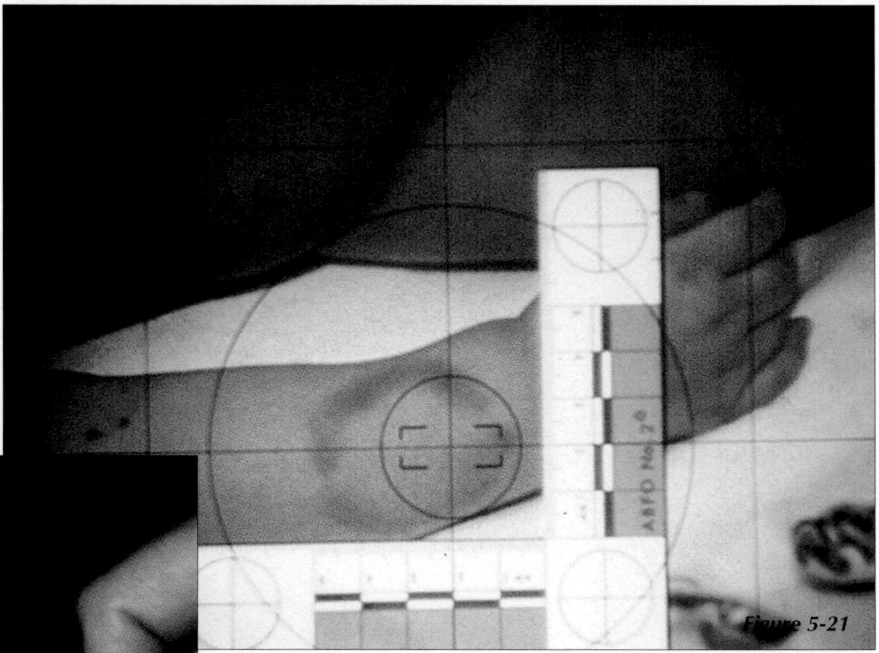

# Bite Marks

## Human Bite Marks

### Case Study 5-23

A sibling of this 11-month-old girl caused these bite marks. The case was reported to CPS for poor supervision. Note the lack of scale in the photo, which is simultaneously the most important factor and most frequent error in photodocumentation.

***Figures 5-23-a, b,*** *and* ***c.*** *Multiple bites on the back, chest, and side of an 11-month-old girl.*

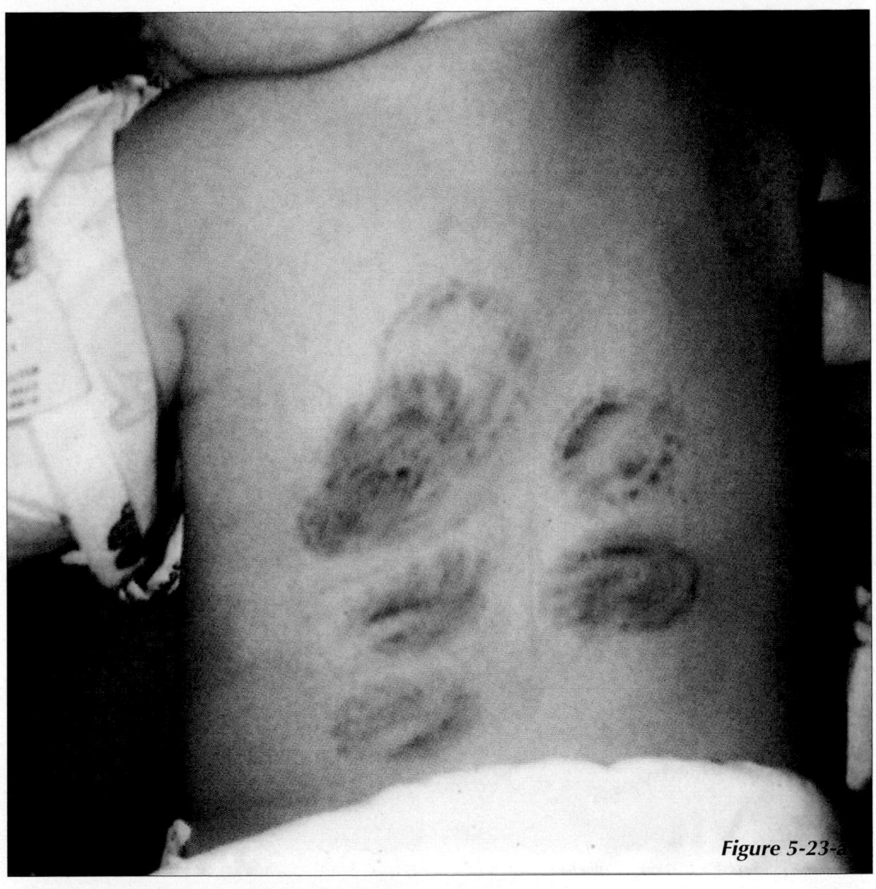

Figure 5-23-a

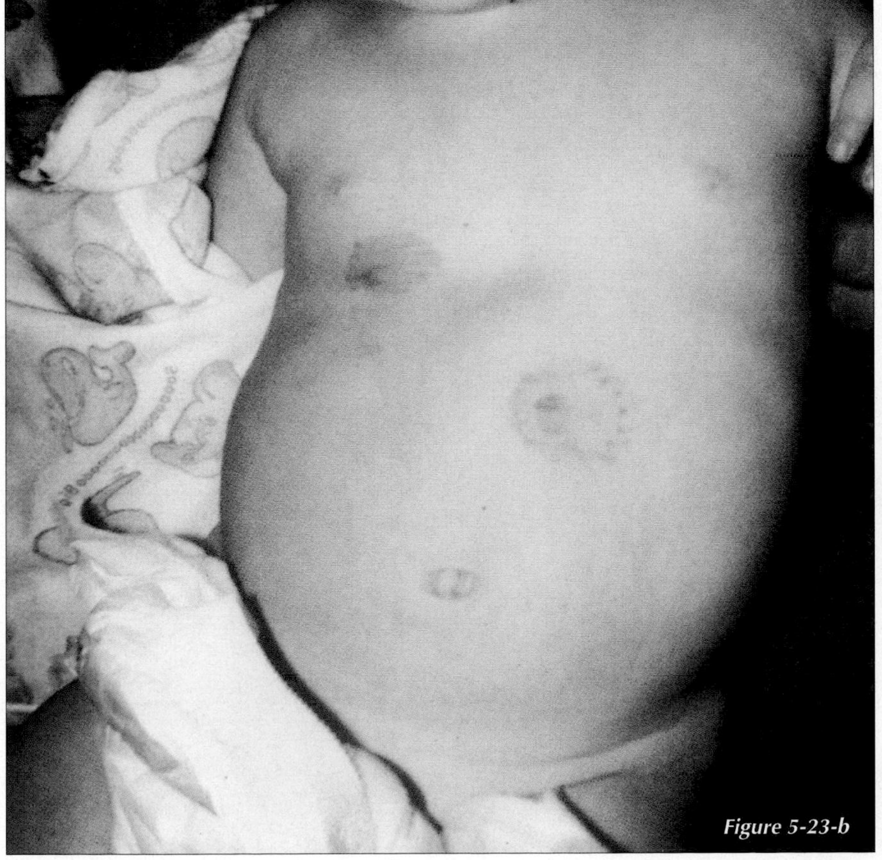

Figure 5-23-b

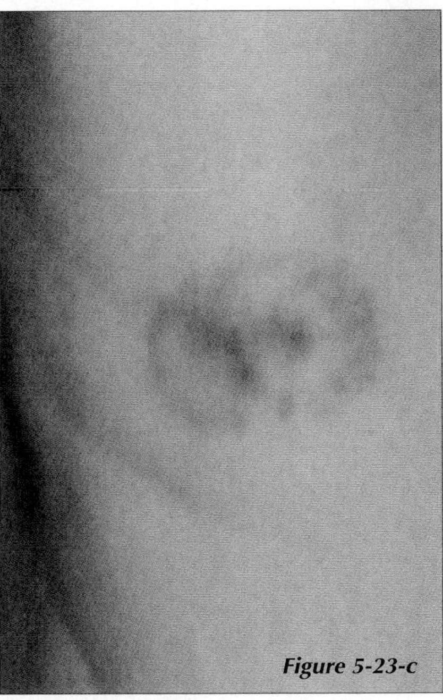

Figure 5-23-c

# Bite Marks

## Human Bite Marks

**Case Study 5-24**

This 15-month-old child was brought to the ER with multiple bite marks to the back, abdomen, chest, and arms.

***Figure 5-24-a.*** *Bite marks to the back of this child.*

***Figure 5-24-b.*** *Note that the outer circle of the bite mark, and the central ecchymotic area. Ecchymoses from suction or tongue thrusting are absent in some of the bites.*

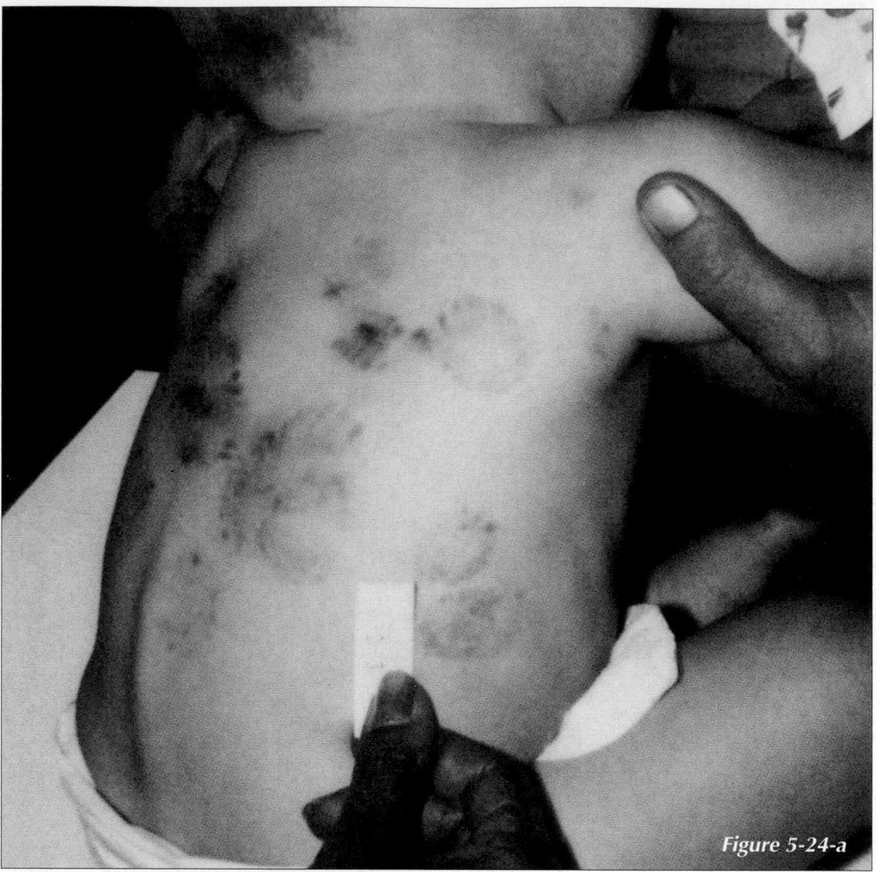

Figure 5-24-a

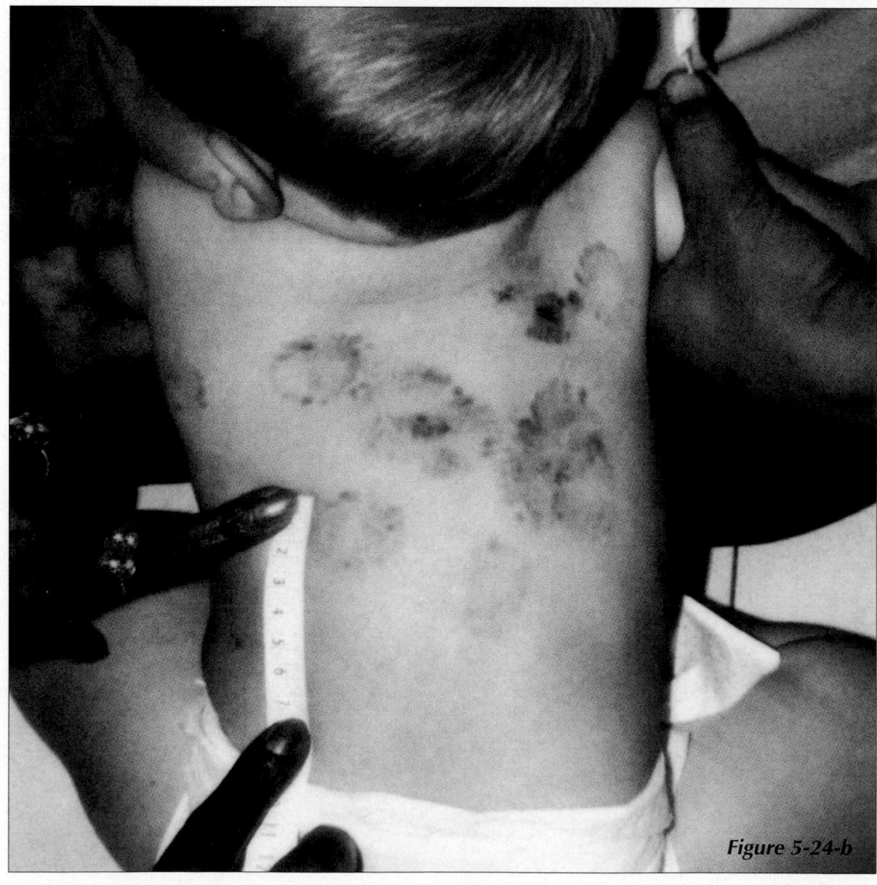

Figure 5-24-b

# Sexual Abuse

## Multiple Injuries

### Case Study 5-25

This girl had a well-documented history of physical abuse and trauma allegedly perpetrated by the mother's boyfriend. The mother had been advised not to allow the boyfriend to have any further contact with the girl; however, the mother chose to allow the situation to continue, which culminated in a fatal attack. The autopsy and subsequent investigation revealed that the mother actually participated in the final attack, which included repeated kicks to the girl's abdomen, bite marks on various parts of the body, self-inflicted bite marks that were caused by forcing the child's own hand into her mouth as a gag, incised and avulsive bite marks to the buttocks, and additional vaginal trauma indicative of sexual abuse. There were also areas on the scalp where the hair had been pulled and later braided over with hair bows to conceal the injuries. The bite marks on the buttocks were determined to have been made by the boyfriend, while the mother inflicted many of the bites on the rest of the girl's body. It took approximately 8 hours to complete the autopsy and thoroughly document all of the injuries. (Photographs courtesy of Cook County Medical Examiner's Office, Chicago.)

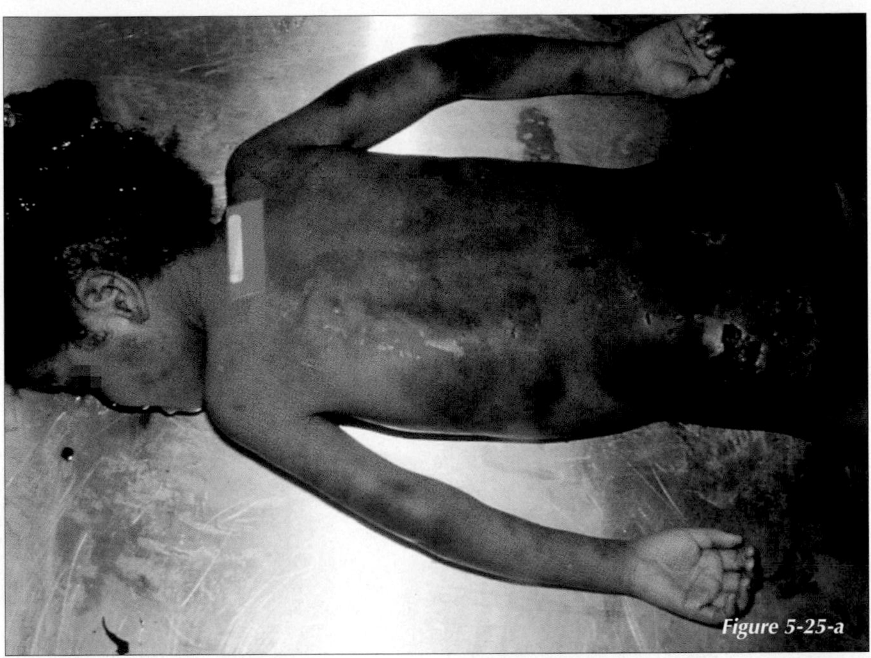

Figure 5-25-a

***Figure 5-25-a.*** *There are at least 24 bite marks shown here, including marks to the back, buttocks, and self-inflicted marks to this girl's wrist.*

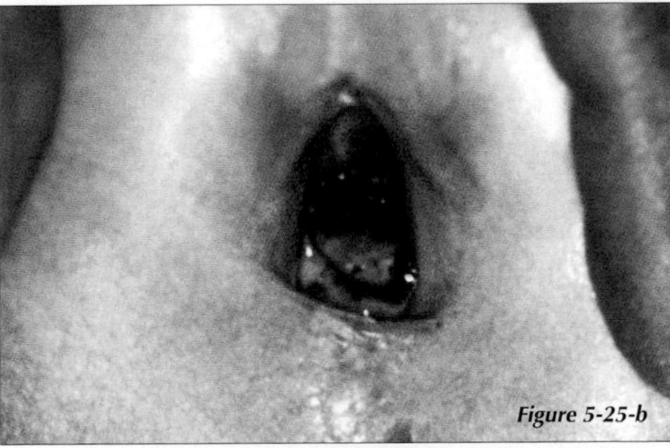

Figure 5-25-b

***Figure 5-25-b.*** *Vaginal trauma is also present.*

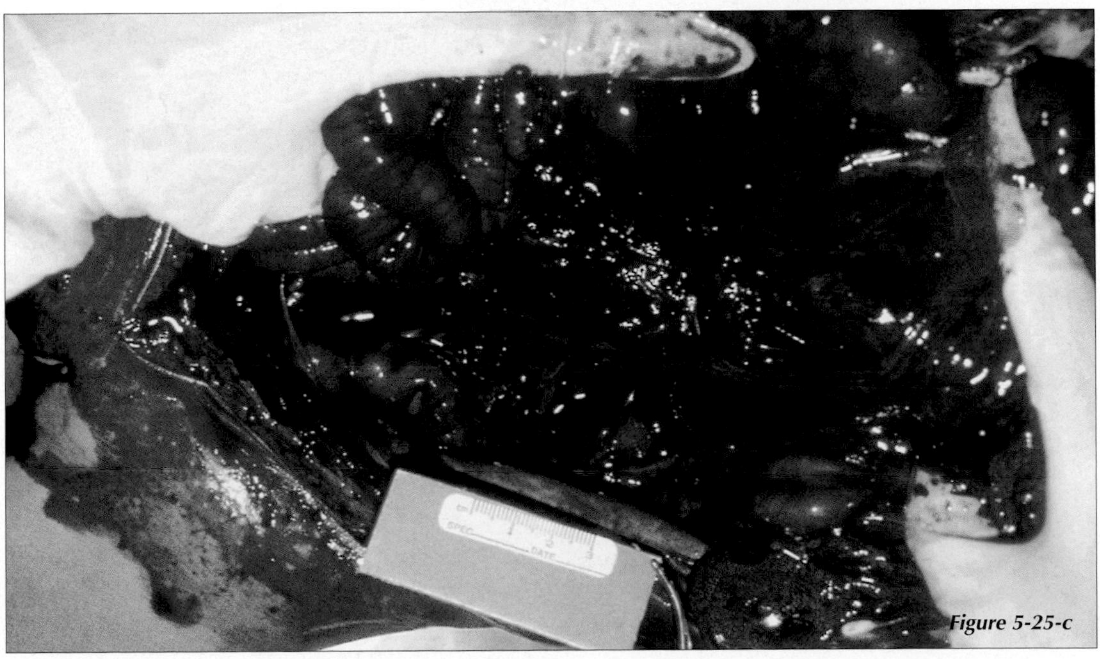

Figure 5-25-c

***Figure 5-25-c.*** *Abdominal trauma due to multiple kicks to the abdomen.*

# Sexual Abuse

## Ecchymosis

### Case Study 5-26

This child was a victim of sexual abuse.

***Figure 5-26.*** *Ecchymosis likely due to suction is present on the neck.*

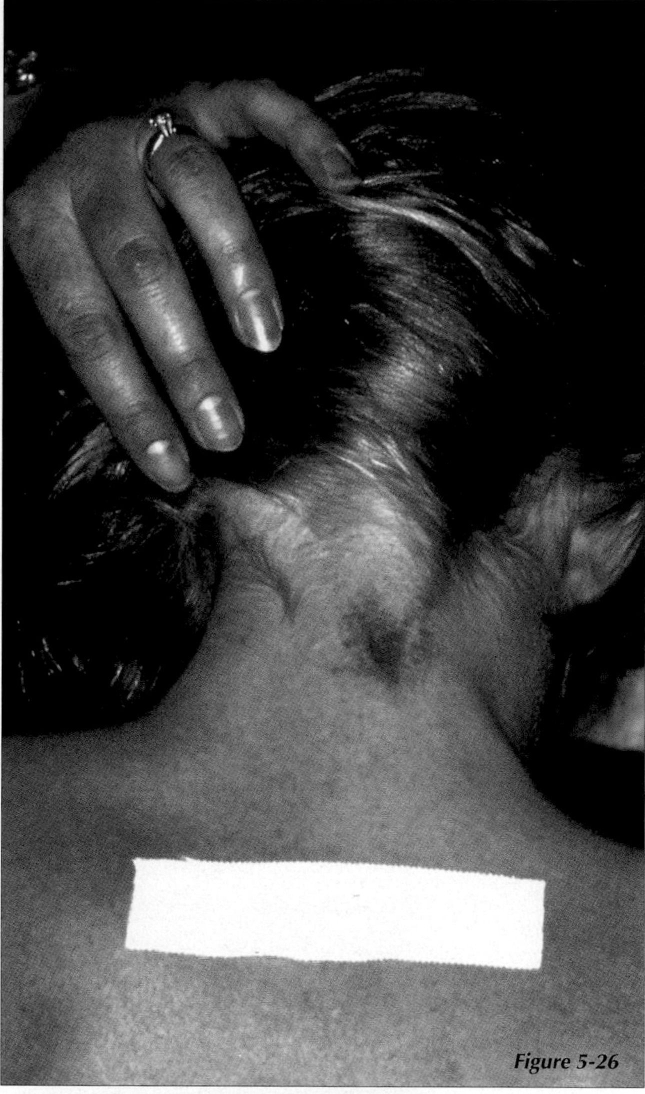

Figure 5-26

# Neglect

## Caries

### Case Study 5-27

This 12-year-old child was seen in the dentist's office for toothaches and bad breath. Examination revealed seven carious teeth, four with draining abscesses. After several broken appointments to complete treatment, the case was reported to CPS. CPS oversaw the remaining treatment over the subsequent 6 weeks.

***Figure 5-27.*** *Rampant caries. Note 3 active abscesses evidenced by gumboils (paruli).*

Untreated rampant caries, which must include the lower anterior teeth to be classified as rampant, with multiply abscessed teeth is a serious medical condition. Ongoing multiple infections in the anterior triangle of the face can progress and become life threatening. This type of chronic neglect can lead to difficulty eating, speaking, and concentrating in school.

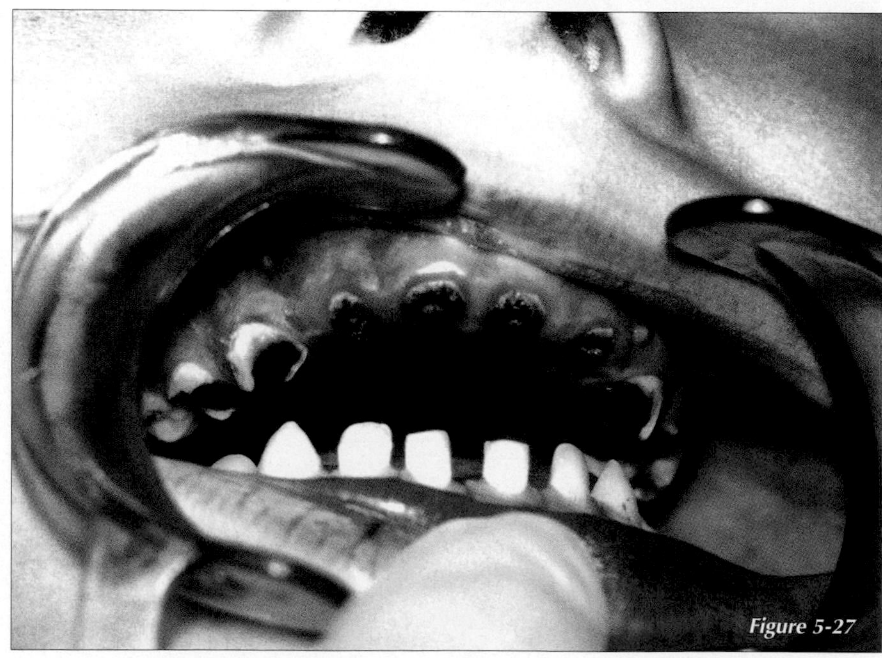

Figure 5-27

Chapter 6

# OPHTHALMOLOGY

Brian Forbes, MD
Randell Alexander, MD, PhD

The eye can be a direct target of assault or it can be injured in the course of more generalized abuse such as shaken baby syndrome (SBS). The eyes should be carefully examined when there is any form of head injury with external indications of periorbital or eye trauma and in situations such as SBS. For infants with broken ribs, SBS has to be considered and appropriate studies must be done to determine if this is present. As part of this examination, a funduscopic eye examination is mandatory.

While a pediatrician or neurologist may detect varying degrees of damage to the eye, such as injuries to the anterior chamber or retina, an ophthalmologist has the advantage of experience and equipment to detect and identify any injuries related to abuse, or to distinguish findings as being secondary to other diseases or conditions. Traditionally, most physicians use direct ophthalmoscopy, while ophthalmologists use indirect ophthalmoscopy to obtain a better view of the retina and other internal structures. For external or anterior structures, a slit lamp in the ER or the ophthalmologist's office can provide excellent magnification.

Direct injuries to the eye can include scratches or trauma to the cornea. Such injuries are painful and can be identified using fluorescein dye and a slit-lamp examination. Direct trauma to the eye can also produce a hyphema. Deeper into the eye, retinal blood vessels can be broken or torn with the repeated violent shakings typical of SBS. Retinal folds and retinoschisis are occasionally seen with SBS, but almost never in other circumstances. Bleeding into the vitreous body can occur with severe retinal hemorrhages.

In addition to location, the pattern of injuries is important when assessing eye trauma. The most important pattern of abusive injury involves retinal hemorrhages. When the examiner looks into the eye, finding one or two spots near the optic nerve is not a specific finding and may represent abuse or other conditions; therefore, it is important to determine the overall extent of retinal bleeding. As with bruises elsewhere on the body, the examiner must determine which layers of the retina are involved, the number of retinal hemorrhages, and their location. Retinal hemorrhages that are numerous, occur in multiple layers, and extend toward the periphery are rarely described in any condition except SBS. Such findings might be slightly less than 100% specific for abuse, but when coupled with other findings and the history, the diagnosis of SBS typically holds. Unilateral retinal hemorrhages are periodically seen in SBS and are not associated with the side where intracranial bleeding is seen. This absence of co-unilaterality is one argument against intracranial pressure causing the multiple retinal hemorrhages commonly seen with SBS.

## Unresponsive Victim of SBS

### Case Study 6-1

Paramedics were called at 4:00 PM to the home of this 13-month-old child who was found breathing irregularly. On arrival they found the child to be limp, pale, and unresponsive to pain. Respirations were 10/minute, pulse rate was 70/minute, and blood pressure was 150/90 mm Hg. No external injuries were evident. The initial history given by the mother was that the child fell off the bed, let out a cry, and then became unconscious. Paramedics noted their concerns regarding the discrepancies between the history, the findings, and the possibility of SBS. The child was intubated and an IV line was started. On arrival at the ER, the pulse rate and blood pressure had improved slightly. The pupils were fixed and dilated and the child remained unresponsive. A computed tomographic (CT) scan revealed a left frontoparietal subdural hematoma with a slight midline shift. There was some lack of gray-white differentiation of the brain, which is a sign of significant swelling or damage.

***Figure 6-1-a.*** *Inferolateral view of the right fundus showing a large retinal fold and retinal hemorrhages.*

***Figure 6-1-b.*** *Medial view of the right fundus showing the head of the optic nerve and numerous retinal hemorrhages.*

***Figure 6-1-c.*** *Lateral view of the right retina illustrating the large retinal fold and more retinal hemorrhages.*

***Figure 6-1-d.*** *View of the superior portion of the right retina. Note the numerous retinal hemorrhages extending out toward the periphery.*

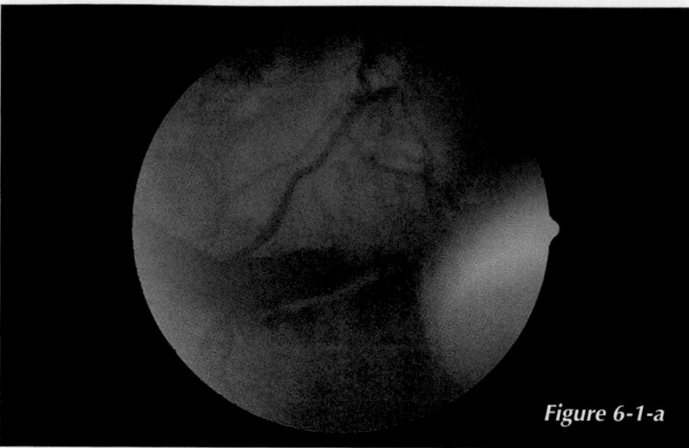

Figure 6-1-a

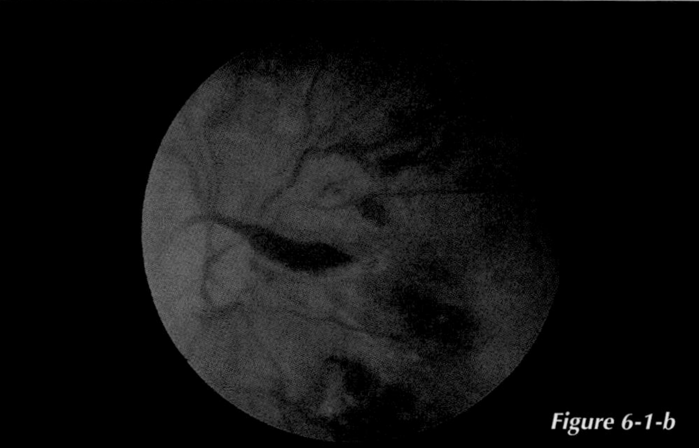

Figure 6-1-b

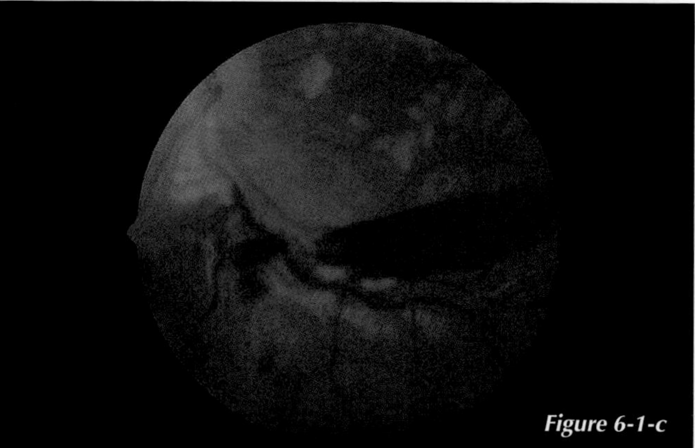

Figure 6-1-c

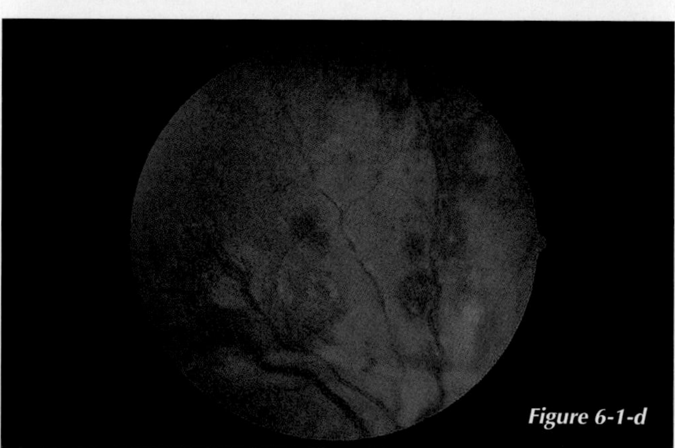

Figure 6-1-d

# Unresponsive Victim of SBS

**Case Study 6-1** *(continued)*

***Figure 6-1-e.*** *View of the superior portion of the left retina showing multiple retinal hemorrhages.*

***Figure 6-1-f.*** *Inferolateral view of the left retina showing an arc of bleeding corresponding to a retinal fold. Note the other hemorrhages.*

***Figure 6-1-g.*** *View of the inferior portion of the left retina showing multiple hemorrhages.*

***Figure 6-1-h.*** *Lateral view of the left eye showing a large fold and multiple hemorrhages.*

***Figure 6-1-i.*** *Centered on the optic nerve, note the many retinal hemorrhages and the fold to the lateral left side.*

Further history confirmed the mother's earlier history of what supposedly happened, and also established that the mother was the only person at home with the child. The child's condition deteriorated further. Various studies showed brain death, and the ventilator was discontinued the next day.

The history is inconsistent with the pattern and severity of the injuries. It was determined that the cause of death was SBS, and the manner was homicide. The mother was arrested.

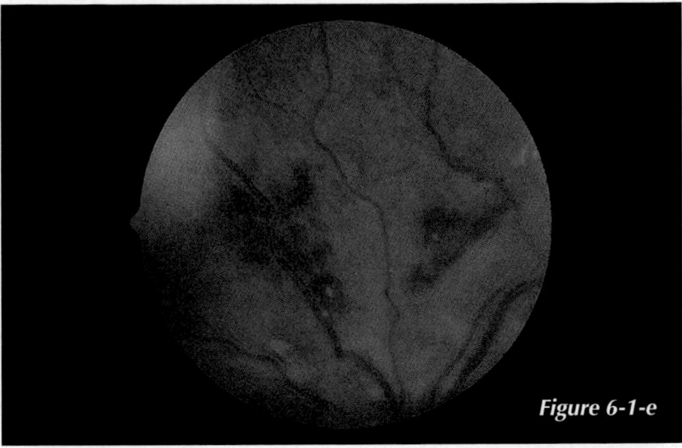

Figure 6-1-e

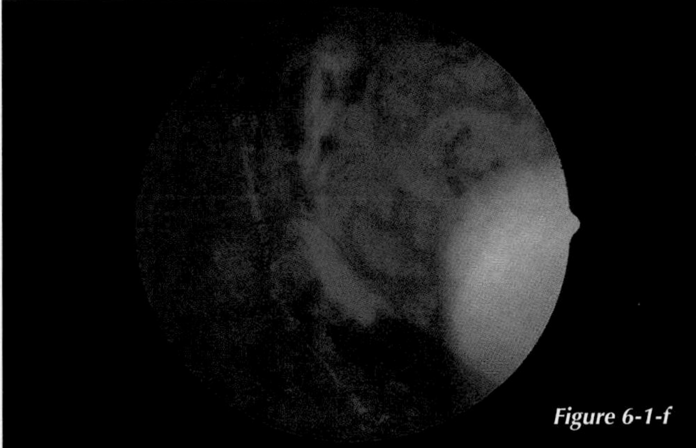

Figure 6-1-f

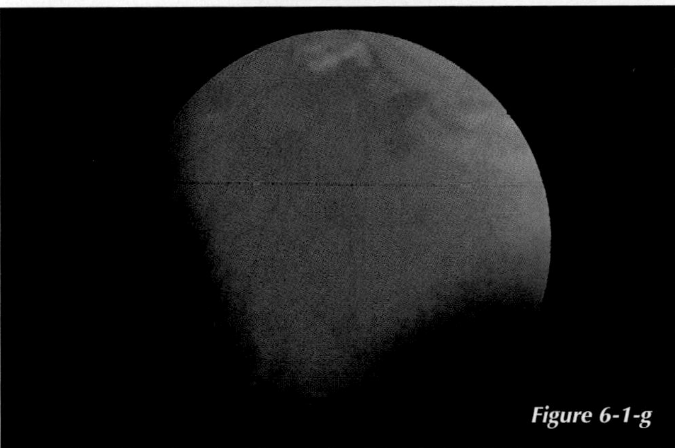

Figure 6-1-g

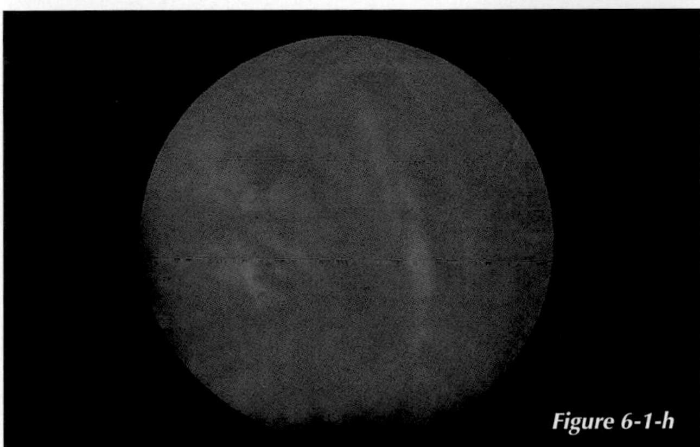

Figure 6-1-h

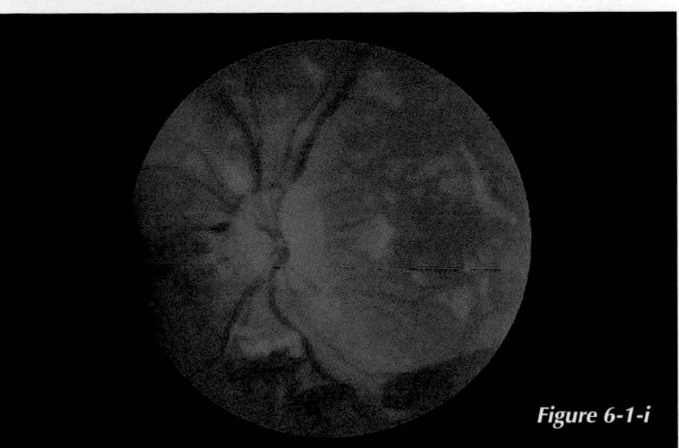

Figure 6-1-i

# Seizures Caused by SBS

**Case Study 6-2**

This 5-month-old girl was brought to the ER by the mother's boyfriend because of an apparent seizure. Medical staff noted she was having continual seizures and administered appropriate medications. The girl had a bulging fontanel and seemed less responsive than could be explained by her postictal state and the medications she received. Examination showed no signs of external trauma. A CT scan revealed acute bilateral thin frontal subdural hemorrhages and an interhemispheric hemorrhage. The results of CT scans of the abdomen, liver and pancreatic enzyme determinations, and a urinalysis were all normal. The skeletal survey revealed no additional injuries. An ophthalmological consultation was obtained. The findings of the examination of the right eye were normal.

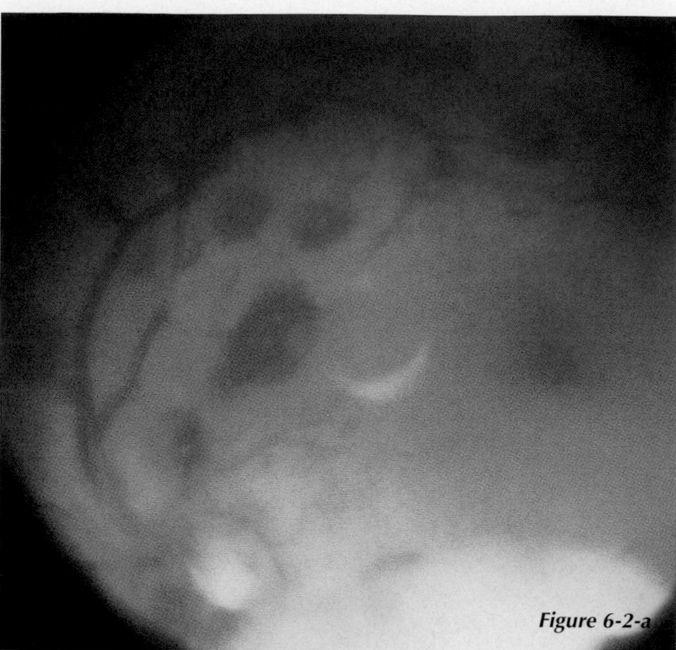

Figure 6-2-a

**Figure 6-2-a.** *The superolateral portion of the left eye showing numerous retinal hemorrhages.*

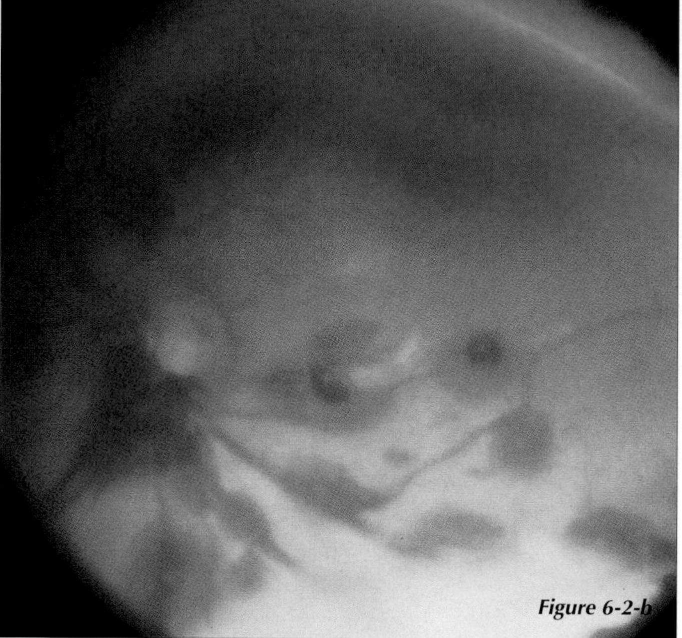

Figure 6-2-b

**Figure 6-2-b.** *The inferior view of the left eye showing numerous retinal hemorrhages, including bleeding partially obscuring the optic nerve.*

# HEMATOMA WITH SBS

**Case Study 6-3**

This 7-month-old child was left with a 24-year-old nanny when both parents left early one day for their jobs as medical residents. The nanny had also worked for the parents' friends who had recently completed their residencies and moved on professionally. During the day, the nanny called the mother at work to tell her that the child was breathing irregularly. The mother asked the nanny to bring the child to the hospital where she worked. On arrival the child was pale and minimally responsive to pain. No external injuries were seen. The nanny gave no history of an injury and the child was suspected of having meningitis. A CT scan revealed a right frontoparietal subdural hematoma with a midline shift. On finding that marked retinal hemorrhages were present, an evaluation for child abuse was initiated. The child's condition eventually stabilized medically but the child exhibited numerous neurological deficits. The nanny later admitted to having shaken the child; she plea-bargained for time served and agreed to cease working as a nanny.

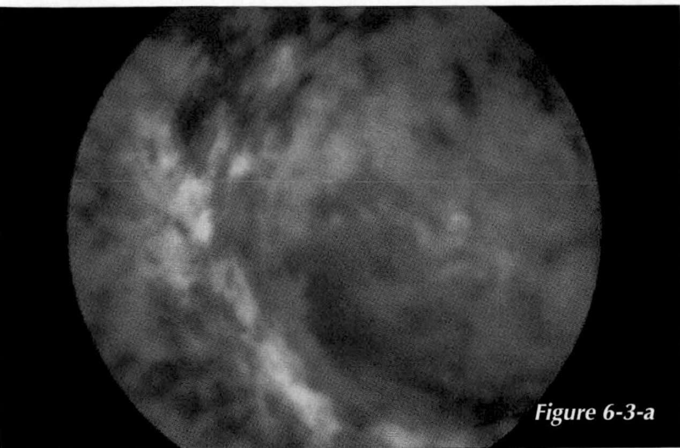
Figure 6-3-a

***Figure 6-3-a.*** *Color funduscopic photograph of the child's retina. Hemorrhages are present in all layers of the retina, including the preretinal, intraretinal, subretinal, and peripapillary areas. It is important to take photographs from multiple angles to ensure proper documentation of the presence of retinal hemorrhages.*

Figure 6-3-b

***Figure 6-3-b.*** *Color funduscopic photograph of the child's retina showing hemorrhages at all layers of the retina as well as a macular fold along the inferotemporal vascular arcade. The latter finding is highly suspicious of SBS in a child of this age.*

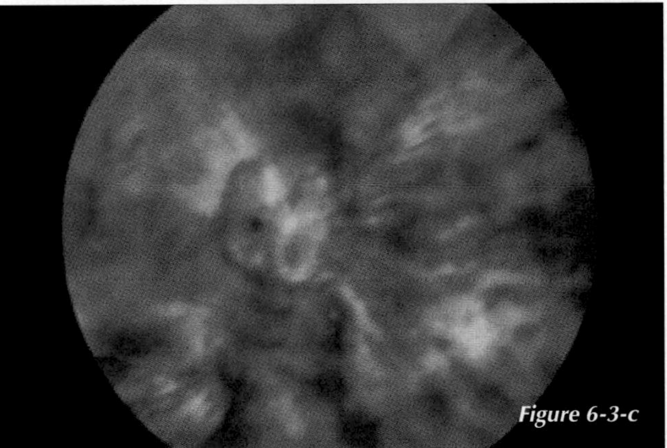
Figure 6-3-c

***Figure 6-3-c.*** *Funduscopic photograph showing hemorrhages at all layers of the retina as well papilledema, which occurs in less than 10% of cases of SBS. Optic nerve hemorrhages are also present, which are frequently associated with optic nerve sheath hemorrhages present in multiple layers with a preponderance of hemorrhaging in the subdural space.*

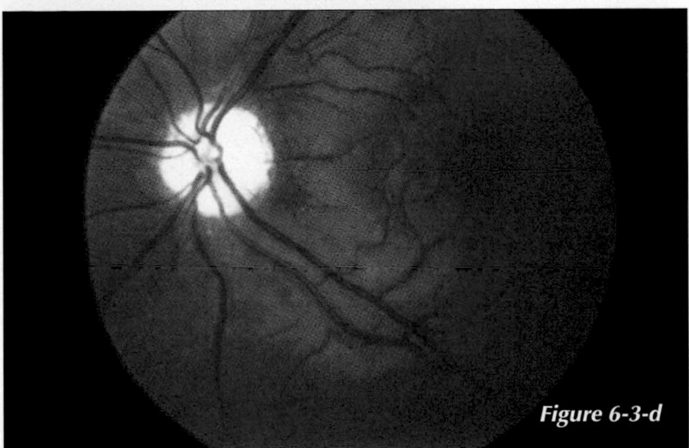
Figure 6-3-d

***Figure 6-3-d.*** *A color funduscopic photograph of the retina of this same child at 6 years old shows profound optic atrophy as a result of having been abused at 11 months old. Such optic atrophy and cortical visual impairment are the primary reasons for decreased vision in victims of SBS.*

## Retinal and Macular Hemorrhages

**Case Study 6-4**

This 10-month-old child was assessed for possible SBS.

***Figure 6-4-a.*** *Retinal hemorrhages, including a macular hemorrhage.*

***Figure 6-4-b.*** *Seven years later this same child later has severe optic nerve atrophy secondary to the nerve fiber layer destruction associated with retinal hemorrhages.*

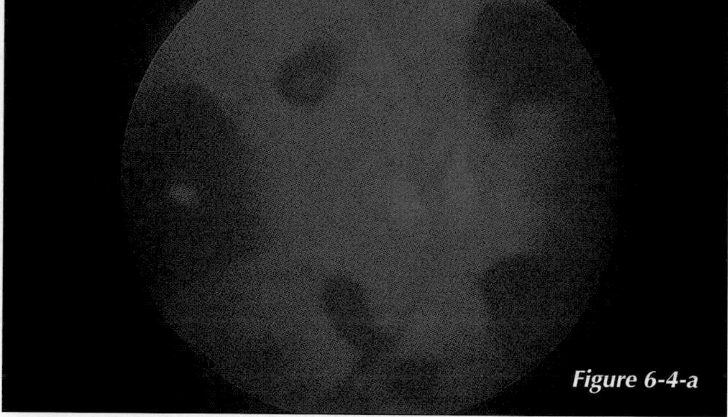

Figure 6-4-a

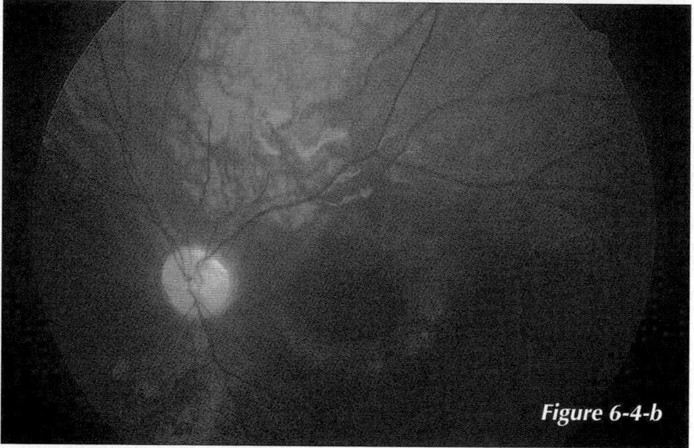

Figure 6-4-b

## Papilledema

**Case Study 6-5**

This 5-month-old infant died from anoxia due to suffocation.

***Figure 6-5.*** *Papilledema secondary to cerebral anoxia caused by suffocation.*

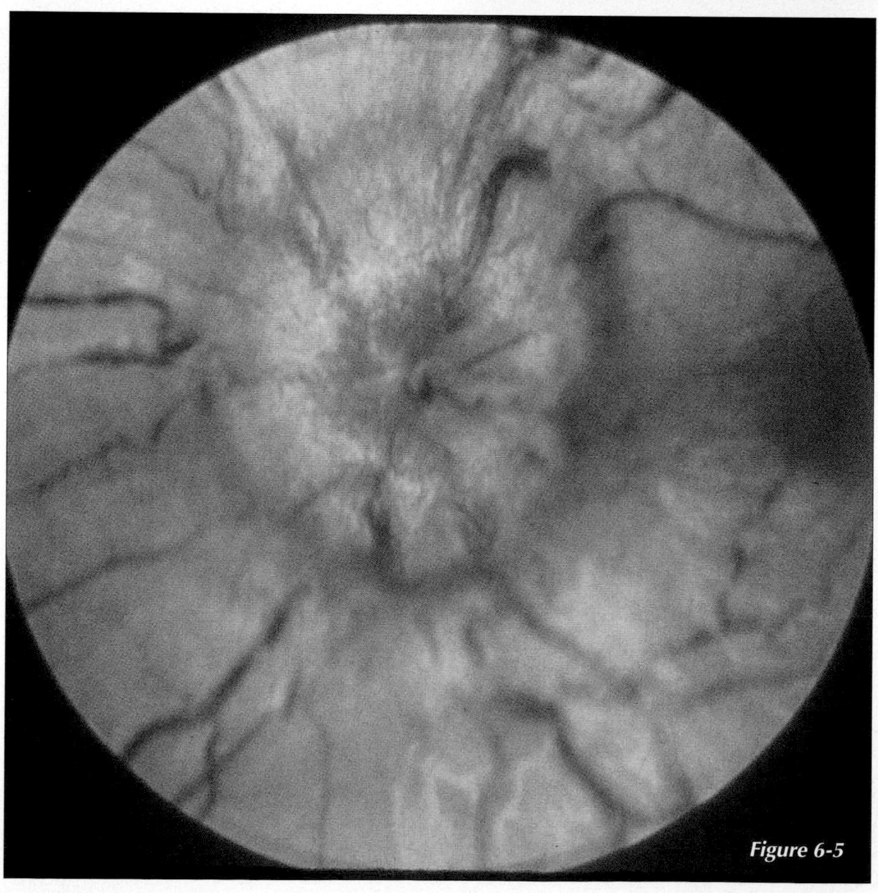

Figure 6-5

# Retinal Hemorrhage

**Case Study 6-6**

These children were examined for retinal hemorrhages. These hemorrhages could consist of breaks in the retinal blood vessels and have different appearances depending upon the size of the hemorrhage, confluence with other hemorrhages, layer in which the retinal hemorrhage is located, and individual variations. The quantity of retinal hemorrhages correlates to the likely severity of brain damage. Examination should document other possible findings such as perimacular folds, vitreous hemorrhaging, retinal detachment, and retinoschisis. (Photographs courtesy of E. Dodson).

***Figure 6-6-a.*** *Scattered retinal hemorrhages.*

***Figure 6-6-b.*** *Large retinal hemorrhage adjacent to the optic nerve.*

***Figure 6-6-c.*** *Several large "blot" retinal hemorrhages are seen.*

***Figure 6-6-d.*** *Numerous, extensive, confluent retinal hemorrhages, which extend outward to the edge of the visible field.*

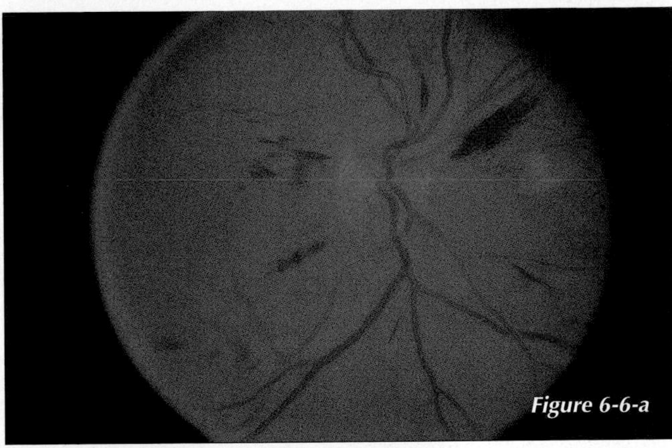

*Figure 6-6-a*

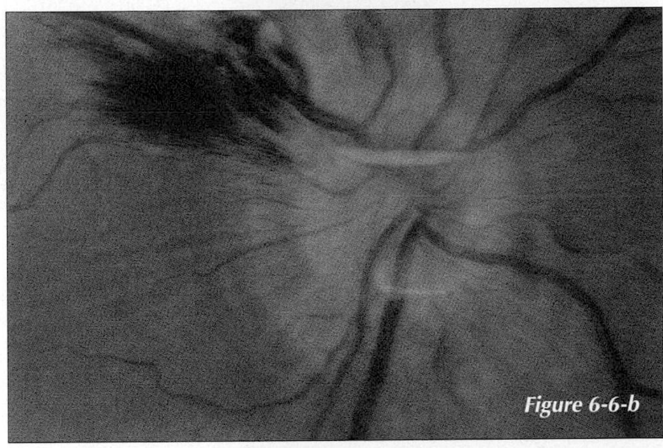

*Figure 6-6-b*

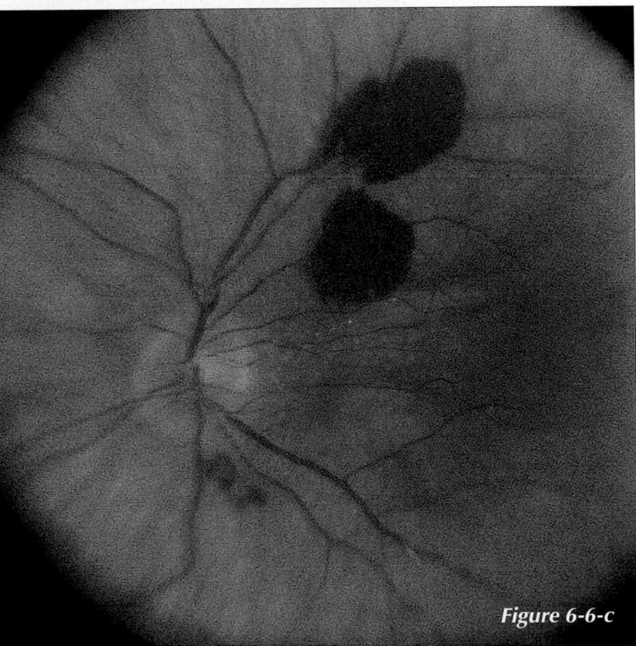

*Figure 6-6-c*

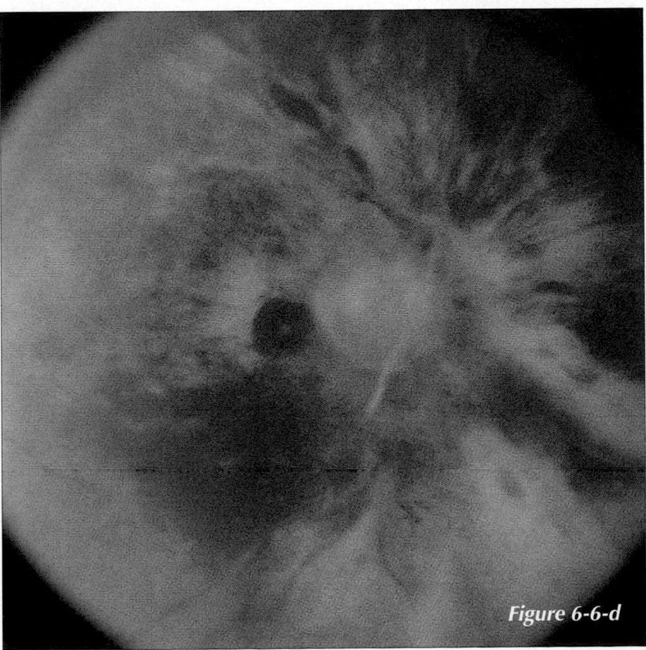

*Figure 6-6-d*

# Residual Findings

**Case Study 6-7**

This child was examined for damage to the optic tract, which can be seen as atrophy of the retina caused by shaken baby syndrome.

***Figure 6-7.*** *The pale optic nerve is a residual effect of retinal hemorrhages caused by abusive shaking.*

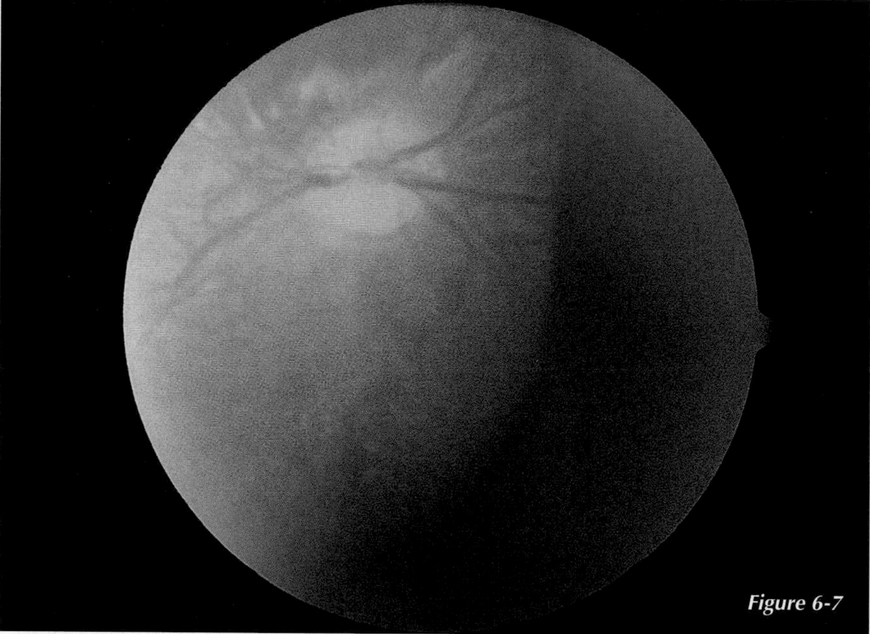

***Figure 6-7***

Chapter 7

# Radiology

Wilbur Smith, MD

Radiological imaging is central to the recognition and diagnosis of child abuse initially involving bone injuries. Clinicians faced with a possible case of abuse involving skeletal injuries must recognize the following 3 major concepts:

1. Any bone can be broken as the result of child abuse. While there are certain fractures that are highly specific for the diagnosis of child abuse, any bone broken without adequate explanation must be considered as possible child abuse.
2. Although it is true that abusers may sometimes break more than 1 bone of a child, abuse cases most commonly exhibit only 1 fracture .
3. It is not reasonable to think that a child could suffer a very painful broken bone without manifesting any symptoms. The biggest problem in diagnosing abusive fractures is the preverbal child who cannot designate the point of pain, requiring the health care provider to rely on testing or screening examinations to reach a precise diagnosis.

There has been considerable discussion of the bone imaging necessary for the adequate diagnosis of child abuse. The practice of taking one x-ray of the whole body as part of a child abuse survey is not recommended both from a radiological safety and a diagnostic standpoint. Although there is still some debate as to the optimal number of images in a survey, focused radiographs of each extremity, rib detail views, spine views, and 2 skull views should be taken at a minimum that is acceptable. The resulting images should be reviewed immediately by an experienced imager and additional views obtained as required. Many authorities advocate follow-up views after 2 weeks, particularly in diagnosing rib fractures.

Although bone scans can show rib fractures with better sensitivity than radiographs, they are not uniformly used to evaluate metaphyseal injuries because the metaphyses are normally very "hot" on bone scans. Some authorities do advocate using bone scans as part of a child abuse examination; however, an alternative is to obtain a follow-up radiograph of the rib fracture 2 weeks after the initial series. On the follow-up radiographs, the evidence of healing will be conspicuous.

The concepts of sensitivity and specificity are important in understanding the interpretations of imaging studies. *Sensitivity* refers to the acceptability of false-positive results. In a screening test, false positives, although not desirable, can be tolerated. X-rays of the skeleton are quite sensitive for showing fractures; however, depending on the clinical setting, these fractures may or may not be related to child abuse.

*Specificity* deals with a high level of true-positive results, a low level of false-positive results, and an acceptance of false-negative results. High specificity for child abuse means that there is a very high likelihood that the findings are attributable to child abuse. The fractures that fall into the high specificity category are frequently seen in child abuse. Other types of fractures may or may not occur with child abuse, depending on the clinical situation.

Bone injuries found to be highly specific for child abuse are as follows:

— Corner fractures

— Bucket-handle fractures

— Traumatic metaphysitis

— Posterior rib fractures

— Periosteal stripping

— Epiphyseal separations

In the spectrum of abusive injury, injuries to the viscera are relatively unusual, comprising approximately 2% of all physical cases of child abuse. Most of these injuries are due to blunt trauma, usually occurring as blows to the thorax or abdomen. Those at or near the body midline can compress abdominal contents against the spine. The maximum effect of these blows appears near the midline, with injuries to the heart, pericardium, solid abdominal organs such as the liver or spleen, urinary bladder, and bowel. Liver hematoma is a very common compression injury. Bowel injuries usually occur in the midline as the bowel crosses the spine; the duodenum is the most common focus of bowel-wall injury. Although most abusive injuries are at or near the midline of the body, abusive injury is not excluded in patients who have non-midline injuries such as kidney lacerations.

Consideration of the structure and the degree of force required to cause injury is included in determining whether an intentional or unintentional injury occurred. For example, the femur is a large bone that takes considerable force to break. Accidents such as trips and falls do not break a normal femur. Several studies show that about one third of femur fractures in children younger than 2 years are caused by abuse. A supracondylar fracture of the humerus can result from impaction or twisting and wrenching. It is an unstable injury and can produce more permanent damage such as loss of pronation and supination if medical treatment is not sought promptly. Fracture of the midshaft of the right clavicle is common in children, although not usually in those who cannot walk or run. When clinical evidence is not considered, a fractured clavicle alone is not very specific for child abuse. However, if it is accompanied by an acute supracondylar fracture of the left elbow, for example, it is no longer an isolated clavicle fracture and is considerably more suspicious of child abuse. If there is not substantiated history of an accidental injury, the likelihood that abuse was involved is even higher.

The type of fracture is also an important consideration in determining whether the injury was intentional. Corner fractures involve a margin of the bone, then extend all the way through the spongiosa or transition point of the calcified portion of the metaphyseal plate. They are similar to the Salter-Harris type of metaphyseal fracture and usually result from a twisting or wrenching force applied to the metaphysis of the bone—thus child abuse is more likely the cause of a corner fracture. *Bucket-handle* fractures are classic injuries that may be seen in cases of child abuse. The "bucket handle" is an extension of the corner fracture, where a rim of curvilinear bone is pulled loose, giving the superficial appearance of a handled bucket above the metaphysis. Roughening of the metaphysis, termed *traumatic metaphysitis*, results from multiple episodes of fracturing and healing along the metaphyseal surface of the bone. The epiphyseal plate is displaced as a result of *epiphyseal separation*. These lesions are highly specific for a diagnosis of child abuse. Chronic metaphysitis can resemble rickets superficially, but on a radiograph the epiphyseal plate is not widened nor is the disease uniform with the other side. This differentiates it from rickets, which is a metabolic disease that affects both sides of the body equally. Metabolic diseases are always symmetrical; traumatic lesions are rarely symmetrical.

When there are rib fractures in child abuse, it is typical to see multiple rib fractures of the same series of ribs. These are most likely the result of severe squeezing and compression during shaking. Rib fractures are seen throughout the length of the rib, but the most common injuries are posterior rib fractures, lateral rib fractures, and fractures of the costochondral junction.

Although it is not strictly a fracture, periosteal stripping that causes hemorrhage beneath the periosteum is quite painful. Severe wrenching and grasping of the extremity are required and cause the periosteal membrane and its emissary veins to tear. The hemorrhage calcifies beginning 10 to 14 days after injury, making the diagnosis clear.

A combination of new and old injuries, especially if an explanation for the fractures is lacking or improbable, is very characteristic of child abuse. Healing is determined by the amount of callus formation or white density shown on radiographs. This represents newly laid down matrix bone and is associated with the healing process of the fracture. Finding fractures of different dates along with specific and less specific fractures makes child abuse highly likely.

The following are case studies of commonly occurring fractures owing to child abuse. While these examples show characteristic injuries, the axiom that any bone can be fractured as the result of child abuse and the inconsistency of the clinical history of the injury and findings are the most important criteria in determining if a child has been abused.

# Spiral Femoral Fracture

**Case Study 7-1**

This 15-month-old child was brought for care after refusing to walk for 10 days. The child was walking previously and began refusing to walk after a "play day" with the mother's paramour. No history of trauma was given initially. However, after physical examination revealed a swollen thigh and radiographs were obtained, the story of a trip over a playground object was offered as an explanation.

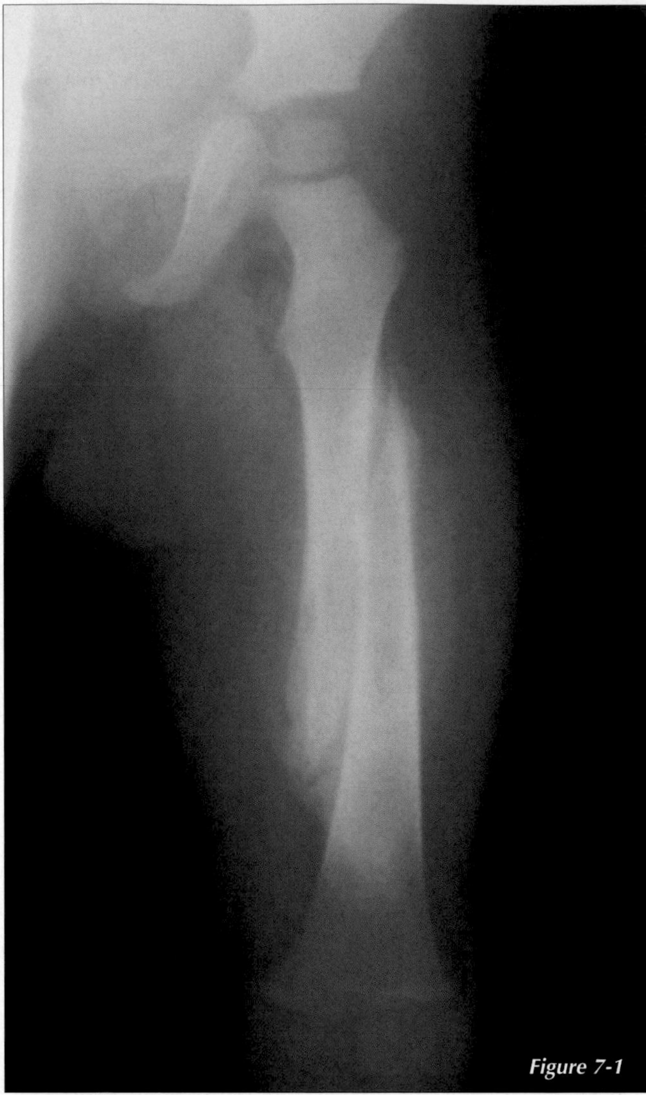
Figure 7-1

***Figure 7-1.*** *There is a spiral fracture of the right femur. The fracture margins are not sharp and there is fine periosteal reaction suggesting that this fracture is not new. This is consistent with a 1- to 2-week-old fracture.*

The x-ray showed no evidence of any bone tumor or other abnormality of the femur that would suggest the femur was prone to pathological fracture. The highly specific connection between such a fracture and abuse plus the delay and lack of an adequate clinical history was sufficient to document this femur fracture as abusive even though it was the only fracture that the child suffered.

# Supercondylar Humeral Fracture

**Case Study 7-2**

This 14-month-old nonverbal child was brought for evaluation of a swollen and painful arm. No initial history of trauma was given and physical examination revealed swelling about the elbow and limited pronation and supination. The child did not appear to be in acute distress unless the elbow was moved.

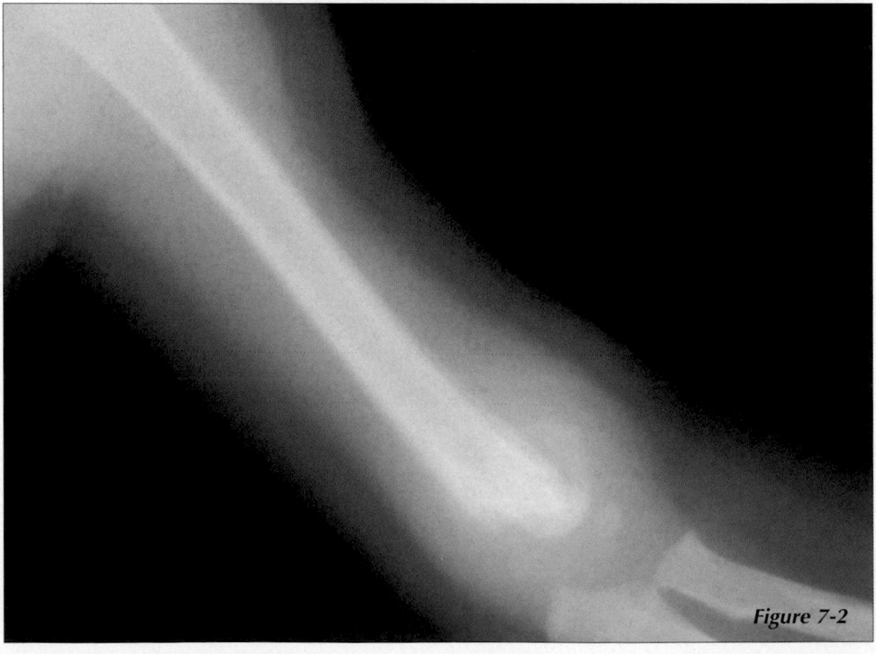
Figure 7-2

***Figure 7-2.*** *Radiograph of the left elbow showing a supercondylar fracture of the humerus with periosteal elevation along the humerus. The fracture itself is not clearly identified because a considerable portion of the fracture extends through the nonradiopaque cartilage about the elbow.*

Further investigation revealed that this child existed in a very chaotic environment with multiple caregivers, episodic use of illegal substances, and lack of effective adult control. When referred to the child abuse center, evidence of an older healed fracture and a new fracture elsewhere in the body was found.

# Multiple Fractures of Ribs, Clavicle, and Left Elbow

**Case Study 7-3**

This 3-month-old child was brought to the hospital due to the inability to move his arms. A fracture of the midshaft of the right clavicle was identified, which, although common in children, is unusual in a 3-month-old child who cannot walk or run. An acute supracondylar fracture of the left elbow was also found, which, along with the absence of any history given, makes this case suspicious for abuse.

***Figure 7-3-a***. *A new fracture of the midshaft of the right clavicle.*

***Figure 7-3-b.*** *Radiograph showing an acute supracondylar fracture of the left elbow.*

Ultimately, this was shown to be a case of child abuse with multiple rib fractures and a head injury.

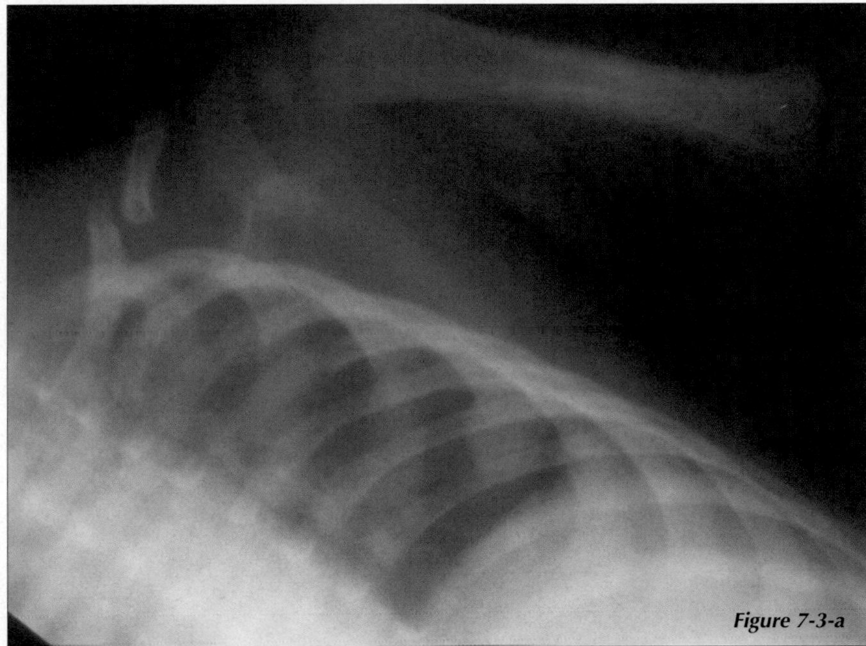

**Figure 7-3-a**

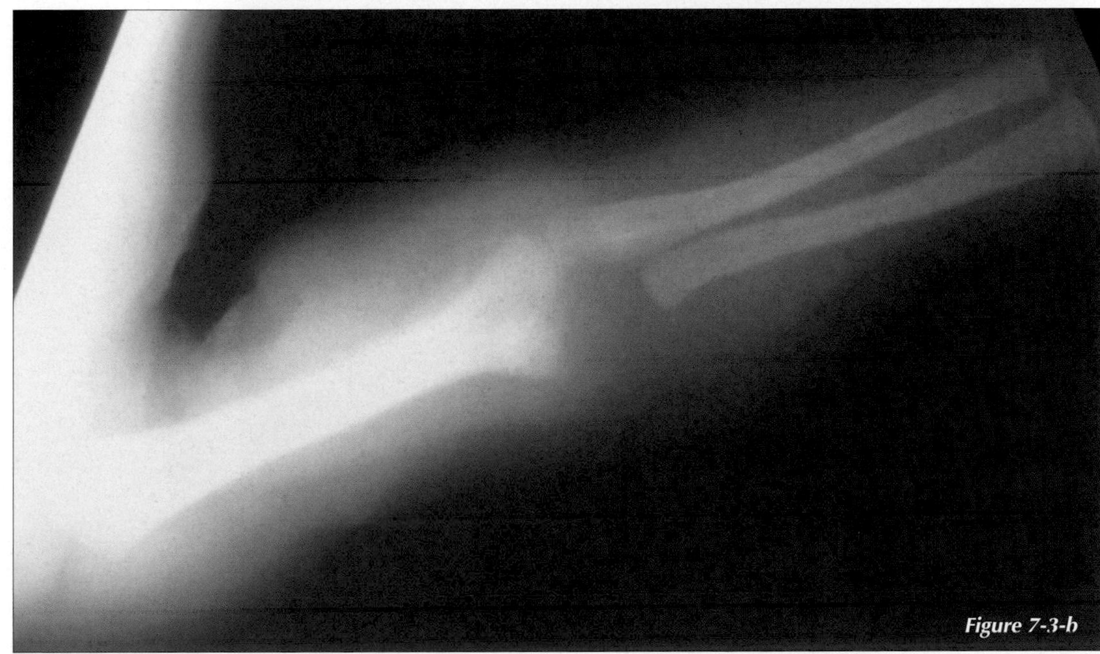

**Figure 7-3-b**

# Bucket-Handle Fracture

**Case Study 7-4**

This 5-month-old child was irritable and cried incessantly the week before suffering a major head injury. Bone radiographs, obtained as part of the child abuse evaluation, showed classical metaphyseal injuries from child abuse.

***Figure 7-4-a.*** *Anteroposterior view of the knees showing a classic "bucket handle" rim of bone protruding from the left proximal tibia.*

***Figure 7-4-b.*** *Lateral view of the left knee showing the loose rim of bone on the proximal tibia.*

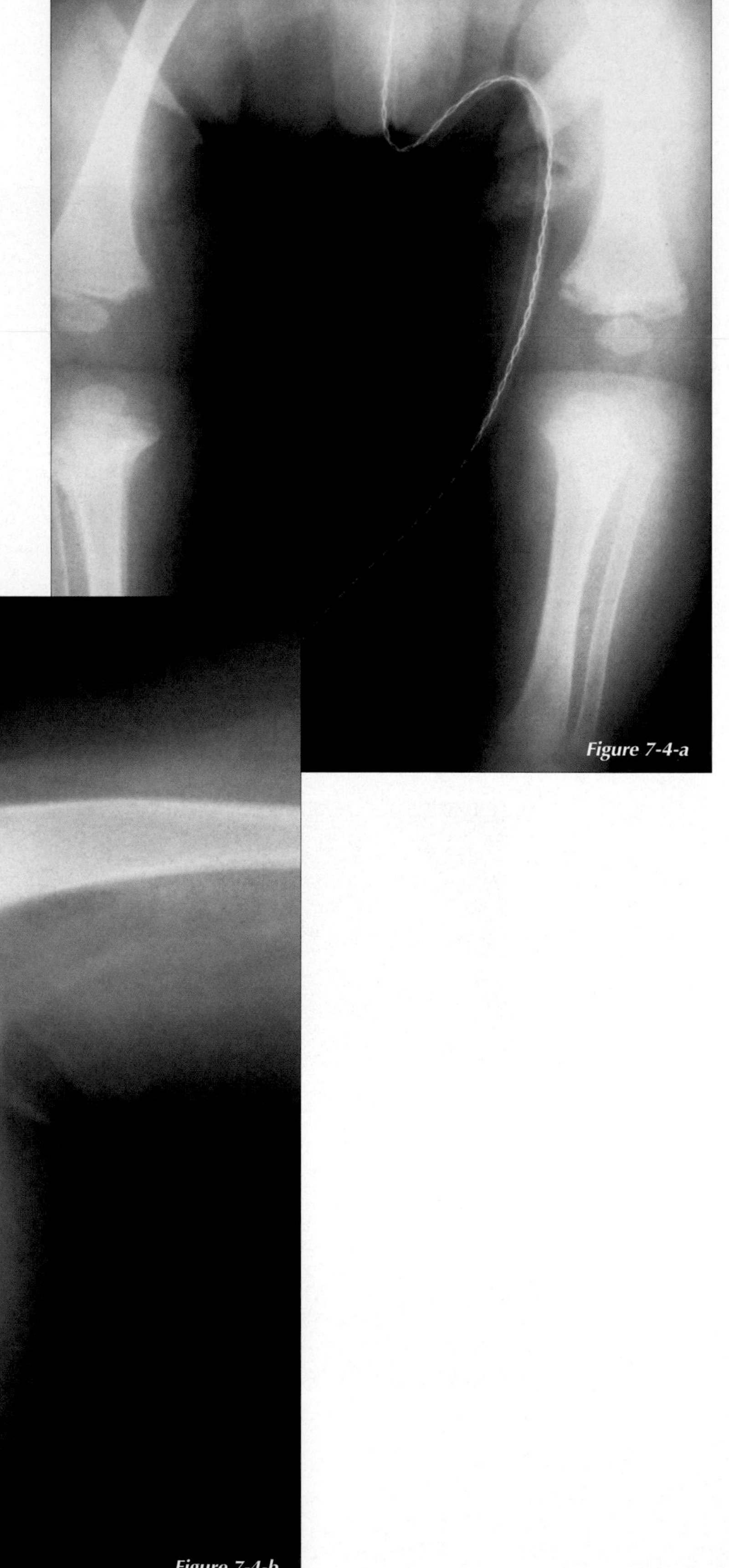

**Figure 7-4-a**

**Figure 7-4-b**

# Chronic Fracture

**Case Study 7-5**

This 5-month-old child was irritable, particularly when the mother handled the right leg.

***Figure 7-5.*** *The right proximal tibia shows a chronic fracture with periosteal elevation and metaphyseal widening. This is markedly asymmetrical compared to the changes on the left, indicative of an abusive injury.*

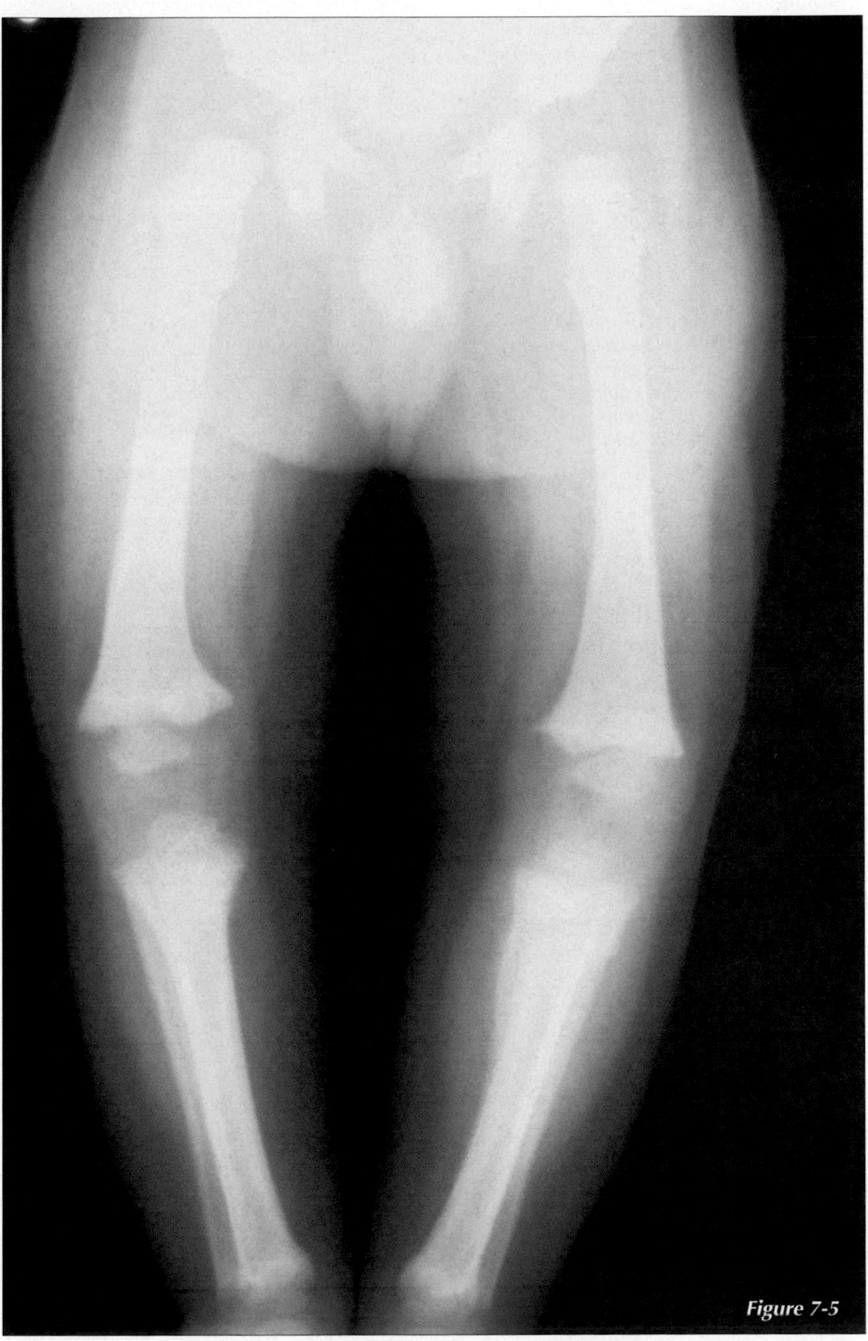

*Figure 7-5*

# Specific and Less Specific Fractures for Abuse Diagnosis

**Case Study 7-6**

This 11-month-old child presented with irritability and healed fractures of the radius and ulna, which could be explained by child abuse or an accident. Subsequent radiographs showed corner fractures of the distal femur and proximal tibia.

***Figure 7-6-a.*** *Sclerotic lines through the midshaft of the radius and ulna represent healed fractures. These fractures are approximately 6 weeks old.*

***Figure 7-6-b.*** *Anteroposterior view of the left knee showing corner fractures of the left distal femur and the left proximal tibia. These corner fractures are new.*

This case illustrates the significance of fractures of different dates as well as the combination of specific and less specific fractures for the diagnosis of child abuse. This was determined to be a case of child abuse.

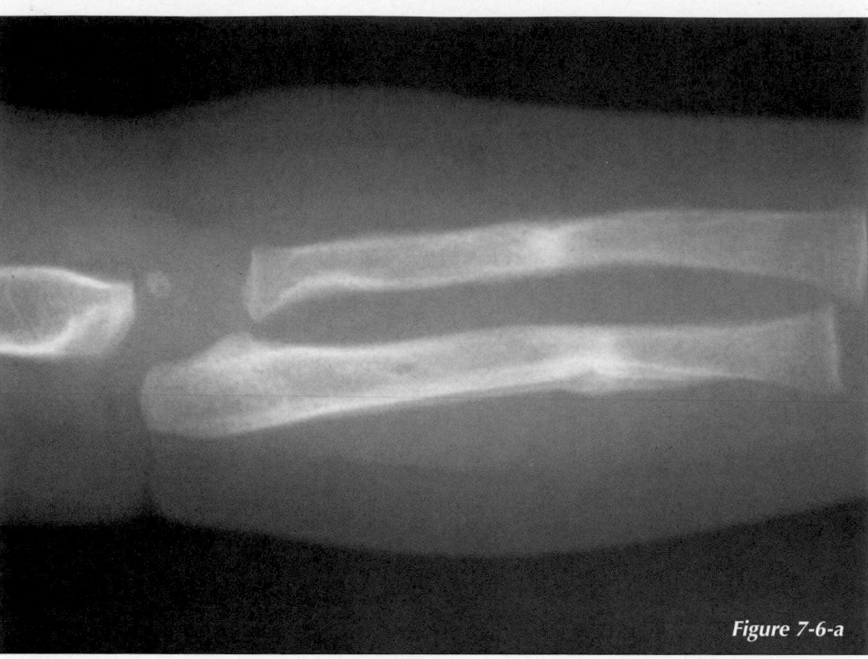

*Figure 7-6-a*

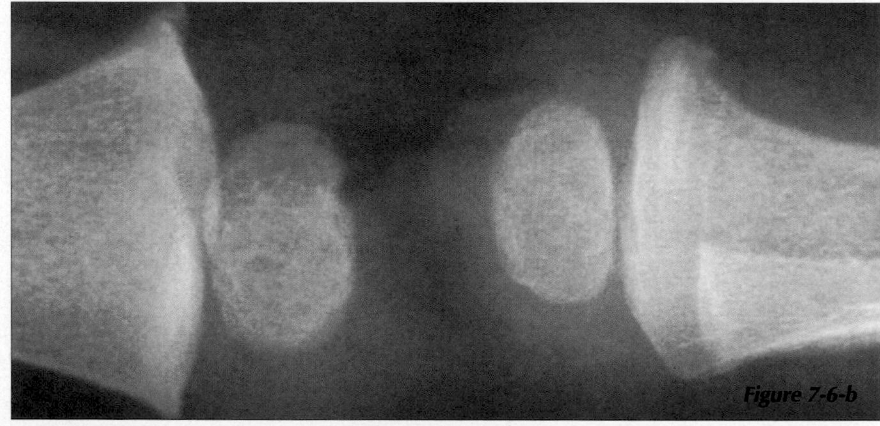

*Figure 7-6-b*

# Multiple Fractures of Various Ages

**Case Study 7-7**

This 3-month-old child presented with pulmonary edema and a massive head injury.

***Figure 7-7.*** *The ribs show multiple fractures of different ages, particularly evident in the left posterior ribs near the spine.*

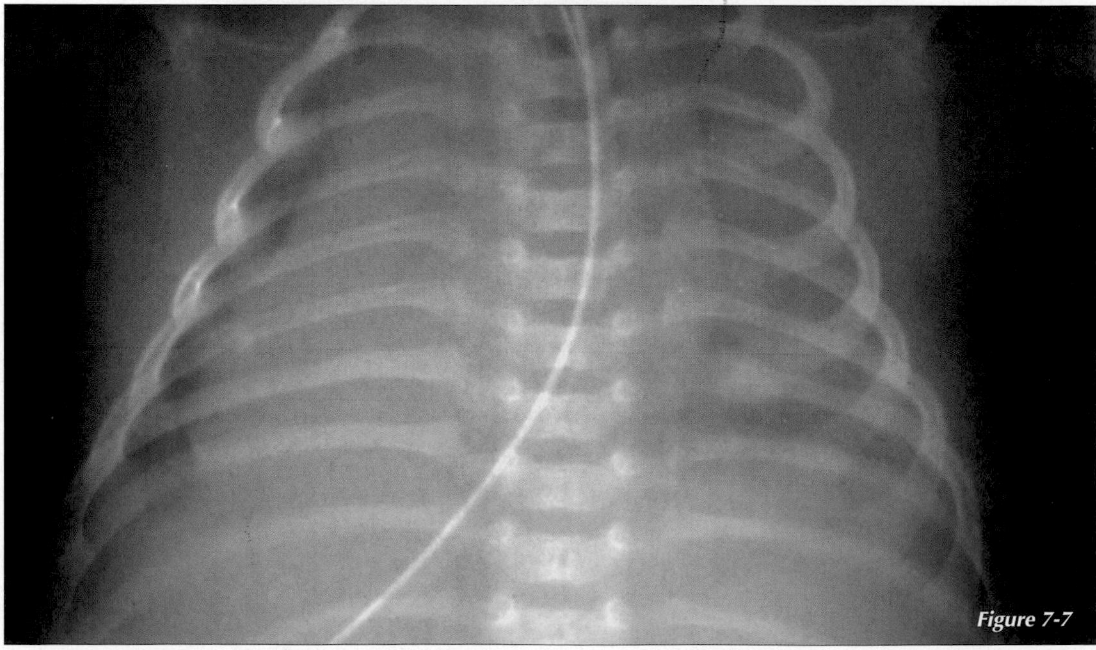

*Figure 7-7*

# Stomping Injuries

**Case Study 7-8**

This child died after being "stomped" in the chest and abdomen. The patient suffered a ruptured bowel and went into shock.

***Figure 7-8.*** *Radiograph showing a tear of the costochondral junction of the lower rib due to the severe compressive force applied to this child's abdomen.*

Figure 7-8

# Multiple Rib Fractures of Various Ages

**Case Study 7-9**

This 4-month-old child suffered a severe head injury as well as rib fractures.

***Figure 7-9.*** *Oblique chest radiograph showing multiple left-sided rib fractures in varying degrees of healing. Healing is judged by the amount of callus formation or white density shown on the radiograph, which represents newly laid matrix bone associated with the healing process of fractures. Some of the rib fractures show very dense callus while others show minimal callus. This documents that these ribs were fractured at different times, likely with repeated episodes of abuse.*

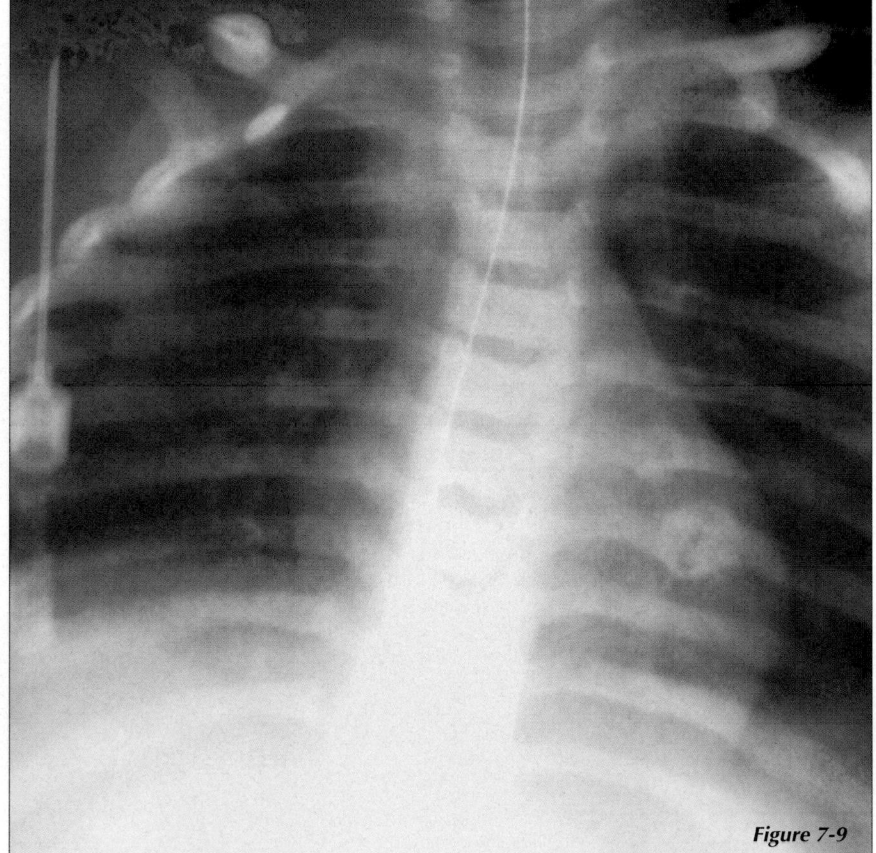

Figure 7-9

## Rib Fractures on a Nuclear Medicine Bone Scan

**Case Study 7-10**

This child was a victim of abuse. A nuclear medicine bone scan was able to show rib fractures more clearly than radiographs.

***Figure 7-10.*** *Nuclear medicine bone scan showing multiple very intensely enhanced areas in the ribs, denoting rib fractures.*

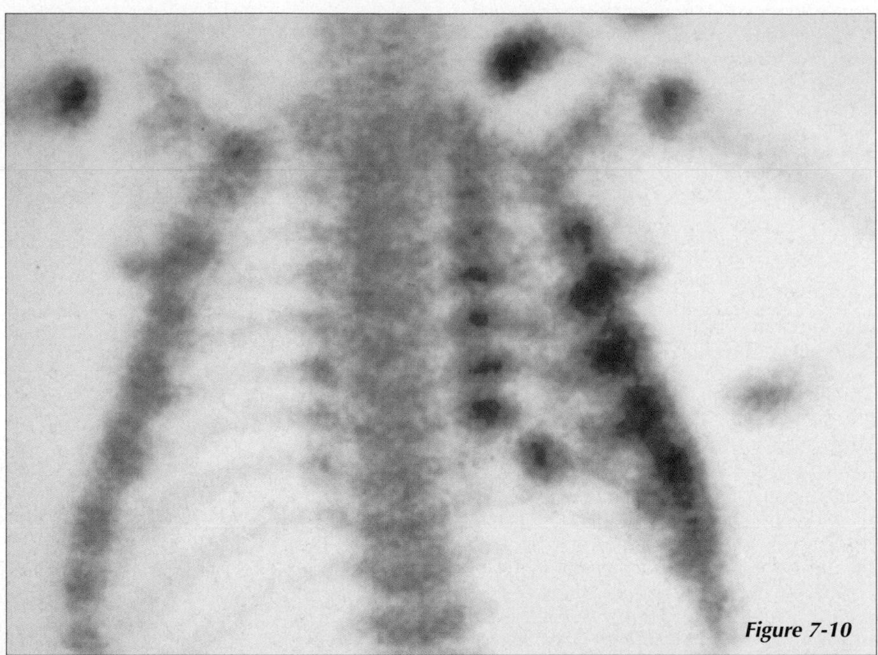

Figure 7-10

## Punching Injuries

**Case Study 7-11**

This infant was repeatedly punched in the abdomen by his father.

***Figure 7-11.*** *CT scan with contrast of this infant's abdomen. Note the low-density liver laceration and hematoma extending through the left lobe of the liver just off the midline and just anterior to the spine.*

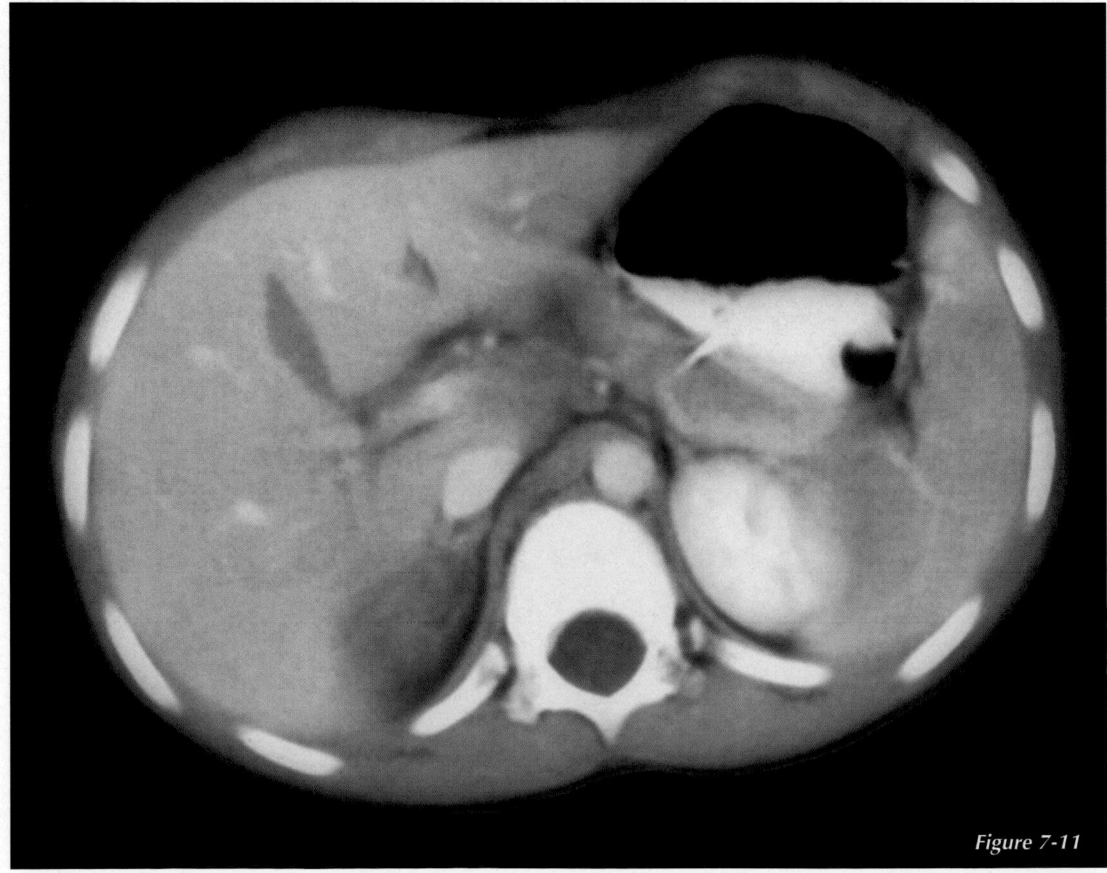

Figure 7-11

# Ruptured Pancreas

**Case Study 7-12**

This 18 month old presented with pernicious vomiting. This child was punched repeatedly by the mother's paramour.

***Figure 7-12-a.*** *Abdominal film clearly showing a large mid-abdominal soft tissue mass.*

***Figure 7-12-b.*** *CT scan through the level of the pancreas showing a multi-lobulated pancreatic pseudocyst from rupture of the pancreas due to repeated blows.*

A bone survey (not shown) showed anterior costochondral rib fractures.

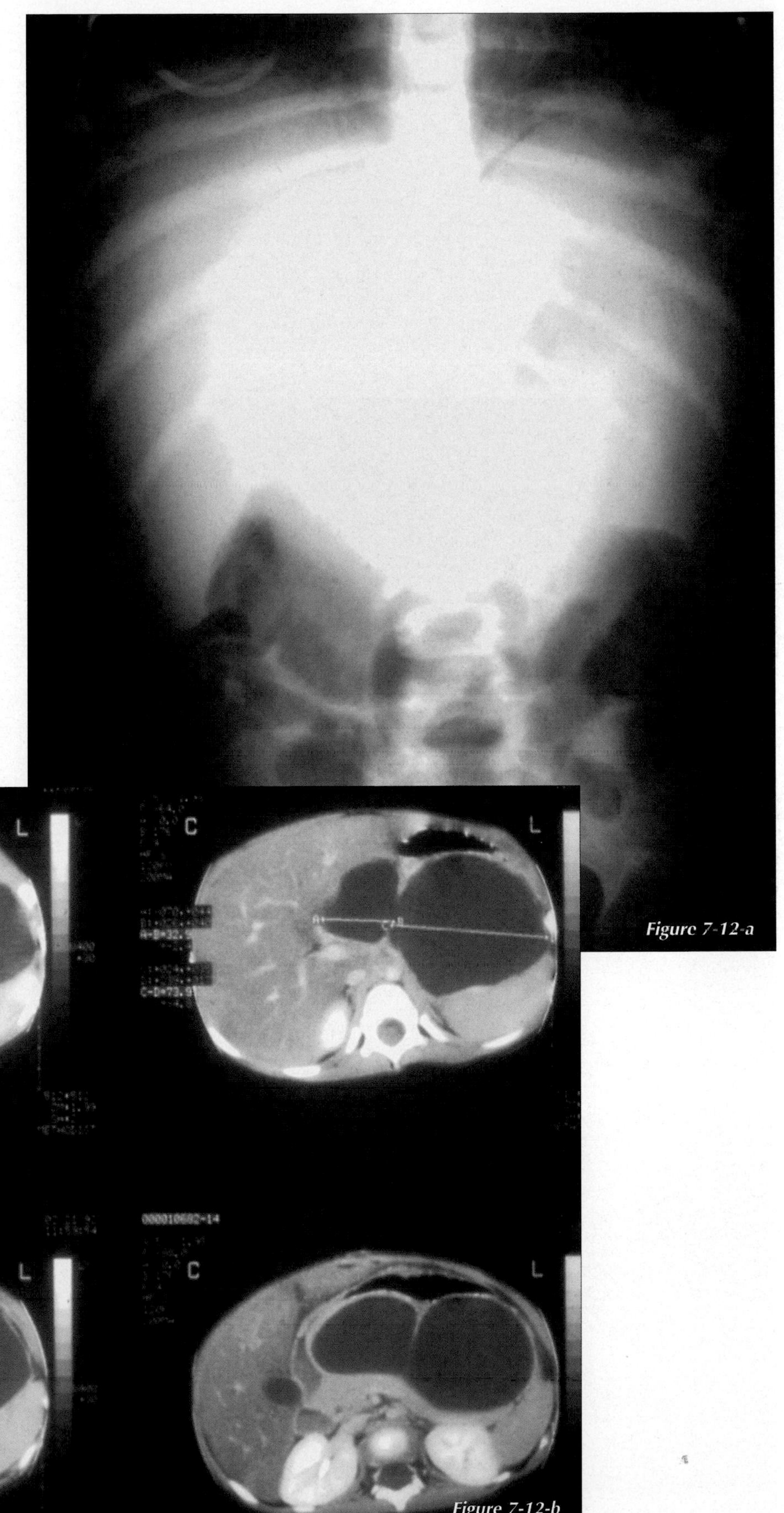

Figure 7-12-a

Figure 7-12-b

# Death From Stomping

**Case Study 7-13**

This 1-year-old child was admitted to the ER in shock after being "stomped" by his inebriated father; the injury was fatal.

***Figure 7-13.*** *A triangular air collection beneath the liver, representing a pneumoperitoneum due to rupture of the duodenum.*

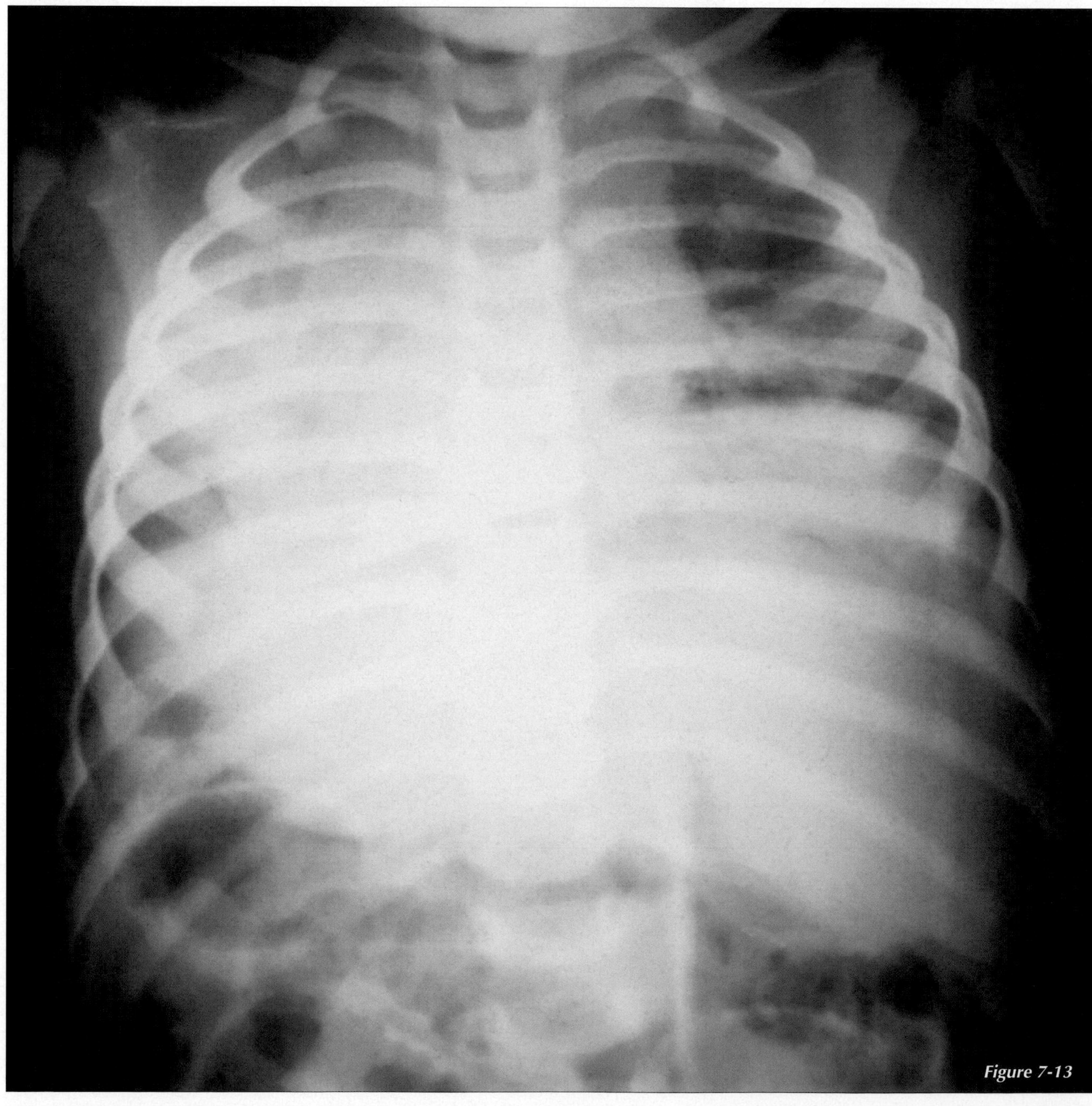

*Figure 7-13*

# Common Injuries Associated With Abuse

**Case Study 7-14**

This collection of radiographs illustrates some of the more common injuries found in cases of abuse.

***Figure 7-14-a.*** *Corner fracture of the left distal tibia at the ankle.*

***Figure 7-14-b.*** *Corner fractures of both sides of a metaphysis of the distal femur of a 6-month-old abused child.*

***Figure 7-14-c.*** *This case illustrates 2 specific types of injury due to child abuse. Note how the metaphysis of the proximal humerus is very rough and irregular, and the epiphyseal growth center is displaced inferiorly and medially. This traumatic metaphysitis results from multiple episodes of fracturing and healing along the metaphyseal surface of the bone. Both of these lesions are highly specific for the diagnosis of child abuse.*

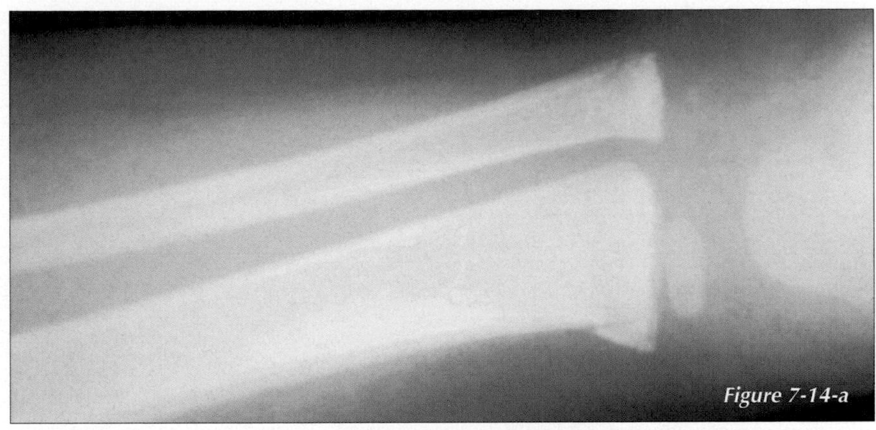

Figure 7-14-a

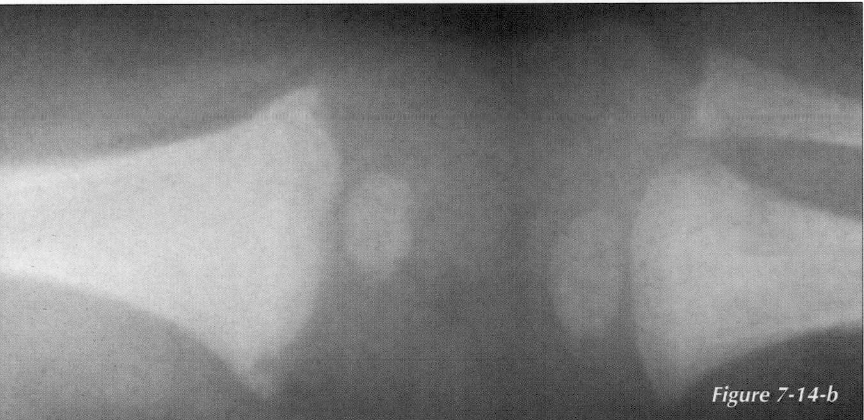

Figure 7-14-b

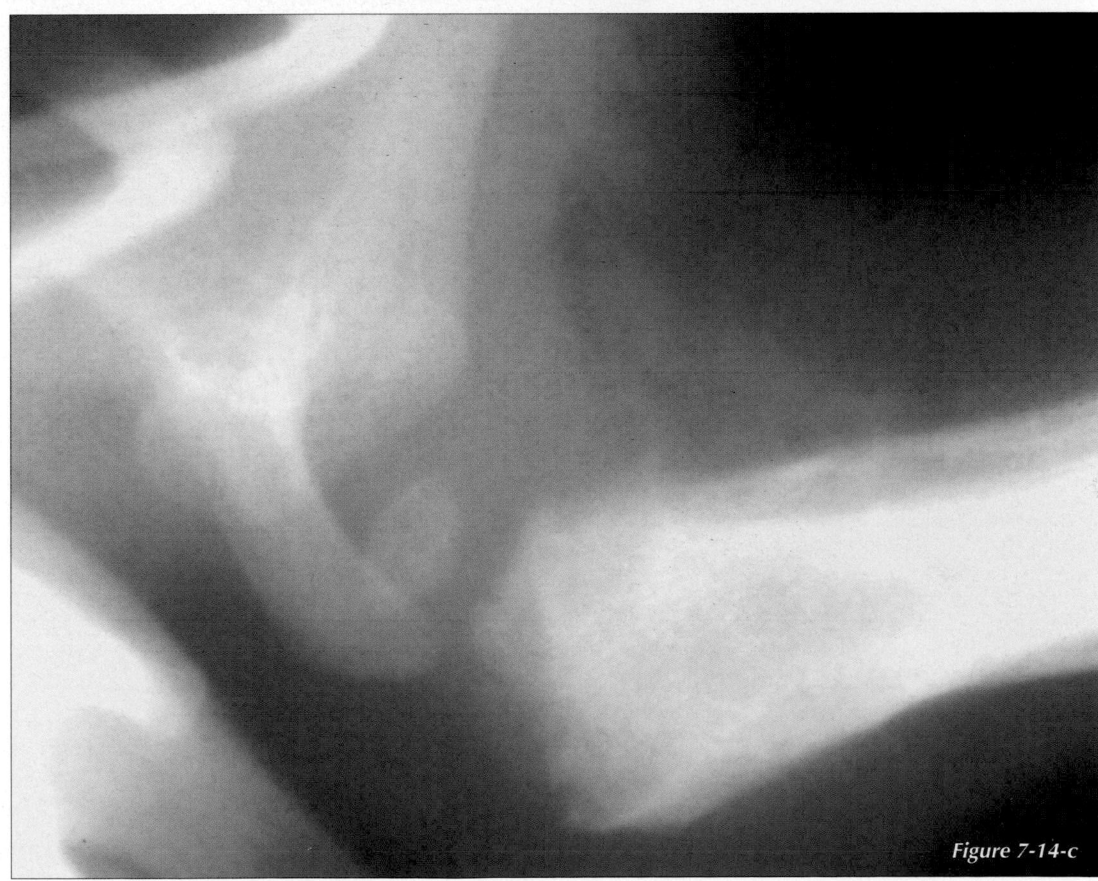

Figure 7-14-c

# Common Injuries Associated With Abuse

**Case Study 7-14** *(continued)*

***Figure 7-14-d.*** *Another example of traumatic metaphysitis. Note how the metaphyseal surface of the left femur is irregular. There is also a corner fracture with considerably more irregularity than ascribable to a corner fracture alone.*

***Figure 7-14-e.*** *Example of periosteal stripping causing hemorrhage beneath the periosteum. This injury is best seen in the thickened periosteum over the right distal femur of this child.*

***Figure 7-14-f.*** *Multiple ribs resected at autopsy from this abused child. The spine is hemisected, and the posterior rib is attached to the larger block of bone on the right. Fractures are present in the posterior aspect of the ribs, the mid aspect of the ribs, and the anterior aspect of the ribs at the costochondral junction.*

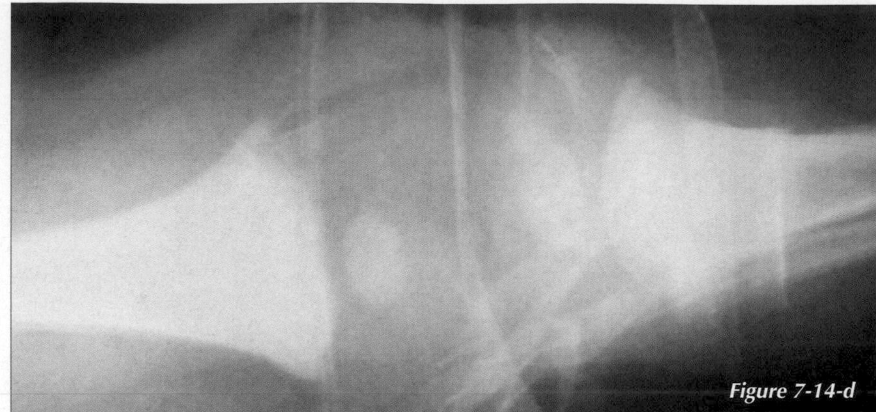

*Figure 7-14-d*

*Figure 7-14-e*

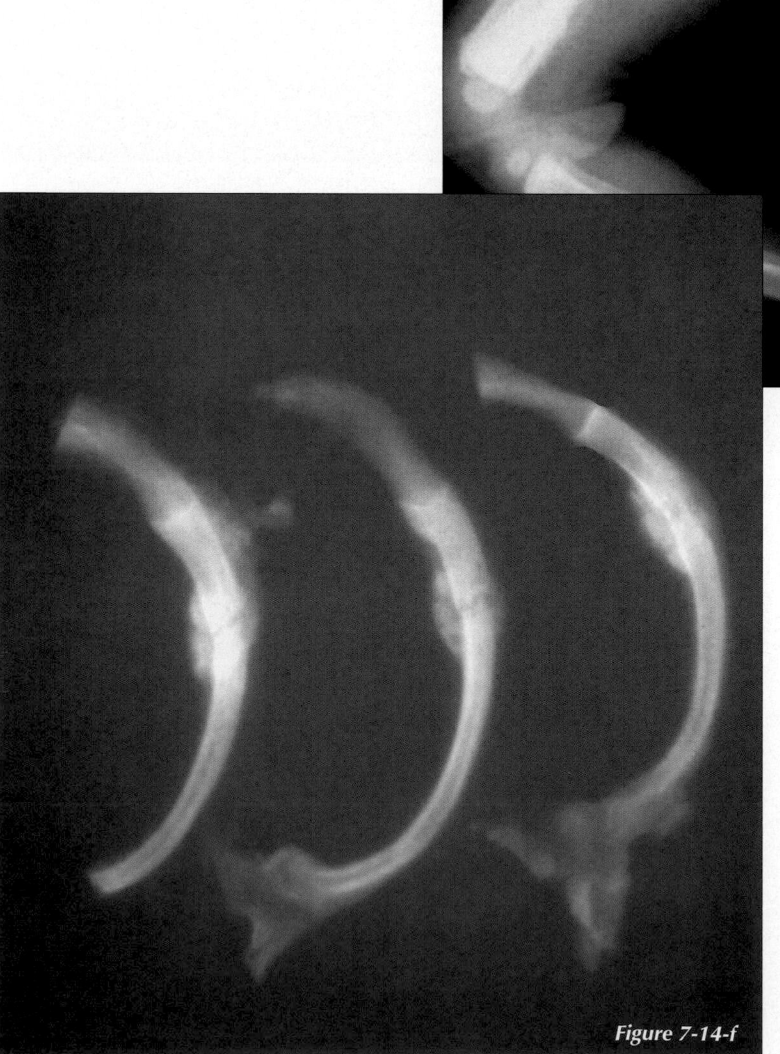

*Figure 7-14-f*

Chapter 8

# Sexual Abuse

Jay Whitworth, MD
Lori Frasier, MD

The medical examination of children with allegations of sexual abuse is a complex process that tests the skills of the most accomplished practitioner. While pediatricians usually recognize the importance of a history in any case, there is no more important factor than the history from the child in evaluating sexual abuse. Since the general approach to every child is to determine the total health status, an examination cannot be performed with the sole focus on evidence collection or the chief complaint. Since the medical history is only one type of interview the child will undergo, it is important to avoid suggesting answers to children by the format of certain questions, or by any subtle indication of the right answer. Not only is it important to collect information in a manner that is sensitive to the needs of a traumatized child, but it must be collected in a manner that is legally sufficient to anticipate future challenges in the courtroom. As children are seen with allegations of sexual abuse, practitioners must always be aware of resources in the community where more definitive forensic interviews can be done as well as the reporting laws relating to abuse, which vary from state to state. It is a practitioner's responsibility to protect children; reports and referrals are essential to the safety of the child, but the practitioner must stay involved to ensure that the results of the examination are addressed in the proper context.

A photographic atlas of child sexual abuse may suggest to some that abnormal findings are common in sexually abused children. In fact, the opposite is true. Most findings in children alleging abuse are actually variants of normal. Many of the photographs in this chapter document these variations so as to keep the examiner from overinterpreting findings as being indicative of abuse. Examiners are still learning the broad limits of "normal" and the extent to which acute injuries can heal without demonstrable scars. It is also known that injuries can heal very quickly, and it is essential that medical examinations are performed as close to an incident as possible. It is extremely common to see children who have had severe genital injuries due to abuse, and who have healed completely with no definitive findings.

It is still commonly believed that doctors can tell by a physical examination whether someone has been sexually abused or is sexually active. While this may be true if certain definitive findings are present or if the patient is seen acutely, it is also true that sexual abuse and consensual sexual activity most often leave no definitive evidence. This fact underscores the importance of the history given by a child. If a child says they have been sexually abused, it is generally safe to assume the allegation is true. In most cases, there is a clear history but no physical findings. To adequately pursue the case, the involvement of many disciplines is essential. The involvement of forensic interviewers, investigators, psychologists, and prosecutors is critical to lead to a positive outcome for the child. In the context of court testimony, the task of the practitioner is to explain that children generally tell the truth about sexual abuse and how abuse can occur and not leave definitive physical evidence.

This chapter is not designed to be exhaustive; it has been designed to show the most common findings that can be misdiagnosed as abnormal in addition to some of the more common injuries seen in sexually abused children. The chapter includes accidental injuries that can be mistaken for abuse and a section on sexually transmitted diseases seen in children. Less-experienced examiners should develop a relationship with an experienced examiner in their region, and all examinations should be photographed for ease of consultation. Peer review is essential for all new and experienced examiners in the field.

## Techniques and Basic Skills

The supine frog-leg position is the most common position for examination as it is the most comfortable for the child (**Figure 8-1-a**). The child lays on her back with her feet close to the buttocks. The knees can be spread by the child simply relaxing. In older children, a sheet can be draped over the knees for a better feeling of modesty. Younger children may be more at ease lying in the frog-leg position while sitting on their caregiver' s lap (**Figure 8-1-b**).

Since it can be difficult to assess the hymen when the child is supine, the prone knee-chest position is sometimes necessary for adequate visualization of the posterior rim of the hymen (**Figure 8-2**). As might be expected, some younger children and many older children feel vulnerable in this position. While the knee-chest position does not add much if the hymen is normal and well-visualized in the supine position, it is helpful if results in the supine position are abnormal or equivocal (**Figure 8-3**). The knee-chest position is also helpful to assess whether the hymen is folded onto itself and therefore merely looks abnormal.

Distractions can help children going through the examination. Examples include reading a book (**Figure 8-4**), watching television, or engaging in conversation about the child's favorite subjects.

In applying labial traction, the examiner gently pulls outward and downward on the labia majora with gloved hands (**Figure 8-5**). Labial separation is another acceptable technique for examination, but it does produce tension on the posterior fourchette and occasionally results in an iatrogenic injury (**Figure 8-6**).

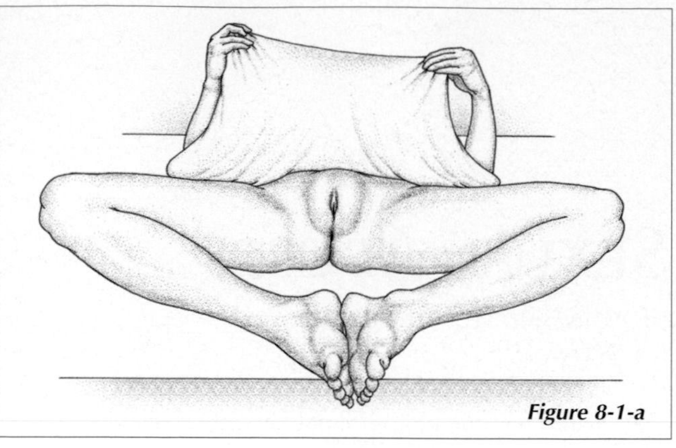

*Figure 8-1-a*

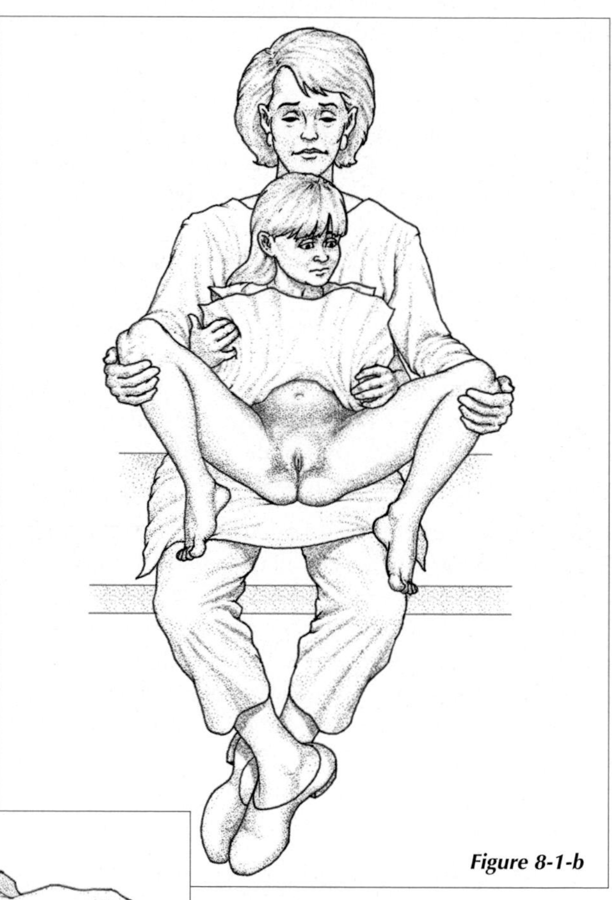

*Figure 8-1-b*

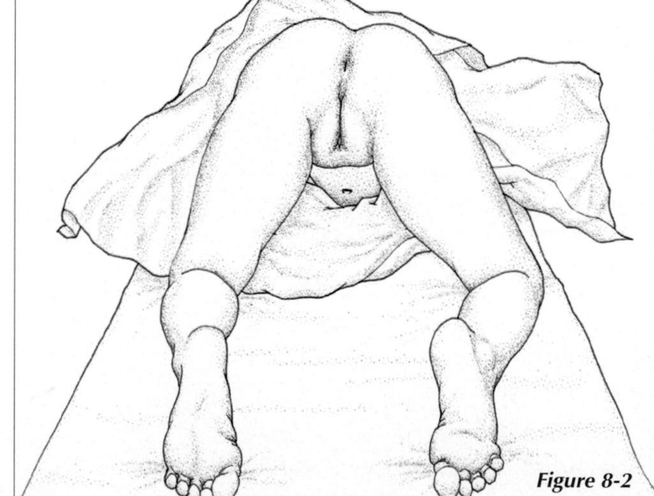

*Figure 8-2*

***Figure 8-1-a.*** *A child examined in the frog-leg position.*

***Figure 8-1-b.*** *The examination done with the patient in frog-leg position sitting on the caregiver's lap.*

***Figure 8-2.*** *Prone knee-chest position.*

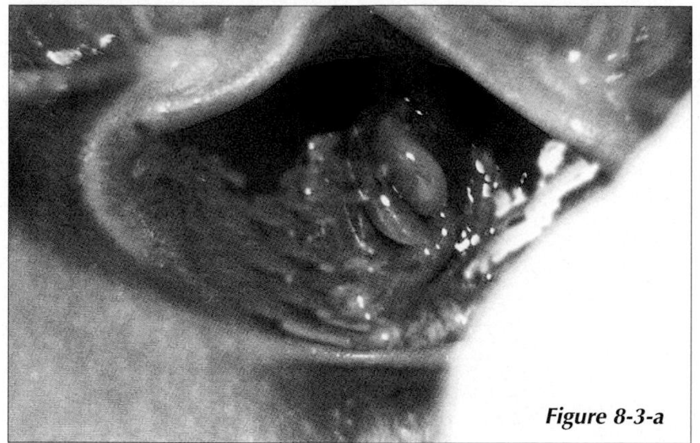

Figure 8-3-a

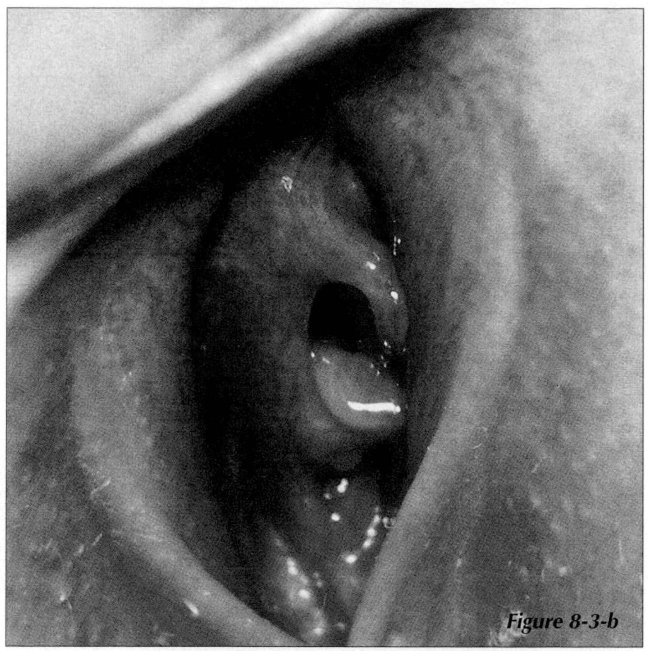

Figure 8-3-b

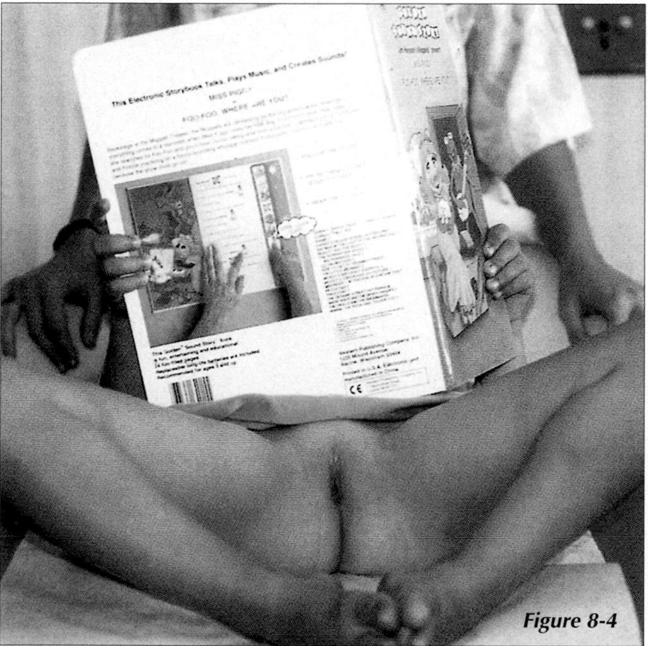

Figure 8-4

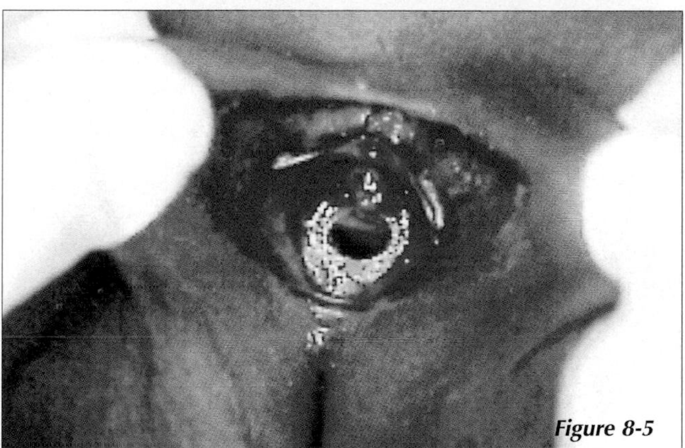

Figure 8-5

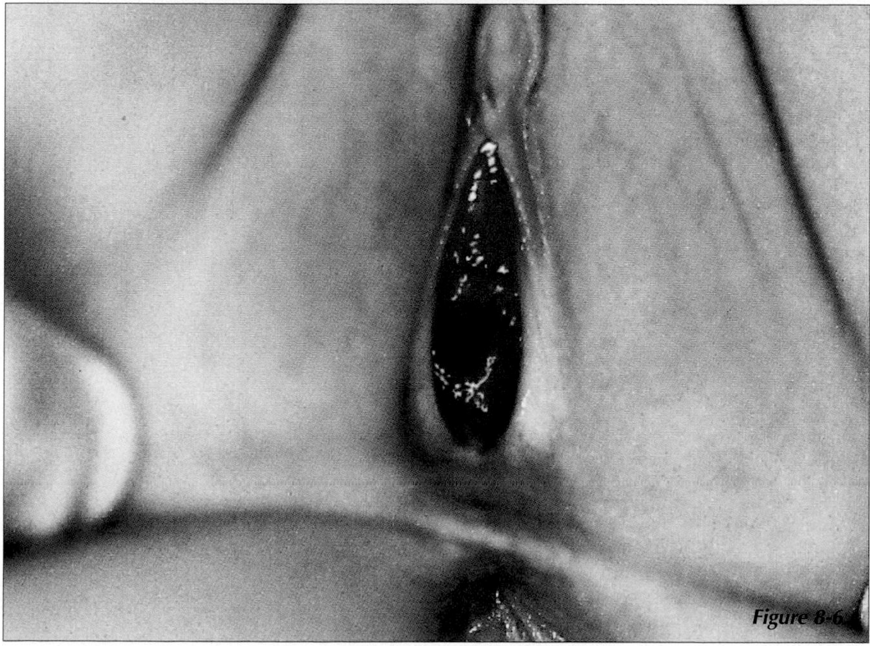

Figure 8-6

***Figures 8-3-a** and **b.** Supine (a) and knee-chest (b) views of a Tanner-stage-1 hymen. In the prone knee-chest position, the hymen is seen to be slightly redundant and annular, with a tag present at the 6-o'clock position. This is a normal examination.*

***Figure 8-4.** Child in a frog-leg supine position with a book on her abdomen to distract her attention away from the examination.*

***Figure 8-5.** Labial traction for a child in the supine frog-leg position reveals the normal crescentic hymen of a Tanner-stage-1 girl. The hymen has attachments at the 11- and 1-o'clock positions without visible tissue being present between the two attachments.*

***Figure 8-6.** Labial separation for a child in the prone knee-chest position. The examiner is gently pushing the labia majora upward and outward.*

## Hymenal Configurations

The annular hymen is the most common hymenal configuration in the first years of life (**Figure 8-7**). Many girls' hymens evolve into a more lacunar configuration as they get older. Estrogenization produces changes such as a thickening of the hymen (**Figure 8-8**) or a redundant or sleeve-like hymen (**Figure 8-9**), but these are normal alterations. The interior of the vagina normally has extensive folding and may have some rugal folds with lateral or vertical configurations (**Figure 8-10**). These folds can move during the examination.

To better visualize the hymen, a few milliliters of water may be squirted onto the hymen to make it float (**Figure 8-11**). This technique is a well-accepted practice.

Current data strongly suggest that anal dilatation of up to 2 cm can occur in normal children simply through relaxation (**Figure 8-12**).[2] Sometimes the technique of examination creates artifacts (**Figure 8-13**).

A septum dividing the hymenal opening is one of the most common normal variants in children (**Figure 8-14**). Most septae spontaneously lyse and leave a septal remnant usually described as a hymenal projection or bump. Whether the result of embryonic arrest or fusion, there is no association with allegations of sexual abuse or with abnormal function. Septal remnants also occur normally (**Figure 8-15**).

Vaginal discharge in children is extremely common and is usually physiological (**Figure 8-16**). If associated with fever, an unusual smell, or itching, further testing may be required.

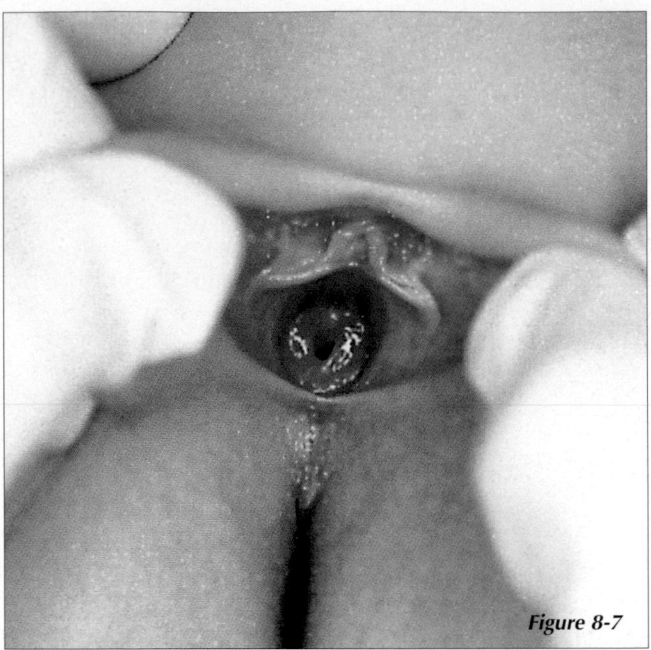

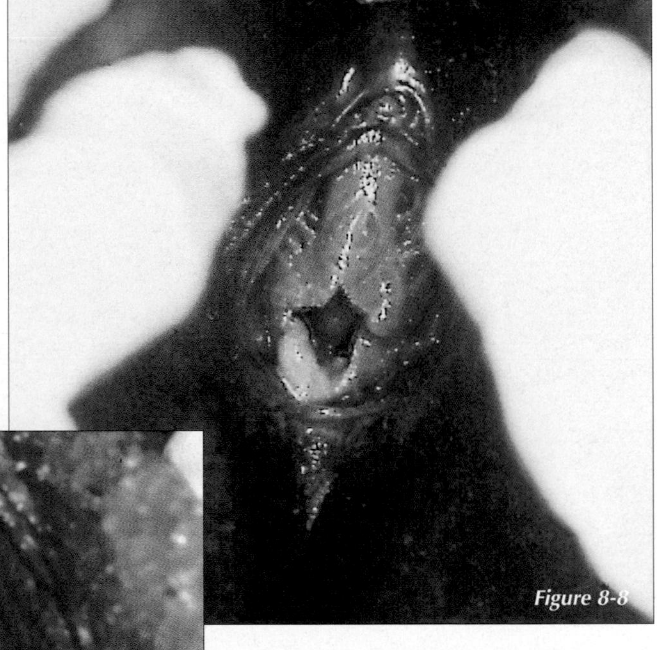

***Figure 8-7.*** *Annular hymen in a Tanner-stage-1 girl. Hymenal tissue extends circumferentially around the entire vaginal orifice.*

***Figure 8-8.*** *Thickened hymen as the result of estrogenization in a Tanner-stage-3 girl. The hymen appears not only thickened but also pale in the patient as a result of estrogen changes. Clefts at the 3- and 9-o'clock positions and periurethral bands are present here as well. Clefts anterior to the 3- and 9-o'clock positions as well as periurethral bands are normal findings.*

***Figure 8-9.*** *A redundant, or sleeve-like, hymen is common with early estrogenization, often shortly before puberty.*

Figure 8-10

Figure 8-11

Figure 8-12

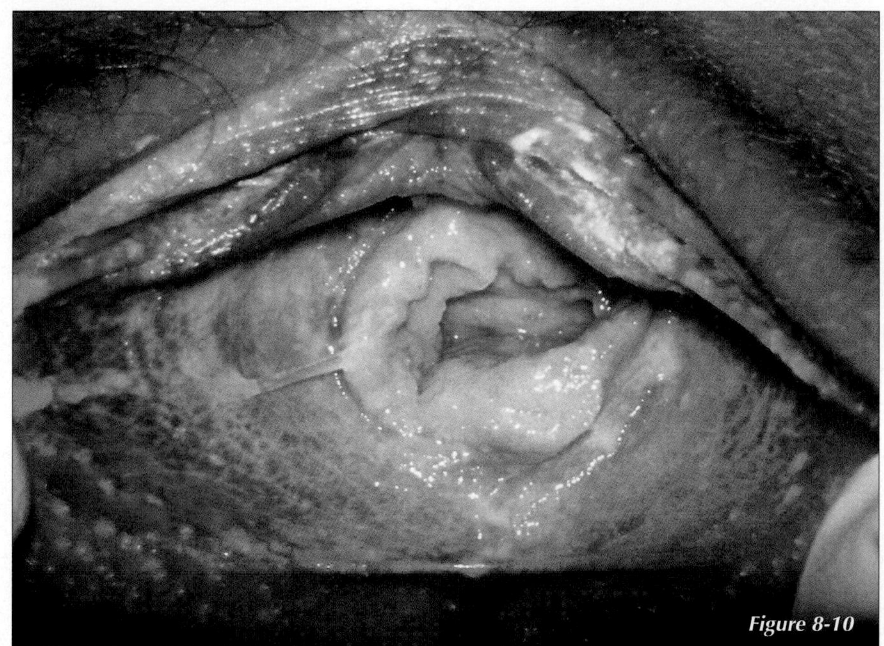

***Figure 8-10.*** *Fully estrogenized child with prominent intravaginal rugae and a small hymenal notch.*

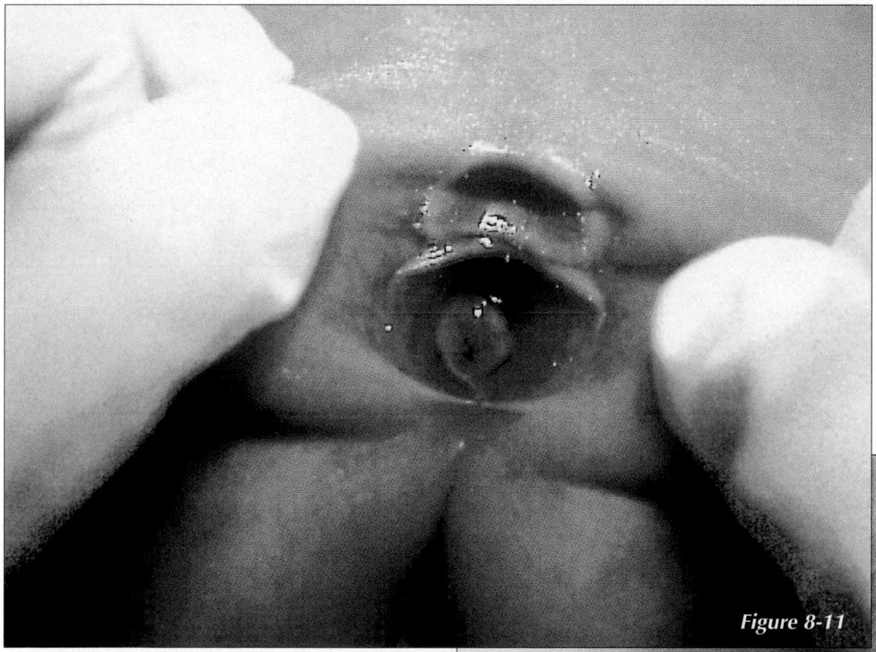

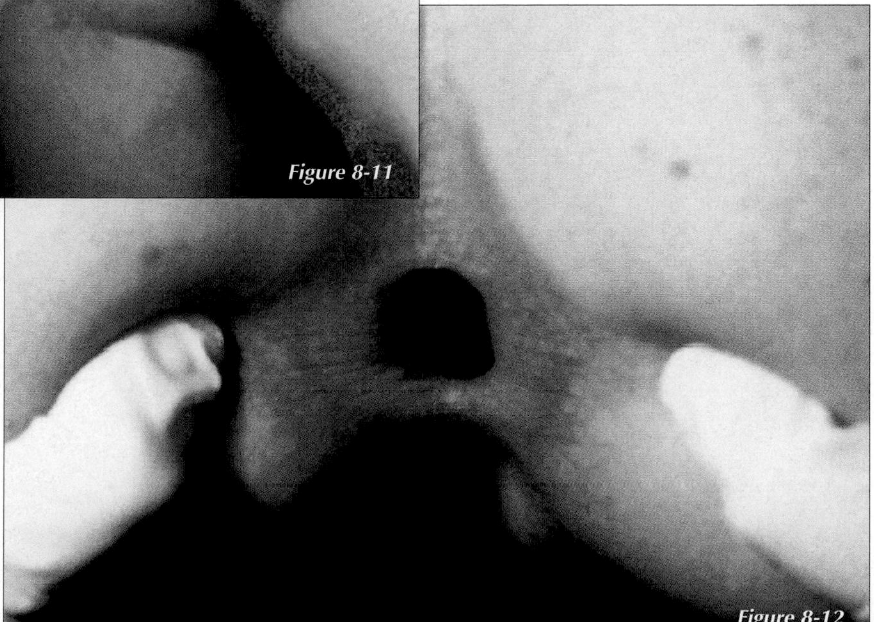

***Figure 8-11.*** *Fimbriated or denticular hymen with multiple projections and indentations along its edge, creating a ruffled appearance.*

***Figure 8-12.*** *Anal dilatation without stool visible in the rectum.*

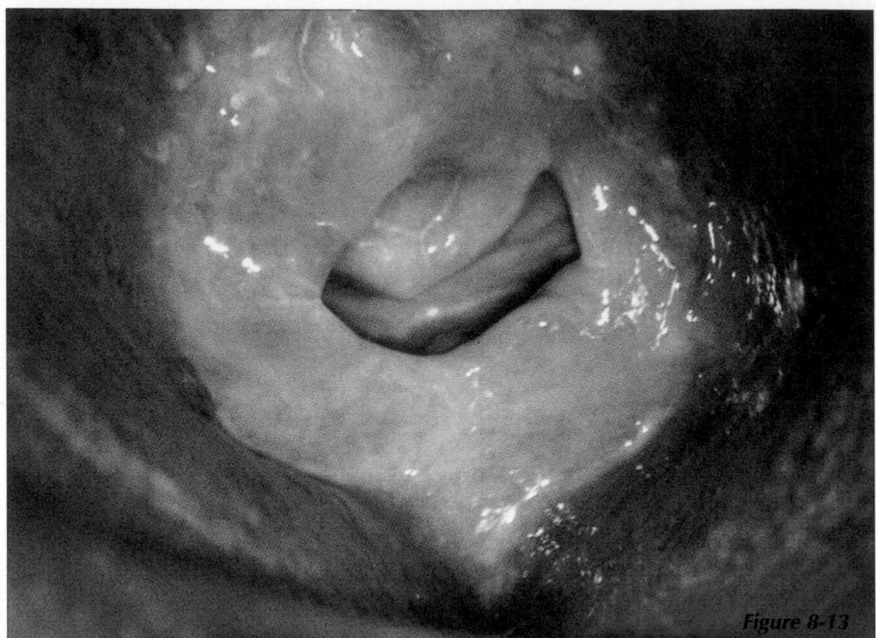

**Figure 8-13.** Normal early pubertal changes of an annular hymen in a 13-year-old girl. There might be a question of the status of the hymen at the 2-o'clock position, where there is an artifact of the technique of examination.

**Figure 8-14.** A septate hymen seen with the child in knee-chest position.

**Figure 8-15.** A septal remnant in a 4-year-old girl who was taken to the ER by her mother, who was concerned that she might have been abused because "she had something hanging out of her." The rest of the examination was not remarkable, and the child denied abuse.

**Figure 8-16.** Vaginal discharge in a prepubertal child.

Figure 8-13

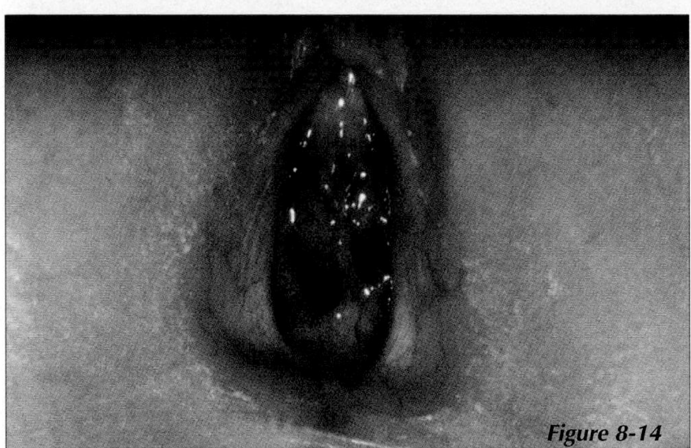

Figure 8-14

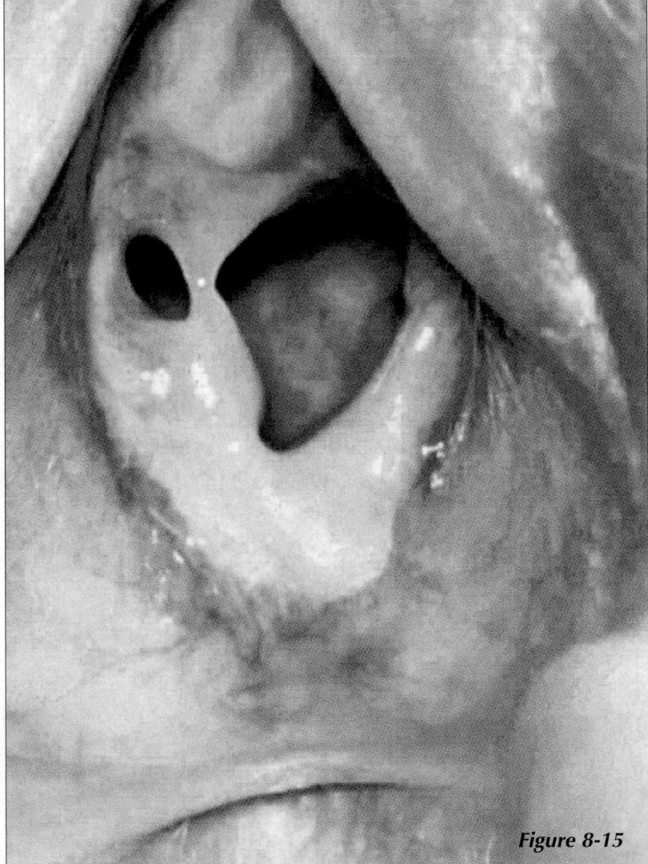

Figure 8-15

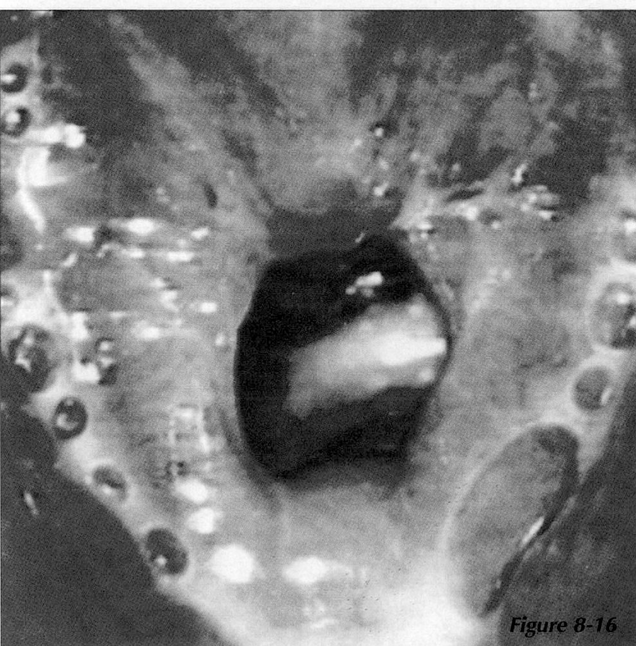

Figure 8-16

# Findings Confused With Abuse

## Imperforate Hymen

**Case Study 8-17**

This 2-month-old girl was evaluated for an abdominal mass. The initial physical examiner failed to note the imperforate hymen. Ultrasound showed a large cystic mass with a small uterus atop it. Subsequent physical examination revealed the imperforate hymen. Two hundred fifty milliliters of mucus was drained from the vagina after surgical hymenectomy.

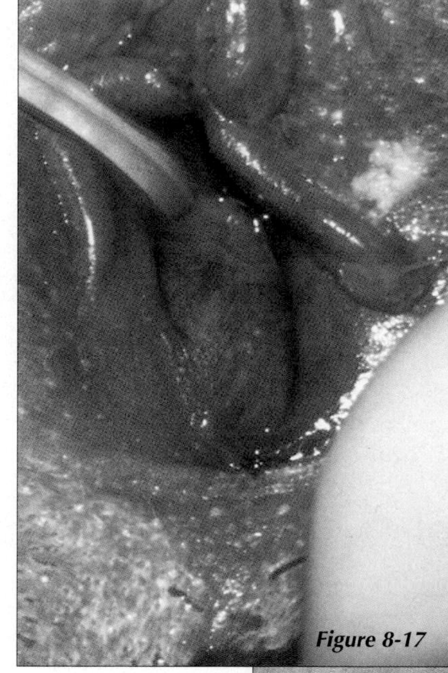

Figure 8-17

***Figures 8-17.*** *Imperforate hymen. The Foley catheter marks the urethral opening.*

## Lichen Sclerosis

**Case Study 8-18**

This 3-year-old girl contracted lichen sclerosis, which is a poorly understood skin condition and not related to sexual trauma. Treatment can be a significant challenge and recurrence is very common.

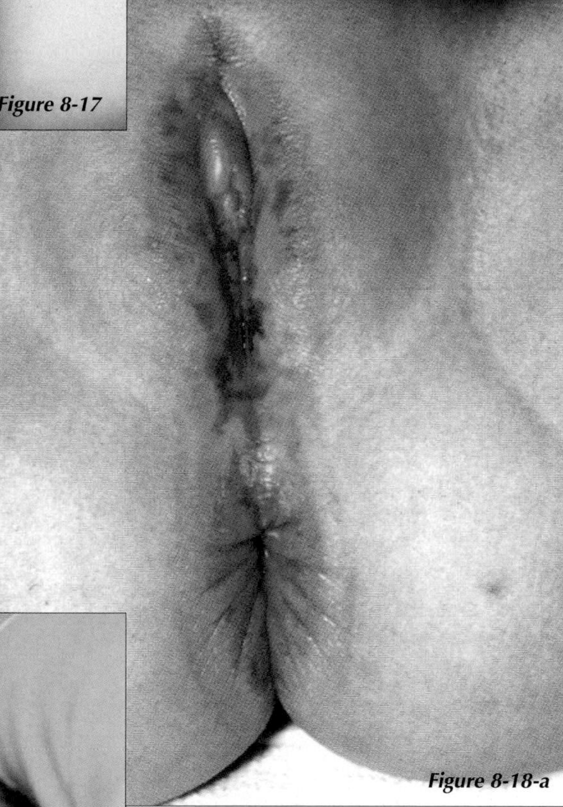

Figure 8-18-a

***Figure 8-18-a.*** *Lichen sclerosis manifested by the white "hourglass" around the vaginal opening and extending down toward the anus. Highly friable skin can be seen along the inner left labia majora, which is a source of bleeding.*

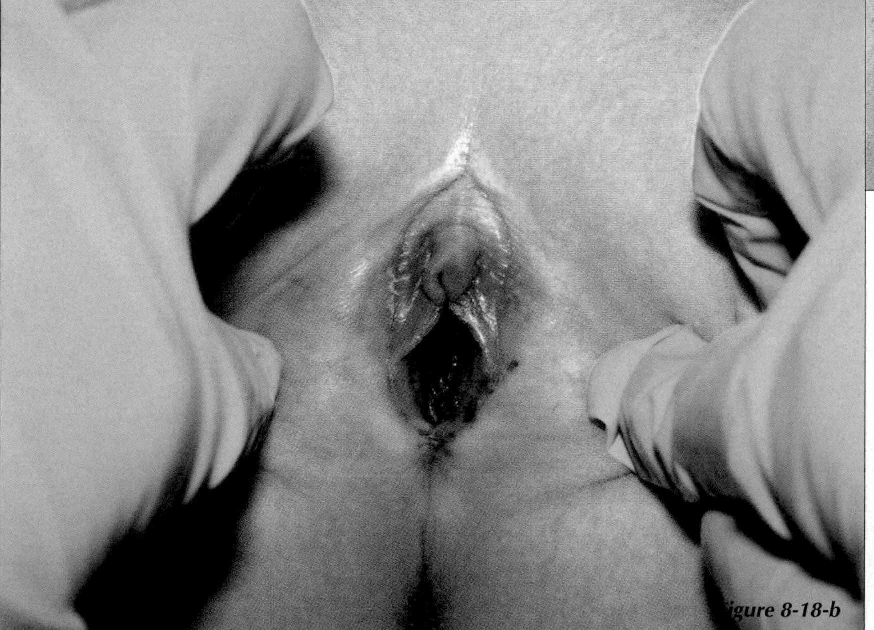

igure 8-18-b

***Figure 8-18-b.*** *A typical presentation of lichen sclerosis. Note the hourglass-shaped white patch and the areas of excoriation, leading to bleeding.*

# Findings Confused With Abuse

## Prolapsed Uterus

### Case Study 8-19

This 6-year-old white girl had an unusual protuberance from her urethra. Prolapsed uterus is more commonly seen in black girls and is not related to sexual trauma. In many children a prolapsed uterus resolves spontaneously.

***Figure 8-19.*** *An early presentation of a prolapsed urethra, prior to the development of bleeding and edema of the prolapsed tissue, which can occlude the vagina.*

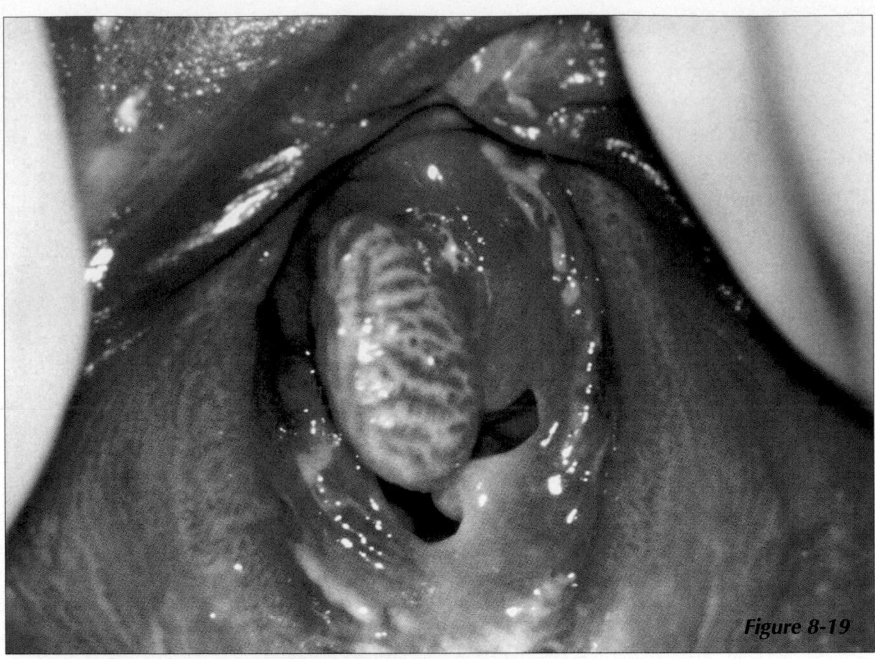

Figure 8-19

## Failure of Midline Fusion

### Case Study 8-20

This 4-year-old boy was brought for evaluation of a possible anal scar found by his pediatrician. Failure of midline fusion can occur anywhere in the midline, but it is most commonly between the anus and vagina or is seen as a perianal midline avascular area.

***Figure 8-20.*** *A small area anterior to the anus that represents a failure of midline fusion—a normal variant.*

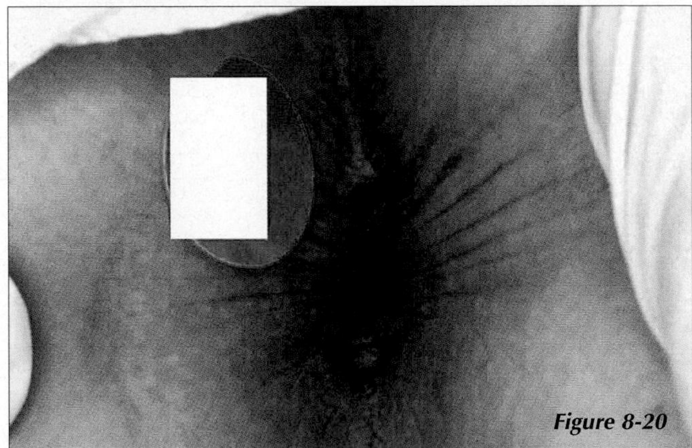

Figure 8-20

## Labial Fusion

### Case Study 8-21

This 4-year-old girl came to her local family practitioner for a school physical. Her vaginal examination revealed severe labial fusion, which is commonly caused by irritation along the labia from nonsexual causes that leads to adhesion of the labial tissues. There was no concern about sexual abuse.

***Figure 8-21.*** *Severe labial fusion both anteriorly and posteriorly. Some practitioners would treat this with topical estrogen, while some would await spontaneous resolution.*

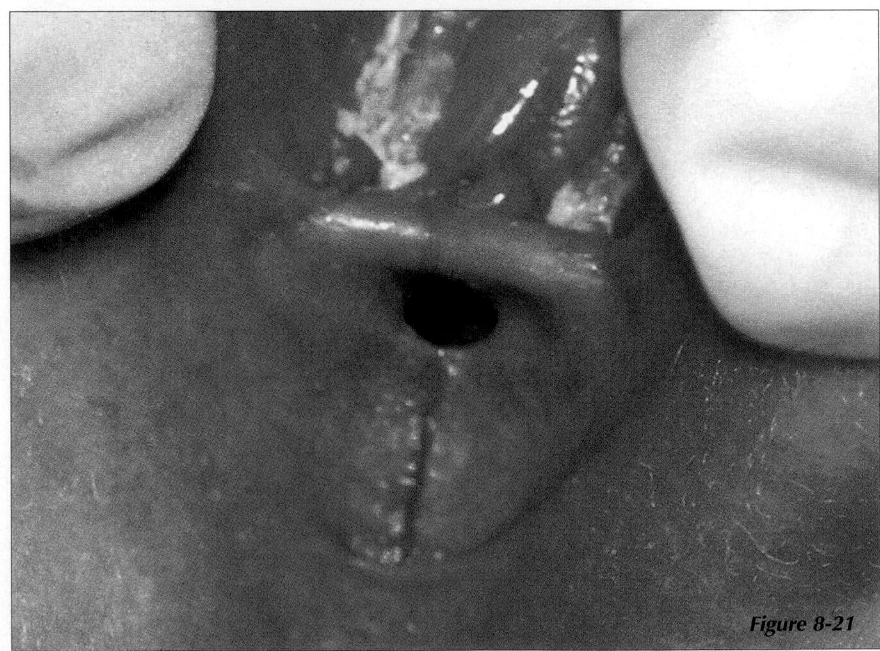

Figure 8-21

# Findings Confused With Abuse

## Straddle Injury

**Case Study 8-22**

This 4-year-old girl had a history of a straddle fall on her bicycle. Her only injury was an interlabial contusion on the examiner's right. Straddle injuries tend to be anterior, while injuries from sexual abuse tend to be posterior. Hymenal straddle injuries are extremely rare.

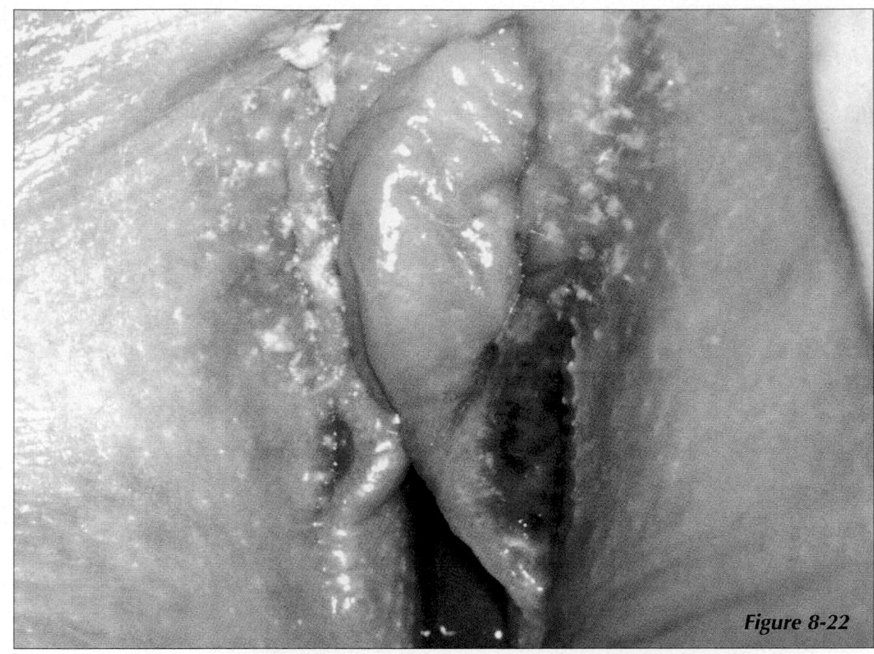

***Figure 8-22.*** *An interlabial contusion on the examiner's right caused by a straddle fall.*

## Vaginal Duplication

**Case Study 8-23**

This 8-year-old girl made allegations of sexual abuse. On examination she was found to have an abnormality of the hymen, evidenced by an apparent band of vertically oriented tissue. On further examination she was found to have duplication of the vagina (ie, 2 vaginas, 2 cervices, and a bicornuate uterus), which is a very rare congenital defect requiring the care of a skilled specialist.

***Figure 8-23.*** *Duplication of the vagina and cervix.*

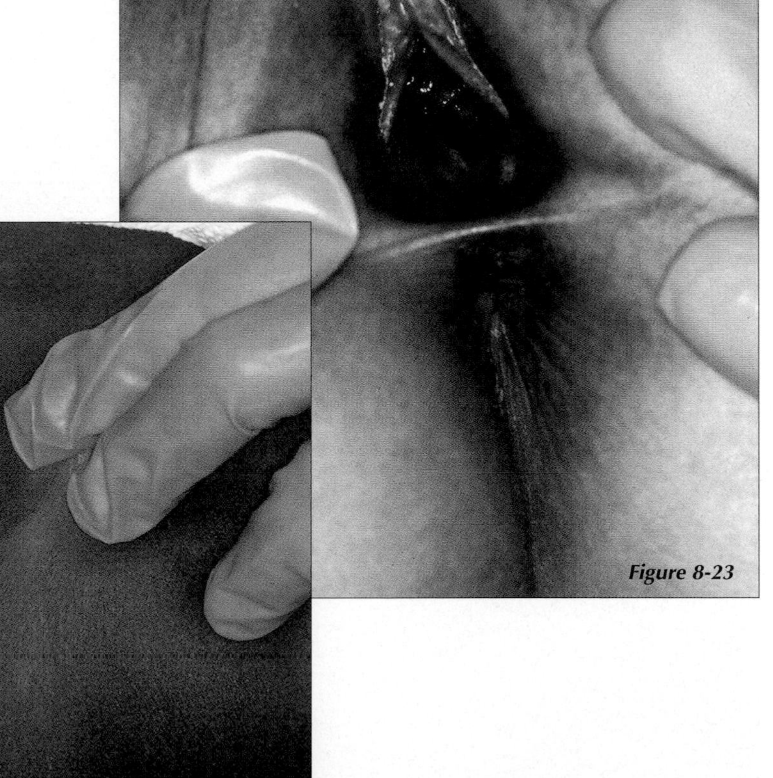

## Vitiligo

**Case Study 8-24**

This 8-year-old was examined for concerns about possible sexual abuse based on an abnormal examination. There was a history for possible sexual abuse as well as the findings depicted. This girl exhibited typical vitiligo, which is not related to sexual abuse.

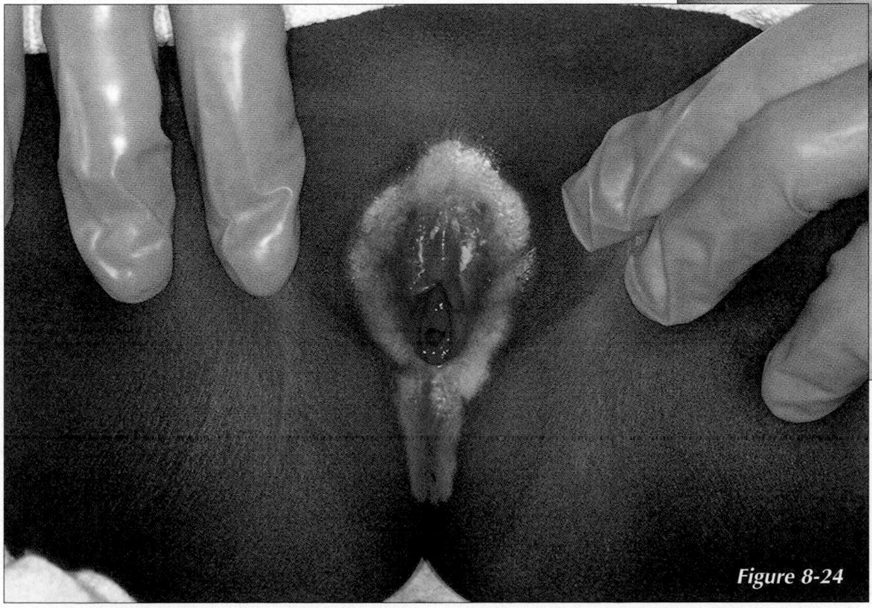

***Figure 8-24.*** *Vitiligo. There is no evidence of excoriation that might indicate lichen sclerosis.*

# Findings Confused With Abuse

## Foreign Body

### Case Study 8-25

This 7-year-old had been experiencing foul-smelling bloody vaginal discharge for 2 months. She had been prescribed several courses of antibiotics. Vaginal cultures grew pure *Staphylococcus aureus*. On examination, a hard green object was noted at the hymenal level within the vagina. A foreign body was removed from the patient while under anesthesia. The foreign body turned out to be a cap from a tube of lip balm. The girl denied any history of sexual abuse. She even denied that she had put anything in her vagina. The most common vaginal foreign body is toilet tissue. In general, toilet tissue can be removed with a warm saline lavage using a small infant feeding tube. Larger objects may require anesthesia and removal by a surgeon.

***Figure 8-25-a.*** *Foreign body removed from a child with a vaginal discharge. The object is the cap from a tube of lip balm.*

***Figure 8-25-b.*** *Appearance of the hymen after removal of the foreign body.*

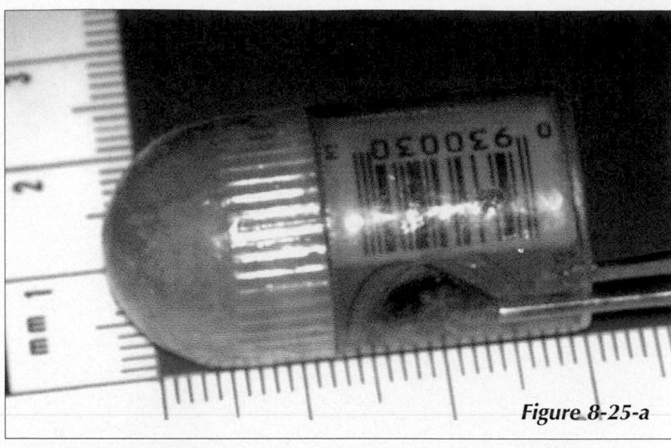

Figure 8-25-a

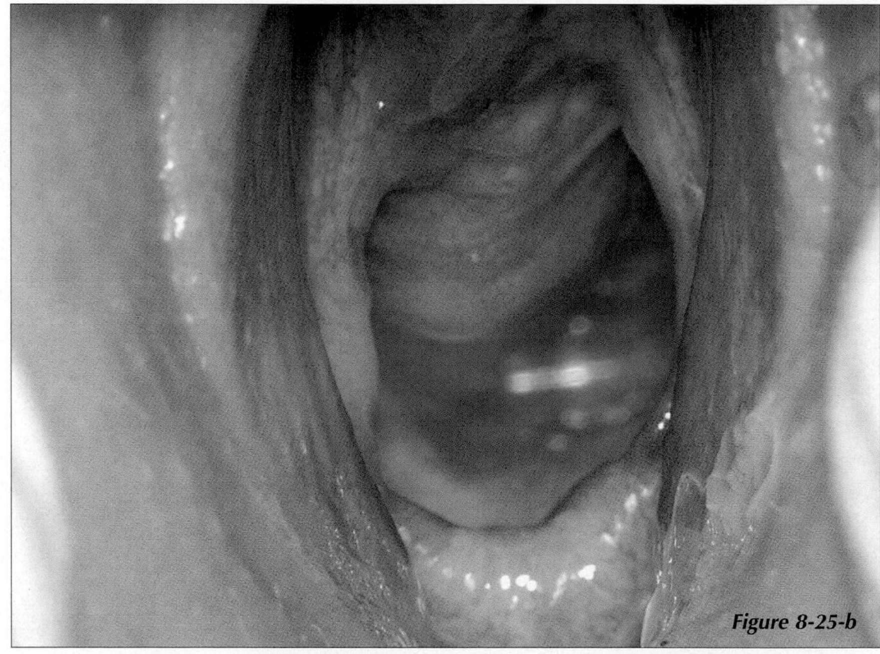
Figure 8-25-b

## Hymenal Projection

### Case Study 8-26

During examination, this 17-year-old girl gave a history of consensual sexual activity with her 32-year-old boyfriend.

***Figure 8-26-a.*** *The hymen is highly estrogenized posteriorly with a very prominent hymenal projection. It is difficult to determine the origin of the projection, but the intact hymen makes trauma unlikely.*

***Figure 8-26-b.*** *The projection after manipulation with a probe. Note that the hymen is intact.*

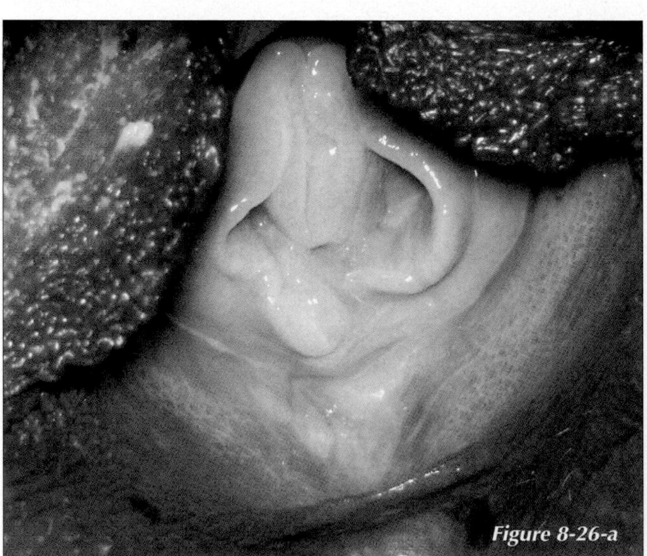
Figure 8-26-a

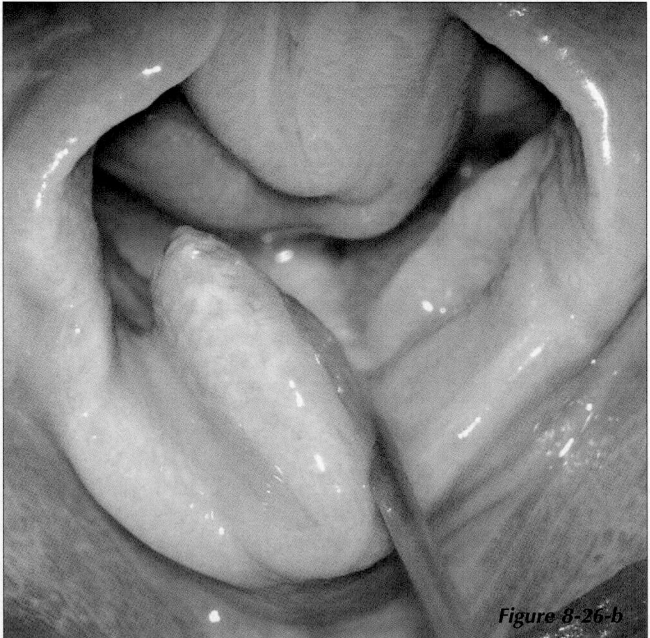
Figure 8-26-b

# Findings Confused With Abuse

## External Hymenal Midline

**Case Study 8-27**

This 3-year-old girl had a wide posterior hymen showing a prominent midline, which is a normal finding and is also termed an external hymenal ridge. The origin was unknown and was explained as a developmental variant.

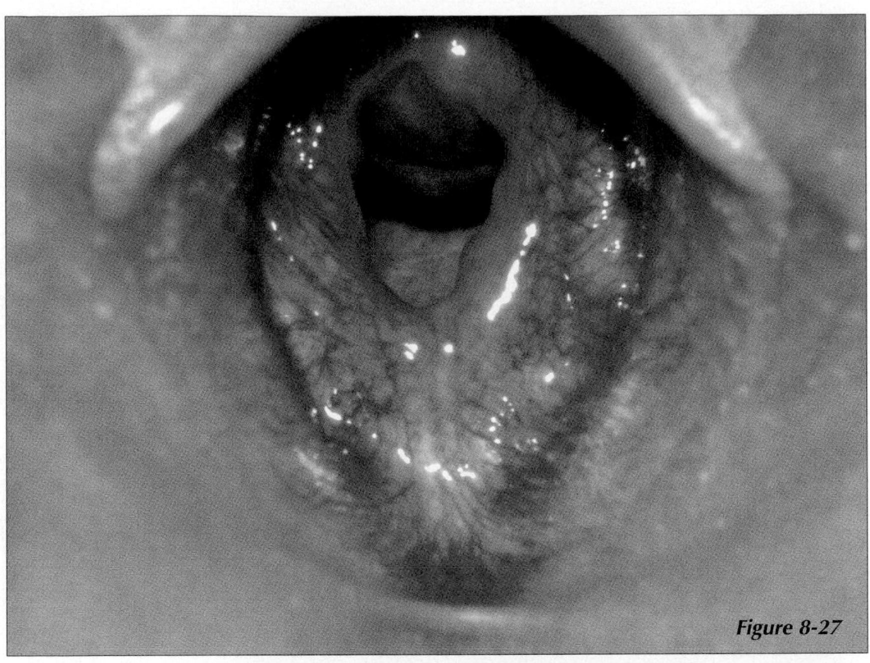

***Figure 8-27.*** *Wide posterior hymen showing a prominent midline.*

## Extensive Labial Fusion

**Case Study 8-28**

This 9-month-old girl had extensive labial fusion, which is a common finding in normal children. While there have been reports of fusion after severe sexual abuse and female circumcision, it was determined that this was a case of typical fusion in infancy and was not an indicator of abuse.

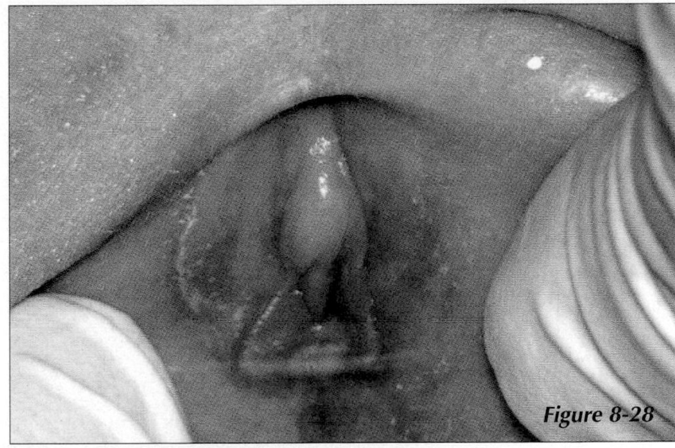

***Figure 8-28.*** *Normal findings of extensive labial fusion.*

## Failed Midline Fusion

**Case Study 8-29**

This 5-year-old girl had a failure of midline fusion between the anal and vaginal openings. It was considered not to be associated with abuse since it was a variation of a common defect.

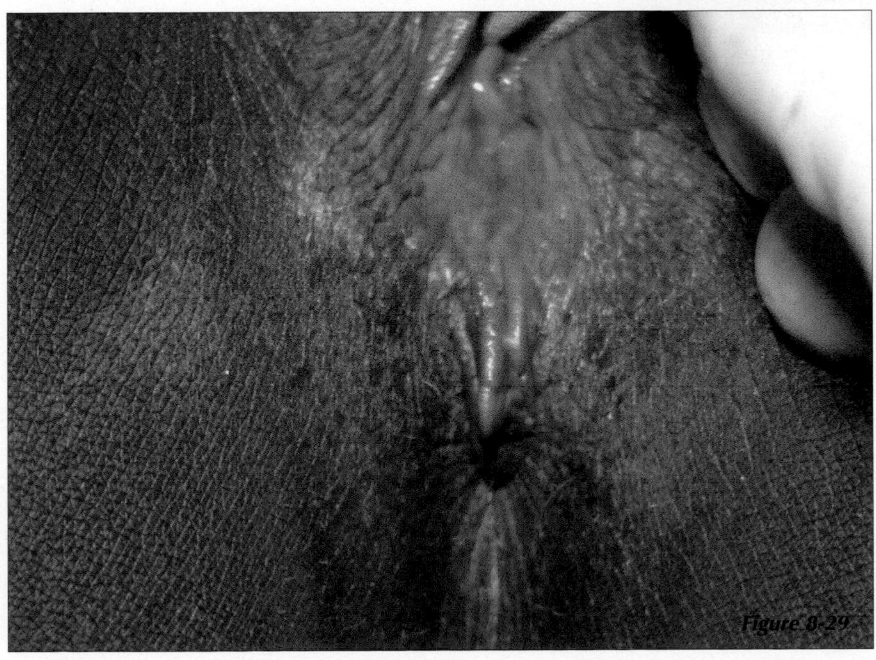

***Figure 8-29.*** *Midline fusion failure between the anal and vaginal openings.*

# Findings Confused With Abuse

## Possible Foreign Body

### Case Study 8-30

This 5-year-old girl had vaginal discharge and a description of a foul smell. The examiner noted a possible foreign body. If the sequential photographs are reviewed, the area of injury can be identified. Without the sequential photographs, the examination shows no indication of prior injury. This case demonstrates that full transections can heal completely without residua.

***Figure 8-30-a.*** *Foreign body suspected in 5-year-old girl because of a vaginal discharge.*

***Figure 8-30-b.*** *Three foreign bodies removed from the girl while under anesthesia: a doll shoe, a bead, and the back of an earring.*

***Figure 8-30-c.*** *A laceration of the hymen at the 5-o'clock position, which was inadvertently caused during the extraction procedure.*

***Figure 8-30-d.*** *A normal posterior hymenal rim 5 months after the extraction procedure.*

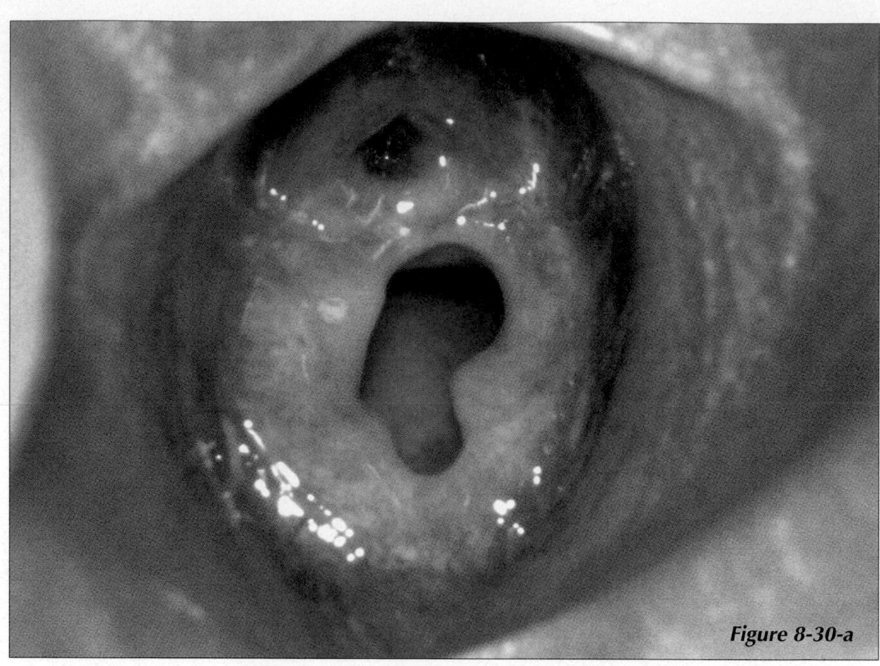

Figure 8-30-a

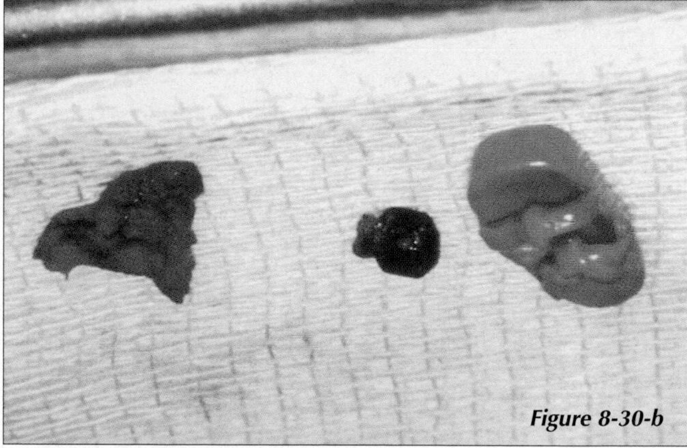

Figure 8-30-b

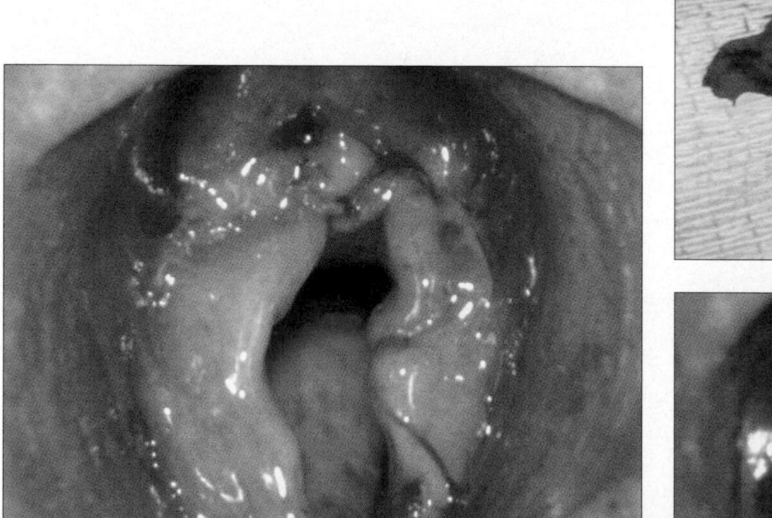

Figure 8-30-c

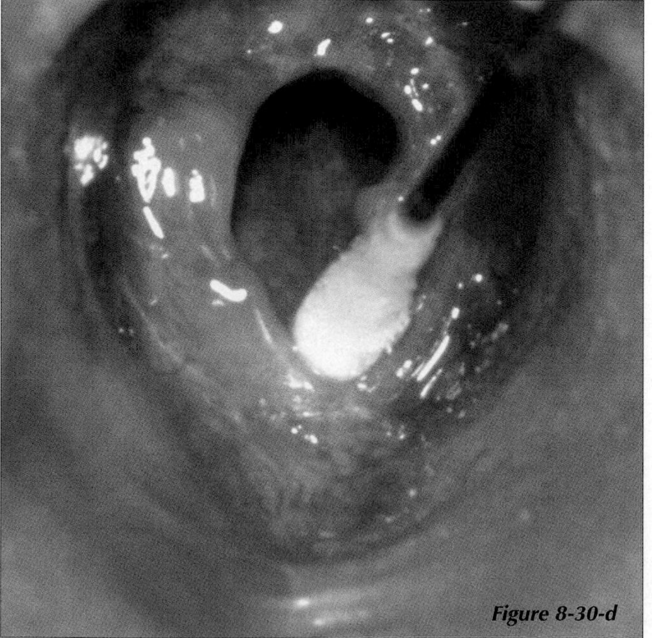

Figure 8-30-d

# Findings Confused With Abuse

## Lichen Sclerosis Causing Bleeding

**Case Study 8-31**

This 7-year-old girl had blood in her underwear. There was no suggestion of sexual abuse. She was diagnosed with lichen sclerosis.

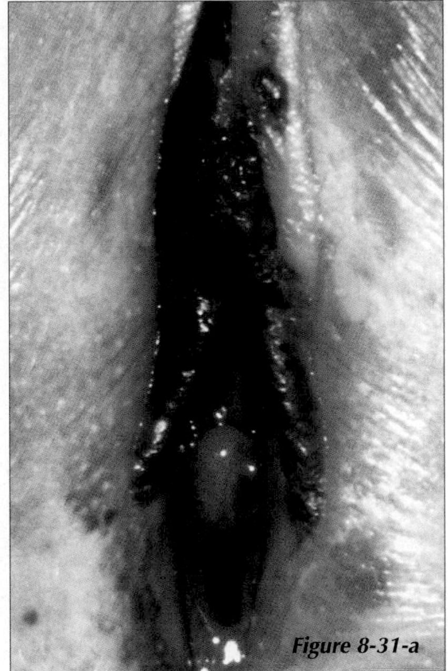

*Figure 8-31-a*

***Figure 8-31-a.*** *A clear white band is exterior to the vaginal opening and excoriations are around the vaginal opening.*

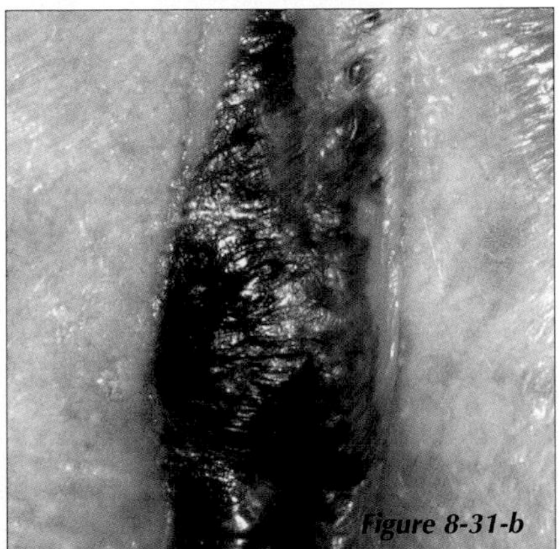

*Figure 8-31-b*

***Figure 8-31-b.*** *The labia minora have extensive subcutaneous bleeding and a surrounding white patch.*

## Labial Bruising

**Case Study 8-32**

This 2-year-old girl had a lesion on her labia majora. Examination revealed a lesion to the clitoral hood and a tiny laceration anterior to the clitoral hood. Follow-up examination revealed the lesion was a stable finding and most likely a vascular malformation. The laceration anterior to the clitoral hood was gone. It was believed to result from friability of the tissue due to poor hygiene.

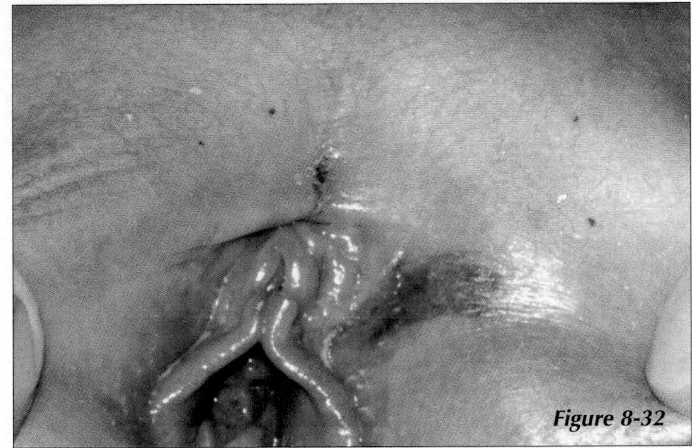

*Figure 8-32*

***Figure 8-32.*** *Clitoral hood lesion and a small anterior laceration.*

## Duplication of Reproductive Structures

**Case Study 8-33**

This 9-year-old girl complained of chronic abdominal pain. Her vaginal examination was abnormal and eventually led to a diagnosis of duplication of all of her reproductive structures. The vaginal division was differentiated from a simple septum of the hymen by the extension vertically into the vagina.

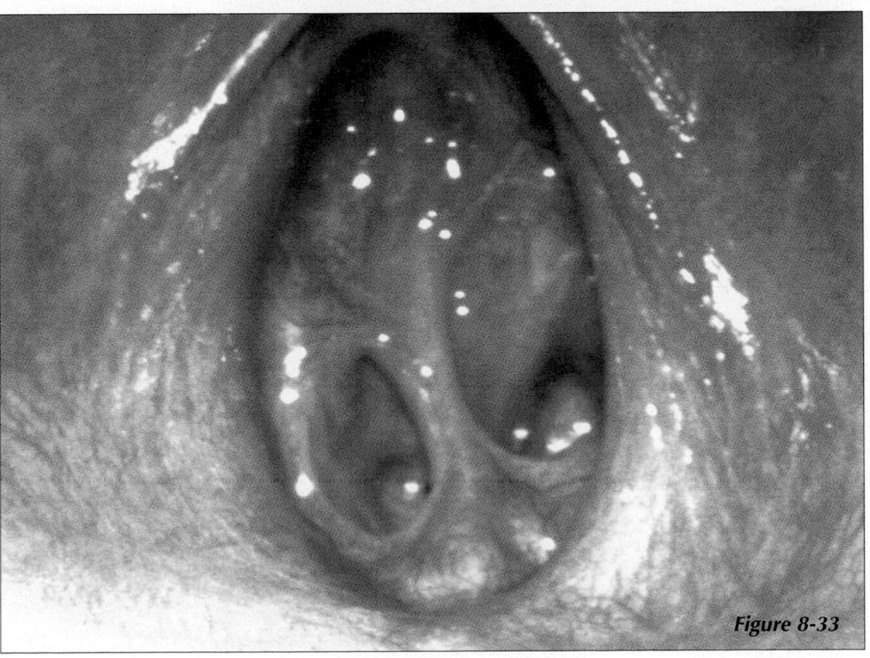

*Figure 8-33*

***Figure 8-33.*** *Vaginal division with duplication of all reproductive structures.*

# Findings Confused With Abuse

## Pinworm

**Case Study 8-34**

The patient complained of severe anal itching and inability to sleep. Examination revealed a pinworm.

***Figure 8-34.*** *A pinworm. Actual demonstration of a pinworm is rare, and the diagnosis is usually made by demonstrating eggs on the perianal skin or mucosa.*

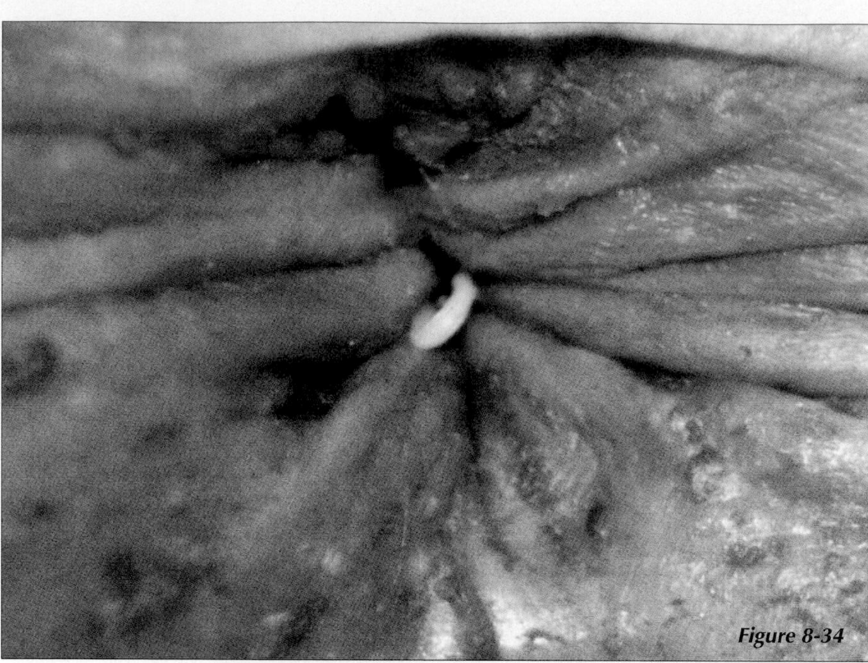

Figure 8-34

## Hemangioma

**Case Study 8-35**

This obvious hemangioma required no treatment.

***Figure 8-35.*** *Hemangioma.*

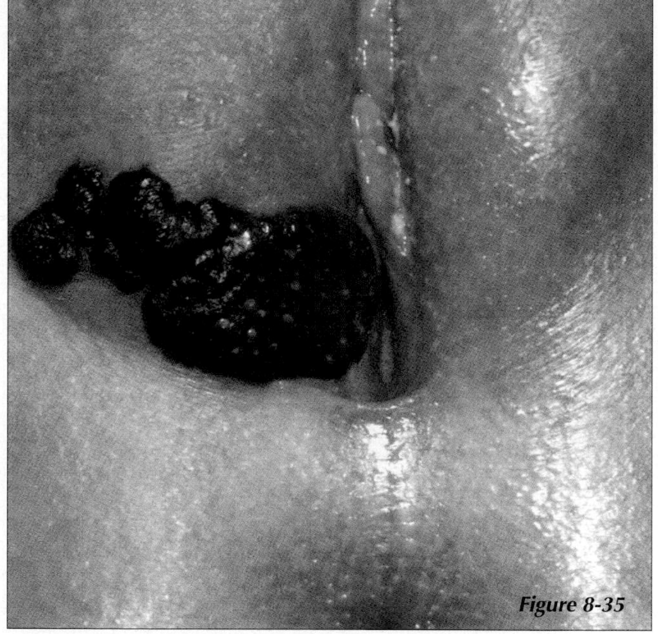

Figure 8-35

## Perianal Vitiligo

**Case Study 8-36**

This patient was referred for unexplained pigment changes. The diagnosis was vitiligo.

***Figure 8-36.*** *Pigment change indicating perianal vitiligo.*

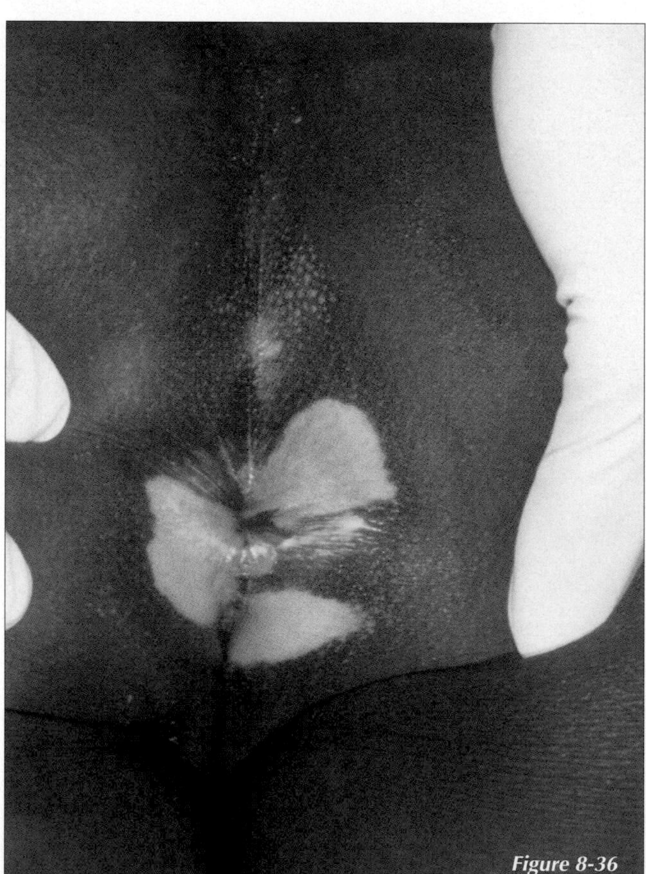

Figure 8-36

# Normal Findings

## Crescentic Hymen

**Case Study 8-37**

This 10-year-old girl was examined with a normal crescentic hymen.

***Figure 8-37.*** *Normal crescentic hymen with a slight notch at the 3-o'clock position.*

When an examination is interpreted as normal, one can never extrapolate the lack of findings to mean that sexual abuse did not occur. Many types of sexual abuse, including penetration, can occur or heal without scarring.

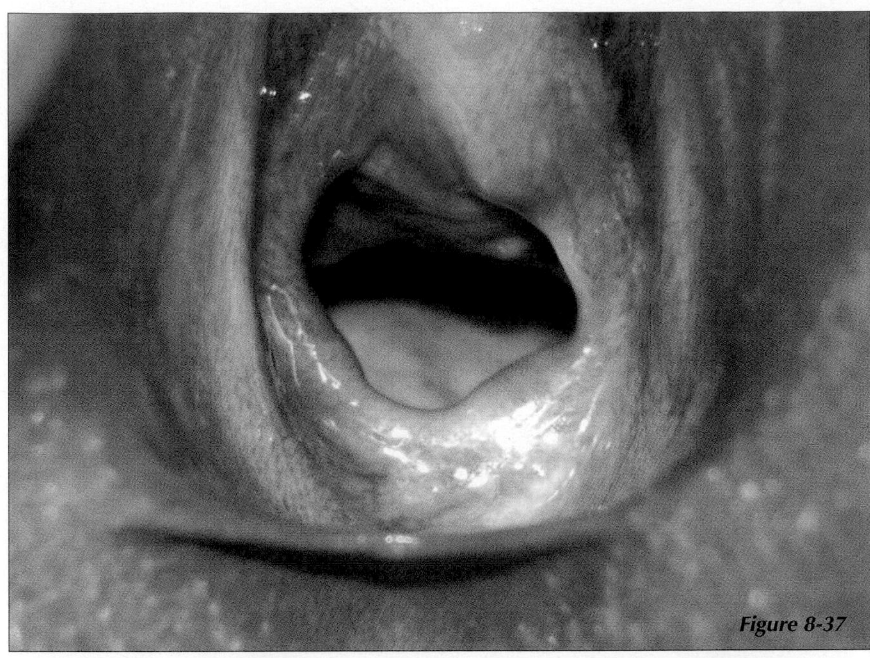

Figure 8-37

## Annular Hymen

**Case Study 8-38**

This 5-year-old girl was referred for allegations of genital contact with an adult. The findings of the examination were typical of a fully relaxed child in the examination environment.

***Figure 8-38.*** *An annular hymen with minimal width at all points. It is within normal limits. Note a prominent posterior vaginal column.*

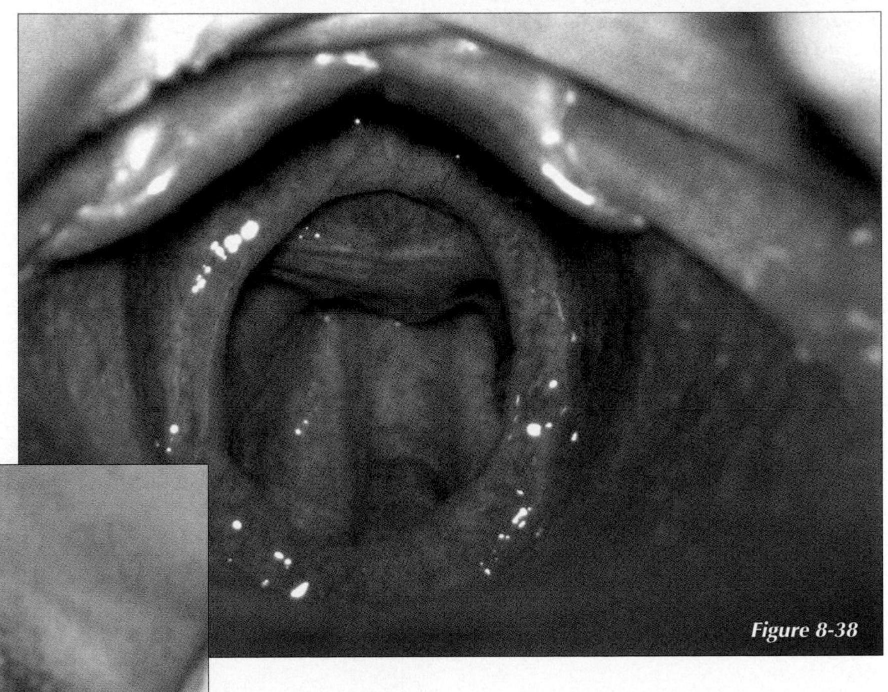

Figure 8-38

## Large Urethral Opening Above Normal Hymen

**Case Study 8-39**

This asymptomatic 3-year-old girl with no allegations of abuse had a large urethral opening above a normal hymen. This finding is common during labial traction and is of no clinical significance.

***Figure 8-39.*** *Large urethral opening located above a normal hymen.*

Figure 8-39

# Normal Findings

## Normal Intact Hymen

**Case Study 8-40**

This 15-year-old sexually active girl alleged penile penetration. She had a fully estrogenized hymen without any signs of trauma. The examination was interpreted as normal.

***Figure 8-40.*** *Intact hymen in sexually active adolescent.*

Normal intact hymens in sexually active adolescents are quite common and, in fact, intact hymens are commonly found in pregnant teenagers.

## Anal Tag

**Case Study 8-41**

This normal 4-year-old boy alleged anal-digital penetration. The examination results were normal, except for the presence of an anal tag. While anal penetration may have occurred, the anal tag was not the result of it.

***Figure 8-41.*** *Anal tag at the 12-o'clock position.*

## Normal Intact Annular Hymen

**Case Study 8-42**

This 5-year-old was referred to the sexual abuse evaluation clinic with an allegation of vaginal penetration with a foreign body by a teenage neighbor. While genital contact may have occurred, there was no evidence of penetration, which is sometimes alleged with genital contact because children have no experiential frame of reference for penetration.

***Figure 8-42.*** *A normal, intact annular hymen.*

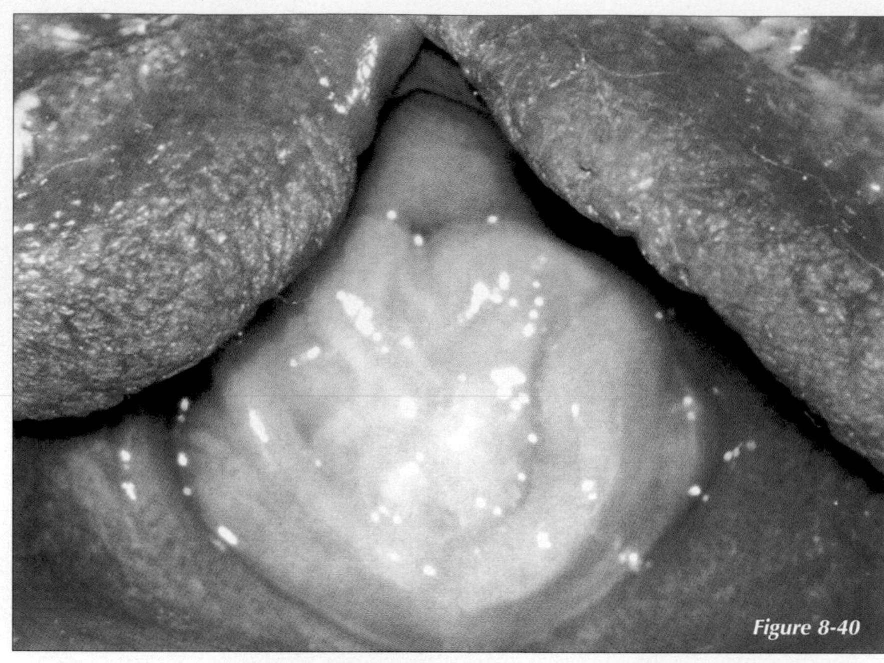

*Figure 8-40*

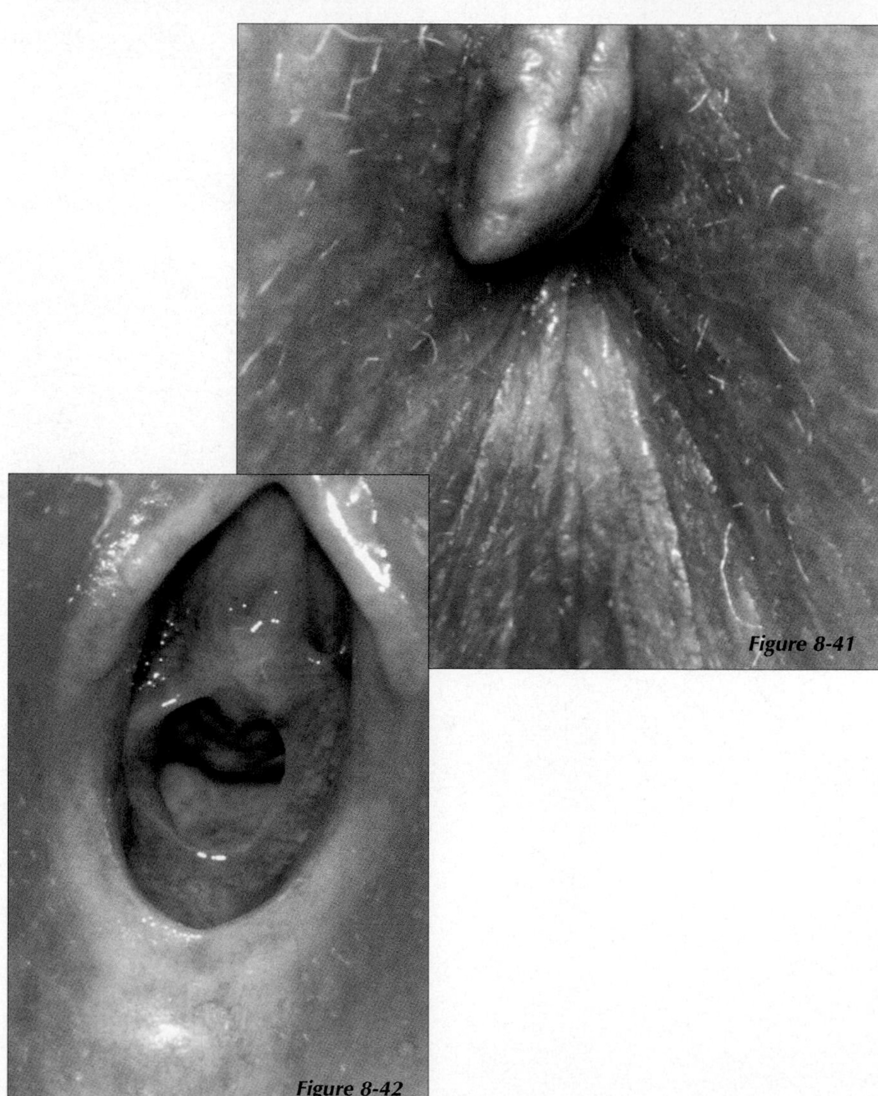

*Figure 8-41*

*Figure 8-42*

# Normal Findings

## Intravaginal Ridge

**Case Study 8-43**

This 10-year-old female has a normal hymen.

***Figure 8-43.*** *The child is in the knee-chest position. The magnified view shows a normal hymen with a mound at the 10-o'clock position.*

A mound may be created by a hymenal attachment of a longitudinal intravaginal ridge.[3]

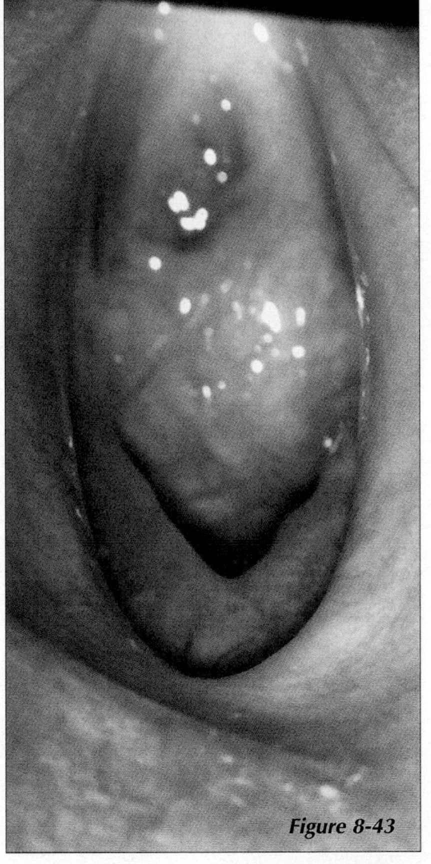

Figure 8-43

## Normal Examination

**Case Study 8-44**

This 12-year-old girl reportedly was sexually assaulted by an older male. Genital-to-genital contact was alleged.

***Figure 8-44-a.*** *Examined in the supine position, the girl has pubertal development with estrogenized tissues. The hymen appears normal.*

***Figure 8-44-b.*** *After several minutes of relaxation, the structures are much better visualized. The hymen is crescentic and an intravaginal ridge is seen at the 5-o'clock position.*

This examination is normal and neither confirms nor disconfirms the clear history of abuse given by the child.

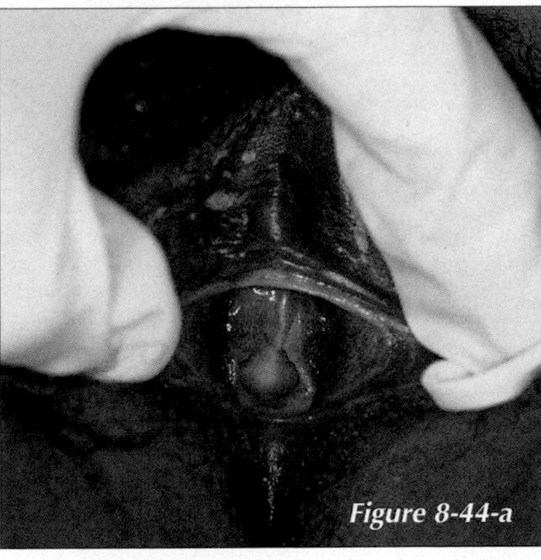

Figure 8-44-a

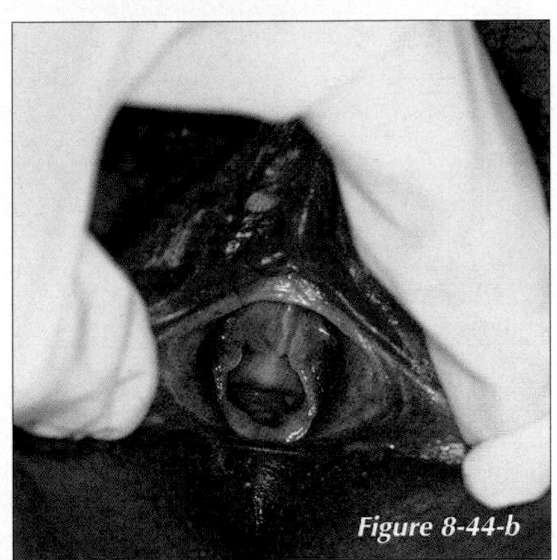

Figure 8-44-b

## Normal Anal Findings

**Case Study 8-45**

This infant was brought in for evaluation because of a suspicion of sexual abuse in an older sibling. The findings of the examination were normal. The case was referred for a forensic interview.

***Figure 8-45.*** *Normal appearance of the anus in an infant.*

## Thickened Crescentic Hymen

**Case Study 8-46**

This 4-year-old girl had a history of possible vaginal penetration by an adult male. The findings of the examination were normal.

***Figure 8-46.*** *A slightly thickened crescentic hymen.*

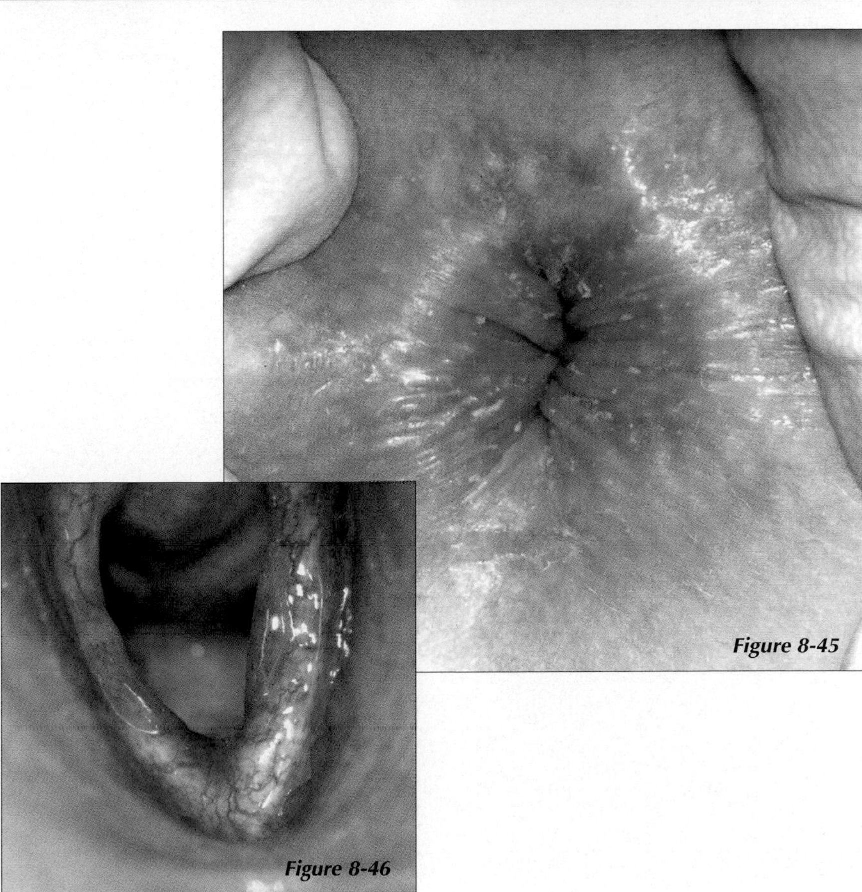

Figure 8-45

Figure 8-46

# Normal Findings

## Circumferential or Annular Hymen

**Case Study 8-47**

This 6-year-old child was evaluated after disclosing genital "touching" by her mother's boyfriend.

***Figure 8-47.*** *A normal circumferential or annular hymen. Note the absence of any abnormality.*

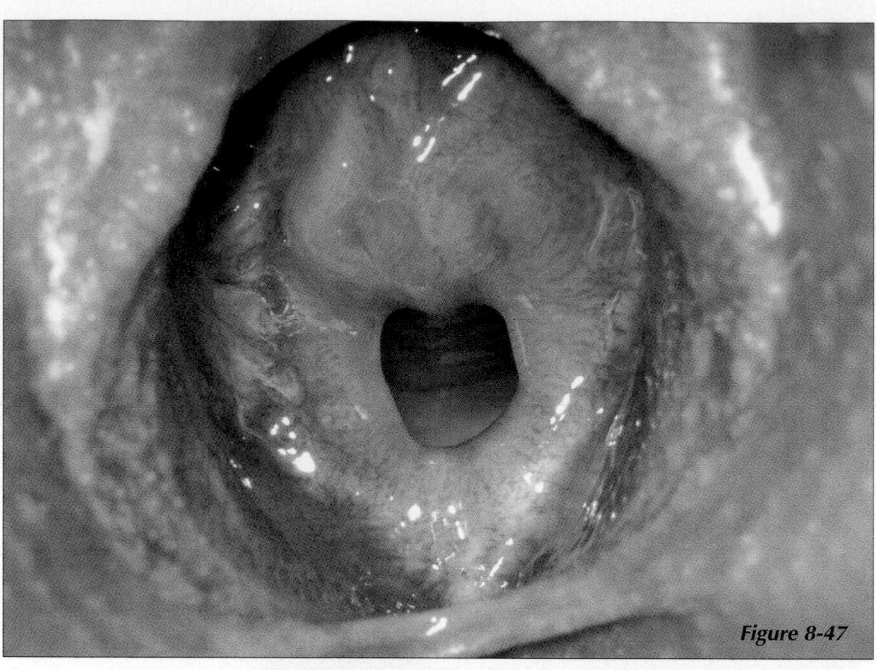

**Figure 8-47**

## Anterior Anal Venous Pooling

**Case Study 8-48**

This 5-year-old child was evaluated for sexual abuse involving anal contact.

***Figure 8-48.*** *Anterior venous pooling noted on anal examination.*

Anterior venous pooling on anal examination is common among normal children, and therefore cannot be used as an indicator of sexual abuse.

**Figure 8-48**

## Extensive Anal Pooling

**Case Study 8-49**

This 7-year-old was evaluated for anal penetration on one or two occasions several months before this examination.

***Figure 8-49.*** *Extensive anal pooling in a 7-year-old. This is considered a normal finding.*

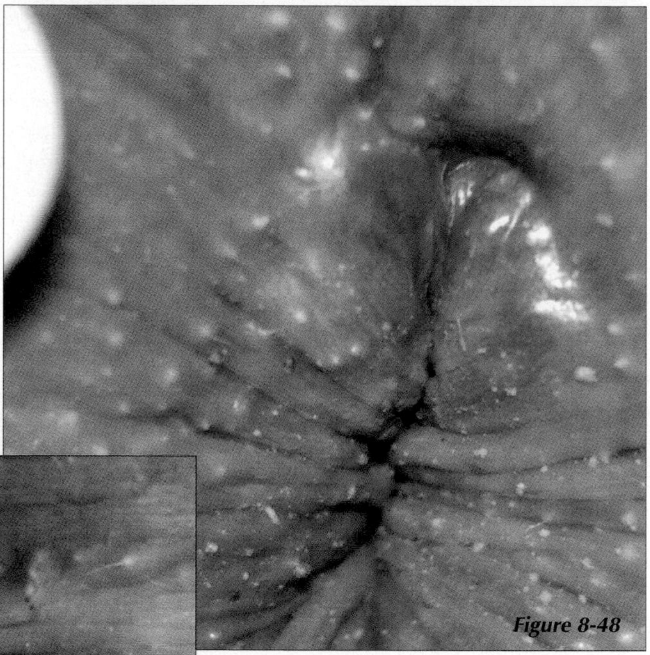

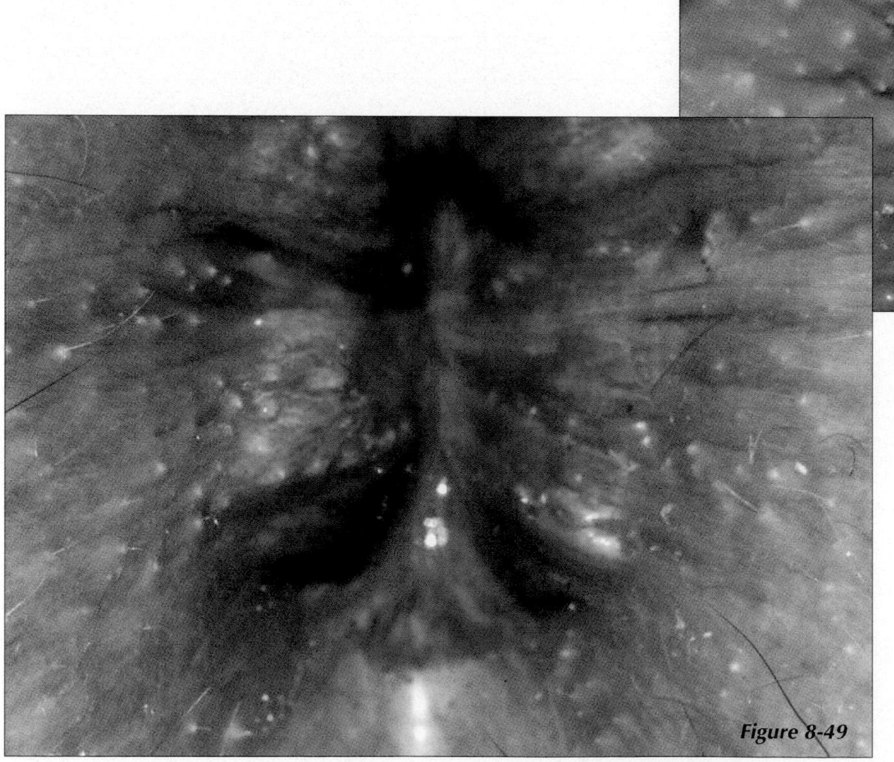

**Figure 8-49**

# Normal Findings

## Midline White Line

**Case Study 8-50**

This 2-year-old girl was referred for suspected sexual abuse of unknown nature. She had a prominent white line extending up the posterior hymen in the midline.

***Figure 8-50.*** *White line extends up the midline of the posterior hymen. This is a common midline finding and is not indicative of a scar. The key to a differential diagnosis is the midline location and the absence of any palpated scar.*

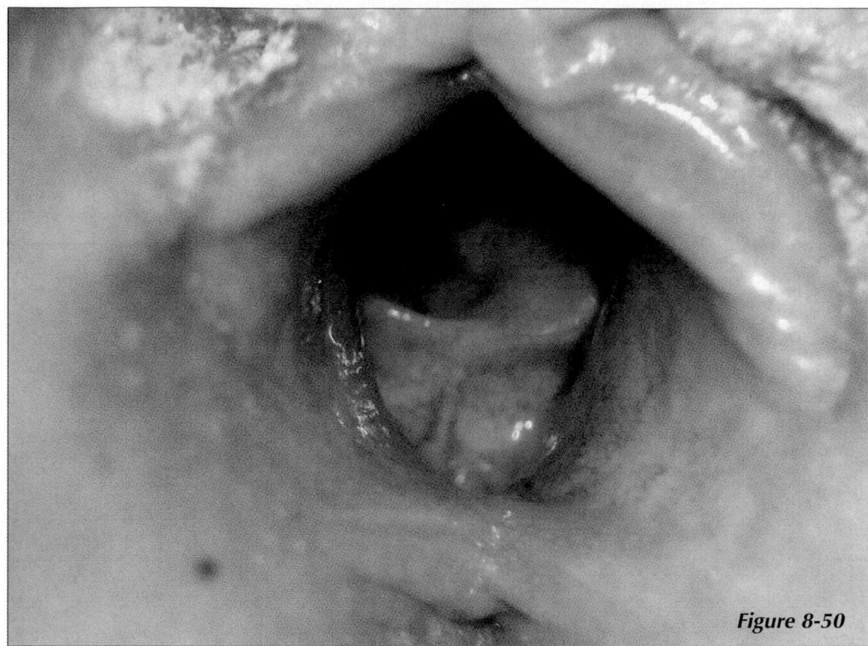

Figure 8-50

## Normal Examination After Sexual Assault

**Case Study 8-51**

This 17-year-old girl had a history of sexual assault 1 month prior to this examination. She had a normal, fully estrogenized hymen and a normal examination.

***Figure 8-51.*** *Hymen is fully estrogenized, constituting a normal examination.*

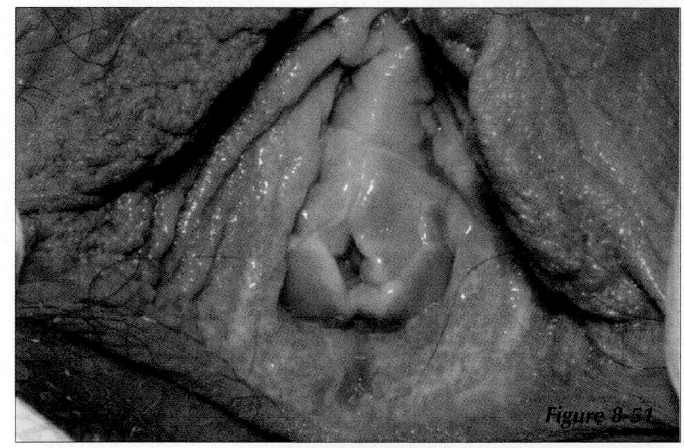

Figure 8-51

## Smooth Avascular Posterior Area

**Case Study 8-52**

This 8-year-old boy was examined after alleging anal penetration involving a teenage cousin.

***Figure 8-52.*** *Common smooth avascular area in anal area. The common smooth avascular area posteriorly is a normal variant that should not be confused with a scar.*

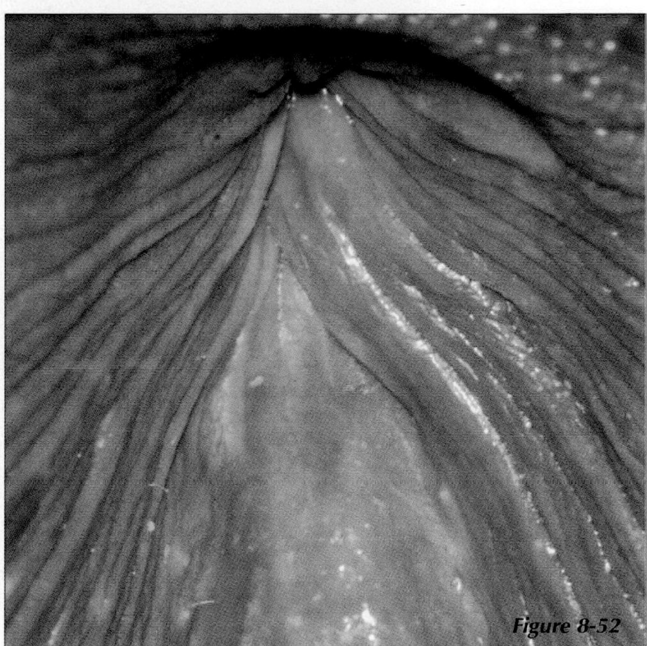

Figure 8-52

## Hymenal Projection

**Case Study 8-53**

This 6-year-old girl had a hymenal projection at the 6-o'clock position, accentuated by demonstration with a cotton swab.

***Figure 8-53.*** *Hymenal projection at the 6-o'clock position.*

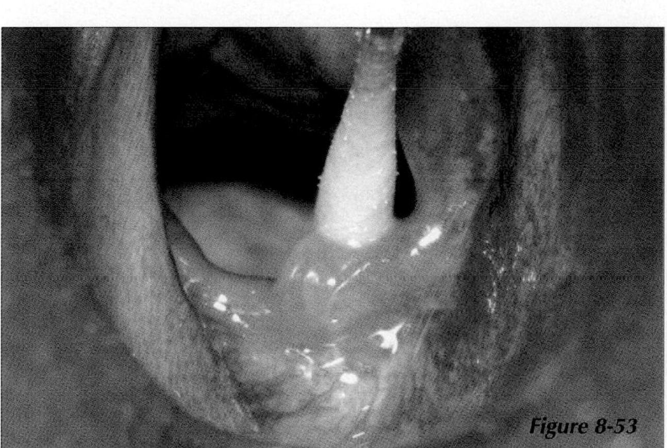

Figure 8-53

# Normal Findings

## Integrity of Hymen

**Case Study 8-54**

This 16-year-old girl had a fully estrogenized hymen on examination.

***Figure 8-54.*** *The technique of using a cotton swab to determine the integrity of the hymen is shown. In older girls, the hymen loses most of its sensitivity to touch and should be explored with a swab to look for old or new transections.*

## Hymenal Mound

**Case Study 8-55**

This 4-year-old girl was not able to understand the concept of abnormal touching on questioning by her mother. She had a hymenal mound, which is a normal finding.

***Figure. 8-55.*** *Hymenal mound at the 8-o'clock position.*

## Anterior Intravaginal Ridge

**Case Study 8-56**

This 3-year-old girl had a prominent anterior intravaginal ridge that was found incidentally during a routine pediatric examination and was indicated by a vaginal discharge.

***Figure 8-56.*** *Prominent intravaginal ridge is present anteriorly.*

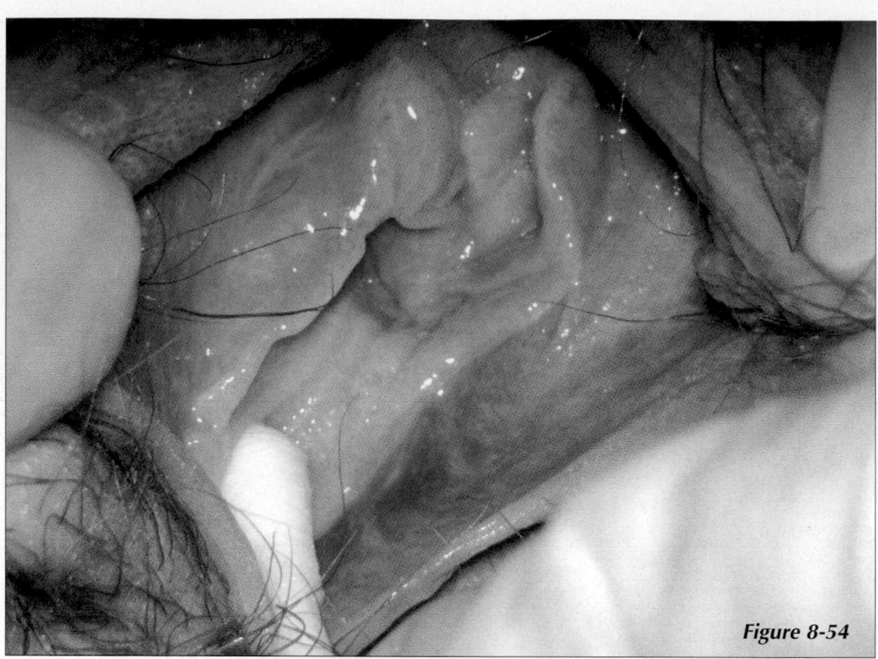

**Figure 8-54**

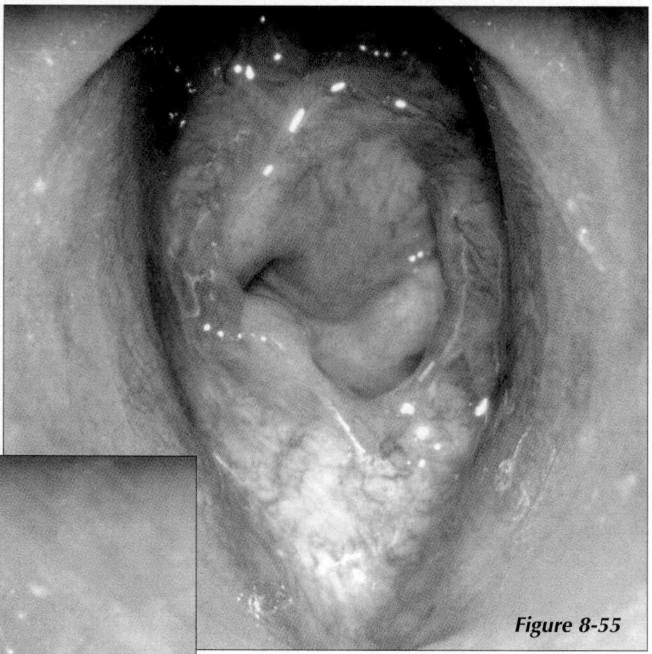

**Figure 8-55**

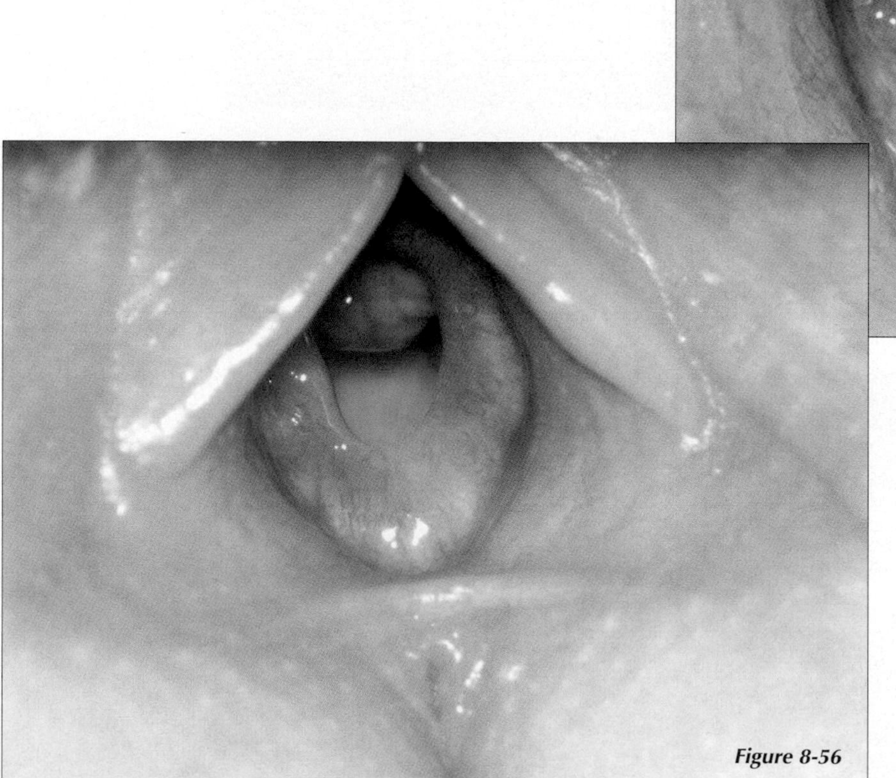

**Figure 8-56**

# Normal Findings

## Knee-Chest Position

**Case Study 8-57**

This 14-year-old girl was evaluated in the knee-chest position. This position is often invaluable to demonstrate the posterior rim, but is often very difficult to accomplish in a girl this age.

***Figure 8-57.*** *Cotton swab indicates intact posterior hymen in a 14-year-old girl.*

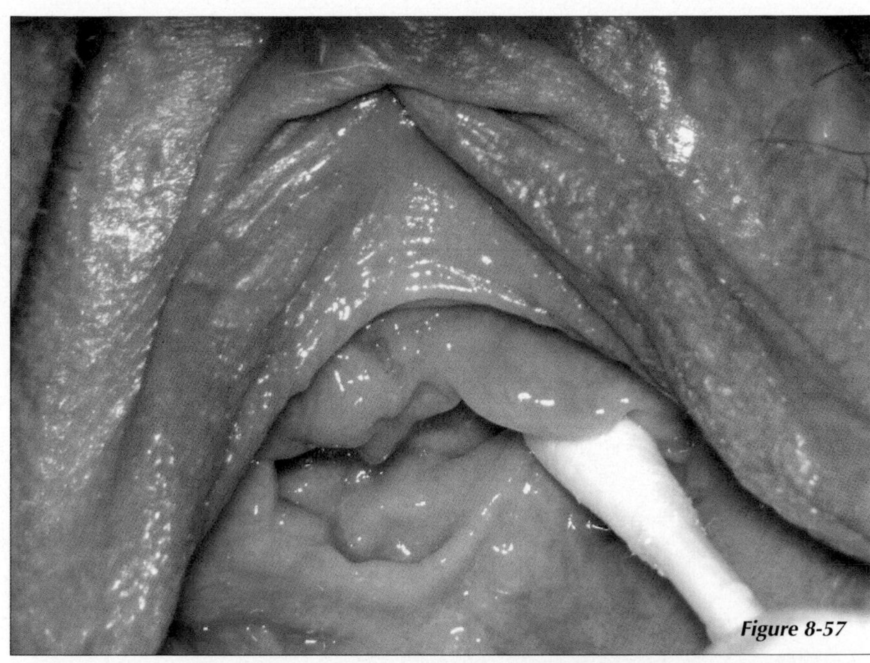

**Figure 8-57**

## Intact Posterior Rim

**Case Study 8-58**

This 7-year-old girl was allegedly fondled by her brother. Her pediatrician was concerned because she was so willing to be examined. There was no indication of abuse in the forensic interview.

***Figure 8-58.*** *A 7-year-old girl in the knee-chest position showing an intact posterior rim.*

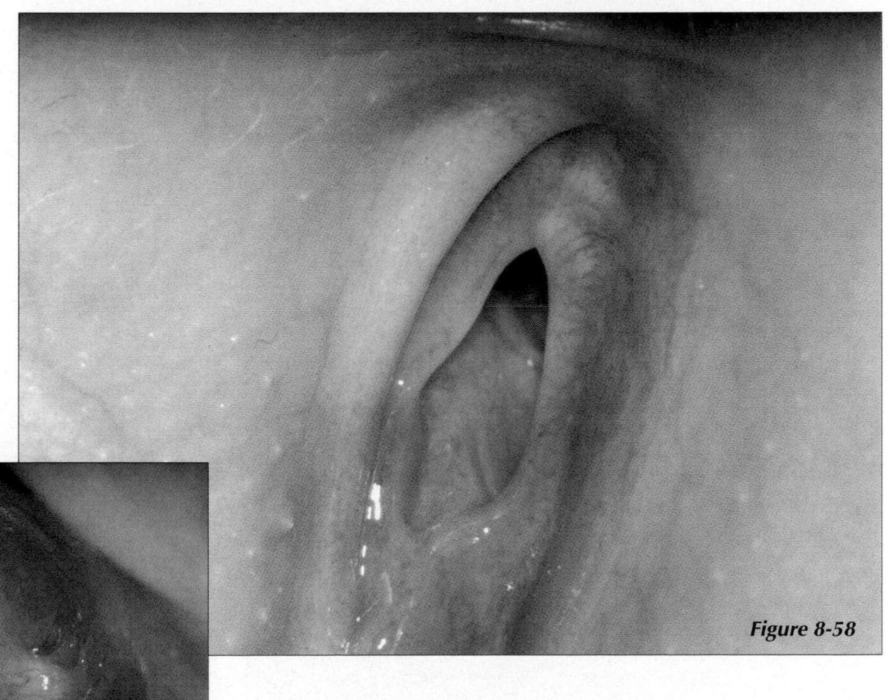

**Figure 8-58**

## Prominent Urethral Support Structures

**Case Study 8-59**

This 3-year-old girl was referred for examination because of the prominent support structures around the urethra. The final interpretation was normal.

***Figure 8-59.*** *A normal asymmetrical crescentic hymen with prominent urethral support structures.*

**Figure 8-59**

# Normal Findings

## Hymenal Tag

**Case Study 8-60**

This 4-year-old girl was examined with a hymenal tag, which may have been a septal remnant or simply asymmetry in the hymen.

***Figure 8-60.*** *Hymenal tag at the 7-o'clock position.*

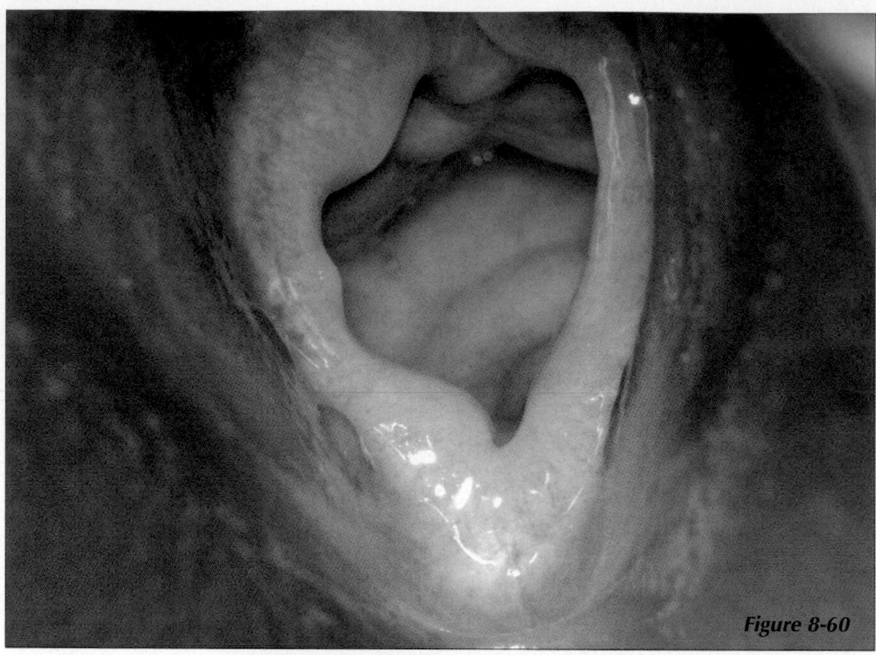

Figure 8-60

## Normal Posterior Hymenal Rim

**Case Study 8-61**

This 7-year-old was brought in for treatment with an allegation of fondling.

***Figure 8-61.*** *This is an examination in knee-chest position showing a normal posterior hymenal rim.*

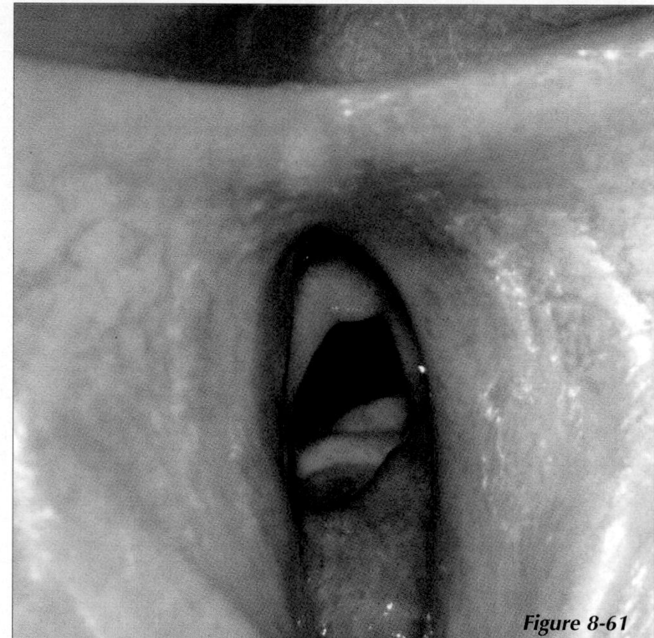

Figure 8-61

## Hymenal Projection

**Case Study 8-62**

This 9-year-old girl was examined for evidence of vaginal discharge.

***Figure 8-62.*** *A hymenal projection was found in the 10-o'clock position.*

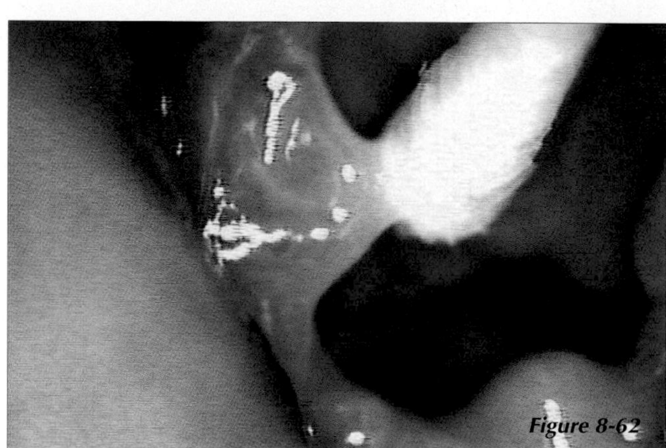

Figure 8-62

## Intravaginal Rugae and Normal Hymen

**Case Study 8-63**

This 5-year-old girl had a normal hymen and typically configured intravaginal rugae.

***Figure 8-63.*** *The hymen is normal and the intravaginal rugae are in a typical configuration.*

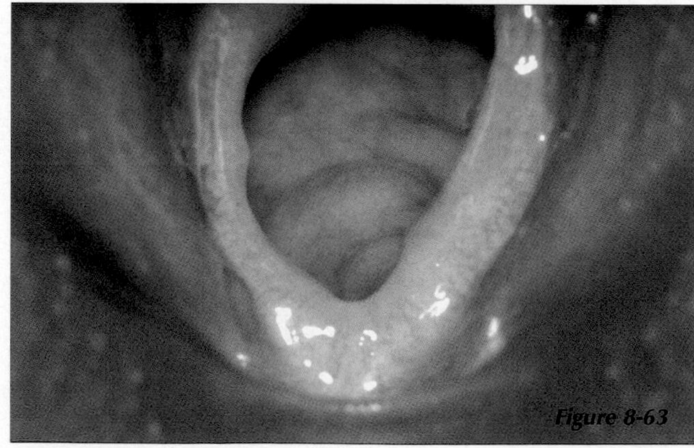

Figure 8-63

## Normal Findings

### Estrogenized Hymen in Abused Girl

**Case Study 8-64**

There had been an allegation of sexual abuse with attempted penetration by the father of this 11-year-old girl. He confessed and was jailed.

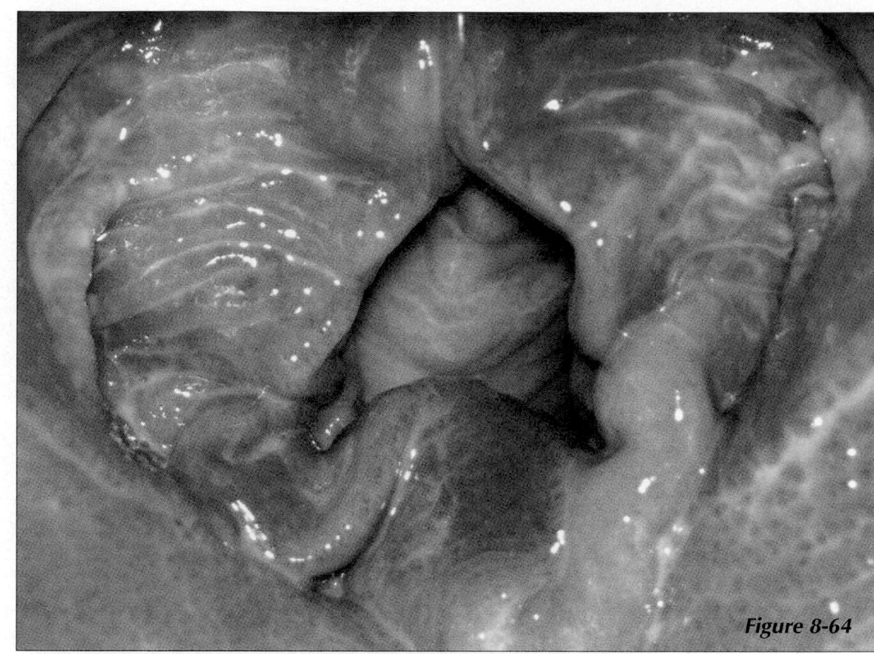

***Figure 8-64.*** *The estrogenized hymen has typical folds.*

Further evaluation with a cotton swab was normal.

### Normal Hymenal Mound

**Case Study 8-65**

This 3-year-old girl was examined with a hymenal mound at the 6-o'clock position, which is a normal finding.

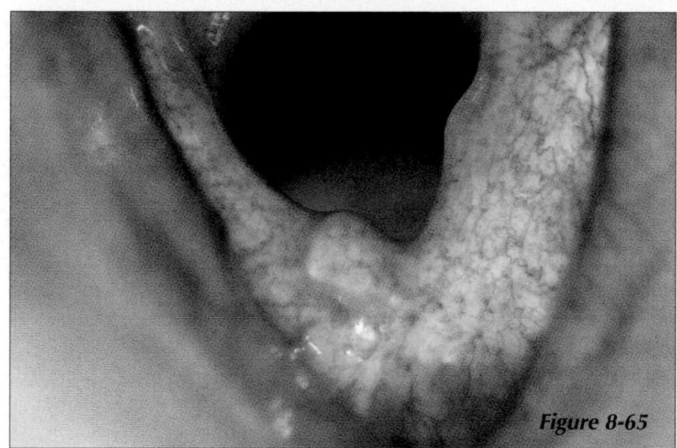

***Figure 8-65.*** *Hymenal mound at the 6-o'clock position.*

### Posterior Mound with Cleft

**Case Study 8-66**

This examination of a girl in the knee-chest position produced normal findings.

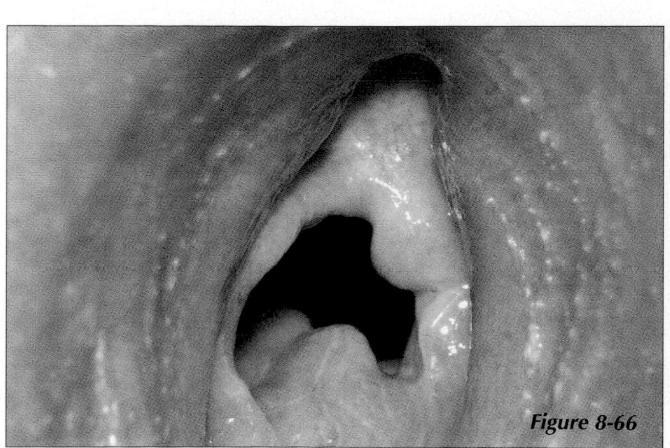

***Figure 8-66.*** *A normal posterior rim as well as a normal cleft at the 3-o'clock position.*

### Possible Precocious Puberty

**Case Study 8-67**

This 9-year-old was just entering puberty and was examined because of abnormal periods and as part of an evaluation for precocious puberty.

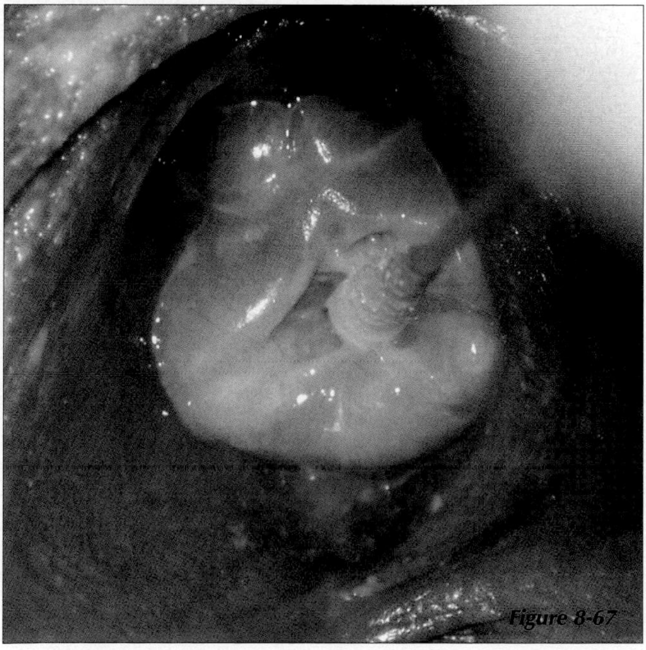

***Figure 8-67.*** *Normal estrogenization.*

# Normal Findings

## Cribriform Hymen

**Case Study 8-68**

This asymptomatic 3-year-old girl underwent examination because her pediatrician noted an "unusual" hymen. Examination revealed a typical cribriform hymen.

***Figure 8-68.*** *Typical cribriform hymen, which is a normal variant that rarely results in a functional problem.*

## Estrogenization and Intravaginal Rugae

**Case Study 8-69**

This 13-year-old girl was examined with estrogenization and intravaginal rugae.

***Figure 8-69.*** *Note well-demonstrated intravaginal rugae.*

## Vascularization

**Case Study 8-70**

Although there was no allegation of abuse in this child, the pediatrician mistakenly thought the extensive vascularization was an indicator of trauma. Vascularization alone is not an indicator of an abnormality.

***Figure 8-70.*** *Posterior of the hymen shows extensive vascularization.*

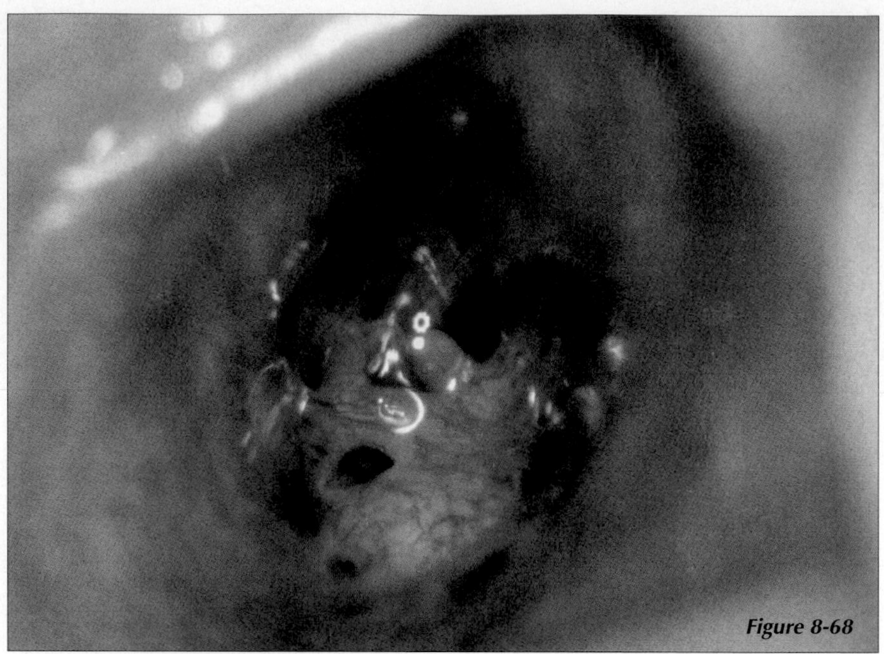

*Figure 8-68*

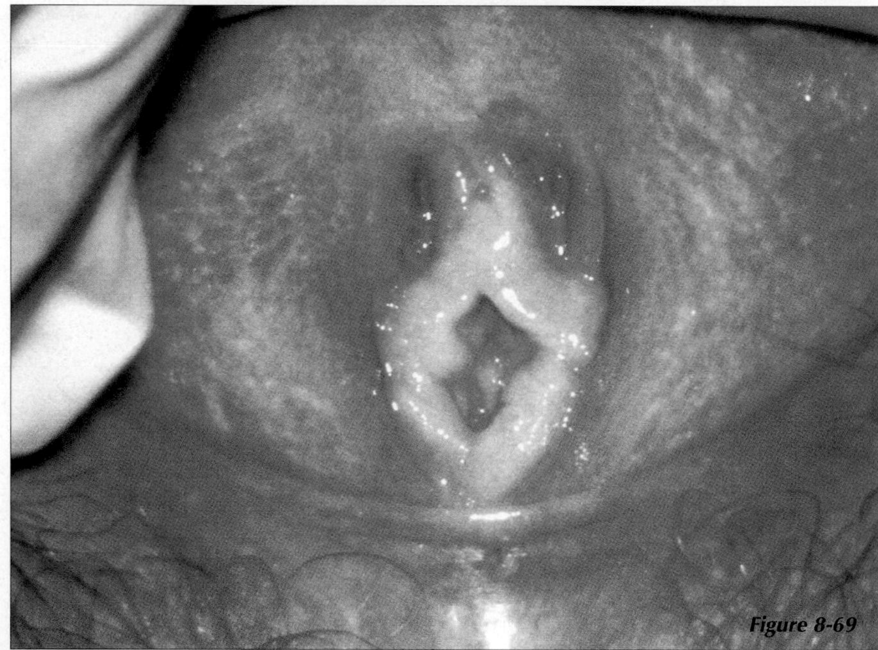

*Figure 8-69*

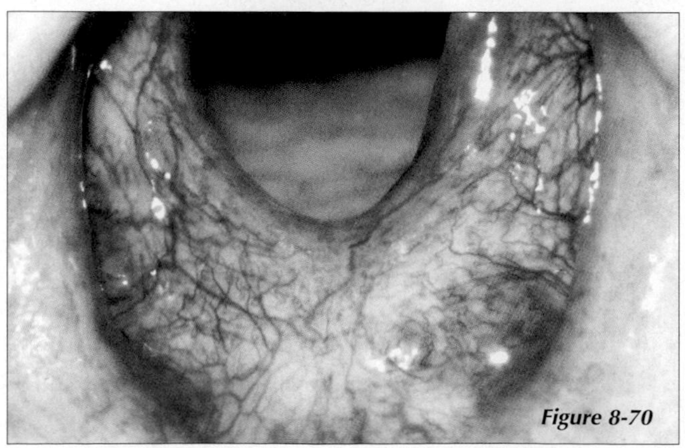

*Figure 8-70*

# Normal Findings

## Examination With and Without Traction

**Case Study 8-71**

This 3-year-old girl was examined in a pediatrician's office.

***Figure 8-71-a.*** *Findings typical of examination without traction.*

***Figure 8-71-b.*** *The same 3-year-old with appropriate moderate traction showing a normal hymen.*

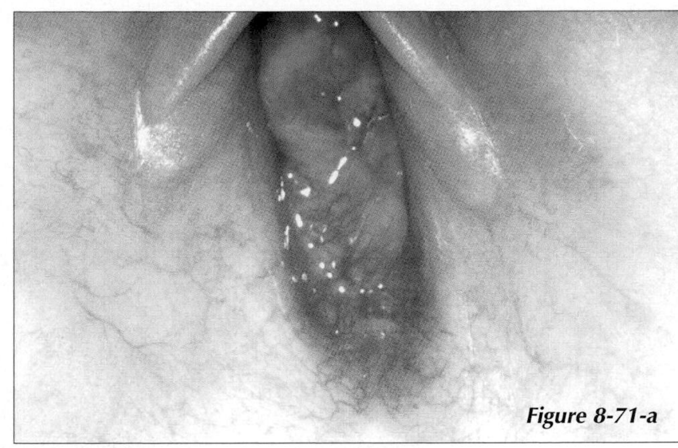

Figure 8-71-a

## Hymenal Pit

**Case Study 8-72**

This 6-year-old was examined because of a hymenal tag or projection.

***Figure 8-72.*** *Note the area of the hymen at about the 7-o'clock position, which is sometimes referred to as a hymenal pit; it is considered a normal variant.*

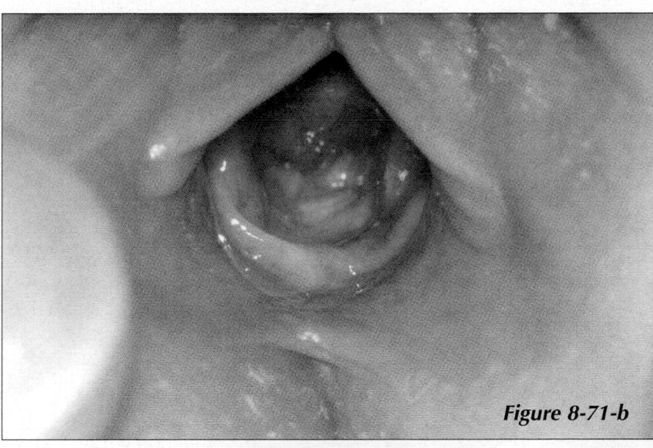

Figure 8-71-b

## Normal Cribriform Hymen in Alleged Abuse

**Case Study 8-73**

This 4-year-old girl underwent a routine examination because of an allegation of abuse in her daycare facility.

***Figure 8-73.*** *Cribriform hymen. Although not common, the cribriform hymen is a normal variant that generally has no functional significance.*

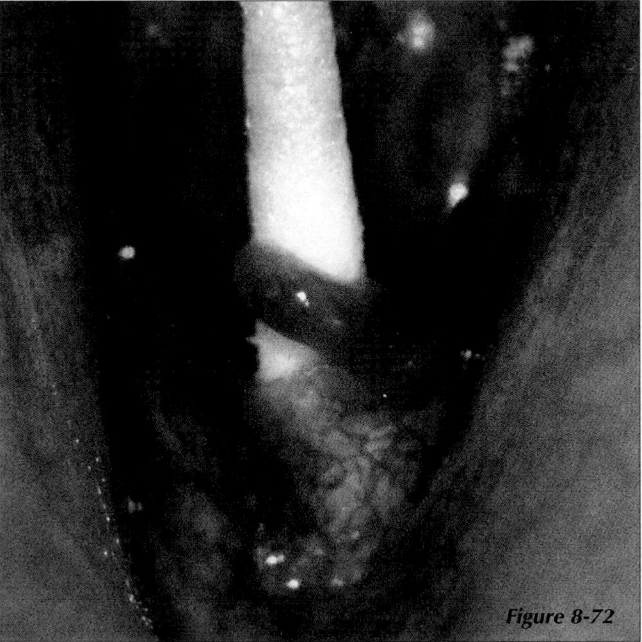

Figure 8-72

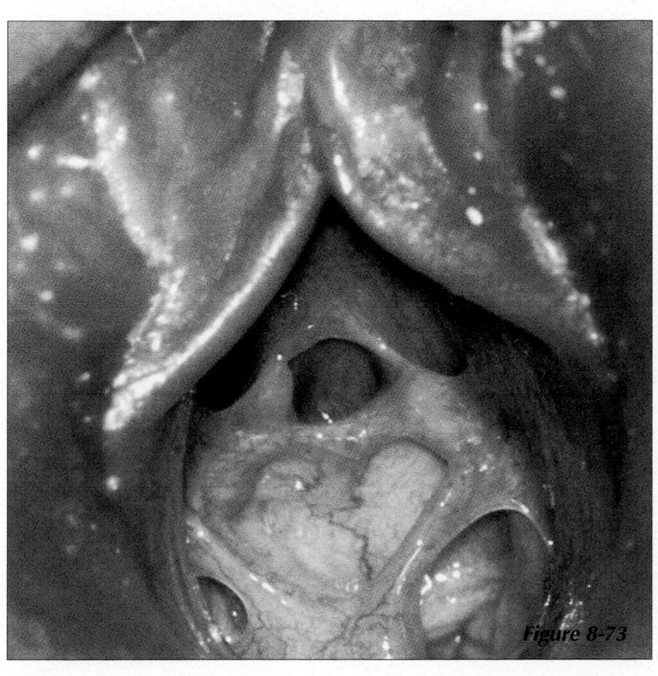

Figure 8-73

# Normal Findings

## Penetration

### Case Study 8-74

This 9-year-old girl gave a credible history of vaginal penetration and possible anal penetration. On examination of the hymen, a separation was apparent at the anterior column. The separation was called a tear by the individual viewing it under colposcopy and a band by those viewing the photographs.

***Figure 8-74-a.*** *On simple labial separation the vaginal examination was not remarkable.*

***Figure 8-74-b.*** *With labial traction the hymen initially appeared normal.*

***Figures 8-74-c*** *and* ***d.*** *With relaxation, a separation becomes obvious at the anterior column.*

***Figure 8-74-e.*** *Moderate anal dilation considered to be a nonspecific finding.*

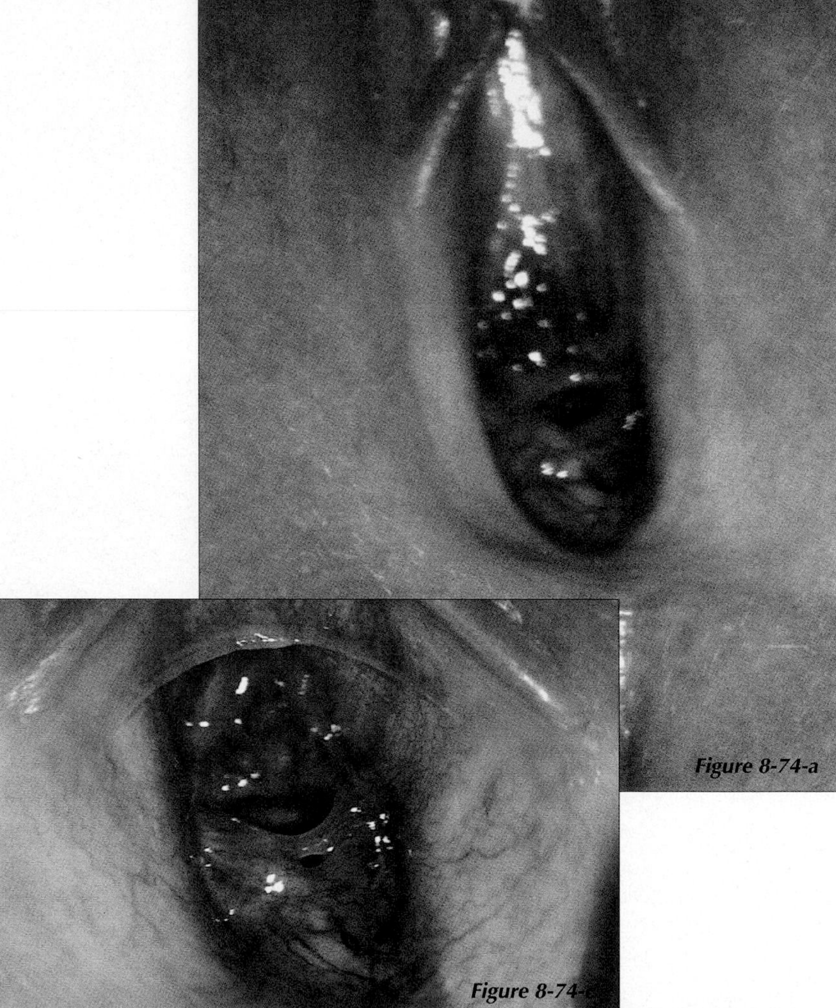

*Figure 8-74-a*

*Figure 8-74-*

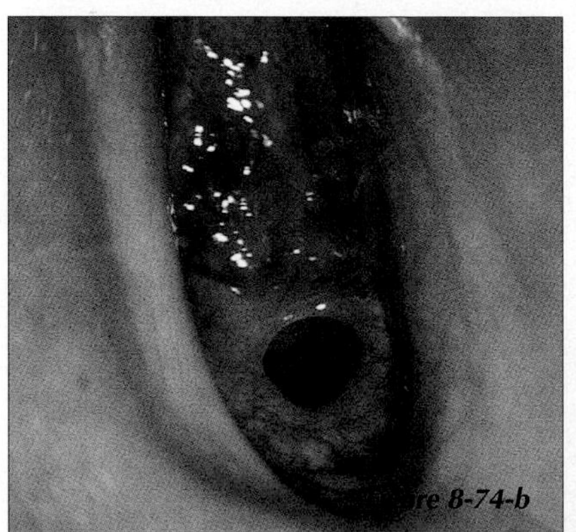

*re 8-74-b*

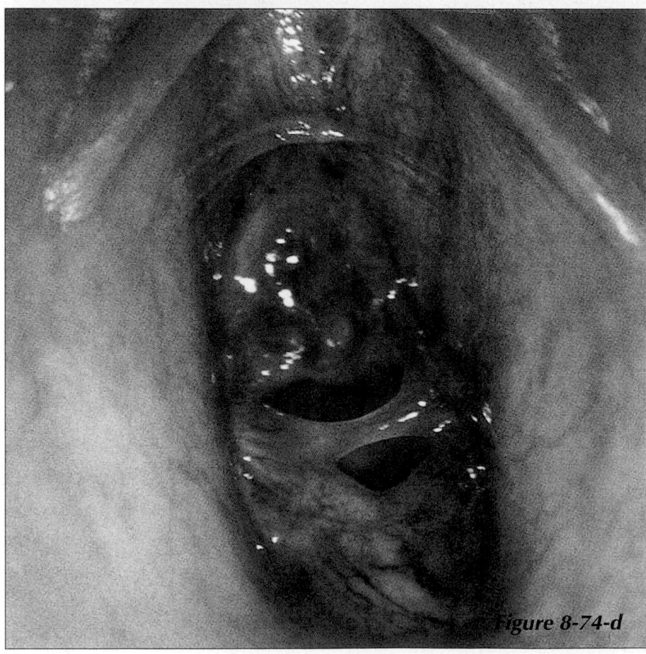

*igure 8-74-d*

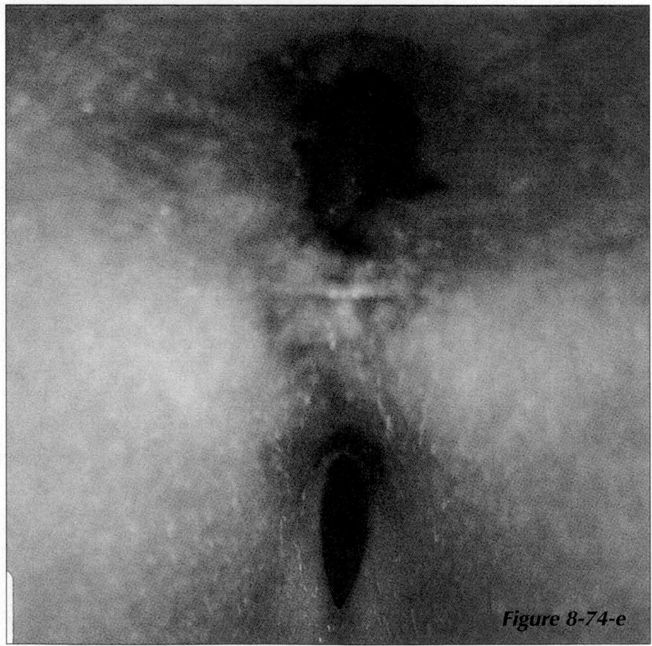

*Figure 8-74-e*

# Acute Findings

## Hematoma and Hymenal Tear

**Case Study 8-75**

This 13-year-old came to the ER 4 hours after a sexual assault that included penile penetration.

***Figure 8-75.*** *A hematoma and tearing of the hymen at the 4-o'clock position, consistent with acute trauma.*

## Partial Healing After Transection of the Hymen

**Case Study 8-76**

This 8-year old girl was seen 1 week after having a complete transection of the hymen.

***Figure 8-76.*** *Note partial healing with granulation tissue on the edges of the transection.*

## Anal Tears

**Case Study 8-77**

This male infant was being watched by a male neighbor while the mother was at work. When the mother returned home, the child was fussy and was not acting like himself. The mother found that there was a large quantity of blood in the child' s diaper. Examination revealed rectal tears consistent with anal sodomy. The neighbor later confessed to the incident.

***Figure 8-77-a.*** *Anal tears are seen at the 7- and 2-o'clock positions.*

***Figure 8-77-b.*** *Further examination shows that the tearing extends into the rectum.*

***Figure 8-77-c.*** *The same infant 2 weeks later. The examination is normal and would neither confirm nor disconfirm the history of abuse had the child only been seen at this time.*

Anal and rectal injuries heal quickly and children with such injuries should be examined immediately. The earlier examination is abnormal and is consistent with the history.

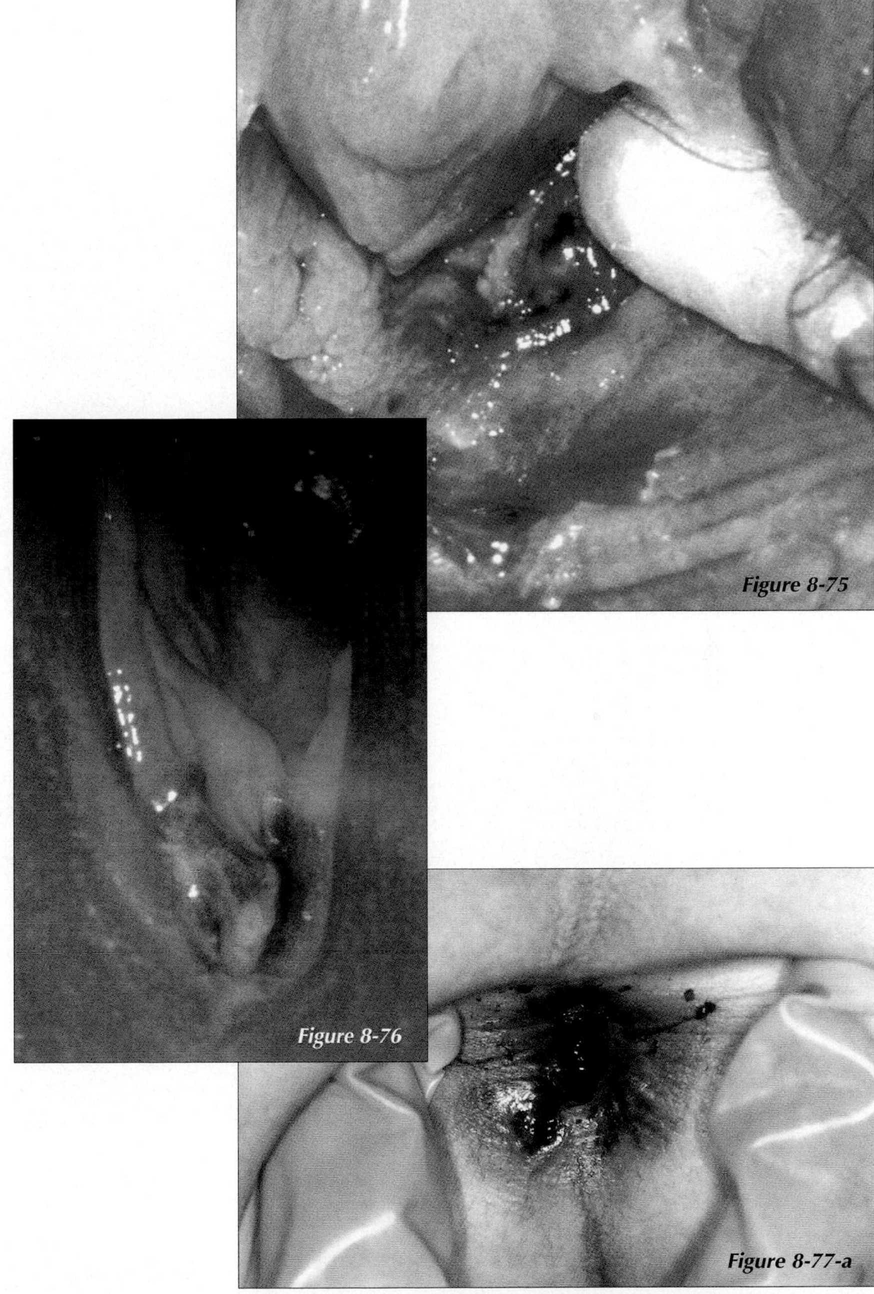

**Figure 8-75**

**Figure 8-76**

**Figure 8-77-a**

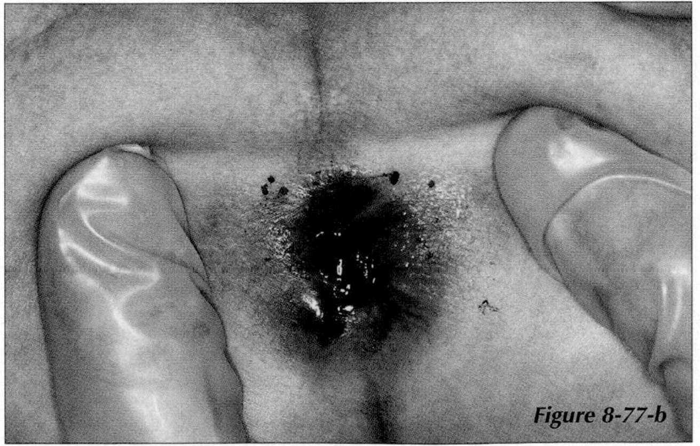

**Figure 8-77-b**

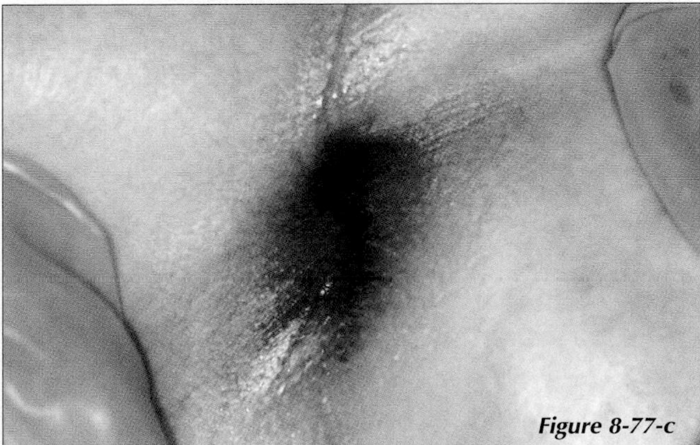

**Figure 8-77-c**

# ACUTE FINDINGS

## LACERATIONS

### Case Study 8-78

This 6-year-old girl was found alone in a house in a pool of blood. On examination she was found to be bleeding from the genital area. A 16-year-old male caregiver was responsible for the injuries.

***Figure 8-78-a.*** *Extensive superficial and deep lacerations with complete loss of integrity of the posterior vaginal wall and extension down through the rectal mucosa.*

***Figure 8-78-b.*** *Another view of the same patient shows the injury requires extensive surgical repair.*

***Figures 8-78-c*** *and* ***d.*** *Follow-up photographs at the child's 3-week post-repair examination under anesthesia show extensive healing of the fourth-degree laceration.*

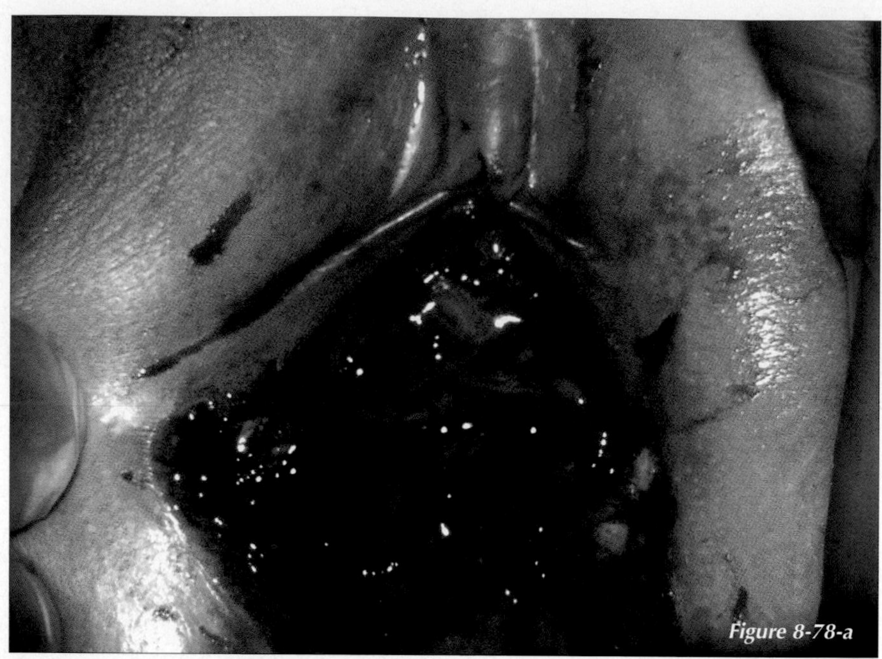

Figure 8-78-a

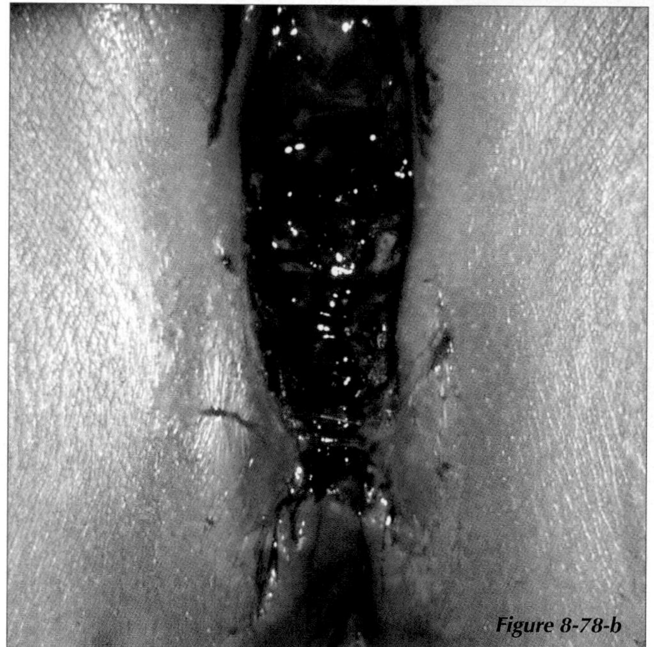

Figure 8-78-b

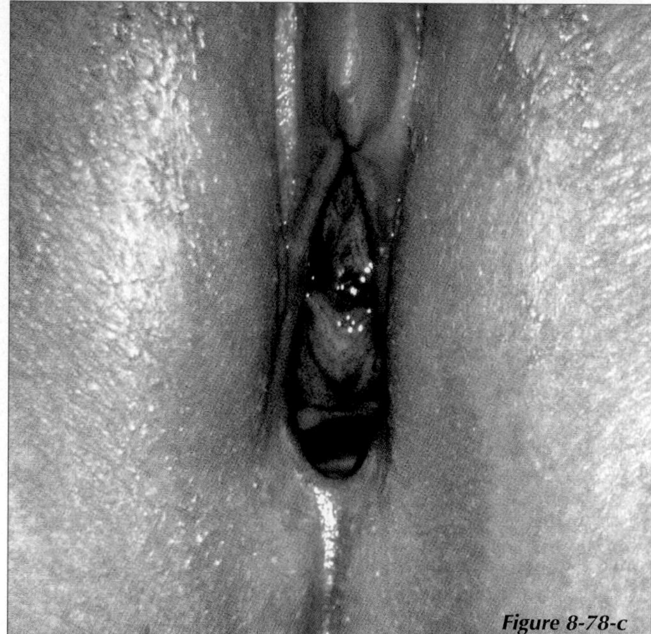

Figure 8-78-c

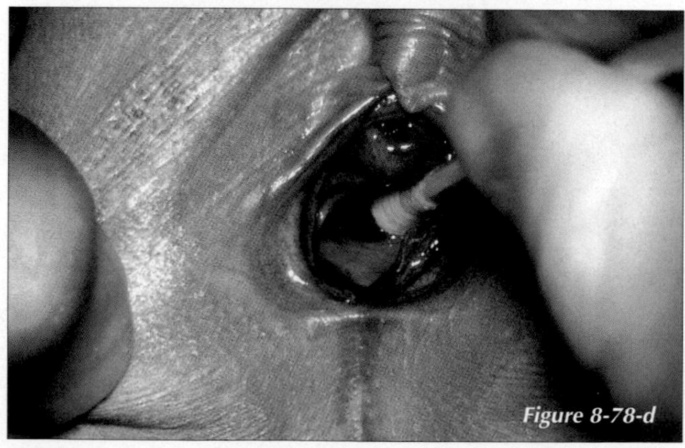

Figure 8-78-d

# Acute Findings

## Unexplained Genital Bleeding

**Case Study 8-79**

This 5-year-old girl had unexplained genital bleeding.

***Figure 8-79-a.*** *On initial appearance, before good labial traction, the hymen appears crescentic and uninjured.*

***Figure 8-79-b.*** *With improved traction and with the camera showing the inner labia minora, several superficial mucosal lacerations are seen external to the hymen.*

***Figure 8-79-c.*** *A slight angulation of the camera also shows superficial abrasions on the hymen and the inner surface of the right labia minora.*

***Figure 8-79-d.*** *A different camera angle shows remarkably prominent periurethral support structures, which is a normal variant.*

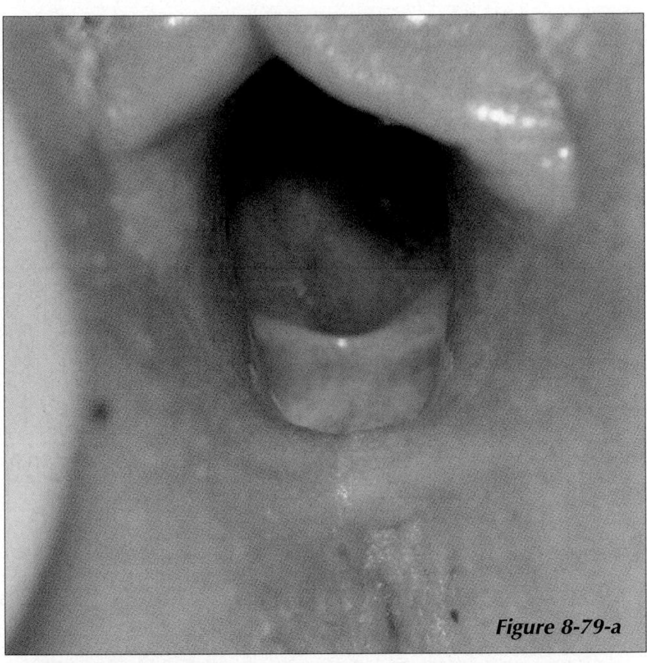

**Figure 8-79-a**

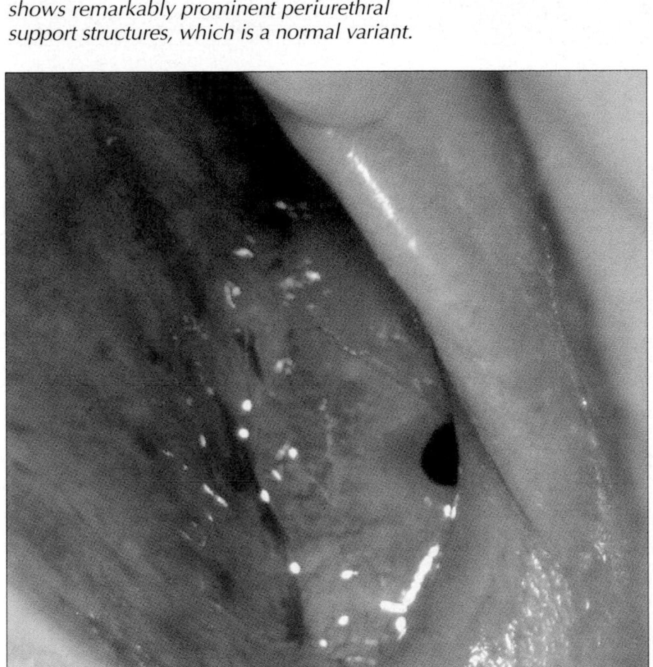

**Figure 8-79-b**

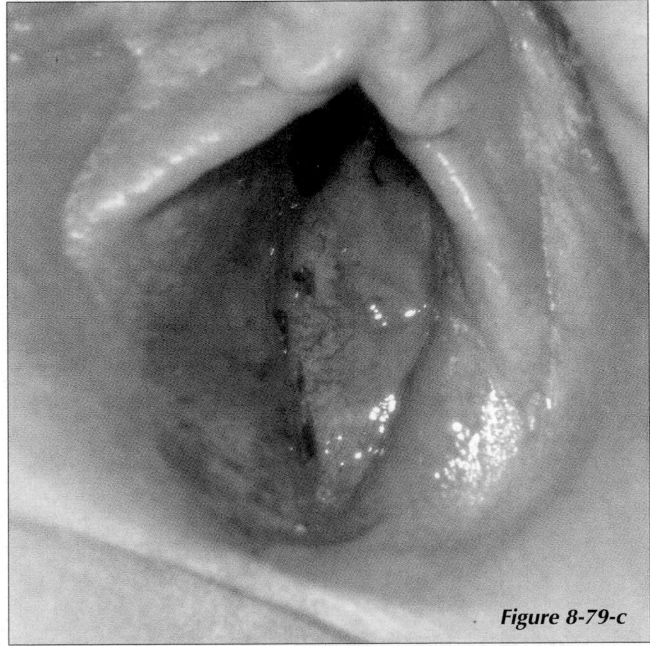

**Figure 8-79-c**

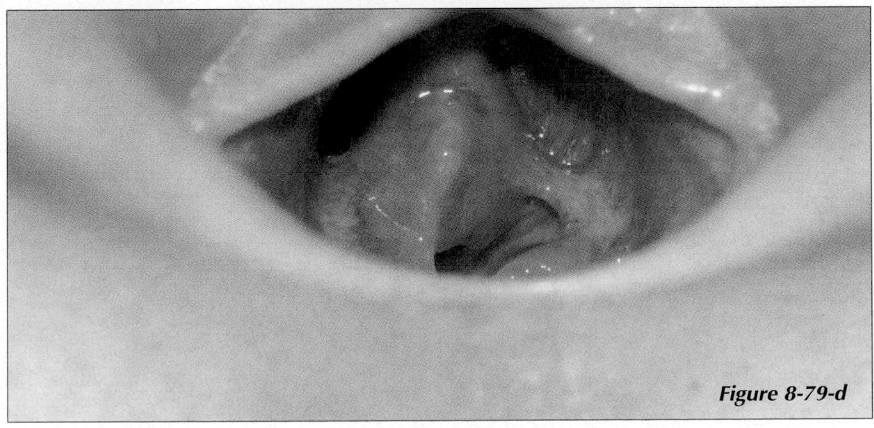

**Figure 8-79-d**

# Acute Findings

## Acute Penetration

**Case Study 8-80**

This 15-year-old girl with a history of acute penetration was examined with a technique of introducing a Foley catheter into the vaginal canal, with slow withdrawal to assess the hymen.

***Figure 8-80.*** *Note the small laceration at the 7-o'clock position.*

## Traumatic Superficial Hymenal Laceration

**Case Study 8-81**

This 13-year-old girl had a history of attempted penetration.

***Figure 8-81.*** *An acute superficial hymenal laceration indicative of trauma.*

## Anal Laceration

**Case Study 8-82**

This 8-year-old boy alleged that he had been anally penetrated by a hanger. He was examined with a large laceration at the 12-o'clock position.

***Figures 8-82-a** and **b.** An example of an acute anal laceration with differing degrees of traction by the examiner.*

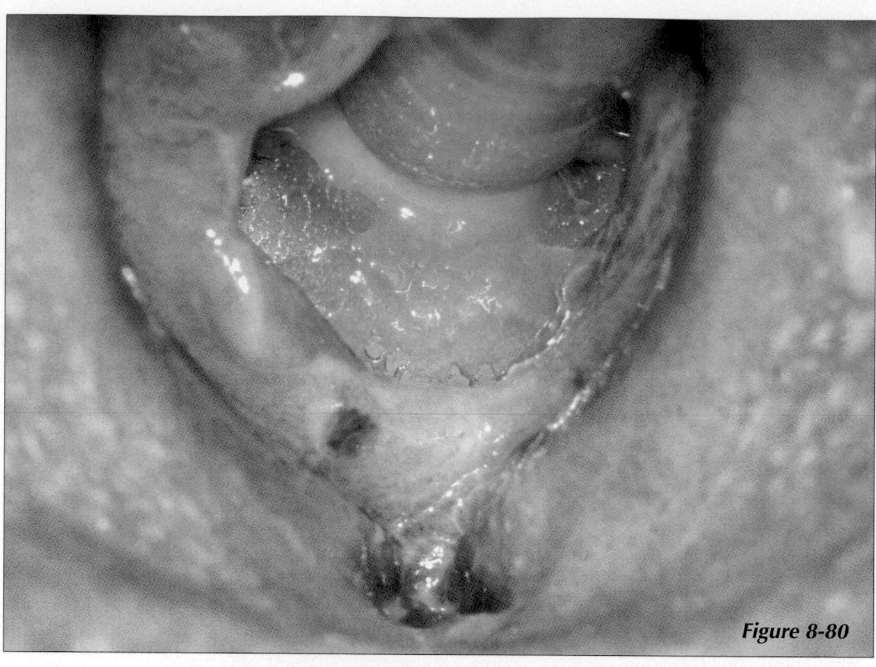

**Figure 8-80**

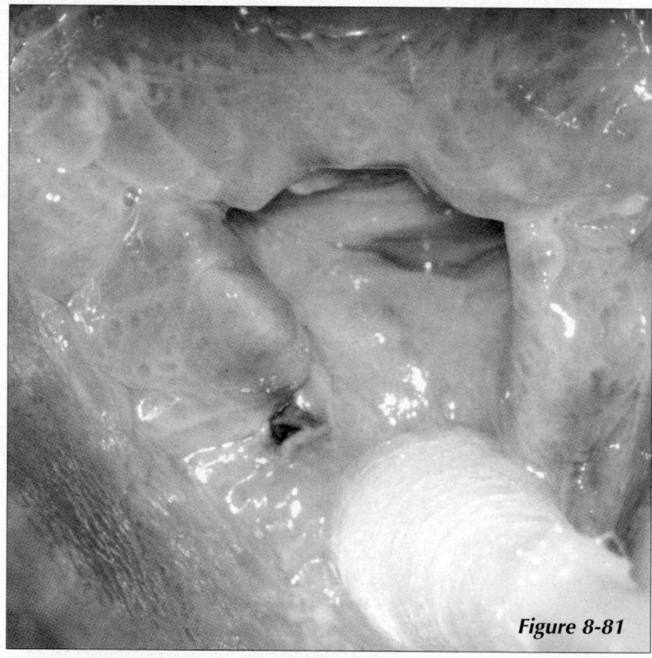

**Figure 8-81**

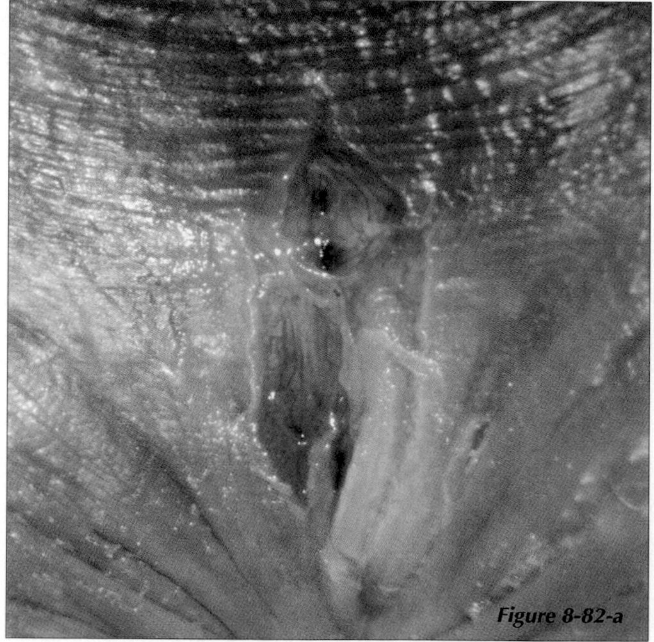

**Figure 8-82-a**

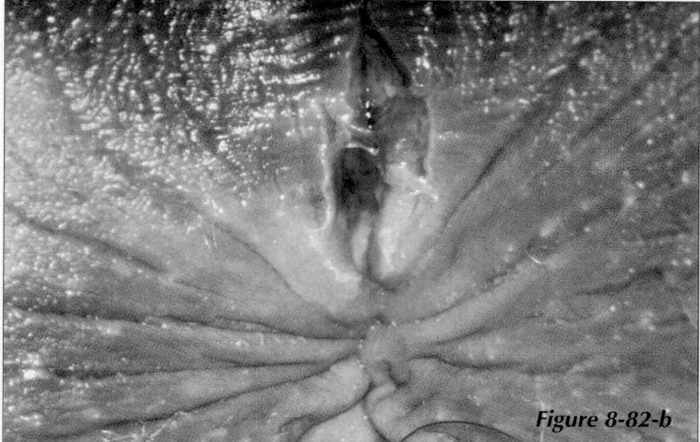

**Figure 8-82-b**

# Acute Findings

## Laceration With Bruising

**Case Study 8-83**

This 5-year-old girl had significant vaginal bleeding and no history of injury or sexual abuse. Investigation revealed her injury was caused by digital penetration by a 16-year-old babysitter.

***Figure 8-83-a.*** *There appears to be an acute laceration at the 6-o'clock position as well as hymenal bruising from the 2- to 10-o'clock positions.*

***Figure 8-83-b.*** *Follow-up examination performed 3 months later shows healing of the laceration located at about the 5-o'clock position.*

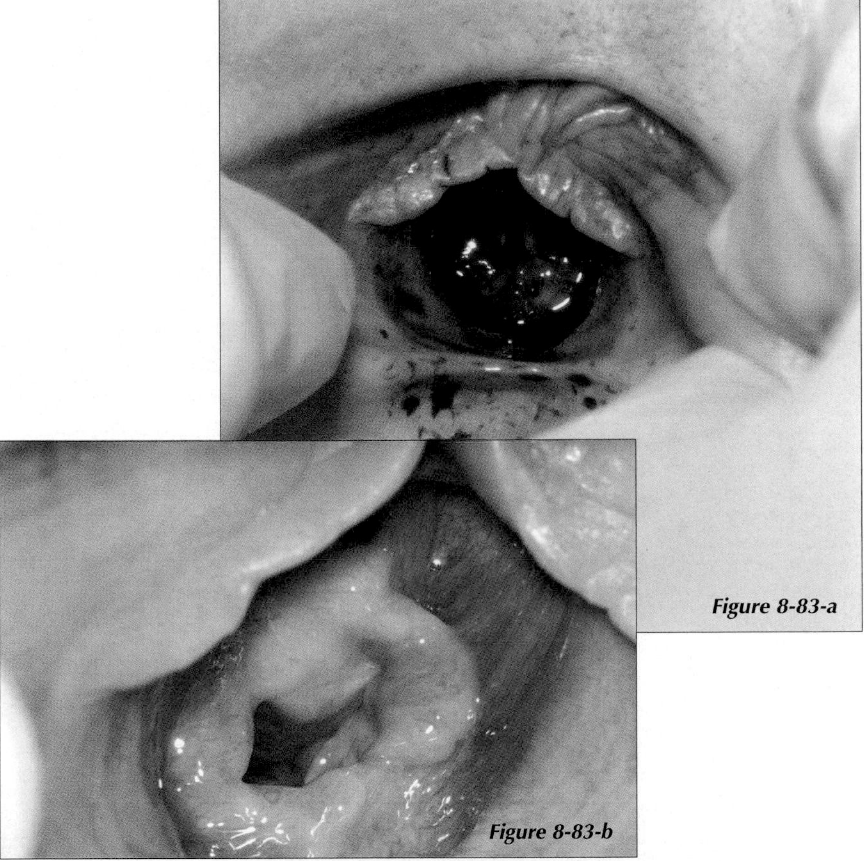

Figure 8-83-a

Figure 8-83-b

## Perianal Laceration

**Case Study 8-84**

This 3-year-old boy alleged that he was anally penetrated by his older brother.

***Figure 8-84.*** *There is a linear perianal laceration at the 11-o'clock position.*

## Acute Laceration After Penile Penetration

**Case Study 8-85**

This 13-year-old girl alleged penile penetration by her boyfriend while on a date. She sustained an acute laceration of the hymen at the 4-o'clock position.

***Figure 8-85.*** *Acute laceration at about the 4-o'clock position, with a cotton swab next to the laceration.*

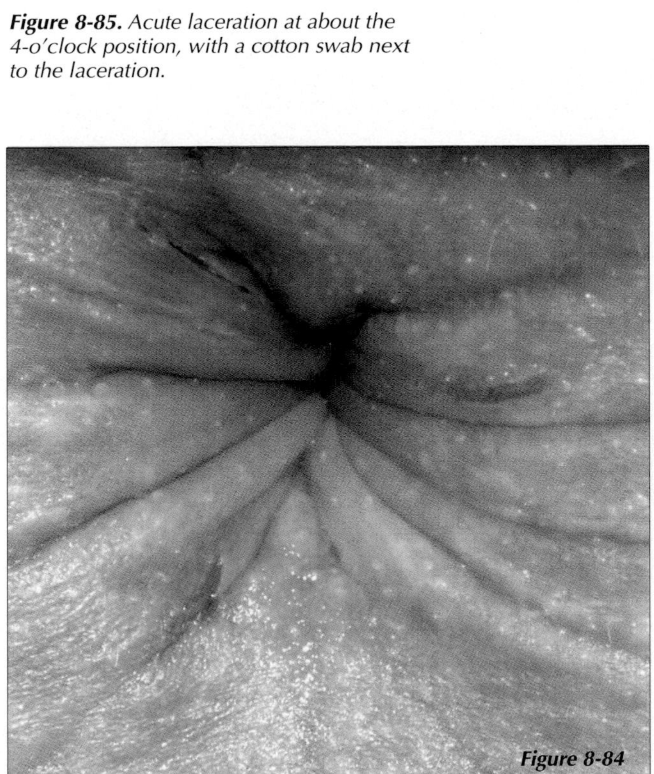

Figure 8-84

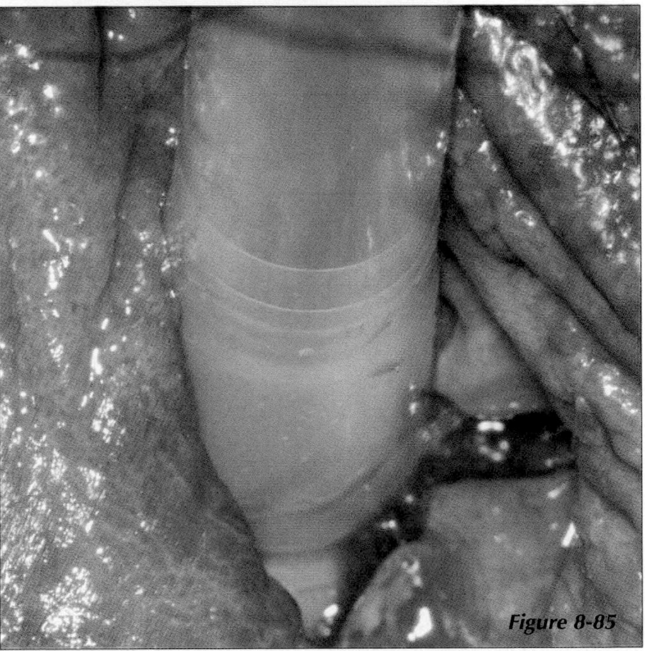

Figure 8-85

# Acute Findings

## Vaginal Bleeding After Penile Penetration

**Case Study 8-86**

This 3-year-old girl had acute-onset vaginal bleeding that was later determined to be the result of penile penetration.

***Figure 8-86.*** *A hymenal laceration is at the 6-o'clock position along with remarkable bruising of the fossa navicularis.*

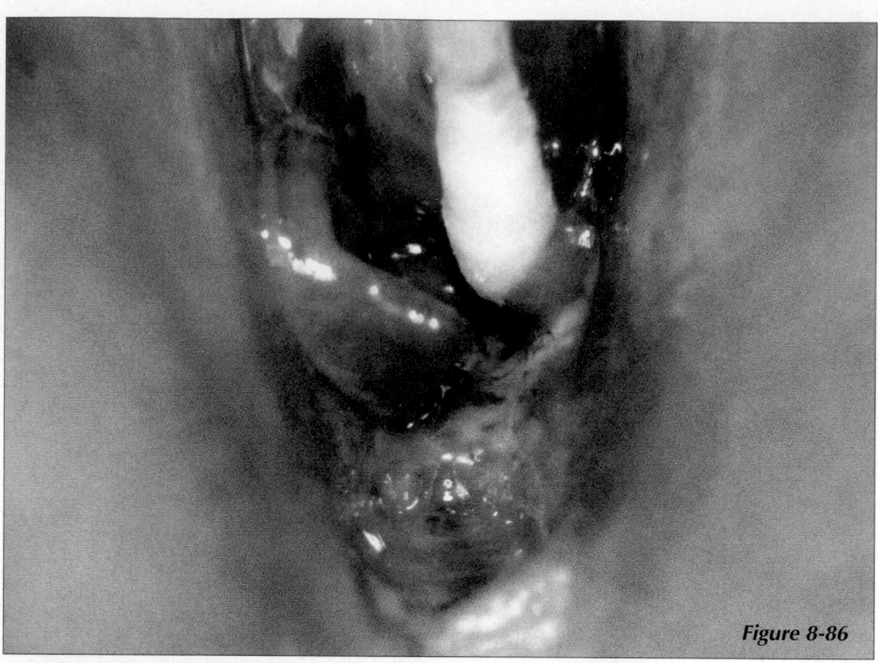

Figure 8-86

## Labial Intercourse

**Case Study 8-87**

This 5-year-old girl was evaluated because of an extensive history of sexual abuse. Her findings were limited to the interior of the labia majora.

***Figure 8-87.*** *Lacerations of the labia, which are commonly seen with labial intercourse.*

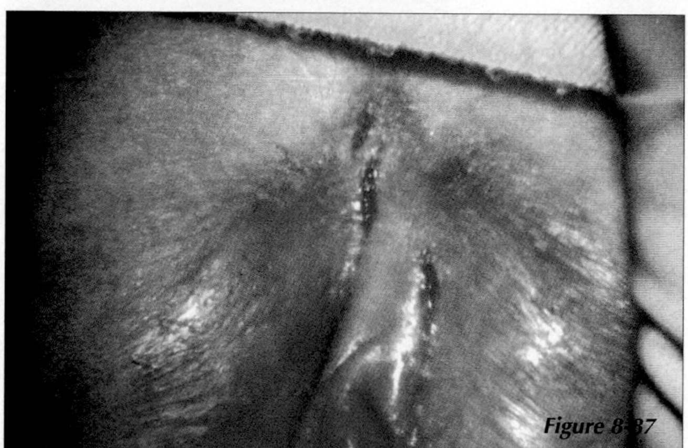

Figure 8-87

## Straddle Injury–Related Bruising

**Case Study 8-88**

This 4-year-old girl was learning to ride her brother's bicycle and sustained a straddle injury when she fell on the crossbar.

***Figure 8-88-a.*** *Extensive bruising of the patient's left labia majora and bruising of the clitoral hood.*

***Figure 8-88-b.*** *An abrasion anterior to the hymen as part of a straddle injury.*

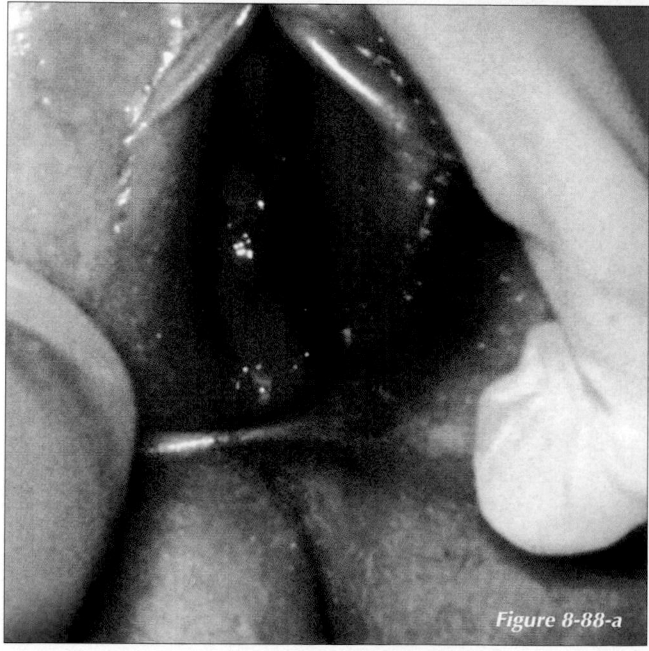

Figure 8-88-a

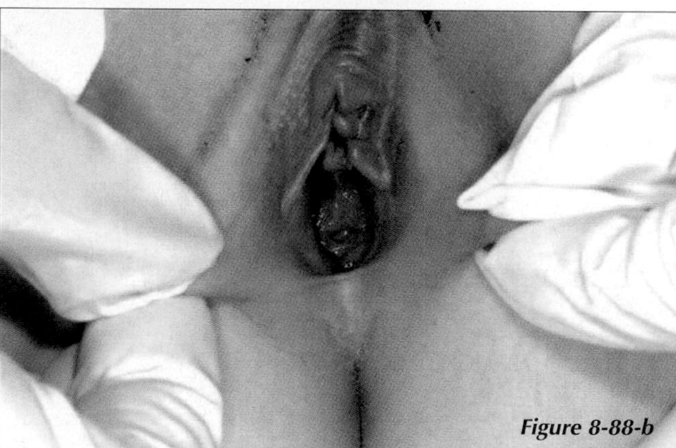

Figure 8-88-b

# Acute Findings

## Alleged Rape

**Case Study 8-89**

This 16-year-old girl came to the ER stating that she had been raped.

***Figure 8-89.*** *A very small laceration at the 7-o'clock position consistent with vaginal penetration.*

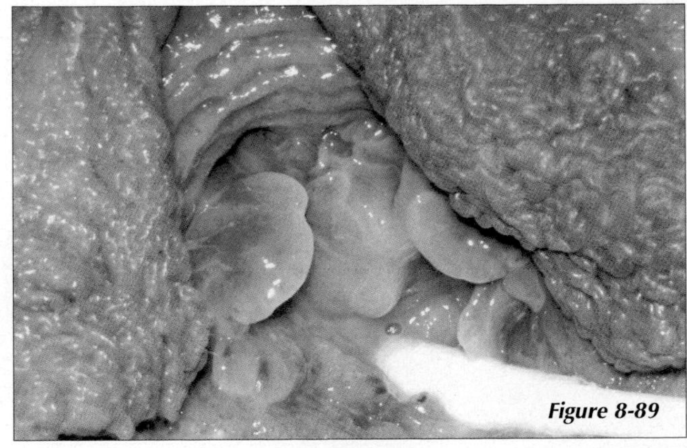

Figure 8-89

## Perianal Bruising

**Case Study 8-90**

This 2-year-old girl was unconscious when she was brought to the ER. She had a massive head injury and extensive body bruising.

***Figure 8-90.*** *Perianal bruising consistent with attempted or successful penetration.*

Figure 8-90

## Bruising of Penis

**Case Study 8-91**

This boy's penis was bruised by his father, who pinched it in an attempt to deter the boy's bedwetting.

***Figure 8-91.*** *Bruising of the penis from pinching.*

Figure 8-91

## Burned Penis

**Case Study 8-92**

This boy's penis was burned by his father as punishment for failing at toilet training.

***Figure 8-92.*** *Burn to the tip of the penis.*

Figure 8-92

## Perianal Laceration Caused by Penetration

**Case Study 8-93**

This 5-year-old was anally penetrated by a 14-year-old neighbor and sustained a perianal laceration.

***Figure 8-93.*** *Perianal laceration at the 1-o'clock position.*

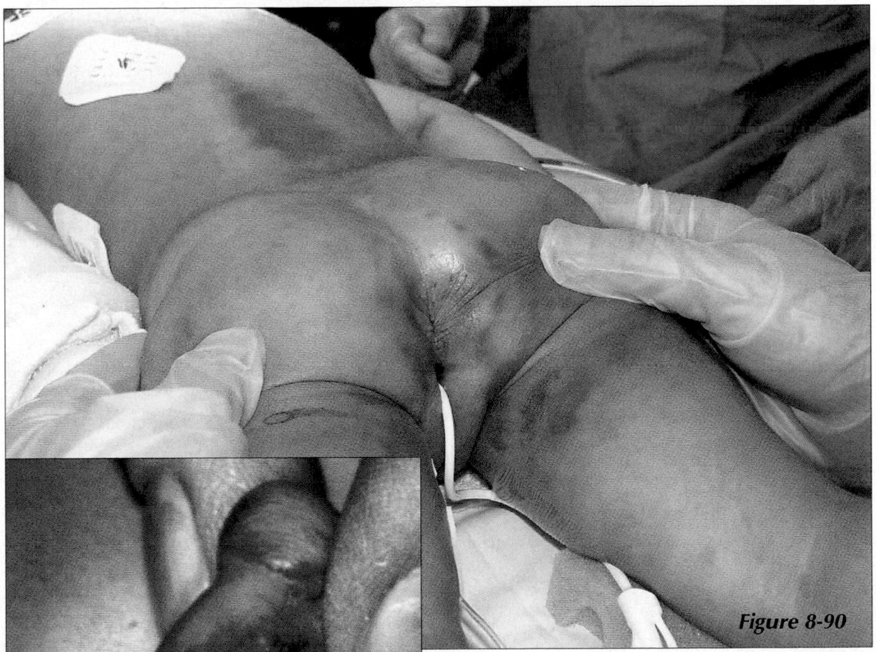

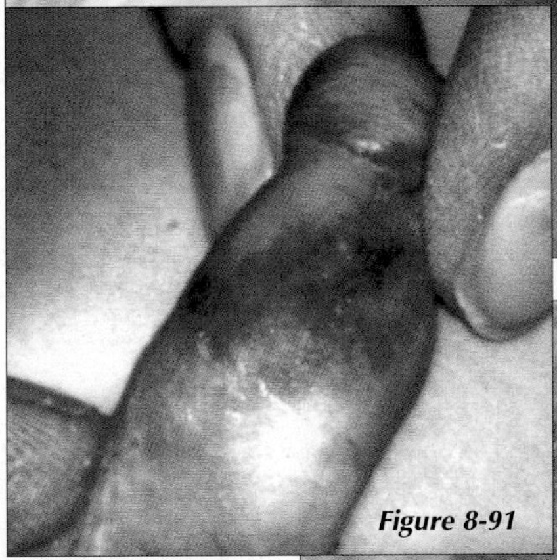

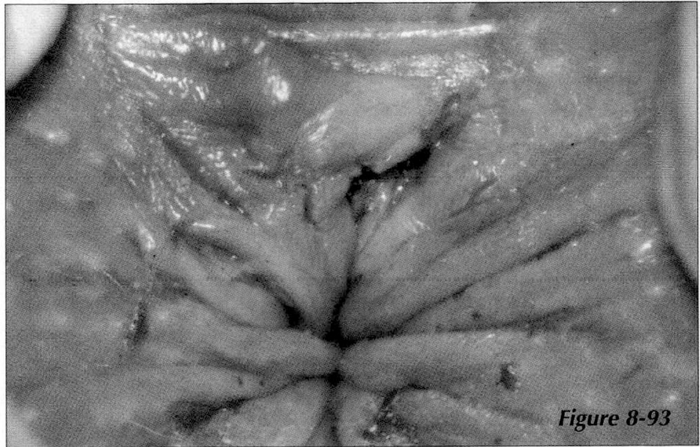

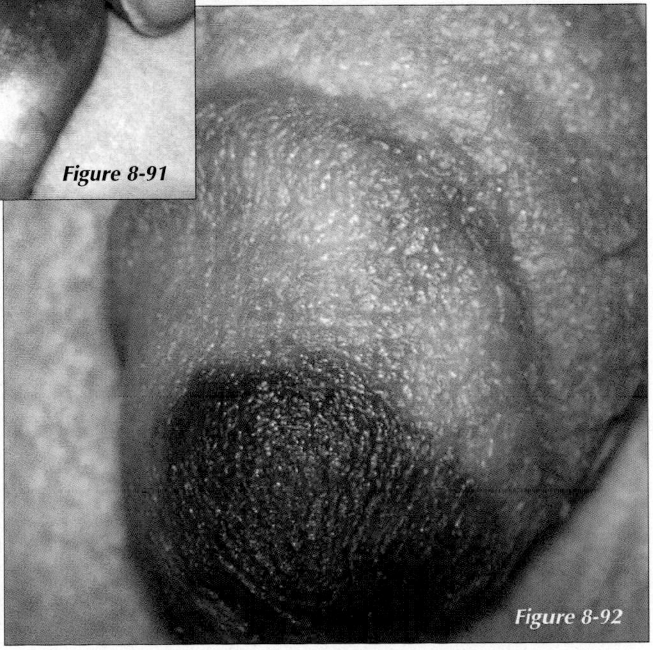

Figure 8-93

# Acute Findings

## Accidental Anal Hematoma

**Case Study 8-94**

This child sustained an acute anal hematoma after a bicycle accident.

***Figure 8-94-a.*** *Acute anal hematoma.*

***Figure 8-94-b.*** *The bicycle seat that caused the injury.*

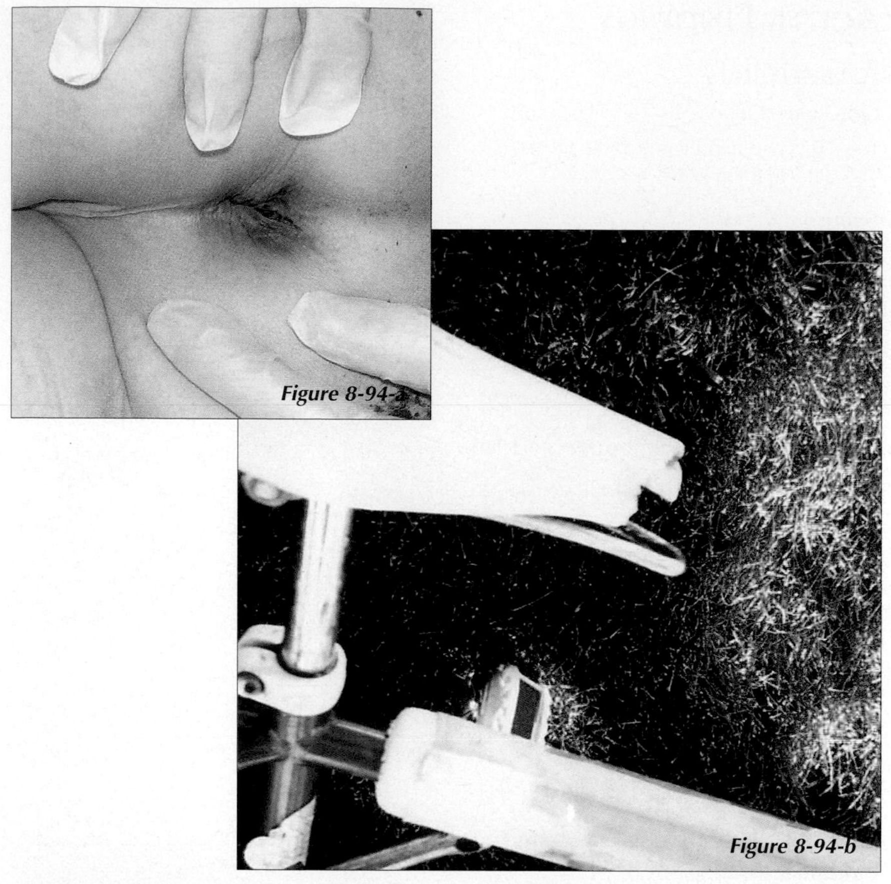

Figure 8-94-a

Figure 8-94-b

# Sexually Transmitted Diseases

## Perianal Herpes

**Case Study 8-95**

This boy, with no history of sexual abuse, contracted type 1 herpes simplex virus (HSV-1) in the perianal area. Autoinoculation was probable because the child had a herpetic lesion on his lip 3 weeks previously.

***Figure 8-95.*** *Herpes type 1 infection around anus.*

This child is in the transition phase between having pustular and crusted lesions and exhibits systemic symptoms. In the past, HSV-1 was thought to have a predilection for the upper body and HSV-2 was generally genital. In fact, both types can be sexually transmitted and both can be autoinoculated.

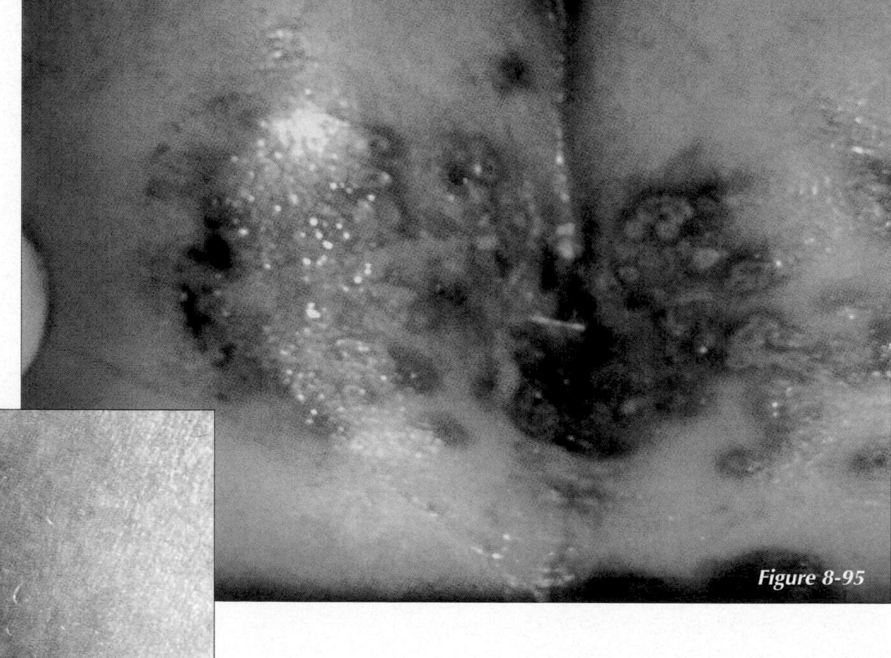

Figure 8-95

## Condyloma Acuminata

**Case Study 8-96**

This 2-year-old child contracted anal warts even though there was no suggestion of sexual abuse and the mother had no history of warts. Vertical transmission was possible, since asymptomatic adults can still shed the virus.

***Figure 8-96.*** *Condyloma acuminata extending posteriorly from the anus.*

Figure 8-96

# Sexually Transmitted Diseases

## Hemorrhagic Herpes

**Case Study 8-97**

This 3-year-old girl had no history of genital herpes but had a herpetic lesion on her lip. When she was examined with hemorrhagic herpes on the genitalia, it likely represented a case of autoinoculation.

***Figure 8-97.*** *Hemorrhagic herpes.*

## Scrotal Condyloma Acuminata

**Case Study 8-98**

There was a convincng history of sexual abuse in this child, but transmission from an adult individual could not be proved.

***Figure 8-98.*** *Scrotal condyloma acuminata.*

## Cylindrical Perianal Condylomata

**Case Study 8-99**

A biopsy from this child tested positive for Bowenoid papulosis, a condition that is considered carcinoma in situ and caused by the human papillomavirus.

***Figure 8-99.*** *Perianal condylomata in a somewhat cylindrical form. Note the brownish lesion.*

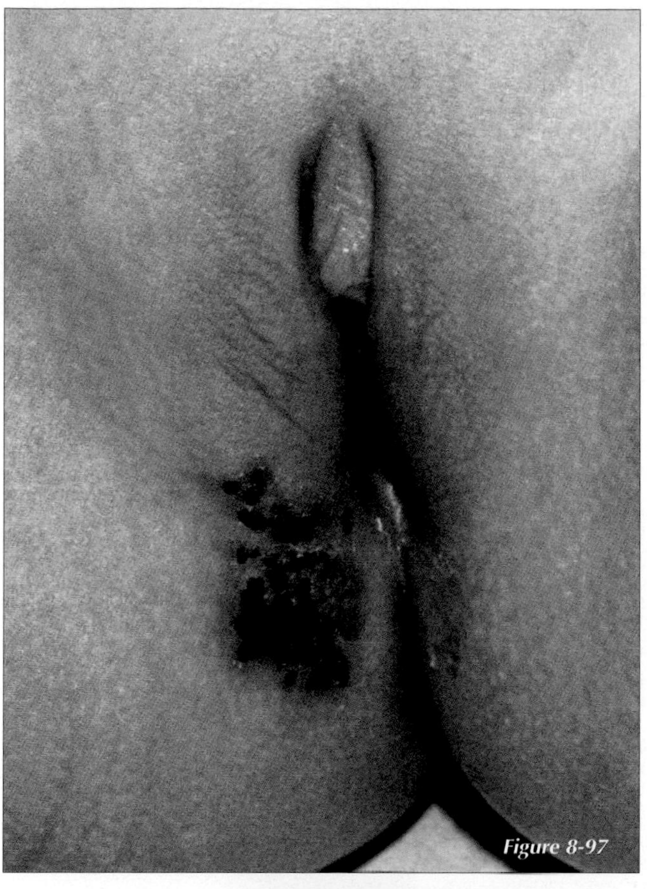

Figure 8-97

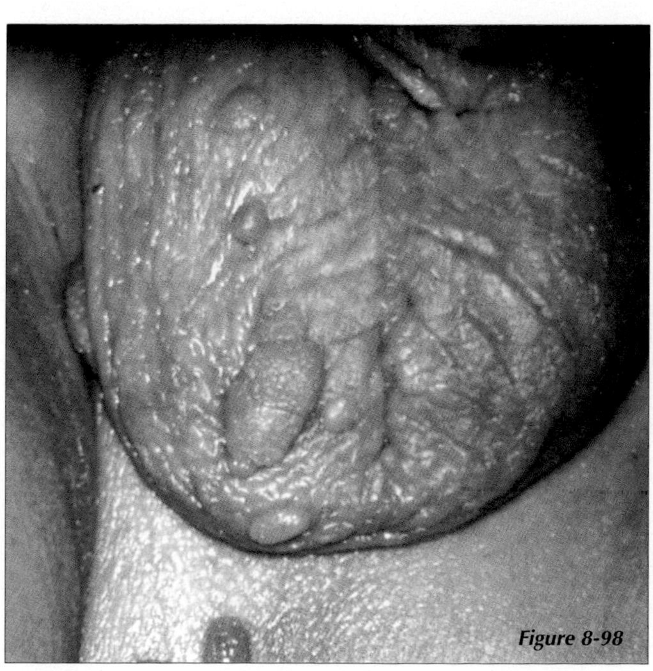

Figure 8-98

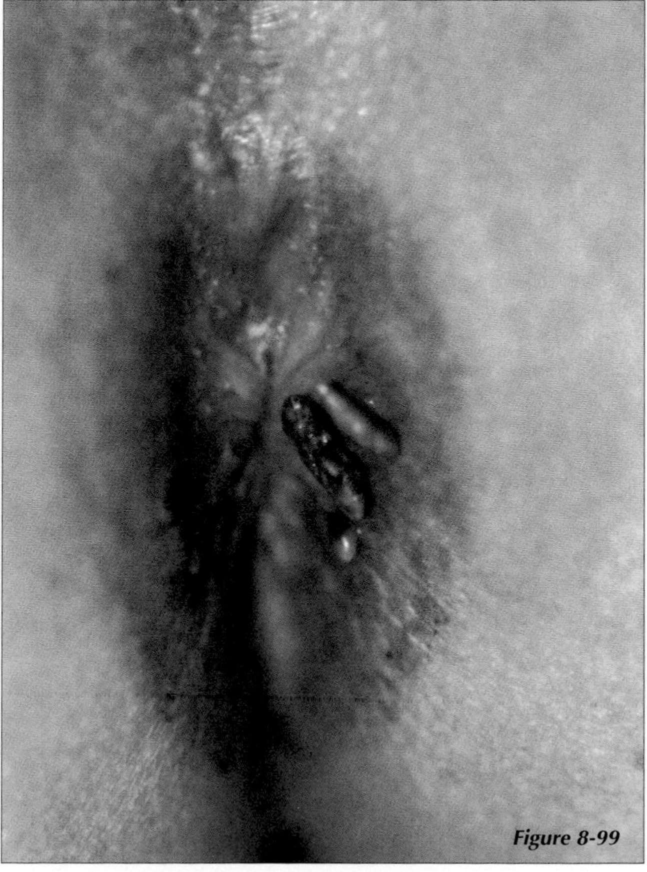

Figure 8-99

# Sexually Transmitted Diseases

## Perianal Streptococcal Infection

**Case Study 8-100**

This 7-year-old girl was examined with a history of painful defecation. Sexual abuse was suspected and a test for perianal streptococcal infection was positive.

***Figure 8-100.*** *Perianal group A streptococcal infection.*

Perianal streptococcal infection can be mistaken for trauma or bruises. The infection responds well to appropriate antibiotic treatment.

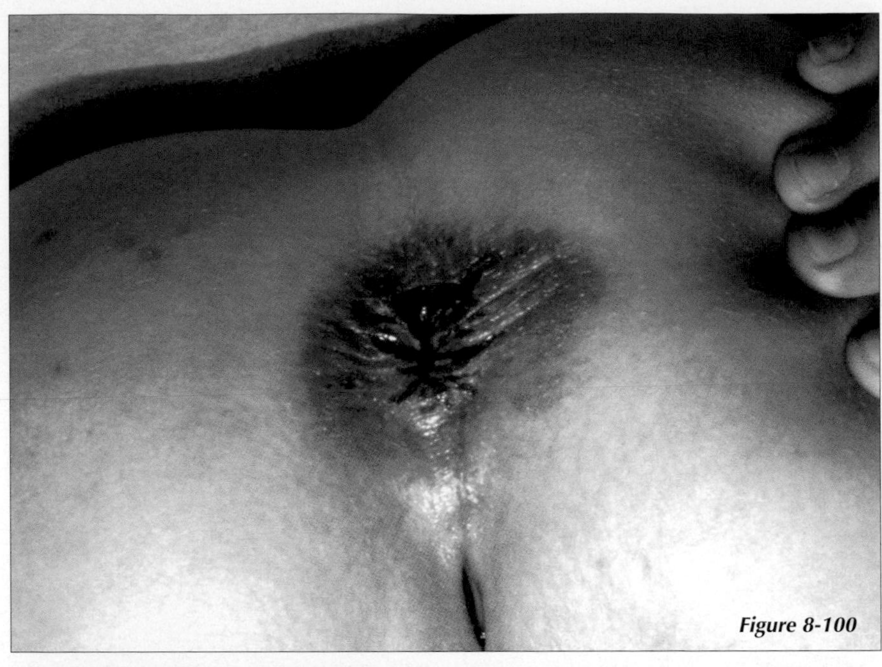

**Figure 8-100**

## Penile Lichen Planus

**Case Study 8-101**

This 6-year-old boy was referred because of a nonpainful genital plaque. Consultation with a dermatologist resulted in a diagnosis of lichen planus, which is related to sexual abuse.

***Figure 8-101.*** *Penile lichen planus.*

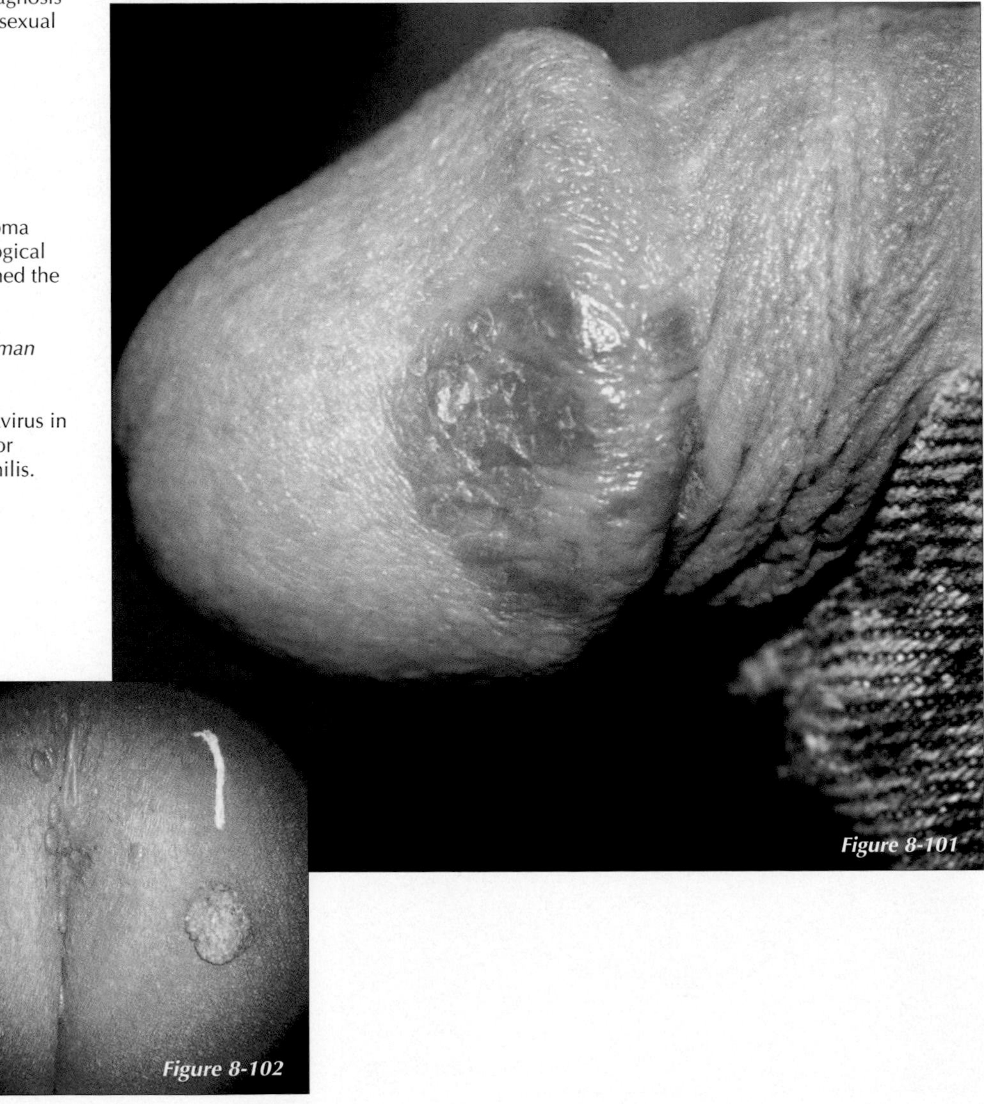

**Figure 8-101**

## Flat Warts

**Case Study 8-102**

This patient was referred for condyloma acuminata. She had a positive serological test for syphilis and a biopsy confirmed the diagnosis of condyloma lata.

***Figure 8-102.*** *Perianal flat warts (human papillomavirus).*

Lesions caused by human papillomavirus in this configuration can be mistaken for condyloma lata, an indicator of syphilis. Biopsy may be necessary.

**Figure 8-102**

# Sexually Transmitted Diseases

## Molluscum Contagiosum

**Case Study 8-103**

This child was referred for an "itchy" rash. The diagnosis was made by observation of umbilicated lesions.

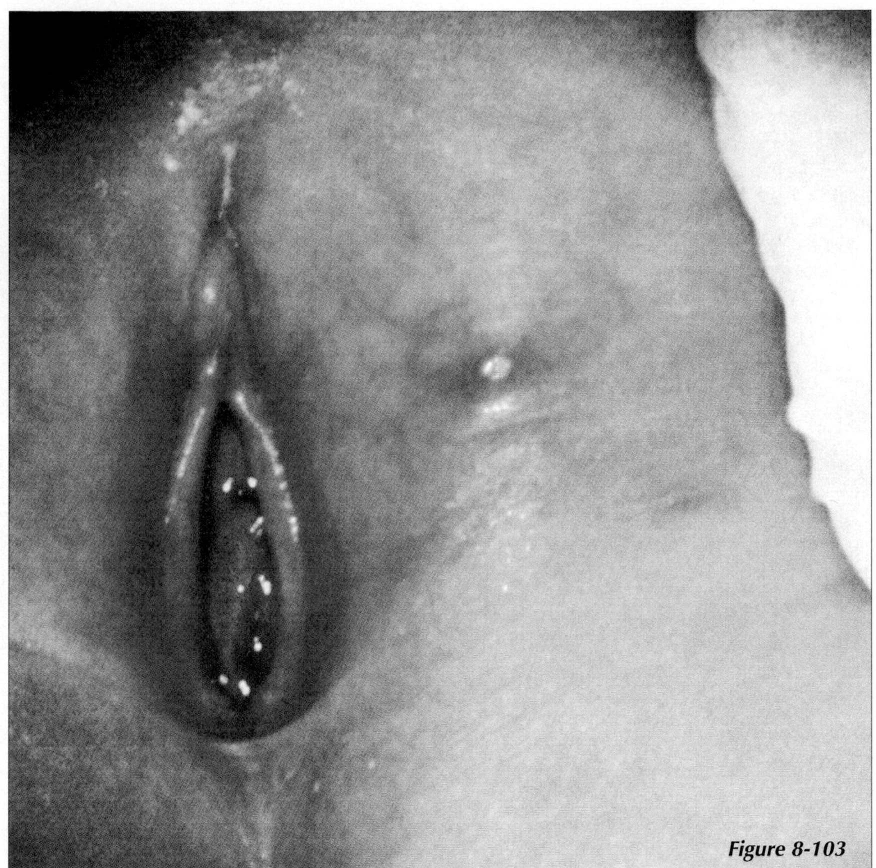

***Figure 8-103.*** *Lesions of molluscum contagiosum.*

Molluscum contagiosum is a very common pediatric disease that is highly contagious and rarely transmitted sexually.

# Old Injuries

## History of Penile Penetration

**Case Study 8-104**

This 8-year-old girl had a history of penile penetration 8 months before examination. Interpretation of a deep notch is controversial and some examiners would interpret the results of the evaluation as a normal finding.

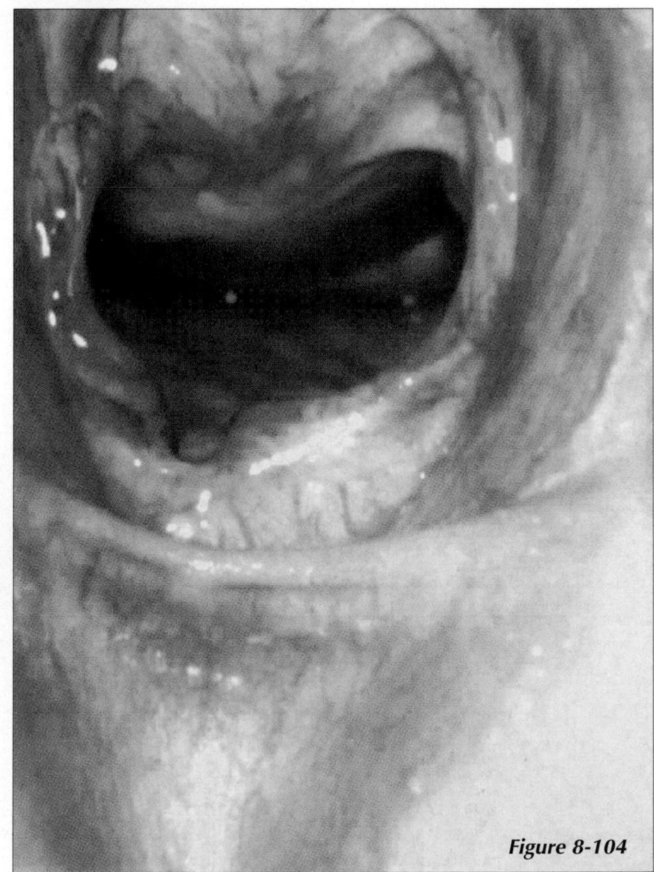

***Figure 8-104.*** *Partial transection of the hymen at the 7-o'clock position that is consistent with the history.*

## Previous Vaginal Penetration

**Case Study 8-105**

This 17-year-old girl was sexually abused and vaginally penetrated 5 months before this examination.

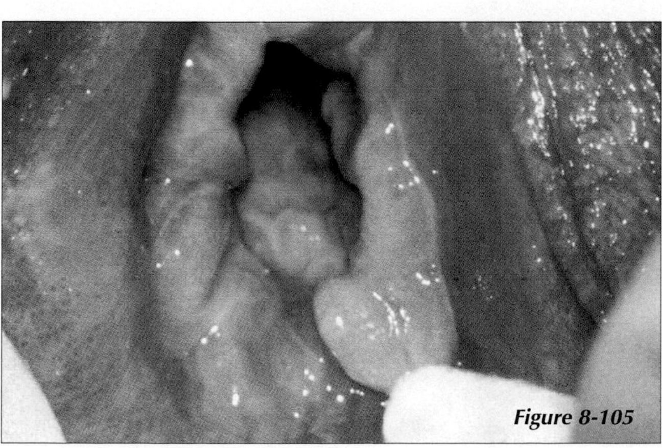

***Figure 8-105.*** *Healed complete transection of the hymen at the 6-o'clock position.*

A complete transection of the hymen refers to a transection that extends to the vaginal wall. This transection has healed, leaving an interrupted hymen. This is consistent with the girl's history.

# Old Injuries

## Digital Penetration

**Case Study 8-106**

This 6-year-old girl was digitally penetrated by an adult male about 5 months before this examination.

***Figure 8-106.*** *Healed complete transection at the 5-o'clock position.*

This transection has healed, leaving an interrupted hymen. This finding is consistent with the girl's history.

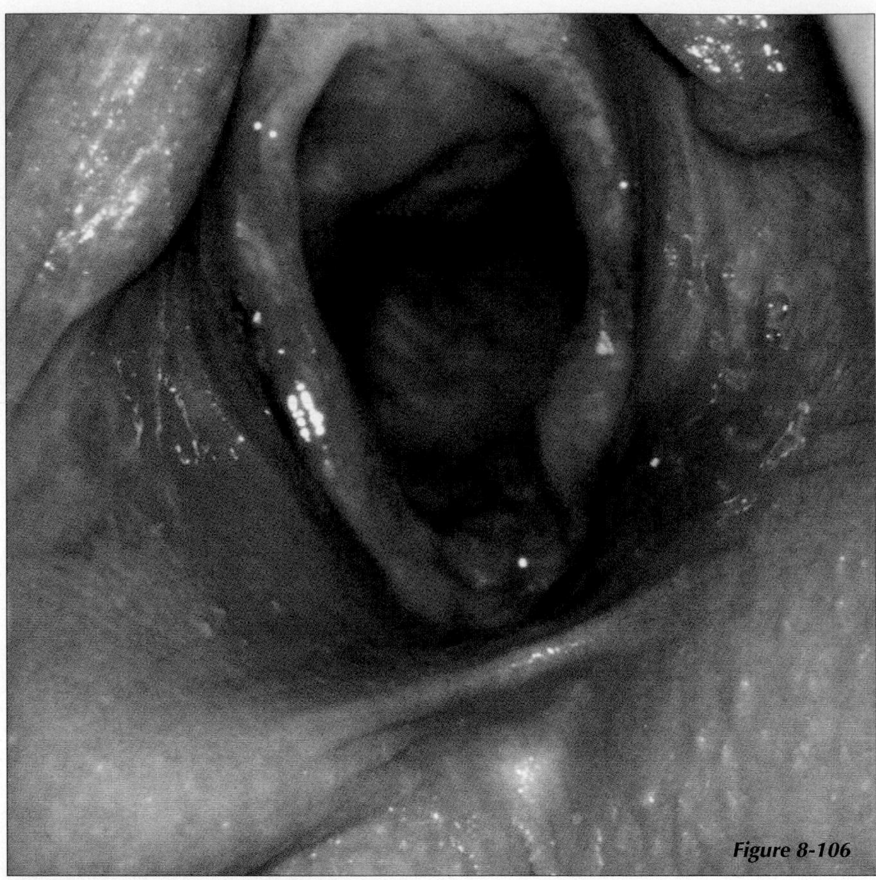

Figure 8-106

## Healed Transection

**Case Study 8-107**

This 6-year-old girl had a well-healed transection of the hymen but no history consistent with penetration. This finding without a history suggested abuse. Further investigation failed to find a perpetrator.

***Figure 8-107.*** *Well-healed transection hymen at the 6-o'clock position.*

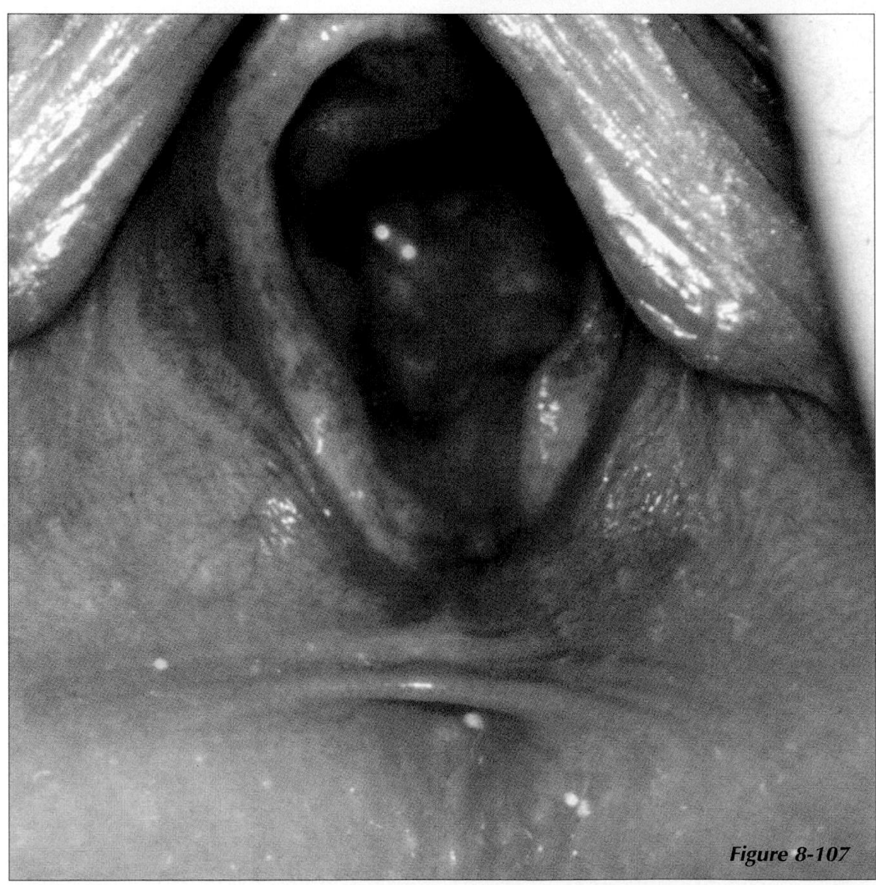

Figure 8-107

Chapter 9

# NEGLECT

Edward Goldson, MD
Andrew P. Sirotnak, MD

The National Child Abuse and Neglect Data System (NCANDS) reports neglect as the most common form of child maltreatment, accounting for more than 50% of all child abuse reported and substantiated in the United States in 2001. At the same time, neglect is not frequently considered as serious as nonaccidental trauma (NAT) and sexual abuse. Issues of neglect are often overlooked and underinvestigated. The various forms of neglect are: physical, emotional, educational, supervisory, and nutritional. Since educational and emotional neglect are difficult to portray graphically, this chapter presents examples consisting of supervisory, environmental, medical, and nutritional neglect.

Supervisory neglect reflects circumstances in which children are not appropriately cared for and are placed in danger of injuring themselves or others. In the case of environmental neglect, children's surroundings are unsafe. Medical and dental neglect contribute to significant health problems, morbidity, and potentially death. Nutritional neglect often results in the failure to gain weight and, ultimately, failure to thrive, which involves inadequate weight gain in addition to developmental and behavioral disturbances.

# Supervisory Neglect

**Case Study 9-1**

Supervisory neglect involves a lack of oversight and intervention on behalf of children's safety, increasing the risk of situations that are potentially harmful or deadly.

These photos were staged by the photographer and were supervised by the subject's caretaker.

***Figure 9-1-a*** *Caregivers may leave children unattended in cars for prolonged periods of time in either extremely cold or hot weather, thereby endangering their lives.*

***Figure 9-1-b.*** *Leaving a child unattended in an automobile represents a significant danger to children because they may inadvertently start the automobile.*

***Figure 9-1-c.*** *Child looking at window cleaner. Young children are at risk of opening containers of toxic cleaning agents and ingesting, absorbing, or aspirating their contents, which are often petroleum based. All cleaning agents should be secured in a location where the child will not see or have access to them. All containers should have safety covers.*

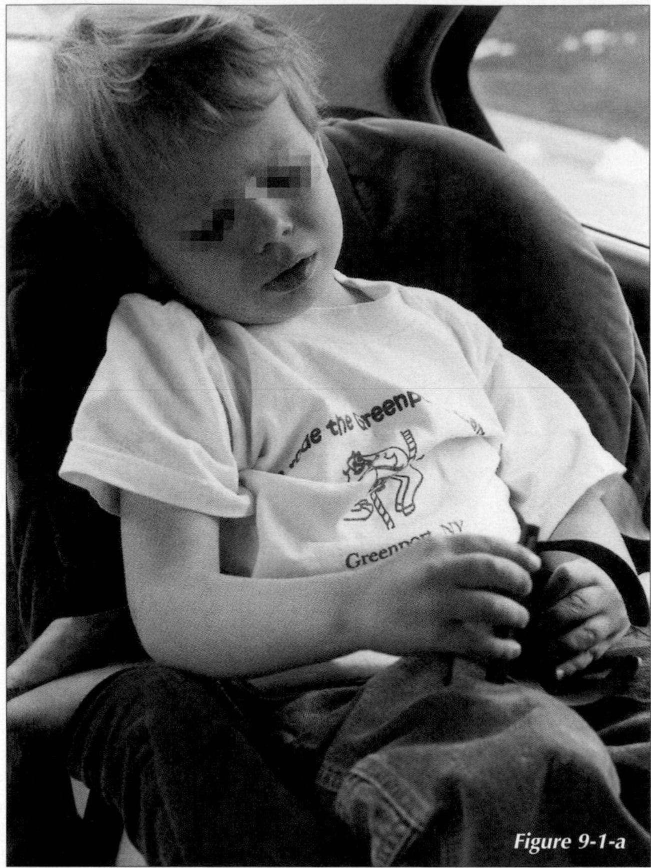

**Figure 9-1-a**

**Figure 9-1-b**

**Figure 9-1-c**

## SUPERVISORY NEGLECT

**Case Study 9-1** *(continued)*

***Figure 9-1-d.*** *Many children are "climbers" and the availability of a ladder and an absent caretaker is an invitation for an accident. All ladders should be stored away from children, closed, and secured.*

***Figure 9-1-e.*** *Although knives are important utensils, they can be extraordinarily dangerous and even lethal. They should never be left where children may find them.*

***Figure 9-1-f.*** *Scissors are important and useful household tools, but they can be lethal in the hands of inexperienced children. Scissors should always be stored where children cannot reach them.*

**Figure 9-1-d**

**Figure 9-1-e**

**Figure 9-1-f**

# Supervisory Neglect

**Case Study 9-1** *(continued)*

***Figure 9-1-g.*** *Children should never be left unattended in a bathtub and should never be allowed to play or be around electrical appliances unattended. Drownings in the family bathtub are one of the most common causes of death in young children. Many times caregivers report that they left their child for only a moment to answer the phone, put something away, or attend to another child. In this time, a young child can easily drown.*

***Figure 9-1-h.*** *Ingestions are also one of the more common causes of morbidity and mortality among young children. Medications should always be stored out of sight of children in locked or secured places.*

***Figures 9-1-i** and **j.*** *Guns should never be left where children can find them. If families decide to keep guns in the home, they should be stored out of the sight of children and should have a safety device on them. Ammunition should be stored in a separate, safe, and hidden location.*

Figure 9-1-g

Figure 9-1-h

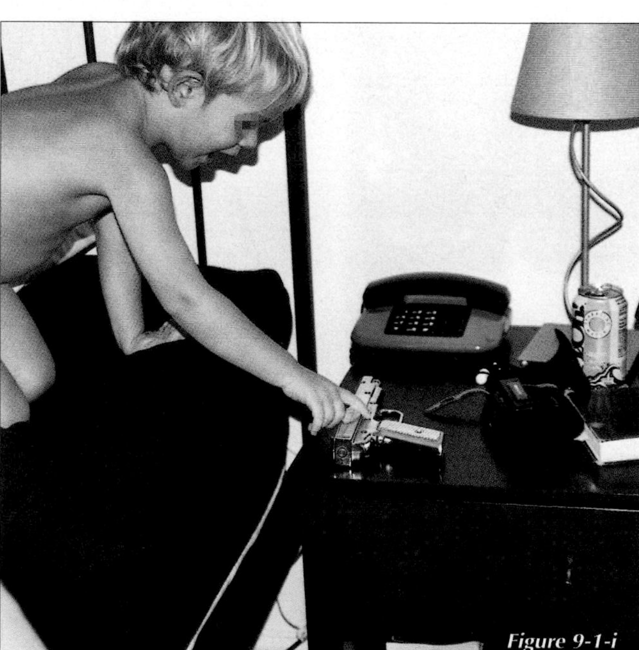
Figure 9-1-i

Figure 9-1-j

# Environmental Neglect

**Case Study 9-2**

A social worker accompanied by police officers went to remove the children from this home because of the parents' parole violations. There were 4 children in the home, aged 9, 13, 14, and 16 years. Dog and cat feces covered the floor and human waste was in the bathtub and on the bathroom floor. There was no heat, electricity, or water in the building. All of the children had head lice.

***Figure 9-2-a.*** *Unsanitary toilet and bathroom floor.*

***Figure 9-2-b*** *and* ***c.*** *Debris and belongings, including cans of fuel for the portable stove, are scattered throughout the house.*

***Figure 9-2-d.*** *A portable stove, which is sitting on the floor, is the primary heat source for the home.*

Figure 9-2-a

Figure 9-2-b

Figure 9-2-c

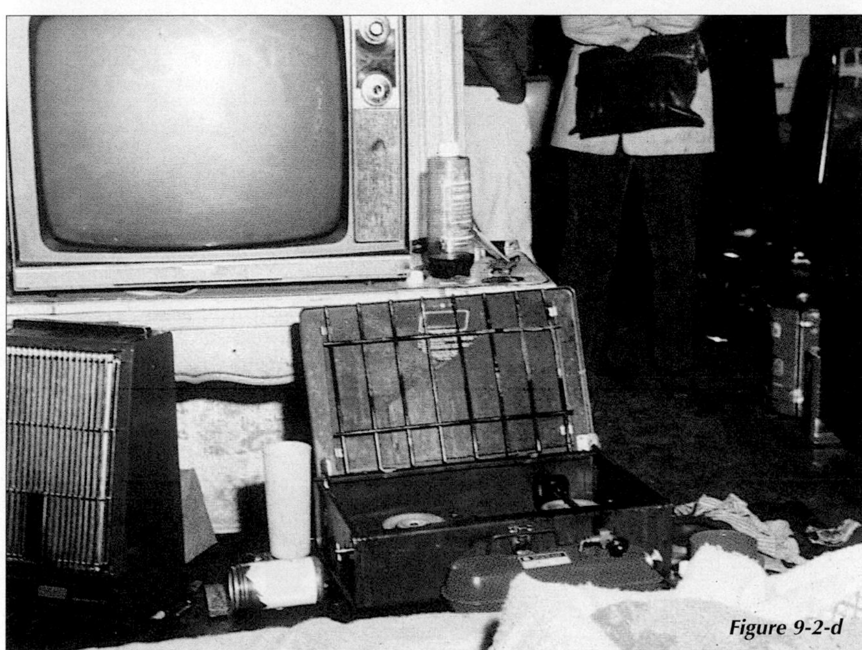

Figure 9-2-d

# Environmental Neglect

**Case Study 9-3**

This case involved a drug raid. Five children, aged 2, 5, 7, 9, and 10 years, were found in the home with 6 adults who were arrested on drug charges.

***Figures 9-3-a** and **b.** Evidence of drugs in the home.*

***Figure 9-3-c.** Trash is scattered in this room and throughout the house. Although clutter does not constitute neglect, filth may harbor bacteria such as* E. Coli, Salmonella, *and other pathogens.*

***Figures 9-3-d** and **e.** The tub is clogged and filled with waste, as is the toilet and a 5-gallon plastic container under the bathroom sink.*

Figure 9-3-a

Figure 9-3-b

Figure 9-3-d

Figure 9-3-c

Figure 9-3-e

# Environmental Neglect

**Case Study 9-3** *(continued)*

***Figure 9-3-f.*** *Open and full gasoline can within reach of the children.*

***Figure 9-3-g.*** *The crib is next to a space heater.*

Figure 9-3-f

Figure 9-3-g

# Environmental Neglect

### Case Study 9-4

This home was littered with garbage, dirt, and objects, such as broken glass and animal feces, which was not conducive to the safety and well-being of the children in the home.

***Figure 9-4.*** *Stairway in a home that is unfit for children and characteristic of environmental neglect.*

Figure 9-4

### Case Study 9-5

The police were called to investigate the possible abandonment of 9 children; they found a small apartment housing the children, ranging in age from 5 to 10 years. They were the children of 2 mothers who were living in a separate and well-kept apartment with their boyfriends. The mothers were collecting welfare subsistence and occasionally dropped off food for the children.

***Figures 9-5-a*** *and* ***b.*** *The apartment housing the children is not heated and has only one source of electricity: an extension cord stretched down the hall and out of the bedroom window to another apartment.*

***Figure 9-5-c.*** *There is little food in the house; the refrigerator is not working and is essentially empty.*

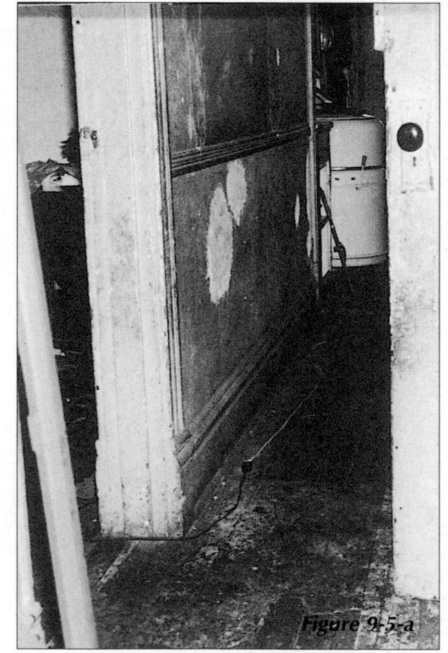
Figure 9-5-a

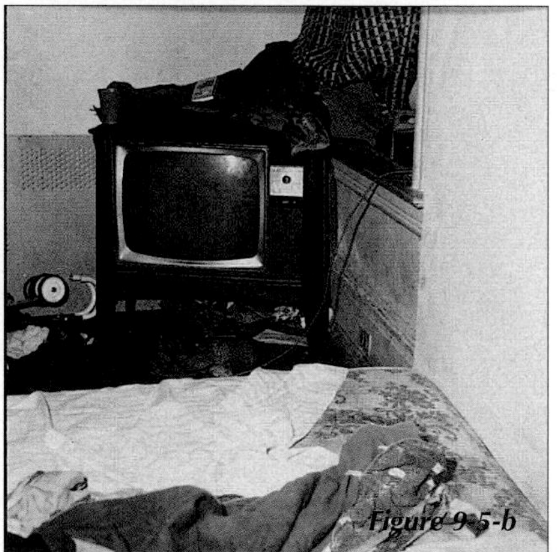
Figure 9-5-b

Figure 9-5-c

# Environmental Neglect

**Case Study 9-4** *(continued)*

***Figure 9-5-d.*** *The children's food consists of a combination of grease, potatoes, and pork and beans.*

***Figure 9-5-e.*** *A frying pan missing a handle with old grease still in it and evidence of rat footprints in the grease.*

***Figure 9-5-f.*** *The cupboard under the stove is full of rat feces.*

***Figure 9-5-g.*** *Trash is strewn about in one of the rooms.*

***Figure 9-5-h.*** *Several of the mattresses are severely damaged.*

Figure 9-5-d

Figure 9-5-e

Figure 9-5-f

Figure 9-5-g

Figure 9-5-h

# Medical Neglect

**Case Study 9-6**

This 18-month-old girl was seen in the free clinic with a monilial rash but missed 2 subsequent appointments. In a telephone follow-up by the clinic's nurse, the grandmother stated that the mother never applied the medication given to her as a starter and did not fill the prescription. The mother was reported for medical neglect. The rash had progressed, and the child was found to have a healing ecchymotic area on the dorsum of the right hand.

***Figures 9-6-a** and **b.*** *Progressed monilial rash.*

***Figure 9-6-c.*** *Healing ecchymosis on the dorsum of the right hand.*

The Division of Family Services assigned a visiting nurse to check in on the home twice daily for the application of medication. The rash cleared promptly. A counselor was also assigned to the case to teach parenting skills to the mother.

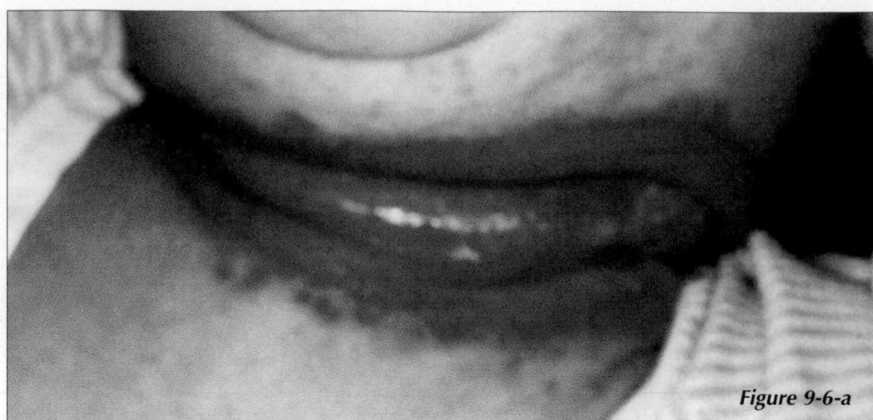

**Figure 9-6-a**

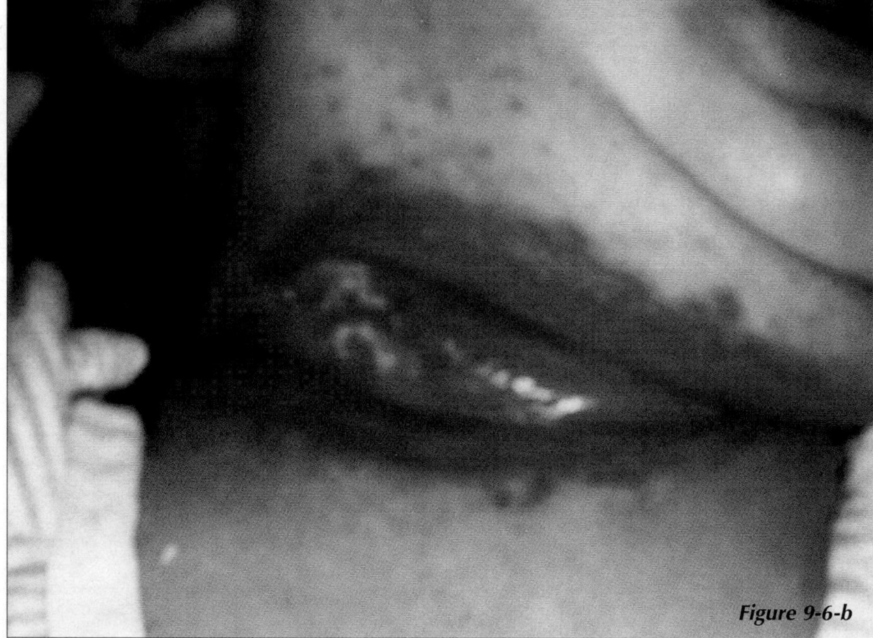

**Figure 9-6-b**

**Figure 9-6-c**

# Nutritional Neglect

**Case Study 9-7**

This 11-month-old female infant was admitted to the hospital for profound malnutrition and global developmental delay. A former 32-week, premature, 1.56-kg infant with minimal newborn complications, she reached a maximum weight of 4.2 kg at 4 months, at which point she stopped growing. Subsequent evaluation for poor growth led to gastroesophageal reflux treatment with a feeding tube. Her measurements at 11 months (weight of 3.54 kg, length of 60.5 cm, and head circumference of 40.5 cm) were all below the 5th percentile for her age.

***Figure 9-7-a.*** *Malnourished at 11 months, posterior view of infant shows loss of fat tissue, poor muscle tone, and hair loss.*

Hospitalization for 2 months was required for nutritional rehabilitation, which included stomach tube feedings, physical therapy including oro-motor and swallowing studies, and monitoring of the parent-child interaction.

***Figures 9-7-b*** *and* ***c.*** *After 1 month, anterior and posterior views of the infant show weight gain, increased fat and muscle tissues, and increased muscle tone.*

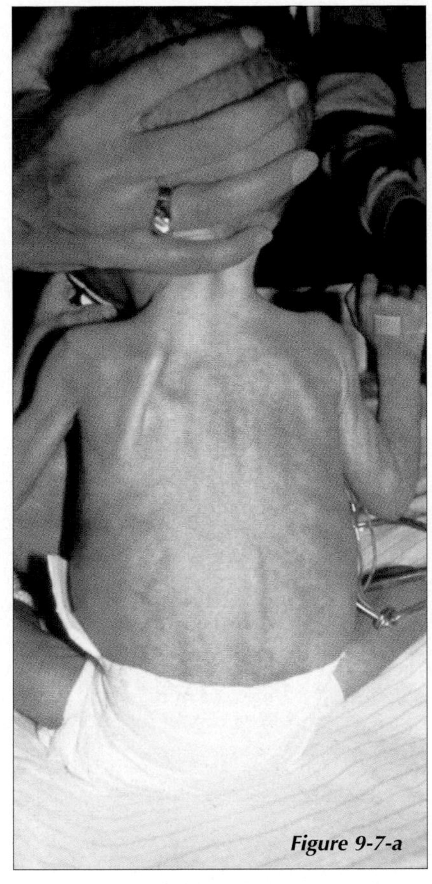

**Figure 9-7-a**

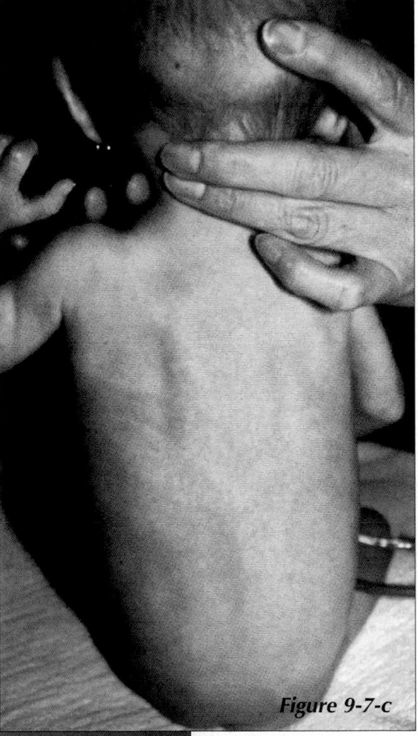

**Figure 9-7-c**

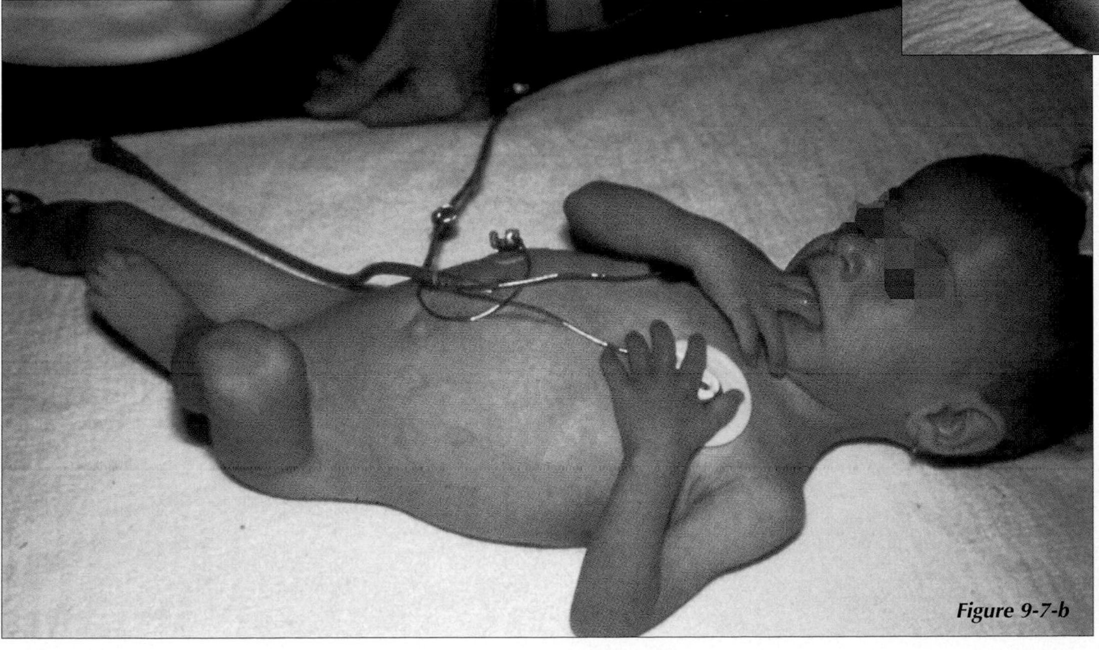

**Figure 9-7-b**

# Nutritional Neglect

**Case Study 9-7** *(continued)*

The family history was striking for many risk factors that led to the poor attachment and neglect. The infant was born unexpectedly to a mother who had prior stillborns, was physically isolated from her adoptive family, had an emotionally distant spouse, and whose church leader had told her that she was never destined to become a mother. Fear that the infant would eventually die led to poor attachment and to the inability of the mother to respond to the infant's basic needs for nurturing.

***Figures 9-7-d*** *and* ***e.*** *After 2 months, remarkable weight gain and growth is evident.*

Temporary foster care placement was required. With intensive psychiatric intervention, court-ordered family treatment, and in-home services, the infant was eventually reunited with her parents. Mild cognitive and motor delays developed and persisted through early childhood.

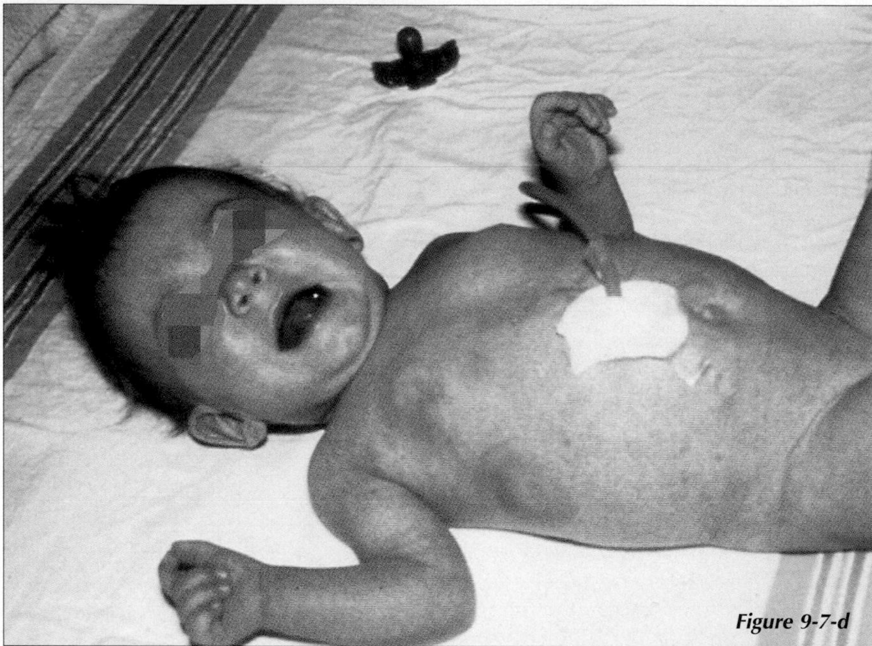

**Figure 9-7-d**

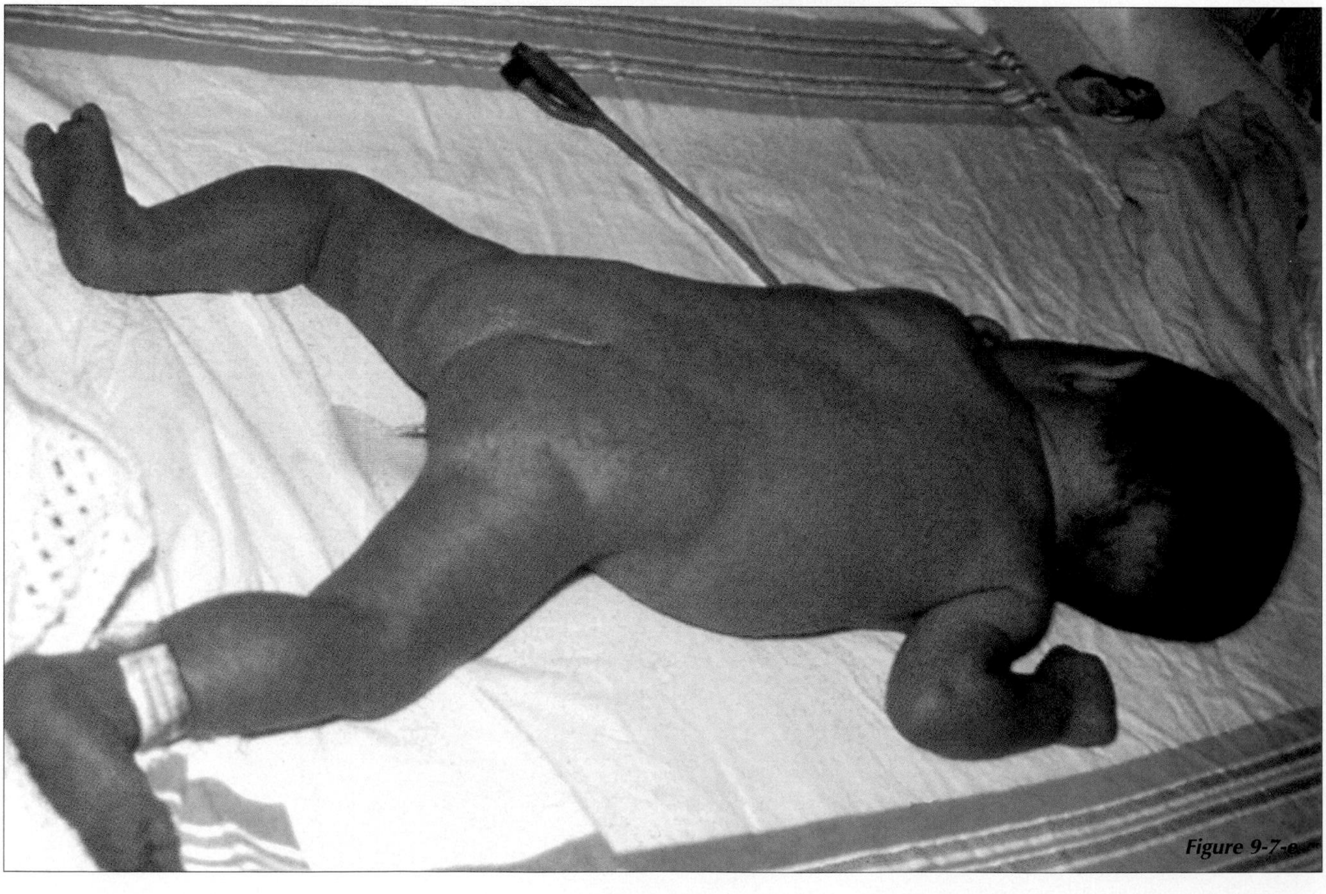

**Figure 9-7-e**

# Nutritional Neglect

**Case Study 9-8**

This 2½-year-old male was admitted in cardiac arrest after having been found unresponsive at home. On admission to intensive care, he was cachectic and had multiple bruises, abrasions, and bite marks consistent with chronic physical abuse. His head and abdominal trauma evaluations were negative. Markedly abnormal laboratory studies—electrolyte imbalance, liver dysfunction, anemia, and vitamin deficiency—all confirmed severe malnutrition.

***Figure 9-8-a.*** *Critically ill toddler suffering from chronic physical and emotional neglect and repeated physical abuse.*

***Figure 9-8-b.*** *Posterior view showing bite and scratch marks, unusual pattern injury on neck, and hair loss from malnutrition.*

***Figure 9-8-c.*** *Leg showing animal scratch marks and marked wasting of muscle and fat tissue.*

***Figure 9-8-d.*** *View of back showing multiple abuse marks with ribs and scapula protruding due to wasting of muscle and fat tissue.*

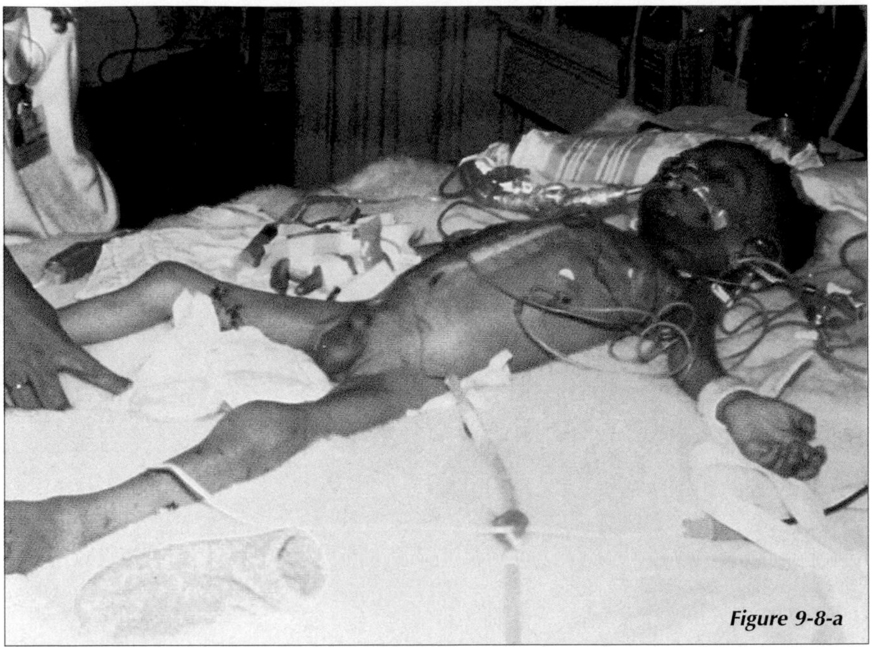
Figure 9-8-a

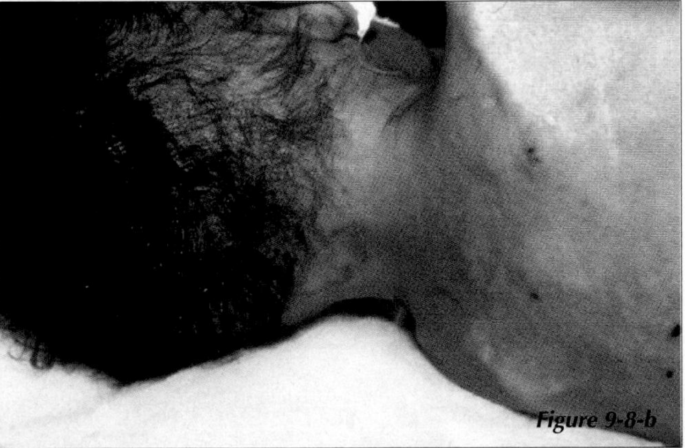
Figure 9-8-b

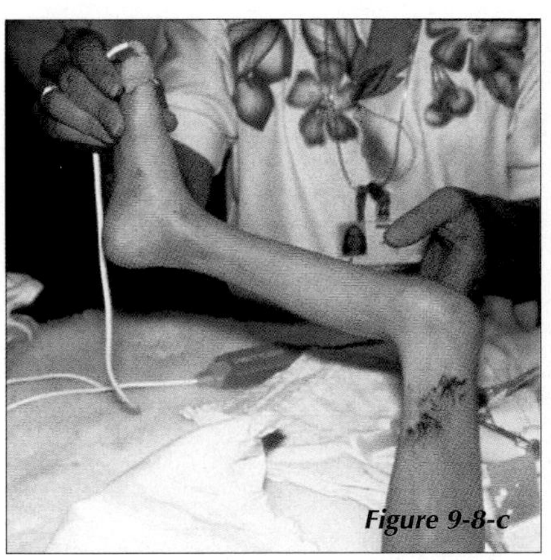
Figure 9-8-c

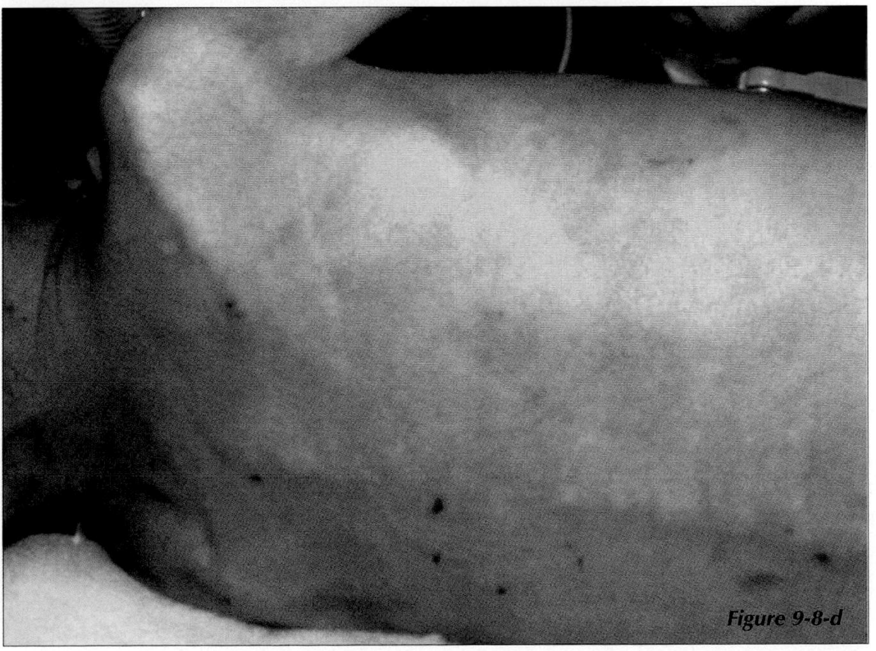
Figure 9-8-d

# Nutritional Neglect

**Case Study 9-8** *(continued)*

After 2 weeks in intensive care, he was transferred to a medical rehabilitation service. Global delays required intensive interventions. He was incapable of speech. Physical therapy for gross motor skills was complicated by his poor muscle bulk and tone. His inability to eat required gastrostomy tube feedings and oral-motor therapy. Play therapy was needed to address his behavioral disturbances. He was fearful of caregivers, had angry outbursts in physical and play therapies, and had frequent night terrors.

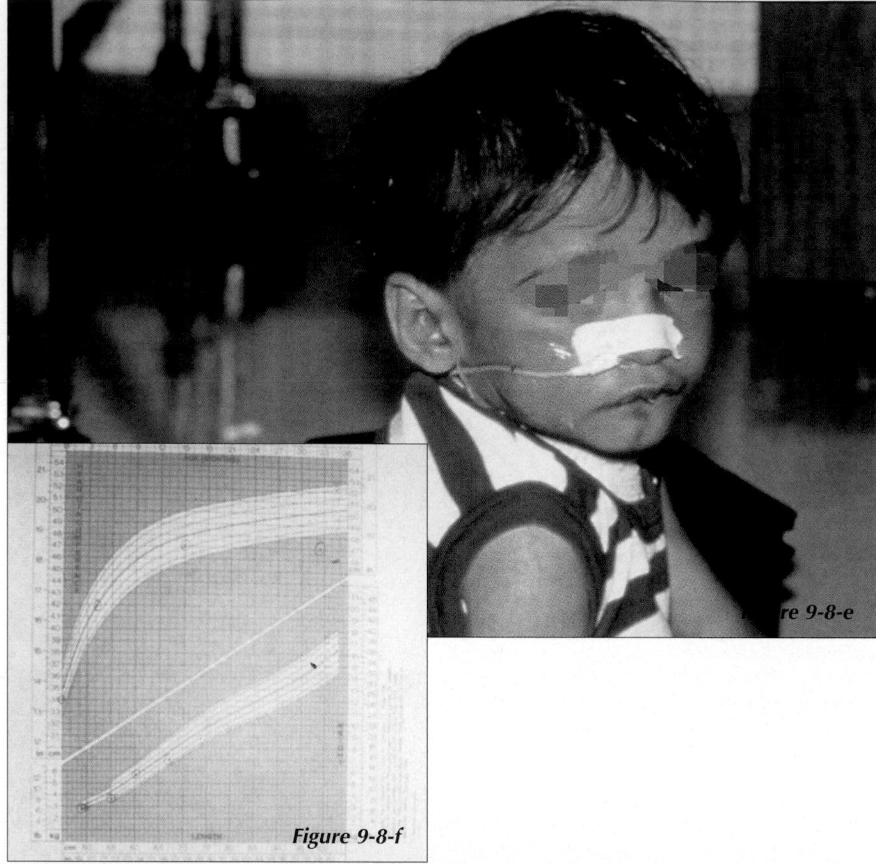


***Figure 9-8-e.*** *After 1 month of hospitalization with intensive therapies and a feeding tube in place, he was slowly gaining weight and strength.*

The child had been placed in a relative's care at the age of 15 months when his mother could no longer care for him. The child experienced immediate separation anxiety behaviors. Relatives were so overwhelmed by the care of his 3 siblings and their own children that they put the child in an attic room and ultimately ignored him, except for periodic meals and repeated beatings.

***Figure 9-8-f.*** *Review of his previous medical records and growth chart showed that he began to fall off growth chart on weight, height, and head circumference within months of placement, and eventually was lost to medical care follow-up.*

Placement in foster care after discharge led to several foster home changes due to his behavioral disturbances. He was eventually adopted and has grown into an emotionally healthy child with mild residual motor and cognitive delays.

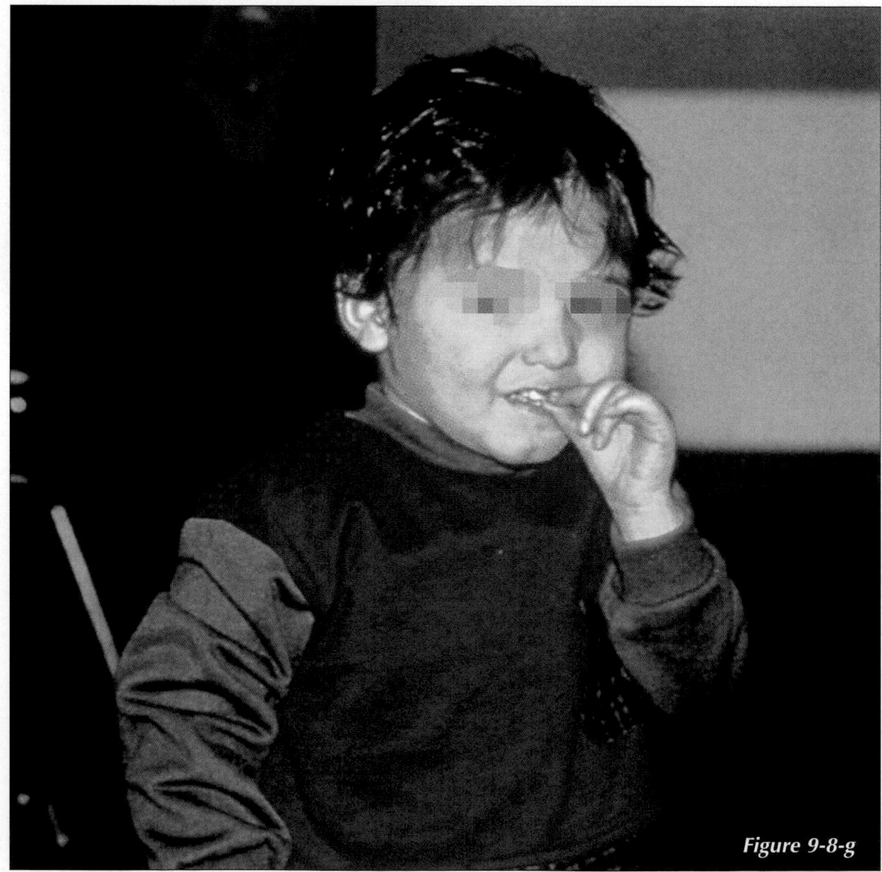


***Figure 9-8-g.*** *Six months after hospitalization, at 3 years of age, he is still small for his age but is healthy and happy in a now-stable environment.*

# Nutritional Neglect

**Case Study 9-9**

This 7-month-old boy was seen in the ER. He had diarrhea for 2 days, was unresponsive, and could not eat. He was well below the third percentile for both height and weight.

***Figures 9-9-a, b, c,*** *and* ***d.*** *The child is dehydrated and emaciated with no subcutaneous fat. His abdomen is protuberant, and numerous cutaneous lesions are present.*

Following rehydration and resolution of the diarrhea, he thrived while in the hospital. He was placed in a foster home and continued to thrive. After 5 months in foster care, his height and weight measurements were in the tenth percentile.

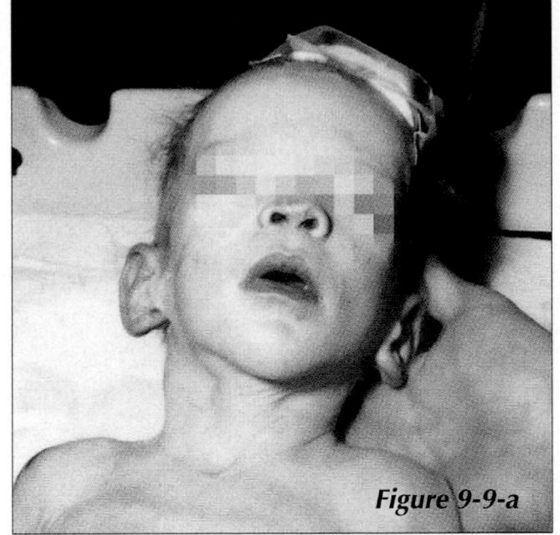

**Figure 9-9-a**

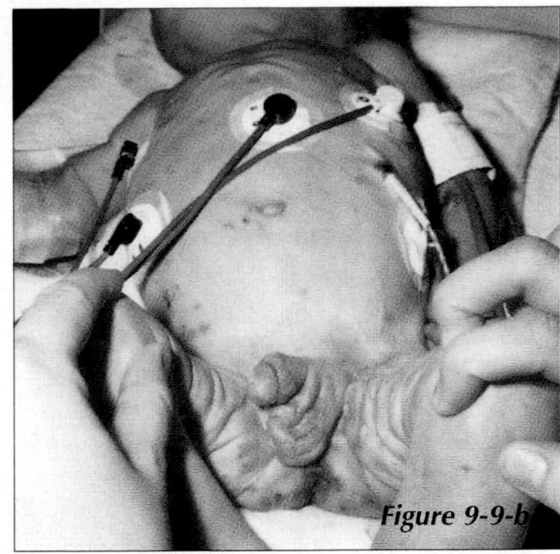

**Figure 9-9-b**

**Figure 9-9-c**

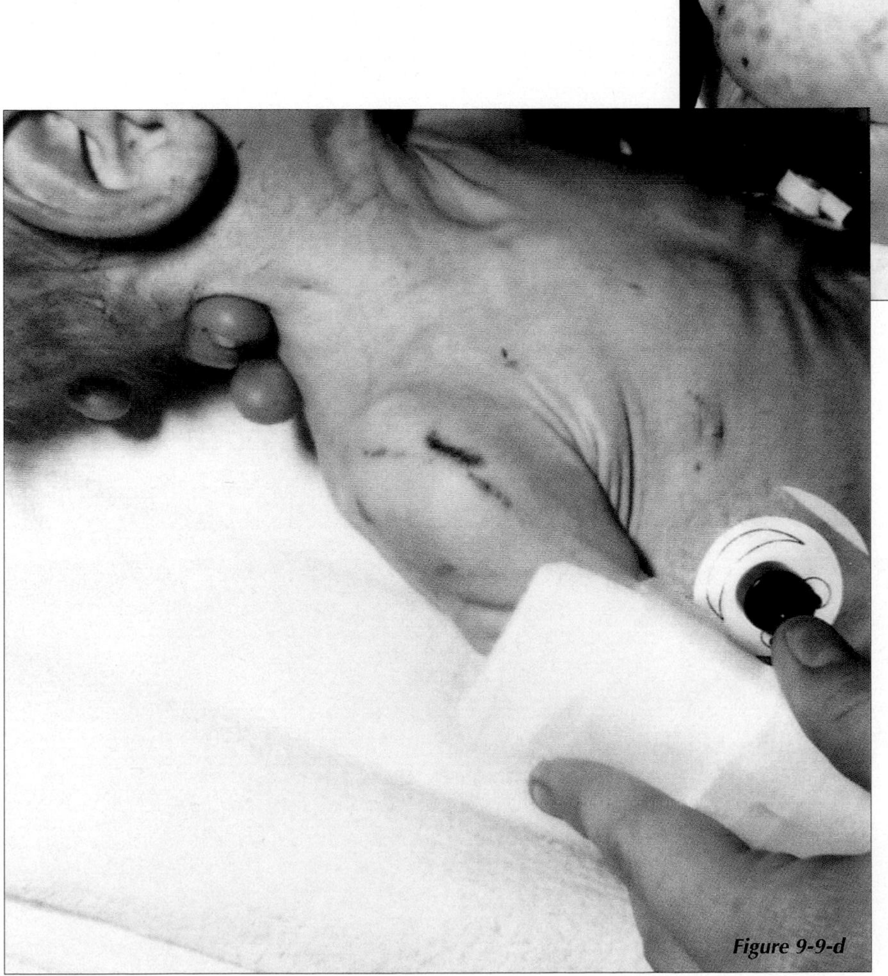

**Figure 9-9-d**

# Nutritional Neglect

**Case Study 9-10**

This 4-year-old girl was severely neglected.

***Figure 9-10-a.*** *Note the lack of subcutaneous fat, protuberant abdomen, and passive flat affect.*

***Figures 9-10-b*** *and* ***c.*** *She is still in a diaper and has diaper-area lesions.*

She thrived in a foster home.

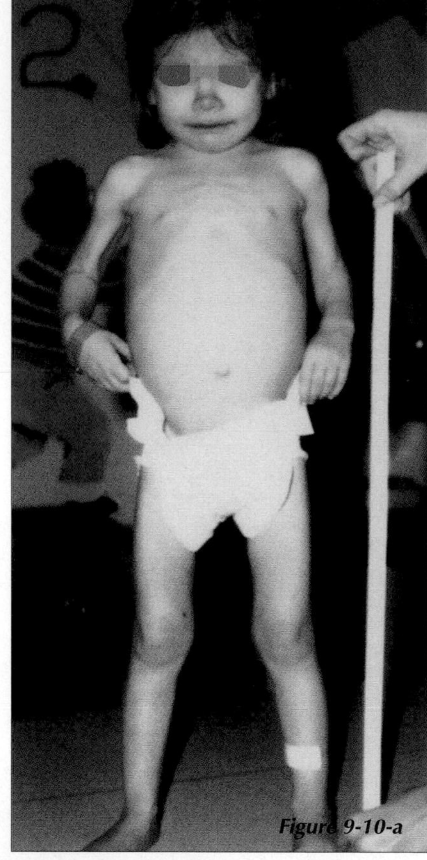

Figure 9-10-a

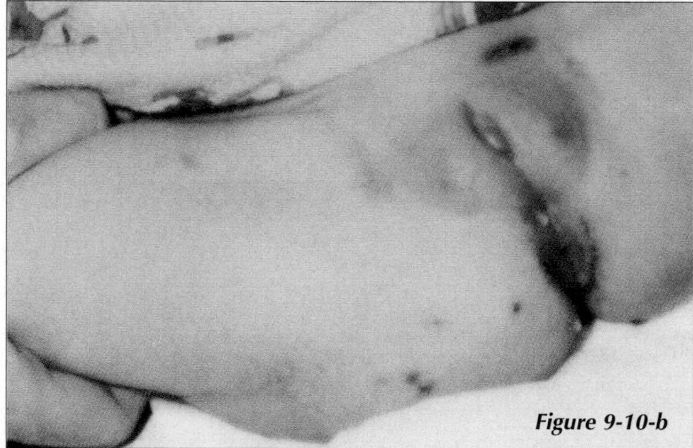

Figure 9-10-b

**Case Study 9-11**

This severely malnourished 7-year-old boy was taken to the ER by an ambulance. The child's mother found him unresponsive in bed and not breathing. The mother stated that the child had had a cold for the past few days and appeared to be recovering. He was emaciated and dirty. Attempts at resuscitation were successful; he was intubated and given fluids and antibiotics to treat severe bilateral pneumonia. After several hours in the hospital he suffered cardiac arrest and died. The other 3 children in the family were well nourished and healthy and the school reported that they attended school regularly. The 7-year-old had been absent for a significant number of days, including the 2 weeks prior to his death, and teachers reported several instances when he had come to school in obvious distress; he was dirty, malnourished, and unable to work on his assignments. On one occasion, he was so weak that he had to crawl up the stairs. While it was suggested that the child be reported to the Division of Family Services, the principal decided that such action was not needed since the siblings were doing well.

***Figure 9-11.*** *The soles of his feet are encrusted with dirt and, when cleaned, they exhibit several infected wounds; one of the wounds resembles a cigarette burn.*

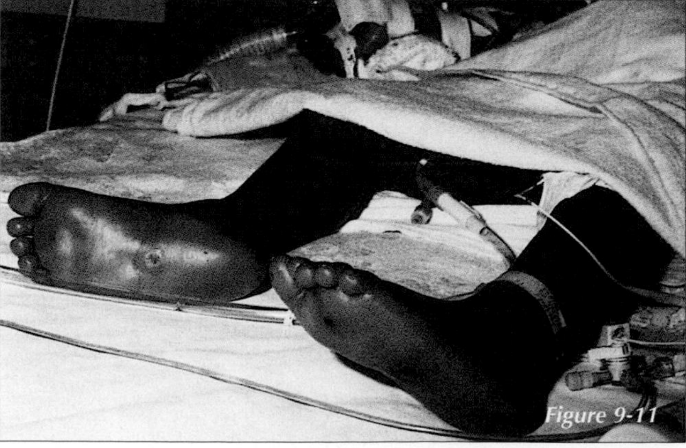

Figure 9-11

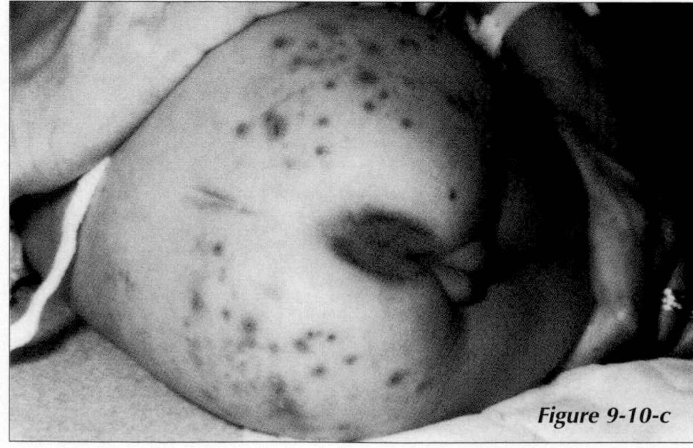

Figure 9-10-c

# Nutritional Neglect

**Case Study 9-12**

This 11-year-old boy with cerebral palsy was taken from a foster home. The foster parents ran a child daycare center. A second child, also with cerebral palsy, had been in the same foster care and was found dead with evidence of severe malnutrition. The foster parents initially denied neglect, stating that the child was difficult to feed because of the cerebral palsy. The boy's rapid weight gain in the hospital was attributed by the foster parents to the specialized care provided by an experienced nursing staff. Employees in the daycare center said the 2 children were kept alone in a secluded room all day. Feeding was done by the foster parents. The foster father confessed that the children were often poorly fed. He also admitted that when the boy was in the home, he was often locked in a closet.

***Figures 9-12-a, b,** and **c.** The boy is severely malnourished.*

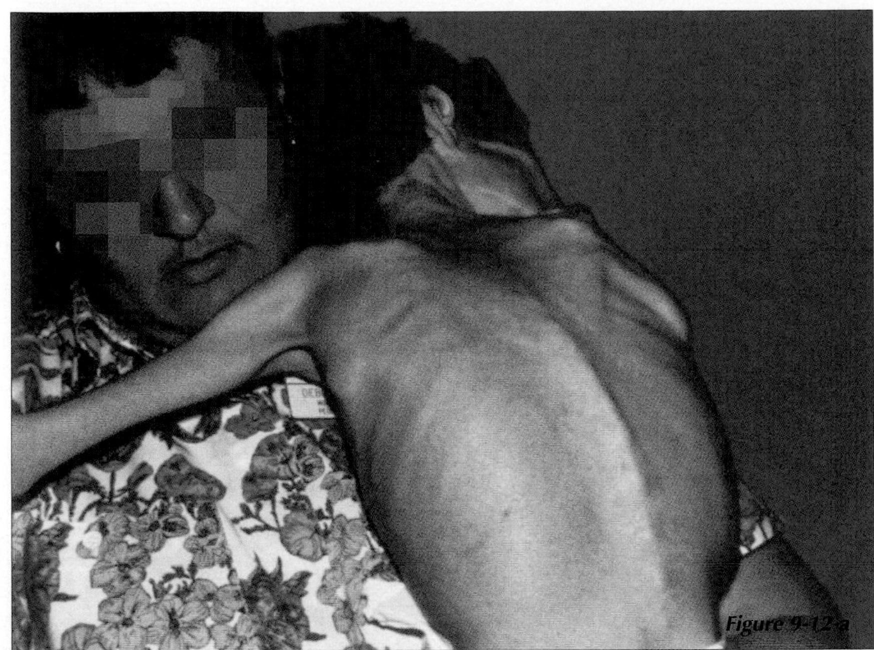

*Figure 9-12-a*

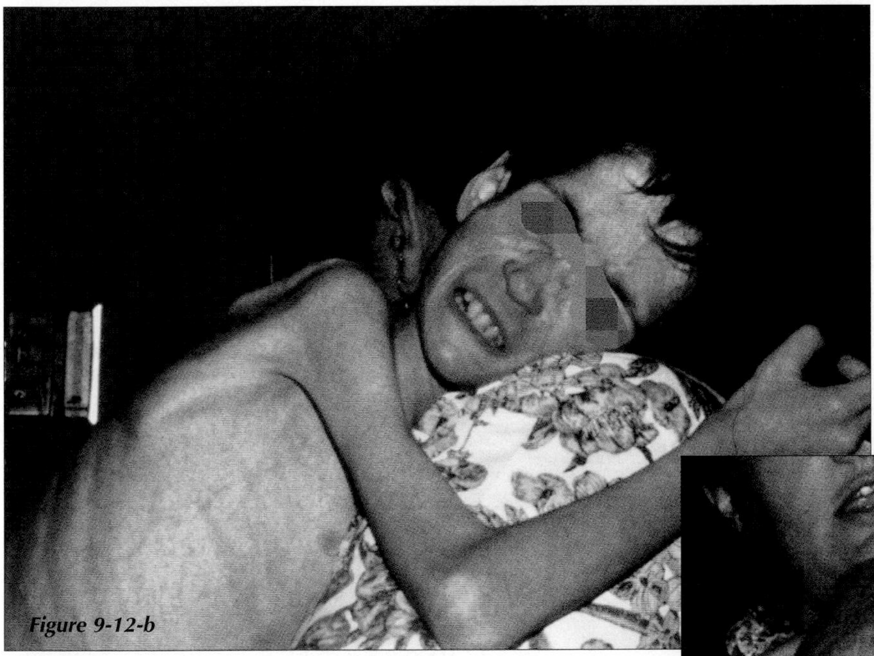

*Figure 9-12-b*

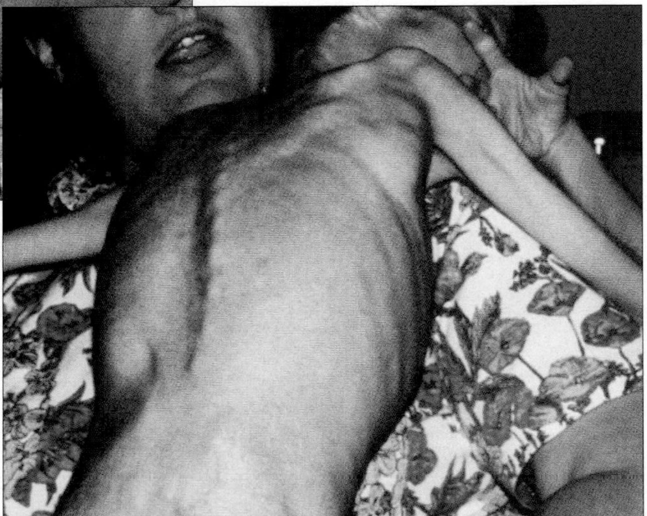

*Figure 9-12-c*

# Nutritional Neglect

**Case Study 9-12** *(continued)*

***Figures 9-12-d*** *and* ***e.*** *Photographs taken during his recovery.*

***Figure 9-12-f.*** *Growth chart illustrating conditions of severe nutritional neglect. It is important to document weight gain when foster parents have little or no experience feeding children with limitations. Such growth in these circumstances signifies that that child was simply lacking regular nutrition.*

***Figure 9-12-g.*** *A picture of the child before he entered into foster care is of value in assessing the severity of the neglect.*

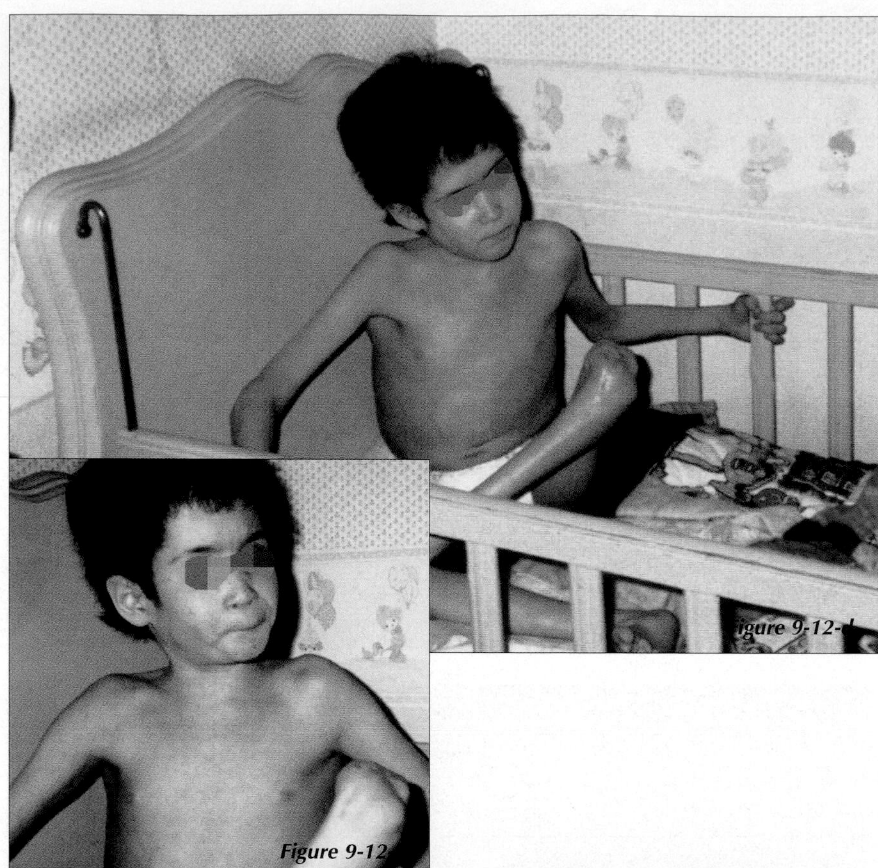

igure 9-12-

Figure 9-12

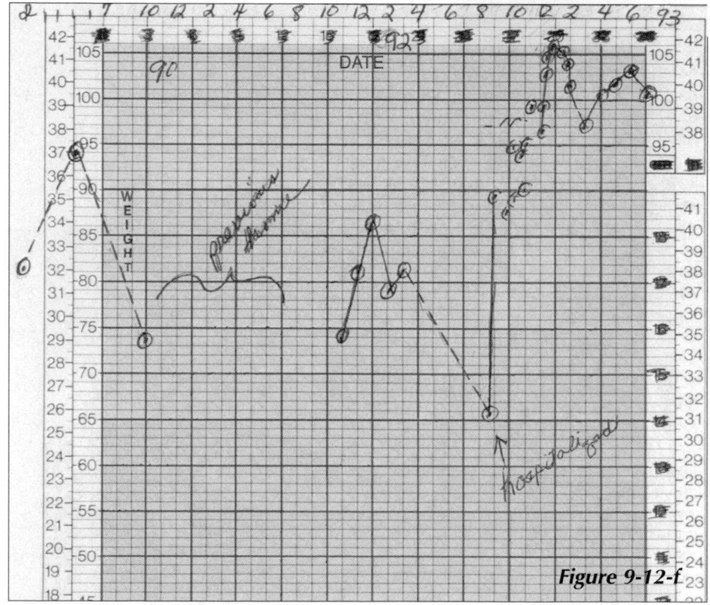


Figure 9-12-f

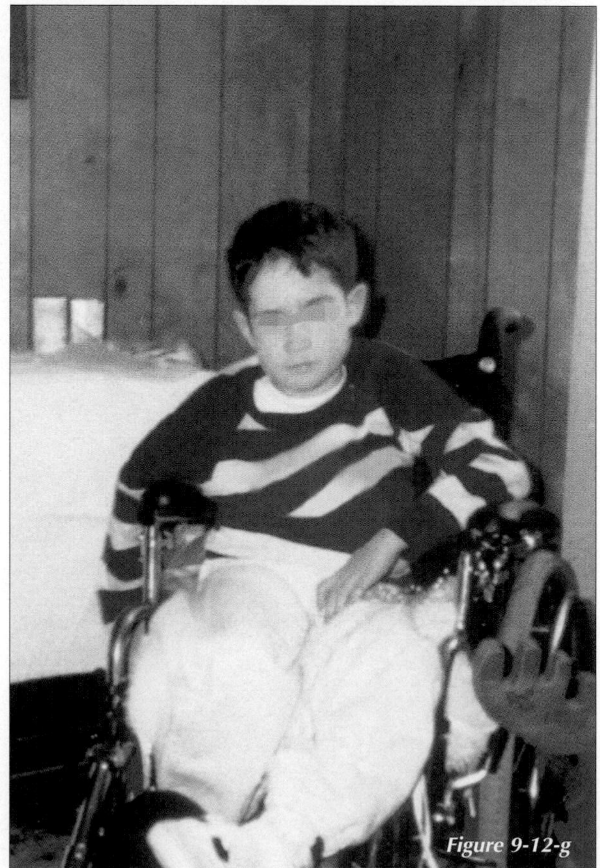

Figure 9-12-g

# Nutritional Neglect

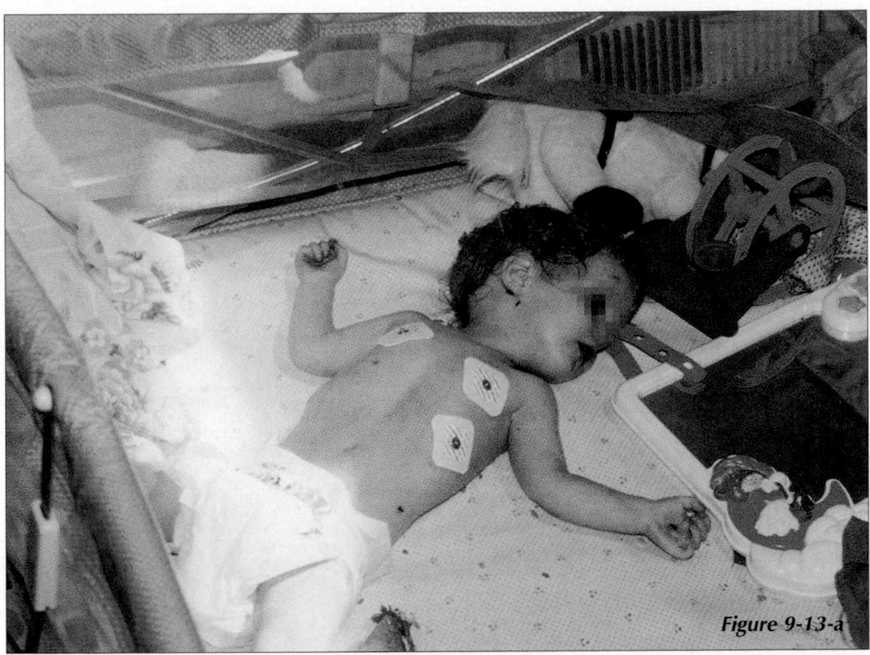


### Case Study 9-13

This 2-year-old girl was found dead in a portable playpen, which also served as her bed. The cardiac leads were placed by Emergency Medical Services (EMS). It was learned later that the parents attempted to clean the area and the child, as well as the other children before calling for EMS and that the other 4 children were usually locked in the bedroom that they shared. There was no food in the house; however, there was ample food for the dog and rabbit. The parents stated that they could not afford baby food; they were well nourished, as were the dog and rabbit. The girl was a twin, and neither she nor her sister had demonstrated an ability to stand without support. They were severely delayed socially and physically. All of the children had been examined previously for failure to thrive. There had been 14 calls to the hotline, which were investigated and unsubstantiated, due to manipulation by the parents and grandparents. When the police arrived at the house, the parents were on the front stoop giving the twin sister water from an outdoor water hose. The police officer stated that the twin sister voraciously consumed five bottles of water while he was there. The older children asked not to be sent back to live with their parents.

***Figures 9-13-a** and **b.** The girl, as found dead, in the portable playpen.*

***Figure 9-13-c.** The bedroom shared by the girl and her 4 siblings.*

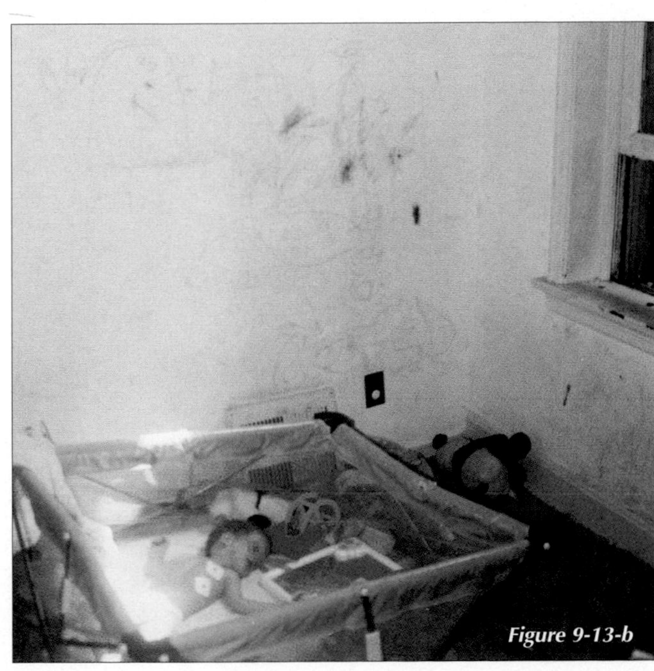

# NUTRITIONAL NEGLECT

**Case Study 9-13** *(continued)*

***Figures 9-13-d, e,** and **f.*** *The girl's head is matted with dirt and old food. Dried feces is present in the diaper area.*

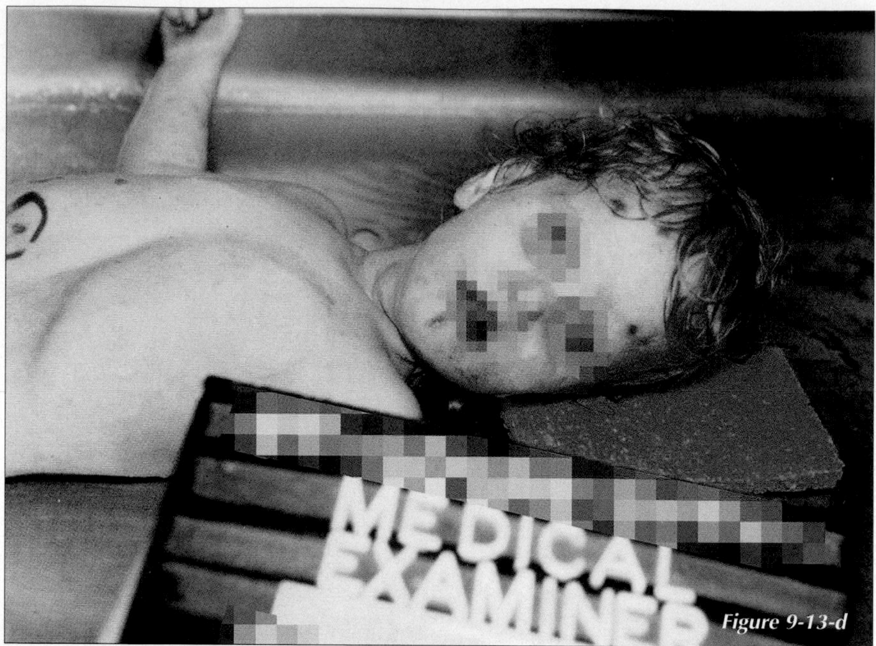

Figure 9-13-d

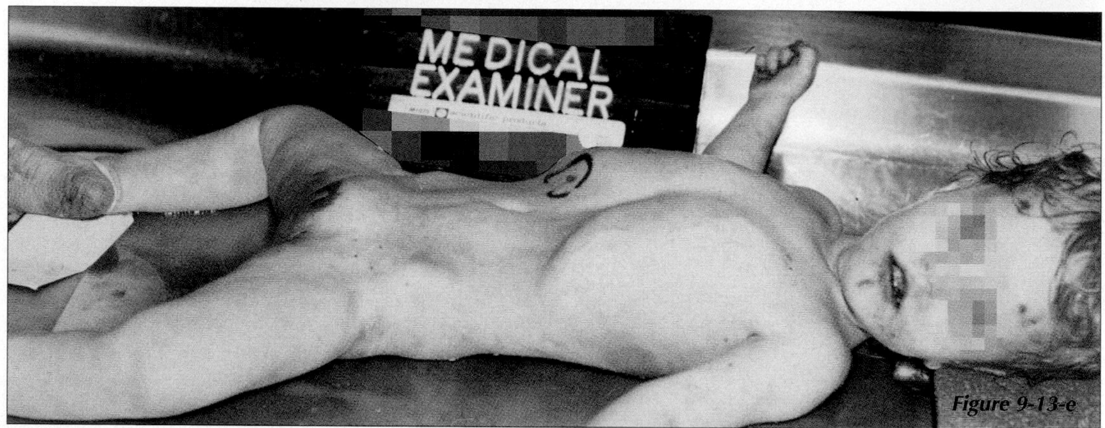

Figure 9-13-e

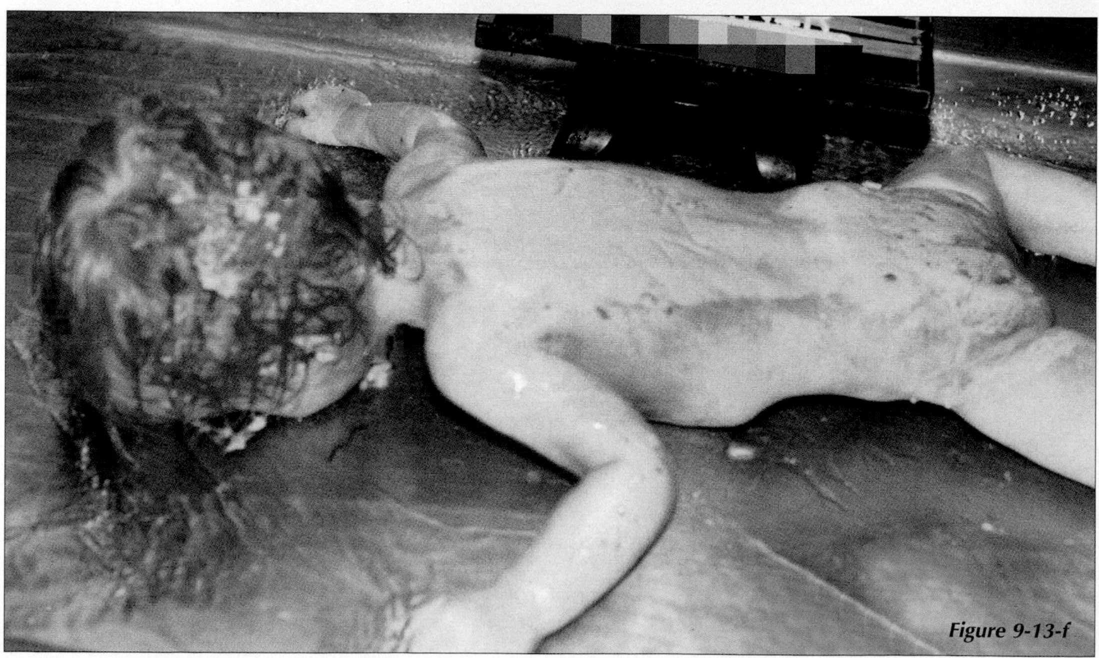
Figure 9-13-f

# Nutritional Neglect

**Case Study 9-13** *(continued)*

***Figure 9-13-g.*** *The house is unsanitary with dog feces, which can transmit worms and harbor harmful bacteria.*

***Figure 9-13-h.*** *The bathroom is dirty, the toilet does not work, and there is no hot water available.*

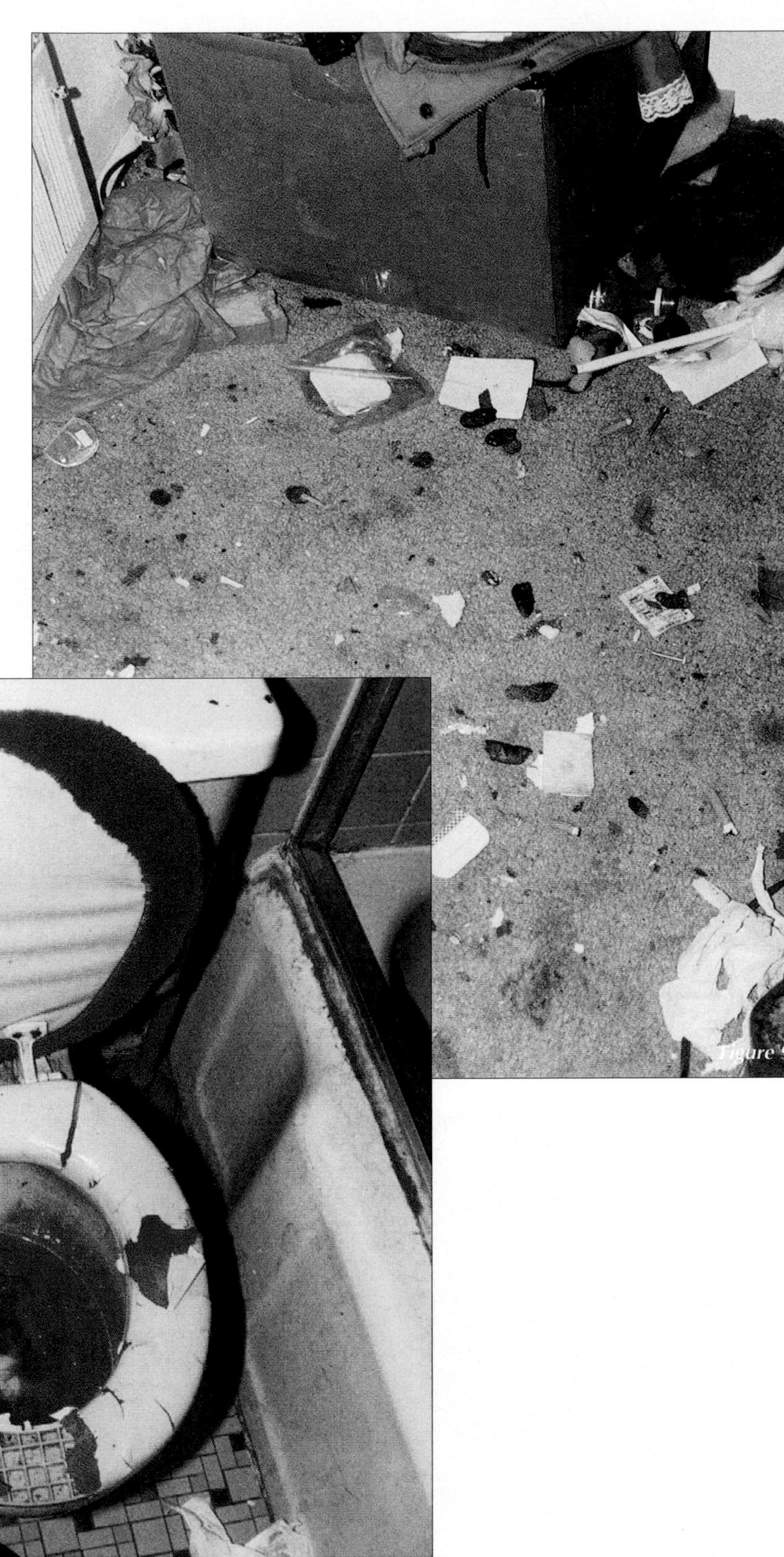

Figure 9-13-g

Figure 9-13-h

# Nutritional Neglect

**Case Study 9-13** *(continued)*

***Figures 9-13-i, j, k,* and *l.*** *Numerous empty beer cans, soft drink cans, and empty beer cases are infested with roaches and strewn about the house.*

***Figure 9-13-m.*** *The mother, father, and 2 of the children as found on the front stoop of the home when police arrived on the scene.*

The autopsy report included findings of severe malnutrition, dehydration, poor hygiene, and wasting. The cause of death was determined to be severe malnutrition and dehydration. All of the remaining children were placed in foster care, where they thrived. The parents were found guilty of child abuse and sent to prison.

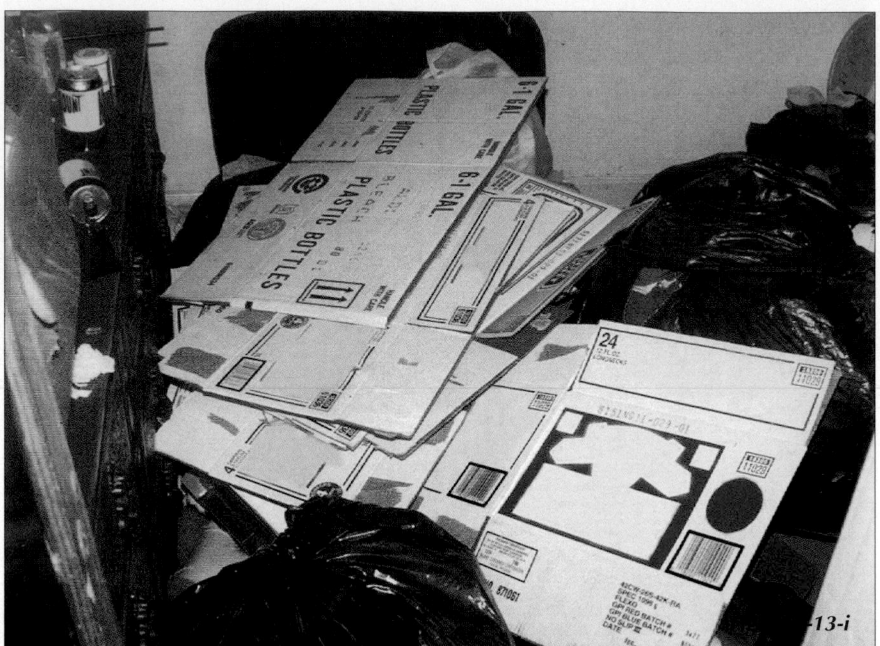

-13-i

Figure 9-1

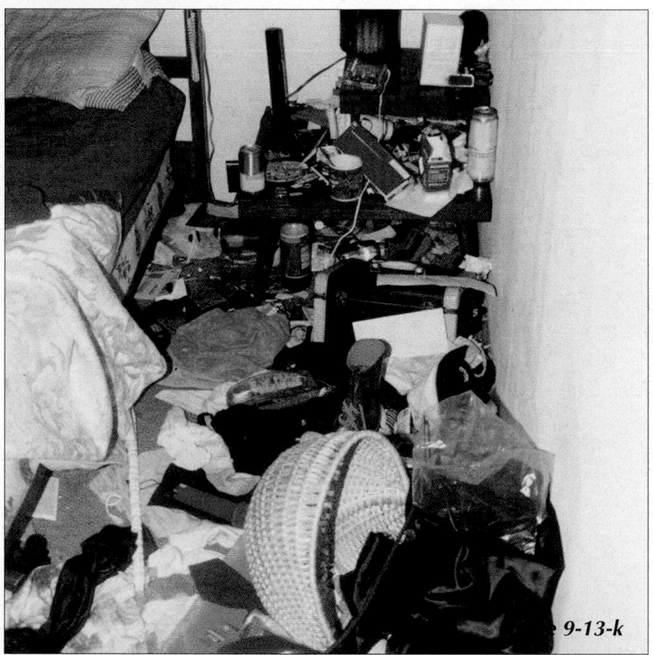
9-13-k

Figure 9-13-l

Fi 13-

Chapter 10

# THE MEDICAL EXAMINER

Tom Bennett, MD
Angelo P. Giardino, MD, PhD
Michael Graham, MD

The medical examiner plays several roles in the evaluation of a patient's death. In cases of suspected child abuse and neglect, the medical examiner is asked to: (1) determine the cause and manner of death to a reasonable degree of medical certainty; (2) provide expert evaluation of the presence, absence, nature, and significance of injuries and disease; (3) collect and preserve evidence; (4) correlate clinical and pathological findings; and (5) present expert opinions and testimony in appropriate forums. Medical examiners are expected to have a background in the basics of child abuse and neglect owing to their training as physicians. It is generally expected that additional training will occur as well in the areas of mechanisms of trauma and injury, dynamics of child maltreatment, and common as well as unusual presentations and manifestations of child abuse and neglect. Additionally, with the growing focus on death scene investigations related to possible sudden infant death syndrome (SIDS) deaths, the medical examiner typically gains experience and expertise at crime scene evidence collection and re-enactments to determine plausibility for the history provided.

The involvement of the medical examiner in child abuse and neglect traditionally begins at the time of death. With the advent of multidisciplinary child fatality review teams the medical examiner may be part of community-wide efforts directed at preventing child deaths as well. The appropriately trained forensic pathologist becomes involved with any sudden and unexpected death or any death suspected to be caused or contributed to by an injury or nonnatural condition which is reported to the medicolegal authority having jurisdiction where death was pronounced.

The medical examiner's role goes beyond the autopsy room, although the performance of an accurate autopsy remains central. To be most effective, medical examiners must work closely with law enforcement personnel and clinicians involved with each case. Once an opinion is rendered, they must communicate with the prosecuting attorney, as appropriate.

The cases shown in this chapter illustrate the types of injuries that fall into the jurisdiction of the medical examiner.

# Crime Scene Reconstruction

### Case Study 10-1

A potential crime scene reconstruction was used to explore the possibility of a reported injury mechanism. A 13-month-old child was being cared for at a home daycare center. On the day of the injuries, he was reportedly on the second floor playing with a family pet and was able to ambulate over to the stairwell, which had a railing and balusters that were fairly widely spaced. It was reported that he fell through the balusters while toddling around. The scene was visited, and the area of potential injury was looked at using a doll as a marker for what was alleged to have happened.

***Figure 10-1-a.*** *The stairwell with the railing surrounding it, descending from the second floor to the first floor.*

***Figure 10-1-b.*** *The stair balusters are separated by a distance of about 14 cm.*

***Figure 10-1-c.*** *The flight of stairs contains 13 steps; each step is 20 cm high and 13 cm long, producing a vertical drop of 2.6 m.*

***Figure 10-1-d.*** *An infant-sized doll lodged between the balusters demonstrates consistency with the history.*

***Figure 10-1-e.*** *A different orientation showing the doll potentially falling through the 2 stair balusters.*

Figure 10-1-a

Figure 10-1-b

Figure 10-1-c

Figure 10-1-d

Figure 10-1-e

## Crime Scene Reconstruction

**Case Study 10-1** *(continued)*

***Figure 10-1-f.*** *A demonstration of what was alleged to have occurred when the child fell through the balusters.*

***Figure 10-1-g.*** *A representation of the child as found at the base of the steps.*

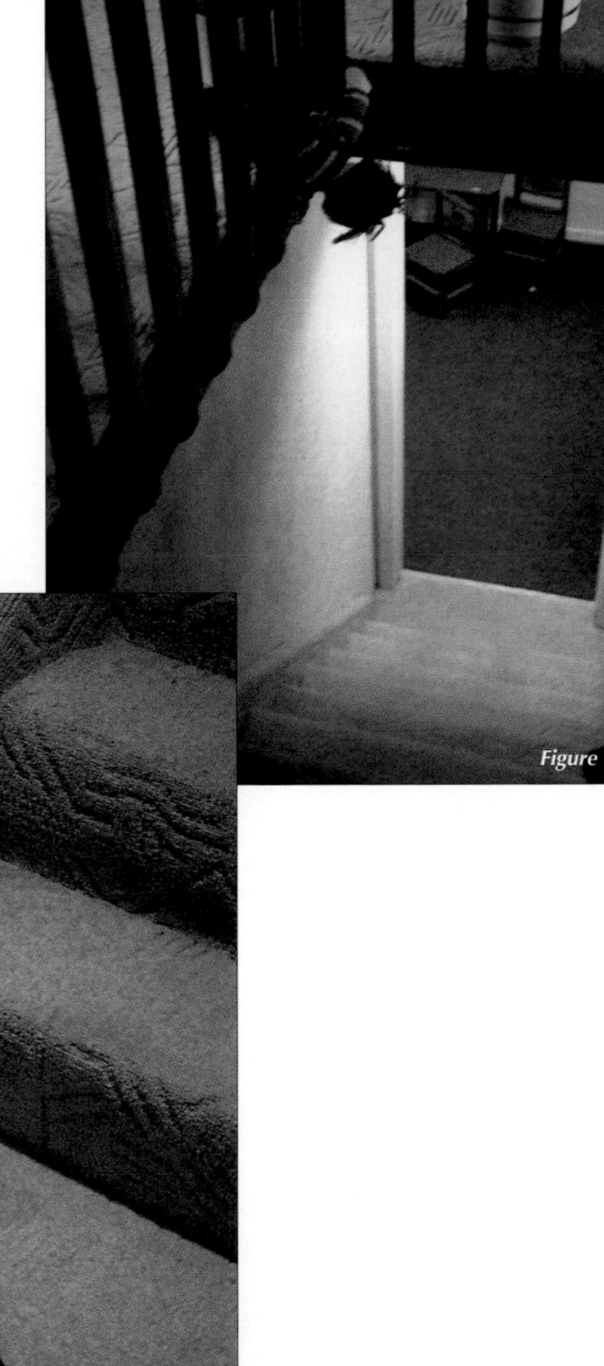

*Figure 10-1-f*

*Figure 10-1-g*

# Suspicious Injuries

## Penile Laceration

### Case Study 10-2

This 2-year-old boy was brought to the ER by his father with a complaint of a "cut on his penis." The boy was apparently well and went into the bathroom alone. He was heard crying out in pain, but came out of the bathroom in no apparent pain. He had soiled his pants, so his father went in the bathroom to clean him. While the father was cleaning the boy with baby wipes, he began to cry out in apparent pain. The father checked the boy's bottom and genital area and noticed a cut across the base of his penis. The father found no sharp objects and no blood in the bathroom. In the ER, the child appeared to be well. The findings of the genital examination were significant for a laceration at the base of the penis, extending along the dorsum of the penis from the left side and proceeding along the right lateral edge onto the ventral surface of the penis, down virtually to the midline. The injury was clinically estimated as a nearly 75% circumferential laceration with sharp edges throughout its entirety and a minuscule amount of tissue—less than 0.05 cm wide and 0.5 cm long—interposed between the two margins at one edge. The entire laceration was 4.5 cm long, and total penile circumference was 7.5 cm. The wound extended into the superficial subcutaneous tissue, but did not appear to lacerate any major nerves, vascular structures, or musculotendinous structures. The distal penis and the penile shaft appeared to have no traumatic injury, with no ecchymosis, abrasion, contusion, erythema, or edema. Immediately superolateral to the midline of the penile shaft on the mons pubis was a 0.1 x 1 cm contusion, indicating deep bleeding beneath the skin. The testes were descended bilaterally and did not appear tender. In the ER the laceration was sutured with a 6-0 suture, a p3 needle, and a locking running suture.

**Figure 10-2-a.** *Laceration at the base of the penis several days after the injury. Note the running suture line on this en face orientation.*

**Figure 10-2-b.** *Lateral view of the wound photographed from the child's left side. The beginning of the laceration margin can be seen.*

**Figure 10-2-c.** *Laceration from the child's right side. Note how the laceration crosses the midline and extends in a semicircular fashion down to the ventral surface of the penis.*

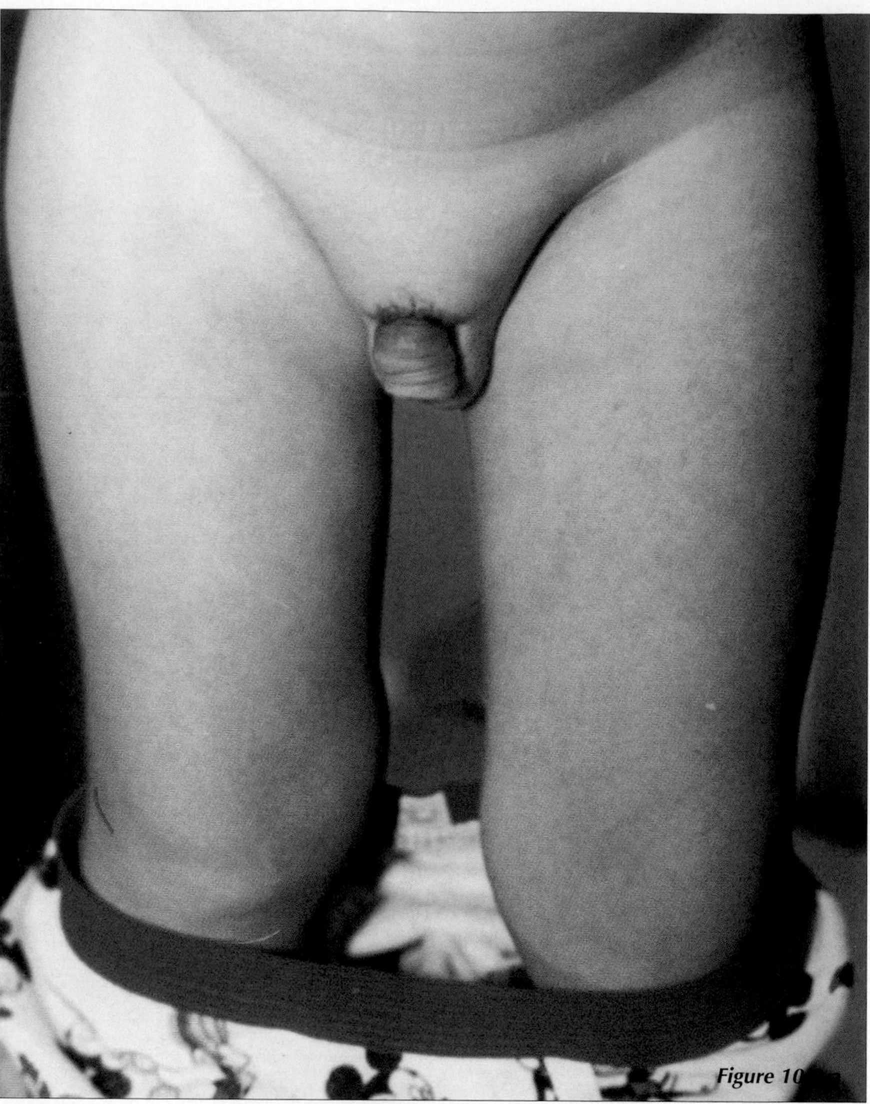

Figure 10-2-a

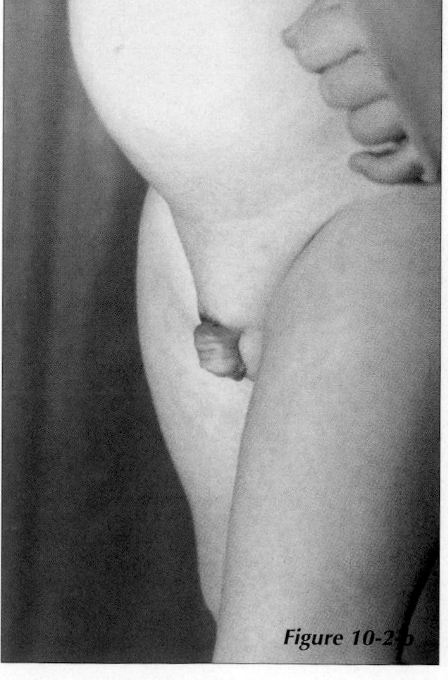

Figure 10-2-b

Figure 10-2-c

# Suspicious Injuries

## Penile Laceration

**Case Study 10-2** *(continued)*

***Figure 10-2-d.*** *Again in the en face orientation, photograph demonstrates the small contusion on the mons pubis, just superolateral to the base of the penis.*

***Figure 10-2-e.*** *Taken from the child's left side, photograph demonstrates the contusion right above the base of the penis on the mons pubis.*

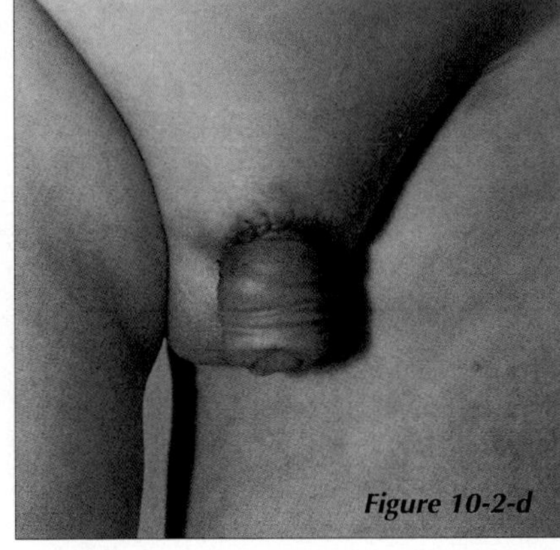

Figure 10-2-d

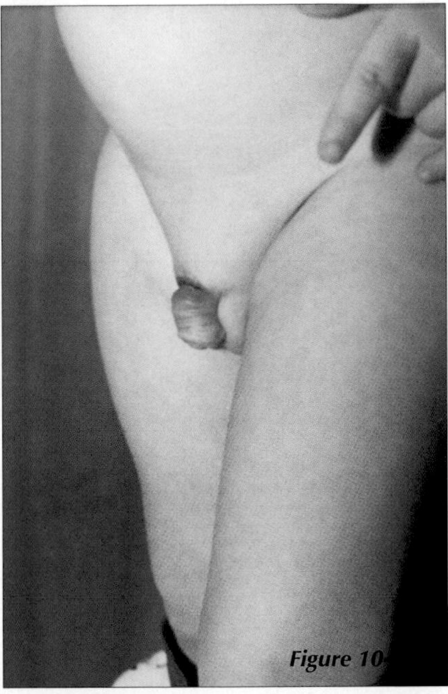

A crushing or biting type injury was excluded as a possibility because there were no injuries to internal structures. The laceration appeared very clean. It was thought that the most likely mechanism of the injury was forcible stretching of the penile skin; a rapid jerking motion essentially tore the skin at the base of the penis.

## Squeezing

**Case Study 10-3**

This 7-month-old boy was brought in for evaluation by his mother who was concerned that the father had squeezed the boy around his chest and thrown him against the wall. The boy's behavior was reported as normal, and he had been eating and sleeping normally. On examination, chest skin surfaces were intact, but both lateral chest walls had linear blue ecchymotic areas over the midlateral area measuring about 8 × 5 cm. No other bruises were noted. The boy's head had a flattened occiput, and the child was active and cooperative during the entire examination. There were some bluish, slate-colored discolorations over the boy's mid back that were determined to be Mongolian spots. The investigators concluded that the bilateral ecchymotic areas were caused by crushing-type injuries during forceable squeezing.

***Figure 10-3-a.*** *The right lateral chest wall with the ecchymosis in the mid axillary line.*

***Figure 10-3-b.*** *The right chest wall.*

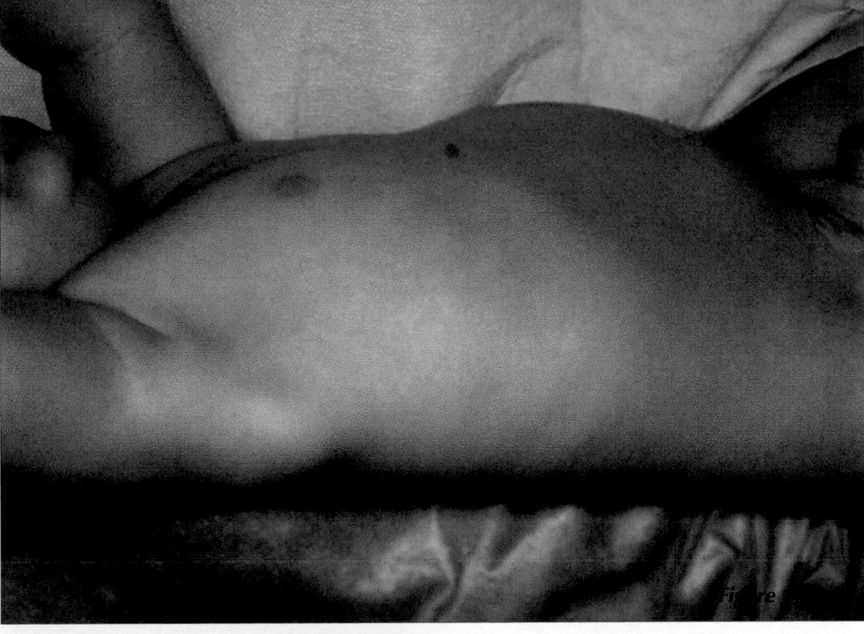

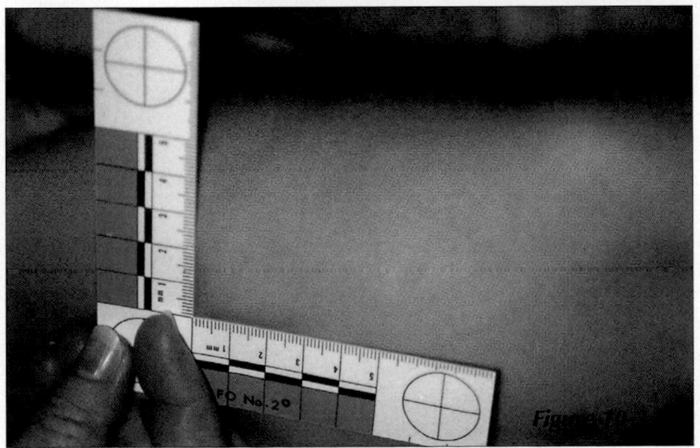

# Suspicious Injuries

## Squeezing

**Case Study 10-3** *(continued)*

***Figure 10-3-c.*** *The left lateral chest wall with the ecchymosis between the anterior and mid axillary lines.*

***Figure 10-3-d.*** *The left lateral chest wall.*

***Figure 10-3-e.*** *The boy's back with the bluish, slate-colored markings in the middle area.*

***Figure 10-3-f.*** *A similar view of the boy's back with the scale in the picture.*

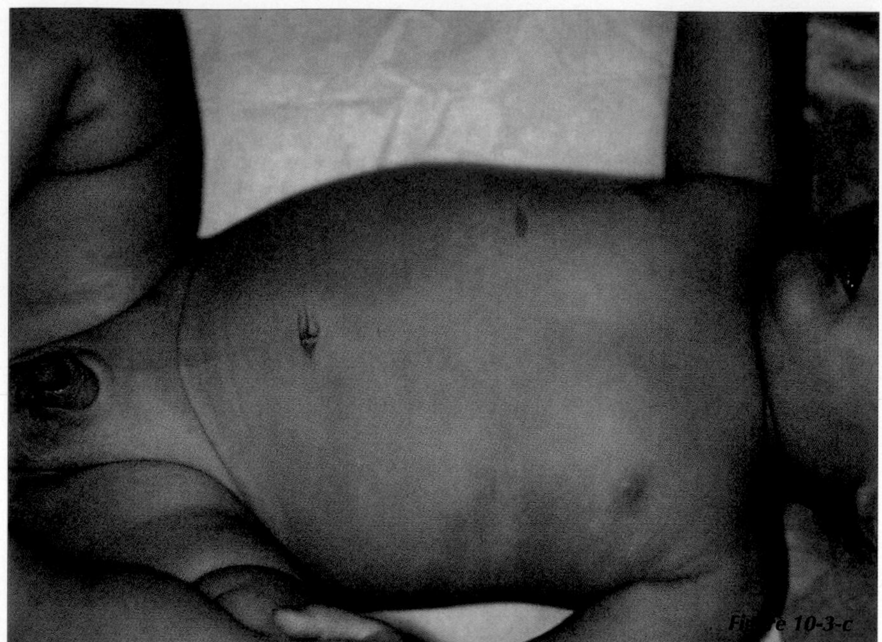

Figure 10-3-c

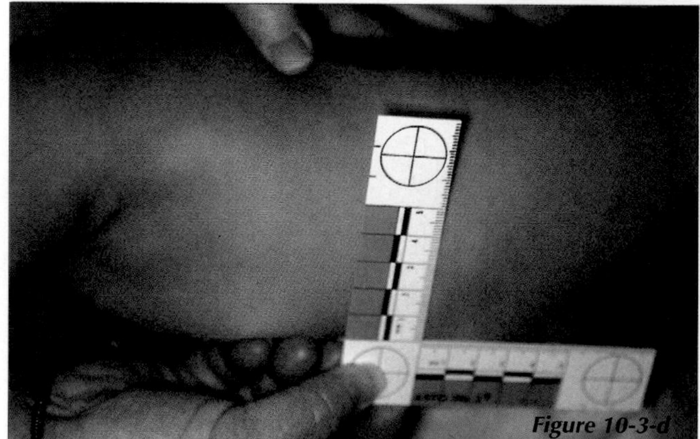

Figure 10-3-d

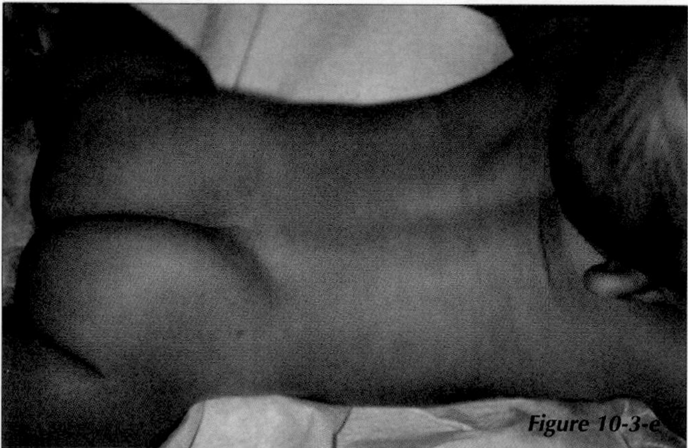

Figure 10-3-e

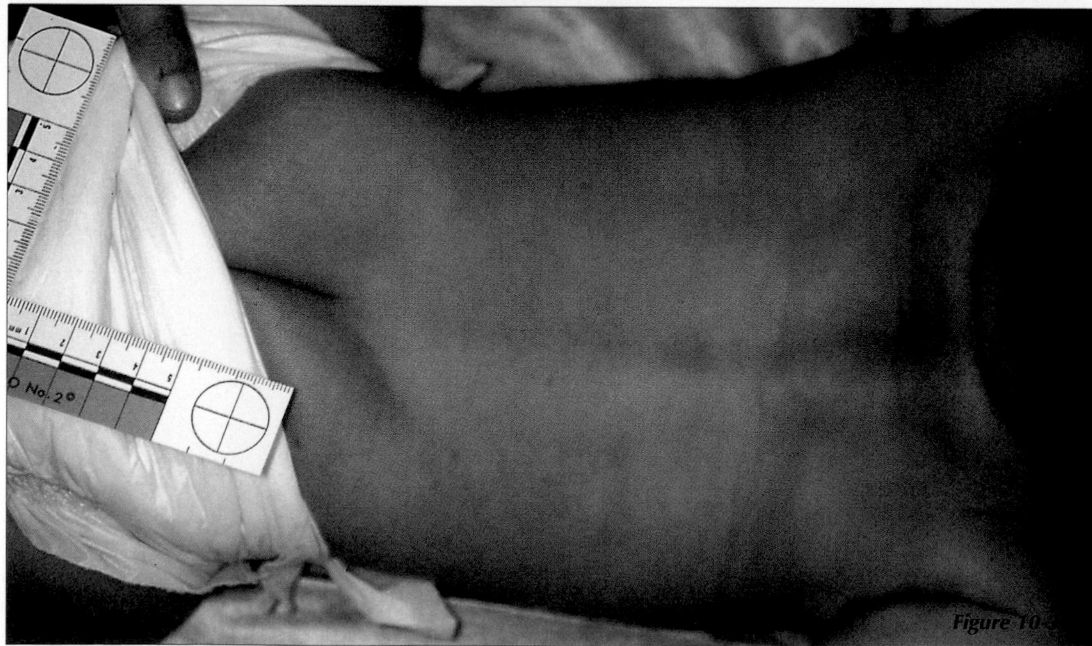

Figure 10-3-f

# Suspicious Injuries

## Nonabusive Skin Lesions

### Case Study 10-4

This 2½-year-old boy was brought in by his new foster parent for assessment of various skin lesions. His foster mother was particularly concerned about the number of scratches primarily over the bony prominences of the boy's extremities, and she noted pigmentated marks on the child's back. The history revealed that the skin lesions were primarily on the child's bony prominences. The marks on the child's back were described as unchanging, bluish-colored marks that extended from the lower back, right above the buttock, up to the scapula. The child was cooperative for the examination. There were various well-healed scratches and scars on the boy's bony prominences, notably the knees and shins. On examination of the back, bluish slate-colored macules were found from the mid back down to the buttocks. These macules were uniformly bluish slate-colored; no green, yellow, or brown discoloration was present. The skin findings on the bony prominences were believed consistent with normal childhood bumps and scrapes. There were no similar findings in more protected areas, such as the axilla or inner thigh, and the bluish slate-colored macules on the boy's back were believed to be Mongolian spots. Several lesions were photographed in black and white as well as through an ultraviolet filter. The ultraviolet light filter accentuated the scratches and well-healed scars on the skin surface and made the Mongolian spots seem to disappear.

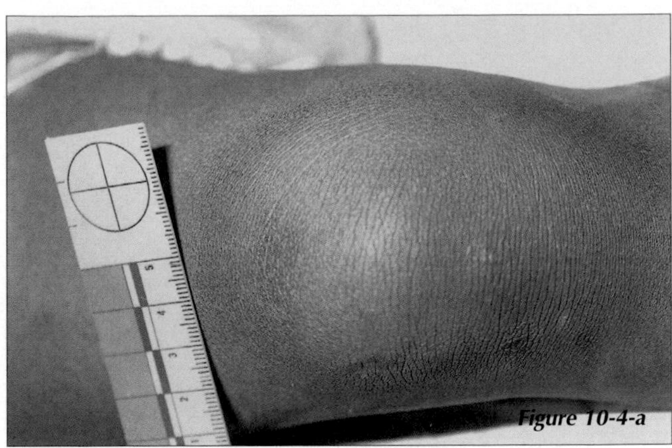
Figure 10-4-a

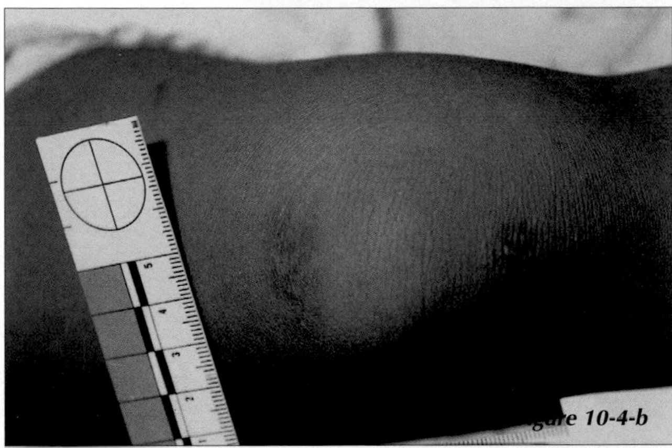
Figure 10-4-b

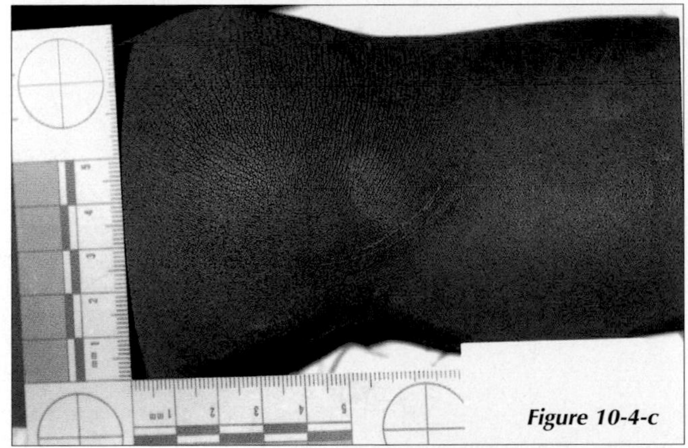
Figure 10-4-c

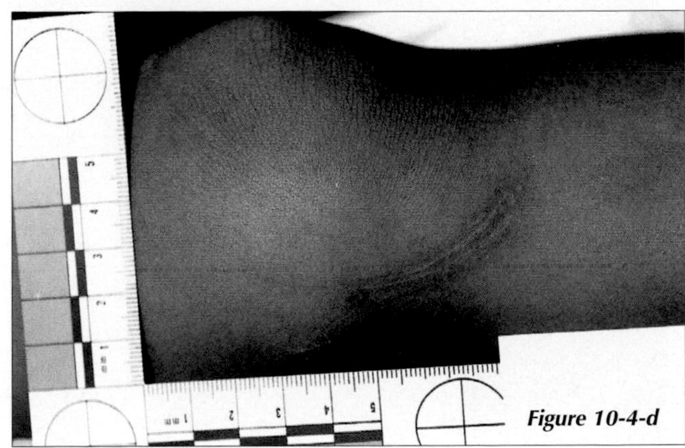
Figure 10-4-d

***Figure 10-4-a.*** *Black-and-white photograph of the boy's knee showing several well-healed abrasions on the bony prominences.*

***Figure 10-4-b.*** *Photograph of the knee under ultraviolet light with accentuation of the well-healed abrasions over the mid-patella and at the distal thigh right above the patella.*

***Figure 10-4-c.*** *Lateral aspect of the boy's knee demonstrating a set of curvilinear scratches.*

***Figure 10-4-d.*** *Photograph taken with an ultraviolet light filter, which accentuates the margins of the curvilinear scratches on the lateral aspects of the knee.*

# Suspicious Injuries

## Nonabusive Skin Lesions

**Case Study 10-4** *(continued)*

***Figure 10-4-e***. *Pretibial area. The skin appears to be dry with several well-healed abrasions on the anterior surface of the shins.*

***Figure 10-4-f.*** *This photograph of the tibial area taken with an ultraviolet light filter shows an accentuation of various abrasions of the child's shin.*

***Figure 10-4-g*** *and* ***h.*** *A series of irregularly shaped bluish slate-colored macules on the child's mid back.*

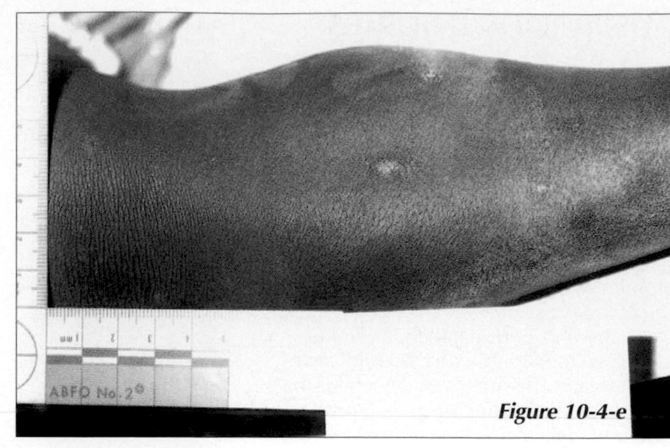


**Figure 10-4-e**

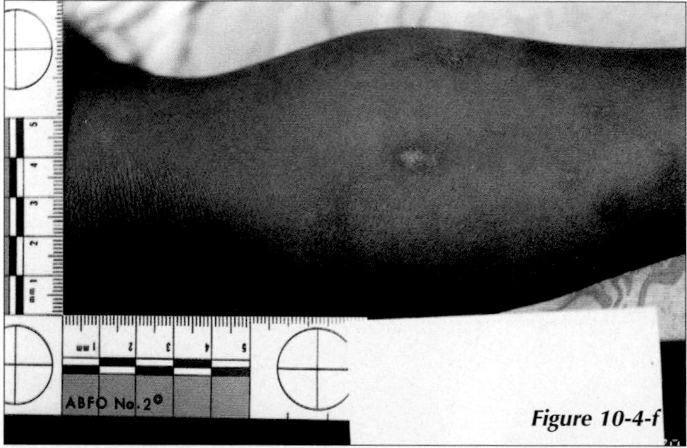


**Figure 10-4-f**

**Figure 10-4-g**

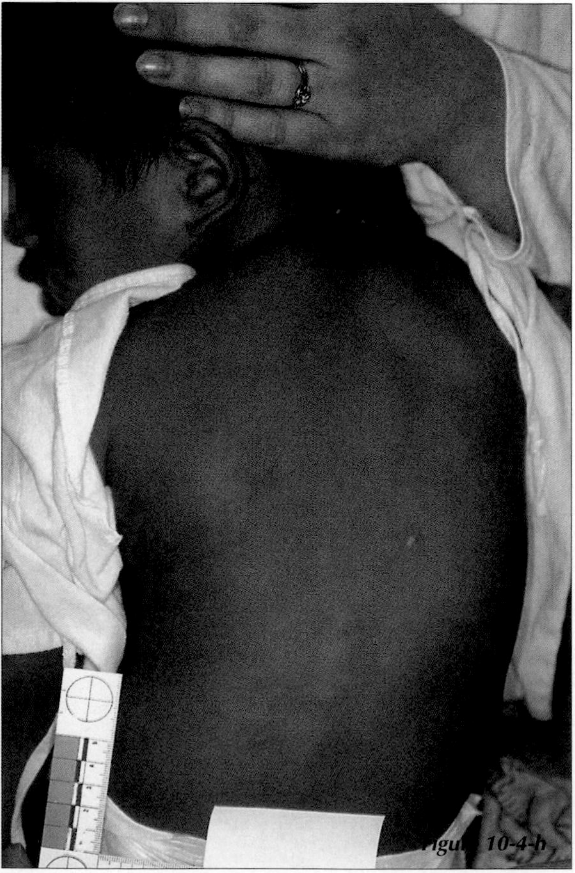

**Figure 10-4-h**

# Suspicious Injuries

## Nonabusive Skin Lesions

**Case Study 10-4** *(continued)*

***Figure 10-4-i.*** *Irregularly shaped macules of the mid back and buttocks.*

***Figure 10-4-j.*** *Black-and-white photograph taken with an ultraviolet light filter illustrates how the macules seem to disappear, supporting the diagnosis of Mongolian spots.*

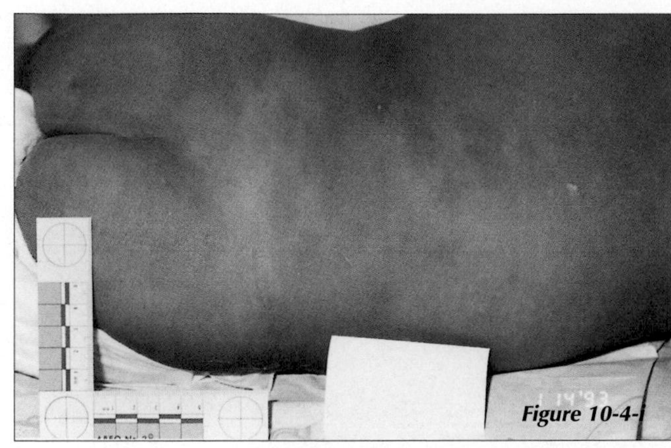
Figure 10-4-i

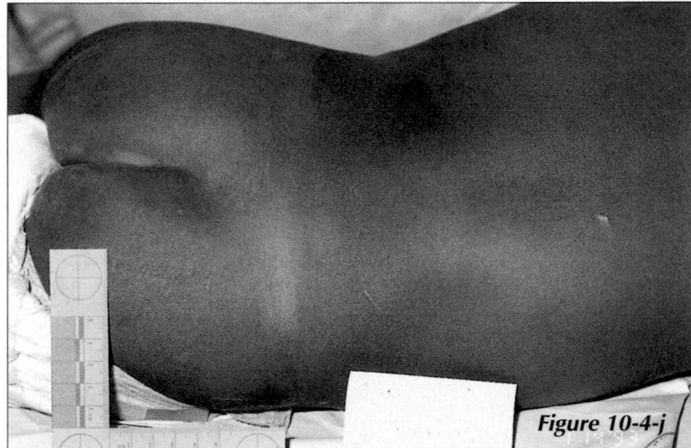
Figure 10-4-j

## Skin Discoloration

**Case Study 10-5**

This 4-year-old girl was brought in by her foster mother for evaluation after she became concerned about some discolorations over the girl's back, which consisted of several circular and ovoid bluish discolorations extending from the mid back down to the sacrum. The child also had some scratches on her back, purportedly from rough play. The child was cooperative during the examination, and the circular and oval bluish discolorations on the back were determined to be Mongolian spots. Additionally, the scratches were evaluated and were believed to be consistent with normal childhood activity. The back was photographed using black-and-white photography and separately with an ultraviolet light filter. The scratches, thought to be fingernail scratches, were accentuated by the ultraviolet light filter. The discolorations believed to be Mongolian spots essentially disappeared.

***Figure 10-5-a.*** *Bluish slate-colored oval and circular macules extending from the mid back down to the sacrum.*

***Figure 10-5-b.*** *The child's back with a measuring device. Notice possible fingernail scratches on the child's left upper back and right mid back on the right side. Mongolian spots are evident; the macule on the lumbar and sacral region is the most prominent.*

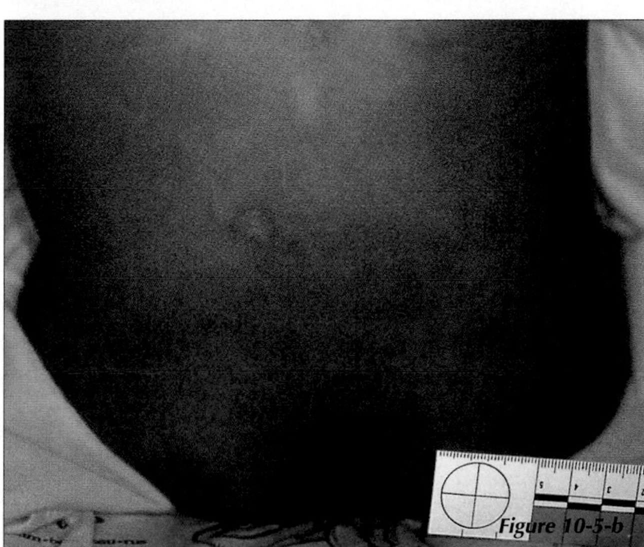
Figure 10-5-b

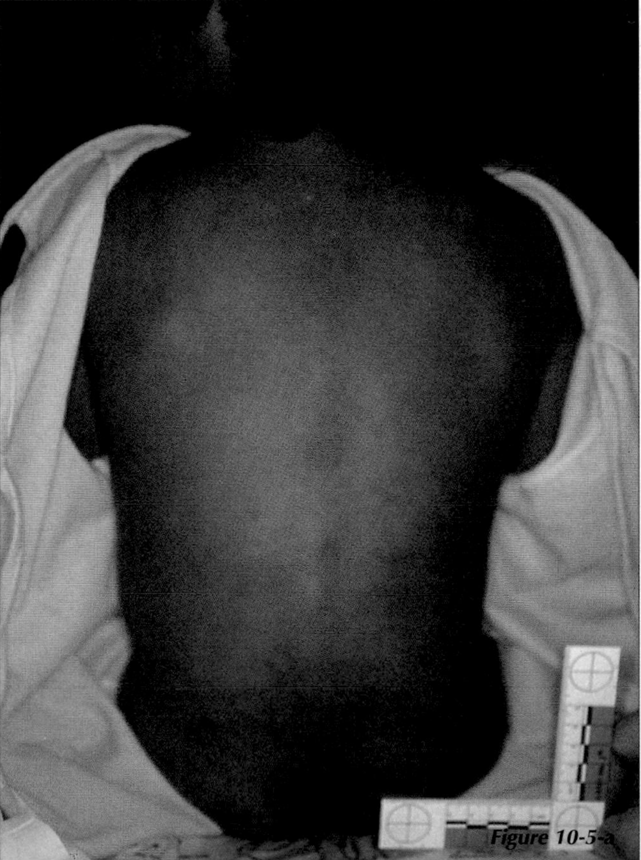
Figure 10-5-a

# Suspicious Injuries

## Skin Discoloration

**Case Study 10-5** *(continued)*

***Figures 10-5-c** and **d.** With the ultraviolet light filter, the scratches in the left upper back and mid back area become accentuated and the discolorations believed to be Mongolian spots essentially disappear.*

***Figure 10-5-e.** A close-up photograph of the child's upper back in black and white.*

***Figure 10-5-f.** The same area of the child's upper back under the ultraviolet light, which demonstrates how scratches can be accentuated using this method of photography.*

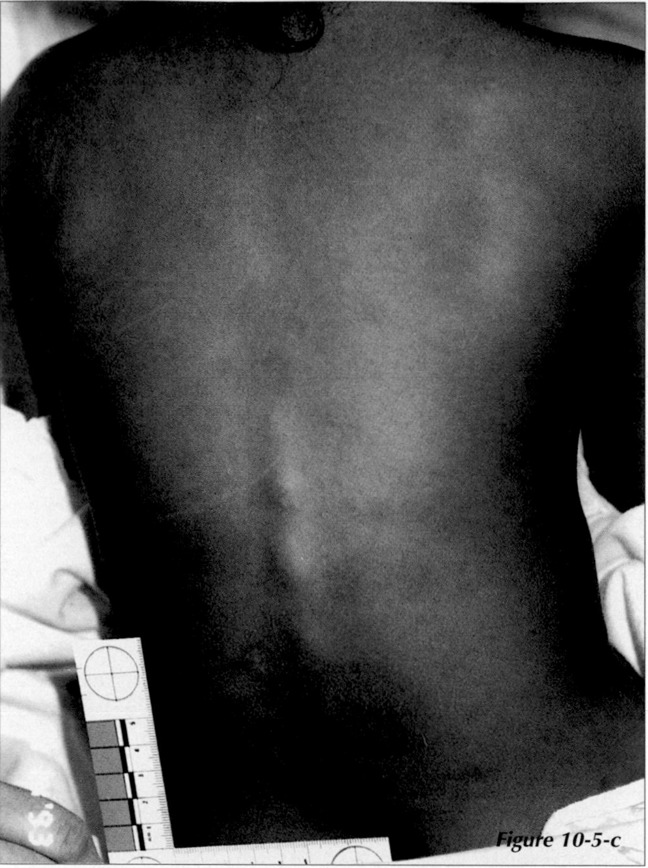

**Figure 10-5-c**

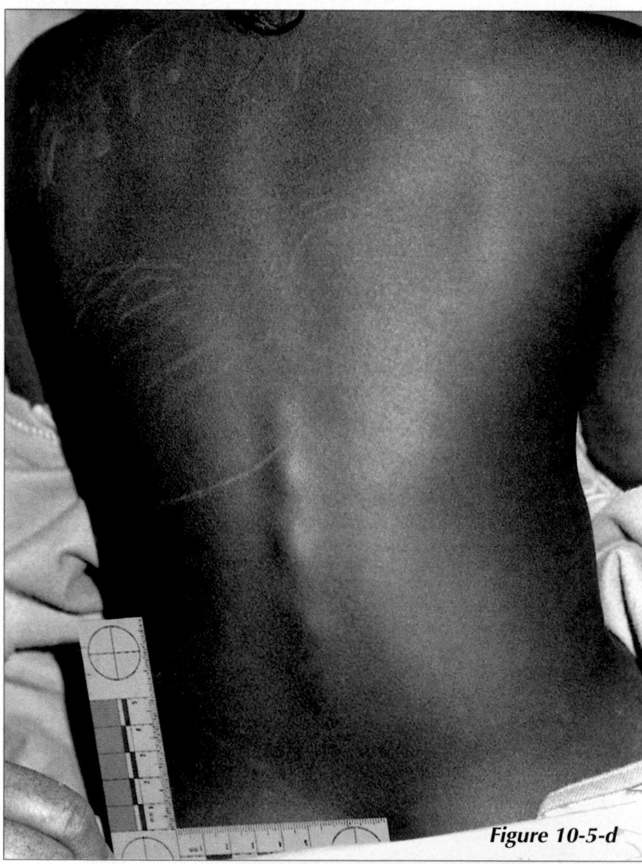

**Figure 10-5-d**

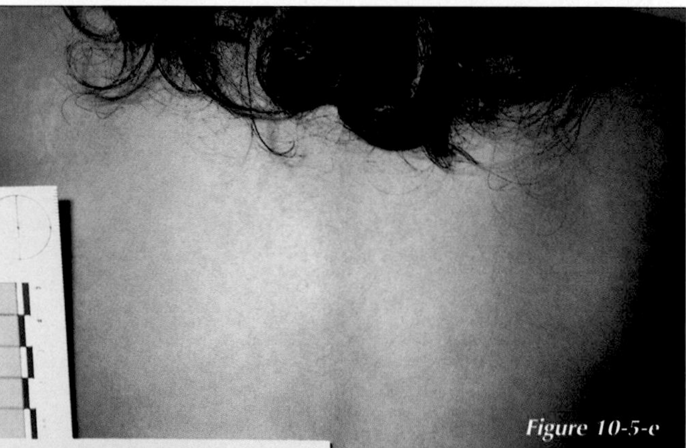

**Figure 10-5-e**

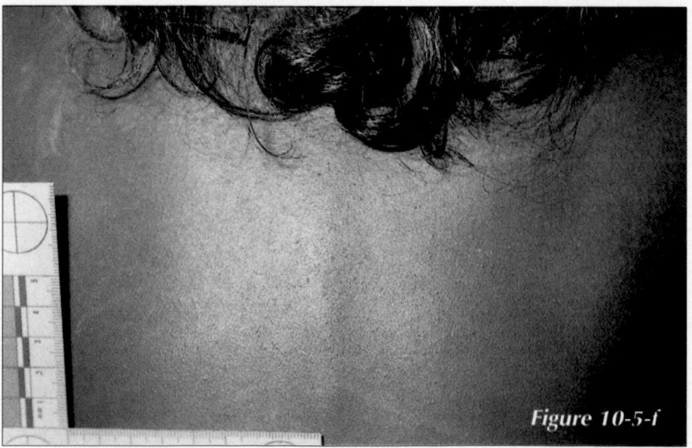

**Figure 10-5-f**

# Suspicious Injuries

## Bite Marks

### Case Study 10-6

This 2-year-old boy was taken in for evaluation after lesions suspicious for bite marks were noted on his face, abdomen, arms, and buttocks. On evaluation, he weighed 13 kg, placing him at about the 70th percentile for weight; he was 82.5 cm tall, or about the fifth percentile for his height. He had not gained weight in about 4 months. His immunizations were current, and he was cooperative for the examination. His skin examination revealed at least 19 paired arc-shaped irregular abrasions and bruises, interpreted as bite marks that were adult in character, owing to the measurement between the canine teeth. A diagram of the bite marks was drawn, and color photographs were obtained. An investigation ensued to determine who had harmed the child.

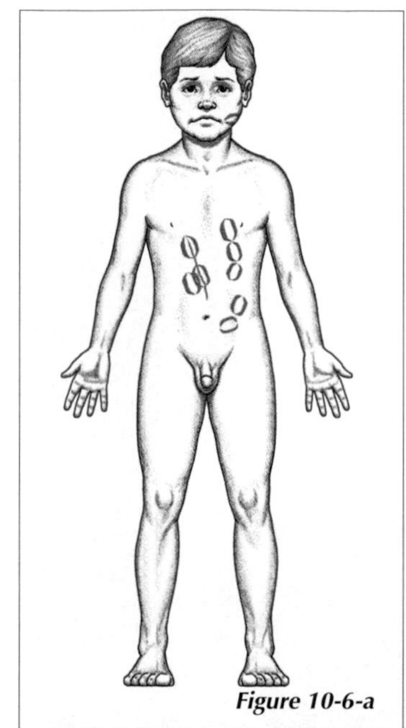

Figure 10-6-a

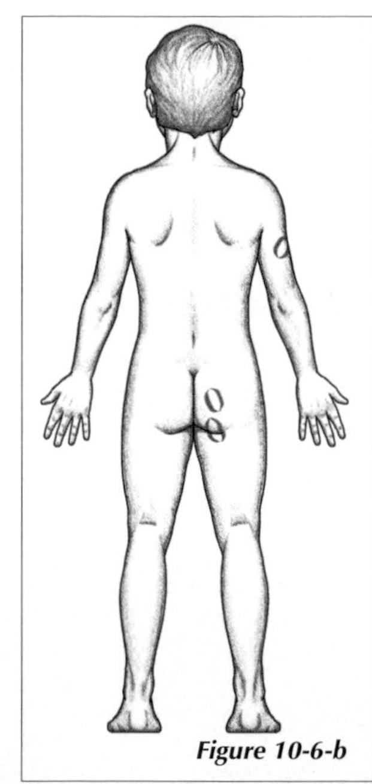

Figure 10-6-b

***Figures 10-6-a** and **b**. Diagram showing the location of the bite marks. All bite injuries appear to be of a similar character and age, judging by the coloration.*

***Figure 10-6-c.** The child's abdomen had multiple bite marks with a linear abrasion on the right side.*

***Figure 10-6-d.** Bites to the abdomen.*

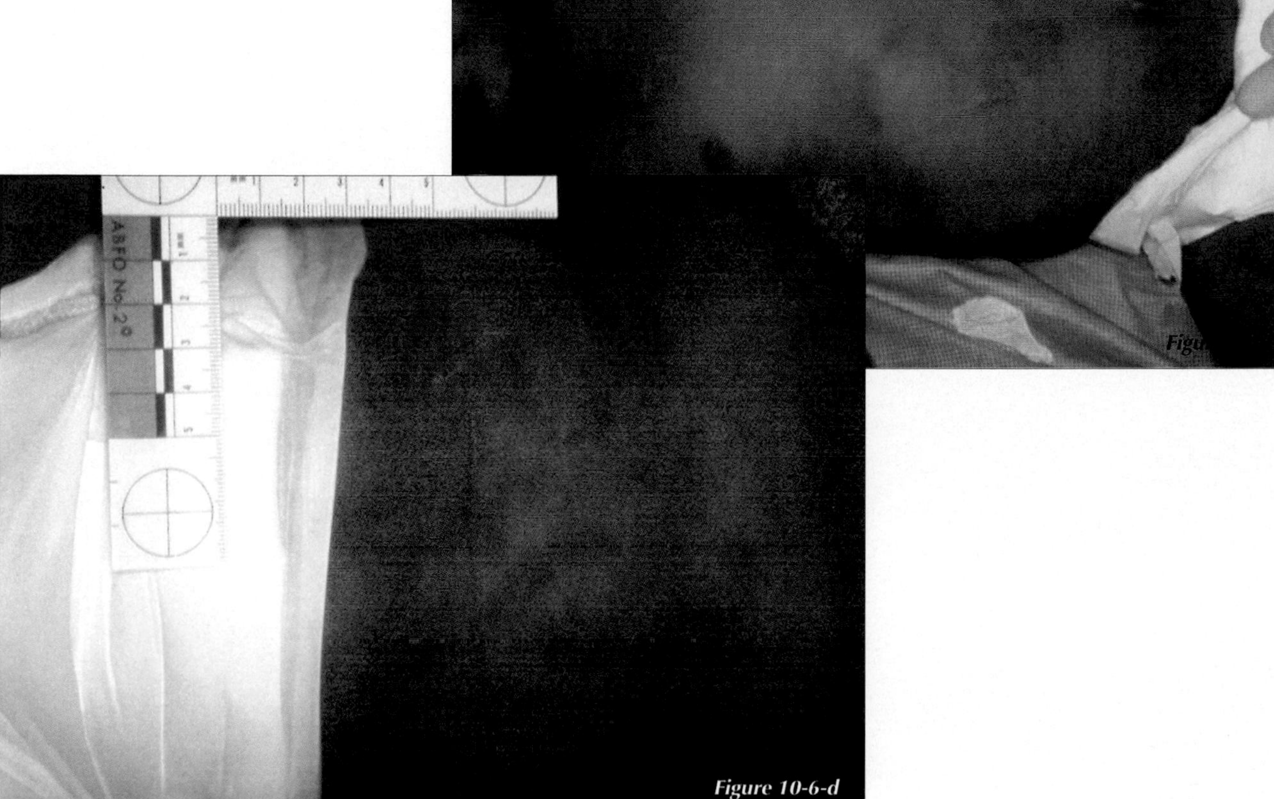


Figure 10-6-d

# Suspicious Injuries

## Bite Marks

**Case Study 10-6** *(continued)*

***Figure 10-6-e.*** *Close-up of a bite mark that also shows a linear abrasion, along with the measuring device.*

***Figure 10-6-f.*** *Several other bite marks on the abdomen.*

***Figure 10-6-g.*** *Bite marks on the child's lower back.*

***Figure 10-6-h.*** *The child's left upper arm, with curved bruises consistent with bite marks.*

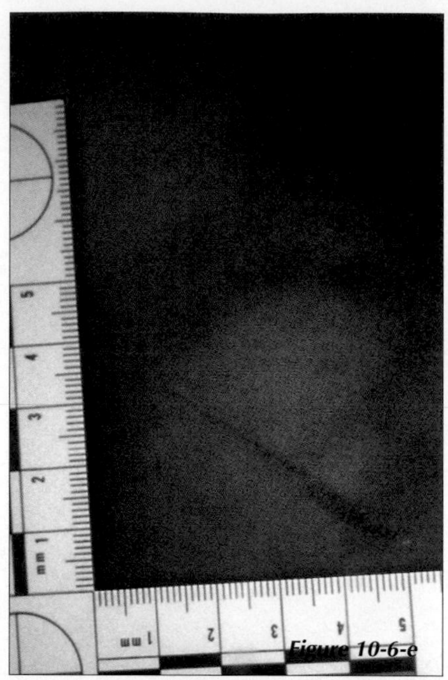

Figure 10-6-e

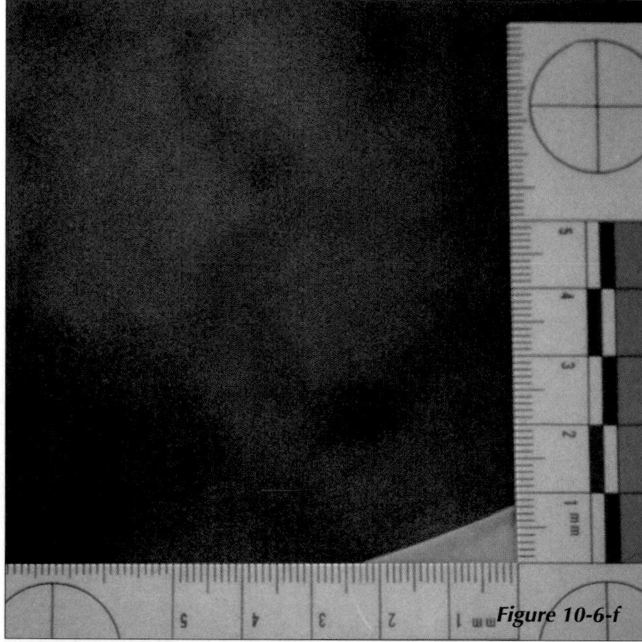

Figure 10-6-f

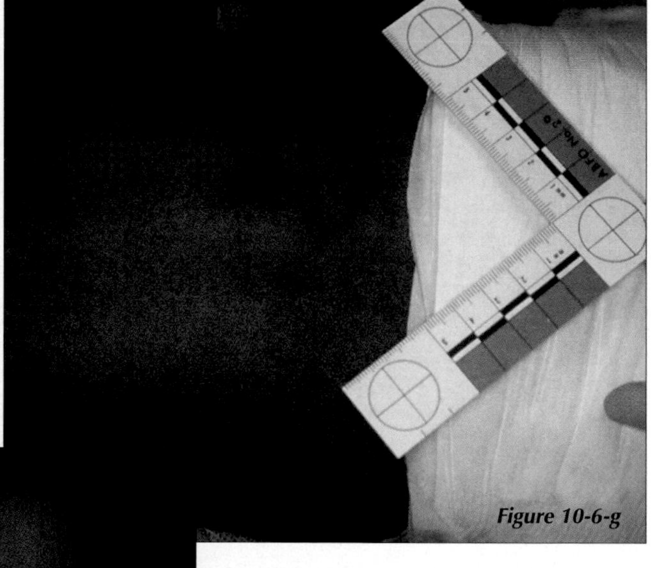

Figure 10-6-g

Figure 10-6-h

# Suspicious Injuries

## Bite Marks

**Case Study 10-6** *(continued)*

***Figure 10-6-i.*** *Close-up photograph of the bite marks on the child's upper arm.*

***Figure 10-6-j.*** *The bite mark on the child's thigh.*

***Figure 10-6-k.*** *The child's buttocks.*

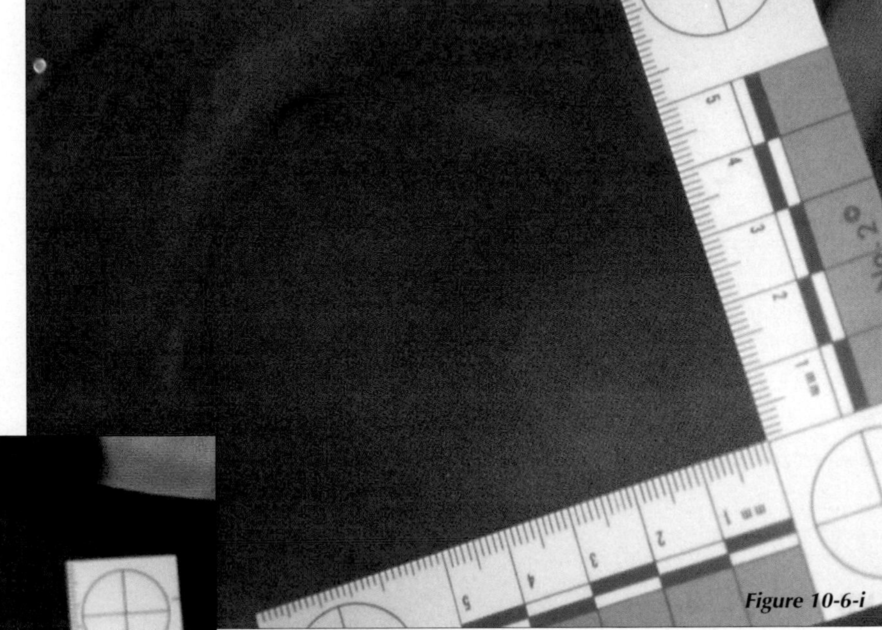

Figure 10-6-i

Figure 10-6-j

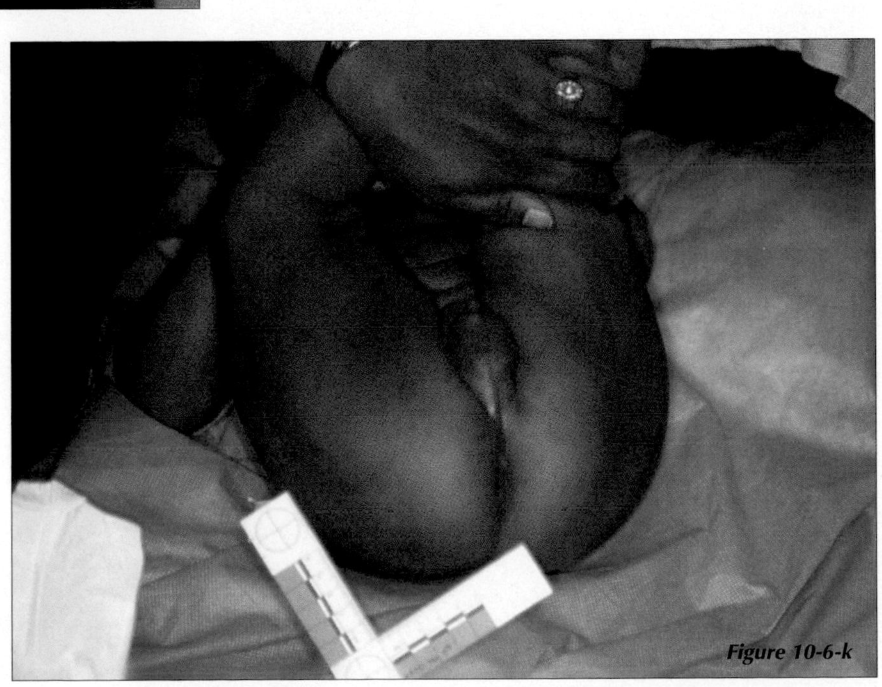

Figure 10-6-k

# Suspicious Injuries

## Evidence of Ongoing Maltreatment

### Case Study 10-7

This 4-year-old boy sustained central nervous system injuries and had several bone fractures. There were also a number of cutaneous findings. Looking at the various injuries and providing ranges for when these injuries would have been sustained suggested that the child was subjected to an extended pattern of maltreatment.

*Figure 10-7-a. Note the approximately 1-cm crusted abrasion at the hairline.*

*Figure 10-7-b. A bruise at the hairline.*

*Figure 10-7-c. The child in the right lateral decubitus position with a number of quarter- to half-dollar–sized brownish bruises.*

*Figure 10-7-d. With the child in the left lateral decubitus position, brownish bruises are seen over his buttocks bilaterally.*

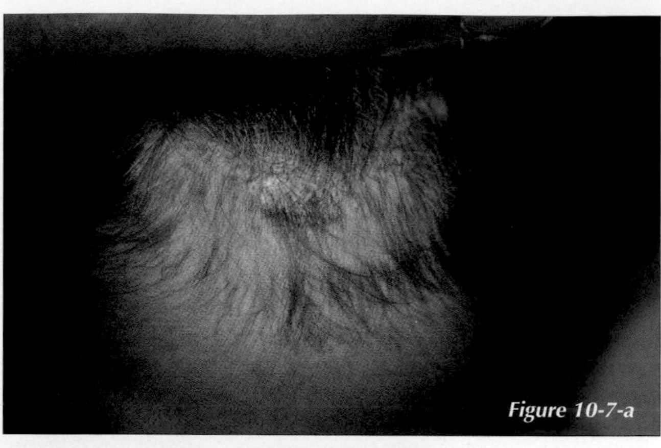


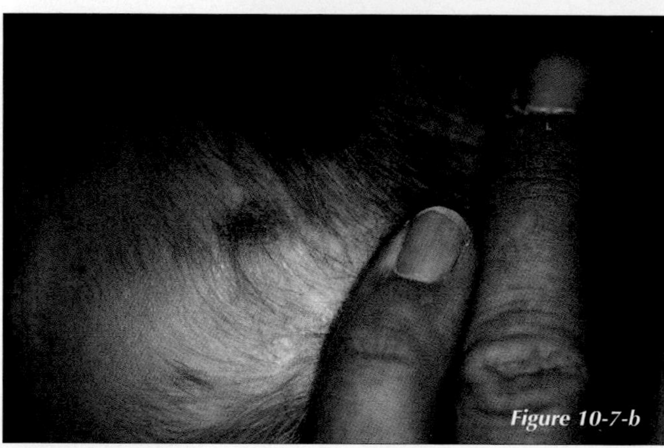


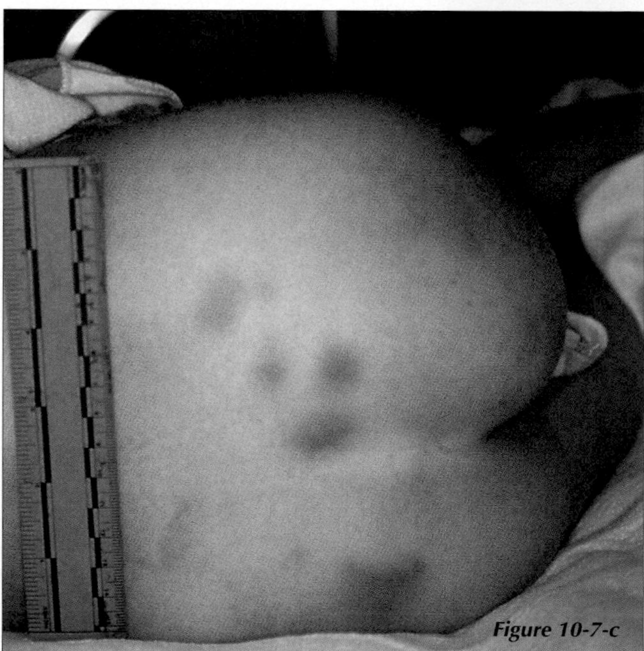


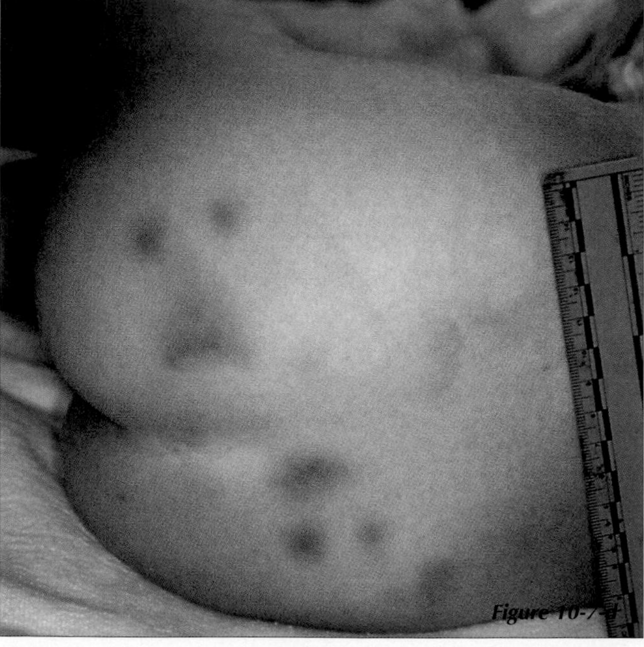

# Suspicious Injuries

## Evidence of Ongoing Maltreatment

**Case Study 10-7** *(continued)*

***Figure 10-7-e.*** *An approximately 5 x 4 cm yellow-green bruise over the child's sternum extending to the nipple line.*

***Figure 10-7-f.*** *The yellow-green lesion on the child's sternum.*

***Figure 10-7-g.*** *The child's left anterior thigh has a yellow-violet bruise, about 2½ cm in diameter.*

***Figure 10-7-h.*** *A lesion on the right thigh.*

Fig… 0-7-f

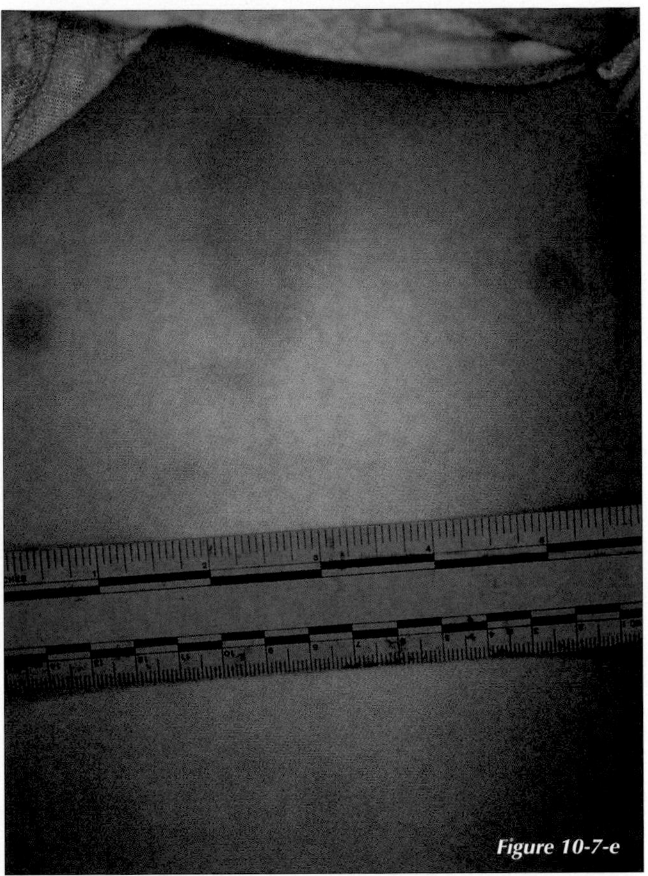

Figure 10-7-e

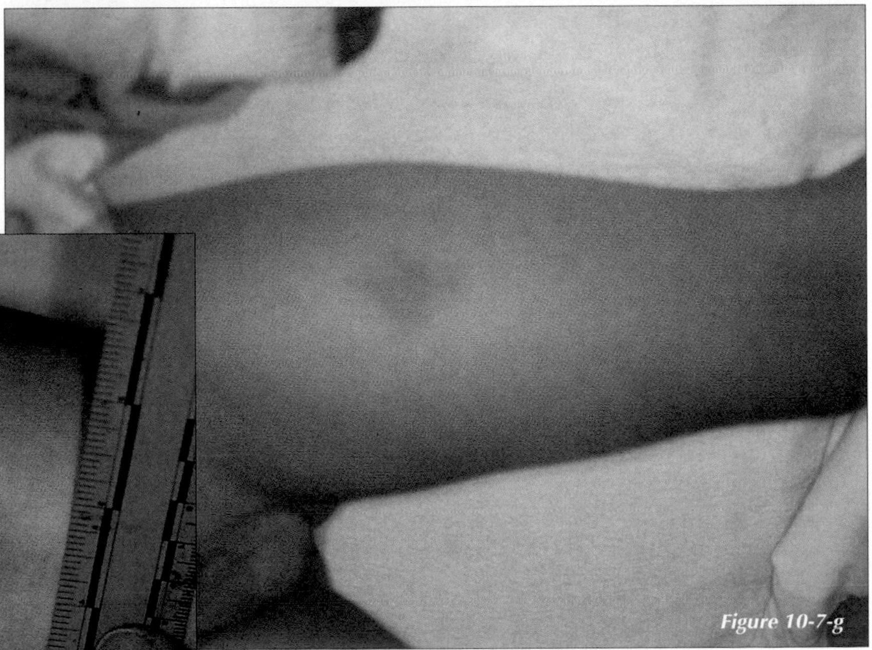

Figure 10-7-g

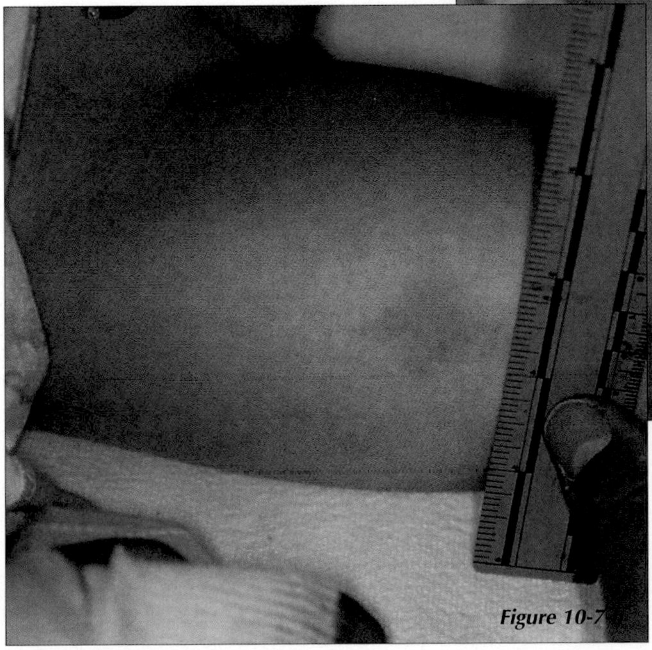

Figure 10-7

# Suspicious Injuries

## Evidence of Ongoing Maltreatment

**Case Study 10-7** *(continued)*

***Figure 10-7-i.*** *Close-up photograph of the lesion on the child's left thigh.*

***Figure 10-7-j.*** *Child's right knee with a tender dusky violet bruise.*

***Figure 10-7-k.*** *Close-up view of the right knee.*

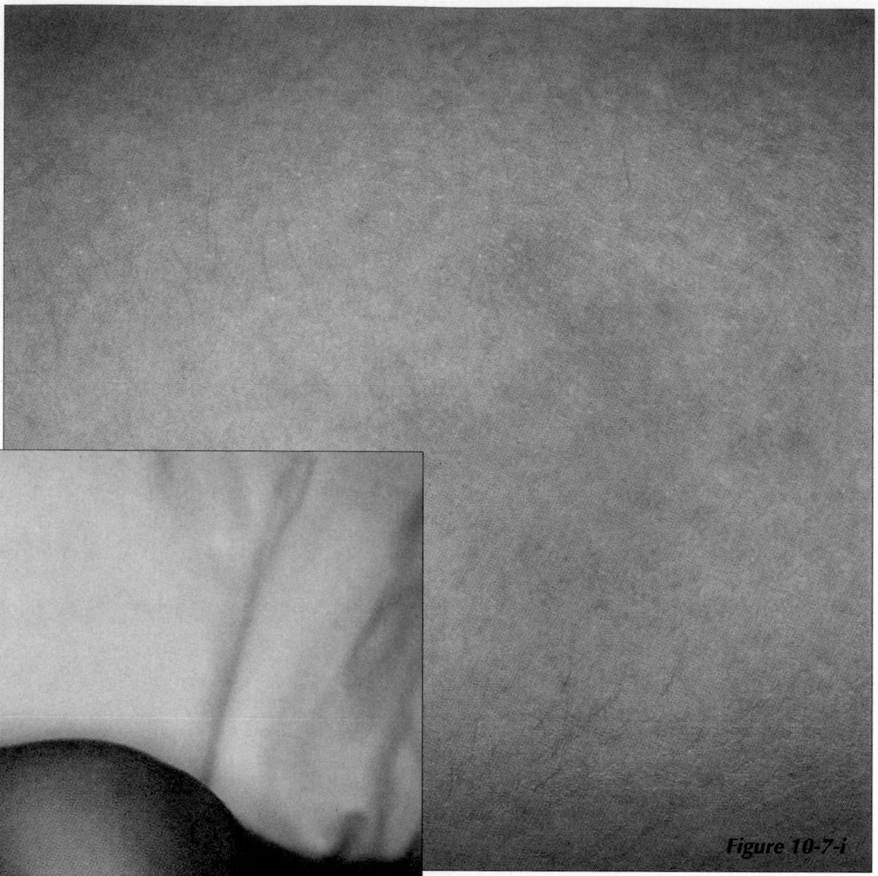

Figure 10-7-i

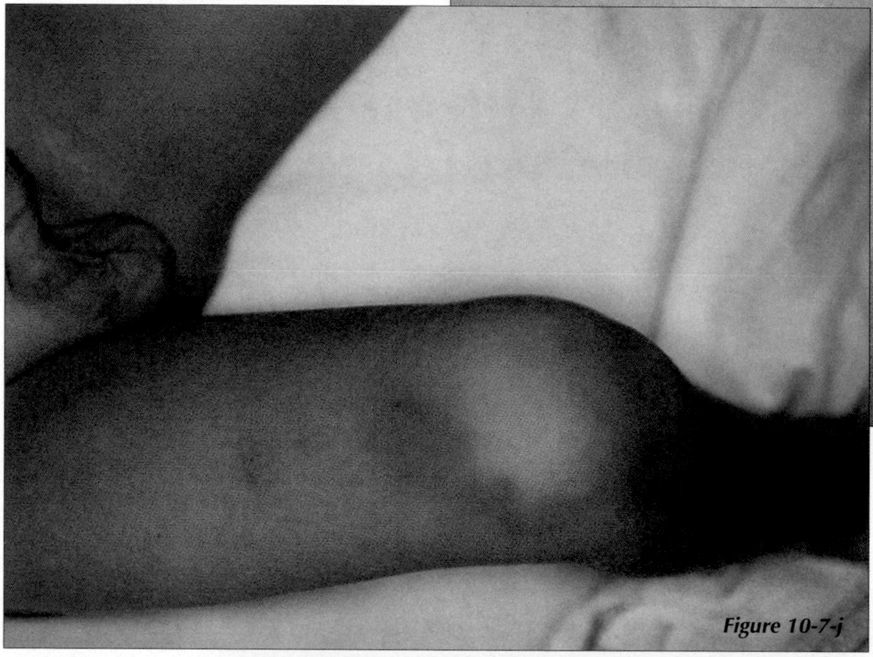

Figure 10-7-j

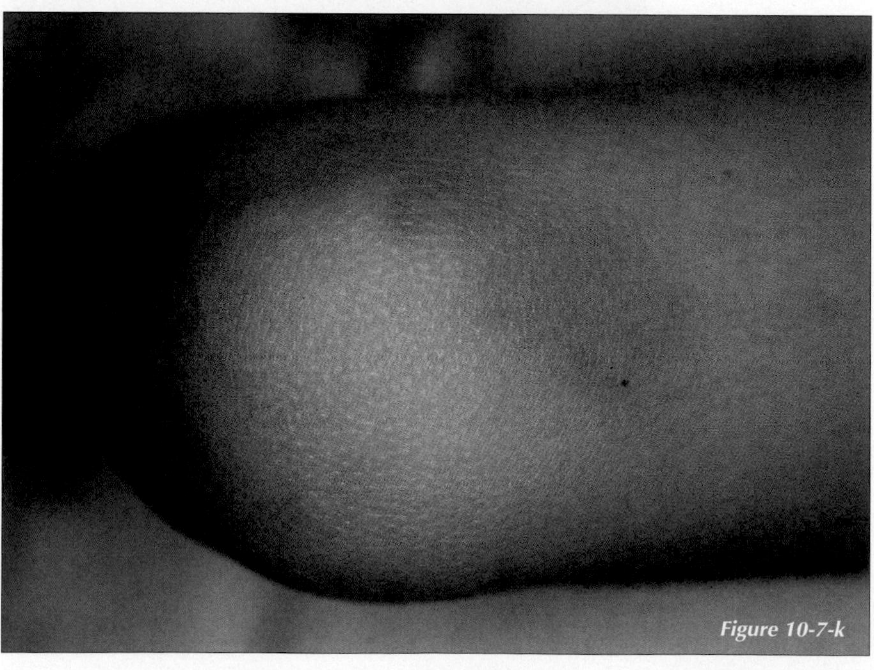

Figure 10-7-k

# Suspicious Injuries

## Evidence of Ongoing Maltreatment

**Case Study 10-7** *(continued)*

***Figure 10-7-l.*** *Closer view of the bruise over the child's right knee.*

***Figure 10-7-m.*** *The child's right hand has a violet contusion over the dorsum, just below the fingers.*

***Figure 10-7-n.*** *Several violet linear bruises over the right forearm dorsal surface, each 2-3 cm apart.*

***Figure 10-7-l***

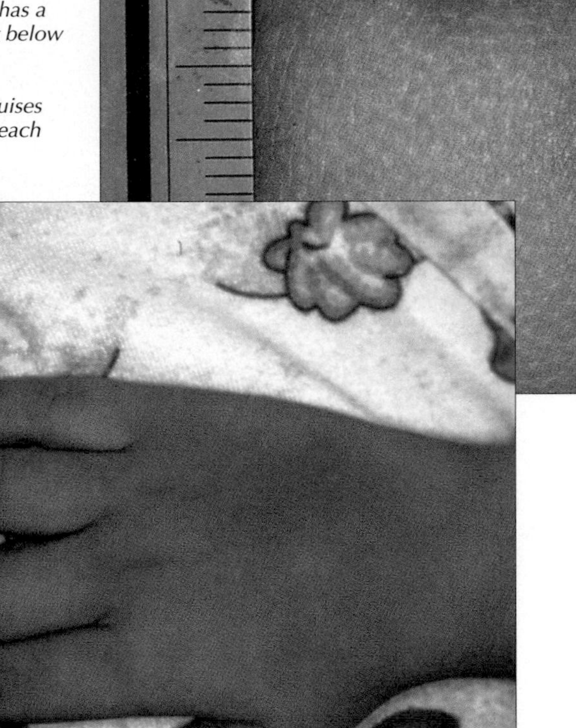

***Figure 10-7-m***

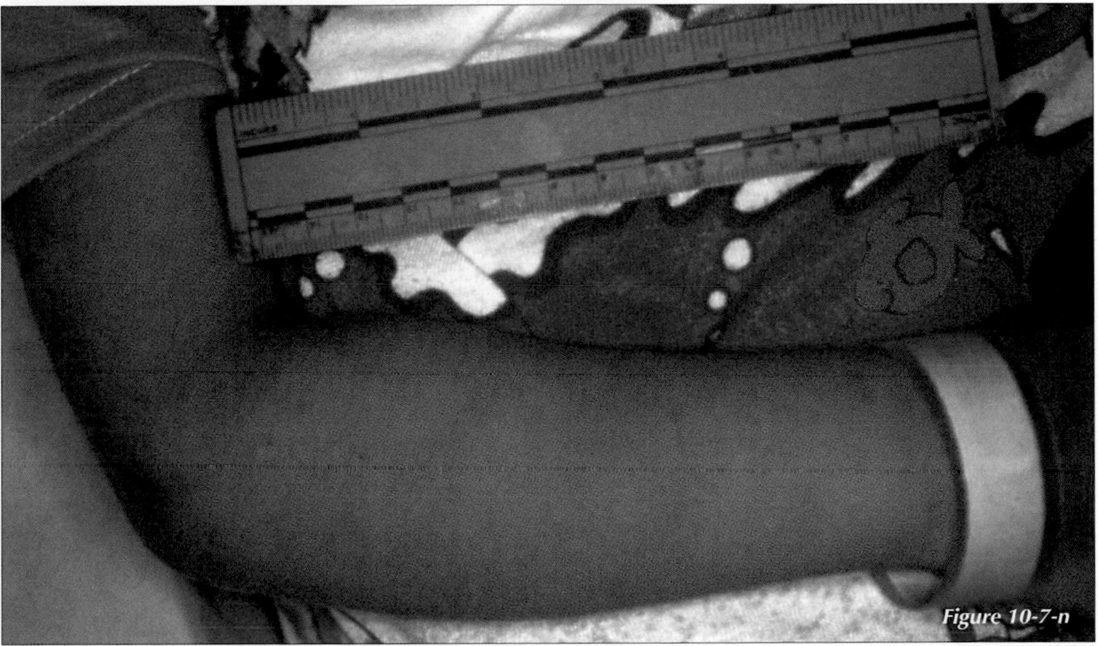

***Figure 10-7-n***

# Suspicious Injuries

## Multiple Fractures

### Case Study 10-8

This 7-month-old girl was found to have 3 fractures. According to the history given, the child was healthy and playful the morning she was dropped off at her babysitter's. However, throughout the day at the babysitter's house, the girl was uncharacteristically irritable. When left alone to play on the floor, she would be quiet but would cry if she was picked up and handled for feeding. She drifted off to sleep but woke tearful. At some point, the babysitter called the mother at work and asked her to come pick up the child because something was not right with her. At the ER, radiographs were obtained, showing a left clavicular fracture and greenstick fractures of the left radius and ulna. Additionally, a left radial head subluxation was found and manually reduced. There was no injury reported by the babysitter. The mother recalled that 2 days earlier the child fell out of a bed 2 feet above a carpeted surface. The child's medical history was notable for a left clavicular fracture at birth. The injuries were suspicious since there was no history that could explain the fractures.

***Figure 10-8-a.*** *Radiograph demonstrating a left clavicular fracture.*

***Figure 10-8-b.*** *Radiograph demonstrating a midshaft greenstick fracture on the child's left radius and ulna.*

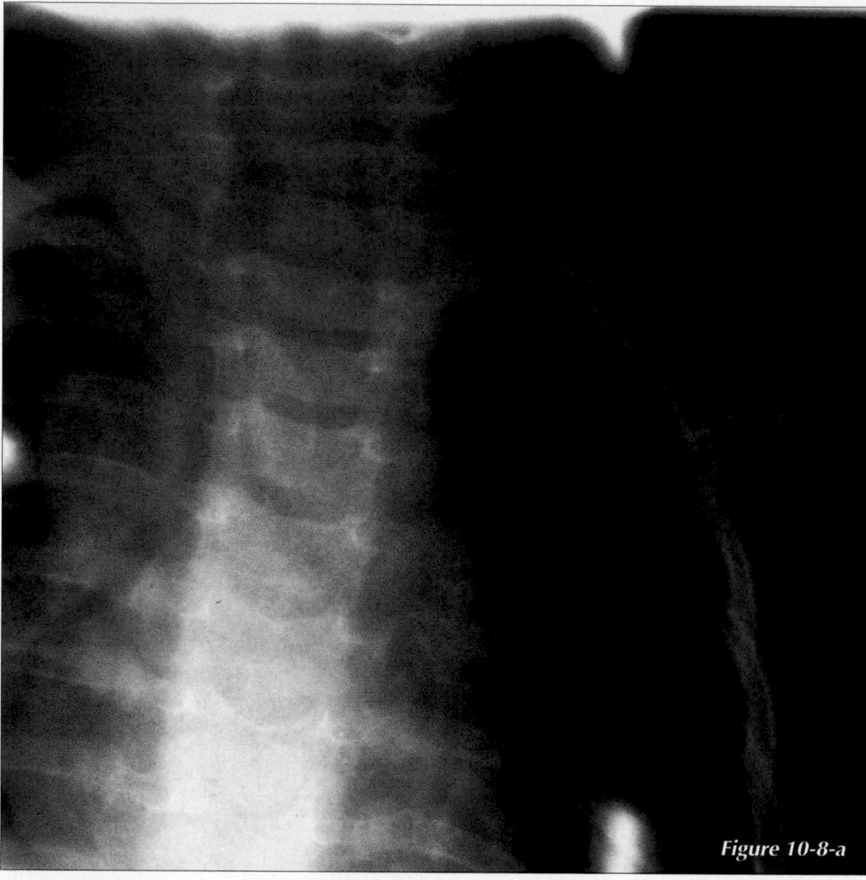

Figure 10-8-a

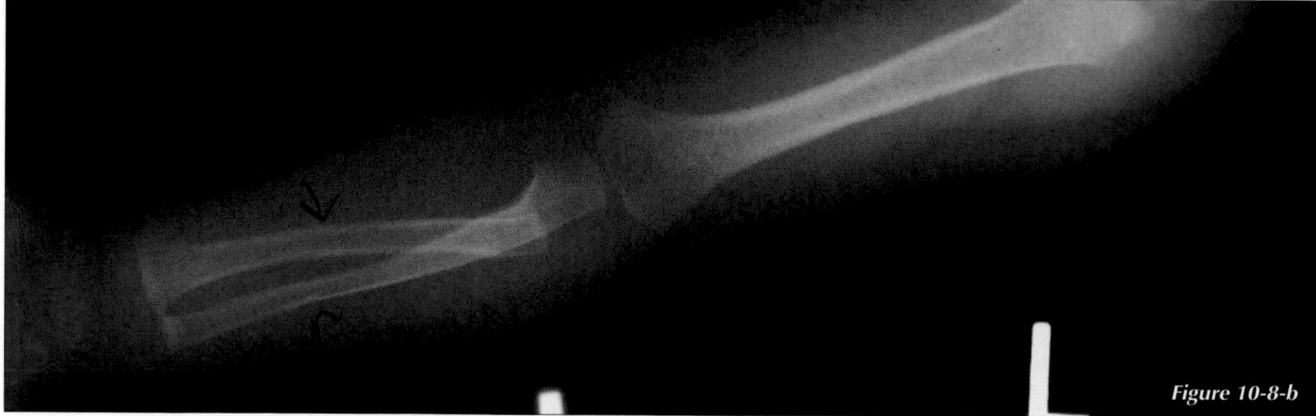

Figure 10-8-b

# Suspicious Injuries

## Abused Siblings

**Case Study 10-9**

This 23-month-old girl was brought to the ER, accompanied by her mother and 6-month-old sister. The mother reported that the children were victimized by their father during a 3-day weekend. The mother was a victim of intimate partner violence and was unable to protect the children during that weekend. On the Monday following the weekend, the mother escaped with the children and brought them to the ER. Examination of the 23 month old revealed multiple contusions, abrasions, and probable cutaneous bite marks on both girls.

***Figure 10-9-a.*** *A bruise over the right cheek.*

***Figure 10-9-b.*** *A bruise anterior to the left ear.*

***Figure 10-9-c.*** *Bruises and abrasions on the back and buttocks.*

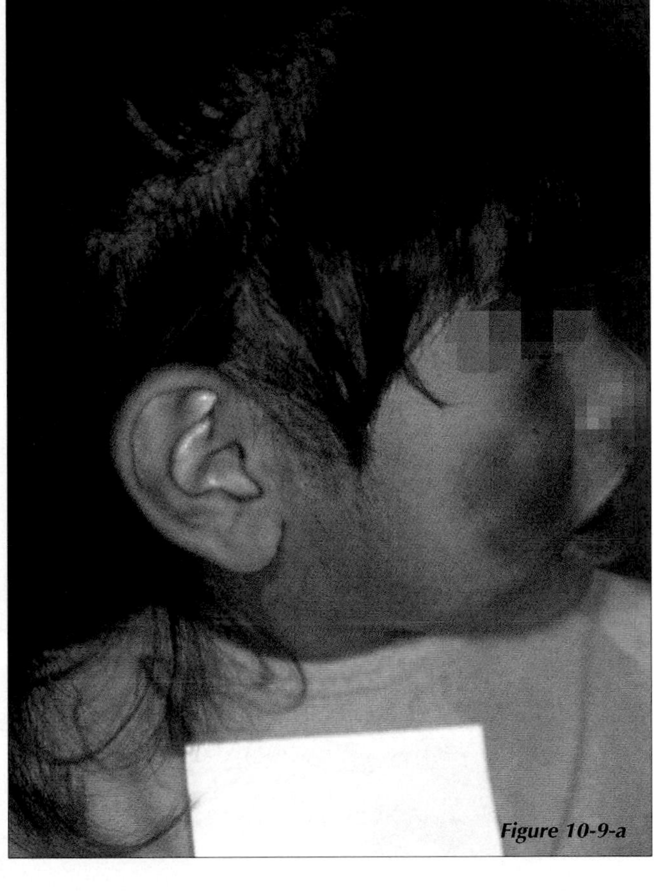

**Figure 10-9-a**

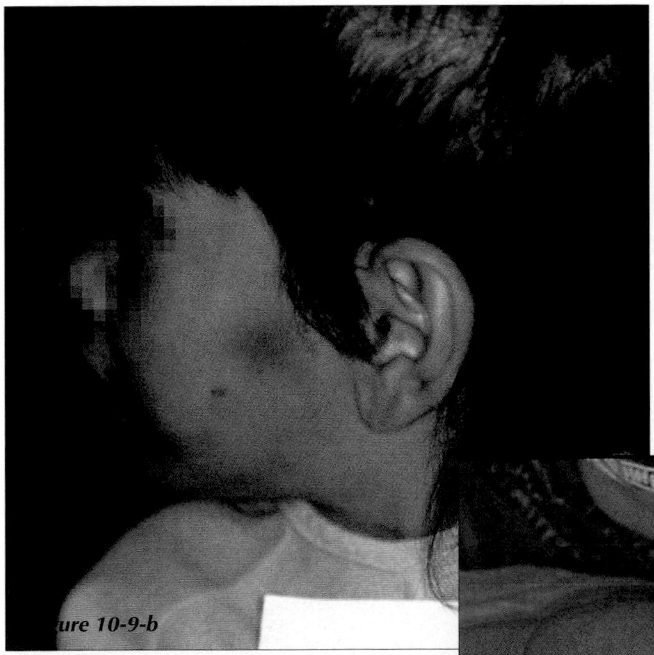

**ure 10-9-b**

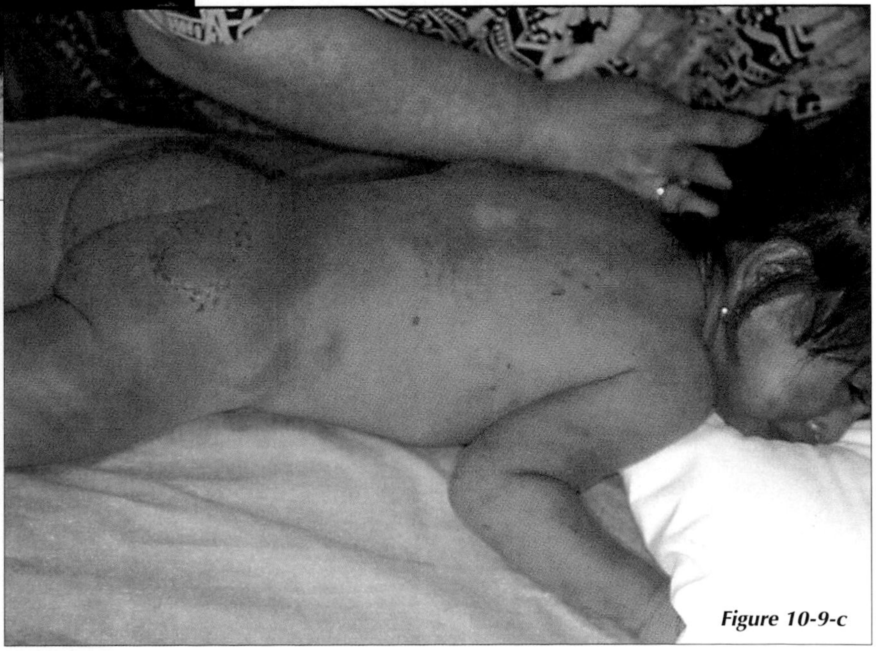

**Figure 10-9-c**

# Suspicious Injuries

## Beating

### Case Study 10-10

This 13-year-old boy was beaten with a fiberglass radio antenna during an episode of corporal punishment.

***Figure 10-10-a.*** *Bilateral bruises on the child's buttocks, illustrating multiple parallel pairs of fresh discrete red-violet bruising with some petechiae. The linear bruises do not appear to wrap around the contours of the body. Skin surfaces are mostly intact with tender areas on the left side.*

***Figures 10-10-b, c,*** *and* ***d.*** *These injuries are over the left buttock and thigh. The photographs get progressively closer. There is an area on the posterolateral aspect that also has characteristics of an abrasion.*

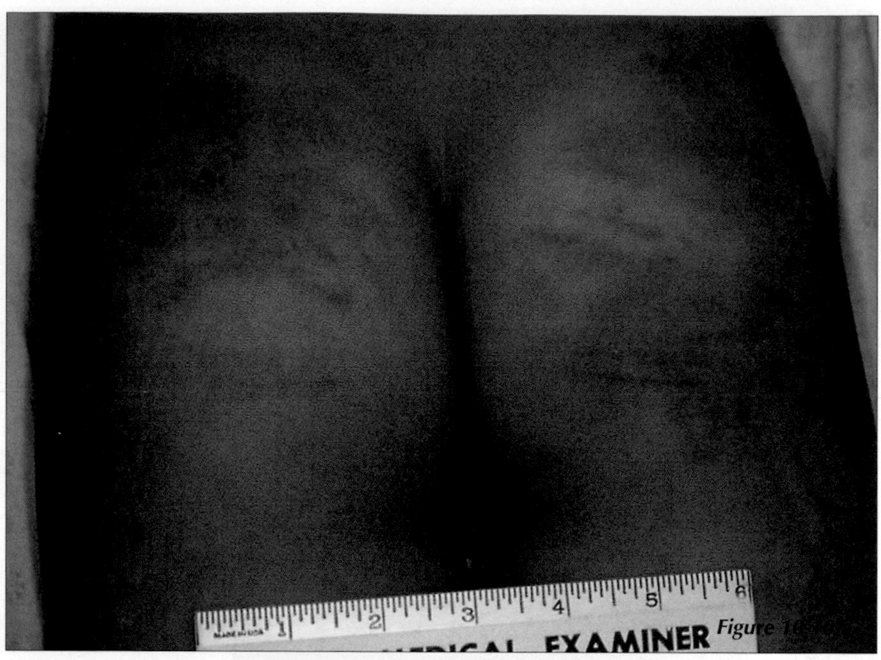


Figure 10-10-a

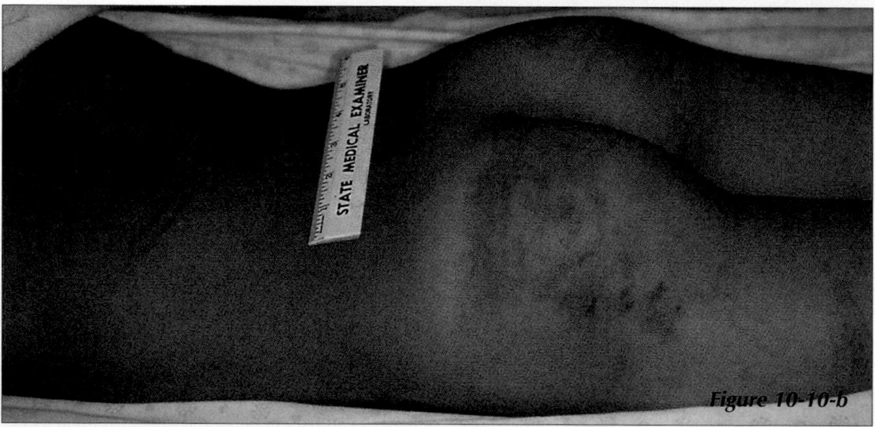


Figure 10-10-b

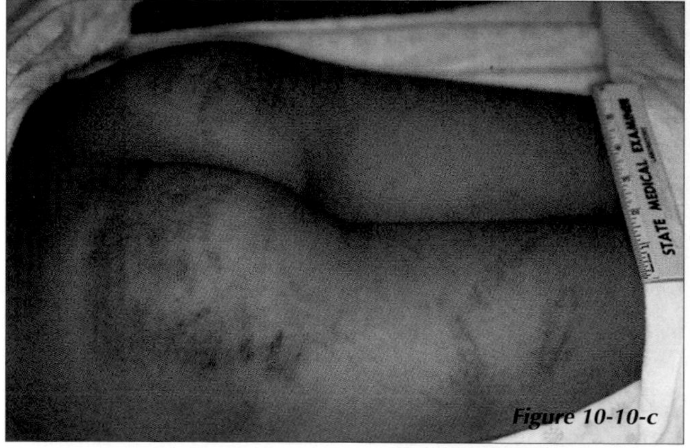


Figure 10-10-c

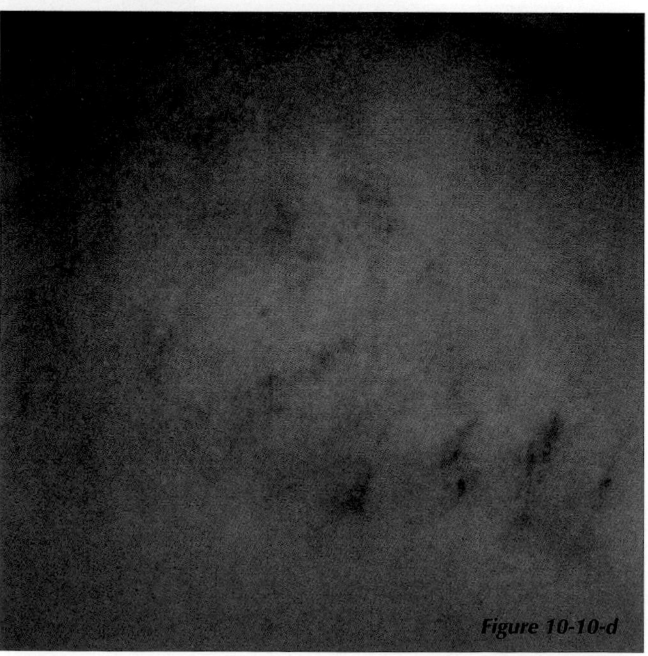

Figure 10-10-d

# Suspicious Injuries

## Beating

**Case Study 10-10** *(continued)*

***Figure 10-10-e.*** *Linear reddish-violet bruises over the thigh. Note that many of the bruises appear to have a thin curved bruise connecting their ends.*

***Figures 10-10-f, g,*** *and* ***h.*** *Posterior and right-sided injuries to the buttock and thigh. Note that the more superficial bruises are reddish-violet, distinct and thin, and are surrounded by a background of larger, more diffuse, bluish-violet deep tissue bruises.*

***Figure 10-10-i.*** *Note the 2 parallel markings over the left back. They are red-violet and discrete, separated by about 1 cm.*

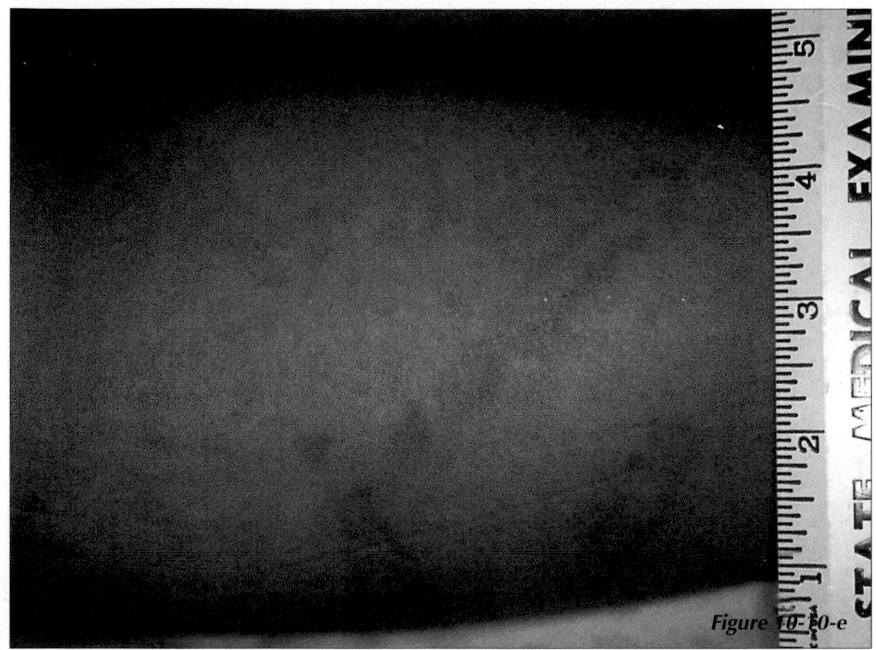
Figure 10-10-e

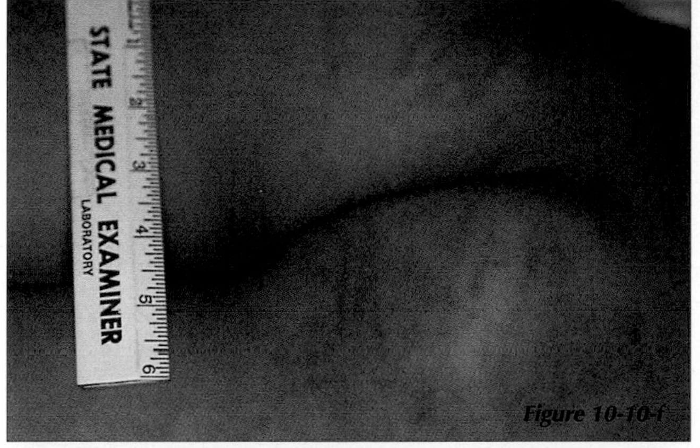

Figure 10-10-f

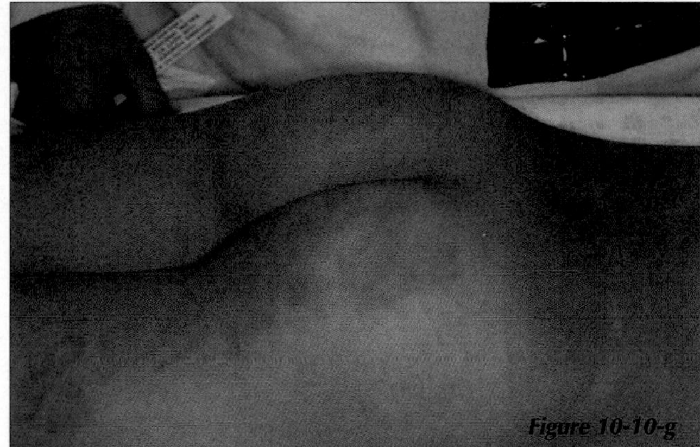
Figure 10-10-g

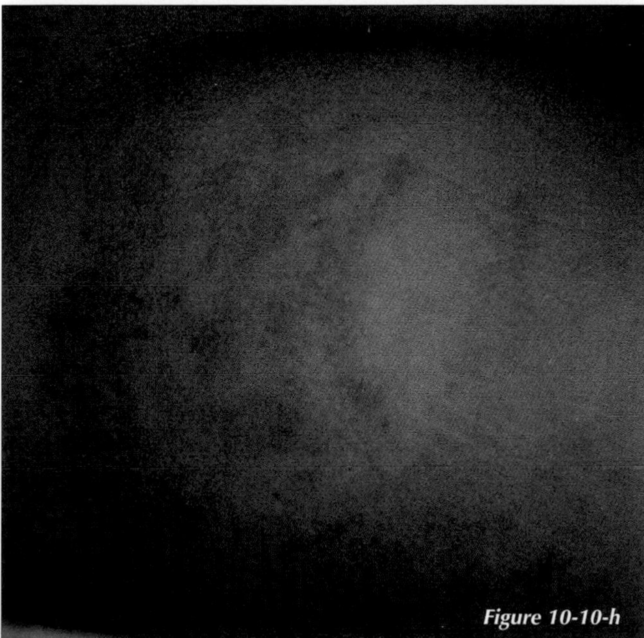
Figure 10-10-h

Figure 10-10-i

# Suspicious Injuries

## Beating

**Case Study 10-10** *(continued)*

***Figures 10-10-j*** *and* ***k.*** *A series of bruises on the left thigh.*

***Figures 10-10-l*** *and* ***m****. Dusky, violet, and tender ecchymotic areas on the dorsa of both hands.*

Figure 10-10-j

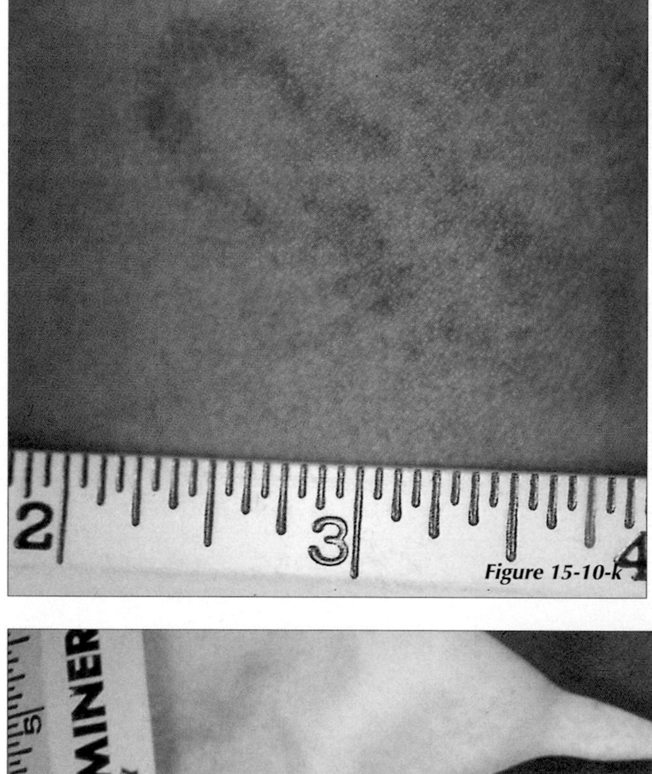

Figure 15-10-k

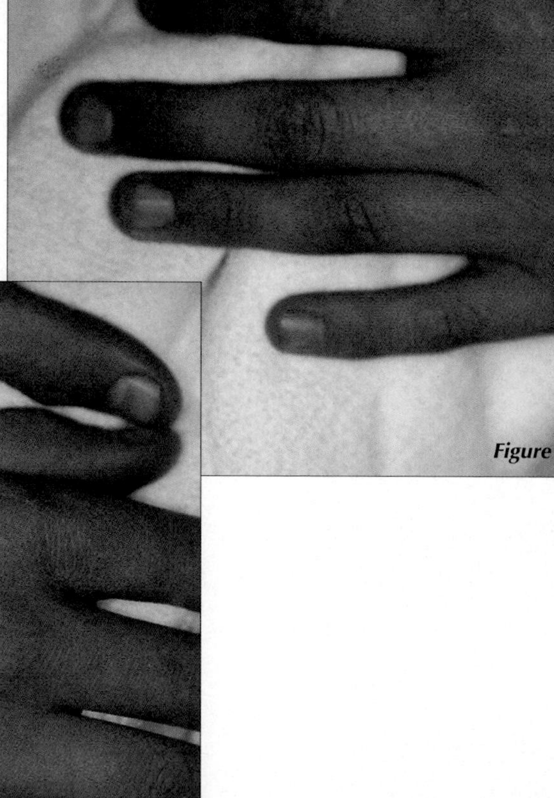

Figure 10-10-l

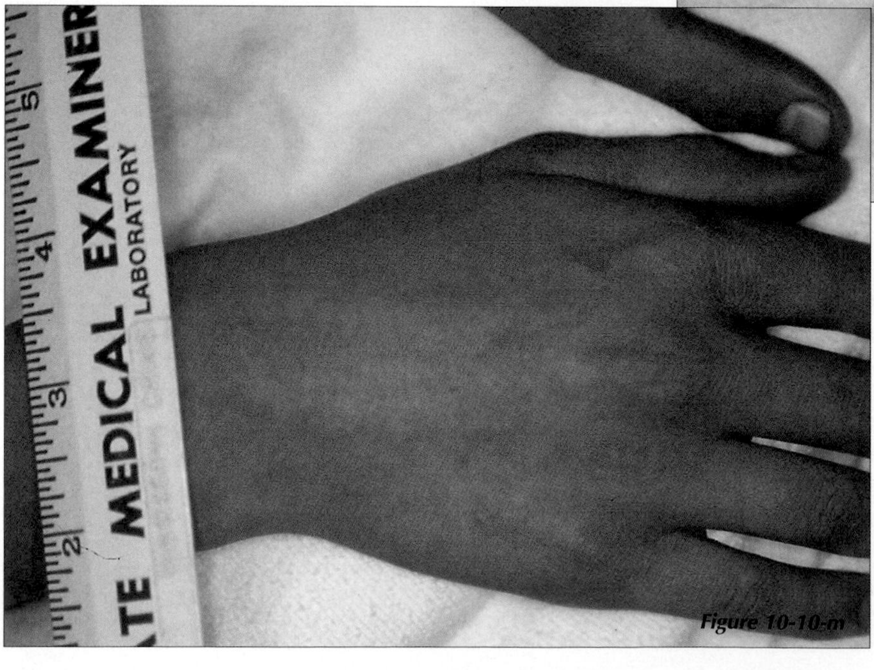

Figure 10-10-m

# Suspicious Injuries

## Distinctive Injuries

### Case Study 10-11

Various individuals with injuries indicative of the device used.

***Figure 10-11-a.*** *A child beaten with a cue stick. Note the characteristic pattern of 2 parallel erythematous areas bordering a blanched area, which indicate an area of impact.*

***Figures 10-11-b*** *and* ***c.*** *Genital injuries in the same child.*

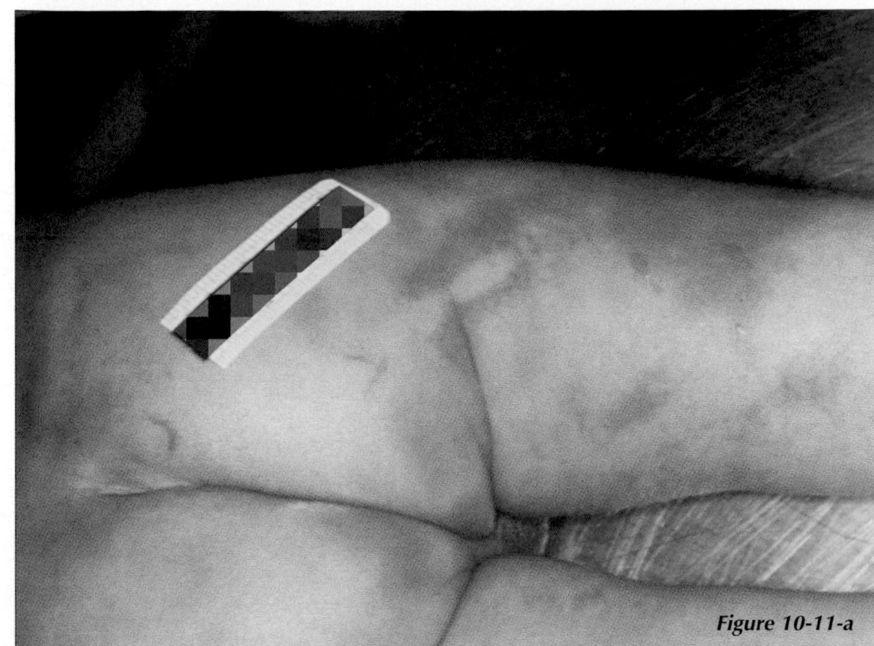

Figure 10-11-a

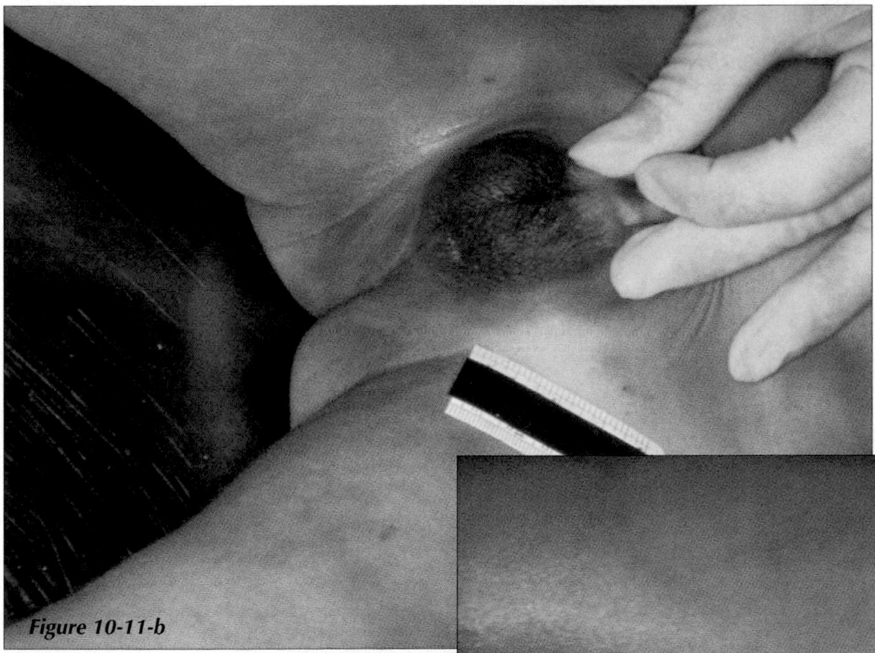

Figure 10-11-b

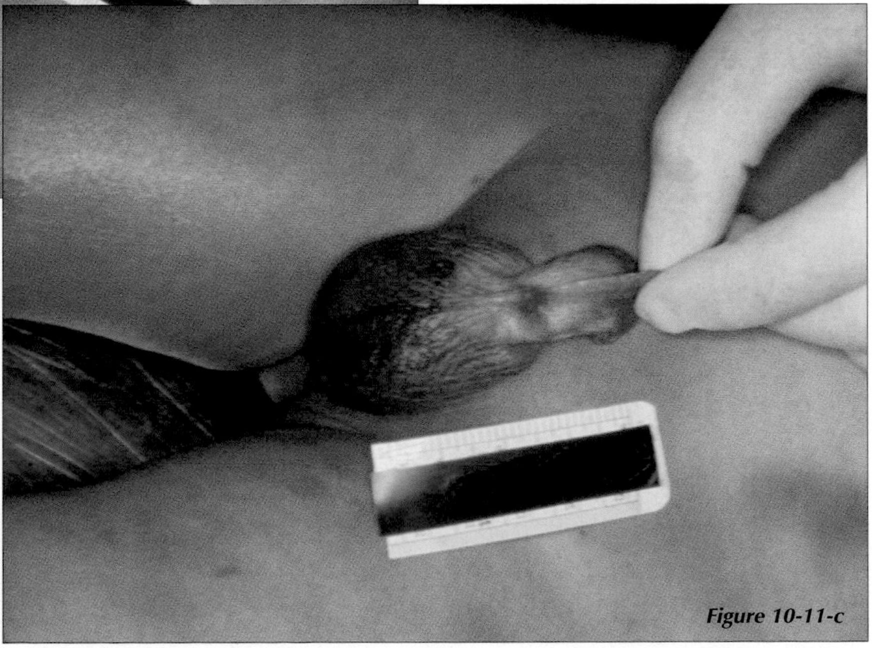

Figure 10-11-c

# Suspicious Injuries

## Distinctive Injuries

**Case Study 10-11** *(continued)*

***Figure 10-11-d.*** *An adult beaten with a cane.*

***Figure 10-11-e.*** *Marks left on a child from being beaten with a switch.*

***Figures 10-11-f** and **g.** Self-inflicted scratching injuries to the forearm; these are not abusive.*

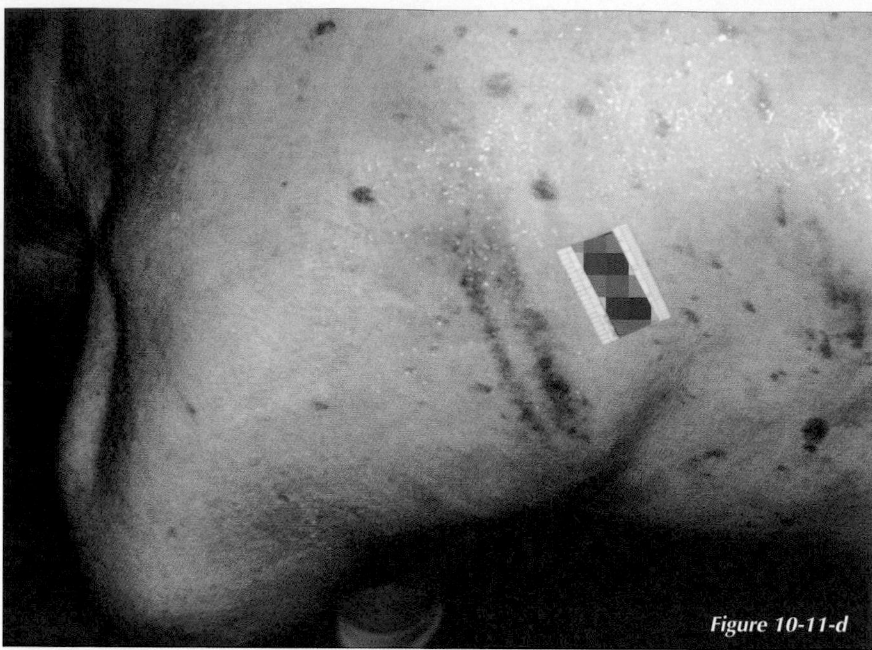

**Figure 10-11-d**

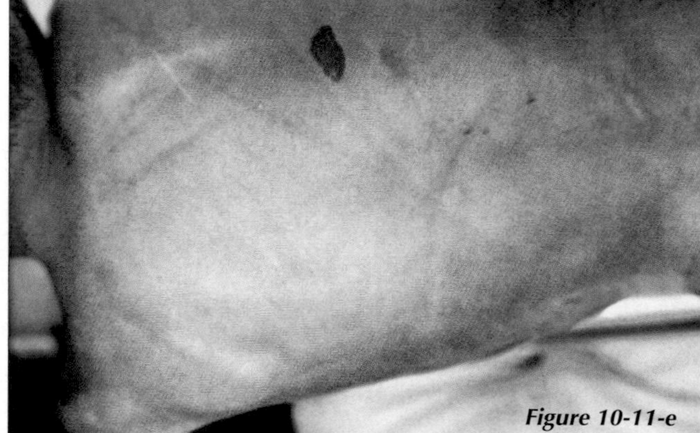

**Figure 10-11-e**

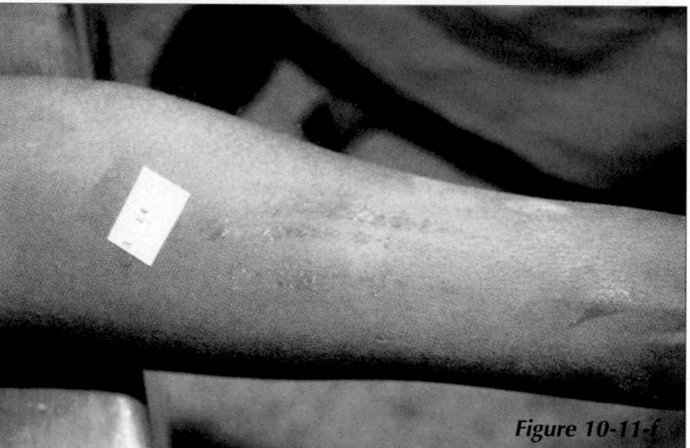

**Figure 10-11-f**

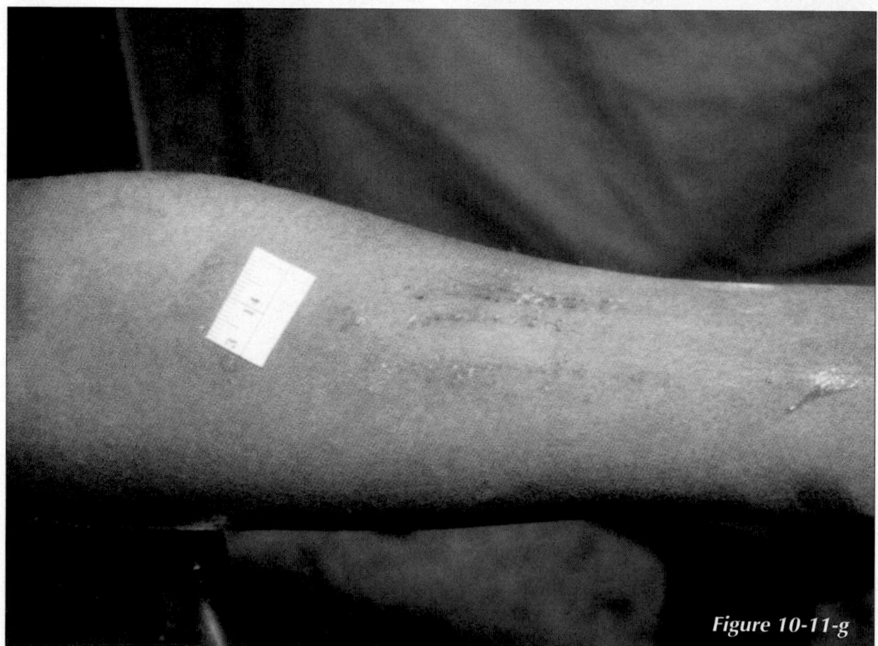

**Figure 10-11-g**

# Suspicious Injuries

## Sexual Assault

**Case Study 10-12**

This adolescent girl was the victim of sexual assault, examined several hours after the initial trauma.

***Figures 10-12-a** and **b**. Evidence of perineal injury, anal bruising and dilatation, and abrasions on the backs of her legs.*

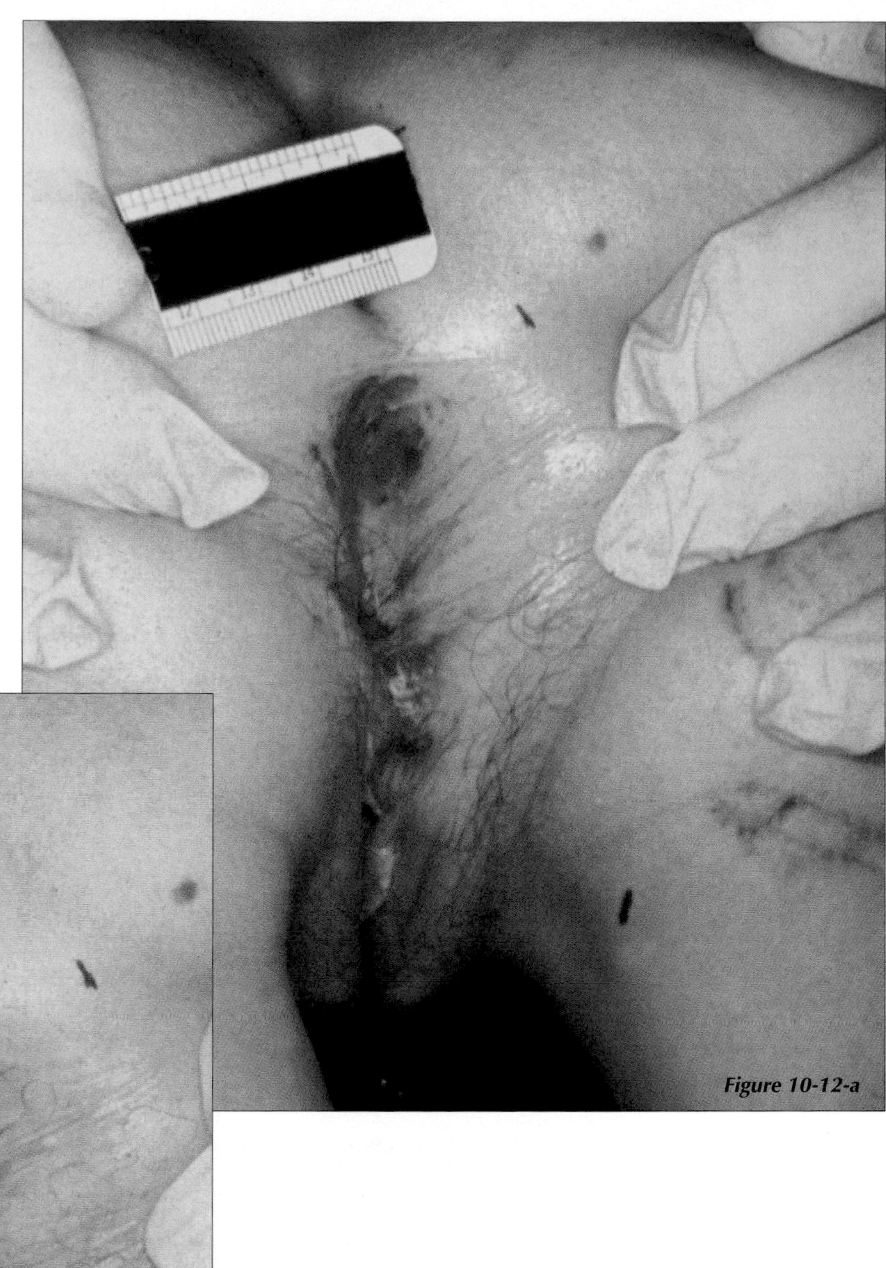

Figure 10-12-a

Figure 10-12-b

# Deaths

## Infant Found Buried

### Case Study 10-13

This nearly full-term infant was found near a construction site. The Infant was determined by height, length, and external body features to be consistent with 36 to 38 weeks' gestation. There was no evidence of traumatic injury to explain the death. Puncture wounds to the head and skull were believed to be inflicted postmortem, possibly by a carnivore that may have found the infant's body and dragged it to where the body was found. The infant was believed to have been born alive, as evidenced by the well-aerated lungs. Several possible mechanisms of death were considered, including: exsanguination from the cut umbilical cord, hypothermia from exposure to the environment, and potential asphyxiation. The degree of autolysis/dehydration of the body and the fact that it was found covered in mud and gravel suggested that it had been buried. The autopsy findings concluded that death occurred shortly after delivery. Death was estimated to have occurred about 4 to 6 weeks before the autopsy, based on the ratios used by forensic pathologists that suggest 1 week of exposure in open air is roughly equivalent to 2 weeks of exposure in water and to 8 weeks buried in soil.

***Figure 10-13-a.*** *Forensic entomology investigation sample format and report.*

***Figure 10-13-b.*** *The child's body at examination. The body is unwashed, with residual dirt and mud as well as plant material (sticks, twigs, and branches) covering the body.*

**Forensic Entomology Investigation Sample Format & Report**
(as follows discussion of climatological data)

Sample Submitted

Sample #1
(date & time) — Preserved larvae (ETOH) — from large clear plastic bag which had contained the infants remains — from morgue cooler.

Sample #2
(date & time) — collected live larvae — most of the larvae were dead and placed into KAAD on (date) — from large clear plastic bag which has contained the infant remains.

CLIMATOLOGICAL DATA
NATIONAL WEATHER SERVICE STATION DATA
(closest to site where body found)
The temperature data, the degree day (DD) and accumulated degree day (ADD) calculation on a base temperature of 6° C (DD-B6) are found in Table ________.
The degree-day calculations are daily heat unit values calculated on maximum and minimum temperatures for assessment of energy unit requirements for development of calliphorids (blow flies) or other insects. Table ________ lists several species of calliphorids with their accompanying accumulated degree day (ADD) requirements for development of different stages of their life cycle.

Summary & Conclusion
Given the location and habitat where the remains were discovered, the season, the prevailing temperatures for the period, and the species of calliphorids found to have colonized the remains (mature 3rd instars larvae from the species of Calliphoridae; Calliphorini; likely either Calliphora vicina, Calliphora livida, or Cynomyopsis cadaverina, but not Calliphor avamitoria), colonization of the body would have taken place sometime between (date) as the latest date for colonization to as early as (date) with colonization occurring during the intermediate hours (blow flies are not active during darkness). In addition, only days when the maximum temperature for the day was in excess of 50° - 55° F would the colonization (egg laying) have occurred due to exclusion of flight and oviposition activity below these temperatures. Death of the individual would have preceded the insect colonization. For the three blue bottle fly species and the prevailing low temperatures for the period, death could have occurred hours to days before the colonization.

**Figure 10-13-a**

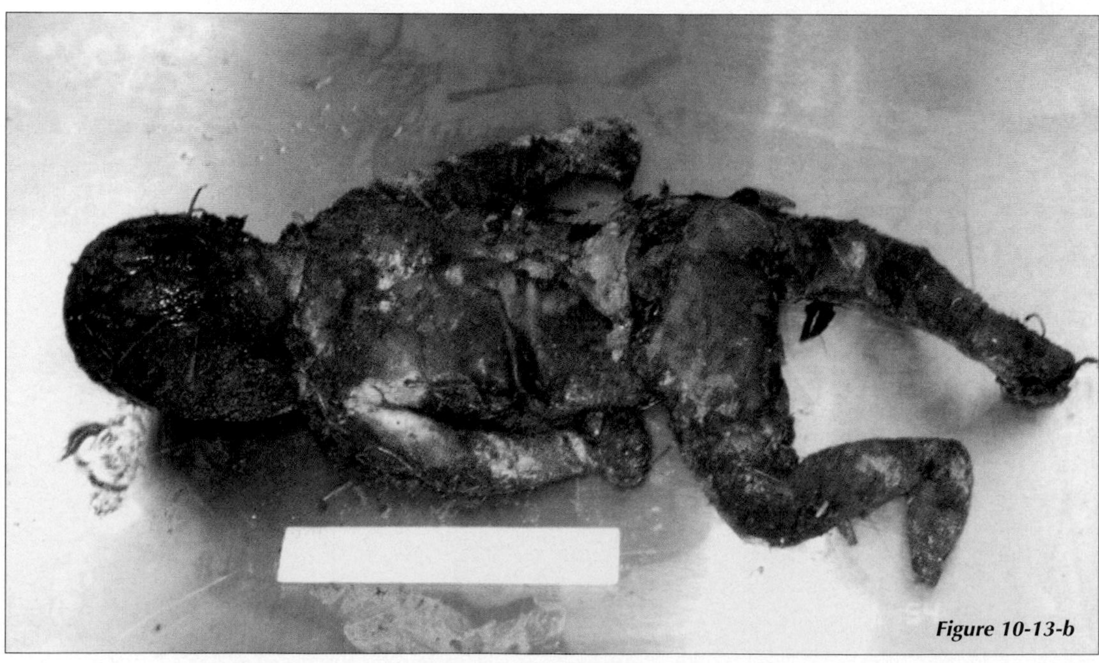

**Figure 10-13-b**

# Deaths

## Infant Found Buried

**Case Study 10-13** *(continued)*

***Figure 10-13-c.*** *The infant's body during the postmortem examination after being washed.*

***Figure 10-13-d.*** *The infant's right shoulder area, which demonstrates some of the puncture wounds believed to have been caused postmortem by a carnivore.*

***Figure 10-13-e.*** *A close-up view of the puncture wounds.*

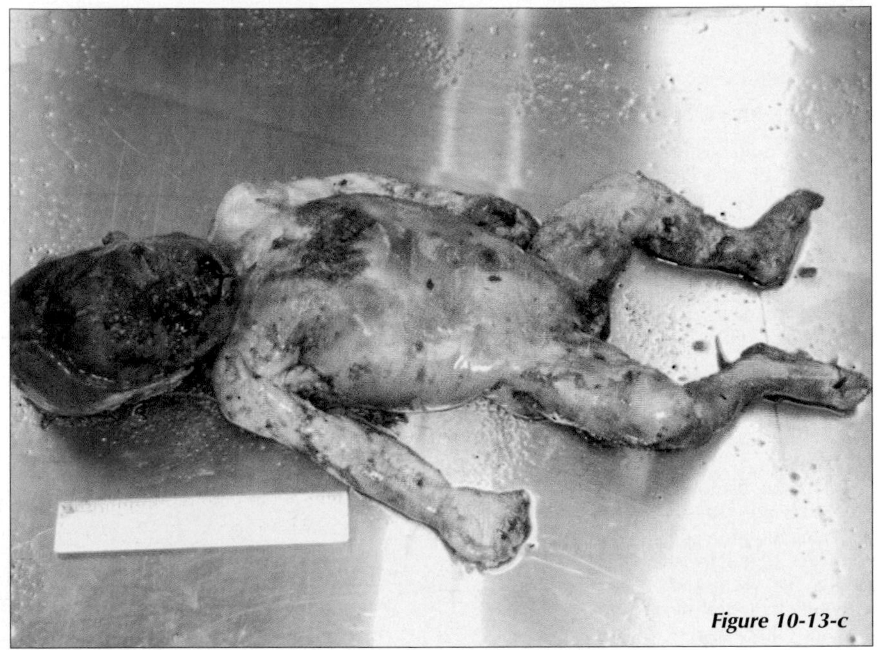

**Figure 10-13-c**

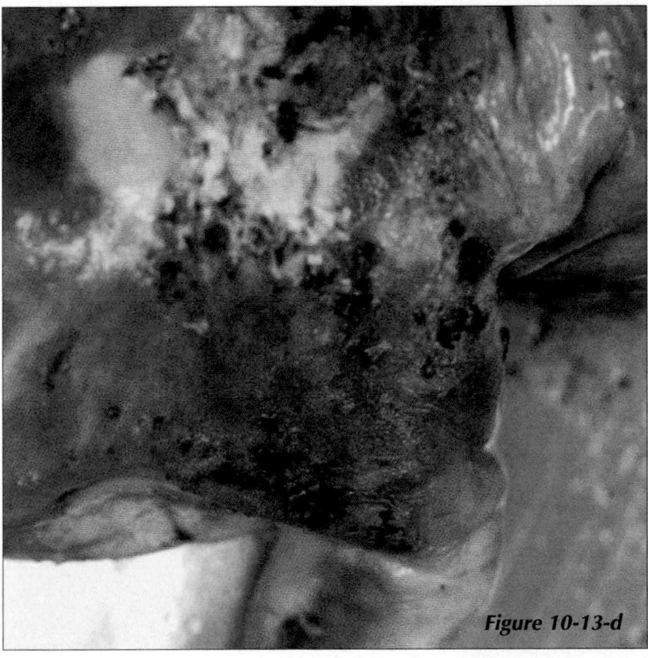

**Figure 10-13-d**

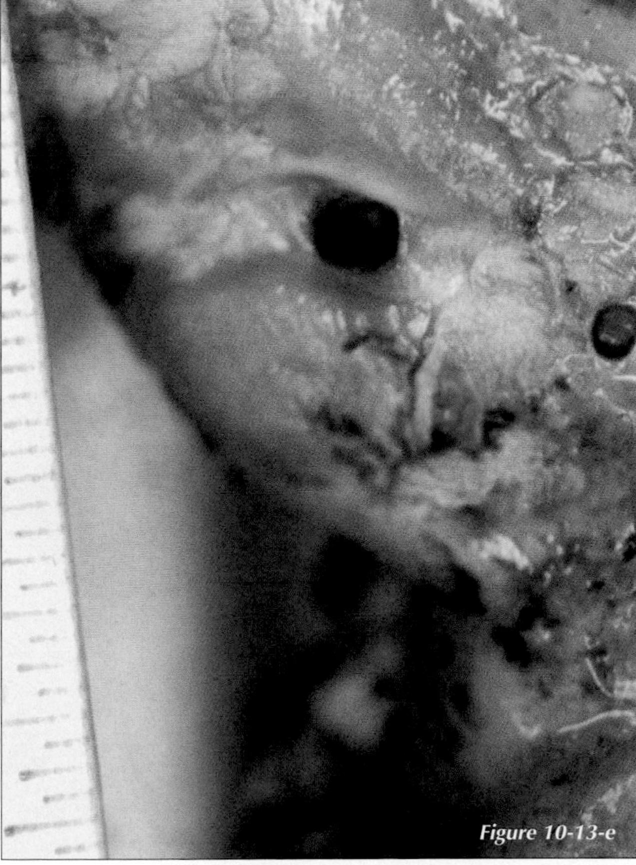

**Figure 10-13-e**

# Deaths

## Starvation

### Case Study 10-14

This 5-year-old boy had cerebral palsy and was 1 of 8 children, ranging in age from 2 months to 14 years. The boy was unable to feed himself, was not ambulatory, and required constant care. Shortly after the birth of the last child and 2 months before this boy's death, his health and feeding progressively deteriorated. Police were called to the residence and found the boy dead in his bed and covered with urine-soaked sheets. He weighed 14 pounds but his expected weight, given his age and height, was 25 pounds. The family could not remember him eating for the last 3 days. He had marked cachexia, dehydration, hemoconcentration, and extremely poor hygiene with urine and feces covering his groin and perineum, in addition to maceration of the skin. There were abdominal, groin, and left back extremity decubiti, including ulceration into the left posterior iliac crest. He also had chronic extremity flexure contractures. The probable cause of death was starvation from severe child neglect.

***Figure 10-14-a.*** *Body diagram done during the postmortem examination, which is used to track the obvious external lesions or injuries noted on the gross examination.*

***Figure 10-14-b.*** *Posterior view postmortem.*

***Figure 10-14-c.*** *Anterior view postmortem.*

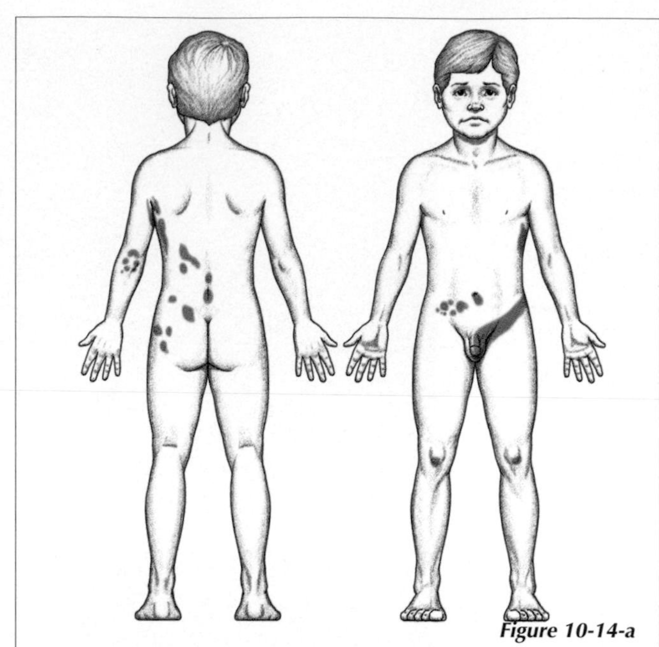

*Figure 10-14-a*

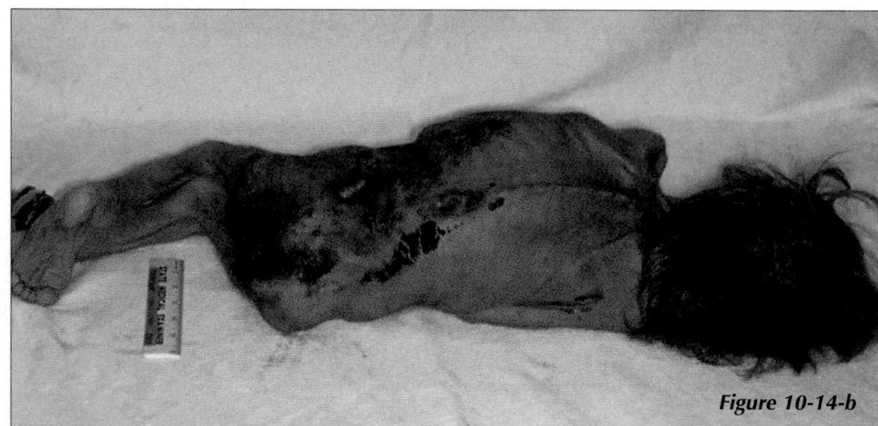

*Figure 10-14-b*

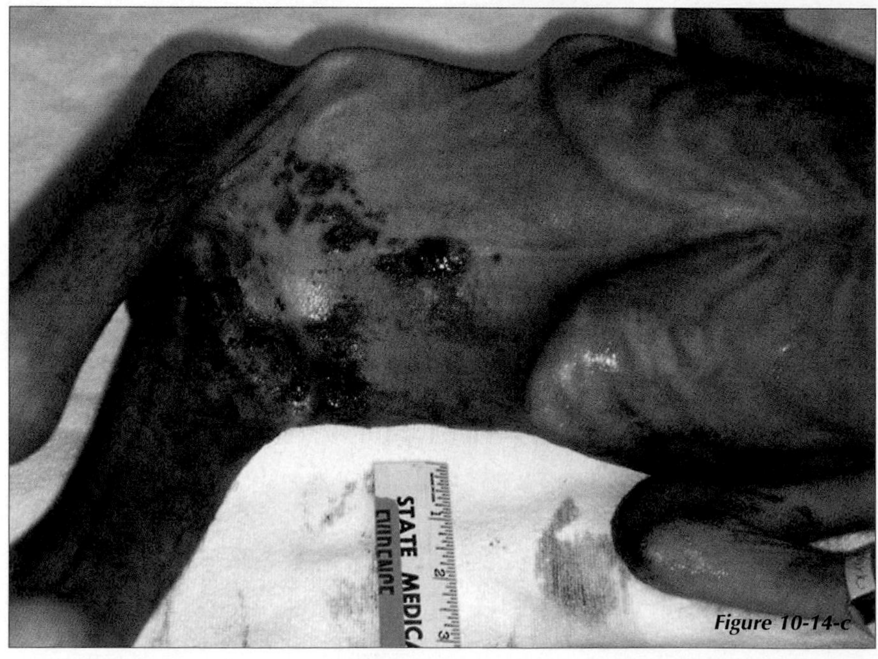


*Figure 10-14-c*

# Deaths

## Starvation

**Case Study 10-14** *(continued)*

***Figure 10-14-d.*** *Various lesions (decubiti) and macerated skin on the mid-back and lower left back areas.*

***Figure 10-14-e.*** *Macerated skin and decubiti over the child's iliac crest.*

***Figure 10-14-f.*** *Note significant extremity wasting and various lesions on the wasted musculature.*

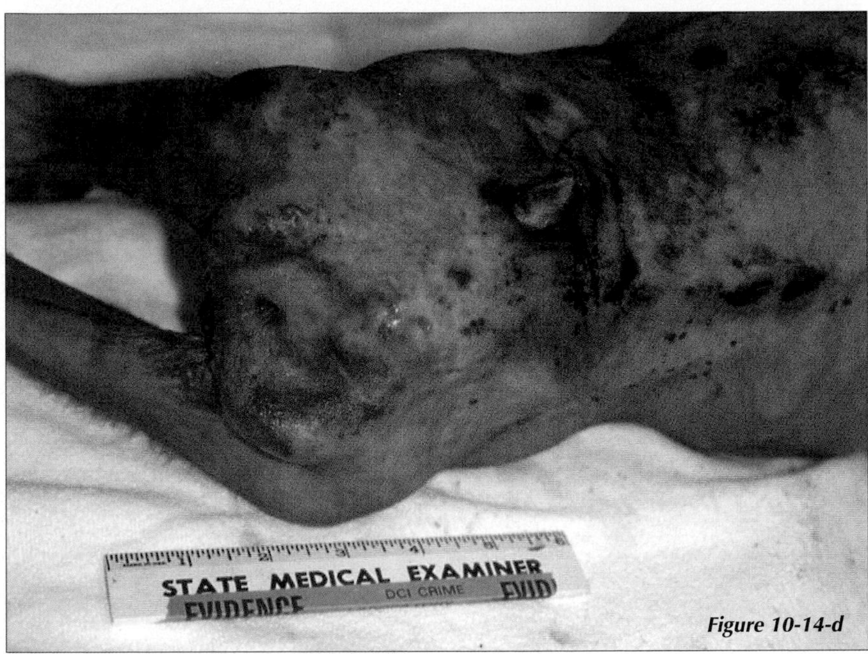


**Figure 10-14-d**

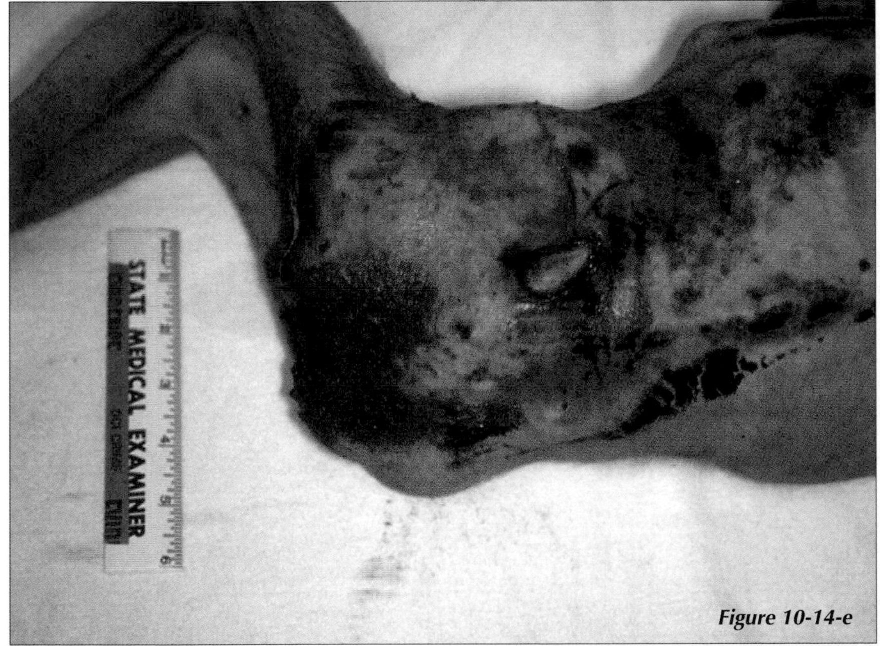


**Figure 10-14-e**

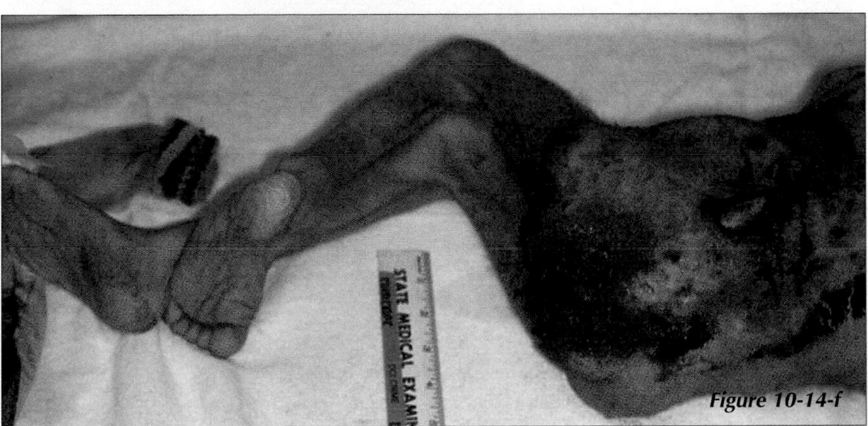

**Figure 10-14-f**

# DEATHS

## STARVATION

**Case Study 10-14** *(continued)*

***Figure 10-14-g.*** *Peripheral sores and macerated skin on the lower abdomen and groin.*

***Figure 10-14-h.*** *Close-up view of the groin area showing skin maceration and pressure sores.*

***Figure 10-14-i.*** *Significant muscle wasting in the buttock area.*

***Figure 10-14-j.*** *Significant wasting of the lower extremities.*

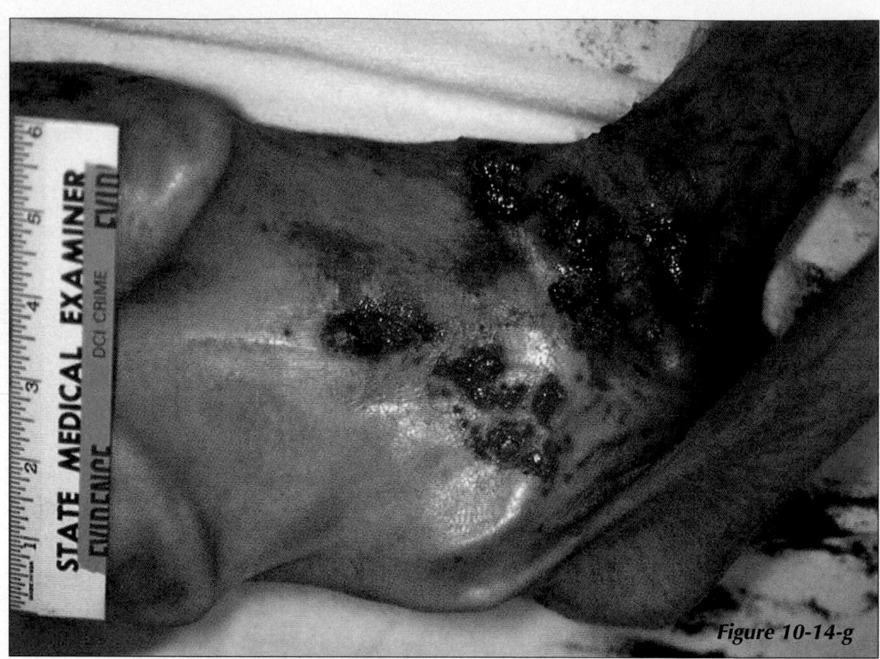

*Figure 10-14-g*

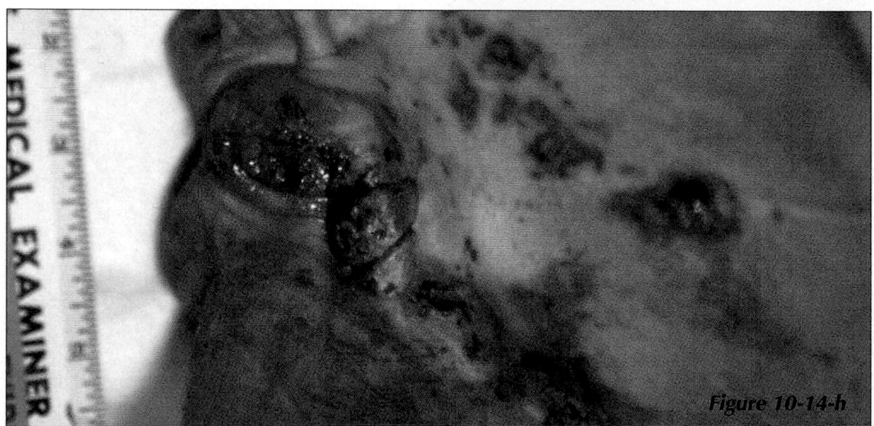

*Figure 10-14-h*

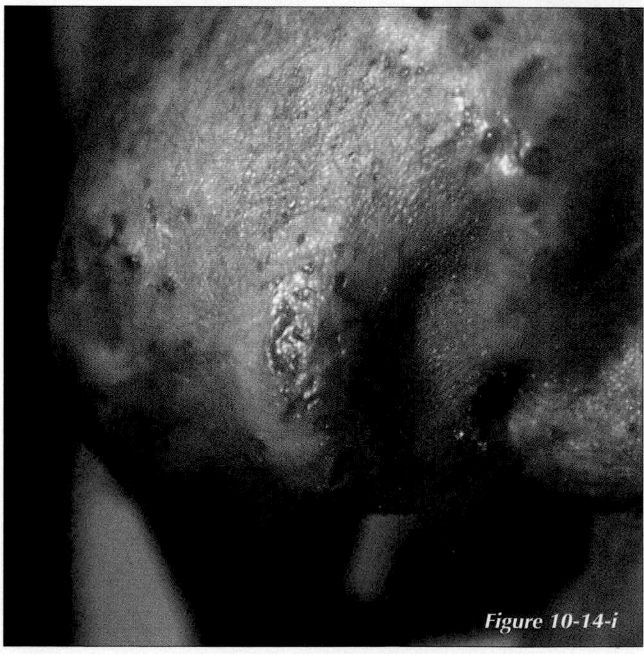
*Figure 10-14-i*

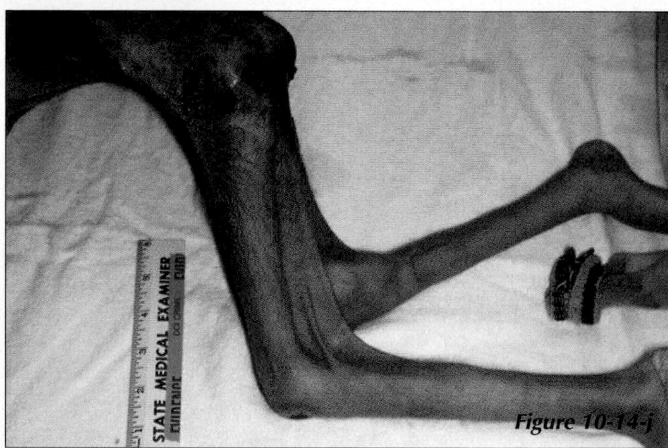

*Figure 10-14-j*

# Deaths

## Impaction

### Case Study 10-15

This 11-year-old boy had a long-standing history of gastrointestinal complaints. He died of severe megacolon with fecal impaction and retention as well as subsequent peritonitis with free intraperitoneal air. At autopsy, he was found to have extreme abdominal distention, very little subcutaneous fat, and cachexia. He was reported to have suffered from chronic bowel problems and had become progressively sicker over the year before his death. As his condition worsened, his weight dropped dramatically, and his abdomen began to swell. He had been receiving medical care, but several appointments with his doctor had been cancelled, which was a significant finding for the investigation of neglect as the possible cause of death. There were no neurological or congenital reasons found in the intestinal exam to account for why the colon had become so distended.

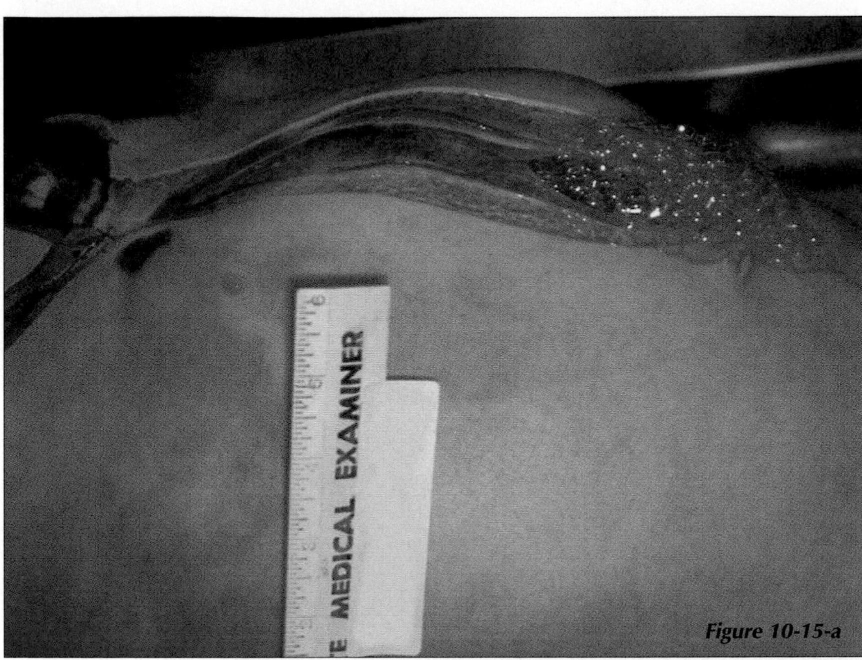


*Figure 10-15-a.* The distended abdomen with several of the postmortem examination incisions made.

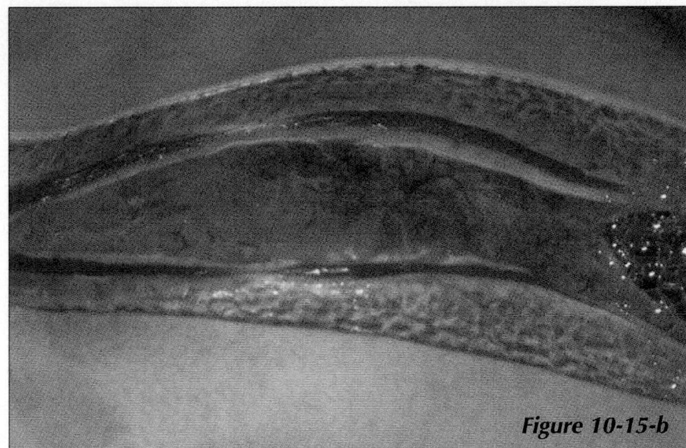


*Figure 10-15-b.* The midline incision made to the abdomen reveals that the abdominal contents appear to be rather tense underneath the distended skin.

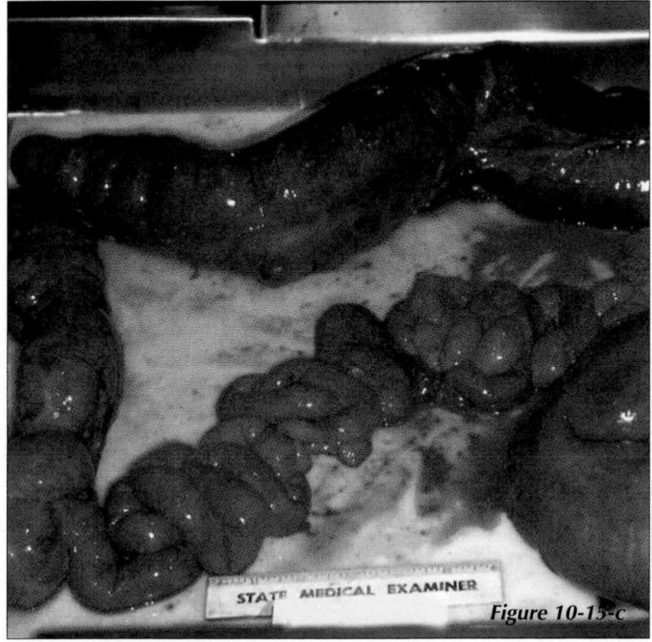


*Figure 10-15-c.* Note the extent of the fecal retention in the colon, with an average of 12 cm in diameter at autopsy.

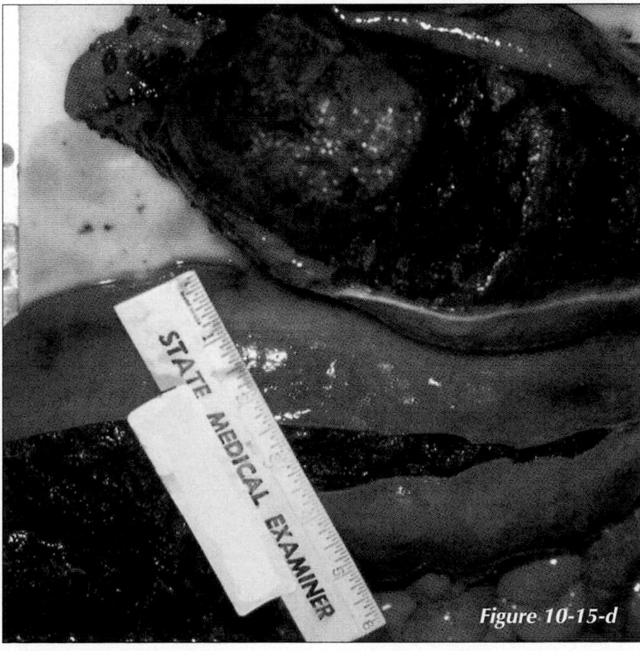


*Figure 10-15-d.* The colon is incised, demonstrating the massive amount of impacted and inspissated feces.

# Deaths

## Severe Neglect

### Case Study 10-16

This child was malnourished and found nearly dead in his bed, having been there unattended overnight. He was alleged to have been ill for several days. He eventually died from a ruptured retropharyngeal abscess. He had attended school earlier that week and was sent home because he could barely walk. The school did not report the case to the hotline.

***Figure 10-16.*** *The lesions on the bottoms of the boy's feet are abscesses. It took several washings in the hospital to remove the dirt from his soles in order to expose these lesions.*

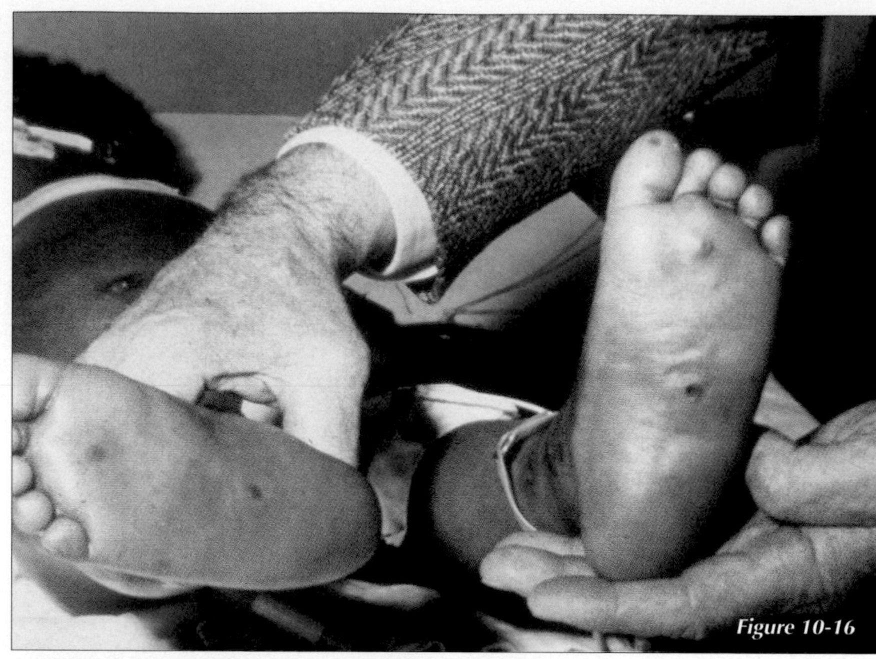

Figure 10-16

## Asphyxia

### Case Study 10-17

This 2-year-old girl and her mother were visiting from another city and staying with friends. The child was sleeping on a sofa in the living room and was found dead in the morning.

***Figure 10-17-a.*** *Petechial hemorrhages over the eyelids and beneath the eyes.*

***Figure 10-17-b.*** *Petechial hemorrhages on the palpebral conjunctiva.*

***Figure 10-17-c.*** *Petechial hemorrhages on the gingiva of the upper gum.*

***Figure 10-17-d.*** *Petechial hemorrhages along the left side of the neck.*

A male member of the host family eventually admitted to lying down on top of the child to keep her from crying. He said that after about 15 minutes the child appeared to be sleeping. The cause of death was traumatic asphyxia.

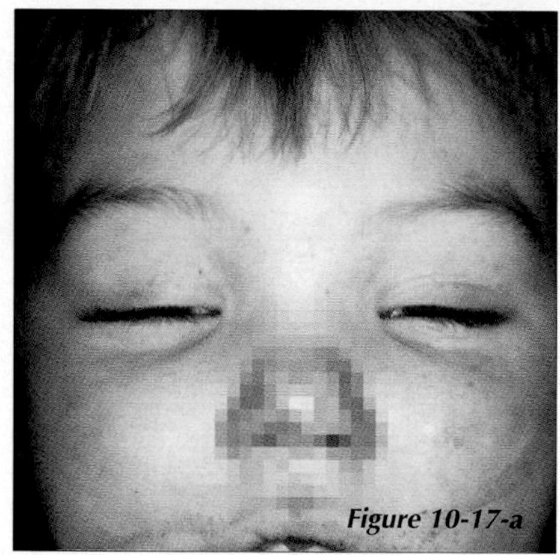

Figure 10-17-a

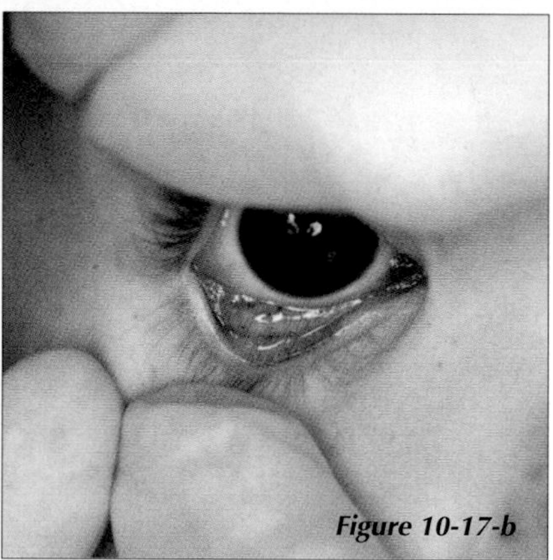

Figure 10-17-b

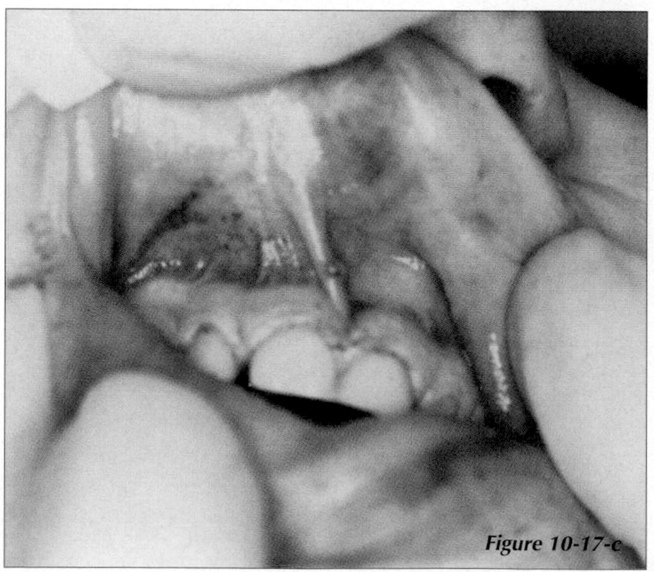

Figure 10-17-c

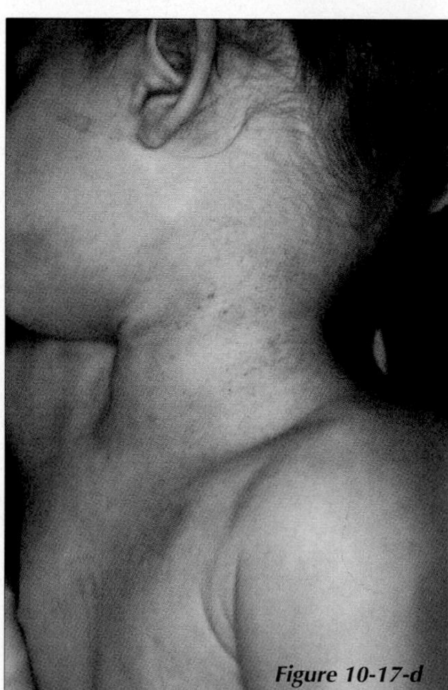

Figure 10-17-d

# Deaths

## Asphyxia

### Case Study 10-18

This infant was asphyxiated. The presence of subconjunctival petechial hemorrhages was unusual since they are not normally present in mechanically asphyxiated infants less than 1 year old.

***Figure 10-18.*** *Subconjunctival petechial hemorrhages secondary to asphyxia. Bruising of the neck may be present in some cases when pressure applied is in that area.*

## Multiple Bruises

### Case Study 10-19

This 7-month-old boy was found dead in his crib. He had multiple bruises to his head and face.

***Figure 10-19.*** *Note the additional bruising in the right chest area.*

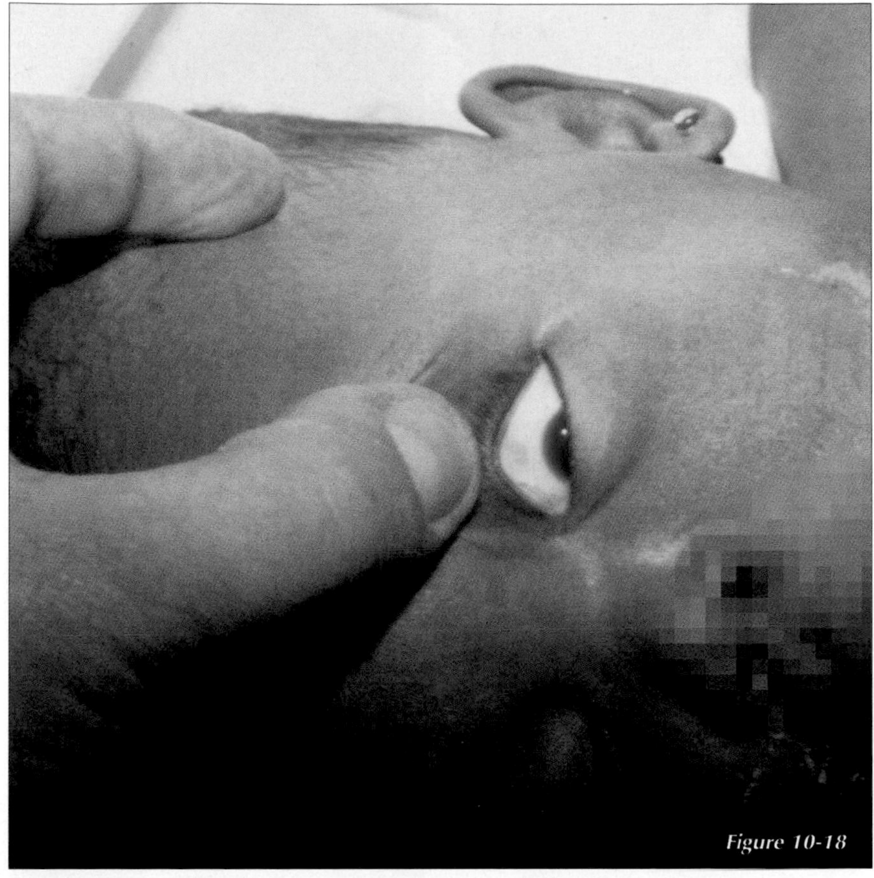

Figure 10-18

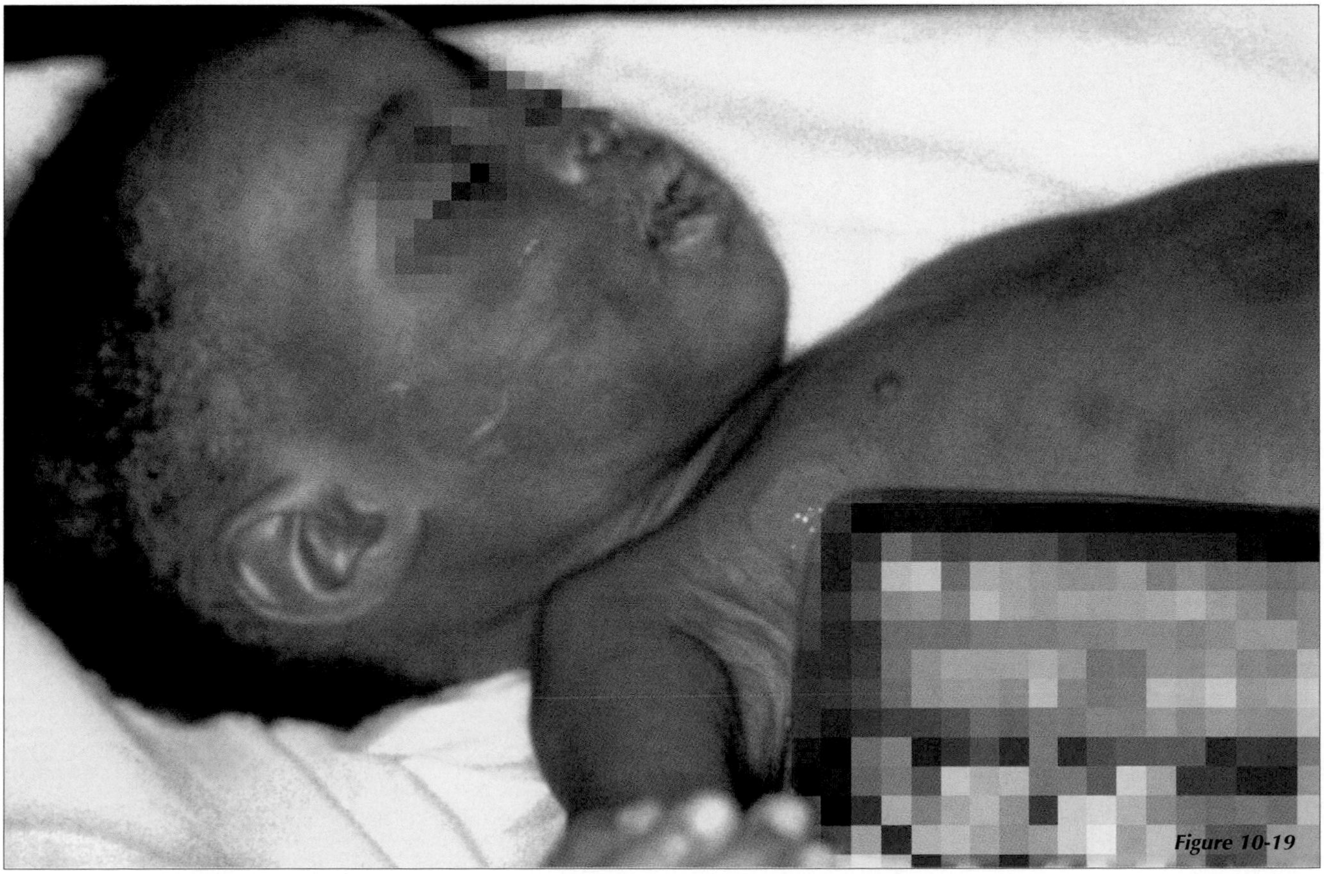

Figure 10-19

# Deaths

## Oral Injuries

### Case Study 10-20

This 5-month-old boy was found dead at home. He had a torn frenulum, most likely caused by a blow to the mouth or by an object being forced into his mouth. The mouth was thoroughly examined since oral lesions may be the only evidence of injury in suffocation homicides.

***Figure 10-20-a.*** *Note the separation of the mucosa at the gum line. This is caused by forcing an object such as a spoon or nipple into the mouth.*

***Figures 10-20-b, c, d,*** *and* ***e.*** *Other oral injuries with little external evidence of their existence.*

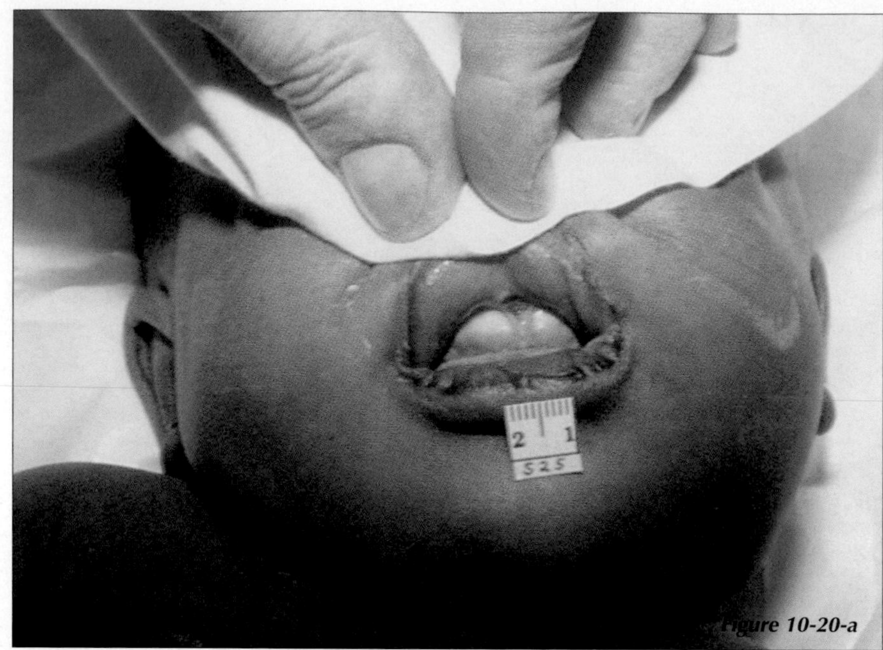

Figure 10-20-a

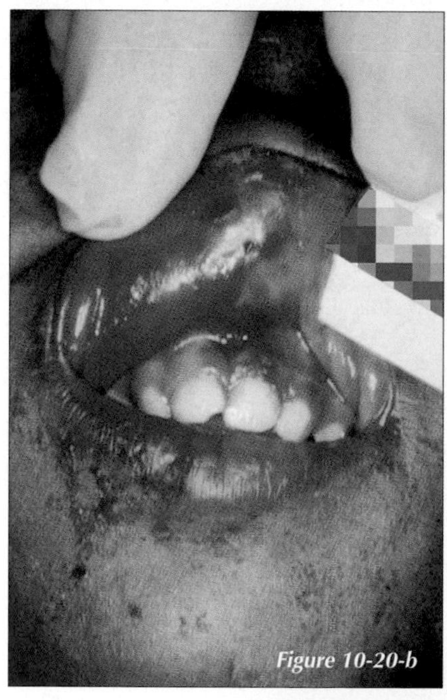
Figure 10-20-b

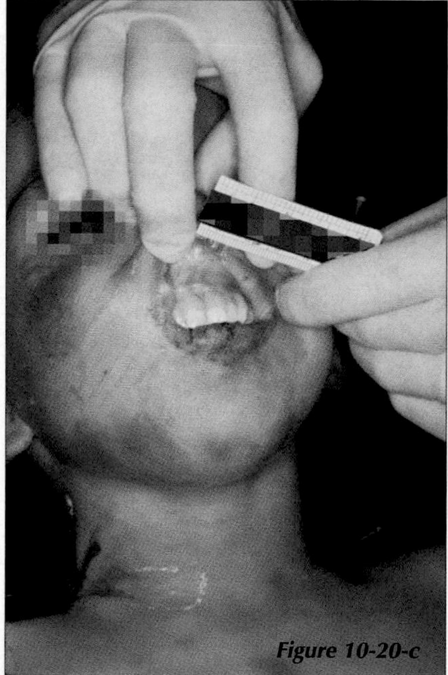
Figure 10-20-c

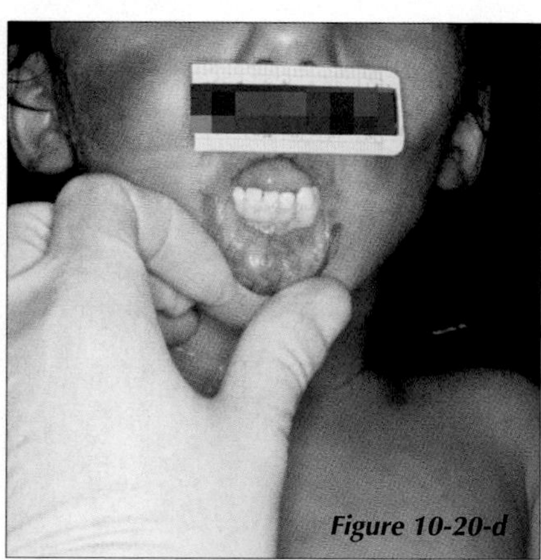
Figure 10-20-d

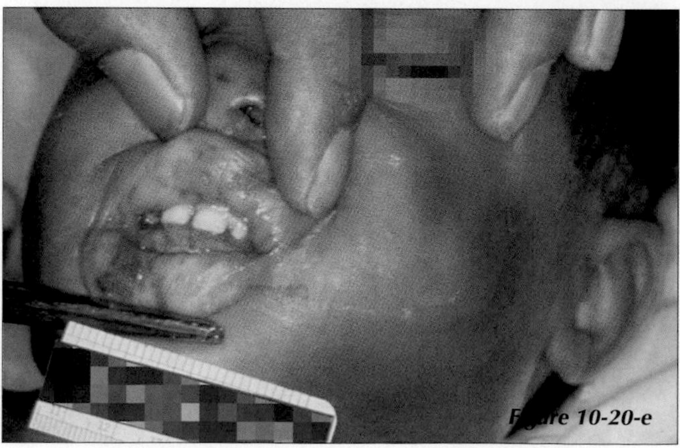
Figure 10-20-e

# Deaths

## Teenage Death

**Case Study 10-21**

This teenage prostitute was found dead.

***Figure 10-21.*** *The fingernails are broken as the result of a fight. The circled wound on the abdomen is postmortem and is the result of a temperature probe.*

## Forced Feeding

**Case Study 10-22**

This 9-year-old boy was killed by his mother's boyfriend. He had refused to eat and the boyfriend force-fed him hot dogs and buns by using the handle of a hammer as a ramrod.

***Figures 10-22-a*** *and* ***b.*** *Alimentary bolus obstructing the airway at the glottic opening.*

***Figure 10-22-c.*** *Stomach contents.*

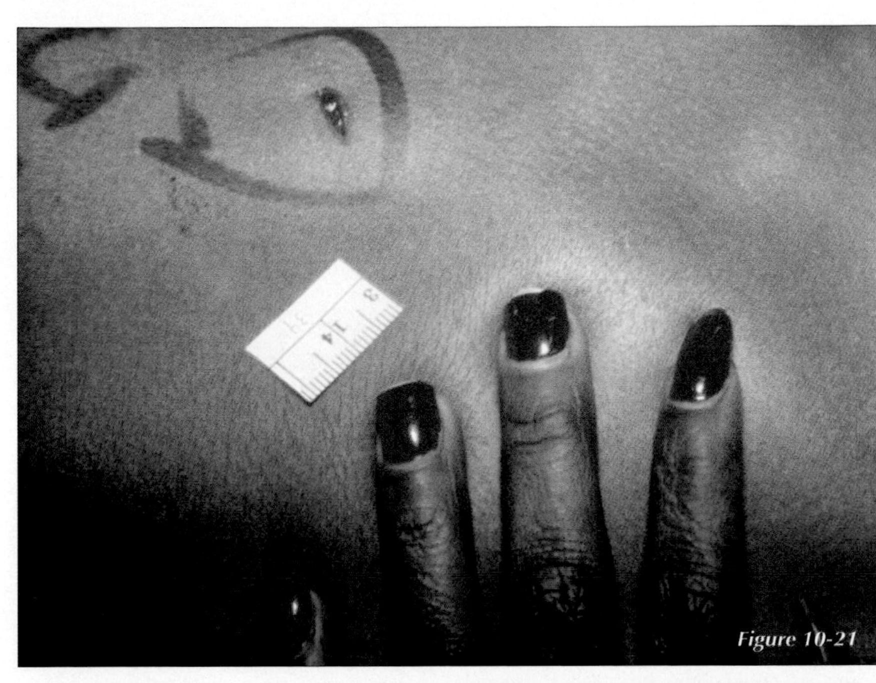

Figure 10-21

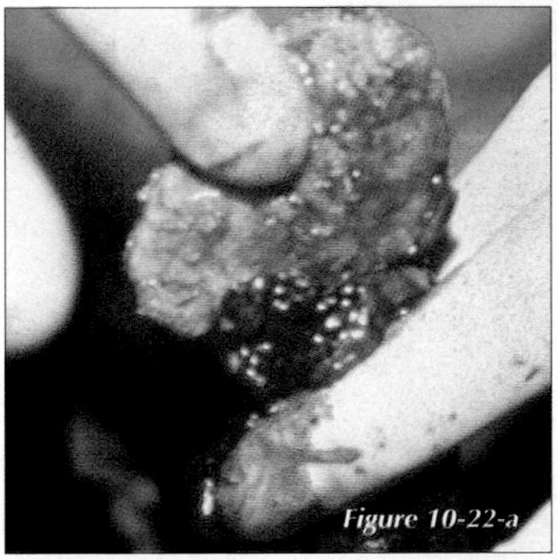

Figure 10-22-a

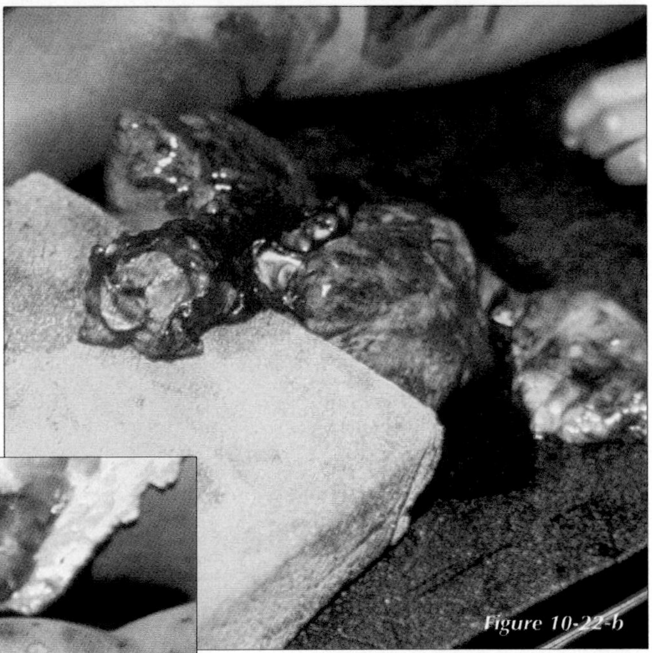

Figure 10-22-b

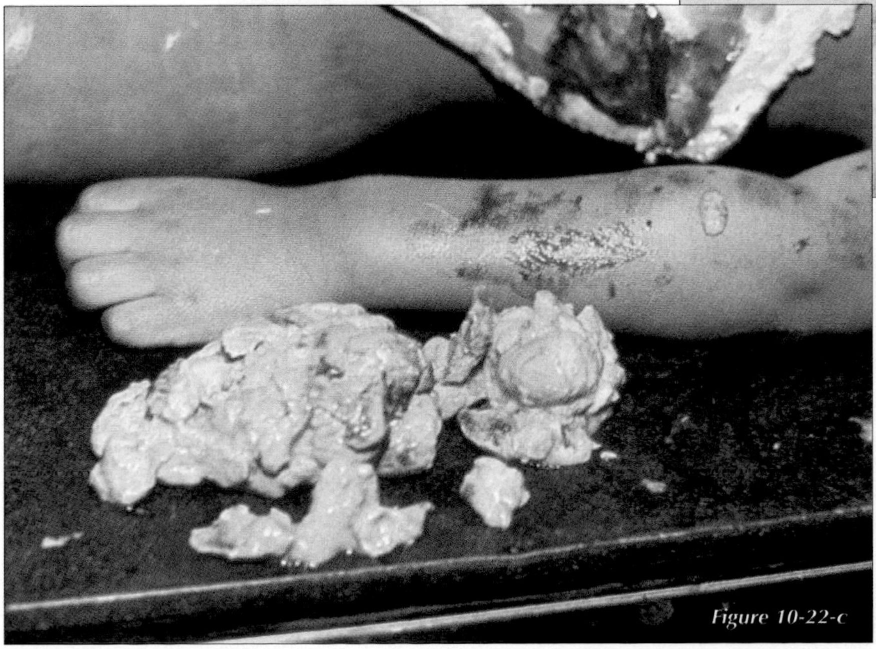

Figure 10-22-c

# Deaths

## Gunshot Wounds

**Case Study 10-23**

This 9-year-old boy was playing with a loaded .38 caliber handgun. He placed it in his mouth and pulled the trigger. ER personnel thought incorrectly that the lesions around the mouth were caused by abuse, but they were actually characteristic lesions secondary to the force of a gun blast. This death was determined to be accidental, although neglect on the part of the caregivers was apparent.

***Figure 10-23.*** *Note external perioral lacerations.*

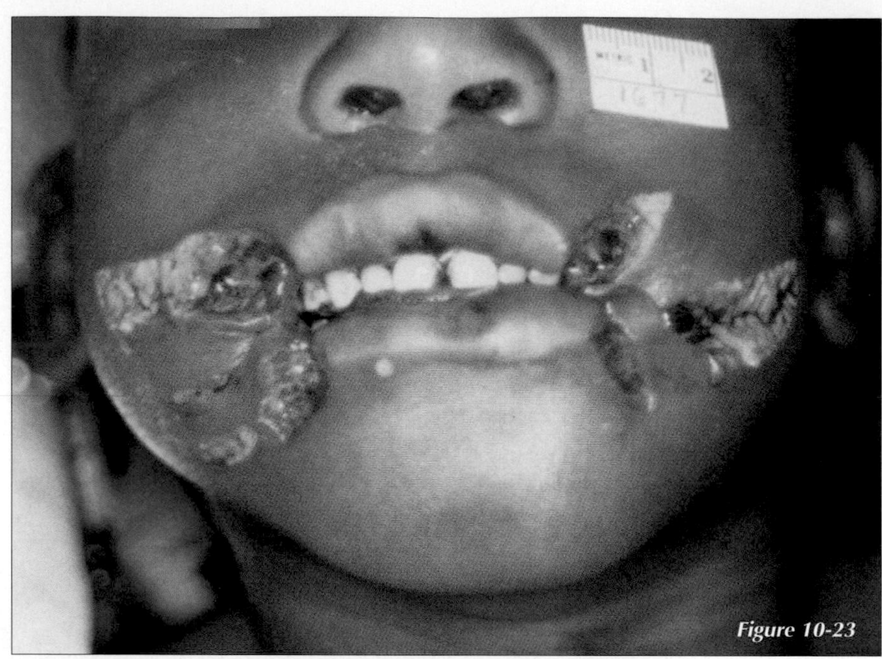

Figure 10-23

## Bruising with Closed Head Injury

**Case Study 10-24**

This abused infant died of a fresh closed head injury. Many bruises predated the head injury and could not be attributed to a single incident.

***Figure 10-24-a.*** *Bruises on neck area.*

***Figure 10-24-b.*** *Head injury.*

***Figure 10-24-c.*** *Trunk bruising.*

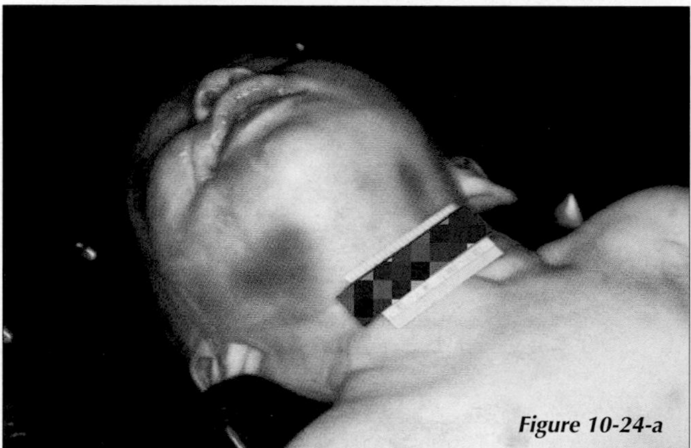

Figure 10-24-a

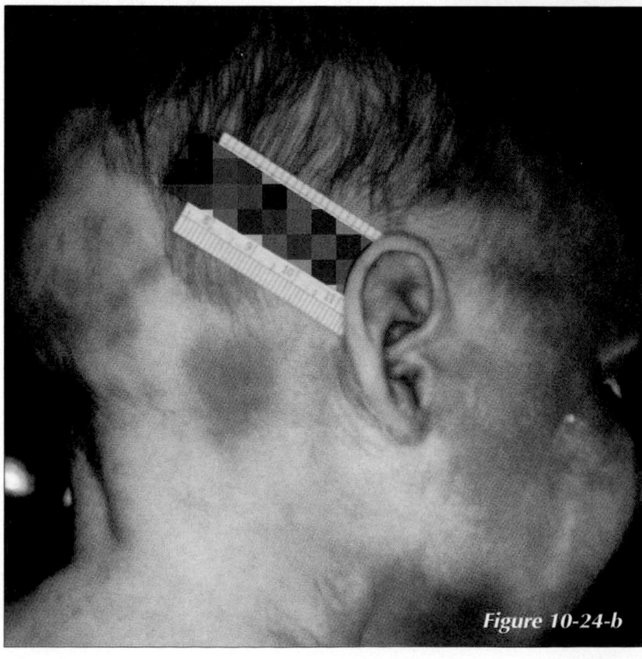

Figure 10-24-b

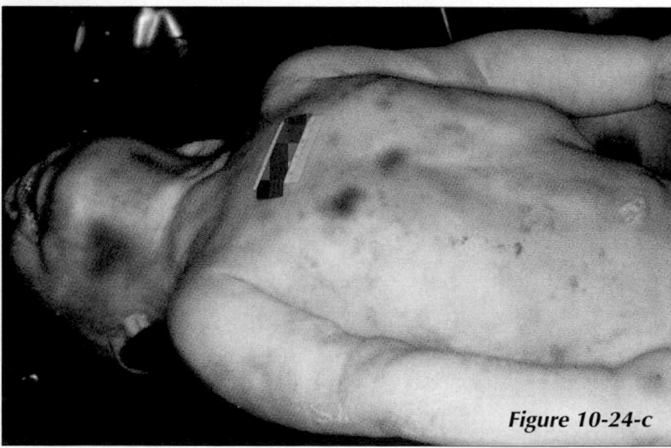

Figure 10-24-c

# Deaths

## Soft Tissue Injuries

**Case Study 10-25**

These infants had severe soft tissue trauma.

***Figure 10-25-a.*** *Bruising of back, buttocks, and legs.*

***Figures 10-25-b*** *and* ***c.*** *The extent of the deep bleeding in this child is not visible until exposed.*

## Rib Fractures

**Case Study 10-26**

This 2-month-old infant had rib fractures.

***Figures 10-26-a*** *and* ***b.*** *Fresh rib fractures. Bleeding into the pleural soft tissues indicates that the fractures are premortem.*

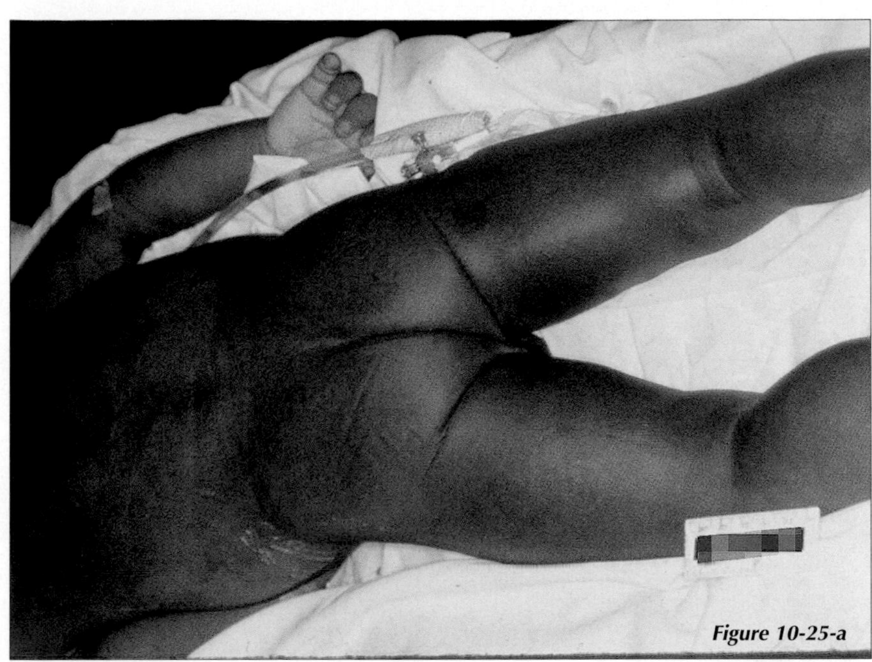

Figure 10-25-a

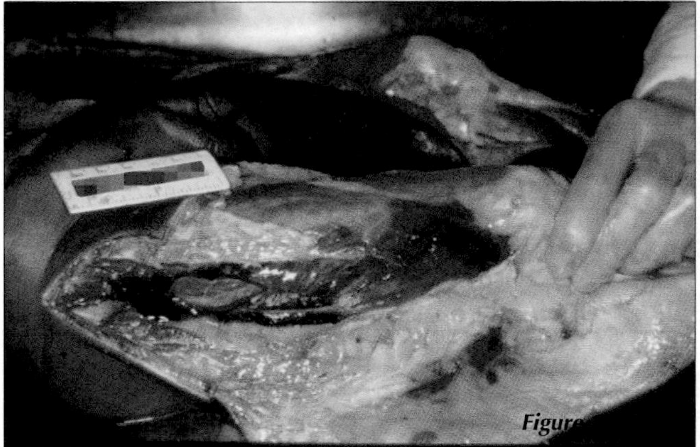

Figur

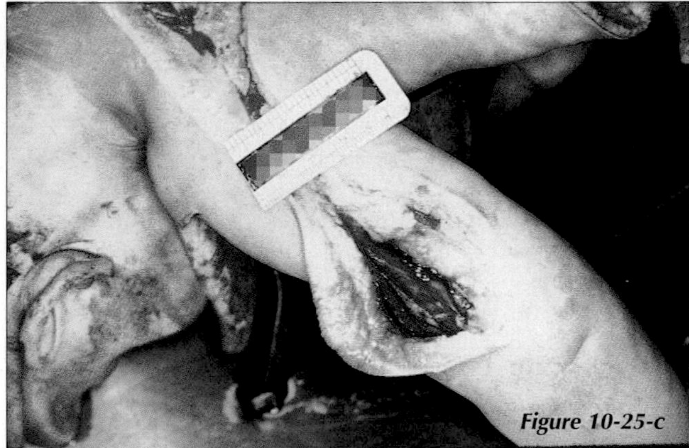

Figure 10-25-c

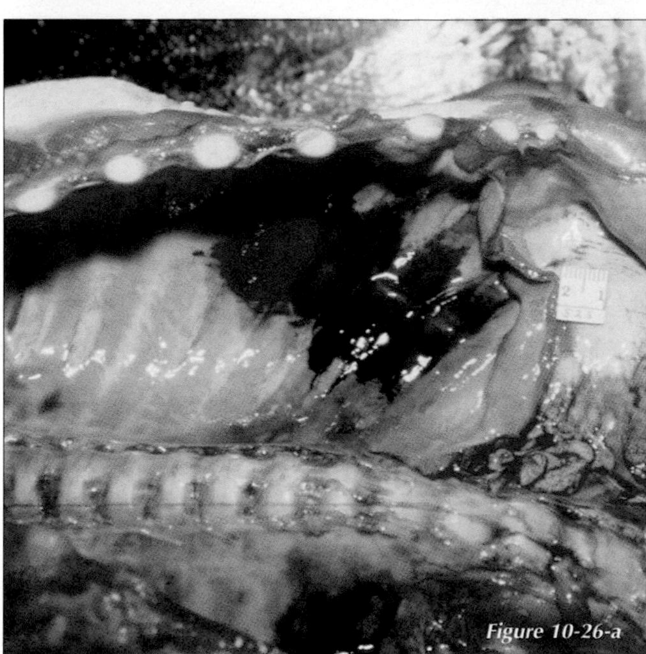

Figure 10-26-a

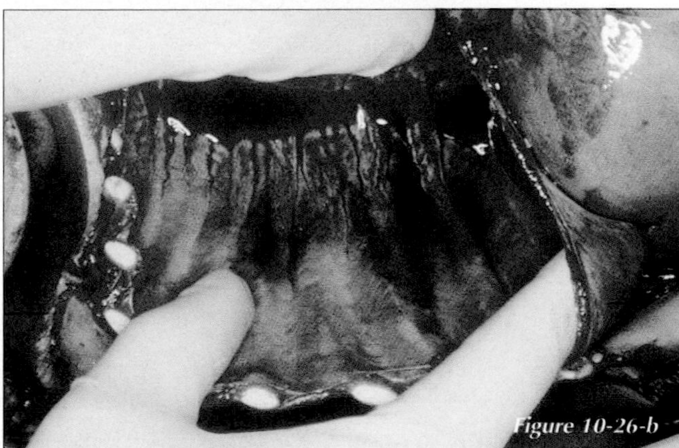

Figure 10-26-b

# Deaths

## Blunt Abdominal Trauma

**Case Study 10-27**

These 2 children had blunt trauma to the abdomen resulting in massive visceral bleeding.

***Figures 10-27-a** and **b**. Retroperitoneal, mesenteric, and intraperitoneal bleeding found at autopsy.*

## Blunt Chest Trauma

**Case Study 10-28**

This infant sustained abusive blunt trauma to the chest that resulted in lung contusions.

***Figures 10-28-a** and **b**. Lung contusions revealed at autopsy.*

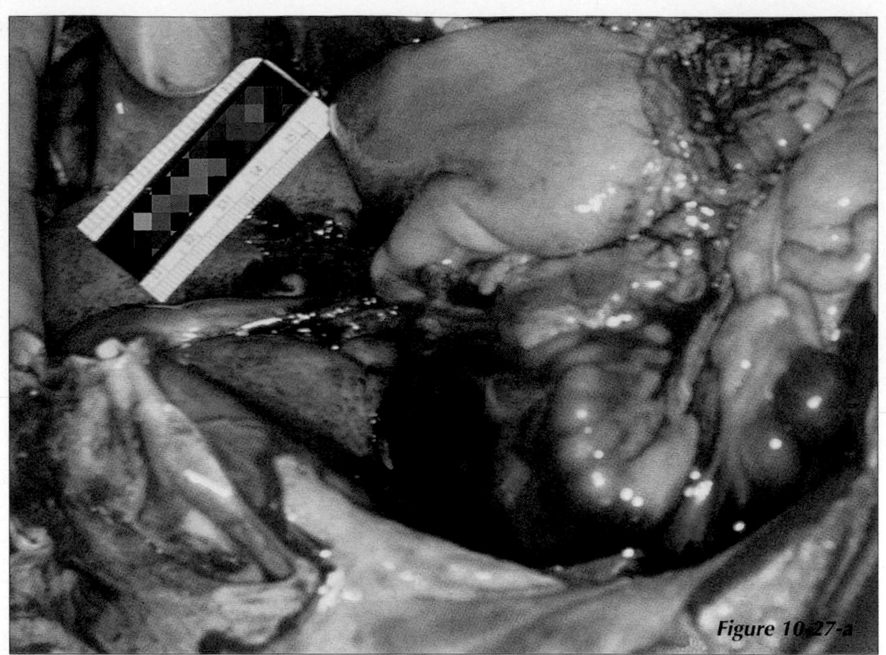

**Figure 10-27-a**

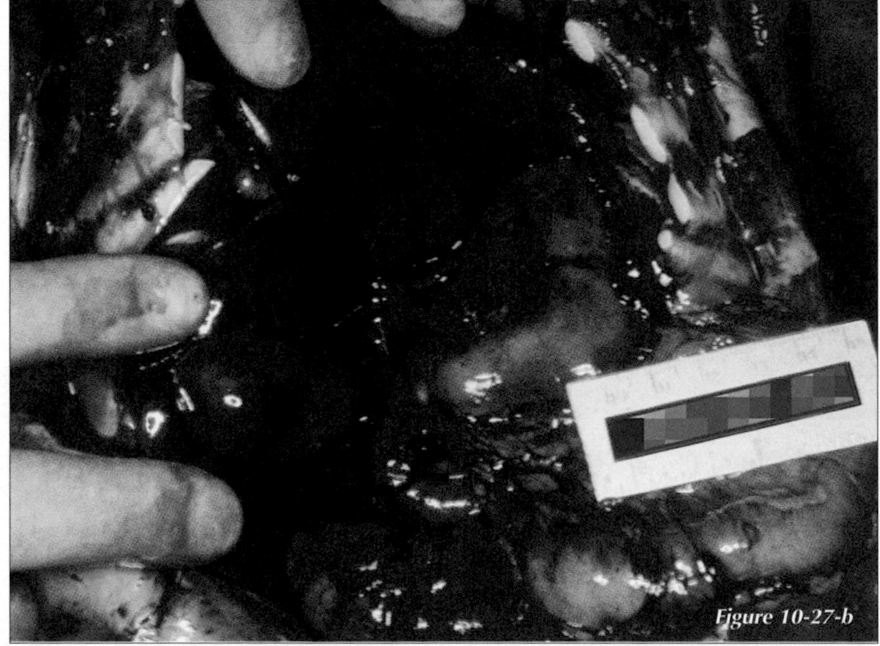

**Figure 10-27-b**

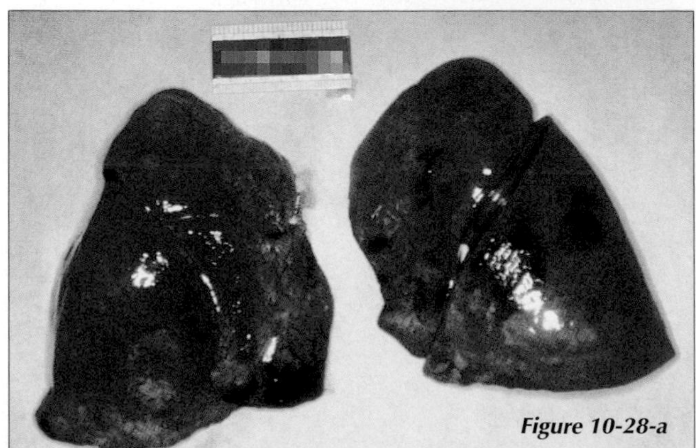

**Figure 10-28-a**

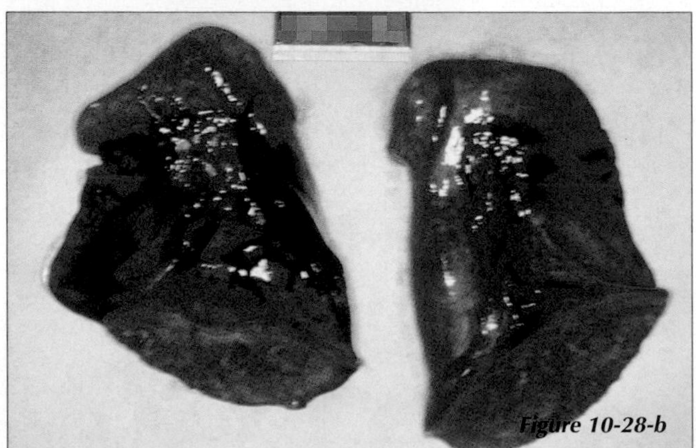

**Figure 10-28-b**

# Deaths

## Closed Head Injury Deaths

**Case Study 10-29**

These 2 deaths were caused by closed head injuries.

***Figure 10-29-a.*** *Widening of the sutures secondary to cerebral edema and increased intracranial pressure in a case of shaken baby syndrome.*

***Figure 10-29-b.*** *The result of impact is a fracture of the left posterior parietal bone. Note that the fracture stops at the suture line. When suture lines are unossified, fracture lines in a bone do not tend to continue to an adjacent bone because the unossified suture line serves as a cushion and dissipates the force of a blow. Only a direct blow in the vicinity of the unossified suture line itself may cause a fracture in 2 adjacent bones. Otherwise, a fracture of the adjacent bone would require a second blow. When suture lines are ossified, however, a fracture can continue to an adjacent bone.*

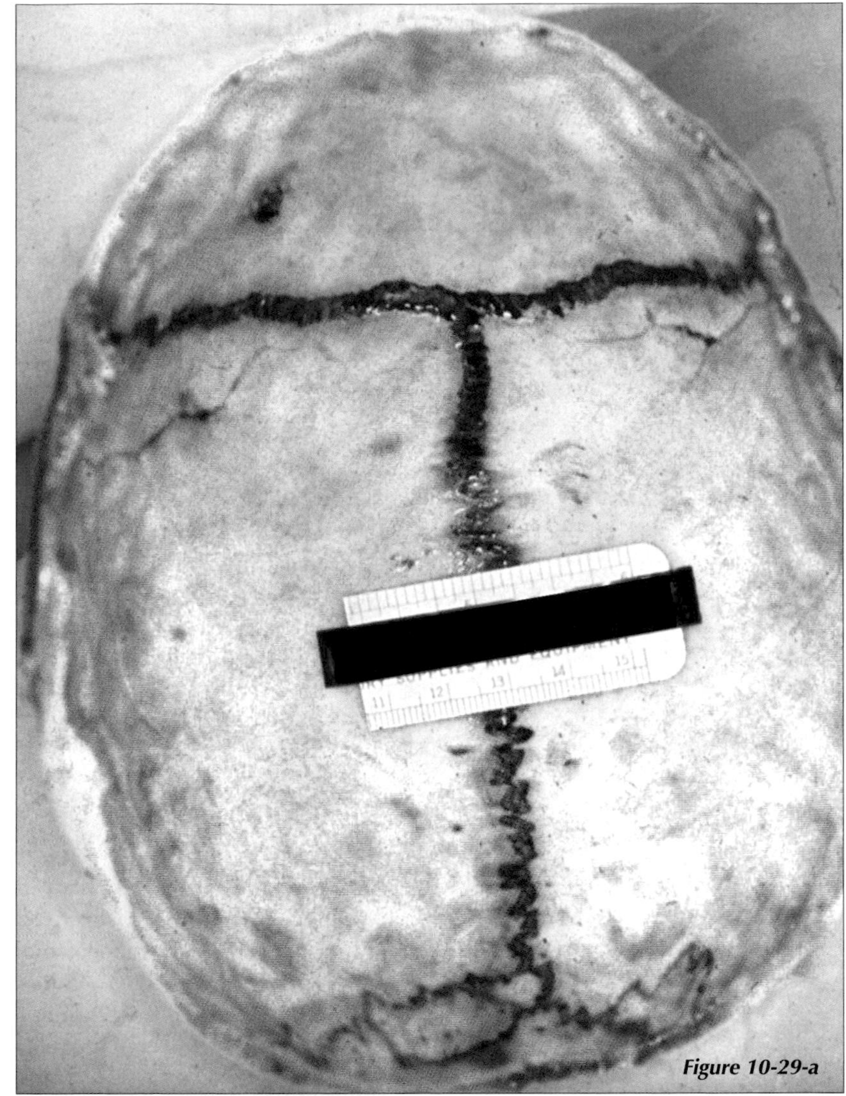

**Figure 10-29-a**

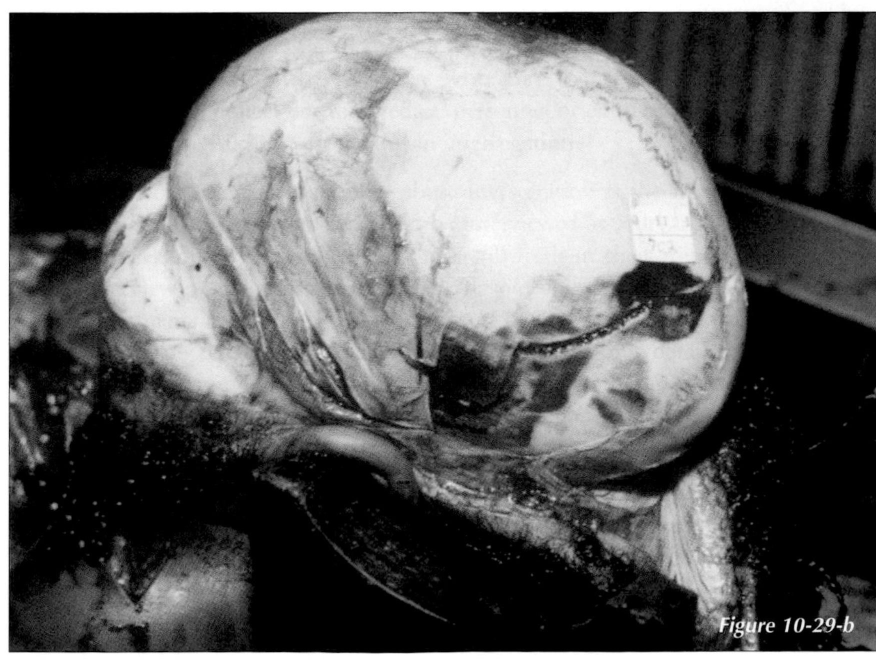

**Figure 10-29-b**

# Reports of Child Maltreatment

**Case Study 11-1** *(continued)*

***Figure 11-1-e.*** *Blood in the ear of this child.*

***Figure 11-1-f.*** *The dead child with his gastric tube attached.*

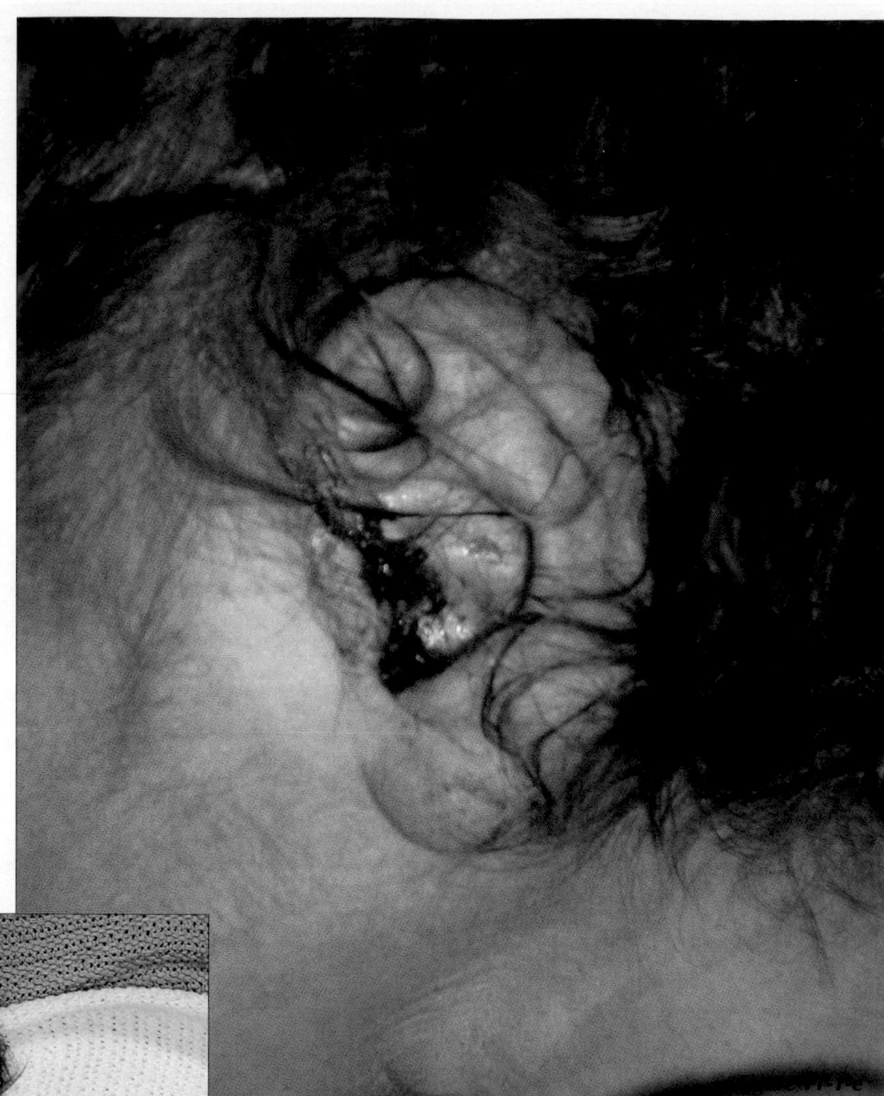

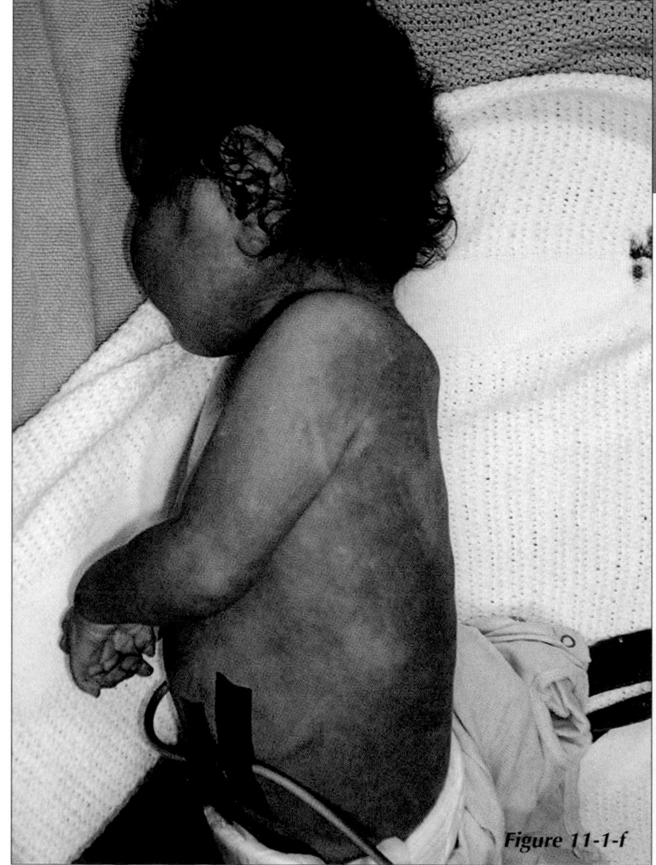
Figure 11-1-f

# Reports of Child Maltreatment

**Case Study 11-2**

This 18-month-old boy was brought into the hospital with a suspicious bruise and cut to his back. The father of the child was a substance abuser with a criminal record for assault. Both he and the mother refused to give statements relating to this injury. Investigators eventually located the maternal grandmother who was more forthcoming. She stated that the child had fallen against the glass door of a cabinet at her home. The non-tempered glass shattered and cut the child. An examination of the grandmother's home revealed a cabinet with broken glass. The dimensions of the glass chards matched the size of the child's injury.

***Figure 11-2-a.*** *Injuries to this child's back.*

***Figure 11-2-b.*** *The injuries to the child's back with a ruler for scale, which is required for the analysis of photodocumentation.*

The cause of this child's injuries was determined to be accidental.

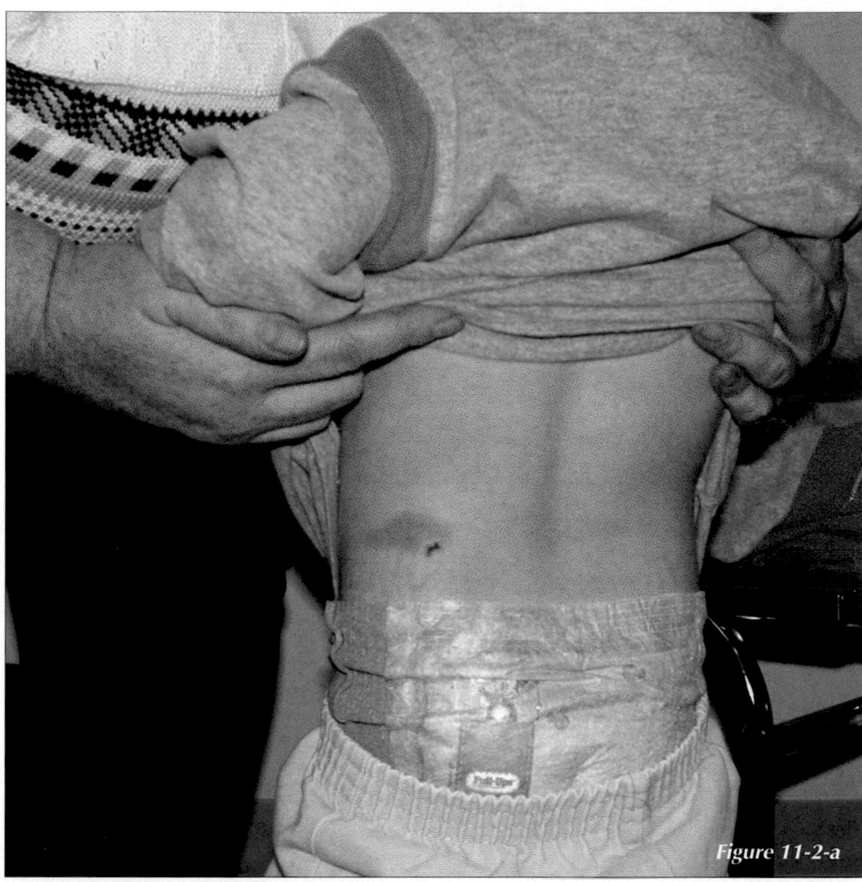

Figure 11-2-a

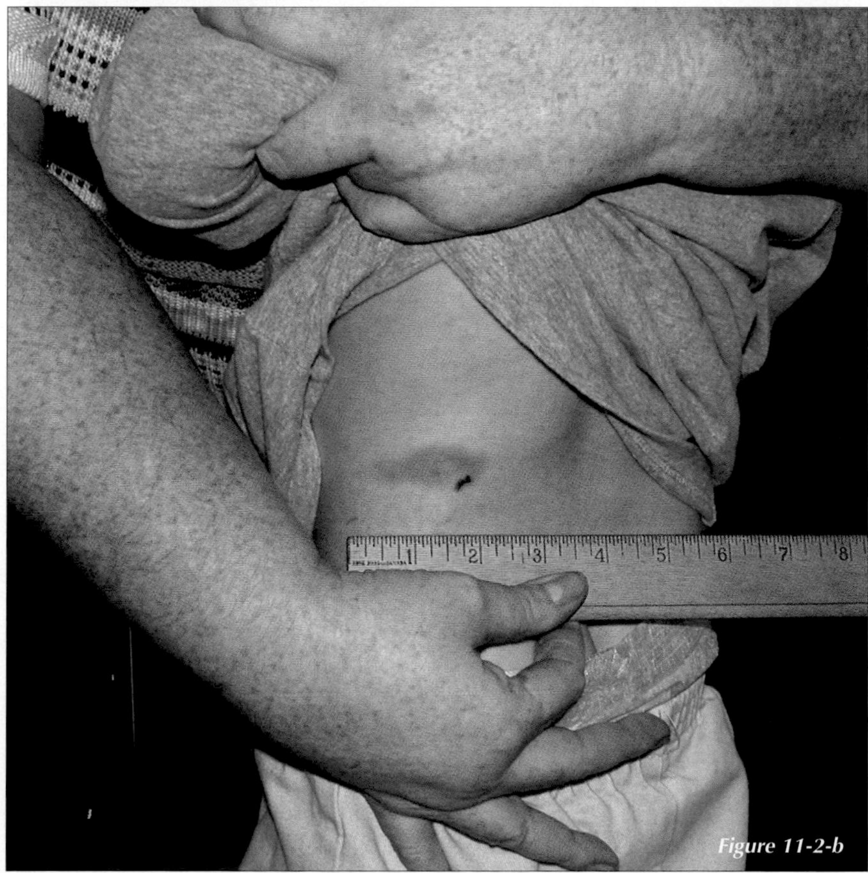


Figure 11-2-b

## Reports of Child Maltreatment

**Case Study 11-3**

This 10-year-old mentally handicapped girl was brought into a medical facility with a severe burn to her left knee. Police and child protection workers were notified because the injury initially appeared to have been abusive in nature. The child was able to explain that she had accidentally spilled hot chocolate on her leg. Her explanation was consistent with the findings of the attending physician.

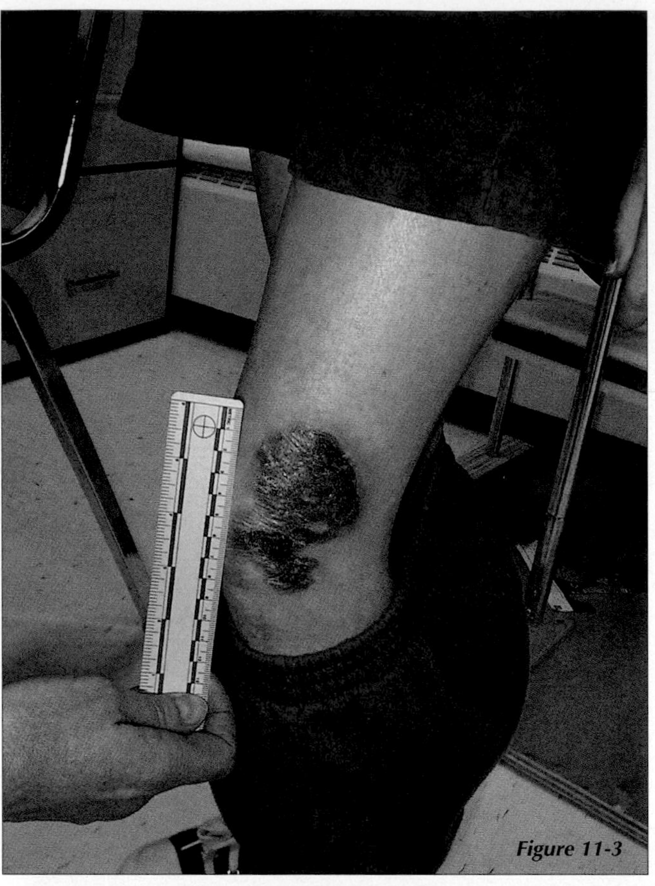

***Figure 11-3.*** *The localized scalding pattern is consistent with her explanation. There is no sign of bruising or other injury that would have accompanied a deliberate infliction of a scald burn of this severity.*

The cause of this injury was determined to be accidental and consistent with the history given by the child.

**Case Study 11-4**

This 2-year-old girl was brought into the hospital with severe scald burns. Investigators individually questioned a house full of witnesses who consistently stated that the child had been left unattended for a moment and climbed into a sink and turned on the hot water, scalding herself. A check of the hot water tank showed that it was set to a maximum temperature of 130 degrees Fahrenheit.

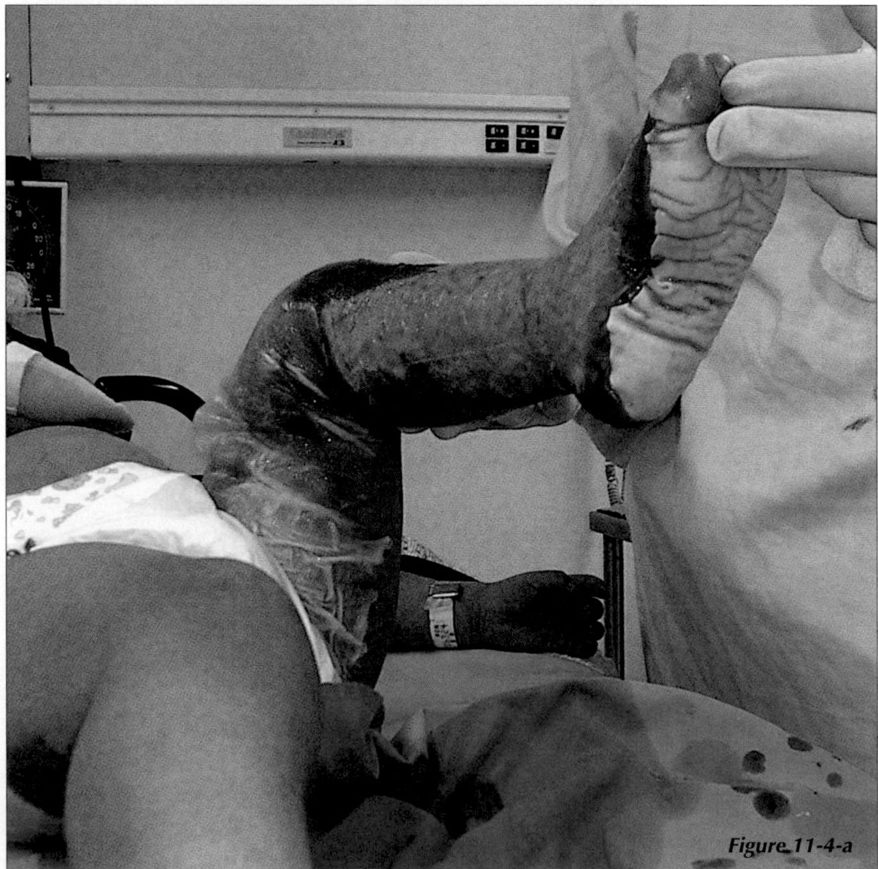

***Figure 11-4-a.*** *Note the total scald damage to this child's left leg, while portions of the right upper thigh are undamaged.*

## Reports of Child Maltreatment

**Case Study 11-4** *(continued)*

***Figure 11-4-b.*** *This child's right heel and upper right thigh are thoroughly scalded, but the right calf and lower right thigh have been spared.*

***Figure 11-4-c.*** *Had this been a deliberate immersion burn, this child's upper right thigh would have more spared skin as the lower leg flexed into a fetal position. The disparity of the burn patterns is consistent with an unintentional injury. These injuries were determined to be accidental, though a result of neglect on the part of the caregiver.*

**Case Study 11-5**

This 12-year-old female was whipped with a belt. The child disclosed that her mother had inflicted the injury and the mother subsequently confessed to police and was charged with assault.

***Figure 11-5.*** *Pattern bruises from the belt to the left leg of this child.*

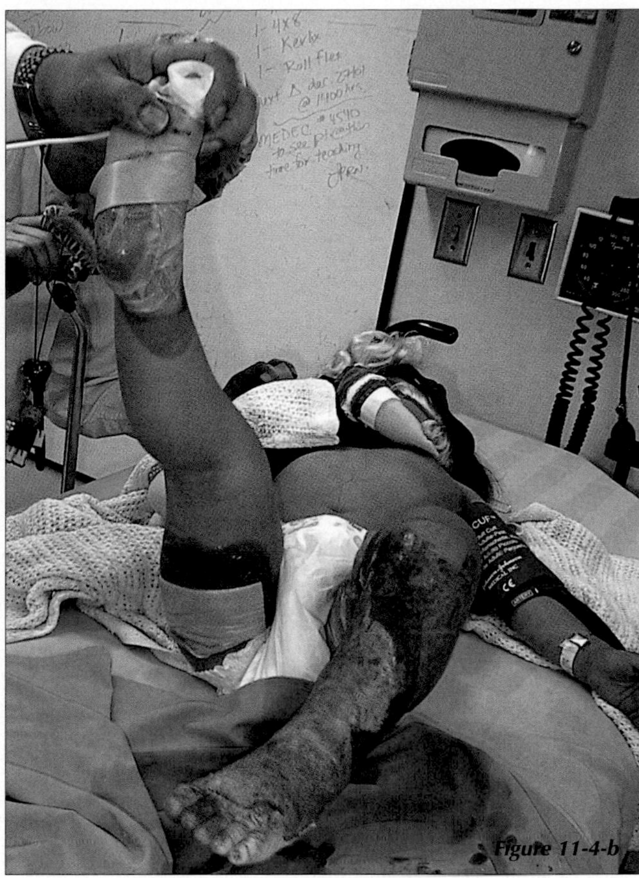

Figure 11-4-b

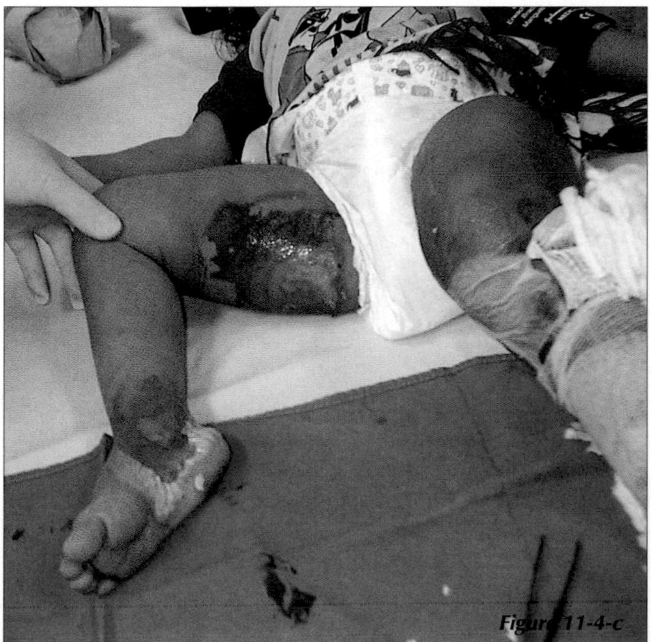

Figure 11-4-c

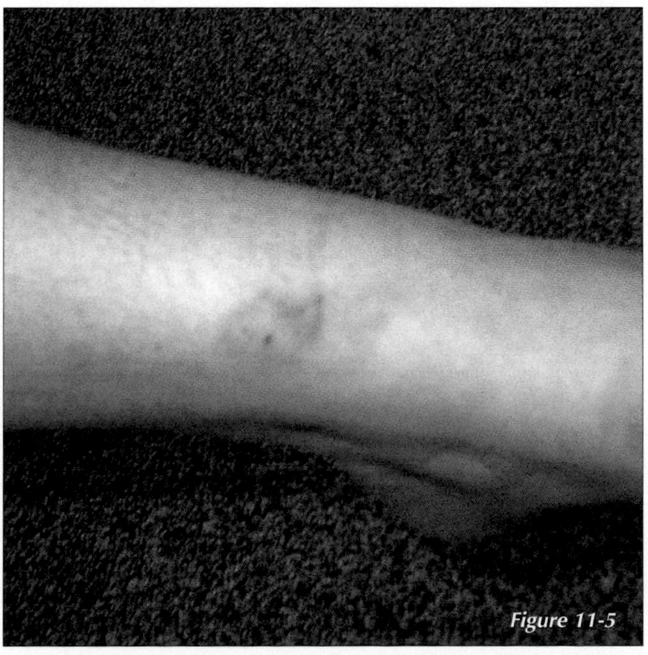

Figure 11-5

## Reports of Child Maltreatment

**Case Study 11-6**

This 12-year-old girl's mother beat her with a wooden spoon. During the assault the spoon broke, yet the mother continued to beat the child with the broken handle. When police interviewed the mother, she confessed and was charged with assault.

***Figure 11-6.*** *Distinctive pattern bruises on this 12-year-old girl's shoulder. The round mark on the shoulder matches the head of the spoon while the linear marks underneath support the child's story that she was beaten with the handle after the spoon broke.*

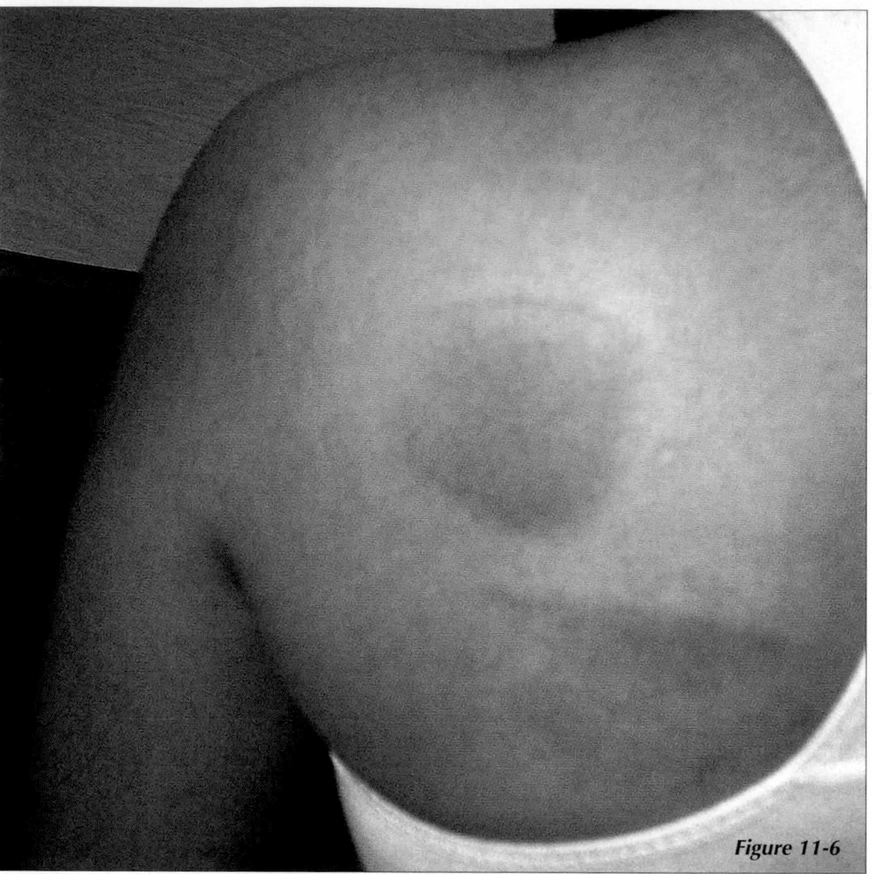

Figure 11-6

**Case Study 11-7**

This 3-year-old boy claimed that his teenaged babysitter spanked and pinched him. The suspect was questioned but would not admit to causing the injuries.

***Figure 11-7.*** *Bruising to the buttocks of the 3-year-old boy.*

These injuries occurred due to high-velocity forces. Suspicions were raised, but charges were not pressed.

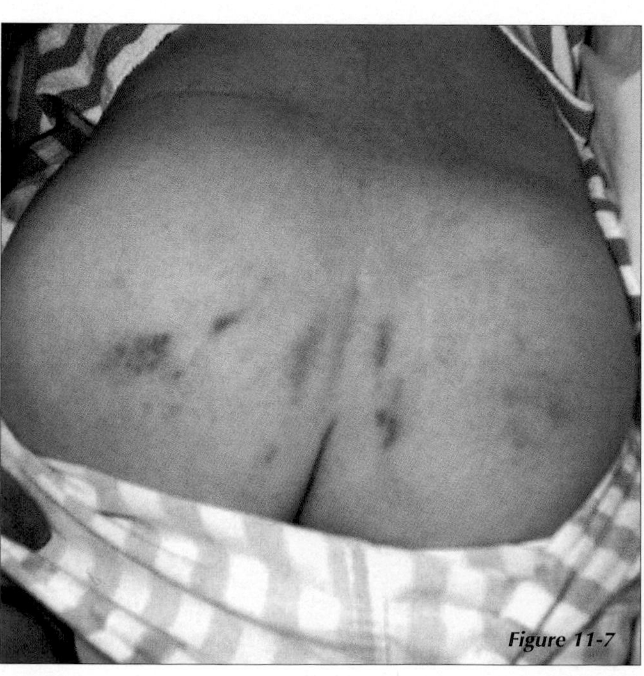

Figure 11-7

**Case Study 11-8**

This 5-year-old boy was beaten with a broom handle. The perpetrator confessed and was charged with assault.

***Figure 11-8.*** *Distinctive pattern bruise on the back of the child.*

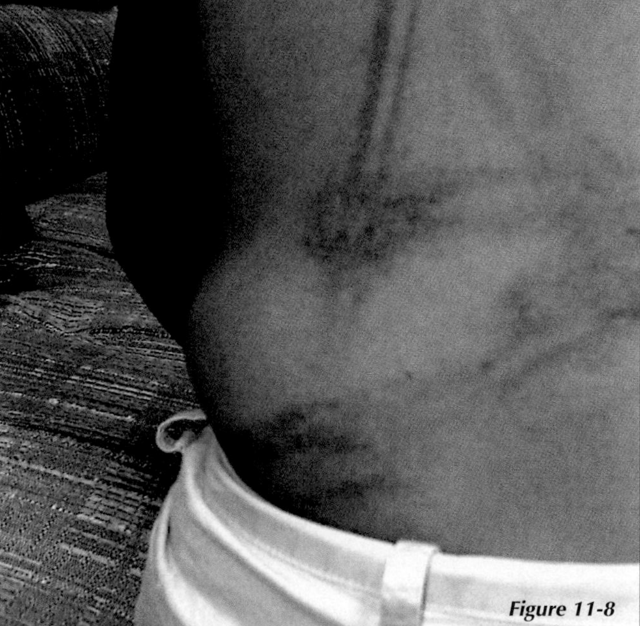

Figure 11-8

## Reports of Child Maltreatment

**Case Study 11-9**

The mother and father were arguing over their 7-month-old son. The father, who was intoxicated at the time, grabbed the child from the mother and both parents fell down the cement stairs in front of their house and landed on top of the child. The child died the day after his fall due to the massive trauma associated with the fall and from being crushed by the weight of his parents. While the death was certainly suspicious, there was insufficient evidence to proceed with charges.

***Figures 11-9-a** and **b.** Outside views of the townhouse. The parents fell down the five cement stairs and landed on the child.*

***Figure 11-9-c.** Minor injuries suffered by the mother during the fall.*

***Figure 11-9-d.** The child on the autopsy table.*

Figure 11-9-a

Figure 11-9-b

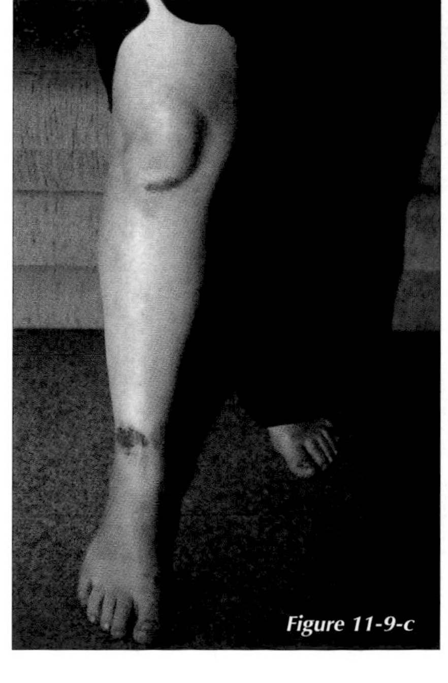
Figure 11-9-c

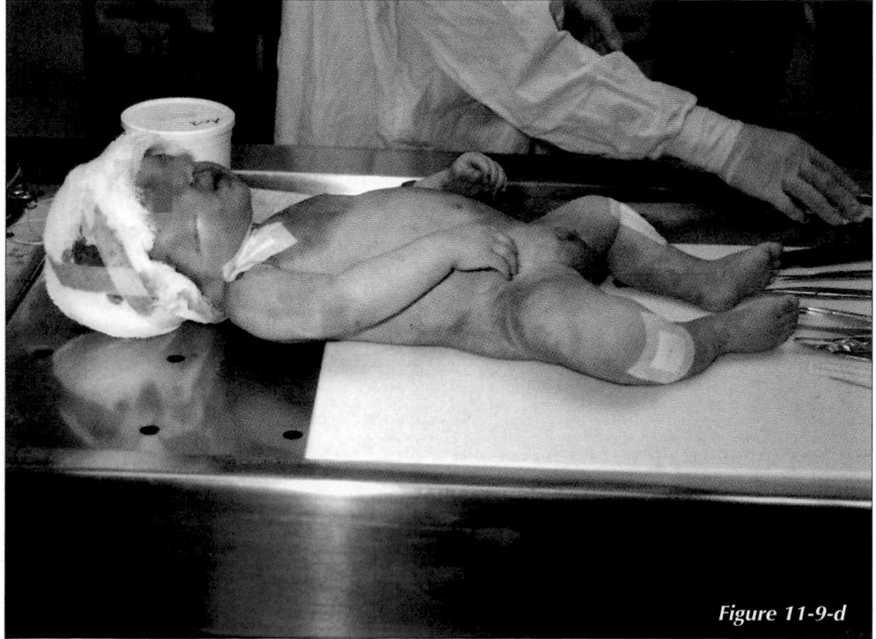
Figure 11-9-d

# Differentiating Between Inflicted and Accidental Injuries

**Case Study 11-11**

This 7-week-old boy was observed with a bruise on his face. The mother said that the child injured himself while holding his bottle and striking his own face with the nipple end of the bottle. This statement is false, since the actions described are beyond a 7-week-old's developmental level.

***Figure 11-11.*** *Facial injury to the child.*

**Case Study 11-12**

This boy was admitted for examination with bruising around the legs and genital area.

***Figures 11-12-a*** *and* ***b.*** *Pattern bruises in the shape of loop marks made by an extension cord.*

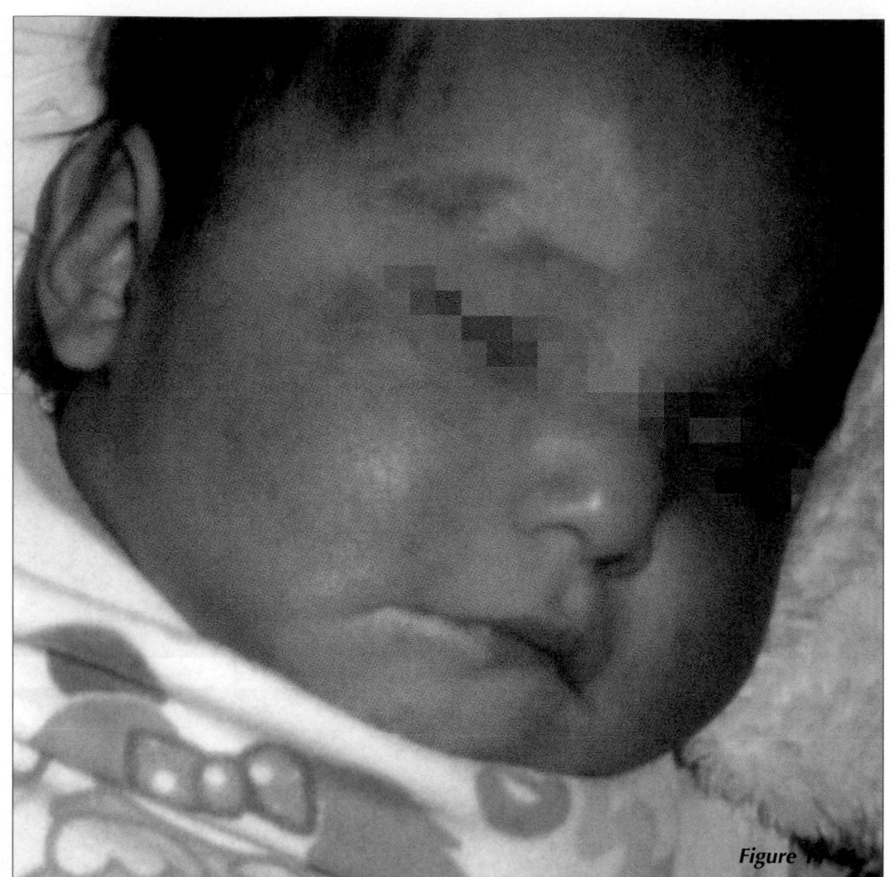

Figure 11-11

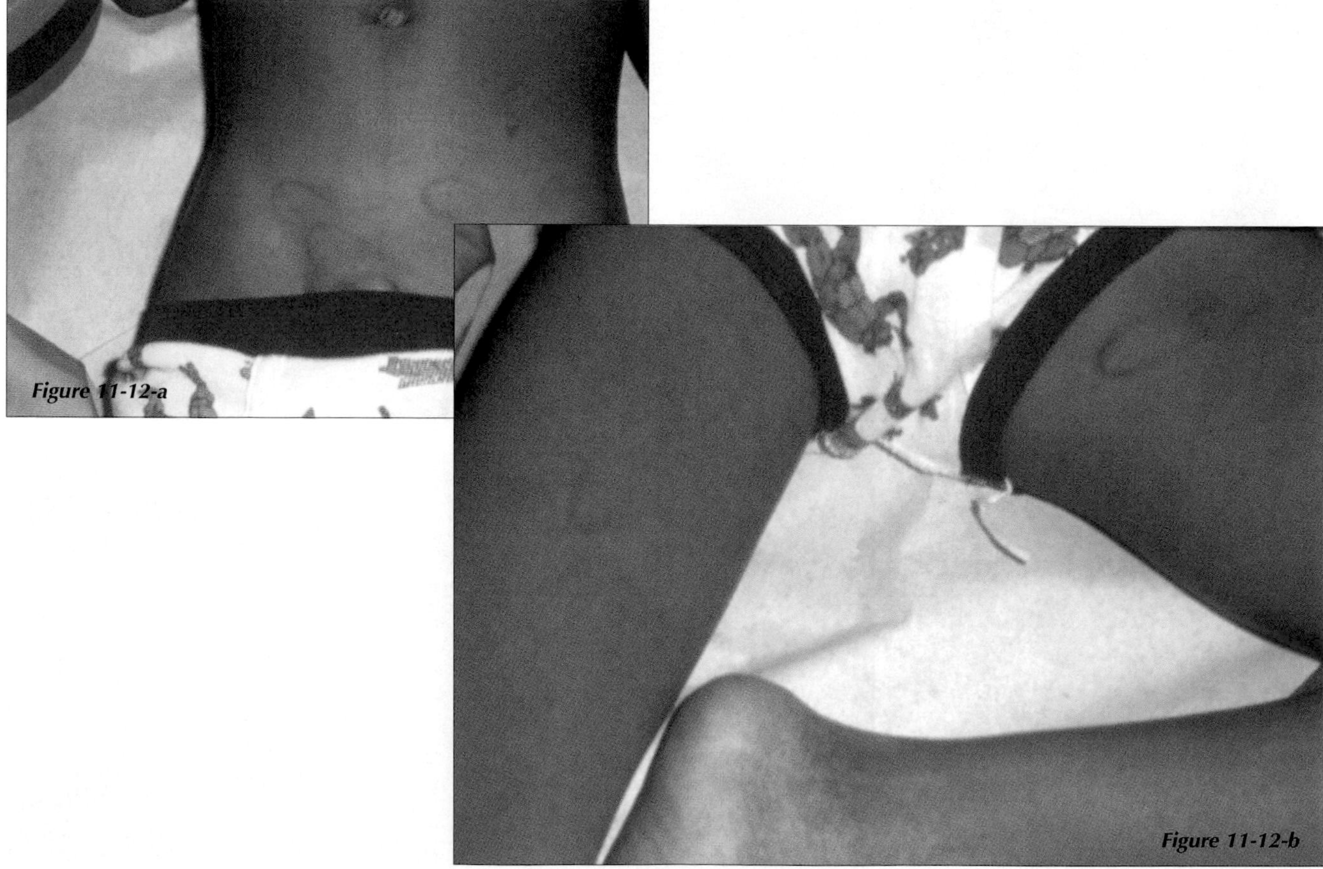

Figure 11-12-a

Figure 11-12-b

# Differentiating Between Inflicted and Accidental Injuries

**Case Study 11-13**

This boy was examined with human bite marks near his armpit.

***Figures 11-13-a** and **b.** Note the central ecchymoses accompanying the bite marks. This child also has grab bruises on his arm.*

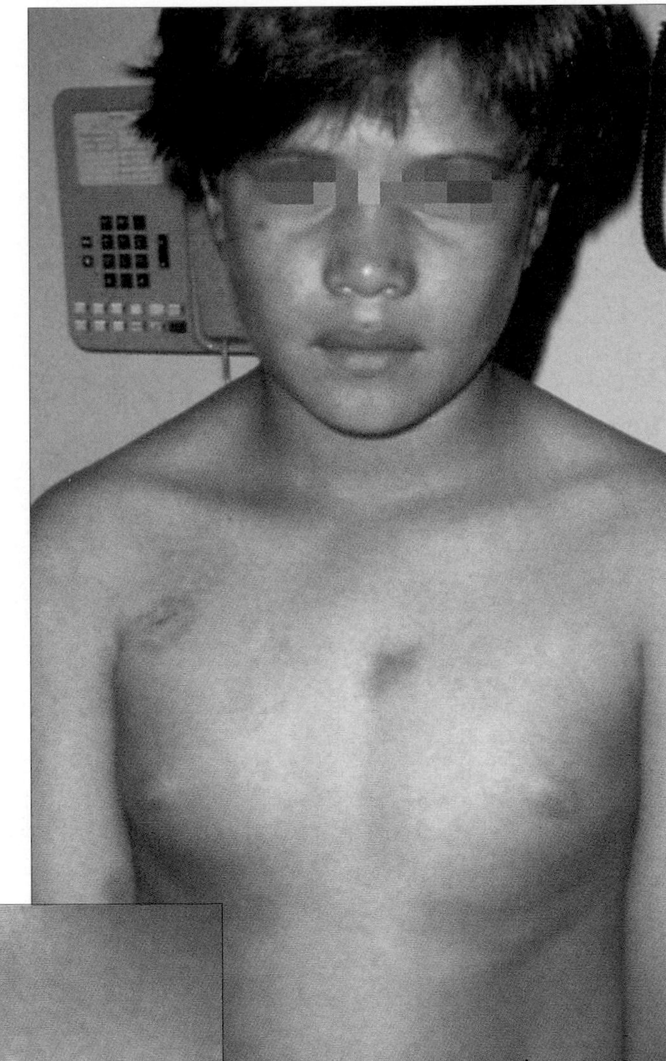

***Figure 11-13-a***

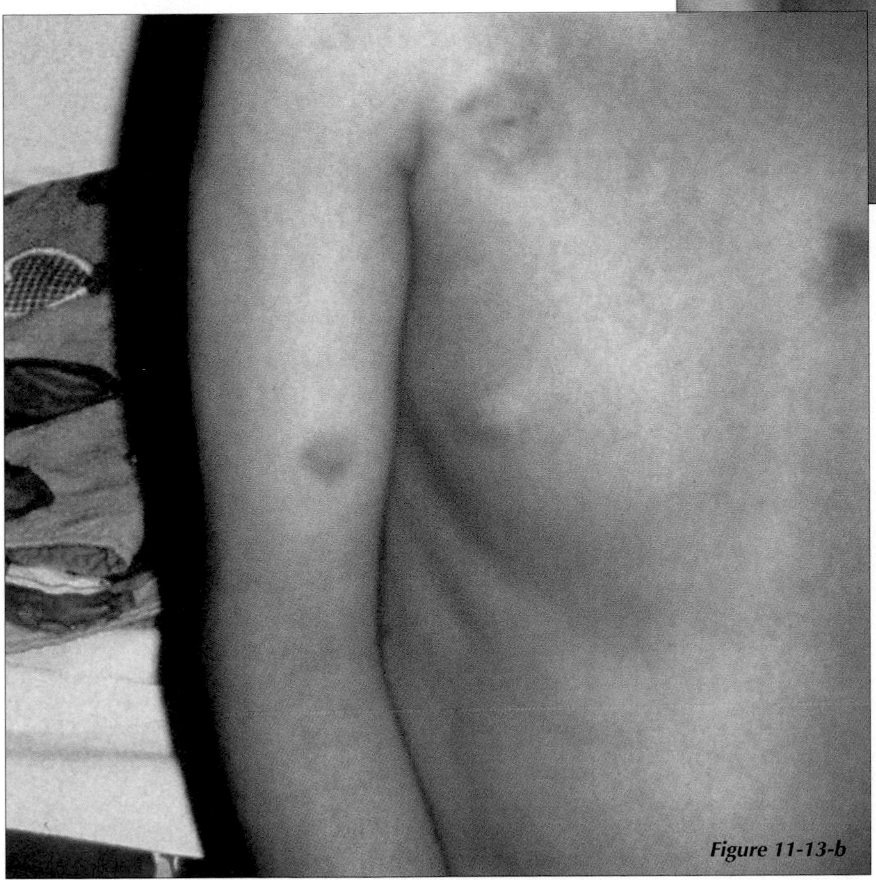

***Figure 11-13-b***

# Differentiating Between Inflicted and Accidental Injuries

**Case Study 11-14**

This child was admitted for examination with pattern bruises to the buttocks. The child had been struck by a belt buckle.

***Figure 11-14.*** *Note the bruises that resulted from being beaten with a belt buckle in the shape of a dollar sign. This is a clear example of a pattern bruise.*

**Case Study 11-15**

This 8-month-old child suffered flame burns after being left alone in a crib at home. The caregiver explained that the child pulled a lamp into the crib and the bedding caught fire. Scene examination confirmed this explanation. It was determined that there was negligence on the part of the caregiver, but not a deliberate assault.

***Figure 11-15-a.*** *Note the burns to the arm, chest, and legs of this child.*

***Figure 11-15-b.*** *The burns also appeared on the back of the child's legs.*

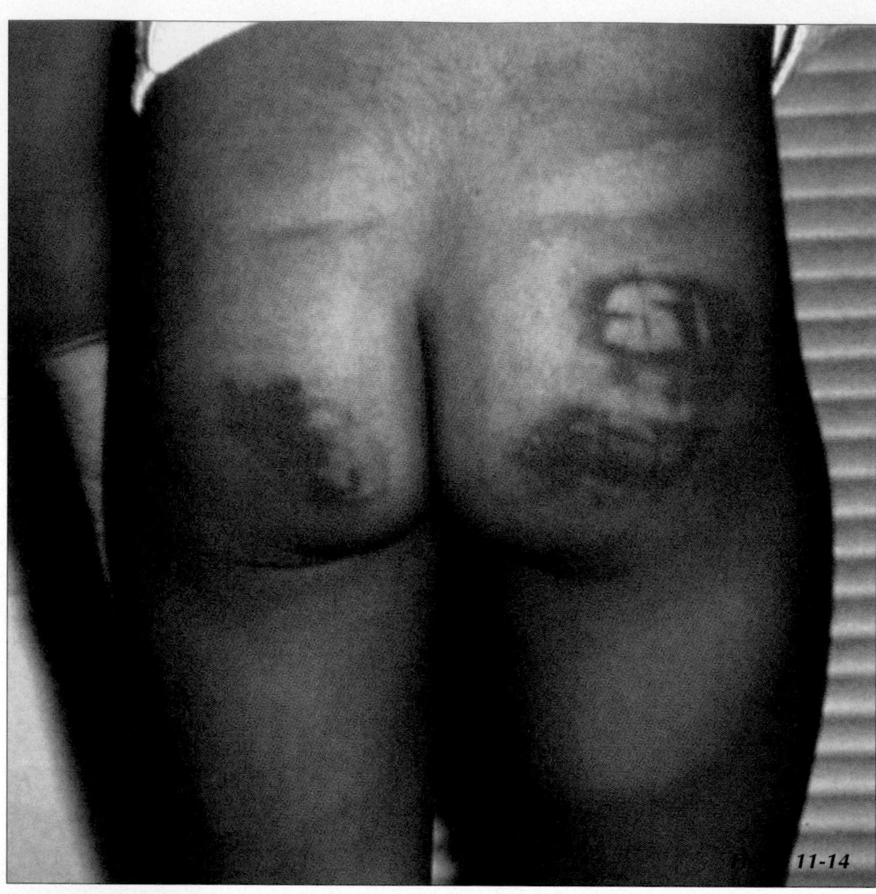

11-14

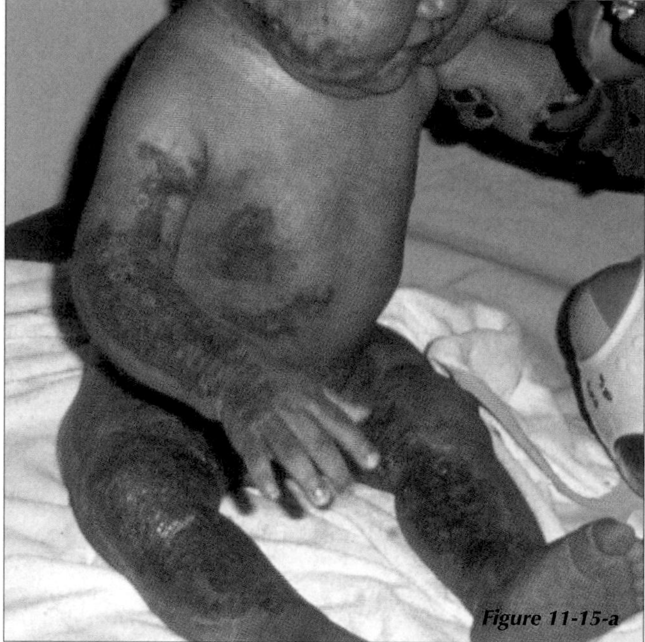

Figure 11-15-a

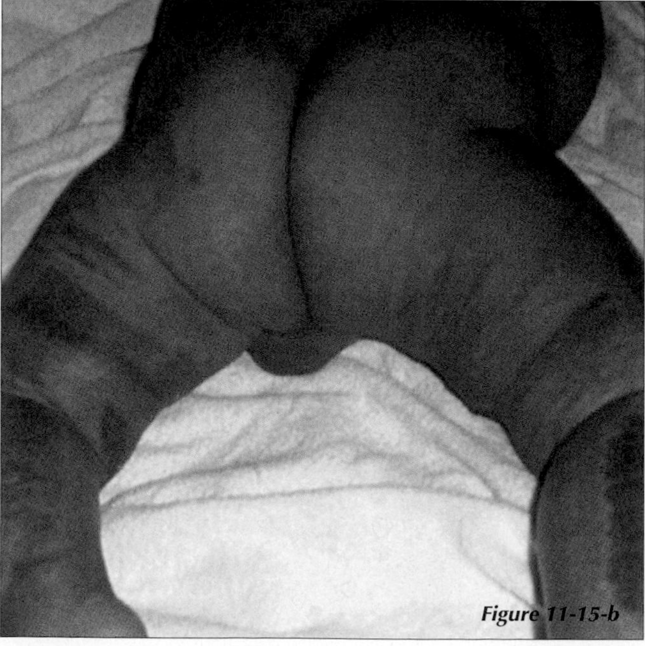

Figure 11-15-b

# Differentiating Between Inflicted and Accidental Injuries

**Case Study 11-16**

This child was immersed in scalding water. Examination of the damaged and undamaged areas of the body can reveal whether the child was wearing a diaper at the time of the incident and whether the child fell into the scaling water or was deliberately immersed. Children with a uniform pattern of scalding, no splash burns, and protected areas of the body where they attempted to pull away from the pain are all indicative of a deliberate assault.

***Figure 11-16.*** *Note that portions of the child's legs that have been spared the most severe damage. These unaffected areas of skin indicate an attempt on the part of the child to escape from the injury, as well as deliberate force on the part of the adult abusing the child to hold the child in the scalding water.*

**Case Study 11-17**

This 4-year-old girl presented with a slap mark to the face. The father stated that a cat had scratched the child.

***Figure 11-17.*** *The injury shows linear bruising rather than the broken skin that would be indicative of a scratch.*

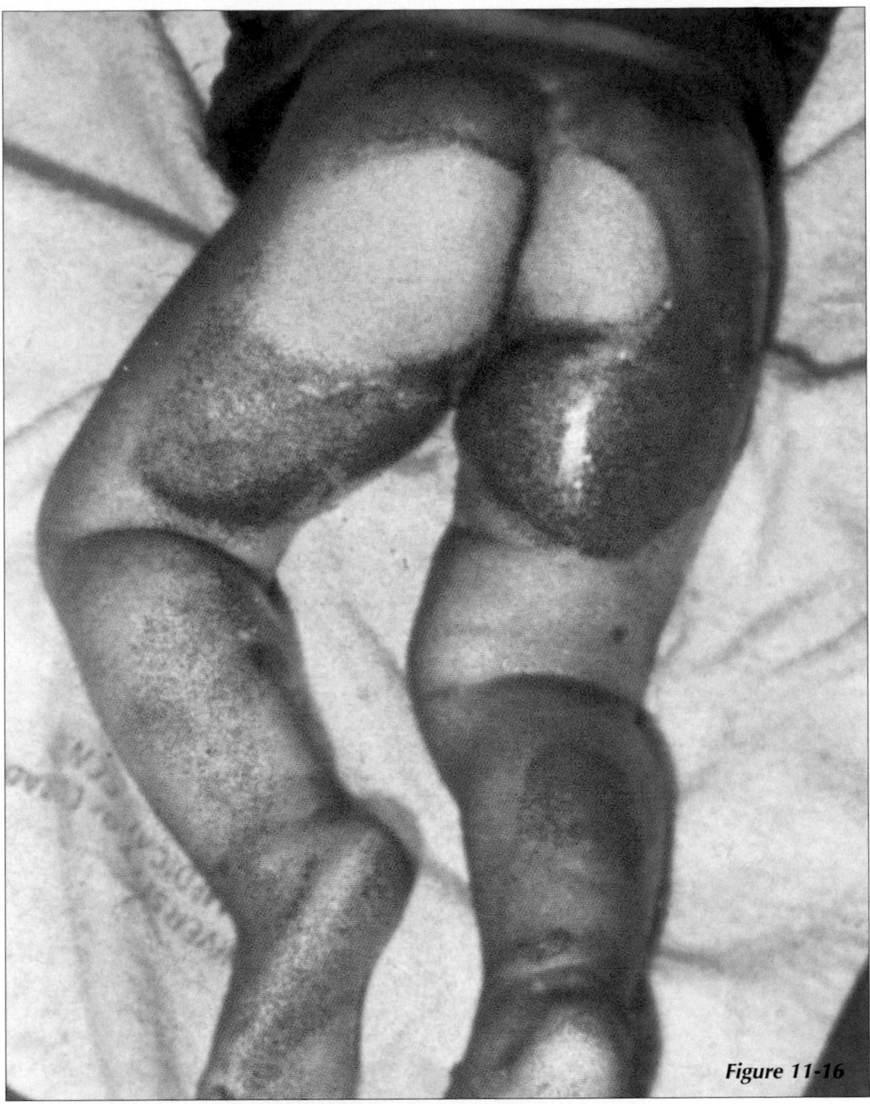

Figure 11-16

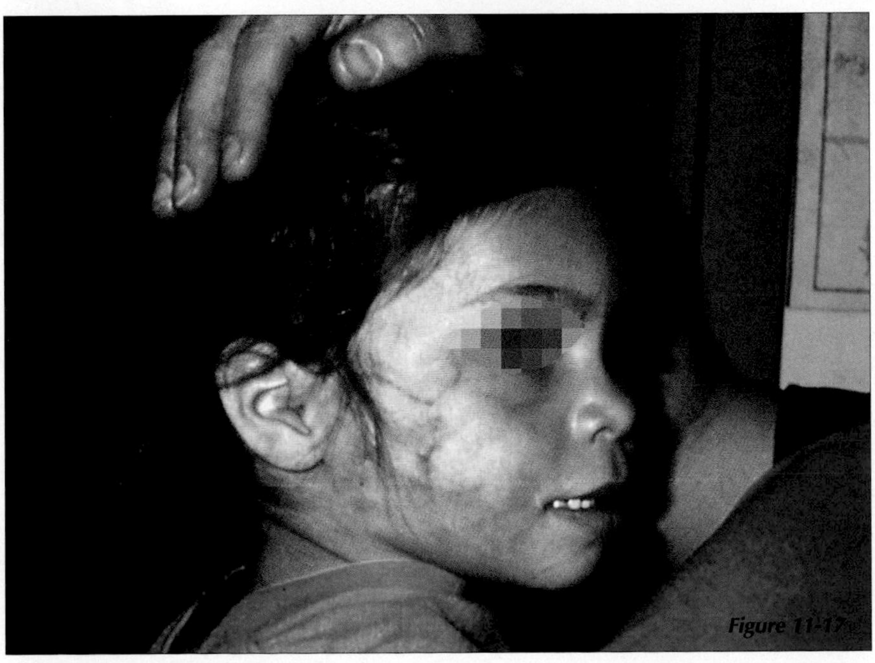

Figure 11-17

## Differentiating Between Inflicted and Accidental Injuries

**Case Study 11-18**

This child is shown with a number of new bruises as well as injuries in different stages of healing. It is often difficult to determine the exact age of a bruise or the cause of an injury. Detailed statements from witnesses and caregivers not only provide verifiable stories for innocent injuries, but can also be used to develop a timeline to discern when the injury could have occurred.

***Figure 11-18.*** *A number of bruises and other injuries of various ages can be seen on the back of this child.*

**Case Study 11-19**

This boy has pattern bruises caused by a belt. The caregiver stated that the child received these injuries from a fall.

***Figure 11-19.*** *The location of the marks is not consistent with injuries usually received from a fall.*

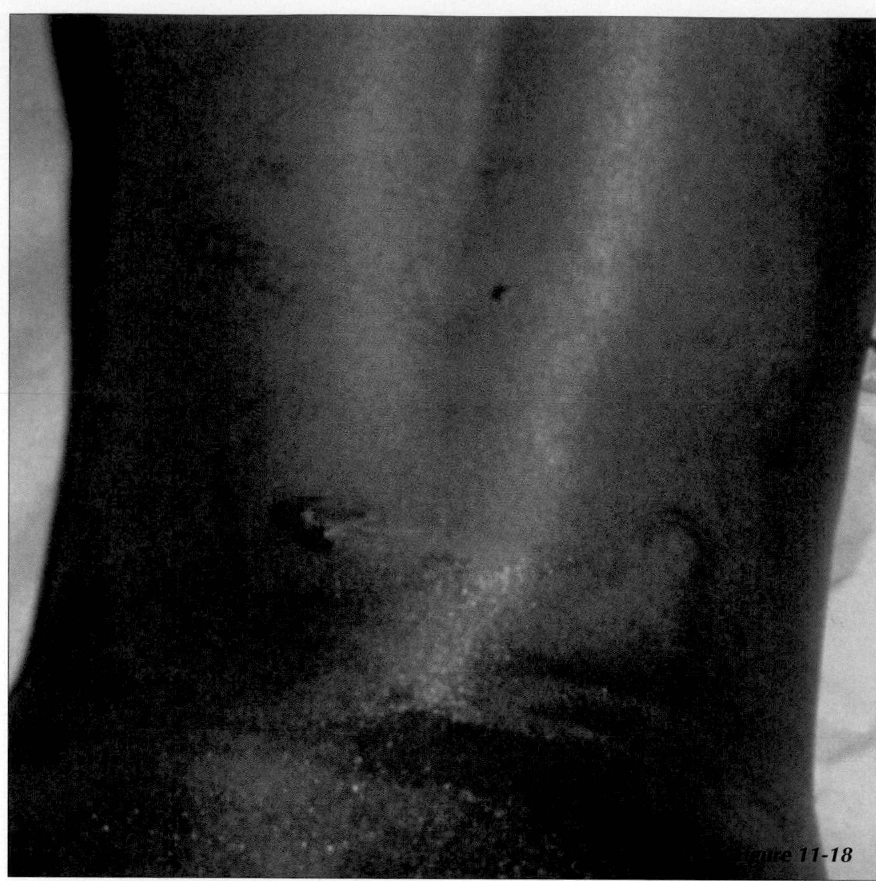

**Figure 11-18**

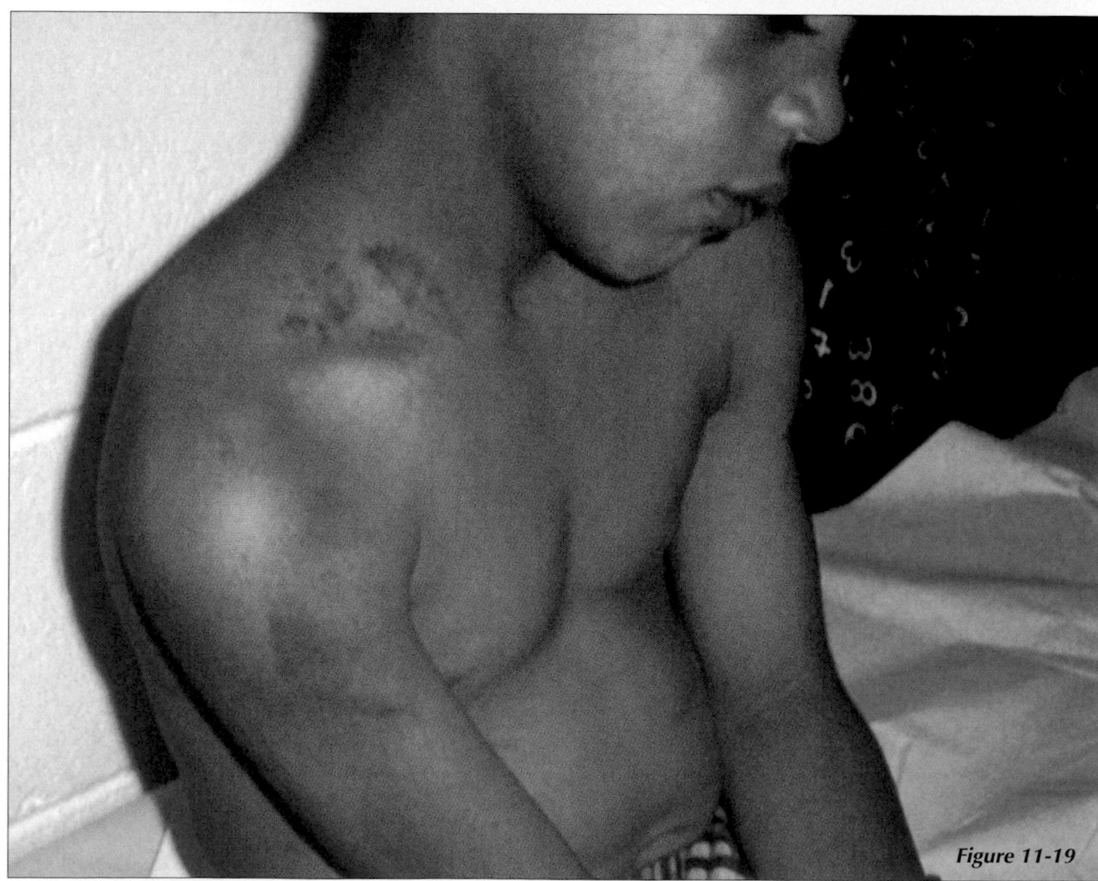

**Figure 11-19**

## Differentiating Between Inflicted and Accidental Injuries

**Case Study 11-20**

This child's legs have been beaten with a belt.

***Figure 11-20.*** *Pattern bruises from a belt curve around the legs in a manner far different than bruising as a result of a fall.*

**Case Study 11-21**

This 1-month-old Native American child died of SIDS. Investigators were initially suspicious of this death because the biological parents, who were both teenagers, had been fighting several hours before the child was found dead in his crib. Both parents were interviewed in a non-confrontational manner and were quite cooperative. A thorough scene examination was completed, which gave the parents the opportunity to outline small details, which confirmed their story that the child had been in another room during their fight and his death was unrelated.

***Figures 11-21-a*** *and* ***b.*** *This child was placed faced down at bedtime as can be seen by the lividity around the chest and shoulder.*

***Figure 11-21-c.*** *A slightly bloody froth at the nose and mouth is a common artifact in SIDS cases.*

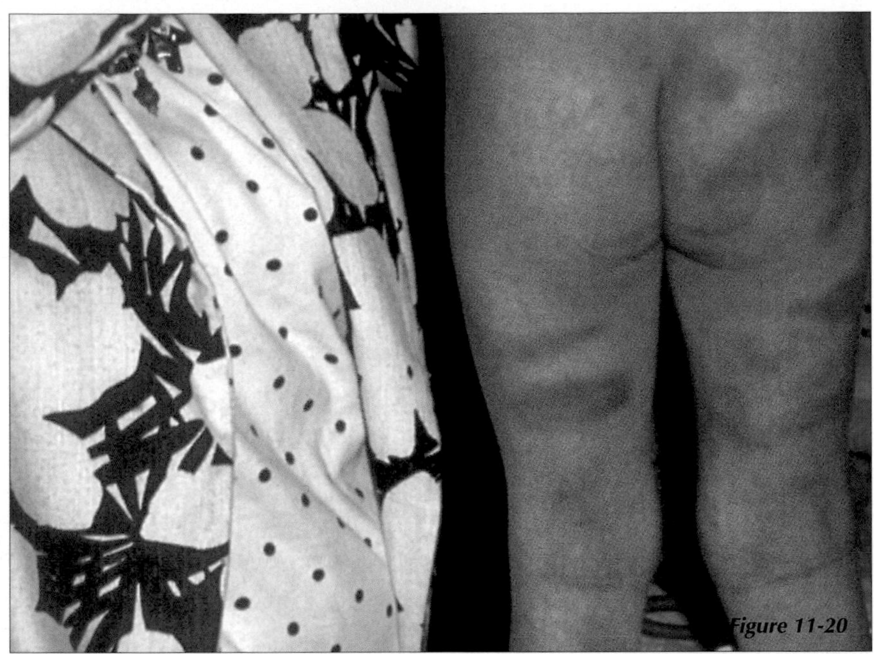

Figure 11-20

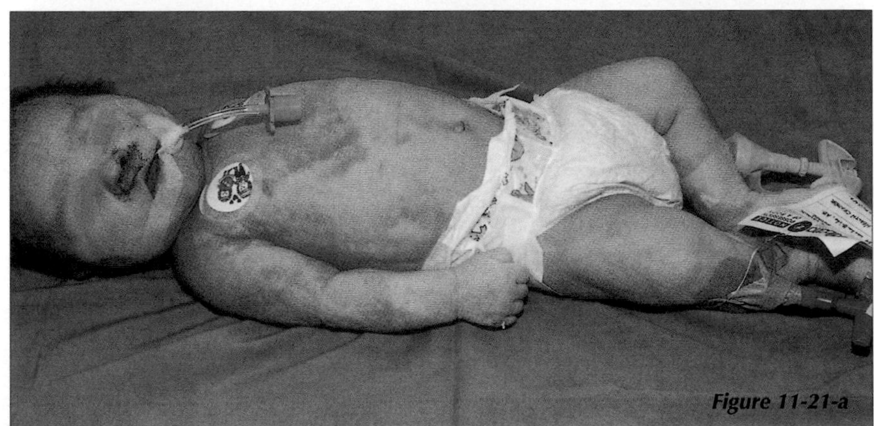

Figure 11-21-a

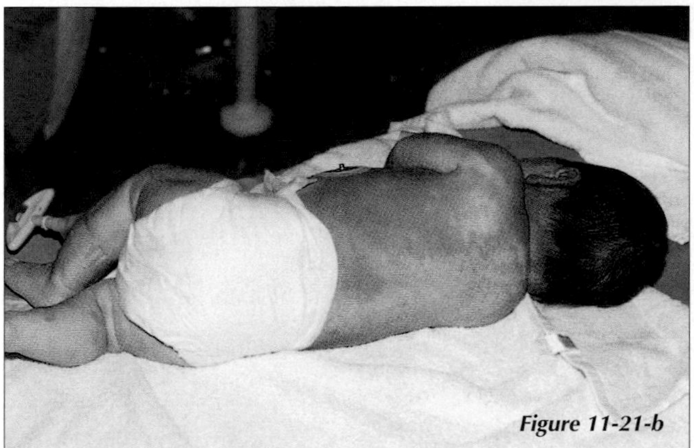

Figure 11-21-b

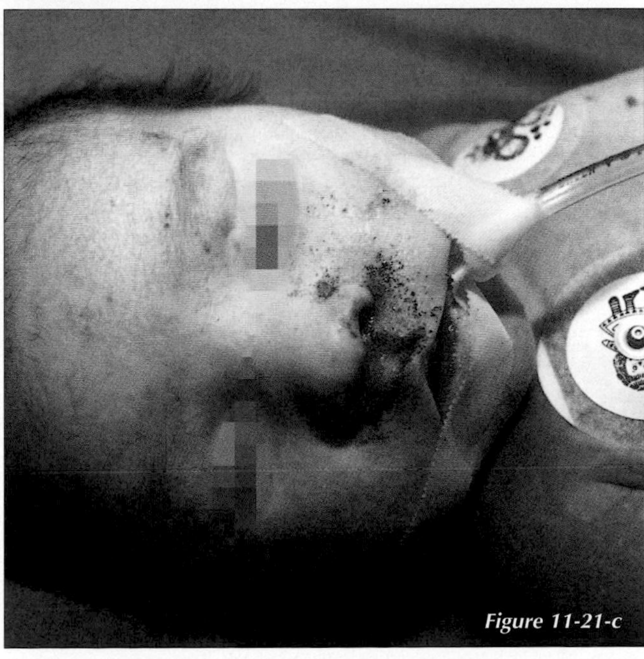

Figure 11-21-c

# Thorough Documentation and Investigation of the Scene

**Case Study 11-22**

This case involved the neglect and subsequent abuse of 5 children. The age of the children at the time of the investigation ranged from 10 months to 8 years. This case came to the attention of the police department after being alerted by school officials.

**11-22-a.** This 8-year-old boy and his 6-year-old brother were acting out angrily in school. An observant teacher noticed pattern marks resembling those from a cord or belt. A closer examination revealed some of the marks to be of a width consistent with a belt, and others to be the width of a common electrical cord.

***Figures 11-22-a.1*** *and* ***a.2.*** *The back of the 6-year-old child.*

***Figure 11-22-a.3.*** *The right shoulder and shoulder blade of the 6-year-old bears marks from abuse.*

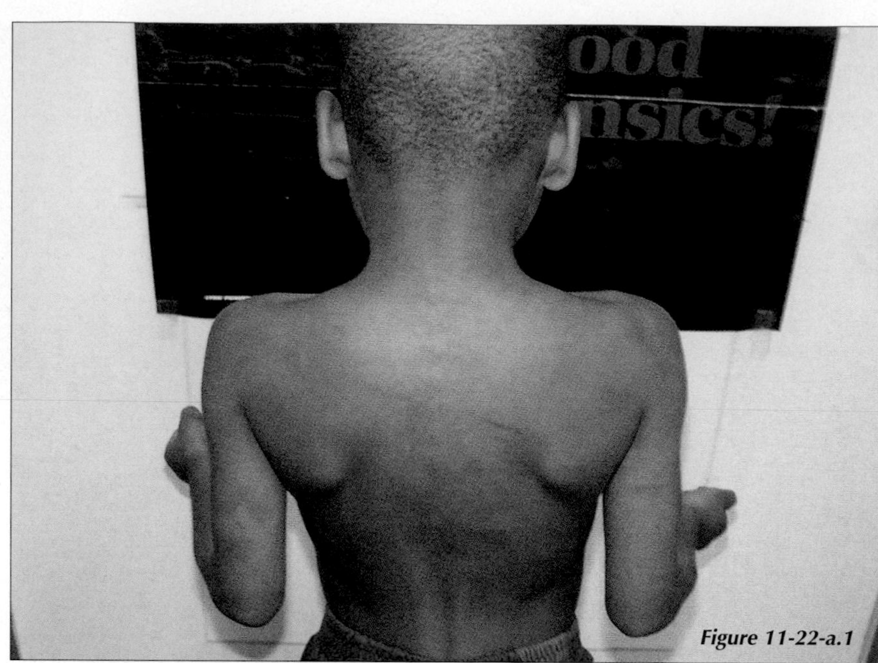

**Figure 11-22-a.1**

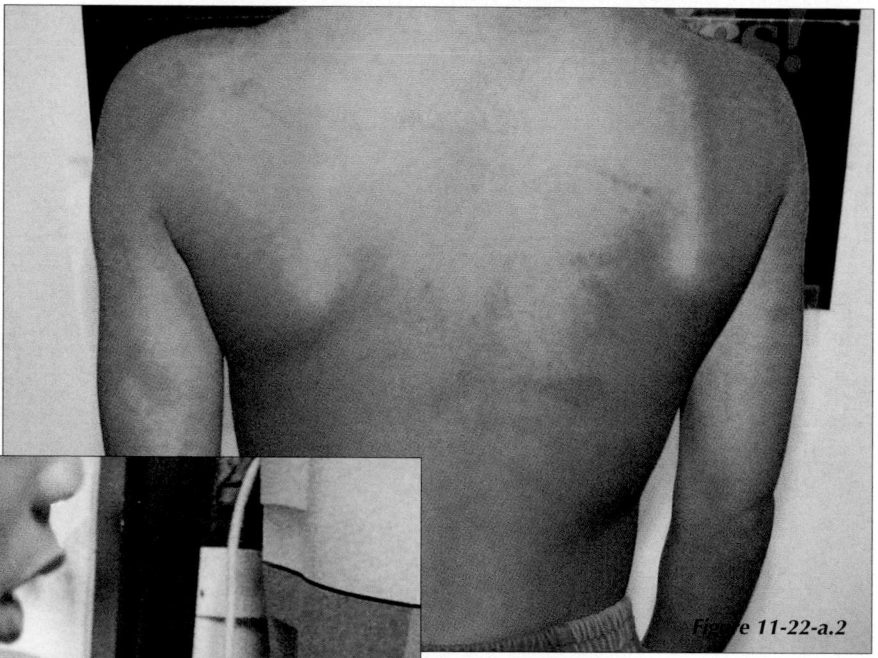

**Figure 11-22-a.2**

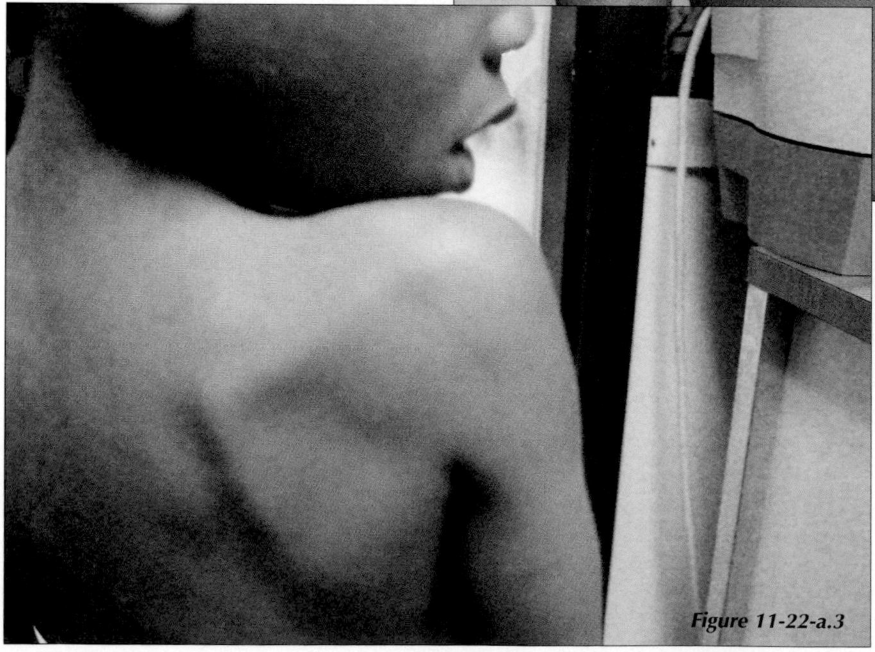

**Figure 11-22-a.3**

# Thorough Documentation and Investigation of the Scene

**Case Study 11-22** *(continued)*

***Figures 11-22-a.4*** *and* ***a.5.*** *Patterned marks can clearly be seen on the back of the 8-year-old.*

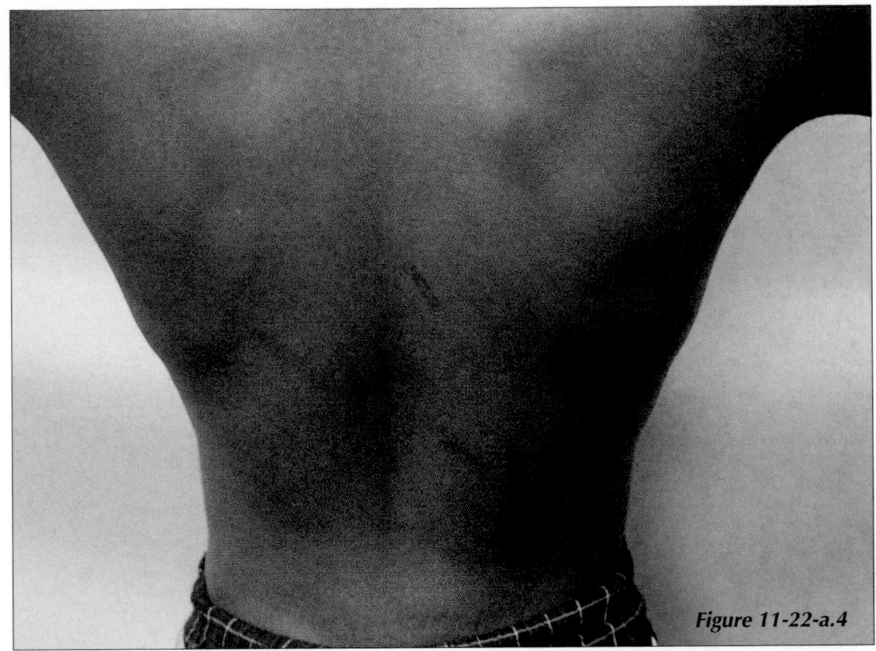

**Figure 11-22-a.4**

**Figure 11-22-a.5**

# Thorough Documentation and Investigation of the Scene

**Case Study 11-22** *(continued)*

***Figures 11-22-a.6, a.7,*** *and* ***a.8.*** *Marks can clearly be seen near the base of the neck and down the back of the 8-year-old.*

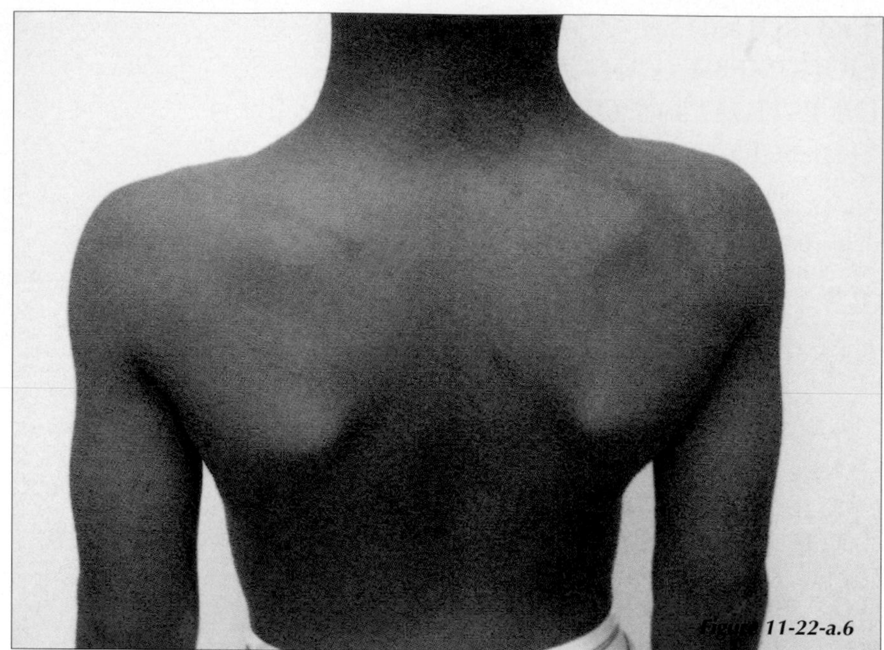

Figure 11-22-a.6

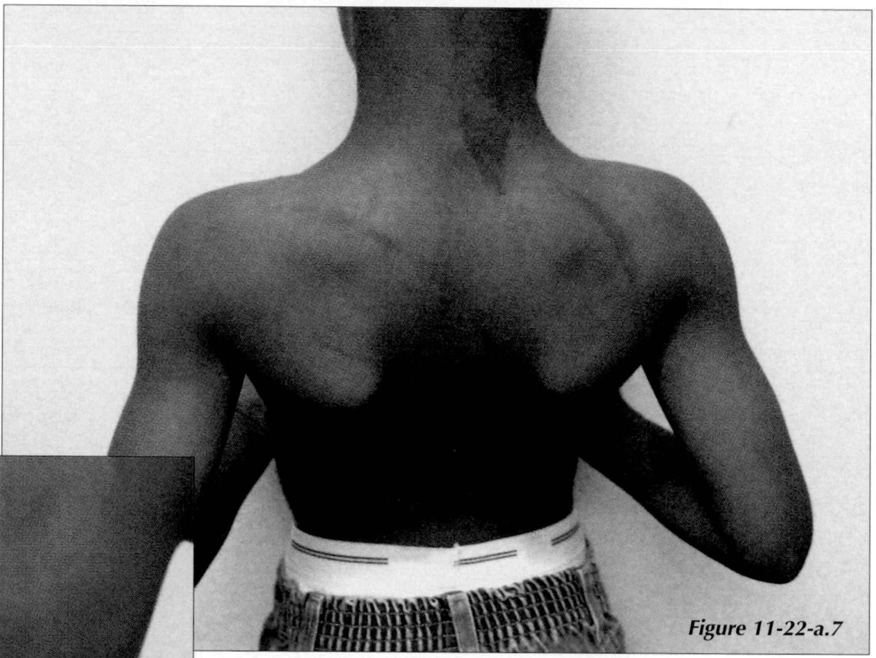

Figure 11-22-a.7

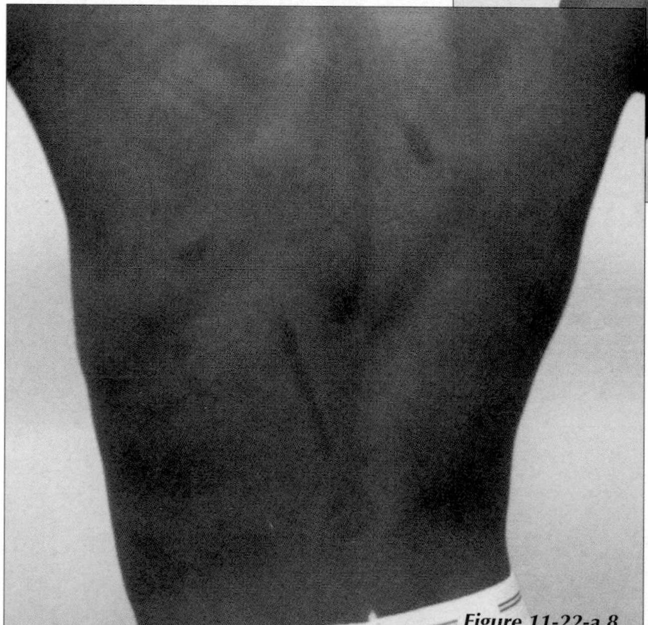

Figure 11-22-a.8

# Thorough Documentation and Investigation of the Scene

**Case Study 11-22** *(continued)*

Other marks were found on the children consistent with a strike to the face and forceful gripping of the upper arm. The marks were too prevalent to have been acquired by accidental means as first stated by the boys.

***Figure 11-22-a.9.*** *Strike to the face caused a noticeable mark on the 6-year-old.*

***Figure 11-22-a.10.*** *Forceful gripping caused a mark on the arm of the 6-year-old.*

It was determined that some intervention was needed. The investigation took place starting at the outside of the apartment and gradually working into the inside. Upon the investigators' arrival, the 5-year-old boy was changing the diaper of the 10-month-old. The 6- and 8-year-old boys were in police custody and the 2-year-old was shopping with the mother.

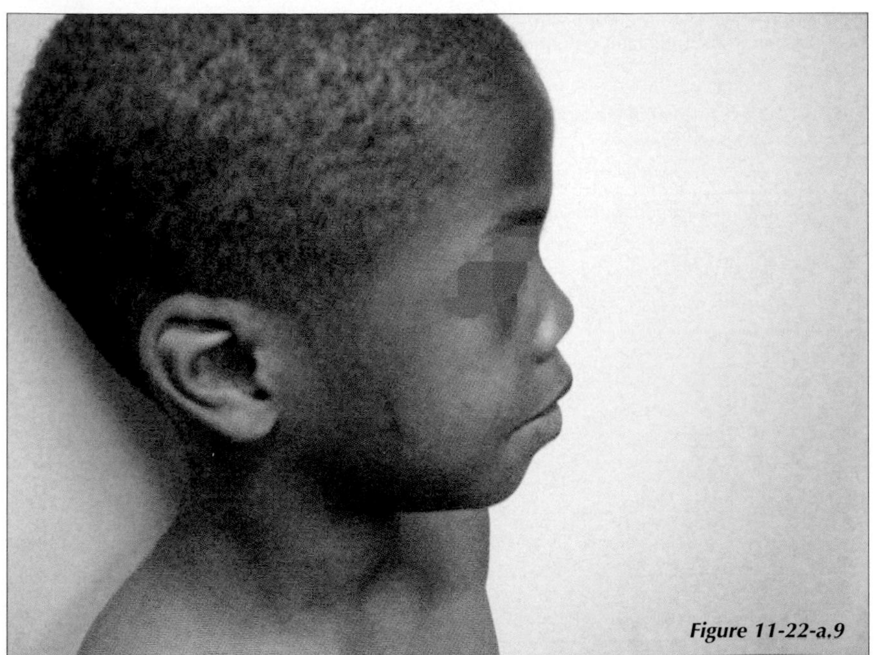

**Figure 11-22-a.9**

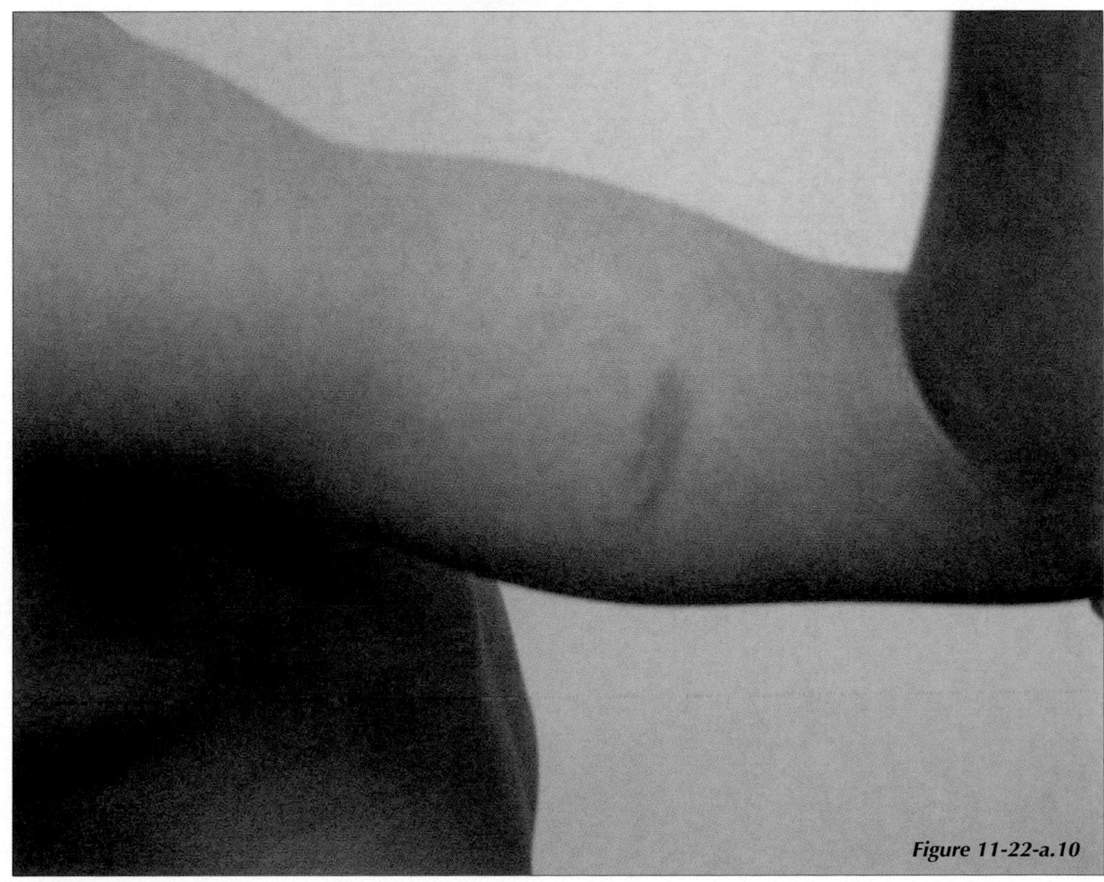

**Figure 11-22-a.10**

# Thorough Documentation and Investigation of the Scene

**Case Study 11-22** *(continued)*

***11-22-b.*** The investigation starts with an overall view of the area later determined to be the crime scene.

***Figure 11-22-b.1.*** *Overall view of the entrance to the apartment.*

***Figure 11-22-b.2.*** *Interior view of the entrance to the apartment, including a view of the closet.*

**Figure 11-22-b.1**

**Figure 11-22-b.2**

# Thorough Documentation and Investigation of the Scene

**Case Study 11-22** *(continued)*

***11-22-c***. As the investigation continued into the apartment, photos document the findings of each individual room.

***Figure 11-22-c.*** *Dining area.*

***11-22-d.*** Investigators moved into the living room area of the apartment.

***Figure 11-22-d.1.*** *Couch and coffee table.*

***Figure 11-22-d.2.*** *Stereo and fan.*

***Figure 11-22-d.3.*** *Entertainment center with dolls.*

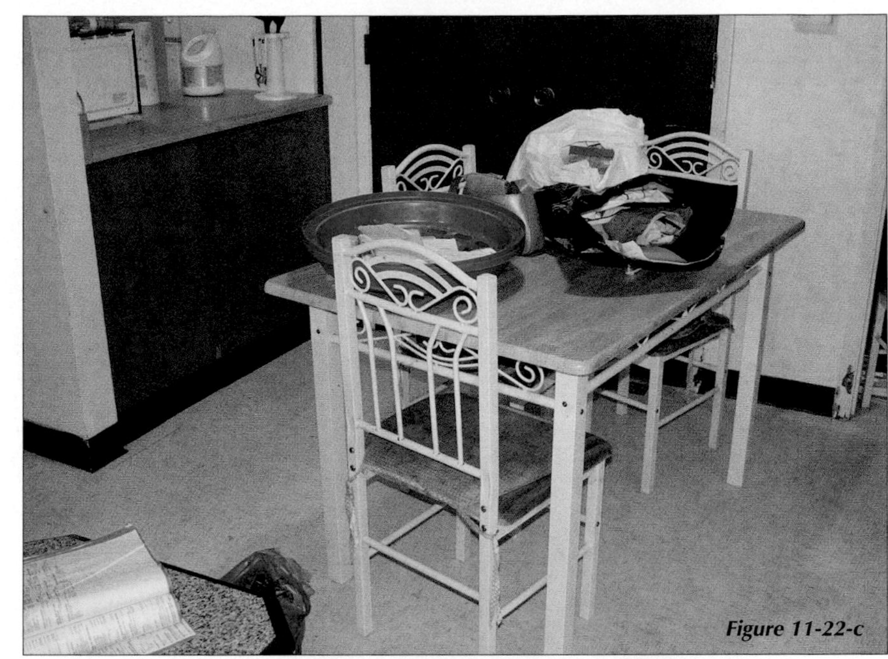

**Figure 11-22-c**

**igure 11-22-d.1**

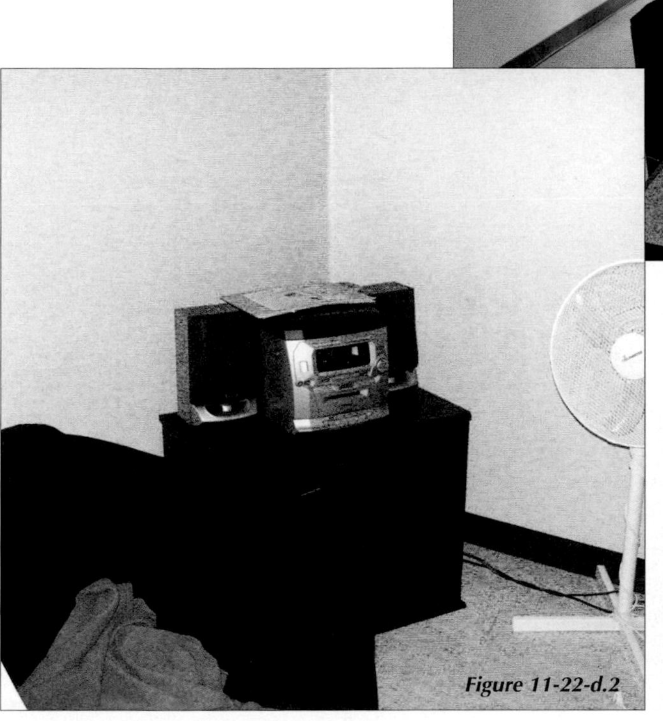

**Figure 11-22-d.2**

**Figure 11-22-d.3**

# Thorough Documentation and Investigation of the Scene

**Case Study 11-22** *(continued)*

***Figures 11-22-d.4*** *and* ***d.5.*** *Dresser that housed a variety of items, including alcohol and prescription medications within reach of the children.*

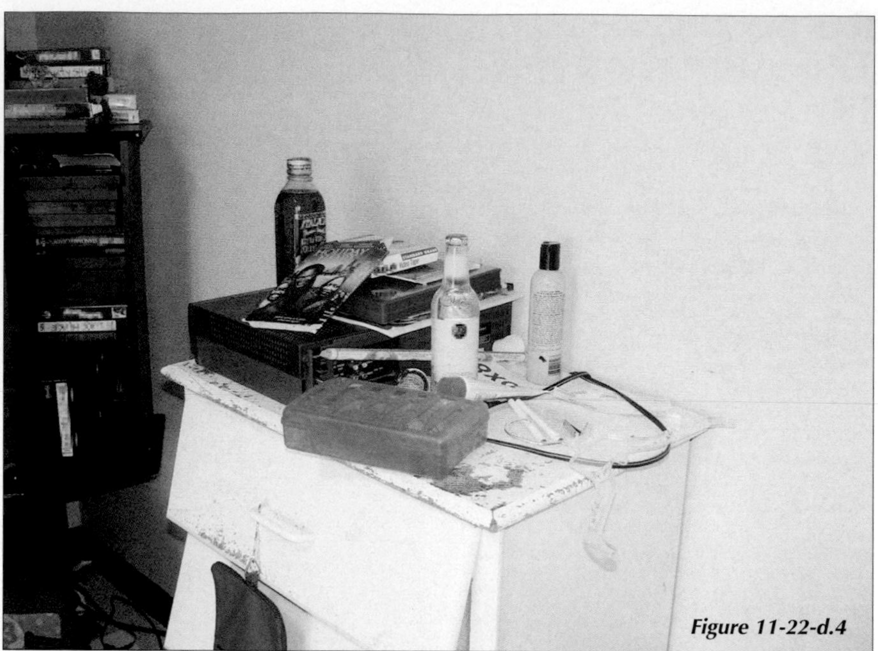

**Figure 11-22-d.4**

**Figure 11-22-d.5**

# Thorough Documentation and Investigation of the Scene

**Case Study 11-22** *(continued)*

***11-22-e.*** Investigators then turned to the kitchen area.

***Figure 11-22-e.1.*** *Entrance to the kitchen.*

***Figure 11-22-e.2.*** *Stove and dirty dishes were left unattended.*

***Figure 11-22-e.3.*** *Refrigerator, counter, and cabinets.*

***Figure 11-22-e.4.*** *Bleach within easy access of the children.*

***Figure 11-22-e.5.*** *Drawer located in the kitchen. Inside the drawer and easily accessible to the abuser is a piece of coaxial cable used to strike the children.*

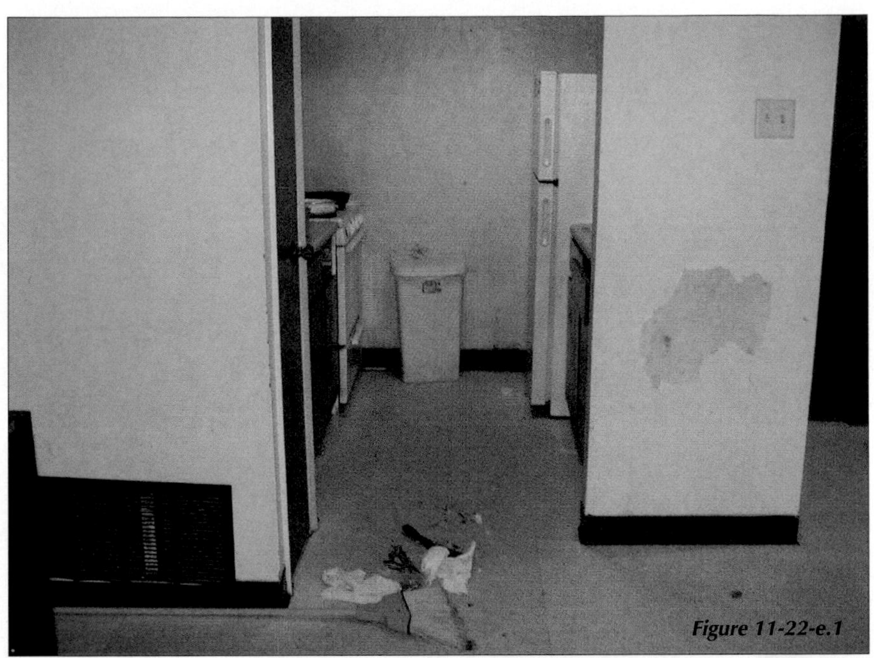

Figure 11-22-e.1

Figure 11-22-e.2

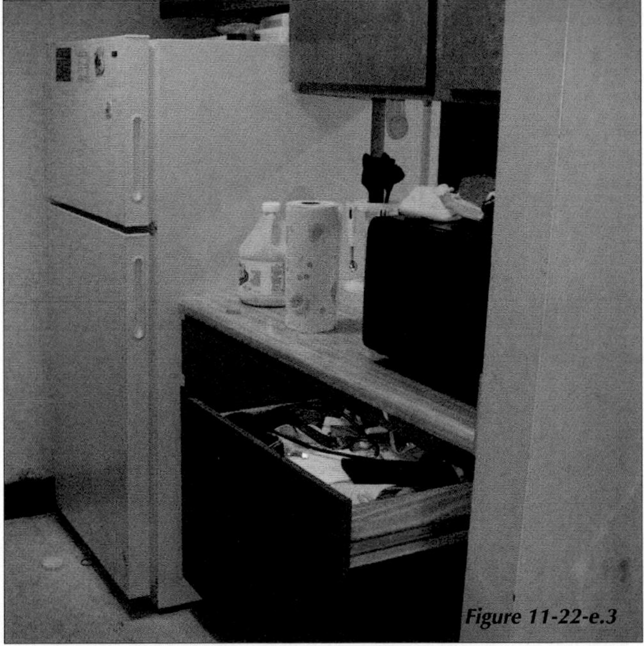

Figure 11-22-e.3

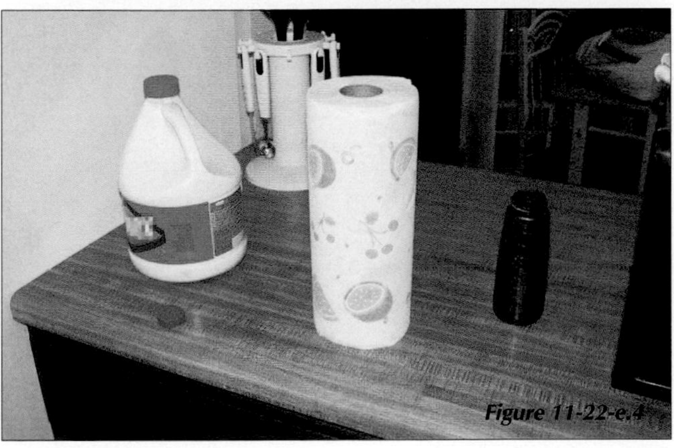

Figure 11-22-e.4

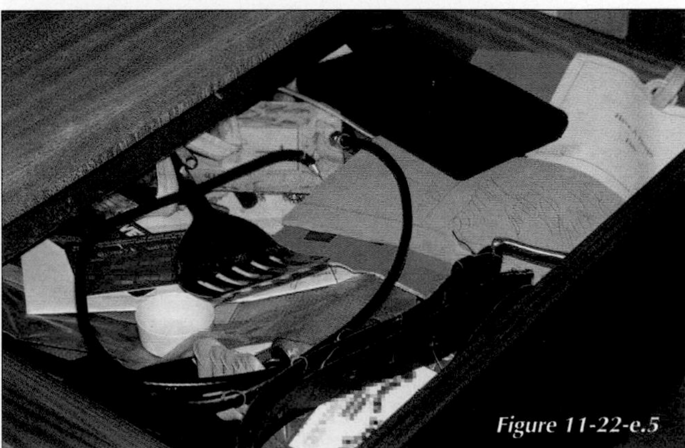

Figure 11-22-e.5

# Thorough Documentation and Investigation of the Scene

**Case Study 11-22** *(continued)*

***11-22-f.*** Photographs of the bathroom.

***Figure 11-22-f.1.*** *View of the bathroom from the entrance.*

***Figure 11-22-f.2.*** *Medicine cabinet containing unprotected razors and medication.*

Figure 11-22-f.1

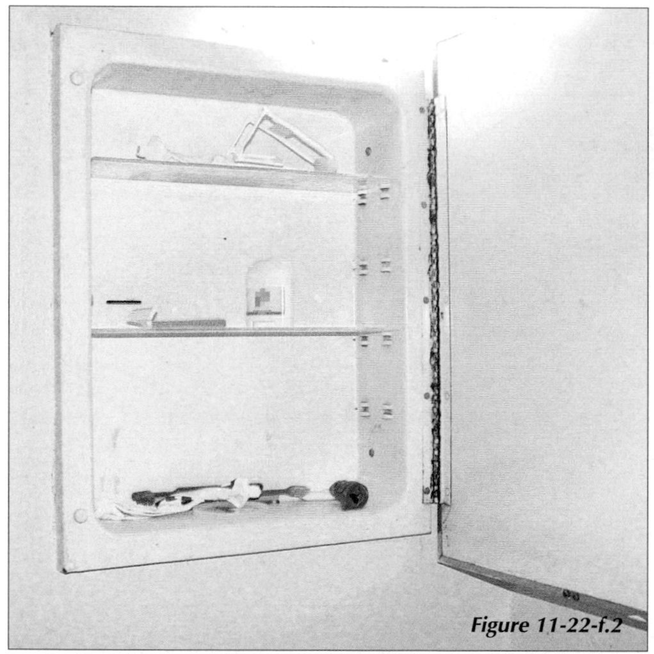

Figure 11-22-f.2

***11-22-g.*** The children's bedroom was found in complete disarray.

***Figure 11-22-g.1.*** *Remnant of wooden door that was torn from its hinges. Note the exposed nails.*

***Figure 11-22-g.2.*** *Overall view of bedroom.*

Figure 11-22-g.1

Figure 11-22-g.2

# Thorough Documentation and Investigation of the Scene

**Case Study 11-22** *(continued)*

***Figure 11-22-g.3.*** *Clutter at the entrance complicates entering and navigating the bedroom.*

***Figure 11-22-g.4.*** *Bed frame and mattress are overturned, with the box springs propped against the wall.*

***Figure 11-22-g.5.*** *Closet area with dresser. One drawer is missing from the dresser, and another portion of the bed frame is propped against the wall. Blinds are broken and nonfunctional.*

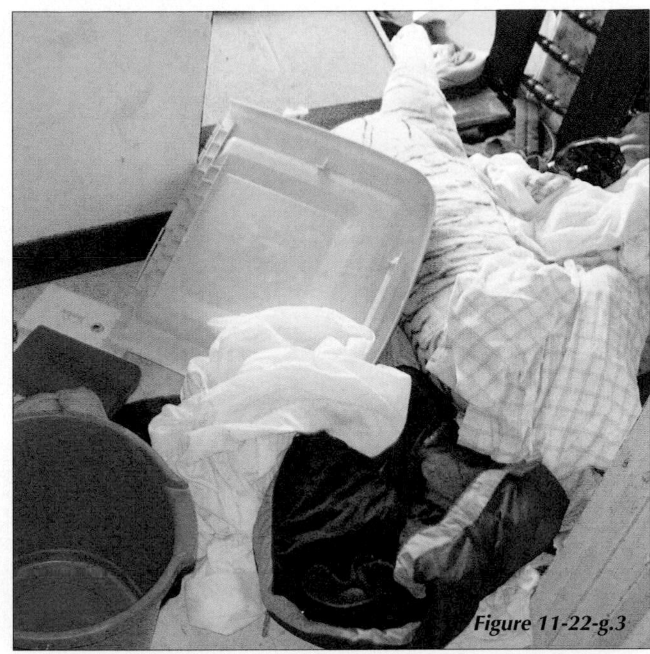

Figure 11-22-g.3

Figure 11-22-g.5

Figure 11-22-g.4

# Thorough Documentation and Investigation of the Scene

**Case Study 11-22** *(continued)*

***11-22-h.*** Further investigation revealed additional evidence of substandard living conditions in the mother's bedroom, which also housed the 10-month-old child.

***Figure 11-22-h.1.*** *Entrance to the bedroom. Includes the mother's bed, an overturned trashcan, and a bassinet covered in clothes.*

***Figure 11-22-h.2.*** *Bedside table with phone.*

***Figure 11-22-h.3.*** *Interior view of the bedroom. Closet includes clothes for the infant, whose crib is found to the left.*

**Figure 11-22-h.1**

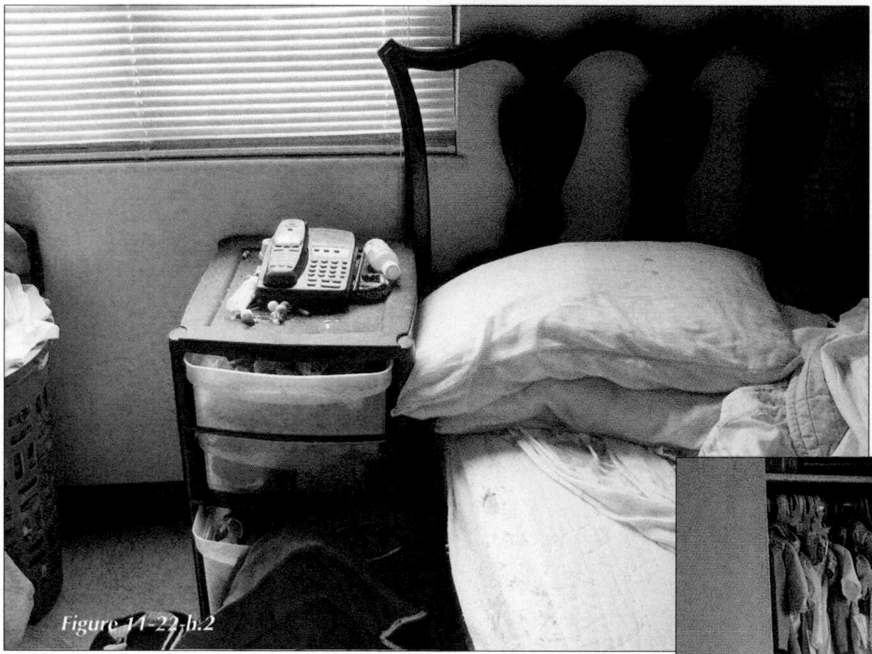

Figure 11-22-h.2

Figure 11-22-h.3

# Thorough Documentation and Investigation of the Scene

**Case Study 11-22** *(continued)*

***Figure 11-22-h.4.*** *10-month-old baby's crib is filled with toys, stuffed animals, and dolls.*

***Figure 11-22-h.5.*** *A box of garbage bags inside the crib.*

***Figure 11-22-h.6.*** *Closet containing the mother's clothes.*

Figure 11-22-h.4

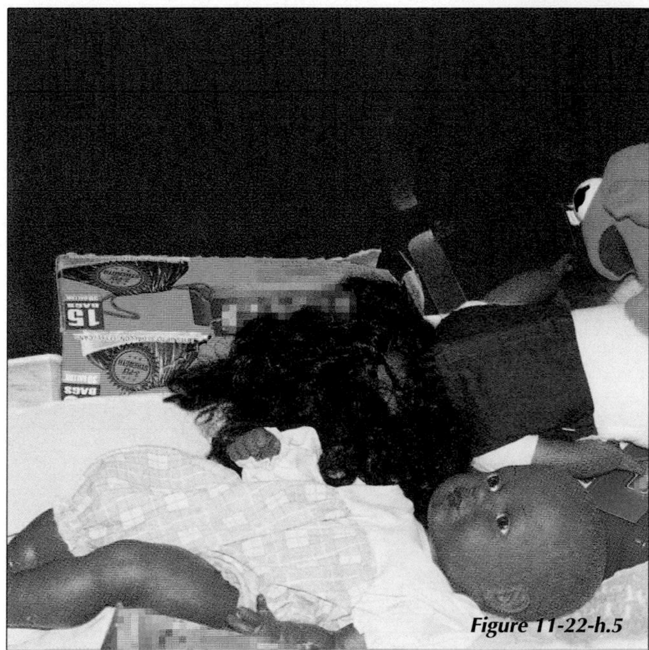

Figure 11-22-h.5

Figure 11-22-h.6

# Thorough Documentation and Investigation of the Scene

**Case Study 11-22** *(continued)*

***Figure 11-22-h.7.*** *Plastic container full of clothes and containing other miscellaneous items.*

***Figure 11-22-h.8.*** *Items on the plastic container include the other instrument of abuse: a belt with a width matching the pattern marks on the children.*

***11-22-i.*** Investigation proceeded through the sliding back doors of the apartment.

***Figure 11-22-i.1.*** *Sliding glass doors leading behind the apartment complex.*

***Figure 11-22-i.2.*** *Rear view of the apartment complex.*

***Figure 11-22-i.3.*** *The outside temperature exceeded 85 degrees Fahrenheit and the chicken on the air conditioning unit was spoiled. This plate was later determined to have come from the children's apartment.*

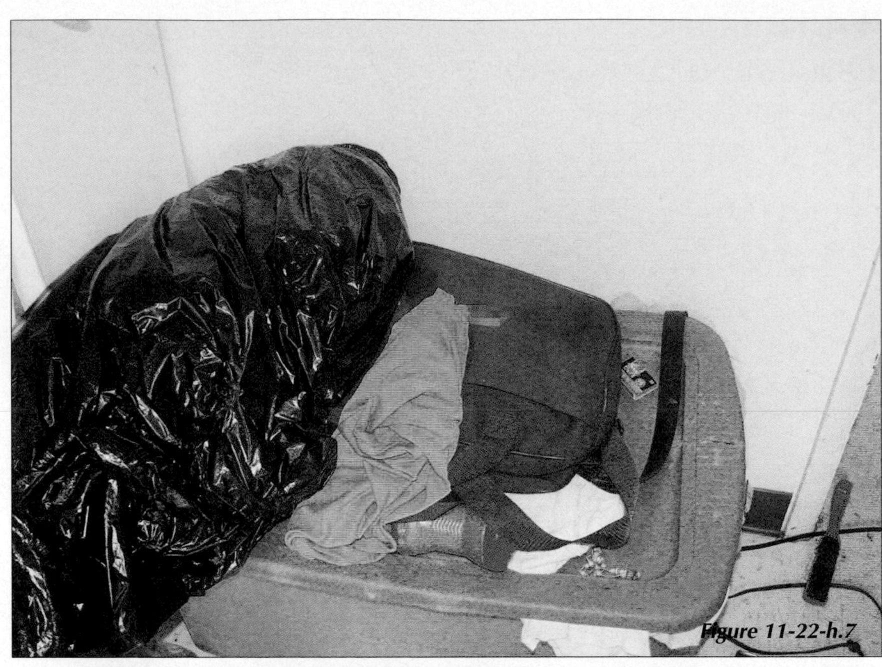

Figure 11-22-h.7

Figure 11-22-h.8

Figure 11-22-i.1

Figure 11-22-i.2

Figure 11-22-i.3

# Thorough Documentation and Investigation of the Scene

**Case Study 11-22** *(continued)*

***11-22-j.*** Photos were also taken to document the car of the perpetrator, or the children's biological mother, when she arrived home. It was later determined that the children had 3 different fathers.

***Figure 11-22-j.1.*** *The mother's car as it arrived at the house.*

***Figure 11-22-j.2.*** *Rear view of the car.*

***Figure 11-22-j.3.*** *The front interior of the car.*

As the documented photos from the investigation reveal, the living conditions of these children and their mother were substandard. This evidence alone was not sufficient to make a case for neglect. The children's situation upon police arrival clearly indicated neglect. The 5-year-old boy was left at home alone with the 10-month-old child without adult supervision. Additionally, the case was made for abuse because the mother could not handle the stress of caring for 5 children and seeing multiple boyfriends without a job. She admitted to taking out her frustration on the children by using the belt and cable as instruments of abuse.

**Figure 11-22-j.1**

**Figure 11-22-j.2**

**Figure 11-22-j.3**

# Thorough Documentation and Investigation of the Scene

**Case Study 11-23**

This case was the result of a domestic dispute. The mother lived with her boyfriend and four other men in a small three-bedroom home. During the disturbance call, it was determined that the boyfriend was wanted on a bench warrant. Officers responding to the call noticed a disturbing mess and odor. Closer inspection found the upstairs of the house to be unsuitable for living, evidenced by the amount of dirt, debris, flies, fecal matter, and damaged utilities. It was determined that 2 children lived there with their mother. One was an infant and the other was in the third grade. The mother was dirty, dishevelled, and appeared to be under the influence of drugs. The investigation revealed that she was. When detectives arrived, they also noted that one of the residents living downstairs had tarantulas, scorpions, and a large boa constrictor within easy access of the children. These children lived in a house that created substantial risk to their well-being. In accordance with the statutes on child endangerment and neglect, child protective services and the police subsequently removed them from the deplorable living conditions of the home. After months of rehabilitation, the mother and her children were reunited. The house was a rental property and the remaining residents were evicted.

***11-23-a.*** The front of the home documented at the beginning of the investigation.

***Figure 11-23-a.1.*** *An overall front view of the home.*

***Figure 11-23-a.2.*** *The mailbox denoting the house number.*

***Figure 11-23-a.3.*** *Trashcans in the front yard.*

***Figure 11-23-a.4.*** *The perpetrator's vehicle.*

Figure 11-23-a.1

Figure 11-23-a.2

Figure 11-23-a.3

Figure 11-23-a.4

# Thorough Documentation and Investigation of the Scene

**Case Study 11-23** *(continued)*

***11-23-b.*** Photographers went on to document the living room and dining room. There were in excess of 100 cigarette butts in and about the living room along with lighters, alcohol, and feces.

***Figure 11-23-b.1.*** *An overall view of the living room.*

***Figure 11-23-b.2.*** *One of 4 dogs in the house.*

***Figure 11-23-b.3.*** *A turtle living in a fish tank, which is growing mold.*

***Figure 11-23-b.4.*** *One of 2 cats found in the residence.*

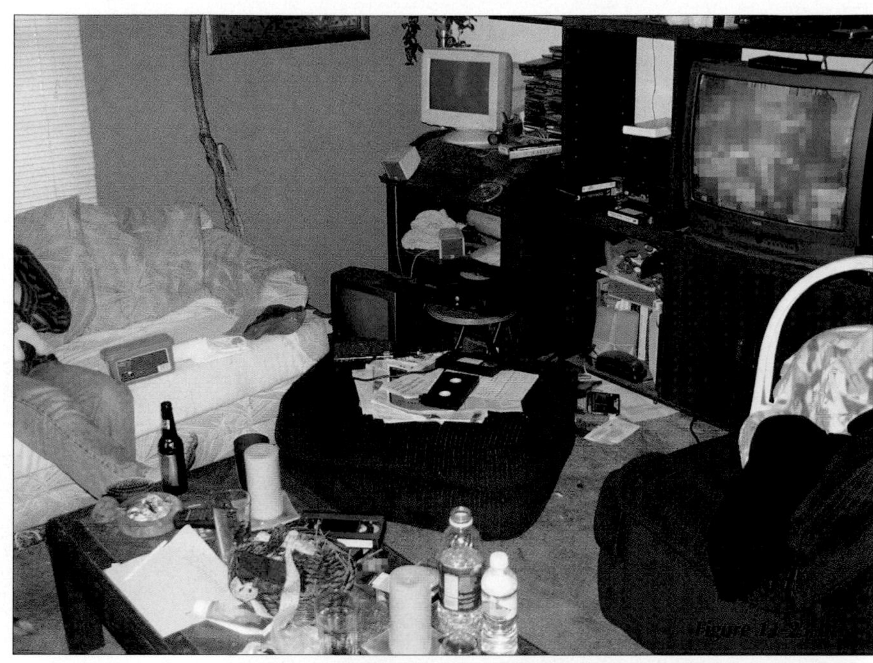

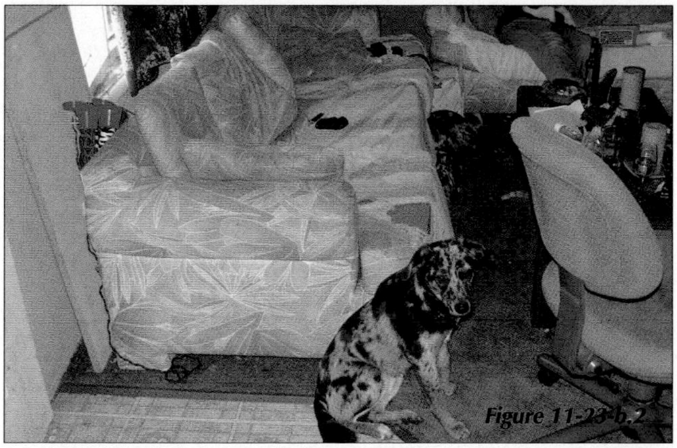

Figure 11-23-b.2

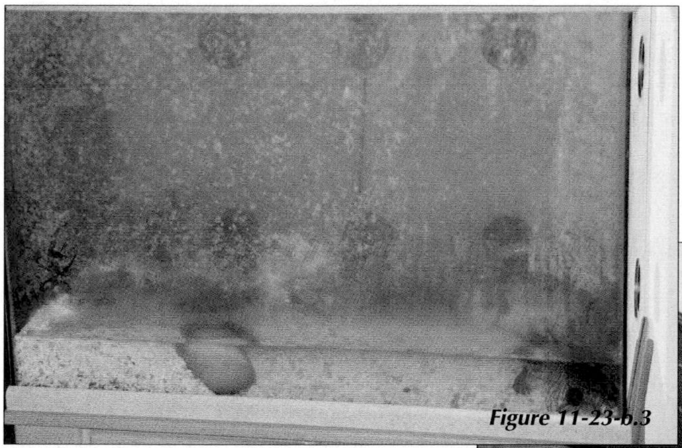

Figure 11-23-b.3

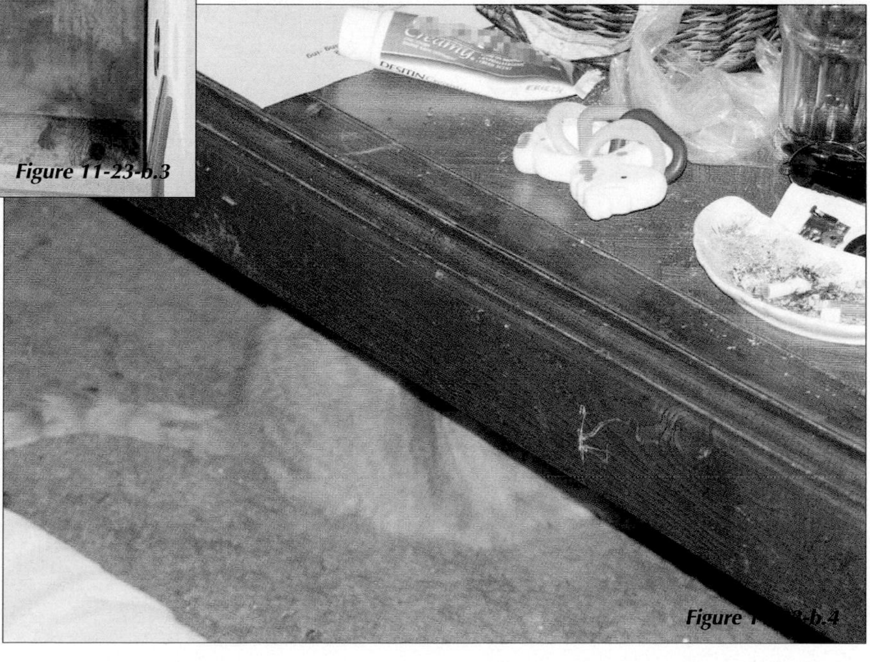

# Thorough Documentation and Investigation of the Scene

**Case Study 11-23** *(continued)*

***Figures 11-23-b.5, b.6,*** and ***b.7.*** Photo documentation of the dining area.

Figure 11-23-b.5

Figure 11-23-b.6

Figure 11-23-b.7

## Thorough Documentation and Investigation of the Scene

**Case Study 11-23** *(continued)*

***Figure 11-23-b.8.*** *Abandoned plate of food with the appearance of flies.*

***Figure 11-23-b.9.*** *Jar of baby food with flies.*

Figure 11-23-b.8

Figure 11-23-b.9

# THOROUGH DOCUMENTATION AND INVESTIGATION OF THE SCENE

**Case Study 11-23** *(continued)*

***11-23-c.*** Photographers then documented the kitchen. There was spoiled food in the refrigerator and on the counter tops. The stove also had spoiled food on it.

***Figure 11-23-c.1.*** *An overall view of the kitchen*

***Figure 11-23-c.2.*** *Dishes in the sink and on the counter containing spoiled food and flies.*

***Figure 11-23-c.3.*** *Food is crusted in dishes on the stove and on the stove itself.*

***Figure 11-23-c.4.*** *Trash piled in the kitchen.*

Figure 11-23-c.1

Figure 11-23-c.3

Figure 11-23-c.2

Figure 11-23-c.4

## Thorough Documentation and Investigation of the Scene

**Case Study 11-23** *(continued)*

***Figures 11-23-c.5, c.6,*** *and* ***c.7.*** *The refrigerator is full of food that has long expired.*

Figure 11-23-c.5

Figure 11-23-c.6

Figure 11-23-c.7

# Thorough Documentation and Investigation of the Scene

**Case Study 11-23** *(continued)*

***11-23-d.*** The child's room had not been cleaned for some time. She kept a ferret as a pet. The cage was filled with feces and there was debris strewn about the room.

***Figure 11-23-d.1.*** *An overall view of the child's room.*

***Figure 11-23-d.2.*** *The child's bed. Note the dirty dishes on the adjacent shelf.*

***Figure 11-23-d.3.*** *The floor of the child's room.*

***Figure 11-23-d.4.*** *The ferret's cage.*

Figure 11-23-d.1

Figure 11-23-d.2

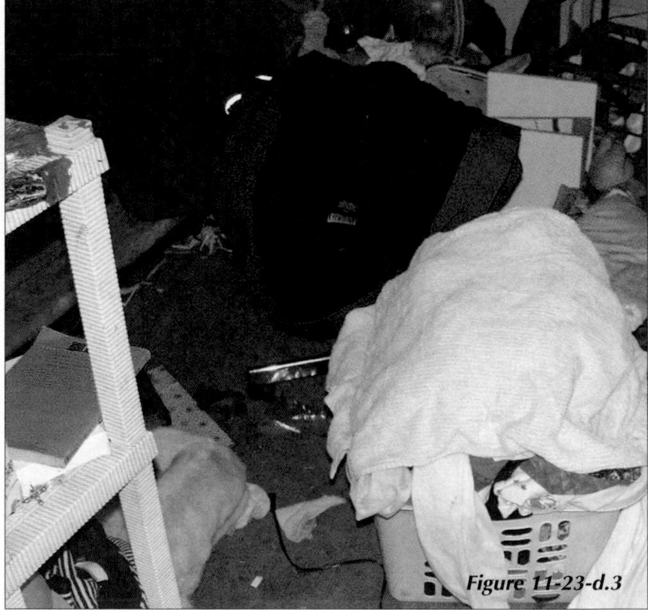
Figure 11-23-d.3

Figure 11-23-d.4

# Thorough Documentation and Investigation of the Scene

**Case Study 11-23** *(continued)*

***Figure 11-23-d.5.*** *The pet ferret.*

***Figure 11-23-d.6.*** *The litter box for the ferret, evidence that the cage has not been cleaned adequately or recently enough.*

***Figure 11-23-d.7.*** *Child's belongings on the floor at the base of the ferret cage, providing a receptacle for additional feces.*

***Figure 11-23-d.8.*** *The child's desk, covered in horse figurines.*

Figure 11-23-d.5

Figure 11-23-d.6

Figure 11-23-d.7

Figure 11-23-d.8

# Thorough Documentation and Investigation of the Scene

**Case Study 11-23** *(continued)*

***Figure 11-23-d.9.*** *Belongings of the child at the base of the desk.*

***Figure 11-23-d.10.*** *A smaller cage housing the child's pet frog.*

***Figure 11-23-d.11.*** *Drawers in the child's dresser.*

Figure 11-23-d.9

Figure 11-23-d.10

Figure 11-23-d.11

## Thorough Documentation and Investigation of the Scene

**Case Study 11-23** *(continued)*

***Figures 11-23-d.12, d.13,*** *and* ***d.14.***
*Contents of the closet in the child's room. Note the additional pet carrier and cage.*

Figure 11-23-d.12

Figure 11-23-d.13



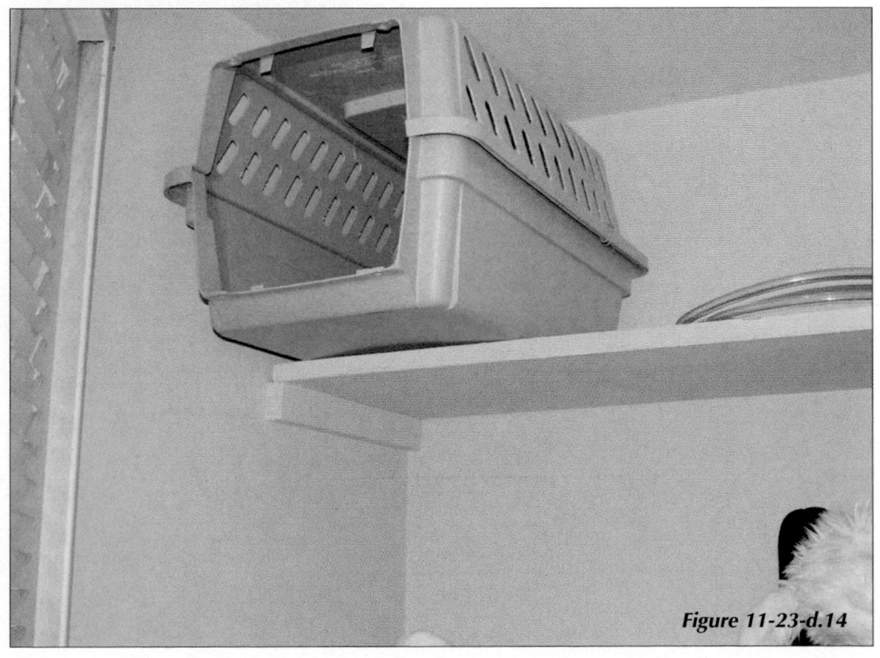

Figure 11-23-d.14

# Thorough Documentation and Investigation of the Scene

**Case Study 11-23** *(continued)*

***11-23-e***. Investigators then turned to the mother's room.

***Figure 11-23-e.1.*** *The view of the mother's room that investigators saw from the hallway.*

***Figure 11-23-e.2.*** *The changing table for the infant.*

***Figures 11-23-e.3*** *and* ***e.4.*** *A significant number of items obstruct the baby bed, preventing its use.*

*Figure 11-23-e.1*

*Figure 11-23-e.2*

*Figure 11-23-e.3*

*Figure 11-23-e.4*

# Thorough Documentation and Investigation of the Scene

**Case Study 11-23** *(continued)*

***Figure 11-23-e.5.*** *The baby sleeps on the mother's bed instead of in a crib.*

***Figure 11-23-e.6.*** *Second cat of 2 in the house.*

***Figure 11-23-e.7.*** *Table with additional belongings of the mother.*

**Figure 11-23-e.5**

**Figure 11-23-e.6**

**Figure 11-23-e.7**

# Thorough Documentation and Investigation of the Scene

**Case Study 11-23** *(continued)*

***Figures 11-23-e.8*** *and* ***e.9.*** *Fecal matter found on the carpeting in the mother's bedroom. The room contains some human feces, but mostly animal feces.*

***Figures 11-23-e.10*** *and* ***e.11.*** *Additional belongings of the mother piled on the floor.*

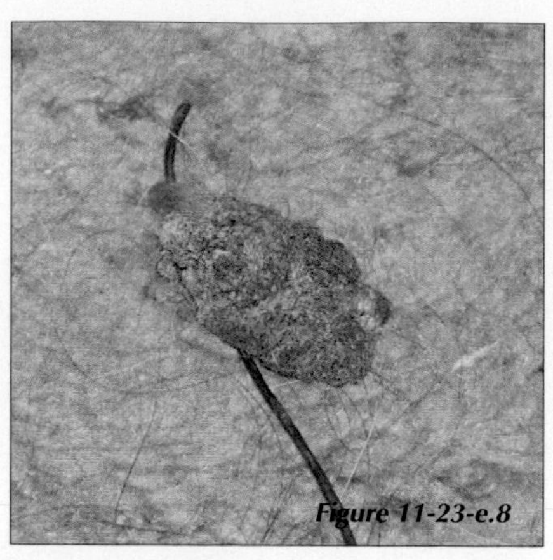

Figure 11-23-e.8

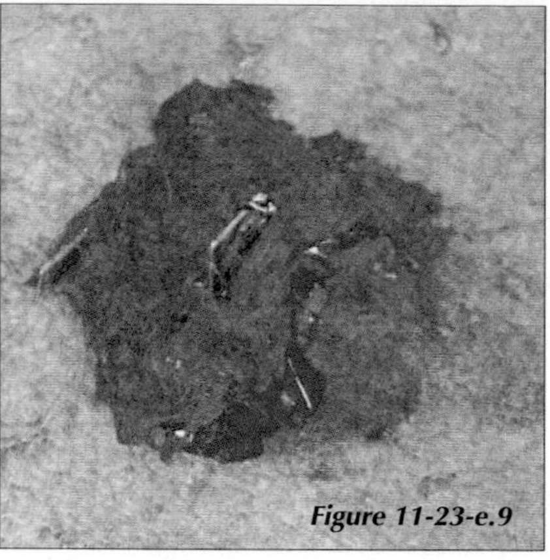

Figure 11-23-e.9

Figure 11-23-e.10

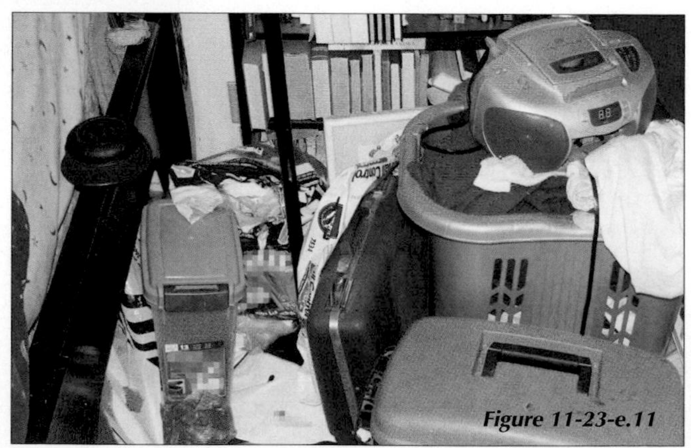

Figure 11-23-e.11

# Thorough Documentation and Investigation of the Scene

**Case Study 11-23** *(continued)*

***Figure 11-23-e.12.*** *The top of the mother's dresser.*

***Figure 11-23-e.13.*** *The contents of a small refrigerator discovered in the mother's bedroom.*

***Figure 11-23-e.14.*** *The mother's bathroom, connected to the bedroom.*

Illicit drugs were found in the mother's room, within easy reach of the children.

***Figure 11-23-e.15.*** *Marijuana, pipes, scales, and other paraphernalia discovered by investigators.*

Figure 11-23-e.12

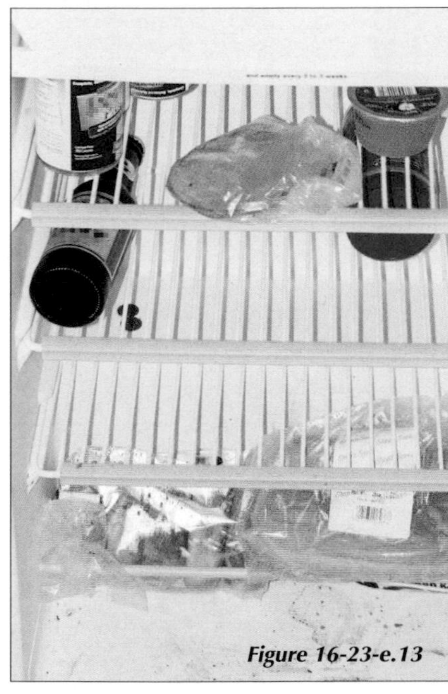
Figure 16-23-e.13

Figure 11-23-e.14

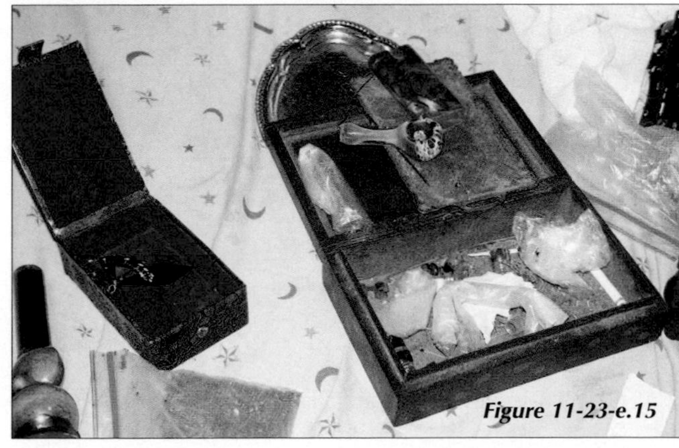
Figure 11-23-e.15

# Thorough Documentation and Investigation of the Scene

**Case Study 11-23** *(continued)*

***11-23-f.*** Further investigation lead to the hallway and the entrance to the basement, where another tenant lived.

***Figure 11-23-f.1.*** *Hallway where vacuum, litter box, and miscellaneous other household items are stored.*

***Figure 11-23-f.2.*** *The litter box and surrounding area for the cats has not been adequately cleaned recently.*

***Figure 11-23-f.3.*** *Crossbow hanging in the hallway, within access and sight of the children.*

Figure 11-23-f.1

Figure 11-23-f.2

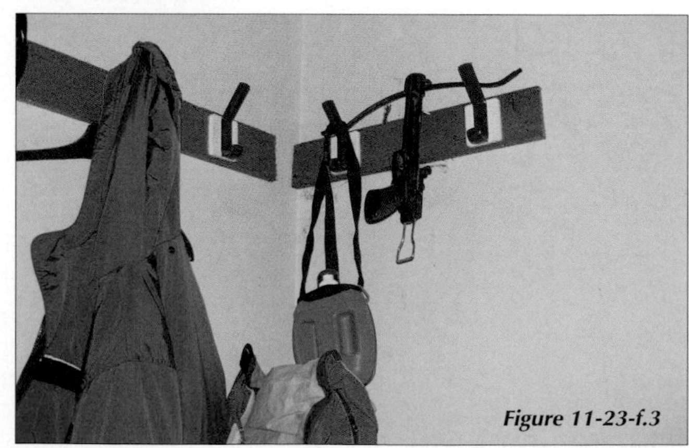

Figure 11-23-f.3

# Thorough Documentation and Investigation of the Scene

**Case Study 11-23** *(continued)*

***Figures 11-23-f.4*** *and* ***f.5.*** *Entrance to the basement. Note the recently lit stick of incense hanging over the steps.*

***Figures 11-23-f.6*** *and* ***f.7.*** *Exposed wiring within reach of the children.*

***Figure 11-23-f.4***

***Figure 11-23-f.5***

***Figure 11-23-f.6***

***Figure 11-23-f.7***

# Thorough Documentation and Investigation of the Scene

**Case Study 11-23** *(continued)*

***11-23-g.*** Investigators documented the interior of the basement, including the downstairs living area.

***Figure 11-23-g.1***. *Overall view of the downstairs living room.*

***Figures 11-23-g.2*** *and* ***g.3.*** *Coffee table with beer and various other items within easy reach of the children.*

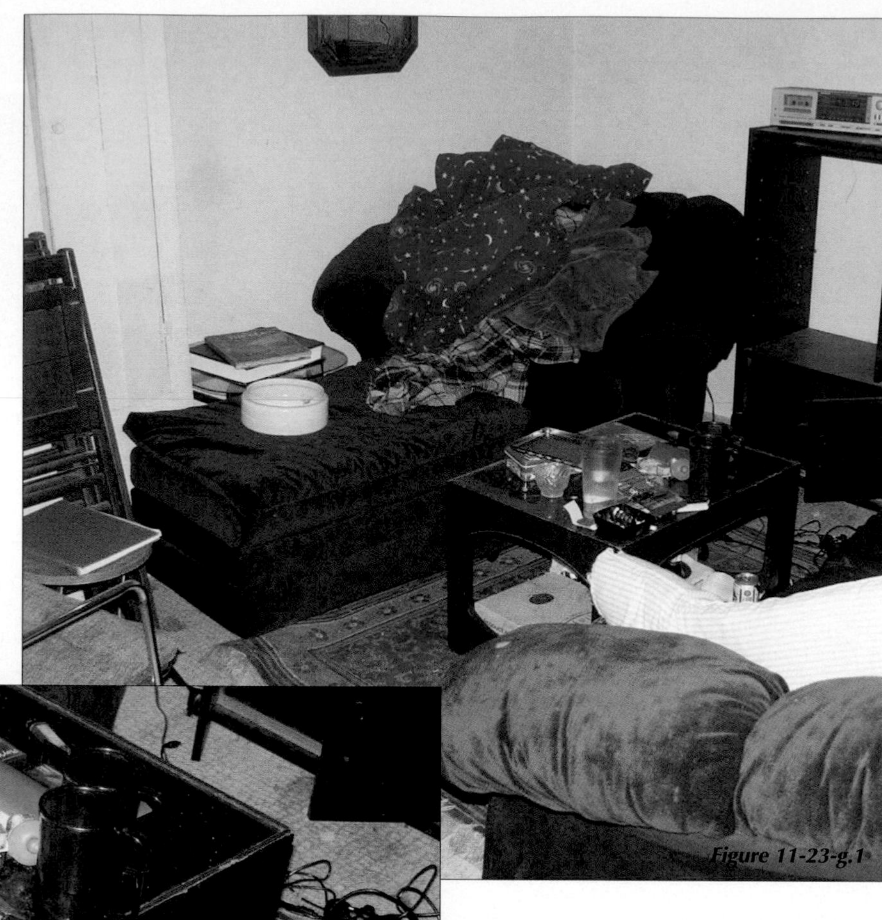

**Figure 11-23-g.1**

**Figure 11-23-g.2**

**Figure 11-23-g.3**

## Thorough Documentation and Investigation of the Scene

**Case Study 11-23** *(continued)*

***Figures 11-23-g.4, g.5,*** *and* ***g.6.*** *The coffee table also contains more drug paraphernalia. Note the presence of paraphernalia used for smoking crack cocaine.*

***Figure 11-23-g.7.*** *Prescription medication on the floor.*

Figure 11-23-g.4

Figure 11-23-g.5

Figure 11-23-g.6

Figure 11-23-g.7

# Thorough Documentation and Investigation of the Scene

**Case Study 11-23** *(continued)*

***Figure 11-23-g.8.*** *Additional belongings piled on the floor in the basement.*

***Figures 11-23-g.9*** *and* ***g.10.*** *Investigation of the hot water heater revealed flammable trash in close proximity to the heater.*

*Figure 11-23-g.8*

*Figure 11-23-g.9*

*Figure 11-23-g.10*

# Thorough Documentation and Investigation of the Scene

**Case Study 11-23** *(continued)*

***11-23-h.*** Further investigation of the downstairs kitchen revealed additional evidence of unsanitary and unsafe living conditions.

***Figures 11-23-h.1*** *and* ***h.2.*** *The gas stove in the kitchen. Note the pile of beer caps and other miscellaneous non–cooking-related items.*

***Figure 11-23-h.3.*** *The gas line to the gas stove downstairs is in disrepair.*

***Figure 11-23-h.4.*** *Kitchen sink filled with dirty dishes.*

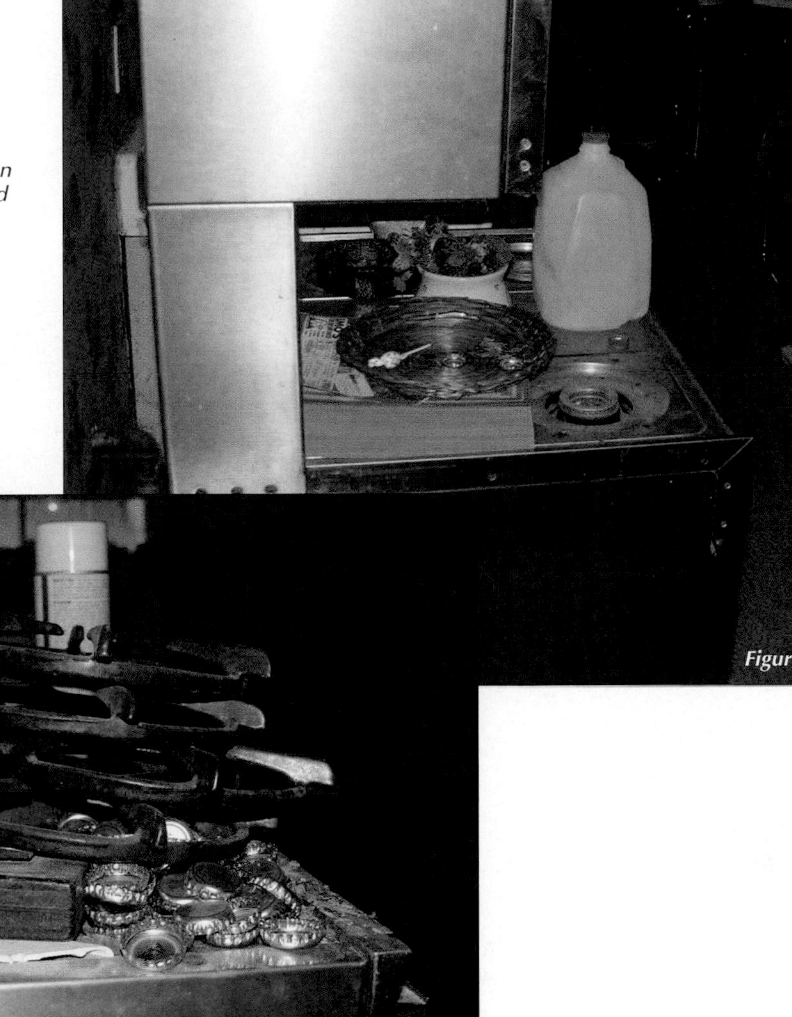

**Figure 11-23-h.1**

**Figure 11-23-h.2**

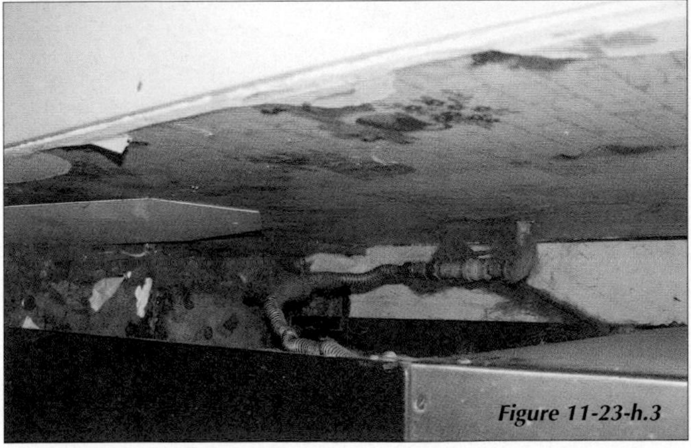

**Figure 11-23-h.3**

**Figure 11-23-h.4**

# Thorough Documentation and Investigation of the Scene

**Case Study 11-23** *(continued)*

***Figure 11-23-h.5.*** *Overfilled trashcan in the kitchen.*

***Figure 11-23-h.6.*** *The child's high chair is littered with a knife, beer bottles, beer caps, and a variety of other small items.*

***Figures 11-23-h.7*** *and* ***h.8.*** *Refrigerator containing spoiled foods.*

Figure 11-23-h.5

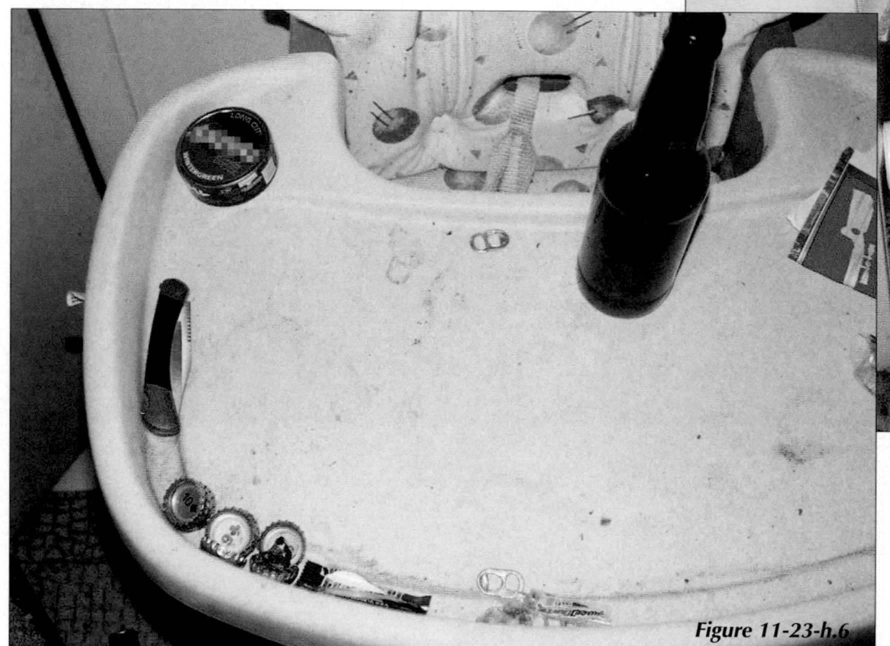

Figure 11-23-h.6

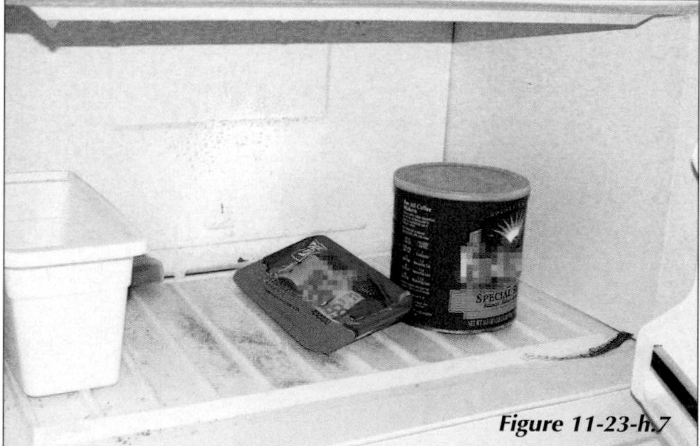

Figure 11-23-h.7

Figure 11-23-h.8

# Thorough Documentation and Investigation of the Scene

**Case Study 11-23** *(continued)*

***11-23-i.*** The downstairs bedroom was further investigated to find caged tarantulas, scorpions, and a boa constrictor cage, along with other items that are unsafe for children.

***Figure 11-23-i.1.*** *Paraphernalia from ritualistic practice on an end table.*

***Figure 11-23-i.2.*** *Knife found on another table, along with alcohol.*

***Figure 11-23-i.3.*** *View of the shelving unit housing scorpions and tarantulas.*

Figure 11-23-i.1

Figure 11-23-i.2

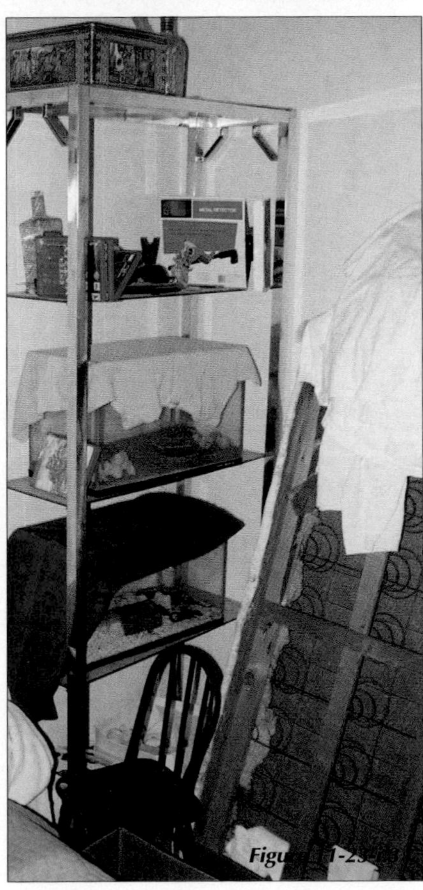

Figure 11-23-i.3

# Thorough Documentation and Investigation of the Scene

**Case Study 11-23** *(continued)*

***Figures 11-23-i.4, i.5,*** *and* ***i.6.*** *Caged scorpions. The cage is covered with only a shirt.*

***Figure 11-23-i.7.*** *Cage for the boa constrictor. The boa was unable to be located as it was loose somewhere in the house.*

Figure 11-23-i.4

Figure 11-23-i.5

Figure 11-23-i.6

Figure 11-23-i.7

# Thorough Documentation and Investigation of the Scene

**Case Study 11-23** *(continued)*

***11-23-j.*** The investigation of the premises closed with documentation of the rear of the house.

***Figure 11-23-j.1.*** *View of the fence and side entrance to the house.*

***Figure 11-23-j.2.*** *View of the backyard and patio furniture belonging to the residents of the house.*

This investigation is a clear case of abuse and neglect by virtue of the unsafe conditions, the presence of narcotics, and the unsanitary and unsafe living quarters.

Figure 11-23-j.1

Figure 11-23-j.2

Chapter 12

# Drawing

Paul Clements, PhD, APRN, BC, DF-IAFN
Kathleen M. Benasutti, MCAT, ATR, BC, LPC
Gloria C. Henry

Through drawing, children can learn to understand the world around them, even if that world is chaotic and abusive. By encouraging and guiding abused or traumatized children through drawing, clinicians can gain access into thoughts and feelings to enhance assessment and guide intervention. Simultaneously, clinicians can promote a normal trajectory of development, including the vital skills needed for relearning the world in light of traumatic events that have occurred. Drawing is frequently overlooked as an assessment tool because it does not appear to be a process concerned with the attainment of specific goals. It is actually a helpful tool to understand the concerns and perceptions of children who have been exposed to traumatic events. For some children, coloring and drawing can be a natural and enjoyable process. For troubled children, especially those living in a chaotic world of distress, violence, or loss, their natural artistic ability can be supported as a life-saving intervention.[4] It can be a powerful tool for children to connect with themselves and reach out to others.[5,6]

The combined use of clinical interviews and drawings can promote the elicitation of sensory information surrounding the traumatic event and can provide insight into the effect of the event on child behaviors and emotions in the chaotic aftermath.[7-9] The realization that violence and abuse are the results of the actions of another human being, usually someone in a position of power or inherent trust, can result in the disruption and derailment of the normal developmental trajectory of children's emotional constructs.

In order to determine the range of emotions felt by victimized children, clinicians are frequently confronted with the task of interpreting words and behaviors, which entails a process of looking for clues that may explain a child's thoughts and perceptions. A commonly overlooked step in this process is the analysis of clues in a child's drawings. These clues often facilitate conversation that may tell a clinician what the child is feeling.[5] Additionally, drawings may convey what is happening but not necessarily why it is happening.[10,11] When used in conjunction with talk therapy or other modalities, drawings can provide insight into the thoughts and perceptions of children who have been exposed to traumatic events. Of importance to community and healthcare practitioners is the tenet that drawings can evoke questions and eventually answers that will guide assessment and intervention.[5,8]

Imagination and artwork lead children to think about painful or anxiety-provoking situations through imitation. Children can take on personalities, act out situations, and provide information about their innermost thoughts, feelings, and concerns. This may seem aimless or merely a display of childhood; however, it can be a constructive way of trying to understand a child's world. Children may also develop their egos and self-confidence by being in command of the situation, and by feeling like the hero versus feeling out of control and vulnerable.

There is no right or wrong way to draw a picture, and drawings will vary based on age, skill, and inherent artistic abilities. The one commonality is the potential for enhancing and enriching communication with adults. Drawing can be a very significant and helpful pathway for children exposed to traumatic events (eg, parental loss, accidents, interpersonal violence, and sudden and traumatic death) to express memories, thoughts, and fears.

Malchiodi[12] notes that children who have witnessed violence or experienced a traumatic event are often silent in their suffering, but art can be used to create a concrete expression of what may seem secret or confusing. Johnson writes that:

> Aside from the therapeutic benefits of nonverbal communication of thoughts and feelings, one of the most impressive aspects of the art process is its potential to achieve or restore psychological equilibrium. This use of the art process as intervention is not mysterious or particularly novel; it may have been one of the reasons that humankind developed art in the first place—to alleviate or contain feelings of trauma, fear, anxiety, and psychological threat to the self and community.[4]

Many studies have successfully used drawings with traumatized children. These studies support the use of child drawings to express sensory images, ideas, and feelings surrounding stressful and traumatic experiences, such as sexual abuse, neglect, violent or chaotic households, courtroom testimony and proceedings, and anxiety-causing dental procedures.[7,10,12-19]

There is a natural cognitive response that attempts to avoid painful and traumatic thoughts by putting them out of the mind, which is often insufficient and results in children trying other coping mechanisms; drawing can be used to explore this cognitive defense.[15,20,21] Communication with children is critical in the assessment and treatment phases of care. During this process, clinicians must convince children that they are trustworthy, that they can ensure safety, and that it is safe to talk about what happened.

Levick[10,11] posits that, for a healthy child, art is a way to chart intellectual and emotional growth, and for the emotionally disturbed child whose fantasies or perceptions seem very real, art provides a way to separate fantasy from fact. Relating specifically to traumatic death, drawing can provide an open atmosphere that can help children explore their feelings surrounding the death and the accompanying trauma. It can create an environment in which the following occurs: the child's feelings are accepted, both the child and the clinician can openly discuss these feelings, the child has an opportunity to ask questions of the clinician, and the child subsequently can receive support and guidance from the clinician.

It is important for clinicians to avoid trying to interpret a child's words or feelings. Rather, it is more important to ask children what they are feeling and to explore the context within which they are explaining their feelings. The subject matter in the drawings may vary from themes of customary childhood topics, such as friendship and homework, to circumstances of confusion and frustration.[22] Questions that are structured in a supportive and open-ended manner will most likely elicit responses without leading children to give explanations thought to be desired by interviewers.

Children react differently to interpersonal violence and other traumatic events, sometimes resulting in varying responses among multiple siblings who experience the same traumatic event. They may appear calm and aloof, stoic, hyperactive, or angry, sometimes manifesting as perceived inappropriate behavior toward those attempting to provide assistance or support. It is important for clinicians not to personalize the actions of children.

Support, education, and genuine appreciation of a child's situation are the most effective means of achieving healthy grieving and integration of a loss. The versatility of artwork for assessment and intervention allows for application in a wide range of therapeutic settings and allows for cultural, ethnic, and gender differences. The intrinsic qualities of this modality, such as its ability to provide structure and promote free expression, can be drawn on to meet the varied needs of clients and to establish effective treatment approaches.[23] The self-expression facilitated by artwork provides a platform for communication and results in the sharing of experiences, feelings, and hopes in ways free of rigid systemic limitations.[241]

Although the use of artwork is somewhat magical in its ability to provide a safe and effective method of understanding the effect of sudden traumatic death in the life of a child, there is truly no magic in the process itself. Drawing is a natural activity by which children explore and express their world, whether that world is peaceful and happy or chaotic and sad. The process allows children to control the amount and content of their expression while affording themselves the opportunity to feel a sense of mastery over a situation in which there is typically a sense of total loss of control. Discussion of drawings provides insight into children's thoughts and feelings in addition to an opportunity to ask questions and seek guidance from adults.[3]

# Reflective Representations

## Variant Artistic Expression

**Case Study 12-1**

This 11-year-old boy, whose brother was beaten to death by their stepfather, expressed his thoughts and feelings in words instead of pictures. He had lost a brother to violent death and a stepfather to incarceration and expressed his ongoing worries about "someone else dieing [sic]." The absence of drawing can say as much as, if not more than, an elaborate drawing. While not doing a drawing can sometimes represent resistance, it also can be representative of a child who is not ready to completely realize or confront the full impact of the traumatic situation.

When asked to describe his current worries after the murder of his older brother, the boy expressed a pervasive, and not necessarily logical, fear that someone else in the family was going to die, as is typical in children exposed to interpersonal violence and sudden traumatic death.

*Figure 12-1. This "drawing" demonstrates that artistic expression comes in many forms and presentations that should be supported and encouraged.*

I worry about...

I worry about someone else dieing.

20. Worries need to be shared with someone!

**Figure 12-1**

## Client's Attitudes

**Case Study 12-2**

Participants were asked to share their feelings about art therapy in a drawing.

*Figure 12-2. This picture represents a response to a structured activity asking participants to make a drawing showing how they feel about art therapy.*

The red and orange X across the mouth represents the mother's messages to "shut up" and "quit complaining." The mother is shown as the red and orange lightning bolt at the top left of the picture. The brown and black X across the mouth comes from her father's message to "never speak to me unless you have something decent to say." He is represented as the black and brown lightning bolt at the top right of the picture.

**Figure 12-2**

# Reflective Representations

## Aspects Charts

### Case Study 12-3

This 12-year-old child was subjected to emotional abuse in the form of isolation, rejection, and duress during visits to a noncustodial parent. Although no overt sexual activities were reported, age-inappropriate bathing activities occurred and covert sexual activities abounded within the home. The child often dissociated during visits and reported experiencing a see-through barrier.

***Figure 12-3-a.*** *Aspects chart, showing the various aspects of the personality.*

***Figure 12-3-b.*** *An aspects chart created by the child. Note the lack of body-specific features in the physical areas, with colors surrounding the form. Although the mental aspect appears ordered with bricks neatly in place, the window could be broken. The child wrote that, "In the top part of my chart [creative], I drew a plant with buds on it. To me that symbolizes my creative self really growing and full. I feel that at the present time I am trying to work more with that section and make it as big as the other parts have been. In the past I think that it has been smaller than some of the other parts, but now I think it is equal. In the right part of my chart [mental] I drew a clear window, with a brick wall around it. I think that that section is very strong and also very clear. Sometimes my mental side can be 'out of it,' [ie, she dissociates] but it seems to always stay clear. In the bottom part of my chart [physical] I drew an outline of a human body with many colors. I think that I am starting to show how great I am on the inside as well as the out-side. In the left part of my chart [emotions] I drew a heart with half of the background green and the other half blue. The heart symbolizes that I am starting to be able to show my emotions, but yet they aren't as sad and dreary as they have been in the past. The green and blue is to symbolize how much I love the earth and how happy I feel outside and on the earth. In the center part of my chart [integration] I drew scribbles, but I used all the colors that I used in the loops and I made them flow in a nice even circle that started in the center and worked its way out. I feel that this symbolizes all of them working together and making me 'even.'"*

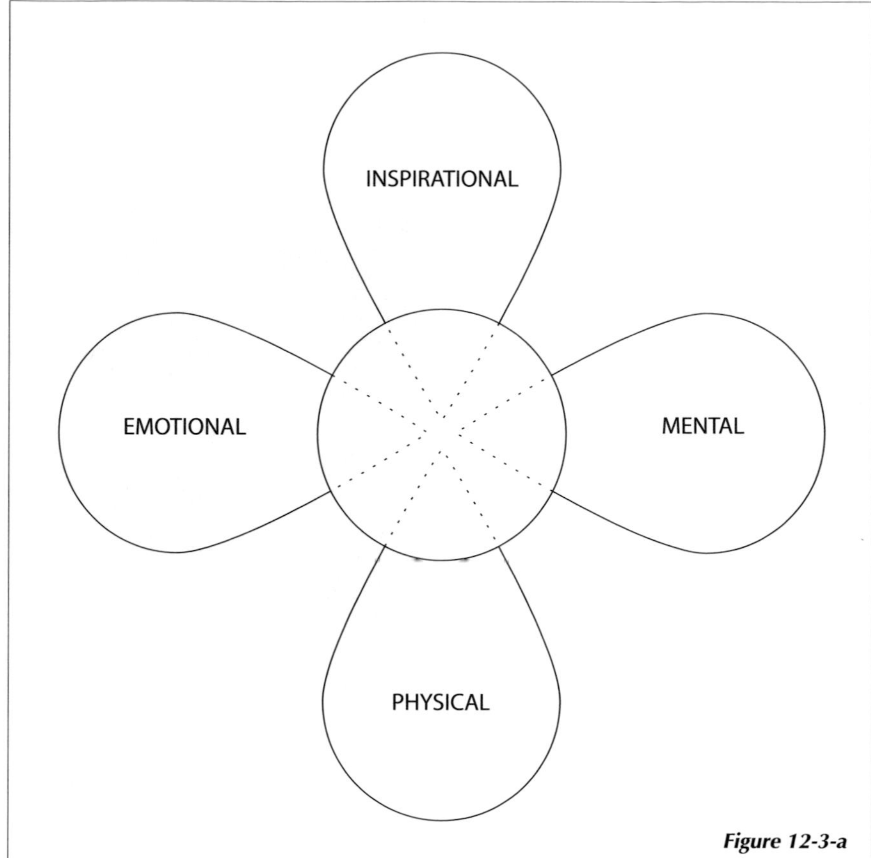


**Figure 12-3-a**

**Figure 12-3-b**

## Illness and Death

### Emotional Attachment

**Case Study 12-8**

This drawing by an 11-year-old boy who lost his mother to cancer provided insight into his emotional attachment to her. This insight provided an opportunity for the therapist to maximize the positive memories of the child's deceased mother as a method of adaptive coping and grief during the initial months after her death.

***Figure 12-8.*** *Drawing by an 11-year-old boy of his deceased mother.*

Figure 12-8

### Insight for Therapeutic Intervention

**Case Study 12-9**

This 8-year-old boy's mother was terminally ill when he wrote, "I think about my mom I feel as I will see her and get scared."

***Figure 12-9.*** *This "drawing" provides another example about the "lived experience" of a child confronted by the terminal illness and impending death of a family member. It provides insight for therapeutic intervention with children confronted by the iatrogenic effects of medical interventions and the certain death of a loved one.*

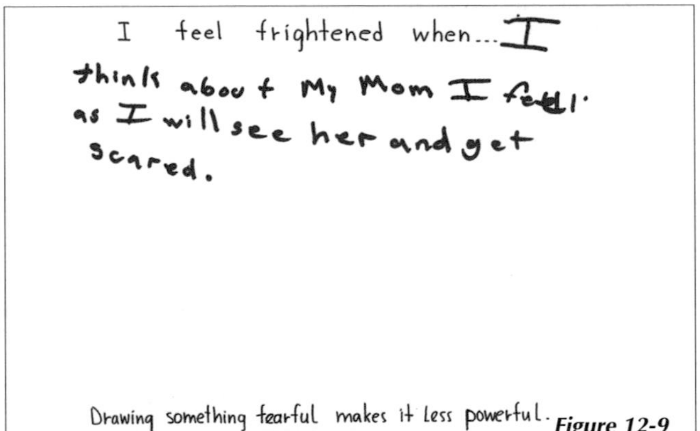

I feel frightened when... I
think about My Mom I feel.
as I will see her and get
Scared.

Drawing something fearful makes it less powerful.

Figure 12-9

### Prenatal Memory

**Case Study 12-10**

The client who created this drawing stated, "The fires hurt the baby. She feels the fires."

***Figure 12-10.*** *This drawing represents a prenatal memory.*

Figure 12-10

# Illness and Death

## Three-Dimenstional Representations

### Case Study 12-11

This woman attended group therapy sessions for a number of years and spoke very rarely in the group. When asked specifically if she preferred to discontinue therapy or be moved to another group, she stated that she wanted to stay. Eventually an art activity was suggested to which she responded with noticeable interest. When asked to make an object that would represent her siblings, she created masks. Her therapeutic journey became more fluid after these masks were done. She was raised in a family where children were never to speak unless spoken to first by an adult. She was supposed to sit still and not move whenever she was at home. If she did express herself or move, her brothers verbally assaulted her. She was isolated from other children and rejected and ignored by other members of her family. She could not recall if she was physically or sexually assaulted.

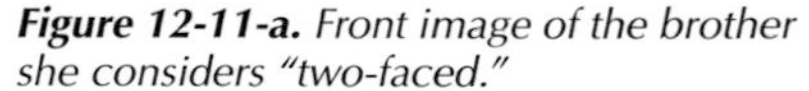

**Figure 12-11-a.** *Front image of the brother she considers "two-faced."*

**Figure 12-11-b.** *Back image of same mask.*

**Figure 12-11-c.** *Mask of the brother who never spoke to the woman.*

Figure 12-11-a

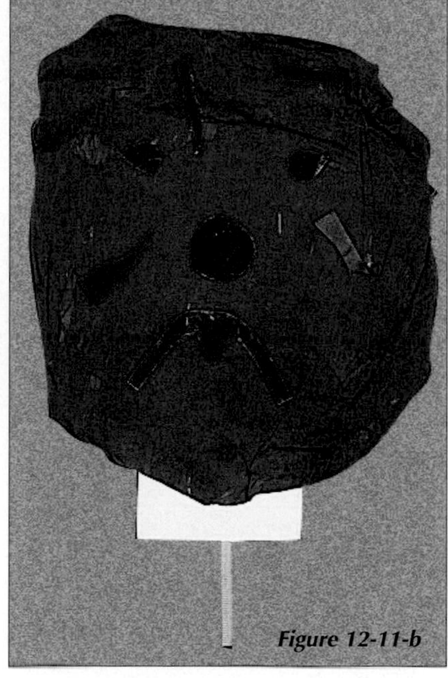

Figure 12-11-b

Figure 12-11-c

## World Events

### September 11

**Case Study 12-12**

This 5-year-old boy drew about what he believed to have happened during the terrorist attacks of September 11, 2001.

***Figure 12-12.*** *The drawing includes "planes" and "bombs" falling on people's houses.*

**Figure 12-12**

## Foundation for Storytelling

### Avoiding Abuse

**Case Study 12-13**

This drawing by a 10-year-old boy provided a foundation for storytelling about how, in the winter, he would run from and avoid his abusive father by getting on a sled and "sledding fast."

***Figure 12-13.*** *Drawing of the boy and his sled.*

**Figure 12-13**

## Sexual Abuse

### Regression and Agitation Signaling Sexual Abuse

**Case Study 12-14**

Drawn by an 11-year-old boy during a therapeutic session with a nurse, this drawing revealed an episode of sexual abuse by a male relative who was spending the night at his house.

***Figure 12-14.*** *This artwork is very regressed for an 11-year-old child and has an agitated line quality and overly exaggerated size of the offending arm and hand.*

**Figure 12-14**

### Sexual Abuse By a Grandfather

**Case Study 12-15**

This 5-year-old girl was sexually abused by her grandfather, who happened to be an amputee with only one leg. When she stated that she had been abused on the couch, the interviewer drew a picture of a couch and asked the girl to show her what happened. When asked what the object on the floor was, she responded that it was "grandpa's leg."

***Figure 12-15-a.*** *A picture the girl drew of her grandfather with and without his artificial leg.*

***Figure 12-15-b.*** *The picture the girl drew of the incident that occurred on the couch.*

picture of grandpa with his leg on

grandpa with his leg off

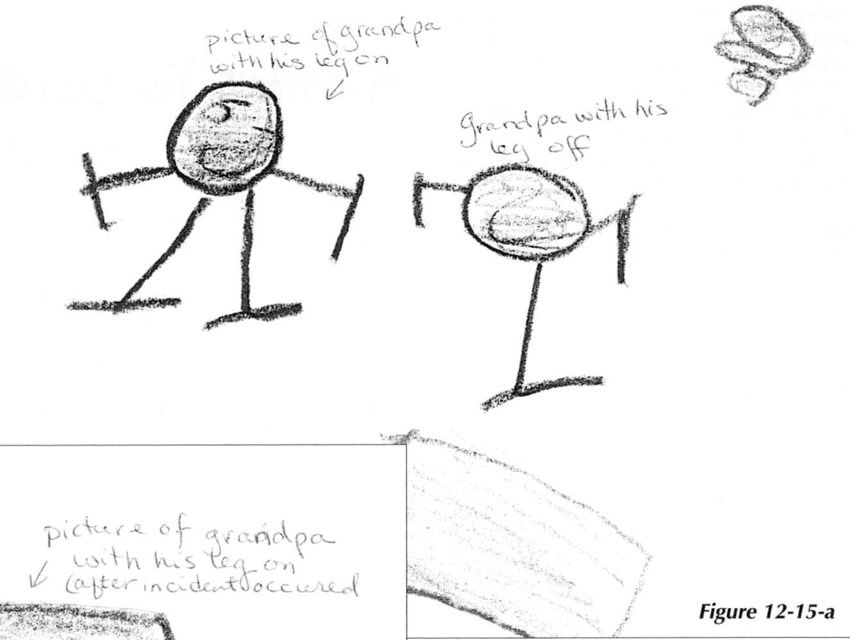

**Figure 12-15-a**

A picture of me with grandpa laying on top of me (without his leg)

picture of grandpa with his leg on (after incident occured)

couch

grandpa's leg

**Figure 12-15-b**

# Interpersonal Violence

## Progression From Abuse To Killing the Abuser

**Case Study 12-24** *(continued)*

***Figures 12-24-c, d, e, f,*** *and* ***g.*** *Note the recurrent theme of encapsulation.*

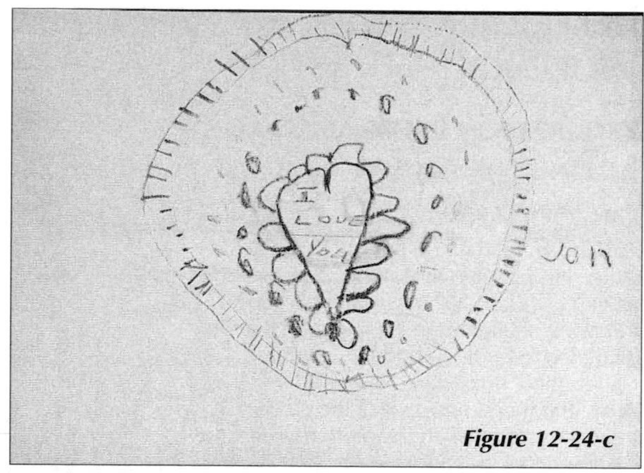

**Figure 12-24-c**

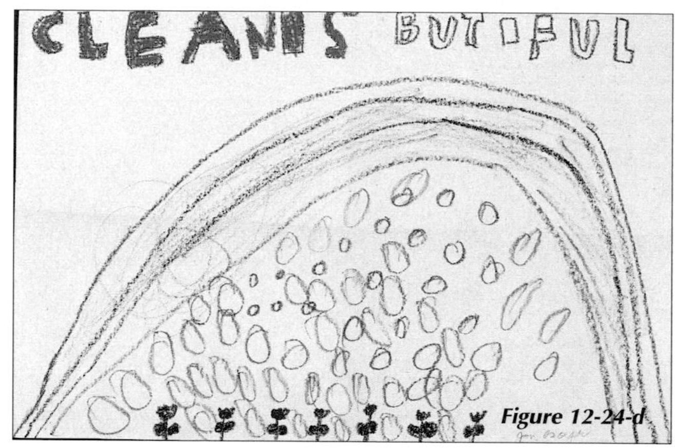
**Figure 12-24-d**

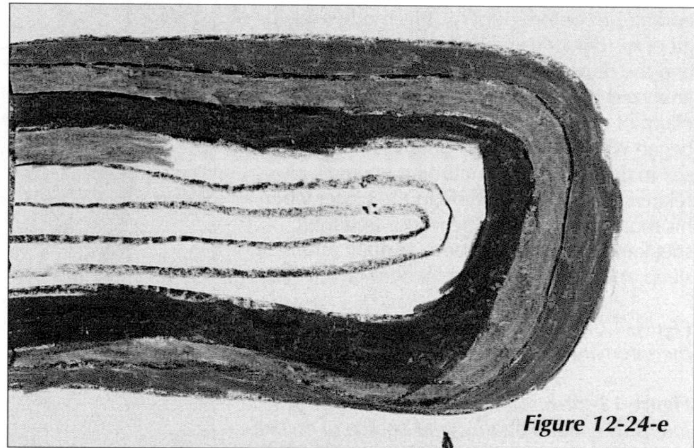
**Figure 12-24-e**

**Figure 12-24-f**

**Figure 12-24-g**

# Interpersonal Violence

## Progression From Abuse To Killing the Abuser

**Case Study 12-24** *(continued)*

***Figures 12-24-h*** *and* ***i.*** *Self-portraits.*

***Figures 12-24-j, k, l, m, n,*** *and* ***o.*** *Latency age drawings. There is a more sophisticated demonstration of encapsulation and intrusion. Often the pictures are chaotic and primitive.*

**Figure 12-24-j**

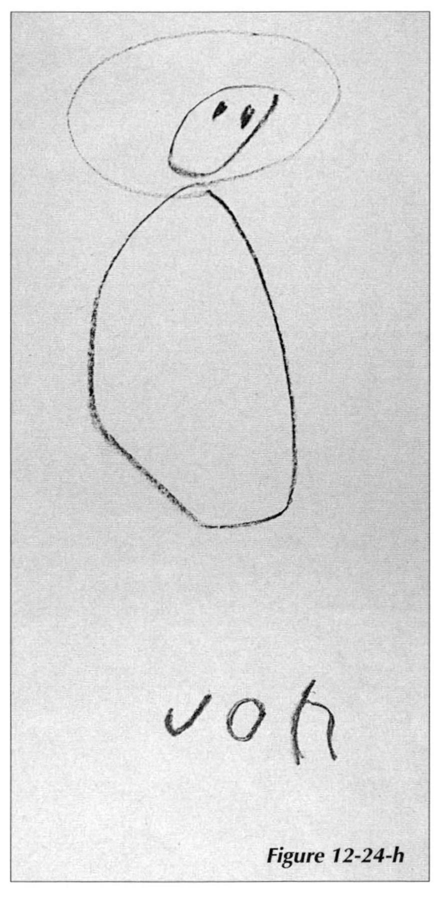


**Figure 12-24-h**

**Figure 12-24-k**

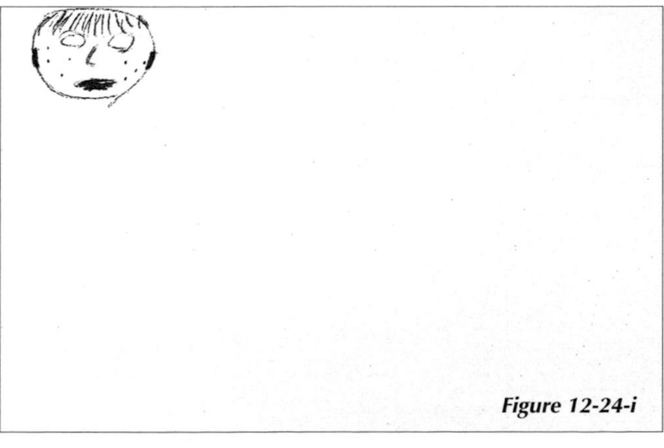

**Figure 12-24-i**

**Figure 12-24-l**

# Interpersonal Violence

## Progression From Abuse To Killing the Abuser

**Case Study 12-24** *(continued)*

***Figure 12-24-p.*** *Art therapy drawing in which he depicts his family. Note the church and dove in the background.*

**Figure 12-24-m**

**Figure 12-24-n**

**Figure 12-24-o**

**Figure 12-24-p**

# Interpersonal Violence

## Progression From Abuse To Killing the Abuser

**Case Study 12-24** *(continued)*

***Figure 12-24-q.*** *Art therapy drawing in which he describes the abuse.*

***Figures 12-24-r** and **s.** Art therapy drawing where he describes his feelings about himself and his father and what had happened.*

***Figure 12-24-t.*** *Art therapy drawing in which he depicts his life in prison.*

This sampling demonstrates fragmentation, intrusion, and encapsulation. Some are intense, some chaotic. His age is not always noted with the drawings. Several were made as an adult in art therapy. (Drawings courtesy of the artist's mother, Joan M. Boyer.)

**Figure 12-24-q**

**Figure 12-24-r**

**Figure 12-24-s**

**Figure 12-24-t**

# Drugs and Alcohol

## Death of Adult

**Case Study 12-25**

At the time of the interview, this 10-year-old girl's aunt had died as the result of the accidental adverse effects of drugs. The children in the household found the aunt dead on the couch in the morning hours as they prepared to leave for school. The girl shared the story of how her aunt died in her sleep on the couch, making it clear that she was aware of her aunt's use of illicit substances and that she believed that her aunt had died from an unanticipated overdose of these drugs.

*Figure 12-25.* A picture of the girl's aunt sitting on the couch.

## Child's Understanding of Aspects of Behavior

**Case Study 12-26**

This 12-year-old boy found his younger sister bound with duct tape and phone cords and stuffed in a closet. She had been raped, beaten, and asphyxiated. The offender was the mother's new boyfriend. In this drawing the boy reflected that he knew drugs and alcohol were abused by the boyfriend and probably contributed to his sister's death.

*Figure 12-26.* Note the "no drugs" t-shirt being worn by the figure, even while he is smoking marijuana and drinking beer (on the table).

**Figure 12-25**

**Figure 12-26**

# Sudden Traumatic Deaths

## Memories of Deceased

### Case Study 12-27

This 8-year-old boy heard about the death of his uncle on the television news while eating lunch in his elementary school cafeteria. The uncle was murdered during an argument while sweeping the sidewalk in front of the store where he worked. The newscast showed his uncle's body, dead, on the street, and covered by a bloodstained sheet. During therapeutic interactions, the child drew this picture about how he would rather remember his "favorite uncle." The child demonstrated his memories of watching his uncle sweeping the sidewalk and how he would "keep the streets clean" when he was still alive.

*Figure 12-27. The child's drawing of the uncle who was murdered.*

Figure 12-27

## Multiple Witnesses of the Same Event

### Case Study 12-28

This 8-year-old boy and his three other siblings were being watched by their uncle while their mother was out shopping. Another uncle and his girlfriend came into the house, had an argument, and "clubbed," repeatedly stabbed, and then shot the first uncle in the head. The perpetrators used a weapon of opportunity to kill the child's uncle who was babysitting that evening. During these events, the child and his siblings were all hiding behind the couch or other chairs in the living room. The child also described how the girlfriend was laughing and smiling throughout the beating and the murder.

***Figure 12-28-a.** "He 'clubbed' him" is the phrase used to describe this drawing. In the hand of the perpetrator is "The Club," a device that is used to lock automobile steering wheels to prevent theft. This drawing depicts "The Club," the bloodstained knife, and the smiling perpetrators.*

***Figure 12-28-b.** This drawing is from the 11-year-old sibling of the boy. It provides an example of drawings from multiple child witnesses of the same event or experience. Note the emergent depiction of both "The Club" in the hands of the perpetrator and the smiling faces during the attack.*

Figure 12-28-a

Figure 12-28-b

# Sudden Traumatic Deaths

## Hypervigilant Attention After Brother's Murder

**Case Study 12-29**

This 9-year-old boy provides his interpretation of the homicide of his brother through drawing. It was immediately noticeable that the boy created the entire drawing in a monochromatic approach, using only a brown marker; but then, taking a red marker, he commented as he drew in on the decedent, "Oh, I forgot something . . . the blood!" The blood of the brother's death, in bright red, represented the expression of feeling and environmental cueing. In the drawing there were three figures: his brother, the brother's girlfriend, and the perpetrator. During the discussion of this drawing of the shooting death of his brother, the child shared that "the guy who shot my brother didn't like him. My brother and his girlfriend were riding in the car. The guy who killed my brother told her [the girlfriend] to duck down because he wanted to shoot my brother and not her."

**Figure 12-29**

***Figure 12-29.*** *In this drawing there is a noticeable incongruity between the appropriate affective response of fear, anger, and terror on the figure of the brother, his girlfriend, and the perpetrator; instead they are all smiling. Only in the portrayal of the brother bleeding and dying is the appropriate affect of sadness depicted on both John and the girlfriend, in the form of a frown-like face. Also noticeable in this picture is the depiction of the "action" of the bullets as they exit the gun and are targeted directly toward the left side of the chest. The trajectory of the bullets is quite accurate based on the cause of death reported by the police of a penetrating gunshot wound to the left side of the chest. Even though the child was not present during the attack, he correctly portrays the cause and manner of death in the correct location. This supports the child's own description of his hypervigilant attention to adult conversation regarding his brother's death.*

# Sudden Traumatic Deaths

## Generalized Fear for Safety and Bodily Integrity

### Case Study 18-30

When asked to describe what was happening in the drawing, this child reported that Uncle Mike and "the guy" were fighting. "He [Uncle Mike] went down there to get some drugs. He had a lot of money . . . so the guy hit him with a little gun. Uncle Mike fell down and when he tried to get up, he [the guy] shot him."

In the drawing, it was clear that the male figure on the left, described as Uncle Mike, had received a gunshot wound to the upper left quadrant of the torso. This was of note because, although the child was not a direct witness to the shooting, he had placed the bullet wound and blood in the correct region of the bullet entry. The figure clearly looked helpless, with no hands to defend himself, no feet to escape, and his arms raised in an open-armed posture of vulnerability. However, incongruent to this depiction was the displaced smile on the face of the victim.

The other figure, described as "the guy" who committed the murder, was clearly holding a gun that was aimed at, and had obviously shot, the figure known as Uncle Mike. This figure was much smaller in body size. The child corroborated this accuracy during his interview, describing that his Uncle Mike was a "big man." When looking at the figure of the perpetrator, it was noted that there were no facial features. During his discussion of the perpetrator the child expressed his anxiety that someone would come and hurt someone else in his family. This anxiety was amorphous, and when asked about the specifics of what he feared would happen, he displayed generalized fear for the safety and bodily integrity of himself and his family, just as the perpetrator is vague and faceless, but deadly.

***Figure 12-30.*** *In this drawing there are two figures, described as Uncle Mike and "the guy who shot him."*

**Figure 12-30**

## Sudden Traumatic Deaths

### Hypervigilance and Fear After Brother's Murder

**Case Study 12-31**

This 9-year-old boy's brother was the victim of a drug-related homicide. Although the offender was incarcerated, the boy continued to worry that a "druggie" or "someone like that" would come and shoot him through the front window. In the drawing, the boy depicted himself standing helpless in his living room as a gun and an arm were above him, outside the house, preparing to shoot him.

Figure 12-31

***Figure 12-31.*** *This drawing reflects the hypervigilance and fear felt after the murder of the boy's brother.*

## Shaken Baby Syndrome

### Fear and Sadness After Infant's Death

**Case Study 12-32**

This drawing was created by a 6-year-old boy to express his fears and sadness after the shaken baby syndrome death of his infant brother.

Figure 12-32

***Figure 12-32.*** *Note the small figures in the adult hands of the perpetrator as well as the affective incongruence of a smiling face during the assault.*

## Shaken Baby Syndrome

### Witness To Death of Infant Sister

**Case Study 12-33**

This 6-year-old boy witnessed the shaken baby syndrome death of his infant sister.

***Figure 12-33-a.*** *This is the boyfriend approaching the infant before he "threw her hard on the bed and her head hit the wall."*

***Figure 12-33-b.*** *This is the drawing of the funeral for the baby killed as a result of shaken baby syndrome. The baby is in the grave, with the shovel and removed dirt nearby. The boy is surrounded by cousins, with whom, he was told, he would be living.*

**Figure 12-33-a**

**Figure 12-33-b**

# Facial Findings

**Case Study 13-1**

This 6-month-old girl was examined approximately 3 days after injury. The father acknowledged "hurting" the baby but did not say how. Photographs were taken with a Nikon Coolpix 950 2-megapixel digital camera with flash at highest resolution UXGA (1600 x 1200) and at lowest compression JPEG (Fine), resulting in an approximately 1-megabyte file.

***Figure 13-1-a.*** *The lesion on the neck is a chronic rash, probably from drooling in the context of significant environmental neglect issues.*

***Figure 1-13-b.*** *Extensive bruising and swelling involve the right cheek.*

***Figures 1-13-c*** *and* ***d.*** *The pattern is not very specific, although consistent with blows to the face or, as the history suggests, forceful pinching of the face.*

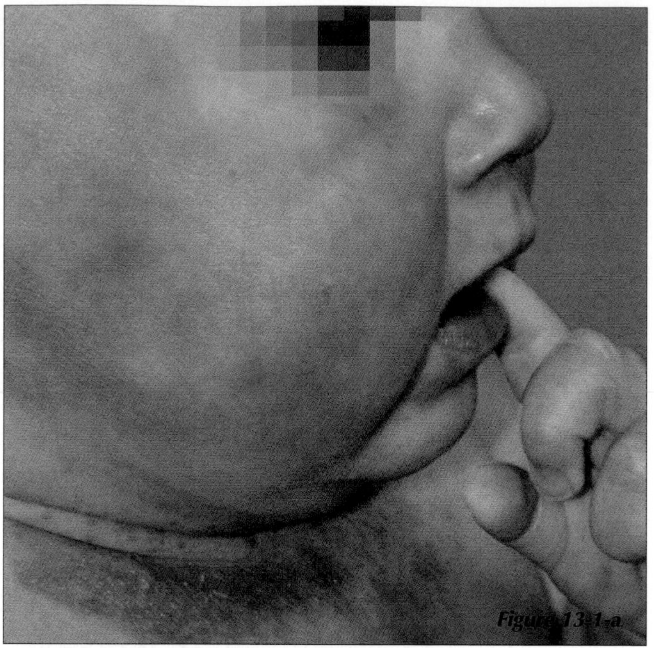

Figure 13-1-a

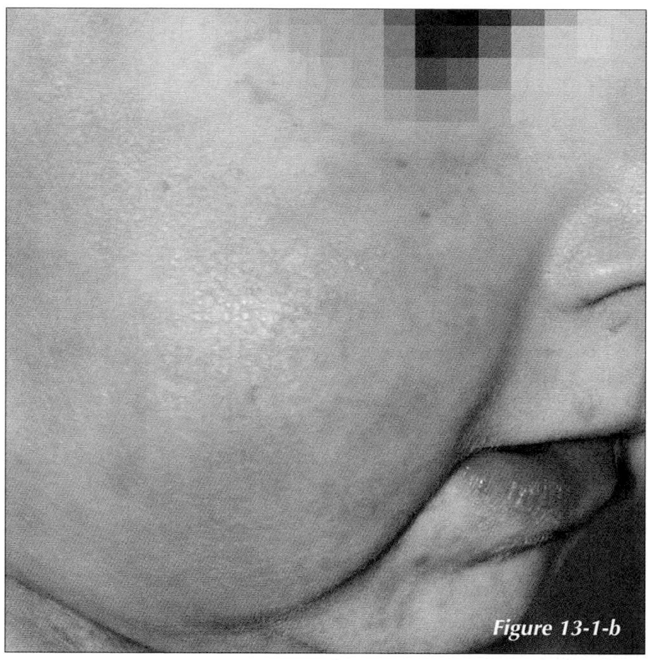

Figure 13-1-b

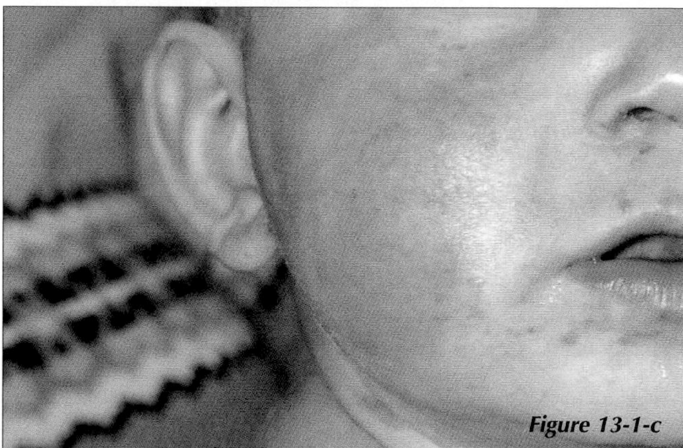

Figure 13-1-c

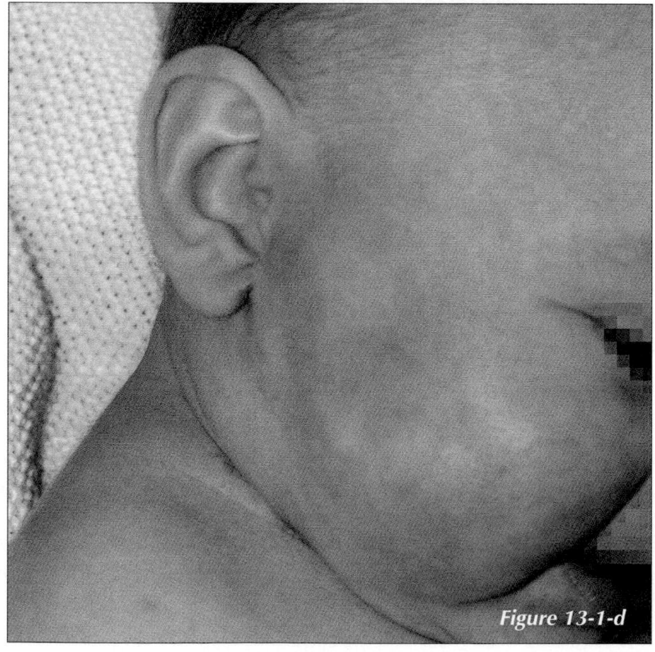

Figure 13-1-d

# Possible Bruising

**Case Study 13-2**

This 3-month-old girl was examined for possible bruising on the back and labia. The examining physician felt that the findings were not significant, and the child went home, returning 1 month later with subdural hematomas and retinal hemorrhages. All images were scanned as low-resolution and high-compression jpegs. All of the photographs were taken at the same time. A consulting physician asked to review only the very limited instant photos could easily be persuaded that the findings were not significant.

***Figure 13-2-a.*** *This scanned instant photo shows erythema and/or hyperpigmentation of the labia. The finding on the left heel is a bandage.*

***Figure 13-2-b.*** *This scanned instant photo shows erythema and/or hyperpigmentation.*

***Figure 13-2-c.*** *The bruise clearly evident on this 35-mm print is not evident on the instant photo.*

***Figure 13-2-d.*** *This 35-mm print shows the bruise not evident on the instant photo.*

***Figure 13-2-e.*** *Instant photos were not taken of the jaw bruise evident on this 35-mm print.*

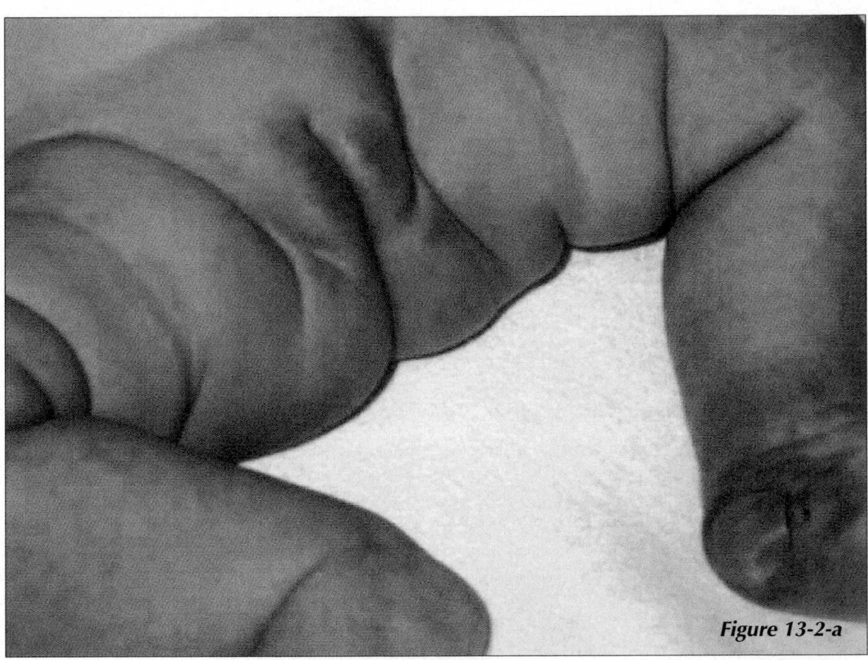
Figure 13-2-a

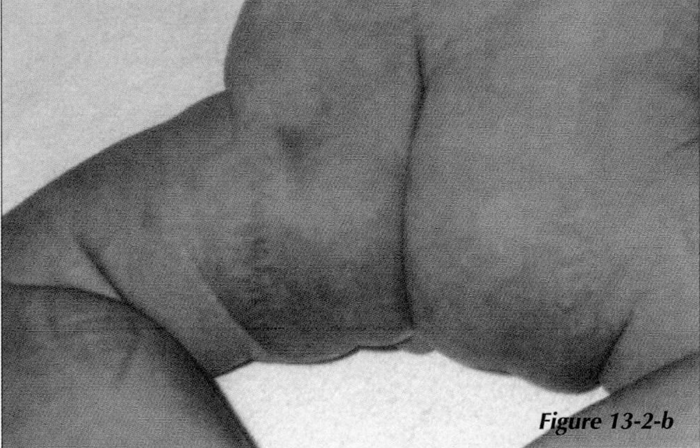
Figure 13-2-b

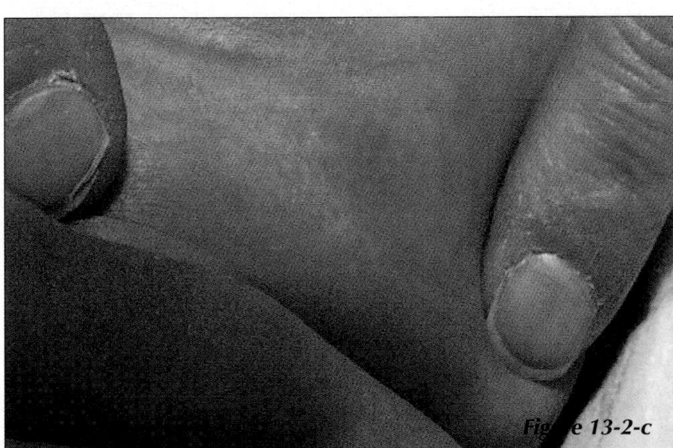
Figure 13-2-c

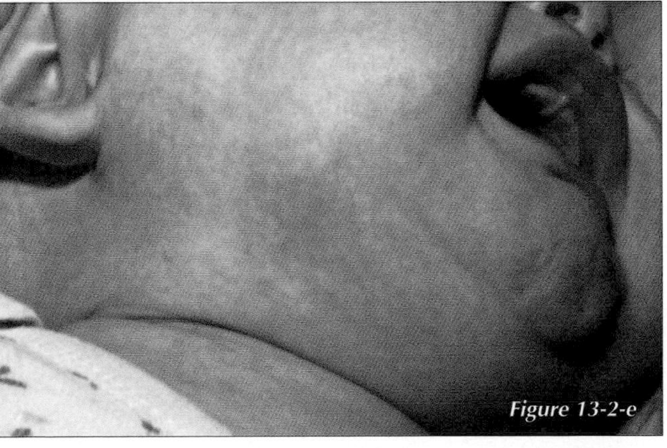
Figure 13-2-e

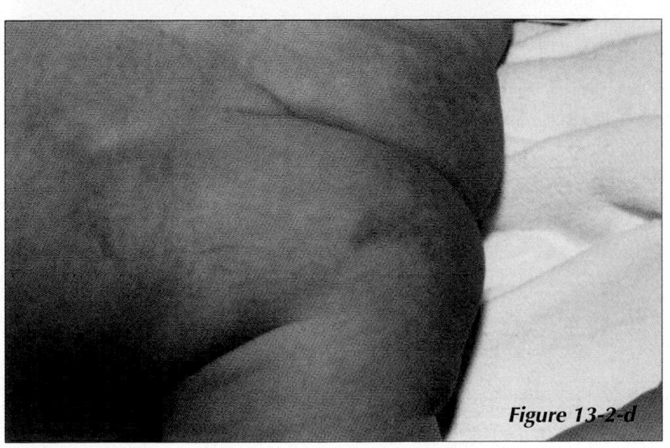
Figure 13-2-d

# Faded and Fresh Bruising

**Case Study 13-3**

This 14-month-old girl was photographed 3 days after first being seen for bruising of the face and ears. The child was babysat by the mother's boyfriend, who had stated that he had slapped the child 1 month earlier. Photographs were taken with a Nikon Coolpix 950 2-megapixel digital camera with the flash at highest resolution UXGA (1600 x 1200) and at lowest compression JPEG (Fine), resulting in an approximately 1-megabyte file.

***Figure 13-3-a.*** *Faded bruising of the anterior chest area.*

***Figure 13-3-b.*** *The child has fresh bruising of the left ear.*

***Figure 13-3-c.*** *A large faded bruise appears on the child's right cheek.*

***Figure 13-3-d.*** *The child has bruising of the pinna of the right ear similar to that of the left ear. Examination also revealed bruising of the scalp behind the ear associated with boggy swelling.*

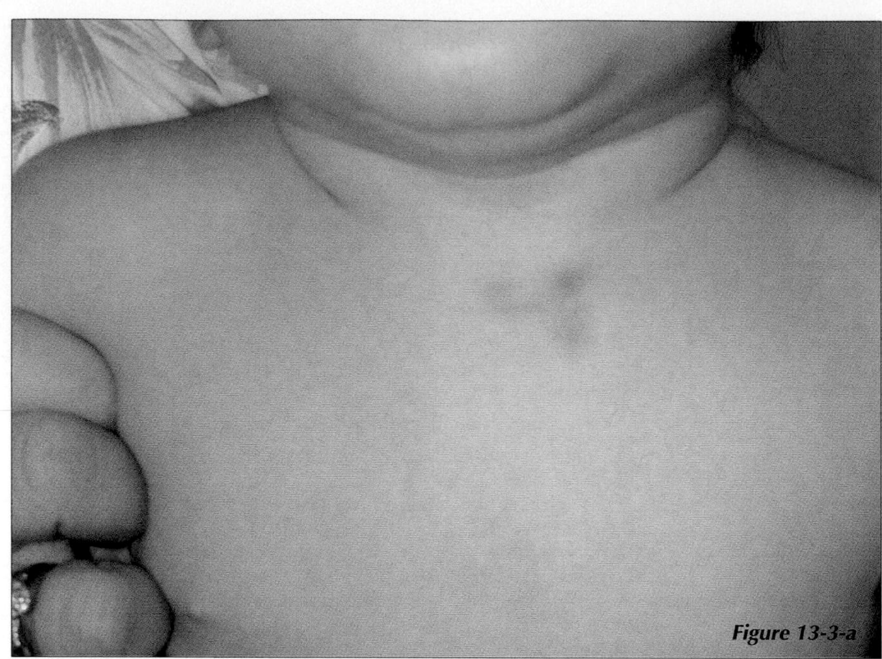

Figure 13-3-a

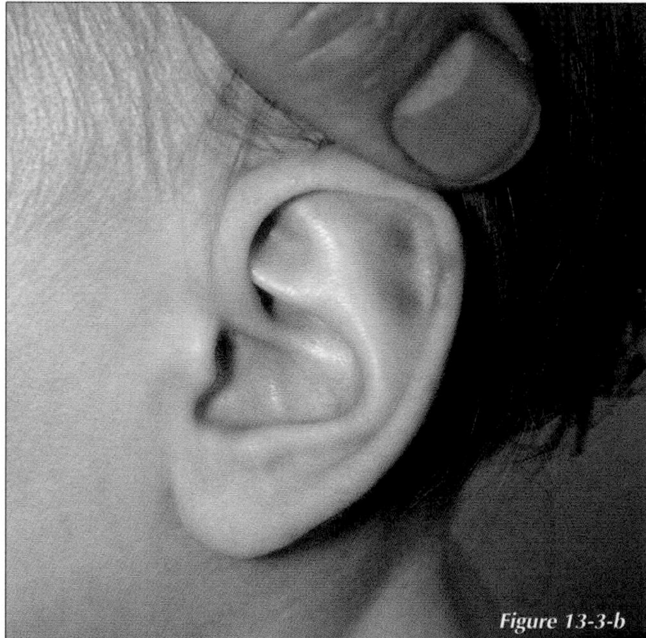

Figure 13-3-b

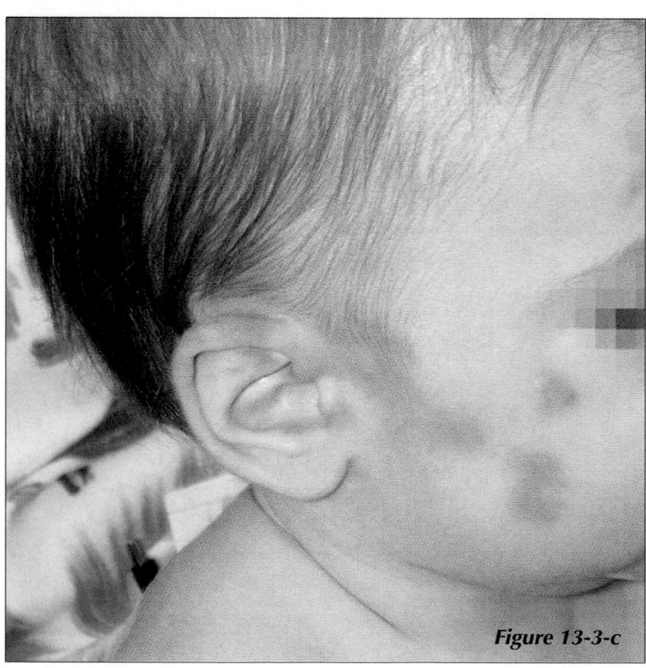

Figure 13-3-c

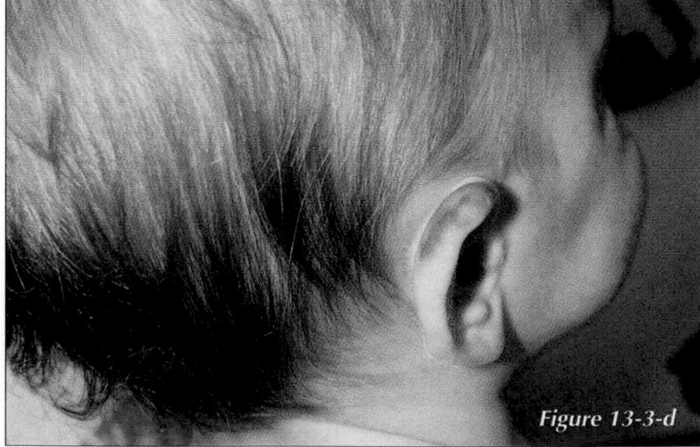

Figure 13-3-d

# Lesion Differentiation

**Case Study 13-4**

This 15-year-old male was examined because of concern over possible inflicted scars on the back. The adolescent and family credibly denied abuse. He had grown 11 inches in the previous 18 months. Photographs were taken with a Nikon Coolpix 950 2-megapixel digital camera with the flash at highest resolution UXGA (1600 x 1200) and at lowest compression JPEG (Fine), resulting in an approximately 1-megabyte jpeg file.

***Figure 13-4-a.*** *These lesions are classic stretch marks.*

***Figure 13-4-b.*** *This image has been enhanced by increasing contrast by 50% and decreasing brightness by 20% so that the findings become much more visible.*

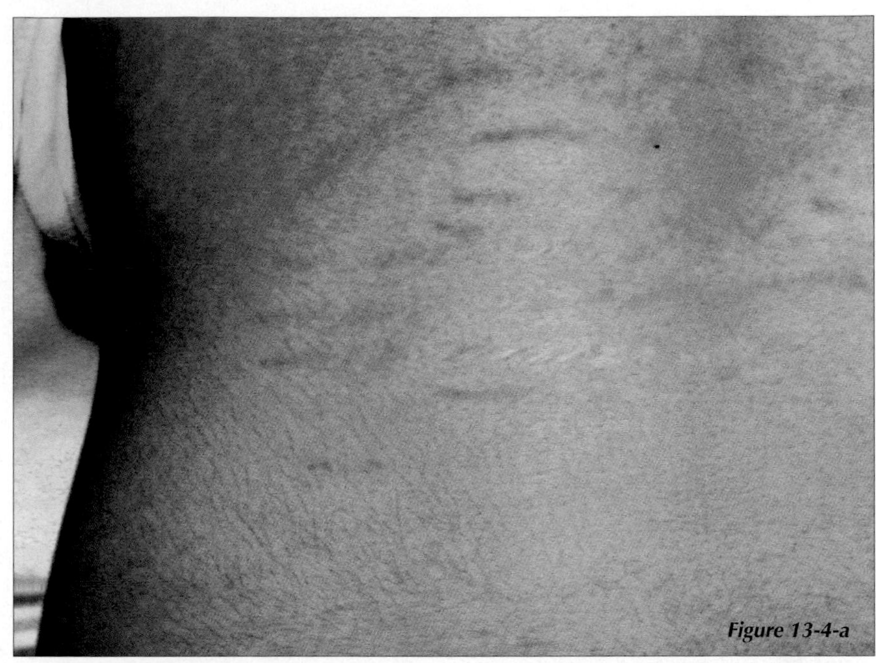

**Figure 13-4-a**

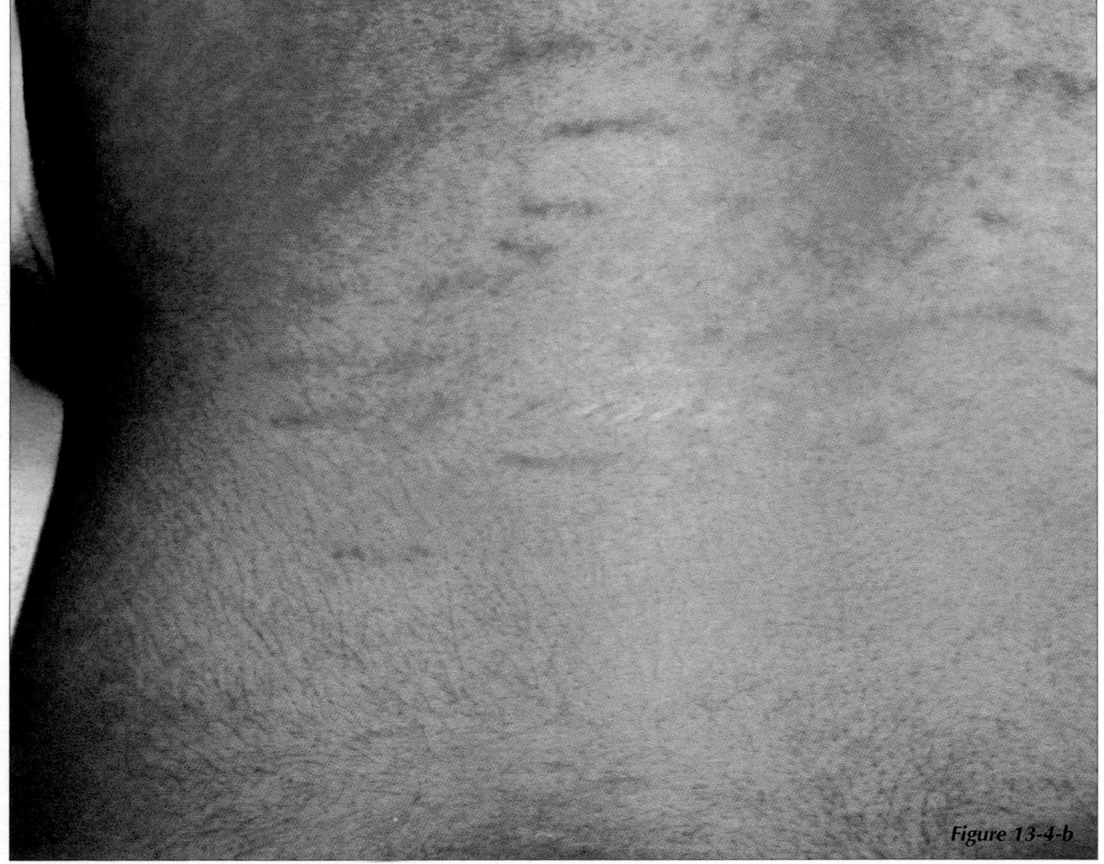

**Figure 13-4-b**

# Scleral Hemorrhage and Bruising

**Case Study 13-5**

This 4-week-old male infant was examined with bilateral scleral hemorrhages and bruising of the lower left leg. Ultimately, the father described holding the child tightly against his chest in frustration while the infant cried. The resulting Valsalva effect likely accounted for the scleral and orbital bruising, and the father clutching the leg with his hand accounted for the bruising on the leg. Photographs were taken with a Nikon Coolpix 950 2-megapixel digital camera with the flash at highest resolution UXGA (1600 x 1200) and at lowest compression JPEG (Fine).

***Figure 13-5-a.*** *Bilateral scleral hemorrhages in this 4-week-old infant.*

***Figure 13-5-b.*** *Bilateral scleral hemorrhages and orbital bruising.*

***Figure 13-5-c.*** *The father's hand clutching the infant resulted in this bruising of the lower left leg.*

***Figure 13-5-d.*** *Bruising of infant's leg caused by father's hand.*

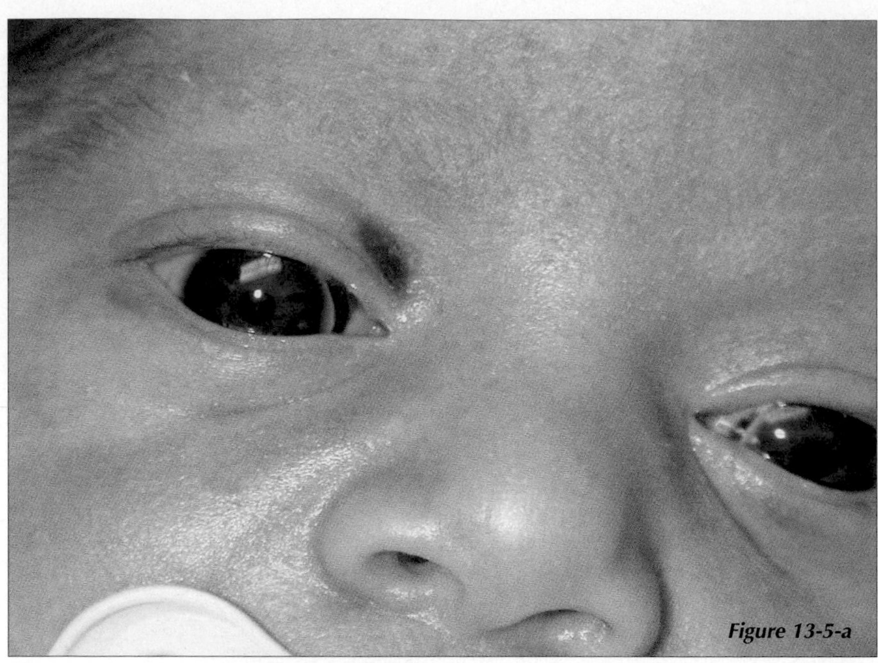

Figure 13-5-a

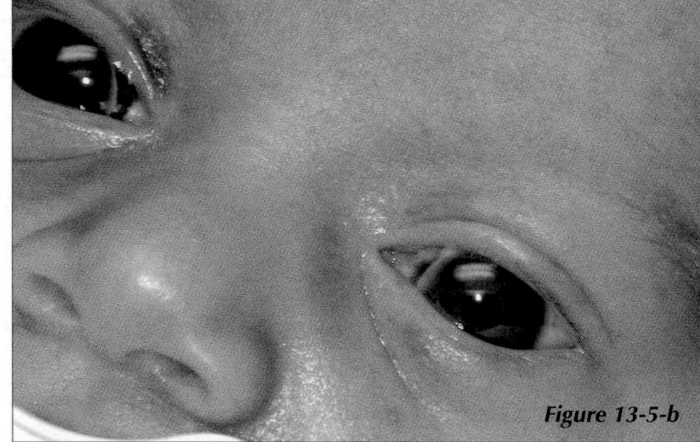

Figure 13-5-b

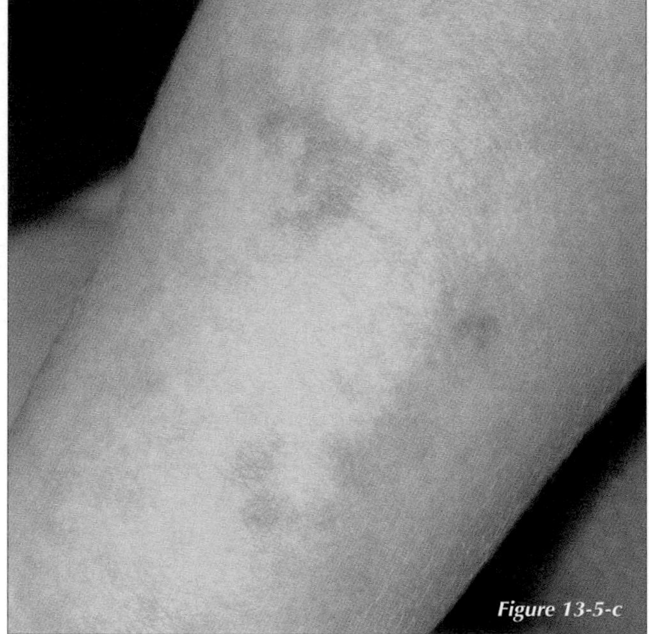

Figure 13-5-c

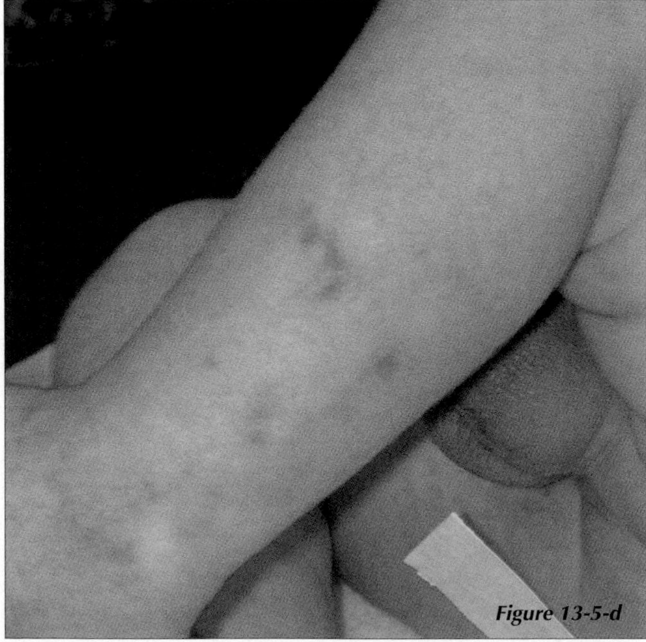

Figure 13-5-d

# Multiple Injuries

**Case Study 13-6**

This 7-month-old child was examined after an alleged fall with extensive facial bruising, an acute fractured femur, as well as older rib fractures. Photographs were taken with a Sony CD Mavica 2048 x 1536 1.22-MB JPEG. The CD Mavica records images on a CD, which allows easy storage and file transfer. Flash was not used, leading to poor color balance from indoor lighting. Flash should always be used indoors.

***Figure 13-6-a.*** *This child experienced facial bruising allegedly as a result of a fall.*

***Figure 13-6-b.*** *Extensive facial bruising was among the injuries experienced by this infant.*

***Figure 13-6-c.*** *Facial and neck bruises were revealed on examination of this 7-month-old infant.*

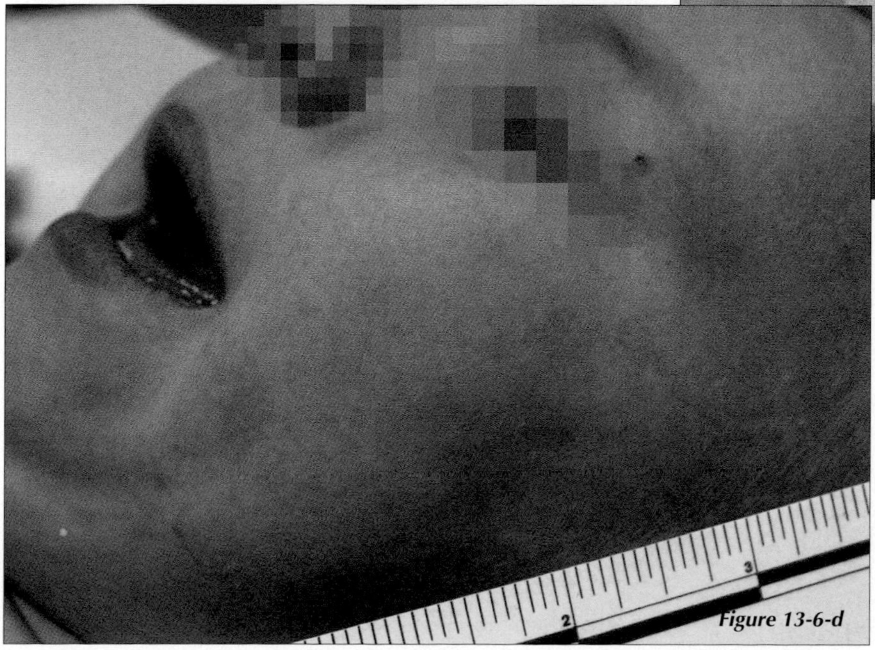

***Figure 13-6-d.*** *Facial bruises examined with scale.*

**Figure 13-6-a**

**Figure 13-6-b**

**Figure 13-6-c**

**Figure 13-6-d**

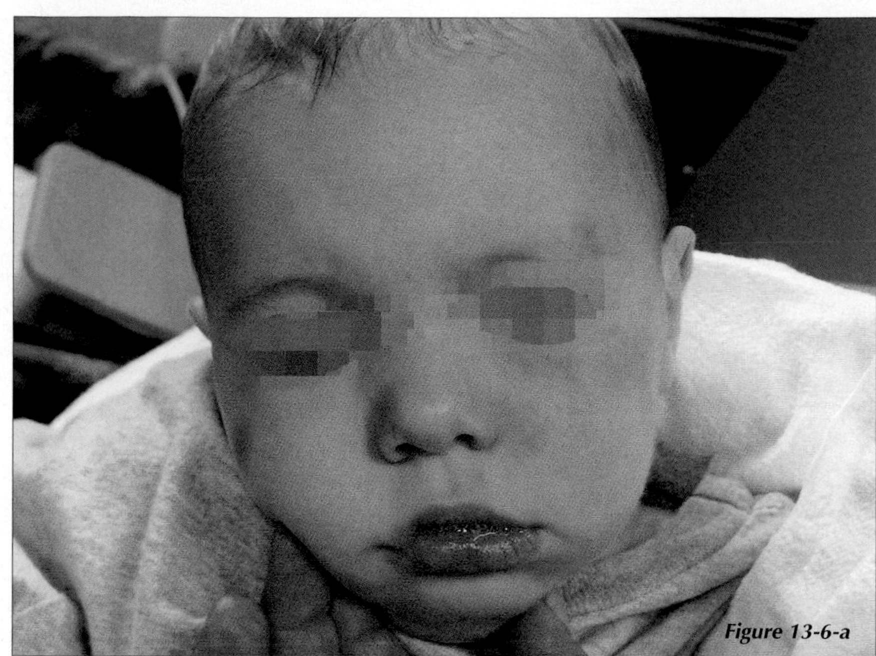

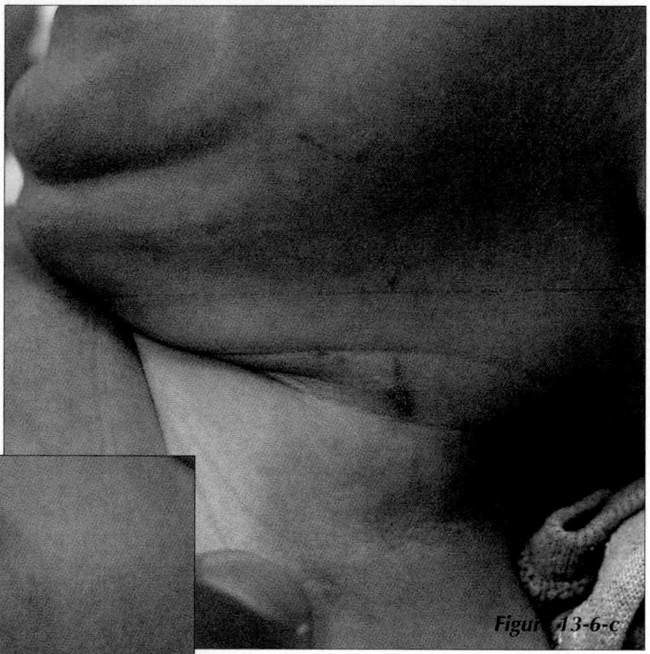

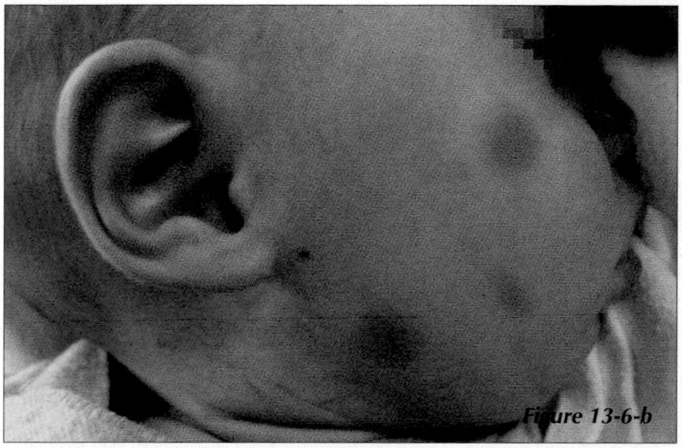

# FACIAL BRUISING

**Case Study 13-7**

This 5-year-old girl and her 3-year-old brother were examined 24 hours after an assault by the mother's boyfriend. Photographs were taken with a Nikon Coolpix 950 2-megapixel digital camera with flash at highest resolution UXGA (1600 x 1200) and at lowest compression JPEG (Fine).

***Figures 13-7-a, b, c,** and **d.** Note classic hand imprint facial bruising on the left side of the face consistent with a slap with a right hand. Bruises may be washed out by close-up flash, but, in general, high-quality digital and film cameras capture such findings well.*

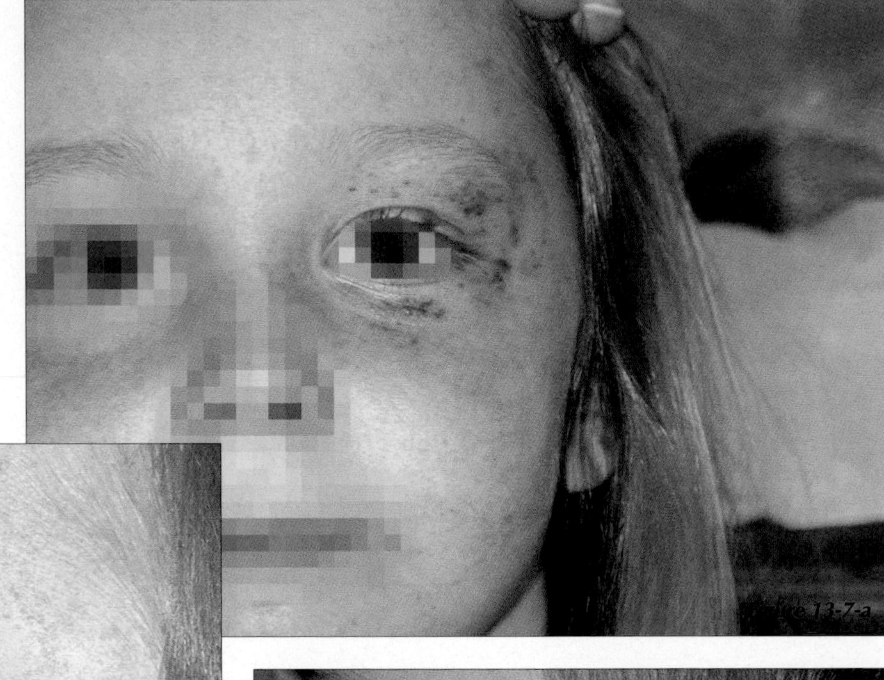

**Figure 13-7-a**

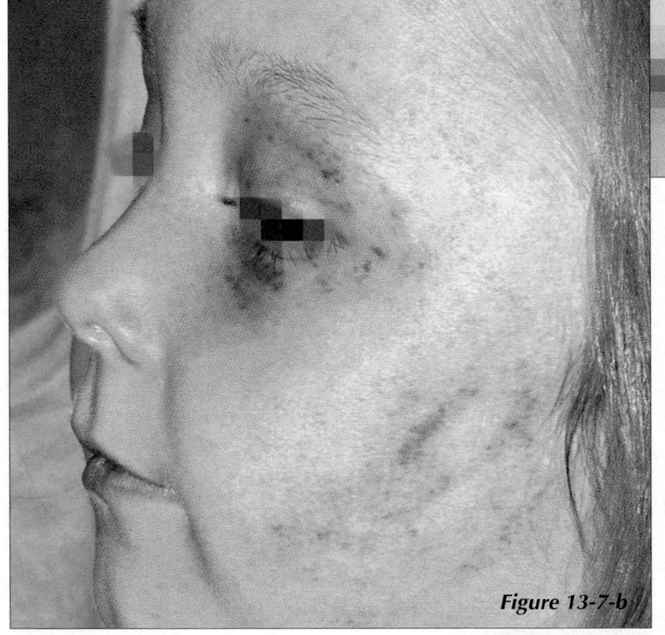

**Figure 13-7-b**

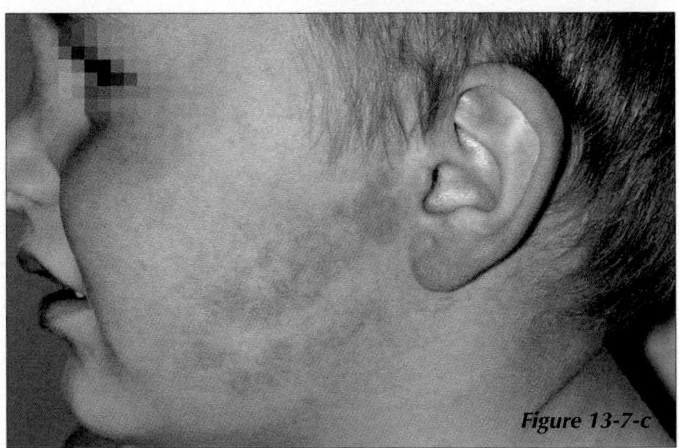

**Figure 13-7-c**

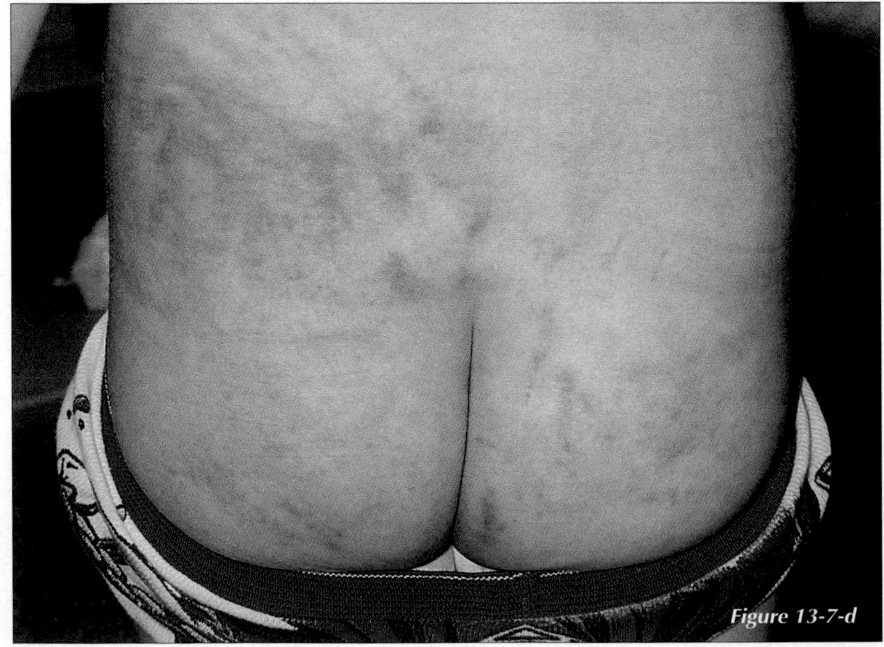

**Figure 13-7-d**

# Grab Marks

**Case Study 13-8**

These photographs of this 3-month-old infant were taken with a Nikon Coolpix 950 2-megapixel digital camera with flash at highest resolution UXGA (1600 x 1200) and at lowest compression JPEG (Fine). The injuries were most consistent with grab marks.

***Figures 13-8-a** and **b.** Bruises on the back of this infant.*

***Figures 13-8-c** and **d.** Photographs of the same infant that are out of focus. Focusing problems are common, particularly if the photographer gets too close, does not change camera settings for close-up work, or does not wait for the autofocus mechanism to lock on.*

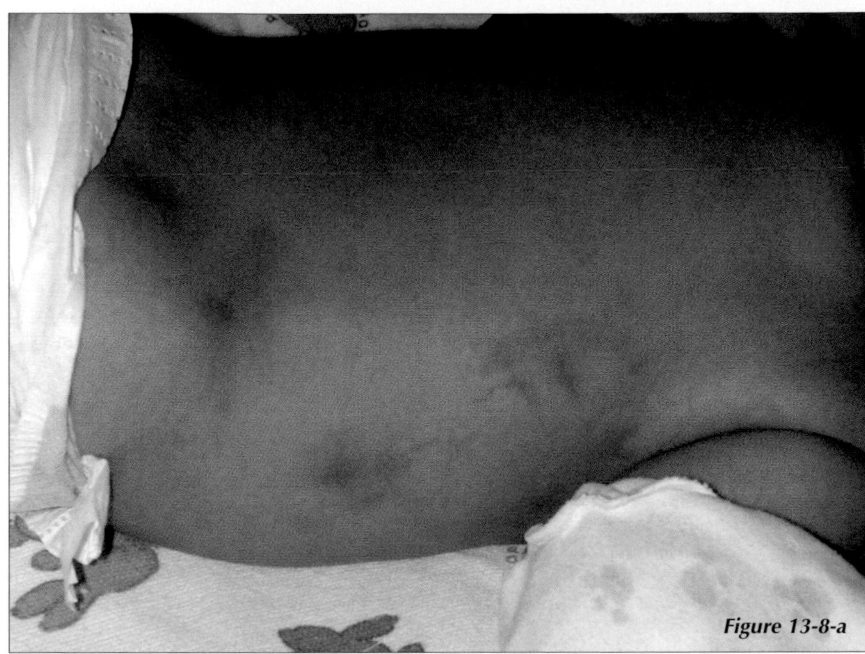

Figure 13-8-a

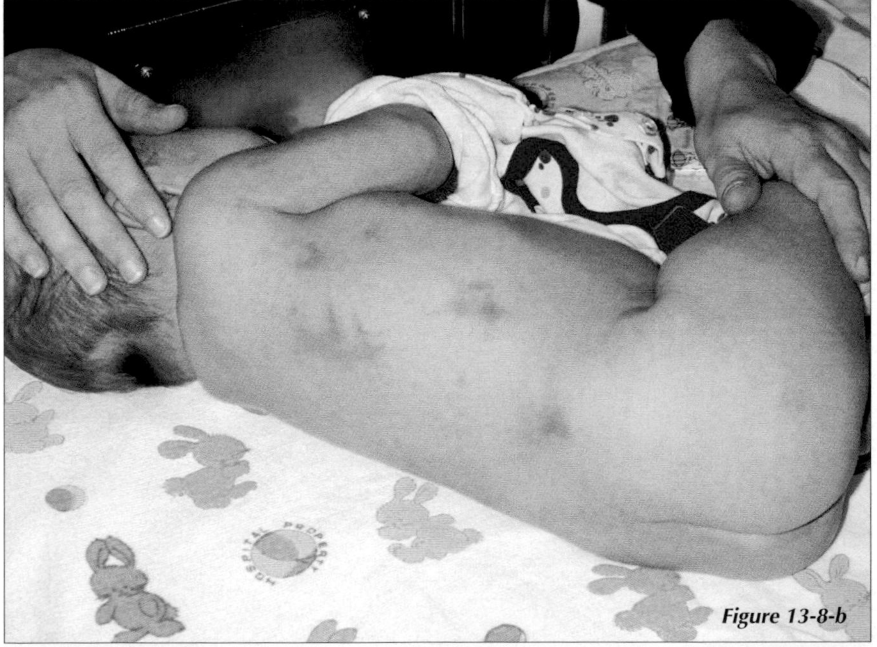

Figure 13-8-b

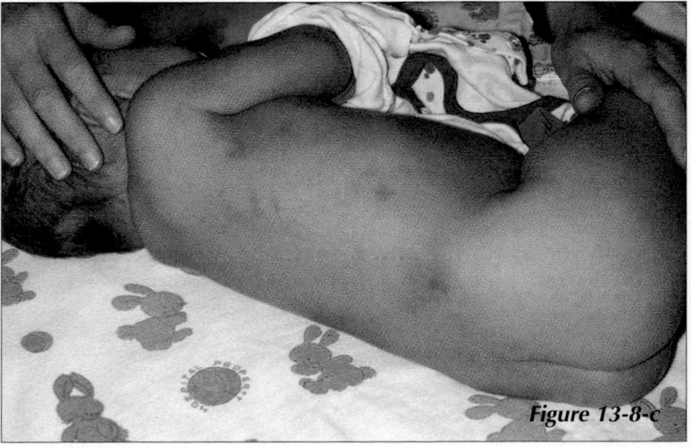

Figure 13-8-c

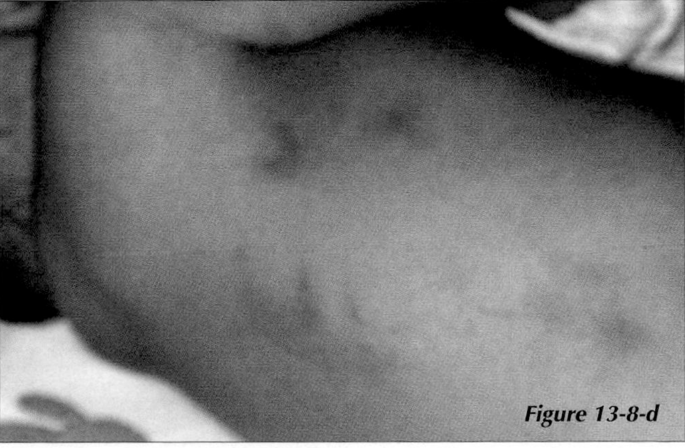

Figure 13-8-d

# Magnification

**Case Study 13-9**

These photographs were taken with the Polaroid Macro 5 SLR-1200 and scanned. This instant camera is specifically designed for dental and medical documentation and provides reproductions at 0.2X, 0.4X, 1X, 2X, and 3X magnification. It has a dual-light rangefinder for focusing. Varying magnifications are very important. A distant image should locate the finding on the child, whereas closer images should clarify the finding. (Photographs and technical discussion courtesy of Samuel H. Moorer, Jr, MD.)

***Figure 13-9-a.*** *Teeth marks inside the lip.*

***Figure 13-9-b.*** *Black-and-white colposcopic image. Note the toluidine blue, which appears as dark stain in the fossa.*

***Figure 13-9-c.*** *Instant photo of the same image shown in **Figure 13-10-b**. Note the toluidine blue in the fossa.*

***Figure 13-9-d.*** *Dry contact burn.*

***Figure 13-9-e.*** *Increased magnification of the dry contact burn in **Figure 13-10-d**.*

***Figure 13-9-f.*** *Further increased magnification of dry contact burn.*

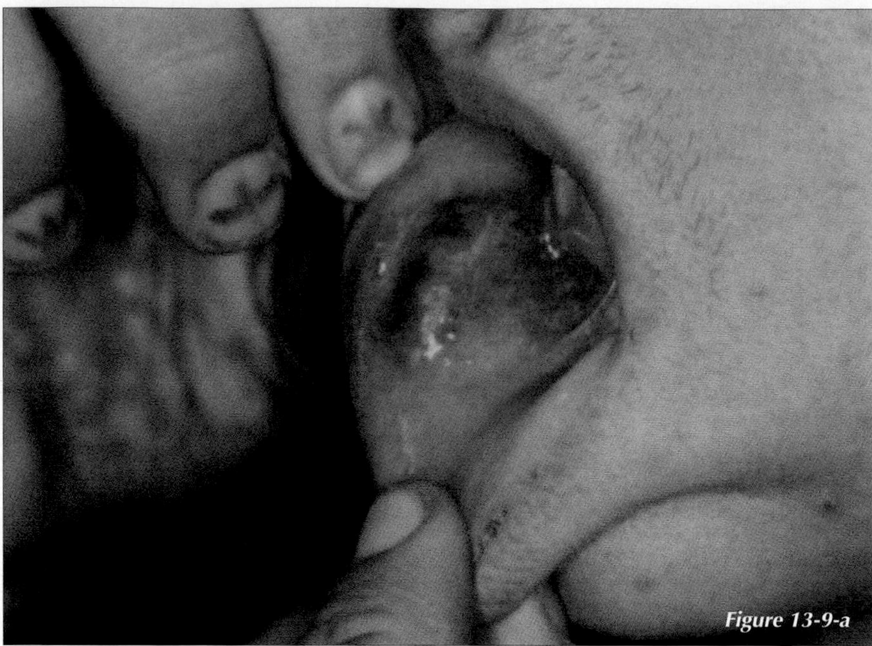

Figure 13-9-a

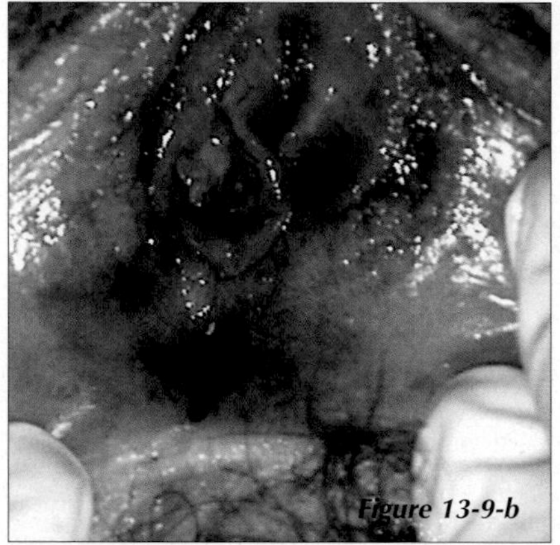

Figure 13-9-b

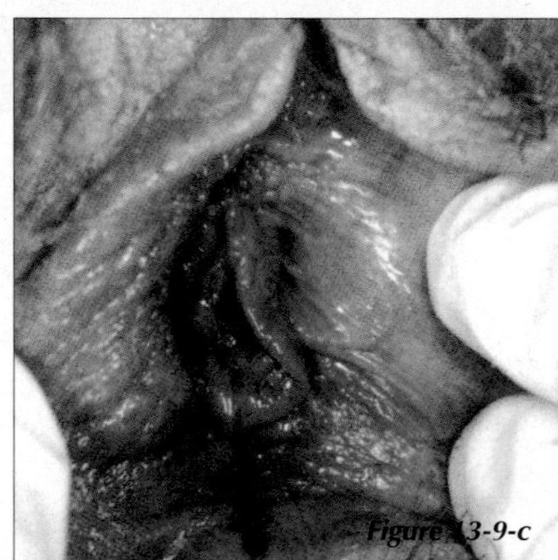

Figure 13-9-c

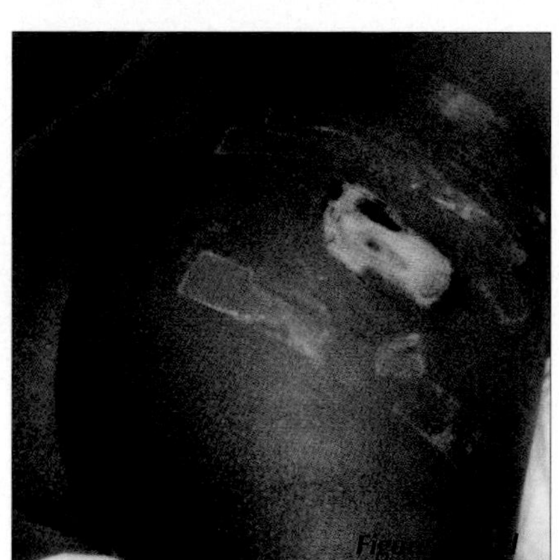

Figure 13-9-d

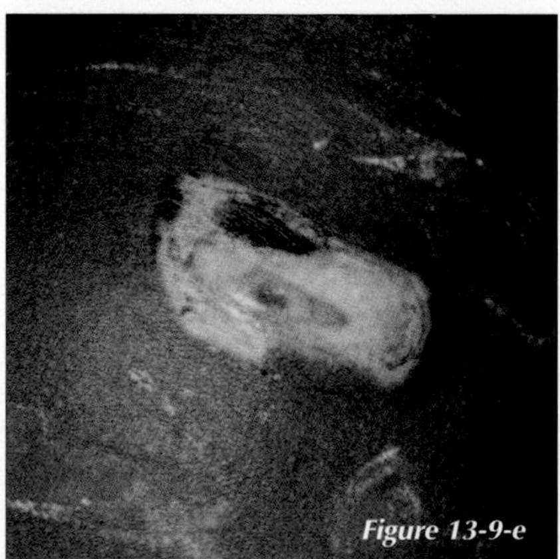

Figure 13-9-e

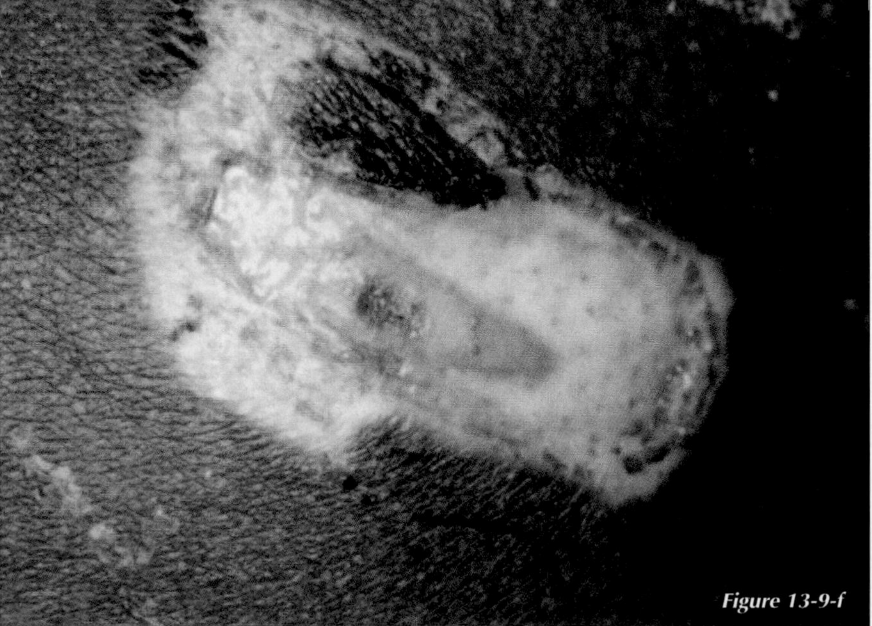

Figure 13-9-f

## Lash Marks

**Case Study 13-10**

Photographs of the linear lash marks were taken with a Poloroid Macro 5 SLR-1200, which includes a contrast-enhancing feature.

***Figure 13-10-a.*** *This unenhanced images suffers from overexposure and washout.*

***Figure 13-10-b.*** *This contrast-enhanced image provides greater detail of the injuries.*

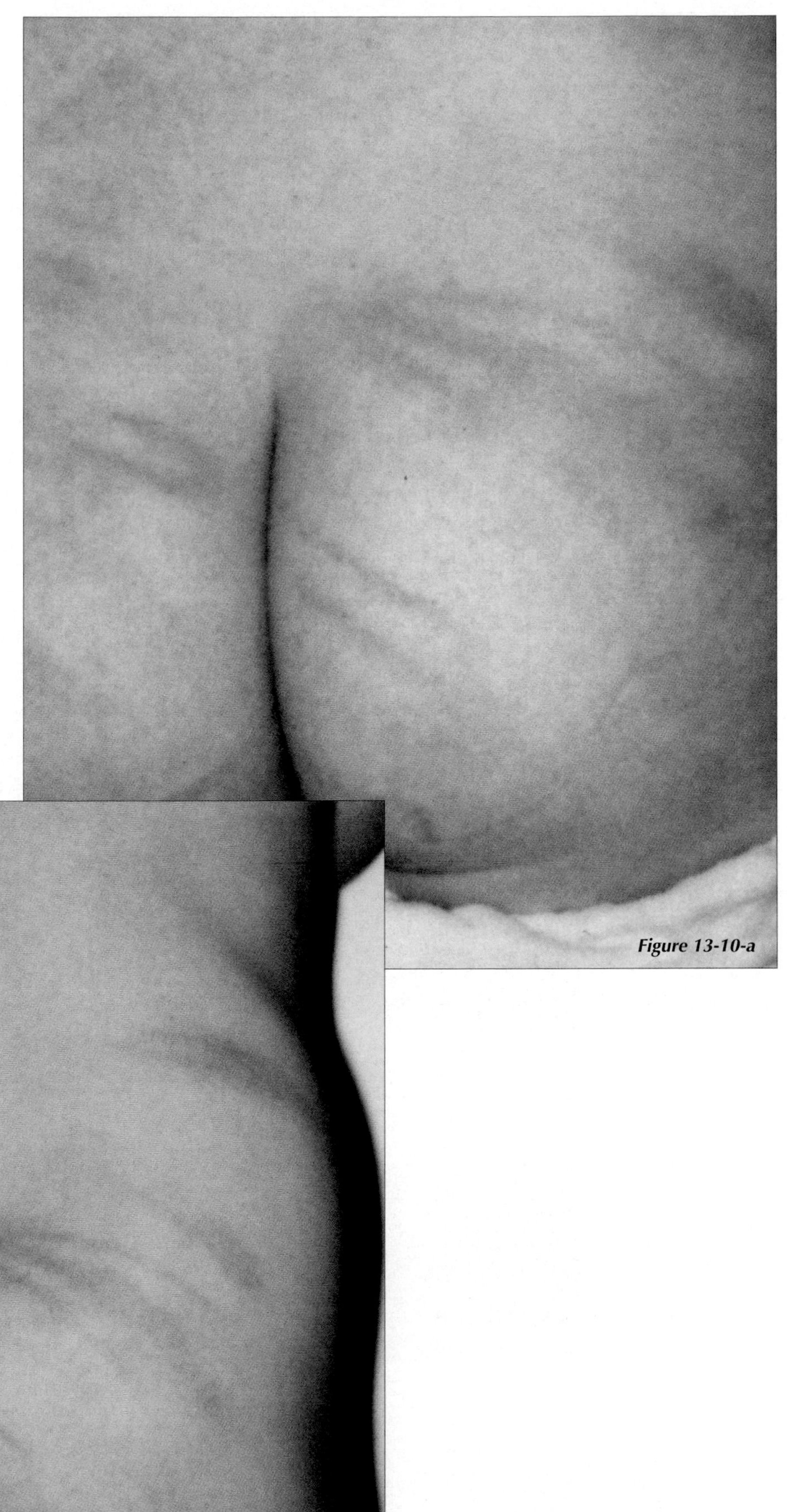

**Figure 13-10-a**

**Figure 13-10-b**

# Hot Water Burn Injury

**Case Study 13-11**

This 11-month-old infant suffered severe hot water burns. The father purportedly caused the burns while bathing the child and pouring hot water over the child's head. The question was whether these burns were most consistent with a pour or an immersion. (Drawings courtesy of James Lauridson, MD.)

***Figure 13-11-a.*** *Hot water burns from liquid poured over the child's head.*

***Figure 13-11-b.*** *Hot water burn injury.*

***Figure 13-11-c.*** *Note the sparing of the axilla.*

***Figure 13-11-d.*** *Digital drawing showing frontal view of burn pattern when liquid is poured over a child's head.*

***Figure 13-11-e.*** *Digital drawing of liquid pour burn on a child's head and back. These drawings illustrate that this child's burns appear to be consistent with hot liquid being poured over the child's head.*

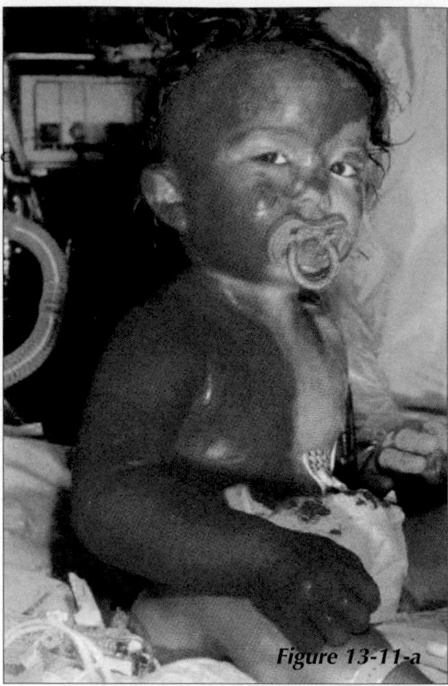

Figure 13-11-a

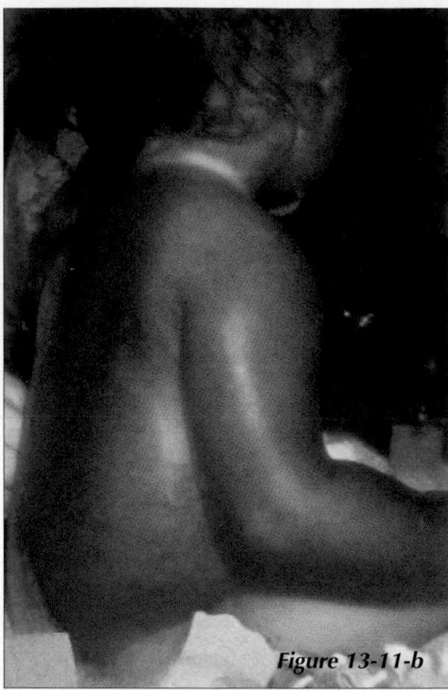

Figure 13-11-b

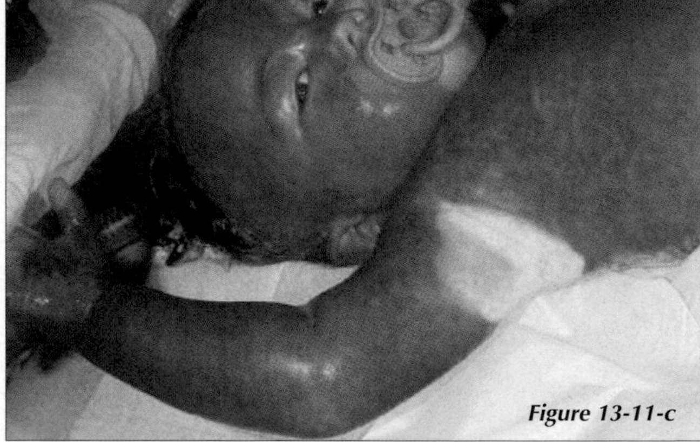

Figure 13-11-c

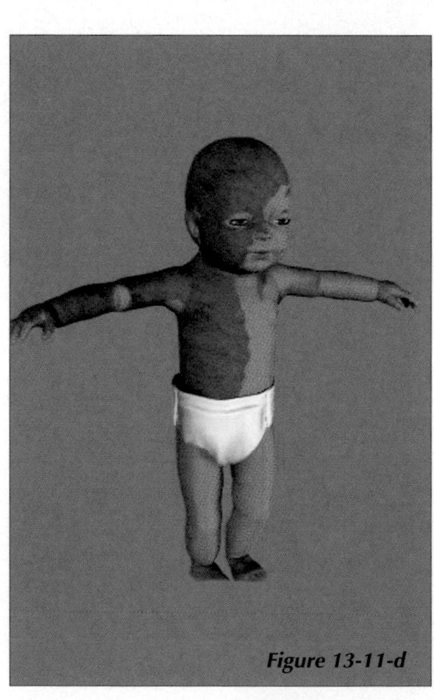

Figure 13-11-d

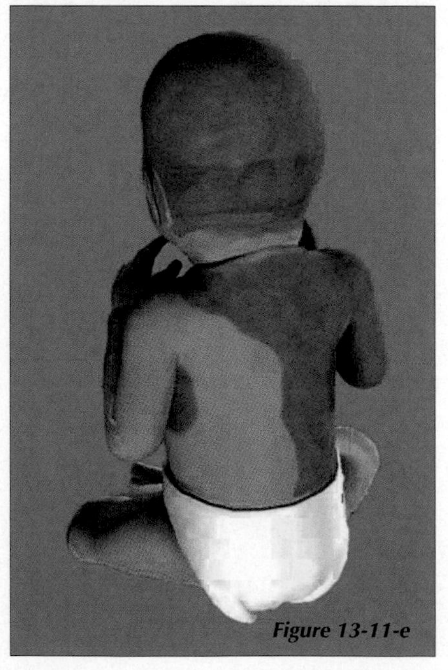

Figure 13-11-e

## Burn Injury

### Case Study 13-12

This 8-year-old girl was examined for a burn on her calf. The girl originally stated that she was burned in the shower, but when confronted with the evidence of the match between the holes in the iron and the burn marks, she stated that the burn was self-inflicted accidentally. While the girl's final story was questionable, it was apparent that the iron was the cause of the burn. Preliminary photographs were taken 1 week after the injury while **Figures 13-12-b, c, d, e,** and **f** were taken 1 month later using a Nikon Coolpix 950 2-megapixel digital camera.

***Figure 13-12-a.*** *This image, taken a week after the injury, is an instant photo that was scanned and digitized as a relatively low-resolution JPEG.*

***Figure 13-12-b.*** *Close-up view of the contact appearance of the burn.*

***Figure 13-12-c.*** *The iron was the instrument of injury.*

***Figure 13-12-d.*** *This image illustrates the 3 circles imbedded in the burn.*

***Figure 13-12-e.*** *A ruler in place allows the magnifications to be matched.*

***Figure 13-12-f.*** *The 3 holes in this iron exactly match the burn circles on the girl's calf.*

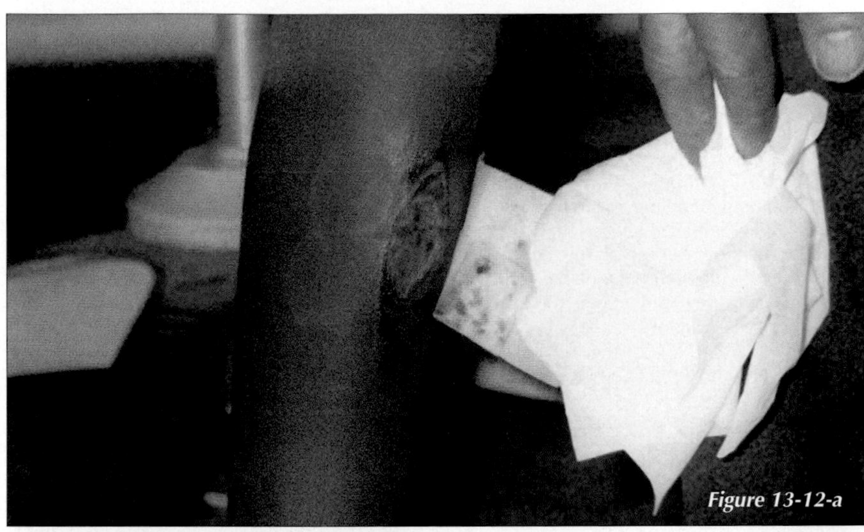
Figure 13-12-a

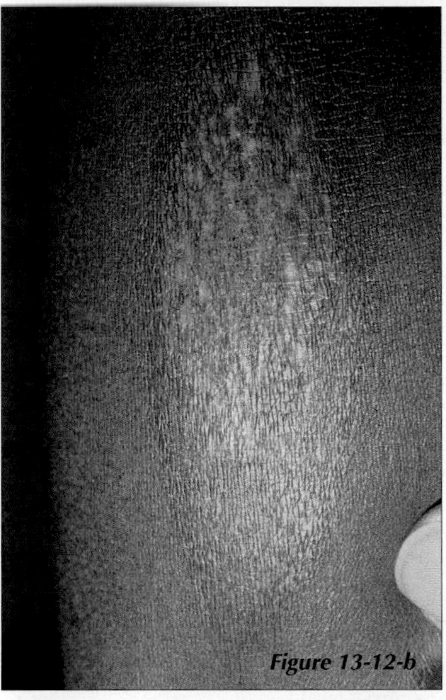
Figure 13-12-b

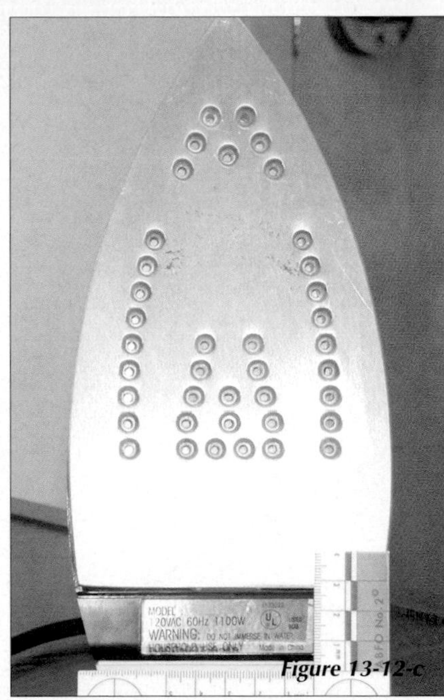
Figure 13-12-c

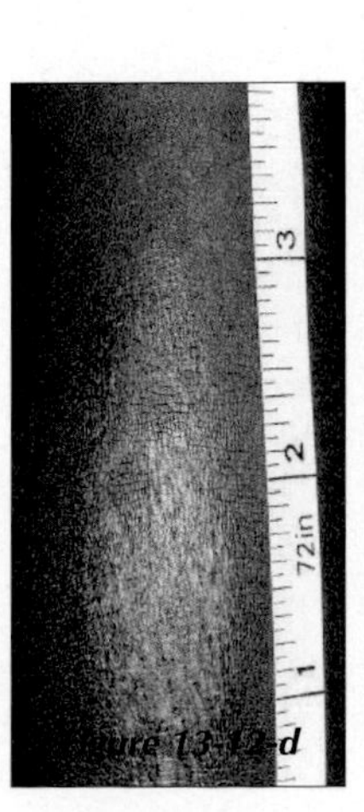
Figure 13-12-d

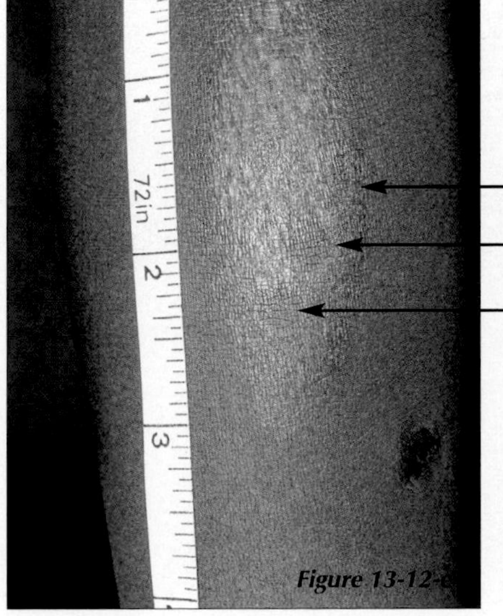
Figure 13-12-e

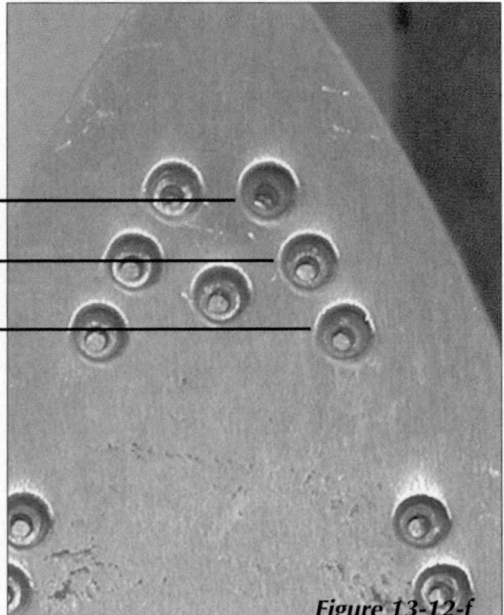
Figure 13-12-f

# Burn Injury and Implement

**Case Study 13-13**

This 3-month-old child was intentionally burned in the mandibular area with a utility lighter. The original lighter was never recovered, but at least one model clearly matched the injury as seen on the lighter and a burn from the lighter on a piece of cloth. These images were taken with Nikon Coolpix 950 2-megapixel digital camera with flash at highest resolution UXGA (1600 x 1200) and at lowest compression JPEG (Fine).

***Figure 13-13-a.*** *Burn seen on the mandibular area.*

***Figure 13-13-b.*** *This style of lighter may have been used to injure the child. The ceramic tip of this type of lighter requires prolonged exposure to the flame before becoming hot enough to burn skin.*

***Figure 13-13-c.*** *The tip of this lighter matches the burn injury on the child.*

***Figure 13-13-d.*** *Example of burn mark made on a piece of cloth.*

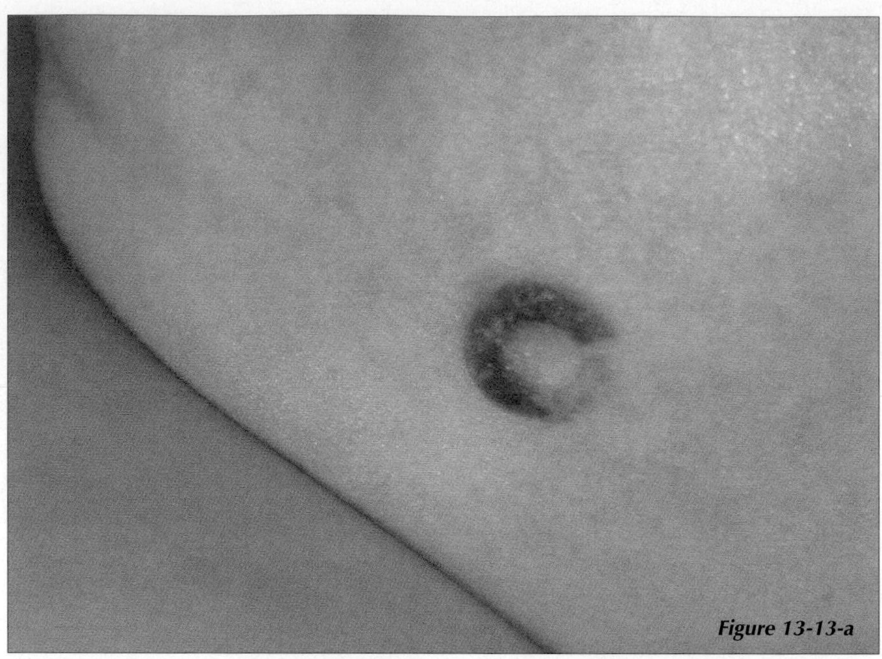

**Figure 13-13-a**

**Figure 13-13-c**

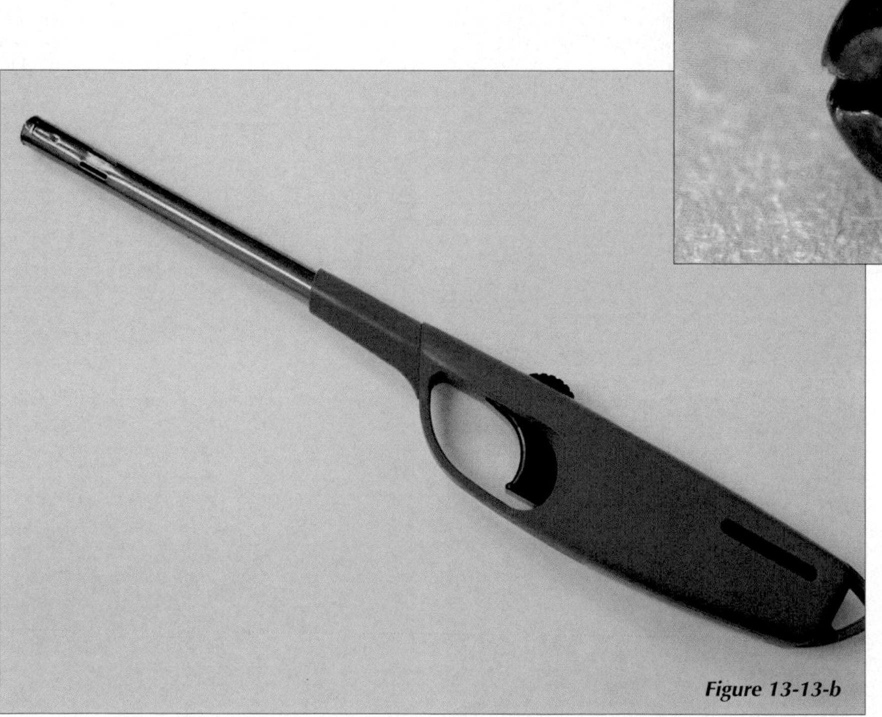

**Figure 13-13-b**

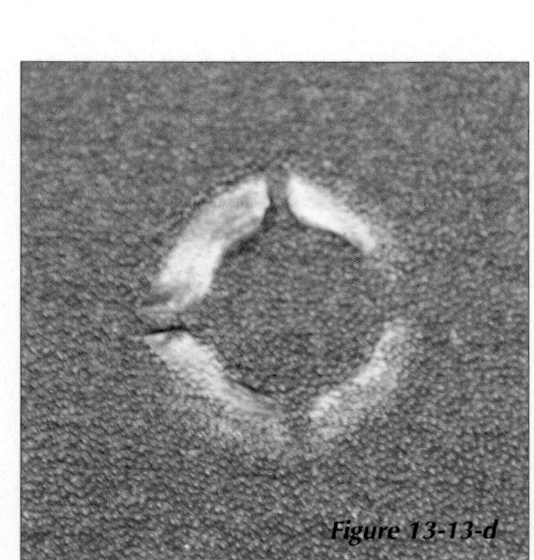

**Figure 13-13-d**

## Abdominal Bruise

**Case Study 13-14**

This infant sustained a small abdominal bruise that was noticed during treatment for a respiratory syncytial virus infection. The bruise was possibly caused by the knot in the monitor cord.

***Figure 13-14-a.*** *Bruise on infant's abdomen.*

***Figure 13-14-b.*** *The knot in the monitor cord that may have caused the bruise.*

## Wrist Splint

**Case Study 13-15**

This male infant suffered from bruises on his right leg. He was in the care of his grandmother, who wore a metal wrist splint for carpal tunnel syndrome. When photographed together, it was apparent that the splint was the possible cause of the bruising.

***Figure 13-15-a.*** *This image shows bruising on an infant's leg.*

***Figure 13-15-b.*** *The wrist splint worn by the grandmother may have caused the bruising on the infant's leg.*

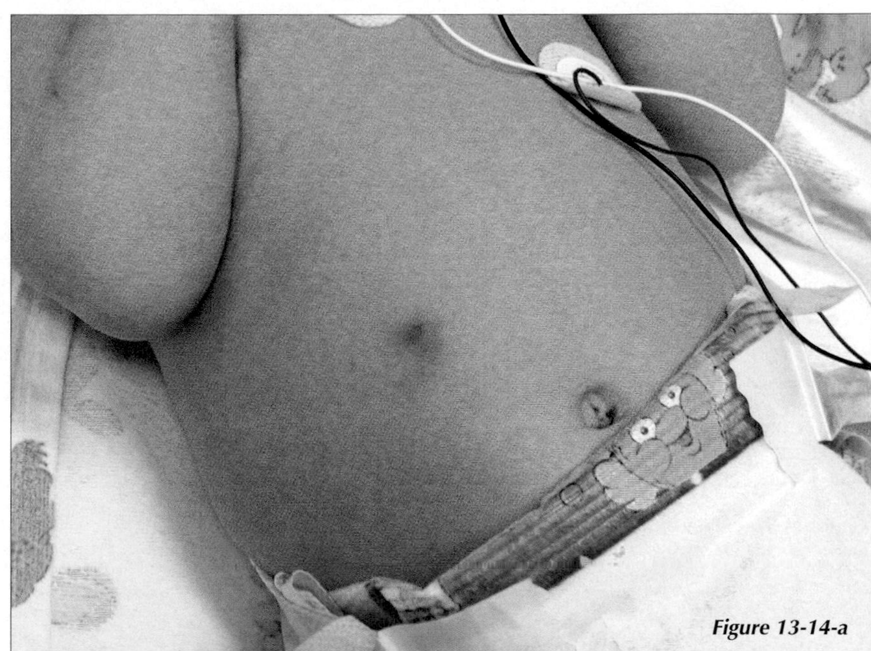

**Figure 13-14-a**

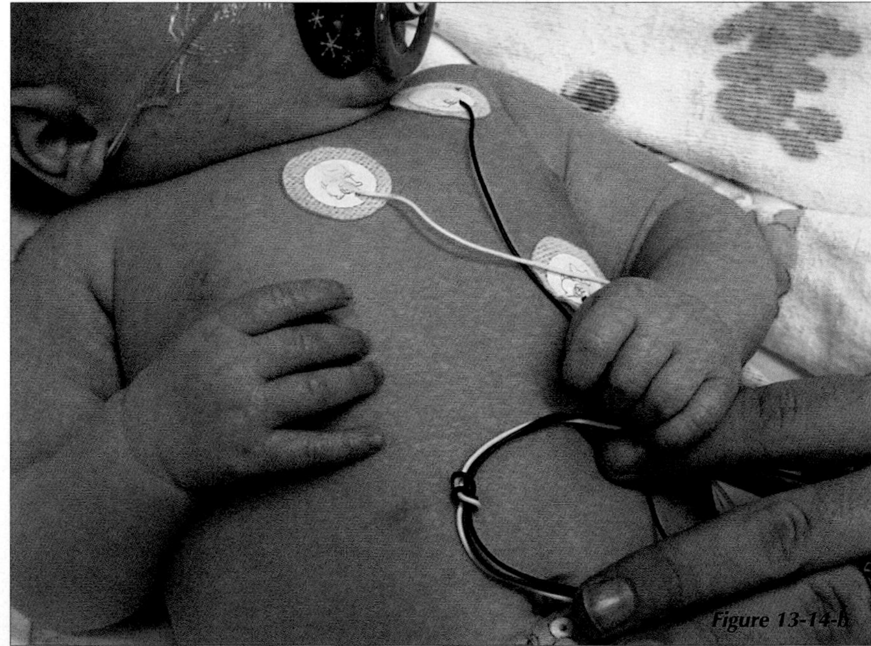

**Figure 13-14-b**

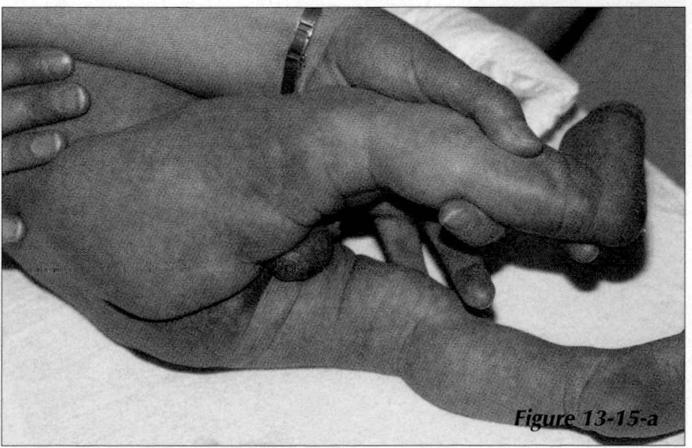

**Figure 13-15-a**

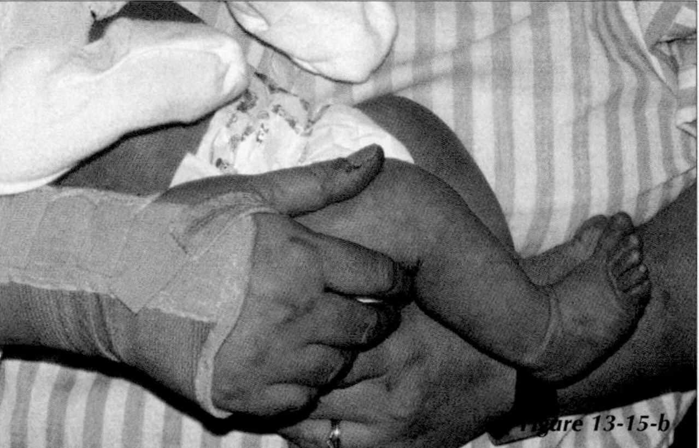

**Figure 13-15-b**

# Fracture

**Case Study 13-16**

This infant sustained an unusual intertrochanteric fracture of the right femur. The scene photograph was taken by a child protective services worker using a doll. The daycare provider positioned the doll in the way she found the infant and suggested that the injury was self-inflicted. It was more likely that the child was found in this position and then violently pulled up, resulting in the fracture.

***Figure 13-16-a.*** *The scene of the injury with a doll positioned as the infant was found.*

***Figure 13-16-b.*** *Digital photograph of a radiograph of an intertrochanteric fracture of right femur.*

***Figure 13-16-c.*** *Digital photograph of a radiograph of an intertrochanteric fracture.*

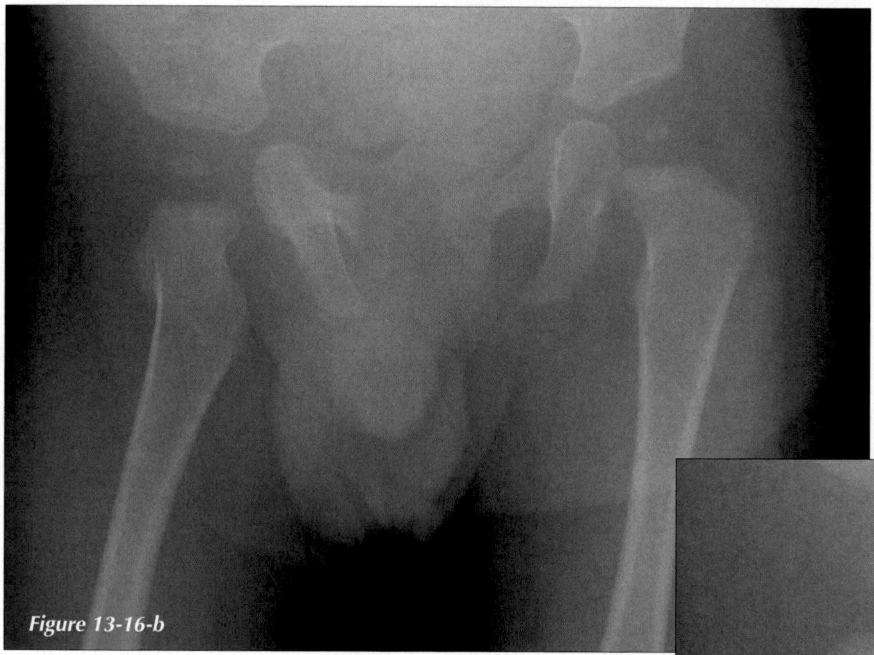

*Figure 13-16-b*

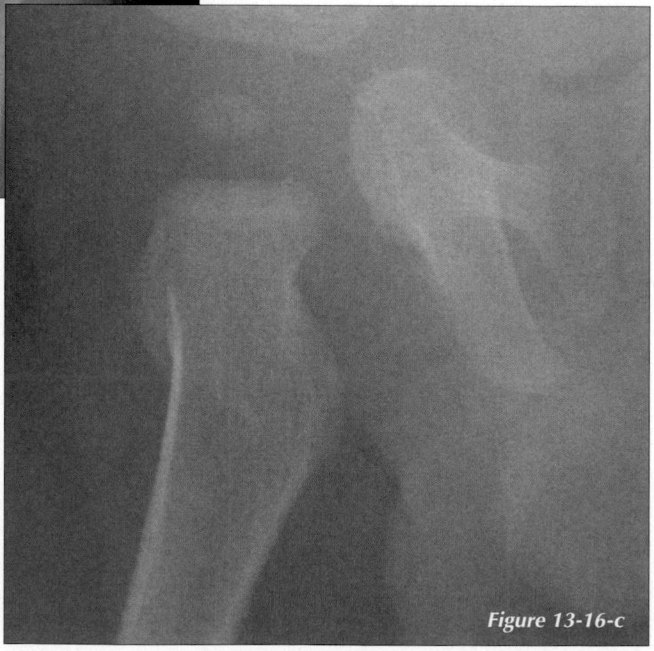

*Figure 13-16-c*

# Fracture

**Case Study 13-17**

This child was examined with a fracture of the right radius and ulna in addition to 3 rib fractures. Digital photographs of the radiographs were taken with a Nikon Coolpix 950 2-megapixel digital camera at highest resolution UXGA (1600 x 1200) and at lowest compression JPEG (Fine) with the flash off. The radiographs were illuminated by a light box.

***Figure 13-17-a.*** *Radiograph showing fracture of the right radius and ulna.*

***Figure 13-17-b.*** *A slight callous formation of the left radius and ulna in addition to a more mature callus formation and a possibly fresh fracture over the callus.*

***Figures 13-17-c*** *and* ***d.*** *Three right rib fractures with some callus formation.*

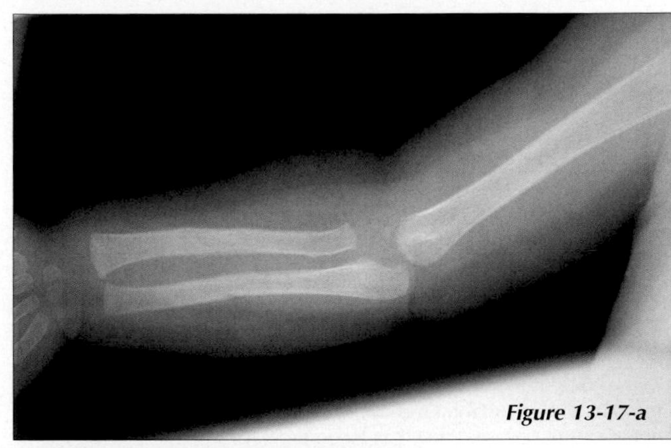

Figure 13-17-a

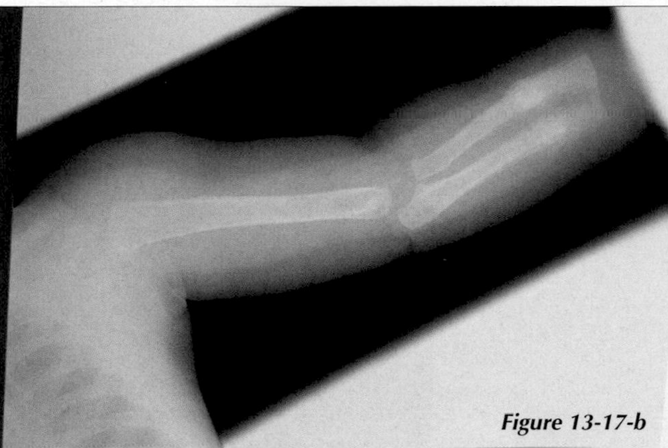

Figure 13-17-b

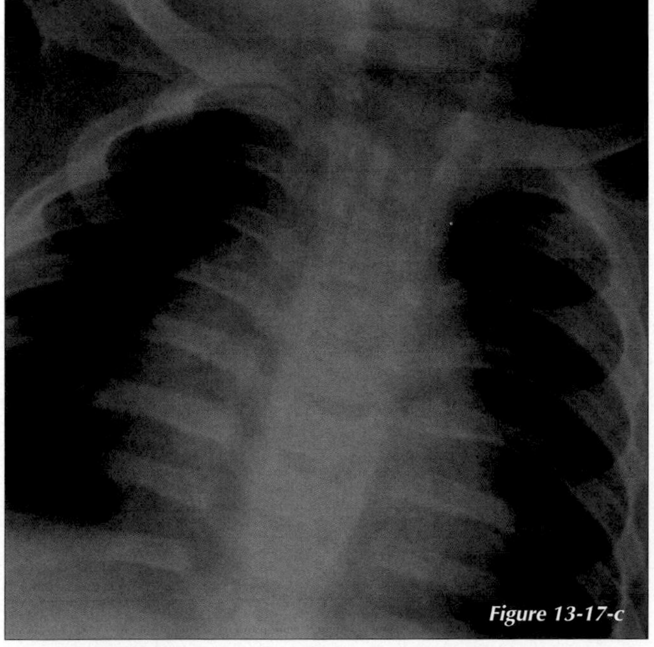

Figure 13-17-c

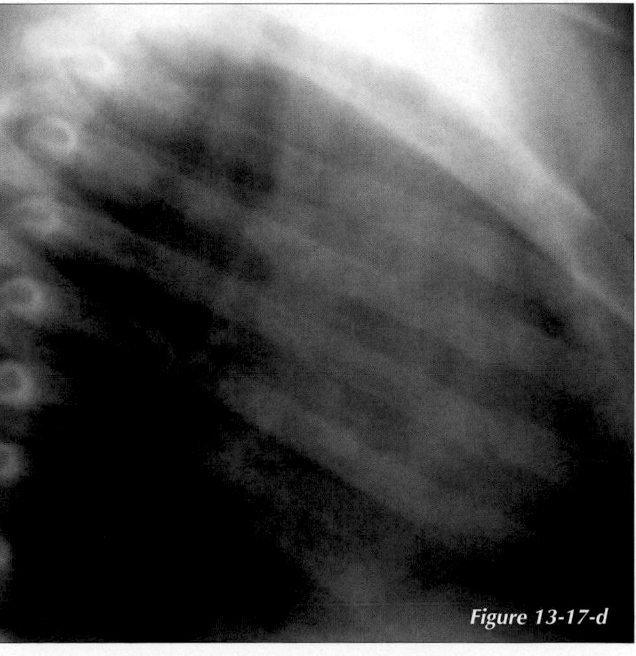

Figure 13-17-d

# Facial Injuries

**Case Study 13-18**

This 6-year-old boy had extensive bruises and abrasions of the face from a purported fall from a top bunk bed onto a chair then onto the floor. It was more likely that the child's face was struck and/or rubbed into the bottom mattress. Photographs were taken at the scene by law enforcement personnel and digitized.

When digitizing photographs or slides, not only should scanning resolution be considered, but format for saving and compression are also important. One can scan an image at 600 DPI, yet save it as a compressed JPEG, resulting in a low-resolution image of limited utility.

**Figure 13-18-a.** *Bruising on the face of child reported to have fallen from the top of a bunk bed.*

**Figures 13-18-b** and **c.** *Bruising and abrasions on the child's face.*

**Figure 13-18-d.** *Blood on one of the boy's pillows.*

**Figure 13-18-e.** *A blood stain can be seen on the bed.*

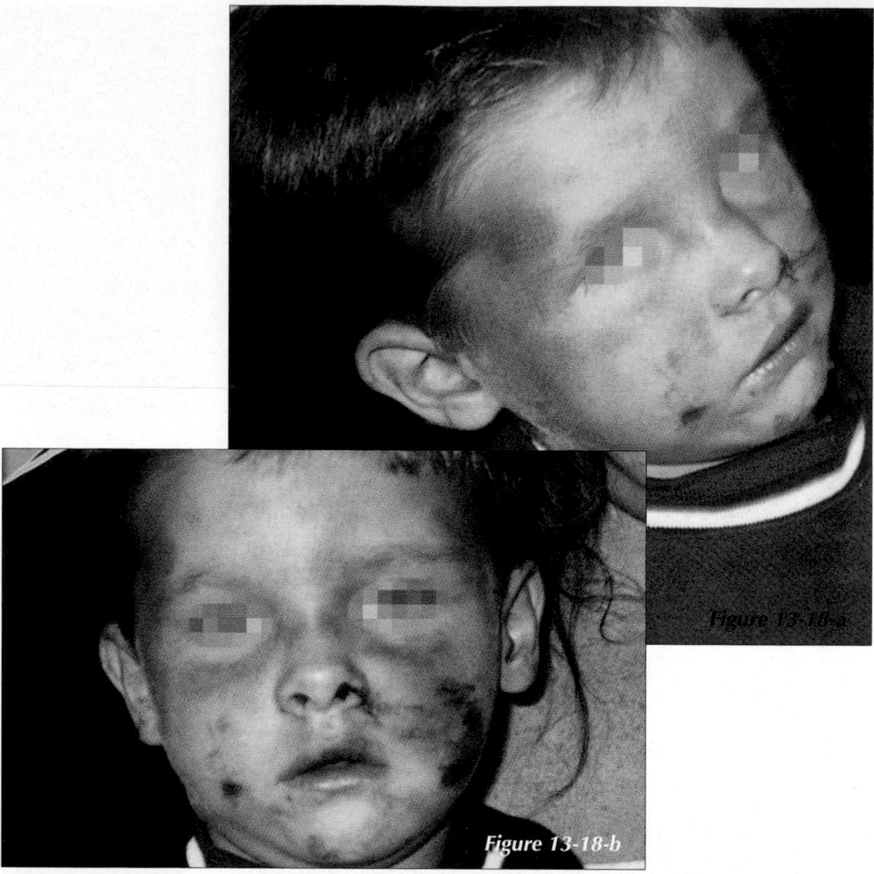

Figure 13-18-a

Figure 13-18-b

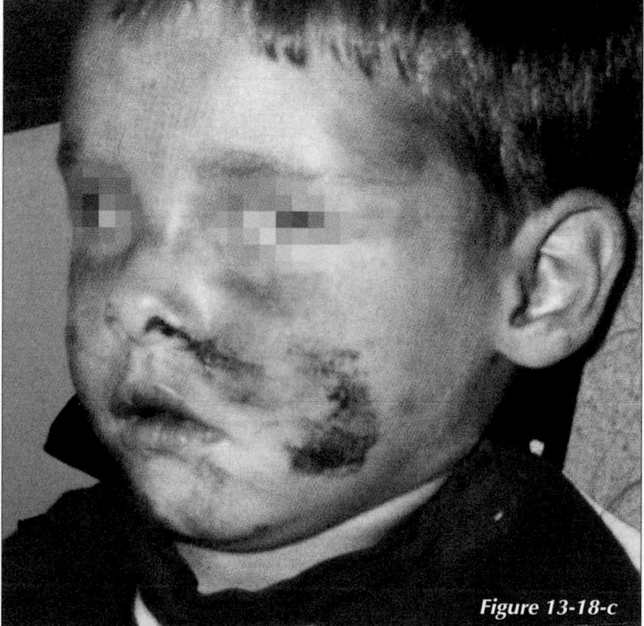

Figure 13-18-c

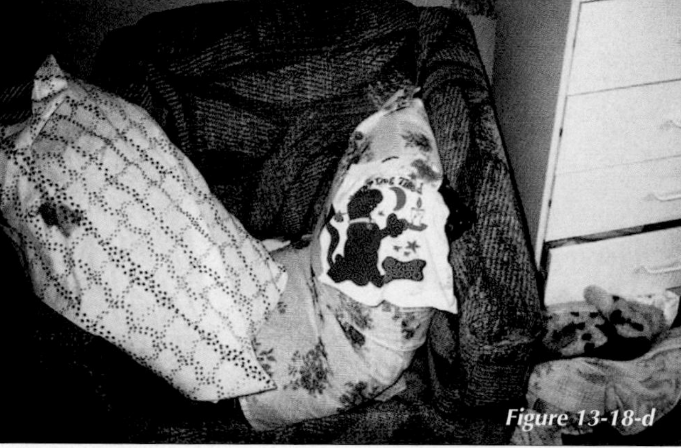

Figure 13-18-d

-18-e

## Injury From a Fall

**Case Study 13-19**

This 15-month-old boy was examined with a history of a fall from a bunk bed at daycare. A computed tomography (CT) scan showed a left parietal subdural hematoma, and eye examination showed extensive bilateral retinal hemorrhages. Photographs were taken with a Nikon Coolpix 950 2-megapixel digital camera with flash at highest resolution UXGA (1600 x 1200) and at lowest compression JPEG (Fine).

***Figure 13-19-a.*** *Curving abrasion of the scrotum is visible. It is consistent with a fingernail scratch.*

***Figure 13-19-b.*** *Nonspecific anal friability can be seen at the 11-o'clock position.*

***Figure 13-19-c.*** *This photograph of a CT scan, taken with the Nikon without the flash, illustrates a left parietal subdural hemorrhage with an apparent midline shift.*

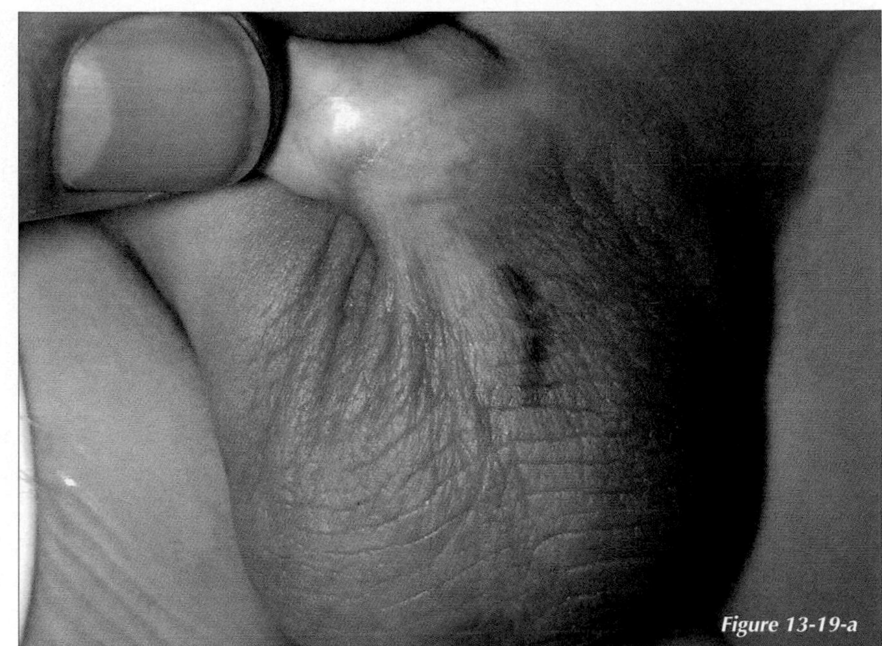

Figure 13-19-a

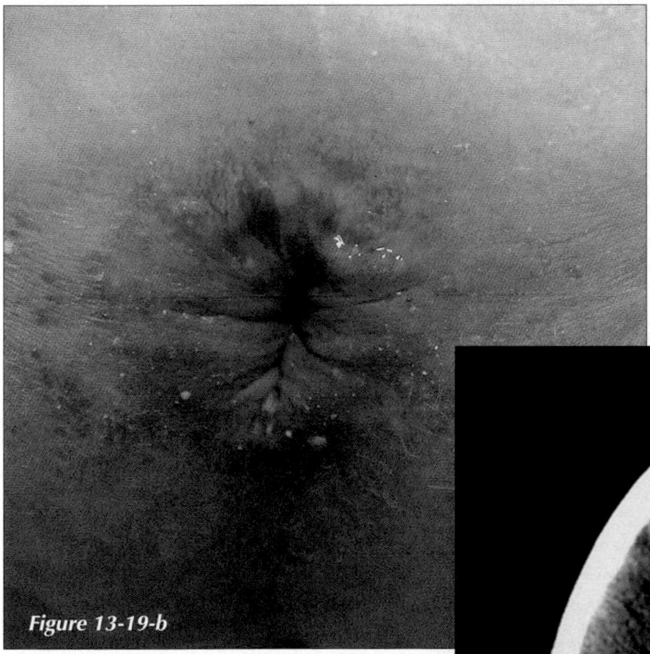

Figure 13-19-b

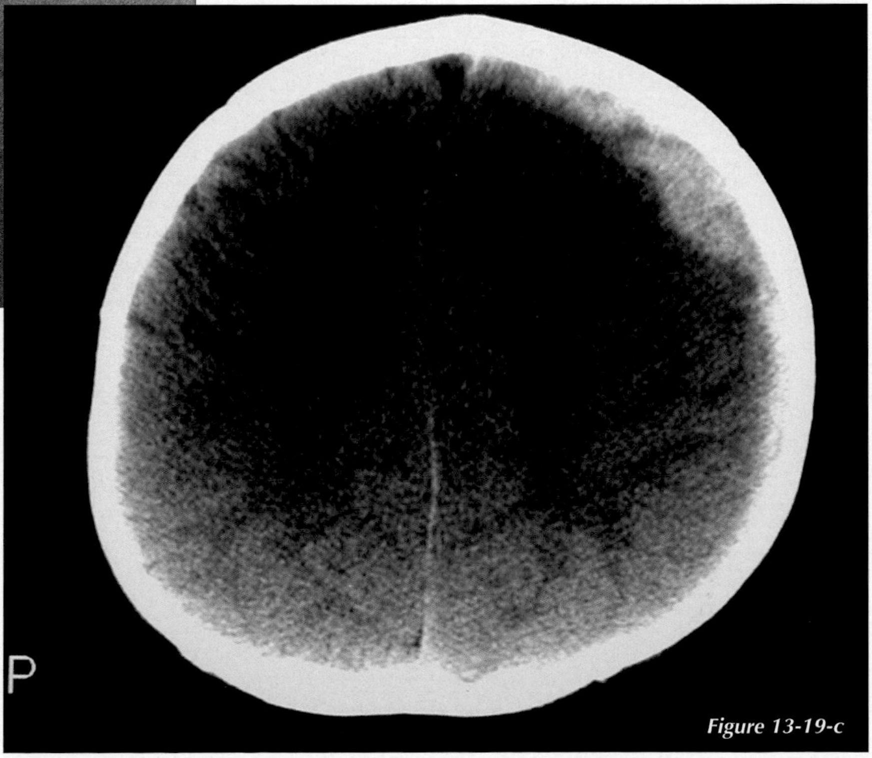

P

Figure 13-19-c

# Genital Injury

### Case Study 13-20

This 11-month-old girl was examined for vaginal bleeding after being babysat by an adult male who later confessed to forceful digital vaginal penetration. Operating room photographs taken with Nikon Coolpix 950 2-megapixel digital camera with flash at highest resolution UXGA (1600 x 1200) and at lowest compression JPEG (Fine) show a large laceration transecting the hymen at the 6-o'clock position down to the rectal sphincter but without injury to the posterior fourchette. There was also a longitudinal laceration of the internal vaginal wall at the 9-o'clock position not visualized here. The speculum that was used to look for the bleeding source was inserted after the initial pictures were taken.

**Figure 13-20-a.** *Vaginal bleeding resulting from forceful digital penetration.*

**Figure 13-20-b.** *Vaginal bleeding.*

**Figure 13-20-c.** *Laceration of the hymen.*

**Figure 13-20-d.** *The cervix is visualized by speculum.*

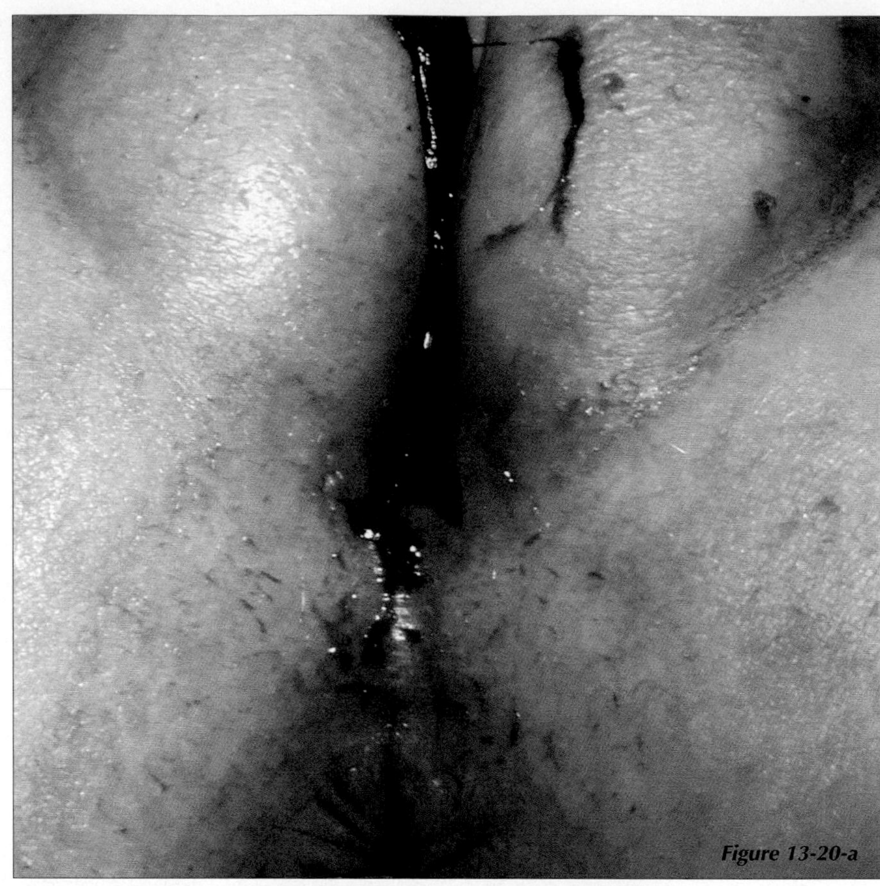

Figure 13-20-a

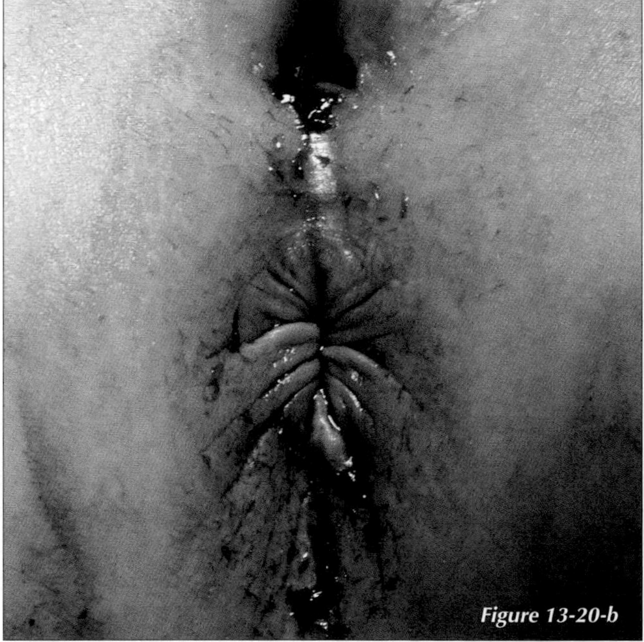

Figure 13-20-b

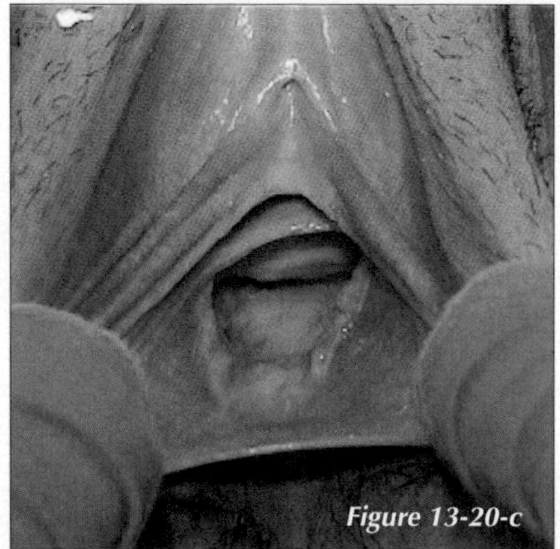

Figure 13-20-c

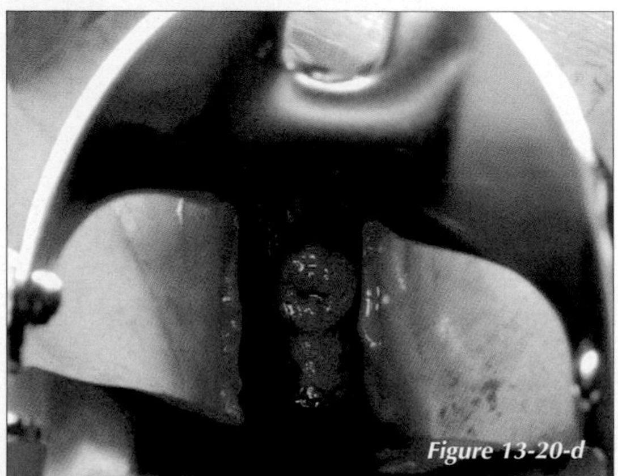

Figure 13-20-d

# Still Images from Digital Video

**Case Study 13-21**

These images were captured from digital video photographed directly with a Sony DV Handicam model DCR-TRV9 NTSC with attached Sony model HVL-S3D 3W video light. The stills were captured with common digital video software after a file transfer to a computer via FireWire interface.

***Figures 13-21-a** and **b.** Normal findings on examination of an 8 year old.*

***Figures 13-21-c** and **d.** Examination of a sexually active 15 year old. Note defects at the 5- and 7-o'clock position with a remnant of hymen in between.*

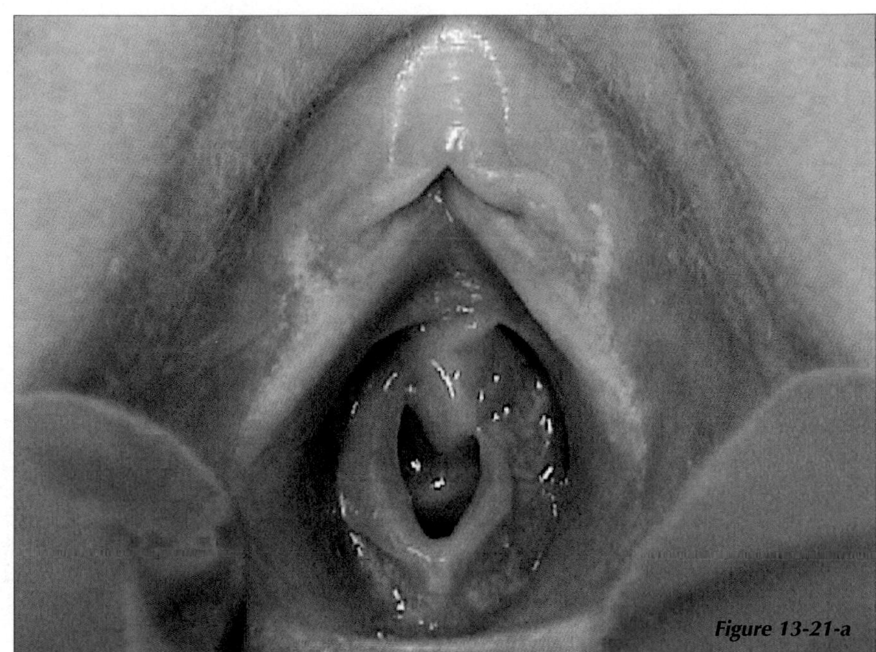

Figure 13-21-a

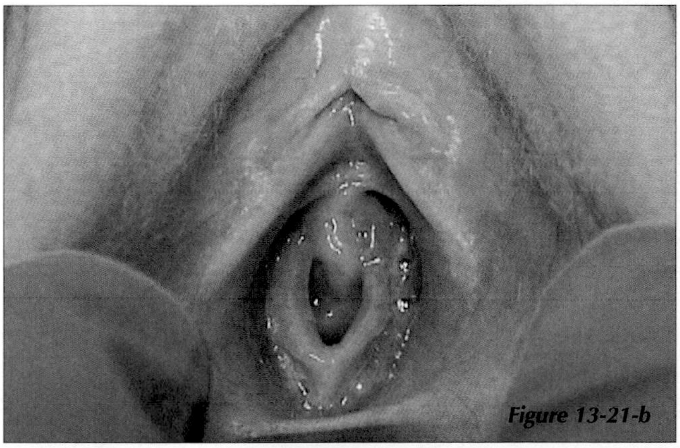

Figure 13-21-b

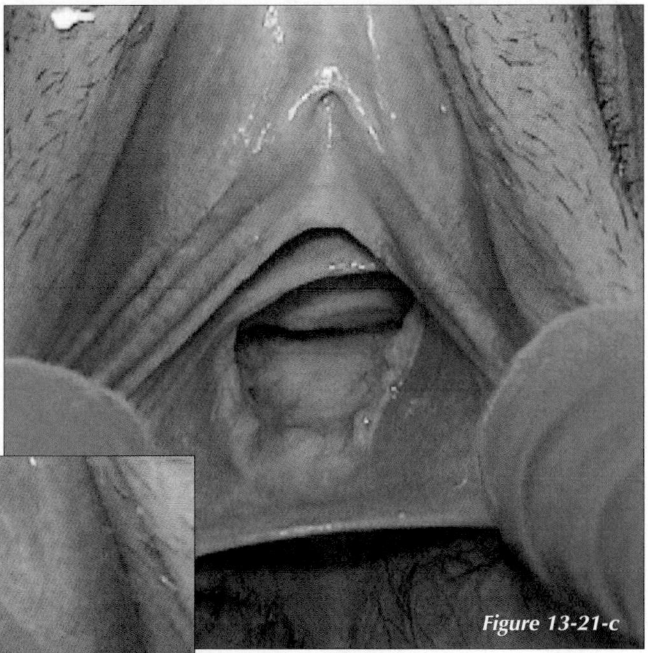

Figure 13-21-c

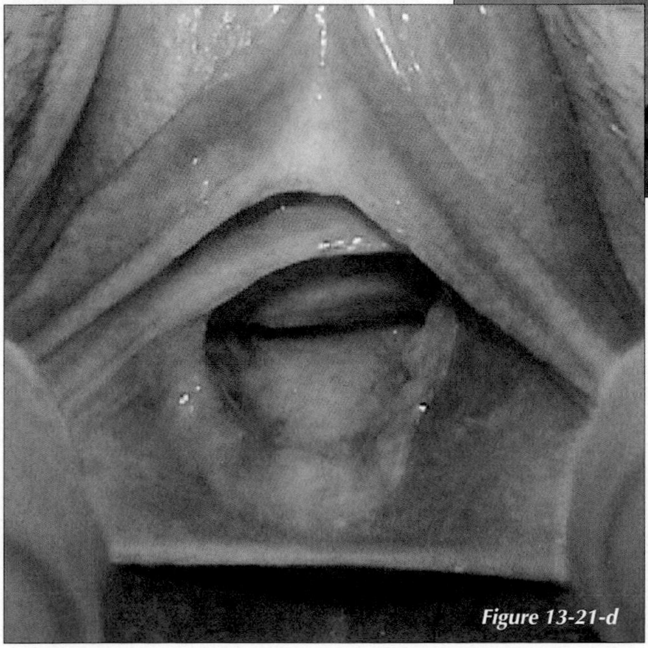

Figure 13-21-d

## Genital Injury

**Case Study 13-22**

This still image was captured from a digital video of an acute injury to the vagina of a 14-year-old girl.

***Figure 13-22.*** *There is submucosal hemorrhage, with a hymenal laceration at the 9-o'clock position and a large avulsion from the 3- to 5-o'clock position. Arrows show the separated borders of the hymen, which are better visualized on video.*

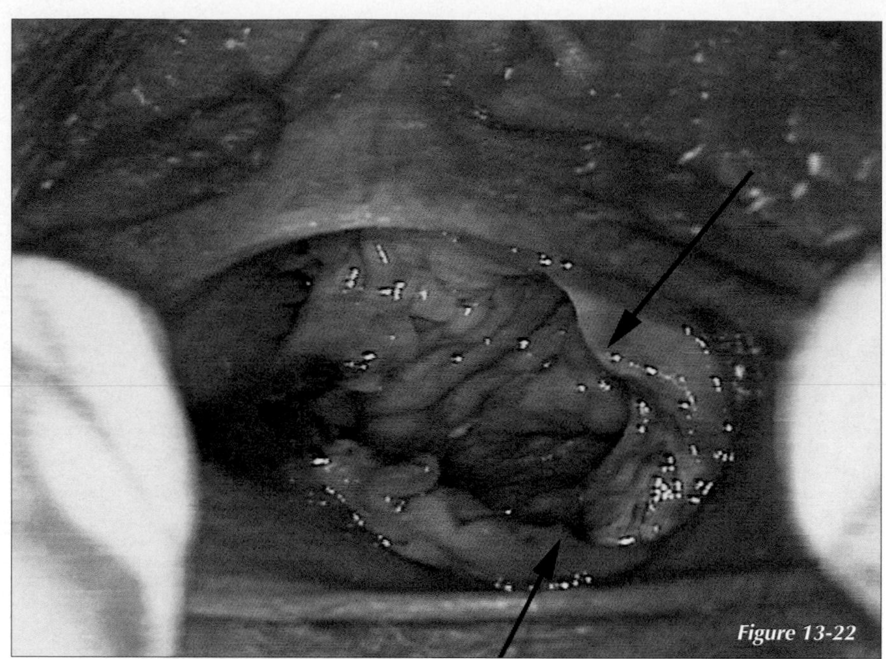

Figure 13-22

## LR Setup

**Case Study 13-23**

This equipment was used to document Case Study 13-21.

***Figures 11-23-a, b,*** *and* ***c.*** *For this setup, the tripod should have a leveling bubble and the legs should lock in partially extended position. Advantages include autofocus, variable zoom, excellent digital video capability, fair digital still capability, and it is significantly less expensive than most other systems. It can also capture video to included DV tape or to a separate VHS, S-VHS, or DV recorder. A separate monitor is essential because the included LCD displays images at low resolution. An attached hotshoe-mounted light is also essential. A ringlight is not needed because the camera's greater distance from the subject allows the hotshoe-mounted light to sufficiently illuminate the subject. The major disadvantage may be appearance, which is that of a home video camera.*

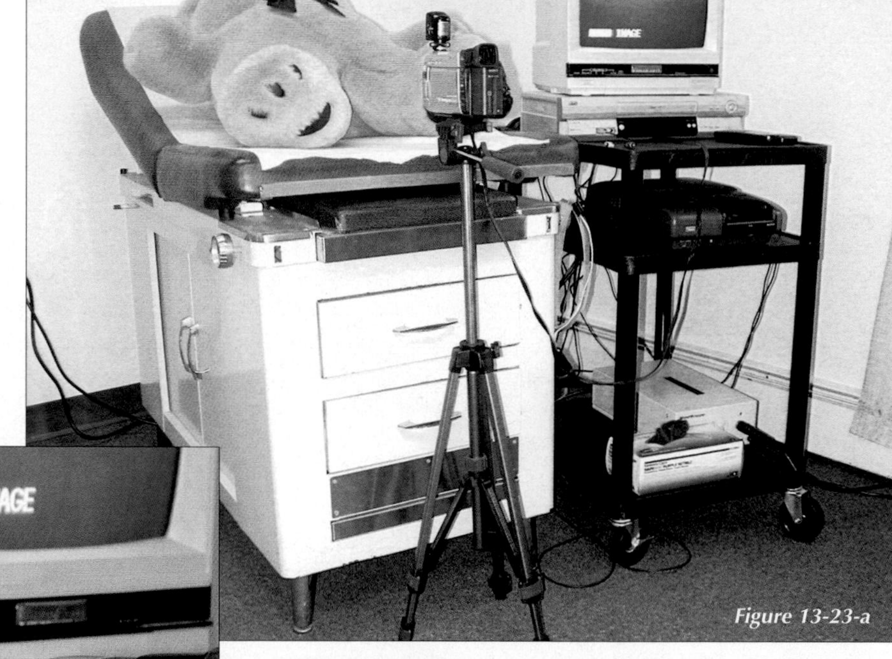

Figure 13-23-a

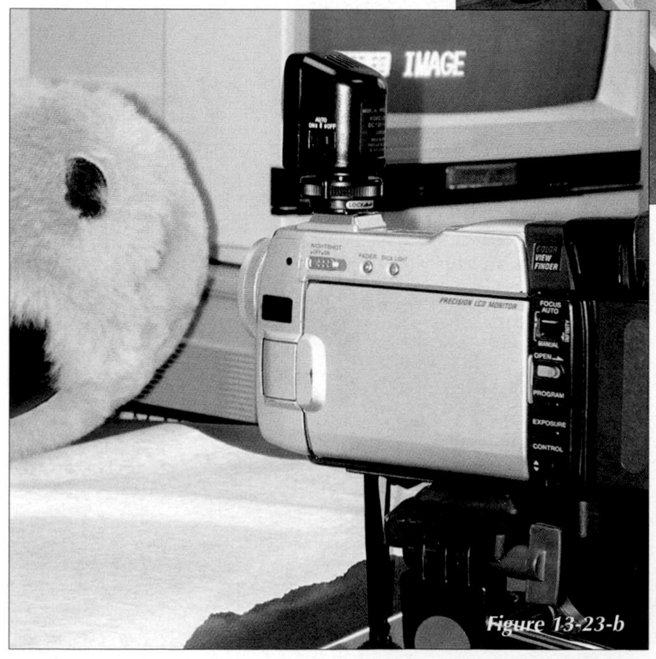


Figure 13-23-b

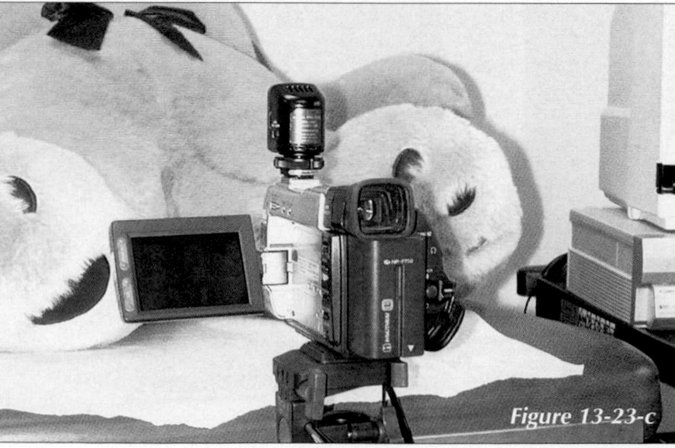

Figure 13-23-c

## Postmortem Rectal Image

**Case Study 13-24**

This photograph was taken with a 35-mm camera with a 105-mm macro lens and ring flash. The slide was scanned at very high resolution and saved as a Kodak PCD file.

***Figure 13-24.*** *Dilated rectal sphincter with protruding rectal mucosa of an accidentally drowned child.*

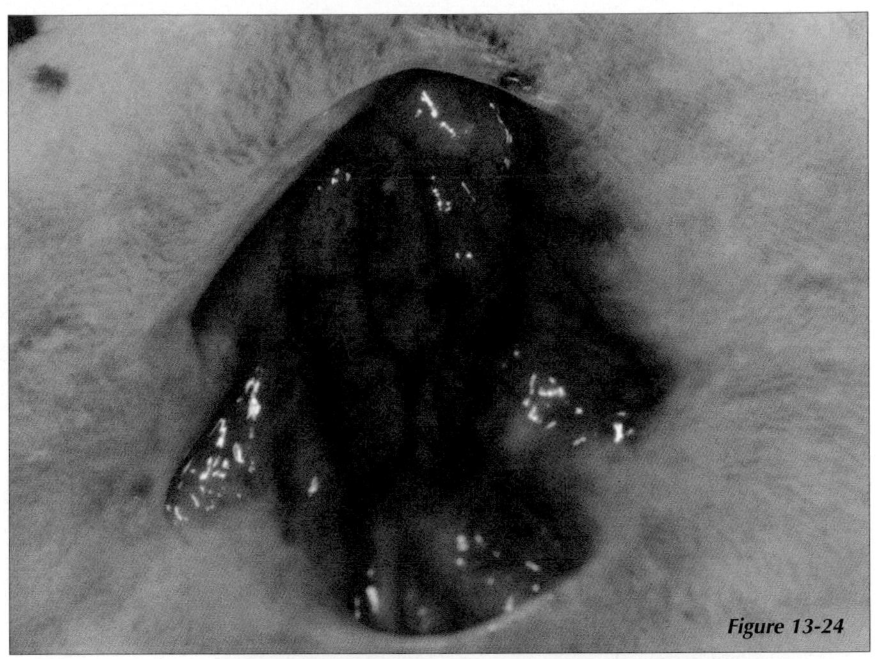

Figure 13-24

## Colposcopic Photographs

**Case Study 13-25**

These scanned 35-mm slides were taken through a colposcope. (Photographs courtesy of Nancy Kellogg, MD.)

***Figure 13-25-a.*** *Colposcopic image of a 15-year-old girl in the supine position with traction. Note the hymenal cleft at the 9-o'clock position.*

***Figure 13-25-b.*** *A balloon-covered swab is used to better visualize the hymenal cleft.*

***Figure 13-25-c.*** *Same 15-year-old in prone knee-chest position.*

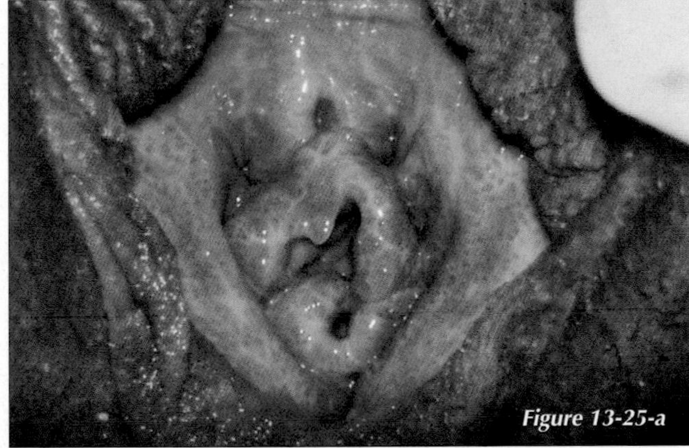

Figure 13-25-a

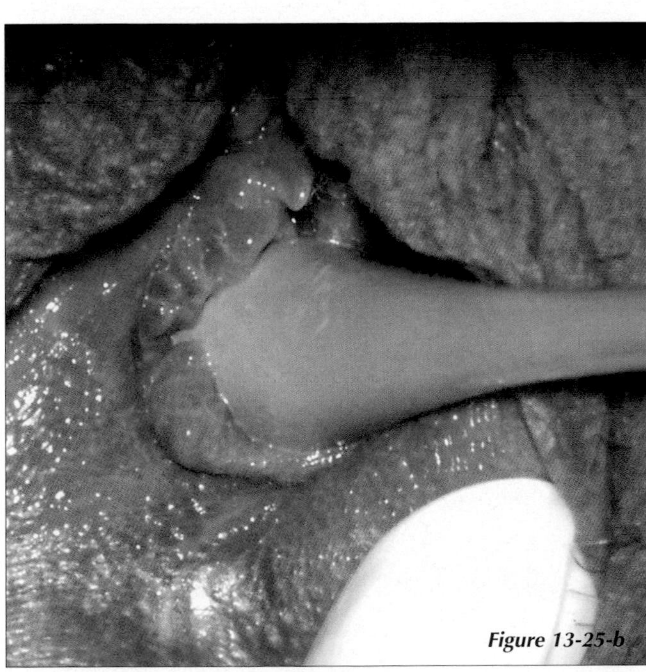

Figure 13-25-b

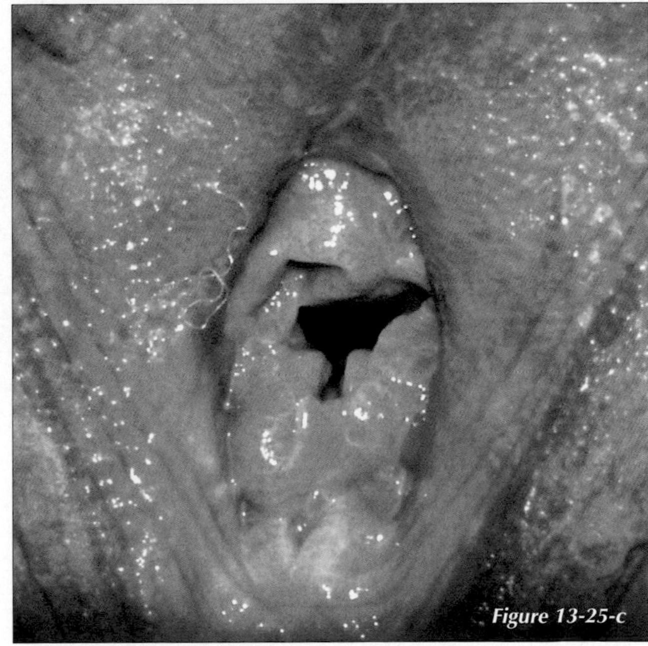

Figure 13-25-c

# Colposcopic Photographs

**Case Study 13-26**

These scanned 35-mm slides were taken with a camera attached to the colposcope in the hymenal examination of a sexually active 16-year-old girl.

***Figure 13-26-a.*** *In this image the defect in the hymeneal edge is not apparent with just the use of traction.*

***Figure 13-26-b.*** *A moistened cotton-tipped applicator used to separate the folds allows visualization of the defect at the 7-o'clock position.*

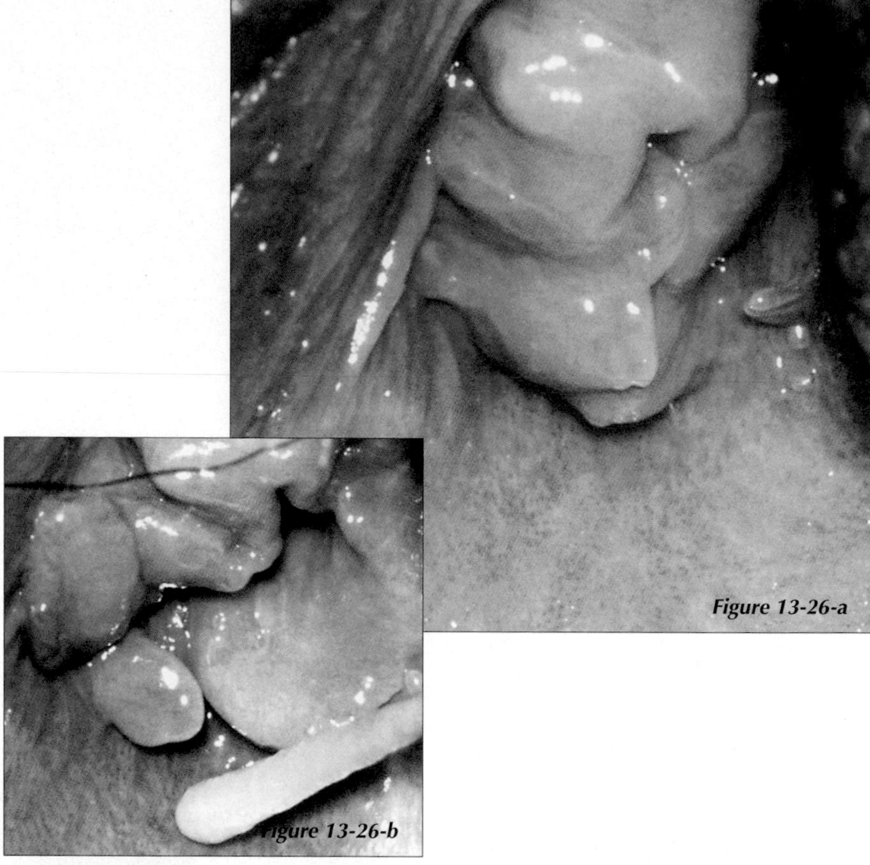

Figure 13-26-a

# Use of Video

**Case Study 13-27**

These photographs of the anal area (**Figures 13-27-a** and **b**) were taken during separate examinations. The photograph in **Figure 13-27-a**, taken with a video camera and transmitted in an email, seemed to show a fissure, but the resolution was too low for a conclusive finding. The photograph in **Figure 13-27-b**, taken 4 weeks later with a 35-mm camera attached to a colposcope, clearly demonstrated the absence of any fissure.

The photograph in **Figure 13-27-c**, taken during a hymenal examination with a video camera and transmitted in an e-mail, appeared to demonstrate a cleft at the 4-o'clock position. However, the photograph in **Figure 13-27-d**, taken 10 days later by another physician, demonstrated that the apparent cleft was actually a normal intravaginal ridge. (Photographs courtesy of Nancy Kellogg, MD.)

***Figure 13-27-a.*** *This image appears to show a fissure, but the resolution is very poor.*

***Figure 13-27-b.*** *This higher quality image demonstrates that there is no fissure.*

***Figures 13-27-c** and **d**. The apparent cleft at the 4-o'clock position is actually a normal intravaginal ridge.*

Figure 13-26-b

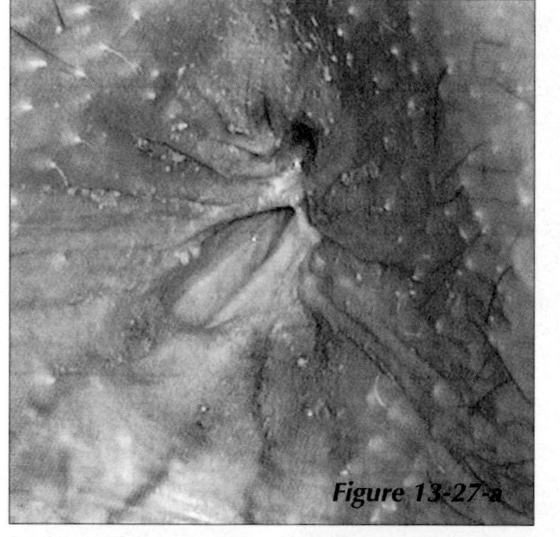

Figure 13-27-a

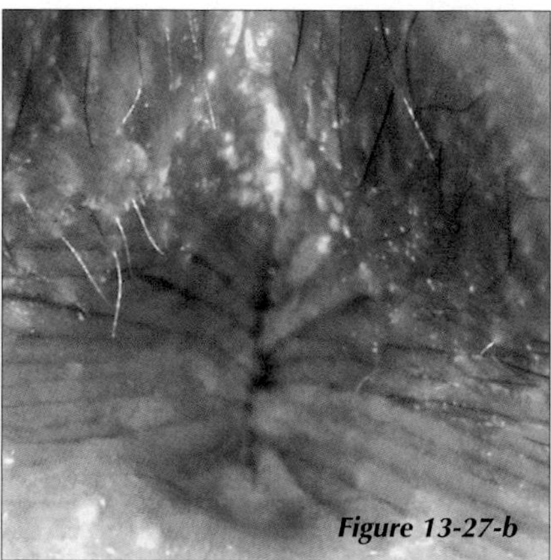

Figure 13-27-b

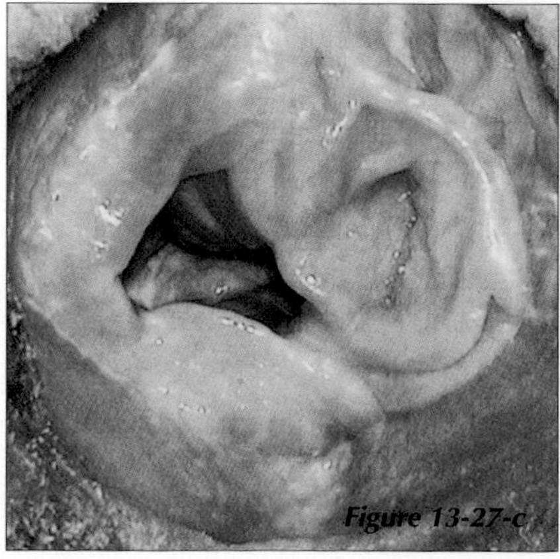

Figure 13-27-c

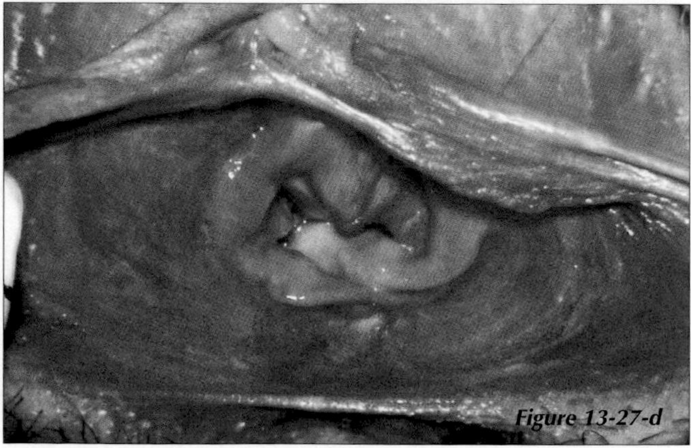

Figure 13-27-d

# Genital Injury

**Case Study 13-28**

This child was examined several hours after an assault. (Photographs courtesy of Robert Shapiro, MD.)

***Figures 13-28-a, b,*** *and* ***c.*** *The examination room used for this case. The setup in this room is described in* ***Table 13-1****.*

***Figure 13-28-d.*** *A normal prepubertal hymen.*

***Figure 13-28-e.*** *A complete acute transection of the hymen at the 6-o'clock position and abrasions of the perineum/ posterior fourchette area.*

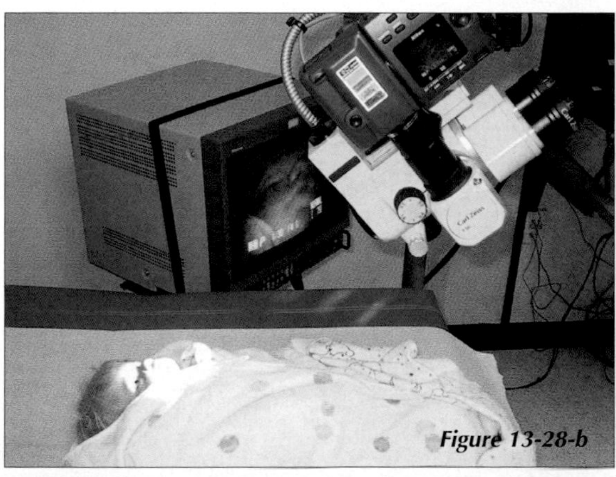

Figure 13-28-b

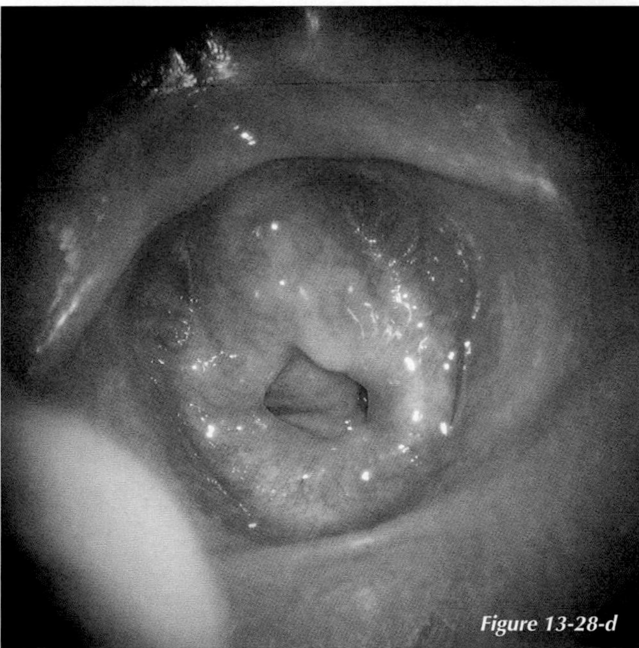

Figure 13-28-d

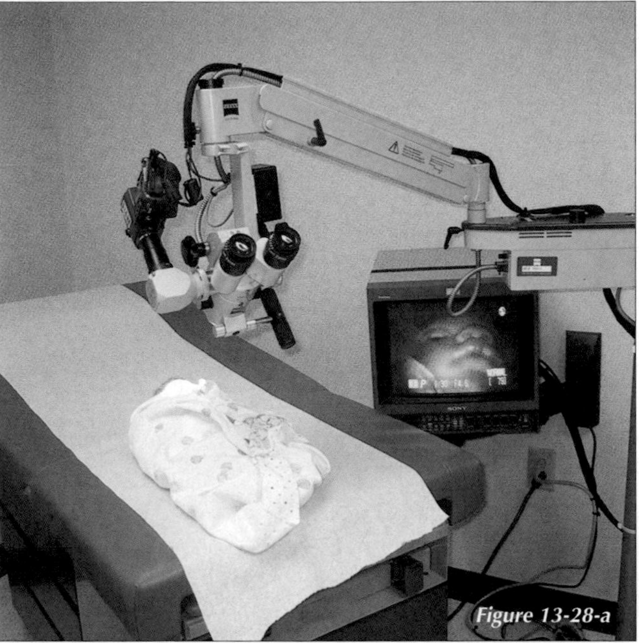

Figure 13-28-a

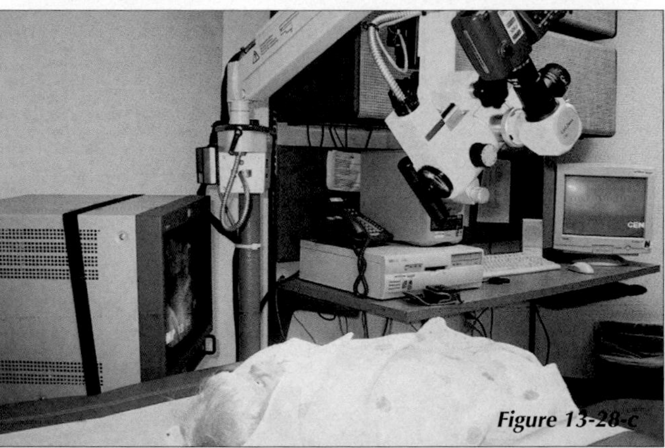

Figure 13-28-c

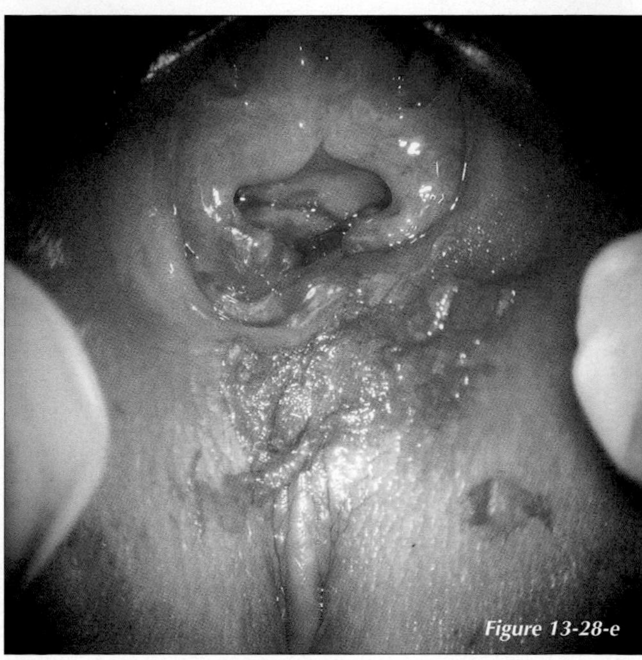

Figure 13-28-e

# Appendix 13-1

## Additional Resources

American Professional Society on the Abuse of Children. Photodocumentation Subcommittee of the APSAC Task Force on Medical Evaluation of Suspected Child Abuse. *APSAC Guidelines for Practice: Photographic Documentation of Child Abuse.* Chicago, Ill: American Professional Society on the Abuse of Children; 1995.

Finkel MA, Ricci LR. Documentation and preservation of visual evidence in child abuse. *Child Maltreat.* 1997;2:322-330.

Ford RJ, Smistek BS. Photography of the maltreated child. In: Ellerstein NS, ed. *Child Abuse and Neglect: A Medical Reference.* New York, NY: John Wiley; 1981:315-325.

McCann J. Use of the colposcope in childhood sexual abuse examinations. *Pediatr Clin North Am.* 1990;37:863-880.

Reeves C. Pediatric photography. *J Audiov Media Med.* 1986;9:131-134.

Ricci LR. Medical forensic photography of the sexually abused child. *Child Abuse Negl.* 1988;12:305-310.

Ricci LR. Photographing the physically abused child: principles and practice. *Am J Dis Child.* 1991;145:275-281.

Ricci LR. Photodocumentation of the abused child. In: Reece RM, ed. *Child Abuse: Medical Diagnosis and Management.* Philadelphia, Pa: Lea & Febiger; 1994:248-265.

Siegel RM, Hill TD, Henderson VA, Daniels K. Comparison of an intra-oral camera with colposcopy in sexually abused children. *Clin Pediatr (Phila).* 1999;38:375-376.

Smistek BS. Photography of the abused and neglected child. In: Ludwig S, Kornberg AE, eds. *Child Abuse: A Medical Reference.* 2nd ed. New York, NY: Churchill Livingstone; 1992:467-477.

Soderstrom RM. Colposcopic documentation: an objective approach to assessing sexual abuse of girls. *J Reprod Med.* 1994;39:6-8.

Spring GE. Evidence photography: an overview. *J Biol Photogr.* 1987;55:129-132.

Chapter 14

# Physical Abuse Documentation

Randell Alexander, MD, PhD
Wilbur Smith MD

The documentation of child abuse is necessary for several purposes other than the obvious means of building a forensic case: photodocumentation enables further reflection on an examination long after a child has left; other examiners are able to assess the examination without reexamining the child; some examination findings change over time and it is possible to preserve the child's condition for later viewing; and photodocumentation can add visual nuances to the findings that words alone may describe inadequately. Documentation can involve the measurement of physical dimensions, quantities, and qualities in a manner that may be reproducible or more understandable. Thus, a fall off of a bed may invoke a mental image of the likely height, but measurement of the actual height removes any guesswork.

## Eye Examination

Eye examinations of children can be very difficult, especially without means to dilate the eyes, or if the child is alert. The retinal examination is therefore easier for a nonophthalmologist in cases of severe head trauma because children with serious head trauma often have dilated pupils and are frequently unresponsive. However, an ophthalmologist should be called in nevertheless.

Most physicians evaluate the retina with a direct ophthalmoscope (**Figures 14-1-a** and **b**), which may be handheld or mounted on the wall. Ophthalmologists use indirect ophthalmoscopy, which involves a handheld lens positioned in front of the eye. Photodocumentation can be created with special imaging cameras that provide views of much of the retina. Some of these cameras provide a field of view ranging up to 180 degrees.

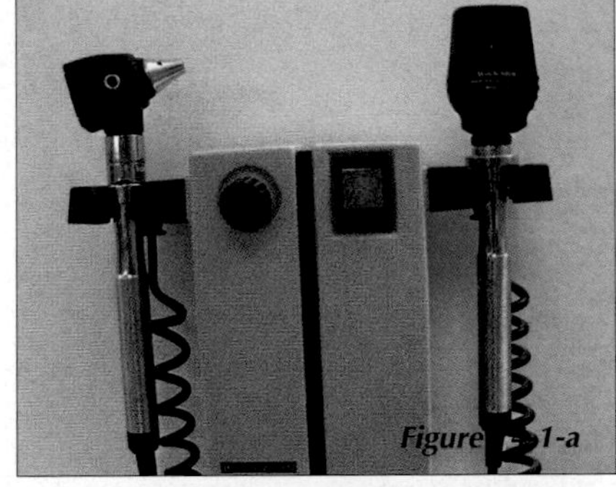

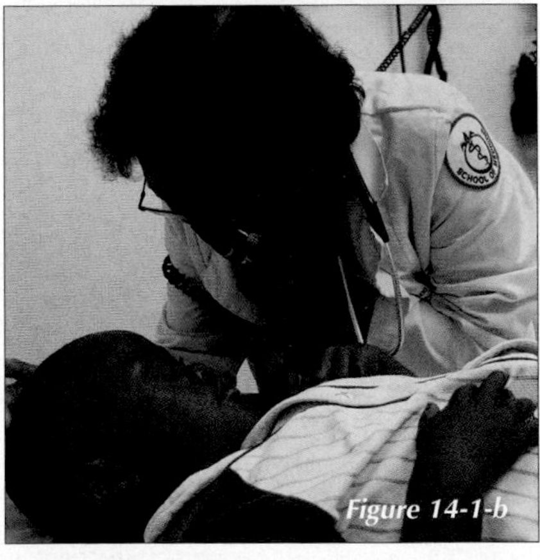

***Figure 14-1-a.*** *Ophthalmoscope mounted on the wall.*

***Figure 14-1-b.*** *Examiner using a direct ophthalmoscope to examine a child.*

## Cameras

Cameras are an important part of the documentation process. They facilitate documentation of the injuries and provide a record for review by others (eg, peer review, second opinions); however, any camera may fail, so it is imperative that examiners diagram injuries and provide extensive written descriptions. Even the best camera does not have the dynamic range of the human eye; therefore, subtle details may not be recovered by photographic processes. The shortfalls of cameras are illustrated by the case of a 2-year-old child with extensive bruising; excellent photographs of the child revealed approximately 40 bruises; however, a pediatric resident made a careful visual inspection of the same areas of the body and counted 67 bruises, aiding in the conviction of the perpetrator.

Improvements in the design of traditional 35-mm cameras have lead to more automation and better photography for most users, but it is in the area of digital photography that the most explosive advancements are being made. A 2-megapixel camera would have been considered of the highest quality available 5 years ago, but it is now considered to be a relatively inexpensive family camera. Cameras with 4 or 5 megapixels yield excellent detail that rivals 35-mm film; yet, 6- and 8-megapixel cameras exist, and predictions include the development of cameras with 18 megapixels in the near future.

Although some object that digital camera photographs might be easily manipulated, 35-mm photographs also may be manipulated easily using digital technology. The key in legal proceedings is whether the photograph accurately depicts what was seen, regardless of the particular method of imaging.

Most cameras on the market (**Figures 14-2-a** and **b**) can be used to obtain excellent-quality photography; however, ongoing advances in technology will eventually render the most advanced cameras obsolete. Resources such as a local camera store or consumer magazines should be consulted before making a purchase.

## Investigational Tools

The most simple investigational tools used in documentation include various types of rulers and thermometers. While it is important to document the circumstances of the event with quantitative measurements, it is perhaps even more important to use measurements to ascertain whether the proposed mechanism of injury is possible. It is important to create comprehensive and detailed documentation during the initial visit to a crime scene, since it may not be possible to view a crime scene on multiple occasions, and the scene will inevitably change over time due to weather, tampering, or other causes.

A straight ruler is useful in many instances, but setting up the photograph is important to avoid distortions. A familiar object, such as a coin, can be placed in the frame to help establish a relative scale for comparing injuries (**Figures 14-3-a** and **b**).

Figure 14-2-a

Figure 14-2-b

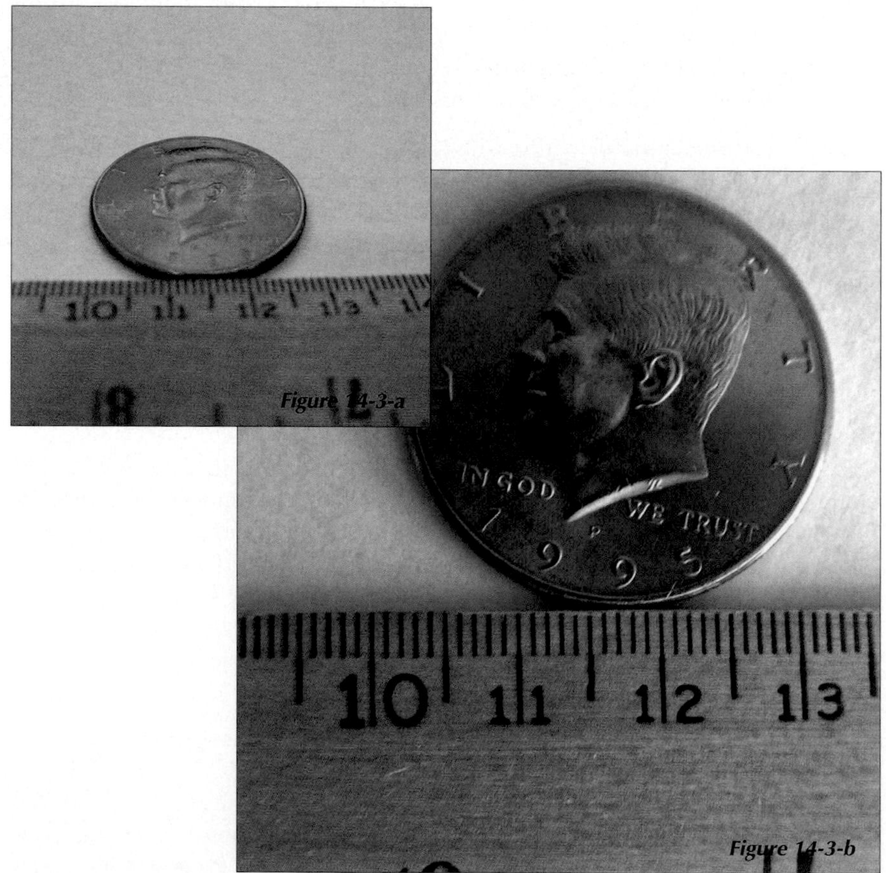


Figure 14-3-a

Figure 14-3-b

***Figure 14-2-a.*** *This high-end 8-megapixel amateur camera yields high-quality images that rival 35-mm film.*

***Figure 14-2-b.*** *The camera on the left is a 5-megapixel camera that will produce excellent quality prints of up to16x20 inches. It has a standard viewfinder as well as an LCD screen. The camera on the right is a more affordable and more compact 6.2-megapixel camera. It is very light and has only an LCD screen.*

***Figure 14-3-a.*** *The object may be correctly measured horizontally, but the vertical dimension is distorted, creating an elliptical appearance.*

***Figure 14-3-b.*** *The same object when viewed directly from above is obviously round.*

To avoid unintended distortions, investigators often use an L-shaped ruler, commonly known as a square. If foreshortening of the vertical dimension of the object or mark in question occurs, it also occurs for the ruler and allows for accurate readings (**Figures 14-4-a** and **b**). A tape measure is handy for measuring many objects and surfaces likely to be named in cases of alleged falls (**Figure 14-5**).

Family members frequently give estimates of height or size that are incorrect. The degree of error is sometimes considerable, frequently owing to the difficulty some people encounter when estimating units of length, and sometimes owing to a deliberate effort to mitigate the circumstances in favor of the perpetrator. For example, if the initial history provided is that a child fell off a bed and extensive skull fractures are subsequently discovered, a perpetrator might think it is in their best interests to overestimate the height by describing the distance as 3 feet high instead of 2 feet, although such an exaggeration does little to help to the perpetrator in this case.

Infants with head or bone injuries are commonly said to have rolled off a sofa. If no object other than the floor is impacted, falls from sofas of normal height should not cause any serious injury (**Figure 14-6**). Either no injury, or a bruise is the expected result. It would be very uncommon to see a skull fracture or another broken bone with a fall from a sofa.

Another common claim is that the infant rolled off the bed. Some beds may be higher than the fairly standard 24 inches (**Figure 14-7**), but falls from such heights generally lead to little or no injury. Older children may jump from beds, adding the height of the bed to the height of the child and perhaps some additional distance for the jump. Toddlers may sustain an accidentally fractured clavicle (collarbone) when they land on their shoulder on the floor.

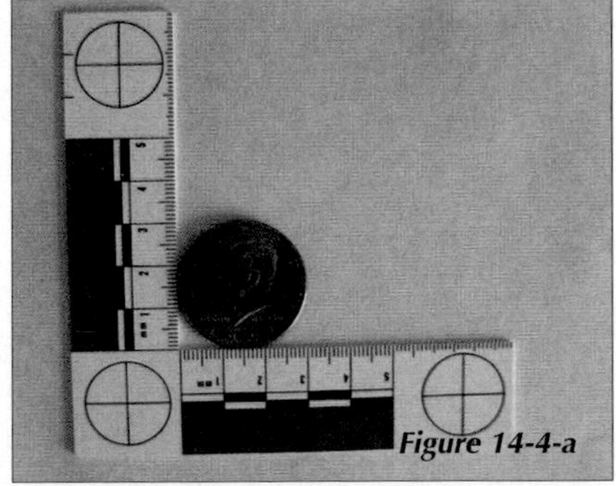
Figure 14-4-a

Figure 14-4-b

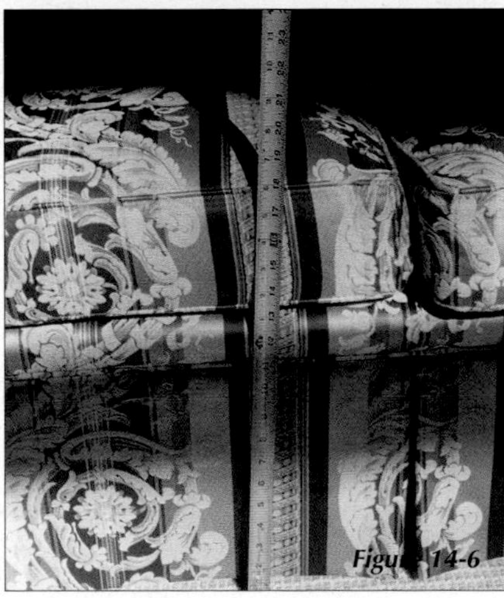
Figure 14-6

Figure 14-5

Figure 14-7

***Figure 14-4-a.*** *This ruler is an ABFO No. 2 Bitemark Scale.*

***Figure 14-4-b.*** *When an object is photographed at an angle, the scale accurately represents horizontal and vertical dimensions.*

***Figure 14-5.*** *Many chairs are about 18 inches high from the floor to the seat. Any calculations should account for whether a child was sitting or standing on the chair when they fell.*

***Figure 14-6.*** *A typical sofa measuring 18 inches high.*

***Figure 14-7.*** *This bed measures 29 inches, which is higher than the more standard 24 inches.*

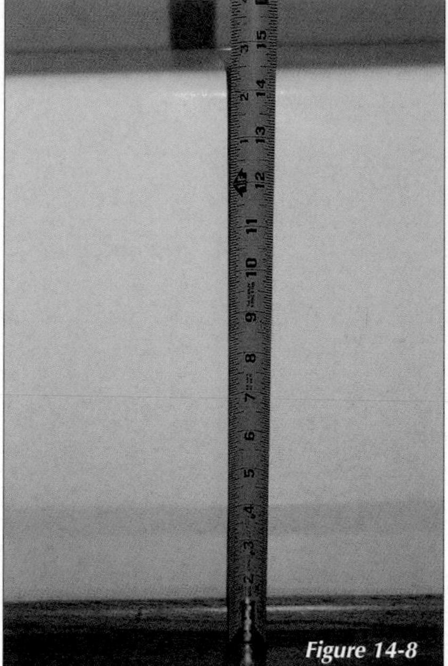


Infants and toddlers are sometimes said to have climbed into a bathtub. The claim might be that they either fell into hot water or they turned on the hot water once in the bathtub. Occasionally, a child who drowns or nearly drowns will be said to have fallen into the bathtub. Whether it is possible that the child could climb into the bathtub depends upon the height of the child, the developmental motor abilities of the child, any possible step up, and the height of the bathtub (**Figure 14-8**).

Sometimes children fall from windows, decks, and other elevated surfaces. This may be accidental, the result of parental or design negligence, or deliberate caregiver behavior. Sometimes a fall is claimed when in fact some other mechanism is responsible for the child's injuries. Careful on-site documentation involving the measurement of the distance between the landing surface and origin of the claimed fall is vital (**Figures 14-9-a** and **b**). In a study of children seen in a hospital after falling from 10 to 45 feet, only 1 of 117 died (the result of a third story fall of about 30 feet).[25]

Temperature measurements help to understand the circumstances of how burns occur. Cigarette burns are instantaneous burns occurring at several hundred degrees Fahrenheit, which is well above the threshold for burning skin. Contact burns usually result from contact with surfaces that conduct heat well (eg, metal, glass) at temperatures that cause instantaneous burns. Liquid burns often occur at temperatures that range from slightly uncomfortable for an adult to scalding, usually resulting in instantaneous burns for a child or infant.

In burn cases, evidence worksheets enable documentation of the temperature of water at different times and circumstances (**Figure 14-10**). Such information is very helpful when assessing whether the history accurately accounts for the injury. Accurately completing such worksheets ensures that all relevant data is collected, and eliminates the possibility that a relevant piece of information will be forgotten. Because water temperature can be easily changed, it is important to obtain these measures before anyone has a chance to tamper with the water heater.

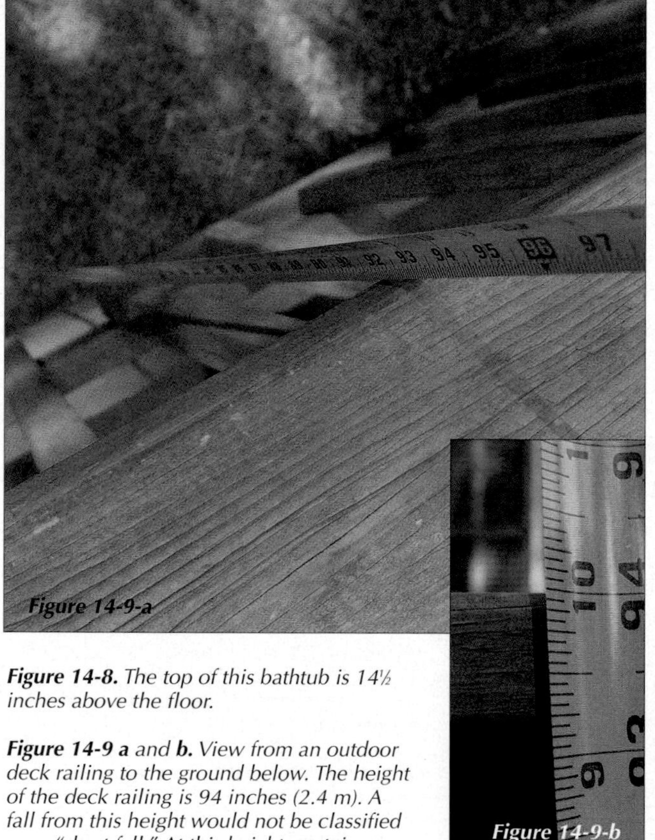


*Figure 14-8.* *The top of this bathtub is 14½ inches above the floor.*

*Figure 14-9* ***a*** *and* ***b****. View from an outdoor deck railing to the ground below. The height of the deck railing is 94 inches (2.4 m). A fall from this height would not be classified as a "short fall." At this height, certain fractures may occur (eg, skull, arm, and leg) but others (eg, posterior rib fractures and fractures of the sternum) are unlikely; serious injury would be uncommon.*

*Figure 14-10.* *This worksheet is adapted from similar ones used in San Diego and Georgia.*

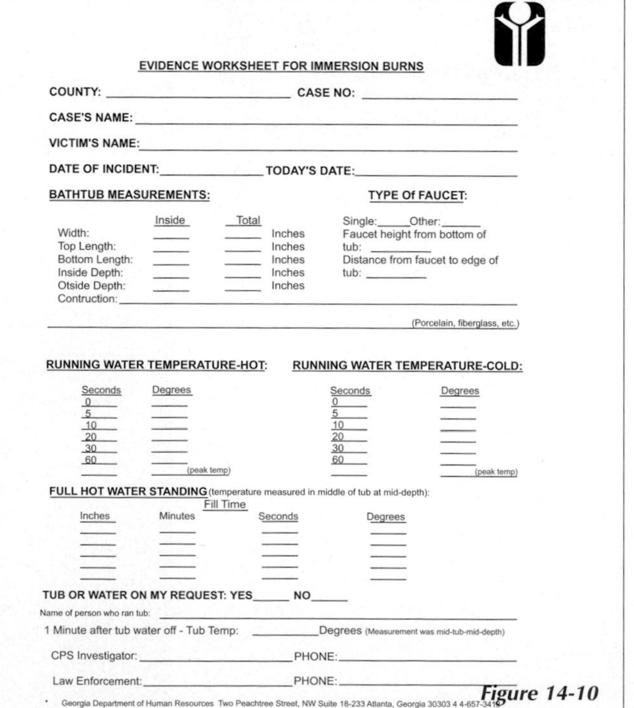

**EVIDENCE WORKSHEET FOR IMMERSION BURNS**

COUNTY: ____________ CASE NO: ____________

CASE'S NAME: ____________

VICTIM'S NAME: ____________

DATE OF INCIDENT: ____________ TODAY'S DATE: ____________

**BATHTUB MEASUREMENTS:**

| | Inside | Total | |
|---|---|---|---|
| Width: | ____ | ____ | Inches |
| Top Length: | ____ | ____ | Inches |
| Bottom Length: | ____ | ____ | Inches |
| Inside Depth: | ____ | ____ | Inches |
| Otside Depth: | ____ | ____ | Inches |

Contruction: ____________

____________ (Porcelain, fiberglass, etc.)

**TYPE Of FAUCET:**

Single: ____ Other: ____

Faucet height from bottom of tub: ____

Distance from faucet to edge of tub: ____

**RUNNING WATER TEMPERATURE-HOT:**

| Seconds | Degrees |
|---|---|
| 0 | ____ |
| 5 | ____ |
| 10 | ____ |
| 20 | ____ |
| 30 | ____ |
| 60 | ____ |
| ____ | ____ (peak temp) |

**RUNNING WATER TEMPERATURE-COLD:**

| Seconds | Degrees |
|---|---|
| 0 | ____ |
| 5 | ____ |
| 10 | ____ |
| 20 | ____ |
| 30 | ____ |
| 60 | ____ |
| ____ | ____ (peak temp) |

**FULL HOT WATER STANDING** (temperature measured in middle of tub at mid-depth):

| Inches | Fill Time Minutes | Fill Time Seconds | Degrees |
|---|---|---|---|
| ____ | ____ | ____ | ____ |
| ____ | ____ | ____ | ____ |
| ____ | ____ | ____ | ____ |
| ____ | ____ | ____ | ____ |
| ____ | ____ | ____ | ____ |

**TUB OR WATER ON MY REQUEST: YES____ NO____**

Name of person who ran tub: ____________

1 Minute after tub water off - Tub Temp: ________ Degrees (Measurement was mid-tub-mid-depth)

CPS Investigator: ____________ PHONE: ____________

Law Enforcement: ____________ PHONE: ____________

- Georgia Department of Human Resources Two Peachtree Street, NW Suite 18-233 Atlanta, Georgia 30303 4 4-657-341

Common household thermometers are insufficient for gathering evidence since they are usually not capable of reading temperatures in excess of 110°F (43°C). The water temperature of hot tubs and hot baths usually will not exceed 105°F (41°C), which may temporarily redden skin after prolonged exposure, but will not ordinarily cause burns. Water temperatures that need to be measured in suspected child abuse cases tend to be in the range of 120°F-180°F (49°C-82°C), requiring the use of thermometers capable of measuring temperatures in this range.

## Radiology Evaluation

Since the early days of child abuse assessment, a key tool for investigators has been the ***skeletal survey***, which consists of radiographs of essentially all bones in the body. The goal of the survey is to look for occult fractures, other bony injuries, soft tissue injuries, foreign bodies, and other signs that may be significant with respect to abuse or other medical conditions. Oblique views enhance the potential for visualizing rib fractures, allowing optimal viewing of different segments of the ribs.

A ***long bone survey*** includes the arms, legs, and ribs, but not all bones. A ***whole body roentgenogram***, often referred to as a ***babygram***, is an attempt to capture an infant's skeleton on one or two photographic plates, and is too broad and not technically acceptable. Such imaging does not allow for centering over each major joint, which is the only way to assure the best possible focus for detection of subtle metaphyseal fractures. A ***bone scan*** is created when a child is injected with a radioisotope and a photographic plate is exposed. While a bone scan is a useful study to detect certain conditions, such as additional rib fractures, it tends to have too many false positives and generally is not a first-line study.

The sequence of images taken during a skeletal survey includes an anteroposterior (AP) view of the chest area (**Figure 14-11-a**), an oblique view of the chest for rib details (**Figure 14-11-b**), lateral and AP skull films (**Figures 14-11-c** and **d**), AP pelvic films (**Figure 14-11-e**), AP and lateral lumbar spine views (**Figures 14-11-f** and **g**), AP view of the upper and lower extremities (**Figures 14-11-h, i,** and **j**), and sacral radiographs (**Figure 14-11-k**).

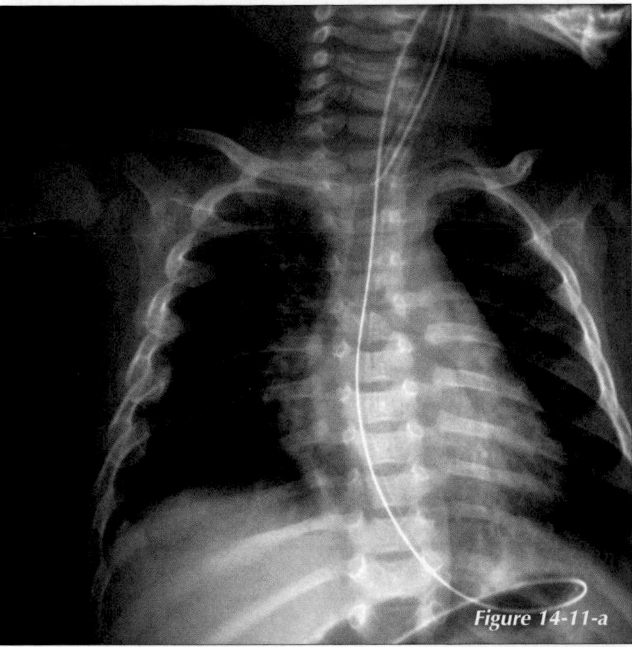


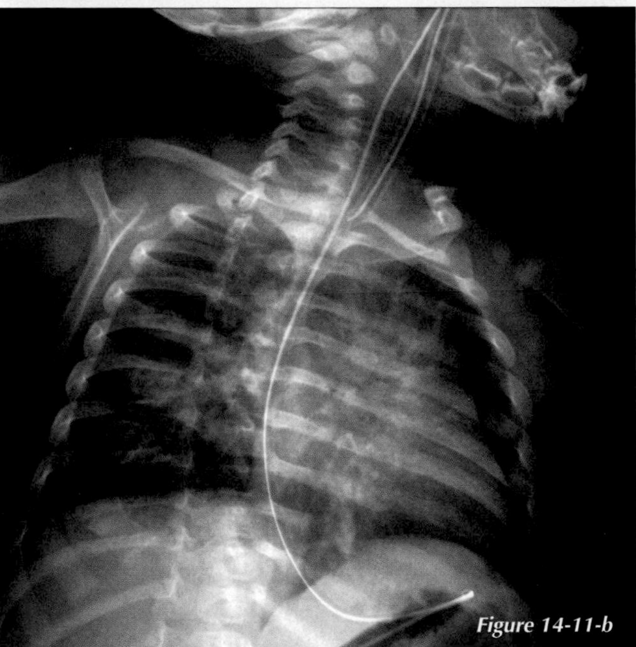


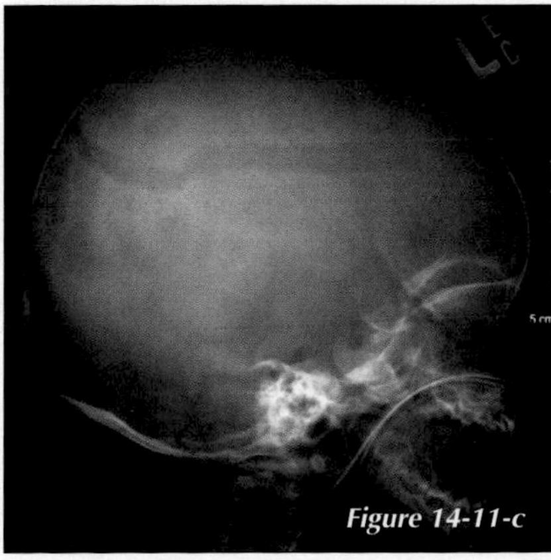


***Figure 14-11-a.*** *AP chest radiograph of an abused child who is comatose with a massive head injury. The lung markings are partially obliterated because this radiograph has been created with a technique designed to accentuate the bones; bone surveys are done with this technique rather than a lung technique. Note the multiple right-sided rib fractures.*

***Figure 14-11-b.*** *Oblique view of the chest for rib detail. Both oblique views are obtained as a standard study; however, only one oblique is shown in this example. Once again, note the right-sided rib fractures.*

***Figure 14-11-c.*** *Lateral skull film shows a diastatic skull fracture in this severely abused patient. The standard is a minimum of an AP and lateral skull film as part of a bone survey.*

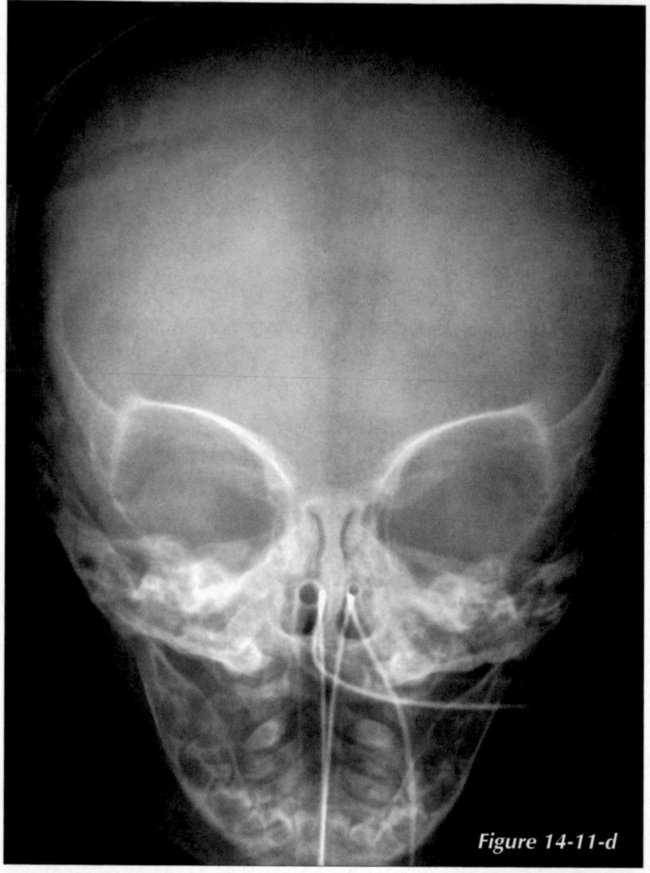


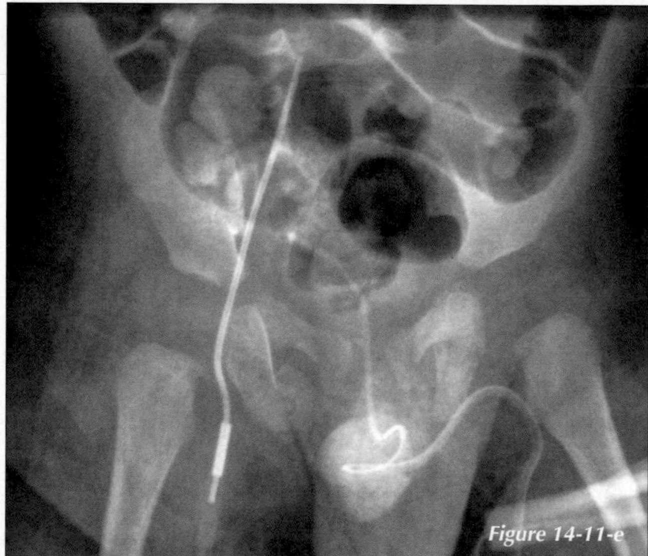


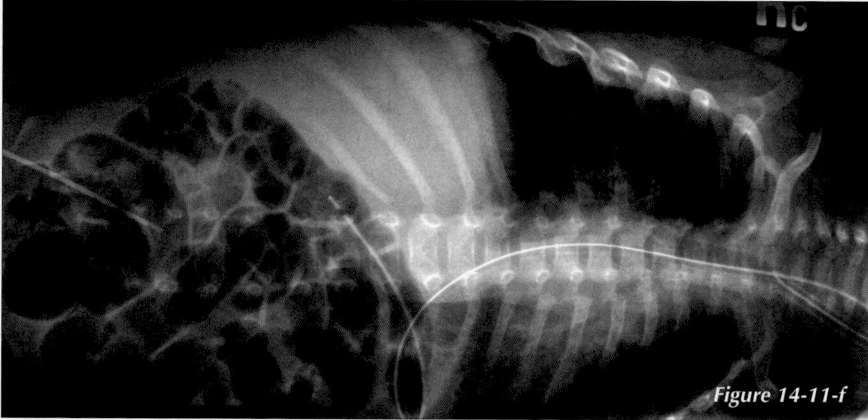


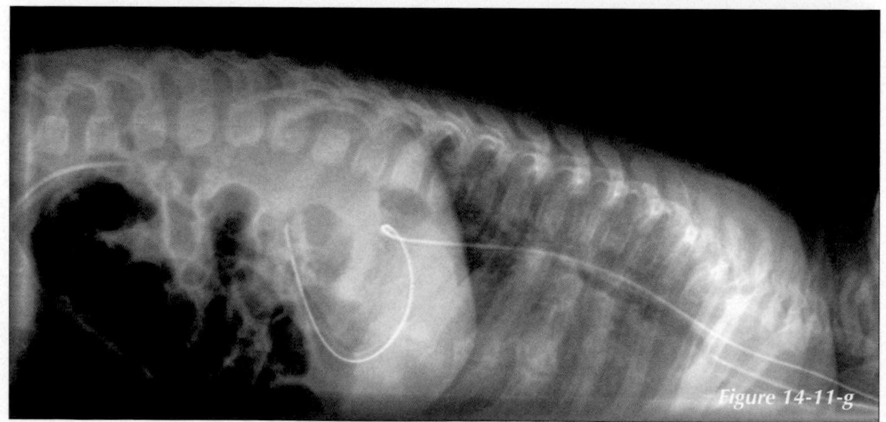


***Figure 14-11-d.*** *AP skull film of this child showing the severely diastatic skull fracture.*

***Figure 14-11-e.*** *AP pelvic view of an abused child. It is important to entirely cover the long bones. The proximal femurs are well visualized. Pelvic fractures are unusual in child abuse but are identified occasionally.*

***Figure 14-11-f.*** *AP view of the lumbar spine. AP and lateral views of the lumbar spine are important in child abuse to reveal flexion fractures, particularly when the infant is severely shaken.*

***Figure 14-11-g.*** *Lateral lumbar spine view. When combined with the AP lumbar spine view, a complete evaluation of the thoracic and lumbar spine is obtained.*

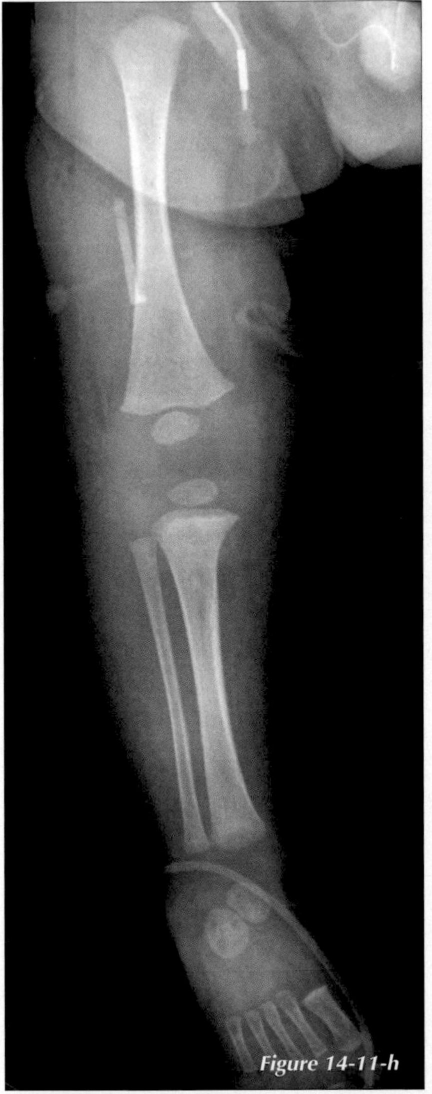


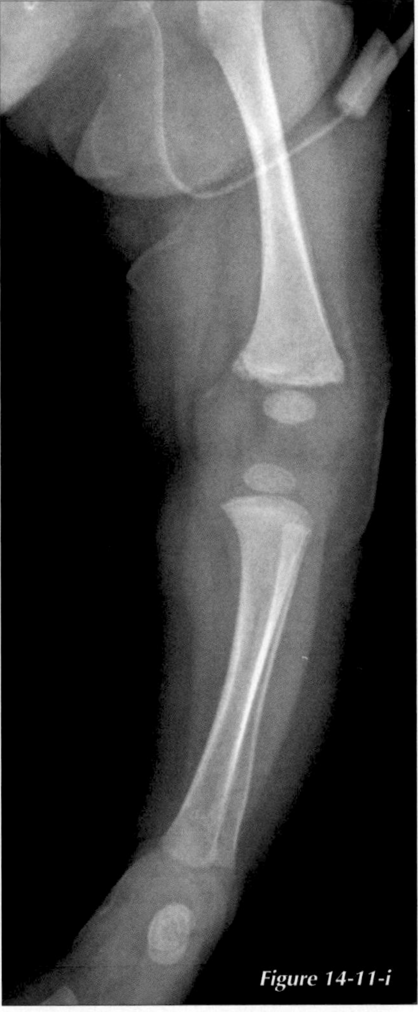


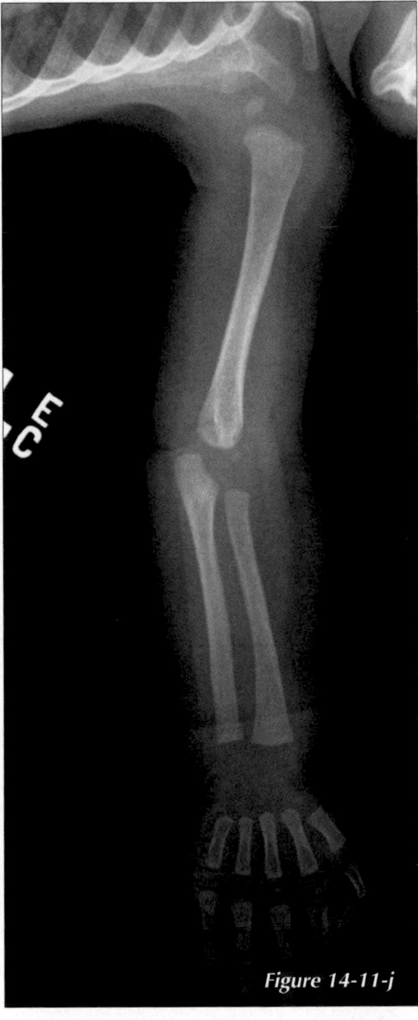


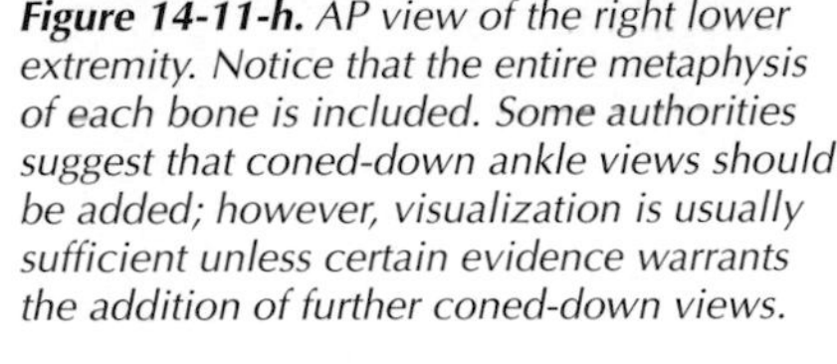
***Figure 14-11-h.*** *AP view of the right lower extremity. Notice that the entire metaphysis of each bone is included. Some authorities suggest that coned-down ankle views should be added; however, visualization is usually sufficient unless certain evidence warrants the addition of further coned-down views.*

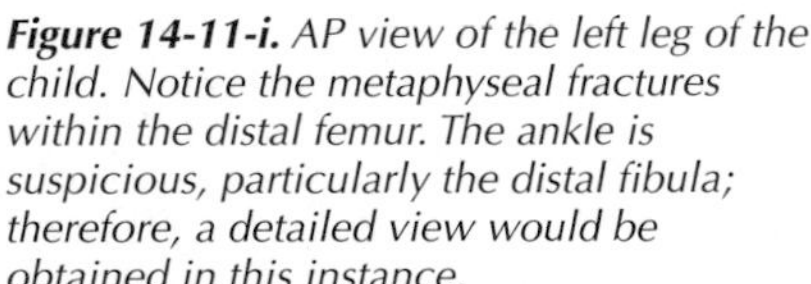
***Figure 14-11-i.*** *AP view of the left leg of the child. Notice the metaphyseal fractures within the distal femur. The ankle is suspicious, particularly the distal fibula; therefore, a detailed view would be obtained in this instance.*

***Figure 14-11-j.*** *View of the right arm of this infant. Note again that all of the epiphyses and metaphyses are included on the examination.*

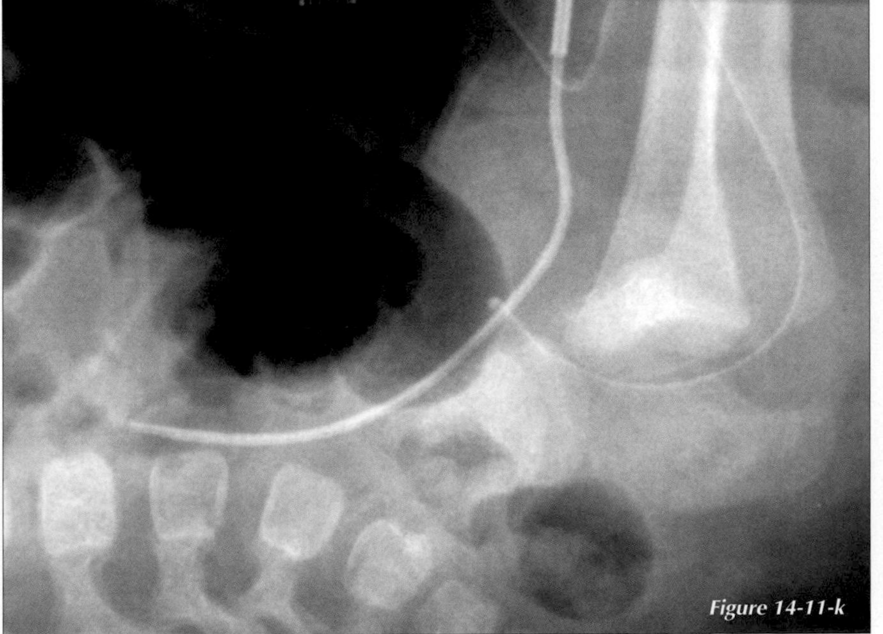


***Figure 14-11-k****. Lower lumbar and sacral radiograph from a severely abused infant. Note the fine details of the bones. This area is not clearly illustrated on the overall lateral view of the thoracolumbar spine, so this second spot view is necessary.*

Chapter 15

# Equipment for the Documentation of Sexual Abuse

Jay Whitworth, MD

Historically, children's genitalia have been examined for a variety of purposes, such as attempting to determine whether a girl is a virgin and for performing circumcision. However, it is only in the last 30 years that more careful examination and documentation of physical findings has been applied to cases of alleged sexual abuse, and only in the last 20 years that photographic equipment, such as the colposcope, has been used. The intricacies of interpreting sexual abuse examinations continue to evolve as practitioners further delineate how an individual finding differs from the norm. In other words, contemporary practices mandate that examiners photodocument all examinations for peer review, analysis, consensus decisions, and inclusion in a data-base for future reference. In addition to these reasons for photodocumentation, there is also the issue of archiving the examination for future comparison as well as avoiding the need for secondary examinations that may be traumatizing to children. In some programs, it is standard practice to document only the abnormal examinations, which raises questions about errors in the interpretation of what is normal.

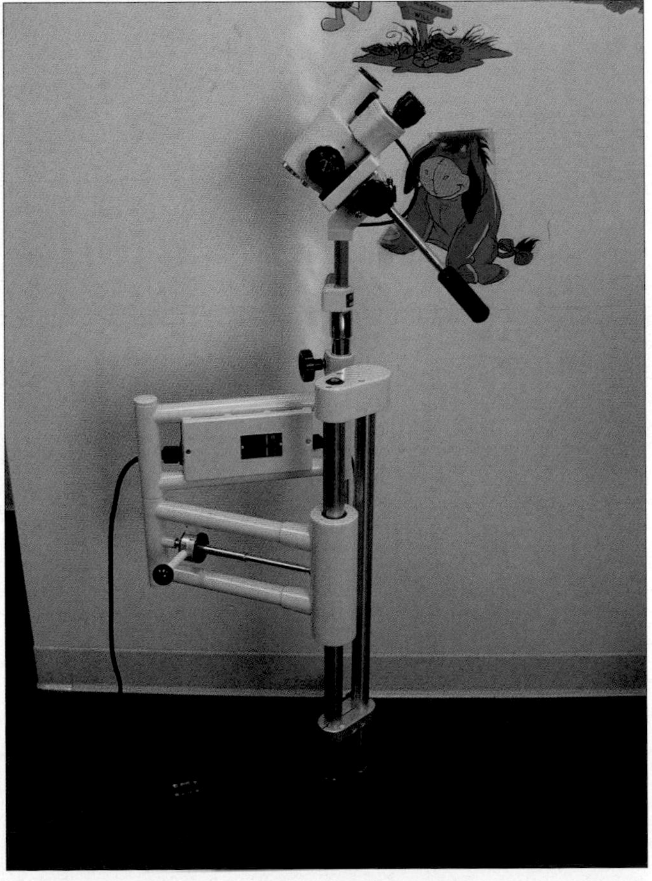

*Figure 15-1. This colposcope is made by Cooper Surgical Products. It does not have a mounted camera because image capturing is facilitated by an attached computer.*

The advent of the colposcope was a major step forward in standardizing equipment for the evaluation of sexually abused children (**Figure 15-1**), although the use of a colposcope is not mandatory. Quality photodocumentation can be produced using a broad range of equipment, if properly focused, lit, and magnified. The lack of funding to buy a colposcope should never be a reason to fail to photodocument cases. Examination rooms can be designed to provide a comfortable setting while creating conditions that lead to ideal photodocumentation (**Figures 15-2** and **15-3**).

Practitioners can take excellent quality images using 35-mm film cameras, but storage of slides and scanning for sharing of images presents challenges. Most examiners opt for the use of digital cameras (**Figures 15-4** and **15-5**), which can be free-standing or attached to a colposcope. To ensure quality images, a camera with a resolution of at least 3 megapixels is advised. Still images can be captured from these cameras and transferred to a computer using free software designed for that purpose. Images can be stored on a computer hard drive indefinitely for printing or transmission to others for review. Due to security concerns, images should be

*Disclaimer: All product recommendations and descriptions listed herein are those of the author.*

**Figure 15-2.** *This setup is typical of rooms used for examinations of children and adolescents. There is a movable evidence collection cart for adolescents.*

**Figure 15-3.** *Note the colposcope and computer photodocumentation equipment in this child-friendly environment. This examination room is set up for prepubertal children in the Swainsboro, Georgia, Children's Advocacy Center. This facility is equipped with Image-quest to generate medical records and encrypt photographs for transmission.*

**Figure 15-4.** *A hand-held camera can produce an analog signal that can be transmitted or captured as a digital image and is very useful for facilities without a colposcope. By capturing through an analog/digital converter, digital images can be stored on any computer.*

**Figure 15-5.** *A portable camera can be used as an additional patient or room camera for telemedicine transmissions. This equipment can also transmit real-time images to a distant site for remote evaluations.*

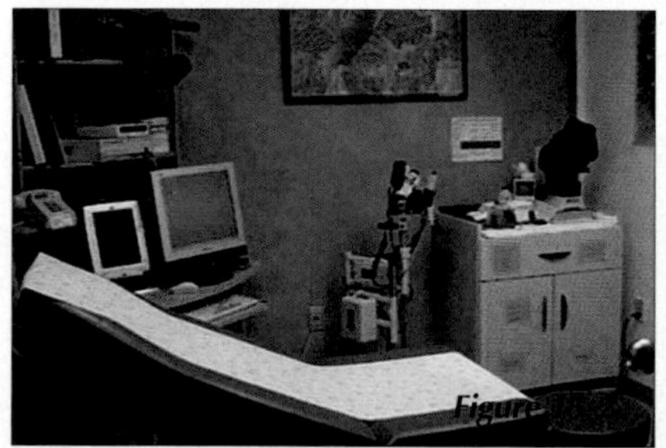

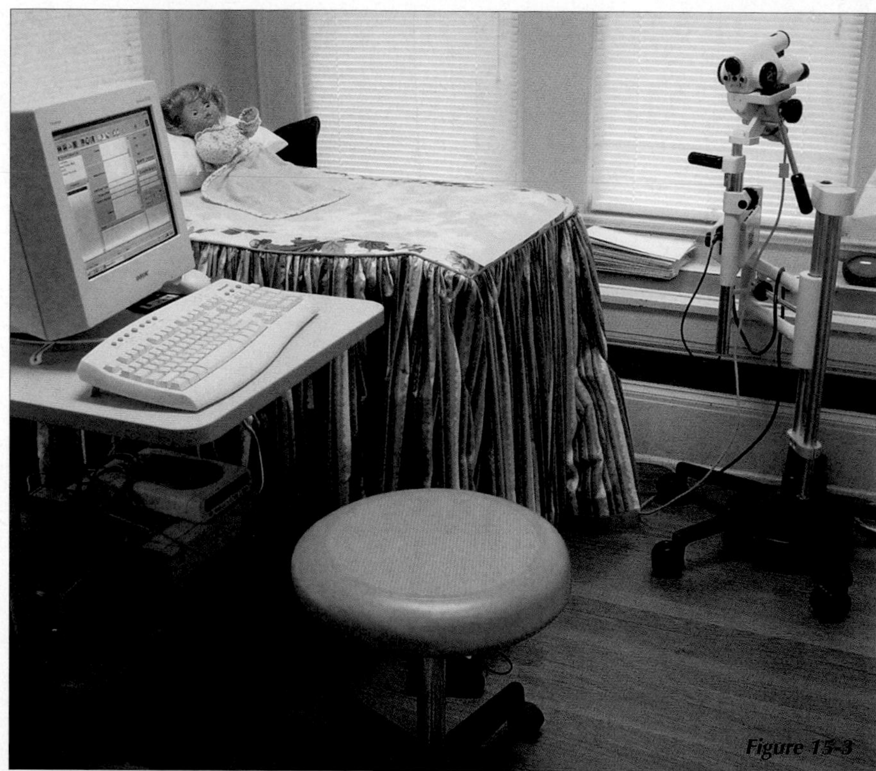

Figure 15-3

Figure 15-4

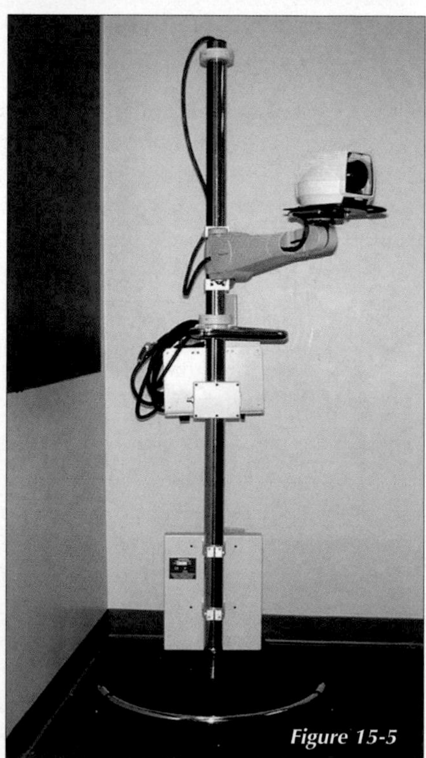

Figure 15-5

password-protected and depersonalized, and their distribution should be allowed only with patient, parental, or court permission. In some states, permission is not necessary to share information with law enforcement officers.

Some examiners prefer to use videoclips for photodocumentation since the camera that is attached to the colposcope is also a digital video camera. Video is transferred to a computer with video capture software, and individual images can be isolated from the video. Lengthy video clips can present a challenge in terms of storage space. Free-standing video cameras can also be used, supported by a tripod for stability. The use of cameras that only provide instant prints should be avoided.

Once the capture series have been developed by individual examiners, the issue of transmitting images for consultation, peer review, and supervision still remains. When images and data are transmitted to distant sites for any medical purpose, the process is called ***telemedicine***. Telemedicine is generally defined as the use of telecommunications and information technology to provide clinical data to individuals at a distance. It can be as simple as a telephone call, or as complex as virtual surgery. There are many choices for transmission available to examiners, many of which require no significant investment beyond access to the Internet. The Internet is not inherently secure for private transmissions, so attention to depersonalizing case details and photographs is essential. Alternatively, records and photographs can be encrypted. Software for encryption is embedded in proprietary products such as Imagequest or Second Opinion; it may also be available in certain Web browsers, or downloadable from other sources. In most cases, depersonalization is easier and less expensive. As an alternative, examiners who communicate on a regular basis can form a listserv so that only recognized members can access records. Communication with a colleague or multiple colleagues can be accomplished by creating an e-mail with a brief history and sending the photograph as an attachment. Photographs usually need to be resized to about 500 kilobytes to be efficiently transmitted as an attachment. Resizing can be accomplished with any photoediting program, and the recipient can then reply with comments. With e-mail as a resource, there is no reason for an examiner to not have access to peer review or consultation. These activities are essential to every examiner seeing sexually abused children.

**Figure 15-6.** *This office setup for teleconferencing has a unit that is reasonably priced and can be used for one participant in a multisite case review or in peer review arrangements. A standard computer with Internet access is seen on the left. On the right is a telemedicine unit, consisting of a Codec and monitor, that uses Internet Protocol technology over commercial cable.*

Electronic technology in sexual abuse cases can also be used as a means for solving problems related to training and access to quality care. Many areas of the country need high-quality services for abused children, but local resources are not always available to provide such services. Geographical considerations often interfere with the availability of medical services by an expert when time may be of the essence. Telemedicine technology has provided a solution to this problem. The profusion of equipment, high-speed transmission lines, and new technology has also reduced the cost of this type of service so that it is within the reach of many. Reimbursement from third-party payers has also made these programs feasible in recent years.

Design of a telemedicine program requires that an established center with extensive experience in the evaluation of sexual abuse determines the needs of a geographical area that is underserved. These needs may only require the provision of occasional consultation on individual cases. Under these circumstances, an e-mail consultative relationship between the center and the peripheral site may solve the problem. If peer review is determined to be needed, a similar e-mail system may neet to be used to exchange cases between sexual examiners. When visual communication between the expert and a peripheral site is needed, a larger investment is necessary (**Figure 15-6**). In this installation, a telemedicine unit uses Internet Protocol technology over commercial cable and allows the expert and peripheral examiner to see each other and share images in real time. This equipment can be purchased at a reasonable cost.

The center may invest in more elaborate transmission equipment that will allow an experienced examiner of record to visually supervise examiners at peripheral sites (**Figure 15-7**). Equipment must, at a minimum, allow the expert to be seen at a peripheral site, allow the expert to see the examination at the peripheral site, and allow audio communication between the 2 sites (**Figure 15-8**). There must be a means of recording images from the peripheral site, such as findings from the examination. By using this equipment, experts can train and supervise peripheral examiners while offering criticism in real time. After the patient has left, the same equipment can be used to review examinations and for peer review. Equipment can be purchased to allow for simultaneous transmission between multiple sites and for PowerPoint presentations. The medical record can be generated at either the peripheral site or the expert site. Evidence collection is, of course, provided at the peripheral site (**Figure 15-9**).

The use of this equipment has been so productive and successful that it has been employed for purposes other than medical examinations. Several areas have developed virtual teams for case review and delivery of highly specialized evaluative services. Some teams have begun to study the use of the tech-nology to provide forensic interviews and psychiatric treatment to peripheral sites.

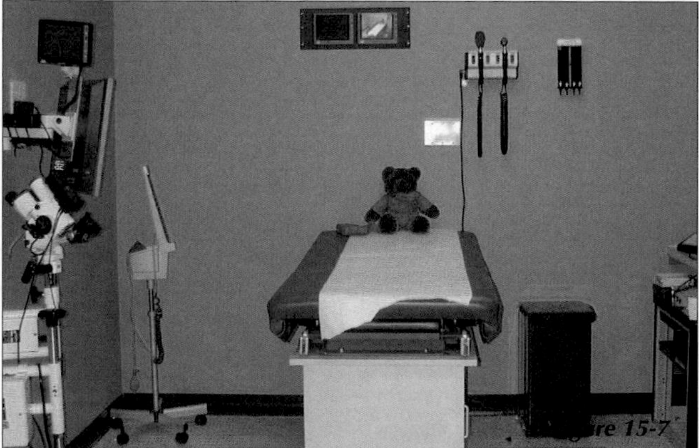

***Figure 15-7.*** *In the examination room, video monitors are placed unobtrusively. In this application, the equipment is installed at the Florida School for the Deaf and Blind. A trained nurse can perform the examination while being supervised in real time by an off-site pediatric examiner. All equipment is linked with the center site so that the camera and video capture is controlled by the off-site expert.*

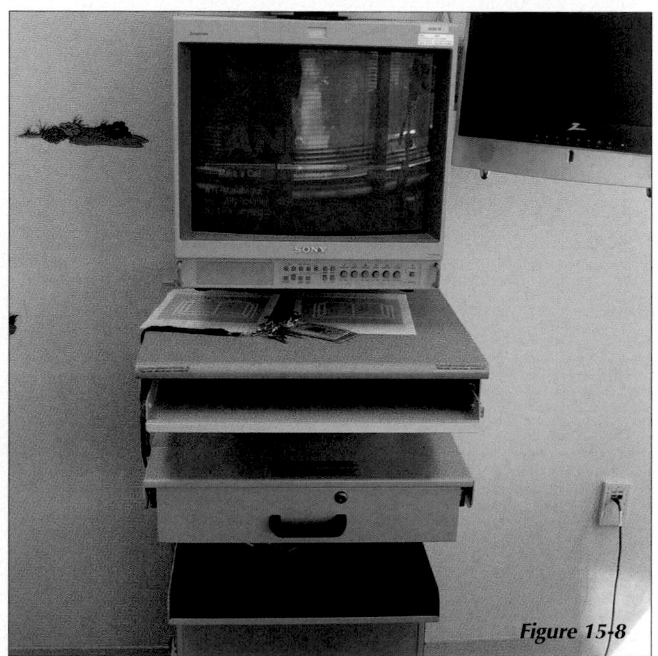

***Figure 15-8.*** *The Tandberg HCS 3 is used for real-time telemedicine examinations. Transmission equipment is hidden in the body of the unit, and it uses either telephone lines or Ethernet connections to transmit data. The upper 2 monitors are used to see the view being transmitted as well as the view being received.*

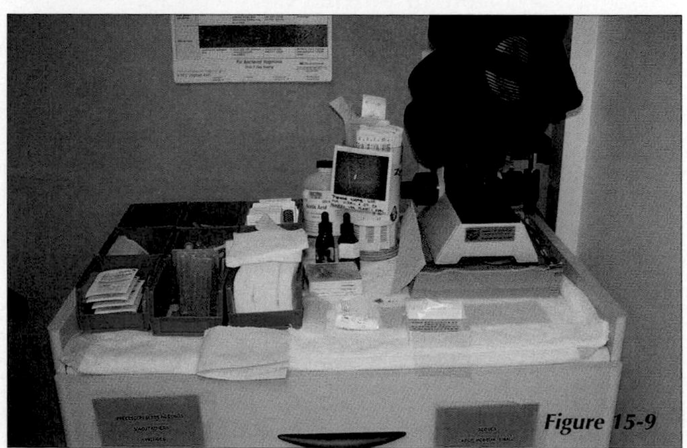

***Figure 15-9.*** *Evidence collection supplies can be transported by cart, which is especially useful for adolescent evaluations.*

Chapter 16

# Documentation of Neglect

Randell Alexander, MD, PhD

Neglect is the most common type of child abuse documented by child protective services. Unlike physical and sexual abuse, neglect does not typically occur as a discrete episode. Instead, it is more chronic and pervasive. Injuries from neglect tend to be developmental and emotional. As a result, they are harder to document and diagnose visually. Neglect is difficult to define since many aspects of neglect depend upon cultural definitions. For example, if a small child who was not properly restrained were injured in an automobile crash, this child would be considered a victim of neglect. However, 40 years ago, restraining a small child in a moving vehicle was not the cultural expectation and the same injury would be considered an accident. Neglect consists of, but is not limited to: denial of proper food, clothing, and shelter; lack of proper supervision; failure to seek or follow through with significant medical care; emotional abuse or neglect; improper restraint (eg, chemical restraint such as medicines to make a child sleepy); and educational neglect.

Investigations of neglect may reveal unsanitary living conditions and practices, such as the use of old formula in baby bottles. These types of conditions can be photographed. Sometimes video documentation is preferred since a 2-dimensional picture rarely conveys information as well as moving images. This is especially true for issues of depth, in which a heightened appreciation of all 3 dimensions is necessary. The other advantage of video is that it records dynamic change over time. For example, a videotape of a chronically neglected child seen in the ER may show the apparent depression, flat affect, and delayed responsiveness that may not be conveyed in photographs.

However, supervisory neglect, administration of medicines to alter behavior (chemical restraint), emotional neglect/abuse, and medical neglect are not conducive to visual diagnosis or documentation. The means to document them is almost entirely written or verbal—by interview, psychological testing, or review of the medical, service, or educational records. The inherent difficulty of visually documenting these types of neglect make them more problematical for others to appreciate. For example, in court, jurors may not gain a firm understanding of the lack of supervision in the home and its significance, even though it was readily apparent to the Child Protective Services worker. Tools to better document these forms of neglect await further development, but understanding of all forms of neglect are generally aided by prompt assessment and whatever forms of documentation that can be employed.

When neglected children are initially discovered, it should be a common practice to obtain a detailed developmental assessment by a knowledgeable and qualified team. While in foster care or the hospital, accelerated development can be the key to documenting harm suffered by children, providing measurable evidence that supports prosecution. When careful developmental documentation is not obtained in the early stages of development, many children remain in neglectful home situations or in foster care. Younger children exhibit more visible signs of neglect than older children.

For example, the neglect of 3-year-old children is much more salient than that of 8 year olds who have the ability to tend to themselves to a larger degree. These children can find food for themselves but younger children depend upon their parents for nourishment. By taking care of their basic needs to some degree, older children have the ability to ward off some of the most obvious signs of neglect.

Growth is more commonly documented visually. While failure to thrive (FTT) means far more than failure to grow, growth can be an excellent indicator of maltreatment. The most recent growth charts by the Centers for Disease Control and Prevention (CDC) can be obtained from their Web site: www.cdc.gov/growthcharts. The Web site contains individual as well as clinical charts that combine multiple charts on the same sheet of paper. Although the figures in this chapter represent ranges from the 5th to 95th percentiles, charts can also be obtained from the CDC Web site illustrating ranges from the 3rd to 97th percentiles.

## Normative Charts

The standardized chart for boys and girls in **Figures 16-1** and **16-2** records weight and length for age cycle from birth to 36 months. Infants must be measured by length, since they cannot stand and must be lain down to record their length. Length is slightly longer than height because of gravity but the difference between them is most noticeable in adults. It is important to note that health care providers must not round infants' ages to the nearest month because the growth of infants is very fast in this stage. However, an age adjustment is required for premature children; for example, a child who was born 8 weeks premature and is now 6 months old should be plotted for an adjusted age of 4 months.

Boys and girls do not grow at the same rate, as indicated in a comparison of **Figures 16-1** and **16-2**. This trend of growing at different rates is magnified in adolescence. Values are shown for the percentiles between the 5th and 95th but certain children who are normal will exceed or fall short of these ranges. Consideration of parental height, siblings, and other medical factors is necessary to determine whether values outside of the standard range are normal. Definitions for FTT that refer to crossing 2 or more percentile lines on these charts are unscientific and should be replaced with more meaningful language.

Plotting of head circumference for age and weight for length is necessary (**Figures 16-2** and **16-3**). While sometimes overlooked, a rapidly increasing head size may be a sign of an intracranial process such as a chronic subdural hemorrhage. Weight for length is important because analyzing weight for age or length for age alone merely compares against a normative sample of other children of the same age. For FTT, the issue is usually whether the child's weight fits the child's length (ie, the child is too thin or too fat), which can usually be seen in trends over time. In rare instances, neglect may be present when parents of an obese child do not cooperate with medical efforts to lose weight and reduce/avoid medical complications. The weight-for-length chart is useful in illustrating this problem as well as failure to grow, particularly if it shows the trend over time.

There are no known charts that document head circumference for length or height alone. Although head size contributes significantly to the length of infants, a small or large head is not an adequate measure of comparison among similarly aged children. A more accurate measurement would reflect whether children's heads fit their own skeletons in terms of length or height or deviate from their overall skeletal growth.

The corresponding stature-for-age and weight-for-age charts for older children overlap the previously discussed charts that go to 36 months, as seen in **Figures 16-5** and **16-6**, which show boys and girls from age 2 through 20 years old. However, there may be slight differences when plotted on one chart or the other. The charts for children up to 36 months of age are primarily based on length while the child is lying down, while the corresponding charts for children over the age of 36 months are based on height while the child is standing up. Note that the difference between measuring in height and measuring in length is significantly exhibited when plotted (see **Figures 16-7** and **16-8** for the corresponding weight-for-stature chart in boys and girls over 36 months of age).

In using normative charts for children from the age of 2 years through 20, it is important to fully understand the difference in the data for boys and girls. While girls' charts usually correspond to boys' charts, weight and stature at 20 years of age are considerably less for girls.

Charts documenting body mass index (BMI) for age (**Figures 16-9** and **16-10**) are an alternative to documenting weight for stature. Although it incorporates age as a parameter, it uses BMI for measurement, which is expressed as a relationship of height and weight. BMI = $m/h^2$ where $m$ is weight in kilograms and $h$ is height in meters. The CDC recommends that the BMI charts be used for all children older than 5 years. However, the weight-for-stature charts are intuitive for juries since weight for stature can be read directly off the chart, rather than calculated, as BMI must be. For example, for consideration of obesity in teenage girls, the chart in **Figure 16-10** is helpful by showing representations of normal ranges sufficiently broad to enable comparison to likely presentations of obese teens.

***Figure 16-1.*** *Length- and weight-for-age percentiles for boys from birth to 36 months.*

***Figure 16-2.*** *Length-for-age and weight-for-age percentiles in girls from birth to 36 months.*

***Figure 16-3.*** *Head circumference-for-age and weight-for-length percentiles for boys from birth to 36 months.*

***Figure 16-4.*** *Head circumference-for-age and weight-for-length percentiles in girls from birth to 36 months.*

***Figure 16-5.*** *Stature-for-age and weight-for-age percentiles in boys from 2 to 20 years.*

***Figure 16-6.*** *Stature-for-age and weight-for-age percentiles in girls from 2 to 20 years.*

***Figure 16-7.*** *Weight-for-stature percentiles in boys from 2 to 20 years.*

***Figure 16-8.*** *Weight-for-stature percentiles in girls from 2 to 20 years.*

***Figure 16-9.*** *Body mass index-for-age percentiles for boys from 2 to 20 years.*

***Figure 16-10.*** *Body mass index-for-age percentiles in girls from 2 to 20 years.*

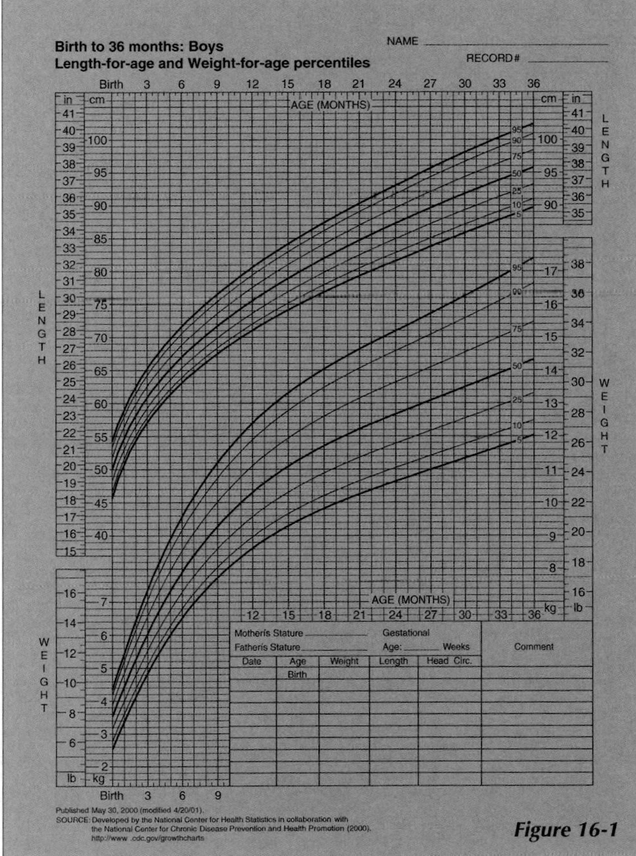


***Figure 16-1***

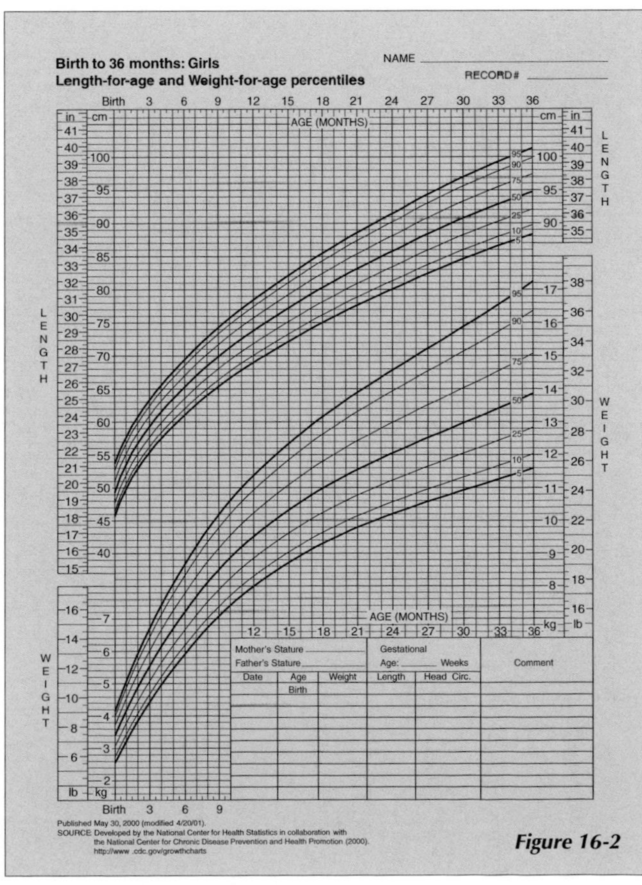


***Figure 16-2***

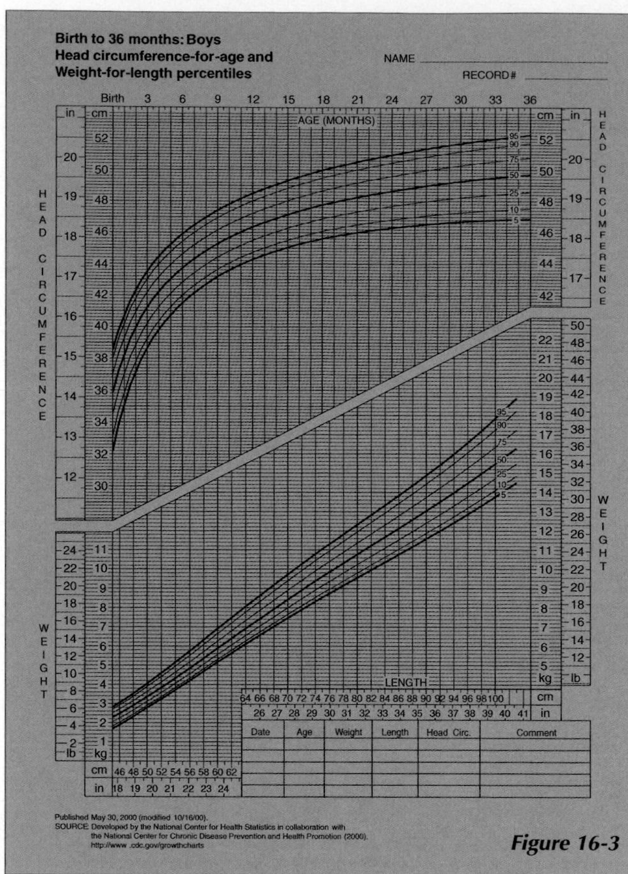

Figure 16-3

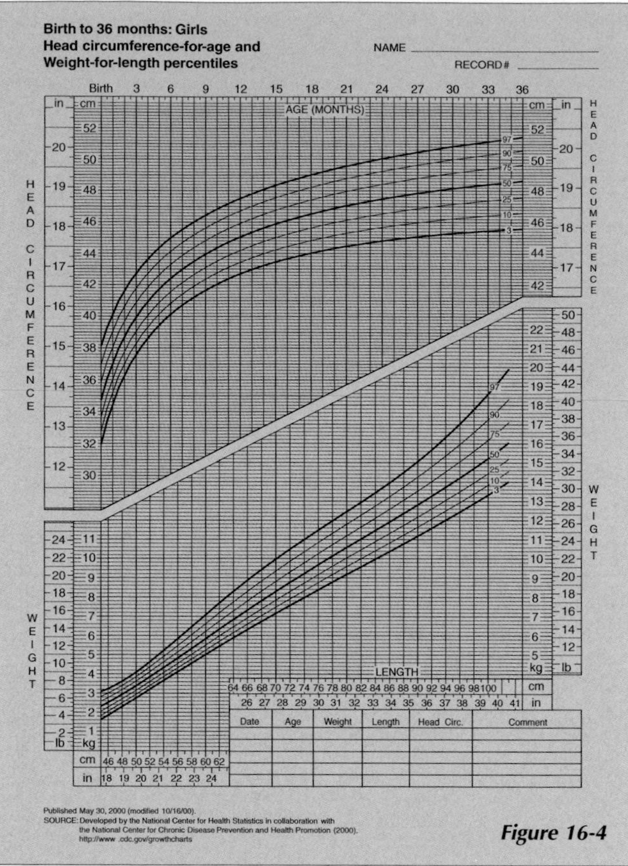

Figure 16-4

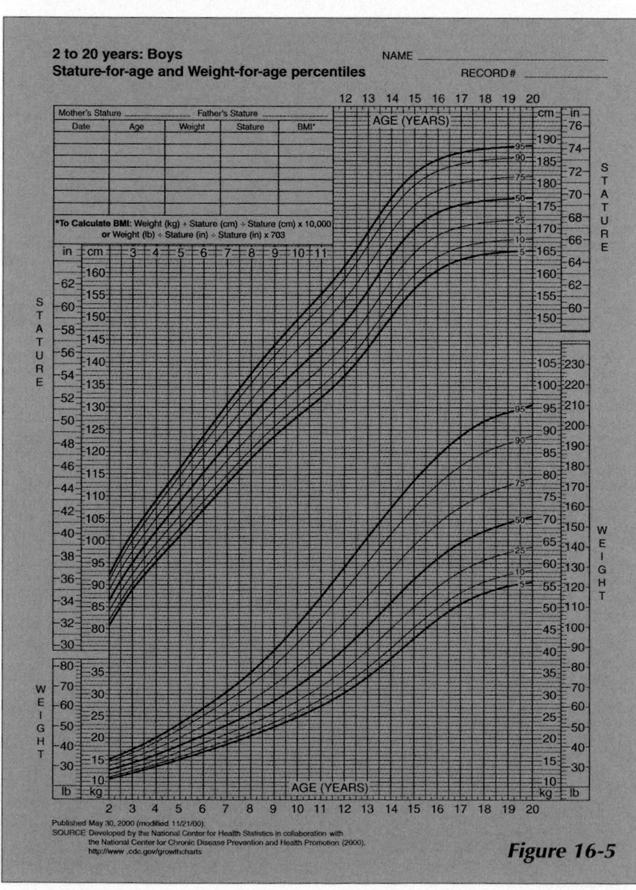

Figure 16-5

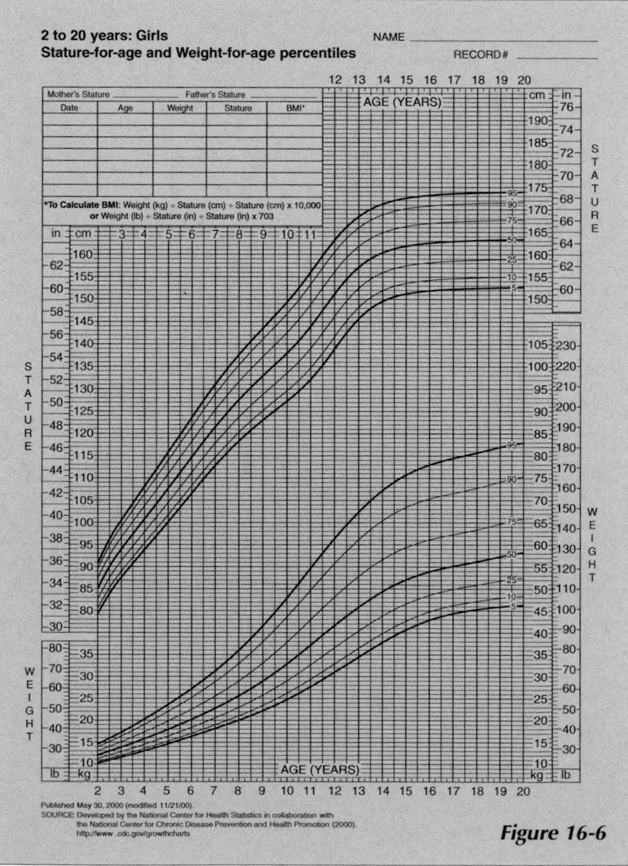

Figure 16-6

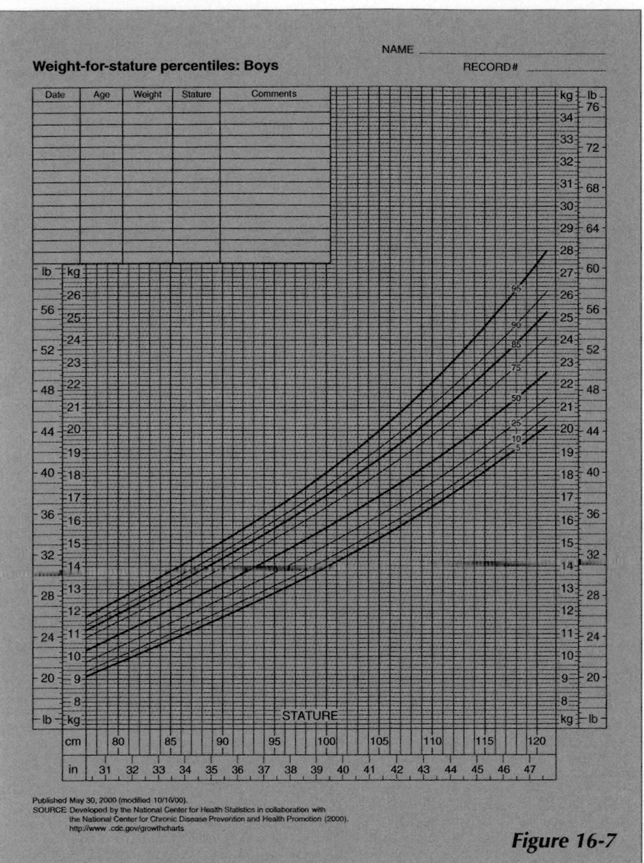


Figure 16-7

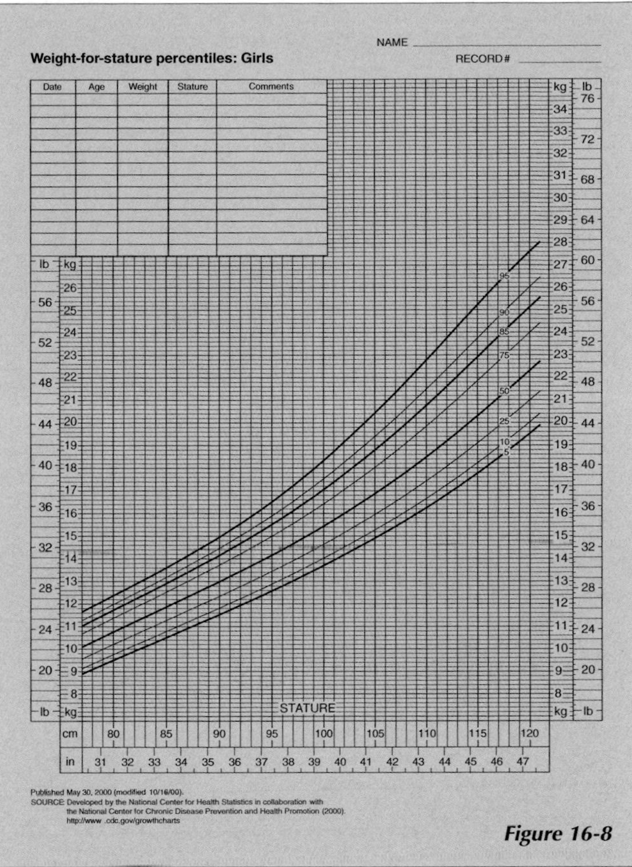


Figure 16-8

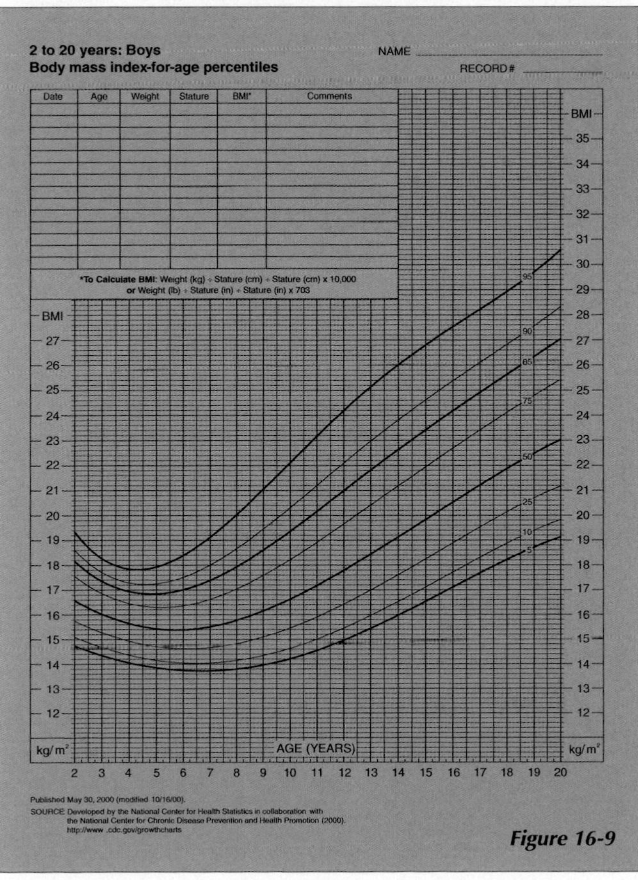


Figure 16-9

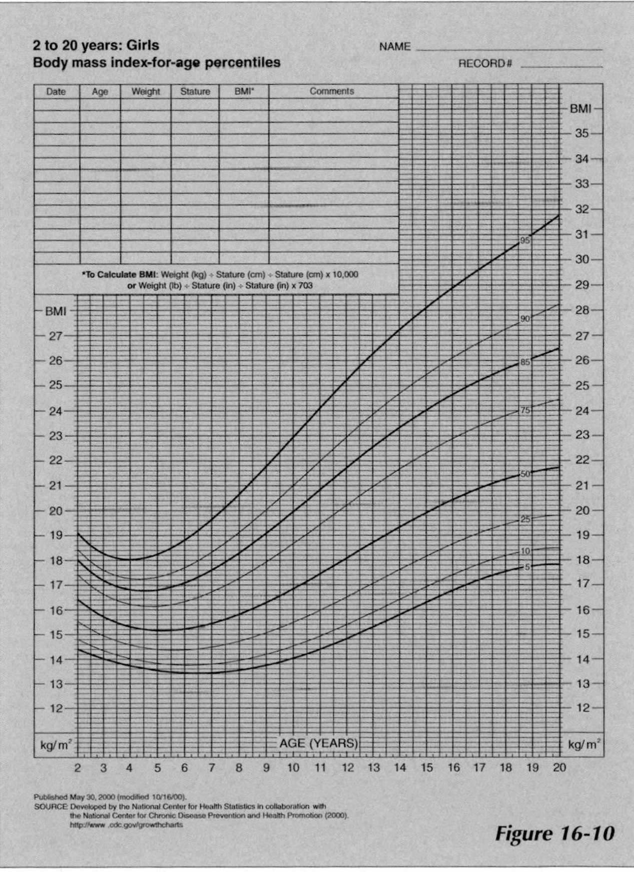


Figure 16-10

# Using charts

**Case Study 16-11**

This 27-month-old child was referred to a forensic pediatrician for FTT. The pediatric resident noted that the child's weight was about three standard deviations below the mean (considerably below the 5th percentile) of weight for age. The first step in the investigation was to verify the figures and the growth chart.

The weight was indeed about 3 standard deviations below the mean. Using the 5th percentile as being approximately 2 standard deviations below the mean, the mean being the 50th percentile, a vertical measurement along the line for 27 months shows that if the distance from the 50th percentile of weight for age to the 5th is 2 standard deviations, then the point labeled A is about 3 standard deviations below the mean. That is, the distance from the average to the 5th percentile should be thought of as approximately 2 units of standard deviation. By extrapolation, the point labeled A would be about 3 units below the average. Whereas many physicians may indicate that FTT is determined by a weight for age below the 5th percentile, the circumstances and extent of this condition may vary considerably. Other factors than weight-for-age percentiles should be considered in the diagnosis of FTT.

In **Figure 16-11-a**, point A represents the weight-for-age measurement of this child. The weight age was determined by drawing a horizontal line to the left until it intersected the 50th percentile at point B. By using this method, the child was determined to have a weight age of 11 months, meaning that the child's weight was that of an average 11-month-old. Noting that the child's length-for-age measurement (point C) was well below the 5th percentile, it was necessary to use a similar method to determine the child's length age, which was determined to be 13 months (point D). By using these additional metrics, it was determined that the child's weight of 10 kilograms was between the 25th and 50th percentiles for a 13-month-old. While the child's weight seemed well below normal for its age, the child was not underweight for length.

**Figure 16-11-b** illustrates an alternative method for evaluating this data. By plotting the weight-for-length measurement as point *E* on the bottom chart, the child was determined to be at an ideal weight for length since the measurements intersected at the 50th percentile.

By using the upper chart, the head circumference-for-age measurement (point *F*) was determined to be below the 5th percentile and possibly abnormal. By using the same method described to discern the weight age, the head circumference age was determined to be about 11 months (point *G*). When compared to the length age of 13 months, the child's head circumference of 46 centimeters fell between the 25th and 50th percentiles.

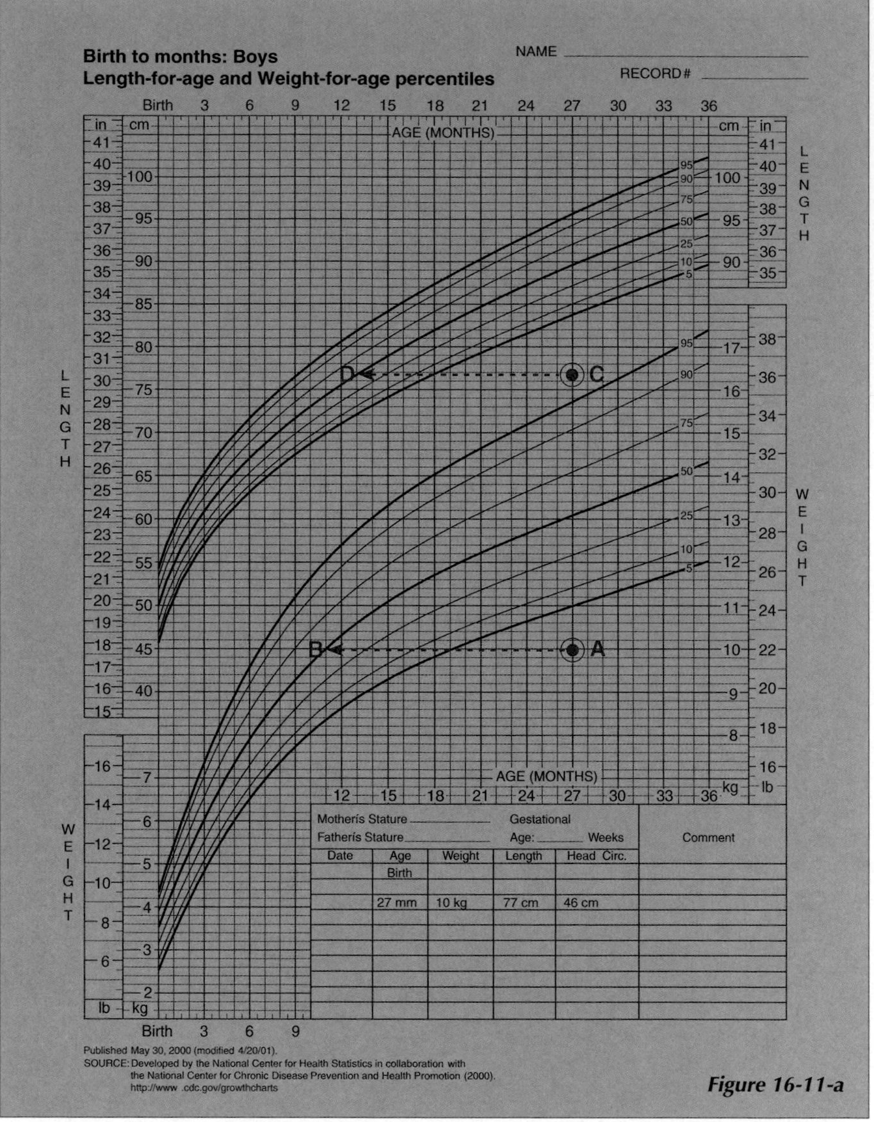


*Figure 16-11-a*

# USING CHARTS

**Case Study 16-11** *(continued)*

The pediatric resident erroneously relied on one calculation: weight for age. An initial inspection of the graphs might have indicated that the child's weight, length, and head circumference are all below normal, but this was only in relationship to age. The comparisons of head circumference, weight-for-length age, and direct plotting of weight-for-length revealed that weight and head circumference were well within the mid-range for the child's length. Trends should have been checked with any available prior growth measurements taken in a clinic or primary care physician's office.

The problem with this child was most likely not FTT, but short stature. The differences in the medical workup and social implications between FTT and short stature are considerable and merited analysis of additional growth parameters.

***Figure 16-11-a.*** *Length-for-age and weight-for-age percentiles for the 27-month-old subject.*

***Figure 16-11-b.*** *Head circumference-for-age and weight-for-length percentiles for 27-month-old subject.*

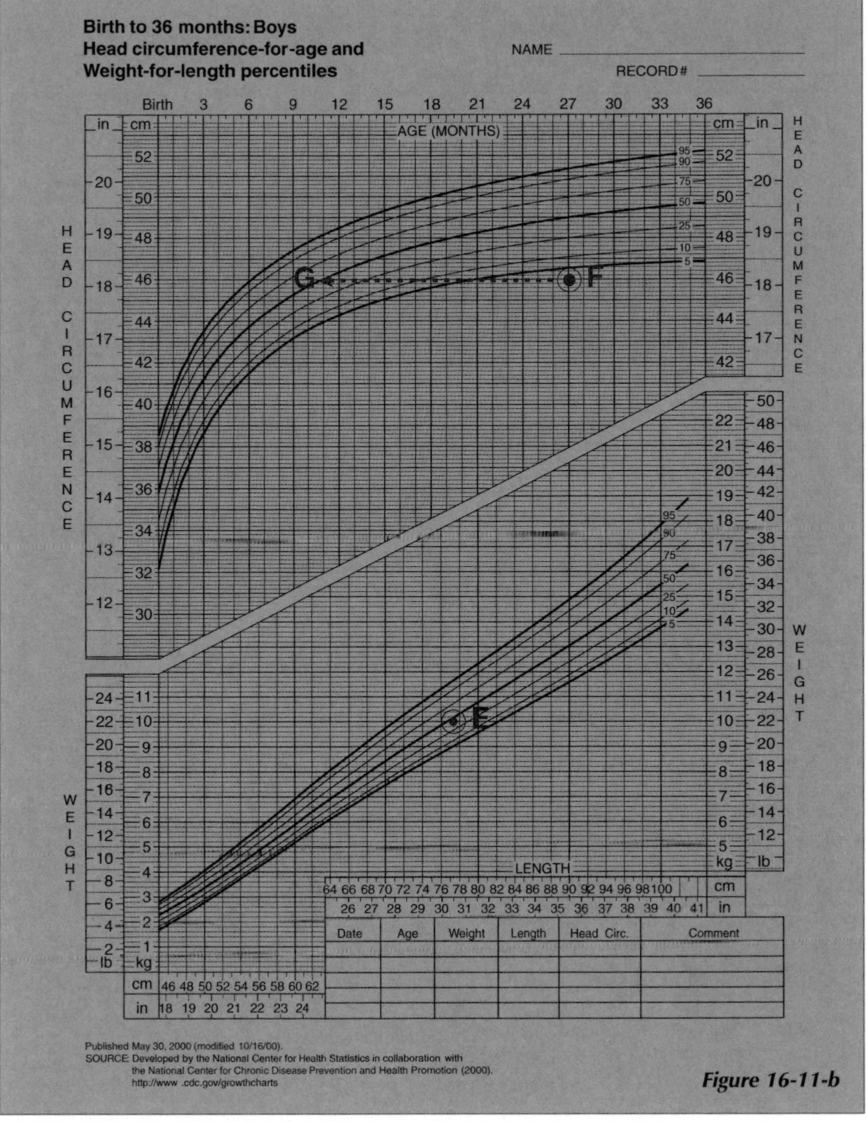

*Figure 16-11-b*

# USING CHARTS

**Case Study 16-12**

This girl was originally thought to be underweight or suffering from FTT as a result of only one measurement of weight-for-age at the age of 6 months.

Two important analyses contradicted this interpretation. A first analysis of the weight-for-length chart (not shown) illustrated that the child's weight was within the normal range, a trend not especially consistent with FTT. The weight gain had been constant and paralleled the standard growth rates of other children. When reviewed over a 36-month period, the child's weight was determined to be "constitutionally" at these particular percentile lines. That is, this child was innately lightweight compared to other children her age—possibly because of genetic or normal variations. In cases of FTT, most analyses of weight gain will produce a fluctuating, flat, or downward trendline, and not a smooth upward curve (**Figure 16-12**).

A second analysis of length for age revealed a similar pattern of parallel growth falling beneath the 5th percentile, indicating constitutional (ie, inherent) short stature that might have normalized at a later age, or that the child would grow to be a short adult. Subsequent decreases in the rate of linear growth warranted consultation with Pediatric Endocrinology.

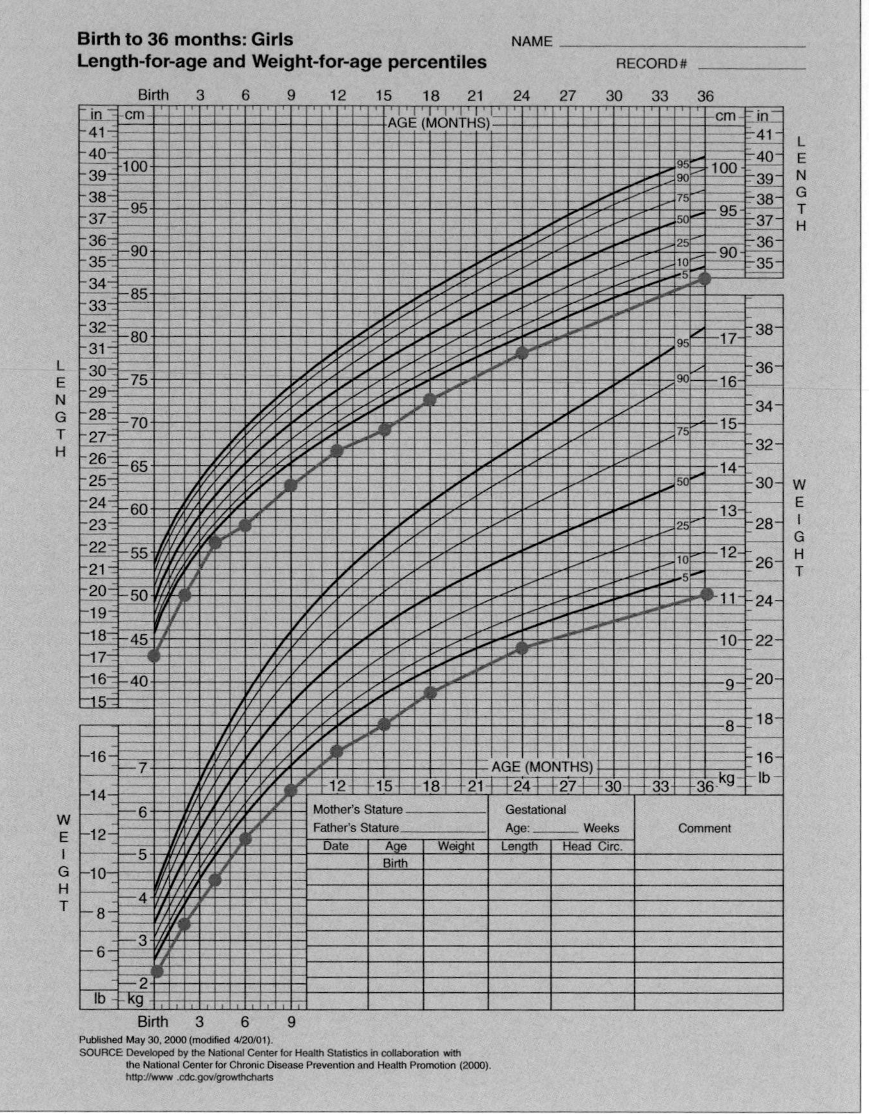


***Figure 16-12.*** *Length-for-age and weight-for-age percentile analyses for subject.*

# USING CHARTS

### Case Study 16-13

By 18 months of age, weight-for-age for this child increased at a much slower rate than expected from approximately 9 months of age. However, when replotted as weight-for-length (not shown), the weight was slightly above the 50th percentile. It was initially hypothesized that this case could have been the result of physiological or parental problems; however, this decline in the rate of weight gain is a relatively common pattern seen in pediatrics.

By 9 to 12 months of age, most children will exert increasing control over their bottle and other oral intake, which will subvert a parent that frequently uses the bottle to quiet a crying child. Once children gain this degree of control, the weight-for-age percentile begins to normalize to the child's genetic predisposition, which may be around the 25th percentile. Although it is common to see a child drop down in percentiles by 9 to 12 months of age, careful monitoring is necessary to ensure normal behavioral adjustment rather than medical concern.

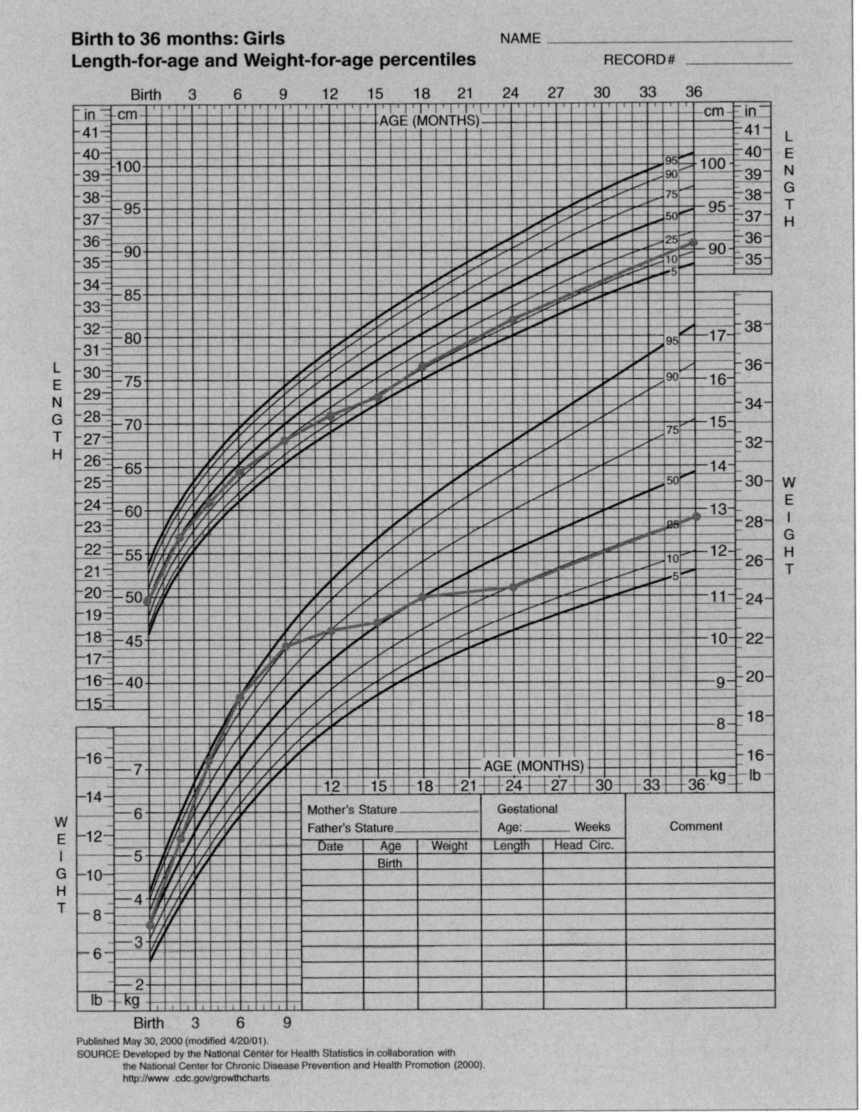


***Figure 16-13.*** *Length-for-age and weight-for-age percentiles in this girl from birth to 36 months.*

# Using charts

### Case Study 16-14

The length-for-age measurement for this infant was relatively normal and constant over time; however, the weight-for-age measurement showed marked peaks and valleys.

In the parent's care, the infant failed to gain weight after 2 months of age—a medically dangerous situation. Admitted to the hospital (point *A*), the child gained weight with normal nursing care. The child was sent home with instructions for the parent regarding feeding. By point *B*, the child had lost most of the weight gained in the hospital. Admitted again, the child experienced extraordinary catch-up weight gain with normal feeding. At this point, the child should have been placed in foster care as a result of 2 failed attempts by the parents to feed the child adequately. Instead, the child was sent home and again lost weight. Admitted a third time (point *C*), the child flourished in the hospital and was then sent to foster care. In this case, a period of observation and normal feeding proved to be more beneficial than a battery of laboratory tests.

When the weight gain for a child with FTT significantly exceeds the normal rate seen in other children of the same age, abnormal weight gain is known as *catch-up growth.* When children feed in the hospital but gain weight slowly, they may require more than the calculated number of calories. Instead of 120 kcal/kg/day, they may need 150, 170, or even up to 200 kcal/kg/day to begin growing. This sometimes entails feeding children all they want until either good growth occurs or just short of the point that may induce vomiting or diarrhea. The goal is to exceed normal intake by whatever means necessary to induce growth.

In this case, the presence of a physiological problem of consequence was irrelevant. Since the child could grow at a normal rate with normal feeding, parental inadequacy was evident and physiological problems were not investigated. In such cases of FTT, significant harm is possible, including a high risk of brain damage and/or death. This type of case represents a serious medical problem that should be addressed by Child Protective Services (CPS) immediately.

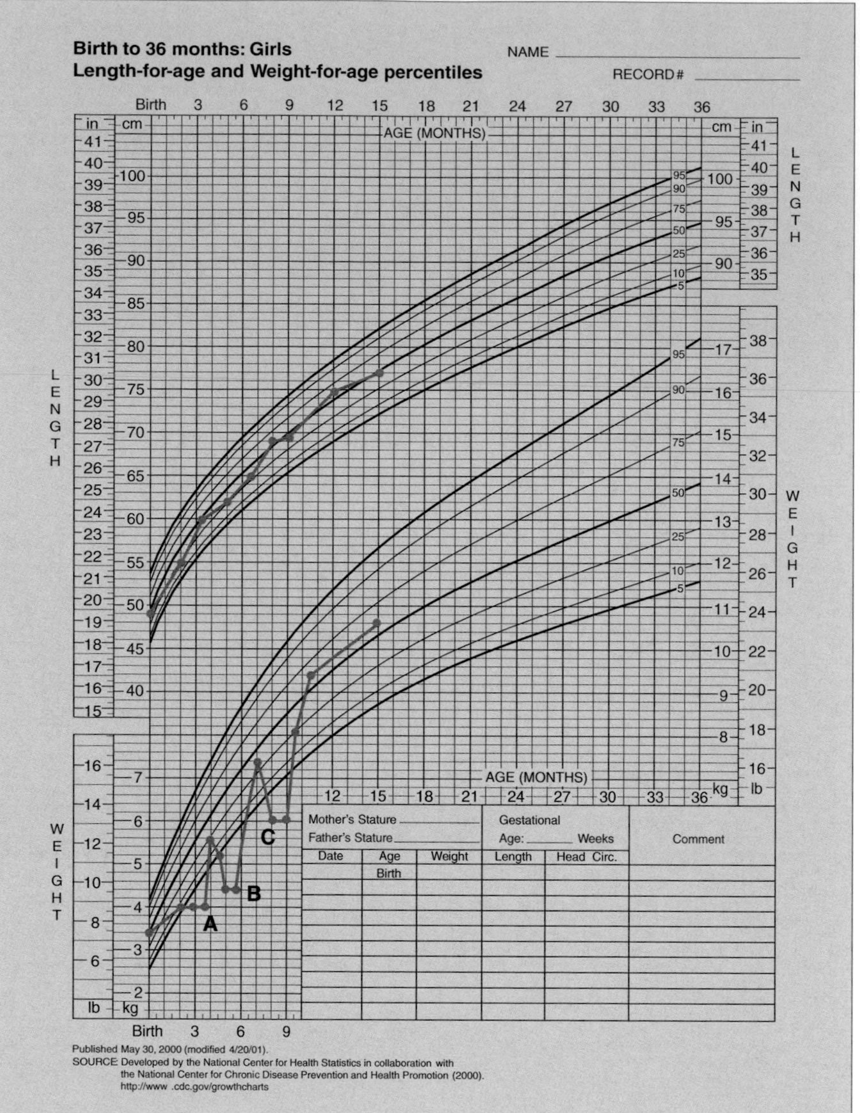


***Figure 16-14.*** *Length-for-age and weight-for-age percentiles in this girl.*

Chapter 17

# DEMONSTRATIONS

Randell Alexander, MD, PhD

Demonstrations are useful in a variety of contexts. They can be very helpful in teaching students and professionals who are not knowledgeable of child abuse issues. Demonstrations may also be useful in the courtroom to help teach the judge or jury about concepts that are difficult to describe. A key concept is that words do not convey some information as well as a visual demonstration.

Dr. Charles Johnson developed a demonstration in which a pretzel is used to illustrate the effect of different forces in causing types of bone fractures (**Figures 17-1-a, b, c,** and **d**). Note that transverse and spiral fractures are not predictive of whether the cause is abusive or accidental. The history for the injury must be compared against the medical and developmental findings.

Lawyers frequently use posters that enlarge a photograph, piece of text, or other key points for the jury. In some courts, electronic imaging is used to display an image on a television set or large screen. Computers are increasingly being employed for PowerPoint presentations of photographs and text. A few courtrooms have added small television screens for each juror, similar to what is available in some first-class seating on airplanes. The usage of such demonstrations is likely to increase as they have proven to be effective.

Using a doll in court to demonstrate shaking can be very helpful. Words and pictures understate the degree of violence and force, which is a very important consideration for jurors. Judges, jurors, and medical students frequently think in terms of "jiggle" baby syndrome and seriously underestimate the forces involved in shaken baby syndrome (SBS).

In doll demonstrations, experts attempt to convey what they feel is important in SBS (**Figures 17-2-a, b,** and **c**); therefore, they are accurate for that purpose. These demonstrations, however, merely illustrate a concept, and are not exact replications of what may occur in a specific case. The jury must still decide if they believe any portion of a witness's testimony. Physicians should not perform doll demonstrations unless they are experts in SBS.

A teddy bear may also be employed to approximate the motions that occur in SBS while not resembling an actual child (**Figures 17-3-a, b,** and **c**). This substitution may be more emotionally palatable, but the ease of the demonstration is possibly achieved at the expense of not thoroughly conveying the traumatic nature of the event for the child.

Should a prosecutor elect to use such a demonstration, it is important to correctly frame the questions to the expert to avoid any misrepresentation of what is being offered. It must be made clear that the demonstration is not an exact replica of the events that took place, but rather a visual representation of a concept that applies to the events of the case. In cases of SBS, experts must deal with the range of the number of shakes that are required to produce an injury and cannot know exactly how many occur in a specific instance. The following example illustrates the limitations in the phrasing of the questions that can be asked:

Q: Doctor, are mere words alone sufficient to convey the nature of the forces involved in shaken baby syndrome?

A: No. It is common that the forces are underestimated when only a verbal description of shaken baby syndrome is offered.

Q: Doctor, would a doll demonstration help the jury to better understand the nature of the forces involved in shaken baby syndrome?

A: Yes.

Q: Please demonstrate to the jury using this doll.

A: {*Witnesses may then hold a doll, teddy bear, or other representation of an infant, and may then gently shake the doll, toss it in the air, and bounce it on their knee while describing that this type of activity does not cause the injuries being discussed. The doll is then shaken* violently *5 to 10 times back and forth. Witnesses should emphasize in their remarks that the nature of the forces involved in shaken baby syndrome would be similar to this.*}

Q: Doctor, in this case, would the forces have been similar to what you just demonstrated?

A: Yes.

Note that the first three questions refer to the general concept of the forces, while the last asks for similarity to the case in question. Because it is not a duplication of what occurred, it is not necessary for the doll to be the same weight and length as the infant in question, nor is it necessary for the doll to have a circulating blood stream or resemble any biological functions. Numerous courts have upheld these demonstrations, but it is suggested that only qualified doctors familiar with SBS perform them.

***Figure 17-1-a.*** *The pretzel is being held with pressure at the ends with the thumb opposing this force by pushing the other way.*

***Figure 17-1-b.*** *The result is a break straight across the pretzel. This corresponds to a transverse fracture of a bone, such as an infant femur, in which each end of the bone may be held, or one end suddenly flexed as the rest of the body acts as inertial weight.*

***Figure 17-1-c.*** *This time the pretzel is being twisted at each end.*

***Figure 17-1-d.*** *The result is an oblique fracture of the pretzel, which corresponds to a spiral fracture of a bone. Some element of twisting is present when falling onto an outstretched leg or arm (eg, falling from a large height and trying to land standing up on a leg). The torque induced by the body not being centered along the long axis of the bone causes a twist. In young children a child might be yanked up by an extremity and, with the body as a counterweight, a fracture may occur. Considerable force, not just rough handling, would be needed to cause this type of fracture.*

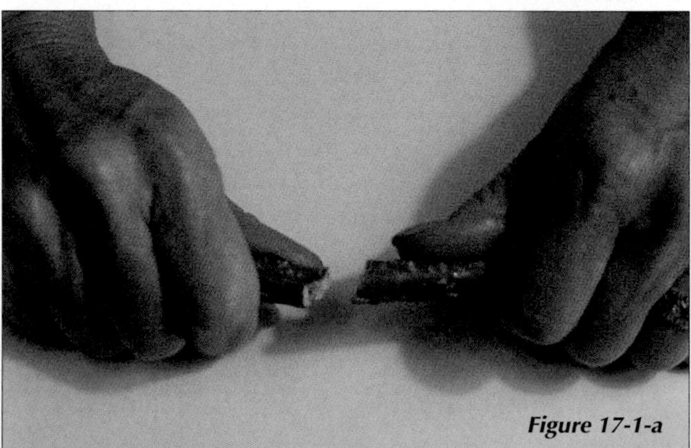

**Figure 17-1-a**

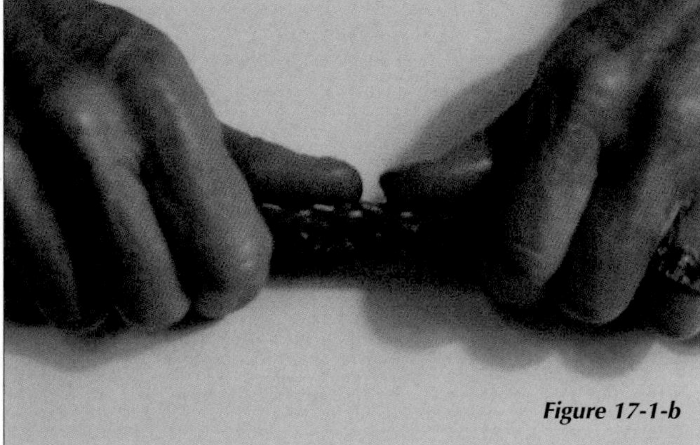

**Figure 17-1-b**

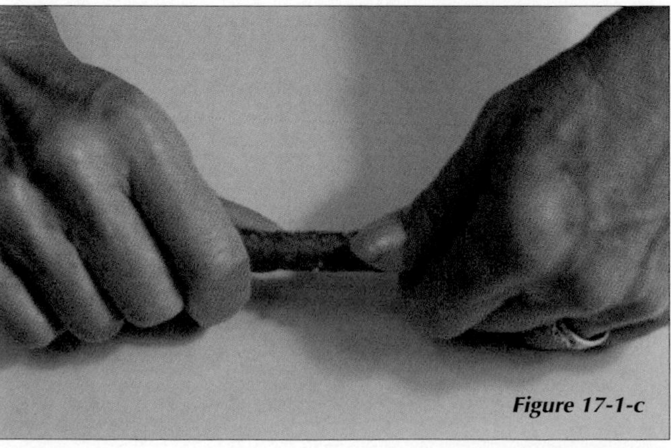

**Figure 17-1-c**

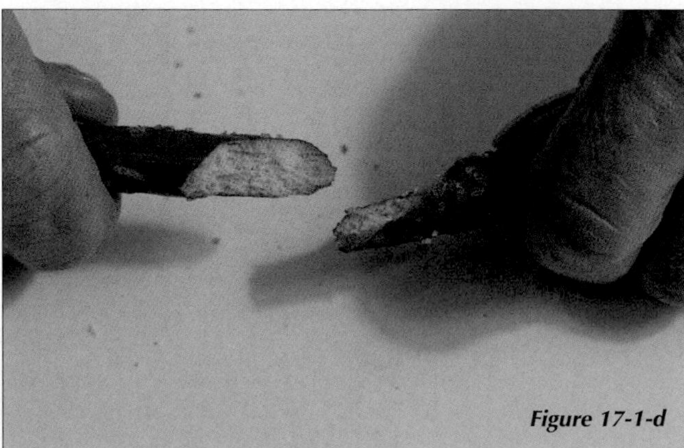

**Figure 17-1-d**

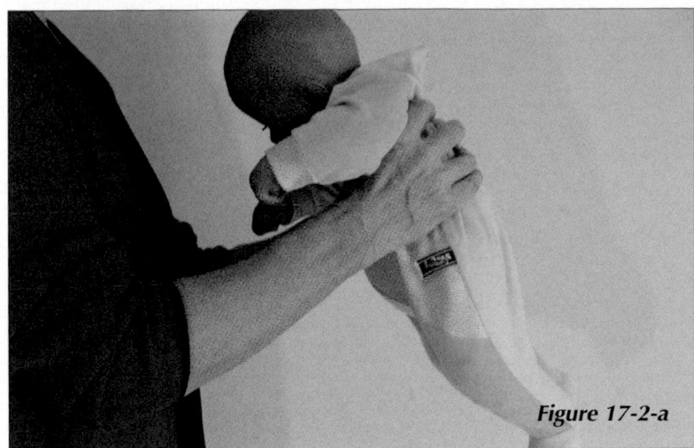
Figure 17-2-a

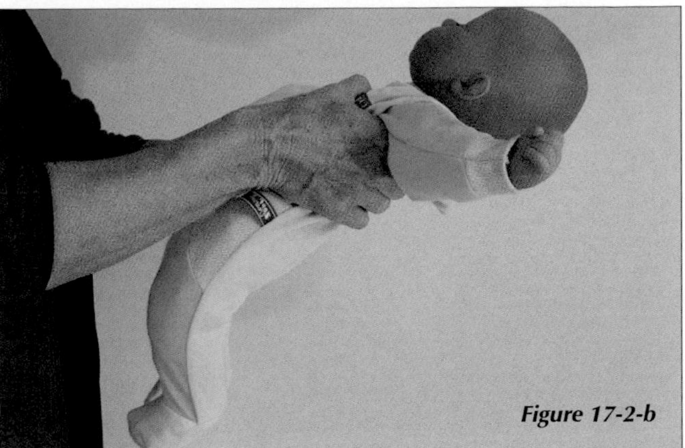
Figure 17-2-b

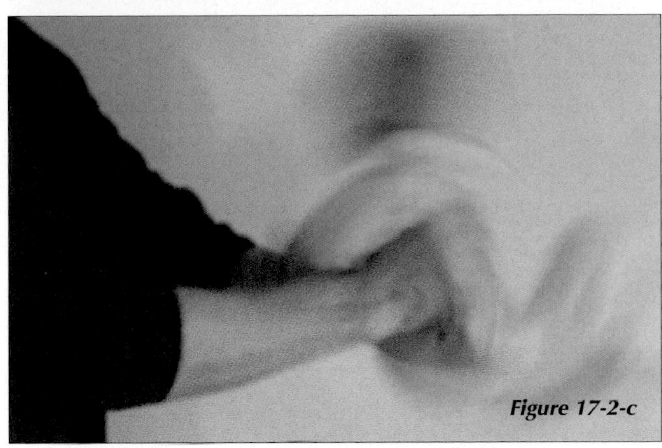
Figure 17-2-c

***Figure 17-2-a.*** *During shaking, the child is almost always held under the arms facing the perpetrator. In this position, the child is held close to the perpetrator's chest.*

***Figure 17-2-b.*** *During shaking, the child is extended away from the perpetrator. Complex, multidirectional motions of the head and movement of the child's body during the course of being shaken make 2-dimensional biomechanical representations simplistic and erroneous.*

***Figure 17-2-c.*** *Properly weighted dolls tend to be shaken about 2½ to 3 cycles per second, with a full shaking cycle being one complete motion back and forth.*

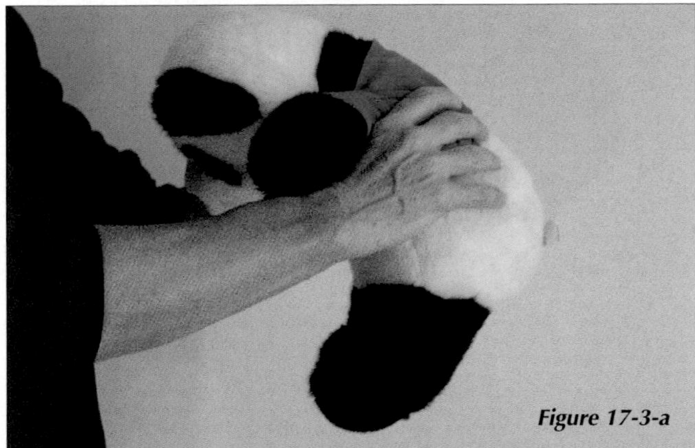
Figure 17-3-a

***Figure 17-3-a.*** *Teddy bear held close, as a child would be in preparation for shaking.*

***Figure 17-3-b.*** *Teddy bear held away.*

***Figure 17-3-c.*** *Teddy bear illustrating the shaking motion.*

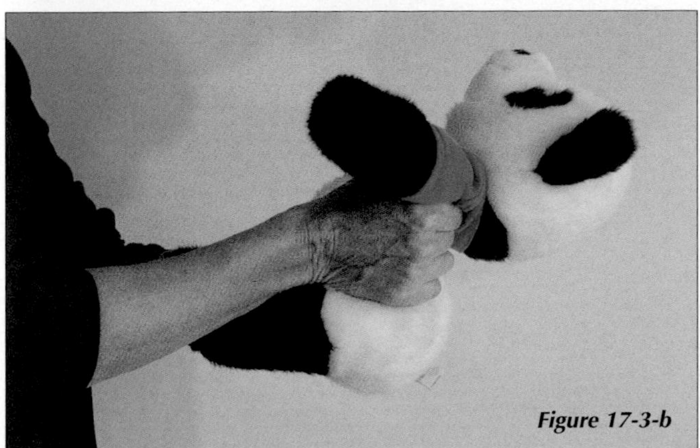
Figure 17-3-b

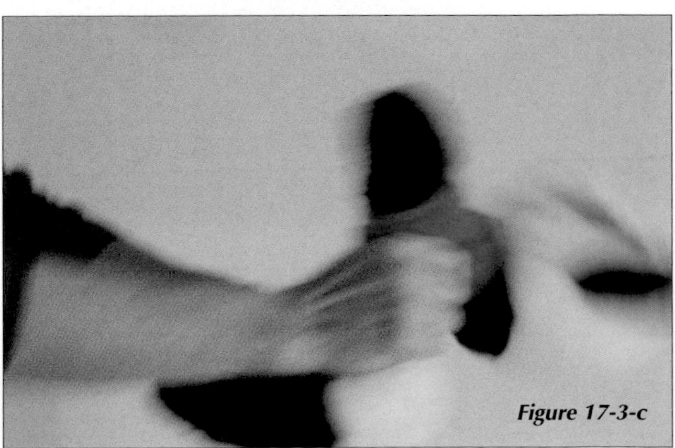
Figure 17-3-c

Chapter 18

# PREVENTION

Sandra Alexander, MEd

## THE PROMISE OF PREVENTION: CHALLENGES AND APPROACHES

Across the country, day after day, thousands of children are abused and neglected physically, sexually, and emotionally. They are hit, kicked, burned, shaken, fondled, threatened, belittled, starved, ignored, and left alone. Child abuse is robbing children of their childhood, shattering their self-esteem, and sometimes taking their lives. Abuse teaches children that it is acceptable to hurt other people, particularly those who are smaller and weaker, and it fosters the development of the next generation of abusive and emotionally harmed adults as well as adults with a host of health problems and early mortality.[26,27] Additionally, child abuse costs billions of dollars each year to treat and respond to victims while adding to long-term health and social costs in the future.[28] These elements contribute to a vicious and repetitive cycle of abuse. More and more children are robbed of their childhood and their opportunity to reach their full potential as competent, productive members of the community.

How has society responded to this tragedy? Policymakers and the public generally agree that keeping children from being abused in the first place is the best response. For many years, concerned organizations and individuals have experimented with various programs with the goal of preventing abuse. These programs work to teach and support parents, to equip children with personal safety and violence prevention skills, to educate the public about abuse, to advocate for policies and practices that support parents, and to prevent teen pregnancies, among a host of other strategies to prevent abuse. While early efforts are lacking in outcome data, there is now a growing body of data pointing to effective strategies for prevention. Yet, despite these laudable efforts, children continue to be abused and neglected in staggering numbers. The only way to change this predictable cycle is to treat child abuse just as we do other public health problems—with a strong prevention strategy.

### CHALLENGES IN DELIVERY OF PREVENTION PROGRAMS

A number of factors—including the nature of abuse itself, the way prevention is defined, the context in which prevention programs operate, and the way programs have developed—have created challenges for delivering effective prevention programs and provided lessons to guide future prevention endeavors.

While everyone wants to prevent abuse, there is not always a consensus of opinion about what prevention means. For some, prevention is something that happens after a child has been abused to keep abuse from occurring again and to help the child recover from the trauma (***tertiary prevention***). For others, prevention means keeping abuse from happening in the first place by targeting efforts to the general population (***primary prevention***) or to children and families at risk of abuse (***secondary prevention***). Responses to child abuse have been traditionally tertiary in nature, occurring after abuse has occurred with the goal of preventing future abuse. Policy and funding priorities have reflected support for intervention and treatment with only small percentages of federal and state funding to bolster pri-mary and secondary prevention efforts. This imbalance has led to a child protection system that is struggling to keep up with the growing numbers of abused children and is in danger of collapsing on itself. While it is important to prevent children from being reabused, tertiary efforts alone will not solve the problem.

Because the response systems (eg, child protection, law enforcement, juvenile court, mental health) are so overburdened with heavy caseloads, they are too busy dealing with the crisis to focus on building prevention systems. In fact, primary and secondary prevention efforts have sometimes been regarded as "fluff" that must take a back seat to the more important job of diagnosing and treating abuse. When done at all, it has been left up to "those prevention folks," usually small nonprofit organizations with limited resources and influence.

Abuse is a complex and emotionally charged issue. Without a full understanding of this, prevention programs risk oversimplifying, overcommitting, and failing to recognize that negative outcomes for children have multiple and interactive elements.

When an abuse tragedy occurs in the community and receives wide media coverage and public attention, there is a tendency to respond with a "quick fix" or "feel-good" solution that may have limited or no significant impact on preventing abuse. These responses often lead to decisions that are not informed by research and/or the implementation of a proven model with changes that can alter or dilute its effectiveness without objective evaluation.

Many prevention programs are considered effective if they increase knowledge in a particular area. In fact, this is the most easily designed and measured prevention strategy. However, prevention programs with the greatest potential for success are both knowledge- and motivation-based with the goal of influencing and changing behavior.

Because of the nature of funding streams, politics, and the often grass-root development of prevention efforts, programs have developed in a pattern of fragmented, isolated, duplicative, and small short-lived efforts that reach a limited number of people. As a result, numerous pilot programs exist, few of which are ever able to reach enough people to determine if they have a significant impact.

For many years, it was acceptable to simply "do good work" in prevention. Funding was driven into direct services, and accountability for outcomes, while desirable, was not a top priority. This situation led to some ineffective programs that continued to replicate without research to support their effectiveness. At the same time, some programs were labeled ineffective and were defunded or discontinued without ever learning if they had merit. In some cases programs lost funding and support for not producing stellar outcome results, thereby losing the opportunity to use the information learned in the evaluation to increase the potential for positive outcomes for participants.

Public campaigns have increased awareness of the issue and encouraged the reporting of suspected abuse. A remaining challenge is designing campaigns that use strategic framing and social marketing to move beyond awareness and reporting to motivate significant action and behavior change that results in prevention.

### Range of Prevention Programs

Even with significant challenges, creative, determined, and courageous prevention advocates in all kinds of organizations and settings have created and sustained a broad spectrum of prevention programs across the country. These programs include public awareness activities, skill-based curricula for children, parent education programs and support groups, home visitation programs, respite and crisis care programs, and family resource centers. Several organizations and programs—including Prevent

Child Abuse America, Family Support America, Healthy Families America, Parents Anonymous Inc, Minnesota Early Learning Design (MELD), Stop It Now!, The Nurturing Parent Programs by Family Development Resources, The National Center on Shaken Baby Syndrome, the National Exchange Club, and Children's Trust Funds—have taken the lead in making prevention a priority by developing various prevention strategies and supporting prevention programs around the country. Both the US Department of Health and Human Services—through the Children's Bureau, Office of Child Abuse and Neglect (OCAN)—and the US Centers for Disease Control and Prevention (CDC) have recently accelerated efforts to learn more about child abuse prevention and disseminate this information to the field. Organizations such as the American Academy of Pediatrics, Boys and Girls Clubs, Boy Scouts of America, Girl Scouts of the USA, faith-based organizations, coaching organizations for children's sports, and educators have recognized the importance of prevention and have developed specific programs to train their staff and members. Corporations are more aware of the impact of abuse on their workforce and potential customer base, and some are joining foundations such as Freddie Mac and the Doris Duke Charitable Foundation, and others in investing in prevention across the country.

## New Directions in Prevention

As the field evolves and the base of knowledge about abuse and prevention expands, new directions and strategies are taking shape. For example, early child sexual abuse prevention efforts used to focus almost exclusively on teaching children to protect themselves from abuse, but through the leadership and programs of Stop It Now!, there is a growing recognition that stopping abuse is an adult responsibility. There is also a shift from simply trying to change individual behaviors to altering the community and environmental context. Recognizing that parents do best in communities that are strong and have defined and sustained ways of supporting them, new initiatives are being tested to help build these strong communities for prevention. There is also a growing movement to develop and include parent leadership in program design, service delivery, and advocacy. Individuals who have been impacted by abuse are joining together through Authentic Voices and the National Call to Action to mobilize the public to create a greater impact on child abuse prevention.

Child abuse is increasingly recognized as a major public health problem, and a public health approach is being advanced for prevention. There is growing knowledge to support efforts that reach out early to reduce or deter risk factors and promote and build protective factors for prevention. While a majority of prevention efforts have historically focused on changing individual factors and behaviors that result in abuse and violence, there is a growing consensus that prevention must be addressed on all the levels encompassed by the ecological model, which address individuals, relationships, communities and society. The ecological model explores the relationship between these levels and considers abuse as the product of multiple levels of influence on behavior. Understanding how these factors are related to violence is one of the important steps in the public health approach to preventing child abuse and other forms of violence.[29]

Program developers are learning that domestic violence and child abuse cannot be addressed in isolation from one another. The links between early childhood abuse and an increased risk for later violent behavior are solid, and child abuse prevention programming for children now may include teaching empathy, anger management, impulse control, how to deal with bullies, as well as personal safety messages such as "Say no, get away, and tell someone."

Prevention programs are increasingly incorporating evaluation and outcome measures from implementation and are requiring replication that ensures quality and integrity of the model. Existing and developing prevention programs are well served by using the growing body of research to guide their programming.

New knowledge is starting to reshape the way public awareness campaigns reach out to the public and policy makers to engage them in prevention. Studies show that the public is now aware of the prevalence and the seriousness of child abuse on a nationwide basis.[30] Yet, public awareness campaigns have not been successful in motivating individuals or communities to change their behavior to focus on prevention. In 2003 Prevent Child Abuse America initiated a strategic frame analysis of child abuse and neglect. The project examined public opinion, communications research, and media coverage to identify effective communication strategies to use when talking about child abuse and neglect. The findings of this project will be used to reframe the issue for the public.[30]

*Figure 18-1-a*

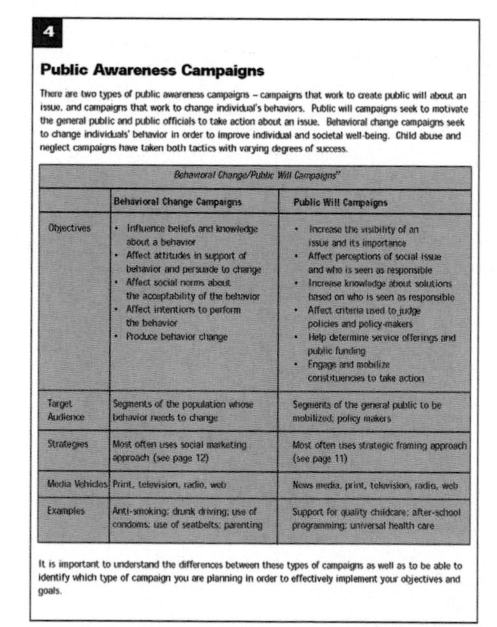

4

**Public Awareness Campaigns**

There are two types of public awareness campaigns – campaigns that work to create public will about an issue, and campaigns that work to change individual's behaviors. Public will campaigns seek to motivate the general public and public officials to take action about an issue. Behavioral change campaigns seek to change individuals' behavior in order to improve individual and societal well-being. Child abuse and neglect campaigns have taken both tactics with varying degrees of success.

| *Behavioral Change/Public Will Campaigns*” | | |
|---|---|---|
| | **Behavioral Change Campaigns** | **Public Will Campaigns** |
| Objectives | • Influence beliefs and knowledge about a behavior<br>• Affect attitudes in support of behavior and persuade to change<br>• Affect social norms about the acceptability of the behavior<br>• Affect intentions to perform the behavior<br>• Produce behavior change | • Increase the visibility of an issue and its importance<br>• Affect perceptions of social issue and who is seen as responsible<br>• Increase knowledge about solutions based on who is seen as responsible<br>• Affect criteria used to judge policies and policy-makers<br>• Help determine service offerings and public funding<br>• Engage and mobilize constituencies to take action |
| Target Audience | Segments of the population whose behavior needs to change | Segments of the general public to be mobilized; policy makers |
| Strategies | Most often uses social marketing approach (see page 12) | Most often uses strategic framing approach (see page 11) |
| Media Vehicles | Print, television, radio, web | News media, print, television, radio, web |
| Examples | Anti-smoking; drunk driving; use of condoms; use of seatbelts; parenting | Support for quality childcare; after-school programming; universal health care |

It is important to understand the differences between these types of campaigns as well as to be able to identify which type of campaign you are planning in order to effectively implement your objectives and goals.

*Figure 18-1-b*

***Figure 18-1-a.*** *Cover page of Prevent Child Abuse North Carolina's Program Advisory Series*—Reframing the Issue: Advice to Professionals on Child Abuse Public Awareness Campaigns.

***Figure 18-1-b.*** *Chart on behavioral change and public will campaigns.*

The way prevention is defined also has been changing in recent years. Researchers in the field of prevention increasingly have turned to a definition of prevention that focuses on the target population instead of or in addition to the traditional primary, secondary and tertiary classification. The new definitional approach groups interventions as either ***universal*** (aimed at the general population or groups without regard to individual risk), ***selected*** (aimed at those considered to be at heightened risk), or ***indicated*** (aimed at those who have already experienced abuse or demonstrated abusive behavior).[29]

This chapter presents only a small sampling of some of the many different programs and strategies that are working to prevent abuse. Readers are encouraged to explore these strategies further as well as inform themselves about other programs that may not be included here.

## PREVENTION STRATEGIES

Public awareness campaigns have long been used to educate the public about child abuse. They take many forms, including public service announcements, print advertisements, press releases, promotional items, videos, special events, and other activities. Generally, public awareness campaigns work to create public will for prevention or work to change individual behaviors.

### PUBLIC AWARENESS AND EDUCATION PREVENTION MESSAGES

The 2004 Program Advisory Series by Prevent Child Abuse North Carolina, *Reframing the Issue: Advice to Professionals on Child Abuse Public Awareness Campaigns* (**Figure 18-1-a**), presents a good summary of past and present public awareness efforts, the differences between behavioral change and public will campaigns (**Figure 18-1-b**), and new directions suggested by the Prevent Child Abuse America reframing project.

### SEXUAL ABUSE

Initial sexual abuse prevention efforts focused on identifying the problem and teaching children to "say no, get away, and tell someone" when confronted with uncomfortable situations. Recognizing that child sexual abuse is an adult problem, Stop It Now! was the first major effort in the country to initiate a campaign identifying the prevention of sexual abuse as an adult responsibility. Through public awareness efforts like the print advertisement in **Figure 18-2**, a toll-free helpline, and other educational and support resources, Stop It Now! reaches out to those who are abusing or know someone who might be abusing. The philosophy of Stop It Now! is being replicated in other sites across the country, including 2 CDC grant pilot sites.

### WARNING SIGNS

Prevent Child Abuse Georgia developed educational pieces as part of a project funded by a CDC grant to develop adult and community responsibility for preventing child sexual abuse. The Stop It Now! Georgia program targets the early identification and treatment of youth and juveniles with sexual behavior problems (**Figures 18-3-a, b,** and **c**).

### Massachusetts—Media Campaign

This poster is the centerpiece of a media campaign on child sexual abuse prevention by Massachusetts Citizens for Children under a grant from the CDC (**Figure 18-4**).

### Georgia—Adult Responsibility Advertisement

This public awareness campaign was developed by Prevent Child Abuse Georgia (formerly known as the Georgia Council on Child Abuse) (**Figure 18-5**).

*Figure 18-2*

*Figure 18-3-a*

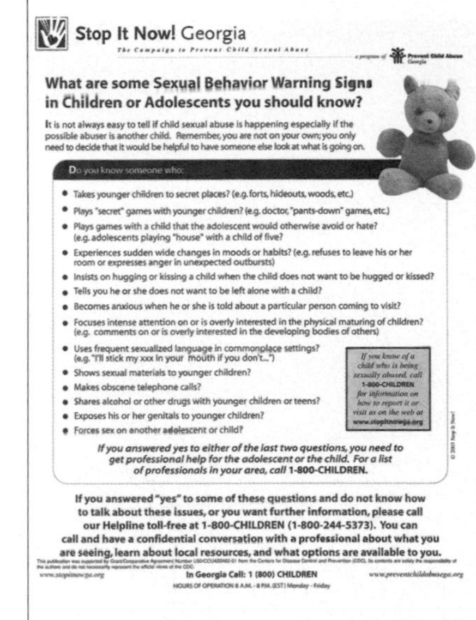


*Figure 18-3-b*

*Figure 18-3-c*

*Figure 18-4*

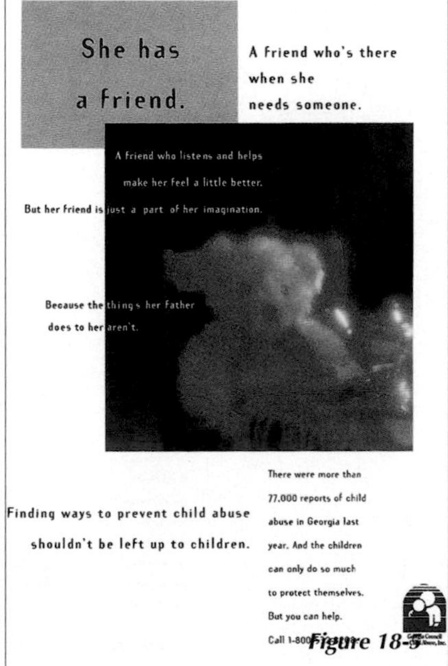


*Figure 18-5*

***Figure 18-2.*** Hide and Seek *print advertisement from Stop It Now!*

***Figure 18-3-a, b,*** *and* ***c.*** *Publications from Stop It Now! Georgia.*

***Figure 18-4.*** Enough *print advertisement from Prevent Child Abuse Massachusetts.*

***Figure 18-5.*** She Has a Friend *print advertisement from Prevent Child Abuse Georgia. This ad is another example of early efforts in the field to focus on adult responsibility in preventing sexual abuse.*

Figure 18-6

## GEORGIA—PRESERVING CHILDHOOD

Childhood is supposed to be a time of growing and learning in a safe and nurturing environment. Childhood is not meant to include abuse. This message is part of the program developed by Prevent Child Abuse Georgia with pro bono help from the Ogilvy & Mather advertising agency (**Figure 18-6**).

## PHYSICAL AND EMOTIONAL ABUSE AND NEGLECT

The long-term negative impact of abuse and neglect on the physical and emotional health of children is well known. The Adverse Childhood Experience study[27] and studies on early brain development,[31] among others, provide significant data supporting the harsh reality of physically and emotionally negative assaults early in life. These advertisements from Prevent Child Abuse Georgia (**Figures 18-7-a, b, c, d, e, f,** and **g**) capture the many "faces of child abuse" while emphasizing the responsibility of adults to "give children back their childhood."

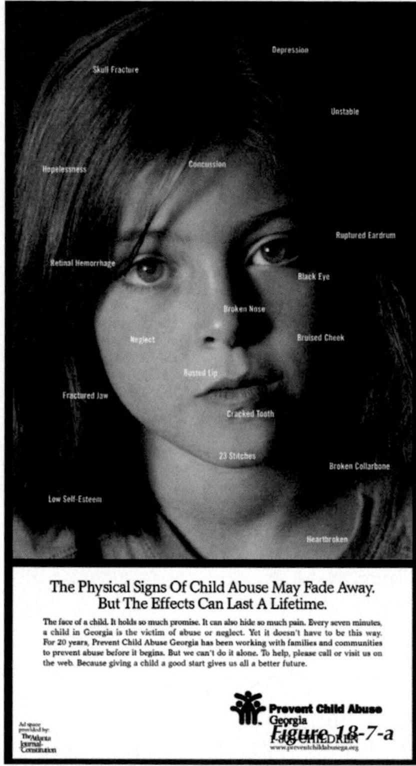

Figure 18-7-a

Figure 18-7-b

Figure 18-7-c

Figure 18-7-d

Figure 18-7-e

***Figure 18-6.*** When She's Only Five, It's Not Sex *print advertisement from Prevent Child Abuse Georgia. This ad is part of a public awareness campaign series with the message "Give Children Back Their Childhood."*

***Figures 18-7-a, b, c, d, e, f,*** *and* ***g.*** *Series of print advertisements from Prevent Child Abuse Georgia.*

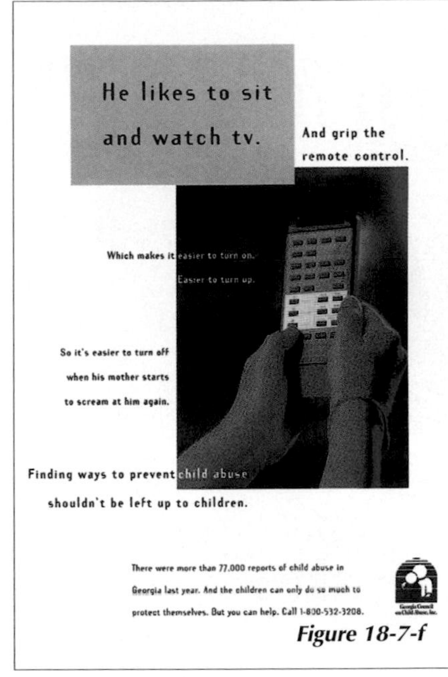


Figure 18-7-f

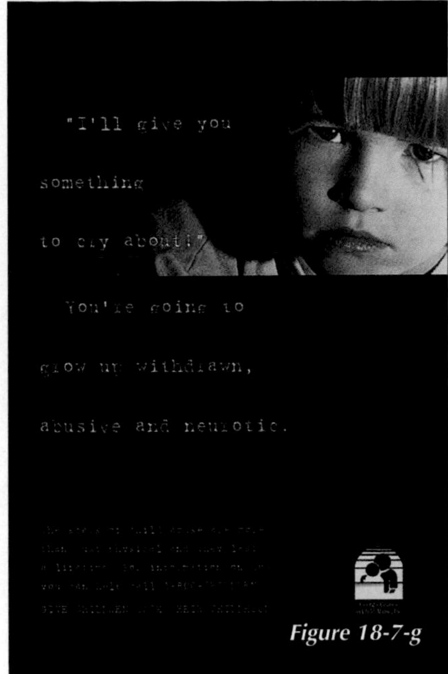


Figure 18-7-g

Figure 18-8

Figure 18-10

Figure 18-9

## Shaken Baby Syndrome

Males perpetrate more than 60% of cases of shaken baby syndrome (SBS).[32] As part of a campaign to prevent SBS, posters produced by the National Center on Shaken Baby Syndrome target males and can be used in schools, pediatrician's offices, hospitals, malls, and sports arenas (**Figure 18-8**).

## Elijah's Story

*Elijah's Story* is a moving documentary showing the devastation that occurs in families affected by SBS (**Figure 18-9**). The video educates about the dangers of shaking an infant or young child and reinforces how important it is to teach anyone who cares for a child to never shake a baby.

## General Prevention Messages

According to Prevent Child Abuse America, 32% of Americans have witnessed physical abuse and 47% report observing neglect, yet nearly half of these Americans also report having done nothing, often because they don't know what to do about it.[33] The advertising campaign *A Child is Helpless—You are Not* from Prevent Child Abuse America (**Figure 18-10**) includes 2 print advertisements, 1 each in Spanish and English, and a brochure that conveys the prevalence of the problem while at the same time giving a sense of hope that family and community members can do something to help stop abuse before it ever starts.

***Figure 18-8.*** Are You Tough Enough to be Gentle *poster from National Center on SBS.*

***Figure 18-9.*** *Cover of* Elijah's Story *video from National Center on SBS.*

***Figure 18-10.*** *Cover of Prevent Child Abuse America brochure,* You Can Help Prevent Child Abuse.

*Figure 18-11*

*Figure 18-12*

### Blue Ribbon Symbol

The blue ribbon is the symbol of child abuse prevention. Many organizations and communities across the country promote wearing and displaying blue ribbons, particularly during April, which is Child Abuse Prevention Month. Someone can wear the blue ribbon to draw attention to the promise of prevention.

*Figure 18-13*

***Figure 18-11.*** Never Leave a Child Alone in a Car *poster from Prevent Child Abuse Missouri.*

***Figure 18-12.*** Take A Stand Against Bullying *poster from Prevent Child Abuse Missouri.*

***Figure 18-13.*** *Georgia Fatality Review Panel Report.*

### Missouri—Car Safety

Young children are often injured, killed, sexually abused, or abducted when they are left alone without adult supervision. Yet, parents often fail to recognize the risks of leaving a child alone in a car. This poster from Prevent Child Abuse Missouri aims to educate parents about the dangers of leaving their children unsupervised (**Figure 18-11**).

### Missouri—Bullying

Threats, intimidation, hitting, pushing, and name-calling are all part of bullying. Recent studies point to the significant number of children who are victims of bullying or witnesses to bullying and the interrelationships between bullying, prior abuse, and future violence.[34] Prevent Child Abuse Missouri's poster calls attention to the need to take bullying seriously (**Figure 18-12**).

## Advocacy

### Building Public and Political Will for Prevention

When a child is dead from abuse or neglect, it is too late for prevention for that child. However, by doing a "social autopsy" in addition to the medical autopsy, much can be learned about how to prevent similar deaths. Like child fatality review teams across the country, the Fulton County Child Fatality Review Committee meets to review child deaths in Fulton County, Georgia, and to make recommendations for practice and policy changes that might prevent future deaths. The State Child Fatality Review Panel then combines the data from across the state into an annual report on the number and causes of child deaths and recommends prevention strategies that could reduce the number of child deaths (**Figure 18-13**). For 2002 in Georgia, child fatality review committees determined that 77% of identified child deaths were definitely or possibly preventable, and 97% of all reviewed child abuse/neglect deaths were determined to be definitely or possibly preventable.[35] The committee recommended the production of public awareness campaigns regarding safe sleeping environments and risk factors associated with infants ***cosleeping***, or sharing a bed with adults or others. The committee also recommended funding for the expansion of home-based family support models that promote and enable appropriate parenting skills for the prevention of child abuse and neglect.

## FIGHT CRIME

The 2003 report, *New Hope for Preventing Child Abuse and Neglect, Proven solutions to save lives and prevent future crime*, produced by Fight Crime: Invest in Kids (**Figure 18-14**), notes, "The crazy quilt of under-funded federal, state, and local abuse and neglect prevention programs is full of gaping holes."[36] The report continues, "Instead of a stitch here and a patch there, the 2000 sheriffs, police chiefs, prosecutors, and victims of violence who make up Fight Crime: Invest in Kids are calling on state and federal officials to fund a comprehensive, research-driven initiative to eliminate most abuse and neglect in high-risk families."[36] The report calls for coaching in parenting skills to all at-risk parents, quality pre-kindergarten programs with parent training for at-risk children, access to drug and alcohol treatment programs for pregnant addicted women, and mental health services for depressed or mentally ill parents.[36]

Figure 18-14

## NURTURING ENVIRONMENTS

The phrase "It takes a village to raise a child" is often used to emphasize the importance of the broader neighborhoods and communities in helping parents provide safe and nurturing environments for their children. Supported by a grant from The Duke Endowment, Strong Communities is a project of the Institute on Family and Neighborhood Life and is a public service activity of Clemson University in collaboration with the Golden Strip Family and Child Development Center in Simpsonville, South Carolina (**Figures 18-15-a, b, c, d, e, and f**). Strong Communities is a comprehensive initiative to build systems of support for families of young children. Strong Communities builds, strengthens, and renews community norms of neighbors' help for each other, which is an important step in preventing child abuse and neglect.

Figure 18-15-a

Figure 18-15-b

Figure 18-15-c

***Figure 18-14.*** FIGHT CRIME: Invest in Kids *report cover.*

***Figure 18-15-a.*** *Mr. Ernest N. Irby, Vice President, Central Carolina Bank: "My involvement with Strong Communities has been as diverse as the number of programs they facilitate. Central Carolina Bank purchased Shaken Baby prevention videos used in local high schools to help educate teenagers about the dangers related to this syndrome. We also participated in the Financial Wellness Fair, which provided an opportunity to help community members learn more about their economic future and equip them with the skills needed to make sound financial decisions."*

***Figure 18-15-b.*** *Chief Anthony Segars, Belmont Fire Department: "Serving as fire chief of Belmont means keeping the community safe and keeping kids safe. That is exactly what Strong Communities does; they keep kids safe. Fire stations do more than fight fires; we provide a vital resource for the community. Strong Communities has provided assistance with everything from helping with our new moms program to providing books for the neighborhood children. We work together as a team to look out for our neighbors."*

***Figure 18-15-c.*** *Ms. Mamie Reid, Ministry Development Coordinator, Shady Grove Baptist Church, Pelzer, South Carolina: "Shady Grove Baptist Church became involved with Strong Communities because our missions are similar. We desire for our members and the community to be strong support systems for children. We both believe in the Golden Rule. Strong Communities has enhanced our involvement in community activities, our collaboration efforts, and volunteer efforts in the Pelzer community and our local schools."*

***Figure 18-15-d.*** *The Honorable Patricia Thomas, Mayor Pro Tem, City of Simpsonville, South Carolina: "I have worked with Strong Communities from the very beginning. During one of the initial meetings with the community, we all agreed that the citizens of Simpsonville and the Golden Strip area needed recognition for all their hard work. Out of that meeting, the Champions for Children program began a recognition given to family-friendly organizations, businesses and individuals. Relatively speaking, our community may be small, but our concern for our children is great."*

***Figure 18-15-e.*** *Ms. Tracy Mitchell, Community Volunteer, Fountain Inn, South Carolina: "I saw a flyer in my church bulletin about needing volunteers to get toys together. I called community outreach worker Janine Sutter and told her that as a single mom with a baby I didn't have a lot of time or money. We realized that the Granny Ellisor Toy Lending Library would be the perfect place for me because I could take my son with me. Now that I know more about Strong Communities, I see it as more than just a way to help out; it brings the citizens of Fountain Inn together."*

***Figure 18-15-f.*** *Pledge Card for Community Members from Strong Communities Program in South Carolina.*

***Figures 18-15-a, b, c, d, e,*** *and* ***f.*** *Photographs courtesy of Strong Communities for Children in the Golden Strip and Clemson Photographic Services.*

Figure 18-15-d

Figure 18-15-e

**Strong Communities**
for Children in the Golden Strip

Thank you for helping to keep kids safe in our community.

Golden Strip Family
and Child Development Center
1102 Howard Drive
Simpsonville, SC 29681

(864) 967-2022 ext.39
www.clemson.edu/strongcommunities

Please remove this quick reference card before mailing

**Keep Kids Safe**

- ☐ **I will watch out for the children in my community.**
  Following the Golden Rule, I will do my best to listen and respond to the needs and concerns of neighbors, friends, relatives, co-workers, and fellow worshippers who have young children.
- ☐ **I will do my best to notice and show that I care when a child or the child's family has reason to rejoice, worry, or grieve.**
- ☐ **I will learn the names of the children in the 10 homes closest to by own.**
- ☐ **I will regularly take time to help a family with young children.**

Signature

Printed Name

Address

Phone Number

E-mail Address

**How did you learn about the Strong Communities campaign to "Keep Kids Safe"?**

Figure 18-15-f

## Child Abuse Prevention Month

Most people believe that child abuse is bad and want to protect children, but many do not know how they can help. Each year, Prevent Child Abuse America produces a Child Abuse Prevention Month packet. Distributed around the country with the help of Prevent Child Abuse America's network of state chapters, the packet includes concrete ways that individuals, organizations, and communities can help prevent child abuse. In 2003 the packet *What Everyone Can Do to Prevent Child Abuse* (**Figure 18-16-a**) was produced jointly by Prevent Child Abuse America and the Children's Bureau of the US Department of Health and Human Services. The 2004 packet, *In Loving Hands Kids Blossom* (**Figure 18-16-b**), is the result of a partnership between Prevent Child Abuse America and Foresters, which is a financial services organization. These 2 efforts also highlight the importance of public and private partnerships in preventing abuse (**Figures 18-16-c** and **d**).

## Prioritizing

Preventing child abuse cannot be just the priority of child abuse organizations and agencies. Making prevention everyone's priority requires many different outreach and public awareness strategies. With the pro bono design and production assistance of see see eye/Atlanta, a graphic design and communications firm, Prevent Child Abuse Georgia's 2002 annual report challenged the legislature and the community to look at their priorities while at the same time communicating the programmatic and fi-

Figure 18-16-a

Figure 18-16-b

***Figure 18-16-a.*** What Everyone Can Do to Prevent Child Abuse. *2003 Child Abuse Prevention Month Packet. Reprinted with permission from Prevent Child Abuse America and Children's Bureau, HHS.*

***Figure 18-16-b.*** In Loving Hands Kids Bloom. *Prevent Child Abuse America 2003 Child Abuse Prevention Month Packet.*

***Figures 18-16-c** and **d.*** How You Can Take Part in Prevention Efforts *big book mark from 2004 Child Abuse Prevention Month Packet.*

***Figures 18-17-a, b,** and **c.*** What Are Your Priorities, Here Are Our Priorities, Prevention Must Be Everyone's Priority. *The Prevent Child Abuse Georgia 3-booklet annual report covers from 2002.*

Figure 18-17-a

Figure 18-17-b

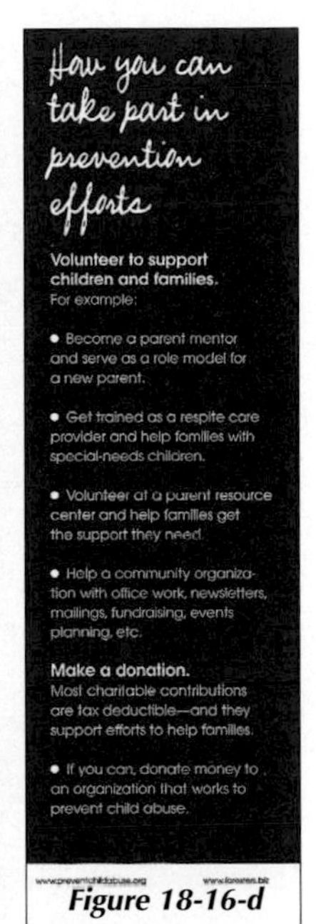

Figure 18-16-d

nancial report of the organization (**Figures 18-17-a, b,** and **c**).

### Louisiana—Advocacy Summits

Through the leadership of Executive Director Marketa Gautreau, Prevent Child Abuse Louisiana brought community members and stakeholders from across the state together to develop *The Platform for Children and Youth.* Community members volunteered countless hours to ensure that every aspect of life was considered in the development of their advocacy platform (**Figures 18-18**).

### Louisiana—Advocacy Platform

The Platform for Children and Youth, developed through the leadership of Prevent Child Abuse Louisiana, put the needs of Louisiana's children on the agenda for the gubernatorial candidates (**Figures 18-19**). Never before had the key issues and the critical lack of resources been addressed in a political campaign for the state's highest office.

### Authentic Voices

Statistics and policies can convey the scope of the problem of child abuse and neglect. However, nothing catches the attention of policymakers or the public more than the voice of someone who has been impacted by abuse or who has struggled but is

Figure 18-17-c

Figure 18-15-f

Figure 18-20-a

Figure 18-19

Figure 18-20-b

Figure 18-21-a

*Figures 18-18.* Prevent Child Abuse Louisiana advocacy summit meeting.

*Figures 18-19.* Prevent Child Abuse Louisiana advocacy platform.

*Figures 18-20-a and b.* Two pictures from National Call To Action. Mobilizing to Prevent Child Abuse: National Call To Action and Authentic Voices are grassroots campaigns to gather signatures for a petition and to enlist member advocates.

*Figure 18-21-a.* Tanya Long, Parents Anonymous National Parent Leadership Team member.

overcoming the challenges of being a parent. Organized efforts have recently formed to use their voices, skills, and leadership to advocate for the prevention of child abuse. An example of these efforts includes Authentic Voices. Authentic Voices grew out of The National Call To Action: A Movement to End Child Abuse and Neglect, which is a coalition of over 25 national organizations and individual members working to prevent abuse. By mobilizing the general public in an effort to reach critical mass, the National Call To Action and Authentic Voices are working to increase support for key legislation and investment in prevention (**Figures 18-20-a** and **b**).

### Parents Anonymous Leadership

Parents Anonymous Inc is committed to ensuring that the voices of parents are heard in local, state, and national discussions of issues that affect families and children. Tanya Long (**Figure 18-21-a**), who is a member of the Parents Anonymous National Leadership Team (**Figure 18-21-b**), testified at a congressional briefing titled *Child Abuse and Neglect: How This Public Health Problem Affects Women and Children.* The Parents Anonymous Inc National Parent Leadership Team is composed of a diverse group of mothers, fathers, grandparents, and kinship care providers who have demonstrated leadership in their local Parents Anonymous groups and have expressed interest in expanding their leadership beyond the group.

## Professional Education

Selecting the most effective prevention strategy can be a difficult task. A growing body of resources is available to help communities and organizations choose wisely and implement effectively. Similarly, a number of publications exist to inform professionals working in the field about best practices, current research, and tools to help them provide the most effective response to the prevention and treatment of abuse.

### Emerging Practices

As part of a larger child abuse prevention initiative of OCAN, the *Emerging Practices in the Prevention of Child Abuse and Neglect* project was initiated to identify effective and innovative programs in child abuse and neglect prevention and disseminate the findings to the professional community. Nominations of programs and initiatives were reviewed by an advisory group of experts in the field of child abuse prevention. This report presents the outcomes of both the literature review and the nomination process (**Figure 18-22**).

### Standards for Prevention Programs

The cornerstone of many child abuse prevention efforts is the promotion of opportunities to gain knowledge and skills that make a family more competent, thus strengthening family functioning. The New Jersey Task Force on Child Abuse and Neglect developed *Standards for Prevention Programs: Building Success through Family Support* (**Figure 18-23-a**). The report provides broad standards, rather than a critique of model programs, to provide professionals with information to evaluate a variety of programs serving diverse populations. The information is organized under 3 headings: conceptual standards, practice standards, and administrative standards (**Figures 18-23-b, c,** and **d**).

### Parent Training

Parent training is a core component of most prevention efforts. Many such programs are replicated on a large scale, yet there is little, and in general, very poor evaluation of these services. *Reducing Child Maltreatment: A Guidebook for Parent Services* (**Figure 18-24**) is intended as a resource and manual for professionals who may wish to apply the programs described, and it can be used as a supplementary text in classes dealing with parent training or other similar social services. It is based on more than 20 years of professionally validating, revalidating, and replicating the protocols presented in the book. It is not considered a panacea, but it is a presentation of procedures that can be very effective in giving skills to parents.

***Figure 18-21-b.*** *Parents Anonymous National Leadership Team picture.*

***Figure 18-22.*** *Front cover of* Emerging Practices in the Prevention of Child Abuse and Neglect.

Figure 18-23-a

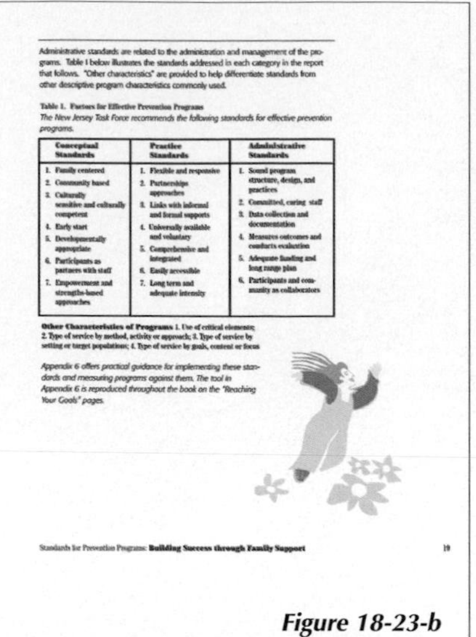

Figure 18-23-b

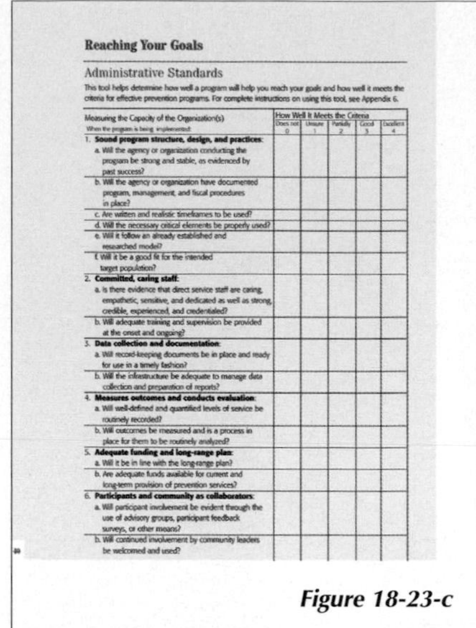

Figure 18-23-c

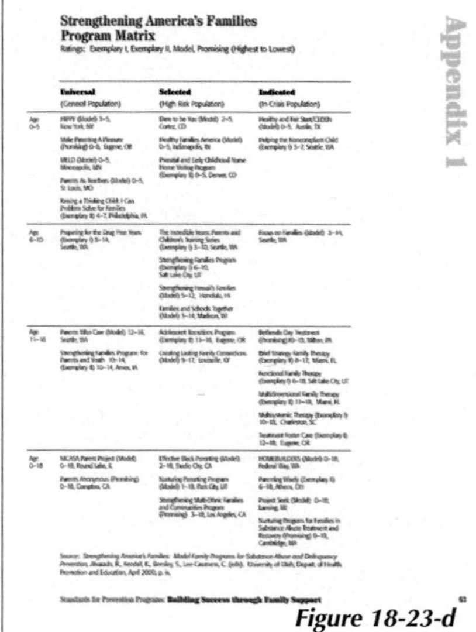

Figure 18-23-d

Figure 18-24

Figure 18-25

***Figure 18-23-a.*** Building Success through Family Support, *developed by the New Jersey Task Force on Child Abuse and Neglect.*

***Figure 18-23-b.*** Factors for Effective Prevention Programs.

***Figure 18-23-c.*** Reaching Your Goals: Administrative Standards.

***Figure 18-23-d.*** Strengthening America's Families Program Matrix.

***Figure 18-24.*** Reducing Child Maltreatment: A Guidebook for Parent Services.

***Figure 18-25.*** Advice to Professionals on Child Sexual Abuse Prevention Programs for Preschoolers and Elementary-Aged Children.

## Advice to Professionals

The publication *Advice to Professionals on Child Sexual Abuse Prevention Programs for Preschoolers and Elementary-Aged Children* (**Figure 18-25**) offers a summary of the current research about child sexual abuse prevention programs. It details trends and innovations in prevention programming and also offers a list of recommendations for any organizations offering child sexual abuse prevention programming.

## Right on Course

Teachers are in a unique position not only to identify potential abuse and neglect, but also to help a child overcome the effects of trauma and thrive academically. *Right on Course: How Trauma and Maltreatment Impact Children in the Classroom and How You Can Help*, a Civitas initiative, provides the guidance and teaching tools to help educators respond to the needs of children who have experienced trauma (**Figures 18-26-a, b, c, d,** and **e**).

## Spider-Man and an Approach to Bullying

The Spider-Man resource on bullying provides guidance to teachers on how to use this comic book (**Figure 18-27**) to help children learn nonviolent ways to deal with

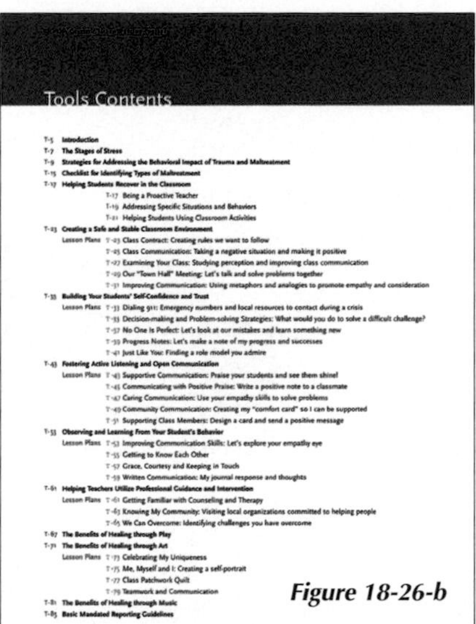

Tools Contents



***Figure 18-26-b***

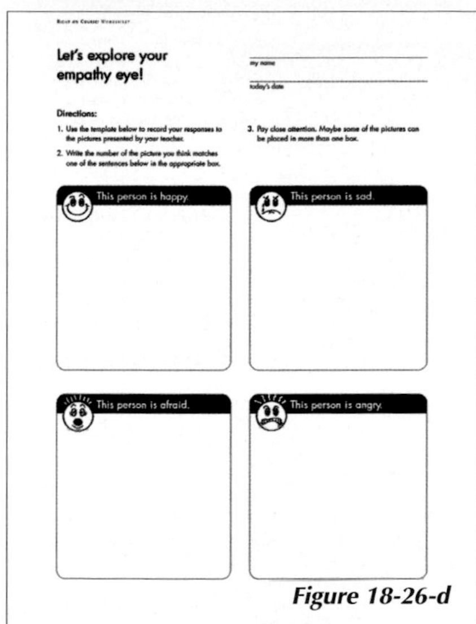

**Let's explore your empathy eye!**

my name

today's date

**Directions:**

1. Use the template below to record your responses to the pictures presented by your teacher.
2. Write the number of the picture you think matches one of the sentences below in the appropriate box.
3. Pay close attention. Maybe some of the pictures can be placed in more than one box.

This person is happy.

This person is sad.

This person is afraid.

This person is angry.

***Figure 18-26-d***

Observing and Learning from Your Students' Behavior

**Lesson Plan** – Improving Communication Skills: Let's explore your empathy eye

The purpose of this activity is to focus on the observation and empathy abilities of your students.

**Grade:** Kindergarten to 3rd grade
**Time:** 25 to 30 minutes
**Materials:** **Worksheet** on the back of this lesson plan, magazines, construction paper, loose-leaf paper, pencils/pens

**Steps:**

1. Prior to the lesson, cut out pictures from magazines that show people expressing different emotions in their facial expressions or body language. Mount the images on construction paper and try to pick images that are large enough for the class to see.
2. At the beginning of the activity, pass around the different pictures (prepare at least 10 to 15 different visuals) and ask the children to try and identify how a particular person might be feeling or what they might be doing in the photo. Make sure to number each picture. Ask the students to write the picture's number in the boxes provided on the worksheet.
3. Next, collect the pictures and show the class one from the pile, asking for their opinion about how the person might be feeling. For the first example, choose a picture that shows clear emotion, like happiness or sadness, to help guide the conversation. Ask the children what they think.
4. As the children respond, give them supportive feedback and ask them to tell you specific gestures or postures that signal the person's state. For example, you might point to the picture of a child and say, "What about this boy tells you he is sad?" Challenge them to differentiate between positive and negative characteristics whenever possible (frowning, wrinkling the forehead, smiling, looking distant).
5. You can finish the activity by reviewing their observations about the images and praising them on their ability to empathize with the characters.

**Extensions:**

- Create a word wall of characteristics and observations given by students.
- Continue the activity at home. Ask them to find another picture and write observation notes about the people depicted, describing their emotions and actions. Have them bring in and share their stories and images with the class.
- Stretch the activity across subject areas such as art. Students can explore their artwork in the same manner.
  - *How does the color _____ make you feel? What else do we know is that color?*
  - *What is happening in this picture? I see (point to a specific detail or object that appears often).*
  - *Why did you draw that there?*
  - *How many people do you see? I see (describe the people you can identify).*
  - *There is a lot of free space in your drawing. Can you add to the space? How?*
  - *Where did you get the idea for this picture? Tell me the story happening in it.*
  - *If this character could speak, what would he say? What would his voice sound like?*
  - *Can anyone in class tell me what they see in this student's drawing?*
  - *What do you like about this picture? I like (give an example of something you find special).*

***Figure 18-26-e***

***Spider-Man®: How to Beat the Bully! and Jubilee™: Peer Pressure***

A Teacher's Guide to Violence Prevention and Conflict Resolution
Kathleen Kostelny, Ph.D.

***Spider-Man: How to Beat the Bully!*** and ***Jubilee: Peer Pressure*** are stories written to help children deal with the conflict, peer pressure, and violence they experience in their lives, and to teach them ways to resolve differences without resorting to violence. The reading level is appropriate for children in grades four through six, but the message is appropriate for both younger children (where the teacher can read to the class) and older children.

Published by the National Committee to Prevent Child Abuse

The National Committee to Prevent Child Abuse acknowledges the support and generosity of Toyota for making this material possible.

©1996 by the National Committee to Prevent

***Figure 18-27***

bullying and peer pressure. This resource was produced by Prevent Child Abuse America.

## Colleagues for Children

Published by Prevent Child Abuse Missouri, *Colleagues for Children* keeps professionals informed and engaged in prevention (**Figure 18-28**).

## Missouri—Mandated Reporters

The *Mandated Reporters Guide* outlines what mandated reporters need to know and is provided as a service by Prevent Child Abuse Missouri (**Figures 18-29-a** and **b**).

## The Quarterly Update: Reviews of Current Child Abuse Medical Research

*The Quarterly Update: Reviews of Current Child Abuse Medical Research* summarizes relevant research articles selected from nearly 1000 peer-reviewed medical journals to help professionals prevent, diagnose, treat, and understand child maltreatment.

## American Professional Society on the Abuse of Children Publications

The American Professional Society on the Abuse of Children (APSAC) is a multi-

***Figure 18-26-a.*** *Front cover of* Right on Course *handbook for educators.*

***Figure 18-26-b.*** *Table of contents for* Right on Course *handbook.*

***Figure 18-26-c.*** *Back cover of* Right on Course *handbook.*

***Figure 18-26-d.*** Let's Explore Your Empathy Eye.

***Figure 18-26-e.*** Observing and Learning from Your Students' Behavior. Lesson Plan: Improving Communication Skills.

***Figure 18-27.*** Spider-Man: How to Beat the Bully! *and* Jubilee: Peer Pressure—A Teacher's Guide to Violence Prevention and Conflict Resolution, *produced by Prevent Child Abuse America and Marvel Comics.*

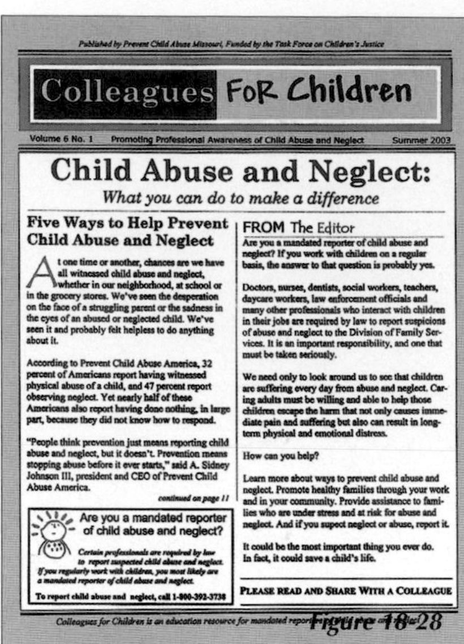

Published by Prevent Child Abuse Missouri, Funded by the Task Force on Children's Justice

Colleagues For Children

Volume 6 No. 1 Promoting Professional Awareness of Child Abuse and Neglect Summer 2003

Child Abuse and Neglect:

*What you can do to make a difference*

**Five Ways to Help Prevent Child Abuse and Neglect**

At one time or another, chances are we have all witnessed child abuse and neglect, whether in our neighborhood, at school or in the grocery stores. We've seen the desperation on the face of a struggling parent or the sadness in the eyes of an abused or neglected child. We've seen it and probably felt helpless to do anything about it.

According to Prevent Child Abuse America, 32 percent of Americans report having witnessed physical abuse of a child, and 47 percent report observing neglect. Yet nearly half of these Americans also report having done nothing, in large part, because they did not know how to respond.

"People think prevention just means reporting child abuse and neglect, but it doesn't. Prevention means stopping abuse before it ever starts," said A. Sidney Johnson III, president and CEO of Prevent Child Abuse America.

*continued on page 11*

Are you a mandated reporter of child abuse and neglect?

*Certain professionals are required by law to report suspected child abuse and neglect. If you regularly work with children, you most likely are a mandated reporter of child abuse and neglect.*

To report child abuse and neglect, call 1-800-392-3738

**FROM The Editor**

Are you a mandated reporter of child abuse and neglect? If you work with children on a regular basis, the answer to that question is probably yes.

Doctors, nurses, dentists, social workers, teachers, daycare workers, law enforcement officials and many other professionals who interact with children in their jobs are required by law to report suspicions of abuse and neglect to the Division of Family Services. It is an important responsibility, and one that must be taken seriously.

We need only to look around us to see that children are suffering every day from abuse and neglect. Caring adults must be willing and able to help those children escape the harm that not only causes immediate pain and suffering but also can result in long-term physical and emotional distress.

How can you help?

Learn more about ways to prevent child abuse and neglect. Promote healthy families through your work and in your community. Provide assistance to families who are under stress and at risk for abuse and neglect. And if you supect neglect or abuse, report it.

It could be the most important thing you ever do. In fact, it could save a child's life.

PLEASE READ AND SHARE WITH A COLLEAGUE

*Colleagues for Children is an education resource for mandated report...*

Figure 18-28

APSAC ADVISOR

Volume 15, Number 2, SPRING 2003

AMERICAN PROFESSIONAL SOCIETY ON THE ABUSE OF CHILDREN

SPECIAL ISSUE

PREVENTING PHYSICAL CHILD ABUSE AND NEGLECT

Guest Editors:
John K. Holton, PhD
Neil B. Guterman, PhD



APSAC: Ensuring that everyone affected by child abuse and neglect receives the best possible professional response.

Figure 18-30-a

**Figure 18-28.** Colleagues for Children.

**Figures 18-29-a** *and* **b.** Mandated Reporters Guide.

***Figure 18-30-a.*** *Front cover of the* APSAC Advisor. *Reprinted with permission from American Professional Society on the Abuse of Children.*

***Figure 18-30-b.*** *Front cover of* APSAC Publications Catalog.

***Figure 18-31-a.*** *Cover of Prevent Child Abuse Georgia 2004 Conference brochure.*

***Figure 18-31-b.*** *Cover of Prevent Child Abuse America 2004 Conference brochure.*

disciplinary professional organization that is focused on meeting the needs of professionals engaged in all aspects of child maltreatment. APSAC disseminates state-of-the-art practices through its quarterly newsletter, *The Advisor* (**Figure 18-30-a**), and other publications (**Figure 18-30-b**), conferences, and institutes around the country.

### Conferences and Training to Equip Professionals to Work in Prevention

Prevent Child Abuse America and its network of state chapters offer a variety of conferences for volunteers and professionals working in the field of prevention (**Figures 18-31-a** and **b**).

### Shared Leadership

Parents Anonymous Inc and its parent leaders design and conduct *Shared Leadership in Action* trainings and technical assistance targeted to meet the needs of community-based organizations and government agencies.

## Programs to Support and Educate Parents

### Universal Parental Support Programs

Designed for all new parents, First Steps (**Figures 18-32-a** and **b**) is a program of Prevent Child Abuse Georgia that has been replicated in sites across the country, often in conjunction with Healthy Families America home visiting programs for more vulnerable families. First Steps is a cost-effective, highly replicable, and adaptable model for reaching a significant number of families. By visiting with parents immediately before or after giving birth, and by providing sustained follow-up, First Steps offers support when vulnerability is high and when parents are most approachable. One of the resources shared with parents is the First Steps developmental calendar (**Figure 18-32-c**), which provides developmental information and allows parents to track developmental milestones.

### Georgia—Crying Program

Crying is commonly a trigger for abuse, including SBS, in infants and young children. Several new prevention initiatives are designed to target crying. Developed as a partnership between Prevent Child Abuse Georgia and the Georgia Chapter of the American Academy of Pediatrics, and supported by a grant from Prevent Child Abuse America as part of their Stages program, the Georgia program targeting crying is designed for implementation in the pediatrician's office at the 2-week, 2-month, and 4-month postnatal visits. With a focus on coping with crying, the program includes an educational session for all members of the pediatric practice staff. Materials for parents include educational cards on crying (**Figures 18-33-a, b,** and **c**), a magnet (**Figure 18-33-d**), and a parent pledge card (**Figure 18-33-e**).

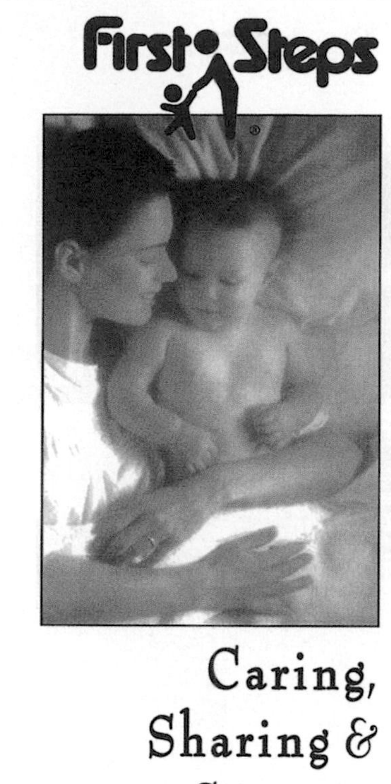

Figure 18-32-a

**Figures 18-32-a** and **b.** First Steps Program brochure from Prevent Child Abuse Georgia.

**Figure 18-32-c.** Cover of First Steps Program Developmental calendar.

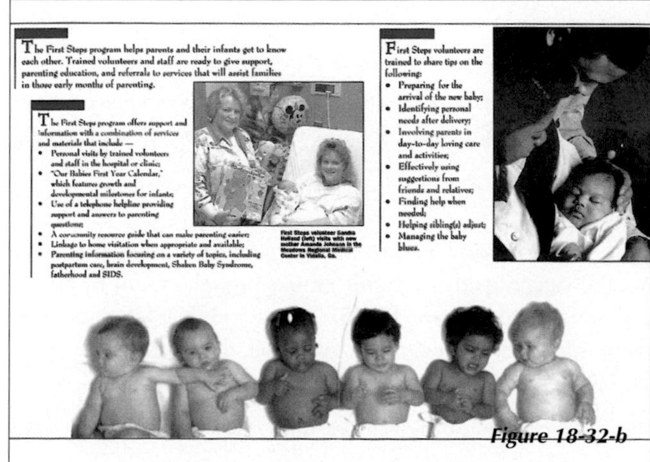

Figure 18-32-b

Figure 18-32-c

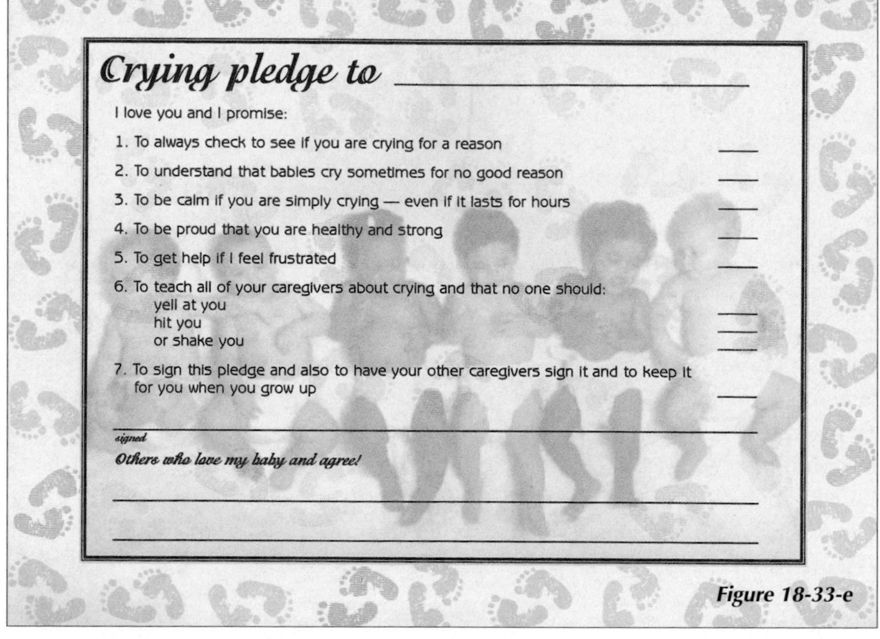

*Crying pledge to* ________________

I love you and I promise:

1. To always check to see if you are crying for a reason ___
2. To understand that babies cry sometimes for no good reason ___
3. To be calm if you are simply crying — even if it lasts for hours ___
4. To be proud that you are healthy and strong ___
5. To get help if I feel frustrated ___
6. To teach all of your caregivers about crying and that no one should:
   yell at you ___
   hit you ___
   or shake you ___
7. To sign this pledge and also to have your other caregivers sign it and to keep it for you when you grow up ___

________________
*signed*

*Others who love my baby and agree!*

________________

________________

Figure 18-33-e

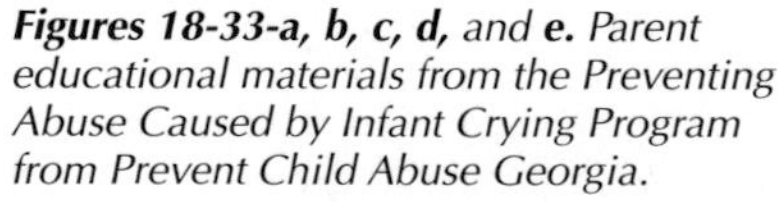

***Figures 18-33-a, b, c, d,** and **e.*** *Parent educational materials from the Preventing Abuse Caused by Infant Crying Program from Prevent Child Abuse Georgia.*

### Stages Crying Program

One of the brochures in the Stages *Understanding Your Child's Development* series created by Prevent Child Abuse America offers tips to parents on dealing with crying (**Figure 18-34**).

### Period of PURPLE Crying

The National Center on Shaken Baby Syndrome's *Period of PURPLE Crying* materials remind parents and caregivers that the frustrations brought about by crying are normal and will come to an end (**Figure 18-35**). The acronym PURPLE helps describe the characteristics of infant crying, with the belief that knowledge helps combat parental frustration[37]:

— *Peak of crying.* Babies may cry increasingly more until they reach the age of 8 weeks.

— *Unexpected.* There may be no discernible reason for a baby crying.

— *Resists soothing.* It may be difficult or even impossible to quiet a crying baby.

— *Pain-like face.* A crying baby's face may belie pain, when not actually experienced by the baby.

— *Long lasting.* Babies can cry for 30-40 minutes or more.

— *Evening.* Crying is more likely to occur in the late afternoon and evening.

### Helpline

The Prevent Child Abuse Helpline provides anonymous support, information, and referral to other services for parents, children, and professionals across the state of Georgia (**Figure 18-36**).

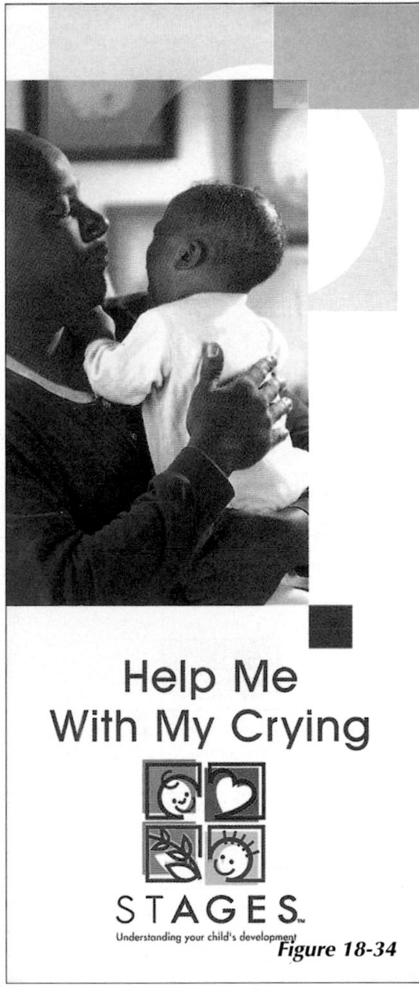


Figure 18-34

Figure 18-35

Figure 18-36

***Figure 18-34.*** *Stages brochure,* Help Me With My Crying.

***Figure 18-35.*** Period of PURPLE Crying *material from National Center on Shaken Baby Syndrome.*

***Figure 18-36.*** *Cover of Prevent Child Abuse Georgia Helpline brochure.*

Figure 18-37-a

Figure 18-37-b

Figure 18-37-c

Figure 18-37-d

Figure 18-37-e

***Figure 18-37-a.*** *Stages brochure,* I'm Ready to Use the Potty.

***Figure 18-37-b.*** *Stages brochure,* Help Me Learn Self Control.

***Figure 18-37-c.*** Great Beginnings Start Before Birth.

***Figure 18-37-d.*** Great Beginnings With Your Baby: A Guide for Teen Parents.

***Figure 18-37-e.*** Terrific Toddlers: Whoever Said That Two-Year-Olds Were Terrible?

### New Parent Materials

Various other materials have been developed for new parents by Prevent Child Abuse America (**Figures 18-37-a, b, c, d,** and **e**).

### Circle of Parents

Outreach brochures have been developed by the Circle of Parents, a mutual support and self-help program for parents (**Figures 18-38-a** and **b**). The program represents a collaboration between Prevent Child Abuse America and the National Family Support Roundtable. Circle of Parents is modeled on the philosophical framework of shared leadership, mutual respect, shared ownership, and inclusiveness. This brochure is also available in Spanish.

### Parents Anonymous Groups

In weekly Parents Anonymous groups, parents find a caring and supportive en-

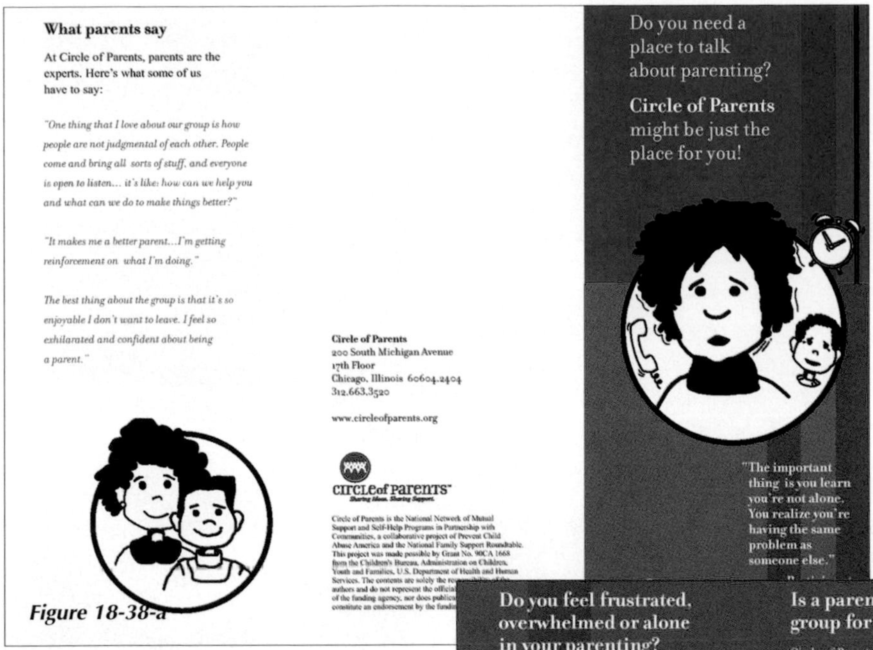

**What parents say**

At Circle of Parents, parents are the experts. Here's what some of us have to say:

*"One thing that I love about our group is how people are not judgmental of each other. People come and bring all sorts of stuff, and everyone is open to listen… it's like: how can we help you and what can we do to make things better?"*

*"It makes me a better parent…I'm getting reinforcement on what I'm doing."*

*The best thing about the group is that it's so enjoyable I don't want to leave. I feel so exhilarated and confident about being a parent."*

**Circle of Parents**
200 South Michigan Avenue
17th Floor
Chicago, Illinois 60604.2404
312.663.3520

www.circleofparents.org

circle of parents®
Sharing Ideas. Sharing Support.

Circle of Parents is the National Network of Mutual Support and Self-Help Programs in Partnership with Communities, a collaborative project of Prevent Child Abuse America and the National Family Support Roundtable. This project was made possible by Grant No. 90CA 1668 from the Children's Bureau, Administration on Children, Youth and Families, U.S. Department of Health and Human Services. The contents are solely the re… authors and do not represent the officia… of the funding agency, nor does publica… constitute an endorsement by the fundi…

Do you need a place to talk about parenting?

**Circle of Parents** might be just the place for you!

**"The important thing is you learn you're not alone. You realize you're having the same problem as someone else."**

**Figure 18-38-a**

**Do you feel frustrated, overwhelmed or alone in your parenting?**

**Or do you just need to talk?**

We all know parenting can be hard.

Kids depend on us, and sometimes it seems like none of us could possibly have enough time, strength or wisdom to give them everything they need.

But help is available – help from other parents who might have a good idea of what you're going through.

**We'll listen to you, talk about it, and offer our own ideas and support.**

**Is a parent support group for you?**

Circle of Parents offers free meetings for anyone in a parenting role. Parents lead the groups with the help of a trained facilitator.

In groups we talk about anything related to raising kids: discipline, school, health, safety.

We meet weekly and keep information shared in the group **confidential** – within the limits of the law.

And, we **never judge** other people's situations or stories.

**We know how it feels… We're parents too.**

**Parent Leadership**

At Circle of Parents, parents decide the topics, lead the discussions and are involved in all levels of decision-making.

Circle of Parents encourages the development of parents' leadership skills – not just as parents and group leaders, but in all aspects of their lives.

**Children's Programs**

Many groups provide children's programs or childcare – usually free of charge. These programs are a safe place for children to play and interact while their parents are in a group.

**Join Us!**

Please see the back of this brochure for contact information for the national office or a program near you.

**Or go to our website at** *www.circleofparents.org.*

**We look forward to seeing you!**

**Figure 18-38-b**

PROGRAM SERIES

Best Practices for Parents Anonymous® Group Facilitators

PARENTS anonymous

**Figure 18-39-a**

***Figure 18-38-a.*** Circle of Parents Mutual Self-Help Support Groups *brochure.*

***Figure 18-38-b.*** Circle of Parents *brochure.*

***Figure 18-39-a.*** *Cover of* Best Practices for Parents Anonymous Group Facilitators.

***Figure 18-39-b.*** *Cover of* Innovative Practices for Parents Anonymous Parent Group Leaders.

vironment where they can learn new parenting strategies to provide a safe and nurturing home environment, develop their leadership skills, and create long-lasting positive changes in their families (**Figures 18-39-a** and **b**).

## Programs Targeting High-Risk Parents

Families with multiple problems and high levels of risk need more intensive and specialized support programs. Many of these programs, like Healthy Families America, provide long-term home visiting services for some of the most vulnerable families.

### Hawaii—Hana Like Home Visitor Program

The Hana Like Home Visitor program in Honolulu, Hawaii, provides group outings to new parents and their young children to expand learning experiences and encourage socialization (**Figure 18-40-a**). This program also offers infant massage classes to new parents (**Figure 18-40-b**). Infant massage promotes bonding and attachment, stimulates the baby's brain and motor development, and provides an enjoyable, soothing experience for parent and child.

Figure 18-40-a

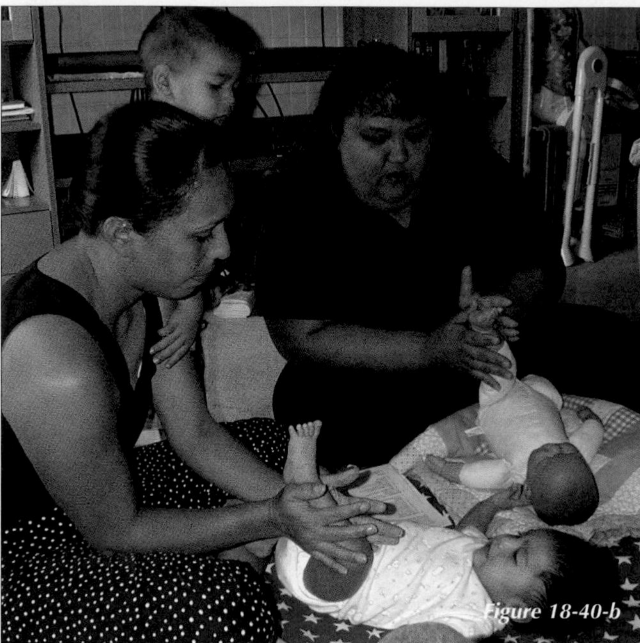
Figure 18-40-b

***Figure 18-40-a.*** *A new mom and her children enjoy seeing the animals up close at the petting zoo.*

***Figure 18-40-b.*** *Parents participating in infant massage class.*

***Figures 18-41-a*** *and* ***b.*** Healthy Families Georgia Fact Sheet, *pages 1 and 2.*

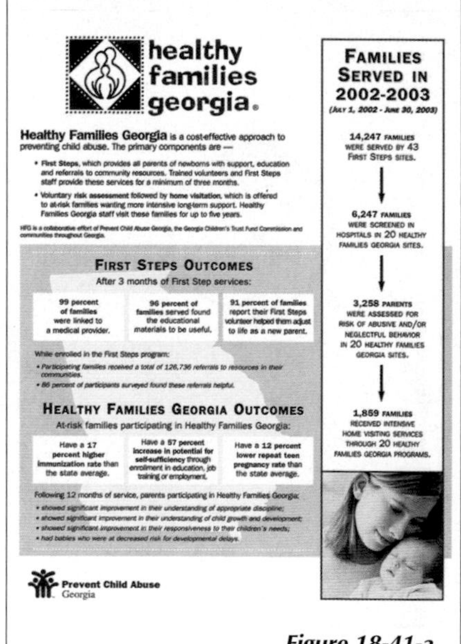

**healthy families georgia.**

**Healthy Families Georgia** is a cost-effective approach to preventing child abuse. The primary components are —

- **First Steps**, which provides all parents of newborns with support, education and referrals to community resources. Trained volunteers and First Steps staff provide these services for a minimum of three months.
- Voluntary **risk assessment** followed by **home visitation**, which is offered to at-risk families wanting more intensive long-term support. Healthy Families Georgia staff visit these families for up to five years.

HFG is a collaborative effort of Prevent Child Abuse Georgia, the Georgia Children's Trust Fund Commission and communities throughout Georgia.

**FIRST STEPS OUTCOMES**

After 3 months of First Step services:

- **99 percent of families** were linked to a medical provider.
- **96 percent of families** served found the educational materials to be useful.
- **91 percent of families** report their First Steps volunteer helped them adjust to life as a new parent.

While enrolled in the First Steps program:

- *Participating families received a total of 126,736 referrals to resources in their communities.*
- *86 percent of participants surveyed found these referrals helpful.*

**HEALTHY FAMILIES GEORGIA OUTCOMES**

At-risk families participating in Healthy Families Georgia:

- Have a **17 percent higher immunization rate** than the state average.
- Have a **57 percent increase in potential for self-sufficiency** through enrollment in education, job training or employment.
- Have a **12 percent lower repeat teen pregnancy rate** than the state average.

Following 12 months of service, parents participating in Healthy Families Georgia:

- *showed significant improvement in their understanding of appropriate discipline;*
- *showed significant improvement in their understanding of child growth and development;*
- *showed significant improvement in their responsiveness to their children's needs;*
- *had babies who were at decreased risk for developmental delays.*

**FAMILIES SERVED IN 2002-2003**
*(JULY 1, 2002 - JUNE 30, 2003)*

**14,247** FAMILIES WERE SERVED BY 43 FIRST STEPS SITES.

↓

**6,247** FAMILIES WERE SCREENED IN HOSPITALS IN 20 HEALTHY FAMILIES GEORGIA SITES.

↓

**3,258** PARENTS WERE ASSESSED FOR RISK OF ABUSIVE AND/OR NEGLECTFUL BEHAVIOR IN 20 HEALTHY FAMILIES GEORGIA SITES.

↓

**1,859** FAMILIES RECEIVED INTENSIVE HOME VISITING SERVICES THROUGH 20 HEALTHY FAMILIES GEORGIA PROGRAMS.

**Prevent Child Abuse** Georgia

***Figure 18-41-a***

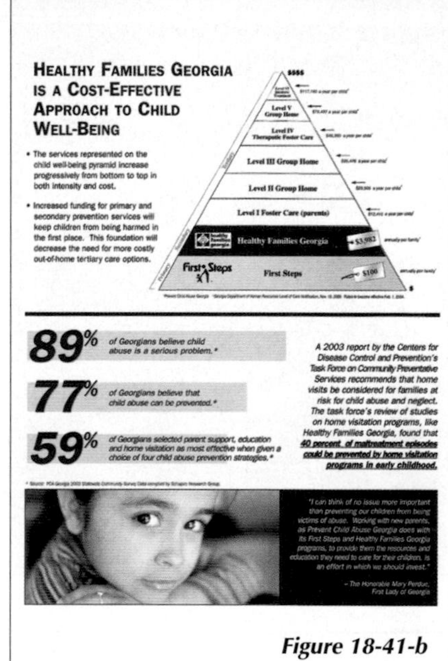

**HEALTHY FAMILIES GEORGIA IS A COST-EFFECTIVE APPROACH TO CHILD WELL-BEING**

- The services represented on the child well-being pyramid increase progressively from bottom to top in both intensity and cost.
- Increased funding for primary and secondary prevention services will keep children from being harmed in the first place. This foundation will decrease the need for more costly out-of-home tertiary care options.



**89%** *of Georgians believe child abuse is a serious problem.**

**77%** *of Georgians believe that child abuse can be prevented.**

**59%** *of Georgians selected parent support, education and home visitation as most effective when given a choice of four child abuse prevention strategies.**

*A 2003 report by the Centers for Disease Control and Prevention's Task Force on Community Preventative Services recommends that home visits be considered for families at risk for child abuse and neglect. The task force's review of studies on home visitation programs, like Healthy Families Georgia, found that* ***40 percent of maltreatment episodes could be prevented by home visitation programs in early childhood.***

*"I can think of no issue more important than preventing our children from being victims of abuse. Working with new parents, as Prevent Child Abuse Georgia does with its First Steps and Healthy Families Georgia programs, to provide them the resources and education they need to care for their children, is an effort in which we should invest."*

*– The Honorable Mary Perdue, First Lady of Georgia*

***Figure 18-41-b***

## HEALTHY FAMILIES GEORGIA

The Healthy Families Georgia Program Fact Sheet (**Figures 18-41-a** and **b**) provides legislators, funders, and community members information about the positive outcomes for participants and the cost effectiveness of investing in prevention.

## FAMILY CONNECTIONS

Family Connections is a community-based program of the University of Maryland, Baltimore, Center for Families. The primary goal is to develop, implement, and evaluate the effectiveness of early intervention models of community-based neglect prevention and psychosocial service programs for families who are struggling to meet their children's needs. The program is built around 9 practice principles: community outreach, family assessment and customized interventions, helping alliance, empowerment approaches, strengths' perspective, cultural competence, developmental appropriateness, outcome-driven service plans, and emphasis on positive attitudes and the qualities of helpers. Family Connections is the only program in the Emerging Practices in Child Abuse and Neglect project that has met the standards for a demonstrated effective program, and the model is being implemented in additional sites around the country (**Figures 18-42-a, b,** and **c**).

## Oklahoma—SafeCare Program

The Oklahoma High-Risk Prevention Pilot Study (OHRAPPS) is funded by the state of Oklahoma to evaluate the feasibility and outcome of a home-based service for young children who are at high risk for abuse and neglect because of factors such as parental drug and/or alcohol abuse, mental illness, mental and/or physical disability, and domestic violence. The OHRAPPS service model is a home-based intervention known as SafeCare, which has been well researched and has been found to reduce child maltreatment in child welfare populations.[38-41] The service model is an enhancement of SafeCare (SafeCare+) that includes motivational interviewing to address parents' motivation to change, a structured problem-solving program to improve caregivers problem solving skills, and safety-planning for intimate partner violence. Preliminary outcome data suggest that SafeCare+ families have greater reductions in child abuse potential, parental depression, and family violence, as well as fewer child welfare reports (**Figures 18-43-a** and **b**).[42]

***Figure 18-42-a.*** *Family Connections staff and interns share information about the program at a community outreach fair.*

***Figures 18-42-b** and **c.** Family Connections participants at multifamily events that are held several times a year to connect and engage families and offer opportunities for learning and socialization. Themes for the events include "Nurturing Day," "Back to School," and "Black History Month."*

***Figure 18-43-a.*** *SafeCare Program Prevention Specialist models parent-child interaction to a parent with a 4-year-old son during a parent-child interaction skills training session.*

***Figure 18-43-b.*** *SafeCare Program Prevention specialist models an outside play activity.*

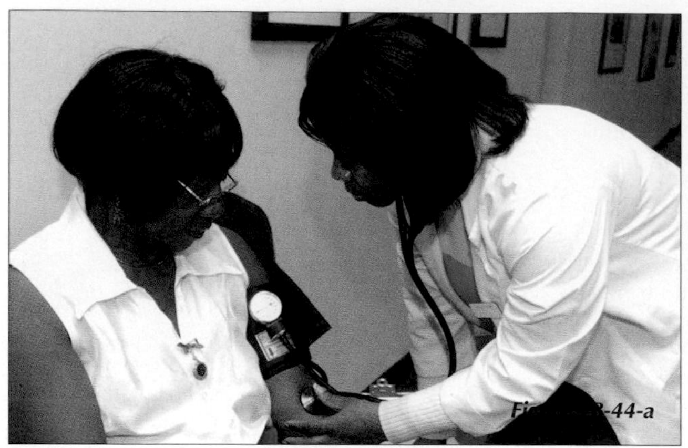

***Figure 18-44-a.*** *A Project Healthy Grandparents nurse taking a grandmother's blood pressure.*

***Figure 18-44-b.*** *A Project Healthy Grandparents support group meeting for grandparents.*

***Figure 18-45.*** *Cover of* Parenting From Prison: A Handbook for Incarcerated Mothers.

***Figure 18-46.*** *Parents participating in First Steps, a component of the Family Program Services of the Muscatine YMCA, meet together to discuss budgeting and the importance of credit while their children are cared for by YMCA staff.*

## Project Healthy Grandparents Program

Increasing numbers of children are being cared for by their grandparents because their parents are absent, often due to substance abuse, incarceration, or death. Many of the children have been abused and come into intergenerational care with multiple developmental and mental health needs. Often the grandparents are also in need because of their age, health, or economic situation. Project Healthy Grandparents at Georgia State University supports grandparent caregivers and their grandchildren through a combination of home visitation services and interactive group sessions (**Figures 18-44-a** and **b**).

## Aid to Children of Imprisoned Mothers

Aid to Children of Imprisoned Mothers provides a self-help manual for mothers in prison (**Figure 18-45**). This manual is only one of the services of this Atlanta-based organization that addresses the critical needs of children of imprisoned mothers and their families.

## Iowa—First Steps

The Iowa First Steps program, delivered through the Muscatine YMCA, is offered for young parents with children of any age (**Figure 18-46**). Parenting education is offered as well as support for individual needs. This effort is one of the local projects receiving financial support through Iowa's child abuse prevention programs, under the direction of Prevent Child Abuse Iowa.

## Iowa—Stork's Nest Program

The Nest Program is a prenatal and parenting program that teaches parents about early childhood development and parenting (**Figure 18-47**). Expectant parents can remain in the program until their children are 3 years old. Incentives such as vouchers

for diapers are provided if parents-to-be or parents in the program take certain positive steps such as going to prenatal exams, parenting classes, or well-baby visits. The Nest Program is a locally run program that receives financial support through Iowa's child abuse prevention programs, which are under the direction of Prevent Child Abuse Iowa.

## Programs Targeting Fathers

This curriculum from the National Center on Shaken Baby Syndrome addresses virtually every topic a new father will need to know and understand (**Figure 18-48**). A key element is SBS prevention. The reality of infant crying, skills to cope with crying, and effective ways to deal with the frustration that can occur are all covered.

## Fathers and Children Together

The Fathers and Children Together (FACT) Program is a prison-based parenting program located at a state minimum-security correctional facility. Backburn Correctional Complex in Lexington, Kentucky, was established in 1992 at the request of inmate fathers who were concerned about the effects of incarceration on their ability to parent from a distance and when they return home. As a program of Prevent Child Abuse Kentucky, the goal of FACT is to reduce the potential for child abuse and neglect and to promote fathers' involvement in the lives of their children during incarceration. Through a 13-week classroom-based curriculum, special father-child visitation sessions (**Figures 18-49-a** and **b**), family outreach efforts, and leadership opportunities, FACT aims to prevent child abuse and neglect while striving to reduce recidivism among incarcerated fathers. FACT was among the innovative programs cited in the Department of Health and Human Services publication *Emerging Practices in the Prevention of Child Abuse and Neglect.*

*Figure 18-47.* Participants in the Lucas County Iowa Nest Program celebrate the holiday season together.

*Figure 18-48.* Dads 101 *curriculum from National Center on Shaken Baby Syndrome.*

*Figures 18-49-a* and *b.* Participants in the Fathers and Children Together Program enjoy time with their children as part of the program activities.

Figure 18-50. Tips For Life in the Parent'Hood *brochure from the Georgia Department of Human Resources (GA DHR).*

Figure 18-51. *Spider-Man "Fatherhood" comic book.*

Figure 18-52. *Cover of* How to Help Kids Stay Safe *brochure.*

### Georgia—Fathers Program

This educational brochure was developed for fathers by the Georgia Department of Human Resources (**Figure 18-50**).

### Iowa—Fathers Program

The Dads Make a Difference Too program is offered through the Young Women's Christian Association (YWCA) in Fort Dodge, Iowa, and receives financial support through Iowa's child abuse prevention programs, under the direction of Prevent Child Abuse Iowa. The group offers fathers the opportunity to learn new skills through group topics, sharing concerns, and networking with other fathers in a confidential setting.

### Spider-Man Fathers Resource

The stories in this Spider-Man comic book demonstrate how important fathers are to their children (**Figure 18-51**). These comic books were produced by Prevent Child Abuse America and Marvel Comics, and they are a resource for both fathers and children.

## Resources to Help Parents Keep Children Safe

### How to Help Kids Stay Safe

This brochure offers parents tips on protecting children from sexual abuse, ideas on communicating about sexual abuse, signs of sexual abuse, and what to do if abuse is suspected (**Figure 18-52**). It is one of the prevention resources produced by Prevent Child Abuse North Carolina.

### What Do I Say Now?

Produced by the Committee for Children, the *What Do I Say Now?* video talks to parents about how to keep their children safe from child sexual abuse (**Figure 18-53**).

### Before You Leave Your Kids with Your Boyfriend

After identifying a significant number of children that were abused by mothers' boyfriends, the Department of Family and Children Services of the Georgia Department of Human Resources developed an informational piece to encourage mothers to evaluate their boyfriend's caregiving skills and temperament before leaving their child with him (**Figure 18-54**).

### Children Home Alone

Many parents struggle with childcare options and this brochure helps parents evaluate their child's capabilities and their environment to make informed decisions about when it is acceptable to leave a child alone. This is a prevention resource produced and distributed by Prevent Child Abuse Indiana (**Figure 18-55**).

### Report Card Time

Report card time is often stressful for parents and children and sometimes results in physical or emotional abuse. Prevent Child Abuse Georgia distributes tips to help reduce the risk of maltreatment around report card time (**Figure 18-56**).

Figure 18-53

DON'T TAKE A CHANCE

Before you leave your kids with your boyfriend — ASK YOURSELF

- Does he get mad easily?
- Does he expect children to act right all the time?
- Does he drink too much or do drugs?

If you answer "yes" to any of these questions, it's probably safer to find someone else to babysit for you.

Kids are going to cry, wet their pants, throw up. But these aren't reasons to spank or hurt them.

You need someone watching them who doesn't expect too much. Is the man you're with that kind of person?

DHR

The Georgia Department of Human Resources
Division of Family and Children Services

Figure 18-54

*Figure 18-53.* What Do I Say Now? *video from the Committee for Children.*

*Figure 18-54.* Before You Leave Your Kids With Your Boyfriend *brochure from GA DHR.*

*Figure 18-55.* When Is It OK for Your Children to be Home Alone? *from Prevent Child Abuse Indiana.*

Figure 18-55

## Personal Safety and Support/Education Progams for Children

### Parents Anonymous Children's Program

While parents are meeting in weekly Parents Anonymous groups, their children find a safe, warm, predictable, and structured setting where they learn and practice ways of interacting, problem solving, and supporting one another. Children also develop and practice leadership skills and become leaders within the program (**Figure 18-57**).

### Circle of Parents Children's Program

Offered in conjunction with Circle of Parents parent support groups, the children's programs are a safe place for children to play and interact while their parents are in a group (**Figure 18-58**). Circle of Parents Program is a collaboration between Prevent Child Abuse America and the National Family Support Roundtable.

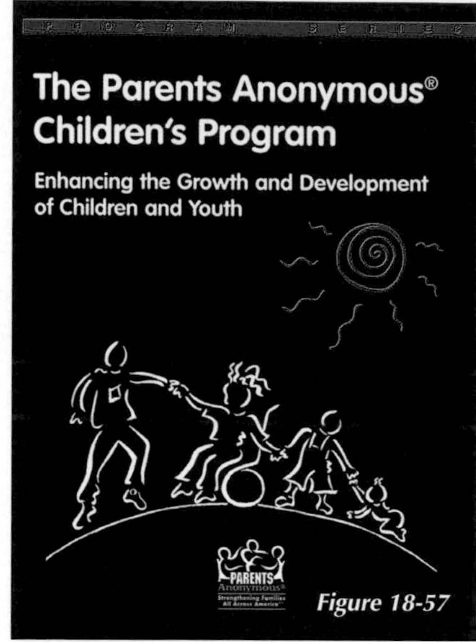


Figure 18-57

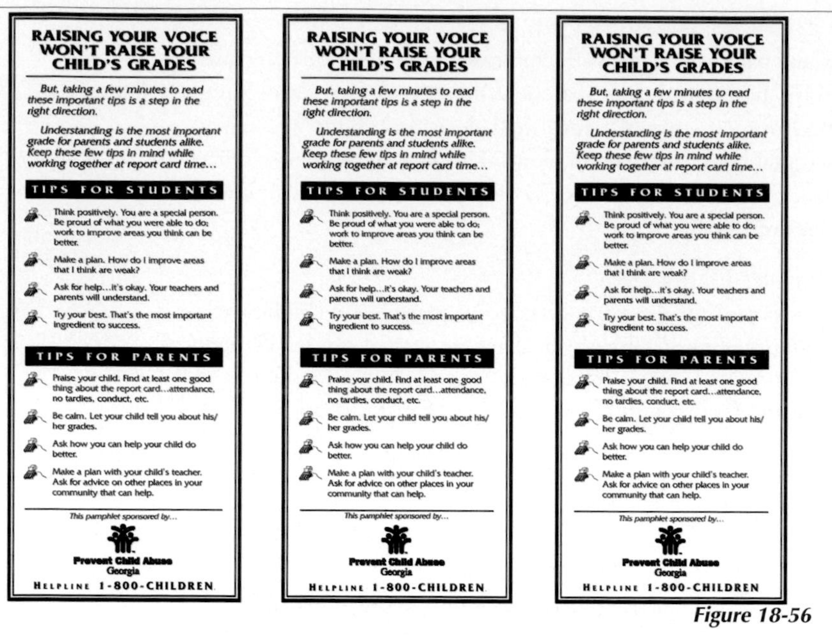

RAISING YOUR VOICE WON'T RAISE YOUR CHILD'S GRADES

*But, taking a few minutes to read these important tips is a step in the right direction.*

*Understanding is the most important grade for parents and students alike. Keep these few tips in mind while working together at report card time...*

TIPS FOR STUDENTS

- Think positively. You are a special person. Be proud of what you were able to do; work to improve areas you think can be better.
- Make a plan. How do I improve areas that I think are weak?
- Ask for help...it's okay. Your teachers and parents will understand.
- Try your best. That's the most important ingredient to success.

TIPS FOR PARENTS

- Praise your child. Find at least one good thing about the report card...attendance, no tardies, conduct, etc.
- Be calm. Let your child tell you about his/her grades.
- Ask how you can help your child do better.
- Make a plan with your child's teacher. Ask for advice on other places in your community that can help.

*This pamphlet sponsored by...*

Prevent Child Abuse Georgia

HELPLINE 1-800-CHILDREN

Figure 18-56

Figure 18-58

***Figure 18-56.*** Raising Your Voice Won't Raise Your Child's Grades *from Prevent Child Abuse Georgia.*

***Figure 18-57.*** *Cover of* Parents Anonymous Children's Program *manual.*

***Figure 18-58.*** *Cover of* Circle of Parents Children's Program Manual.

### Georgia—Need to Talk Helpline

"Need To Talk?" gives young people between the ages of 10 and 18 years in Georgia an opportunity to speak confidentially to the Prevent Child Abuse Georgia Helpline whenever they have concerns. The cards are distributed in schools after key educational staff members receive an orientation to the program (**Figures 18-59-a** and **b**).

### Aid to Children of Imprisoned Mothers

Aid to Children of Imprisoned Mothers (AIM) in Atlanta, Georgia, works to inspire hope in the children of imprisoned mothers and their families by providing programs and services that lessen the impact of the mother's incarceration. On a weekly basis, children are matched one-on-one with volunteers in AIM's after-school and teen programs where they receive help with homework and computer training. The children participate in a curriculum designed to promote academic, personal, and professional development. The program also has field trips, a summer camp, Camp AIM High, monthly year-round transportation, and volunteer supervision so that children may visit their mothers in prison.

### Project Healthy Grandparents—Children's Program

Growing numbers of children are being raised by their grandparents due to the absence of their parents, most often because of substance abuse, incarceration, or death. Supported in part by Georgia State University, Project Healthy Grandparents (PHG) works to strengthen intergenerational families and to improve the quality of life by providing grandparents and grandchildren with comprehensive services and improved access to community services. PHG offers a Saturday Youth Academy to provide children aged 5 to 16 years with psychoeducational group therapy; cultural/recreational activities; and time to socialize with each other, build positive self-images, and reduce their sense of isolation. The Early Childhood Intervention Program serves children 0-5 years old who are at risk for developmental delay due to maternal substance abuse and/or HIV/AIDS.

## Programs to Teach Violence Prevention Skills

There is increasing recognition of the relationship between abuse in the early years and an increased risk of being a perpetrator of violence or a victim of violence as a juvenile or adult. Teaching violence prevention skills to children may be a vital cornerstone for preventing future child abuse and neglect.

### Second Step Violence Prevention Program

The Second Step Violence Prevention Program produced by the Committee for Children offers violence prevention curricula for all grade levels (**Figures 18-60-a, b, c, d,** and **e**). The program teaches empathy, anger management, impulse control, and assertiveness.

### Violence Prevention Skills

These Spider-Man comics were produced by Prevent Child Abuse America and Marvel Comics to teach violence prevention skills to children (**Figures 18-61-a, b,** and **c**).

### Steps to Respect Kit

The Steps to Respect kit is a bullying prevention program from the Committee for Children (**Figure 18-62**).

### Personal Safety Curriculum

One of the first strategies to prevent sexual abuse is teaching children about body safety and how to protect themselves. Some programs focus exclusively on these skills while others offer a broader look at personal safety skills. The *Talking About Touching* personal safety curriculum was produced by the Committee for Children (**Figures 18-63-a** and **b**).

### Spider-Man Personal Safety Material

In these comic books, Spider-Man teaches children about sexual (**Figure 18-64-a**), physical (**Figure 18-64-b**), and emotional abuse (**Figure 18-64-c**), and how to protect themselves and get help if they need it. Prevent Child Abuse America and Marvel Comics produced this Spider-Man series on abuse.

***Figures 18-59-a** and **b**. Front and back of the* Need to Talk *card from the Prevent Child Abuse Georgia Helpline.*

### QuickThink

Children learn best through play. QuickThink, a board game from Prevent Child Abuse Georgia, helps children learn how to make safe and smart decisions about potentially dangerous situations including child abuse, fire, strangers, bullies, Internet predators, and guns (**Figure 18-65**). Blank decision cards allow families to create situations specific to their family.

### HOPE! Drama Troupe

HOPE! Drama Troupe is a child abuse prevention program in which peers educate their peers about child abuse. Under the guidance of professional directors and the Child Abuse Prevention Council in Des Moines, Iowa, the troupe writes and performs message-oriented vignettes. Because the performances are written and performed by young people, they effectively connect with their target audience of middle and high school students. Troupe members emphasize to young people that the problems they face will not change, and the healing will not begin until they tell someone they trust—a friend, a teacher, or a counselor. HOPE! Drama Troupe performs for more than 3000 students each school year in the Des Moines area (**Figure 18-66**).

### Woven Word Family Book

For children aged 3 to 5 years, the Woven Word program stories and books use dialogical reading to increase emerging literary skills and teach social and emotional skills that include waiting, sharing, taking turns, simple planning, and empathy (**Figure 18-67**). The lessons dovetail with the Second Step program lessons and include a parent component. The program was developed by the Committee for Children.

Figure 18-60-a

Figure 18-60-b

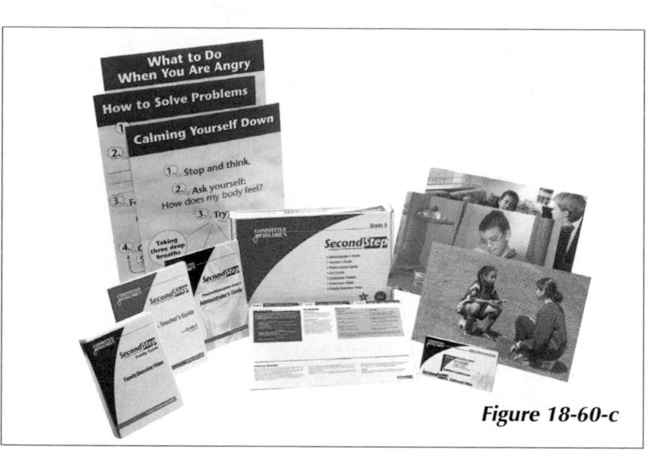


Figure 18-60-c

Figure 18-60-d

**_Figure 18-60-a._** *The* Second Step Preschool/ Kindergarten *kit includes materials for use with children, parents, and teachers.*

**_Figure 18-60-b._** *Kindergarten children learn violence prevention skills in the Second Step Program.*

**_Figure 18-60-c._** *Like the preschool kit, the Grade 3 Second Step kit offers a variety of resources for teaching violence prevention skills.*

**_Figure 18-60-d._** *Children participate in a Second Step Program lesson.*

**_Figure 18-60-e._** *The Second Step Program kit for middle school students.*

Figure 18-60-e

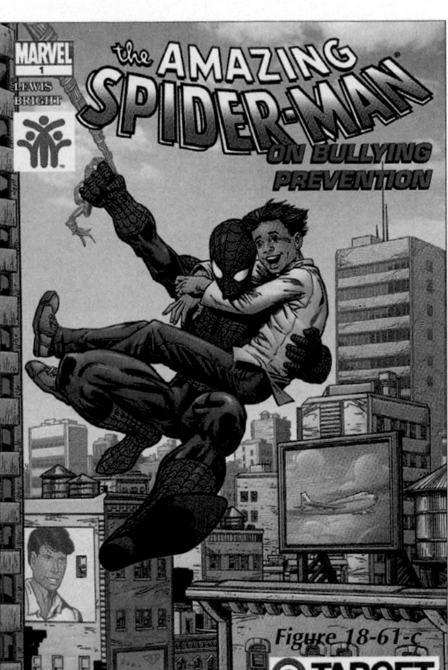

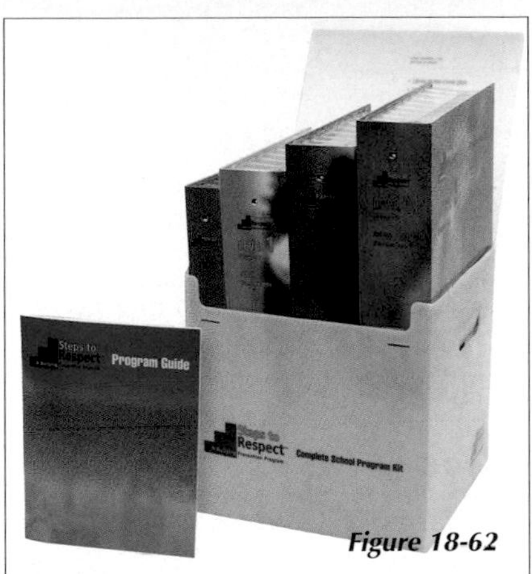

***Figure 18-61-a.*** *Spider-Man comic book,* How to Beat the Bully.

***Figure 18-61-b.*** Jublilee: Peer Pressure. *This is the back cover of* ***Figure 18-61-a****, creating 2 stories in 1 comic book.*

***Figure 18-61-c.*** *Spider-Man comic book addressing bullying prevention.*

***Figure 18-62.*** Steps to Respect *kit from the Committee for Children.*

***Figure 18-63-a.*** *Talking About Touching Personal Safety Curriculum for preschool and kindergarten children.*

***Figure 18-63-b.*** *Grade 3 lesson picture for* Talking About Touching. *Lessons in the grade 3 curriculum engage children in discussing how to handle potentially dangerous situations.*

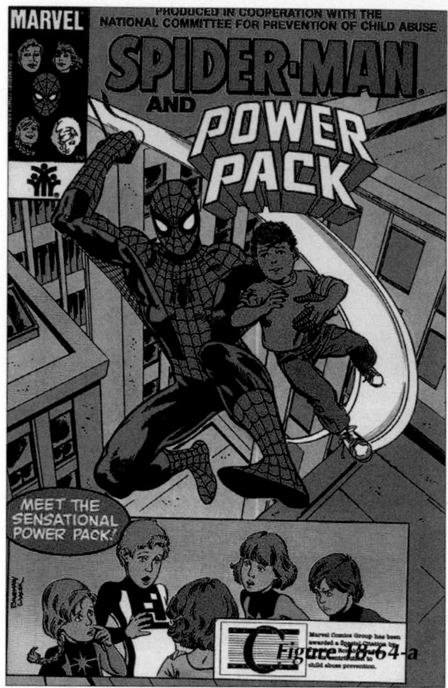

**Figure 18-64-a.** *Front cover of a Spider-Man and Power Pack comic book addressing sexual abuse.*

**Figure 18-64-b.** *Front cover of Spider-Man and the New Mutants comic book addressing physical abuse.*

**Figure 18-64-c.** *Front cover of Spider-Man comic book addressing emotional abuse.*

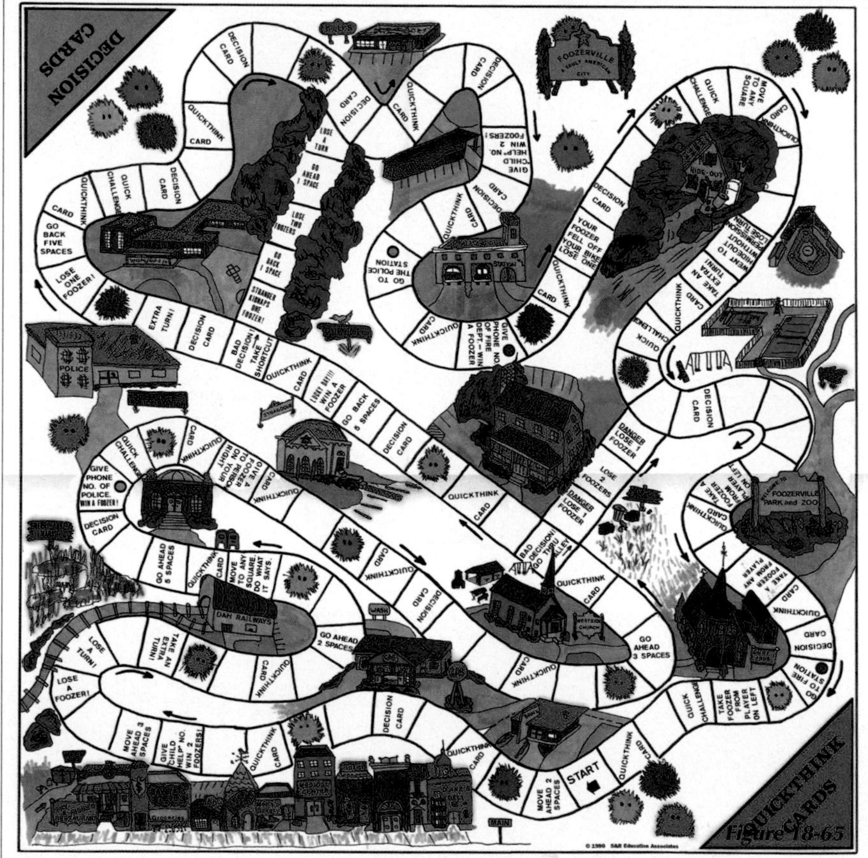


**Figure 18-65.** *QuickThink board game.*

**Figure 18-66.** *David Van Cleve (left) and Glenn Burmeister perform at a HOPE! Drama Troupe presentation at the Prevent Child Abuse Iowa Conference.*

**Figure 18-67.** Woven Word Family book.

Chapter 19

# Resources and Settings in the Field of Child Maltreatment

Randell Alexander, MD, PhD

The field of child maltreatment consists of physical findings, histories, interventions, treatments, and prevention as well as the people who work to accomplish these endeavors. Child maltreatment is one of many fields that use interdisciplinary and multidisciplinary teams and organizations. Such contacts are essential for the protection and advancement of children's safety, thus it is important to be aware of others who function outside of one's own discipline and to appreciate the important organizations, conferences, and settings that exist. Some examples of resources and settings within the field of child abuse are listed in this chapter. For those new to the field, it is important to learn about these components of child abuse and others that will benefit child maltreatment casework.

## Professional Organizations

Within professional organizations colleagues can learn from each other, attend advanced training, share research, and affect public policy. There are a number of key organizations; some are discipline specific and others include multiple disciplines. Such organizations not only help advance the cause of abused children, they also can be very useful for professional development and even emotional support for those working in difficult situations. Some organizations and resources are listed here, along with adapted versions of some of their promotional materials.

### National Clearinghouse on Child Abuse and Neglect Information

One organization that collects, classifies, and distributes information for several entities is the National Clearinghouse on Child Abuse and Neglect Information. This is an excellent resource for child abuse information. The Office of Child Abuse and Neglect is a government entity that awards grants for child abuse research. In addition, it is responsible for a national conference on child abuse every 2 years. The National Clearinghouse can be contacted at:

National Clearinghouse on Child Abuse and Neglect Information
330 C Street, SW
Washington, DC 20447
Phone: (800) 394-3366 or (703) 385-7565
Fax: (703) 385-3206
E-mail: nccanch@caliber.com
http://nccanch.acf.hhs.gov

### American Professional Society on the Abuse of Children

The American Professional Society on the Abuse of Children (APSAC) (**Figure 19-1**) is a membership society consisting of approximately 2500 top professionals from nearly all disciplines of child abuse (eg, law enforcement, medicine, social services,

***Figure 19-1.*** *APSAC logo. Reprinted with permission from APSAC.*

law, mental health, education, and allied professions). This is an organization that nearly every professional working within the field of child abuse wants to join. The goals of APSAC include professional education and advancement of the field of child abuse in general as well as the promotion of research and practice guidelines to inform all forms of professional practice in child maltreatment. Its mission is to improve the quality of practice provided by professionals who work within the field of child abuse and neglect by providing them education that promotes effective, culturally sensitive, and interdisciplinary approaches to the identification, intervention, treatment, and prevention of child abuse and neglect. APSAC provides information via publications such as the *APSAC Advisor*, the organization's official newsletter that is issued quarterly; *Child Maltreatment*, a quarterly peer-reviewed scientific journal containing articles aimed at various practitioners; the *APSAC Study Guides; The APSAC Handbook on Child Maltreatment;* and *Guidelines for Practice*. The APSAC Annual Colloquium brings professionals together to hear the latest research findings and share points of view and expertise. Training also includes the innovative Forensic Interview Clinics and the Maui Child Abuse/Child Trauma Seminar. APSAC has a number of state chapters where professionals within a state work on training and other child abuse issues. APSAC is primarily a North American professional organization.

Information about APSAC and membership applications can be obtained from:

APSAC
PO Box 30669
Charleston, SC 29417
Phone: (877) 40-APSAC
Fax: (803) 753-9823
E-mail: apsac@comcast.net.
http://www.apsac.org

***Figure 19-2.*** *ISPCAN logo. Reprinted with permission from ISPCAN.*

## International Society for Prevention of Child Abuse and Neglect

The International Society for Prevention of Child Abuse and Neglect (ISPCAN) (**Figure 19-2**), founded in 1977, is the only multidisciplinary international organization that brings together a worldwide cross-section of committed professionals to work toward the prevention and treatment of child abuse, neglect, and exploitation. Its mission is to support individuals and organizations working to protect children from abuse and neglect worldwide.

ISPCAN targets the prevention of any form of cruelty to children in every nation. Among the areas addressed by ISPCAN are physical abuse, sexual abuse, neglect, street children, child fatalities, child prostitution, children of war, emotional abuse, and child labor. ISPCAN is committed to: (1) increasing public awareness of violence against children; (2) developing activities to prevent such violence; and (3) promoting the rights of children throughout the world. ISPCAN members employ the use of their journal (*The International Journal of Child Abuse & Neglect*) and periodic newsletter updates as a forum for discussion. ISPCAN hosts an international child abuse conference every 2 years at sites around the world.

The contact information for ISPCAN is as follows:

The International Society for Prevention of Child Abuse and Neglect
245 W. Roosevelt Road, Bldg. 6, Suite 39
West Chicago, IL 60185
Phone: (630) 876-6913
Fax: (630) 876-6917
E-mail: ispcan@ispcan.org or exec@ispcan.org
http://www.ispcan.org

## Prevent Child Abuse America

Prevent Child Abuse America (PCA America) (**Figure 19-3**) is essentially the American equivalent of ISPCAN. It is open to professionals and nonprofessionals, and coordinates many child abuse initiatives through its state chapters. PCA America has worked with numerous organizations to spread the word about child abuse prevention, including Marvel Comics (through a Spiderman series on child abuse prevention) and the National Basketball Association. PCA America has chapters in virtually every state. Professionals and the public are invited to participate in local volunteer efforts to dramatically reduce child abuse and enrich the lives of children. Prevention is the ultimate solution to child abuse, but it is often overlooked in the rush to deal with current cases.

Figure 19-3

Further information can be found at:

Prevent Child Abuse America
200 S. Michigan Avenue, 17th Floor
Chicago, IL 60604-2404
Phone: (312) 663-3520
Fax: (312) 939-8962
E-mail: mailbox@preventchildabuse.org
http://www.preventchildabuse.org

## National Children's Alliance

National Children's Alliance (NCA) (**Figure 19-4**), formerly the National Network of Children's Advocacy Centers, is a nationwide not-for-profit membership organization whose mission is to promote and support communities in providing a coordinated investigation and comprehensive response to victims of severe child abuse. Children's Advocacy Centers (CACs)—the primary location for forensic interviewing of children in many locales—are NCA accredited members. CACs bring together professionals and agencies as a multidisciplinary team in an attempt to improve the response to cases of child abuse.

Figure 19-4

National Children's Alliance can be contacted at:

National Children's Alliance
1612 K Street, NW, Suite 500
Washington, DC 20006
Phone: (800) 239-9950 or (202) 452-6001
Fax: (202) 452-6002
E-mail: info@nca-online.org
http://www.nca-online.org

## National Center on Shaken Baby Syndrome

The National Center on Shaken Baby Syndrome (NCSBS) (**Figure 19-5**) collects information about shaken baby syndrome and is a superb resource for information and referral on such matters. The NCSBS hosts North American and international conferences every year.

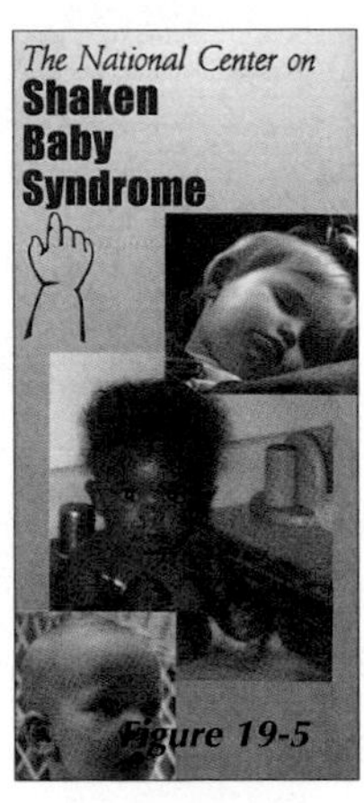


Figure 19-5

Contact information is as follows:

National Center on Shaken Baby Syndrome
2955 Harrison Blvd., Suite 102
Ogden, UT 84403
Phone: (888) 273-0071
Fax: (801) 627-3321
E-mail: mail@dontshake.com
http://www.dontshake.com

***Figure 19-3.*** *PCA America logo. Reprinted with permission from PCA America.*

***Figure 19-4.*** *NCA logo. Reprinted with permission from NCA.*

***Figure 19-5.*** *National Center on Shaken Baby Syndrome brochure.*

## Conferences

Conferences are a valuable way to meet colleagues, share cases and frustrations, and learn new developments in one's own discipline and others. There are a number of excellent local, state, and regional conferences.

### ISPCAN Conference

ISPCAN holds the biannual European Regional Conference on Child Abuse and Neglect and a separate international conference in different locations around the world (**Figure 19-6**). Themes are focused on prevention with a truly international emphasis.

Figure 19-6

Figure 19-7

### APSAC Conference

APSAC hosts a yearly conference in various US cities (**Figure 19-7**). All disciplines are represented in this practice, research, and state-of-the-art conference. About 500 to 800 professionals attend.

### Children's Hospital of San Diego Conference

A popular conference is the one hosted by Children's Hospital of San Diego each year at the end of January (**Figures 19-8-a** and **b**). This multidisciplinary conference is known for its high-quality presentations to the nearly 2000 professionals who attend. Traditionally, it

Figure 19-8-a

Figure 19-8-b

***Figure 19-6.*** *ISPCAN conference brochure.*

***Figure 19-7.*** *APSAC conference brochure.*

***Figures 19-8-a*** *and* ***b.*** *San Diego conference brochure and site.*

has strong medical and mental health components, but all of the disciplines are well represented.

## National Conference on Child Abuse and Neglect

Boston, Massachusetts, is where the 15th National Conference on Child Abuse and Neglect (NCCAN) will be held in April 2005 (**Figure 19-9**). The conference theme promotes interagency and interdisciplinary collaboration to make the best use of available resources and provide more effective services for the protection of children and the strengthening of families. Both beginners and advanced professionals can find beneficial support at this conference. The US Office of Child Abuse and Neglect hosts the conference every 2 years.

*Figure 19-9*

## Crimes Against Children Conference

Interdisciplinary, but with special emphasis for law enforcement, the annual Crimes Against Children conference is held in Dallas, Texas, each August (**Figure 19-10**). Top professionals in a variety of fields help to educate approximately 2000 fellow professionals about the newest developments in combating the various forms of crimes against children.

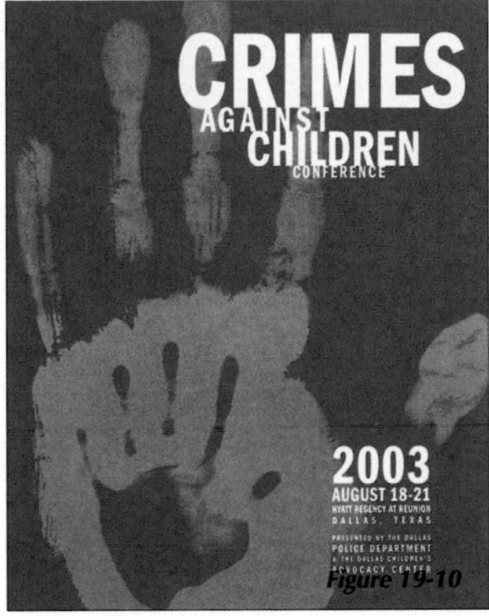

*Figure 19-10*

## Huntsville Conference

Held at the site of the original CAC, the interdisciplinary Huntsville conference (as it is commonly known) is held in mid-March each year (**Figures 19-11-a** and **b**). Invariably, it is an excellent program consisting of top experts and a large group of attendees.

*Figure 19-11-a*

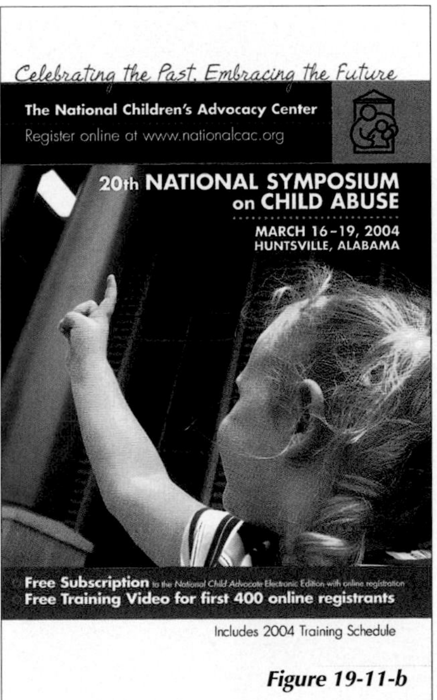

*Figure 19-11-b*

***Figure 19-9.*** *NCCAN conference program.*

***Figure 19-10.*** *Crimes Against Children Conference brochure.*

***Figures 19-11-a*** *and* ***b.*** *Huntsville conference brochure.*

*Figure 19-12-a*

The National Australian
Conference on
Shaken Baby Syndrome

The Regent Hotel, Sydney
3-4 September 2001
Sydney, Australia

*Figure 19-12-b*

**Figures 19-12-a, b, c,** and **d.** *Several program brochures representing previous shaken baby syndrome conferences.*

**Figure 19-13.** The Quarterly Update. *Reprinted with permission from The Quarterly Update.*

### Conference on Shaken Baby Syndrome

Each Conference on Shaken Baby Syndrome (**Figures 19-12-a, b, c,** and **d**) draws from 400 to over 600 participants to hear state-of-the-art discussions of all aspects of abusive head trauma. Caregivers who have been affected by shaken baby syndrome (eg, the Shaken Baby Alliance) have been active participants, and special sessions are set aside for them. Previous sites for the conference include: Salt Lake City, Sydney, Edinburgh, and Montreal.

## Publications

Publications are another important way to keep informed. Some publications are linked to organizations, but others are not. Following is a list of periodicals that form an excellent basis for understanding the field of child abuse.

### The Quarterly Update

*The Quarterly Update* (**Figure 19-13**) is an invaluable means to stay current with the latest information regarding the field of child abuse. Articles appearing in a wide range of journals are abstracted every 3 months in this publication, with commentary by experts in the field. For up-to-date information about child abuse literature, *The Quarterly Update* is an incomparable resource.

### Child Maltreatment

*Child Maltreatment* is the journal for APSAC. It covers a wide range of topics appealing to those in the field of child abuse.

*Figure 19-12-d*

EUROPEAN CONFERENCE ON
SHAKEN BABY SYNDROME
19-20 May 2003
Edinburgh
Scotland

*Figure 19-12-c*

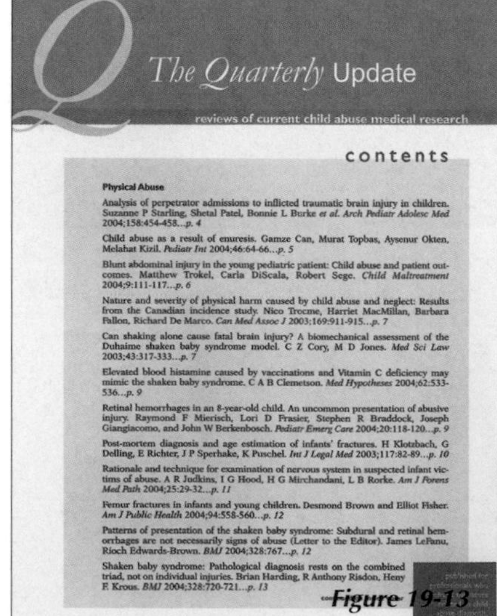
The *Quarterly* Update
reviews of current child abuse medical research

contents

**Physical Abuse**

Analysis of perpetrator admissions to inflicted traumatic brain injury in children. Suzanne P Starling, Shetal Patel, Bonnie L Burke *et al. Arch Pediatr Adolesc Med* 2004;158:454-458...*p. 4*

Child abuse as a result of enuresis. Gamze Can, Murat Topbas, Aysenur Okten, Melahat Kizil. *Pediatr Int* 2004;46:64-66...*p. 5*

Blunt abdominal injury in the young pediatric patient: Child abuse and patient outcomes. Matthew Trokel, Carla DiScala, Robert Sege. *Child Maltreatment* 2004;9:111-117...*p. 6*

Nature and severity of physical harm caused by child abuse and neglect: Results from the Canadian incidence study. Nico Trocme, Harriet MacMillan, Barbara Fallon, Richard De Marco. *Can Med Assoc J* 2003;169:911-915...*p. 7*

Can shaking alone cause fatal brain injury? A biomechanical assessment of the Duhaime shaken baby syndrome model. C Z Cory, M D Jones. *Med Sci Law* 2003;43:317-333...*p. 7*

Elevated blood histamine caused by vaccinations and Vitamin C deficiency may mimic the shaken baby syndrome. C A B Clemetson. *Med Hypotheses* 2004;62:533-536...*p. 9*

Retinal hemorrhages in an 8-year-old child. An uncommon presentation of abusive injury. Raymond F Mierisch, Lori D Frasier, Stephen R Braddock, Joseph Giangiacomo, and John W Berkenbosch. *Pediatr Emerg Care* 2004;20:118-120...*p. 9*

Post-mortem diagnosis and age estimation of infants' fractures. H Klotzbach, G Delling, E Richter, J P Sperhake, K Puschel. *Int J Legal Med* 2003;117:82-89...*p. 10*

Rationale and technique for examination of nervous system in suspected infant victims of abuse. A R Judkins, I G Hood, H G Mirchandani, L B Rorke. *Am J Forens Med Path* 2004;25:29-32...*p. 11*

Femur fractures in infants and young children. Desmond Brown and Elliot Fisher. *Am J Public Health* 2004;94:558-560...*p. 12*

Patterns of presentation of the shaken baby syndrome: Subdural and retinal hemorrhages are not necessarily signs of abuse (Letter to the Editor). James LeFanu, Rioch Edwards-Brown. *BMJ* 2004;328:767...*p. 12*

Shaken baby syndrome: Pathological diagnosis rests on the combined triad, not on individual injuries. Brian Harding, R Anthony Risdon, Heny F Krous. *BMJ* 2004;328:720-721...*p. 13*

*Figure 19-13*

## APSAC Advisor

The *APSAC Advisor* (**Figure 19-14**) is much more than just a newsletter. Some of the latest developments in practice are first discussed here. The range of topics reflects the diversity of the organization itself.

## APSAC Guidelines

*APSAC Practice Guidelines* (**Figures 19-15-a, b, c, d, e,** and **f**) represent state-of-the-art thinking about various practice areas. The guidelines are not rigid "standards" but have proved helpful to those in the field. Further information about these guidelines can be found at http://www.apsac.org.

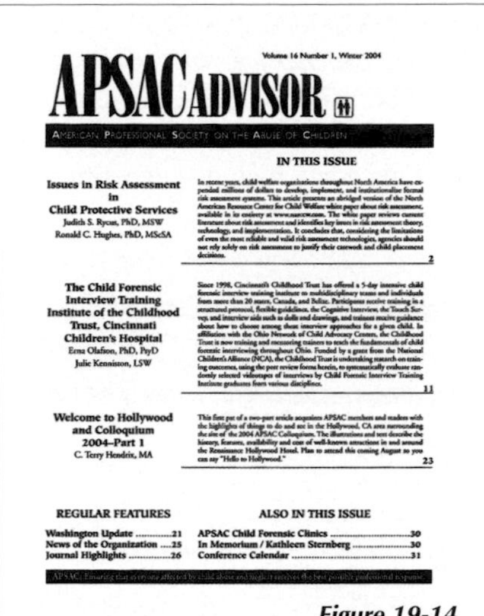

Volume 16 Number 1, Winter 2004

APSAC ADVISOR

AMERICAN PROFESSIONAL SOCIETY ON THE ABUSE OF CHILDREN

IN THIS ISSUE

**Issues in Risk Assessment in Child Protective Services**
Judith S. Rycus, PhD, MSW
Ronald C. Hughes, PhD, MScSA

**The Child Forensic Interview Training Institute of the Childhood Trust, Cincinnati Children's Hospital**
Erna Olafson, PhD, PsyD
Julie Kenniston, LSW

**Welcome to Hollywood and Colloquium 2004–Part 1**
C. Terry Hendrix, MA

REGULAR FEATURES

Washington Update ..... 21
News of the Organization ..... 25
Journal Highlights ..... 26

ALSO IN THIS ISSUE

APSAC Child Forensic Clinics ..... 30
In Memorium / Kathleen Sternberg ..... 30
Conference Calendar ..... 31

*Figure 19-14*

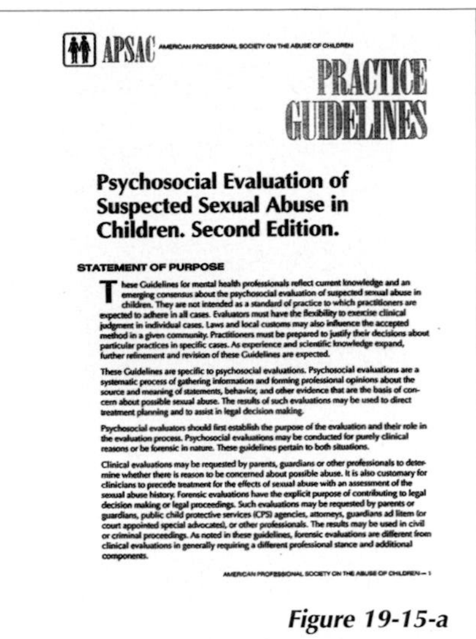

APSAC AMERICAN PROFESSIONAL SOCIETY ON THE ABUSE OF CHILDREN

PRACTICE GUIDELINES

**Psychosocial Evaluation of Suspected Sexual Abuse in Children. Second Edition.**

STATEMENT OF PURPOSE

*Figure 19-15-a*

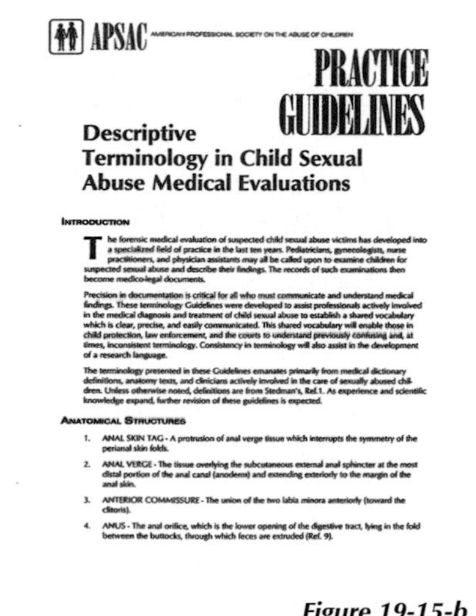

APSAC AMERICAN PROFESSIONAL SOCIETY ON THE ABUSE OF CHILDREN

PRACTICE GUIDELINES

**Descriptive Terminology in Child Sexual Abuse Medical Evaluations**

INTRODUCTION

ANATOMICAL STRUCTURES

*Figure 19-15-b*

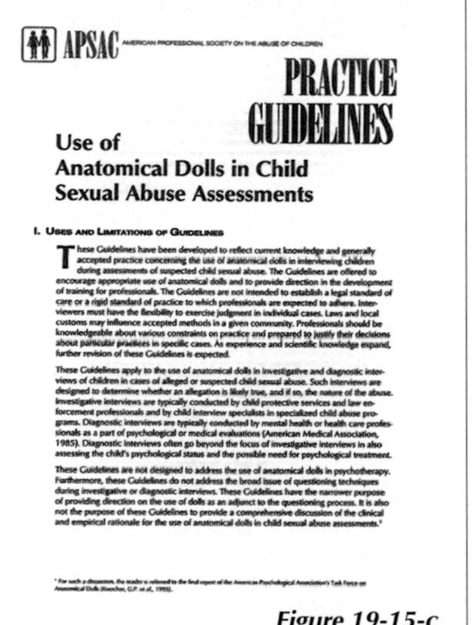

APSAC AMERICAN PROFESSIONAL SOCIETY ON THE ABUSE OF CHILDREN

PRACTICE GUIDELINES

**Use of Anatomical Dolls in Child Sexual Abuse Assessments**

I. USES AND LIMITATIONS OF GUIDELINES

*Figure 19-15-c*

APSAC AMERICAN PROFESSIONAL SOCIETY ON THE ABUSE OF CHILDREN

PRACTICE GUIDELINES

**Photographic Documentation of Child Abuse**

STATEMENT OF PURPOSE

*Figure 19-15-d*

APSAC AMERICAN PROFESSIONAL SOCIETY ON THE ABUSE OF CHILDREN

PRACTICE GUIDELINES

**Investigative Interviewing in Cases of Alleged Child Abuse**

*Figure 19-15-e*

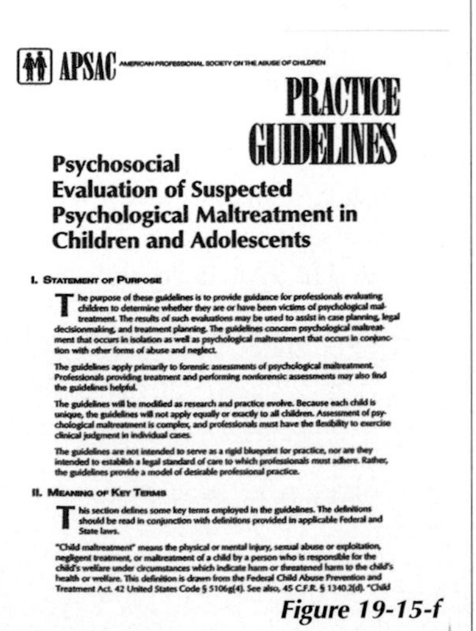

APSAC AMERICAN PROFESSIONAL SOCIETY ON THE ABUSE OF CHILDREN

PRACTICE GUIDELINES

**Psychosocial Evaluation of Suspected Psychological Maltreatment in Children and Adolescents**

I. STATEMENT OF PURPOSE

II. MEANING OF KEY TERMS

*Figure 19-15-f*

***Figure 19-14.*** The APSAC Advisor. *Reprinted with permission from APSAC.*

***Figures 19-15-a, b, c, d, e,** and **f.*** APSAC Practice Guidelines. *Reprinted with permission from APSAC.*

Figure 19-16

**Figure 19-16.** *The* International Journal of Child Abuse & Neglect. *Reprinted with permission from Elsevier.* Int J Child Abuse Neglect. *2003;28(3).*

**Figure 19-17.** The Link. *Reprinted with permission from ISPCAN.*

## International Journal of Child Abuse & Neglect

*The International Journal of Child Abuse & Neglect* (**Figure 19-16**) is the journal for ISPCAN. With some focus on prevention, its topics cover all facets of child abuse in articles from around the world. This was the first journal in the field of child abuse, and it maintains high-quality writing and editing.

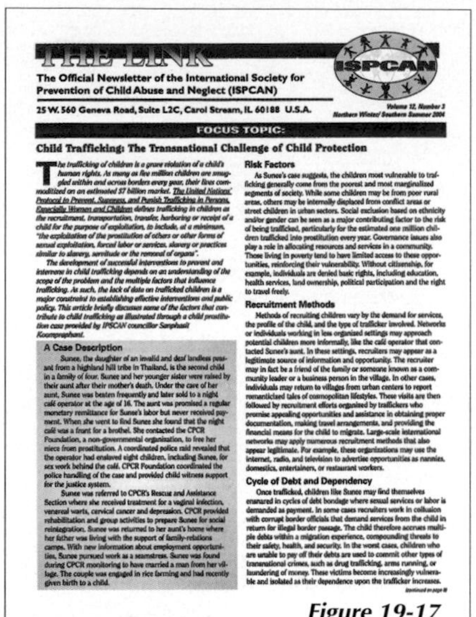

THE LINK

The Official Newsletter of the International Society for Prevention of Child Abuse and Neglect (ISPCAN)

ISPCAN

25 W. 560 Geneva Road, Suite L2C, Carol Stream, IL 60188 U.S.A.

Volume 12, Number 3
Northern Winter/ Southern Summer 2004

FOCUS TOPIC:

**Child Trafficking: The Transnational Challenge of Child Protection**

*The trafficking of children is a grave violation of a child's human rights. As many as five million children are smuggled within and across borders every year, their lives commoditized on an estimated $7 billion market. The United Nations' Protocol to Prevent, Suppress, and Punish Trafficking in Persons, Especially Women and Children defines trafficking in children as the recruitment, transportation, transfer, harboring or receipt of a child for the purpose of exploitation, to include, at a minimum, "the exploitation of the prostitution of others or other forms of sexual exploitation, forced labor or services, slavery or practices similar to slavery, servitude or the removal of organs".*

*The development of successful interventions to prevent and intervene in child trafficking depends on an understanding of the scope of the problem and the multiple factors that influence trafficking. As such, the lack of data on trafficked children is a major constraint to establishing effective interventions and public policy. This article briefly discusses some of the factors that contribute to child trafficking as illustrated through a child prostitution case provided by IPSCAN councillor Sanphasit Koompraphant.*

**A Case Description**

Sunee, the daughter of an invalid and deaf landless peasant from a highland hill tribe in Thailand, is the second child in a family of four. Sunee and her younger sister were raised by their aunt after their mother's death. Under the care of her aunt, Sunee was beaten frequently and later sold to a night café operator at the age of 16. The aunt was promised a regular monetary remittance for Sunee's labor but never received payment. When she went to find Sunee she found that the night café was a front for a brothel. She contacted the CPCR Foundation, a non-governmental organization, to free her niece from prostitution. A coordinated police raid revealed that the operator had enslaved eight children, including Sunee, for sex work behind the café. CPCR Foundation coordinated the police handling of the case and provided child witness support for the justice system.

Sunee was referred to CPCR's Rescue and Assistance Section where she received treatment for a vaginal infection, venereal warts, cervical cancer and depression. CPCR provided rehabilitation and group activities to prepare Sunee for social reintegration. Sunee was returned to her aunt's home where her father was living with the support of family-relations camps. With new information about employment opportunities, Sunee pursued work as a seamstress. Sunee was found during CPCR monitoring to have married a man from her village. The couple was engaged in rice farming and had recently given birth to a child.

**Risk Factors**

As Sunee's case suggests, the children most vulnerable to trafficking generally come from the poorest and most marginalized segments of society. While some children may be from poor rural areas, others may be internally displaced from conflict areas or street children in urban sectors. Social exclusion based on ethnicity and/or gender can be seen as a major contributing factor to the risk of being trafficked, particularly for the estimated one million children trafficked into prostitution every year. Governance issues also play a role in allocating resources and services in a community. Those living in poverty tend to have limited access to these opportunities, reinforcing their vulnerability. Without citizenship, for example, individuals are denied basic rights, including education, health services, land ownership, political participation and the right to travel freely.

**Recruitment Methods**

Methods of recruiting children vary by the demand for services, the profile of the child, and the type of trafficker involved. Networks or individuals working in less organized settings may approach potential children more informally, like the café operator that contacted Sunee's aunt. In these settings, recruiters may appear as a legitimate source of information and opportunity. The recruiter may in fact be a friend of the family or someone known as a community leader or a business person in the village. In other cases, individuals may return to villages from urban centers to report romanticized tales of cosmopolitan lifestyles. These visits are then followed by recruitment efforts organized by traffickers who promise appealing opportunities and assistance in obtaining proper documentation, making travel arrangements, and providing the financial means for the child to migrate. Large-scale international networks may apply numerous recruitment methods that also appear legitimate. For example, these organizations may use the internet, radio, and television to advertise opportunities as nannies, domestics, entertainers, or restaurant workers.

**Cycle of Debt and Dependency**

Once trafficked, children like Sunee may find themselves ensnared in cycles of debt bondage where sexual services or labor is demanded as payment. In some cases recruiters work in collusion with corrupt border officials that demand services from the child in return for illegal border passage. The child therefore accrues multiple debts within a migration experience, compounding threats to their safety, health, and security. In the worst cases, children who are unable to pay off their debts are used to commit other types of transnational crimes, such as drug trafficking, arms running, or laundering of money. These victims become increasingly vulnerable and isolated as their dependence upon the trafficker increases.

Figure 19-17

## The Link

*The Link* (**Figure 19-17**) is the official newsletter from ISPCAN and complements the *International Journal of Child Abuse & Neglect* by covering more topical information.

# Settings

Child abuse victims are seen in homes, clinics, hospitals, offices, and some, unfortunately, in the morgue. Two settings, CACs and the court, are experienced by a number of children, but not by all professionals who work with them. CACs were developed to provide a place where children could be interviewed by experienced professionals (usually social workers or psychologists). Such centers have reduced the number of interviews a child has to endure and enhanced the quality of the interviews. Some centers record a video of the interviews, and others do not. In addition, CACs frequently serve as a site for multidisciplinary case staffing with interviewers, medical personnel, law enforcement, prosecutors, and other involved professionals. Medical examinations may be on-site in some locales, but often are coordinated with other facilities. CACs provide a professional but child-friendly environment to provide the child and family with an opportunity to report any child abuse concerns they may have. Equally as important as obtaining information from children about child abuse is skillfully determining whether or not child abuse occurred. The NCA helps to set standards and supplies funding for the hundreds of CACs in the United States.

Figure 19-18

## CACs

The small CAC in Brunswick, Georgia (**Figure 19-18**), exemplifies the concept of a CAC as a separate house. However, a small number of CACs are located within hospitals. The type of location is not as significant as much as the ambience and dedication of the staff. The CAC in Swainsboro, Georgia (**Figure 19-19**), is also contained within a house but has a separate small conference building as well. The exterior of the moderate-size DeKalb County CAC in Decatur, Georgia, belies that it actually occupies the basement of a church (**Figure 19-20**). Modern renovations and a separate entrance make this a strong community resource.

**Figure 19-18.** *CAC in Brunswick.*

**Figure 19-19.** *CAC in Swainsboro, Georgia.*

**Figure 19-20.** *Exterior of the CAC in DeKalb County.*

Green Cove Springs is a relatively small child abuse examination center (**Figure 19-21**) that is a local extension of the Jacksonville Child Protection Team (one of Florida's 21 Child Protection Teams that cover the entire state). The floor plan for this center shows the different functions that occur here (**Figure 19-22**). Note the observation rooms used by police and child protective service workers while the child is being interviewed. One-way mirrors and/or discreet cameras enable the observers to view the examination without being in the same room. A medical examination room, conference room (for multidisciplinary staff meetings), and offices are other key areas. When designing a center, it is also desirable to have a bathroom immediately adjacent to the medical examination room so that the child does not need to go into a hallway.

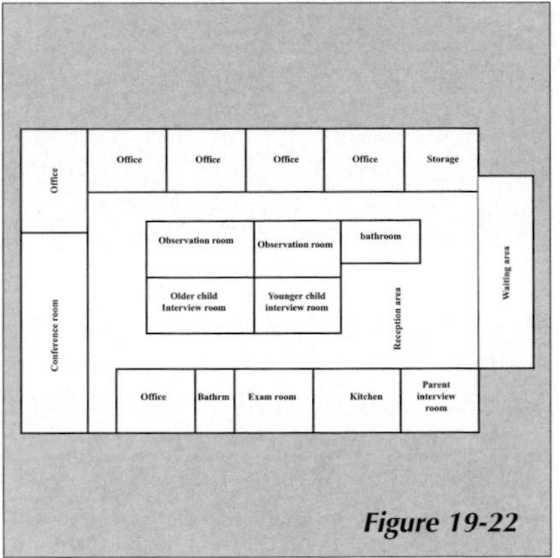

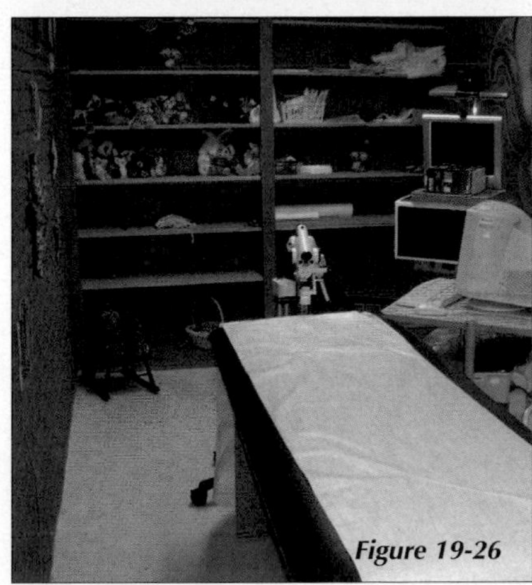

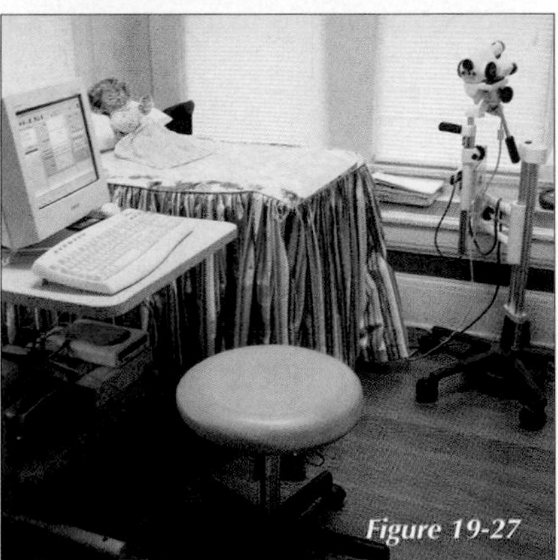

*__Figure 19-21.__ The front of the Green Cove Springs CAC.*

*__Figure 19-22.__ Floor plan for the CAC center in Green Cove Springs.*

*__Figure 19-23.__ Reception area of the Green Cove Springs CAC.*

*__Figure 19-24.__ Waiting room with toys, a big-screen television, and a bathroom.*

*__Figure 19-25.__ Model waiting room for a CAC.*

*__Figure 19-26.__ Child-friendly examination room.*

*__Figure 19-27.__ Setting for medical examination of children.*

## Reception to the Center

Comfortable seating in the reception area enhances the family's experience (**Figure 19-23**). The waiting room for a CAC should have a variety of toys and other diversions to keep children and adults comfortable before the interview or therapy session begins (**Figure 19-24**). A model waiting room is light and child friendly and accommodates a range of ages (**Figure 19-25**).

## The Examination

The examination room for forensic medical examinations should be child friendly (**Figure 19-26**). Bright colors and designs may help to put the patient at ease and serve as a distraction. In larger centers, decorations may be different in rooms used to examine teenagers than in rooms used to examine younger children. Medical examinations can also be conducted in a homey setting (**Figure 19-27**).

## The Interview

Children are interviewed in rooms that may be equipped with small wall-mounted cameras to record the conversation (**Figure 19-28**). Interview rooms can be tailored for the developmental interests of younger or older children by changing the furniture and décor of the room (**Figures 19-29** and **19-30**). Law enforcement personnel and others can observe the interview in a room separate from the child and interviewer (**Figure 19-31**). Some CACs have equipment so that police and others can make suggestions to the interviewer via an unobtrusive earpiece. Seen in **Figure 19-31** is equipment that allows the interview to be simultaneously recorded on videotape (copy goes with the police) and DVD (copy kept by the CAC).

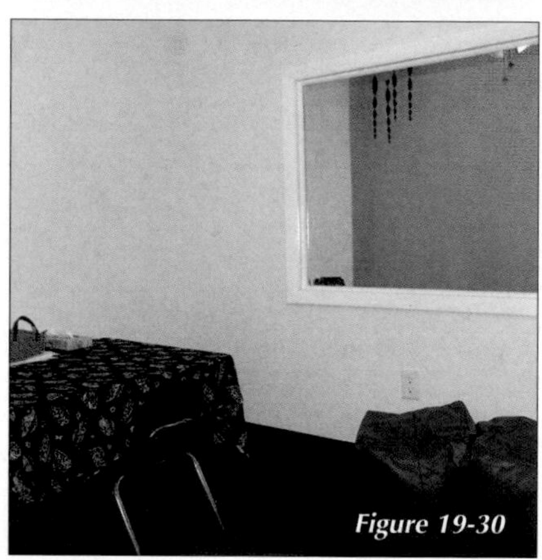

## Therapy

Therapy is offered on-site in some CACs. Therapy rooms can be adapted for a range of ages (**Figure 19-32**).

***Figure 19-28.*** *Interview room.*

***Figure 19-29.*** *Interview room for a younger child.*

***Figure 19-30.*** *Interview room for an older child.*

***Figure 19-31.*** *Observation room.*

***Figure 19-32.*** *Therapy room.*

## Meetings

After a child is interviewed, a small meeting room is used to review the interview and immediate aspects of the case (**Figure 19-33**). Weekly multidisciplinary staff meetings are typically held in another room (**Figures 19-34** and **19-35**). Attendees include CAC staff, child protective services, police, hospital personnel, and representatives of the prosecutor's office.

**Figure 19-33.** Meeting room.

**Figure 19-34.** Multidisciplinary staff meeting room.

**Figure 19-35.** Conference room for multidisciplinary staff meetings.

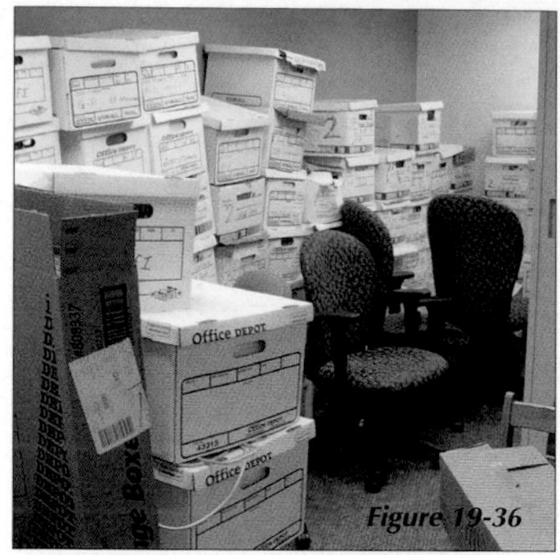

Figure 19-36

## Storage

Finding sufficient storage space is always difficult (**Figure 19-36**). With hundreds of interviews each year, videotapes consume a great deal of space. The use of DVDs as a recording mechanism has improved storage considerations (**Figure 19-37**). Some centers record multiple interviews on such a medium, enabling even greater space reduction.

## Estonian Child Sexual Abuse Interview Center, Tartu, Estonia

This interview center was developed through the office of the prosecutor, but is at a separate site within a larger building (**Figure 19-38**). The interview rooms (**Figures 19-39-a** and **b**) were constructed according to a description heard by one of the staff at an international conference without ever having seen such a room.

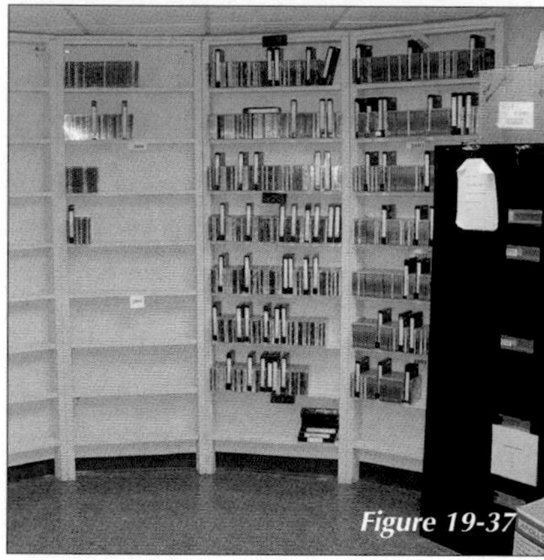
Figure 19-37

Figure 19-38

***Figure 19-36.*** *Storage space.*

***Figure 19-37.*** *DVD storage.*

***Figure 19-38.*** *Interview center in Tartu, Estonia.*

***Figures 19-39-a** and **b.** Interior views of the Estonian interview room.*

Figure 19-39-a

Figure 19-39-b

## Courtrooms

Most child abuse cases do not involve courtrooms. However, both children and professionals may attend court when the case cannot be addressed through social service approaches alone. Courts in the United States operate on a federal and state level. Federal courts consist of district courts, the circuit courts of appeal, and the US Supreme Court. State court systems vary from state to state, but typically include local courts with authority on specific issues and jurisdictions (eg, justice of the peace, police court, and probate court), county courts, and appellate courts. Courtrooms differ from location to location, depending on the size of its jurisdiction and the types of cases it sees (**Figures 19-40-a, b, c,** and **d**). Many courts throughout the world follow a similar system (**Figures 19-41-a** and **b**).

***Figure 19-40-a.*** *Atlanta, Georgia, has a large criminal court where felony child abuse cases are decided along with other crimes.*

***Figure 19-40-b.*** *Atlanta's modern juvenile court occupies a large city building devoted to child abuse cases.*

***Figure 19-40-c.*** *Mason City, Iowa, has a small city court that hears both juvenile and criminal child abuse cases along with various other criminal cases.*

***Figure 19-40-d.*** *This suburban criminal court in DuPage County (Wheaton, Illinois) is part of a large government complex. (Photograph courtesy of Jeff Kendall, JD.)*

Figure 19-41-a

Figure 19-41-b

Figure 19-42

## Courtroom Organization

Within the courtroom, the judge typically sits in the middle on a raised platform. The clerk sits to the judge's left and the witness to the right (**Figure 19-42**). Many courtrooms have a microphone for the witness for recording purposes and so that his/her voice may be heard. The 2 tables in the courtroom are for the defense and the prosecution (**Figure 19-43**). The position of the prosecution and defense varies depending on which side the jury occupies. The jury usually sits along one side of a courtroom (**Figure 19-44**). There are often 12 jurors in US criminal courts, but the number can vary. Military courts have "panels" instead of "juries" and have some other procedural differences compared to civilian courts.

*__Figure 19-41-a.__ The court in Tartu, Estonia, is a modern building that meets European Community standards, an organization that Estonia recently joined.*

*__Figure 19-41-b.__ The prosecutor's office in Tartu has developed operational information in different languages and tries to be user friendly to children.*

*__Figure 19-42.__ Interior of DuPage County courtroom. (Photograph courtesy of Jeff Kendall, JD.)*

*__Figure 19-43.__ The prosecution sits on the right side of the defense and the left of this court. (Photograph courtesy of Jeff Kendall, JD.)*

*__Figure 19-44.__ Jury location in this courtroom. (Photograph courtesy of Jeff Kendall, JD.)*

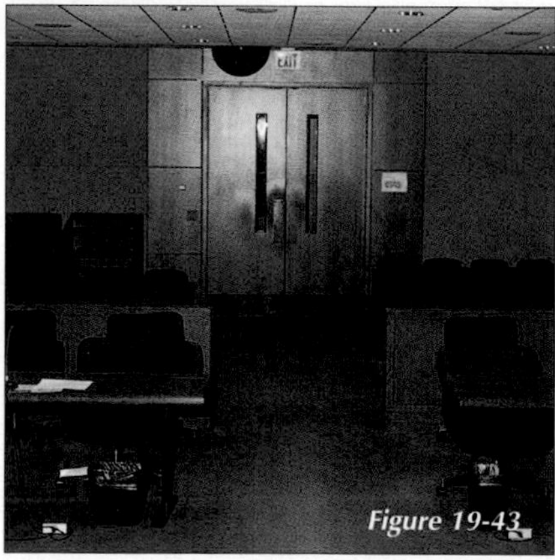

Figure 19-43

Figure 19-44

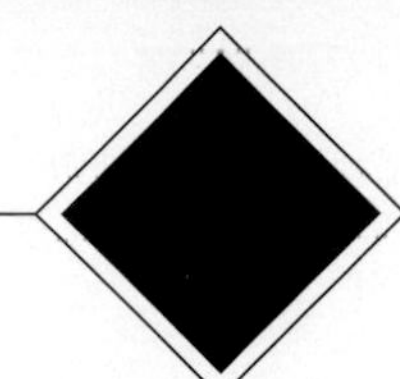

# REFERENCES


1. Cohle SD, Trestail JD III, Graham MA, Oxley DW, Walp B, Jachimczyk J. Fatal Pepper Aspiration. *Am J Dis Child.* 1988;142:633-636.

2. McCann J. Voris J. Simon M. and Wells R. Perianal Findings in Prepubertal Children Selected for Non-Abuse: A Descriptive Study. *Child Abuse Negl.* 1989;13:179-193

3. American Professional Society on the Abuse of Children (APSAC). *Glossary of Terms and the Interpretations of Findings for Child Sexual Abuse Evidentiary Examintaions.* Chicago, Ill: APSAC; 1998.

4. Johnson A. The role of the creative arts therapies in the diagnosis and treatment of psychological trauma. *Arts Psychother.* 1987;14:7-13.

5. Clements PT, Benasutti KM, Henry GC. Drawing from experience: utilizing drawings to facilitate communication and understanding with children exposed to sudden traumatic deaths. *J Psychosoc Nurs.* 2001;39:12-20.

6. Steinberg D. Book, exhibit look at mental illness in children. *The Albuquerque Sunday Journal.* February 11, 2001:F7-F8.

7. Clements P. *Traumatic Presentations and Behaviors in Children Exposed to Homicide* [dissertation]. Philadelphia, Pa: University of Pennsylvania; 2000.

8. Clements PT, Burgess AW. Children's responses to family member homicide. *Fam Community Health.* 2002;25:1-11.

9. Clements PT, Weisser S. Cries from the morgue: guidance for assessment, evaluation and intervention with children exposed to homicide of a family member. *J Child Adolesc Psychiatr Nurs.* 2003;16:153-161.

10. Levick M. *Mommy, Daddy, Look What I'm Saying: What Children Are Telling You Through Their Art.* New York, NY: M Evans and Company; 1986.

11. Levick M. *See What I'm Saying: What Children Tell Us Through Their Art.* DuBuque, Iowa: Islewest Publishing; 1998.

12. Malchiodi C. *Breaking the Silence.* New York, NY: Brunner/Mazel; 1990.

13. Benasutti K. *Childhood Psychological Maltreatment and the Use of Art Expressions* [master's thesis]. Philadelphia, Pa: Hahnemann University; 1993.

14. Blandford-Bynoe T. *On My Way to the Courthouse: A Child's Guide to What Happens in Court.* Trenton, NJ: State Office of Victim-Witness Advocacy Division of Criminal Justice; 1996.

15. Burgess E. Sexually abused children and their drawings. *Arch Psychiatr Nurs.* 1988;2:65-73.

16. Burgess A, Hartman C, Wolbert W, Grant C. Child molestation: assessing impact in multiple victims (Part I). *Arch Psychiatr Nurs.* 1987;1:33-39.

17. Burgess A, McCausland M, Wolbert W. Children's drawings as indicators of sexual trauma. *Perspect Psychiatr Care.* 1981;19:50-58.

18. Buschel B. Trauma, children, and art. *Am J Art Ther.* 1990;29:48-52.

19. Sheskin R, Klein H, Lowental U. Assessment of children's anxiety throughout dental treatment by their drawings. *ASDC J Dent Child.* 1982;49:99-106.

20. Burgess A, Clements P. Stress, coping and defensive functioning. In: Burgess AW, ed. *Psychiatric Nursing: Promoting Mental Health.* Stamford, Conn: Appleton & Lange; 1997:77-90.

21. Burgess A, Hartman C, Clements P. Biology of memory and childhood trauma. J *Psychosoc Nurs.* 1995;33:16-26.

22. Koplewicz H, Goodman R, eds. *Childhood Revealed: Art Expressing Pain, Discovery and Hope.* New York, NY: Abrams; 1999.

23. Belnick J. A crisis intervention model for family art therapy. In: Linesch D, ed. *Art Therapy With Families in Crisis: Overcoming Resistance Through Nonverbal Expression.* New York, NY: Brunner/Mazel; 1993; 23-45.

24. Linesch D. Family systems and the creative process: the second look. In: Linesch D, ed. *Art Therapy With Families in Crisis: Overcoming Resistance Through Nonverbal Expression.* New York, NY: Brunner/Mazel; 1993; 155-160.

25. Chadwick DL, Chin S, Salerno C, Landsverk J, Kitchen L. Deaths from falls in children: how far is fatal? *J Trauma.* 1991;31:1353-1355.

26. The Effects of Adverse Childhood Experiences on Adult Health and Well Being. The Adverse Childhood Experiences Study Web site. Available at: http://www.acestudy.org. Accessed February 4, 2005.

27. Felitti VJ, Anda RF, Nordenberg D, et al. The relationship of adult health status to childhood abuse and household dysfunction. *Am JPrev Med.* 1998;14:245-258.

28. Fromm S.Total Estimated Cost of Child Abuse and Neglect In the United States: Statistical Evidence. Prevent Child Abuse America Web Site. Available at: http://www.preventchildabuse.org/learn_more/research.html. Accessed February 4, 2005.

29. Krug EG, Dahlberg LL, Mercy JA, Zwi A, Lozano R, eds, for the World Health Organization Global Consultation on Violence and Health. *World Report on Violence and Health.* Geneva, Switzerland: WHO, 2002.

30. Kilpatrick KT, for Prevent Child Abuse America. *Reframing Child Abuse and Neglect for Increased Understanding and Engagement: Defining the Need for Strategic Reframing.* Chicago, Ill: PCA America; 2004.

31. Perry BD, Marcellus J. The Impact of Abuse and Neglect on the Developing Brain. *Colleagues For Children.* 1997;7:1-4.

32. Starling SP, Holden JR, Jenny C. Abusive head trauma: the relationship of perpetrators to their victims. *Pediatrics.* 1995;95:259-62.

33. Prevent Child Abuse America. Top Five Ways to Prevent Child Abuse and Neglect [press release]. Chicago, Ill: PCA America; Feb. 25, 2002.

34. Nansel TR, Overpeck MD, Haynie DL, Ruan WJ, Scheidt PC. Relationships between bullying and violence among US youth. *Arch Pedtr Adolesc Med.* 2003;157:348-353.

35. Criminal Justice Coordinating Council. Partners in Justice: Georgia Child Fatality Review Panel Annual Report, 2002. Available at: http://www.cjcc.georgia.gov. Accessed February 4, 2005.

36. Alexander RA, Baca L, Fox JA, et al, for Fight Crime: Invest in Kids. New Hope for Preventing Child Abuse and Neglect: Proven Solutions to Save Lives and Prevent Future Crime. Washington, DC: FIGHT CRIME: Invest in Kids; 2003. Available at: http://www.fightcrime.org. Accessed February 4, 2005.

37. Understanding Infant Crying: Period of PURPLE Crying. National Center on Shaken Baby Web site. Available at: http://www.dontshake.com/Subject.aspx?categoryID=13&PageName=UnderstandInfantCrying.htm. Accessed February 7, 2005.

38. Lutzker JR, Rice JM. Project 12-ways: Measuring outcome of a large in-home service for treatment and prevention of child abuse and neglect. *Child Abuse Negl.* 1984;8:519-524.

39. Lutzker JR, Bigelow KM. *Reducing Child Maltreatment: A Guidebook for Parent Services.* New York, NY: Guilford Publications Inc; 2002.

40. Lutzker JR, Bigelow KM, Doctor RM, Kessler ML. Safety, health care and bonding within an ecobehavioral approach to treating and preventing child abuse and neglect. *J Fam Violence.* 1998;13(pt 2):163-185.

41. Lutzker JR, Rice JM. Using recidivism data to evaluate Project 12-Ways: An ecobehavioral approach to the treatment and prevention of child abuse and neglect. *J Fam Violence.* 1987;2(pt 4):283-290.

42. Chaffin M, Silovsky JF, Funderburk B, et al. Parent-child interaction therapy with physically abusive parents: efficacy for reducing future abuse reports. *J Consult Clin Psychol.* 2004;72:500-510.

# B

# C

# D

## E

# G

# J



# K



# L

# M

# Q



# R

## S

## U



## V



## W



## Y



## Z